Intermediate Accounting

Comprehensive Volume **Twelfth Edition**

Jay M. Smith, PhD, CPA
Brigham Young University

K. Fred Skousen, PhD, CPA
Brigham Young University

Earl K. Stice, PhD
Rice University

James D. Stice, PhD
Brigham Young University

SOUTH-WESTERN College Publishing

An International Thomson Publishing Company

Acquisitions Editor: Dave Shaut
Developmental Editor: Linda A. Spang
Production Editors: Robin Schuster, Gail L. Strietmann
Designer: Joseph M. Devine
Marketing Manager: Sharon Oblinger
Internal Art Illustration: Hans and Cassady, Inc.

AC92LA

1 2 3 4 5 KI 8 7 6 5 4

Printed in the United States of America

This book is printed on recycled, acid-free paper that meets Environmental Protection Agency standards.

PREFACE

We are very appreciative of the many positive comments made about our eleventh edition. In this, the twelfth edition, we have refined many of the innovations introduced in the eleventh edition. We also have added material that reflects changing accounting standards and the movement toward integration in many accounting curricula. The Brigham Young University AECC-sponsored curriculum change is now entering its fourth year of full implementation. Students who entered the program in its first class are now graduated and working in their chosen jobs. The enthusiasm of recruiters, graduating students, and incoming students continues to convince the BYU faculty of the effectiveness of the integrated curriculum. We encourage you at your schools to take advantage of the pioneering work done at many universities to examine your curriculum, including Intermediate Accounting, and adapt ideas to your specific needs. We attest to the excitement that comes from this approach. We continue to keep these varied approaches to accounting education in mind as we revise our text and make it as timely and flexible as we can. We welcome your ideas.

SIGNIFICANT CHANGES IN THE TWELFTH EDITION

As is true with every edition of INTERMEDIATE ACCOUNTING, many changes are made because of new accounting standards issued by the Financial Accounting Standards Board. This is certainly true of this edition. The following topics have been substantially revised to reflect relevant new standards and proposals for new standards.

1. Debt and equity investments, FASB Statement Nos. 114 and 115 (Chapter 17)
2. Accounting for income taxes, FASB Statement No. 109 (Chapter 20)
3. Proposed changes in accounting for stock-based compensation plans (Chapter 16)
4. Proposed changes in reporting earnings per share (Chapter 23)

Other major changes include extensive revision of material covering pension accounting in Chapter 21, integration of ratio analysis throughout the text, and many new end-of-chapter cases, exercises, and problems.

New Chapter on Investments

Since the last edition of the text was published, the FASB has been busy in the area of accounting for investments. The Board made a significant step away from historical cost and toward market value with the issuance of FASB Statement No. 115. As a result of this new standard, many debt and equity securities purchased as investments are adjusted to market value at the end of each accounting period. Depending on the classification of the security, the change in value is disclosed on the income statement or directly in a stockholders' equity account. Chapter 17 has been updated to address the issues presented by this new standard.

Accounting for Income Taxes

Chapter 20 on income taxes has been completely revised to reflect the provisions mandated in FASB Statement No. 109. The chapter begins with a basic illustration that outlines the important aspects of accounting for deferred tax assets and liabilities. The chapter continues with a number of more complex examples that highlight the sticky conceptual issues underlying the controversy that has surrounded the accounting for income taxes in recent years.

Stock-Based Compensation Plans

The issue of how to account for stock-based compensation plans exploded on the scene in 1993. The FASB has proposed greatly expanding the circumstances in which stock-based compensation awards would be considered an expense. The proposal has prompted a cry of alarm from many in the business community. One Congress person accused the FASB of trying to "change reality" and of causing suffering among growth companies. As this book goes to press, the FASB has not yet issued a final pronouncement. Chapter 15 compares the FASB's Exposure Draft to existing standards and illustrates the conceptual issues and practical difficulties underlying this important topic.

Accounting for Pensions

Chapter 21 now includes a simple example that allows students to get inside the black box of pension computations and actually see how different factors, such as employee turnover and expected future salary growth, impact a company's pension obligation. This simple example is followed by a multi-year illustration using a spreadsheet framework that introduces and explains the infamous intricacies of pension accounting.

Earnings Per Share

In 1994 the topic of earnings per share was added to the FASB's agenda. Anticipated changes will make EPS reporting by U. S. companies more comparable to companies in other countries. In effect, the primary earnings per share computation would be replaced by basic earnings per share. Chapter 23 has been revised and reorganized to reflect the expected changes.

Integration of Ratio Analysis Throughout the Text

In this edition, we have moved much of the ratio analysis from the back of the text to appropriate places in various chapters. For example, in Chapter 4 on the income statement, we present and discuss the uses of gross profit percentage and net profit percentage; in Chapter 9, we discuss inventory turnover and days' sales in inventory; and in Chapter 14, we introduce students to the debt-to-equity ratio and its uses. In the last chapter of the text, all the ratios are tied together in a summary, but students do not have to wait until the end of the text to get a feel for the uses of accounting information.

Additional Cases, Exercises, and Problems in Each Chapter

Many new cases, exercises, and problems have been added to the text. Many of these new end-of-chapter materials require students to review the Microsoft annual report that is featured at the end of the text. In addition, numerous cases involving real-world examples have been included in this edition. The emphasis of many of these new end-of-chapter materials is to focus on a student's developing the analytical tools necessary to succeed in his or her chosen profession.

OTHER IMPORTANT FEATURES

Several changes made in the eleventh edition made our text distinctive. We have been encouraged by the response to these changes, and have retained them in this edition with some revisions to make them even more valuable.

New Opening Scenarios and Boxed Items

Each chapter of the text has a real-world opening scenario that suggests why the topics covered in the chapter are relevant to what the students will be doing when they graduate. Each chapter of the text also includes at least one boxed item, derived from current literature, that describes recent events and asks the student to consider various policy and conceptual issues related to the material. Students can consider these "asides" as they read the text material, and instructors can use this material in class discussion to broaden the student's understanding. Suggested solutions to the questions in the boxed items are included in the Solutions Manual. A sampling of opening scenarios and boxed items is given below.

Opening Scenarios:

- IBM: Its Rise, Its Fall, and Its Creative Accounting (Chapter 1)
- The Balance Sheet of the Boston Celtics (Chapter 5)
- Blockbuster Video: Garbage, Videos, and Depreciation Policy (Chapter 12)
- Net Assets in the U.S. Federal Government—Negative $3.1 Trillion (Chapter 21)

Boxed Items:

- Russian Accounting (Chapter 3)
- Phar-Mor and the World Basketball League (Chapter 4)
- Asset Revaluations: Daimler-Benz and Grand Metropolitan (Chapter 11)
- BASF Aktiengesellschaft: German Liabilities (Chapter 13)

Early Cash Flow Chapter With More Complex Items Covered in Later Chapters

We feel that the movement of the cash flows chapter from the back of the text to the front is very significant. For several years, especially since the FASB adopted its conceptual framework, the importance of reporting cash flows has been stressed. No longer can the statement of cash flows be looked upon as a "supplemental statement." It reports information that is vital for many decisions, and the usefulness of this information was enhanced significantly by the revised format prescribed by FASB Statement No. 95. We feel that placement of the statement of cash flows with the income statement and the balance sheet conveys this importance to students and assists them in gaining a broader understanding of the impact of business events, not only on net income and the balance sheet, but also on cash flows.

Recognizing that students would have difficulty understanding some complex transactions at this early stage of their study of intermediate accounting, we omit unnecessary complexities from Chapter 6. We include discussion of their impact on cash flows as appropriate throughout the text. Thus, the treatment of the allowance for doubtful accounts is covered in Chapter 8, the cash effects of bond premium and discount amortization are discussed in Chapter 14, and the complexities of cash flows for lease arrangements are explained in Chapter 19. With these complexities removed from Chapter 6, we feel that the format for the statement of cash flows, which is more understandable than the old funds statement, makes it possible to teach both the indirect and direct methods at this earlier time. We have elected to stress the T-account approach in the chapter because it is less complicated than the work sheet approach. The latter approach is retained, however, in an appendix to Chapter 6 for those who wish to use it. A comprehensive cash flow review problem is included as an appendix to Chapter 25.

We recognize that some users of our text will want to continue teaching the statement of cash flows later in the course. As users of the eleventh edition have pointed out, the text provides flexibility that allows individual instructors to determine when their students should study the statement of cash flows. The Instructor's Resource Manual that accompanies the text explains how the cash flow material in Chapter 6 and subsequent chapters can be used by those who prefer later coverage.

International Topics and Illustrations Integrated Throughout the Text

Accounting and business students need more exposure to international issues. This conclusion is stressed by all groups that have been studying accounting and business education. In the past, international issues have been taught mainly in the advanced accounting course. Because many accounting graduates do not take an advanced course, we feel it is important that some international issues be covered in an intermediate text. We have carefully added many examples and topics to achieve this goal.

The movement to coordinate the establishment of accounting standards internationally is presented in Chapter 1. Throughout the text, examples of international variations in the treatment of business events are presented. For example, look at the international items included in the sampling of boxed items presented earlier. Chapter 11 includes a section dealing with the accounting for sales and purchases of goods in foreign markets, and the foreign exchange adjustments necessary at the time of sale or purchase, subsequent reporting, and settlement of the transaction. In Chapter 24, we cover the process of adjusting financial statements with different currencies, a process that is similar to that for constant-dollar adjustments.

Annotated Instructor's Edition

The introduction of our annotated instructor's edition was well-received by adopters of the eleventh edition, and annotations are again included in the twelfth edition. Four types of annotated notes are included throughout the text: (1) enrichment examples, (2) points to stress, (3) teaching tips, and (4) historical notes. We have included these annotations to provide instructors with additional information that should prove useful and interesting.

SUPPLEMENTARY MATERIALS

A comprehensive package of supplementary materials is provided with the twelfth edition to assist both instructors and students.

Available to Instructors

Solutions Manual. This manual contains independently verified answers to all end-of-chapter questions, cases, and problems, and suggested solutions to questions that accompany the boxed items in the text.

Solutions Transparencies. Transparencies of solutions for all end-of-chapter exercises and problems are available to adopters.

Instructor's Resource Manual, prepared by David M. Cottrell, Brigham Young University. This manual contains objectives, chapter outlines, teaching suggestions and strategies, topical overviews of end-of-chapter materials, assignment classifications with level of difficulty and estimated completion time, suggested readings on chapter topics, and teaching transparency masters. The text of the Instructor's Resource Manual is available on diskette.

Test Bank, prepared by David M. Cottrell, Brigham Young University. The revised and expanded test bank is available in both printed and computer (MicroExam) versions. Test items include multiple choice questions and short examination problems for each chapter, accompanied by solutions.

Template Diskette. The diskette is used with Lotus® 1-2-3®* for solving selected end-of-chapter exercises and problems that are identified in the textbook with the symbol at the right. The diskette may be ordered free of charge from South-Western College Publishing by instructors who have adopted the textbook for their courses.

Available to Students

Study Guide, prepared by Sara York Kenny, University of Utah. Each chapter of this all-new study guide includes learning objectives, a study outline, self-testing questions, and study group activities. Most chapters also include activities relating to the 1993 annual report of Campbell Soup Company, which is included in the study guide.

Working Papers. Forms for solving end-of-chapter exercises and problems are contained in a single bound volume and are perforated for easy removal.

Practice Set, "Bright Landscapes, Inc.," prepared by J. Gregory Bushong and Jane B. Wells, University of Kentucky. This case provides a comprehensive review of introductory financial accounting. The number of routine transactions is minimized, allowing students to concentrate more on the overall accounting process and less on the details. Students can use their social security numbers to change transaction amounts, thus creating a unique solution. The instructor's manual includes a diskette that generates each student's solution.

ACKNOWLEDGEMENTS

Relevant pronouncements of the Financial Accounting Standards Board and other authoritative publications are paraphrased, quoted, discussed, and referenced throughout the text. We are indebted to the American Accounting Association, the American Institute of Certified Public Accountants, the Financial Accounting Standards Board, and the Securities and Exchange Commission for material from their publications. Also, we gratefully acknowledge the American Institute of Certified Public Accountants for permission to use questions from the Uniform CPA Examination.

We wish to thank the following faculty who reviewed manuscript for this edition and provided many helpful suggestions.

Kenneth H. Johnson
Georgia Southern University
David J. Karmon
Central Michigan University
William Kross
Purdue University
David Mautz
University of North Carolina-Greensboro
E. James Meddaugh
Ohio University
Tina Y. Mills
Miami University
Kermit Natho
Georgia State University
Gale E. Newell
Western Michigan University
Dave Nichols
University of Mississippi
Marcia S. Niles
University of Idaho
Barbara W. Scofield
University of Kentucky
Nancy Wagner
Georgia Southern University
Gary L. Waters
Troy State University

We would like to thank Cathy Xanthaky Larson, Middlesex Community College, who served as verifier for the text and solutions manual. Her careful editing helped us attain a high level of quality and accuracy.

Finally, we extend our thanks to the many instructors and students who have used INTERMEDIATE ACCOUNTING and volunteered their comments and suggestions.

Jay M. Smith
K. Fred Skousen
Earl K. Stice
James D. Stice

ABOUT THE AUTHORS

This edition of INTERMEDIATE ACCOUNTING marks the addition of two new authors. Earl K. Stice and James D. Stice are outstanding young faculty at Rice University and Brigham Young University, respectively. They are brothers and are realizing a long-time goal of working together professionally, combining their expertise and enthusiasm for the field of accounting. Together with senior authors, Jay M. Smith and K. Fred Skousen, they have introduced many innovative changes in the text—changes that reflect their creative approach to education. A brief educational and professional profile is presented below for each member of the author team.

Jay M. Smith is Professor of Accounting at the School of Accountancy and Information Systems, Brigham Young University. He holds a bachelor's and master's degree from BYU and a PhD from Stanford University. He has over thirty years' teaching experience at BYU, Stanford, the University of Minnesota, and the University of Hawaii. Dr. Smith has received numerous awards and recognitions in accounting including teaching excellence awards from BYU and the Utah Association of CPAs. He served as a faculty resident at Arthur Andersen & Co.'s professional education center and also as a member of the Faculty Advisory Group working with Coopers & Lybrand in their Excellence in Auditing educational project. Dr. Smith also served as project coordinator for the AECC grant received by BYU to restructure the accounting junior year curriculum. He is a member of the American Institute of CPAs and the American Accounting Association and has served on numerous committees of these organizations.

K. Fred Skousen is Dean of the Marriott School of Management, Brigham Young University. He has a bachelor's degree from BYU and master's and PhD degrees from the University of Illinois. Dr. Skousen has taught at the University of Illinois, the University of Minnesota, the University of California at Berkeley, and the University of Missouri, as well as BYU. He received Distinguished Faculty Awards at the University of Minnesota and at BYU and was recognized as the National Beta Alpha Psi Academic Accountant of the Year in 1979. Dr. Skousen is the author or coauthor of over 50 articles, research reports, and books. He has held leadership positions in the American Accounting Association, the American Institute of CPAs, and the Utah Association of CPAs. He has been a consultant to the Controller General of the United States, the Federal Trade Commission, and several large companies. He was a Faculty Resident with the Securities and Exchange Commission and a Faculty Fellow with Price Waterhouse and Co.

Earl K. Stice is Assistant Professor of Accounting at the Jones Graduate School of Administration, Rice University. He holds bachelor's and master's degrees from Brigham Young University and a PhD from Cornell University. Dr. Stice has taught at the University of Arizona and at Cornell University as well as Rice University. He has published papers in the *Journal of Financial and Quantitative Analysis, The Accounting Review,* and *Issues in Accounting Education* and is co-author of *Readings and Applications in Financial Accounting,* second edition. Dr. Stice has presented research papers at a number of professional meetings, including conferences in Finland, Taiwan, and Australia. He has twice served as co-chairperson of the Membership and Subscriptions Committee of the American Accounting Association.

James D. Stice is the Price Waterhouse Research Fellow and an Associate Professor in the School of Accountancy and Information Systems (SOAIS) at Brigham Young University. He holds a bachelor's and master's degree from BYU and a PhD in accounting from the University of Washington. He received the Outstanding Faculty Award from the SOAIS in 1990 and was selected by graduating students as "Teacher of the Year" in both 1992 and 1993. Articles by Dr. Stice have appeared in *The Accounting Review, Decision Sciences, The CPA Journal,* and other professional journals. In addition to teaching and research, he has served as a consultant for companies in the computer and banking industries.

BRIEF CONTENTS

CONTENTS

PART 3 SPECIAL PROBLEMS IN INCOME DETERMINATION

PART 4 OTHER DIMENSIONS OF FINANCIAL REPORTING

Overview of Accounting and Its Theoretical Foundation

CHAPTER 1

Financial Reporting and the Accounting Profession

CHAPTER TOPICS

- Financial Reporting to Users of Accounting Information
- Components of the Accounting Profession
- Role of the FASB and Various Governmental and Professional Organizations in the Development of Accounting Standards
- Conflict Between Public and Private Sectors in Establishing Accounting Standards

Analysis of the data gathered in the United States Census of 1880 took almost ten years. For the census of 1890, the U.S. government commissioned Herman Hollerith to provide data tabulation machines in an attempt to speed the process. Hollerith's machines used cards with holes punched in them to represent the census data. This system of mechanized data handling saved the census bureau $5 million and slashed the data analysis time by two years.[1] In 1911, Hollerith's company was merged with two firms that made scales and time clocks, forming the Computing-Tabulating-Recording Company. In 1924, this combined company changed its name to the International Business Machines Corporation (IBM). Under the leadership of Thomas J. Watson, Sr., who had come to IBM from the National Cash Register Company (NCR) in 1914, IBM became the largest office machine producer in the U.S. with sales of over $180 million in 1949.

In 1950, resistance to the idea of electronic computers was high inside IBM. IBM's engineers were specialists in electromechanical devices and were uncomfortable working with vacuum tubes, diodes, and magnetic recording tapes.[2] In addition, there were many

1. Cortada, James W. *Before the Computer*. Princeton, NJ: Princeton University Press, 1993.
2. Fisher, Franklin M., James W. McKie, and Richard B. Mancke. *IBM and the U.S. Data Processing Industry*. New York, NY: Praeger, 1983.

questions about the customer demand for electronic computers. One IBM executive forecast that the size of the total worldwide market for computers was about five. Following significant internal debate, Thomas J. Watson, Jr. authorized development of IBM's first electronic computer, the 701. Through the 1960s and 70s, with its aggressive leasing program, emphasis on sales and service, and continued investment in research and development, IBM established a dominant (some claimed a monopolistic) position in the mainframe computer market.

IBM was not the first company to produce a personal computer, but when the IBM PC was released in 1981, it quickly became the industry standard. Other machines came to be described as "IBM compatible" or "clones." By 1986, IBM held 40% of the PC market.[3] Amid this success, IBM made what, in retrospect, was a crucial error — it chose to focus on producing and selling hardware and to leave the software, by and large, to others. In fact, IBM did not develop the operating system for its first PC, instead electing to use a system called "DOS" developed by a small, 32-person company named Microsoft. In the early 1990s, as profits of software developers like Microsoft and Novell exploded, the profits of IBM slumped badly. In 1990, IBM reported an operating profit of $11 billion. Operating profit in 1991 fell to $942 million, and operations showed a loss of $45 million in 1992, IBM's first operating loss ever. As of December 31, 1992, the total market value of IBM stock was $28.8 billion, down from $105.8 billion in 1987 when IBM was the most valuable company in the world.

As is always the case when stockholders lose money, analysts are taking another look at IBM's financial statements to determine whether accounting techniques were used to artificially inflate IBM's reported performance. The following two examples illustrate the types of questions that have been raised about IBM's accounting.[4]

Revenue Recognition. In response to increased competition in the computer market, IBM's sales force devised new payment plans to spur sales. They offered stretched out payment plans, no money down "try and buy" plans, and "price protection" plans, guaranteeing refunds if prices dropped subsequent to a customer's purchase. Salespeople are certainly free to concoct any gimmicks they wish, but these creative payment plans then present the thorny accounting question of when to recognize the revenue from these sales. As explained more fully in Chapter 18 of this text, revenue should not be recorded until the earnings process is substantially complete — that is, until the seller has done essentially everything promised to the buyer. For some of its mainframe computers, IBM records the revenue when the machine is shipped, asserting that the earnings process is complete at that point. In other cases, IBM recognizes the revenue when the machine is merely transferred to IBM's own warehouse for temporary storage en route to the customer. By comparison, Amdahl, one of IBM's competitors, records no revenue until its field engineering group makes sure the machine is installed and running.

Leasing. Historically, IBM has leased, rather than sold, most of its mainframe computers. This policy goes back to Herman Hollerith who leased his tabulating machines to the Census Bureau in 1890. Accounting for leases is fascinating — it includes elements of historical controversy, subtlety and complexity, possibility for manipulation, and vast potential impact on the reported financial statements. (Note: The full story is in Chapter 19.) To prevent companies from reporting that they have sold a computer when in fact they have only rented it, the Financial Accounting Standards Board (FASB) has estab-

3. Carroll, Paul B. "Giant Missteps: How an IBM Attempt to Regain PC Lead Has Slid Into Trouble," *The Wall Street Journal*, December 2, 1991, p. Al.

4. Miller, Michael W. and Lee Berton. "As IBM's Woes Grew, Its Accounting Tactics Got Less Conservative." *The Wall Street Journal*, April 7, 1993, p. A1.

lished strict rules governing lease accounting. One stipulation is that a lease deal is accounted for as a sale if the value of the lease payments, plus the anticipated salvage value of the computer at the end of the lease term, are equal to at least 90% of the cash price of the computer. In its efforts to ensure it could account for computer leases as sales, IBM arranged a unique deal with Merrill Lynch, the financial services firm. Merrill Lynch sold IBM an insurance contract guaranteeing to pay a certain amount for computers returned to IBM at the end of their lease terms. These guaranteed salvage amounts were calculated to be just sufficient to allow IBM to satisfy the 90% requirement and thus be able to account for the original computer leases as outright sales. Illegal? Certainly not. Clever? Absolutely.

Arguments over appropriate accounting, like these disputes raised about IBM's accounting, are a fact of life because accounting involves judgment. Before the financial statements of a company are released, the management of the company is likely to have a host of accounting disagreements with the independent auditor. If a company falters, as IBM has in the last few years, outside analysts are sure to find accounting judgments with which, in retrospect, they disagree. If the FASB proposes a new accounting rule, it is certain that some business executives will proclaim the rule to be utterly absurd. This is not because managers are sleezy, conniving, and self serving (although such managers certainly exist); it is because the business world is a complex place filled with complex transactions and reasonable people can disagree about how to account for those transactions.

Your introductory accounting course gave you an overview of the primary financial statements and touched briefly on such topics as revenue recognition, depreciation, leases, pensions, deferred taxes, LIFO, and marketable securities. In intermediate accounting, all these topics are back, bigger and better than ever. But now, instead of getting an overview, you will actually get the nuts and bolts. Yes, some of these topics are complex — as mentioned above, they have to be complex because the business world is a complex place. When you complete your course in intermediate accounting, you will be the type of person who doesn't need to be reminded to look at the notes when evaluating a set of financial statements. You will not only be aware of the large impact that accounting assumptions can have but will also be able to quantify that impact. And you will better understand the important role accountants have in preparing the financial statements that are so vital to the smooth functioning of both the U.S. and the global economy.

ACCOUNTING AND FINANCIAL REPORTING

The overall objective of **accounting*** is to provide information that can be used in making economic decisions.

Accounting is a service activity. Its function is to provide quantitative information, primarily financial in nature, about economic entities that is intended to be useful in making economic decisions—in making reasoned choices among alternative courses of action.[5]

Several key features of this definition should be noted. First, accounting provides a vital service in today's business environment. Economists and environmentalists remind us constantly that we live in a world with limited resources. We must use our natural resources, our labor, and our financial wealth wisely so as to maximize their benefits to society. The better the accounting system that measures and reports the costs of using these

*A glossary of key terms appears in Appendix B at the end of the text. The terms included in the glossary are printed in color and are listed at the end of each chapter.

5. *Statement of the Accounting Principles Board No. 4,* "Basic Concepts and Accounting Principles Underlying Financial Statement of Business Enterprises" (New York: American Institute of Certified Public Accountants, 1970), par. 40.

Exhibit 1–1
Internal and External Users of Accounting Information

Internal users	External users
Company management	Creditors and potential creditors
Company employees	Investors and potential investors
Board of directors	Financial analysts
	Governmental agencies
	Other interested parties

resources, the better the decisions that are made for allocating them. Second, accounting is concerned primarily with quantitative financial information that is used in conjunction with qualitative evaluations in making judgments. Finally, although accountants place much emphasis on reporting what has already occurred, this past information is intended to be useful in making economic decisions about the future.

Users of Accounting Information

If accounting is to meet its objective of providing useful information for economic decision making, the following questions must be answered: (1) Who are the users of accounting information? and (2) What information do they require to meet their decision-making needs?

User groups are normally divided into two major classifications: (1) **internal users,** who make decisions directly affecting the internal operations of the enterprise, and (2) **external users,** who make decisions concerning their relationship to the enterprise. Major internal and external user groups are listed in Exhibit 1–1.

Internal users need information to assist in planning and controlling enterprise operations and managing (allocating) enterprise resources. The accounting system must provide timely information needed to control day-to-day operations and to make major planning decisions, such as: Do we make this product or another one? Do we build a new production plant or expand existing facilities? Must we increase prices or can we cut costs?

The types of decisions made by external users vary widely; thus, their information needs are highly diverse. Considerable time and effort have been devoted to studying the information needs of external users. As a result, two groups, creditors and investors, have been identified as the principal external users of financial information. Two reasons cited for the importance of these groups are:[6]

1. Their decisions significantly affect the allocation of resources in the economy.
2. Information provided to meet investors' and creditors' needs is likely to be generally useful to members of other groups who are interested in essentially the same financial aspects of business enterprises as investors and creditors.

Creditors need information about the profitability and stability of the enterprise to answer such questions as: Do we lend the money? And, if so, with what provisions? Investors (both existing stockholders and potential investors) need information concerning the safety and profitability of their investment. Stockholders must decide whether to increase, decrease, terminate, or maintain their interest in an enterprise.

Financial Reporting

The two major classifications of users, internal and external, have led to a distinction between two major areas of accounting. **Management accounting** (sometimes referred to

6. *Statement of Financial Accounting Concepts No. 1*, "Objectives of Financial Reporting by Business Enterprises" (Stamford: Financial Accounting Standards Board, 1978), par. 30.

as managerial or cost accounting) is concerned primarily with financial reporting for internal users. Internal users, especially management, have control over the accounting system and can specify precisely what information is needed and how the information is to be reported. **Financial accounting** focuses on the development and communication of financial information for external users primarily in the form of **general-purpose financial statements.** These statements include a balance sheet, income statement, statement of cash flows, and usually a statement of changes in retained earnings or in owners' equity.

Most accounting systems are designed to generate information for both internal and external reporting. Generally, the external information is much more highly summarized than the information reported internally. The internal decisions made by management require information regarding, for example, specific product lines, specific financing alternatives, individual sales territories, detailed expense classifications, and differences between actual and budgeted revenues and costs. The decisions made by external users require broader indications of overall profitability and financial stability.

While internal financial reporting is governed by the needs of management, external financial reporting is governed by an established body of standards or principles[7] that are designed to reflect the external users' needs. The development of these standards is discussed in some detail later in this chapter.

This textbook focuses on financial accounting and external reporting. The remaining chapters present the concepts, standards, and procedures applied in the development of the basic financial statements.

THE ACCOUNTING PROFESSION

Professional accountants perform their work in many different roles and environments. To meet its various reporting needs, a business enterprise may employ **financial accountants,** who are primarily concerned with external financial reporting; **management accountants,** who are primarily concerned with internal financial reporting; and **tax accountants,** who prepare the necessary federal, state, and local tax returns and advise management in matters relating to taxation. In smaller organizations, there is less specialization and more combining of responsibility for the various accounting functions.

Larger business enterprises typically employ **internal auditors** who review the work performed by accountants and others within the enterprise and report their findings to management. In addition to auditing financial reports generated by the accounting system, they review the operational policies of the company and make recommendations for improving efficiency and effectiveness. Although internal auditors are employees of the enterprise, they must be independent with respect to the employees whose work they review. Thus, internal auditors generally report to top management or a special audit committee of the board of directors.

Some accountants, known as **Certified Public Accountants (CPAs),** do not work for a single business enterprise. Rather, they provide a variety of services for many different individual and business clients. With respect to external financial reporting, the most important service provided by CPAs is the independent audit of financial statements.

The Independent Audit Function

As independent auditors, CPAs play a critical role in the reporting of financial information to external users. In performing an **independent audit,** their responsibility is to examine

7. The terms "standards" and "principles" are used interchangeably by the accounting profession and in this text.

the financial statements to be furnished to external users and to express an opinion as to the fairness of the statements in adhering to generally accepted accounting principles. The auditor's opinion is communicated in a report that accompanies the financial statements. The opinion is based on evidence gathered by the auditor from the detailed records and documents maintained by the company and from a review of the controls over the accounting system. A revised three-paragraph auditor's report was adopted by the accounting profession in 1988. This report form replaced a standard two-paragraph report that had been used for fifty years. The revision emphasizes the separate responsibilities that management and the auditors have for the accounting system and for the information in the financial statements. An example of the standard report form is included in the 1993 annual report of The Procter & Gamble Company and is reproduced in Exhibit 1—2.[8] The report of Procter & Gamble's auditor is an example of an unqualified, or "clean", opinion. Modifications to the standard report are required in some cases, for example, when the auditor determines that the financial statements contain a departure from generally accepted accounting principles. Another type of modification is necessary when, because of circumstances, no opinion is possible. As an example, consider the following excerpt from the 1992 auditor's report for The Circle K Corporation, a large convenience store chain operating primarily in the southwestern United States.

> *[O]n May 15, 1990, the Company filed a voluntary petition for relief under Chapter 11 of the U.S. Bankruptcy Code... As a result of the reorganization proceedings, the Company may sell or otherwise dispose of assets and liquidate or settle liabilities for amounts other than those reflected in the financial statements... The accompanying consolidated financial statements do not give effect to all adjustments to the carrying value of assets, or amounts and classification of liabilities that might be necessary as a consequence of these bankruptcy proceedings... [C]ertain litigation claims have been filed against the Company, the outcome of which are uncertain at this time. Because of the possible material effect of the matters discussed in the preceding paragraphs, we are unable to express, and we do not express, an opinion on the consolidated financial statements...*

The need for independent audits resulted from the emergence of the corporate form of business and the resulting separation of ownership and management. A significant proportion of the productive activity in the United States is conducted by publicly held corporations; that is, by corporations whose securities are sold to the general public. The stockholders who own the corporations are primarily investors and are generally not involved in enterprise operations. These investor-owners rely on management to operate the business and report periodically on the performance and financial status of the enterprise. Those companies registered nationally with the Securities and Exchange Commission are *required* to have an annual independent audit as an assurance to the stockholders.

Management has control over the information reported to stockholders and other external users and is responsible for the content of the financial statements. A statement emphasizing this responsibility is included in the annual report to stockholders, as illustrated for The Procter & Gamble Company in Exhibit 1—3. Management is also accountable for the profitability and financial condition of the enterprise as reflected in the statements. Obviously, there is a motivation on the part of management to present the financial information in the most favorable manner possible. It is the responsibility of the auditors to review management's reports and to independently decide if the reports are indeed representative of the actual conditions existing within the enterprise. The auditor's opinion adds credibility to the financial statements of enterprises, whether large or small, or privately or publicly held.

8. See also the auditor's report that accompanies the financial statements of Microsoft Corporation, reproduced in Appendix A at the end of the book.

Exhibit 1-2 The Procter & Gamble Company—Auditors' Report

Report Of Independent Accountants

Deloitte & Touche

250 East Fifth Street
Cincinnati, Ohio 45202

To the Board of Directors and Shareholders of The Procter & Gamble Company:

We have audited the accompanying consolidated balance sheets of The Procter & Gamble Company and subsidiaries as of June 30, 1993 and 1992, and the related consolidated statements of earnings, retained earnings, and cash flows for each of the three years in the period ended June 30, 1993. These financial statements are the responsibility of the companies' management. Our responsibility is to express an opinion on these financial statements based on our audits.

We conducted our audits in accordance with generally accepted auditing standards. Those standards require that we plan and perform the audits to obtain reasonable assurance about whether the financial statements are free of material misstatement. An audit includes examining, on a test basis, evidence supporting the amounts and disclosures in the financial statements. An audit also includes assessing the accounting principles used and significant estimates made by management, as well as evaluating the overall financial statement presentation. We believe that our audits provide a reasonable basis for our opinion.

In our opinion, the financial statements referred to above present fairly, in all material respects, the financial position of the companies at June 30, 1993 and 1992, and the results of their operations and their cash flows for each of the three years in the period ended June 30, 1993, in conformity with generally accepted accounting principles.

As discussed in Note 1 to the financial statements, effective July 1, 1992, the Company changed its methods of accounting for other post retirement benefits and income taxes.

Deloitte & Touche

August 10, 1993

Exhibit 1-3 The Procter & Gamble Company—Statement of Management Responsibility

Responsibility For The Financial Statements

The financial statements of The Procter & Gamble Company and its subsidiaries are the responsibility of, and have been prepared by, the Company in accordance with generally accepted accounting principles. To help insure the accuracy and integrity of its financial data, the Company has developed and maintains internal accounting controls which are designed to provide reasonable assurances that transactions are executed as authorized and accurately recorded, and that assets are properly safeguarded. These controls are monitored by an extensive program of internal audits.

The financial statements have been audited by the Company's independent public accountants, Deloitte & Touche. Their report is shown on the following page.

The Board of Directors has an Audit Committee composed entirely of outside Directors. The Committee meets periodically with representatives of Deloitte & Touche and financial management to review accounting, control, auditing, and financial reporting matters. To help assure the independence of the public accountants, Deloitte & Touche regularly meets privately with the Audit Committee.

Other Services Provided by CPAs

In addition to performing independent audits, CPAs assist clients in **tax planning** and reporting to various government entities. CPAs also function as management consultants, offering advice to clients in such areas as systems design, organization, personnel, finance, internal control, and employee benefits. These services are frequently referred to as **management advisory services.** Various accounting services are also provided for smaller, privately owned businesses.

Slow growth in the market for audit services has caused public accounting firms to earn an increasing share of their revenue doing consulting work. In fact, it has been suggested, only partly in jest, that the large accounting firms are becoming consulting firms which do a little auditing on the side. Increased consulting is both good and bad: consulting work typically is more profitable than are traditional audit services, but the sight of auditors doing consulting for the same clients they audit has caused some to question the independence of the auditor.

The Practice of Public Accounting

CPAs practice either individually or in firms. Because of the importance of personal liability for professional conduct, public accounting firms are generally organized as either proprietorships or partnerships. Most state laws now permit CPAs to be organized as professional corporations. These corporations provide many of the benefits of the corporate structure, but still retain personal liability for the professionals involved.

Almost all big, publicly held corporations are audited by a few large CPA firms. Listed in alphabetical order, the six largest firms are Arthur Andersen & Co.; Coopers & Lybrand; Deloitte & Touche; Ernst & Young; KPMG Peat Marwick; and Price Waterhouse & Co. Each of these firms is an international organization with many offices in the United States and abroad.

Many small businesses and nonprofit entities are serviced by regional and local CPA firms, including a large number of sole practitioners. In these firms, the role of auditing is often less important than the areas of tax reporting and planning and systems consulting. A CPA in a smaller firm is expected to be something of an accounting generalist, as opposed to the more specialized positions of CPAs in large regional and national firms.

No discussion of the public accounting profession in the 1990s is complete without treatment of the legal liability crisis. Litigation against public accountants is not a new concern; the number of suits filed against accountants during the 1970s and 1980s exceeded the number filed in the entire previous history of the profession. What is new is the astronomical amounts of the judgments levied against auditors. Among the most notorious of these is the $338 million jury verdict handed down in May 1992 against the auditor of United Bank of Arizona. In 1987, Standard Chartered, a British bank, acquired the Arizona bank and then discovered that some of the bank's large loans were uncollectible. In the classic American tradition, the British bank sued the auditor and won. The jury verdict has subsequently been thrown out on appeal and a new trial ordered, but the possibilities suggested by the $338 million amount have sent a chill through the accounting profession. The boxed item on page 10 discusses auditor liability in more detail.

THE DEVELOPMENT OF ACCOUNTING STANDARDS

Accounting principles and procedures have evolved over hundreds of years. The formal standard-setting process that exists today, however, has developed in the past fifty years. Because accounting grew so rapidly with the advent of the Industrial Revolution, accounting procedures were often developed without extended debate or discussion. Accountants developed methods that seemed to meet the needs of their respective companies, resulting in diverse procedures among companies in accounting for similar activities. The comparability of the resulting financial reports, therefore, was often questionable.

During the 1920s, these differences led to financial statements that were often inflated in value. Market values of stocks rose higher than the underlying real values warranted until the entire structure collapsed in the stock market crash of 1929. The government of the United States attacked the ensuing depression and, among other things, created the Securities and Exchange Commission (SEC). This new agency was given the responsibility to protect the interests of investors by ensuring full and fair disclosure in the regulation of the capital markets. The broad power granted to the SEC by Congress will be more fully discussed in a separate section. The emergence of the SEC forced the accounting profession in the U.S. to unite and to become more diligent in developing accounting principles and ethics to govern the profession. This led over time to the formation of several different private sector organizations, each having the responsibility of issuing accounting standards. These organizations, their publications, and the time they were in existence are identified in Exhibit 1—4 and discussed in subsequent sections of the chapter.

In the previous pages, three important groups that are involved with general-purpose financial statements were identified: users, managers of business enterprises, and independent auditors. As has been demonstrated, each of these groups has its own specific function to perform in the complex business environment that constitutes our economy. In many instances, these functions may be in conflict with each other. This condition provides another reason for the establishment of accounting standards—to resolve those different points of view that lead to different accounting methods being applied in similar circumstances.

Standards are designed to help accountants apply consistent principles for different businesses. They are recognized by the profession as representing the generally accepted position of the profession, and must be followed in the preparation of financial statements unless circumstances warrant an exception to a standard. These standards are commonly referred to as **generally accepted accounting principles (GAAP).** If the management of an enterprise feels the circumstances do not warrant compliance with the standard, an exception can be taken. Under these circumstances, the auditor's report must clearly disclose the nature of and the reason for the exception in the financial statements.[9]

Financial Accounting Standards Board

The **Financial Accounting Standards Board (FASB)** is an independent organization consisting of seven full-time members drawn from professional accounting, business, government, and academia. The members are required to sever all connections with their firms or institutions prior to assuming membership on the Board. Members are appointed for five-year terms and are eligible for reappointment to one additional term. Headquartered in Norwalk, Connecticut, the Board has its own research staff and had an operating fund exceeding $15 million in 1992.

Exhibit 1—4 U.S. Accounting Standard-Setting Bodies

Standard-Setting Body	Date	Authoritative Publications
AICPA Committee on Accounting Procedure	1939-1959	Accounting Research Bulletins
Accounting Principles Board	1959-1973	APB Opinions
Financial Accounting Standards Board	1973-present	Statements of Financial Accounting Standards Interpretations

9. American Institute of Certified Public Accountants, *Code of Professional Conduct,* Rule 203.

Public Accounting and Legal Liability

During 1991, the Big Six public accounting firms paid $477 million to settle and defend against lawsuits. This amount equaled nine percent of total U.S. accounting and auditing revenues for these firms. And the amounts continue to climb. In May 1992, Price Waterhouse was hit with a $338 million judgment in the United Bank of Arizona case. Fortunately for the partners of Price Waterhouse, this judgment was reversed on appeal. Not so fortunate was the firm of Ernst & Young, which, in November 1992, agreed to pay $400 million to settle claims that it had improperly audited a number of failed savings and loan institutions. As of August 1992, it was estimated that the public accounting profession faced a total of $30 billion in damage claims.

Critics of public accounting hail these judgments. Stephen Gillers, a professor of legal ethics at New York University, said: "This represents a new magnitude of exposure for professional firms. Now maybe we'll get auditors who audit." Defenders of the profession suggest that the large judgments against auditors are not a sign of negligence, but instead a sign that investors who have lost money will bring suit against anyone with "deep pockets" to pay. In addition, auditors suffer because the public mistakenly perceives an audit as a guarantee that the audited firm is solvent, well managed, and free of fraud.

Not surprisingly, as a result of these large judgments against auditors, audit fees are going up. Forty percent of CPA firms are operating without legal liability insurance because the premiums have skyrocketed, tripling since 1985 for some firms. Because of the liability risk, some companies are finding it difficult to hire a public accounting firm willing to perform an audit. Companies having particular difficulty finding an auditor are small banks and companies preparing to issue stock for the first time.

The auditing profession is anxiously seeking a solution to this liability crisis, but none has been found to date. Some of the possibilities being considered are as follows:

- **Proportionate liability.** Auditors are typically found jointly and severally liable for losses suffered by investors. Joint and several liability means that if the auditor is found one percent responsible for a $100 million loss, but those responsible for the other 99% (i.e., the failed company's management and board of directors) are unable to pay, then the "deep pockets" auditor must come up with the whole $100 million. Proportionate liability would limit an auditor's obligation to the appropriate share of the total loss.
- **Quasi-limited liability.** CPA firms are required by law in many states to be organized as partnerships. This means that all of the partners are legally liable for the damages caused by the actions of one partner. An alternative, currently allowable in a few states like Texas, is to organize as a limited liability partnership (LLP). In an LLP, each partner has unlimited liability for the general debts of the business, but is not responsible for legal liabilities associated with the negligent actions of other partners.
- **Trade-off with the federal authorities.** Many members of Congress, most conspicuously Representative Ron Wyden of Oregon, have issued calls for the auditors to be required to report any fraud they discover to the approriate legal authorities. The auditing profession has generally opposed this proposal, but a grand compromise might involve increased fraud detection duties for auditors in exchange for limited immunity from lawsuits.

Questions:

1. The public mistakenly perceives an audit as a guarantee that the audited firm is solvent, well managed, and free of fraud. What assurance is actually given by an unqualified audit opinion?
2. Why might an audit firm shy away from auditing a small bank or a company preparing to issue stock for the first time?
3. As an investor, would you place more reliance on financial statements audited by a firm organized as an ordinary partnership or as a limited liability partnership? Why?

Sources:

"The Liability Crisis in the United States: Impact on the Accounting Profession." A Statement of Position by Arthur Andersen & Co., Coopers & Lybrand, Deloitte & Touche, Ernst & Young, KPMG Peat Marwick, and Price Waterhouse. August 6, 1992.

Kelley Holland and Larry Light. "Big Six Firms are Firing Clients." *Business Week*, March 1, 1993, p. 76.

John H. Cushman, Jr. "$400 Million Paid by S.& L. Auditors, Settling U.S. Case." *The New York Times*, November 24, 1992.

Funding for the FASB is obtained through the **Financial Accounting Foundation (FAF),** an organization that is also responsible for selecting members of the FASB and its Advisory Council. (See Exhibit 1—5 for the Financial Accounting Foundation organization

Exhibit 1—5 Financial Accounting Foundation Organizational Chart

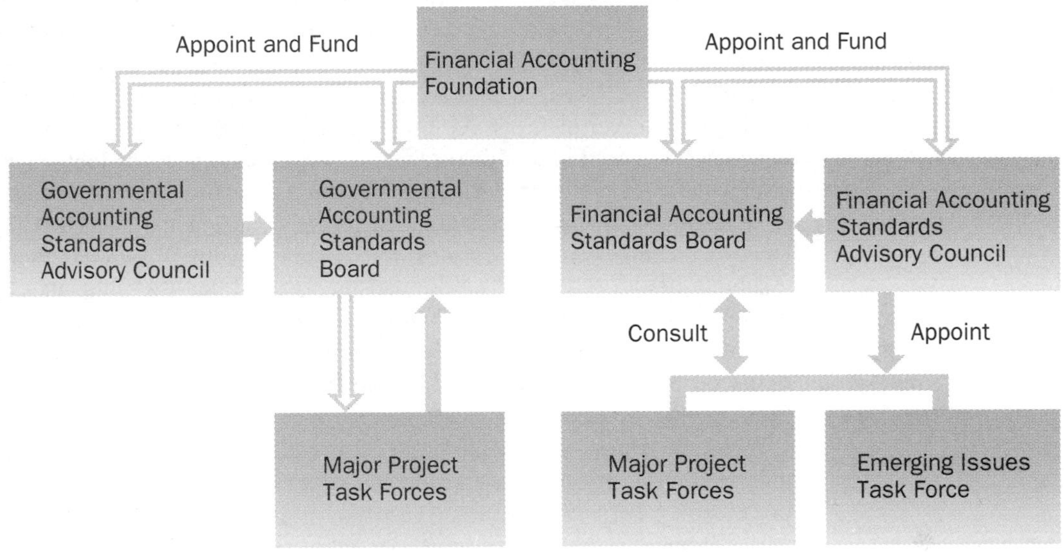

chart.) The **Financial Accounting Standards Advisory Council** consults with the Board on major policy questions, selects task forces to work on specific major projects, and conducts such other activities as may be requested by the FASB. The Foundation is administered by a Board of Trustees whose 16 members are made up of representatives from the accounting profession, the business world, government, and academia. In 1992, Trustees of the Foundation included chief executive officers from three of the Big Six accounting firms, vice presidents of Citicorp and General Electric, the comptroller of the state of Tennessee and the attorney general of Illinois, and William H. Beaver, a noted accounting professor from Stanford University.

In addition to funding and overseeing the FASB, the FAF is also responsible for selecting and supporting members of the **Governmental Accounting Standards Board (GASB).** The GASB was established in 1984 and sets financial accounting standards for state and local government entities.

The Standard-Setting Process

The major function of the FASB is to study accounting issues and establish accounting standards. These standards are published as **Statements of Financial Accounting Standards.** The FASB also issues **Statements of Financial Accounting Concepts.** The concepts identified in the statements are intended as guides for establishing standards. That is, they provide a framework within which specific accounting standards can be developed.[10]

Because the actions of the FASB have an impact on many individuals and groups within the economy, the Board follows a standard-setting process that is open to public observation and participation. The Board separates the topics it deals with into two areas: (1) Major Projects and (2) Implementation and Practice Problems. The process for the first area is very

10. The conceptual framework of the FASB is discussed fully in Chapter 2.

extensive and often requires from two to four years or more to complete. For example, significant events in the development of FASB Statement No. 87, "Employers' Accounting for Pensions," issued in 1985, and FASB Statement No. 106, "Employers' Accounting for Postretirement Benefits Other Than Pensions," issued in 1990, are listed in Exhibit 1—6.

Controversial issues, such as accounting for pensions, generate extensive debate and lobbying on the part of firms. As might be expected, the lobbying behavior of firms for and against proposed accounting standards is not random; firms lobby against standards that they perceive will have a negative impact on their financial statements. For example, 218 industrial companies that submitted letters opposing the FASB's 1982 Preliminary Views document relating to pensions were compared with 582 similar companies that did not submit opposing letters. The comparison revealed that the companies opposed to the proposed pension accounting standard were more likely to be adversely affected by it (in terms of lower earnings or higher liabilities). One letter read: "Including the net pension liability on the balance sheet...could result in even higher borrowing costs and possibly jeopardize loan covenants and other regulatory requirements."[11]

While the sixteen years required to complete the pensions project exceed the normal period for Major Projects, this example illustrates how difficult it is to resolve some of the more complex accounting issues. The process for the second area, Implementation and Practice Problems, though still subject to public input, is designed for completion within a six- to twelve-month period.

Major Projects. For each major project undertaken by the Board, a task force of outside experts is appointed to study the existing literature. When available literature is deemed insufficient, additional research is conducted. Subsequently, the Board issues a **Discussion Memorandum** that identifies the principal issues involved with the topic. This document includes a discussion of the various points of view as to the resolution of the issues, but does not include specific conclusions. An extensive bibliography is usually included. Readers of the discussion memorandum are invited to comment either in writing or orally at a public hearing. Sometimes a topic is not identified well enough to issue a discussion memorandum, and the FASB issues a preliminary document identified as an "Invitation to Comment." The topic is briefly discussed in the document, and readers are encouraged to send their comments to the FASB for more definite formulation of specific issues.

Exhibit 1—6
Significant Events in the Development of FASB Statements No. 87, "Employers' Accounting for Pensions," and No. 106, "Employers' Accounting for Postretirement Benefits Other Than Pensions"

1974	Pensions added to FASB agenda
1975	Task force appointed
1975	Discussion Memorandum #1 issued
1976	Public hearing #1 held
1977	Exposure Draft #1 issued
1979	Exposure Draft #1 revised; other postretirement benefits added to project
1980	FASB background paper issued
1981	Discussion Memorandum #2 issued
1981	Public hearing #2 held
1982	Preliminary Views document issued
1983	Supplement to Discussion Memorandum #2 issued
1984	Public hearing #3 held; other postretirement benefits made a separate project
1985	Exposure Draft #2 issued
1985	Public hearing #4 held
1985	Statement No. 87 issued in December
1989	Exposure Draft on other postretirement benefits issued and public hearing held
1990	Statement No. 106 issued in December

11. Jere R. Francis. "Lobbying Against Proposed Accounting Standards: The Case of Employers' Pension Accounting," *Journal of Accounting and Public Policy*, (Spring 1987), p. 35.

After a Discussion Memorandum has been issued and comments from interested parties have been evaluated, the Board meets as many times as necessary to resolve the issues. These meetings are open to the public, and the agenda is published in advance. From these meetings, the Board develops an **Exposure Draft** of a Statement that includes specific recommendations for financial accounting and reporting. Prior to 1991, a majority of the 7-member board (4 members) was the minimum requirement for approval of an exposure draft or a final statement of standards. This requirement was changed effective January 1, 1991, to a minimum approval of 5 members, or to what has been referred to as a "super majority."[12] After the exposure draft has been issued, reaction to the new document is again requested from the accounting and business community. At the end of the exposure period, usually 60 days or more, all comment papers are reviewed by the staff and the Board. Further deliberation by the Board leads to either the issuance of a **Statement of Financial Accounting Standards,** to a revised Exposure Draft, or in some cases to abandonment of the project.

The final statement not only sets forth the actual standards, but also establishes the effective date and method of transition, and gives pertinent background information and the basis for the Board's conclusions, including reasons for rejecting significant alternative solutions. If any members dissent from the majority view, they may include the reasons for their dissent as part of the document.

Implementation and Practice Problems. The second category of issues dealt with by the Board involves implementation and practice problems that relate to previously issued standards. Depending on the nature of a problem, the Board may issue a Statement of Financial Accounting Standards or an **Interpretation of a Statement of Financial Accounting Standards.** The interpretation may be issued without appointing a task force, issuing a Discussion Memorandum, or holding public hearings. Exposure of these publications, however, to either the public or the Advisory Council is required as part of the due process followed by the Board.

Problems that arise in practice are also addressed in **Technical Bulletins** prepared and issued by the staff of the FASB. The Bulletins, which are reviewed by the Board prior to being issued, provide guidance for particular situations that arise in practice.

Emerging Issues Task Force. The long-term nature of the standard-setting process has been one of the principal points of criticism of the FASB. There seems to be no alternative to the lengthy process, however, given the philosophy that arriving at a consensus among members of the accounting profession and other interested parties is important to the Board's credibility.

In an effort to overcome this criticism and provide more timely guidance on issues, in 1984 the FASB established the **Emerging Issues Task Force (EITF).** The Task Force assists the FASB in the early identification of emerging issues that affect financial reporting. Members of the EITF include the senior technical partners of the major national CPA firms plus representatives from major associations of preparers of financial statements, such as the Institute of Management Accountants (IMA) and the Financial Executives Institute (FEI). They meet approximately every six weeks.

As an emerging issue is discussed, an attempt is made to arrive at a consensus treatment for the issue. If no more than two members disagree with a position, a consensus is reached that defines the generally accepted accounting treatment until the FASB considers

12. A number of close 4-3 votes that resulted in standards not favored by many businesspeople led to strong pressure on the Financial Accounting Foundation to change the voting requirements. Although not favored by members of the FASB, the change was made in 1990.

the issue. The EITF not only helps the FASB and its staff to better understand emerging issues, but in some cases the Task Force determines that no immediate FASB action is necessary because a diversity in practice is not likely to evolve.[13]

Abstracts of the FASB Emerging Issues Task Force are published periodically—the *Journal of Accountancy* includes a regular "EITF Update" section. The abstracts are identified by a two-part number; the first part represents the year the issue was discussed, and the second part identifies the issue number for that year. As of March 15, 1992, 157 EITF Consensuses were outstanding, ranging from 84-18, "Stock Option Pyramiding," to 91-1, "Hedging Intercompany Foreign Currency Risks."[14] Although many of the issues are very specialized by topic and industry, the importance of the EITF to the standard-setting process cannot be overemphasized. Because discussions rarely last more than a day or two, and a consensus is reached on a majority of the issues discussed, timely guidance is provided to the accounting profession without the often lengthy due process of the FASB.

The standard-setting procedures of the FASB are intended to help accomplish its mission, which is to establish and improve standards of financial accounting and reporting. The credibility of the Board has fluctuated through the years as different issues have been resolved. The FASB has no legislative power, but must depend on the general acceptance of its pronouncements by the accounting profession and other interested groups. This acceptability is directly influenced by two other organizations: the AICPA and the SEC.

American Institute of Certified Public Accountants

The **American Institute of Certified Public Accountants (AICPA)** is the professional organization of practicing CPAs in the United States. The organization was founded in 1887, and it publishes a monthly journal, the *Journal of Accountancy*. Membership in the AICPA is voluntary, and over 300,000 CPAs are members. The AICPA has several important responsibilities, including standard-setting, quality control, and certification and continuing education for CPAs.

Standard-Setting Responsibilities. Prior to the formation of the FASB, accounting principles were established under the direction of the AICPA. From 1939-1959, principles were formed by the AICPA's **Committee on Accounting Procedure (CAP).** Their pronouncements were known as **Accounting Research Bulletins (ARBs).** From 1959 to 1973, accounting principles were formed by another AICPA committee, the **Accounting Principles Board (APB),** and issued as **Opinions.** Dissatisfaction with the part-time nature of these committees, their failure to react quickly to some issues, and the lack of broad representation on the committees because of their direct relationship to the AICPA led to the formation of the FASB in 1973.

Although the FASB replaced the APB as the official standard-setting body for the profession, the AICPA continues to influence the establishment of accounting standards through its issuance of **Accounting and Audit Guides** and **Statements of Position (SOPs).** The Guides are issued by specially appointed committees of the AICPA and relate to specific industries, such as construction, insurance, banking, and real estate. These Guides contain information concerning the auditing of these entities, and also discuss alternative accounting methods that may be employed by the industry. The Guides often recommend a preferred accounting method. The SOPs were issued by the Accounting Standards Executive Committee (AcSEC), an AICPA committee established when the FASB assumed the standard-setting role. SOPs often dealt with emerging issues that had

13. *EITF Abstracts*, October 26, 1989 (Norwalk: Financial Accounting Standards Board, 1989), p. i.
14. "Financial Accounting: EITF Update," *Journal of Accountancy*, May 1992, p. 103.

not yet been placed on the FASB agenda but needed to be addressed by the profession for improved comparability in financial reporting.

The FASB became concerned about this growing volume of "other" standards, and in 1979 adopted the Guides and SOPs as officially preferred accounting principles subject to their review and possible subsequent issuance as FASB Statements.[15] Beginning in the early 1980s, many specialized industry guides were adopted as FASB standards. (See list of FASB standards in Appendix C of the text). Although SOPS are now being issued only to amend audit guides, AcSEC still helps the FASB identify emerging issues and communicates the concerns of CPAs on accounting issues to the FASB. Thus, the AICPA continues to influence the establishment of accounting standards.

In addition to influencing the establishment of accounting standards, the AICPA assumes direct responsibility for the establishment of auditing standards. The Auditing Standards Board is a part-time board composed of members from public accounting practice with responsibility for establishing guidelines for the proper conduct of audits.

Quality Control. The AICPA is also concerned with maintaining the integrity of the profession through its Code of Professional Conduct and through a quality control program that includes a process of peer review of CPA firms conducted by other CPAs. Although membership in the AICPA traditionally has been individual, the influence of the firm has become increasingly important. In the late 1970s, the AICPA instituted a firm membership in one of two sections: (1) the **SEC Practice Section (SECPS)** for firms that have clients subject to government regulation through the Securities and Exchange Commission (SEC), and (2) the **Private Companies Practice Section (PCPS)** for firms that do not have clients regulated by the SEC. The SEC practice firms are subject to more stringent regulation than the private companies practice firms, although a high quality of performance is expected of all firms.

In late 1989, the AICPA membership voted by a more than six-to-one margin to make membership in the SECPS a requirement for all firms that audit any companies that are SEC registrants. Before this vote, membership in both sections was voluntary. A firm may belong to both sections, and most of the larger firms do. Both sections require periodic peer reviews of all its members. In addition, since 1988, the AICPA has required a quality review program of all its members. While this review is not as extensive as a peer review, it is designed to upgrade the quality of work done in the profession. Thus, those members without SEC clients who do not join the PCPS must still submit to periodic quality reviews.

The quality review requirement was only one of several requirements approved by the AICPA membership to address an issue that arose primarily in the 1980s referred to as the "expectation gap." This gap is identified as the difference between how users of financial statements interpreted the auditor's responsibilities and how auditors themselves viewed their responsibilities. Users felt auditors should alert them earlier to a firm's financial difficulties, and thus protect their investments from loss. The auditing profession addressed this problem and issued a group of ten new auditing standards in mid-1988 to identify more clearly the auditor's responsibilities for detection of fraud, evaluation of a company's internal control, and identification of companies unlikely to be able to continue operations.

As part of its quality control and peer review programs, the AICPA established the Public Oversight Board in 1977. The Board is an independent body composed of "prominent individuals of high integrity and reputation." In 1993, the five members of the Board

15. *Statement of Financial Accounting Standards No. 32,* "Specialized Accounting and Reporting Principles and Practices in AICPA Statements of Position and Guides on Accounting and Auditing Matters" (Stamford: Financial Accounting Standards Board, 1979).

were: A.A. Sommer, Jr., former Commissioner of the SEC; Robert K. Mautz, professor emeritus of the University of Illinois and the University of Michigan; Robert F. Froehlke, former Secretary of the Army; Melvin Laird, former Secretary of Defense; and Paul W. McCracken, former Chairman of the President's Council of Economic Advisers. This Board issued a special report in 1993 outlining what it views as crucial issues facing the accounting profession and warranting the attention of business groups and government agencies.[16] These issues are:

1. Auditor legal liability and the need for litigation reform.
2. The need for improved peer review and quality control in the accounting profession to avoid imposition of government regulation.
3. Improvement in financial accounting and auditing standards to bring financial reporting more in line with what the public expects.
4. In order to enhance public confidence, increased professionalism among accountants and increased willingness by auditors to uncover fraud.

Certification and Continuing Education. Another important function of the AICPA is preparation and grading of the Uniform CPA examination. This examination is given simultaneously in all fifty states and the U.S. territories twice each year—in May and November.

To emphasize the importance of good writing skills to a practicing accountant, portions of the CPA exam are graded for both technical content and written quality. Writing samples are judged on the following six criteria: coherent organization, conciseness, clarity, use of standard English, sticking to the point, and appropriately writing for the intended audience.[17]

One controversy that has perenially surrounded the CPA examination is that graduating students spend their final semester cramming for the May CPA exam and ignoring their academic coursework. Professors teaching seniors graduating in accounting are met with apathy when they try to discuss open-ended, conceptual issues because students doubt that those things will be on the CPA exam. One suggested way to keep student attention focused on their academic coursework until after graduation is to require candidates for the CPA exam to complete their education before applying to take the exam.[18] This means that someone graduating from college in May would not be able to take the exam until the following November. Such a requirement has already passed in some states.

In addition to passing the examination, an individual must meet the state education and experience requirements in order to obtain state certification as a CPA. Most states now require CPAs to meet continuing education requirements in order to retain their licenses to practice. The AICPA assists its members in meeting these requirements through an extensive Continuing Professional Education (CPE) program that includes courses offered throughout the United States.

Securities and Exchange Commission

The **Securities and Exchange Commission (SEC)** was created by an act of Congress in 1934. Its primary role is to regulate the issuance and trading of securities by corporations to the general public. Prior to offering securities for sale to the public, a company must file

16. "In the Public Interest: A Special Report by the Public Oversight Board of the SEC Practice Section, AICPA," (Stamford, CT: Public Oversight Board, March 5, 1993).

17. Susan Menelaides, "Writing Skills: What They're Looking For," *Journal of Accountancy*, October, 1991, p. 39.

18. Accounting Education Change Commission (AECC), "AECC Urges Decoupling of Academic Studies and Professional Accounting Examination Preparation: Issues Statement No. 2," *Issues in Accounting Education*, Fall 1991, p. 313.

a registration statement with the Commission that contains financial and organizational disclosures. In addition, all publicly held companies are required to furnish annual and other periodic information to the Commission and to have their external financial statements examined by independent accountants.

The Commission's intent is not to prevent the trading of speculative securities, but to insist that investors have adequate information. As a result, the SEC is vitally interested in financial reporting and the development of accounting standards. The Commission carefully monitors the standard-setting process and responds to Discussion Memorandums and Exposure Drafts issued by the FASB. The Commission also brings to the Board's attention emerging problems that need to be addressed and sends observers to meet with the Emerging Issues Task Force.

When the Commission was formed, Congress gave it power to establish accounting principles as follows:

The Commission may prescribe, in regard to reports made pursuant to this title, the form or forms in which the required information shall be set forth, the items or details to be shown in the balance sheet and the earning statement, and the methods to be followed in the preparation of reports, in the appraisal or valuation of assets and liabilities . . .[19]

The Commission has generally refrained from fully using these powers, preferring to work through the private sector in the development of standards. Throughout its existence, however, the Commission has issued statements pertaining to accounting and auditing issues. Most of them are quite specific in nature and deal with a particular company or a specific situation. At present, SEC statements are referred to as either **Financial Reporting Releases (FRRs)** or **Accounting and Auditing Enforcement Releases (AAERs).** Prior to 1982, they were referred to as **Accounting Series Releases (ASRs).** Although the SEC is generally supportive of the FASB, there have been disagreements between the two bodies. One of the most public of these disagreements occurred in the late 1970s and concerned the accounting for oil and gas exploratory costs. The FASB issued a standard in 1977, the SEC publicly opposed the standard, and the FASB finally succumbed to the pressure and reversed its position in 1979. (See Statements No. 19 and 25 in the list of FASB Statements in Appendix C.) In recent years, the SEC and FASB have increased their efforts at behind-the-scenes coordination and consultation.

What is GAAP?

With all of these different bodies (FASB, EITF, AICPA, and SEC) establishing accounting standards, what is GAAP? The Auditing Standards Board of the AICPA has defined GAAP in the context of the phrase included in the auditor's opinion: "present fairly. . . in conformity with generally accepted accounting principles."[20] The hierarchy of pronouncements is as follows:

1. FASB Statements and Interpretations, APB Opinions, and CAP Accounting Research Bulletins.
2. FASB Technical Bulletins, AICPA Industry Audit and Accounting Guides, and AICPA Statements of Position.
3. Consensus positions of the FASB Emerging Issues Task Force and AICPA Practice Bulletins.
4. AICPA accounting interpretations, "Question and Answer" guides published by the FASB staff, and other widely recognized industry practices.

19. Securities Exchange Act of 1934, Section 13(b).

20. *Statement of Auditing Standards No. 69,* "The Meaning of Present Fairly in Conformity With Generally Accepted Accounting Principles in the Independent Auditor's Report," (New York: AICPA, December 1991).

For firms required to file financial statements with the SEC, the SEC rules and interpretive releases have the same authority as the standards listed in category (1). The pronouncements in category (1) are of particular importance to auditors because Rule 203 of the AICPA Code of Professional Conduct specifies that an auditor must not express an unqualified opinion where there is a material departure from category (1) pronouncements.

American Accounting Association

The **American Accounting Association** is primarily an organization for accounting academicians, although practicing professional accountants also belong in large numbers. The oldest regular publication of the AAA is a quarterly research journal, *The Accounting Review*. It has been published since 1926. In 1983, a second journal was added, *Issues in Accounting Education*. Although this educator's journal began as an annual publication, it is now published semiannually. Beginning in March 1987, the AAA began publishing another quarterly general-audience journal, *Accounting Horizons*. This newest journal is designed to address issues of wide interest to both educators and practitioners that stress real-world accounting problems and practices and thus attract a wider readership than *The Accounting Review*.

Several specialized sections have been organized within the AAA, and many of these also publish journals. Accounting academicians are very interested in the development of accounting standards. They have the unique position of being professionals not directly involved with the preparation or audit of financial statements. Thus, they are able to consider objectively the needs of users as well as business enterprises and auditors. The AAA was instrumental in encouraging development by the FASB of a conceptual framework for accounting that would assist in the development of standards to govern financial reporting. AAA committee members review FASB Discussion Memorandums and Exposure Drafts and respond to the proposals of the FASB. Individual members of the association participate actively in research projects that are used by the FASB as the basis for many of its recommendations.[21]

The members of the American Accounting Association hold many different opinions and points of view. One of the major roles of the AAA is to serve as a forum within which educators can express their views, either individually or in specially appointed committees. The AAA, however, does not claim to serve as a majority voice for accounting academicians and, until recently, had a firm policy against taking positions on accounting issues as an association. A new policy was adopted in 1988 that permits the Executive Committee of the AAA to take positions representing its membership as needed. The impact of the academic arm of accounting on the establishment of accounting standards has increased through the years, as evidenced by inclusion of an educator as a member of the FASB and the large number of educators included on FASB task forces and the FASB staff.

One of the most significant actions of the AAA in recent years is the formation of the **Accounting Education Change Commission (AECC).** The AECC was formed to facilitate improvements in accounting education. This is being done through the publication of reports and position statements urging a renewed commitment to quality classroom teaching by professors, and through the funding of innovative curriculum restructuring projects at various colleges and universities in the United States. Much of the AECC funding comes from the large public accounting firms.

21. Indicative of this type of research is the following report; Paul Pacter, Reporting Disaggregated Information (Norwalk: FASB, 1993).

Other Organizations

Although the preceding groups have traditionally exercised the most direct influence upon the regulation of accountants and the development of accounting principles, the influence of other groups has also been felt. Professional accountants from business enterprises are represented on the Board of Trustees of the Financial Accounting Foundation by two organizations, the **Financial Executives Institute (FEI)** and the **Institute of Management Accountants (IMA).**

The FEI is a national organization composed of financial executives employed by large corporations. The FEI membership includes treasurers, controllers, and financial vice-presidents. The FEI has sponsored several research projects through the years related to financial reporting problems.

The IMA is more concerned with the information needs of internal users than with external reporting. Its monthly publication, *Management Accounting*, has traditionally dealt mainly with problems involving information systems and the development and use of accounting data within the business organization. Those management accountants who pass a 2 1/2-day qualifying examination and meet specified experience requirements are designated as Certified Management Accountants (CMAs). Because a firm's information system usually provides data for both internal and external reporting, the IMA is also concerned about the activities of the FASB and responds to its invitations to comment on issues that are related to internal reporting.

The users of external financial reports are also represented on the Financial Accounting Foundation's Board of Trustees by two organizations. The **Financial Analysts Federation** represents the large number of analysts who advise the investing public on the meaning of the financial reports issued by America's businesses. Members of this group have often been critical of corporate financial reporting practices and have continually requested increased disclosure of pertinent financial data. The **Securities Industry Association** is the organization that represents the investment bankers who manage the portfolios of the large institutional investors that have affected the stock market so dramatically in the past decade. The large amount of investment capital controlled by insurance companies and banks has significantly diminished the influence of the small investor in the market. Institutional investors represent a major group of external users of financial information and have become increasingly vocal with regard to financial reporting and the establishment of accounting standards.

Although the preceding discussion of accounting standards has focused on reporting by business enterprises, the accounting profession is also concerned with the reporting by the numerous government institutions in our economy. This includes not only the Federal Government and its agencies, but also the large number of states, counties, and municipal governments. It is estimated that the total expenditures by these government organizations exceed 1.5 trillion dollars per year. Two government organizations were added to the list of sponsors of the FAF in 1984—the **National Association of State Auditors, Treasurers, and Controllers** and the **Government Finance Officers Association.** These organizations are especially interested in the standards issued by the **Governmental Accounting Standards Board,** a companion board to the FASB organized in 1984 to focus on reporting by the public sector of our economy. Although the statements issued by governmental organizations do not have a direct impact on investors, the magnitude of their impact on such vital economic factors as interest rates, tax policies, and employment rates cannot be ignored in any financial planning. Creditors are especially affected by the financial activities of governmental units that require funding through various forms of bonds and long-term notes.

Although the FASB and the GASB are independent boards, their jurisdictional bounds at times have been subject to much discussion. Some types of entities, such as hospitals and universities, exist in both the private and public (government) sectors of our economy. Because the FASB is responsible for establishing accounting standards for these institutions in the private sector, and the GASB is responsible for those in the government sector, a lack of comparability can exist on several issues. In 1989, the Financial Accounting Foundation decided that in these areas with conflicting jurisdictions, the FASB would govern. When the government sector objected strenuously to this proposal, the Foundation reversed itself and left the jurisdiction divided, with a commitment from the public sector to consider more carefully the problem of differing standards for essentially the same type of organization.

Another government unit of great interest to the accounting profession is the **Internal Revenue Service.** Although tax accounting and financial accounting impact one another only indirectly in most cases, the popular perception is that they are one and the same. However, it must be kept in mind that tax accounting and financial accounting were designed with different purposes in mind. In the Thor Power Tool Case (1979), the Supreme Court stated:

The primary goal of financial accounting is to provide useful information to management, shareholders, creditors, and others properly interested; the major responsibility of the accountant is to protect these parties from being misled. The primary goal of the income tax system, in contrast, is the equitable collection of revenue. . .

International Standard-Setting

When the value of a building increases, do accounting standards allow for the recording of the increased value? The answer to that question depends on the country in which it is asked. Is it allowable in the United Kingdom? Certainly. Australia? Yes. Turkey? Absolutely. The United States? No. This is just one of the many examples of diversity in accounting standards across the world. Other examples include goodwill accounting (many countries, including the United Kingdom, allow for the recording of goodwill as a subtraction from equity instead of as an asset) and inventory valuation (LIFO is an American invention and is much less common in other countries).

Just as the FASB establishes accounting standards for U.S. entities, other countries have their own standard-setting bodies. The international differences in standards create many reporting problems for foreign companies doing business in the United States and U.S. companies doing business abroad. In an attempt to harmonize conflicting standards, the International Accounting Standards Committee (IASC) was formed in 1973 to develop worldwide accounting standards. This body now represents more than 100 accountancy bodies from 75 countries. However, formation of a body to promote harmonization is quite different from actually achieving harmonization. Even within the European Community, where great progress has been made at dismantling trade barriers and creating a single market covering 19 countries and 380 million people, there is no reasonable prospect of quickly establishing a single set of common accounting standards.[22]

The SEC has thus far barred foreign companies from listing their shares on U.S. stock exchanges unless those companies agree to provide financial statements in accordance with U.S. GAAP. Disclosure requirements in the U.S. are the strictest in the world, and few foreign companies have submitted to the SEC requirement. Some market observers are predicting that this inability to list the shares of foreign companies will exclude U.S. exchanges from the global market and reduce them to the status of "regional exchanges."[23] Alternatively, pressure from these exchanges, and from the SEC, may be major factors leading to increased harmonization of international accounting standards.

22. Bob Hagerty. "Differing Accounting Rules Snarl Europe," *The Wall Street Journal*, September 4, 1992.
23. Gregg A. Jarrell. "SEC Crimps Big Board's Future," *The Wall Street Journal*, June 19, 1992, p. A12.

Who Hates the FASB?

Some things in life are constant: Texans complain about the summer heat, Minnesotans complain about the winter cold, voters complain about Congress, and accountants and businesspeople complain about the FASB. In recent years, the FASB has been criticized for overly complex deferred tax accounting, market value accounting leading to more volatile earnings, postretirement benefit accounting that has significantly increased reported liabilities, and difficult stock option accounting that many users think is unnecessary. Criticisms of the FASB fall under two general headings:

1. The standards are too theoretical and too costly to implement.
2. The standards negatively impact companies' bottom lines.

The FASB has made a great effort to address the first concern. Proposed standards are often field tested to ascertain how costly they will be to implement. Recent standards, like Statement No. 115 which requires recording most securities at market value, have included explicit discussion of the expected costs and benefits of the standard. The Board views the standard-setting process as a balancing act — balancing the desire to make financial reporting technically and theoretically sound against the need to avoid overly radical and costly changes in the current system.

Although business executives often oppose FASB standards in public by voicing practicality concerns, privately they are more worried about the standards' impact on reported performance. The Business Roundtable, a group of chief executives from 200 major U.S. corporations, complained that the negative impact of FASB standards on reported performance was hampering U.S. competitiveness in global markets. Some financial executives have run out of patience with the FASB and are ready to replace it, perhaps trusting the setting of accounting standards to Congress or the SEC. The FASB must continue to carefully walk the fine line between theory and practice in order to avoid the fate of its predecessors, the APB and the CAP.

Questions:

1. What reasons might a company have for opposing a new accounting standard?
2. What factors favor entrusting the setting of accounting standards to the SEC? To the FASB?
3. What do you think should be the FASB's most important consideration when setting accounting standards?

Sources:

Lee Berton, "Accounting Rules Board Is Under Fire As It Nears Decision on Two Key Issues," *The Wall Street Journal*, April 6, 1993, p. A2.

"A Visit to the FASB," *The CPA Journal*, January 1992, p. 40.

Letter from John S. Reed, Chairman of the Accounting Principles Task Force of The Business Roundtable, to Philip R. Lochner, Jr., Commissioner of the Securities and Exchange Commission: August 20, 1990.

CONFLICT BETWEEN PUBLIC AND PRIVATE SECTOR

As indicated previously, the SEC has historically left the standard-setting process to the private sector. The Commission's influence, however, has often been felt on specific issues. From time to time, Congress has urged the SEC to exercise a more direct role in setting financial accounting standards and in evaluating the independence and quality control of CPA firms. Over the past two decades, there have been many legal actions brought against CPA firms for failure to disclose fairly the financial condition of a company. These legal actions have become more common, and as they arise, Congress, through its committee structure, again raises difficult questions about whether the standard-setting system in the private sector is working for the benefit of the public.

In 1978 there were two significant congressional committees that conducted hearings concerning the accounting profession: the Metcalf Committee, chaired by Senator Lee Metcalf (Montana), and the Moss Committee, chaired by Representative John E. Moss (California). A Senate staff report entitled "The Accounting Establishment" was used extensively by the Metcalf committee as it probed such issues as the possible monopoly position of the largest U.S. accounting firms; the independence of auditors whose firms employ tax consultants and management advisory consultants who work directly with audit clients; and the poor quality of audit work being performed in some instances. Although no definite legislative action was taken, these committees attracted a great deal of attention from the profession, and several changes were made by the AICPA as a result of these hearings, including its establishment of the firm membership divisions. Also, as a result of these hearings, annual reports from the SEC on the auditing profession are now required by Congress. These reports have generally been positive; however, another increase in business failures in the mid and late 1980s, including many savings and loan failures, led to another round of hearings under the direction of Representative John Dingell of Michigan. The SEC commissioned a blue ribbon committee to study the issue of fraudulent financial reporting. Their report, known as the Treadway Report, made several specific recommendations to management, auditors, and educators to help detect and deter management fraud. The congressional Dingell Committee urged the various sectors to study the Treadway Report carefully, and generally agreed with the recommendations to improve audit quality.

Although much attention is paid to the audit function by these congressional committees, there also has been concern over the establishment of accounting standards. Critics of standard-setting in the private sector ask if it is realistic to assume that the profession can establish and administer standards and still retain an independent posture. Congress continues to prod the SEC to exercise a more active role in assuring that financial reporting is adequately measuring and disclosing the true status of companies and their activities. The FASB has responded to this pressure by its open discussion policy and its attempt to arrive at standards that balance theory and varying user needs.

Regardless of who sets accounting standards, the task is difficult. As will be discussed in the next chapter, there are very few absolutes in accounting principles. As evidenced by the voluminous tax legislation and the extreme difficulty in achieving tax simplification, passing the responsibility for accounting standardsetting to the SEC or a similar governmental agency would probably lead to even greater complexity in financial reporting. If accountants are to retain their role as professionals, they must be able to exercise judgment in applying general guidelines to specific problems. Financial statement users, managers of business enterprises, and professional auditors must balance their needs and views and continue to work toward more meaningful accounting and financial reporting. If these users cannot obtain meaningful reports through private sector organizations such as the FASB, there will be increased demand from the public through Congress to do it by legislation.

OVERVIEW OF INTERMEDIATE ACCOUNTING

This first chapter is designed to emphasize the importance of accounting and financial reporting in today's complex business environment and the challenges that face those who are members of the accounting profession. The remaining chapters of the text cover in depth the elements contained in the basic financial statements presented to external users. To help students realize that the issues discussed are not just textbook issues, extensive examples of actual businesses are included throughout the book.

Although there has been a growing body of standards that constitute GAAP, there are many unresolved areas. In some cases, the existing standards have been questioned, and recommendations for revision of the standards have been made. It is important that those who plan to enter the profession of accounting have a foundation as to not only what GAAP currently is, but also have a theoretical understanding of why it developed to its present state.

KEY TERMS

Accounting 3
Accounting and Audit Guides 14
Accounting and Auditing Enforcement Releases (AAERs) 17
Accounting Education Change Commission (AECC) 18
Accounting Principles Board (APB) 14
Accounting Research Bulletins (ARBs) 14
Accounting Series Releases (ASRs) 17
American Accounting Association (AAA) 18
American Institute of Certified Public Accountants (AICPA) 14
Certified Public Accountants (CPAs) 5
Committee on Accounting Procedure (CAP) 14
Discussion Memorandum 12
Emerging Issues Task Force (EITF) 13
Exposure Draft 13
Financial accounting 5
Financial Accounting Foundation (FAF) 10
Financial Accounting Standards Advisory Council 11
Financial Accounting Standards Board (FASB) 9
Financial Analysts Federation 19
Financial Executives Institute (FEI) 19
Financial Reporting Releases (FRRs) 17
Generally accepted accounting principles (GAAP) 9
General-purpose financial statements 5
Governmental Accounting Standards Board (GASB) 11
Independent audit 5
Institute of Management Accountants (IMA) 19
Interpretation of a Statement of Financial Accounting Standards 13
Management accounting 4
Opinions 14
Private Companies Practice Section (PCPS) 15
Securities and Exchange Commission (SEC) 16
SEC Practice Section (SECPS) 15
Securities Industry Association 19
Statements of Financial Accounting Concepts 11
Statements of Financial Accounting Standards 11
Statements of Position (SOPs) 14
Technical Bulletins 13

QUESTIONS

1. Accounting has been defined as a service activity. Who is served by accounting and how are they benefited?
2. Accounting is sometimes characterized as dealing only with the past. Give three examples of how accounting information can be of value in dealing with the future.
3. How does the fact that there are limited resources in the world relate to accounting information?
4. Distinguish between management accounting and financial accounting.
5. Contrast the roles of an accountant and an auditor.
6. Why are independent audits necessary?
7. How has the merger of several large accounting firms improved the ability of these firms to deal with international clients?
8. What conditions led to the establishment of accounting standard-setting bodies?
9. What are the differences in purpose and scope of the FASB's Statements of Financial Accounting Standards, Statements of Financial Accounting Concepts, Interpretations of Statements of Financial Accounting Standards, and Technical Bulletins?
10. What characteristics of the standard-setting process are designed to increase the acceptability of standards established by the FASB?
11. (a) What role does the Emerging Issues Task Force play in establishing accounting standards? (b) Why can it meet this role more efficiently than the FASB?
12. What are the relationships of the AICPA and the AAA to the FASB?
13. What is the purpose of the AICPA peer review program and which firms are required to submit to such a review?
14. How does the SEC influence the accounting profession?
15. Why is standard setting such a difficult and complex task?
16. Why does Congress conduct hearings on the accounting profession? What type of legislation has been proposed to increase control over accounting?

DISCUSSION CASES

Case 1—1 (How should I invest?)

Recent projections suggest that members of the "baby boom" generation will inherit as much as $8 trillion from their parents. Assume that you just inherited $1 million. You are aware that numerous studies have shown that investments in equity securities (stocks) give the highest rate of return over the long run. However, you are not sure which companies you should invest in. You send for and receive the annual reports of several companies in three growth industries.

In making your investment decision, what useful information would you expect to find in:

(a) the balance sheet?
(b) the income statement?
(c) the statement of cash flows?

Case 1—2 (And then there were six!)

The existence of relatively few large CPA firms that service virtually all of the major industrial and financial companies and thus dominate the accounting profession has led to criticism through the years. During 1989, mergers among the large public accounting firms in the United States changed the Big Eight into the Big Six.

(a) What dangers do you see from the emergence of relatively few large CPA firms? What advantages?
(b) One reason offered for the mergers is that they improved the ability of merging firms to provide the broad array of consulting services that provide an increasing share of the revenues of the large accounting firms. What problems might intensify as public accounting firms earn an ever-larger share of their income from consulting?

Case 1—3 (What do users need?)

Emilio Valdez worked for several years as a loan analyst for a large bank. He recently left the bank and took a management position with Positron, a high-tech manufacturing firm. Emilio prepared for his first management meeting by extensively analyzing Positron's external financial statements. However, in the meeting, the other managers referred to lots of information that Emilio hadn't found in the financial statements. In addition to using the financial statements, the other managers were also using computer printouts and reports unlike anything Emilio had seen in his years at the bank. After the meeting, Monique Vo, one of Emilio's associates, offered the following advice: "Emilio, you have to remember that you are an internal user now, not an external user." What does Monique mean?

Case 1—4 (SEC: A necessary evil?)

Annette Wilson and Henry Wall were selected to compete with students from other universities in presenting a case dealing with the need for a government agency with oversight responsibility to monitor the quality of accounting in the private sector.

Prepare an outline showing the points you think Annette and Henry should make.

Case 1—5 (How can accounting standards be taught?)

The FASB issues statements of standards, statements of concepts, interpretations, positions, and technical bulletins. The FASB's Emerging Issues Task Force issues consensus statements. The SEC issues releases. The AICPA produces position statements and audit guides. With this proliferation of authoritative material, some see the practice of accounting becoming more like the practice of law.

Describe some of the difficulties in accounting education that are caused by the complex nature of accounting standards.

Case 1—6 (We aren't getting what we expect.)

Quality Enterprises Inc. issued its 1995 financial statements on February 22, 1996. The auditors expressed a "clean" opinion in the audit report. On July 14, 1996, the company filed for bankruptcy as a result of an inability to meet currently maturing long-term debt obligations. Reasons cited for the action include (1) large losses on inventory due to overproduction of product lines that did not sell, (2) failure to collect on a large account receivable due to the customer's bankruptcy, and (3) a deteriorating economic environment caused by a severe recession in the spring of 1996. Joan Stevens, a large stockholder of Quality, is concerned about the fact that a company with a clean audit opinion could have financial difficulty leading to bankruptcy just four months after the audit report was issued. "Where were the auditors?" she inquired. In reply, the auditors contend that on December 31, 1995, the date of the financial statements, the statements were presented in accordance with GAAP.

What is the auditor's responsibility for protecting users from losses? How does this case illustrate the "expectation gap" issue?

Case 1—7 (Does lobbying improve the quality of accounting standards?)

The "due process" system of the FASB encourages public input into the standard-setting process. Written comments are invited, public hearings are held, and proposed standards are often changed in response to this input. However, some observers have suggested that this process makes the setting of accounting standards less a technical exercise and more a political one. Parties are known to lobby for or against proposed standards according to their economic interests.

(a) How would accounting standard-setting be improved by eliminating lobbying?
(b) How would accounting standard-setting be harmed by eliminating lobbying?

Case 1—8 (But the IRS doesn't call it compensation!)

Business executives are frequently granted options to buy company stock at a stated price that often proves to be far below the increasing market price. One of the incentives for granting these options is a tax deferral on the difference between the option price and the market price until the stock is sold by the business executive. The accounting standards boards also encouraged this type of "deferred compensation" by not recognizing the stock price difference that occurred after the option was granted to the executive but before the option was exercised as compensation expense. In 1993, despite strong pressure from the business community, the FASB voted 5-2 to change the accounting rules and require this difference be recognized as an expense. Some business leaders indicated that the change was without merit, and threatened to withhold funding for the FASB. The board decided to review and perhaps revise the rule as a way to defuse the intense opposition to the standard.

What role should business lobby interests play in establishing accounting standards? Since the IRS granted tax deferral for such items, why shouldn't that decision also govern the accounting standards?

Case 1—9 (Let's expand our services.)

During the early 1990s, audit fees generated a lower percentage of a CPA firm's total revenue than in earlier decades. Increasing tax and consulting revenues accounted for some of this change, however, CPA firms also started offering new services to business clients. What services besides the basic three, auditing, tax, and consulting, are CPA firms beginning to offer? What business risks does a firm face by expanding beyond the traditional services? Should any limits be placed on the activities of CPA firms?

Case 1—10 (Let's play by the IRS rules)

At least three bodies in the United States have authority to establish accounting standards that govern the financial reporting for business entities. They are the FASB, the IRS, and the SEC. Conflicts between SEC requirements and FASB requirements must be resolved since companies must follow the SEC rules if they fall under its jurisdiction. Little attempt is made, however, to reconcile the accounting standard differences between the IRS and the FASB. These differences are recognized as arising from differences in the objectives of the two bodies. However, the existence of differences requires companies to keep two different sets of records in some areas; records that follow the FASB pronouncements and those that follow the IRS rules and regulations. The differences also created the need to introduce deferred income tax accounting in the United States to reflect the tax impacts of the different treatments.

In many foreign countries, such as Japan and Germany, the financial accounting standards closely follow the tax rules established by the respective legislatures. What applies for taxes often applies for the balance sheet and the income statement as well.

Should the United States follow the practice of many foreign competitors? What are the advantages of merging accounting for taxes and financial reporting? What are the disadvantages? What would it take to change a system so deeply ingrained in the business fabric of either the United States or other countries?

Case 1—11 (Why don't the accounting educators lead us?)

The American Accounting Association has been the collective voice of accounting educators for more than 60 years. Several times throughout their history they have published statements of accounting theory that encouraged certain approaches to accounting standards. These statements have often been ignored by professional standard setting boards as being too theoretical for practical purposes. In more recent years, the AAA has limited its standard setting role to responding to exposure drafts of proposed FASB statements and providing, through its magazines, a medium for individual professors to express their views as to existing or proposed standards.

What are the advantages of the academic community issuing statements to direct the profession in its standard setting? What are the difficulties academicians have in arriving at a consensus position that they can promote "as one voice?" Do you think the AAA should assume a more proactive role in standard setting?

Case 1—12 (You need more education!)

For over three decades, accounting professionals, accounting educators, and accounting bodies have debated requiring more education for those entering the public accounting profession. In 1988, the AICPA passed a resolution mandating 150 college credit hours as a minimum educational requirement for all new members of its organization after 1999. This requirement placed added pressure on state legislators to pass new accounting legislation, and during the 1990s an increasing number of states passed the "150-hour rule." Some groups, however, opposed this move and argued that it was restrictive to entry of minority groups and that it would unnecessarily reduce the number of accounting graduates and put accounting educators "out of work" as students opted for less expensive educational alternatives.

Why does the accounting profession recommend more education for new accounting professionals? Why would some groups resist this move? Were you, as an accounting student, deterred in your decision to major in accounting because of the 1999 requirement? Why or why not?

Case 1—13 (Microsoft)

The 1993 financial statements for Microsoft Corporation are included in Appendix A. Locate those financial statements and consider the following questions:

1. How did Microsoft do during the year ended June 30, 1993? Hint: Look at the income statement.
2. Do you notice anything unusual about Microsoft's balance sheet?
3. In 1993, was Microsoft's net cash from operations sufficient to pay for the additions to property, plant, and equipment?

CHAPTER 2

A Conceptual Framework of Accounting

CHAPTER TOPICS

- Need for a Conceptual Framework
- Nature and Components of the FASB'S Conceptual Framework
- Traditional Assumptions of the Accounting Model
- Conceptual Framework Summarized

In reporting financial position and results of operations, companies are sometimes allowed to select alternative accounting methods. The specific reporting procedures used by a company are intended to accurately reflect the economic circumstances of that company with respect to particular transactions or events. The flexibility to choose alternative accounting methods is needed because different companies have different circumstances. This flexibility, however, places an important responsibility on management to select those methods that reflect most fairly the economic results to shareholders and other interested parties. As the following two examples illustrate, the choice between alternative reporting methods can make a significant difference.

In 1987 General Motors elected to change the estimated useful life of its tools and dies. This change resulted in an increase in income from operations of over $1.2 billion, accounting for approximately 25 percent of reported earnings. In 1991 General Motors elected to change its accounting procedures to include general purpose spare parts in inventory; the cost of these parts was previously expensed. This accounting change resulted in a favorable adjustment of $306.5 million in net income for General Motors that year. A basic question is whether accounting standards should allow management such discretion in reporting financial information. A related questions is, if accounting rules allow such flexibility in reporting revenues and expenses, is accounting more an art or a science?

Contrary to the preceding examples, the general public often views accounting as a scientific discipline based on a fixed set of rules and procedures. This is a natural perception since the public's exposure to accounting generally relates to financial statements, tax returns, and other reports showing dollar amounts that give an impression of exactness. Those within the profession, however, recognize that accounting is more an art than a science and that the operating results and other accounting measurements are based on estimates and judgments relative to the measurement and communication of business activity.

Even though professional judgment plays an important role, accounting and financial reporting are governed by a well-established body of "generally accepted accounting principles," referred to as GAAP. As explained in Chapter 1, GAAP includes standards and interpretations issued by the FASB and those pronouncements issued by previous standard-setting bodies that have not been superseded. Underlying these principles or standards are several fundamental concepts and assumptions that collectively provide a theoretical or conceptual framework of accounting. This chapter focuses on the need for such a framework and examines the major components of the FASB's conceptual framework.

NEED FOR A CONCEPTUAL FRAMEWORK

Much has been written about the theoretical foundation or **conceptual framework** that underlies accounting practice. There are several reasons why such a framework is important. One major purpose is to provide broad definitions of the objectives, terms, and concepts involved in the practice of accounting. This definitional aspect of the framework prescribes the boundaries of accounting and financial reporting.

A strong theoretical foundation is essential if accounting practice is to keep pace with a changing business environment. Accountants are continually faced with new situations, technological advances, and business innovations that present new accounting and reporting problems. These problems must be dealt with in an organized and consistent manner. If their impact is sufficiently broad, specific issues may be resolved through the FASB's standard-setting process. The conceptual framework plays a vital role in the development of new standards and in the revision of previously issued standards. Recognizing the importance of this role, the FASB stated that fundamental concepts "guide the Board in developing accounting and reporting standards by providing . . . a common foundation and basic reasoning on which to consider merits of alternatives."[1] In a very real sense, then, the FASB itself is a primary beneficiary of a conceptual framework.

A conceptual framework also brings together the objectives and fundamentals of existing accounting practice and financial reporting. This helps users to better understand the purposes, content, and characteristics of information provided by accounting.

In addition, when accountants are confronted with new developments that are not covered by GAAP, a conceptual framework provides a reference for analyzing and resolving emerging issues. Thus, a conceptual framework not only helps in understanding existing practice, it also provides a guide for future practice.

A conceptual framework is also useful in selecting the most appropriate methods for reporting enterprise activity. Often, there is more than one justifiable or generally accepted reporting alternative for a particular transaction or event, and accountants must use their judgment in selecting among available alternatives. Fundamental concepts provide guidance in choosing the alternative that most accurately reflects the financial position and results of operations for the entity given the specific circumstances involved. If businesses and their activities were identical, reporting alternatives could be eliminated. However, such is not the case. Even within a particular industry, companies are not organized in exactly the same way. They do not produce identical products nor provide identical

1. *Statement of Financial Accounting Concepts No. 6,* "Elements of Financial Statements" (Stamford: Financial Accounting Standards Board, December 1985), p. i.

services, and their accounting systems and the reports generated therefrom are not uniform. Thus, accountants must exercise professional judgment in fulfilling their role as suppliers of useful information for decision makers. A conceptual framework helps make the results of the reporting process more comparable than they would be otherwise.

In summary, a conceptual framework of accounting:

1. Defines the boundaries of accounting by providing definitions of basic objectives, key terms, and fundamental concepts;
2. Assists the FASB in the standard-setting process by providing a basis for developing new and revised accounting and reporting standards;
3. Provides a description of current practice and a frame of reference for resolving new issues not covered by GAAP; and
4. Assists accountants and others in selecting from among reporting alternatives the method that best represents the economic reality of the situation.

If these purposes are accomplished, the overall result should be a reporting of the most useful information for decision-making purposes, which is the ultimate goal of accounting.

NATURE AND COMPONENTS OF THE FASB'S CONCEPTUAL FRAMEWORK

Serious attempts to develop a theoretical foundation of accounting can be traced to the 1930s. Among the leaders in such attempts were accounting educators, both individually and collectively as a part of the American Accounting Association (AAA). In 1936, the Executive Committee of the AAA began issuing a series of publications devoted to accounting theory, the last of which was published in 1965 and entitled "A Statement of Basic Accounting Theory." During the period from 1936 to 1973, there were several additional publications issued by the AAA and also by the American Institute of Certified Public Accountants (AICPA), each attempting to develop a conceptual foundation for the practice of accounting.[2]

While these publications made significant contributions to the development of accounting thought, no unified structure of accounting theory emerged from these efforts. When the Financial Accounting Standards Board was established in 1973, it responded to the need for a general theoretical framework by undertaking a comprehensive project to develop a "conceptual framework for financial accounting and reporting." This project has been described as an attempt to establish a constitution for accounting. The goal of the FASB was to provide "a coherent system of interrelated objectives and fundamentals that is expected to lead to consistent standards and that prescribes the nature, function, and limits of financial accounting and reporting."[3]

The conceptual framework project was one of the original FASB agenda items. It was viewed as a long-term, continuing project to be developed in stages. Because of its significant potential impact on many aspects of financial reporting, and therefore its controversial nature, progress was deliberate. The project had high priority and received a large share of

2. Among the most prominent of these publications were: Maurice Moonitz, *Accounting Research Study No. 1*, "The Basic Postulates of Accounting" (New York: American Institute of Certified Public Accountants, 1961); William A. Paton and A. C. Littleton, *An Introduction to Corporate Accounting Standards*, Monograph 3 (Evanston, Ill.: American Accounting Association, 1940); Thomas H. Sanders, Henry R. Hatfield, and W. Moore, *A Statement of Accounting Principles* (New York: American Institute of Accountants, Inc., 1938); Robert T. Sprouse and Maurice Moonitz, *Accounting Research Study No. 3*, "A Tentative Set of Broad Accounting Principles for Business Enterprises" (New York: American Institute of Certified Public Accountants, 1962); *Statement of the Accounting Principles Board No. 4*, "Basic Concepts and Accounting Principles Underlying Financial Statements of Business Enterprises" (New York: American Institute of Certified Public Accountants, October 1970), *Report of the Study Group on the Objectives of Financial Statements*, "Objectives of Financial Statements" (New York: American Institute of Certified Public Accountants, October 1973).

3. *Statement of Financial Accounting Concepts No. 6*, p. i.

Exhibit 2—1 A Conceptual Framework for Accounting

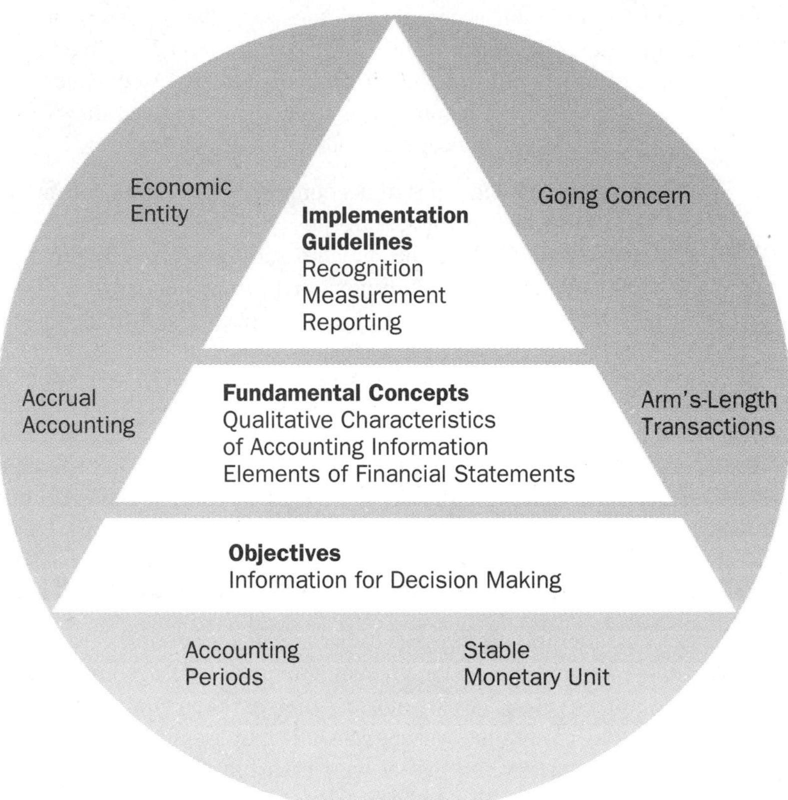

FASB resources. In December 1985, the FASB issued the last of six **Statements of Financial Accounting Concepts** (frequently referred to as Concepts Statements), which provide the basis for the conceptual framework.[4]

The FASB's framework incorporates many widely accepted concepts and principles developed in earlier works. In addition, several traditional assumptions underlying accounting practice are explicitly or implicitly recognized in the framework. The assumptions are discussed later in the chapter and include economic entity, going concern, arm's-length transactions, stable monetary unit, accounting periods, and accrual accounting. The main components of the FASB's conceptual framework, including the underlying assumptions, are presented in Exhibit 2—1.

The first area addressed by the FASB was the basic purposes or **objectives** of financial reporting. The Board sought answers to the questions: Who are the users of accounting information? What kinds of information do they require for decision making? Based on the objectives, the FASB proceeded to develop fundamental concepts that define the important **qualitative characteristics** of useful information and the specific **elements** to be included in financial statements.

4. The six Concepts Statements issued by the FASB are:
   1. Objectives of Financial Reporting by Business Enterprises
   2. Qualitative Characteristics of Accounting Information
   3. Elements of Financial Statements of Business Enterprises
   4. Objectives of Financial Reporting by Nonbusiness Organizations
   5. Recognition and Measurement in Financial Statements of Business Enterprises
   6. Elements of Financial Statements (a replacement of No. 3, broadened to include not-for-profit as well as business enterprises).

Exhibit 2—2
Objectives of Financial Reporting

Overall Objective:	Provide useful information for decision making
Primary Objectives:	Provide information: a. for assessing cash flow prospects b. about financial condition c. about performance and earnings d. about how funds are obtained and used
Additional Objectives:	Provide information: a. that allows managers to make decisions in the best interest of owners b. that allows owners to assess management's performance c. as explanations and interpretations to help users understand the financial information provided

Source: *Statement of Financial Accounting Concepts No. 1*

Building on the objectives and fundamental concepts, the FASB addressed the issues of **recognition, measurement,** and **reporting.** In this final phase of the framework project, the Board established broad implementation guidelines relating to the questions: When should revenues and expenses be recognized? How should revenues and expenses and other financial statement elements be measured (valued)? How should financial information be reported or displayed?

Each of the framework components is discussed in the following sections. In considering the individual components, the interrelationships become apparent. Decisions concerning one part of the framework influence other parts.

Objectives of Financial Reporting

The starting point for the FASB's conceptual framework was to establish the objectives of financial reporting. Without identifying the goals for financial reporting (e.g., who needs what kind of information and for what reasons), accountants cannot determine the recognition criteria needed, which measurements are useful, or how best to report accounting information.

The financial reporting objectives discussed in this chapter and listed in Exhibit 2—2 are summarized and adapted from FASB Concepts Statement No. 1. Some general observations regarding these objectives should be made. First, because the FASB is currently the primary standard-setting body for accounting in the private sector, the Board's objectives should be considered carefully. However, it should also be recognized that another group might identify somewhat different objectives for financial reporting. The objectives, as well as the other components of the conceptual framework, should, therefore, not be interpreted as "universal truths."

A second and related point is that the objectives of financial reporting are directly connected with the needs of those for whom the information is intended and must be considered in their environmental context. Financial reporting is not an end in itself, but is directed toward satisfying the need for useful information in making business and economic decisions. Thus, the objectives of financial reporting may change due to changes in the information needs of decision makers and because of changes in the economic, legal, political, and social aspects of the total business environment.

Third, the objectives of financial reporting are intended to be broad in nature. The objectives must be broadly based to satisfy a variety of user needs. Thus, they are objectives for general-purpose financial reporting, attempting to satisfy the common interests of various potential users rather than to meet the specific needs of any selected group.

Exhibit 2—3 Information Spectrum

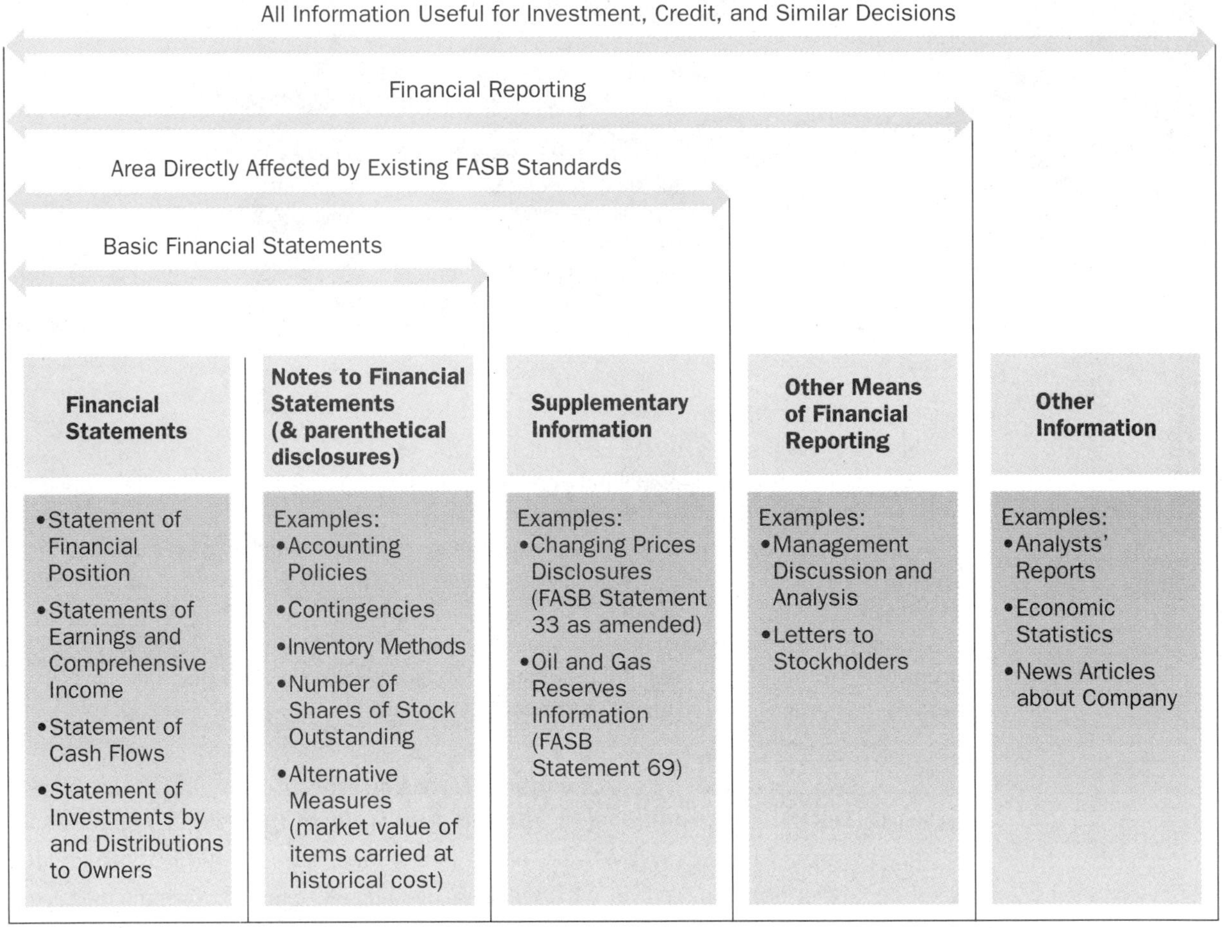

Financial Statements	Notes to Financial Statements (& parenthetical disclosures)	Supplementary Information	Other Means of Financial Reporting	Other Information
• Statement of Financial Position • Statements of Earnings and Comprehensive Income • Statement of Cash Flows • Statement of Investments by and Distributions to Owners	Examples: • Accounting Policies • Contingencies • Inventory Methods • Number of Shares of Stock Outstanding • Alternative Measures (market value of items carried at historical cost)	Examples: • Changing Prices Disclosures (FASB Statement 33 as amended) • Oil and Gas Reserves Information (FASB Statement 69)	Examples: • Management Discussion and Analysis • Letters to Stockholders	Examples: • Analysts' Reports • Economic Statistics • News Articles about Company

Source: Adapted from Statement of Financial Accounting Concepts No. 5, p. 5.

While there are many potential users of financial reports, the objectives are directed primarily toward the needs of those external users of accounting data who lack the authority to prescribe the information they desire. For example, the Internal Revenue Service or the Securities and Exchange Commission can require selected information from individuals and companies. Investors and creditors, however, must rely to a significant extent on the information contained in the periodic financial reports supplied by management and, therefore, are the major users toward which financial reporting is directed.

A fourth point is that the objectives pertain to financial reporting in general, which encompasses not only disclosures in financial statements, but also other information concerning an enterprise's financial condition and earnings ability. While financial statements are a primary means of communicating information to external parties, other forms and sources are also used for decision making. The total information spectrum relative to investment, credit, and similar decisions is presented in Exhibit 2—3. This illustrates the overall focus of financial reporting and, more specifically, the areas of primary concern for financial accounting—the financial statements, the notes to financial statements, and supplementary disclosures directly affected by generally accepted accounting principles.

Information for Decision Making. As discussed in Chapter 1, the **overall objective** of financial reporting is to **provide information that is useful for decision making.** The FASB states:

Financial reporting should provide information that is useful to present and potential investors and creditors and other users in making rational investment, credit, and similar decisions. The information should be comprehensible to those who have a reasonable understanding of business and economic activities and are willing to study the information with reasonable diligence.[5]

The emphasis in this overall objective is on investors and creditors as the primary external users, because in satisfying their needs, most other general-purpose needs of external users will be met. This objective also recognizes a fairly sophisticated user of financial reports, one who has a reasonable understanding of accounting and business and who is willing to study and analyze the information presented.

Cash Flow Prospects. Investors and creditors are interested primarily in a company's future cash flows. Thus, financial reporting should **provide information that is useful in assessing cash flow prospects.** Investment and lending decisions are made with the expectation of eventually increasing cash resources. An investor hopes to receive a return on the investment in the form of cash dividends and ultimately to sell the investment for more than it cost. Creditors seek to recover their cash outlays by repayments of the loans and to increase cash resources from interest payments. In making decisions, investors and creditors must consider the amounts, timing, and uncertainty (risk) of these prospective cash flows.

A company is similar to an investor in desiring to recover its investment plus receive a return on that investment. A company invests cash in noncash resources in order to produce a product or service that it expects to sell for an amount greater than the amount invested, thereby increasing cash resources. To the extent that a company is successful in generating favorable cash flows, it can pay dividends and interest, and the market price of its securities will increase. Thus, as illustrated in Exhibit 2—4, the cash flows to investors and creditors are directly related to the cash flows of business enterprises, and financial reporting should provide information that is useful in assessing the enterprise's prospective cash flows.

Exhibit 2—4
Enterprise Cash Flows To and From Investors and Creditors

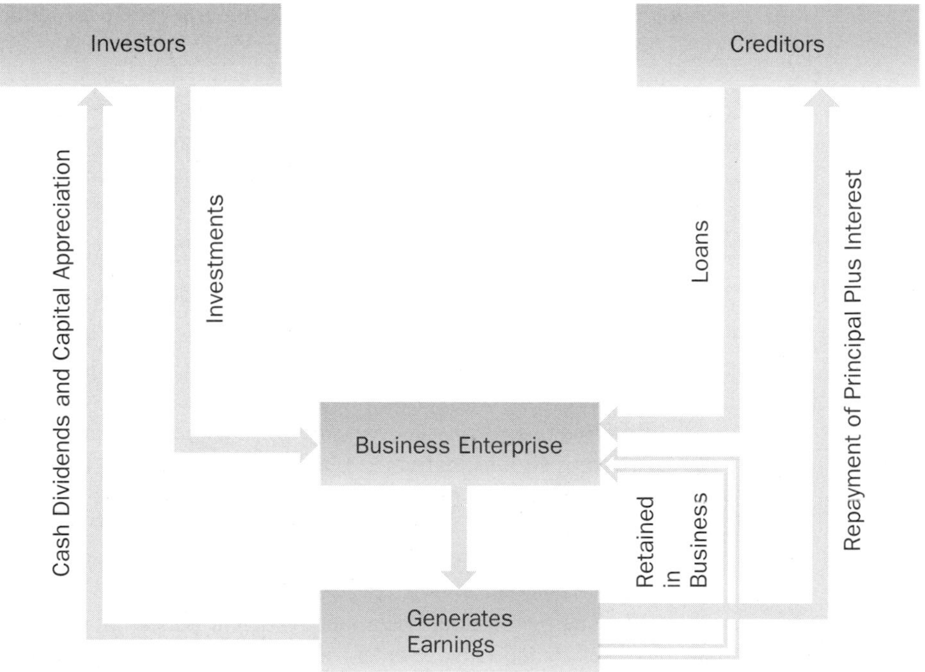

5. *Statement of Financial Accounting Concepts No. 1*, par. 34.

Enterprise Financial Condition. Financial reporting should **provide information about an enterprise's assets, liabilities, and owners' equity** to help investors, creditors, and others evaluate the financial strengths and weaknesses of the enterprise and its liquidity and solvency. Such information will help users determine the financial condition of a company, which, in turn, should provide insight into the prospects of future cash flows. It may also help users who wish to estimate the overall value of a business.

Enterprise Performance and Earnings. Another important objective of financial reporting is to **provide information about an enterprise's financial performance during a period.** Performance is evaluated mainly on the basis of enterprise earnings. In fact, the FASB states that "the primary focus of financial reporting is information about an enterprise's performance provided by measures of earnings and its components."[6] There are several aspects of this important objective. Clearly, investors and creditors are concerned mostly with expectations of future enterprise performance. However, to a large degree, they rely on evaluations of past performance as measures of future performance. The FASB recognizes that investors and creditors want information about earnings primarily as an indicator of future cash-flow potential. The Board concluded, however, that information about enterprise earnings, measured by accrual accounting, generally provides a better indicator of performance than does information about current cash receipts and disbursements.

Investors and creditors use reported earnings and information concerning the components of earnings in a variety of ways. For example, earnings may be interpreted by users of financial statements as an overall measure of managerial effectiveness, as a predictor of future earnings and long-term "earning power," and as an indicator of the risk of investing or lending. The information may be used to establish new predictions, confirm previous expectations, or change past evaluations.

How Funds Are Obtained and Used. Notwithstanding the emphasis on earnings, another objective of financial reporting is to **provide information about an enterprise's cash flows during a period.** This objective encompasses information about the enterprise's borrowing and repayment of borrowed funds; its capital transactions, such as the issuance of stock and payment of dividends; and any other factors that may affect its liquidity and solvency. Much of the information to satisfy this objective is provided in the statement of cash flows, although information about earnings and about assets, liabilities, and owners' equity is also useful in evaluating the liquidity and solvency of a firm.

Additional Objectives. Although the objectives of financial reporting are aimed primarily at the needs of external users, financial reporting should also **provide information that allows managers and directors to make decisions that are in the best interest of the owners.** A related objective is that sufficient **information should be provided to allow the owners to assess how well management has discharged its stewardship responsibility** over the entrusted resources. This requires an additional objective—**financial reporting should include explanations and interpretations to help users understand the financial information provided.**

In summary, if the objectives discussed in the preceding paragraphs are fully attained, the FASB believes those who make economic decisions will have better information upon which to evaluate alternative courses of action and the expected returns, costs, and risks of each. The result should be a more efficient allocation of scarce resources among competing uses by individuals, enterprises, markets, and the government.

6. *Statement of Financial Accounting Concepts No. 1,* par. 43.

Qualitative Characteristics of Accounting Information

Individuals who are responsible for financial reporting should continually seek to provide the best, i.e., most useful, information possible within reasonable cost constraints. The problem is very complex because of the many choices among acceptable reporting alternatives. For example, what items should be capitalized as assets or which items reported as liabilities? Which revenues and costs should be assigned to a particular reporting period and on what basis? What are the attributes to be measured: historical costs, current values, or net realizable values? At what level of aggregation or disaggregation should information be presented? Where should specific information be disclosed—in the financial statements, in the notes to the financial statements, or perhaps not at all? These and similar choices must be made by policymakers, such as members of the FASB or SEC; by management as they fulfill their stewardship roles; and by accountants as they assist management in reporting on a company's activities.

To assist in choosing among financial accounting and reporting alternatives, several criteria have been established by the FASB. These criteria relate to the qualitative characteristics of accounting information. A hierarchy of these qualities is presented in Exhibit 2—5 and will be used as a frame of reference in discussing them.

Decision Usefulness. The overriding quality or characteristic of accounting information is **decision usefulness,** which is central to the hierarchy presented in Exhibit 2—5. All other qualities are viewed in terms of their contribution to decision usefulness. The illustrated hierarchy distinguishes user-specific qualities, such as **understandability,** from qualities inherent in accounting information, such as relevance and reliability. The quality of understandability is essential to decision usefulness. Information cannot be useful to decision makers if it is not understood even though the information may be relevant and reliable. The understandability of information depends on the characteristics of users, e.g., their prior knowledge, and also on the inherent characteristics of the information presented. Hence, understandability can be evaluated only with respect to specific classes of decision makers. As indicated earlier, financial reporting is directed toward those users who have a reasonable understanding of business and economic activities and who are willing to study the information provided with reasonable diligence.

Primary Qualities. In the following statement, the FASB identified **relevance** and **reliability** as the primary qualities inherent in useful accounting information:

The qualities that distinguish "better" (more useful) information from "inferior" (less useful) information are primarily the qualities of relevance and reliability, with some other characteristics that those qualities imply.[7]

Relevance. The relevance of information may be judged only in relation to its intended use. If information is not relevant to the needs of decision makers, it is useless regardless of how well it meets other criteria. The objective of relevance, then, is to select methods of measuring and reporting that will aid those individuals who rely on financial statements to make decisions.

The FASB defines relevant information as that which will "make a difference." Relevant information may confirm expectations or change them. Thus, relevance is related to the **feedback value** and the **predictive value** of information. If the decision maker's expectations are neither confirmed nor changed by certain information, that information is not relevant and therefore is not useful to the decision maker. If a user can better predict future consequences based on information about past events and transactions, then such information is relevant.[8]

7. *Statement of Financial Accounting Concepts No. 2,* "Qualitative Characteristics of Accounting Information" (Stamford: Financial Accounting Standards Board, May 1980), par. 15.

8. *Ibid.,* pars. 46-50.

Exhibit 2—5 A Hierarchy of Accounting Information Qualities

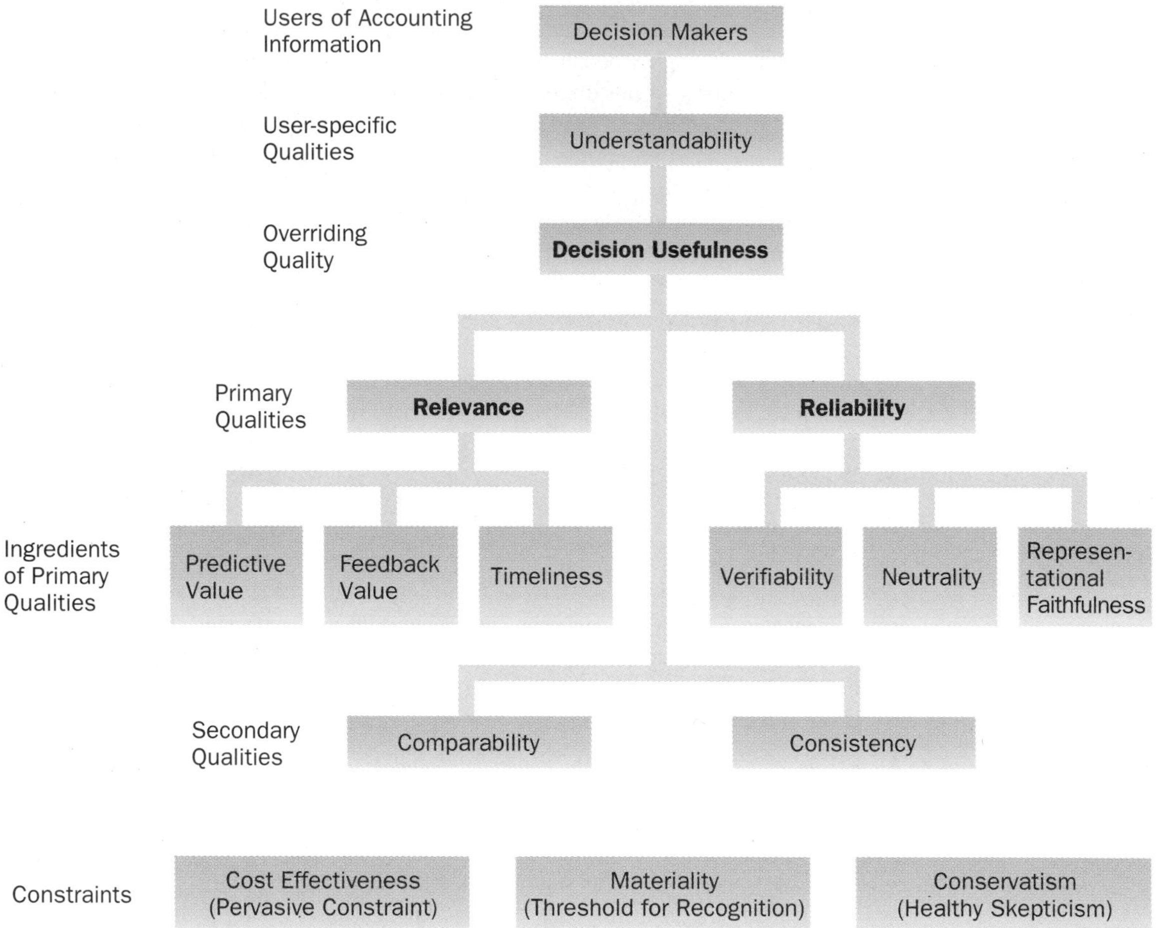

Source: Adapted from FASB *Statement of Financial Accounting Concepts No. 2*, p. 15.

Relevant information normally provides both feedback and predictive value at the same time. Feedback on past events helps confirm or correct earlier expectations. Such information can then be used to help predict future outcomes. For example, when General Motors presents comparative income statements, an investor has information to compare last year's operating results with this year's. This provides a general basis for evaluating prior expectations and for estimating what next year's results might be. The information therefore provides both feedback and predictive value concerning General Motors. As stated by the FASB, "Without a knowledge of the past, the basis for prediction will usually be lacking. Without an interest in the future, knowledge of the past is sterile."[9]

Timeliness is another key ingredient of relevance, relating directly to decision usefulness. Again using General Motors as an example, when the company issues interim financial reports, it is attempting to provide information on a timely basis so that the informa-

9. *Ibid.*, par. 51.

tion will be more relevant. Thus, to be relevant, information must offer predictive or feedback value, and it must be presented to users in a timely manner.

Reliability. The second primary quality of accounting information is reliability. Accounting information is reliable if users can depend on it to be reasonably free from error or bias and to be a faithful representation of the economic conditions or events that it purports to represent.[10] Reliability does not mean absolute accuracy. Information that is based on judgments and that includes estimates and approximations cannot be totally accurate, but it should be reliable. The objective, then, is to present the type of information in which users can have confidence. Such information must contain the key ingredients of reliability: verifiability, neutrality, and representational faithfulness.

Verifiability implies objectivity and consensus. Accountants seek to base their findings on facts that are determined objectively and that can be verified by other trained accountants using the same measurement methods. For example, assume that the amount of depreciation expense reported in the current year's income statement for the SAVE-ON Company is $125,000. That amount can be verified if it is known that the straight-line method of depreciation was applied to depreciable assets totaling $1,250,000 and that the assets had an estimated useful life of 10 years with no salvage value.

Neutrality relates to information being communicated in an unbiased manner. If financial statements are to satisfy a wide variety of users, the information presented should not be biased in favor of one group of users to the detriment of others. In this sense, the concept of neutrality is similar to the all-encompassing concept of "fairness."

The ingredient of **representational faithfulness** means that there is agreement between the information being reported and the actual results of economic activity being measured. Thus, the amounts and descriptions reported in the financial statements should reflect the economic reality of what is being represented. For a company to report sales of $3.4 million when they actually had sales of $2.5 million would not be a faithful representation and would cause the information to be unreliable.

Secondary Qualities. In addition to the primary qualities of relevance and reliability, there are two secondary qualities that affect the usefulness of accounting information: comparability and consistency.

Comparability. The essence of **comparability** is that information becomes much more useful when it can be related to a benchmark or standard. The comparison may be with data for other firms or it may be with similar information for the same firm but for other equivalent periods of time. To illustrate how comparable data can increase the usefulness of information, consider the situation where a company reports current assets of $350,000 and current liabilities of $275,000. The current ratio is 1.27, but does this information reflect a favorable or unfavorable liquidity position? Without knowing comparable data for other companies in the industry or the current ratio of this company for other years, the information is of somewhat limited value. If data were available to show that the average current ratio of all companies in this particular industry is 1.22 and further that this company's current ratio was 1.10 for the previous year, then it would appear that the company's liquidity position has improved and that it is in relatively good shape.

Given that comparability increases the usefulness of information, financial reports should provide data permitting comparisons among companies and comparisons of results of the same company over different time periods. This requires that similar events be accounted for in the same manner on the financial statements of different companies and

10. *Ibid.*, par. 63.

for a particular company for different periods. It should be recognized, however, that uniformity is not always the answer to comparability. Different circumstances may require different accounting treatment.

Still, one of the greatest unsolved problems in accounting is the present acceptance of alternative accounting methods under situations that do not appear to be sufficiently different to warrant different accounting practices. The goal is for basic similarities and differences in the activities of companies to be apparent from the financial statements.

Accounting research is being directed toward identifying circumstances that justify the use of a given method of accounting. If this research is successful, alternative methods can be eliminated where circumstances are found to be the same. In the meantime, current practice requires disclosure of the accounting methods used, as well as the impact of changes in methods when a change can be justified. Although the disclosures currently made do not generally provide enough information for a user to convert the published financial information from one accounting method to another, they do provide information that can assist the user in determining the degree of comparability among enterprises.

Consistency. **Consistency** is another important ingredient of useful accounting information. In view of the number of reporting alternatives, the methods adopted by an enterprise should be consistently employed if there is to be continuity and comparability in the financial statements. In analyzing statements, users seek to identify and evaluate the changes and trends within the enterprise. Conclusions concerning financial position and operations may be materially in error if, for example, accelerated depreciation is applied against the revenue of one year and straight-line depreciation against the revenue of the next year, or if securities are reported under long-term investments in one year and under current assets in the following year.

This is not to suggest that methods once adopted should not be changed. A continuing analysis of the business activities, as well as changing conditions, may suggest changes in accounting methods and presentations leading to more informative statements. These changes should be incorporated in the accounting system and the financial statements. The statements should be accompanied by a clear explanation of the nature of the changes and their effects, where they are material, so that current reporting can be properly interpreted and related to past reporting.

Constraints. Underlying the informational qualities identified in Exhibit 2—5 are three important constraints: (1) cost effectiveness, (2) materiality, and (3) conservatism.

Cost Effectiveness. Information is like other commodities in that it must be worth more than the cost of providing it to consumers. This concept is referred to as **cost effectiveness.** Too often government regulators and others assume that information is a "free" good. Obviously, it is not, and the relationship between costs and benefits must always be kept in mind when selecting or requiring reporting alternatives. To illustrate, in the early 1970s the Federal Trade Commission proposed that large companies be required to disclose information about lines of business. A group of companies brought court action to prohibit the proposed requirement. A major argument of the companies was that the information would be very costly to prepare, because it was not normally generated by the accounting system. The companies also argued that the line-of-business disclosures in the form proposed by the FTC would not be beneficial to users, because the reported segments would be artificial and not those the companies normally used to report on a less-than-company-wide basis. Although the FTC prevailed, primarily because of perceived benefits in regulating anti-trust situations, this case underscores an important point—the cost of producing information (including, for example, modification to the existing accounting system, or even additional printing and mailing costs) must be compared to the extra benefits (generally meaning an improvement in specific decisions of users) to determine if the information should be reported.

The difficulty in assessing cost effectiveness is that the costs and benefits, especially the benefits, are not always evident or easily measured. Notwithstanding this difficulty, cost effectiveness is an important constraint and should be considered when selecting reporting alternatives.

Materiality. Contrary to the belief of many readers of financial statements, the amounts reported in the statements are often not exact. They are based on estimates and are the summarized results of thousands of individual transactions. While for many decisions exactness is not required, there is a point at which information that is inexact does influence a decision. This point defines the boundary between information that is material and information that is immaterial.

Materiality is an overriding concept related to, but distinguishable from, the primary qualities of relevance and reliability. Materiality determines the threshold for recognition of accounting items and is primarily a quantitative consideration. While relevance is directed toward the nature of the information, materiality focuses on the size of a judgment item in a given set of circumstances. Materiality deals with the specific question: Is the item large enough or the degree of the accuracy precise enough to influence the decision of a user of the information? Of course, the degree of influence caused by the size of an item also depends on the nature of the item and the circumstances in which a judgment must be made. For example, a $1 million loss from a product-related lawsuit might be financially devastating for some enterprises, but may not even warrant separate disclosure on Ford Motor Company's financial statements.

At the present time, there are few guidelines to assist preparers of financial reports in applying the concept of materiality. Where materiality guidelines do exist, they are often not uniform. For example, the materiality guideline for reporting by segments of a company suggests that certain information be disclosed for any major segment that accounts for 10% or more of total company sales. On the other hand, for determining the significance of dilution in earnings-per-share computations, the materiality guideline is 3%. Thus for these two different reporting areas, the materiality guideline varies from 10% to 3%. Since quantitative guidance concerning materiality is often lacking, managers and accountants must exercise judgment in determining whether a failure to disclose certain data will influence the decisions of the users of financial statements.

Past court cases can help determine what is material by providing examples of where the lack of disclosure of certain information in the financial statements has been considered a material misstatement. The failure to disclose proper inventory values or pending sales of large amounts of assets, the failure to disclose the imminence of a highly profitable transaction or to disclose a significant downward readjustment of reported earnings are a few examples.[11]

In summary, the following point should be kept in mind in making judgments concerning materiality:

The omission or misstatement of an item in a financial report is material if, in the light of surrounding circumstances, the magnitude of the item is such that it is probable that the judgment of a reasonable person relying upon the report would have been changed or influenced by the inclusion or correction of the item.[12]

11. For additional examples of quantitative materiality considerations, see *Statement of Financial Accounting Concepts No. 2*, Appendix C, par. 165.

12. *Ibid.*, par. 132.

Conservatism. Another constraint associated with the characteristics of useful information is **conservatism.** This means that when accountants have genuine doubt concerning which of two or more reporting alternatives should be selected, users are best served by adopting a conservative approach, that is, by choosing the alternative with the least favorable impact on owners' equity. However, conservatism does not mean deliberate and arbitrary understatement of assets and earnings. On the contrary, use of conservative procedures is motivated by not wanting to overstate assets and earnings when dealing in "gray areas."

Conservatism should be used when a degree of skepticism is warranted. For example, generally accepted accounting principles require the expensing of research and development costs on the basis that the future benefits cannot be accurately determined. Since there is often reasonable doubt as to the existence or amount of future benefits, the costs are expensed, and the amount of income reported currently is reduced. Another example of conservatism in accounting practice is the general guideline of reporting losses as soon as they can be reasonably determined but not reporting gains until there is verification from an arm's-length transaction. Thus, if an asset's value is permanently reduced, a loss should be recognized; but if an asset increases in value, the gain is not generally recognized until that asset is sold and the gain is verified.

The constraint of conservatism is a useful one, but one that should be applied carefully and used only as a moderating and refining influence on the information reported. Essentially, conservatism means prudence in financial accounting and reporting.

Elements of Financial Statements

Having identified the qualitative characteristics of accounting information, the FASB in Concepts Statement No. 3 established definitions for the ten basic elements of financial statements of business enterprises. In Concepts Statement No. 6, the FASB expanded the scope of Statement No. 3 to encompass not-for-profit organizations as well. These elements comprise the building blocks upon which financial statements are constructed. The elements are interrelated and collectively report the performance and status of an enterprise. For reference purposes, the FASB definitions of the ten basic elements are listed in Exhibit 2-6. These definitions and the issues surrounding them are discussed in detail as the elements are introduced in later chapters.

Exhibit 2-6
The 10 Elements of Financial Statements

- **Assets** are probable future economic benefits obtained or controlled by a particular entity as a result of past transactions or events.
- **Liabilities** are probable future sacrifices of economic benefits arising from present obligations of a particular entity to transfer assets or provide services to other entities in the future as a result of past transactions or events.
- **Equity** or **net assets** is the residual interest in the assets of an entity that remains after deducting its liabilities.
- **Investments by owners** are increases in equity of a particular business enterprise resulting from transfers to it from other entities of something valuable to obtain or increase ownership interests (or equity) in it. Assets are most commonly received as investments by owners, but that which is received may also include services or satisfaction or conversion of liabilities of the enterprise.
- **Distributions to owners** are decreases in equity of a particular business enterprise resulting from transferring assets, rendering services, or incurring liabilities by the enterprise to owners. Distributions to owners decrease ownership interests (or equity) in an enterprise.
- **Comprehensive income** is the change in equity of a business enterprise during a period from transactions and other events and circumstances from nonowner sources.

Accounting for an Oil Spill

On January 5, 1993, a Liberian-registered supertanker, Braer, ran aground in heavy seas off Scotland's Shetland Islands. This accident resulted in over 25.5 million gallons of oil being spilled, more than twice as much as the Exxon Valdez spilled in Alaska in 1989. The impact on the environment was similar to that of the Valdez oil spill, as evidenced by hundreds of dying sea birds with blackened feathers drooping under the weight of thick crude oil. Although the tanker company carried insurance against such events, damage from the Shetland oil spill, estimated at roughly the same costs as the Exxon Valdez spill of $3 billion, exceeded policy limits.

The UK government is a member of the International Oil Pollution Compensation Fund (IOPC). This fund will cover damages up to $82.5 million. However, the fund stipulates that any claims that exceed this sum should be covered by the shipowner provided that "fault of privity" can be established. It has not been determined if Braer is at fault.

Questions:

1. From the limited information provided, does it appear that Braer's owners have a liability as a result of this event?
2. If the cleanup of the spill takes several years, would it be likely that Braer's owners could make damage estimates at the end of 1993 that would be reliable enough to allow the liability to be recorded at the end of 1993?
3. If Braer's owners determine that the liability cannot be reliably estimated, should some other type of disclosure be required?

Sources:
Platt's Oilgram News, January 13, 1993, p. 1
Chicago Tribune, January 17, 1993, p. 21

It includes all changes in equity during a period except those resulting from investments by owners and distributions to owners.

- **Revenues** are inflows or other enhancements of assets of an entity or settlement of its liabilities (or a combination of both) from delivering or producing goods, rendering services, or other activities that constitute the entity's ongoing major or central operations.
- **Expenses** are outflows or other using-up of assets or incurrences of liabilities (or a combination of both) from delivering or producing goods, rendering services, or carrying out other activities that constitute the entity's ongoing major or central operations.
- **Gains** are increases in equity (net assets) from peripheral or incidental transactions of an entity and from all other transactions and other events and circumstances affecting the entity except those that result from revenues or investments by owners.
- **Losses** are decreases in equity (net assets) from peripheral or incidental transactions of an entity and from all other transactions and other events and circumstances affecting the entity except those that result from expenses or distributions to owners.

Source: *Statement of Financial Accounting Concepts No. 6,* pp. ix-x.

Recognition, Measurement, and Reporting

FASB Concepts Statement No. 5 builds on the foundation laid by the previously issued concepts statements and provides broad guidelines for implementing or applying the objectives and fundamental concepts discussed thus far. It provides guidance in determining *what* information should be formally incorporated into financial statements and *when.* Specifically, Statement No. 5 sets forth recognition criteria and discusses certain measurement issues that are closely related to recognition. In addition, this statement addresses financial reporting and identifies the financial statements that should be presented in light of the objectives of financial reporting.

Recognition Criteria. **Recognition** is the process of formally recording an item and eventually reporting it as one of the elements in the financial statements. Recognition involves both the initial recording of an item and any subsequent changes related to that item. To qualify for recognition, an item should meet four fundamental criteria: (1) definition, (2) measurability, (3) relevance, and (4) reliability.[13] For an item to be formally recognized, it must meet one of the definitions of the elements of financial statements, as defined in Concepts Statement No. 6. For example, a receivable must meet the definition of an asset to be recorded and reported as such on a balance sheet. The same is true of liabilities, owners' equity, revenues, expenses, and other elements.

In addition to qualifying as an element, an item must be objectively measurable in monetary terms to be recognized. Sometimes an item clearly meets the definition criterion but cannot be measured objectively. For example, in the letter to shareholders in the 1993 annual report of Microsoft Corporation, the Chief Executive Officer mentions the significant value of customer satisfaction. (See Appendix A at the end of the book.) The millions of Microsoft customers around the world definitely have future benefit to Microsoft and may be considered assets of high value to that company. Yet, that value is not recognized explicitly as an asset on the balance sheet, since it cannot be measured in a reliable manner.

Information about an item must be both relevant and reliable in order for the item to be recognized. Since there are often trade-offs between relevance and reliability, consideration of these primary qualities may affect the timing of recognition. For example, information about a pending lawsuit may be relevant, but its recognition usually is delayed until the amounts and circumstances can be determined with sufficient reliability.

The four fundamental recognition criteria apply to all elements of financial statements. However, since one of the major tasks of accounting is to measure and report net income (loss), proper application of the recognition criteria is particularly important when recognizing revenues and expenses. Generally, under the **revenue recognition principle,** revenues for a period are recorded when two conditions are met: (1) the earnings process is substantially complete, and (2) there is receipt of cash or a near-cash asset. These two criteria have led to the conventional recognition of revenue at the point of sale, i.e., at the specific point in the earning process when assets are sold or services are rendered. According to the **matching principle,** expenses for a period are determined by association with specific revenues or a particular time period. The revenue recognition and expense matching principles are discussed and illustrated in Chapter 4.

Measurement Attributes. Closely related to recognition is measurement. There are five different measurement attributes currently used in practice and specifically mentioned in Concepts Statement No. 5.[14]

Historical cost is the cash equivalent price exchanged for goods or services at the date of acquisition. Land, buildings, equipment, and most inventories are common examples of items recognized using the historical cost attribute.

Current replacement cost is the cash equivalent price that would be exchanged currently to purchase or replace equivalent goods or services. Some inventories are recognized at their current replacement costs.

13. *Statement of Financial Accounting Concepts No. 5,* "Recognition and Measurement in Financial Statements of Business Enterprises" (Stamford: Financial Accounting Standards Board, December 1984), par. 63.
14. *Ibid.*, par. 67.

Current market value is the cash equivalent price that could be obtained by selling an asset in an orderly liquidation. Investments in securities often are reported using current market values.

Net realizable value is the amount of cash expected to be received from the conversion of assets in the normal course of business. Generally, this attribute is equal to the sales price less normal costs to sell. Net realizable value is used for recognizing short-term receivables and some inventories.

Present (or discounted) value is the amount of net future cash inflows or outflows discounted to their present value. Long-term receivables and long-term payables use this measurement attribute.

It should be noted that different measurement attributes often have the same monetary value, especially at the point of initial recognition. For example, the historical cost and the current replacement cost of a piece of land are the same at the date of acquisition. The amount would also be the current market value of the land at that point in time, assuming an arm's-length transaction.

The trade-off between relevance and reliability mentioned earlier is also evident in considering which measurement attribute to use. Current accounting practice is said to be based on historical costs, since that is the attribute generally used in the initial recording of transactions. Historical cost is used because it is objective (reliable), being based on an exchange that has taken place between presumably independent parties. In effect, the historical cost is the fair market price of the item involved in the transaction at that date. Many accountants feel that current replacement costs or market values are more relevant than historical costs for future-oriented decisions; yet, those attributes often lack reliability. Because it is both reliable and relevant, historical cost has been the valuation basis most commonly used in accounting practice. However, as indicated above, other measurement attributes are used at times and are expected to continue to be used in the future. The "proper" measurement attribute is the one that under the circumstances provides the most useful (relevant and reliable) information at a reasonable cost.

In using historical cost as one (and perhaps the dominant) measurement attribute, the FASB indicated in Concepts Statement No. 5 that it expects nominal units of money to continue to be used in recognizing items in financial reporting. Nominal units of money are unadjusted for general price changes and therefore fluctuate over time in terms of purchasing power. If there is little or no inflation, measurement using nominal dollars is satisfactory. However, if general price levels change significantly, the FASB will probably have to reconsider this decision.

Financial Reporting. For financial reporting to be most effective, all relevant information should be presented in an unbiased, understandable, and timely manner. This is sometimes referred to as the **full disclosure principle.** Because of the cost-benefit constraint discussed earlier, however, it would be impossible to report *all* relevant information. Further, too much information would adversely affect understandability and, therefore, decision usefulness. Those who provide financial information must use judgment in determining what information best satisfies the full disclosure principle within reasonable cost limitations.

Although guidelines in this area are not well defined, Concepts Statement No. 5 indicates that a "full set of financial statements" is necessary to meet the objectives of financial reporting. Included in the recommended set of general-purpose financial statements are reports that would show:[15]

15. *Statement of Financial Accounting Concepts No. 5*, par. 13.

- Financial position at the end of the period
- Earnings (net income) for the period
- Comprehensive income (total nonowner changes in equity) for the period
- Cash flows during the period
- Investments by and distributions to owners during the period

Current practice generally includes a set of financial statements consisting of: (1) a **balance sheet** reporting the financial position of a business at a certain date; (2) an **income statement** presenting the results of operations of an entity for a reporting period; and (3) a **statement of cash flows** identifying the net cash flows from operating, investing, and financing activities during the reporting period. The three primary statements are referred to as general-purpose financial statements because they are intended for use by a wide variety of external users. Although there has been some discussion as to the need for special-purpose statements directed to specific external users, there has been no significant movement toward this in practice.

Sometimes a **retained earnings statement** is provided, or combined with the income statement, showing the changes in retained earnings for the period. When there are changes in owners' equity other than those affecting retained earnings, a supplemental **statement of changes in owners' equity** may be presented to provide a complete reconciliation of the beginning and ending equity balances.

The current general-purpose statements would seem to satisfy the recommendations of Concepts Statement No. 5 with one exception. **Comprehensive income** is a concept specifically defined in Statement No. 5 as including all changes in owners' equity except investments by and distributions to owners. This concept, which is explained and illustrated in Chapter 4, may eventually require a new statement.

In general, the FASB and other standard-setting bodies have been reluctant to specify exact formats for reporting. Instead, they have allowed and encouraged companies to experiment with various reporting (display) techniques. The results are sometimes quite encouraging as companies voluntarily seek new and better ways to present information. For example, many companies present graphic and various types of pictorial displays in their annual reports to assist users in understanding the information provided in financial statements. The graphs reproduced in Exhibit 2—7 were included in the 1992 annual report of Albertson's, Inc., to supplement the information presented in the financial statements. This is one example of the many ways in which companies are attempting to enhance the usefulness of their financial statements.

TRADITIONAL ASSUMPTIONS OF THE ACCOUNTING MODEL

The FASB's Conceptual Framework described in the preceding sections is influenced by several underlying assumptions. While not addressed explicitly, these traditional assumptions are implicit in the conceptual framework. They, too, help establish generally accepted accounting practice. The following paragraphs briefly describe the six basic assumptions that were identified in Exhibit 2—1.

First, the business enterprise is viewed as a specific **economic entity** separate and distinct from its owners and any other business unit. It is the entity and its activities that receive the focus of attention for accounting and reporting purposes.

Second, in the absence of evidence to the contrary, the entity is viewed as a **going concern.** This continuity assumption provides support for the preparation of a balance sheet that reports costs assignable to future activities rather than market values of properties that would be realized in the event of voluntary liquidation or forced sale. This same assumption calls for the preparation of an income statement reporting only such portions of revenues and costs as are allocable to current activities.

■ **Exhibit 2—7** Supplemental Disclosure of Operating Data

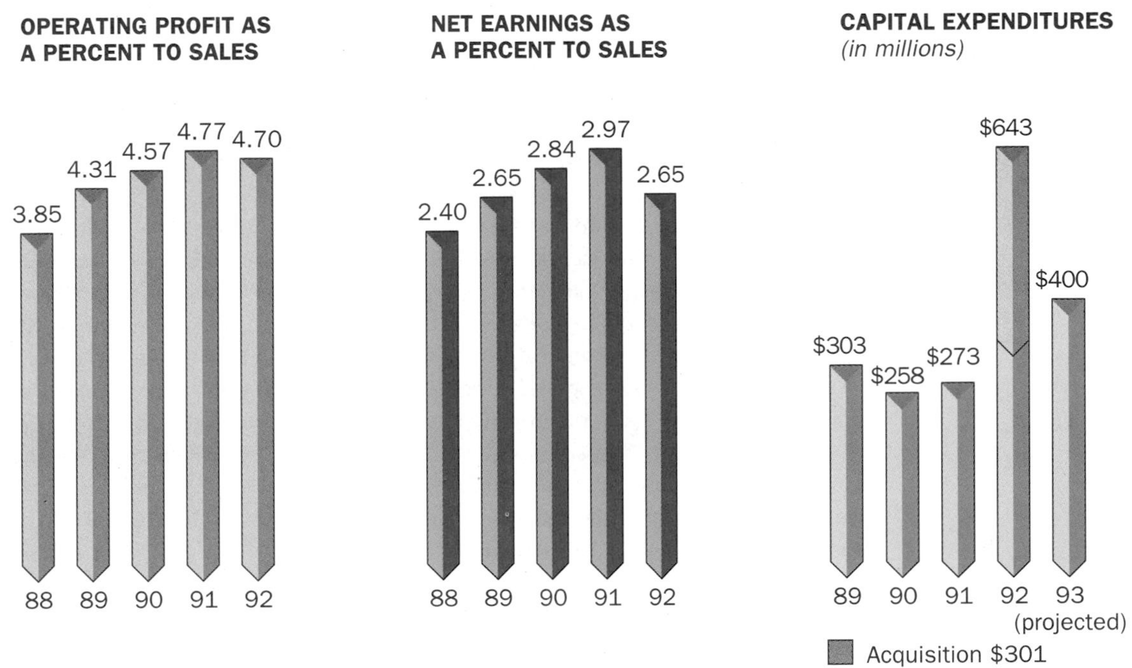

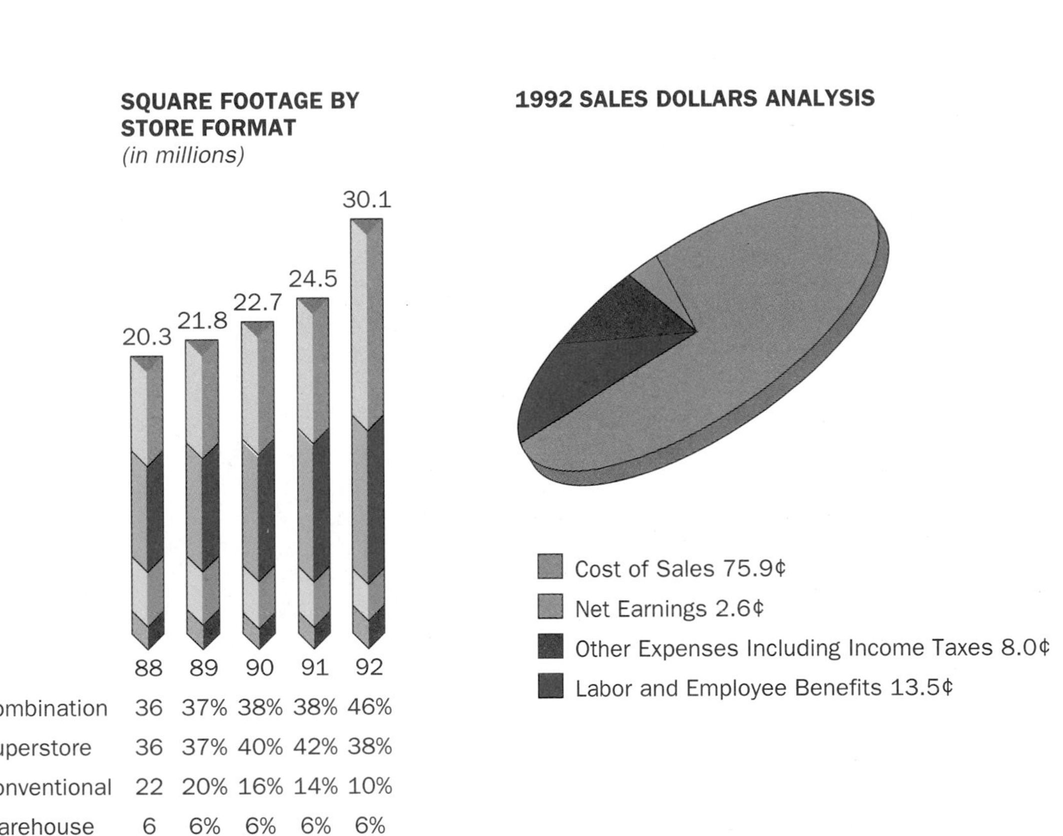

Third, the transactions and events of an entity provide the basis for accounting entries, and any changes in resources and equity values are generally not recorded until a transaction has taken place. Furthermore, transactions are assumed to be **arm's-length transactions.** That is, they occur between independent parties, each of whom is capable of protecting its own interests. If Entity A is selling goods to Entity B, it will try to sell at a sufficiently high price to make a profit. Entity B, on the other hand, will try to purchase those goods at a reasonably low price. The bargained price arrived at in this arm's-length transaction is assumed to be an objective market valuation at that date, and is considered an objective value for measurement purposes.

Fourth, transactions are assumed to be measured in **stable monetary units.** Because of this assumption, changes in the dollar's purchasing power have traditionally been ignored. Thus, financial statements reflect items that are measured in terms of nominal dollars. To many accountants, this is a serious limitation of the accounting model.

Fifth, because accounting information is needed on a timely basis, the life of a business entity is divided into specific **accounting periods.** By convention, the year has been established as the normal period for reporting. Annual statements, as well as statements covering shorter intervals, such as quarters, are provided by entities to satisfy the needs of those requiring timely financial information.

Finally, for each time period, an income measure is determined using **accrual accounting.** This means that revenues are recognized when earned, not necessarily when cash is received; and expenses are recognized when incurred, not necessarily when cash is paid. For most financial reporting purposes, accrual accounting is considered preferable to the cash-basis system of accounting.

In total, these assumptions as well as the concepts discussed earlier in the chapter comprise the current accounting model. They help determine what will be accounted for and in what manner. In effect, they set the boundaries of accounting practice. If these boundaries are violated, additional disclosure in the financial statements is typically required.

CONCEPTUAL FRAMEWORK SUMMARIZED

Exhibit 2—8 summarizes the major components of a conceptual framework of accounting. Such a framework provides a basis for consistent judgments by standard-setters, preparers, users, auditors, and others involved in financial reporting. A conceptual framework will not solve all accounting problems, but if used on a consistent basis over time, it should help improve financial reporting.

Exhibit 2—8 A Conceptual Framework of Accounting

I. Objectives of Financial Reporting

- A. Overall—Provide useful information for decision making
- B. Primary—Provide information:
  1. For assessing cash flow prospects
  2. About financial condition
  3. About performance and earnings
  4. About how funds are obtained and used
- C. Additional—Provide information:
  1. That allows managers to make decisions in the best interest of owners
  2. That allows owners to assess management's performance
  3. As explanations and interpretations to help users understand the information provided

II. Fundamental Concepts

A. Qualitative Characteristics of Accounting Information
  1. Overriding quality—decision usefulness
  2. Primary qualities
    a. Relevance
      • predictive value
      • feedback value
      • timeliness
    b. Reliability
      • verifiability
      • neutrality
      • representational faithfulness
  3. Secondary qualities
    a. Comparability
    b. Consistency
  4. Constraints
    a. Cost effectiveness (pervasive constraint)
    b. Materiality (recognition threshold)
    c. Conservatism (healthy skepticism)

B. Elements of Financial Statements
  1. Assets
  2. Liabilities
  3. Equity
  4. Investments by owners
  5. Distributions to owners
  6. Comprehensive income
  7. Revenues
  8. Expenses
  9. Gains
  10. Losses

III. Implementation Guidelines

A. Recognition Criteria
  1. Definition
  2. Measurability
  3. Relevance
  4. Reliability

B. Measurement Attributes
  1. Historical cost
  2. Current replacement cost
  3. Current market value
  4. Net realizable value
  5. Present (or discounted) value

C. Financial Reporting
  1. Full disclosure
  2. Set of general-purpose financial statements
    a. Financial position
    b. Earnings (net income or loss)
    c. Comprehensive income
    d. Cash flows
    e. Investments by and distributions to owners

IV. Traditional Assumptions of the Accounting Model

A. Economic entity
B. Going concern
C. Arm's-length transactions
D. Stable monetary unit
E. Accounting periods
F. Accrual accounting

The framework discussed in this chapter will be a reference source throughout the text. In studying the remaining chapters, you will see many applications and a few exceptions to the theoretical framework established here. An understanding of the overall theoretical framework of accounting should make it easier for you to understand specific issues and problems encountered in practice.

KEY TERMS

Accounting periods 46
Accrual accounting 46
Arm's-length transactions 46
Balance sheet 44
Comparability 37
Comprehensive income 44
Conceptual framework 28
Conservatism 40
Consistency 38
Cost effectiveness 38
Current market value 43
Current replacement cost 42
Decision usefulness 35
Economic entity 44
Feedback value 35
Full disclosure principle 43
Going concern 44
Historical cost 42
Income statement 44
Matching principle 42
Materiality 39
Net realizable value 43
Neutrality 37
Predictive value 35
Present (or discounted) value 43
Recognition 42
Relevance 35
Reliability 35
Representational faithfulness 37
Retained earnings statement 44
Revenue recognition principle 42
Stable monetary units 46
Statement of cash flows 44
Statement of changes in owners' equity 44
Statements of financial accounting concepts 30
Timeliness 36
Understandability 35
Verifiability 37

QUESTIONS

1. List and explain the main reasons why a conceptual framework of accounting is important.
2. Why is judgment required by accountants in fulfilling their role as suppliers of information?
3. The FASB's Conceptual Framework project has received considerable attention. What is the project expected to accomplish? What is it not likely to do?
4. Identify the major objectives of financial reporting as specified by the FASB.
5. The overriding quality of accounting information is decision usefulness. How does the user-specific quality of "understandability" affect decision usefulness?
6. Distinguish between the primary informational qualities of relevance and reliability.
7. Does reliability imply absolute accuracy? Explain.
8. Define comparability. How does comparability relate to uniformity?
9. Of what value is consistency in financial reporting?
10. Why is it so difficult to measure the cost effectiveness of accounting information?
11. What is the current materiality standard in accounting?
12. Is it possible for information to be immaterial and yet relevant? Explain.
13. What is conservatism in accounting? When does it become a relevant issue? What are some examples of conservatism in accounting practice?
14. Identify the criteria that an item must meet to qualify for recognition.
15. Identify and describe five different measurement attributes.
16. FASB Concepts Statement No. 5 indicates that a full set of financial statements is needed to meet the objectives of financial reporting. What should the reports that constitute a set of general-purpose financial statements show?
17. Identify the six traditional assumptions that influence the conceptual framework, and briefly explain how they affect it.

DISCUSSION CASES

Case 2—1 (The establishment of a conceptual framework)

As a student of accounting, you have noticed that a substantial portion of the literature deals with establishing a theoretical framework upon which accounting practice can be based. This is currently the case and has been for the past 50 years. Yet, in discussions with colleagues and friends, you have to admit that the accounting profession has found it difficult to establish an authoritative set of accounting concepts and principles that are universally accepted within the business community. As you think about this problem, at least two questions come to mind: (1) Is an overall conceptual framework of accounting even needed? and (2) What has the FASB done differently, if anything, to succeed in establishing a conceptual framework for accounting where others have failed? Discuss possible answers to these questions.

Case 2—2 (How important are the economic consequences of accounting principles?)

During the 1980s and 1990s, many savings and loan associations went bankrupt and their assets had to be sold by the government to recoup monies paid to depositors. The accounting profession was criticized for failure to design accounting principles that would give earlier warning signals of impending financial danger. One of the suggested remedies was the requirement for all institutions, including banks, to recognize losses in the value of investments they were holding earlier than was done according to GAAP. Bankers objected to these more stringent requirements, and predicted that the earlier recognition of losses would expand the financial difficulties for both banks and savings institutions and actually contribute to their demise.

At about the same time, the FASB issued standards that required companies to account for unfunded pension costs as liabilities. Executives of several large companies have argued that such accounting will seriously limit the ability of many companies to borrow and will have a serious, negative impact on business activity and, therefore, on society.

Recognizing that accounting rules have an impact on business activity and may affect economic growth, should this result influence the decision by accounting standard-setting bodies as to how transactions should be recorded and reported? Should the impact on society be an important consideration for an accounting principle?

Case 2—3 (Cash flow vs. accrual-based earnings)

The Financial Accounting Standards Board concluded in Concepts Statement No. 1 that investors and creditors are interested "in an enterprise's future cash flows and its ability to generate favorable cash flows leads primarily to an interest in information about its earnings rather than information directly about its cash flows." The Board further states that "information about enterprise earnings and its components measured by accrual accounting generally provides a better indication of enterprise performance than information about current cash receipts and payments." If an investor or creditor is interested in future cash flows, why isn't the focus on an examination of a firm's past cash flows? What are the limitations associated with using cash flows to measure the performance of an enterprise? Conversely, what are the risks to an investor or creditor of focusing solely on accrual-based earnings figures?

Case 2—4 (Trade-offs in providing useful accounting information)

The FASB's conceptual framework is intended to provide guidance in selecting from alternative accounting methods those that are most appropriate under the circumstances. Accountants must exercise judgment in applying the general guidelines in each specific set of circumstances. Often trade-offs exist between different qualitative characteristics of accounting information. For each of the following situations, identify the qualitative characteristics involved and discuss the possible trade-offs that exist.

1. Benavides Company charges to expense all items under $1,000.
2. Do-It-Now Company has recently decided to change its depreciation method to straight line from declining balance.
3. Future, Inc., has decided to use the allowance method for bad debts rather than the direct write-off method.
4. Nights Inn is trying to convince its auditors to allow a restatement of all asset values to their current market values.
5. Forester's Inc. decides to recognize the adjustment of postretirement health care benefits from the cash to the accrual basis as an immediate charge against current net income rather than as a deferral to charge against the next twenty years.

Case 2—5 (Elements of financial statements)

Conserv Corporation, a computer software company, is trying to determine the appropriate accounting procedure to apply to its software development costs. Management is considering capitalizing the development costs and amortizing them over several years. Alternatively, they are considering charging the costs to expense as soon as they are incurred. You, as an accountant, have been asked to help settle this issue. Which definitions of financial statement elements would apply to these costs? Based on this information, what accounting procedure would you recommend and why?

Case 2—6 (Recognition, measurement, and reporting considerations in financial reporting)

Several years ago, the SEC adopted amendments to Regulation S-X, requiring separate disclosure of preferred stock subject to mandatory redemption requirements, often called "redeemable preferred stock." In taking such action, the SEC noted an increase in the use of complex securities—such as redeemable preferred stock—that exhibit both debt and equity characteristics. The question subsequently considered by the FASB was whether or not such securities should be classified as liabilities rather than as equity securities. How might the FASB's guidelines for recognition, measurement, and reporting assist in resolving this or similar issues?

Case 2—7 (Measurement attributes: historical costs vs. current values)

Financial statements rely heavily on historical cost information. In fact, the FASB, in Concepts Statement No. 5, states:

Present financial statements frequently are characterized as being based on the historical cost (historical proceeds) attribute. That no doubt reflects the fact that, for most enterprises, a great many of the individual events recognized in financial statements are acquisitions of goods or services for cash or equivalent that are recorded at historical cost.

However, several industries feel that the information provided using historical costs is not relevant for investors and creditors. As an example, The Rouse Company, a national real estate development firm, provides financial statements using both a historical cost and a current-value basis. In its 1991 annual report, The Rouse Company reported operating property with a current value of just over \$3.6 billion. The property's historical cost was less than \$2.2 billion. Why do accountants focus primarily on historical cost figures? If the \$3.6 billion figure is more relevant for investors and creditors, why don't traditional financial statements reflect current values? What are the risks to investors, creditors, and auditors of presenting current-value information in the body of financial statements?

Case 2—8 (Financial reporting: the difficult task of satisfying diverse informational needs)

Teri Green has recently been promoted. She is now the chief financial officer of Teltrex, Inc., and has primary responsibility for the external reporting function. During the past three weeks, Green has met with: Jeff Thalman, the senior vice president of Westmore First National Bank, where Teltrex has a \$1,000,000 line of credit; Susan Davis, a financial analyst for Stubbs, Jones, and McConkie, a brokerage firm; and Brian Ellis, who is something of a corporate gadfly and who owns 2 percent of the outstanding common stock of Teltrex. Each of these individuals has commented on last year's annual report of Teltrex, pointing out deficiencies and suggesting additional information they would like to see presented in this year's annual report. From Green's point of view, explain the nature of general-purpose financial statements and indicate the informational qualities of the accounting data that she must be concerned with in fulfilling the corporation's external reporting responsibility.

Case 2—9 (Responsibility for financial reporting)

It is apparent from reading *The Wall Street Journal* and other financial publications that an increasing number of lawsuits are being filed each year against independent accountants (CPAs). Most cases involve accountants who audited the financial statements of companies that subsequently went bankrupt. Who is responsible for a company's financial statements, and how might preparers and others use a conceptual framework to fulfill their responsibilities?

Case 2—10 **(The trade-off between relevance and reliability)**

The cable television industry is facing competition from companies using advanced technologies. The use of microwaves allows programs to be beamed, at low cost, to locations not accessed by cable. This technology, if successful, could eliminate the need for the current high-fixed-cost, physically-intrusive cable systems. What information do cable companies need in order to evaluate the potential of microwave TV? What is a limitation associated with estimating demand for microwave TV? Why don't cable companies just wait and see if microwave TV is a success?

Case 2—11 **(Measurement issues associated with a specific liability)**

Companies regularly obtain money through the issuance of bonds. The market value of bonds changes daily and on any given day is a function of many factors including economic variables, industry developments, and firm-specific information. How should bonds be reported on the books of the issuer: at their market value on the balance sheet date? at their historical selling price? at their discounted present value? or at their eventual maturity value? For each of the above measurement attributes, identify and discuss the issues associated with each attribute.

Case 2—12 **(Let's use the FASB conceptual framework world-wide!)**

David Frey and Bertha Lui were discussing the differences in accounting principles used in the United States and other countries. They are aware of the attempt by an international accounting body to arrive at a "harmonization" of these standards; however, they have read a recent article in an accounting journal indicating how difficult it is to achieve this harmonization.

David expressed his view that if all countries accepted the conceptual framework developed by the FASB, the differences in accounting principles would be reduced. Bertha indicated that she understood that the FASB developed its conceptual framework for the United States, not for the world. She further contended that because economic structure and events vary by country, no one conceptual framework can address all situations.

Which viewpoint of the FASB conceptual framework project do you think is correct? What parts of the conceptual framework might be affected by differences in the economic structures of countries?

Case 2—13 **(But we only need one accounting standard—fairness)**

In the 1970s, a leader in the accounting profession proposed that there really only needed to be one underlying standard to govern the establishment of generally accepted accounting principles. That standard was identified as "fairness." Financial statements should be prepared so that they are fair to all users: management, labor, investors, creditors. As changes occur in society, financial reporting should change to fairly reflect each user's needs.

Since the financial statements are the responsibility of management, such a standard would require management to determine what reporting methods would be fair. What advantages do you see to this proposal? What would be management's most serious problem in applying a fairness standard?

EXERCISES

Exercise 2—14 **(Aspects of the FASB's conceptual framework)**

Determine whether the following statements are true or false. If a statement is false, explain why.

1. Comprehensive income includes changes in equity resulting from distributions to owners.
2. Timeliness and predictive value are both characteristics of relevant information.
3. The tendency to recognize favorable events early is an example of conservatism.
4. Objectives of Concepts Statement No. 1 focus primarily on the needs of internal users of financial information.
5. Statements of Financial Accounting Concepts are considered authoritative pronouncements.

6. The overriding objective of financial reporting is to provide information for making economic decisions.
7. Concepts Statement No. 1 seeks to clarify *how* financial statement reporting should be accomplished, and succeeding Concepts Statements clarify *what* should be reported in financial statements.
8. Certain modifying constraints, such as conservatism, can justify departures from GAAP.
9. Under Concepts Statement No. 5, the term "recognized" is synonymous with the term "recorded."
10. Once an accounting method is adopted, it should never be changed.

Exercise 2—15 (Conceptual framework terminology)

Match the statements on the left with the letter of the terms on the right. An answer (letter) may be used more than once and some terms require more than one answer (letter).

1. Key ingredients in quality of relevance.
2. Basic assumptions that influence the FASB's Conceptual Framework.
3. The idea that information should represent what it purports to represent.
4. An important constraint, relating to costs and benefits.
5. An example of conservatism.
6. The availability of information when it is needed.
7. Associating expense with a particular revenue or time period.
8. Determines the threshold for recognition.
9. Implies objectivity and consensus.
10. Transactions between independent parties.

a. Cost effectiveness
b. Representational faithfulness
c. Matching principle
d. Verifiability
e. Time periods
f. Unrealized
g. Completeness
h. Timeliness
i. Materiality
j. Predictive value
k. Economic entity
l. Lower-of-cost-or-market rule
m. Accrual accounting
n. Arm's-length

Exercise 2—16 (Objectives of financial reporting)

For each of the following independent situations, identify the relevant objective(s) of financial reporting that the company may be overlooking. Discuss each of these objectives.

1. The president of Coventry, Inc., feels that the financial statements should be prepared for use by management only, since they are the primary decision makers.
2. Cascade Carpets Co. feels that financial statements should only reflect the present financial standing and cash position of the firm and should not provide any future-oriented data.
3. The vice president of Share Enterprises, Inc., believes that the financial statements are to present only current-year revenues and expenses and not disclose assets, liabilities, and owners' equity.
4. Cruz Co. has a policy of providing disclosures of only its assets, liabilities, and owners' equity.
5. Marty Manufacturing, Inc., always discloses the assets, liabilities, and owners' equity of the firm along with the revenues and expenses. Marty's management believes that these items provide all the information relevant to investing decisions.

Exercise 2—17 (Applications of accounting characteristics and concepts)

For each situation listed, indicate by letter the appropriate qualitative characteristic(s) or accounting concept(s) applied. A letter may be used more than once, and more than one characteristic or concept may apply to a particular situation.

(a) Understandability
(b) Verifiability
(c) Timeliness
(d) Representational faithfulness
(e) Neutrality
(f) Relevance
(g) Going concern
(h) Economic entity
(i) Historical cost
(j) Quantifiability
(k) Materiality
(l) Comparability
(m) Conservatism

1. Goodwill is only recorded in the accounts when it arises from the purchase of another entity at a price higher than the fair market value of the purchased entity's tangible assets.
2. Land is valued at cost.
3. All payments out of petty cash are debited to Miscellaneous Expense.
4. Plant assets are classified separately as land or buildings, with an accumulated depreciation account for buildings.
5. Periodic payments of $1,500 per month for services of H. Hay, who is the sole proprietor of the company, are reported as withdrawals.
6. Small tools used by a large manufacturing firm are recorded as expenses when purchased.
7. Investments in equity securities are initially recorded at cost.
8. A retail store estimates inventory, rather than taking a complete physical count, for purposes of preparing monthly financial statements.
9. A note describing the company's possible liability in a lawsuit is included with the financial statements even though no formal liability exists at the balance sheet date.
10. Depreciation on plant assets is consistently computed each year by the straight-line method.

Exercise 2—18 (Trade-off between qualitative characteristics)

In each of the following independent situations, an example is given requiring a trade-off between the qualitative characteristics discussed in the text. For each situation, identify the relevant characteristics and briefly discuss how satisfying one characteristic may involve not satisfying another.

1. The book value of an office building is approaching its originally estimated salvage value of $200,000. However, its current market value has been estimated at $20 million. The company's management would like to disclose to financial statement users the current value of the building on the balance sheet.
2. MMM Industries has used the FIFO inventory method for the past twenty years. However, all other major competitors use the LIFO method of accounting for inventories. MMM is contemplating a switch from FIFO to LIFO.
3. Stocks Inc. is negotiating with a major bank for a significant loan. The bank has asked that a set of financial statements be provided as quickly after the year-end as possible. Because invoices from many of the company's suppliers are mailed several weeks after inventory is received, Stocks Inc. is considering estimating the amounts associated with those liabilities to be able to prepare their financial statements more quickly.
4. Satellite Inc. produces and sells satellites to government and private industries. The company provides a warranty guaranteeing the performance of the satellites. A recent space launch placed one of their satellites in orbit, and several malfunctions have occurred. At year-end, Satellite Inc.'s auditors would like the company to disclose the potential liability in the notes to the financial statements. Officers of Satellite Inc. believe that the satellite can be repaired in orbit and that disclosure of a contingency such as this would unnecessarily bias the financial statements.

Exercise 2—19 (Application of accounting principles)

John Jewkes, chief accountant for Mountain Springs, Inc., desires your advice on the following accounting transactions. He knows you are majoring in accounting, and wants to be sure the entries he has made reflect generally accepted accounting principles. Evaluate each of his current year entries. Justify your evaluation using the conceptual framework.

1. On December 20, a customer makes a deposit of $10,000 on a $40,000 order for inventory. The order will be filled in the first week of January, the next fiscal year. The cost of the inventory to be sold is $32,000.

Cash	10,000	
Accounts Receivable	30,000	
Cost of Goods Sold	32,000	
Merchandise Inventory		32,000
Sales		40,000

2. During the current year, a lawsuit is filed against Mountain Springs, Inc. for $75,000. Negotiations with the plaintiff have reduced the claim to $40,000. There is still a remote possibility the claim can be further reduced to $25,000 on a technical point. Settlement will not be finalized until next year.

Loss from Lawsuit	25,000	
Estimated Liability from Lawsuit		25,000

3. A stockholder donates equipment to Mountain Springs, Inc. that has a market value of $100,000, but is carried at $30,000 on the stockholder's books.

Equipment	30,000	
Miscellaneous Revenue		30,000

4. The board of directors approve a $40,000 management bonus to be paid next year.

Salaries Expense	40,000	
Salaries Payable		40,000

5. Land purchased for $60,000 is currently worth $200,000.

Land	140,000	
Increase in Equity from Price Change		140,000

Exercise 2—20 (Elements of financial reporting)

For each of the following items, identify the financial statement element being discussed.

1. Changes in equity during a period, except those resulting from investments by owners and distributions to owners.
2. The net assets of an entity.
3. The result of a transaction requiring the future transfer of assets to other entities.
4. An increase in assets from the delivery of goods that constitute the entity's ongoing central operations.
5. An increase in an entity's net assets from incidental transactions.
6. An increase in net assets through the issuance of stock.
7. Decreases in net assets from peripheral transactions of an enterprise.
8. The payment of a dividend.
9. Outflows of assets from the delivery of goods or services.
10. An item offering future value to an entity.

Exercise 2—21 (Assumptions of financial reporting)

In each of the following independent situations, an example is given involving one of the traditional assumptions of the accounting model. For each situation, identify the assumption involved (briefly explain your answer).

1. A subsidiary of Parent Inc. was exhibiting poor earnings performance for the year. In an effort to increase the subsidiary's reported earnings, Parent Inc. purchased products from the subsidiary at twice the normal markup.
2. Johnson Corp. required additional funding to introduce a new product line. Management prepared cash-basis financial statements and presented them to bank officials in order to obtain the loan.
3. When preparing the financial statements for MacNeil & Sons, the accountant included certain personal assets of MacNeil and his sons in preparing the statements.
4. The operations of Uintah Savings & Loan are being evaluated by the federal government. During their investigations, government officials have determined that numerous loans made by top management were unwise and have seriously endangered the future existence of the savings and loan.

5. Pine Valley Ski Resort has experienced a drastic reduction in revenues because of light snowfall for the year. Rather than produce financial statements at the end of the fiscal year, as is traditionally done, management has elected to wait until next year and present results for a two-year period.
6. Colobri Inc. has inventory that was purchased in 1993 at a cost of $150,000. Because of inflation, that same inventory, if purchased today, would cost $225,000. Management would like to report the asset on the balance sheet at its current value.

Exercise 2—22 (Measurement attributes and going concern problems)

One of the underlying assumptions of the accounting model is the "going concern" assumption. When this assumption is questionable, valuation methods used for assets and liabilities may differ from those used when the assumption is viable. For each of the following situations, identify the measurement attribute that would most likely be used if the company is not likely to remain a "going concern."

1. Plant and equipment is carried at an amortized cost on a straight line basis of $1,500,000.
2. Bonds with a maturity price of $2,000,000 and interest in arrears of $500,000 are reported as a noncurrent liability.
3. Accounts receivable are carried at $700,000, the gross amount charged for sales. No allowance for doubtful accounts is reported.
4. The reported LIFO cost of inventory is $300,000.
5. Investments in a subsidiary company are recorded at initial cost plus undistributed profits.

Exercise 2—23 (Theoretical support for corrected balance sheet)

G. Nielsen prepared the following balance sheet for Nielsen Inc. as of December 31, 1996. Review each item listed, and considering the additional data given, prepare a corrected, properly classified balance sheet. Where a change is made in reporting an item, disclose in a separate note the theoretical support for your suggested change. Record any offsetting adjustments in Retained Earnings, except for possible contributed capital changes.

Assets	
Cash	$ 30,000
Trading securities	55,000
Notes receivable	40,000
Accounts receivable	130,000
Inventories	195,000
Land and buildings	520,000
Accumulated depreciation — buildings	(27,000)
Goodwill	40,000
	$983,000

Liabilities	
Accounts payable	$ 85,000
Taxes payable	65,000
Notes payable	120,000
Mortgage payable	273,000
Capital stock	300,000
Retained earnings	140,000
	$983,000

Additional data:

(a) Cash included a bank checking account of $20,000, current checks and money orders on hand of $5,000, and a $5,000 check that could not be cashed. The check was from Davis Co., a customer that had gone out of business. Nielsen feels this $5,000 will probably not be recovered.
(b) Investments in securities are classified as trading securities and reported at year-end market values. They were purchased during 1996 for $66,800.

(c) Nielsen estimates that all receivables are collectible except for a three-year-old, past-due note of $8,000. Past collection experience indicates that two percent of current notes and accounts prove uncollectible.
(d) Land and buildings are recorded at initial cost. At date of acquisition, land was valued at $70,000 and buildings at $450,000. Building depreciation has been correctly recorded.
(e) Goodwill was recorded when Nielsen received an offer of $40,000 more for the business than the recorded asset values.
(f) Of the notes payable, $30,000 will be due in 1997 with the remainder of the notes coming due in 1998 and 1999.
(g) The mortgage is payable in annual payments of $19,500 plus interest.
(h) The capital stock has a par value of $100 per share; 2,500 shares are issued and outstanding.

Exercise 2—24 (Theoretical support for corrected income statement)

Hillstead prepared the following income statement for the calendar year 1996.

Revenues	$80,000
Expenses	50,000
Net income	$30,000

An examination of the records reveals the following:

(a) Hillstead is the sole proprietor.
(b) Business operations include:
1. A catering service
2. An equipment rental shop
3. Rental of a part of Hillstead's home for small receptions

(c) Revenues include:

1. Catering service sales	$50,000
2. Equipment rentals	12,500
3. Reception rental space	17,500
	$80,000

(d) Expenses consisted of:

1. Cost of goods sold (catering)	$15,000
2. Other costs (catering)	11,500
3. Depreciation—equipment rental	1,500
4. Repairs and other costs—equipment rental	2,500
5. Depreciation, $2,000; cleaning, $4,500; and miscellaneous costs, $1,000—reception rental space	7,500
6. Living expenses—family	12,000
	$50,000

Based on the FASB's Conceptual Framework, indicate what changes, if any, you would make in the income statement format and amount of Hillstead's income for 1996 and give theoretical support for your conclusions.

CHAPTER 3

Review of the Accounting Process

CHAPTER TOPICS

- Overview of the Accounting Process
- Recording Phase
- Summarizing Phase
- Accrual Versus Cash-Basis Accounting
- Computers and the Accounting Process
- Special Journals and Subsidiary Ledgers (Appendix 3—1)
- Closing Method for Inventory (Appendix 3—2)

In 1991, 25 Travel was one of Florida's largest travel agencies. Total sales were $68 million, and the company employed 250 people in its 22 independent offices. One year later, 25 Travel was in Chapter 11 bankruptcy.

The size and visibility of 25 Travel agencies made the company's bankruptcy proceedings a hot topic around South Florida. This caused other agencies and the general public to speculate about what went wrong and how the situation might impact tourism in Florida.

Major factors in the bankruptcy included unreported airline ticket sales and sloppy accounting procedures. As one reporter put it, "unreported sales to a national airline ticket clearing house may have been the catalyst leading to the company's failure, but check kiting allegations were the final straw."[1] The check kiting allegations relate to 25 Travel's practice of transferring uncollected funds from one bank account to another in order to keep its operations running smoothly. In addition, 25 Travel's receivables were understated because sales were not properly recorded. Without proper record keeping, many of

1. See "Questions Raised on 25 Travel's Books," *South Florida Business Journal,* November 23, 1992, Sec. 1, p. 1A.

these receivables were never collected. It seems that 25 Travel forgot the cardinal rule of bookkeeping: debits = credits.

As indicated in the above example, all business enterprises, regardless of size or the nature of their operations, need accurate records of business transactions. Businesses that do not keep accurate records will not operate as efficiently and profitably as they could otherwise. In addition, the Foreign Corrupt Practices Act of 1977 requires publicly held companies to keep accurate books and records that fairly reflect business activity.

A variety of reports are prepared from accounting records to assist users in making better economic decisions. As explained in Chapters 1 and 2, general-purpose financial statements are prepared for external user groups, primarily current or potential investors and creditors, who are involved financially with an enterprise but who are not a part of its management team. User groups within organizations, especially those in managerial positions, receive reports to assist them in planning and controlling the day-to-day operations of their organizations. Tax returns and similar reports must be prepared to comply with Internal Revenue Service (IRS) requirements. Special reports are required by various regulatory agencies such as the Securities and Exchange Commission (SEC).

Each of these reports is based on data that are the result of an accounting system and a set of procedures collectively referred to as the **accounting process,** or the **accounting cycle.** While this process follows a fairly standard set of procedures, the exact nature of the **accounting system** used to collect and report the data will depend on the type of business, its size, the volume of transactions processed, the degree of automation employed, and other related factors. The various routines in each system are developed to meet the special needs of the business unit. Every accounting system, however, should be designed to provide accurate information on a timely and efficient basis. At the same time, the system must provide controls that are effective in preventing mistakes and guarding against dishonesty.

Historically, accounting systems were maintained by hand and referred to as **manual systems.** Such systems continue to be used effectively in many situations. In today's business environment, however, most companies use at least some type of automated equipment, such as cash registers or other special-purpose business machines, and many companies have **electronic data processing (EDP) systems** that utilize the capabilities of high-speed computers. Furthermore, the advent of microcomputers has put EDP systems within the reach of almost all smaller companies that previously had to rely on manual or partially mechanized systems. As explained later in the chapter, an EDP system has many advantages and some disadvantages. The important point is that all accounting systems are designed to serve the same information gathering and processing functions. There is no difference in the underlying accounting concepts involved, only in some mechanical aspects of the process and in the appearance of the records and reports. Since it is easier to understand and to illustrate, a manual system will be used for the examples in this chapter and throughout the text.

The purpose of this chapter is to review the basic steps of the accounting process, including a brief review of the mechanics of double-entry accounting. A number of basic accounting terms are presented in the chapter and are included in the glossary at the end of the book.

OVERVIEW OF THE ACCOUNTING PROCESS

The accounting process consists of two interrelated parts: (1) the recording phase and (2) the summarizing phase. The recording phase is concerned with the collection of information about economic transactions and events. For most businesses, the recording function is based on double-entry accounting procedures. In the summarizing phase, the recorded information is organized and summarized, using various formats for a variety of decision-making purposes. There is an overlapping of the two phases, since the recording of transactions is an ongoing activity that does not cease at the end of an accounting period but continues uninterrupted while events of the preceding period are being summarized. The recording and summarizing phases of the accounting process are reviewed and illustrated in this chapter. The form and content of the basic financial statements are discussed in depth and illustrated in Chapters 4, 5, and 6.

The accounting process, illustrated in Exhibit 3-1, generally includes the following steps in well-defined sequence:

Recording Phase

1. Business documents are analyzed. Analysis of the documentation of business activities provides the basis for making an initial record of each transaction.
2. Transactions are recorded. Based on the supporting documents from Step 1, transactions are recorded in chronological order in books of original entry, or journals.
3. Transactions are posted. Transactions, as classified and recorded in the journals, are posted to the appropriate accounts in the general and, where applicable, subsidiary ledgers.

Summarizing Phase

4. A trial balance of the accounts in the general ledger is prepared. The trial balance, usually prepared on a work sheet, provides a summary of the information as classified in the ledger, as well as a general check on the accuracy of recording and posting.
5. Adjusting entries are recorded. Before financial statements can be prepared, all relevant information that has not been recorded must be determined. Often, adjustments are first made on a work sheet and may be formally recorded and posted at any time prior to closing (Step 7). If a work sheet is not used, the adjusting entries must be recorded and posted at this point so the accounts are current prior to the preparation of financial statements.
6. Financial statements are prepared. Statements summarizing operations and showing the financial position and cash flows are prepared from the information on the work sheet or directly from the adjusted accounts.
7. Nominal accounts are closed. Balances in the nominal (temporary) accounts are closed into appropriate summary accounts. As determined in summary accounts, the results of operations are transferred to the appropriate owners' equity accounts.
8. A post-closing trial balance may be taken. A post-closing trial balance is taken to determine the equality of the debits and credits after posting the adjusting and closing entries.
9. Selected accounts may be reversed. Accrued and prepaid balances that were established by adjusting entries may be returned to the nominal accounts that are to be used in recording and summarizing activities involving these items in the new period. This step is not required, but may be desirable as a means of facilitating recording and adjusting routines in the succeeding period.

Recording Phase

Accurate financial statements can be prepared only if transactions have been properly recorded. A **transaction** is an event that involves the transfer or exchange of goods or services between two or more entities. Examples of business transactions include the purchase of merchandise or other assets from suppliers and the sale of goods or services to customers. In addition to transactions, other events and circumstances may affect the assets, liabilities, and owners' equity of the business. Some of those events and circumstances also must be recorded. Examples include the recognition of depreciation on

Exhibit 3-1 The Accounting Process

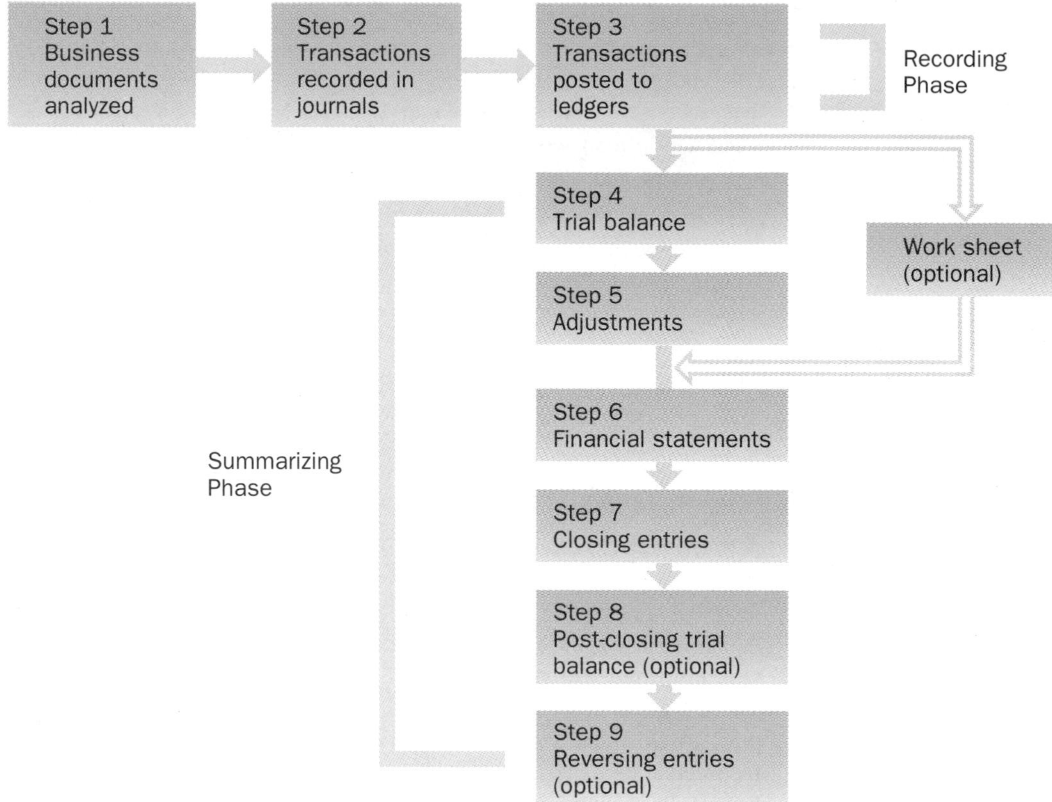

plant assets, a decline in the market value of inventories and investments, or a loss suffered from a flood or an earthquake.

As indicated, the recording phase involves analyzing business documents, journalizing transactions, and posting to the ledger accounts. Before discussing these steps, the system of double-entry accounting will be reviewed, since most businesses use this procedure in recording their transactions.

Double-Entry Accounting. As explained in Chapters 1 and 2, financial accounting rests on a foundation of basic assumptions, concepts, and principles that govern the recording, classifying, summarizing, and reporting of accounting data. **Double-entry accounting** is an old and universally accepted system for recording accounting data. With double-entry accounting, each transaction is recorded in a way that maintains the equality of the basic accounting equation:

Assets = Liabilities + Owners' Equity

To review how double-entry accounting works, recall that a **debit** is an entry on the left side of an account and a **credit** is an entry on the right side. The debit/credit relationships of accounts were explained in detail in your introductory accounting course. Exhibit 3—2 summarizes these relationships for a corporation. You will note that assets, expenses, and dividends are increased by debits and decreased by credits. Liabilities, owners' equity accounts (capital stock and retained earnings), and revenues are increased by credits and decreased by debits.

■ Exhibit 3—2 Debit and Credit Relationships of Accounts

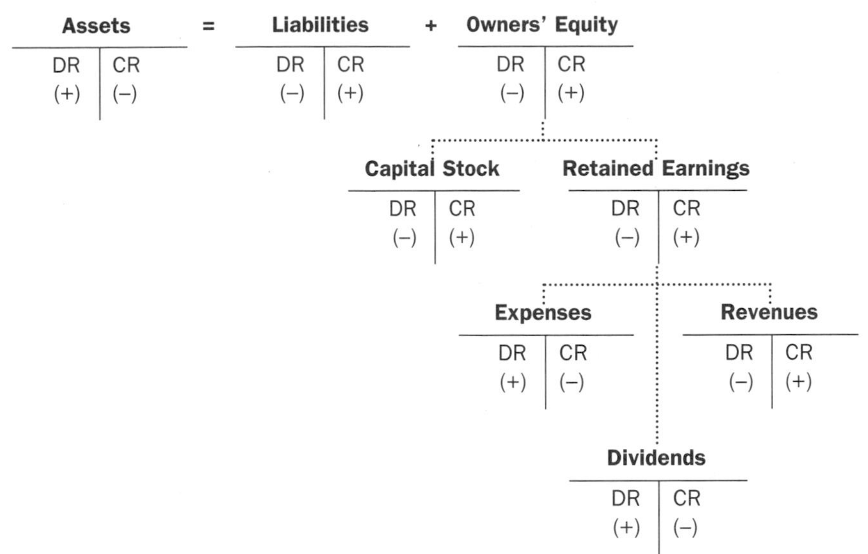

To illustrate double-entry accounting, consider the transactions and journal entries shown in Exhibit 3—3 and their impact on the accounting equation. In studying this illustration, you should note that for each transaction, total debits equal total credits and the equality of the accounting equation is maintained.

To summarize, you should remember the following important features of double-entry accounting:

1. Assets are always increased by debits and decreased by credits.
2. Liability and owners' equity accounts are always increased by credits and decreased by debits.
3. Owners' equity for a corporation includes capital stock accounts and the retained earnings account.
4. Revenues, expenses, and dividends relate to owners' equity through the retained earnings account.
5. Expenses and dividends are increased by debits and decreased by credits.
6. Revenues are increased by credits and decreased by debits.
7. The difference between total revenues and total expenses for a period is net income (loss), which increases (decreases) owners' equity through Retained Earnings.

Analyzing Business Documents. The basic accounting records of a business consist of:

1. Original source materials evidencing transactions, called **business documents** or **source documents,**
2. Records for classifying and recording transactions, known as **journals** or "books of original entry" and,
3. Records for summarizing the effects of transactions upon individual accounts, known as **ledgers.**

The recording phase begins with an analysis of the documentation showing what business activities have occurred. Normally, a business document is the first record of each transaction. Such a document offers detailed information concerning the transaction and also fixes responsibility by naming the parties involved. The business documents provide support for the data to be recorded in the journals. Copies of sales invoices or cash register tapes, for example, are the evidence in support of sales transactions;

■ Exhibit 3—3 Double-Entry Accounting: Illustrative Transactions and Journal Entries

Transaction	Journal Entry			Impact of Transactions on Assets = Liabilities + Owners' Equity
1. Investment by shareholder in a corporation, $10,000	Cash	10,000		+ 10,000 = + 10,000
	Capital Stock		10,000	
2. Purchase of supplies on account, $5,000	Supplies	5,000		+ 5,000 = + 5,000
	Accts. Payable		5,000	
3. Payment of wages expense, $2,500	Wages Expense	2,500		– 2,500 = – 2,500
	Cash		2,500	(Increase in an expense reduces Retained Earnings and, therefore, Owners' Equity)
4. Collection of accounts receivable, $1,000	Cash	1,000		+ 1,000
	Accts. Receivable		1,000	– 1,000 = 0
5. Payment of account payable, $500	Accts. Payable	500		– 500 = – 500
	Cash		500	
6. Sale of merchandise on account for $20,000	Accts. Receivable	20,000		+ 20,000 = +20,000
	Sales		20,000	(Increase in revenue increases Retained Earnings and, therefore, Owners' Equity)
7. Purchase of equipment: $15,000 down payment plus $40,000 long-term note	Equipment	55,000		+ 55,000
	Cash		15,000	– 15,000 = +40,000
	Note Payable		40,000	
8. Payment of cash dividends, $4,000	Dividends	4,000		– 4,000 = – 4,000
	Cash		4,000	(Dividends reduce Retained Earnings and, therefore, Owners' Equity)

purchase invoices support purchase transactions; debit and credit memorandums support adjustments in debtor and creditor balances; check stubs and canceled checks provide data concerning cash disbursements; the corporation minutes book supports entries authorized by action of the board of directors; journal vouchers prepared and approved by appropriate officers are a source of data for adjustments or corrections that are to be reported in the accounts. Documents underlying each recorded transaction provide a means of verifying the accounting records and thus form a vital part of the information and control system.

Journalizing Transactions. Once the information provided on business documents has been analyzed, transactions are recorded in chronological order in the appropriate journals. In some small businesses, all transactions are recorded in a single journal. Most business enterprises, however, maintain various special journals, designed to meet their specific needs, as well as a general journal. A **special journal** is used to record a particular type of frequently recurring transaction. Special journals are commonly used, for example, to record each of the following types of transactions: sales, purchases, cash disbursements, and cash receipts. A **general journal** is used to record all transactions for which a special journal is not maintained. As illustrated, a general journal shows the transaction date and the accounts affected, and allows for a brief description of each transaction. It also provides Debit and Credit columns and a Posting Reference column. When transactions are posted, as explained in the next section, the appropriate ledger account numbers are entered in the Posting Reference column. Special journals are illustrated and explained in Appendix 3—1 at the end of this chapter.

GENERAL JOURNAL **Page** 24

Date		Description	Post. Ref.	Debit	Credit
1996					
July	1	Dividends	330	25,000	
		Dividends Payable	260		25,000
		Declared semiannual cash dividend on common stock.			
	10	Equipment	180	7,500	
		Notes Payable	220		7,500
		Issued note for new equipment.			
	31	Payroll Tax Expense	418	2,650	
		Payroll Taxes Payable	240		2,650
		Recorded payroll taxes for month.			

Posting to the Ledger Accounts. An **account** is used to summarize the effects of transactions on each element of the expanded accounting equation. A **ledger** is a collection of all the accounts maintained by a business and may be in the form of a book or computer files. The specific accounts required by a business unit vary depending on the nature of the business, its properties and activities, the information to be provided on the financial statements, and the controls to be employed in carrying out the accounting functions. The accounts used by a particular business are usually expressed in the form of a **chart of accounts.** This chart lists all accounts in systematic form with identifying numbers or symbols that provide the framework for summarizing business operations.

Information recorded in the journals is transferred to appropriate accounts in the ledger. This transfer is referred to as **posting.** Ledger accounts for Equipment and Notes Payable are presented below, illustrating the posting of the July 10 transaction from the preceding general journal. The posting reference (J24) indicates that the transaction was transferred from page 24 of the general journal. Note that the account numbers for Equipment (180) and Notes Payable (220) are entered in the Posting Reference column of the journal.

It is often desirable to establish separate ledgers for detailed information in support of balance sheet or income statement items. The **general ledger** includes all accounts appearing on the financial statements, while separate **subsidiary ledgers** afford additional detail in support of certain general ledger accounts. For example, a single accounts receivable account is usually carried in the general ledger, and individual customer accounts are recorded in a subsidiary accounts receivable ledger. Also, the capital stock account in the

GENERAL LEDGER

Account EQUIPMENT **Account No.** 180

Date		Item	Post Ref.	Debit	Credit	Balance
1996						
July	1	Balance				10,550
	10	Purchase Equipment	J24	7,500		18,050

Account NOTES PAYABLE **Account No.** 220

Date		Item	Post Ref.	Debit	Credit	Balance
1996						
July	1	Balance				5,750
	10	Purchase Equipment	J24		7,500	13,250

Luca Pacioli

The earliest systematic explanation of modern double-entry accounting is contained in a book on mathematics written in 1494. *Summa de Arithmetica, Geometria, Proportioni et Proportionalita* (Everything about Arithmetic, Geometry, and Proportion) was written by Luca Pacioli, a noted mathematician and a monk of the order of St. Francis. Pacioli was no obscure writer; he once collaborated on a book with Leonardo da Vinci. The bookkeeping portion of *Summa* is called *De Computis et Scripturis* (Of Reckonings and Writings). Pacioli did not invent double-entry accounting; he simply provided an organized treatment of the "method of Venice," which had developed during the fourteenth and fifteenth centuries.

In most respects, the double-entry method explained by Pacioli is the same as that used today. One difference was the use of a third book—the memorial—in addition to the journal and the ledger, which we currently use. The memorial was the book of original entry. Since transactions occurred in a variety of currencies, and also because money was rarely worth its face value, amounts recorded in the memorial were converted to a common working currency before being entered in the journal. In addition, Pacioli didn't outline procedures for the production of periodic financial statements. Business was seen as a succession of individual ventures (like a voyage to trade textiles for spices), and the revenues and expenses for each venture were accounted for separately. Instead of a periodic closing of the nominal accounts, the profit or loss from an individual venture was transferred to the capital account when the venture was completed.

One notable feature of Pacioli's work is that it contains no worked-out examples; the topic of bookkeeping is dealt with strictly in the abstract. Since Pacioli's day, quite a number of accounting students have unsuccessfully tried the same approach in preparing for accounting exams.

Sources:

J. Row Fogo. "History of Bookkeeping." *A History of Accounting and Accountants,* Richard Brown, editor, (London: Frank Cass and Company Limited, 1968): pp. 93-170.

Henry Rand Hatfield. "An Historical Defense of Bookkeeping." *The Journal of Accountancy,* April 1924: pp. 241-253.

general ledger is normally supported by individual stockholder accounts in a subsidiary stockholders ledger. The general ledger account that summarizes the detailed information in a subsidiary ledger is known as a **control account.** Subsidiary ledger accounts are illustrated in Appendix 3—1 at the end of this chapter.

Depending primarily on the number of transactions involved, amounts may be posted to ledger accounts on a daily, weekly, or monthly basis. If a computer system is being used, the posting process may be done automatically as transactions are recorded. At the end of an accounting period, when the posting process has been completed, the balances in the ledger accounts are used for preparing the trial balance.

Summarizing Phase

As noted earlier, the objective of the accounting process is to produce financial statements and other reports that will assist various users in making economic decisions. Once the recording phase is completed, the data must be summarized and organized into a useful format. The remaining steps of the accounting process are designed to accomplish this purpose. These steps will be illustrated using data from Rosi, Inc., a hypothetical merchandising company, for the year ended December 31, 1996.

Preparing a Trial Balance. After all transactions for the period have been posted to the ledger accounts, the balance for each account is determined. Every account will have either a debit, credit, or zero balance. A **trial balance** is a list of all accounts and their balances. The trial balance, therefore, indicates whether total debits equal total credits and thus provides a general check on the accuracy of recording and posting. A trial balance for Rosi, Inc., follows.

Rosi, Inc.
Trial Balance
December 31, 1996

	Debit	Credit
Cash	$ 83,110	
Accounts Receivable	106,500	
Allowance for Doubtful Accounts		$ 1,610
Inventory	45,000	
Prepaid Insurance	8,000	
Interest Receivable	0	
Notes Receivable	28,000	
Land	114,000	
Buildings	156,000	
Accum. Depr.—Buildings		39,000
Furniture & Equipment	19,000	
Accum. Depr.—Furniture & Equipment		3,800
Accounts Payable		37,910
Unearned Rent Revenue		0
Salaries and Wages Payable		0
Interest Payable		0
Payroll Taxes Payable		5,130
Income Taxes Payable		0
Dividends Payable		3,400
Bonds Payable		140,000
Common Stock, $15 par		150,000
Retained Earnings		126,770
Dividends	13,600	
Sales		479,500
Purchases	162,600	
Purchase Discounts		3,290
Cost of Goods Sold	0	
Salaries and Wages Expense	172,450	
Heat, Light, and Power	32,480	
Payroll Tax Expense	18,300	
Advertising Expense	18,600	
Doubtful Accounts Expense	0	
Depr. Exp.—Buildings	0	
Depr. Exp.—Furniture & Equipment	0	
Insurance Expense	0	
Interest Revenue		1,100
Rent Revenue		2,550
Interest Expense	16,420	
Income Tax Expense	0	
Totals	$994,060	$994,060

Preparing Adjusting Entries. In order to report information on a timely basis, the life of a business is divided into relatively short time periods, such as a year, a quarter, or a month. While this is essential for the information to be useful, it does create problems for the accountant who must summarize the financial operations for the designated period and report on the financial position at the end of that period. Transactions during the period have been recorded in the appropriate journals and posted to the ledger accounts. At the end of the period, many accounts require adjustments to reflect current conditions. At this time, too, other financial data, not recognized previously, must be entered in the accounts to bring the books up to date. This requires analysis of individual accounts and various source documents. Based on this analysis, **adjusting entries** are made, and financial statements are prepared using the adjusted account balances.

This part of the accounting process is illustrated using the adjusting data for Rosi, Inc., presented below. The data are classified according to the typical areas requiring adjustment at the end of the designated time period, in this case the year 1996. The accounts listed in the trial balance below do not reflect the adjusting data. The adjusting data must be combined with the information on the trial balance if the resulting financial statements are to appropriately reflect company operating results and financial position.

Adjusting Data for Rosi, Inc.
December 31, 1996

Asset Depreciation:
- (a) Buildings, 5% per year.
- (b) Furniture and equipment, 10% per year.

Doubtful Accounts:
- (c) The allowance for doubtful accounts is to be increased by $1,100.

Accrued Expenses:
- (d) Salaries and wages, $2,150.
- (e) Interest on bonds payable, $5,000.

Accrued Revenues:
- (f) Interest on notes receivable, $250.

Prepaid Expenses:
- (g) Prepaid insurance, $3,800.

Deferred Revenues:
- (h) Unearned rent revenue, $475.

Income taxes:
- (i) Federal and state income taxes, $8,000.

Inventory:
- (j) A periodic inventory system is used; the ending inventory balance is $51,000

Asset Depreciation. Charges to operations for the use of buildings, furniture, and equipment must be recorded at the end of the period. In recording asset depreciation, operations are charged with a portion of the asset's cost, and the carrying value of the asset is reduced by that amount. A reduction in an asset for depreciation is usually recorded by a credit to a contra account, Accumulated Depreciation. A **contra account** (or offset account) is set up to record subtractions from a related account. For example, Allowance for Doubtful Accounts is a contra account to Accounts Receivable. Certain accounts relate to others, but must be added rather than subtracted on the statements, and are referred to as **adjunct accounts.** Examples include Freight-In, which is added to Purchases, and Additional Paid-In Capital, which is added to the capital stock account balance.

Adjustments at the end of the year for depreciation for Rosi, Inc., are as follows:

		Debit	Credit
(a)	Depreciation Expense—Buildings	7,800	
	Accumulated Depreciation—Buildings		7,800
	To record depreciation on buildings at 5% per year.		
(b)	Depreciation Expense—Furniture & Equipment	1,900	
	Accumulated Depreciation—Furniture & Equipment		1,900
	To record depreciation on furniture and equipment at 10% per year.		

Doubtful Accounts. Invariably, when a business allows customers to purchase goods and services on credit, some of the accounts receivable will not be collected, resulting in a charge to income for bad debt expense. Under the accrual concept, an adjustment should be made for the estimated expense in the current period, rather than when specific accounts actually become uncollectible. This produces a better matching of revenues and expenses and therefore a better income measurement. Using this procedure, operations are charged with the estimated expense, and receivables are reduced by means of a contra account, Allowance for Doubtful Accounts. To illustrate, the adjustment for Rosi, Inc., at the end of the year, assuming the allowance account is to be increased by $1,100, would be as follows:

(c)	Doubtful Accounts Expense	1,100	
	Allowance for Doubtful Accounts		1,100
	To adjust for estimated doubtful accounts expense.		

Throughout the accounting period, when there is positive evidence that a specific account is uncollectible, the appropriate amount is written off against the contra account. For example, if a $150 receivable were considered uncollectible, that amount would be written off as follows:

Allowance for Doubtful Accounts	150	
Accounts Receivable		150
To write off an uncollectible account.		

No entry is made to Doubtful Accounts Expense, since the adjusting entry has already provided for an estimated expense based on previous experience for all receivables.

Accrued Expenses. During the period, certain expenses may have been incurred for which payment is not to be made until a subsequent period. At the end of the period, it is necessary to determine and record any expenses not yet recognized. In recording an accrued expense, an expense account is debited and a liability account is credited. The adjusting entries to record accrued expenses for Rosi, Inc., are:

(d)	Salaries and Wages Expense	2,150	
	Salaries and Wages Payable		2,150
	To record accrued salaries and wages.		
(e)	Interest Expense	5,000	
	Interest Payable		5,000
	To record accrued interest on bonds.		

Accrued Revenues. During the period, certain amounts may have been earned, although collection is not to be made until a subsequent period. At the end of the period, it is necessary to determine and record the earnings not yet recognized. In recording accrued revenues, an asset account is debited and a revenue account is credited. The illustrative entry recognizing the accrued revenue for Rosi, Inc., is as follows:

(f)	Interest Receivable	250	
	Interest Revenue		250
	To record accrued interest on notes receivable.		

Prepaid Expenses. During the period, expenditures may have been recorded on the books for commodities or goods that are not to be received or used up currently. At the end of the period, it is necessary to determine the portions of such expenditures that are applicable to subsequent periods, and hence require recognition as assets.

The method of adjusting for prepaid expenses depends on how the expenditures were originally entered in the accounts. They may have been recorded originally as debits to (1) an asset account or (2) an expense account.

Original Debit to an Asset Account. If an asset account was originally debited, the adjusting entry requires that an expense account be debited for the amount applicable to the current period and the asset account be credited. The asset account remains with a debit balance that shows the amount applicable to future periods. An adjusting entry for prepaid insurance for Rosi, Inc., illustrates this situation as follows:

(g) Insurance Expense	4,200	
Prepaid Insurance		4,200
To record expired insurance ($8,000 – $3,800 = $4,200).		

Since the asset account Prepaid Insurance was originally debited, as shown in the trial balance, the amount of the prepayment ($8,000) must be reduced to reflect only the $3,800 that remains unexpired.

Original Debit to an Expense Account. If an expense account was originally debited, the adjusting entry requires that an asset account be debited for the amount applicable to future periods and the expense account be credited. The expense account then remains with a debit balance representing the amount applicable to the current period. For example, if Rosi, Inc., had originally debited Insurance Expense for $8,000, the adjusting entry would be:

Prepaid Insurance ($8,000 – $4,200)	3,800	
Insurance Expense		3,800

Deferred Revenues. Payments may be received from customers prior to the delivery of goods or services. Amounts received in advance are recorded by debiting an asset account, usually Cash, and crediting either a revenue account or a liability account. At the end of the period, it is necessary to determine the amount of revenue earned in the current period and the amount to be deferred to future periods. The method of adjusting for deferred revenues depends on whether the receipts for undelivered goods or services were recorded originally as credits to (1) a revenue account or (2) a liability account.

Original Credit to a Revenue Account. If a revenue account was originally credited, this account is debited and a liability account is credited for the revenue applicable to a future period. The revenue account remains with a credit balance representing the earnings applicable to the current period. As indicated in the trial balance for Rosi, Inc., rent receipts are recorded originally in the rent revenue account. Unearned revenue at the end of 1996 is $475 and is recorded as follows:

(h) Rent Revenue	475	
Unearned Rent Revenue		475
To record unearned rent revenue.		

Original Credit to a Liability Account. If a liability account was originally credited, this account is debited and a revenue account is credited for the amount applicable to the current period. The liability account remains with a credit balance that shows the amount applicable to future periods. For example, if Rosi, Inc., had originally credited Unearned Rent Revenue for $2,550, the adjusting entry would be:

Unearned Rent Revenue	2,075	
Rent Revenue ($2,550 – $475)		2,075

Income Taxes. When a corporation reports earnings, adjustments must be made for federal and state income taxes. Income Tax Expense is debited and Income Tax Payable is credited. The entry to record income taxes for Rosi, Inc., is as follows:

(i) Income Tax Expense	8,000	
Income Taxes Payable		8,000
To record income taxes.		

Note that the above entry assumes a single year-end accrual of income taxes. Most companies record income taxes monthly when estimated payments are made to federal and state taxing authorities.

Adjusting the Inventory Account. The type of adjustment required for the inventory account depends on whether a periodic or a perpetual inventory system is used. When the periodic inventory system is used, physical inventories must be taken at the end of the period to determine the inventory to be reported on the balance sheet and the cost of goods sold to be reported on the income statement. When perpetual inventory records are maintained, the ending inventory and the cost of goods sold balances appear in the ledger. An adjustment is necessary only to correct the recorded balances for any spoilage or theft or bookkeeping errors that may have occurred, as determined by a physical count of the inventory. The inventory procedures for merchandising companies are reviewed in the following paragraphs. Accounting for inventories of manufacturers is explained in a later chapter.

Periodic (Physical) Inventories. When using the **periodic inventory system,** all purchases of merchandise during a period are recorded in a purchases account. At the end of the period, before adjustments are made, the inventory account still reflects the beginning inventory balance. The ending balance, based on a physical count, may be recorded in the inventory account by an adjusting entry. At the same time the inventory account is adjusted, the balance in Purchases and related accounts, such as Purchase Discounts or Freight-In, are transferred to Cost of Goods Sold. In this way, the amount of Cost of Goods Sold is established through a single adjusting entry.

Using the method just described, an adjustment for Rosi, Inc., would be made to the inventory account by debiting it for $6,000 ($51,000 - $45,000), debiting Purchase Discounts for $3,290, crediting Purchases for $162,600, and debiting Cost of Goods Sold for the net amount, $153,310. This would increase Inventory to its ending balance of $51,000, close Purchase Discounts and Purchases, and reflect the amount of Cost of Goods Sold to be reported on the income statement. The adjusting entry would be as follows:

(j)	Inventory	6,000	
	Purchase Discounts	3,290	
	Cost of Goods Sold	153,310	
	Purchases		162,600
	To adjust inventory, cost of goods sold, and related accounts.		

An alternative to the above procedure is illustrated in Appendix 3—2 at the end of this chapter. This alternative is sometimes referred to as the "closing method," while the preceding approach is referred to as the "adjusting method" for a periodic inventory system.

Perpetual Inventories. When a **perpetual inventory system** is maintained, a separate purchases account is not used. The inventory account is debited whenever goods are acquired. When a sale takes place, two entries are required: (1) the sale is recorded in the usual manner, and (2) the merchandise sold is recorded by a debit to Cost of Goods Sold and a credit to Inventory. At any time during the period, Inventory reflects the inventory on hand, and Cost of Goods Sold shows the cost of merchandise sold. At the end of the period, no adjustment is needed for inventory, except to adjust for spoilage or theft as noted earlier. Cost of Goods Sold would be debited and Inventory would be credited for the cost of the spoiled or stolen goods.

Preparing Financial Statements. Once all accounts have been brought up to date through the adjustment process, **financial statements** may be prepared. The data may be taken directly from the adjusted account balances in the ledger, or a work sheet may be used.

Using a Work Sheet. An optional step in the accounting process is to use a **work sheet** to facilitate the preparation of adjusting entries and financial statements. A work sheet is an accounting tool that is often used in organizing large quantities of data. However, preparing a work sheet is not a required step. As indicated, financial statements can be prepared directly from data in adjusted ledger account balances.

When a work sheet is constructed, trial balance data are listed in the first pair of columns. The adjusting entries are listed in the second pair of columns. Sometimes a third pair of columns is included to show the trial balance after adjustment. Account balances, as adjusted, are carried forward to the appropriate financial statement columns. A work sheet for a merchandising enterprise will include a pair of columns for the income statement accounts and a pair for the balance sheet accounts. There are no columns for the statement of cash flows, because this statement requires additional analysis of changes in account balances for the period. The income statement, balance sheet, and statement of cash flows are discussed and illustrated in subsequent chapters. A work sheet for Rosi, Inc., is shown on pages 72 and 73. All adjustments illustrated previously are included.

Closing the Nominal Accounts. Once adjusting entries are formally recorded in the general journal and posted to the ledger accounts, the books are ready to be closed in preparation for a new accounting period. During this closing process, the **nominal (temporary) account** balances are transferred to a **real (permanent) account,** leaving the nominal accounts with a zero balance. Nominal accounts include all income statement accounts plus the dividends account for a corporation or the drawings account for a proprietorship or partnership. The real account that receives the closing amounts from the nominal accounts is Retained Earnings for a corporation or the respective capital accounts for a proprietorship or partnership. Since they are real accounts, these and all other balance sheet accounts remain open and carry their balances forward to the new period.

The mechanics of closing the nominal accounts are straightforward. All revenue accounts with credit balances are closed by being debited; all expense accounts with debit balances are closed by being credited. This reduces these temporary accounts to a zero balance. The difference between the closing debit amounts for revenues and the credit amounts for expenses is net income (or net loss) and is an increase (or decrease) to Retained Earnings. The closing of Dividends reduces Retained Earnings. Thus, the closing entries for revenues, expenses, and dividends may be made directly to Retained Earnings, as follows:

Revenues	xx	
Retained Earnings		xx
To close revenues to Retained Earnings.		
Retained Earnings	xx	
Expenses		xx
To close expenses to Retained Earnings.		
Retained Earnings	xx	
Dividends		xx
To close the dividends account to Retained Earnings.		

An alternative to the closing method described above is to use an **income summary** account. Income Summary is a temporary "clearing" account that is used only to accumulate amounts from the closing entries for revenues and expenses and therefore summarizes the net income or net loss for the period. After revenues and expenses are closed to Income Summary, the balance in that account is then closed to Retained Earnings. Dividends must still be closed directly to Retained Earnings, since dividends do not affect net income and are not closed to Income Summary. If a work sheet is prepared, the balances in the Income Statement columns provide the data for closing revenues and expenses. The **closing**

Closing Entries

1996			
Dec. 31	Sales	479,500	
	Interest Revenue	1,350	
	Rent Revenue	2,075	
	Income Summary		482,925
	To close revenue accounts to Income Summary.		
31	Income Summary	441,710	
	Cost of Goods Sold		153,310
	Salaries and Wages Expense		174,600
	Heat, Light, and Power		32,480
	Payroll Tax Expense		18,300
	Advertising Expense		18,600
	Interest Expense		21,420
	Doubtful Accounts Expense		1,100
	Depreciation Expense—Buildings		7,800
	Depreciation Expense—Furniture and Equipment		1,900
	Insurance Expense		4,200
	Income Tax Expense		8,000
	To close expense accounts to Income Summary.		
31	Income Summary	41,215	
	Retained Earnings		41,215
	To transfer the balance in Income Summary to Retained Earnings.		
31	Retained Earnings	13,600	
	Dividends		13,600
	To close Dividends to Retained Earnings.		

entries for Rosi, Inc., are presented, assuming that an income summary account is used. Note that with the adjusting method illustrated for Inventory, Cost of Goods Sold is already computed. It can then be closed to Income Summary (or directly to Retained Earnings if an income summary account is not used) just like any other operating expense.

Preparing a Post-Closing Trial Balance. After the closing entries are posted, a **post-closing trial balance** may be prepared to verify the equality of the debits and credits for all real accounts. The post-closing trial balance for Rosi, Inc., is on page 74.

Reversing Entries. At the beginning of a new period, the following types of adjusting entries may be reversed:

1. Accrued expenses
2. Accrued revenues
3. Prepaid expenses when the original debit was to an expense account
4. Deferred revenues when the original credit was to a revenue account

Reversing entries are not necessary, but they make it possible to record the expense payments or revenue receipts in the new period in the usual manner. For example, if a reversing entry is not made for accrued expenses, payments in the subsequent period would have to be analyzed as to (1) the amount representing payment of the accrued liability, and (2) the amount representing the expense of the current period. Alternatively, the accrued and deferred accounts could be left unadjusted until the close of the subsequent reporting period when they would be adjusted to their correct balances.

The adjustments establishing accrued and prepaid balances for Rosi, Inc., were illustrated earlier in the chapter. The appropriate reversing entries are shown on page 74.

Rosi.,
Work
December

	Account Title	Trial Balance Debit	Trial Balance Credit	
1	Cash	83,110		1
2	Accounts Receivable	106.500		2
3	Allowance for Doubtful Accounts		1,610	3
4	Inventory	45,000		4
5	Prepaid Insurance	8,000		5
6	Interest Receivable	0		6
7	Notes Receivable	28,000		7
8	Land	114,000		8
9	Buildings	156,000		9
10	Accumulated Depreciation—Buildings		39,000	10
11	Furniture & Equipment	19,000		11
12	Accumulated Depreciation—Furniture & Equipment		3,800	12
13	Accounts Payable		37,910	13
14	Unearned Rent Revenue		0	14
15	Salaries and Wages Payable		0	15
16	Interest Payable		0	16
17	Payroll Taxes Payable		5,130	17
18	Income Taxes Payable		0	18
19	Dividends Payable		3,400	19
20	Bonds Payable		140,000	20
21	Common Stock, $15 par		150,000	21
22	Retained Earnings		126,770	22
23	Dividends	13,600		23
24	Sales		479,500	24
25	Purchases	162,600		25
26	Purchase Discounts		3,290	26
27	Cost of Goods Sold	0		27
28	Salaries and Wages Expense	172,450		28
29	Heat, Light, and Power	32,480		29
30	Payroll Tax Expense	18,300		30
31	Advertising Expense	18,600		31
32	Doubtful Accounts Expense	0		32
33	Depreciation Expense—Buildings	0		33
34	Depreciation Expense—Furniture & Equipment	0		34
35	Insurance Expense	0		35
36	Interest Revenue		1,100	36
37	Rent Revenue		2,550	37
38	Interest Expense	16,420		38
39	Income Tax Expense	0		39
40	Totals	994,060	994,060	40
41	Net Income			41
42				42

Inc.
Sheet
31, 1996

	Adjustments		Income Statement		Balance Sheet		
	Debit	**Credit**	**Debit**	**Credit**	**Debit**	**Credit**	
1					83,110		1
2					106,500		2
3		(c) 1,100				2,710	3
4	(j) 6,000				51,000		4
5		(g) 4,200			3,800		5
6	(f) 250				250		6
7					28,000		7
8					114,000		8
9					156,000		9
10		(a) 7,800				46,800	10
11					19,000		11
12		(b) 1,900				5,700	12
13						37,910	13
14		(h) 475				475	14
15		(d) 2,150				2,150	15
16		(e) 5,000				5,000	16
17						5,130	17
18		(i) 8,000				8,000	18
19						3,400	19
20						140,000	20
21						150,000	21
22						126,770	22
23					13,600		23
24				479,500			24
25		(j) 162,600					25
26	(j) 3,290						26
27	(j) 153,310		153,310				27
28	(d) 2,150		174,600				28
29			32,480				29
30			18,300				30
31			18,600				31
32	(c) 1,100		1,100				32
33	(a) 7,800		7,800				33
34	(b) 1,900		1,900				34
35	(g) 4,200		4,200				35
36		(f) 250		1,350			36
37	(h) 475			2,075			37
38	(e) 5,000		21,420				38
39	(i) 8,000		8,000				39
40	193,475	193,475	441,710	482,925	575,260	534,045	40
41			41,215			41,215	41
42			482,925	482,925	575,260	575,260	42

Rosi, Inc.
Post-Closing Trial Balance
December 31, 1996

	Debit	Credit
Cash	$ 83,110	
Accounts Receivable	106,500	
Allowance for Doubtful Accounts		$ 2,710
Inventory	51,000	
Prepaid Insurance	3,800	
Interest Receivable	250	
Notes Receivable	28,000	
Land	114,000	
Buildings	156,000	
Accumulated Depreciation—Buildings		46,800
Furniture and Equipment	19,000	
Accumulated Depreciation—Furniture and Equipment		5,700
Accounts Payable		37,910
Unearned Rent Revenue		475
Salaries and Wages Payable		2,150
Interest Payable		5,000
Payroll Taxes Payable		5,130
Income Taxes Payable		8,000
Dividends Payable		3,400
Bonds Payable		140,000
Common Stock, $15 par		150,000
Retained Earnings		154,385
	$561,660	$561,660

Reversing Entries

1997			
Jan. 1	Salaries and Wages Payable	2,150	
	Salaries and Wages Expense		2,150
1	Interest Payable	5,000	
	Interest Expense		5,000
1	Interest Revenue	250	
	Interest Receivable		250
1	Unearned Rent Revenue	475	
	Rent Revenue		475

To illustrate accounting for an accrued expense when (1) reversing entries are made and (2) reversing entries are not made, assume that accrued salaries on December 31, 1996, are $350 and on December 31, 1997, are $500. Payment of salaries for the period ending January 4, 1997, is $1,000. Adjustments are made and the books are closed annually on December 31. The possible entries are shown at the top of the next page.

ACCRUAL VERSUS CASH-BASIS ACCOUNTING

The procedures described in the previous sections are those required in a double-entry system based on accrual accounting. **Accrual accounting** recognizes revenues as they are earned, not necessarily when cash is received. Expenses are recognized and recorded when they are incurred, not necessarily when cash is paid. This provides for a better matching of

	(1) Assuming Liability Account is Reversed			(2) Assuming Liability Account is Not Reversed					
				(a) Transaction in Next Period Is Analyzed.			(b) Transaction in Next Period Is Not Analyzed. Adjustment at Close of Next Reporting Period.		
December 31, 1996 Adjusting entry to record accrued salaries.	Salaries Exp. Salaries Payable	350	 350	Salaries Exp. Salaries Payable	350	 350	Salaries Exp. Salaries Payable	350	 350
December 31, 1996 Closing entry to transfer expense to the income summary account.	Income Summary Salaries Exp.	xxx	 xxx	Income Summary Salaries Exp.	xxx	 xxx	Income Summary Salaries Exp.	xxx	 xxx
January 1, 1997 Reversing entry to transfer balance to the account that will be charged when payment is made.	Salaries Payable Salaries Exp.	350	 350	No entry			No entry		
January 4, 1997 Payment of salaries for period ending January 4, 1997.	Salaries Exp. Cash	1,000	 1,000	Salaries Payable Salaries Exp. Cash	350 650	 1,000	Salaries Exp. Cash	1,000	 1,000
December 31, 1997 Adjusting entry to record accrued salaries.	Salaries Exp. Salaries Payable	500	 500	Salaries Exp. Salaries Payable	500	 500	Salaries Exp. Salaries Payable	150	 150

revenues and expenses during an accounting period and generally results in financial statements that more accurately reflect a company's financial position and results of operations.[2]

Some accounting systems are based on cash receipts and cash disbursements instead of accrual accounting. **Cash-basis accounting** procedures frequently are found in organizations not requiring a complete set of double-entry records. Such organizations might include smaller, unincorporated businesses, and some nonprofit organizations. Professionals engaged in service businesses, such as CPAs, dentists, and engineers, also have traditionally used cash accounting systems. Even many of these organizations, however, periodically use professional accountants to prepare financial statements and other required reports on an accrual basis.

Discussion continues as to the appropriateness of using cash accounting systems, especially as a basis for determining tax liabilities. The FASB, in *Concepts Statement No. 1,* indicates that accrual accounting provides a better basis for financial reports than does information showing only cash receipts and disbursements. The AICPA's position, however, is that the cash basis is appropriate for some smaller companies and especially for companies in the service industry. Until this issue is settled, accountants will continue to be asked on occasion to convert cash-based records to generally accepted accrual-based financial statements. The concepts involved are described and illustrated in Chapter 6, which explains the statement of cash flows.

2. In Concepts Statement No. 6, the FASB discusses the concept of accrual accounting and relates it to the objectives of financial reporting. *Statement of Financial Accounting Concepts No. 6,* "Elements of Financial Statements" (Stamford: Financial Accounting Standards Board, December 1985).

Why Doesn't the United States Government Use Accrual Accounting?

In February 1993, the Office of Management and Budget forecast that the budget deficit for the United States government for fiscal 1993 would total $332 billion. The deficit was projected to decrease to only $205 billion in 1996. The continuing inability of the federal government to balance its budget has prompted a flood of proposals, accusations, campaign slogans, and TV infomercials. One suggested remedy is that the U.S. government adopt accrual accounting. The cash basis used by the federal government makes no attempt to differentiate between operating expenditures, such as current period salaries, and capital expenditures, such as amounts spent on interstate highway construction. All cash expenditures are lumped together, the total is subtracted from total cash receipts, and the difference is called the deficit. Accrual accounting, it is claimed, would yield a more accurate picture of the government's financial health.

This call for accrual accounting by the federal government is not a new one. In 1975, Arthur Andersen, the public accounting firm, assisted the U.S. government in preparing a prototype set of financial statements using accrual accounting. These financial statements are still prepared annually, but are not widely disseminated by the government. A look at the 1991 balance sheet reveals why this might be so. Total reported assets were $1.394 trillion while total liabilities were $4.540 trillion, resulting in a negative equity of $3.146 trillion. Thus far, the only national government to adopt the accrual basis for its official accounting system is New Zealand.

Some claim that the use of accrual accounting would make the reported federal budget numbers less subject to manipulation. One of the most blatant acts of manipulation occurred in 1987 when Congress ordered the Department of Defense to change its payday from the last day in September, which is the last day in the federal government's fiscal year, to the first day in October. Since the cash basis requires that expenditures be recognized in the period they are paid instead of when they are incurred, this simple delay in mailing out the paychecks reduced the reported deficit for fiscal 1987 by $1 billion.

The cash basis is certainly subject to some manipulation, but the same can be said of the accrual basis. If the federal government were to adopt the accrual basis, cash outlays would then have to be classified as capital expenditures or operating expenditures. For capital expenditures, lawmakers would be required to estimate depreciable lives. Imagine a Congress empowered to make accounting judgments—scary.

Questions:

1. The "equity" in the 1991 prototype balance sheet of the U.S. federal government was a negative $3.146 trillion. What aspects of the historical cost accounting model might have caused this prototype balance sheet to look worse than it really is?
2. How can Congress take advantage of cash-basis accounting to manipulate the reported deficit? How could Congress use accrual accounting to manipulate the reported deficit?

Sources:

"Clinton's Budget at a Glance," *The Wall Street Journal,* February 19, 1993, p. A4.

"Balancing the Government's Books," *The Economist,* January 25, 1992.

Charles A. Bowsher. "Commentary on the Federal Budget: Presenting and Facing the Facts." *Accounting Horizons,* June 1990, p. 96.

When using an accrual-based system of accounting, it is often necessary to correct the accounts for accrual adjustments not made or made incorrectly. Errors of this type generally involve the failure to record accrued expenses and revenues or the failure to record a prepaid expense or an unearned revenue item. Such errors will result in reported income on the income statement being too high or too low and a corresponding over- or understatement of assets or liabilities on the balance sheet.

To illustrate, assume that at the end of the year $10,000 of sales salaries had been earned but had not been recorded. The failure to record this accrued expense would understate operating expenses and the corresponding payroll liability in the current year. The result of this error would be an overstatement of net income and retained earnings for the current year. Unless corrected, the expenses of the following year would be overstated, resulting in an understatement of net income for that year, which would then correct the retained earnings balance. The topic of error corrections, including those dealing with accrual-based accounting, is discussed fully in a later chapter.

COMPUTERS AND THE ACCOUNTING PROCESS

The usual procedures for recording transactions and the sequence of activities leading to the preparation of financial statements have been briefly reviewed in this chapter. These procedures and activities are referred to collectively as the accounting process or accounting cycle.

As an organization grows in size and complexity, the recording and summarizing processes become more involved, and means are sought for improving efficiency and reducing costs. Some enterprises may find that a system involving primarily manual operations is adequate in meeting their needs. Others find that information processing needs can be handled effectively only through the use of computers.

Companies requiring great speed and accuracy in processing large amounts of accounting data utilize computer systems capable of storing and recalling data, performing many mathematical functions, and making certain routine decisions based on mathematical comparisons. Early business computers were descendants of the scientific computers developed during World War II. Use of computers for accounting purposes was resisted initially because of concerns about high costs. To get a sense for how high the cost was in those early days, consider that it has been estimated that the cost of computing has been cut in half every three years since 1950. That means that to buy the same computing power that one can get for $1,000 in 1995 would have cost approximately $32,768,000 in 1950. Another concern with using those early computers for accounting purposes was reliability. Anyone who has experienced a hard disk crash on the reliable machines of the 1990s can appreciate the apprehension felt by accountants in 1950 who were asked to entrust the bookkeeping function to a roomful of vacuum tubes, wires, and punch cards.

Business computing in the 1960s was characterized by batch computing—all computer jobs were initiated from terminals located near the computer itself, and transactions were processed in batches. The 1970s saw the development of time sharing arrangements where computers were accessed from remote locations and more on-line, real-time processing was done.

Technological advances in integrated circuitry and microchips led to one of the most significant phenomena of the 1980s—the development of *personal computers (PCs)*. These compact, relatively inexpensive computers have changed the way in which many companies and individuals keep track of their business activities. These computers are being used for a variety of activities, including: financial analysis, accounting functions, word processing, data base management, inventory control, and credit analysis of customers. As uses have expanded, software packages have been developed to meet current and future demand. The impact of PCs is felt not only in business, but in education and in family life. Several colleges now require entering freshmen to purchase their own PCs for use in a variety of business, mathematics, and science courses. Exposure to computers, and especially the PC, is also very common in elementary and secondary school curricula.

This computer revolution has rapidly changed society and, along with it, the way business is conducted and, therefore, the way accounting functions are performed. The 1990s are spoken of as the Decade of Networking—indicating that the PCs on everyone's desk in the 1980s have been and will increasingly be interconnected. The opportunities for information exchange will expand exponentially. However, despite their tremendous

Russian Accounting

Were there accountants in the old Soviet Union? Absolutely. A Soviet-style centralized economy requires a sophisticated statistical database for use by central planners. A drawback of a unified information system like this is that it places a premium on ease of aggregation. All firms use a uniform chart of accounts, and accountants are reduced to filling in spaces in government forms instead of using individual judgment to account for unique circumstances. In this type of environment, accountants are, in practice, merely bookkeepers.

With the increase in Western joint ventures and the rise of homegrown Russian enterprises, accounting and accountants in Russia are evolving. One of the most fundamental changes is an increased focus on using accrual accounting to measure income. According to Richard Lewis, partner in the Moscow office of Ernst & Young, "No one in the past was concerned about whether you made a profit. If you made one, it was likely to be taken away, whereas if you made a loss, you would be given money by the government." Formerly, revenues were recognized only when cash was received, partly because of the uncertainty of payment. In addition, bad debt expense was recognized only when there was absolutely no chance of recovery of a debt.

Many accountants from the West have been enlisted in the effort to explain the ins and outs of FIFO, LIFO, goodwill, and dividends to the Russians. However, not all the assistance offered by Western entrepreneurs has been welcomed. Occasionally, consultants from the West have tried to sell complex systems to countries struggling to implement basic accrual accounting. As one Eastern Europe official put it: "You are trying to teach us how to make juice out of oranges. Instead, we need to learn how to make soup from potatoes."

Questions:

1. In the old Soviet Union, a single accounting system was used to generate statistics for use in central planning, to evaluate individual firm performance, and to provide data for taxation. In the United States, separate, though related, systems are used to accomplish these tasks. What advantages do you see in the old Soviet system? In the U.S. system?

2. Accountants in the old Soviet Union possessed little prestige. Why do you think this was so?

3. Do you have any advice to give a budding Russian accountant about the dangers of accrual accounting?

Sources:

Andrew Jack. "Working Russian Model Now in Need of Overhaul." *Financial Times*, July 31, 1992.

Alison Leigh Cowan. "Profit? Loss? A Primer for Soviets." *The New York Times*, September 22, 1990, p. 17.

capabilities, computers cannot replace skilled accountants. In fact, their presence places increased demands on the accountant in directing the operations of the computer systems to assure the use of appropriate procedures. Although all arithmetical operations can be assumed to be done accurately by computers, the validity of the output data depends on the adequacy of the instructions given the computer. Unlike a human accountant, a computer cannot think for itself but must be given explicit instructions for performing each operation. This has certain advantages in that the accountant can be sure every direction will be carried out precisely. On the other hand, this places a great responsibility on the accountant to anticipate any unusual situations requiring special consideration or judgment. Various control techniques also must be developed for checking and verifying data recorded in electronic form.

The significance of the accounting process in our society and its applicability to every business unit, regardless of size, must be appreciated. Although the procedures may be modified to meet special conditions and may be performed through a variety of manual or computer systems, the process reviewed in this chapter is fundamental to the accounting systems of all enterprises.

APPENDIX 3-1

Special Journals and Subsidiary Ledgers

In recording transactions, many companies use **special journals** in addition to the general journal. Special journals eliminate much of the repetitive work involved in recording routine transactions. In addition, they permit the recording functions to be divided among accounting personnel, each individual being responsible for a separate record. This specialization often results in greater efficiency and increased accuracy, as well as a higher degree of control.

Some examples of special journals are the sales journal, the purchases journal, the cash receipts journal, the cash disbursements journal, the payroll register, and the voucher register.

Sales on account are recorded in the **sales journal**. The subsequent collections on account, as well as other transactions involving the receipt of cash, are recorded in the **cash receipts journal**. Merchandise purchases on account are entered in a **purchases journal** or a **voucher register**. Subsequent payments on account, as well as other transactions involving the payment of cash, are recorded in a **cash disbursements journal** or a **check register**. A payroll register may be employed to accumulate payroll information, including payroll deductions and withholdings for taxes.

Column headings in the various journals specify the accounts to be debited or credited; account titles and explanations may therefore be omitted in recording routine transactions. A Sundry column is usually provided for transactions that are relatively infrequent, and account titles must be entered in recording such transactions.

The use of special journals facilitates recording and also simplifies the posting process, because the totals of many transactions, rather than separate data for each transaction, can be posted to the ledger accounts. Certain data must be transferred individually—data affecting individual accounts receivable and accounts payable and data reported in the Sundry columns—but the overall volume of posting is substantially reduced.

The format of a particular journal must satisfy the needs of the individual business unit. For example, with an automated or computerized system, the general journal, any specialized journals, and subsidiary ledgers may be modified or eliminated. Recognizing that modifications are necessary for individual systems, the following sections discuss a voucher system and illustrate some special journals that are commonly used with manual accounting systems.

VOUCHER SYSTEM

Relatively large organizations ordinarily provide for the control of purchases and cash disbursements through adoption of some form of a **voucher system.** With the use of a voucher system, checks may be drawn only upon a written authorization in the form of a **voucher** approved by some responsible official.

A voucher is prepared, not only in support of each payment to be made for goods and services purchased on account, but also for all other transactions calling for payment by check, including cash purchases, retirement of debt, replenishment of petty cash funds, payrolls, and dividends. The voucher identifies the person authorizing the expenditure, explains the nature of the transaction, and names the accounts affected by the transaction. For control purposes, vouchers should be prenumbered, checked against purchase invoices, and compared with receiving reports. Upon verification, the voucher and the related business documents are submitted to the appropriate official for final approval. When approved, the prenumbered voucher is recorded in a voucher register. The voucher register is a book of original entry and takes the place of a purchases journal. Charges on each voucher are classified and recorded in appropriate Debit columns, and the amount to be paid is listed in an Accounts Payable or Vouchers Payable column. After a voucher is entered in the register, it is placed in an unpaid vouchers file together with its supporting documents.

Checks are written in payment of individual vouchers. The checks are recorded in a check register, which is used in place of a cash payments journal, as debits to Accounts Payable or Vouchers Payable and credits to Cash. Since charges to the various asset, liability, or expense accounts were recognized when the payable was recorded in the voucher register, these accounts need not be listed in the payments record. When a check is issued, payment of the voucher is reported in the voucher register by entering the check number and the payment date. Paid vouchers and supporting documents are removed from the unpaid file, marked "paid," and placed in a separate paid vouchers file. The balance of the payable account, after the credit for total vouchers issued and the debit for total vouchers paid, should be equal to the sum of the unpaid vouchers file. The voucher register, while representing a journal, also provides the detail in support of the accounts payable or vouchers payable total.

ILLUSTRATION OF SPECIAL JOURNALS AND SUBSIDIARY LEDGERS

Assume that Central Valley, Inc., maintains the following books of original entry: sales journal, cash receipts journal, voucher register, check register, and general journal. As noted, the format of a particular journal must satisfy the needs of the individual business unit. Those presented for Central Valley, Inc., are illustrative only.

Sales Journal

The sales journal for the month of July 1996 appears as follows:

SALES JOURNAL **Page 6**

Date		Invoice No.	Account Debited	Post. Ref.	Accts. Rec. Dr. Sales Cr.
1996					
July	2	701	The Chocolate Factory	✓	3,450
	6	702	Huffman Company	✓	6,510
	10	703	Stocks and Co.	✓	1,525
	12	704	Bennet, Inc.	✓	4,860
	15	705	The Chocolate Factory	✓	2,000
	18	706	Ridnour Corporation	✓	5,940
	20	707	Hillcrest Sales Co.	✓	1,910
	23	708	Kirstein, Inc.	✓	7,650
	27	709	Datamark Systems Inc.	✓	1,280
	29	710	Fuller Distributing Co.	✓	2,925
	31	711	Stocks and Co.	✓	2,100
					40,150
					(116) (41)

As illustrated, credit sales are recorded by debits to Accounts Receivable and credits to Sales. The sales invoice number provides a reference to the original source document for each transaction. Debits are posted to individual customers' accounts in the accounts receivable subsidiary ledger as indicated by a check (✓) in the Posting Reference column. The total sales for the month ($40,150) are posted to Accounts Receivable and Sales (accounts #116 and #41, respectively).

Cash Receipts Journal

The cash receipts journal for Central Valley, Inc., for July 1996 appears as follows:

CASH RECEIPTS JOURNAL **Page** 8

Date		Account Credited	Post. Ref.	Sundry Accounts Cr.	Accounts Receivable Cr.	Sales Discounts Dr.	Cash Dr.
1996							
July	3	Hamilton Sign Co.	✓		5,650	113	5,537
	7	DataMark Systems Inc.	✓		1,400	28	1,372
	8	Sales	41	365			365
	10	The Chocolate Factory	✓		3,450	69	3,381
	11	Sawyer Co.	✓		2,735		2,735
	14	Rohas, Inc.	✓		4,875		4,875
	16	Milo Company	✓		920		920
	17	Poynter Corp.	✓		6,100		6,100
	21	Earnst Co.	✓		6,870		6,870
	22	Tax Refund Receivable	120	5,780			5,780
	25	Sales	41	440			440
	29	Hillcrest Sales Co.	✓		1,900	38	1,862
	31	The Chocolate Factory	✓		2,000		2,000
	31	Notes Receivable	113	8,500			
		Interest Revenue	72	65			8,565
				15,150	35,900	248	50,802
				(✓)	(116)	(42)	(111)

The cash receipts journal records all receipts of cash. Collections of cash from previously recorded credit sales are posted in total as a credit to Accounts Receivable (account #116) and as debits to Sales Discounts (account #42) and Cash (account #111). The credits to Accounts Receivable are posted to the individual customer accounts in the subsidiary ledger as noted by the check (✓) in the Posting Reference column. Cash sales, e.g., as shown for July 8 and July 25, are posted individually as a credit to Sales (account #41) and as a part of the total debit to Cash. Other transactions involving cash receipts, e.g., the collection of a note receivable on July 31, are posted individually as credits and as a part of the total debit to Cash.

Voucher Register

As noted, the voucher register takes the place of a purchases journal, providing a record of all authorized payments to be made by check. A partial voucher register is presented. For illustrative purposes, separate debit columns are provided for two accounts—Purchases and Payroll. Other items are recorded in the Sundry Dr. column. Additional separate columns could be added for other items, such as advertising, if desired. The total amount of each column is posted to the corresponding account, with the exception of the Sundry Dr. and Cr. columns, which are posted individually.

VOUCHER REGISTER

	Vouch.		Paid		Accounts Payable	Purchases	Payroll			Sundry	
									Post.	Amount	
Date	No.	Payee	Date	Ck. No.	Cr.	Dr.	Dr.	Account	Ref.	Dr.	Cr.
31	7132	Security National Bank	7/31	3106	9,120			Notes Payable	211	9,120	
31	7133	Payroll	7/31	3107	1,640		2,130	FICA Taxes Payable	215		90
								Income Taxes Payable	214		400
31	7134	Far Fabrications			3,290	3,290					
31	7135	Midland Inc.			1,500	1,500					
31	7136	Nyland Supply Co.			5,550	5,550					
31		Total			55,375	24,930	2,130			33,645	5,330
					(213)	(51)	(620)			(✓)	(✓)

Check Register

A partial check register is illustrated below. It accounts for all the checks issued during the period. Checks are issued only in payment of properly approved vouchers. The payee is designated together with the number of the voucher authorizing the payment.

CHECK REGISTER

Date	Check No.	Account Debited	Voucher No.	Accounts Payable Dr.	Purchase Discounts Cr.	Cash Cr.
31	3106	Security National Bank	7132	9,120		9,120
31	3107	Payroll	7133	1,640		1,640
31	3108	Pat Bunnell	7005	1,500	30	1,470
31		Total		61,160	275	60,885
				(213)	(52)	(111)

General Journal

Regardless of the number and nature of special journals, certain transactions cannot appropriately be recorded in the special journals and are recorded in the general journal. A general journal with an illustrative entry during the month of July is illustrated on the next page. This general journal is prepared in two-column form. A pair of Debit and Credit columns is provided for the entries that are to be made to the general ledger accounts.

GENERAL JOURNAL **Page 3**

Date		Description	Post. Ref.	Debit	Credit
1996					
July	31	Allowance for Doubtful Accounts	117	1,270	
		Accounts Receivable	116		1,270
		To write off uncollectible account.			
		(Rit-Z Shop)			

Subsidiary Ledgers

As explained in the chapter, subsidiary ledgers provide the detail of individual accounts in support of a control account in the general ledger. Whenever possible, individual postings to subsidiary accounts are made directly from the business documents evidencing the transactions. This practice saves time and avoids errors that might arise in summarizing and transferring this information. If postings to the subsidiary records and to the control accounts are made accurately, the sum of the detail in a subsidiary record will agree with the balance in the control account. A reconciliation of each subsidiary ledger with its related control account should be made periodically, and any discrepancies found should be investigated and corrected.

As an illustration of the relationship of a general ledger control account to its subsidiary ledger accounts, the accounts receivable control account is shown. Three of the subsidiary accounts are also shown.

GENERAL LEDGER

Account: ACCOUNTS RECEIVABLE **ACCOUNT NO.** 116

Date		Item	Post. Ref.	Debit	Credit	Balance
1996						
July	1	Balance				9,200
	31	Sales on account	S6	40,150		49,350
	31	Collections on account	CR8		35,900	13,450
	31	Write-off of uncollectible account (Rit-Z Shop)	J3		1,270	12,180

Accounts Receivable Subsidiary Ledger

Name: Stocks and Co.
Address: 546 South Fox Rd., Chicago, IL 60665

Date		Item	Post. Ref.	Debit	Credit	Balance
1996						
July	1	Balance				1,000
	10	Purchase	S6	1,525		2,525
	31	Purchase	S6	2,100		4,625

Name: The Chocolate Factory
Address: 7890 Redwood Dr., Pittsburgh, PA 15234

Date		Item	Post. Ref.	Debit	Credit	Balance
1996						
July	2	Purchase	S6	3,450		3,450
	10	Payment	CR8		3,450	–0–
	15	Purchase	S6	2,000		2,000
	31	Payment	CR8		2,000	–0–

Name: The Rit-Z Shop
Address: 789 Cotton Drive, Phoenix, AZ 85090

Date		Item	Post. Ref.	Debit	Credit	Balance
1996						
July	1	Balance				1,270
	31	Write-off of uncollectible account (6 months old)	J3		1,270	–0–

APPENDIX 3-2

Closing Method for Inventory

In the work sheet presented in the chapter, Inventory and related accounts are adjusted through a cost of goods sold account. An alternative approach is to "close" beginning and ending inventory amounts to Income Summary. With this procedure, cost of goods sold appears only as a calculated figure in the income statement; it does not appear in the accounts. This method is illustrated in the work sheet following. Adjusting entries (a) through (i) are the same as those in the earlier example for Rosi, Inc. Using the closing procedure, however, the following entries would be made for Inventory:

		Debit	Credit
(j)	Income Summary	45,000	
	Inventory		45,000
	To close beginning inventory to Income Summary.		
(k)	Inventory	51,000	
	Income Summary		51,000
	To record ending inventory.		

Note that Income Summary shows both a debit and a credit on the income statement section of the work sheet, and no adjustment is made for Purchases and Purchase Discounts. The balances in these accounts are extended to the Income Statement columns in the work sheet. Subsequently, these accounts would be closed to Income Summary as part of the normal closing process.

Other variations of the closing approach to merchandise inventory can be found in practice. Regardless of the approach used, financial statements will reflect the same ending inventory and cost of goods sold amounts.

Rosi.,
Work
December

	Account Title	Trial Balance		
		Debit	**Credit**	
1	Cash	83,110		1
2	Accounts Receivable	106.500		2
3	Allowance for Doubtful Accounts		1,610	3
4	Inventory	45,000		4
5	Prepaid Insurance	8,000		5
6	Interest Receivable	0		6
7	Notes Receivable	28,000		7
8	Land	114,000		8
9	Buildings	156,000		9
10	Accumulated Depreciation—Buildings		39,000	10
11	Furniture & Equipment	19,000		11
12	Accumulated Depreciation—Furniture & Equipment		3,800	12
13	Accounts Payable		37,910	13
14	Unearned Rent Revenue		0	14
15	Salaries and Wages Payable		0	15
16	Interest Payable		0	16
17	Payroll Taxes Payable		5,130	17
18	Income Taxes Payable		0	18
19	Dividends Payable		3,400	19
20	Bonds Payable		140,000	20
21	Common Stock, $15 par		150,000	21
22	Retained Earnings		126,770	22
23	Dividends	13,600		23
24	Income Summary		0	24
25	Sales		479,500	25
26	Purchases	162,600		26
27	Purchase Discounts		3,290	27
28	Salaries and Wages Expense	172,450		28
29	Heat, Light, And Power	32,480		29
30	Payroll Tax Expense	18,300		30
31	Advertising Expense	18,600		31
32	Doubtful Accounts Expense	0		32
33	Depreciation Expense—Buildings	0		33
34	Depreciation Expense—Furniture & Equipment	0		34
35	Insurance Expense	0		35
36	Interest Revenue		1,100	36
37	Rent Revenue		2,550	37
38	Interest Expense	16,420		38
39	Income Tax Expense	0		39
40	Totals	994,060	994,060	40
41	Net Income			41
42				42

Inc.
Sheet
31, 1996

	Adjustments		Income Statement		Balance Sheet		
	Debit	**Credit**	**Debit**	**Credit**	**Debit**	**Credit**	
1					83,110		1
2					106,500		2
3		(c) 1,100				2,710	3
4	(k) 51,000	(j) 45,000			51,000		4
5		(g) 4,200			3,800		5
6	(f) 250				250		6
7					28,000		7
8					114,000		8
9					156,000		9
10		(a) 7,800				46,800	10
11					19,000		11
12		(b) 1,900				5,700	12
13						37,910	13
14		(h) 475				475	14
15		(d) 2,150				2,150	15
16		(e) 5,000				5,000	16
17						5,130	17
18		(i) 8,000				8,000	18
19						3,400	19
20						140,000	20
21						150,000	21
22						126,770	22
23					13,600		23
24	(j) 45,000	(k) 51,000	45,000	51,000			24
25				479,500			25
26			162,600				26
27				3,290			27
28	(d) 2,150		174,600				28
29			32,480				29
30			18,300				30
31			18,600				31
32	(c) 1,100		1,100				32
33	(a) 7,800		7,800				33
34	(b) 1,900		1,900				34
35	(g) 4,200		4,200				35
36		(f) 250		1,350			36
37	(h) 475			2,075			37
38	(e) 5,000		21,420				38
39	(i) 8,000		8,000				39
40	126,875	126,875	496,000	537,215	575,260	534,045	40
41			41,215			41,215	41
42			537,215	537,215	575,260	575,260	42

KEY TERMS

Account 63
Accounting process (cycle) 58
Accounting system 58
Accrual accounting 74
Adjunct accounts 66
Adjusting entries 65
Business (source) documents 61
Cash-basis accounting 75
Chart of accounts 63
Closing entries 70
Contra account 66
Control account 64
Credit 60
Debit 60
Double-entry accounting 60
Electronic data processing (EDP) systems 58
General journal 62
General ledger 63
Income summary 70
Journals 61
Ledgers 61
Nominal (temporary) account 70
Periodic inventory system 69
Perpetual inventory system 69
Post-closing trial balance 71
Posting 63
Real (permanent) account 70
Reversing entries 71
Special journal 62
Subsidiary ledgers 63
Transaction 59
Trial balance 64
Voucher system 79
Work sheet 70

QUESTIONS

1. What type of reports are generated from the accounting system?
2. What are the main similarities and differences between a manual and an automated accounting system?
3. Distinguish between the recording and summarizing phases of the accounting process.
4. List and describe the steps in the accounting process. Why is each step necessary? Which steps are optional?
5. Under double-entry accounting, what are the debit/credit relationships of accounts?
6. Distinguish between: (a) real and nominal accounts, (b) general journal and special journals, and (c) general ledger and subsidiary ledgers.
7. As Beechnut Mining Company's independent certified public accountant, you find that the company accountant posts adjusting and closing entries directly to the ledger without formal entries in the general journal. How would you evaluate this procedure in your report to management?
8. Explain the nature and the purpose of (a) adjusting entries, (b) closing entries, and (c) reversing entries.
9. Give three common examples of contra accounts. Explain why contra accounts are used.
10. Payment of insurance in advance may be recorded in either (a) an expense account or (b) an asset account. Which method would you recommend? What periodic entries are required under each method?
11. Distinguish between the procedures followed by a merchandising enterprise using a periodic (physical) inventory system and one using a perpetual inventory system.
12. Describe the nature and purpose of a work sheet.
13. What effect, if any, does the use of a work sheet have on the sequence of the summarizing phase of the accounting process?
14. The accountant for the Miller Hardware Store, after completing all adjustments except for the merchandise inventory, makes the following entry to close the beginning inventory, to set up the ending inventory, to close all nominal accounts, and to report the net result of operations in the capital account.

Inventory (Dec. 31, 1996)	22,500	
Sales	250,000	
Purchase Discounts	2,500	
Inventory (Jan. 1, 1996)		25,000
Purchases		175,000
Selling Expense		25,000
General and Administrative Expenses		18,750
Interest Expense		1,875
M. Miller, Capital		29,375

(a) Would you regard this procedure as being acceptable?
(b) What alternate procedure could you have followed to close the nominal accounts?

15. From the following list of accounts, determine which ones should be closed and whether each would normally be closed by a debit or by a credit entry.

Cash
Rent Expense
Accounts Receivable
Land
Depreciation Expense
Sales Revenue
Sales Discounts
Purchases
Freight-In
Retained Earnings
Capital Stock
Interest Revenue
Advertising Expense

Purchase Discounts
Notes Payable
Dividends
Accounts Payable

16. Distinguish between accrual and cash-basis accounting.
17. Is greater accuracy achieved in financial statements prepared from double-entry accrual data as compared with cash data? Explain.
18. What are the major advantages of electronic data processing as compared with manual processing of accounting data?
19. One of your clients overheard a computer manufacturer sales representative saying the computer will make the accountant obsolete. How would you respond to this comment?

*20. What advantages are provided through the use of: (a) special journals, (b) subsidiary ledgers, and (c) the voucher system?

*21. The Tantor Co. maintains a sales journal, a voucher register, a cash receipts journal, a check register and a general journal. For each account listed below, indicate the most common journal sources of debits and credits.

(a) Cash
(b) Temporary Investments
(c) Notes Receivable
(d) Accounts Receivable
(e) Allowance for Doubtful Accounts
(f) Merchandise Inventory
(g) Land and Buildings
(h) Accumulated Depreciation
(i) Notes Payable
(j) Vouchers Payable
(k) Capital Stock
(l) Retained Earnings
(m) Sales
(n) Sales Discounts
(o) Purchases
(p) Freight-In
(q) Purchase Returns
(r) Purchase Discounts
(s) Salaries Expense
(t) Depreciation Expense

**22. How does the closing method differ from the adjusting method for Inventory and related accounts in a periodic inventory system?

*Relates to Appendix 3—1
**Relates to Appendix 3—2

DISCUSSION CASES

Case 3—1 (Where is your cash box?)

Consider the following account of a veterinarian attempting to hire his first bookkeeper:

> Miss Harbottle, the prospective bookkeeper, paused at the desk, heaped high with incoming and outgoing bills and circulars from drug firms with here and there stray boxes of pills and tubes of udder ointment.
>
> Stirring distastefully among the mess, she extracted the dog-eared old ledger and held it up between finger and thumb. "What's this?"
>
> Siegfried trotted forward. "Oh, that's our ledger. We enter the visits into it from our day book, which is here somewhere." He scrabbled about on the desk. "Ah, here it is. This is where we write the calls as they come in."
>
> She studied the two books for a few minutes with an expression of amazement that gave way to a grim humor. She straightened up slowly and spoke patiently. "And where, may I ask, is your cash box?"
>
> "Well, we just stuff it in there, you know." Siegfried pointed to the pint pot on the corner of the mantelpiece. "Haven't got what you'd call a proper cash box, but this does the job all right."
>
> Miss Harbottle looked at the pot with horror. Crumpled cheques and notes peeped over the brim at her; many of their companions had burst out on the hearth below. "And you mean to say that you go out and leave that money there day after day?"
>
> "Never seems to come to any harm." Siegfried replied.
>
> "And how about your petty cash?"
>
> Siegfried gave an uneasy giggle. "All in there, you know. All cash—petty and otherwise."

(Excerpted from: James Herriot, *All Creatures Great and Small,* 1972, St. Martin's Press: New York.)

Situations similar to the one described above are not unusual for small businesses. How does a business survive with such bad bookkeeping?

Case 3—2 **(To record or not to record)**

Explain why each of the following hypothetical events would *not* be recorded in a journal entry.

1. A famous and much-beloved movie star is secretly filmed by an investigative news team using your company's product when she in fact has an endorsement contract with your company's major competitor.
2. Two of your firm's top vice presidents have a bitter argument and will probably never speak to one another again.
3. Your company's chief research chemist is killed in a plane crash.
4. Because of unfavorable economic news, consumer confidence is shaken and the stock market falls by 10 percent.
5. You, a small business owner, buy a sofa for your home. You pay with a check drawn on your personal, not your business, checking account.
6. Disney decides to build the next Walt Disney World near a large piece of property you own.

Case 3—3 **(Is it time to revolutionize the recording of business events?)**

Jim Price and Elaine Bijard are taking an accounting systems course at their university. They are intrigued with the rapid advances in technology and communication that are occurring in the computer world. Today's lecture was especially thought-provoking. Professor Hansen stated that it is no longer necessary or even desirable to record business events in sequential order as has been traditionally done in accounting journals. The better approach is to capture all data related to a business event in a computer database, including accounting, marketing, and production data, and to prepare reports for many different users from a single source. The database would be a management information database, not just one for accounting reports.

Jim argues that such an approach would make it more difficult for accountants to keep control of input and assure the integrity of their financial reports, but Elaine feels that the sooner accountants recognize the potential, the better they can serve management's varied needs. What advantages and disadvantages do you see coming from a database approach to recording? How can Jim's objections be met?

Case 3—4 **(When cash basis is different from accrual)**

Alice Guth operates a low-impact aerobics studio. Alice has been in business for three years and has always had her financial statements prepared on a cash basis. This year, Alice's accountant has suggested that accrual-based financial statements would give a more accurate picture of the performance of the business. Alice's friend Frank Geller tells her that, in his experience, accrual-based financial statements tell pretty much the same story as cash-basis statements.

Under what circumstances would the cash basis and the accrual basis of accounting yield quite different pictures of a firm's operating performance? Under what circumstances would the cash basis and the accrual basis show approximately the same picture?

Case 3—5 **(The impact of computers on financial reporting)**

Computers have drastically altered the way accounting records are maintained. Almost all businesses now keep at least some of their accounting records on computer. However, the most visible output of the accounting system, the financial information included in the Annual Report, is still prepared and disseminated the old-fashioned way—on paper. What types of changes in companies' annual reports are likely to occur over the next 10 to 15 years as a result of the increasingly widespread use of computers?

Case 3—6 **(But I need more timely information!)**

Julie is successful in her position as a consultant for Worldwide Enterprises. She has selectively invested her money in stocks of several companies. She receives the annual reports and faithfully analyzes them as she was taught in her university accounting class. She is concerned, however, with the impact that events have on the financial reports between years. Julie understands that quarterly reports are available upon request from the companies, but also understands they are not audited and thus may not be reliable. She wonders if they can be trusted. Even quarterly reports might not be often enough. Wouldn't it be useful if she could use her computer and modem to interrogate the company's computer and obtain information anytime she wanted it?

She decides to write for advice to the chief accountant of the companies in which she holds stock. As chief accountant, how would you address Julie's concerns?

EXERCISES

Exercise 3—7 (Recording transactions in T-accounts)

Alaska Supply Company, a merchandising firm, prepared the following trial balance as of October 1:

	Debit	Credit
Cash	$200,000	
Accounts Receivable	21,540	
Inventory	32,680	
Land	15,400	
Building	9,000	
Accounts Payable		$ 9,190
Mortgage Payable		23,700
Common Stock		185,000
Retained Earnings		60,730
	$278,620	$278,620

Alaska Supply engaged in the following transactions during October 1996. The company records inventory using the perpetual system.

Oct. 1 Sold merchandise on account to the Plough Corporation for $15,000; terms 2/10, n/30, FOB shipping point. Plough paid $200 freight on the goods. The merchandise cost $7,450.

5 Purchased inventory costing $8,350 on account; terms n/30.

7 Received payment from Plough for goods shipped October 1.

15 The payroll paid for the first half of October was $18,000. (Ignore payroll taxes.)

18 Purchased a machine for $10,400 cash.

22 Declared a dividend of $.75 per share on 45,000 shares of common stock outstanding.

27 Purchased building and land for $150,000 in cash and a $250,000 mortgage payable, due in 30 years. The land was appraised at $150,000 and the building at $350,000.

1. Prepare T-accounts for all items in the October 1 trial balance and enter the initial balances.
2. Record the October transactions directly to the T-accounts.
3. Prepare a new trial balance as of the end of October.

Exercise 3—8 (Adjusting entries)

In analyzing the accounts of Loma Corporation, the adjusting data listed below are determined on December 31, the end of an annual fiscal period.

(a) The prepaid insurance account shows a debit of $3,600, representing the cost of a 2-year fire insurance policy dated July 1.

(b) On September 1, Rent Revenue was credited for $3,750, representing revenue from subrental for a 5-month period beginning on that date.

(c) Purchase of advertising materials for $2,475 during the year was recorded in the advertising expense account. On December 31, advertising materials costing $275 are on hand.

(d) On November 1, $3,000 was paid for rent for a 6-month period beginning on that date. The rent expense account was debited.

(e) Miscellaneous Office Expense was debited for office supplies of $1,350 purchased during the year. On December 31, office supplies of $320 are on hand.

(f) Interest of $352 is accrued on notes payable.

1. Give the adjusting entry for each item.
2. What sources would provide the information for each adjustment?

Exercise 3—9 **(Adjusting and correcting entries)**

Upon inspecting the books and records for Beardall Company for the year ended December 31, 1996, you find the following data.

(a) A receivable of $380 from Clarke Realty is determined to be uncollectible. The company maintains an allowance for doubtful accounts for such losses.
(b) A creditor, E. J. Stanley Co., has just been awarded damages of $2,200 as a result of breach of contract during the current year by Beardall Company. Nothing appears on the books in connection with this matter.
(c) A fire destroyed part of a branch office. Furniture and fixtures that cost $10,200 and had a book value of $7,800 at the time of the fire were completely destroyed. The insurance company has agreed to pay $6,500 under the provisions of the fire insurance policy.
(d) Advances of $1,150 to salespersons have been previously recorded as sales salaries expense.
(e) Machinery at the end of the year shows a balance of $18,460. It is discovered that additions to this account during the year totaled $4,460, but of this amount, $800 should have been recorded as repairs. Depreciation is to be recorded at 10% on machinery owned throughout the year, but at one-half this rate on machinery purchased or sold during the year.

Record the entries required to adjust and correct the accounts. (Ignore income tax consequences.)

Exercise 3—10 **(Reconstructing adjusting entries)**

For each of the following situations, reconstruct the adjusting entry that was made to arrive at the ending balance. Assume statements and adjusting entries are prepared only once each year.

1.

Prepaid insurance

Balance beginning of year	$6,500
Balance end of year	7,200

During the year, an additional business insurance policy was purchased. A two-year premium of $2,000 was paid and charged to Prepaid Insurance.

2.

Accumulated Depreciation

Balance beginning of year	$85,200
Balance end of year	89,500

During the year, a depreciable asset that cost $7,500 and had a carrying value of $1,600 was sold for $2,400. The disposal of the asset was recorded correctly.

3.

Unearned Rent

Balance beginning of year	$12,000
Balance end of year	15,000

Warehouse quarterly rent received in advance is $18,000. During the year, equipment was rented to another company at an annual rent of $9,000. The quarterly rent payments were credited to Rent Revenue; the annual equipment rental was credited to Unearned Rent.

4.

Salaries Payable

Balance beginning of year	$31,550
Balance end of year	26,750

Salaries are paid bi-weekly. All salary payments during the year were debited to Salaries Expense.

Exercise 3—11 (Adjusting and closing entries and post-closing trial balance)
Accounts of Pioneer Heating Co. at the end of the first year of operations show the balances listed below. The end-of-the-year physical inventory is $50,000. Prepaid operating expenses are $4,000 and accrued sales commissions payable are $5,900. Investment revenue receivable is $1,000. Depreciation for the year on buildings is $4,500 and on machinery, $5,000. Federal and state income taxes for the year are estimated at $18,100.

	Debit	Credit
Cash	$ 39,000	
Investments	50,000	
Land	70,000	
Buildings	180,000	
Machinery	100,000	
Accounts Payable		$ 65,000
Common Stock		320,000
Additional Paid-In Capital		40,000
Sales		590,000
Purchases	280,000	
Sales Commissions	200,000	
General Operating Expenses	101,000	
Investment Revenue		5,000
	$1,020,000	$1,020,000

1. Prepare the necessary entries to adjust and close the books, assuming use of an income summary account and the adjusting method for inventory.
2. Prepare a post-closing trial balance.

Exercise 3—12 (Adjusting and closing entries and post-closing trial balance)
Below is the trial balance for Feigenbaum Company as of December 31.

	Debit	Credit
Cash	$ 58,000	
Accounts Receivable	402,000	
Inventory	57,000	
Prepaid Expenses	54,000	
Land	65,000	
Plant and Equipment	1,167,000	
Other Assets	1,563,000	
Accounts Payable		$ 147,000
Wages, Interest, and Taxes Payable		215,000
Unearned Revenue		33,000
Long-Term Debt		1,201,000
Other Liabilities		336,000
Common Stock		185,000
Retained Earnings		1,112,000
Sales		2,801,000
Interest Revenue		23,000
Cost of Goods Sold	1,565,000	
Selling, General, and Administrative Expenses	640,000	
Interest Expense	79,000	
Income Tax Expense	264,000	
Dividends	139,000	
	$6,053,000	$6,053,000

Consider the following additional information:

(a) Feigenbaum uses a perpetual inventory system.
(b) The prepaid expenses were paid on September 1 and relate to a 3-year insurance policy that went into effect on September 1.
(c) The unearned revenue relates to rental of an unused portion of the corporate offices. The $33,000 was received on April 1 and represents payment in advance for one year's rental.
(d) Plant and Equipment includes $10,000 for equipment repairs that were erroneously recorded as equipment purchases. The repairs were made on December 30.
(e) Other Assets include $8,000 for miscellaneous office supplies, which were purchased in mid-October. An end-of-year count reveals that only $6,500 of the office supplies remain.
(f) Selling, General, and Administrative Expenses incorrectly includes $15,000 for office furniture purchases (Other Assets). The purchases were made on December 30.
(g) Inventory wrongly includes $6,000 of inventory that Feigenbaum had purchased on account but that was returned to the supplier on December 28 because of unsatisfactory quality.

Based on the above information:

1. Record the entries necessary to adjust the books.
2. Record the entries necessary to close the books. Use an income summary account. Assume the adjustments in (1) do not affect Income Tax Expense.
3. Prepare a post-closing trial balance.

Exercise 3—13 (Analysis of journal entries)

For each of the journal entries below, write a description of the underlying event.

	Account	Debit	Credit
1.	Cash	300	
	Accounts Receivable		300
2.	Accounts Payable	400	
	Inventory		400
3.	Cash	5,000	
	Loan Payable		5,000
4.	Cash	200	
	Accounts Receivable	700	
	Sales Revenue		900
	Cost of Goods Sold	550	
	Inventory		550
5.	Prepaid Insurance	200	
	Cash		200
6.	Dividends	250	
	Dividends Payable		250
7.	Retained Earnings	1,000	
	Dividends		1,000
8.	Insurance Expense	50	
	Prepaid Insurance		50
9.	Inventory	600	
	Cash		150
	Accounts Payable		450
10.	Allowance for Doubtful Accounts	46	
	Accounts Receivable		46
11.	Interest Expense	125	
	Interest Payable		125
12.	Wages Payable	130	
	Wages Expense	75	
	Cash		205
13.	Accounts Payable	500	
	Cash		490
	Purchase Discounts		10

Exercise 3—14 (Adjusting entries)

The following accounts were taken from the trial balance of Cristy Company as of December 31, 1996. Given the information below, make the necessary adjusting entries.

Sales Revenue	$90,000
Interest Revenue	5,000
Equipment	46,000
Accumulated Depreciation—Equipment	12,000
Beginning Inventory	20,000
Advertising Expense	2,000
Selling Expense	6,000
Interest Expense	1,000

(a) The equipment has an estimated useful life of 5 years and a salvage value of $1,000. Depreciation is calculated using the straight-line method.
(b) Ending inventory is $28,000. The adjusting method for inventory is used.
(c) $1,000 of selling expense has been paid in advance.
(d) Interest of $500 has accrued on notes receivable.
(e) $400 of advertising expense was incorrectly debited to selling expense.

Exercise 3—15 (Adjusting entries)

The data listed below were obtained from an analysis of the accounts of Noble Distributor Company as of March 31, 1996, in preparation of the annual report. Noble records current transactions in nominal accounts and *does not* reverse adjusting entries. What are the appropriate adjusting entries?

(a) Prepaid Insurance has a balance of $14,100. Noble has the following policies in force:

Policy	Date	Term	Cost	Coverage
A	1/1/96	2 years	$ 3,600	Shop equipment
B	12/1/95	6 months	1,800	Delivery equipment
C	7/1/95	3 years	12,000	Buildings

(b) Unearned Subscription Revenue has a balance of $56,250. The following subscriptions were collected in the current year. There are no other unexpired subscriptions.

Effective Date	Amount	Term
July 1, 1995	$27,000	1 year
October 1, 1995	22,200	1 year
January 1, 1996	28,800	1 year
April 1, 1996	20,700	1 year

(c) Interest Payable has a balance of $825. Noble owes a 10%, 90-day note for $45,000 dated March 1, 1996.
(d) Supplies has a balance of $2,190. An inventory of supplies revealed a total of $1,410.
(e) Salaries Payable has a balance of $9,750. The payroll for the 5-day workweek ended April 3 totaled $11,250.

Exercise 3—16 (Analyzing adjusting entries)

Computer Consulting Company uses the asset-and-liability approach in accounting for prepaid expenses and unearned revenues. Selected account balances at the end of the current and prior year are presented below. The company does not make reversing entries, and accrued expenses and revenues are adjusted only at year-end.

	Adjusted Balances Dec. 31, 1995	Adjusted Balances Dec. 31, 1996
Prepaid Rent	$ 4,800	$3,600
Salaries and Wages Payable	2,500	4,500
Unearned Consulting Fees	13,000	6,400
Interest Receivable	1,200	1,800

During 1996 Computer Consulting paid $10,000 for rent and $50,000 for wages. $108,000 was received for consulting fees and $2,400 was received as interest.

1. Provide the entries that were made at December 31, 1996, to adjust the accounts to the year-end balances above.
2. Determine the proper amount of Rent Expense, Salaries and Wages Expense, Consulting Fees Revenue, and Interest Revenue to be reported on the current-year income statement.

Exercise 3—17 (Closing entries)

An accountant for Jolley, Inc., a merchandising enterprise, has just finished posting all the year-end adjusting entries to the ledger accounts and now wishes to close the appropriate account balances in preparation for the new period.

1. For each of the accounts listed, indicate whether the year-end balance should be: (a) carried forward to the new period, (b) closed by debiting the account, or (c) closed by crediting the account. Assume Jolley uses a perpetual inventory system.

(a) Cash	$ 25,000	(k) Accounts Payable	$ 12,000
(b) Sales	50,000	(l) Accounts Receivable	140,000
(c) Dividends	3,000	(m) Prepaid Insurance	16,000
(d) Inventory	7,500	(n) Interest Receivable	1,500
(e) Selling Expenses	6,000	(o) Sales Discounts	2,500
(f) Capital Stock	100,000	(p) Interest Revenue	3,500
(g) Income Summary	0	(q) Supplies	8,000
(h) Wages Expense	10,000	(r) Retained Earnings	6,500
(i) Dividends Payable	4,000	(s) Accumulated Depr.	2,000
(j) Cost of Goods Sold	22,500	(t) Depreciation Exp.	1,000

2. Give the necessary closing entries.
3. What was Jolley's net income (loss) for the period?

Exercise 3—18 (Closing entries—proprietorship, partnership, and corporation)

Lennon's Tannery shows a credit balance in the Income Summary account of $67,600 after the revenue and expense items have been transferred to this account at the end of the fiscal year. Give the remaining entries to close the books assuming:

(a) The business is a sole proprietorship: the owner, D. H. Lennon, has made withdrawals of $14,000 during the year, and this is reported in a drawing account.
(b) The business is a partnership: the owners, D. H. Lennon and B. L. Oster, share profits 5:3; they have made withdrawals of $25,000 and $16,000, respectively, and these amounts are reported in drawing accounts.
(c) The business is a corporation: the ledger reports Additional Paid-In Capital, $250,000, and Retained Earnings, $100,000; dividends during the year amounting to $32,500 were recorded in a dividends account.

Exercise 3—19 (Determining income from equity account analysis)

An analysis of Huffman, Inc. disclosed changes in account balances for 1996 and the supplementary data listed below. From these data, calculate the net income or loss for 1996. (Hint: Net income can be thought of as the increase in net assets resulting from operations.)

Cash	$16,000 increase
Accounts receivable	25,000 increase
Inventory	10,000 decrease
Equipment	70,000 increase
Accounts payable	5,000 decrease

Huffman sold 5,000 shares of its $5 par stock for $8 per share and received cash in full. Dividends of $15,000 were paid in cash during the year. Huffman borrowed $50,000 from the bank and made interest payments of $5,000. Huffman had no other loans payable. $1,000 interest was payable at December 31, 1996. There was no interest payable at December 31, 1995. Equipment of $20,000 was donated by stockholders during the year.

Exercise 3—20 (Accrual errors)

Loring Tools, Inc. failed to make year-end adjustments to record accrued salaries and recognize interest receivable on investments over the last three years as follows:

	1994	1995	1996
Accrued salaries	$25,000	$21,000	$32,000
Interest receivable	10,500	8,500	13,200

What impact would the correction of these errors have on the net income for these three years? Ignore income taxes.

***Exercise 3—21 (Special journals)**

Caddy's Inc. uses a general journal, sales journal, cash receipts journal, check register, and a voucher register. For each transaction below, indicate the appropriate journal(s) or register to be used.

(a) Make a credit sale.
(b) Collect cash on an account receivable.
(c) Record bad-debt expense.
(d) Write a check for payroll expense.
(e) Purchase materials on account.
(f) Give a discount on a sale.
(g) Sell equipment on credit.
(h) Make a cash sale.
(i) Borrow $3,000 from the bank.
(j) Record adjusting and closing entries.
(k) Pay a supplier with a check.
(l) Record accrued interest payable.
(m) Sell truck for cash.
(n) Record depreciation expense.
(o) Pay back loan.

*Relates to Appendix 3—1

***Exercise 3—22 (Voucher register)**

On July 15, vouchers for payment of the following items were approved by the chief financial officer of Lorenz Company:

Amount	Payee	Purpose
$1,530	Outland Hardware	Payment for inventory received
4,000	Locker Bank	Repayment of loan principal
350	Thom Insurance	Payment in advance for insurance
8,790	Payroll	Gross pay = $10,000; taxes payable = $1,210
1,240	Better Electric	Last month's utilities
2,600	Rands Supply	Payment for inventory received
670	Frank Elsholz	Customer refund for sales return
1,210	U.S. Government	Remittance of taxes withheld
3,000	Thurston Howell	Advance on salary

Prepare a voucher register and record the approved vouchers described above. The last voucher prepared on July 14 had the number 1022. Lorenz uses a periodic inventory system.

*Relates to Appendix 3—1

***Exercise 3—23 (Voucher register and check register)**

All of the vouchers described in Exercise 3—22 were paid by check on July 16, starting with check number 439. A 2 percent purchase discount was taken on the payment to Rands Supply. Based on the information provided:

1. Complete the voucher register prepared in Exercise 3—22 showing the payment of the vouchers by check.
2. Prepare a check register and enter the checks paid on July 16.

*Relates to Appendix 3-1

*Exercise 3—24 (Cash receipts journal)

Mandelbrot Graphics makes most of its sales on credit. Data from the October sales journal are given below:

Date	Invoice No.	Account Debited	Acct. Rec. (Dr) Sales (Cr)
10/2	9045	Franklin Printing	$1,200
10/8	9046	Simpson Company	2,350
10/15	9047	Midstate University	4,780
10/18	9048	Topper Oil, Inc.	565
10/24	9049	Julia Company	1,700
10/29	9050	Fractal Design	3,675

During November, Mandelbrot received payment for all of the credit sales made in October. Julia Company was given a 3 percent sales discount. Mandelbrot's cash sales during November totaled $380. In addition, during November Mandelbrot received full payment on a $5,000 note receivable, along with $450 in interest. Also, Mandelbrot received a $750 refund for an insurance policy that had been canceled.

Prepare a cash receipts journal for Mandelbrot Graphics for November.

*Relates to Appendix 3—1

*Exercise 3—25 (Closing method for inventory)

The unadjusted balances for inventory and related accounts for Button-Down Corporation as of December 31, 1996, are as follows:

Beginning Inventory	$26,750
Ending Inventory	32,425
Purchases	59,400
Purchase Discounts	2,650
Freight-In	3,115

1. Give the necessary adjusting and closing entries for Inventory and related accounts assuming the "closing method" is used.
2. Determine the amount of cost of goods sold to be reported on the Income Statement.

*Relates to Appendix 3—2

PROBLEMS

Problem 3—26 (Journal entries)

Selfish Gene Company is a merchandising firm. The following events occurred during the month of May. Note: Selfish Gene maintains a perpetual inventory system.

May 1 Received $40,000 cash as new stockholder investment.
3 Purchased inventory costing $8,000 on account from Dawkins Company; terms 2/10, n/30.
4 Purchased office supplies for $500 cash.
4 Held an office party for the retiring accountant. Balloons, hats, and refreshments cost $150 and were paid for with office staff contributions.
5 Sold merchandise costing $7,500 on account for $14,000 to Richard Company; terms, 3/15, n/30.

May	8	Paid employee wages of $2,000. Gross wages were $2,450; taxes totaling $450 were withheld.
	9	Hired a new accountant; agreed to a first-year salary of $28,000.
	9	Paid $1,500 for newspaper advertising.
	10	Received payment from Richard Company.
	12	Purchased a machine for $6,400 cash.
	15	Declared a cash dividend totaling $25,000.
	18	Sold merchandise costing $13,000 for $3,000 cash and $21,000 on account to Feynman Company; terms, n/30.
	19	Paid Dawkins Company account in full.
	22	Company executives appeared on the cover of a national news magazine. Related article extolled Selfish Gene's labor practices, environmental concerns, and customer service.
	23	Market value of Selfish Gene's common stock rose by $150,000.
	25	Purchased a building for $15,000 cash and a $135,000 mortgage payable.
	29	Paid dividends declared on May 15.

Instructions:

1. Record the preceding events in general journal form.
2. Which event do you think had the most significant economic impact on Selfish Gene Company? Are all economically relevant events recorded in the financial records?

Problem 3—27 (Account classification and debit/credit relationship)

Instructions: Using the format provided, identify for each account:

1. Whether the account will appear on a balance sheet (B/S), income statement (I/S), or neither (N);
2. Whether the account is an asset (A), liability (L), owners' equity (OE), revenue (R), expense (E), or other (0);
3. Whether the account is real or nominal;
4. Whether the account will be "closed" or left "open" at year-end; and
5. Whether the account *normally* has a debit (Dr) or a credit (Cr) balance.

Account Title	(1) B/S I/S N	(2) A,L,OE, R,E,O	(3) Real or Nominal	(4) Closed or Open	(5) Debit (Dr) or Credit (Cr)
Example: Cash	B/S	A	Real	Open	Dr

(a) Unearned Rent Revenue
(b) Accounts Receivable
(c) Inventory
(d) Accounts Payable
(e) Prepaid Rent
(f) Mortgage Payable
(g) Sales
(h) Cost of Goods Sold
(i) Dividends
(j) Dividends Payable
(k) Interest Receivable
(l) Wages Expense
(m) Drawings
(n) Supplies
(o) Income Summary
(p) Accumulated Depreciation
(q) Retained Earnings
(r) Discount on Bonds Payable
(s) Goodwill
(t) Additional Paid-In Capital

Problem 3—28 (Adjusting entries)

On December 31, the Philips Company noted the following transactions that occurred during 1996, some or all of which might require adjustment to the books.

(a) Payment to suppliers of $1,200 was made for purchases on account during the year and was not recorded.

(b) Building and land were purchased on January 2 for $175,000. The building's fair market value was $100,000 at the time of purchase. The building is being depreciated over a 20-year life using the straight-line method, and assuming no salvage value.
(c) Of the $34,000 in Accounts Receivable, 2.5% is estimated to be uncollectible. Currently, Allowance for Doubtful Accounts shows a debit balance of $290.
(d) On August 1, $25,000 was loaned to a customer on a 6-month note with interest at an annual rate of 12%.
(e) During 1996, Philips received $2,500 in advance for services, 80% of which will be performed in 1997. The $2,500 was credited to sales revenue.
(f) The interest expense account was debited for all interest charges incurred during the year and shows a balance of $1,100. However, of this amount, $300 represents a discount on a 60-day note payable, due January 30, 1997.

Instructions:

1. Give the necessary adjusting entries to bring the books up to date.
2. Indicate the net change in income as a result of the foregoing adjustments.

Problem 3—29 **(Analysis of adjusting entries)**

The accountant for Save More Company made the following adjusting entries on December 31, 1996:

(a) Prepaid Rent	1,200	
Rent Expense		1,200
(b) Advertising Materials	2,000	
Advertising Expense		2,000
(c) Rent Revenue	500	
Unearned Revenue		500
(d) Office Supplies	1,000	
Office Supplies Expense		1,000
(e) Prepaid Insurance	1,050	
Insurance Expense		1,050

Further information is provided as follows:

(a) Rent is paid every October 1.
(b) Advertising materials are paid at one time (June 1) and are used evenly throughout the year.
(c) Rent is received in advance every March 1.
(d) Office supplies are purchased every July 1 and used evenly throughout the year.
(e) Yearly insurance premium is payable each August 1.

Instructions: For each adjusting entry, indicate the original transaction entry that was recorded.

Problem 3—30 **(Adjusting entries)**

The bookkeeper for the Irwin Wholesale Electric Co. prepares no reversing entries and records all revenue and expense items in nominal accounts during the period. The following balances, among others, are listed on the trial balance at the end of the fiscal period, December 31, 1996, before accounts have been adjusted:

	Dr (Cr)
Accounts Receivable	$152,000
Allowance for Doubtful Accounts	(1,000)
Interest Receivable	2,800
Discounts on Notes Payable	300
Prepaid Real Estate and Personal Property Tax	1,800
Salaries and Wages Payable	(4,000)
Discounts on Notes Receivable	(2,800)
Unearned Rent Revenue	(1,500)

Inspection of the company's records reveals the following as of December 31, 1996:

(a) Uncollectible accounts are estimated at 3% of the accounts receivable balance.
(b) The accrued interest on investments totals $2,400.
(c) The company borrows cash by discounting its own notes at the bank. Discounts on notes payable at the end of 1996 are $1,600.
(d) Prepaid real estate and personal property taxes are $1,800, the same as at the end of 1995.
(e) Accrued salaries and wages are $4,300.
(f) The company accepts notes from customers, giving its customers credit for the face of the note less a charge for interest. At the end of each period, any interest applicable to the succeeding period is reported as a discount. Discounts on notes receivable at the end of 1996 are $1,500.
(g) Part of the company's properties had been sublet on September 15, 1995, at a rental of $3,000 per month. The arrangement was terminated at the end of one year.

Instructions: Give the adjusting entries required to bring the books up to date.

Problem 3—31 (Cash to accrual adjusting entries and income statement)

Gee Enterprises records all transactions on the cash basis. At the end of the year, Greg Gee, company accountant, prepared the following income statement at the end of the company's first year of operations.

Gee Enterprises
Income Statement
For Year Ended December 31, 1996

Sales		$252,000
Selling and administrative expenses		
Salary expense	$ 78,000	
Rent expense	45,000	
Utility expense	29,000	
Equipment	30,000	
Commission expense	37,800	
Insurance expense	6,000	
Interest expense	3,000	
		228,800
Net income		$ 23,200

You have been asked to prepare an income statement on the accrual basis. The following information is given to you to assist in the preparation.

a. Amounts due from customers at year end—$28,000. Of this amount, $3,000 will probably not be collected.
b. Salaries of $5,500 for December 1996 were paid on January 5, 1997. Ignore payroll taxes.
c. Gee rents its building for $3,000 a month payable quarterly in advance. The contract was signed on January 1, 1996.
d. The bill for December's utility costs of $2,700 was paid January 10, 1997.
e. Equipment of $30,000 was purchased on January 1, 1996. The expected life is 5 years, no salvage value. Assume straight-line depreciation.
f. Commissions of 15% of sales are paid on the same day cash is received from customers.
g. A one-year insurance policy was issued on company assets on July 1, 1996. Premiums are paid annually in advance.
h. Gee borrowed $50,000 for one year on May 1, 1996. Interest payments based on an annual rate of 12% are made quarterly, beginning with the first payment on August 1, 1996.
i. The income tax rate is 40%. No prepayments of income taxes were made during 1996.

Instructions:

1. Prepare adjusting entries to convert the books from a cash to an accrual basis.
2. Prepare the income statement for the year ended December 31, 1996 based on the entries in (1).

Problem 3—32 (Preparation of work sheet and adjusting and closing entries)

Account balances taken from the ledger of the Builders' Supply Corporation on December 31, 1996, are listed below. Information relating to adjustments on December 31, 1996, follows:

(a) The inventory on hand is $87,570. Inventory and related accounts are adjusted through Cost of Goods Sold.
(b) Allowance for Doubtful Accounts is to be increased to a balance of $3,000.
(c) Buildings are depreciated at the rate of 5% per year.
(d) Accrued selling expenses are $3,840.
(e) There are supplies of $780 on hand.
(f) Prepaid insurance relating to 1997 totals $720.
(g) Accrued interest on long-term investments is $240.
(h) Accrued real estate and payroll taxes are $900.
(i) Accrued interest on the mortgage is $480.
(j) Income tax is estimated to be 20% of the income before income tax.

Cash	$ 24,000
Accounts Receivable	72,000
Allowance for Doubtful Accounts	1,380
Inventory, Dec. 31, 1995	62,000
Long-Term Investments	15,400
Land	69,600
Buildings	72,000
Accumulated Depreciation—Buildings	19,800
Capital Stock, $10 par	180,000
Retained Earnings, Dec. 31, 1995	14,840
Dividends	13,400
Accounts Payable	35,000
Mortgage Payable	68,800
Sales	246,000
Sales Returns	4,360
Sales Discounts	5,400
Interest Revenue	660
Purchases	138,480
Purchase Discounts	2,140
Freight-In	3,600
Selling Expense	49,440
Office Expense	21,680
Insurance Expense	1,440
Supplies Expense	5,200
Taxes—Real Estate and Payroll	7,980
Interest Expense	2,640

Instructions:

1. Prepare a trial balance.
2. Journalize the adjustments.
3. Journalize the closing entries.
4. Prepare a post-closing trial balance.

Although not required, the use of a work sheet is recommended for the solution of this problem.

Problem 3—33 (Adjusting and closing entries and post-closing trial balance)

Kwon International Corporation
Unadjusted Trial Balance
December 31, 1996

	Debit	Credit
Cash	$ 22,500	
Accounts Receivable	24,000	
Allowance for Doubtful Accounts		$ 240
Inventory	45,300	
Equipment	210,000	
Accumulated Depreciation—Equipment		42,000
Accounts Payable		28,000
Notes Payable		80,000
Wages Payable		10,000
Income Taxes Payable		8,900
Common Stock		50,000
Retained Earnings		27,310
Sales Revenue		270,000
Interest Revenue		8,000
Cost of Goods Sold	171,250	
Wages Expense	28,000	
Interest Expense	1,500	
Utilities Expense	5,000	
Insurance Expense	2,000	
Advertising Expense	6,000	
Income Tax Expense	8,900	
	$524,450	$524,450

Data for adjustments at December 31, 1996, are as follows:

(a) Kwon International uses a perpetual inventory system.
(b) An analysis of Accounts Receivable reveals that the appropriate year-end balance in the Allowance for Doubtful Accounts is $700.
(c) Equipment depreciation for the year totaled $45,000.
(d) A recheck of the inventory count revealed that goods costing $4,300 were wrongly excluded from ending inventory. The goods in question were not shipped until January 3, 1997. A related receivable for $6,000 was also mistakenly recorded.
(e) Interest on the note payable has not been accrued. The note was issued on March 1, 1996, and the interest rate is 15 percent.
(f) The balance in Insurance Expense represents $2,000 that was paid for a one-year policy on October 1. The policy went into effect on October 1.
(g) Dividends totaling $5,600 were declared on December 25. The dividends will not be paid until January 15, 1997.

Instructions:

1. Journalize the necessary adjusting entries.
2. Journalize the necessary closing entries using an income summary account.
3. Prepare a post-closing trial balance.
4. Can a company pay dividends in a year in which it has a net loss? Can a company owe income taxes in a year in which it has a net loss?

Problem 3—34 (Preparation of work sheet)

Account balances taken from the ledger of Royal Distributing Co. on December 31, 1996, are on page 104. Information relating to adjustments on December 31, 1996, follows:

(a) The inventory on hand is $92,000. Inventory and related accounts are adjusted through Cost of Goods Sold.
(b) Allowance for Doubtful Accounts is to be increased by $2,000.
(c) Buildings have a salvage value of $7,500. They are being depreciated at the rate of 10% per year.
(d) Accrued selling expenses are $8,600.
(e) There are supplies of $1,250 on hand.
(f) Prepaid insurance relating to 1997 totals $4,000.
(g) Total interest revenue earned in 1996 is $1,400.
(h) Accrued real estate and payroll taxes are $2,340.
(i) Accrued interest on the mortgage is $1,780.
(j) Income tax is estimated to be 40% of income.

Cash	$ 35,000
Accounts Receivable	91,000
Allowance for Doubtful Accounts	1,800
Inventory, December 31, 1995	84,000
Long-Term Investments	27,500
Land	53,400
Buildings	112,500
Accumulated Depreciation—Buildings	26,780
Accounts Payable	47,300
Mortgage Payable	99,500
Capital Stock, $5 par	175,000
Retained Earnings, 12/31/95	14,840
Dividends	9,670
Sales	359,000
Sales Returns	12,890
Sales Discounts	7,540
Purchases	159,000
Purchases Discounts	6,780
Freight In	6,300
Selling Expense	62,350
Office Expense	38,900
Insurance Expense	14,000
Supplies Expense	4,800
Taxes—Real Estate and Payroll	9,500
Interest Revenue	550
Interest Expense	3,200

Instructions: Prepare a work sheet showing the net income and balance sheet totals for the year ending December 31, 1996.

***Problem 3—35 (Preparation of work sheet and adjusting, closing, and reversing entries)**
The following account balances are taken from the general ledger of the Whitni Corporation on December 31, 1996, the end of its fiscal year. The corporation was organized January 2, 1993.

Cash	$ 40,250
Notes Receivable	16,500
Accounts Receivable	63,000
Allowance for Doubtful Accounts (credit balance)	650
Inventory, January 1, 1996	88,700
Land	80,000
Buildings	247,600
Accumulated Depreciation—Buildings	18,000
Furniture and Fixtures	15,000
Accumulated Depreciation—Furniture and Fixtures	9,000
Notes Payable	18,000
Accounts Payable	72,700

Common Stock, $100 par	240,000
Retained Earnings	129,125
Sales	760,000
Sales Returns and Allowances	17,000
Purchases	479,650
Purchase Discounts	7,850
Heat, Light, and Power	16,700
Property Tax Expense	10,200
Salaries and Wages Expense	89,000
Sales Commissions	73,925
Insurance Expense	18,000
Interest Revenue	2,600
Interest Expense	2,400

Data for adjustments at December 31, 1996, are as follows:

(a) Merchandise inventory, $94,700.
(b) Depreciation (to nearest month for additions):
Furniture and fixtures, 10%; Buildings, 4%.
Additions to the buildings costing $150,000 were completed June 30, 1996.
(c) Allowance for Doubtful Accounts is to be increased to a balance of $2,500.
(d) Accrued expenses:
Sales commissions, $700
Interest on notes payable, $45
Property tax, $6,000
(e) Prepaid expenses: insurance, $3,200.
(f) Accrued revenue: interest on notes receivable, $750.
(g) The following information is also to be recorded:
(1) On December 30, the board of directors declared a quarterly dividend of $1.50 per share on common stock, payable January 25, 1997, to stockholders of record January 15, 1997.
(2) Income tax for 1996 is estimated at $15,000.
(3) The only charges to Retained Earnings during the year resulted from the declaration of the regular quarterly dividends.

Instructions: Using either the adjusting method for inventory or the closing method illustrated in Appendix 3—2:

1. Prepare an eight-column work sheet. There should be a pair of columns each for trial balance, adjustments, income statement, and balance sheet.
2. Prepare all the journal entries necessary to record the effects of the foregoing information and to adjust and close the books of the corporation.
3. Prepare the reversing entries that may appropriately be made.

*Closing method (Appendix 3—2) is optional for this problem.

***Problem 3—36 (Using special journals)**
West Mountain Inc., a fruit wholesaler, records business transactions in the following books of original entry: general journal (J); voucher register (VR); check register (CR); sales journal (SJ); and cash receipts journal (CRJ). West Mountain recorded and filed the following business documents:

(a) Sales invoices for sales on account totaling $4,600.
(b) The day's cash register tape showing receipts for cash sales at $700.
(c) A list of cash received on various customers' accounts totaling $2,930. Sales discounts taken were $30.
(d) The telephone bill for $60 payable in one week.
(e) Vendors' invoices for $5,000 worth of fruit received.
(f) Check stub for payment of last week's purchases from All-Growers Farms, $5,940. Terms were 1/10, n/30, and payment was made within the discount period.

(g) Check stub for repayment of a $10,000, 90-day note to Mercantile Bank, $10,300.
(h) A letter notifying West Mountain that Littex Markets, a customer, has declared bankruptcy. All creditors will receive 10 cents on every dollar due. Littex owes West Mountain $1,300.

Instructions:

1. Indicate the books of original entry in which West Mountain recorded each of the business transactions. (Use the designated abbreviations.)
2. Record the debits and credits for each entry as though only a general journal were used. Use account titles implied by the voucher system.

*Relates to Appendix 3—1

*Problem 3—37 (Using special journals)

A fire destroyed Fong Company's journals. However, the general ledger and accounts receivable subsidiary ledger were saved. An inspection of the ledgers reveals the following information:

General Ledger

Cash (Acct. No. 11)

Debit		
May 1 Bal. 8,200		
31 7,338		

Sales (Acct. No. 41)

	Credit
	May 31 5,050
	31 4,500

Sales Discounts (Acct. No. 42)

Debit	
May 3 12	

Accounts Receivable (Acct. No. 12)

Debit	Credit
May 1 Bal. 3,100	May 31 2,850
31 5,050	

Accounts Receivable Ledger

Customer A

Debit	Credit
May 1 Bal. 290	
5 500	

Customer B

Debit	Credit
May 1 Bal. 1,250	May 13 1,000
5 400	

Customer C

Debit	Credit
May 2 1,450	

Customer D

Debit	Credit
May 1 Bal. 1,560	May 11 650

Customer E

Debit	Credit
May 2 1,200	May 3 1,200
12 1,500	

Fong's credit terms are 1/10, n/30.

Instructions: Reconstruct the sales and cash receipts journals from the information given.

*Relates to Appendix 3—1

*Problem 3—38 (Voucher and check registers)

Prepare a voucher register and a check register for Bethe Company and record the following transactions. The last voucher used was #9847, and the last check used was #562.

June 1 Paid voucher #9846 (for office supplies from JOK Supplies), $560. No discount was taken. (Record this in the check register only.)
2 Purchased inventory on account from Nimitz Company, $1,800; terms, 1/10, n/30. Bethe uses the periodic inventory method.
2 Received utilities bill from NiStar Electric for May, $985; terms, 3/15, n/30.

4 Paid voucher #9847 to the *Archer Journal* for advertising, $400. No discount was taken. (Record this in the check register only.)
8 Paid Nimitz Company account in full.
8 Authorized customer refund to Spruance Company, $1,150.
8 Paid refund to Spruance Company.
9 Authorized payment of cash dividends previously declared, $2,500. (No voucher was prepared at declaration date.)
10 Received notice of mortgage payment due to ATP Financial, $5,000; $4,600 represents interest and $400 represents principal. Payment was authorized.
12 Paid utility bill.
12 Made mortgage payment.
13 Approved loan to Ken Nelson, an officer of the company, $6,000.
15 Disbursed loan to Ken Nelson.
15 Approved payroll: gross pay, $11,000; taxes withheld, $2,000; health insurance premiums withheld, $980.
15 Paid net payroll.
17 Signed a contract for a fire insurance policy with Halsey Casualty. The policy is for one year, costs $4,000, and goes into effect on June 18.
18 Paid for fire insurance.
19 Purchased inventory on account from Wainwright Company, $2,300; terms, 2/10, n/30.
22 Paid cash dividend.
30 Approved payroll: gross pay, $11,500; taxes withheld, $2,200; health insurance premiums withheld, $980.
30 Paid net payroll.
30 Authorized and paid taxes withheld for June to U.S. Government.
30 Authorized and paid health insurance premiums withheld for June to Unicare Insurance.

*Relates to Appendix 3—1

CHAPTER 4

The Income Statement

CHAPTER TOPICS

- Importance of Recognizing, Measuring, and Reporting Income
- Capital Maintenance Concepts of Income Determination
- Transaction Approach to Income Determination
- Reporting Income from Continuing Operations
- Reporting Irregular and Extraordinary Items
- Form of the Income Statement
- Income Reporting Implications of the Conceptual Framework

On Sunday, November 15, 1992, the board of directors of Comptronix Corporation held a special meeting to discuss a mushrooming accounting crisis.[1] As the affair unfolded over the ensuing ten days, the directors of Comptronix, a manufacturer of electronics, learned that the founder and chief executive officer of the firm, William J. Hebding, had masterminded a scheme to inflate reported sales and understate cost of goods sold. The first public announcement of the fraud, on November 25, 1992, caused Comptronix stock to decline in price from $22 to $6.125 in one day, a 72% drop.[2] Investors were reacting to the fact that the impressive track record of Comptronix (fifteenfold increase in sales and tripling of net income over the preceding six years) was partly based on bookkeeping manipulations instead of profitable operations.

The accounting scheme at Comptronix started out as a straightforward overstatement of inventory. Beginning in 1989, fictitious inventory was recorded at the end of each month, decreasing reported cost of goods sold and increasing reported gross profit. Then,

1. Diana B. Henriques. "New Questions on Comptronix," *The New York Times*, December 3, 1992.
2. Helene Cooper. "Comptronix Says 3 Officials Inflated Profits," *The Wall Street Journal*, November 27, 1992.

to avoid the suspicious build-up of inventory, bogus sales of the fictitious inventory were recorded, creating bogus accounts receivable.[3] In the cleverest part of the plan, cash collection of these accounts receivable was faked in the following way:

- Comptronix wrote checks to real equipment suppliers for imaginary equipment purchases.
- Comptronix recorded fake sales of inventory to these same equipment suppliers.
- Through an unusual bank arrangement, Comptronix then deposited its own checks into its own bank account. The checks were those that Comptronix had originally written to the equipment suppliers for the bogus purchases. The deposits were recorded as receipts from the equipment suppliers in payment for the fake sales.

The restatement of the financial statements required when the fraud was uncovered turned the previous four years of profits into four years of losses and cut stockholders' equity by 50%. Where was the auditor during all of this? The auditor, one of the Big Six, claimed to be the victim of a sophisticated scheme. Said a spokesperson: "These are people who knew the accounting rules inside and out and knew what documentation would be needed in a test to fool an auditor."

In this chapter, we focus on one of the primary financial statements — the income statement. By analyzing the various components of the income statement, we will understand how the performance of a business is reported to financial statement users and why some firms, like Comptronix, have gone to such great lengths to falsify their income statements.

IMPORTANCE OF RECOGNIZING, MEASURING, AND REPORTING INCOME

The recognition, measurement, and reporting (display) of business income and its components are considered by many to be the most important tasks of accountants. The users of financial statements who must make decisions regarding their relationship with the company are almost always concerned with a measure of its success in using the resources committed to its operation. Has the activity been profitable? What is the trend of profitability? Is it increasingly profitable, or is there a downward trend? What is the most probable result for future years? Will the company be profitable enough to pay interest on its debt and dividends to its stockholders and still grow at a desired rate? These and other questions all relate to the basic question—What is income?

For many users, only one figure, the "bottom line," is meaningful. They feel uncomfortable trying to analyze additional information. To others, information about the components of income is important and can be used to help predict future income and cash flows. Not only can this information be helpful to a specific user, but it is also of value to the economy. As discussed in Chapter 1, one of the principal tasks facing accountants is to provide information that will assist in allocating scarce resources to the most efficient and effective organizations. If reported income is overstated when compared with the actual underlying situation, a poor allocation will be made. Resources will flow to inefficient entities, while the more efficient entities will suffer due to a lack of resources.

Income figures are also used for purposes other than resource allocation by creditors and investors. Governments, both federal and state, rely heavily on income taxes as a source of their revenues. The income figure used for assessing taxes is based on laws passed by Congress and regulations applied by the IRS and various courts. The income determined for financial reporting, however, is determined by adherence to accounting standards (GAAP) developed by the profession. Thus, the amount of income reported to creditors and investors may not be the same as the income reported for tax purposes. Many

3. Martha Brannigan and Laurie M. Grossman. "Comptronix Fires Its CEO but Keeps Two Other Aids," *The Wall Street Journal*, December 14, 1992.

items are the same for both types of reporting, but there are some significant differences. Most of these differences relate to the specific purposes Congress has for taxing income. Governments use an income figure as a base to assess taxes, but they must use one that relates closely with the ability of the taxpayer to pay the computed tax. For example, accrual accounting requires companies to defer recognition of revenues that are received before they are earned. Income tax regulations, however, require these unearned revenues to be reported as income as soon as they are received in cash.

This text focuses on principles of accounting that are the supporting foundation for financial accounting and reporting. Income for tax purposes will be discussed, but only as it is used to determine the income tax expense and other tax-related amounts reported in the financial statements.

INCOME DETERMINATION

Although there are varying ways to measure income, all of them share a common basic concept: income is a return over and above the investment. One of the more widely accepted definitions of income states that it is the amount that an entity could return to its investors and still leave the entity as well-off at the end of the period as it was at the beginning.[4] But what does it mean to be "as well-off," and how can it be measured? Most measurements are based on some concept of capital or ownership maintenance. Two concepts of capital maintenance were considered by the FASB in its conceptual framework: financial capital maintenance and physical capital maintenance.

Capital Maintenance Concept of Income Determination

The **financial capital maintenance** concept assumes that an enterprise has income "only if the dollar amount of an enterprise's net assets (assets - liabilities, or owners' equity) at the end of a period exceeds the dollar amount of net assets at the beginning of the period *after* excluding the effects of transactions with owners."[5] To illustrate, assume that Kreidler, Inc., had the following assets and liabilities at the beginning and the end of a period:

	Beginning of Period	End of Period
Total assets	$510,000	$560,000
Total liabilities	430,000	390,000
Net assets (owners' equity)	$ 80,000	$170,000

If there were no investments by owners or distributions to owners during the period, income would be $90,000, the amount of the increase in net assets. Assume, however, that owners invested $40,000 in the business and received distributions (dividends) of $15,000. Income for the period would be $65,000, computed as follows:

Net assets, end of period	$170,000
Net assets, beginning of period	80,000
Change (increase) in net assets	$ 90,000
Deduct investment by owners	(40,000)
Add distributions (dividends) to owners	15,000
Income	$ 65,000

4. Although many economists and accountants have adopted this view, a basic reference is J. R. Hicks' widely accepted book, *Value and Capital*, 2nd edition (Oxford University Press, 1946).

5. *Statement of Financial Accounting Concepts No. 5*, "Recognition and Measurement in Financial Statements of Business Enterprises" (Stamford: Financial Accounting Standards Board, 1984) par. 47.

Another way of defining capital maintenance is in terms of **physical capital maintenance.** Under this concept, income occurs "only if the physical productive capacity of the enterprise at the end of a period . . . exceeds the physical productive capacity at the beginning of the same period, also after excluding the effects of transactions with owners."[6] This concept requires that productive assets (inventories, buildings, and equipment) be valued at current cost. Productive capital is maintained only if the current costs of these capital assets are maintained. Thus, if the beginning net asset's value of $80,000 in the above example rose to $100,000 by the end of the year because of rising prices, and new investments and dividends were as shown, income would be $45,000 rather than $65,000. The $20,000 difference would be the amount necessary to "maintain physical productive capacity" and would not be part of income.

The Financial Accounting Standards Board considered carefully these two ways of viewing income, and adopted the financial capital maintenance concept as part of its conceptual framework.

Even with the acceptance of the financial capital maintenance concept, the question of how the net asset balance should be valued must be considered. Many suggest that net assets should be measured at their unexpired historical cost values as is currently being done. Others feel that replacement values or disposal values should be used. Some would include as assets intangible resources, such as human resources, goodwill, and geographical location, that have been attained over time without specifically identified payments. Others feel that only resources that have been acquired in arm's-length exchange activities should be included.

Likewise, controversy has developed over the recognition and measurement of liabilities. Should future claims against the entity for items such as pensions, warranties, and deferred income taxes be valued at their discounted values, at their future cash flow values, or eliminated completely from the financial statements until events clearly define the existence of a specific liability? The reported income under the financial maintenance concept will vary widely depending on when and how the assets, liabilities, and changes in the valuation of assets and liabilities are measured.

Comparing the net assets at two points in time, as was done above, yields a single net income figure. However, no detail concerning the components of income is disclosed. To provide this detail, accountants have adopted a transaction approach to measuring income that stresses the direct computation of revenues and expenses. As long as the same measurement method is used, income will be the same under the transaction approach as with a single income computation.

Transaction Approach to Income Determination

The **transaction approach,** sometimes referred to as the "matching method," focuses on business events that affect certain elements of financial statements, namely, revenues, expenses, gains, and losses. Income is measured as the difference between resource inflows (revenues and gains) and outflows (expenses and losses) over a period of time. Definitions for the four income elements were presented in Chapter 2 and are repeated in Exhibit 4-1 as an aid to the following discussion.

As can be seen from studying these definitions, by defining gains and losses in terms of changes in equity after providing for revenues, expenses, and investments and distributions to the owners, income determined by the transaction approach will be the same income as that determined under financial capital maintenance. However, by identifying intermediate income components, the transaction approach provides detail to assist in predicting future cash flows.

6. *Ibid.*

Exhibit 4-1
Component Elements of Income

- **Revenues** are inflows or other enhancements of assets of an entity or settlements of its liabilities (or a combination of both) from delivering or producing goods, rendering services, or other activities that constitute the entity's ongoing major or central operations.
- **Expenses** are outflows or other using-up of assets or incurrences of liabilities (or a combination of both) from delivering or producing goods, rendering services, or carrying out other activities that constitute the entity's ongoing major or central operations.
- **Gains** are increases in equity (net assets) from peripheral or incidental transactions of an entity and from all other transactions and other events and circumstances affecting the entity except those that result from revenues or investments by owners.
- **Losses** are decreases in equity (net assets) from peripheral or incidental transactions of an entity and from all other transactions and other events and circumstances affecting the entity except those that result from expenses or distributions to owners.

Source: *Statement of Financial Accounting Concepts No. 6,* "Elements of Financial Statements" (Stamford: Financial Accounting Standards Board, 1985), p. x.

The key problem in recognizing and measuring income using the transaction approach is deciding when an "inflow or other enhancement of assets" has occurred and how to measure the "outflows or other using-up of assets." As discussed in Chapter 2, the first issue is identified as "the revenue recognition" problem, and the second issue is identified as the "expense recognition" or "matching" problem.

Revenue and Gain Recognition. The transaction approach requires a clear definition of when income elements should be recognized, or recorded, in the financial statements. Under the generally accepted accounting principle of accrual, **revenue recognition** does not necessarily occur when cash is received. The conceptual framework identifies two factors that should be considered in deciding when revenues and gains should be recognized: **realization** and the **earnings process.** Revenues and gains are generally recognized when:[7]

1. They are realized or realizable, and
2. They have been earned through substantial completion of the activities involved in the earnings process.

In order for revenues and gains to be **realized,** inventory or other assets must be exchanged for cash or claims to cash, such as accounts receivable. Revenues are **realizable** when assets held or assets received in an exchange are readily convertible to known amounts of cash or claims to cash. The **earnings process** criterion relates primarily to revenue recognition. Most gains result from transactions and events, such as the sale of land or a patent, that involve no earnings process. Thus, being realized or realizable is of more importance in recognizing gains.

Application of these two criteria to certain industries and companies within these industries has resulted in recognition of revenue at different points in the revenue-producing cycle. This cycle can be a lengthy one. For a manufacturing company, it begins with the development of proposals for a certain product by an individual or by the research and development department and extends through planning, production, sale, collection, and finally expiration of the warranty period. All of these steps are involved in generating sales revenue. If there is a failure at any step, revenue may be seriously curtailed or even

7. *Statement of Financial Accounting Concepts No. 5*, par. 83.

POLLUTED ACCOUNTING

The solid waste disposal industry has gained much attention as cities and states wrestle with how to dispose of the thousands of tons of garbage produced daily by inhabitants. One "small but formidable player in the solid-waste industry" is Chambers Development Company. Chambers went public in 1985 with three landfills and the capacity to handle 10 million tons of garbage per year. By 1992, Chambers owned 17 landfills with a capacity of 84 million tons of waste. Revenues grew at an annual rate of 51%—rising from $5 million in 1980 to $322 million in 1991.

But revenues weren't the only thing growing at Chambers Development Company. The gap between reported results and reality was increasing at an alarming rate. It seems that increasing pressure from top management to produce profitable results caused many within the company to ignore generally accepted accounting principles. Investigations by Deloitte & Touche revealed that after-tax income had been overstated by $362 million over a seven-year period. These overstatements were accomplished by incorrectly capitalizing such items as: the costs of disposing of waste, interest costs, start-up costs, and certain intangible items.

And where was the independent auditor when all of this was going on? The audit partner who signed off on Chambers' audits through 1990 joined the company as chief financial officer later that same year. In addition, two other employees of the same audit firm were hired by Chambers to fill top finance positions. A new team of auditors from the same firm would not accept Chambers' accounting practices and refused to sign off on the audit report for 1991.

Questions

1. How does capitalizing the costs of disposing of waste, interest costs, start-up costs, and certain intangible items affect the income statement? What journal entries would have been made by Chambers' accountant to capitalize these costs? What journal entries should have been made by the accountant?

2. A former consultant for Chambers stated that the president of Chambers "would not tolerate the presence of persons who would not give him the answers he wanted." As the accountant for Chambers Development Company, what would you have done if you had been asked to make these incorrect journal entries?

3. As a user of a firm's financial statements, would it concern you when the audit partner in charge of the independent audit became the chief financial officer for the company?

Source:
"Polluted Numbers: Audit Report Shows How Far Chambers Would Go for Profits," Gabriella Stern, *The Wall Street Journal,* October 21, 1992, pp. A1, A8.

completely eliminated. Yet, there is only one aggregate revenue amount for the entire cycle, the selling price of the product.

For a service company, the revenue-producing cycle begins with an agreement to provide a service and extends through the planning and performance of the service to the collection of the cash and final proof through the passage of time that the service has been adequately performed. With increasing legal actions being taken against professionals, such as doctors and accountants, one could argue that the revenue-producing cycle does not end until the possibility of legal claims for services performed is remote.

Although some accountants have argued for recognizing revenue on a partial basis over these extended production or service periods, the prevailing practice has been to select one point in the cycle that best meets the revenue recognition criteria. Both of these criteria are generally met at the **point of sale,** which is generally when goods are delivered or services are rendered to customers and payment or a promise of payment is received. Thus, revenue for automobiles sold to dealers by Ford Motor Company will be recognized when the cars are shipped to the dealers. Similarly, Price Waterhouse and Co. will record its revenue from audit and tax work when the services have been performed and billed. In both examples, the earnings process is deemed to be substantially complete, and the cash or receivable from the customer meets the realization criterion. Although the "point-of-sale" practice is the most common revenue recognition point, there are notable variations to this general rule.

1. If products or other assets are readily realizable because they can be sold at reliably determined prices without significant selling effort, revenues may be recognized at the

point of completed production. Examples of this situation may occur with certain precious metals and agricultural products that are supported by government price guarantees. In these situations, the earnings process is considered to be substantially complete when the mining or production of the goods is complete.

2. If a product or service is contracted for in advance, revenue may be recognized as production takes place or as services are performed, especially if the production or performance period extends over more than one fiscal year. The **percentage-of-completion** and **proportional performance** methods of accounting have been developed to recognize revenue at several points in the production or service cycle rather than waiting until the final delivery or performance takes place. This exception to the general point-of-sale rule is necessary if the qualitative characteristics of relevance and representational faithfulness are to be met. Construction contracts for buildings, roads, and dams, and contracts for scientific research are examples of situations where these methods of revenue recognition occur. In all cases where this revenue recognition variation is employed, a firm, enforceable contract must exist to meet the realizability criterion, and an objective measure of progress toward completion must be attainable.
3. If collectibility of assets received for products or services is considered doubtful, revenues and gains may be recognized as the cash is received. Although the earnings process has been substantially completed, the questionable receivable fails to meet the realization criterion. The **installment sales** and **cost recovery methods** of accounting have been developed to recognize revenue under these conditions. Sales of real estate, especially speculative recreational property, are often recorded using this variation of the general rule.

The general point-of-sale rule will be assumed unless specifically stated otherwise. The variations introduced above are discussed fully in a later chapter.

Expense and Loss Recognition. In order to determine income, not only must criteria for revenue recognition be established, but the principles for recognizing expenses and losses must be clearly defined. Some expenses are directly associated with revenues and can thus be recognized in the same period as the related revenues. Other expenses are not associated with specific revenues and are recognized in the time period when paid or incurred. Still other expenditures are not recognized currently as expenses because they relate to future revenues and, therefore, are reported as assets. **Expense recognition,** then, can be divided into three categories: (1) direct matching, (2) systematic and rational allocation, and (3) immediate recognition.

Direct Matching. Relating expenses to specific revenues is often referred to as the "matching" process. For example, the cost of goods sold is clearly a direct expense that can be matched with the revenues produced by the sale of goods and reported in the same time period as the revenues are recognized. Similarly, shipping costs and sales commissions usually relate directly to revenues.[8]

Direct expenses include not only those that have already been incurred, but should also include anticipated expenses related to revenues of the current period. After delivery of goods to customers, there are still costs of collection, bad debt losses from uncollectible receivables, and possible warranty costs for product deficiencies. These expenses are directly related to revenues and should be estimated and matched against recognized revenues for the period.

Systematic and Rational Allocation. The second general expense recognition category involves assets that benefit more than one accounting period. The cost of assets such

8. *Statement of Financial Accounting Concepts No. 6*, par. 144.

as buildings, equipment, patents, and prepaid insurance are spread across the periods of expected benefit in some systematic and rational way. Generally, it is difficult if not impossible to relate these expenses directly to specific revenues or to specific periods, but it is clear that they are necessary if the revenue is to be earned. Examples of expenses that are included in this category are depreciation and amortization.

The methods adopted for recognizing expenses and losses should appear reasonable to an unbiased observer and should be followed consistently unless the underlying conditions surrounding the asset change. Some expenses are related to the goods being produced, and thus may be deferred in inventory values if the goods are unsold at the end of an accounting period. Examples include depreciation on production machinery and plant insurance. Other expenses are related to periods, and are allocated directly as an expense of the immediate time period. Examples of these types of expenses include depreciation of delivery trucks and amortization of bond discount.[9]

Immediate Recognition. Many expenses are not related to specific revenues, but are incurred to obtain goods and services that indirectly help to generate revenues. Because these goods and services are used almost immediately, their costs are recognized as expenses in the period of acquisition. Examples include most administrative costs, such as office salaries, utilities, and general advertising and selling expenses.

Immediate recognition is also appropriate when future benefits are highly uncertain. For example, expenditures for research and development may provide significant future benefits, but these benefits are usually so uncertain that the costs are written off in the period in which they are incurred.

Most losses also fit in the immediate recognition category. Because they arise from peripheral or incidental transactions, they do not relate directly to revenues. Examples include losses from disposition of used equipment, losses from natural catastrophes such as earthquakes or tornadoes, and losses from disposition of investments.

Changes in Estimates. In reporting periodic revenues and in attempting to properly match those expenses incurred to generate current-period revenues, accountants must continually make judgments. The numbers reported in the financial statements reflect these judgments and are based on estimates of such factors as the number of years of useful life for depreciable assets, the amount of uncollectible accounts expected, or the amount of warranty liability to be recorded on the books. These and other estimates are made using the best available information at the statement date. However, conditions may subsequently change, and the estimates may need to be revised. Naturally, if either revenue or expense amounts are changed, the income statement is affected. The question is whether the previously reported income measures should be revised or whether the changes should impact only current and future periods.

The Accounting Principles Board stated in Opinion No. 20 that changes in estimates should be reflected in the current period (the period in which the estimate is revised) and in future periods, if any, that are affected. No retroactive adjustments are to be made for a change in estimate.[10] These changes are considered a normal part of the accounting process and not errors made in past periods. For example, Data General Corporation increased the maximum amortization period for software development costs from two years to three years. The effect of this change in estimate was to decrease cost of sales and increase net income for fiscal 1991 by approximately $11 million or $.34 per share.

9. *Ibid.*, par. 147.

10. *Opinions of the Accounting Principles Board No. 20*, "Accounting Changes" (New York: American Institute of Certified Public Accountants, 1971), par. 31.

To illustrate the computations for a change in estimate, assume that Springville Manufacturing Co., Inc., purchased a milling machine at a cost of $100,000. At the time of purchase, it was estimated that the machine would have a useful life of 10 years. Assuming no salvage value and the straight-line method is used, the depreciation expense is $10,000 per year ($100,000 ÷ 10). At the beginning of the fifth year, however, conditions indicated that the machine would only be used for 3 more years. Depreciation expense in the fifth, sixth, and seventh years should reflect the revised estimate, but depreciation expense recorded in the first four years would not be affected. Since the book value at the end of four years is $60,000 ($100,000 - $40,000 accumulated depreciation), annual depreciation charges for the remaining 3 years of estimated life would be $20,000 ($60,000 ÷ 3). The following schedule summarizes the depreciation charges over the life of the asset:

Year	Depreciation
1	$ 10,000
2	10,000
3	10,000
4	10,000
5	20,000
6	20,000
7	20,000
	$100,000

Effects of Changing Prices. The preceding presentation of revenue and expense recognition has not addressed the question of how, if at all, changing prices are to be recognized under the transaction approach. As indicated in Chapter 2, accountants have traditionally ignored this phenomenon, especially when gains would result from recognition. When an economy experiences high rates of inflation, users of financial statements become concerned that the statements do not reflect the impact of these changing prices. When the inflation rates are lower, this user concern decreases. Glenfed Inc., a financial institution, addresses the effects of inflation and interest rates in its 1992 annual report:

Impact of Inflation and Changing Prices: *The consolidated financial statements and related consolidated financial information have been prepared in accordance with generally accepted accounting principles, which require the measurement of financial position and operating results in terms of historical dollars without considering changes in the relative purchasing power of money over time due to inflation. Unlike most industrial companies, virtually all of the assets and liabilities of a financial institution are monetary in nature. As a result, interest rates have a more significant impact on a financial institution's performance than the effects of general levels of inflation. Interest rates do not necessarily move in the same direction or in the same magnitude as the price of goods and services.*

The Financial Accounting Standards Board in Statement No. 33 required certain large publicly held companies to disclose selected information about price changes on a supplemental basis. The Board did not require this recognition to be reported in the basic financial statements, but in a supplemental note to the financial statements that did not have to be audited. Subsequently, some of the disclosure requirements were eliminated in Statement No. 82, and all price-level disclosures were made voluntary in Statement No. 89.

Generally accepted accounting principles are still based primarily on historical exchange prices, and the transaction approach to income determination in most cases recognizes price changes only when losses in value are indicated.

Phar-Mor and the World Basketball League

Michael "Mickey" Monus, former president of Phar-Mor Inc., a deep-discount drugstore chain, had a keen interest in sports. His interest was such that he purchased a share of the Colorado Rockies major league baseball team and also founded the World Basketball League (WBL) — a league for players 6'7" and under. The Rockies, although suffering from some rocky performances on the field, have done quite well financially, setting attendance records in their first season of play. Unfortunately, Mr. Monus was forced to sell his interest in the Rockies because of financial difficulties touched off by the failure of the WBL. WBL players and referees rebelled in July 1992 because they hadn't been paid in two months. Mr. Monus tried to prop up the league, but it soon suspended operations.

During late July 1992, Phar-Mor received a tip that Mr. Monus had been transferring money from Phar-Mor to the WBL. Investigation revealed that the $10 million in Phar-Mor cash Mr. Monus had used in an attempt to sustain the WBL was just the tip of a large iceberg of accounting irregularities. Payments from large vendors to secure exclusive supply arrangements for a period of time were recorded as revenue at the time of receipt instead of being deferred and recognized over the period of the arrangement. Inventory was overstated by $175 million by keeping items in the inventory records even after they had been sold and also by creating phantom inventory at selected stores. The stores were selected based on the auditor's plan to verify inventory at only a few stores — Mr. Monus and his accomplices allegedly found out which stores those were and made sure not to manipulate inventory in those stores. Mr. Monus faces a 129-count indictment filed by the U.S. attorney general's office. And, in an interesting twist, the remaining management of Phar-Mor and Phar-Mor's auditor are suing one another. Management claims that the auditor was negligent. The auditor claims that Phar-Mor's management should have detected Mr. Monus' fraudulent activities.

Questions:

1. How would overstating inventory and receivables inflate reported income? Why would someone want to inflate reported income?
2. Does the independent auditor have a responsibility for detecting these types of misstatements?
3. Observation of Mr. Monus' woes with the WBL may have given some indication that he was in need of cash. When performing an audit, what evidence should the auditor seek outside the financial records of the firm being audited?

Sources:

Lee Berton. "Inventory Chicanery Tempts More Firms, Fools More Auditors," *The Wall Street Journal,* December 14, 1992, p. A1.

Gabriella Stern and Clare Ansberry, "Fouling Out: A Founder Embezzled Millions for Basketball," *The Wall Street Journal,* August 5, 1992, p. A1.

Gabriella Stern, "Phar-Mor's Profit Growth Since 1989 May Have Been Inflated," *The Wall Street Journal,* August 28, 1992, p. A3.

REPORTING OF INCOME

After recognition and measurement criteria are established, the manner in which income is to be reported (displayed) must be determined. Although GAAP requires disclosure of many specific items of information, there is no standardized form of the income statement or other general-purpose financial statements. The reporting of income thus raises many questions regarding, for example, the format of the income statement, terminology used to describe the items presented, the level of detail in the statement, and income-related disclosures to be presented in notes to the financial statements. In answering these and other questions regarding the reporting of income, the overriding consideration should be the usefulness of the information for decision making.

In the following sections, the content of the income statement will be discussed and illustrated using the statement for Techtronics Corporation, a hypothetical company, presented on page 119. Variations in current reporting practices will be examined and illustrated with income statements of actual companies. Subsequently, the implications of the FASB's conceptual framework for future reporting practices will be considered.

Income from Continuing Operations

The Techtronics Corporation income statement has two major categories of income: (1) income from continuing operations and (2) irregular or extraordinary items. Income from continuing operations includes all revenues and expenses and gains and losses arising from the ongoing operations of the firm. In the Techtronics example, income from continuing operations includes six separate sections:

1. Net sales
2. Cost of goods sold
3. Operating expenses
4. Other revenues and gains
5. Other expenses and losses
6. Income taxes on continuing operations

Also, a review of the Techtronics income statement discloses several subtotals in the income from continuing operations category. These subtotals are identified as follows:

1. Gross profit (Net sales - Cost of goods sold)
2. Operating income (#1 - Operating expenses)
3. Income from continuing operations before income taxes (#2 + Other revenues and gains - Other expenses and losses)
4. Income from continuing operations (#3 - income taxes)

Each of the major sections and related subtotals will be discussed separately as a way to better understand current practices in reporting income from continuing operations. Subsequently, we will examine the irregular and extraordinary components of income.

Net Sales. Revenue from net sales reports the total sales to customers for the period less any sales discounts or returns and allowances. This total should not include additions to billings for sales and excise taxes that the business is required to collect on behalf of the government. These billing increases are properly recognized as current liabilities. Sales returns and allowances and sales discounts should be subtracted from gross sales in arriving at net sales revenue. When the sales price is increased to cover the cost of freight to the customer and the customer is billed accordingly, freight charges paid by the company should also be subtracted from sales in arriving at net sales. Freight charges not passed to the buyer are recognized as selling expenses.

Cost of Goods Sold. In any merchandising or manufacturing enterprise, the cost of goods relating to sales for the period must be determined. As illustrated in the Techtronics Corporation income statement, **cost of goods available for sale** is first determined. This is the sum of the beginning inventory, net purchases, and all other buying, freight, and storage costs relating to the acquisition of goods. The net purchases balance is developed by subtracting purchase returns and allowances and purchase discounts from gross purchases. Cost of goods sold is then calculated by subtracting the ending inventory from the cost of goods available for sale.

When the goods are manufactured by the seller, additional elements enter into the cost of goods sold. Besides material costs, a company incurs labor and overhead costs to convert the material from its raw material state to a finished good. A manufacturing company has three inventories rather than one: raw materials, goods in process, and finished goods. The Techtronics Corporation is a merchandising company. The cost of goods sold for a manufacturing company is illustrated in Chapter 9.

For most merchandising and manufacturing companies, cost of goods sold is the most significant expense on the income statement. Because of its size, firms pay particular attention to changes in cost of goods sold relative to changes in sales. **Gross profit on sales** is the difference between sales and cost of goods sold and **gross profit percentage on sales,** computed by dividing gross profit by net sales, provides a measure of profitability that allows comparisons

Techtronics Corporation
Income Statement
For the Year Ended December 31, 1996

Continuing Operations	Revenue from net sales:			
	Sales		$800,000	
	Less: Sales returns and allowances	$ 12,000		
	Sales discounts	8,000	20,000	$780,000
	Cost of good sold:			
	Beginning inventory		$125,000	
	Net purchases	$630,000		
	Freight-in	32,000	662,000	
	Cost of goods available for sale		$787,000	
	Less ending inventory		296,000	491,000
	Gross profit on sales			$289,000
	Operating expenses:			
	Selling expenses:			
	Sales salaries	$ 46,000		
	Advertising expense	27,000		
	Miscellaneous selling expenses	12,000	$ 85,000	
	General and administrative expenses:			
	Officers' and office salaries	$ 44,000		
	Taxes and insurance	26,500		
	Depreciation and amortization expense	30,000		
	Doubtful accounts expense	8,600		
	Miscellaneous general expense	9,200	118,300	203,300
	Operating income			$ 85,700
	Other revenues and gains:			
	Interest revenue		$ 12,750	
	Gain on sale of investment		37,000	49,750
	Other expenses and losses:			
	Interest expense		$ (18,250)	
	Loss on sale of equipment		(5,250)	(23,500)
	Income from continuing operations before income taxes			$111,950
	Income taxes on continuing operations			44,780
	Income from continuing operations			$ 67,170
Irregular or Extraordinary Items	Discontinued operations:			
	Loss from operations of discontinued business segment (net of income tax savings of $14,000)		$(21,000)	
	Loss on disposal of business segment (net of income tax savings of $6,400)		(9,600)	(30,600)
	Extraordinary gain from early debt extinguishment (net of income taxes of $10,160)			15,240
	Cumulative effect of changing inventory method (net of income tax savings of $3,000)			(4,500)
	Net income			$ 47,310
	Earnings per common share:			
	Income from continuing operations			$ 1.34
	Discontinued operations			(0.61)
	Extraordinary gain			0.31
	Cumulative effect of accounting change			(0.09)
	Net income			$ 0.95

for a firm from year to year. For example, using information from IBM's income statement in Exhibit 4-2, we can compute a gross profit percentage for each type of revenue as follows:

IBM Corporation
Gross Profit Percentage

	1992	1991	1990
Sales	41.6%	49.9%	55.9%
Software	64.7%	63.2%	68.4%
Maintenance	55.1%	54.4%	54.1%
Services	17.7%	18.8%	19.6%
Rentals & financing	58.0%	58.7%	58.3%
Overall Gross Profit	45.6%	50.5%	55.4%

This analysis reveals that IBM's overall gross profit percentage has declined significantly over the three-year period from 1990 through 1992. Couple this decline with declining sales and increasing operating expenses and it is no surprise that IBM is reporting losses.

Operating Expenses. Operating expenses may be reported in two parts: (1) selling expenses and (2) general and administrative expenses. **Selling expenses** include such items as sales salaries and commissions and related payroll taxes, advertising and store displays, store supplies used, depreciation of store furniture and equipment, and delivery expenses. **General and administrative expenses** include officers' and office salaries and related payroll taxes, office supplies used, depreciation of office furniture and fixtures, telephone, postage, business licenses and fees, legal and accounting services, contributions, and similar items. For manufacturing companies, charges related jointly to both production and administrative functions should be allocated in some equitable manner between manufacturing overhead and operating expenses.

Other Revenues and Gains. This section usually includes items identified with the peripheral activities of the company. Examples include revenue from financial activities, such as rents, interest, and dividends, and gains from the sale of assets such as equipment or investments. A gain reported on the income statement represents a net amount, i.e., the difference between selling price and cost. This differs from revenues, which are reported in total separately from related expenses.

Other Expenses and Losses. This section is parallel to the previous one, but results in deductions from, rather than increases to, operating income. Examples include interest expense and losses from the sale of assets. Losses, like gains, are reported at their net amounts.

Income Tax on Continuing Operations. When a company does not report any irregular or extraordinary items, income taxes on continuing operations represents total income tax expense for the period. When irregular or extraordinary items are reported, total taxes for the period must be allocated among the various components of income. One income tax amount is reported for all items included in the income from continuing operations category; it is presented as the last section in the category. In contrast, each item in the irregular or extraordinary items category is reported net of its income tax effect, referred to as "net of tax." This separation of income taxes into different sections of the income statement is referred to as **intraperiod income tax allocation.** Income taxes are a significant factor in the computation of income, and disclosing the amount of taxes related to specific components of income provides more useful information for users of financial statements.

Exhibit 4-2 IBM's Income Statement

Consolidated Statement of Earnings

International Business Machines Corporation and Subsidiary Companies

(Dollars in millions except per share amounts) For the year ended December 31:	1992	1991*†	1990*
Revenue:			
Sales	$ 33,755	$ 37,093	$ 43,959
Software	11,103	10,498	9,865
Maintenance	7,635	7,414	7,198
Services	7,352	5,582	4,124
Rentals and financing	4,678	4,179	3,785
	64,523	64,766	68,931
Cost:			
Sales	19,698	18,571	19,401
Software	3,924	3,865	3,118
Maintenance	3,430	3,379	3,302
Services	6,051	4,531	3,315
Rentals and financing	1,966	1,727	1,579
	35,069	32,073	30,715
Gross Profit	29,454	32,693	38,216
Operating Expenses:			
Selling, general and administrative	19,526	21,375	20,709
Research, development and engineering	6,522	6,644	6,554
Restructuring charges	11,645	3,735	—
	37,693	31,754	27,263
Operating Income	(8,239)	939	10,953
Other Income, principally interest	573	602	495
Interest Expense	1,360	1,423	1,324
Earnings before Income Taxes	(9,026)	118	10,124
Provision for Income Taxes	(2,161)	716	4,157
Net Earnings before Changes in Accounting Principles	(6,865)	(598)	5,967
Effect of Changes in Accounting Principles‡	1,900	(2,263)	—
Net Earnings	$ (4,965)	$ (2,861)	$ 5,967
Per Share Amounts:			
Before Changes in Accounting Principles	$ (12.03)	$ (1.05)	$ 10.42
Effect of Changes in Accounting Principles‡	3.33	(3.96)	—
Net Earnings	$ (8.70)	$ (5.01)	$ 10.42

Average Number of Shares Outstanding:
1992—570,896,489; 1991—572,003,382; 1990—572,647,906

*Restated for the American Institute of Certified Public Accountants Statement of Position, "Software Revenue Recognition."

†Reclassified to conform with 1992 presentation.

‡1992, cumulative effect of Statement of Financial Accounting Standards (SFAS) 109, "Accounting for Income Taxes"; and 1991, transition effect of SFAS 106, "Employers' Accounting for Postretirement Benefits Other Than Pensions."

In the Techtronics illustration, an income tax rate of 40% was assumed. Thus, the amount of income tax related to continuing operations is $44,780 ($111,950 x .40). The same tax rate is applied to all income components in the Techtronics example. In practice, however, intraperiod income tax allocation may involve different rates for different components of income. This results from graduated tax rates and special or alternative rates for certain types of gains and losses.

Irregular and Extraordinary Items

Components of income that are reported separately after income from continuing operations are sometimes called "below-the-line" items. They arise from transactions and events that are irregular or extraordinary *and* material in amount. Reporting these items, and their related tax effects, separately from continuing operations provides more informative disclosure to users of financial statements. Three types of transactions and events are reported in this manner: (1) discontinued operations, (2) extraordinary items, and (3) cumulative effects of changes in accounting principles.

Discontinued Operations. An increasingly common irregular item involves the disposition of a major segment of a business either through sale or abandonment. In 1992, 55 of the 600 surveyed companies in *Accounting Trends & Techniques* reported discontinued operations in their statements. The segment of the company disposed of may be a major line of business, a major class of customer, or a subsidiary company. To qualify as **discontinued operations** for reporting purposes, the assets and related activities of the segment must be clearly distinguishable from other assets, operating results, and general activities of the company, both physically and operationally, as well as for financial reporting purposes. For example, closing down one of three plants making the same product, eliminating *part* of a line of business, or shifting the production or marketing functions from one location to another would not be classified as discontinued operations.

There are many reasons why management may decide to dispose of a segment. For example:

1. The segment may be unprofitable.
2. The segment may be too isolated geographically.
3. The segment may not fit into the long-range plans for the company.
4. Management may need funds to reduce long-term debt or to expand into other areas.
5. Management may be fearful of a corporate take-over by new investors desiring to gain control of the company.

In the 1980s, management of many companies adopted anti-takeover strategies to try to protect their companies. One of the more popular techniques was to sell peripheral operational segments, especially unprofitable ones, that had been acquired during earlier conglomerate years, and to consolidate the company around its principal business operations. As an example, Winnebago, Inc. elected to discontinue its Commercial Vehicle Division. The division, which had lost money for years, manufactured delivery vans and shuttle buses. Winnebago's 1991 income statement is reproduced in Exhibit 4-3, and the note explaining the divestiture is reproduced in Exhibit 4-4.

Many successful takeovers are financed by financial institutions willing to lend billions of dollars to support the buyout of current stockholders. After the new management assumes control of the company, a common strategy is to sell parts of the company to reduce the debt incurred in the takeover. For example, Allied Corporation purchased Bendix Corporation, a $4.1 billion (revenues) automotive parts, aerospace, and machine tool conglomerate. Within two years, Allied liquidated a machine tool company, an earth-moving machine business, and a large pipe-bending business. Similarly, in 1985 W. R. Grace & Co. purchased a 26% interest in a West German group and then made plans to sell over $1 billion of assets, including its retail operations that included sporting goods, home centers, and western wear.[11]

11. "W. R. Grace Plans Asset Sales in 1986 Totaling $1 Billion," *The Wall Street Journal,* February 12, 1986, p. 33.

■ **Exhibit 4-3** Winnebago Industries, Inc. — Income Statement

WINNEBAGO INDUSTRIES, INC. & SUBSIDIARIES

Consolidated Statements of Operations

Dollars in thousands except per share data

Year Ended	August 31, 1991	August 25, 1990	August 26, 1989
Revenues			
Manufactured products	$ 210,438	$ 320,175	$ 422,423
Service	12,210	12,658	15,077
Total net revenues	222,648	332,833	437,500
Costs and Expenses			
Cost of manufactured products	196,584	291,961	380,476
Cost of services	12,623	13,535	15,865
Selling and delivery	20,342	24,387	25,046
General and administrative	14,791	22,852	23,026
Other expense	403	3,981	4,856
Minority interest in net loss of consolidated subsidiary	(766)	(2,087)	—
Total costs and expenses	243,977	354,629	449,269
Operating loss	(21,329)	(21,796)	(11,769)
Financial income (loss)	(340)	(3,946)	6,121
Loss from continuing operations before income taxes	(21,669)	(25,742)	(5,648)
Credits for taxes	(5,398)	(11,176)	(2,470)
Loss from continuing operations	(16,271)	(14,566)	(3,178)
Discontinued Operations:			
Loss from discontinued Commercial Vehicle Division operations (less applicable credits for income taxes of $0, $2,509 and $1,163, respectively)	(4,992)	(3,269)	(1,497)
Loss on disposal of Commercial Vehicle Division, including a provision of $1,042 for operating losses during phase-out period (less applicable income taxes of $0)	(8,118)		
Loss from discontinued operations	(13,110)	(3,269)	(1,497)
Net loss	$ (29,381)	$ (17,835)	$ (4,675)
Loss per common share:			
Continuing operations	$ (.65)	$ (.59)	$ (.13)
Discontinued operations	(.53)	(.13)	(.06)
Net loss	$ (1.18)	$ (.72)	$ (.19)
Weighted average number of shares of stock (in thousands)	24,986	24,748	24,695

See Notes to Consolidated Financial Statements

■ Exhibit 4-4
Winnebago Industries, Inc.—Note Disclosure for Discontinued Operations

NOTES TO CONSOLIDATED FINANCIAL STATEMENTS

In September 1991, the Company adopted a formal plan to discontinue the Commercial Vehicle Division which manufactures delivery vans and shuttle buses. As part of such plan, the Company intends to discontinue production by December 1991 and either sell or liquidate the operations during fiscal 1992.

As a result, the Company recorded a fourth quarter charge of $8.1 million to write-down the division's assets to their estimated net realizable values and to accrue for operating losses through the anticipated phase-out period ($7.1 million and $10.0 million, respectively). No income tax benefits have been allocated to the division's fiscal 1991 losses because there are no realizable taxable benefits available to allocate to the discontinued operation. Such fiscal 1991 losses are included in the Company's net operating loss carryforwards disclosed in Note 11.

Revenues for the discontinued Commercial Vehicle Division were $760,000, $2,265,000 and $0 for fiscal 1991, 1990 and 1989, respectively. The assets and liabilities of the discontinued operations have been reclassified on the balance sheet from their historic classification to separately identify them as net assets of discontinued operations and principally consist of inventory, tooling, equipment and accrued losses for the phase-out period.

Regardless of the reason, the discontinuance of a substantial portion of company operations is a significant event. Therefore, information about discontinued operations should be presented explicitly to readers of financial statements.

Reporting Requirements for Discontinued Operations. When a company discontinues operating a segment of its business, future comparability requires that all elements that relate to the discontinued operation be identified and separated from continuing operations. Thus, in the Techtronics Corporation income statement illustrated earlier in this chapter, the first category after Income From Continuing Operations is Discontinued Operations. The category is further separated into two subdivisions: (1) the current-year income or loss from operating the discontinued segment, or a $21,000 loss, and (2) disclosure of the gain or loss on the actual disposal of the business segment, or a further $9,600 loss.

As previously indicated, the irregular items are all reported net of their respective tax effects. If the item is a gain, it is reduced by the tax on the gain. If the item is a loss, it is deductible against other income and thus its existence *saves* income taxes. The overall company loss can thus be reduced by the tax savings arising from being able to deduct the loss from otherwise taxable income.

The income statement for Techtronics Corporation illustrated earlier in the chapter discloses both of these subdivisions. The income tax rate is 40% on all items. Analysis of the income statement shows that the discontinued segment had an operating loss for the current year of $35,000, but that after a tax savings of $14,000 was deducted, only $21,000 is reported as a loss. The second item discloses that the segment was sold and a loss of $16,000 was experienced on the sale. Application of the income tax rate of 40% reduces this loss to $9,600. If comparative statements are prepared, the same separation between continued and discontinued operations for prior years should be made.

Often a company will decide on a particular date (the **measurement date**) to dispose of a business segment, but will have a phase-out period between that date and the date the segment is actually sold (**disposal date**). The gain or loss on disposal will include any income or loss from operating the segment during the phase-out period. To illustrate using Techtronics Corporation's income statement, assume the company decided on July 1, 1996,

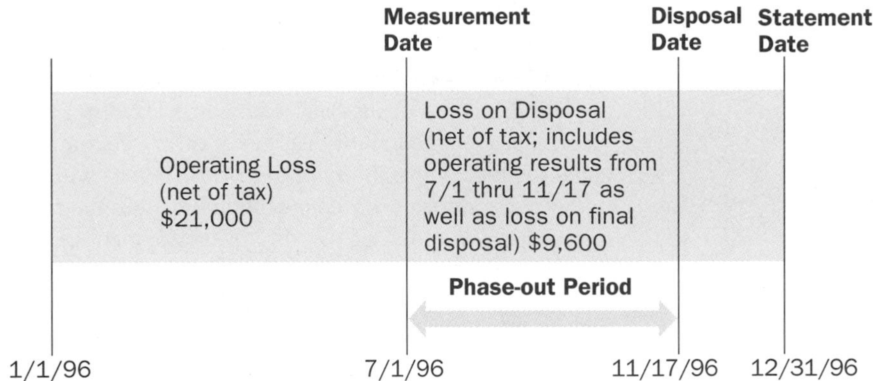

to phase out a segment of its operation. This date is the measurement date and marks the beginning of the phase-out period. Assume also that the segment was disposed of on November 17, 1996. The $9,600 loss on disposal reflects both the operating results during phase-out and the gain or loss on final disposal, net of income taxes. The $21,000 loss represents the operating loss (net of income tax savings of $14,000) for the period January 1, 1996, to July 1, 1996. The time line presented at the top of this page uses the Techtronics example to illustrate the relevant time periods to be considered when accounting for discontinued operations.

If the accounting year ends before the disposal is completed, estimates must be made of the expected gain or loss from final disposal. If the computation indicates an expected loss on disposal, the accounting constraint of conservatism dictates that the loss should be recognized in the current period, not in the later period when the loss actually occurs. If the computation indicates an expected gain on disposal, the gain will not be recognized until it is actually realized in the subsequent period. The information contained in the Winnebago income statement (Exhibit 4-3) and note (Exhibit 4-4) can be used to illustrate the disclosure required when the disposal date occurs after the fiscal year-end. In September 1991, Winnebago decided to discontinue the Commercial Vehicle Division, after its 1991 fiscal year-end (August 31, 1991) but before it issued its 1991 financial statements. Winnebago incurred a loss in fiscal year 1991 of $4,992,000 from operating the division. For the phase-out period, which began and was expected to be completed in the fiscal year ending August 29, 1992, Winnebago estimated an operating loss of $1,042,000 and a loss on disposal of division assets of $7,076,000. The revelant time periods in the Winnebago example are illustrated with the time line at the bottom of this page.

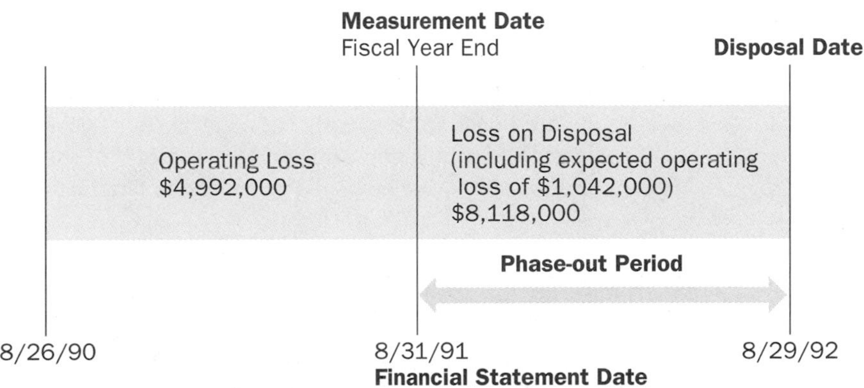

The Winnebago income statement in Exhibit 4—3 illustrates how the two components of discontinued operations (income or loss from operating the segment and gain or loss on disposal) are reported. The first line in the discontinued operations section reports the operating income or loss, net of income taxes, for the discontinued operations for all 3 years. The separation of income from discontinued operations from regular income enhances the comparability of this year's results with those of prior years. The second line in the discontinued operations section indicates the estimated loss (which includes an estimated operating loss) on disposal of the segment in fiscal year 1992.

The reporting requirements for discontinued operations are contained in APB Opinion No. 30, "Reporting the Results of Operations."[12] The reporting of discontinued operations can become complex, and only a summary of the guidelines provided by APB Opinion No. 30 is covered here. Application of the guidelines requires judgment. The goal should be to report information that will assist external users in assessing future cash flows by clearly distinguishing normal, recurring earnings patterns from those activities that are irregular, yet significant in assessing the total company results of operations.

Extraordinary Items. According to APB Opinion No. 30, **extraordinary items** are events and transactions that are both **unusual in nature and infrequent in occurrence.** Thus, to qualify as extraordinary, an item must "possess a high degree of abnormality and be of a type clearly unrelated to, or only incidentally related to, the ordinary and typical activities of the entity . . . [and] be of a type that would not reasonably be expected to recur in the foreseeable future. . . .[13]

The intent of the Accounting Principles Board was to restrict the items that could be classified as extraordinary. The presumption of the Board was that an item should be considered ordinary and part of the company's continuing operations unless evidence clearly supports its classification as an extraordinary item. The Board offered examples of gains and losses that should *not* be reported as extraordinary items. These include:

1. The write-down or write-off of receivables, inventories, equipment leased to others, or intangible assets.
2. The gains or losses from exchanges or remeasurement of foreign currencies, including those relating to major devaluations and revaluations.
3. The gains or losses on disposal of a segment of a business.
4. Other gains or losses from sale or abandonment of property, plant, or equipment used in the business.
5. The effects of a strike.
6. The adjustment of accruals on long-term contracts.

The standard-setting bodies have identified only one major item as extraordinary regardless of whether it meets the dual criteria: a gain or loss from early extinguishment of debt.[14] An example would be a gain or loss on the retirement of bonds before their maturity date. Besides early extinguishment of debt, companies have reported as extraordinary items litigation settlements, write-offs of assets in foreign countries where expropriation risks were high, and pension plan terminations.

12. *Opinions of the Accounting Principles Board No. 30,* "Reporting the Results of Operations" (New York: American Institute of Certified Public Accountants, 1973), par. 20.
13. *Ibid.,* par. 20.
14. *Statement of Financial Accounting Standards No. 4,* "Reporting Gains and Losses From Extinguishment of Debt" (Stamford: Financial Accounting Standards Board, 1975).

Some items may not meet both criteria for extraordinary items, but may meet one of them. Although these items do not qualify as extraordinary, they should be disclosed separately as part of income from continuing operations, either before or after operating income. Examples of these items include strike-related costs, obsolete inventory write-downs, and gains and losses from liquidation of investments. Another example is included in IBM's income statement in Exhibit 4—2. IBM reported restructuring charges in 1992 and 1991 of $11.645 billion and $3.735 billion, respectively. Because these charges were included as part of operating income, they were reported before income taxes.

Cumulative Effects of Changes in Accounting Principles. The last item included in the irregular category of the income statement is the effect of changing accounting principles. Although the profession has recognized the desirability of consistency in application of accounting principles, there are occasions where conditions justify a change from one principle to another. Sometimes this condition arises because the standard-setting body issues a new pronouncement requiring a change in principle. If GAAP is to be followed, the company has no choice but to change to conform with the new standard. IBM reported the combined effects of two such changes when they adopted the FASB standards for deferred income taxes (FASB Statement No. 109) and postretirement benefits other than pensions (FASB Statement No. 106). Sometimes economic conditions change, and a company changes accounting principles so that reporting can be more representative of the actual conditions. For example, when there was double-digit inflation during the late 1970s, many companies changed their inventory methods to LIFO to reduce their income and thus reduce the actual cash payments for income taxes.

Depending on the type of change in accounting principle, the change may be implemented retroactively or it may be reflected only in the current and future periods. If the change arises because of a new FASB standard, the Board designates how the change must be implemented. If the change in accounting principle is made at management's discretion, however, the implementation decision is made by management using guidance provided by accounting standard setters. The Board has recognized two different ways to adjust current statements to reflect the **cumulative effect of a change in accounting principle:** (1) generally, income statements should report the cumulative effect of the change in the current year with no restatement of prior years' figures, (2) special cases require the restatement of financial statements presented for prior years. For example, in the general case, if a company decides to change its depreciation method from straight-line to declining balance for all existing assets, an entry is needed in the current year to adjust the statements for the cumulative effect of the change. In the special cases, the beginning balance of retained earnings for the current year reflects the cumulative effect of the prior year's changes. The Accounting Principles Board specified differrent criteria to help accountants determine which approach should be applied under what circumstances. Further discussion of these criteria is included in a later chapter.

In the income statement illustrated earlier in the chapter, the Techtronics Corporation recorded a $4,500 cumulative loss due to changing inventory principles. The pretax loss to Techtronics was $7,500, but income tax savings reduced the reported loss by $3,000. If Techtronics had met one of the criteria identified by the APB as requiring restatement of the financial statements, the other method of reporting the cumulative effects of the change in accounting principles would have been used. There would have been no adjustment to income; instead, the loss would have been recorded as a charge directly to Retained Earnings.

Net Income or Loss. Income or loss from continuing operations combined with the results of discontinued operations, extraordinary items, and the cumulative effects of changes in accounting principles provides users with a summary measure of the firm's performance for a period — net income or net loss. In order to compare this period's results with prior periods or with the performance of other firms, net income is divided by net sales to determine the **net profit percentage on sales.** This measurement represents the net income percentage per dollar of sales. For example, Microsoft, Inc. (Appendix A) reported the following net profit percentages:

	1993	1992	1991
Net Profit Percentage	25.4%	25.7%	25.1%

Compare these results with a sample of profit percentages from various industries.

Industry (number of firms included)	Median Profit Percentage
Dairy Farms (303)	6.4%
Blast Furnaces and Steel Mills (550)	3.9%
Electric Utilities (2,167)	6.9%
Grocery Stores (2,183)	1.4%
Jewelry Stores (2,319)	5.0%
Legal Services (2,463)	8.3%

Keep in mind, when computing the net profit percentage, that net income may include extraordinary or irregular items that can distort the results and hamper comparability. Adjustments may be needed in the analysis to account for such items.

Earnings Per Share. In 1969, the Accounting Principles Board issued Opinion No. 15 that required all companies to include a section in the income statement converting certain income components to earnings per share. Separate earnings-per-share amounts are computed by dividing income from continuing operations and each irregular or extraordinary item by the weighted average number of shares of common stock outstanding for the reporting period.[15]

For example, the Techtronics Corporation income statement shows earnings per share of $1.34 for income from continuing operations, $.61 for loss from discontinued operations, $.31 for extraordinary gain, and a loss of $.09 for the cumulative effect of a change in accounting principle, for a total of $.95 for net income. These figures were derived by dividing each identified component of net income by 50,000 shares of common stock outstanding during the period. When a company has only common stock outstanding, computing earnings per share is very straightforward. The computations become more complex, however, when a company has certain types of securities outstanding, such as convertible stock and stock options. These and other types of securities are discussed in later chapters.

Earnings per share is often used to calculate a firm's **price-earnings ratio (P/E ratio).** This ratio expresses the market value of common stock as a multiple of earnings and allows investors to evaluate the attractiveness of a firm's common stock. The price-earn-

15. *Opinions of the Accounting Principles Board No. 15,* "Earnings Per Share" (New York: American Institute of Certified Public Accountants, 1969), par. 47.

ings ratio is computed by dividing the market price per share of stock by the annual earnings per share. Instead of using the average market value of shares for the period covered by earnings, the latest market value is normally used. *The Wall Street Journal* reports P/E ratios for most listed companies on a daily basis. Assuming Techtronics Corporation's stock closed with a market value of $14.25 per share on December 31, 1996, the P/E ratio would be computed as follows:

$$\text{P/E ratio} = \frac{\text{Market value per share}}{\text{Earnings per share}} = \frac{\$14.25}{\$0.95} = 15.0$$

Form of the Income Statement

All income statements prepared in accordance with GAAP report the same basic type of information and have certain common display features. Some sections of the income statement, especially irregular and extraordinary items, are specified by FASB pronouncements. Others have become standardized by wide usage.

Traditionally, the income from continuing operations category has been presented in either a single-step or a multiple-step form. With the **single-step form,** all revenues and gains that are identified as operating items are placed first on the income statement followed by all expenses and losses that are identified as operating items. The difference between total revenues and gains and total expenses and losses represents income from operations. If there are no nonoperating, irregular, or extraordinary items, this difference is also equal to net income (or loss). The income statement for the American Stock Exchange in Exhibit 4-5 illustrates the single-step form. Note that income taxes are reported separately from other expenses, which is a common variation of the basic single-step form. With the **multiple-step form,** the income statement is divided into separate sections (referred to as "intermediate components" in Concepts Statement No. 5), and various subtotals are reported that reflect different levels of profitability. The income statement of IBM, Exhibit 4—2, illustrates one form of a multiple-step income statement.[16]

The Techtronics Corporation income statement is also presented in the multiple-step form. This hypothetical income statement contains more categories and more detail than is usually found in actual published financial statements. It has become common practice to issue highly condensed statements, with details and supporting schedules provided in notes to the statements. The potential problem with this practice is that the condensed statements may not provide as much predictive and feedback value as statements that provide more detail about the components of income directly on the statement.

The Techtronics income statement differs from most published statements in other ways. For example, to simplify the illustration of the various income components, only one year is presented for Techtronics. To comply with SEC requirements, income statements of public companies are presented in comparative form for three years (see Exhibits 4-2 and 4-3).[17] **Comparative financial statements** enable users to analyze performance over multiple periods and identify significant trends that might impact future performance.

16. The AICPA's annual survey of reporting practices indicates the multiple-step format has become increasingly popular in recent years. Of the 600 companies surveyed in 1992, 65% used the multiple-step format. *Accounting Trends & Techniques,* 1993 (Jersey City, NJ: American Institute of Certified Public Accountants), p. 273.

17. Note that the American Stock Exchange (Exhibit 4-5) presents comparative statements for only two years. The Exchange is owned by its members and is not a publicly traded company subject to SEC reporting rules.

■ Exhibit 4-5
American Stock Exchange — Single Step Income Statement

CONSOLIDATED STATEMENTS OF INCOME AND EXPENSES

American Stock Exchange, Inc. and Subsidiaries – Years Ended December 31, 1992 and 1991

	1992	1991
Income:		
Transaction and clearance charges	$ 36,113,000	$ 33,197,000
Communication charges	47,639,000	39,898,000
Listing fees	14,159,000	13,691,000
Members' dues and fees	2,768,000	2,744,000
Investment and other income	13,810,000	11,453,000
Total income	114,489,000	100,983,000
Expenses:		
Compensation and benefits	51,218,000	49,375,000
Product services and development project costs	26,635,000	25,855,000
Facilities costs	8,833,000	8,549,000
Professional services	3,753,000	3,746,000
Depreciation and amortization	8,662,000	8,393,000
General and administrative	12,709,000	7,368,000
Total expenses	111,810,000	103,286,000
Income (loss) before income tax (benefit)	2,679,000	(2,303,000)
Income tax (benefit):		
Current	1,099,000	(2,726,000)
Deferred	272,000	1,836,000
	1,371,000	(890,000)
Net income (loss)	$ 1,308,000	$ (1,413,000)

See accompanying notes to consolidated financial statements.

Also note that the Techtronics income statement is for a single business entity, but public companies often present **consolidated financial statements** that combine the financial results of a "parent company," such as IBM, with other companies that it owns, called "subsidiaries." All of the actual company statements illustrated in this chapter, as well as the Microsoft statements in Appendix A, are consolidated statements.

Throughout this text, we will use many actual companies to illustrate financial reporting concepts and practices. You will observe many variations in statement titles, terminology, level of detail, and other aspects of reporting. As a result, you will develop an appreciation of the diversity in financial reporting and the ability to understand financial information presented in a wide variety of terms and formats.

REPORTING CHANGES IN RETAINED EARNINGS

Many corporations include a statement identifying the changes in retained earnings as one of their financial statements. This statement generally begins with the opening balance in the retained earnings account and then shows the additions and deductions to arrive at the ending balance. In many cases, this statement is very simple. Net income is included as an addition, dividend distributions as a deduction, and any special credits or charges are added or subtracted as appropriate. There are two general types of retained earnings adjustments: (1) prior-period adjustments, and (2) as indicated earlier, adjustments arising from some changes in accounting principles. **Prior-period adjustments** arise primarily when an error occurs in one period and is not discovered until a subsequent period.

The retained earnings statement for Techtronics Corporation is illustrated below.

Techtronics Corporation
Retained Earnings Statement
For the Year Ended December 31, 1996

Retained earnings, January 1, 1996	$286,590
Add prior-period adjustment—correction of inventory understatement (net of income taxes of $10,000)	15,000
Adjusted retained earnings, January 1, 1996	$301,590
Add net income from income statement	47,310
	$348,900
Deduct dividends declared	40,000
Retained earnings, December 31, 1996	$308,900

Prior-period adjustments for errors are not reported often, because most errors are discovered and corrected in the year they occur. In some cases, however, a considerable amount of time may elapse before an error is discovered. As an example, in 1987 Matrix Science Corp. discovered revenue recognition errors arising from fraudulent actions by its former management. As a result, the following adjustment was made to restate retained earnings as of June 30, 1984:

Retained earnings, June 30, 1984	$28,534,300
Less prior-period adjustment (see accompanying note)	1,207,500
Adjusted retained earnings, June 30, 1984	$27,326,800

The accompanying note presented in the 1987 annual report, and reproduced in Exhibit 4—6, is revealing in its specificity as to the cause of the prior-period errors.

REPORTING IMPLICATIONS OF THE CONCEPTUAL FRAMEWORK

The Financial Accounting Standards Board recommended new terminology to report the changes in owners' equity. One of the ten elements defined in Concepts Statement No. 6 and presented in Chapter 2 was **"Comprehensive income."** The Board defined this term as follows:

Comprehensive income is the change in equity of a business enterprise during a period from transactions and other events and circumstances from nonowner sources. It includes all changes in equity during a period except those resulting from investments by owners and distributions to owners.[18]

18. *Statement of Financial Accounting Concepts No. 6*, par. 70.

■ **Exhibit 4—6**
Matrix Science Corp.—Disclosure of Prior-Period Adjustment

NOTES TO CONSOLIDATED FINANCIAL STATEMENTS

2. *Special Investigation and Accounting Practices*

In August 1987, it became known that the Company had followed a practice of recording sales prior to the shipment of goods. In connection therewith, the Board of Directors engaged special legal counsel and the Company's auditors to conduct an investigation of the Company's accounting practices. Additionally, in September 1987, it was determined that substantial amounts of credit memorandums, primarily for customer returns, had not been processed in a timely manner.

The above practices involved certain senior officers and other employees of the Company. In October 1987, the former president, executive vice president, and chief financial officer resigned their positions and entered into consulting agreements as of the date of their resignations with the Company. The consulting agreement with the former president ended on January 8, 1988, and the other two agreements are on a month-to-month basis.

The results of the investigation concluded that the sales recording and credit memo practices discussed above resulted in the incorrect recording of sales. While the Company does not believe the resulting adjustments were material to its financial statements, when taken as a whole in any prior year, the Company has determined that a restatement of prior years' financial statements is appropriate. . . .

At June 30, 1984, retained earnings as previously reported, was $28,534,300. Retained earnings, as restated, was $27,326,800.

The Board also defined a new term for the bottom line of an income statement. As discussed in the chapter, the last figure on an income statement is usually labeled "Net income." The Board did not define net income; however, they did recommend adoption of the term "earnings." As defined in the Statement, **earnings** is identical with net income as that term is used in practice except that the last irregular item discussed, "Cumulative Effects of Changes in Accounting Principles," is not included in earnings. Thus, the earnings amount for the Techtronics Corporation would be $51,810 ($47,310 + $4,500). In addition to an earnings statement, the Board suggested that a new comprehensive income statement should be prepared. This statement would start with the earnings amount and include all other nonowner changes to owners' equity. This statement would include the cumulative effects of changes in accounting principles. Also included would be any recognized changes in values, such as market value adjustments of some investment securities and foreign currency translation adjustments.

The Board did not include a display of a suggested statement of comprehensive income in Concepts Statement No. 5, but stated: "This Statement does not consider details of displaying those different kinds of information and does not preclude the possibility that some entities might choose to combine some of that information in a single statement."[19] An example of how a statement of comprehensive income might appear for Techtronics Corporation is included on the next page.

It is important to recognize that the terms "earnings" and "comprehensive income" recommended in the concepts statements are not presently part of GAAP. Not until they are incorporated into a statement of standards will they be required of business management and auditors.

A review of the 1993 edition of *Accounting Trends & Techniques* indicates very little change in terminology has occurred as a result of Concepts Statement No. 5. "Income" is still the most widely used, with "earnings" being only half as popular. None of the 600 reporting companies surveyed by *Accounting Trends & Techniques* in 1992 adopted the comprehensive income concept.

19. *Statement of Financial Accounting Concepts No. 5*, par. 14.

Techtronics Corporation
Statement of Comprehensive Income
For the Year Ended December 31, 1996

Earnings per earnings statement	$51,810
Cumulative effect of changing inventory method (net of income tax savings of $3,000)	(4,500)
Prior-period adjustment—correction of inventory understatement (net of income taxes of $10,000)	15,000
Foreign currency translation adjustment	30,000
Comprehensive income	$92,310

CONCLUDING COMMENT

As indicated in the Comptronix case that began this chapter, one "bottom line" figure for income can often be misleading and result in an inefficient allocation of resources. Standard-setting bodies have been concerned with the ingredients that enter income measurement. The FASB has tried to address the related problems of income recognition, measurement, and reporting in their concepts statements. Decision usefulness will be improved if some of these recommendations are incorporated into practice. However, change is always slow, especially when the changes involve entrenched terminology and formats. Many of the income components introduced in this chapter will be explored in greater depth in later chapters of the text. A summary of the treatment of the special items discussed in this chapter is presented in Exhibit 4—7.

Exhibit 4—7 Summary of Procedures for Reporting Irregular, Non-recurring, or Unusual Items*

Where Reported	Category	Description	Examples
Part of income from continuing operations	Changes in estimates	Normal recurring changes in estimating future amounts. Included in normal accounts.	Changes in building and equipment lives, changes in estimated loss from uncollectible accounts receivable, changes in estimate of warranty liability.
	Unusual gains and losses, not considered extraordinary	Unusual or infrequent, but not both. Related to normal operations. Material in amount. Shown in other revenues and gains or other expenses and losses.	Gains or losses from sale of assets, investments, or other operating assets. Write-off of inventories as obsolete.
On income statement, but after income from continuing operations	Discontinued operations	Disposal of completely separate line of business. Include gain or loss from sale or abandonment.	Sale by conglomerate company of separate line of business, such as milling company selling restaurant segment.
	Extraordinary items	Both unusual and infrequent. Not related to normal business operations. Material in amount.	Material gains and losses from early extinguishment of debt, from some casualties or legal claims if meet criteria.
	Changes in accounting principles—general case	Change from one accepted principle to another.	Change from one method of inventory pricing to another, change in depreciation method.

continued

Where Reported	Category	Description	Examples
As adjustments to retained earnings on the balance sheet	Prior-period adjustment and special case changes in accounting principles	Material correction of errors, changes in accounting principles that require retroactive adjustment.	Failure to depreciate fixed assets, mathematical error in computing inventory balance, retroactive adjustment for new FASB standard.

*This chart describes the usual case. Exceptions to the descriptions occasionally do occur.

KEY TERMS

Comparative financial statements 129
Comprehensive income 131
Consolidated financial statements 130
Cumulative effect of a change in accounting principle 127
Discontinued operations 122
Earnings 132
Expense recognition 114
Expenses 112
Extraordinary items 126
Financial capital maintenance 110
Gains 112
Gross profit on sales 118
Gross profit percentage on sales 118
Intraperiod income tax allocation 120
Losses 112
Net profit percentage on sales 128
Physical capital maintenance 111
Price earnings ratio (P/E ratio) 128
Prior-period adjustments 131
Revenue recognition 112
Revenues 112
Transaction approach 111

QUESTIONS

1. FASB Concepts Statement No. 1 states, "The primary focus of financial reporting is information about an enterprise's performance provided by measures of earnings and its components." Why is it unwise for users of financial statements to focus too much attention on the income statement?
2. Income as determined by income tax regulations is not necessarily the same as income reported to external users. Why might there be differences?
3. After the necessary definitions and assumptions have been made that support the determination of income, what are the two methods of income measurement that may be used to determine income? How do they differ?
4. What different measurement methods may be applied to net assets in arriving at income under the capital maintenance approach?
5. How are revenues and expenses different from gains and losses?
6. What two factors must be considered in deciding the point at which revenues and gains should be recognized? At what point in the revenue cycle are these conditions usually met?
7. Name three exceptions to the general rule that assumes revenue is recognized at the point of sale. What is the justification for these exceptions?
8. What guidelines are used to match costs with revenues in determining income?
9. What are some possible disadvantages of a multiple-step income statement and of a single-step statement?
10. Identify the major sections (components of income) that are included in a multiple-step income statement.
11. What is the meaning of "intraperiod" income tax allocation?
12. The Pop-Up Company has decided to sell its lid manufacturing division even though the division is expected to show a small profit this year. The division's assets will be sold at a loss of $10,000 to another company. What information (if any) should Pop-Up disclose in its financial reports with respect to this division?
13. Which of the following would *not* normally qualify as an extraordinary item?
    (a) The write-down or write-off of receivables.
    (b) Major devaluation of foreign currency.
    (c) Loss on sale of plant and equipment.
    (d) Gain from early extinguishment of debt.
    (e) Loss due to extensive flood damage to an asphalt company in Las Vegas, Nevada.
    (f) Loss due to extensive earthquake damage to a furniture company in Los Angeles, California.
    (g) Farming loss due to heavy spring rains in the Northwest.
14. Explain briefly the difference in accounting treatment of (a) a change in accounting principle, and (b) a change in accounting estimate.
15. What is the general practice in reporting earnings per share?
16. Define comprehensive income. How does it differ from net income?

DISCUSSION CASES

Case 4—1 (Are we really better off?)

The Plath Company Board of Directors finally receives the income statement for the past year from management. Board members are initially pleased to see that after three years of losses, the company will be reporting a profit for the current year. Further investigation reveals that depreciation expense is significantly lower than it was last year. Company management, concerned by the losses, decided to change its method of reporting depreciation from an accelerated method to straight-line. If the depreciation method had not been changed, a loss would have resulted for the fourth consecutive year. When questioned by the Board about the accounting change, management replied that the majority of companies in the industry use the straight-line depreciation method, and thus the change makes Plath's income statement more comparable to the other companies.

Since comparability is an important qualitative characteristic of accounting information, should the Board accept the explanation of management? How should the information about the change in the depreciation method be displayed in the financial statements?

Case 4—2 (How can my company have income but no cash?)

Max Stevenson owns a local drug store. During the past few years the economy has experienced a period of high inflation. Stevenson has had the policy of withdrawing cash from his business equal to 80% of the company's reported net income. As the business has grown, he has had a CPA prepare the company's financial statements and tax returns. The following is a summary of the company's income statement for the current year:

Revenue	$565,000
Cost of goods sold (drugs, etc.)	395,000
Gross profit on items sold	$170,000
Operating expenses (including taxes)	110,000
Net income	$ 60,000

Even though the business has reported net income each year, it has experienced severe cash flow shortages. The company has had to pay higher prices for its inventory as the company has tried to maintain the same quantity and quality of its goods. For example, last year's cost of goods sold had a historical cost of $250,000 and a replacement cost of $295,000. The current year's cost of goods sold has a replacement cost of $440,000. Stevenson's personal cash outflows have also grown faster than his withdrawals from the company due to increasing personal demands.

Stevenson asks you as a financial advisor how the company can have income of $60,000, but how he and the company can still have a shortage of cash.

Case 4—3 (When should revenue be recognized?)

Stan Crowfoot is a renowned sculptor who specializes in American Indian sculptures. Typically, a cast is prepared for each work to permit the multiple reproduction of the pieces. A limited number of copies are made for each sculpture, and the mold is destroyed after the number is reached. Limiting the number of pieces enhances the price, and most of the pieces have initially sold for $2,000 to $4,000. To encourage sales, Stan has a liberal return policy that permits customers to return any unwanted piece for a period of up to one year from the date of sale and receive a full refund.

Do you think Stan should recognize revenue: (1) when the piece is produced and cast in bronze, (2) when the goods are delivered to the customer, or (3) when the period of return has passed? Justify your answer in terms of the conceptual framework.

Case 4—4 (When should revenue be recognized?)

You are engaged as a consultant to Skyways Unlimited, a manufacturer of satellite dishes for television reception. Skyways sells its dishes to dealers who in turn sell them to customers. As an inducement to carry sufficient inventory, the dealers are not required to pay for the dishes until they have been sold. There is no formal provision for return of the dishes by the dealers; however, Skyways has requested returns when a dealer's sales activity is considered to be too low. Overall, returns have amounted to less than 10% of the dishes sent to dealers. No interest is charged to the dealers on their balances unless they do not remit promptly upon the sale to a customer.

At what point would you recommend that Skyways recognize the revenue from the sale of dishes to the dealers?

Case 4—5 (We just changed our minds.)

Management for Marlowe Manufacturing Company decided in 1996 to discontinue one of its unsuccessful product lines. (The product line does not meet the definition of a business segment.) The planned discontinuance involved obsolete inventory, assembly lines, and packaging and advertising supplies. It was estimated that a loss of $250,000 would result from the decision, and this estimate was recorded as a loss in the 1996 income statement. In 1997, new management was appointed and it was decided that maybe the unsuccessful product line could be turned around with a more aggressive marketing policy. The change was made, and indeed the product began to make money. The new management wants to reverse the adjustment made the previous year and remove the liability for the estimated loss.

How should the 1996 estimated loss be reported in the 1996 income statement? How should the 1997 reversal of the 1996 action be reported in the 1997 financial statements?

Case 4—6 (The sure-fire computer software)

The Flexisoft Company has had excellent success in developing business software for microcomputers. Management has followed the accounting practice of deferring the development costs for the software until sufficient sales have developed to cover the software cost. Because of past successes, management feels it is improper to charge software costs directly to expense as current GAAP requires.

What are the pros and cons of deferring or expensing immediately these developmental costs?

Case 4—7 (Deferred initial operating losses)

Small loan companies often experience losses in the operation of newly opened branch loan offices. Such results usually can be anticipated by management prior to making a decision on expansion. It has been recommended by some accountants that the operating losses of newly opened branches should be reported as deferred charges during the first twelve months of operation or until the first profitable month occurs. Such deferred charges would then be amortized over a five-year period.

Would you support this recommendation? Justify your answer.

Case 4—8 (What was last year's income?)

The Walesco Corporation has decided to discontinue an entire segment of its business effective November 1, 1996. It hopes to sell the assets involved and convert the physical plant to other uses within the manufacturing division. The CPA auditing the books indicates that GAAP requires separate identification of the revenues and expenses related to the segment to be sold and their removal from the continuing revenue and expense amounts. The controller objects to this change. "We have already distributed last year's numbers. If we change them now, one year later, confidence in our financial statements will be greatly eroded."

What are the pros and cons of identifying separately the costs related to the discontinued segment?

Case 4—9 (Accrual accounting)

The stock market crash of October 1987 caused many businesses to rethink the manner in which they operate. The crash caused at least one business to consider the way it recognized revenues and expenses. The Boston Company, Inc., a money managing unit of Shearson Lehman Hutton

Holdings Inc., reported that pretax profits for the first nine months of 1988 had been overstated by an estimated 40%. Being a subsidiary of another company, Boston does not disclose separate earnings. However, the company admits that 1988 profits were overstated by $44 million.

In danger of not meeting corporate performance goals, top executives at Boston deferred many expenses "beyond accepted accounting norms, and revenue was inappropriately booked far in advance." These practices had the effect of "making the current quarter look more profitable." Boston Co. was hoping that a decline in short-term interest rates would provide additional profits to cover the deceptive accounting practices. (Boston Co. funds its long-term mortgages with short-term deposits in its banking units, so the firm benefits when short-term rates drop.)

Sources:
George Anders, *The Wall Street Journal*, January 23, 1989.
Christopher J. Chipallo & George Anders, *The Wall Street Journal*, January 30, 1989.

1. How are expenses deferred and revenues booked (recorded) in advance? What would the journal entries be?
2. Why would top executives encourage these misleading accounting practices?
3. None of the top executives who ordered the misstatements actually made the journal entries. If you were Boston Co.'s accountant, what would you have done?
4. Is Boston's independent auditor responsible for detecting these types of misstatements?

Case 4—10 (Revenue recognition)

A common method for inflating revenues and profits is to ship more inventory to customers than they order. *Business Week* illustrates two instances where the revenue recognition criteria may have been compromised. Using a practice known as "trade loading," RJR Nabisco, the second largest cigarette producer in America, would ship more inventory to wholesalers than the wholesalers could resell. The excess inventory would eventually be returned, but RJR would book the revenue and profit when the cigarettes were originally shipped. Management stopped this practice in 1988, and the result was a $360 million decrease in operating profits for 1989.

Another company, Regina Co., took trade loading several steps further. In a hurried effort to compete in the upright vacuum cleaner market, Regina skipped proper testing of its product, the Housekeeper. The result: 40,000 units, or 16% of sales, were returned. Regina's solution: lease a building to store the returned items and make no entries to record the returns. In a continued effort to make Regina's stock attractive, the firm began to record sales when goods were ordered, not when they were shipped. Further, to ensure that projected sales figures were achieved for the fiscal year ending June 30, 1988, the company generated $5.4 million of fictitious sales invoices for the last three business days of the year.

Sources:
Wafecia Konrad, "RJR Nabisco," *Business Week*, February 19, 1990.
John A. Byrne, "Regina," *Business Week*, February 12, 1990.

1. Do the above transactions of RJR Nabisco and Regina satisfy the revenue recognition criteria as set forth by the FASB?
2. If RJR Nabisco has open contracts with distributors that require distributors to attempt to sell all inventory shipped to them, does trade loading violate the revenue recognition criteria?
3. Regina recorded revenue when goods were ordered rather than when the goods were shipped. Does it really make a difference when the journal entry is made?
4. As Regina's accountant, what could you do if the president of the company (who was fined $50,000 and sentenced to one year in jail) asked for your assistance in "cooking the books?"

Case 4—11 (Financial statement analysis—ratios)

Shawn O'Neil owns two businesses: a drug store and a retail department store.

	Drug Store	Department Store
Net Sales	$1,050,000	$670,000
Cost of Goods Sold	950,000	560,000
Other Expenses	39,500	66,500

Which business earns more income? Which business has the higher gross profit percentage? Net profit percentage? Which business would you consider more profitable?

Case 4—12 (Analysis of financial statements — Microsoft Corporation)

Refer to the financial statements of Microsoft Corporation in Appendix A in answering the following questions:

1. Of Microsoft's three divisions — applications, hardware, and systems — which generated the most revenue in 1993?
2. Microsoft's operating income increased from $996 million in 1992 to $1.326 billion in 1993. Identify the major reasons for the increase. (Search the notes to the financial statements for additional information.)
3. Does Microsoft generate most of its revenue within the United States or outside the United States? What is the trend for Microsoft regarding international sales?
4. How does Microsoft recognize revenue?
5. Does Microsoft expense its research and development costs using direct matching, systematic and rational allocation, or immediate recognition?
6. How does Microsoft expense buildings, leasehold improvements, and computer equipment?

EXERCISES

Exercise 4—13 (Calculation of net income)

Changes in the balance sheet account balances for the Smite Sales Co. during 1996 are shown below. Dividends declared during 1996 were $40,000. Calculate the net income for the year assuming there were no transactions, other than the dividends, affecting retained earnings.

	Increase (Decrease)
Cash	$ 95,500
Accounts Receivable	92,000
Inventory	(30,000)
Buildings and Equipment (net)	$190,000
Patents	(5,000)
Accounts Payable	(75,000)
Bonds Payable	150,000
Capital Stock	100,000
Additional Paid-In Capital	50,000

Exercise 4—14 (Revenue recognition)

For each of the following transactions, events, or circumstances, indicate whether the recognition criteria for revenues and gains are met and provide support for your answer.

(a) An order of $25,000 for merchandise is received from a customer.
(b) The value of timberlands increases by $40,000 for the year due to normal growth.
(c) Accounting services are rendered to a client on account.
(d) A 1985 investment was made in land at a cost of $80,000. The land currently has a fair market value of $107,000.
(e) Cash of $5,600 is collected from the sale of a gift certificate that is redeemable in the next accounting period.
(f) Cash of $7,500 is collected from subscribers for subscription fees to a monthly magazine. The subscription period is 2 years.
(g) You owe a creditor $1,500, payable in thirty days. The creditor has cash flow difficulties and has agreed to allow you to retire the debt in full with an immediate payment of $1,200.

Exercise 4—15 **(Revenue recognition)**

Indicate which of the following transactions or events gives rise to the recognition of revenue in 1996 under the accrual basis of accounting. If revenue is not recognized, what is the account, if any, that is credited?

(a) On December 15, 1996, Howe Company received $20,000 as rent revenue for the six-month period beginning January 1, 1997.
(b) Monroe Tractor Co., on July 1, 1996, sold one of its tractors and received $10,000 in cash and a note for $50,000 at 12% interest, payable in one year. The fair market value of the tractor is $60,000.
(c) Oswald, Inc., issued additional shares of common stock on December 10, 1996, for $30,000 above par value.
(d) Balance Company received a purchase order in 1996 from an established customer for $10,200 of merchandise. The merchandise was shipped on December 20, 1996. The company's credit policy allows the customer to return the merchandise within 30 days, and a 3% discount is allowed if paid within 20 days from shipment.
(e) Gloria, Inc., sold merchandise costing $2,000 for $2,500 in August 1996. The terms of the sale are 15% down on a 12-month conditional sales contract, with title to the goods being retained by the seller until the contract price is paid in full.
(f) On November 1, 1996, Jones & Whitlock entered into an agreement to audit the 1996 financial statements of Lehi Mills for a fee of $35,000. The audit work began on December 15, 1996, and will be completed around February 15, 1997.

Exercise 4—16 **(Expense recognition)**

For each of the following items, indicate whether the expense should be recognized using (1) direct matching, (2) systematic and rational allocation, or (3) immediate recognition. Provide support for your answer.

(a) Johnson & Smith, Inc., conducts cancer research. The company's hope is to develop a cure for the deadly disease. To date, their efforts have proven unsuccessful. They are testing a new drug, Ebzinene, which has cost $400,000 to develop.
(b) Sears, Roebuck and Co. warranties many of the products it sells. Although the warranty periods range from days to years, Sears can reasonably estimate warranty costs.
(c) Stocks Co. recently signed a two-year lease agreement on a warehouse. The entire cost of $15,000 was paid in advance.
(d) John Clark assembles chairs for the Stone Furniture Company. The company pays Clark on an hourly basis.
(e) Hardy Co. recently purchased a fleet of new delivery trucks. The trucks are each expected to last for 100,000 miles.
(f) Taylor Manufacturing Inc. regularly advertises in national trade journals. The objective is to acquire name recognition, not to promote a specific product.

Exercise 4—17 **(Change in estimate)**

The Swalberg Corporation purchased a patent on January 2, 1991, for $375,000. The original life of the patent was estimated to be 15 years. However, in December of 1996, the controller of Swalberg received information proving conclusively that the product protected by the Swalberg patent would be obsolete within three years. Accordingly, the company decided to write off the unamortized portion of the patent cost over four years beginning in 1996. How would the change in estimate be reflected in the accounts for 1996 and subsequent years?

Exercise 4—18 **(Classification of income statement items)**

Where in a multiple-step income statement would each of the following items be reported?

(a) Purchase discounts
(b) Gain on early retirement of debt
(c) Interest revenue
(d) Loss on sale of equipment

(e) Casualty loss from hurricane
(f) Sales commissions
(g) Loss on disposal of segment
(h) Income tax expense
(i) Gain on sale of land
(j) Sales discounts
(k) Loss from long-term investments written off as worthless
(l) Depletion expense
(m) Cumulative effect of change in depreciation method
(n) Vacation pay of office employee
(o) Ending inventory

Exercise 4—19 (Analysis and preparation of income statement)

The selling expenses of Caribou Inc. for 1996 are 13% of sales. General expenses, excluding doubtful accounts, are 25% of cost of goods sold, but only 15% of sales. Doubtful accounts are 2% of sales. The beginning inventory was $136,000, and it decreased 30% during the year. Income from operations for the year before income tax of 30% is $160,000. Extraordinary gain, net of tax of 30%, is $21,000. Prepare an income statement, including earnings-per-share data, giving supporting computations. Caribou Inc. has 110,000 shares of common stock outstanding.

Exercise 4—20 (Intraperiod income tax allocation)

The Brigham Corporation reported the following income items before tax for the year 1996:

Income from continuing operations before income tax	$210,000
Loss from operations of a discontinued business segment	50,000
Gain from disposal of a business segment	20,000
Extraordinary gain on retirement of debt..	100,000

The income tax rate is 35% on all items. Prepare the portion of the income statement beginning with "Income from continuing operations before income tax" for the year ended December 31, 1996, after applying proper intraperiod income tax allocation procedures.

Exercise 4—21 (Discontinued operations)

On June 30, 1996, top management of Garrison Manufacturing Co. decided to dispose of an unprofitable business segment. A loss of $80,000 associated with the segment was incurred during the first six months of 1996, prior to management's decision. Between July 1 and November 30, an additional $20,000 loss was incurred in phasing out the segment. The plant facilities associated with the business segment were sold on December 1, and a $15,000 gain was realized on the sale of the plant assets.

(a) Assuming a 30% tax rate, what will be the gain or loss from operating the discontinued segment?
(b) What will be the gain or loss on disposal of the business segment?
(c) Prepare the discontinued operations section of Garrison Manufacturing Co.'s income statement for the year ending December 31, 1996.

Exercise 4—22 (Discontinued operations)

For the following independent cases, compute (1) the gain (loss) from operations of a discontinued segment, and (2) the gain (loss) from disposal of a discontinued segment. Ignore income taxes.

	Case A	Case B	Case C	Case D
Operating gain (loss) of discontinued segment to measurement date.	$1,000	$(3,000)	$(5,000)	$6,000

	Case A	Case B	Case C	Case D
Operating gain (loss) of discontinued segment from measurement date to end of fiscal year or disposal date, whichever comes first.	2,000	1,000	6,000	(3,000)
Operating gain (loss) expected from discontinued segment in subsequent year until disposal date, if applicable	1,000	NA	(4,000)	(5,000)
Gain or (loss) on disposal of net assets	(6,000)	2,500	8,000	(3,000)

Exercise 4—23 (Change in accounting principle)

In 1988, Sears, Roebuck and Co. changed its method of accounting for income taxes. The FASB required the new principle to be applied retroactively, but prior years' financial statements were not required to be restated. The change decreased 1988 income from continuing operations by $177.6 million. However, the cumulative effect on prior years was a gain of $544.2 million (net of taxes).

Assuming income from continuing operations for 1988 was $1,032.3 million, complete Sears' income statement for 1988, assuming no other irregular or extraordinary items. Assume 400 million shares of common stock were outstanding during the period.

Exercise 4—24 (Reporting items on financial statements)

Under what classification would you report each of the following items on the financial statements?

(a) Revenue from sale of obsolete inventory.
(b) Loss on sale of the fertilizer production division of a lawn supplies manufacturer.
(c) Material penalties arising from early payment of a mortgage.
(d) Gain resulting from changing asset balances to adjust for the effect of excessive depreciation charged in error in prior years.
(e) Loss resulting from excessive accrual in prior years of estimated revenues from long-term contracts.
(f) Costs incurred to purchase a valuable patent.
(g) Net income from the discontinued dune buggy operations of a custom car designer.
(h) Costs of rearranging plant machinery into a more efficient order.
(i) Error made in capitalizing advertising expense during the prior year.
(j) Gain on sale of land to the government.
(k) Loss from destruction of crops by a hailstorm.
(l) Cumulative effect of changing depreciation method.
(m) Additional depreciation resulting from a change in the estimated useful life of an asset.
(n) Gain on sale of long-term investments.
(o) Loss from spring flooding.
(p) Sale of obsolete inventory at less than book value.
(q) Additional federal income tax assessment for prior years.
(r) Loss resulting from the sale of a portion of a line of business.
(s) Costs associated with moving an American business to Japan.
(t) Loss resulting from a patent that was recently determined to be worthless.

Exercise 4—25 (Multiple-step income statement)

From the following list of accounts, prepare a multiple-step income statement in good form showing all appropriate items properly classified, including disclosure of earnings-per-share data. (No monetary amounts are to be recognized.)

Accounts Payable
Accumulated Depreciation—Office Building
Accumulated Depreciation—Office Furniture and Fixtures
Advertising Expense
Allowance for Doubtful Accounts
Cash
Common Stock, $1 par (10,000 shares outstanding)
Depreciation Expense—Office Building

Depreciation Expense—Office Furniture and Fixtures
Dividend Revenue
Dividends Payable
Dividends Receivable
Doubtful Accounts Expense
Extraordinary Gain (net of income taxes)
Freight-In
Federal Unemployment Tax Payable
Goodwill
Income Tax Expense
Income Tax Payable
Insurance Expense
Interest Expense—Bonds
Interest Expense—Other
Interest Payable
Interest Receivable
Interest Revenue
Inventory
Loss From Discontinued Operations (net of income taxes)
Miscellaneous General Expense
Miscellaneous Selling Expense
Office Salaries Expense
Office Supplies
Office Supplies Used
Officers' Salaries Expense
Property Taxes Expense
Purchases
Purchase Discounts
Purchase Returns and Allowances
Retained Earnings
Royalties Received in Advance
Royalty Revenue
Salaries and Wages Payable
Sales
Sales Discounts
Sales Returns and Allowances
Sales Salaries and Commissions
Sales Tax Payable

Exercise 4—26 (Single-step income statement and statement of retained earnings)

The Pensacola Awning Co. reports the following for 1996:

Retained earnings, January 1	$ 444,500
Selling expenses	288,720
Sales revenue	1,380,000
Interest expense	13,390
General and administrative expenses	236,400
Cost of goods sold	765,000
Dividends declared this year	32,000
Tax rate for all items	40%
Average shares of common stock outstanding during the year	25,000

Prepare a single-step income statement (including earnings-per-share data) and a statement of retained earnings for Pensacola.

Exercise 4—27 (Correction of retained earnings statement)

M. Taylor has been employed as a bookkeeper at the Losser Corporation for a number of years. With the assistance of a clerk, Taylor handles all accounting duties, including the preparation of financial statements. The following is a statement of earned surplus prepared by Taylor for 1996.

Losser Corporation
Statement of Earned Surplus For 1996

Balance at beginning of year		$ 85,949
Additions:		
Change in estimate of 1995 amortization expense	$ 2,800	
Gain on sale of land	18,350	
Interest revenue	4,500	
Profit and loss for 1996	13,680	
Total additions		39,330
Total		$125,279
Deductions:		
Increased depreciation due to change in estimated life	$ 5,000	
Dividends declared and paid	10,000	
Loss on sale of equipment	3,860	
Loss from major casualty (extraordinary)	27,730	
Total deductions		46,590
Balance at end of year		$ 78,689

Instructions:

1. Prepare a schedule showing the correct net income for 1996. (Ignore income taxes.)
2. Prepare a retained earnings statement for 1996.
3. Explain why you have changed the retained earnings statement.

PROBLEMS

Problem 4—28 **(Single-step income statement)**
The Payette Co. on June 30, 1996, reported a retained earnings balance of $1,525,000. The books of the company showed the following account balances on June 30, 1996:

Sales	$2,380,000
Inventory: July 1, 1995	160,000
June 30, 1996	170,000
Sales Returns and Allowances	30,000
Purchases	1,497,000
Purchase Discounts	24,000
Dividends Paid	260,000
Selling and General Expenses	238,000
Interest Revenue	42,000
Income Taxes	262,800

Instructions: Prepare a single-step income statement and a retained earnings statement. The Payette Co. has 325,000 shares of common stock outstanding.

Problem 4—29 **(Revenue recognition and preparation of income statement)**
The Richmond Company manufactures and sells robot-type toys for children. Under one type of agreement with the dealers, Richmond is to receive payment upon shipment to the dealers. Under another type of agreement, Richmond receives payments only after the dealer makes the sale. Under this latter agreement, toys may be returned by the dealer. The president of Richmond desires to know how the income statement would differ under these two methods over a two-year period.

The following information is made available for making the computations:

Sales price per unit:	
If paid after shipment	$5
If paid after sale, with right of return	$6
Cost to produce per unit (assume fixed quantity of toys is produced)	$3
Expected bad debt percentage of sales if revenue recognized at time of shipment	5%
Expected bad debt percentage of sales if revenue recognized at time of sale	1/2%
Selling expense—1996	$25,000
Selling expense—1997	$15,000
General and administrative expenses—1996 and 1997	$20,000

Quantity Shipped and Sold

	1996	*1997*
Units shipped to dealers	25,000	30,000
Units sold by dealers	14,000	22,000

Instructions:

1. Prepare comparative income statements for 1996 and 1997 for each of the two types of dealer agreements assuming the company began operations in 1996.

2. Discuss the implications of the revenue recognition method used for each of the dealer agreements.

Problem 4—30 **(Revenue and expense recognition)**

On December 31, 1996, The Hadley Company provides the following pre-audit income statement for your review:

Sales	$185,000
Cost of goods sold	(94,000)
Gross margin	$ 91,000
Rent expense	(18,000)
Advertising expense	(6,000)
Warranty expense	(8,000)
Other expenses	(20,000)
Net income	$ 39,000

The following information is also available:

(a) Many of Hadley's customers pay for their orders in advance. At year-end, $18,000 of orders paid for in advance of shipment have been included in the sales figure.

(b) Hadley introduced and sold several products during the year with a 30-day, money-back guarantee. During the year, customers seldom returned the products. Hadley has not included in revenue or in cost of goods sold those items sold within the last 30 days that included the guarantee. The revenue is $16,000, and the cost associated with the products is $7,500.

(c) On January 1, 1996, Hadley prepaid its building rent for 18 months. The entire amount paid, $18,000, was charged to Rent Expense.

(d) On July 1, 1996, Hadley paid $24,000 for general advertising to be completed prior to the end of 1996. Hadley's management estimates that the advertising will benefit a two-year period and, therefore, has elected to charge the costs to the income statement at the rate of $1,000 a month.

(e) Hadley has collected current cost information relating to its inventory. The cost of goods sold, if valued using current costing techniques, is $106,000.

(f) In past years, Hadley has estimated warranty expense using a percentage of sales. Hadley estimates future warranty costs relating to 1996 sales will amount to five percent of sales. However, during 1996, Hadley elected to charge costs to warranty expense as costs were incurred. Hadley spent $8,000 during 1996 to repair and replace defective inventory sold in current and prior periods.

Instructions:

1. For each item of additional information, identify the revenue or expense recognition issue.
2. Prepare a revised income statement using the information provided.

Problem 4—31 **(Intraperiod income tax allocation)**

The following information relates to Delaney Manufacturing Inc. for the fiscal year ended July 31, 1997. Assume there are no tax rate changes, a 30% tax rate applies to all items reported in the income statement, and there are no differences between financial and taxable income.

Taxable income, year ending July 31, 1997	$ 975,000
Nonoperating items included in taxable income:	
Extraordinary gain	101,000
Loss from disposal of a business segment	(140,000)
Prior-year error resulting in income overstatement for fiscal year 1996; tax refund to be requested	75,000
Retained earnings, August 1, 1996	2,750,000

Instructions: Prepare the income statement for Delaney Manufacturing Inc. beginning with "Income from continuing operations before income taxes" and the retained earnings statement for the fiscal year ended July 31, 1997. Apply intraperiod income tax allocation procedures to both statements.

Problem 4—32 (Reporting special income items)

Radiant Cosmetics Inc. shows a retained earnings balance on January 1, 1996, of $620,000. For 1996, the income from continuing operations was $210,000 before income tax. Following is a list of special items:

Income from operations of a discontinued cosmetics division	$18,000
Loss on the sale of the cosmetics division	50,000
Gain on extinguishment of long-term debt	25,000
Correction of sales understatement in 1995 (net of income taxes of $21,000 to be paid when amended 1995 return is filed)	39,000
Omission of depreciation charges of prior years (a claim has been filed for an income tax refund of $8,000)	20,000

Income tax paid during 1996 was $82,000, which consisted of the tax on continuing operations, plus $8,000 resulting from operations of the discontinued cosmetics division and $10,000 from the gain from extinguishment of debt, less a $20,000 tax reduction for the loss on the sale of the cosmetics division. Dividends of $30,000 were declared by the company during the year (50,000 shares of common stock are outstanding).

Instructions: Prepare the income statement for Radiant Cosmetics Inc. beginning with "Income from continuing operations before income taxes." Include an accompanying retained earnings statement.

Problem 4—33 (Discontinued operations in process)

In 1996, Laetner Industries decided to discontinue its Laminating Division, an identifiable segment of Laetner's business. The measurement date for the discontinuance is August 1. At December 31, Laetner's year-end, the Division has not been sold, however, negotiations for the sale are progressing in a positive manner. Analysis of the records for the year disclosed the following relative to the Laminating Division:

Loss for period, January 1 to August 1, 1996	$28,600
Loss for period, August 1 to December 31, 1996	51,300
Expected loss in 1997 preceding disposal	25,000
Expected gain on disposal of Division	60,000

(a) Assuming a 35% tax rate, what will be the 1996 reported gain or loss from operating the discontinued division?

(b) What will be the 1996 reported gain or loss from disposal of the division?

(c) Prepare the discontinued operations section of Laetner Industries' income statement for the year ending December 31, 1996.

Problem 4—34 (Financial statement analysis — ratios)

The following financial statement information for RoboCon Inc. is available for the years 1994 through 1996.

(in thousands)	1996	1995	1994
Sales	$5,346	$5,127	$4,982
Cost of Goods Sold	2,780	2,461	2,292
Operating Expenses	2,031	1,985	1,768
Income Taxes	160	204	277

The following information relates to the firm's common stock for the same 3-year period:

	1996	1995	1994
Shares Outstanding	1,000	1,000	1,000
Market Value Per Share at Year-End	$4.125	$8.625	$13.50

Instructions:

1. For each year compute:
   (a) gross profit percentage on sales
   (b) net profit percentage on sales
   (c) price/earnings ratio.
2. Do you notice any significant trends as a result of this analysis?

Problem 4—35 (Income and retained earnings statements)

Selected account balances of Connell Company for 1996 along with additional information as of December 31 are as follows:

Contribution to Employee Pension Fund	$ 190,000
Delivery Expense	425,000
Depreciation Expense—Delivery Trucks	29,000
Depreciation Expense—Office Building	25,000
Depreciation Expense—Office Equipment	10,000
Depreciation Expense—Store Equipment	25,000
Dividends	150,000
Dividend Revenue	35,000
Doubtful Accounts Expense	32,000
Freight-In	145,000
Gain on Sale of Office Equipment	8,000
Income Taxes, 1996	397,425
Interest Revenue	10,000
Loss on Sale of Investment Securities	20,000
Loss on Write-Down of Obsolete Inventory	75,000
Inventory, January 1, 1996	775,000
Miscellaneous General Expenses	45,000
Miscellaneous Selling Expenses	50,000
Officers' and Office Salaries	550,000
Property Taxes	100,000
Purchase Discounts	47,700
Purchases	4,633,200
Retained Earnings, January 1, 1996	550,000
Sales	8,125,000
Sales Discounts	55,000
Sales Returns and Allowances	95,000
Sales Salaries	521,000

(a) Inventory was valued at year-end as follows:

Cost	$ 825,000
Write-down of obsolete inventory	75,000
	$ 750,000

(b) Number of Connell shares of stock outstanding: 60,000

Instructions: Prepare a multiple-step income statement and statement of retained earnings for the year ended December 31, 1996.

Problem 4—36 (Corrected income statement)

The pre-audit income statement of Jericho Recreation Incorporated was prepared by a newly hired staff accountant for the year ending December 31, 1996.

Net revenues	$797,000
Cost of goods sold	320,800
Gross profit	$476,200

Expenses:		
Sales salaries and commissions	$160,000	
Officers' and office salaries	210,000	
Depreciation	56,000	
Advertising expense	13,400	
Other general and administrative expenses	38,800	
		478,200
Net loss from continuing operations		$ (2,000)
Discontinued operations:		
Gain on disposal of business segment		40,000
Income before income taxes		$ 38,000
Income taxes (30%)		11,400
Net income		$ 26,600
Earnings per common share (10,000 shares outstanding)		$2.66

The following information was obtained by Jericho's independent auditor:

(a) Net revenues in the income statement included the following items:

Sales returns and allowances	$ 9,500
Interest revenue	6,600
Interest expense	10,600
Loss on sale of short-term investment	3,000
Gain on early extinguishment of debt	16,000

(b) Jericho changed its method of inventory costing in 1996. The staff accountant correctly determined that the cumulative effect of the change, before any tax considerations, was a reduction in current-year income of $18,000. In preparing the income statement, the accountant added the $18,000 to cost of goods sold.

(c) Of the total depreciation expense reported in the income statement, 60% relates to stores and store equipment, 40% to office building and equipment.

(d) At the beginning of 1996, management decided to close one of Jericho's retail stores. The inventory and equipment were moved to another Jericho store, and the land and building were sold on July 1, 1996, at a pretax gain of $40,000. This amount has been reported under discontinued operations.

(e) The income tax rate is 30%.

Instructions: Prepare a corrected multiple-step income statement for the year ended December 31, 1996.

Problem 4—37 **(Analysis of income items—multiple-step income statement preparation)**

On December 31, 1996, analysis of the Rollins Sporting Goods' operations for 1996 revealed the following:

(a) Total cash collections from customers, $107,770.
(b) December 31, 1995, inventory balance, $10,020.
(c) Total cash payments, $96,350.
(d) Accounts receivable, December 31, 1995, $20,350.
(e) Accounts payable, December 31, 1995, $9,870.
(f) Accounts receivable, December 31, 1996, $15,780.
(g) Accounts payable, December 31, 1996, $5,175.
(h) General and administrative expenses total 25% of sales. This amount includes the depreciation on store and equipment.
(i) Selling expenses of $11,661 total 20% of gross profit on sales.
(j) No general and administrative or selling expense liabilities existed at December 31, 1996.
(k) Wages and salaries payable at December 31, 1995, $3,750.
(l) Depreciation expense on store and equipment total 12.0% of general and administrative expenses.

(m) Shares of stock issued and outstanding, 6,000.
(n) The income tax rate is 40%.

Instructions: Prepare a multiple-step income statement for the year ended December 31, 1996.

Problem 4—38 **(Corrected income and retained earnings statements)**
Selected preadjustment account balances and adjusting information of Sunset Cosmetics Inc. for the year ended December 31, 1996, are as follows:

Retained Earnings, January 1, 1996	$440,670
Sales Salaries and Commissions	35,000
Advertising Expense	16,090
Legal Services	2,225
Insurance and Licenses	8,500
Travel Expense—Sales Representatives	4,560
Depreciation Expense—Sales/Delivery Equipment	6,100
Depreciation Expense—Office Equipment	4,800
Interest Revenue	700
Utilities	6,400
Telephone and Postage	1,475
Supplies Inventory	2,180
Miscellaneous Selling Expenses	2,200
Dividends	33,000
Dividend Revenue	7,150
Interest Expense	4,520
Allowance for Doubtful Accounts (Cr. balance)	370
Officers' Salaries	36,600
Sales	495,200
Sales Returns and Allowances	11,200
Sales Discounts	880
Gain on Sale of Assets	18,500
Inventory, January 1, 1996	89,700
Inventory, December 31, 1996	20,550
Purchases	173,000
Freight-In	5,525
Accounts Receivable, December 31, 1996	261,000
Gain From Discontinued Operations (before income taxes)	40,000
Extraordinary Loss (before income taxes)	72,600
Shares of common stock outstanding, 39,000	

Adjusting information:

(a) Cost of inventory in the possession of consignees as of December 31, 1996, was not included in the ending inventory balance	$33,600
(b) After preparing an analysis of aged accounts receivable, a decision was made to increase the allowance for doubtful accounts to a percentage of the ending accounts receivable balance	3%
(c) Purchase returns and allowances were unrecorded. They are computed as a percentage of purchases (not including freight-in)	6%
(d) Sales commissions for the last day of the year had not been accrued. Total sales for the day	$ 3,600
Average sales commissions as a percent of sales	3%
(e) No accrual had been made for a freight bill received on January 3, 1997, for goods received on December 29, 1996	$ 800

(f) An advertising campaign was initiated November 1, 1996. This amount was recorded as "prepaid advertising" and should be amortized over a six-month period. No amortization was recorded	$ 1,818
(g) Freight charges paid on sold merchandise and not passed on to the buyer were netted against sales. Freight charge on sales during 1996.	$ 4,200
(h) Interest earned but not accrued	$ 690
(i) Depreciation expense on a new forklift purchased March 1, 1996, had not been recognized. (Assume all equipment will have no salvage value and the straight-line method is used. Depreciation is calculated to the nearest month.)	
Purchase price	$ 7,800
Estimated life in years	10
(j) A "real" account is debited upon the receipt of supplies. Supplies on hand at year-end	$ 1,600
(k) Income tax rate (on all items)	35%

Instructions: Prepare a corrected multiple-step income statement and a retained earnings statement for the year ended December 31, 1996. Assume all amounts are material.

Problem 4—39 (Comprehensive income statement)

The Blacksburg Company decides to follow the FASB recommendations and prepare both an earnings statement and a statement of comprehensive income. The following information for the year ending December 31, 1996, has been provided for the preparation of the statements:

Sales	$450,000
Cost of goods sold	263,000
Foreign translation adjustment (net of income taxes)	33,000 (cr.)
Selling expenses	63,900
Extraordinary gain (net of income taxes)	39,400
Correction of inventory error (net of income taxes)	28,680 (cr.)
General and administrative expenses	58,720
Cumulative effect of change in depreciation method (net of income tax savings)	18,380 (dr.)
Income tax expense	21,500
Gain on sale of investment	6,700
Proceeds from sale of land at cost	75,000
Dividends	8,900

Instructions: Prepare the two statements for the company. Use a single-step approach for the earnings statement.

CHAPTER 5

The Balance Sheet

CHAPTER TOPICS

- Usefulness of the Balance Sheet
- Elements of the Balance Sheet
- Form of the Balance Sheet
- Additional Disclosure to the Balance Sheet
- Limitations of the Balance Sheet

In 1946, the Boston Celtics were one of the original 11 teams of the Basketball Association of America, predecessor of the National Basketball Association (NBA). The Celtics enjoyed limited success until the 1956-57 season when they added center Bill Russell to the team. The Russell-led Celtics won 11 of the next 13 NBA championships. The Celtics won five more championships in the 1970s and 80s with players such as Dave Cowens, John Havlicek, Larry Bird, and Robert Parish.

Shares in the Boston Celtics are publicly traded on the New York Stock Exchange (ticker symbol "BOS"). Accordingly, the Celtics are an unusual professional sports team from an accounting standpoint because they are required to file an annual financial report with the Securities and Exchange Commission. Most other teams are owned by private individuals or partnerships that are not legally required to make any public financial disclosures. This annual report filed with the SEC, called Form 10-K, contains the Celtics' financial statements, the notes, and a description of the Celtics' business operations. In addition to the standard information about amortization periods and lease terms, the Celtics 1992 Form 10-K also included note disclosure of the playoff record of the Celtics for the past 15 years and of the fact that Larry Bird had announced his retirement from the NBA on August 18, 1992 after 13 seasons and three NBA championships with the Celtics.

The balance sheet is sometimes spoken of as a "snapshot" of the company. When do companies choose to have this snapshot taken? In the United States, the majority of companies choose December 31. The 1992 balance sheet of the Boston Celtics is dated June 30. Why? June 30 corresponds to a natural lull in the business cycle of a professional basketball team. The playoffs are over, and the next season doesn't start again until the fall. In fact, in the three months of July, August, and September, the Celtics report no revenue at all.

The 1992 balance sheet of the Celtics (see Exhibit 5-1) is interesting, more for what it excludes than for what it includes. Consider the following items:

- The Celtics report total assets of $15,378,331. At first glance, this is puzzling since the market value of the team is said to be in excess of $100 million. How can a company be worth seven times the reported value of its total assets? Recall that balance sheets in the United States include only the historical costs of assets. The most valuable asset of the Celtics, or any other NBA team, is membership in the NBA. The Celtics balance sheet does include a $4.8 million asset entitled "National Basketball Association Franchise," but that amount reflects what was paid for the franchise by the current owners of the Celtics when they acquired the team in August 1983. Try to buy an NBA franchise for $4.8 million now.
- What asset would you expect to see in the Property, Plant, and Equipment section of the Celtics balance sheet? If you are a basketball fan, you answered, "The Boston Garden." The Boston Garden, with its famous parquet floor, is the site of the Celtics home games. However, it is nowhere in the Celtics balance sheet. The facilities are leased under long-term agreements and, according to U.S. GAAP, the leased asset and corresponding liability for lease payments for this type of lease are not included in the balance sheet. (Note: Be patient; you will be treated to more detail about lease accounting in Chapter 19.)
- Are the players recorded as assets? No. For most service organizations, like the Celtics, the employees are the most valuable assets of the organization. One challenge for future accountants, as service organizations assume an increasingly large economic role, is to determine how to best reflect these human resources in the financial statements. The Celtics do disclose in Note F to the financial statements that guaranteed future payments to players, coaches, and officers total over $60 million.

The balance sheet is the fundamental financial statement. The income statement and statement of cash flows can be thought of as simply detailed descriptions of the changes in certain balance sheet accounts (i.e., retained earnings and cash). For many years, however, the income statement has been the dominant financial statement for external decision making. *The Wall Street Journal* regularly reports quarterly earnings of large corporations as newsworthy events. The income statement, however, tells only part of the financial story. It does not answer questions such as: What is the company doing with the income? How is the company being financed? How far in debt is the company? How liquid are its assets? To answer these questions, an external user has to consider the balance sheet, or statement of financial position. This statement reports information that is very important for a user in evaluating the ability of a company to continue in operation.

Over the past several years the financial community has expressed increased interest in the financial conditions of reporting entities, especially their liquidity. The Financial Accounting Standards Board also has devoted considerable attention to evaluating how its standards affect the balance sheet. The increased interest in the balance sheet is partially related to the significant number of companies that have been experiencing financial difficulty. This chapter focuses on the strengths and limitations of the balance sheet and describes how companies report their assets, liabilities, and owners' equity.

Exhibit 5-1

Balance Sheets
BOSTON CELTICS LIMITED PARTNERSHIP

	June 30, 1992	June 30, 1991
ASSETS		
CURRENT ASSETS		
Cash and cash equivalents	$ 4,728,584	$11,218,185
Due from Boston Celtics Communications Limited Partnership	2,741,880	86,430
Accounts receivable	2,106,927	1,759,910
Current portion of notes receivable from players	585,000	1,068,000
Prepaid expenses	123,454	30,195
TOTAL CURRENT ASSETS	10,285,845	14,162,720
NOTES RECEIVABLE FROM PLAYERS, less current portion	165,286	447,286
FRANCHISE AND OTHER RELATED ASSETS		
National Basketball Association franchise, less amortization of $1,388,160 in 1992 and $1,233,920 in 1991	4,781,421	4,935,661
Deferred player acquisition costs, less amortization of $112,500 in 1991		337,500
Other costs, less amortization of $296,944 in 1991		15,556
	4,781,421	5,288,717
EQUIPMENT AND IMPROVEMENTS — at cost, less allowances for depreciation and amortization of $172,131 in 1992 and $109,340 in 1991	145,779	208,570
OTHER ASSETS		28,577
	$15,378,331	$20,135,870
LIABILITIES AND PARTNERS' CAPITAL (DEFICIT)		
CURRENT LIABILITIES		
Accounts payable and accrued expenses	$ 4,992,845	$ 3,230,725
Ticket refunds payable	1,917,151	1,585,123
Current portion of deferred compensation	691,000	5,160,000
TOTAL CURRENT LIABILITIES	7,600,996	9,975,848
DEFERRED REVENUE		20,000
DEFERRED COMPENSATION, less current portion	8,828,299	4,285,765
PARTNERS' CAPITAL (DEFICIT)		
General partner	(10,509)	58,543
Limited partners	(1,040,455)	5,795,714
	(1,050,964)	5,854,257
	$15,378,331	$20,135,870

See notes to financial statements.

USEFULNESS OF THE BALANCE SHEET

The **balance sheet** reports, as of a given point in time, the resources of a business (**assets**), its obligations (**liabilities**), and the residual ownership claims against its resources (**own-**

ers' equity). By analyzing the relationships among these items, investors, creditors, and others can assess a firm's **liquidity,** i.e., its ability to meet short-term obligations, and **solvency,** i.e., its ability to pay all current and long-term debts as they come due. The balance sheet also shows the composition of assets and liabilities, the relative proportions of debt and equity financing, and how much of a firm's earnings have been retained in the business. Collectively, this information can be used by external parties to help assess the financial status of a firm at a particular date.

Following the traditional accounting model, the balance sheet is a historical report presenting the cumulative results of all past transactions of a business measured primarily in terms of historical costs. It is an expression of the basic accounting equation: **Assets = Liabilities + Owners' Equity.** The balance sheet shows both the character and the amount of the assets, liabilities, and owners' equity.

Balance sheets, especially when compared over time and with additional data, provide a great deal of useful information to those interested in analyzing the financial well-being of a company. Specific relationships, such as a company's current ratio, its debt-to-equity ratio, and its rate of return on investment can be highlighted. Future commitments, favorable and unfavorable trends, problem areas in terms of collection patterns, and the relative equity positions of creditors and owners can also be analyzed, all of which assist in evaluating the financial position of a company.

Of special interest to both creditors and investors in analyzing the balance sheet is the company's **financial flexibility.** For example, how well could the company weather unexpected losses in assets, damage claims arising from its operations, or significant reductions in sales? Often, the negative impact on net assets from such events is so material that the existence of the company is threatened unless it can enter the capital markets for additional funds from either creditors or investors. The problem is that obtaining funds becomes difficult once a company is in trouble. Terms for borrowing, including high interest rates, may be so unfavorable that they create further difficulty for a company. Additional stock issues may only sell at decreased prices, diluting the equity of existing shareholders.

Even large companies are not immune to financial crisis. In January 1990, two giant U.S. retailing corporations, Allied Stores Corp. and Federated Department Stores, Inc., filed for bankruptcy protection. These corporations were part of Canadian Robert Campeau's real estate and investment holdings. Extensive borrowing by Campeau to acquire such prominent retail chains as Bloomingdale's and Abraham & Straus in New York and Seattle's Bon Marche led to a $7.5 billion debt that required massive cash payments for principal and interest.[1] Other prominent companies, such as Greyhound, Inc., Circle K, and the many holdings of New York real estate developer Donald Trump, were faced with burgeoning debt and extremely high cash flow requirements in the early 1990s. Severe restrictions by creditors were necessary to try to save these companies from collapse. The impact of high debt was observable on the balance sheets as companies lost their financial flexibility.

ELEMENTS OF THE BALANCE SHEET

The three elements found on the balance sheet were defined in Chapter 2. These definitions, which are part of FASB Concepts Statement No. 6, are repeated below.[2]

- **Assets** are probable future economic benefits obtained or controlled by a particular entity as a result of past transactions or events.

1. "It'll Be a Hard Sell," *Business Week,* January 29, 1990, pp. 30-31.
2. *Statement of Financial Accounting Concepts No. 6,* "Elements of Financial Statements" (Stamford: Financial Accounting Standards Board, 1985), par. 25, 35, and 49.

- **Liabilities** are probable future sacrifices of economic benefits arising from present obligations of a particular entity to transfer assets or provide services to other entities in the future as a result of past transactions or events.
- **Equity** or **net assets** is the residual interest in the assets of an entity that remains after deducting its liabilities. In a business enterprise, the equity is the ownership interest.

Assets are the resources owned or controlled by an entity. They include cash and other highly liquid resources, such as claims against others (receivables) and investments in debt and equity securities. Assets also include costs that are expected to provide future economic benefits. For example, expenditures made for inventories, prepaid insurance, equipment, and patents are recoverable costs that will be recognized as expenses and matched against revenues of future periods.

Liabilities measure the claims of creditors against entity resources. As indicated by the FASB's definition, the method for settlement of liabilities varies. A liability may call for settlement by cash payment or settlement through goods to be delivered or services to be performed.

Owners' equity measures the interest of the ownership group in the total resources of the enterprise. It equals the **net assets** of an enterprise, or the difference between total assets and total liabilities. This interest arises from investment by owners, and is increased by net income and decreased by net losses and distributions to owners. An ownership interest does not call for settlement on a certain date; in the event of business dissolution, it represents a claim on assets only after creditors have been paid in full.

Classified Balance Sheets

Balance sheet items are generally classified in a manner that facilitates analysis and interpretation of financial data. Information of primary concern to all parties is the business unit's liquidity and solvency—its ability to meet current and long-term obligations. Accordingly, assets and liabilities are classified as (1) **current** or **short-term** items and (2) **noncurrent** or **long-term** items. When assets and liabilities are so classified, the difference between current assets and current liabilities may be determined. This is referred to as the company's **working capital**—the liquid buffer available in meeting financial demands and contingencies of the near future.

The importance of an adequate working capital position cannot be minimized. A business may not be able to survive in the absence of a satisfactory relationship between current assets and current liabilities. Furthermore, its ability to prosper is largely determined by the composition of the current asset pool. There must be a proper balance between liquid assets in the form of cash and temporary investments, and receivables and inventories. Activities of the business revolve around these assets. Cash and temporary investments, representing immediate purchasing power, are used to meet current claims and purchasing, payroll, and expense requirements; receivables are the outgrowth of sales effort and provide cash in the course of operations; inventory is also a source of cash as well as the means of achieving a profit. Management, in setting policies with respect to selling, purchasing, financing, expanding, and the paying of dividends, must work within the limitations set by the company's working capital position.

The division of assets and liabilities into just two categories — current and noncurrent — is in some sense an arbitrary partition. Users of financial statements may desire a different partition. For example, some users exclude inventory when evaluating a company's working capital position. Users are certainly free to recast the balance sheet in whatever manner they wish. However, although there is some arbitrariness in the current/noncurrent classifications, the popularity among users of the current ratio (current assets divided by current liabilities) as a measure of liquidity suggests that the classification does meet the test of decision usefulness and should be retained.[3]

Although there are no standard categories that must be used, the general framework for a balance sheet shown in Exhibit 5-2 is representative and will be used in this chapter. The different sections of the classified balance sheet will be discussed in detail below. The components of working capital, current assets and current liabilities, will be discussed first, followed by noncurrent assets and noncurrent liabilities. The hypothetical balance sheet of Techtronics Corporation will be used to illustrate each section.

Current Assets

Current assets include cash and resources that are reasonably expected to be converted into cash during the normal operating cycle of a business or within one year, whichever period is longer. As depicted on the next page, the **normal operating cycle** is the time required for cash to be converted to inventories, inventories into receivables, and receivables ultimately into cash. When the operating cycle exceeds twelve months, for example, in the tobacco, distillery, and lumber industries, the longer period is used.

Some exceptions to the general definition of current assets should be noted. Cash that is restricted as to use, e.g., designated for the acquisition of noncurrent assets or for the liquidation of noncurrent debts, should not be included in current assets. Also, in classifying

Exhibit 5—2
General Form for a Classified Balance Sheet

Assets

Current assets:
- Cash
- Investment securities
- Accounts and notes receivable
- Inventories
- Other current assets, such as prepaid expenses

Noncurrent assets:
- Investments
- Land, buildings, and equipment
- Intangible assets
- Other noncurrent assets

Liabilities

Current liabilities:
- Accounts and notes payable
- Accrued expenses
- Current portion of long-term obligations
- Other current liabilities, such as unearned revenues

Noncurrent liabilities:
- Long-term debt, such as notes, bonds, and mortgages payable
- Long-term lease obligations
- Deferred income tax liability
- Other noncurrent liabilities

Owners' Equity

Contributed capital:
- Capital stock
- Additional paid-in capital

Retained earnings

3. One writer has suggested that since any classification scheme for assets and liabilities is arbitrary, attempts at classification should be abandoned. Assets and liabilities could simply be listed in order of their liquidity, leaving users to impose a classification scheme of their own. Loyd Heath. "Is Working Capital Really Working?" *Journal of Accoutancy* (August 1980), pp. 55-62.

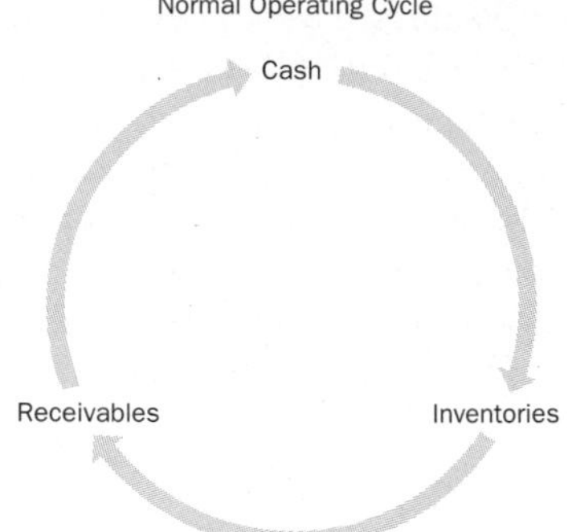

assets not related to the operating cycle, a one-year period is always used as the basis for current classification. For example, a note receivable due in 15 months that arose from the sale of land previously held for investment would be classified as noncurrent even if the normal operating cycle exceeds 15 months.

In addition to cash, receivables, and inventories, current assets typically include such resources as prepaid expenses and investments in debt and equity securities. Prepayments of such items as insurance and rent are not current assets in the sense that they will be converted into cash but on the basis that, if they had not been prepaid, the use of cash or other current assets during the operating cycle period would have been required. Long-term prepayments should be reported as noncurrent assets and charged to the operations of several years. Debt and equity securities that are purchased mainly with the intent of reselling them in the short term are called **trading securities** and are classified as current assets. Other investments in debt and equity securities are classified as current or noncurrent depending on whether management intends to convert them into cash within one year, or within one operating cycle if the length of the cycle exceeds a year.[4]

Current assets are normally listed on the balance sheet in the order of their liquidity. These assets, with the exception of investment securities and inventories, are usually reported at their estimated realizable values. Thus, current receivable balances are reduced by allowances for estimated uncollectible accounts. Investments in debt and equity securities are reported, in most cases, at current market value.[5] Inventories may be reported at cost or on the basis of "cost or market, whichever is lower."

The current asset section of the balance sheet for Techtronics Corporation is illustrated below.

Current assets:		
Cash	$ 52,650	
Investment securities (reported at market; cost, $72,600)	67,350	
Receivables (net of allowance for doubtful accounts)	363,700	
Inventories (reported at FIFO cost or market, whichever is lower)	296,000	
Prepaid expenses and other	32,900	
Total current assets		$812,600

4. *Statement of Financial Accounting Standards No. 115*, "Accounting for Certain Investments in Debt and Equity Securities" (Norwalk: Financial Accounting Standards Board, 1993), par. 17.
5. Ibid., par. 1.

Current Liabilities

Current liabilities are those obligations that are reasonably expected to be paid using current assets or by creating other current liabilities. Generally, if a liability is reasonably expected to be paid within 12 months, it is classified as current. As with receivables, payables arising from the normal operating activities may be classified as current even if they are not to be paid within 12 months, as long as they are to be paid within the operating cycle, which may exceed 12 months.

In addition to accounts payable and short-term borrowings, current liabilities also include amounts for accrued expenses. Common accruals include salaries and wages, interest, and taxes. The current liabilities section also includes amounts representing the portion of the long-term obligations due to be satisfied within one year, or within one operating cycle if the length of the cycle exceeds one year.

The current liability classification generally does not include the following items, since these do not require the use of resources classified as current.

1. Debts to be liquidated from funds that have been accumulated and are reported as noncurrent assets. These funds are often called "sinking funds."
2. Short-term obligations to be refinanced, assuming certain criteria are met as discussed below.[6]

Short-Term Obligations to Be Refinanced. The FASB has concluded that short-term obligations that are expected to be refinanced, i.e., replaced by the issuance of new obligations, should be excluded from current liabilities if the following conditions are met: (1) the intent of the company is to refinance the obligations on a long-term basis, and (2) the company's intent is evidenced by an actual refinancing after the balance sheet date but before the financial statements are finalized, or by the existence of an explicit refinancing agreement.[7] In effect, the FASB is recognizing that certain short-term obligations will not require the use of current assets during a period even though they are scheduled to mature during that period. Thus, they should not be classified as current liabilities.

Callable Obligations. Classification problems can arise when an obligation is **callable** by a creditor, because it is difficult to determine exactly when the obligation will be paid. A **callable obligation** is one that is either (1) payable on demand (has no specified due date) or (2) has a specified due date, but is callable if the debtor violates the provisions of the debt agreement. Any obligation that is due on demand or will become due on demand within one year from the balance sheet date (or operating cycle if longer) should be classified as current.[8]

In addition, a long-term obligation should be classified as current if it is callable at the balance sheet date because the debtor is in violation of a contract provision. For example, some instruments have a specific clause identifying conditions that can cause the debt to be immediately callable, e.g., failure to earn a certain return on assets or failure to make an interest payment. These clauses are referred to as **objective acceleration clauses.** The FASB has stated that if conditions that make the obligation callable have occurred, the debt should be classified as a current debt unless (1) the creditor has waived the right to demand payment for more than one year (or normal operating cycle if longer) from the balance sheet date, or (2) the debtor has cured the deficiency after the balance sheet date

6. *Statement of Financial Accounting Standards No. 6,* "Classification of Short-Term Obligations Expected to Be Refinanced" (Stamford: Financial Accounting Standards Board, 1975).
7. *Statement of Financial Accounting Standards No. 6,* pars. 9-11.
8. *Statement of Financial Accounting Standards No. 78,* "Classification of Obligations That Are Callable by the Creditor" (Stamford: Financial Accounting Standards Board, 1983), par. 5.

but before the statements are issued, and the debt is not callable for a period that extends beyond the debtor's normal operating cycle.[9]

In some cases, the contract does not specifically identify the circumstances under which a payment will be accelerated, but it does indicate some general conditions that permit the lender to unilaterally accelerate the due date. This type of provision is known as a **subjective acceleration clause** because, although the clause may specify certain conditions under which the obligation may be called, the violation of the conditions cannot be objectively determined. Examples of the wording in such clauses might be, "if the debtor fails to maintain satisfactory operations," or "if a material adverse change occurs." The FASB has recommended that if invoking of the clause is deemed probable, the liability should be classified as a current liability. If invoking of the clause is considered to be reasonably possible but not probable, only a footnote disclosure is necessary, and the liability continues to be classified as noncurrent.[10]

The current liability section of the balance sheet for Techtronics Corporation is illustrated below:

Current liabilities:		
Notes payable	$ 75,000	
Accounts payable	312,700	
Accrued expenses	46,200	
Current portion of long-term debt	62,000	
Other current liabilities	28,600	
Total current liabilities		$524,500

Evaluating Liquidity

The relationship between current assets and current liabilities can be used to evaluate the liquidity of a company. Liquidity is the ability of a firm to satisfy its short-term obligations. Many companies with fantastic long-run potential have been killed by short-run liquidity problems.

A common indicator of the overall liquidity of a company is the current ratio. The **current ratio** is computed by dividing total current assets by total current liabilities. For Techtronics Corporation, the current ratio is 1.55 ($812,600 / $524,500). A rule of thumb is that a current ratio below 2.0 is an indication of uncertainty about a company's ability to satisfy its obligations in the short run. Note that this is just a rule of thumb; proper evaluation of a company's liquidity would involve comparing the current year's current ratio to current ratios in prior years, and also comparing the company's current ratio to those for other companies in the same industry.

Minimum current ratio requirements are frequently included in loan agreements. For example, the notes to the 1991 financial statements of Chiles Offshore Corporation, an offshore oil drilling company, contain the following:

The . . . Loan Agreement . . . requires the Company to maintain a current ratio of not less than 1.0 in 1992, not less than 1.5 in 1993, and not less than 2.0 thereafter.

If the current ratio of Chiles is below the required level, the company's lender has the right to declare the loan in default and can require immediate repayment, or renegotiation of the loan at a higher interest rate. This minimum current ratio restriction forces Chiles to maintain its liquidity and gives the lender an increased assurance that the loan will be repaid.

9. *Ibid.*

10. *FASB Technical Bulletin, 79-3,* "Subjective Acceleration Clauses in Long-Term Debt Agreements" (Stamford: Financial Accounting Standards Board, December 1979), par. 003.

Another ratio used to measure a firm's liquidity is the **quick ratio,** also known as the **acid-test ratio.** This ratio is computed as total quick assets divided by total current liabilities, where quick assets are defined as cash, marketable securities, and net receivables. For Techtronics Corporation, the quick ratio is 0.92 [($52,650 + $67,350 + $363,700] / $524,500). The quick ratio indicates how well a firm can satisfy existing short-term obligations with assets that can be converted into cash without difficulty. For a bank considering a three-month loan, or for a supplier considering selling to a company on short-term credit, the quick ratio yields some information about the likelihood of being repaid.

A lender wants to lend on a short-term basis to a company with high current and quick ratios, thus ensuring repayment. However, maintaining an excessively high current ratio is an inefficient use of company resources. Having excess marketable securities will increase a company's current and quick ratios and give comfort to lenders, but the resources used to buy those excess marketable securities might be better utilized by buying trucks, or buildings, or paying off debts, or, if nothing else, returning the cash to the owners for their personal use. A common characteristic of almost all financial ratios is that a ratio that deviates too much from the norm, either high or low, is an indication of a possible problem.

Noncurrent Assets

Assets not qualifying for presentation under the current heading are classified under a number of noncurrent headings. Noncurrent assets may be listed under separate headings, such as "Investments," "Land, buildings, and equipment," "Intangible assets," and "Other long-term assets."

Investments. Investments held for such long-term purposes as regular income, appreciation, or ownership control are reported under the heading "Investments." Examples of items properly reported under this heading are stocks, bonds, and mortgage holdings; securities of affiliated companies and advances to such companies; fund assets consisting of cash and securities held for the redemption of bonds or stocks, the replacement of buildings, or the payment of pensions; land held for investment purposes; the cash surrender value of life insurance; and other miscellaneous investments not used directly in the operations of the business. Although many long-term investments are reported at cost, there are modifications to the valuation of some investments that will be discussed in later chapters.

Land, Buildings, and Equipment. Properties of a tangible and relatively permanent character that are used in the normal business operations are reported under "Land, buildings, and equipment" or other appropriate headings, such as "Property and equipment." Land, buildings, machinery, tools, furniture, fixtures, and vehicles are included in this section of the balance sheet. Most tangible properties, except land, are normally reported at cost less accumulated depreciation.

Intangible Assets. The long-term rights and privileges of a nonphysical nature acquired for use in business operations are often reported under the heading "Intangible assets." Included in this class are such items as goodwill, patents, trademarks, franchises, copyrights, formulas, leaseholds, and organization costs. Intangible assets are normally reported at cost less amounts previously amortized.

Other Noncurrent Assets. Those noncurrent assets not suitably reported under any of the previous classifications may be listed under the general heading "Other noncurrent assets" or may be listed separately under special descriptive headings. Such assets include, for example, long-term advances to officers, long-term receivables, deposits made with taxing authorities and utility companies, and deferred income tax assets.

Prepayments for services or benefits to be received over a number of periods are properly regarded as noncurrent. Among these are such items as plant rearrangement costs and developmental and improvement costs. These long-term prepayments are frequently reported under a "Deferred costs" or "Deferred charges" heading. However, objection can be raised to a deferred costs category since this designation could be applied to all costs assignable to future periods including inventories, buildings and equipment, and intangible assets. The deferred costs heading may be avoided by reporting long-term prepayments within the other noncurrent assets section or under separate descriptive headings.

A deferred income tax asset account may be shown under "Other noncurrent assets" or may be reported separately. In general, deferred income tax balances result from temporary differences between taxable income (the income subject to tax on the tax return) and income before taxes reported on the income statement. **Deferred income tax assets** arise when taxable income exceeds reported income for the period and the difference is expected to "reverse" in future periods. These assets are similar to prepaid expenses, but the computation and reporting of deferred income tax assets is much more complex.

The noncurrent assets section of the balance sheet for Techtronics Corporation is illustrated below:

Noncurrent assets:		
Investments	$128,000	
Land	76,300	
Buildings and equipment (net of accumulated depreciation of $228,600)	732,900	
Intangible assets	165,000	
Other noncurrent assets	37,800	
Total noncurrent assets		$1,140,000

Noncurrent Liabilities

Obligations not reasonably expected to be paid or otherwise satisfied within 12 months (or within the operating cycle if it exceeds 12 months) are classified as noncurrent liabilities. Noncurrent liabilities are generally listed under separate headings, such as "Long-term debt," "Long-term lease obligations," "Deferred income tax liabilities," and "Other noncurrent liabilities."

Long-Term Debt. Long-term notes, bonds, mortgages, and similar obligations not requiring the use of current funds for their retirement are generally reported on the balance sheet under the heading "Long-term debt."

When an amount borrowed is not the same as the amount ultimately required in settlement of the debt and the debt is stated in the accounts at its maturity amount, a discount or premium is reported. The discount or premium should be related to the debt item; a discount, then, should be subtracted from the amount reported for the debt, and a premium should be added to the amount reported for the debt. The debt is thus reported at its present value as measured by the proceeds from its issuance.

When a note, a bond issue, or a mortgage formerly classified as a long-term obligation becomes payable within a year, it should be reclassified and presented as a current liability, except when the obligation is to be refinanced, as discussed earlier, or is to be paid out of a fund classified as noncurrent.

Long-Term Lease Obligations. Some leases of land, buildings, and equipment are financially structured so that they are in substance debt-financed purchases. The FASB has established criteria to determine which leases are in effect purchases, or capital leases, rather than ordinary operating leases. In accounting for capital leases, the present value of the future minimum lease payments is recorded as a long-term liability. That portion of the present value due within the next year or normal operating cycle, whichever is longer, is classified as a current liability.

Deferred Income Tax Liability. The credit balance in this account indicates that, due to temporary differences between taxable income and financial income, a future tax liability may have to be paid. The most common temporary difference occurs in computing depreciation expense for book and tax purposes. Generally, the tax regulations permit a faster write-off of asset cost than is used for financial reporting purposes.

Almost all large companies include a **deferred income tax liability** in their balance sheets. This liability can be thought of as the income tax expected to be paid in future years on income that has already been reported in the income statement but which, because of the tax law, has not yet been taxed. The liability is valued using the income tax rates expected to prevail in the future when the income is taxed. However, since the liability is not reported at its present (discounted) value, some analysts disregard it when evaluating a company's debt position. In summary, the accounting for deferred income taxes is very complex and controversial and has been the subject of considerable debate in recent years.

Other Noncurrent Liabilities. Those noncurrent liabilities not suitably reported under the separate headings may be listed under this general heading or may be listed separately under special descriptive headings. Such liabilities could include long-term obligations to company officers or affiliated companies, matured but unclaimed bond principal and interest obligations, long-term liabilities under pension plans, unearned revenues, and obligations for advance collections on contracts that will not be completed within one year.[11]

Contingent Liabilities. Past activities or circumstances may give rise to possible future liabilities, although legal obligations do not exist on the date of the balance sheet. These possible claims are known as **contingent liabilities.** They are potential obligations involving uncertainty as to possible losses. As future events occur or fail to occur, this uncertainty will be resolved. Thus, a contingent liability is distinguishable from an **estimated liability.** The latter is a definite obligation with only the amount of the obligation in question and subject to estimation at the balance sheet date. There may not be any doubt as to the amount of a contingent liability, for example, a pending lawsuit, but there is considerable uncertainty as to whether the obligation will actually materialize.

In the past, contingent liabilities were not recorded in the accounts nor presented on the balance sheet. When they were disclosed, it was in the notes to the financial statements. As indicated in Chapter 1, FASB Statement No. 5 states that if a future payment is considered probable, the liability should be recorded by a debit to a loss account and a credit to a liability account.[12] Otherwise, the contingent nature of the loss may be disclosed in a note to the financial statements as discussed later in this chapter. The noncurrent liabilities section of Techtronics Corporation's balance sheet is illustrated below.

Noncurrent liabilities:		
Notes payable	$ 75,000	
Bonds payable	165,000	
Long-term lease obligations	135,000	
Deferred income tax liability	126,700	
Other noncurrent liabilities	72,500	
Total noncurrent liabilities		$574,200

11. *Accounting Research and Terminology Bulletins—Final Edition, No. 43,* "Restatement and Revision of Accounting Research Bulletins" (New York: American Institute of Certified Public Accountants, 1961), Chapter 3, par. 8 and footnotes 2 and 3.

12. *Statement of Financial Accounting Standards No. 5,* "Accounting for Contingencies" (Stamford: Financial Accounting Standards Board, 1975), pars. 8-13.

Evaluating Solvency

Comparing the amount of liabilities to the amount of assets held by a business gives an indication of whether the business can be expected to be able to pay off its debts. This comparison, called the **debt ratio,** is of great importance to a firm's creditors. A debt ratio is computed as total liabilities divided by total assets. The debt ratio is frequently used as an indicator of the overall ability of a company to repay its debts. An intuitive interpretation of the debt ratio is that it represents the proportion of borrowed funds used to acquire the company's assets. For Techtronics Corporation, the debt ratio is 0.56 ([$524,500 + $574,200] ÷ [$812,600 + $1,140,000]). In other words, Techtronics borrowed 56% of the money it needed to buy its assets. The higher the debt ratio, the higher the likelihood that some of the debt might not be repaid. The general rule of thumb is that debt ratios should be below 50%. Again, this varies widely from one industry to the next. A bank, for example, could easily have a debt ratio in excess of 95%.

Owners' Equity

The method of reporting the owners' equity varies with the form of the business unit. Business units are typically divided into three categories: (1) **proprietorships,** (2) **partnerships,** and (3) **corporations.** In the case of a proprietorship, the owner's equity in assets is reported by means of a single capital account. The balance in this account is the cumulative result of the owner's investments and withdrawals as well as past earnings and losses. In a partnership, capital accounts are established for each partner. Capital account balances summarize the investments and withdrawals and shares of past earnings and losses of each partner, and thus measure the partners' individual equities in the partnership assets.

In a corporation, the difference between assets and liabilities is referred to as **owners' equity, shareholders' equity,** or simply, **capital.** In presenting the owners' equity on the balance sheet, a distinction is made between the equity originating from the stockholders' investments, referred to as **contributed capital** or **paid-in capital,** and the equity originating from earnings, referred to as **retained earnings.**

The relationship and distinction between the amount of capital contributed or paid in by the owners of the corporation relative to the amount the company has earned and retained in the business is a significant one. Such disclosure helps creditors and investors assess the long-term ability of a company to internally finance its own operations. If the contributed capital of a corporation is large relative to the total owners' equity, it means the corporation has been financed primarily from external sources, usually from the sale of stock to investors. If the earned capital of a corporation is large relative to the total owners' equity, it means the company has been profitable in the past and has retained those earnings in the business to help finance its activities. This distinction between earned and contributed capital is not as important for a proprietorship or partnership because the owners of those types of businesses generally are also involved in their management and therefore are aware of how the company activities are being financed.

Contributed Capital. Contributed (or paid-in) capital is generally reported in two parts: (1) **capital stock** and (2) **additional paid-in capital.** The amount reported on the balance sheet as **capital stock** usually reflects the number of shares issued multiplied by the par value or stated value per share. When the stock does not have a par or stated value, capital stock is reported at the amount received on its original sale or at some other value as stipulated by law or assigned by the corporation's board of directors. When more than one class of stock has been issued, the stock of each class is reported separately.

Additional paid-in capital represents investments by stockholders in excess of the amounts assignable to capital stock. It may also reflect transactions other than the sale of stock, such as the sale of treasury stock at more than cost. **Treasury stock** is stock that has been issued but subsequently reacquired by the corporation and is being held for possible future reissuance or retirement.

Additional paid-in capital balances are added to capital stock so that the total amount of contributed capital is reported on the balance sheet. Treasury stock is usually subtracted from the sum of contributed capital and retained earnings balances. Contributed capital is discussed in detail in Chapter 15.

Retained Earnings. The amount of undistributed earnings of past periods is reported as **retained earnings.** An excess of dividends and losses over earnings results in a negative retained earnings balance called a **deficit.** The balance of retained earnings is added to the contributed capital total in summarizing the stockholders' equity; a deficit is subtracted.

Portions of retained earnings are sometimes reported as restricted and unavailable as a basis for dividends. Restricted earnings may be designated as *appropriations*. Appropriations are sometimes made for such purposes as sinking funds, plant expansion, loss contingencies, and the reacquisition of capital stock. Often such appropriations are disclosed in a note rather than in the accounts. When appropriations have been made in the accounts, retained earnings on the balance sheet consists of an amount designated as appropriated and a balance designated as *unappropriated* or *free*. The term "reserve" should not generally be used to designate appropriations. Retained earnings are discussed in detail in Chapter 16.

The Owners' Equity section of the balance sheet of Techtronics Corporation is illustrated as follows:

Contributed capital:		
Preferred stock, $50 par, 20,000 shares authorized, 2,500 shares issued and outstanding	$125,000	
Common stock, $5 par, 100,000 shares authorized, 50,000 shares issued and outstanding	250,000	
Additional paid-in capital	170,000	$545,000
Retained earnings		308,900
Total owners' equity		$853,900

Offsets on the Balance Sheet

As illustrated in the preceding discussion, a number of balance sheet items are frequently reported at gross amounts calling for the recognition of offset balances in arriving at proper valuations. Such offset balances are found in asset, liability, and owners' equity categories. In the case of assets, for example, an allowance for doubtful accounts is subtracted from the sum of the customer accounts in reporting the net amount estimated as collectible; accumulated depreciation is subtracted from the related buildings and equipment balances in reporting the costs of the assets still assignable to future revenues. In the case of liabilities, reacquired bonds or *treasury* bonds are subtracted from bonds issued in reporting the amount of bonds outstanding; a bond discount is subtracted from the face value of bonds outstanding in reporting the net amount of the debt. In the stockholders' equity section of the balance sheet, treasury stock is deducted in reporting total stockholders' equity.

The types of offsets described above, utilizing contra accounts, are required for proper reporting of particular balance sheet items. Offsets are improper, however, if applied to different asset and liability balances or to asset and owners' equity balances even when there is some relationship between the items. For example, a company may accumulate cash in a special fund to discharge certain tax liabilities; but as long as control of the cash is retained and the liabilities are still outstanding, the company should continue to report both the asset and the liabilities separately. Or a company may accumulate cash in a special fund for the

Today's Balance-Sheet Tilt

The following is condensed from an article by Ray Groves, Co-Chief Executive of Ernst & Young, one of the six largest U.S. public accounting firms.

If there is a theme for the future for financial executives, public accountants, and the users of financial statements, it may be summed up in two words: complexity and volatility. A major reason for the increase in complexity and volatility is the shift that has been in process for some time and promises to accelerate—the shift in emphasis from the income statement to the balance sheet.

The FASB spent a good bit of its first decade developing a conceptual framework. This conceptual framework has a significant leaning toward the balance sheet. There is a feeling that any changes in valuation of assets and liabilities should be reflected in the financial statements, regardless of whether there has been a transaction that causes that change. The result is a movement toward more market-value accounting and reporting. In the view of some, the emphasis today on balance-sheet accounting recalls a similar emphasis of 50 years ago.

This balance-sheet tilt shows up in recent FASB statements on pensions and on income taxes. We are moving toward an era in which the income statement reflects not just operating results, but all changes in the values of assets and liabilities.

This shift in emphasis is not only from the income statement to the balance sheet; it is also away from supplemental disclosure off the balance sheet and toward integrated disclosure on the balance sheet. For example, automotive and other large manufacturing companies that have financial subsidiaries must now fully disclose the assets and liabilities of those subsidiaries on the parent balance sheets.

The theme of complexity and volatility is reflective of the society in which we live. It is an increasingly complex world in which money moves in different forms very quickly. Obviously, given this volatility, our financial reporting does have to mirror what is going on, whether it's in the economic environment or the political environment. What we need is realistic and useful financial information that is complete but not too complex, and subject to change but not too volatile. We have an accounting model that, with continual improvements, will achieve just that.

Questions:

1. How do you think the balance-sheet tilt has affected the valuation of marketable securities owned by a company?
2. How can the balance sheet reflect changes in value without greatly affecting the income statement?
3. Does an emphasis on balance-sheet valuation automatically mean a change in the income statement?

Source:
Ray Groves. "What Today's Balance-Sheet Tilt Means," *Financial Executive*, September/October 1989: pp. 26-30.

redemption of preferred stock outstanding; but until the cash is applied to the reacquisition of the stock, the company must continue to report the asset as well as the owners' equity item. A company may have made advances to certain salespersons while at the same time reporting accrued amounts payable to others; but a net figure cannot be justified here, just as a net figure cannot be justified for the offset of trade receivables against trade payables.

The offset criteria came under scrutiny in the mid 1980s when a new standard for pension accounting was issued by the FASB. The FASB faced a major question concerning whether pension assets should be reported separately from pension liabilities or whether the past practice of allowing pension assets to be offset against pension liabilities should be continued. The Board elected to allow offsets of pension assets and liabilities, but the topic of offsetting is likely to be revisited in the future.

FORM OF THE BALANCE SHEET

The form of the balance sheet presentation varies in practice. Its form may be influenced by the nature and size of the business, by the character of the business properties, by requirements set by regulatory bodies, or by display preferences in presenting key relationships. The balance sheet is prepared in one of two basic forms: (1) the **account form,** with assets being reported on the left-hand side and liabilities and owners' equity on the right-hand side, or (2) the **report form,** with assets, liabilities, and owners' equity sections appearing in vertical arrangement.[13]

13. These two forms have been equally popular; however, the report form has been increasing in popularity. *Accounting Trends & Techniques* reported that in 1992, 421 of 600 companies used the report form and 178 the account form. *Accounting Trends & Techniques* (Jersey City, NJ: AICPA, 1993), p. 125.

The order of asset and liability classifications may vary, but most businesses emphasize working capital position and liquidity, with assets and liabilities presented in the order of their liquidity. An exception to this order is generally found in the land, buildings, and equipment section where the more permanent assets with longer useful lives are listed first. The balance sheet for Techtronics Corporation reproduced on page 167 illustrates the account form reported in order of liquidity. The balance sheet of Microsoft Corporation, reproduced in Appendix A, is an example of the report form. The categories used by individual companies vary widely; however, the basic format and structure remain the same.

In some industries, the investment in plant assets is so significant that these assets are placed first on the balance sheet. Also, the equity capital and long-term debt obtained to finance plant assets are listed before current liabilities. The utility industry is a good example of this situation. A balance sheet for Yankee Energy System is illustrated in Exhibit 5—3.

Exhibit 5—3
Yankee Energy System, Inc.—Consolidated Balance Sheet

Yankee Energy System, Inc. and Subsidiaries
Consolidated Balance Sheets

At September 30,	(Thousands of Dollars) 1992	1991
ASSETS		
Utility Plant, at original cost	**$432,764**	$400,633
Less: Accumulated provision for depreciation	**134,101**	126,620
	298,663	274,013
Construction work in progress	**5,052**	13,828
Total Net Utility Plant	**303,715**	287,841
Other Property and Investments	**24,217**	20,114
Current Assets:		
Cash	**462**	593
Accounts receivable, less accumulated provision for uncollectible accounts of $4,298,000 in 1992 and $4,191,000 in 1991	**18,330**	13,789
Fuel, materials and supplies	**14,269**	11,667
Accrued utility revenues	**4,728**	5,439
Recoverable gas costs	–	4,804
Other	**6,723**	2,443
Total Current Assets	**44,512**	38,735
Deferred Gas Costs and Other	**5,783**	9,579
Recoverable Environmental Cleanup Costs	**15,000**	–
Total Assets	**$393,227**	$356,269
CAPITALIZATION AND LIABILITIES		
Capitalization (see accompanying statements):		
Common shareholders' equity	**$114,891**	$108,662
Preferred stock subject to mandatory redemption	**15,000**	15,000
Long-term debt	**147,500**	126,350
Total Capitalization	**277,391**	250,012
Current Liabilities:		
Notes payable to banks	**15,300**	36,385
Long-term debt – current portion	**15,550**	550
Accounts payable	**12,543**	10,522
Accrued interest	**4,348**	4,379
Refundable gas costs	**3,936**	–
Other	**6,895**	10,440
Total Current Liabilitics	**58,572**	62,276
Accumulated Deferred Income Taxes	**27,048**	26,029
Accumulated Deferred Investment Tax Credits	**10,589**	10,967
Reserve for Environmental Cleanup Costs	**15,000**	–
Other Deferred Credits	**4,627**	6,985
Commitments and Contingencies (Note 6)		
Total Capitalization and Liabilities	**$393,227**	$356,269

The accompanying notes are an integral part of these financial statements.

Balance sheets are generally presented in comparative form. With comparative reports for two or more dates, information is made available concerning the nature and trend of financial changes taking place within the periods between balance sheet dates. Currently, a minimum of two years of balance sheets and three years of income statements and cash flow statements are required by the SEC to be included in the annual report to shareholders.

ADDITIONAL DISCLOSURE TO THE BALANCE SHEET

Regardless of which form of balance sheet is used, the basic statement does not provide all the information desired by users. Among other things, creditors and investors need to know what methods of accounting were used by the company to arrive at the balances in the accounts. The users often feel they need more information than just account titles and amounts. Sometimes the additional information desired is descriptive and is reported in narrative form. In other cases, additional numerical data are reported.

There are at least three methods commonly used by companies to provide additional disclosure:

1. Parenthetical notations in the body of the statement.
2. Notes to the basic financial statements.
3. Separate schedules furnished by management that supplement the basic financial statements.

It is generally felt that readers of financial statements are more likely to see the additional information if it is included on the face of the financial statement in a parenthetical notation. However, if the data are lengthy or complex, it is generally better to provide the detail in notes that are recognized as being an integral part of the statements themselves. Unless specifically excluded, notes are covered by the auditor's opinion. In some instances, the notes include detailed schedules that provide additional information to the serious user. Several parenthetical notations are included in the balance sheet for Techtronics Corporation. For example, in current assets, there are parenthetical comments concerning valuation. In each case, the same data could have been disclosed in notes.

The following types of notes are typically included by management as support to the basic financial statements:

1. Summary of significant accounting policies.
2. Additional information (both numerical and descriptive) to support summary totals found on the financial statements, usually the balance sheet. This is the most common type of note used.
3. Information about items that are not reported on the basic statements because the items fail to meet the recognition criteria, but are still considered to be significant to users in their decision making.
4. Supplementary information required by the FASB or the SEC to fulfill the full-disclosure principle.

Each of these classifications is briefly discussed in the following paragraphs.

Summary of Significant Accounting Policies

GAAP requires that information about the accounting principles and policies followed in arriving at the amounts in the financial statements be disclosed to the users. The Accounting Principles Board concluded in APB Opinion No. 22:

. . . When financial statements are issued purporting to present fairly financial position, changes in financial position, and results of operations in accordance with generally accepted accounting

Techtronics Corporation
Balance Sheet
December 31, 1996

Assets			Liabilities		
Current assets:			Current liabilities:		
Cash	$ 52,650		Notes payable	$ 75,000	
Investment securities (reported at market; cost, $72,600)	67,350		Accounts payable	312,700	
Receivables (net of allowance for doubtful accounts)	363,700		Accrued expenses	46,200	
Inventories (reported at FIFO cost or market, whichever is lower)	296,000		Current portion of long-term debt	62,000	
Prepaid expenses and other	32,900		Other current liabilities	28,600	
Total current assets		$ 812,600	Total current liabilities		$ 524,500
			Noncurrent liabilities:		
			Notes payable	$ 75,000	
			Bonds payable	165,000	
			Long-term lease obligations	135,000	
			Deferred income tax liability	126,700	
			Other noncurrent liabilities	72,500	
			Total noncurrent liabilities		574,200
			Total liabilities		$1,098,700
			Owners' Equity		
Noncurrent assets:			Contributed capital:		
Investments	$ 128,000		Preferred stock, $50 par, 20,000 shares authorized, 2,500 shares issued and outstanding	$125,000	
Land	76,300		Common stock, $5 par, 100,000 shares authorized, 50,000 shares issued and outstanding	250,000	
Buildings and equipment (net of accumulated depreciation of $228,600)	732,900		Additional paid-in capital	170,000	$ 545,000
Intangible assets	165,000		Retained earnings		308,900
Other noncurrent assets	37,800		Total owners' equity		$ 853,900
Total noncurrent assets		1,140,000			
Total assets		$1,952,600	Total liabilities and owners' equity		$1,952,600

principles, a description of all significant accounting policies of the reporting entity should be included as an integral part of the financial statements.[14]

14. *Opinions of the Accounting Principles Board, No. 22,* "Disclosure of Accounting Policies" (New York: American Institute of Certified Public Accountants, 1972), par. 8.

The Board further stated:

> *. . . In general, the disclosure should encompass important judgments as to appropriateness of principles relating to recognition of revenue and allocation of asset costs to current and future periods; in particular, it should encompass those accounting principles and methods that involve any of the following: (a) A selection from existing acceptable alternatives; (b) Principles and methods peculiar to the industry in which the reporting entity operates, even if such principles and methods are predominantly followed in that industry; (c) Unusual or innovative applications of generally accepted accounting principles (and, as applicable, of principles and methods peculiar to the industry in which the reporting entity operates).*[15]

Examples of disclosures of accounting policies required by this opinion would include, among others, those relating to depreciation methods, amortization of intangible assets, inventory costing methods, the recognition of profit on long-term, construction-type contracts, and the recognition of revenue from leasing operations.[16]

The exact format for reporting the summary of accounting policies was not specified by the APB. However, the Board recommended such disclosure be included as the initial note or as a separate summary preceding the notes to the financial statements. The summary of significant accounting policies for Microsoft Corporation is presented in Appendix A.

Additional Information to Support Summary Totals

In order to prepare a balance sheet that is brief enough to be understandable but complete enough to meet the needs of users, notes are sometimes added that provide either quantitative or narrative information to support the statement amounts. The Microsoft Corporation notes in Appendix A include a number of examples of this type of note, e.g., Cash and Short-term Investments, Property, Plant, and Equipment, Leases, and Income Taxes all provide additional numerical information to support the statement totals. Much of this detail is provided in response to specific disclosure requirements of either the SEC or the FASB. The specific format for the schedules is generally left to management's discretion. Some of the notes that support amounts in the financial statements are primarily descriptive in nature. Examples of this type in the Microsoft statements include notes on Common Stock and Employee Stock and Savings Plans.

Information About Items Not Included in Financial Statements

As discussed in Chapter 2, items included in the financial statements must meet certain recognition criteria. Even though an item might not meet the criteria for recognition in the statements, information concerning the item might be relevant to the users. Gain and loss contingencies are good examples of this type of item. A **gain contingency** exists when a company has a potential claim to receive assets, but the actual receipt of the assets is uncertain, pending the outcome of some future event, such as a possible favorable court settlement in a lawsuit. A **loss contingency** relates to a possible claim against the company that might require an outflow of assets. In Statement No. 5, the FASB indicated that if the incurrence of a loss is "reasonably possible," the contingency should be disclosed in the notes to the financial statements. The information provided should include as much data as possible to assist the user in evaluating the risk of the loss contingency.[17]

Supplementary Information

The FASB and SEC both require supplementary information that must be reported in separate schedules. For example, the FASB requires the disclosure of quarterly information for

15. *Ibid.*, par. 12.
16. *Ibid.*, par. 13.
17. *Statement of Financial Accounting Standards No. 5*. Further discussion of loss contingencies and disclosure examples are presented in Chapter 13.

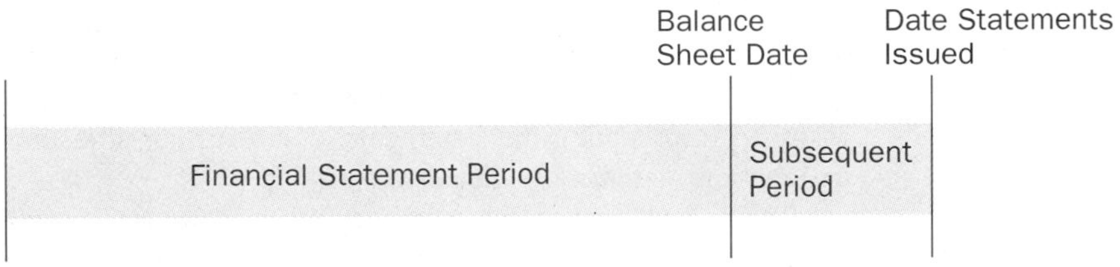

Balance Sheet Date | Date Statements Issued

Financial Statement Period | Subsequent Period

certain companies. While the information in these notes is important to the users, it may not be covered by the auditors' opinion. A note that is not covered by the opinion should be clearly marked "unaudited."

Another category of supplementary information is business segment information. For companies with geographically dispersed operations, this segment information outlines the results for the different geographic segments. For firms with diverse product lines (like PepsiCo, with substantial operations in soft drinks, fast food outlets, and snack foods), segment information for the different product lines is presented.[18] The Microsoft Corporation notes in Appendix A include information about the geographic distribution of Microsoft's revenues, operating income, and assets. It is interesting to observe that if one combines the sales of Microsoft's foreign subsidiaries with the export sales of Microsoft's U.S. operation, over 55% of Microsoft's 1992 revenue was from non-U.S. markets.

Subsequent Events

Although a balance sheet is prepared as of a given date, it is usually several weeks and sometimes even months after that date before the financial statements are issued and made available to external users. During this time, the accounts are analyzed, adjusting entries are prepared, and for many companies, an independent audit is completed. Events may take place during this "subsequent period" that have an impact upon the balance sheet and the other basic financial statements for the preceding year. Some of these events may even affect the amounts reported in the statements. These events are referred to in the accounting literature as **subsequent events** or **post-balance sheet events.**

There are two different types of subsequent events that require consideration by management and evaluation by the independent auditor:[19]

1. Those that affect the amounts to be reported in one or more of the financial statements for the preceding accounting period.
2. Those that do not affect the amounts in the financial statements for the preceding accounting period, but that should be reported in the notes to these financial statements.

The first type of subsequent event usually provides additional information that affects the amounts included in the financial statements. The reported amounts in several accounts, such as Allowance for Doubtful Accounts, Warranty Liability, and Income Taxes Payable, reflect estimates of the expected value. These estimates are based on information available as of a given date. If a subsequent event provides information that shows that the conditions existing as of the balance sheet date were different from those assumed when making the estimate, a change in the amount to be reported in the financial statements is required.

To illustrate this type of event, assume that a month after the balance sheet date it is learned that a major customer has filed for bankruptcy. This information was not known as of the balance sheet date, and only ordinary provisions were made in determining the

18. *Statement of Financial Accounting Standards No. 14,* "Financial Reporting for Segments of a Business Enterprise" (Stamford: Financial Accounting Standards Board, 1976).

19. *AICPA Professional Standards,* AU Section 560, "Subsequent Events" (Chicago: Commerce Clearing House, 1985), pars. .02-.05.

Allowance for Doubtful Accounts. In all likelihood, the customer was already in financial difficulty at the balance sheet date, but it was not general knowledge. The filing of bankruptcy reveals that the conditions at the balance sheet date were different than those assumed in preparing the statements, and a further adjustment to both the balance sheet and income statement is indicated.

The second type of subsequent event does not reveal a difference in the conditions as of the balance sheet date, but involves an event that is considered so significant that its disclosure is highly relevant to readers of the financial statements. These events will usually affect the subsequent year's financial statements and thus may affect decisions currently being made by users. Examples of such events include a casualty that destroys material portions of a company's assets, acquisition of a major subsidiary, sale of significant amounts of bonds or capital stock, and losses on receivables when the cause of the loss occurred subsequent to the balance sheet date. Information about this type of event is included in the notes to the financial statements and serves to notify the reader that the predictive value of the statements may be affected by the subsequent event. The Clorox Company reported this type of subsequent event in its 1990 financial statements as shown in Exhibit 5-4.

The most common types of subsequent events reported by companies include events associated with debt refinancing, debt reduction, or incurring significant amounts of new debt; post-balance-sheet developments associated with litigation; and changes in the status of a proposed business combination. There are, of course, many business events that occur during this subsequent period that are related only to the subsequent year and therefore have no impact on the preceding year's financial statements.

The overall objective of note disclosure is clarification of the information presented in the financial statements. Disclosure requirements are so extensive that they cannot be completely discussed in any single chapter. Specific requirements will be noted as appropriate throughout the text.

LIMITATIONS OF THE BALANCE SHEET

Notwithstanding its usefulness, the balance sheet has some serious limitations. External users often need to know a company's worth. The balance sheet, however, does not generally reflect the current values of a business. Instead, the entity's resources and obligations are usually shown at historical costs based on past transactions and events. The historical cost measurements represent market values existing at the dates the transactions or events occurred. However, when the prices of specific assets increase significantly after the acquisition date, as has certainly been the case recently in the United States, then the balance sheet numbers are not relevant for evaluating a company's current worth.

A related problem with the balance sheet is the instability of the dollar, the standard accounting measuring unit in the United States. Because of general price changes in the economy, the dollar does not maintain a constant purchasing power. Yet the historical costs of resources and equities shown on the balance sheet are not adjusted for changes in the purchasing power of the measuring unit. The result is a balance sheet that reflects assets, liabilities, and equities in terms of unequal purchasing power units. Some elements, for example, may be stated in terms of 1960 dollars and some in terms of current-year dollars. The variations in purchasing power of the amounts reported in the balance sheet make comparisons among companies, and even within a single company, less meaningful.

An additional limitation of the balance sheet, also related to the need for comparability, is that all companies do not classify and report all like items similarly. For example, titles and account classifications vary; some companies provide considerably more detail

Exhibit 5—4
The Clorox Company —Disclosure of Subsequent Event (June 30, 1990 Financial Statements)

Subsequent Event—Acquisition

On August 1, 1990, the Company completed its purchase of American Cyanamid Company's household products brands for $465,000,000. With this acquisition, which will be accounted for as a purchase, the Company acquired the *Pine-Sol* cleaner and *Combat* insecticide brands, including a primary manufacturing facility and a small amount of working capital. An amount in excess of $400,000,000 of the purchase price will be allocated to trademarks, goodwill and other intangibles to be amortized over the estimated useful lives which are yet to be determined.

The acquisition is being funded with cash and up to $400,000,000 in debt initially placed through a syndication of banks. Repayment of refinancing of half the amount borrowed must occur within one year and the balance within five years. The debt agreement includes covenants among which are limitations on the amount of future indebtedness and required maintenance of a minimum net worth of $550,000,000.

than others; and some companies with apparently similar transactions report them differently. Such differences make comparisons difficult and diminish the potential value of balance sheet analysis.

The balance sheet may be considered deficient in another respect. Due primarily to measurement problems, some entity resources and obligations are not reported on the balance sheet. For example, as mentioned at the beginning of the chapter in connection with The Boston Celtics, the employees of a company may be one of its most valuable resources; yet, they are not shown on the balance sheet because their future service potentials are not measurable in monetary terms. Similarly, a company's potential liability for polluting the air would not normally be shown on its balance sheet. The assumptions of the traditional accounting model identified in Chapter 2, specifically the requirements of arm's-length transactions or events measurable in monetary terms, add to the objectivity of balance sheet disclosures but at the same time cause some information to be omitted that is likely to be relevant to certain users' decisions.

One author, reflecting on these limitations, wrote the following:

The current balance sheet published by most corporations is a pathetic financial representation of a company's real resources and obligations. It is a dumping ground for dangling debit and credit entries and a listing of dollar values determined by different, often outmoded, accounting concepts. Users find that the face of such statements often excludes more relevant data than it includes.[20]

This dim view of the balance sheet is not shared by many accountants and users of financial statements. The balance sheet is an important statement for investors and creditors. While its limitations must be understood, it can still provide a user with valuable information for decisions.

The conceptual framework established by the FASB stresses the objective of usefulness of accounting information. During the past few years, the Board has considered several issues that directly affect the balance sheet, using the conceptual framework as a guide in the development of new standards. In some instances, the new standards have a direct impact on the amounts reported on the balance sheet. Notable examples include pensions, receivables with right of return, deferred income tax accounting, and interest capitalization. In other instances, the impact has been on required disclosure in notes, such as the requirement for some companies to disclose segment data and off-balance-sheet financing arrangements. These and other examples will be discussed throughout the text.

20. David E. Hawkins. "Towards the New Balance Sheet." *Harvard Business Review,* November–December 1984, p. 156.

KEY TERMS

Account form 164
Acid-test ratio 159
Additional paid-in capital 162
Assets 153
Balance sheet 152
Callable obligation 157
Capital stock 162
Contingent liabilities 161
Contributed capital 162
Current assets 155
Current liabilities 157
Current ratio 158
Debt ratio 162
Deferred income tax assets 160
Deferred income tax liability 161
Deficit 163
Liabilities 154
Liquidity 153
Net assets 154
Normal operating cycle 155
Objective acceleration clauses 157
Owners' equity 154
Paid-in capital 162
Post-balance sheet events 169
Quick (acid test) ratio 159
Report form 164
Retained earnings 162
Solvency 153
Subjective acceleration clause 158
Subsequent events 169
Trading securities 156
Treasury stock 163
Working capital 154

QUESTIONS

1. In what way is the balance sheet useful to decision makers?
2. What three elements are contained in the balance sheet?
3. What are the major classifications of (a) assets, (b) liabilities, and (c) owners' equity? Indicate the nature of the items reported within each major classification.
4. (a) Why is the distinction between current assets/liabilities and noncurrent assets/liabilities considered to be important? (b) What arguments are there for not making a distinction?
5. What criteria are generally used (a) in classifying assets as current or noncurrent? (b) in classifying liabilities as current or noncurrent?
6. (a) What is a subjective acceleration clause? (b) An objective acceleration clause? (c) How do these clauses in debt instruments affect the classification of a liability?
7. Indicate under what circumstances each of the following can be considered noncurrent: (a) cash (b) receivables.
8. Distinguish between the following: (a) contingent liabilities and estimated liabilities (b) appropriated retained earnings and unappropriated retained earnings.
9. Under what circumstances may offset balances be properly recognized on the balance sheet?
10. What are the major types of notes attached to the financial statements?
11. Under what circumstances might a parenthetical notation on the balance sheet be preferred to a note?
12. What are some examples of supplementary information included in the notes to financial statements?
13. Under what circumstances does a subsequent event lead to a journal entry for the previous reporting period?

DISCUSSION CASES

Case 5—1 (What do the figures mean?)

Listed below are some of the largest corporations in the world.

	(in millions of U.S. dollars)			
Company Name	*Country*	*Market Value*	*Total Assets*	*Net Income*
Nippon Telegraph and Telephone (telecommunications)	Japan	77,603	86,070	1,432
Dai-Ichi Kangyo Bank (banking)	Japan	34,712	426,858	626
Toyota Motor Corp. (automobiles)	Japan	44,018	65,178	3,145
Tokyo Electric Power (utilities)	Japan	29,276	78,638	565

Royal Dutch/Shell (energy)	Netherlands	77,898	105,582	4,237
Wal-Mart Stores (retail)	U.S.	76,176	20,565	1,995
General Motors (automobiles)	U.S.	37,606	190,908	(2,621)
Exxon (energy)	U.S.	80,264	85,030	4,810
American Telephone and Telegraph (telecommunications)	U.S.	78,415	57,188	3,807
Citicorp (banking)	U.S.	10,582	213,701	722

Sources: *Forbes,* Apr. 26, 1993 and *Forbes,* July 20, 1992.

As an analyst for a securities broker, you are asked the following questions concerning some of the figures:

1. Wal-Mart Stores has total assets of $21 billion, but a stock market value of $76 billion. How can a company be worth more than its total assets?
2. Citicorp and Dai-Ichi Kangyo Bank have the highest total assets on the list and yet their net incomes are exceeded by many of the other companies. Why do you think this is?
3. The price/earnings ratio, often called the PE ratio, is defined as: market price per share divided by earnings per share. Alternatively, the PE ratio can be computed as: total market value divided by net income. Compute the PE ratios for the companies listed above. What factors do you think determine PE ratios?

Case 5—2 (We've got you now!)

The Piedmont Computer Company has brought legal action against ATC Corporation for alleged monopolistic practices in the development of software. The claim has been pending for two years, with both sides accumulating evidence to support their positions. The case is now ready for trial. ATC Corporation has offered to settle out of court for $500,000, but Piedmont is asking for $5,000,000. Piedmont's attorneys feel an award of $2,500,000 from the court is very likely.

If financial statements must be issued prior to the court action, how should Piedmont reflect this contingent claim? Support your decision where possible from the conceptual framework.

Case 5—3 (But what is our liability?)

The Ditka Engineering Co. has signed a third-party loan guarantee for Liberty Company. The loan is from the National Bank of Illinois for $500,000. Liberty has recently filed for bankruptcy, and it is estimated by the company's auditors that creditors can expect to receive no more than 40% of their claims from Liberty. The treasurer of Ditka feels that because of the high uncertainty of final settlement, a liability should be recorded for the entire $500,000. The chief accountant, on the other hand, feels the 40% collection figure is reasonable and proposes that a $300,000 liability be recorded. The president of Ditka does not think a reasonable estimate can be made at this time, and proposes that nothing be accrued for the contingent liability, but that a note be added to the financial statements explaining the situation.

As an independent outside auditor, what position would you take? Why?

Case 5—4 (Aren't the financial statements enough?)

Excello Corporation's basic financial statements for the year just ended have been prepared in accordance with GAAP. During the current year, management changed the accounting method for computing depreciation; a major competitor constructed a new plant in the area; three separate lawsuits were brought against the corporation that are not expected to be settled for two years or more; and the corporation continued to use an acceptable revenue recognition principle that differs from that used by most other companies in the industry. Also, after the end of the year, but before the statements were issued, Excello issued additional shares of common stock.

Excello has recently applied for a large bank loan, and the bank has requested a copy of the financial statements. The auditors for Excello have prepared several notes, some quite lengthy, to accompany the financial statements, but Excello's management does not think the loan officer at the bank would understand them and therefore submits the statements without the notes. The bank accepts the statements as submitted.

Which of the events described above should be included in notes to the financial statements? Do you think it is acceptable to delete notes when submitting financial statements to third parties? Substantiate your position.

Case 5—5 (Which company is which?)

Below are summaries of the balance sheets of five companies. The amounts are all stated as a percentage of total assets. The five companies are:

BankAmerica, a large bank.
Kelly Services, a firm that provides temporary employees.
Sears (just the merchandise group).
Sears (consolidated, including the financial subsidiaries).
Consolidated Edison, a utility serving New York City.

	A	B	C	D	E
Receivables	36.8	61.1	41.5	69.1	3.9
Inventories	4.8	15.7	0.0	0.0	3.3
Other current assets	9.7	4.9	48.0	25.0	4.6
Land, buildings, and equipment	6.6	15.7	8.7	1.9	84.5
Other long-term assets	42.1	2.6	1.8	4.0	3.7
Short-term payables	9.6	15.3	29.6	1.3	4.2
Other current liabilities	37.0	26.2	0.0	89.3	3.2
Long-term liabilities	35.4	35.7	0.0	6.5	41.9
Equity	18.0	22.8	70.4	2.9	50.7

1. Match each of the balance sheet summaries (A through E) with the appropriate company. Justify your choices.
2. How does consolidation improve the usefulness of financial statements? What are some disadvantages of consolidated financial statements?

Case 5—6 (How can we live with debt covenant requirements?)

Bohr Company has a credit agreement with a syndicate of banks. In order to impose some limitations on Bohr's financial riskiness, the credit agreement requires Bohr to maintain a current ratio of at least 1.4 and a debt ratio of .55 or less. The following summary data reflect a projection of Bohr's balance sheet for the coming year-end:

Current assets	$1,200,000
Long-term assets	1,800,000
Current liabilities	900,000
Long-term liabilities	800,000
Equity	1,300,000

The following information has also been prepared:

(a) If Bohr were to use FIFO instead of LIFO for inventory valuation, ending inventory would increase by $50,000.
(b) The amounts listed for long-term assets and liabilities include the anticipated purchase (and associated mortgage payable) of a building costing $100,000. Bohr can lease the building instead; the lease would qualify for treatment as an operating lease.
(c) The projected amounts include a planned declaration of cash dividends totaling $40,000 to be paid next year. Bohr has consistently paid dividends of equivalent amounts.

As a consultant to Bohr, you are asked to respond to the following two questions:

1. What steps can Bohr take to avoid violating the current-ratio constraint?
2. What steps can Bohr take to avoid violating the debt-ratio constraint?

Of the steps that you propose, which ones do you think the banks had in mind when they imposed the loan covenants? If you had assisted the banks in drawing up the loan covenants, how would you have written them differently to avoid unintended consequences?

Case 5—7 (Are current values necessary for valuing investment assets?)

First Federal Finance Co. carries several different types of investment assets on its balance sheet. Equity securities have historically been carried at the lower of cost or market. Debt securities, including real estate mortgages, have been carried at cost unless a permanent impairment of the cost value occurred. During the past few years, many of the real estate values against which the mortgages are held have declined in value, sometimes significantly. Because this has been true throughout the banking and finance community, the FASB has adopted a standard (Statement No. 115) that moves toward a current market valuation on the balance sheet. The SEC has also encouraged this change. As a banker, however, you do not see this change as being necessary, and indeed, feel it will be threatening to your existence if it were to be required. (1) As a banker, why would current value accounting be threatening to you? (2) How would you respond to these reasons if you were a member of the FASB?

Case 5—8 (What should we tell the stockholders?)

Technology Unlimited, Inc. uses a fiscal year ending June 30. The auditors completed their review of the 1996 financial statements on September 8, 1996. They discovered the following subsequent events between June 30 and September 8.

1. Technology split its common stock 2 for 1 on August 15. Prior to the split, Technology had outstanding 100,000 shares of $10 par common stock.
2. A major customer, Diatride Company, declared bankruptcy on August 1. The customer owed Technology $75,000 on June 30. No payment has been received as of September 8. It is estimated that creditors will receive only 15% of outstanding claims.
3. Technology completed negotiations to purchase Liston Development Labs on July 18. The purchase price was $525,000 in cash and a 4-year, $250,000 10% note.
4. A $750,000 lawsuit against Technology was filed on August 15. It is too early to measure the loss potential.
5. A general decline in stock market values for technology stocks occurred during the first week of September. Technology Unlimited's market value dropped from $42.50 to $28.00 in this week.

The auditors have requested that you prepare the "Subsequent Event" note that should accompany the financial statements for the year ending June 30, 1996. Only those events that require disclosure should be included in your note. Justify the exclusion of any events from your note.

Case 5—9 (What does this British balance sheet mean?)

Jonathan Atwood, a student from England, shows you the following balance sheet from his father's British company. Jonathan knows you are majoring in accounting and asks you to look at the statement. You immediately recognize some differences between this statement and the ones you have been studying in your textbook. (1) Identify the differences that exist between this British statement and those prepared using the standards and conventions of the United States. (2) Evaluate the differences, identifying strengths and weaknesses of each nation's approach.

		Group		Company	
		31 December		31 December	
	NOTES	1996 £m	1995 £m	1996 £m	1995 £m
Fixed Assets					
Intangibles	13	**304.0**	307.4	**—**	—
Tangible assets	14	**978.8**	822.5	**16.8**	16.2
Investments	15	**16.7**	25.2	**938.9**	679.3
		1,299.5	1,155.1	**955.7**	695.5
Current Assets					
Stock	16	**328.2**	334.8	**—**	—
Debtors	17	**554.1**	548.2	**113.4**	210.8
Investments — short term loans and deposits		**118.0**	33.3	**5.1**	23.5
Cash at bank and in hand		**62.6**	57.4	**—**	—
		1,062.9	973.7	**118.5**	234.3
Creditors: amounts falling due within one year					
Borrowings	18	**(136.3)**	(133.7)	**(175.0)**	(74.6)
Other	19	**(825.9)**	(809.2)	**(98.4)**	(234.7)
Net Current Assets (Liabilities)		**100.7**	30.8	**(154.9)**	(75.0)
Total Assets less Current Liabilities		**1,400.2**	1,185.9	**800.8**	620.5
Other Liabilities					
Creditors: amounts falling due after more than one year					
Borrowings	18	**(407.9)**	(381.4)	**(54.2)**	(80.4)
Other	19	**(12.0)**	(8.5)	**(26.4)**	(42.1)
Provisions for liabilities and charges	20	**(96.4)**	(115.5)	**0.5**	1.2
		(516.3)	(505.4)	**(80.1)**	(121.3)
		883.9	680.5	**720.7**	499.2
Capital and Reserves					
Called up share capital	21	**174.7**	173.6	**174.7**	173.6
Share premium account	22	**381.6**	217.4	**381.6**	217.4
Revaluation reserve	22	**95.8**	36.7	**2.4**	1.1
Profit and loss account	22	**115.8**	167.6	**162.0**	107.1
		767.9	595.3	**720.7**	499.2
Minority Interests		**116.0**	85.2	**—**	—
		883.9	680.5	**720.7**	499.2

Case 5—10 (Analysis of financial statements—Microsoft Corporation)

Refer to the financial statements of Microsoft Corporation in Appendix A in answering the following questions:

1. How did the liquidity of Microsoft change between 1992 and 1993?
2. What was unusual about Microsoft's long-term debt at the end of 1993?
3. What method of inventory valuation does Microsoft use?
4. What method of depreciation does Microsoft use?
5. Commitments and contingencies shows a -0- balance on the balance sheet. What reasonably possible contingency losses does Microsoft have at the end of 1993?
6. How much accumulated depreciation does Microsoft report as of the end of 1993?
7. How much computer equipment does Microsoft own at the end of 1993?

EXERCISES

Exercise 5—11 (Balance sheet classification)

A balance sheet contains the following classifications:

(a) Current assets
(b) Investments
(c) Land, buildings, and equipment
(d) Intangible assets
(e) Other noncurrent assets
(f) Current liabilities
(g) Long-term debt
(h) Other noncurrent liabilities
(i) Capital stock
(j) Additional paid-in capital
(k) Retained earnings

Indicate by letter how each of the following accounts would be classified. Place a minus sign (–) for all accounts representing offset or contra balances.

1. Discount on Bonds Payable
2. Stock of Subsidiary Corporation
3. 12% Bonds Payable (due in six months)
4. U.S. Treasury Notes
5. Income Tax Payable
6. Sales Tax Payable
7. Estimated Claims Under Warranties for Service and Replacements
8. Par value of Stock Issued and Outstanding
9. Unearned Rent Revenue (six months in advance)
10. Long-Term Advances to Officers
11. Interest Receivable
12. Preferred Stock Retirement Fund
13. Trademarks
14. Allowance for Doubtful Accounts
15. Dividends Payable
16. Accumulated Depreciation
17. Petty Cash Fund
18. Prepaid Rent
19. Prepaid Insurance
20. Organization Costs

Exercise 5—12 (Balance sheet classification)

State how each of the following accounts should be classified on the balance sheet:

(a) Treasury Stock
(b) Retained Earnings
(c) Vacation Pay Payable
(d) Retained Earnings Appropriated for Loss Contingencies
(e) Allowance for Doubtful Accounts
(f) Liability for Pension Payments
(g) Investment Securities (Trading)
(h) Paid-In Capital From Sale of Stock at More Than Stated Value
(i) Leasehold Improvements
(j) Goodwill
(k) Receivables—U.S. Government Contracts
(l) Advances to Salespersons
(m) Premium on Bonds Payable
(n) Inventory
(o) Patents
(p) Unclaimed Payroll Checks
(q) Employees' Income Tax Payable
(r) Subscription Revenue Received in Advance
(s) Interest Payable
(t) Deferred Income Tax Asset
(u) Tools
(v) Deferred Income Tax Liability

Exercise 5—13 (Asset definition)

Using the definition of an asset from FASB Concepts Statement No. 6, indicate whether each of the following should be listed as an asset by DeBroglie Company:

(a) DeBroglie has legal title to a silver mine in a remote location. Historically, the mine has yielded over $100 million in silver. Engineering estimates suggest that no further minerals are economically extractable from the mine.
(b) DeBroglie is currently negotiating the purchase of an oil field with proven oil reserves totaling 2 billion barrels.
(c) DeBroglie employs a team of five geologists who are widely recognized as the worldwide leaders in their field.

(d) DeBroglie claims ownership of a large piece of real estate in a foreign country. The real estate has a current market value of over $650 million. The country expropriated the land 35 years ago, and no representative of DeBroglie has been allowed on the property since.
(e) Several years ago, DeBroglie purchased a large meteor crater on the advice of a geologist who had developed a theory claiming that vast deposits of iron ore lay underneath the crater. The crater has no other economic use. No ore has been found and the geologist's theory is not generally accepted.

Exercise 5—14 (Liability definition)

Using the definition of a liability from FASB Concepts Statement No. 6, indicate whether each of the following should be listed as a liability by Pauli Company:

(a) Pauli was involved in a highly publicized lawsuit last year. Pauli lost and was ordered to pay damages of $125 million. The payment has been made.
(b) In exchange for television advertising services that Pauli received last month, Pauli is obligated to provide the television station with building maintenance service for the next four months.
(c) Pauli contractually guarantees to replace any of its stain-resistant carpets if they are stained and can't be cleaned.
(d) Pauli estimates that its total payroll for the coming year will exceed $35 million.
(e) In the past, Pauli has suffered frequent vandalism at its storage warehouses. Pauli estimates that losses due to vandalism during the coming year will total $3 million.

Exercise 5—15 (Balance sheet preparation—account form)

From the following list of accounts, prepare a balance sheet in account form showing all balance sheet items properly classified. (No monetary amounts are to be recognized.)

Accounts Payable
Accounts Receivable
Accumulated Depreciation—Buildings
Accumulated Depreciation—Equipment
Advertising Expense
Allowance for Doubtful Accounts
Bonds Payable
Buildings
Cash
Common Stock
Cost of Goods Sold
Deferred Income Tax Liability
Depreciation Expense—Buildings
Dividends
Doubtful Accounts Expense
Equipment
Estimated Warranty Expense Payable (current)
Gain on Sale of Land
Gain on Sale of Investment Securities
Goodwill
Income Summary
Income Tax Expense
Income Tax Payable
Interest Receivable
Interest Revenue
Inventory
Investment in Bonds
Land
Loss on Purchase Commitments
Investment Securities (Trading)
Miscellaneous General Expense
Notes Payable
Paid-In Capital From Sale of Common Stock at More Than Stated Value
Paid-In Capital From Sale of Treasury Stock
Patents
Pension Fund
Premium on Bonds Payable
Prepaid Insurance
Property Tax Expense
Purchases
Purchase Discounts
Retained Earnings
Salaries Payable
Sales
Sales Salaries
Travel Expense

Exercise 5—16 (Computation of working capital)

From the following data, compute the working capital for Benson Equipment Co. at December 31, 1996:

Cash in general checking account	$ 10,000
Cash in fund to be used to retire bonds in 2000	50,000
Cash held to pay sales taxes	18,000
Notes receivable—due February 1998	100,000
Trade accounts receivable	125,000
Inventory	75,000
Prepaid insurance—for 1997 and 1998	15,000
Vacant land held as investment	300,000
Used equipment to be sold	25,000
Deferred tax asset—to be recovered in 1998	10,000
Trade accounts payable	80,000
Note payable—due July 1997	33,000
Note payable—due January 1998	10,000
Bonds payable—maturity date 2000	210,000
Salaries payable	20,000
Sales tax payable	23,000
Goodwill	37,000

Exercise 5—17 (Preparation of corrected balance sheet)

The following balance sheet was prepared for Jared Company as of December 31, 1996:

Jared Company
Balance Sheet
December 31, 1996

Assets		Liabilities and Owner's Equity	
Current assets		Current liabilities:	
Cash	$ 12,500	Accounts payable	$ 3,400
Investment securities	8,000	Other current liabilities	2,000
Accounts receivable, net	21,350	Total current liabilities	$ 5,400
Inventory	31,000		
Other current assets	14,200	Long-term liabilities	32,750
Total current assets	$ 87,050	Total liabilities	$ 38,150
Noncurrent assets:			
Land, buildings, and equipment, net	$ 64,800	Owners' equity:	
		Common stock	$ 50,000
Treasury stock	4,500	Retained earnings	81,800
Other noncurrent assets	13,600	Total owners' equity	$131,800
Total noncurrent assets	$ 82,900		
Total assets	$169,950	Total liabilities and owners' equity	$169,950

The following additional information relates to the December 31, 1996, balance sheet:

(a) Cash includes $3,000 that has been restricted to the purchase of manufacturing equipment (a noncurrent asset).

(b) Investment securities include $2,750 of stock that was purchased in order to give the company significant ownership and a seat on the board of directors of a major supplier.

(c) Other current assets include a $4,000 advance to the president of the company. No due date has been set.

(d) Long-term liabilities include bonds payable of $10,000. Of this amount, $2,500 represents bonds scheduled to be redeemed in 1997.

(e) Long-term liabilities also include a $7,000 bank loan. On May 15, the loan will become due on demand.

(f) Retained earnings in the amount of $5,300 has been restricted and is unavailable for dividends.

(g) On December 21, dividends in the amount of $15,000 were declared to be paid to shareholders of record on January 25. These dividends have not been reflected in the financial statements.

(h) Cash in the amount of $19,000 has been placed in a restricted fund for the redemption of preferred stock in 1997. Both the cash and the stock have been removed from the balance sheet.

(i) Land, buildings, and equipment includes land costing $8,000 that is being held for investment purposes and that is scheduled to be sold in 1997.

Based on the information provided, prepare a corrected balance sheet as of December 31, 1996.

Exercise 5—18 (Balance sheet relationships)

For each of the items, (a) through (o) on the Faevero and Company Inc. balance sheet, indicate the amount that should appear on the balance sheet.

Faevero and Company Inc.
Consolidated Balance Sheet
December 31, 1997

Assets			
Current assets:			
Cash		$ 13,185	
Investment securities		(a)	
Accounts and notes receivable	$ (b)		
Allow. for doubtful accounts and notes receivable	9,622	165,693	
Inventories		235,813	
Other current assets		10,419	
Total current assets			$ (c)
Noncurrent assets:			
Land, buildings, and equipment	$771,604		
Accumulated depreciation	(d)	$419,418	
Other noncurrent assets		15,631	
Total noncurrent assets			435,049
Total assets			$885,312
Liabilities and Owners' Equity			
Current liabilities:			
Accounts payable		$ (e)	
Payable to banks		22,858	
Income taxes payable		8,328	
Current installments of long-term debt		5,720	
Accrued expenses		6,610	
Total current liabilities			$ (f)
Noncurrent liabilities:			
Long-term debt		$ (g)	
Deferred income tax liability		40,406	
Minority interest in subsidiaries		3,309	
Total noncurrent liabilities			175,469
Total liabilities			$317,655
Contributed Capital:			
Preferred stock, no par value (authorized 1,618 shares; issued 1,115 shares)		$ 16,596	
Common stock, $1 par value per share (authorized 60,000 shares, issued 25,939 shares)	$ (h)		
Additional paid-in capital	(i)	(j)	
Total contributed capital		$ (k)	

Retained earnings:			
Appropriated	$100,000		
Unappropriated	(l)	504,744	
Total contributed capital and retained earnings		$ (m)	
Less treasury stock, at cost (1,236 shares)		26,688	
Total owners' equity			(n)
Total liabilities and owners' equity			$ (o)

Exercise 5—19 (Balance sheet schedules)

In its annual report to stockholders, Crantz Inc. presents a condensed balance sheet with detailed data provided in supplementary schedules. (1) From the adjusted trial balance of Crantz, prepare the following schedules, properly classifying all accounts as to balance sheet categories:

(a) Current assets
(b) Land, buildings, and equipment
(c) Intangible assets
(d) Total assets
(e) Current liabilities
(f) Noncurrent liabilities
(g) Owners' equity
(h) Total liabilities and owners' equity

(2) Compute the current ratio and debt ratio for Crantz.

Crantz Inc.
Adjusted Trial Balance
December 31, 1996

	Debit	Credit
Cash	$ 28,900	
Investment Securities (trading)	20,000	
Notes Receivable—trade debtors	18,000	
Accrued Interest on Notes Receivable	1,800	
Accounts Receivable	88,400	
Allowance for Doubtful Accounts		$ 4,300
Inventory	56,900	
Prepaid Expenses	6,100	
Accounts Payable		26,500
Notes Payable—trade creditors		16,000
Accrued Interest on Notes Payable		800
Land	80,000	
Buildings	170,000	
Accumulated Depreciation—Buildings		34,000
Equipment	48,000	
Accumulated Depreciation—Equipment		7,600
Patents	15,000	
Franchises	10,000	
Bonds Payable, 8%—issue 1 (mature 12/31/98)		50,000
Bonds Payable, 12%—issue 2 (mature 12/31/02)		100,000
Accrued Interest on Bonds Payable		8,000
Premium on Bonds Payable—issue 1		1,500
Discount on Bonds Payable—issue 2	10,500	
Mortgage Payable		57,500
Accrued Interest on Mortgage Payable		2,160
Capital Stock, par value $25, 10,000 shares authorized, 4,000 shares issued		100,000
Additional Paid-In Capital		16,800
Retained Earnings Appropriated for Bond Redemption		35,000
Unappropriated Retained Earnings		104,440
Treasury Stock—at cost (500 shares)	11,000	
	$564,600	$564,600

Exercise 5—20 **(Classification of subsequent events)**

The following events occurred after the end of the company's fiscal year, but before the annual audit was completed. Classify each event as to its impact on the financial statements, i.e., (1) reported by changing the amounts in the financial statements, (2) reported in notes to the financial statements, (3) does not require reporting. Include support for your classification.

(a) Major customer went bankrupt due to a deteriorating financial condition.
(b) Company sustained extensive hurricane damage to one of its plants.
(c) Company settled a major lawsuit that had been pending for two years.
(d) Increasing U.S. trade deficit may have impact on company's overseas sales.
(e) Company sold a large block of preferred stock.
(f) Preparation of current year's income tax return disclosed an additional $25,000 is due on last year's return.
(g) Company's controller resigned and was replaced by an audit manager from the company's audit firm.

Exercise 5—21 **(Reporting financial information)**

For each of the items below, indicate whether the item should be reflected in the 1996 financial statements for Rutherford Company. If the item should be reflected, indicate whether it should be reported in the financial statements themselves or by note disclosure.

(a) During 1996, the company had a gain on the sale of manufacturing assets.
(b) As of December 31, 1996, the company was in violation of certain loan covenants. The violation does not cause the loans to be callable immediately, but does increase the interest charge by 1.5%.
(c) The company uses straight-line depreciation for all tangible, long-term assets.
(d) As of December 31, 1996, accounts receivable in the amount of $6.7 million are estimated to be uncollectible.
(e) The Environmental Protection Agency is investigating the company's procedures for disposing of toxic waste. Outside consultants have estimated that the company may be liable for fines of up to $8 million.
(f) The company's reported Provision for Income Taxes includes $3.6 million in current taxes and $7.3 million in deferred taxes.
(g) During 1996, a long-term insurance agreement was signed. The company paid five years' insurance premiums in advance.
(h) As of December 31, 1996, the company holds $11.2 million of its own stock that it purchased in the open market and is holding for possible reissuance.
(i) During 1996, the company hired three prominent research chemists away from its chief competitor.
(j) Reported long-term debt is composed of senior subordinated debentures, convertible debentures, junior subordinated debentures, and capital lease obligations.
(k) Early in 1997, a significant drop in raw materials prices caused the company's stock price to rise in anticipation of sharply increased profits for the year.

Exercise 5—22 **(Preparation of notes to financial statements)**

The following information was used to prepare the financial statements for Delta Chemical Company. Prepare the necessary notes to accompany the statements.

Delta uses the LIFO inventory method on its financial statements. If the FIFO method were used, the ending inventory balance would be reduced by $50,000, and net income for the year would be reduced by $35,000 after taxes. Delta depreciates its equipment using the straight-line method. Revenue is generally recognized when inventory is shipped unless it is sold on a consignment basis. The current value of the equipment is $525,000 as contrasted to its depreciated cost of $375,000.

Delta has borrowed $350,000 on 10-year notes at 14% interest. The notes are due on July 1, 2006. Delta's equipment has been pledged as collateral for the loan. The terms of the note prohibit additional long-term borrowing without the express permission of the holder of the notes. Delta is planning to request such permission during the next fiscal year.

The board of directors of Delta is currently discussing a merger with another chemical company. No public announcement has yet been made, but it is anticipated that additional shares of stock will be issued as part of the merger. Delta's balance sheet will report receivables of $126,000. Included in this figure is a $25,000 advance to the president of Delta, $30,000 of notes receivable from customers, $10,000 in advances to sales representatives, and $70,000 of accounts receivable from customers. The reported balance reflects a deduction for anticipated collection losses.

PROBLEMS

Problem 5—23 (Computing balance sheet components)

Denton Equipment Inc. furnishes you with the following list of accounts:

Account	Amount	Account	Amount
Accounts Payable	$ 66,000	Investment in Siebert Co. Stock (current investment securities)	$21,000
Accounts Receivable	40,000	Paid-In Capital in Excess of Par	42,500
Accumulated Depreciation	44,000	Premium on Bonds Payable	6,000
Advances to Salespersons	10,000	Prepaid Insurance	6,000
Advertising Expense	72,000	Rent Revenue	37,000
Allowance for Doubtful Accounts	10,000	Rent Revenue Received in Advance (4 months)	12,000
Bonds Payable	80,000	Retained Earnings	57,500
Cash	22,000	Retained Earnings Appropriated for Loss Contingencies	40,000
Certificates of Deposit	16,000	Taxes Payable	10,000
Common Stock (par)	100,000	Tools	52,000
Deferred Income Tax Liability	46,000		
Equipment	215,500		
Inventory	55,000		
Investment in Rowe Oil Co. Stock (40% of outstanding stock owned for control purposes)	76,500		

Instructions: From the above list of accounts, determine working capital, total assets, total liabilities, and owners' equity per share of stock (75,000 shares outstanding).

Problem 5—24 (Classified balance sheet)

Below is a list of account titles and balances for Zaldo Investment Corporation as of January 31, 1996.

Account	Amount	Account	Amount
Accounts Payable	$ 75,900	Income Taxes Payable	$ 29,200
Accounts Receivable	153,100	Interest Payable	5,390
Accumulated Depreciation—Buildings	151,700	Interest Receivable	900
Accumulated Depreciation—Machinery and Equipment	127,000	Inventory	201,300
Additional Paid-In Capital—Common Stock	62,000	Investment Securities (current)	102,500
Allowance for Doubtful Notes and Accounts Receivable	16,500	Investments in Undeveloped Properties	175,000
Buildings	410,000	Land	188,000
Cash in Banks	9,120	Machinery and Equipment	145,000
Cash on Hand	97,300	Miscellaneous Supplies Inventory	6,200
Cash Fund for Stock Redemption	17,500	Notes Payable (current)	58,260
Claim for Income Tax Refund	4,500	Notes Payable (due in 2001)	38,000
Common Stock, $20 par	650,000	Notes Receivable (current)	22,470
Employees' Income Tax Payable	4,780	Preferred Stock, $5 par.	320,000
		Prepaid Insurance	3,500
		Retained Earnings (debit balance)	11,740
		Salaries and Wages Payable	9,400

Instructions:

(1) Prepare a properly classified balance sheet in report form.
(2) Compute current ratio and debt ratio.

Problem 5—25 (Classified balance sheet—account form including notes)

Adjusted account balances and supplemental information for Brockbank Research Corp. as of December 31, 1996, are as follows:

Accounts Payable	$ 32,160	Cash Fund for Bond Retirement	$ 3,600
Accounts Receivable—Trade	57,731	Common Stock	175,000
Accumulated Depreciation—Leasehold Improvements and Equipment	579,472	Deferred Income Tax Liability	45,000
Additional Paid-In Capital	125,000	Dividends Payable	37,500
Furniture, Fixtures, and Store Equipment	769,000	Franchises	12,150
Inventory	201,620	Leasehold Improvements	65,800
Investment in Unconsolidated Subsidiary	80,000	7 1/2%-12% Mortgage Notes	200,000
Insurance Claims Receivable	120,000	Notes Payable—Banks (due in 1997)	17,000
Land	6,000	Notes Payable—Trade	63,540
Allowance for Doubtful Accounts	1,731	Patent Licenses	57,402
Automobiles	132,800	Prepaid Insurance	5,500
Cash	30,600	Profit Sharing, Payroll, and Vacation Payable	40,000
		Retained Earnings	225,800

Supplemental information:

(a) Depreciation is provided by the straight-line method over the estimated useful lives of the assets.
(b) Common stock is $5 par, and 35,000 of the 100,000 authorized shares were issued and are outstanding.
(c) The cost of an exclusive franchise to import a foreign company's ball bearings and a related patent license are being amortized on the straight-line method over their remaining lives: franchise, 10 years; patents, 15 years.
(d) Inventories are stated at the lower of cost or market; cost was determined by the specific identification method.
(e) Insurance claims based on the opinion of an independent insurance adjustor are for property damages at the central warehouse. These claims are estimated to be 2/3 collectible in the following year and 1/3 collectible thereafter.
(f) The company leases all of its buildings from various lessors. Estimated fixed lease obligations are $50,000 per year for the next ten years. The leases do not meet the criteria for capitalization.
(g) The company is currently in litigation over a claimed overpayment of income tax of $13,000. In the opinion of counsel, the claim is valid. The company is contingently liable on guaranteed notes worth $17,000.

Instructions: Prepare a properly classified balance sheet in account form. Include all notes and parenthetical notations necessary to properly disclose the essential financial data.

Problem 5—26 (Classification of liabilities)

The accountant for Sierra Corp. prepared the following schedule of liabilities as of December 31, 1996:

Accounts payable	$ 65,000
Notes payable—trade	12,000
Notes payable—bank	80,000
Wages and salaries payable	1,500
Interest payable	14,300
Mortgage note payable—10%	60,000
Mortgage note payable—12%	150,000
Bonds payable	200,000
Total	$582,800

The following additional information pertains to these liabilities:

(a) All trade notes payable are due within six months of the balance sheet date.
(b) Bank notes payable include two separate notes payable to First Interstate Bank:
  (1) A $30,000, 8% note issued March 1, 1994, payable on demand. Interest is payable each six months.
  (2) A 1-year, $50,000, 11 1/2% note issued January 2, 1996. On December 30, 1996, Sierra negotiated a written agreement with First Interstate Bank to replace the note with a 2-year, $50,000, 10% note to be issued January 2, 1997.
(c) The 10% mortgage note was issued October 1, 1993, with a term of 10 years. Terms of the note give the holder the right to demand immediate payment if the company fails to make a monthly interest payment within 10 days of the date the payment is due. As of December 31, 1996, Sierra is three months behind in paying its required interest payment.
(d) The 12% mortgage note was issued May 1, 1990, with a term of 20 years. The current principal amount due is $150,000. Principal and interest are payable annually on April 30. A payment of $22,000 is due April 30, 1997. The payment includes interest of $18,000.
(e) The bonds payable are 10-year, 8% bonds, issued June 30, 1987.

Instructions: Prepare the liabilities section of the December 31, 1996, classified balance sheet for Sierra Corp. Include notes as appropriate. Assume the interest payable accrual has been computed correctly.

Problem 5—27 (Corrected balance sheet)

The following balance sheet was prepared by the accountant for Rowley Company.

Rowley Company
Balance Sheet
June 30, 1996

Assets	
Cash	$ 25,500
Investment securities—trading (includes long-term investment of $250,000 in stock of Oak Mountain Developers)	312,000
Inventories (net of amount still due suppliers of $85,000)	624,600
Prepaid expenses (includes a deposit of $10,000 made on inventories to be delivered in 18 months)	33,000
Land, buildings, and equipment (excluding $60,000 of equipment still in use, but fully depreciated)	220,000
Goodwill (based on estimate by the president of Rowley Company)	70,000
Total assets	$1,285,100
Liabilities and Owners' Equity	
Notes payable ($75,000 due in 1998)	$ 135,000
Accounts payable (not including amount due to suppliers of inventory—see above)	142,000
Long-term liability under pension plan	60,000
Appropriation for building expansion	105,000
Accumulated depreciation	73,000
Taxes payable	44,500
Bonds payable (net of discount of $10,000)	290,000
Deferred income tax liability	68,000
Common stock (10,000 shares, $20 par)	200,000
Additional paid-in capital	50,500
Unappropriated retained earnings	117,100
Total liabilities and owners' equity	$1,285,100

Instructions: Prepare a corrected classified balance sheet in report form using appropriate account titles.

Problem 5—28 **(Classified balance sheet—report form)**

The financial position of St. Charles Ranch is summarized in the following letter to the corporation's accountant.

Dear Dallas:

The following information should be of value to you in preparing the balance sheet for St. Charles Ranch as of December 31, 1996. The balance of cash as of December 31 as reported on the bank statement was $43,825. There were still outstanding checks of $9,320 that had not cleared the bank, and cash on hand of $5,640 was not deposited until January 4, 1997.

Customers owed the company $40,500 at December 31. We estimated 6% of this amount will never be collected. We owe suppliers $32,000 for poultry feed purchased in November and December. About 75% of this feed was used before December 31.

Because we think the price of grain will rise in 1997, we are holding 10,000 bushels of wheat and 5,000 bushels of oats until spring. The market value at December 31 was $3.50 per bushel of wheat and $1.50 per bushel of oats. We estimate that both prices will increase 15% by selling time. We are not able to estimate the cost of raising this product.

St. Charles Ranch owns 1,850 acres of land. Two separate purchases of land were made as follows: 1,250 acres at $200 per acre in 1979, and 600 acres at $400 per acre in 1984. Similar land is currently selling for $800 per acre. The balance of the mortgage on the two parcels of land is $250,000 at December 31; 10% of this mortgage must be paid in 1997.

Our farm buildings and equipment cost us $176,400 and on the average are 40% depreciated. If we were to replace these buildings and equipment at today's prices, we believe we would be conservative in estimating a cost of $300,000.

We have not paid property taxes of $5,500 for 1997 billed to us in late November. Our estimated income tax for 1996 is $18,500. A refund claim for $2,800 has been filed relative to the 1994 income tax return. The claim arose because of an error made on the 1994 return.

The operator of the ranch will receive a bonus of $9,000 for 1996 operations. It will be paid when the entire grain crop has been sold.

As you will recall, we issued 14,000 shares of $10 par stock upon incorporation. The ranch received $290,000 as net proceeds from the stock issue. Dividends of $30,000 were declared last month and will be paid on February 1, 1997.

The new year appears to hold great promise. Thanks for your help in preparing this statement.

Sincerely,
Frank K. Santiago
President—St. Charles Ranch

Instructions: Based on this information, prepare a properly classified balance sheet in report form as of December 31, 1996.

Problem 5—29 **(Corrected balance sheet—report form)**

The bookkeeper for Dependable Computers Inc. reports the following balance sheet amounts as of June 30, 1996:

Current Assets	$264,050
Other Assets	628,550
Current Liabilities	158,600
Other Liabilities	90,000
Capital	644,000

A review of account balances reveals the following data:

(a) An analysis of current assets discloses the following:

Cash	$ 62,250
Investment securities—trading	60,000
Trade accounts receivable	56,800
Inventories, including advertising supplies of $2,000	85,000
	$264,050

(b) Other assets include:

Land, buildings, and equipment:	
Depreciated book value (cost, $656,000)	$549,000
Deposit with a supplier for merchandise ordered for August delivery	2,150
Goodwill recorded on the books to cancel losses incurred by the company in prior years	77,400
	$628,550

(c) Current liabilities include:

Payroll payable		$ 7,150
Taxes payable		4,150
Rent payable		11,400
Trade accounts payable:		
Total owed to suppliers on account	$101,400	
Less 6-month note received from a supplier who purchased some used equipment on June 29, 1996	1,500	99,900
Notes payable		36,000
		$158,600

(d) Other liabilities include:

9% mortgage on land, buildings, and equipment, payable in semiannual installments of $9,000 through June 30, 2001	$ 90,000

(e) Capital includes:

Preferred stock: 19,000 shares outstanding ($20 par value)	$380,000
Common stock: 160,000 shares at stated value	264,000
	$644,000

(f) Common shares were originally issued for full consideration, but the losses of the company for the past years were charged against the common stock balance.

Total consideration at time of issuance	$391,000

Instructions: Using the account balances and related data, prepare a corrected balance sheet in report form showing individual asset, liability, and capital balances properly classified.

Problem 5—30 **(Corrected balance sheet—report form)**

The following balance sheet is submitted to you for inspection and review.

Appalachian Freight Company
Balance Sheet
December 31, 1996

Assets		Liabilities and Owners' Equity	
Cash	$ 45,050	Miscellaneous liabilities	$ 3,600
Accounts receivable	112,500	Loan payable	76,200
Inventories	204,000	Accounts payable	75,250
Prepaid insurance	8,800	Capital stock	215,000
Land, buildings, and equipment	376,800	Paid-in capital	377,100
	$747,150		$747,150

In the course of the review, you find the data listed below.

(a) The possibility of uncollectible accounts on accounts receivable has not been considered. It is estimated that uncollectible accounts will total $4,800.
(b) $45,000 representing the cost of a large-scale newspaper advertising campaign completed in 1996 has been added to the inventories, since it is believed that this campaign will benefit sales of 1997. It is also found that inventories include merchandise of $16,250 received on December 31 that has not yet been recorded as a purchase.
(c) The books show that land, buildings, and equipment have a cost of $556,800 with depreciation of $180,000 recognized in prior years. However, these balances include fully depreciated equipment of $85,000 that has been scrapped and is no longer on hand.
(d) Miscellaneous liabilities of $3,600 represent salaries payable of $9,500, less noncurrent advances of $5,900 made to company officials.
(e) Loan payable represents a loan from the bank that is payable in regular quarterly installments of $6,250.
(f) Tax liabilities not shown are estimated at $18,250.
(g) Deferred income tax liability arising from temporary differences totals $44,550. This liability was not included in the balance sheet.
(h) Capital stock consists of 6,250 shares of preferred 6% stock, par $20, and 9,000 shares of common stock, stated value $10.
(i) Capital stock had been issued for a total consideration of $283,600, the amount received in excess of the par and stated values of the stock being reported as paid-in capital.
(j) Net income and dividends were recorded in Paid-In Capital.

Instructions: Prepare a corrected balance sheet in report form with accounts properly classified.

Problem 5—31 (Corrected balance sheet—report form)

The accountant for the Delicious Bakery prepares the following condensed balance sheet.

Delicious Bakery
Condensed Balance Sheet
December 31, 1996

Current assets	$53,415
Less current liabilities	29,000
Working capital	$24,415
Add other assets	75,120
	$99,535
Deduct other liabilities	3,600
Investment in business	$95,935

A review of the account balances disclosed the following data:

(a) An analysis of the current asset grouping revealed the following:

Cash	$10,600
Trade accounts receivable (fully collectible)	12,500
Notes receivable (notes of customer who has been declared bankrupt and is unable to pay anything on the obligations)	1,000
Investment securities—trading, at cost (market value $2,575)	4,250
Inventory	20,965
Cash surrender value of insurance on officers' lives	4,100
Total current assets	$53,415

The inventory account was found to include supplies costing $425, a delivery truck acquired at the end of 1996 at a cost of $2,100, and fixtures at a depreciated value of $10,400. The fixtures had been acquired in 1993 at a cost of $12,500.

(b) The total for other assets was determined as follows:

Land and buildings at cost of acquisition, July 1, 1994	$92,000
Less balance due on mortgage, $16,000, and accrued interest on mortgage, $880 (mortgage is payable in annual installments of $4,000 on July 1 of each year together with interest for the year at that time at 11%)	16,880
Total other assets	$75,120

It was estimated that the land, at the time of the purchase, was worth $30,000. Buildings as of December 31, 1996, were estimated to have a remaining life of 17 1/2 years.

(c) Current liabilities represented balances that were payable to trade creditors.

(d) Other liabilities consisted of withholding, payroll, real estate and other taxes payable to the federal, state, and local governments. However, no recognition was given the accrued salaries, utilities, and other miscellaneous items totaling $350.

(e) The company was originally organized in 1992 when 5,000 shares of no-par stock with a stated value of $5 per share were issued in exchange for business assets that were recognized on the books at their fair market value of $55,000.

Instructions: Prepare a corrected balance sheet in report form with the items properly classified.

Problem 5—32 (Classified balance sheet—account form)

Tony Akea incorporated his concrete manufacturing operations on January 1, 1996, by issuing 10,000 shares of $10 par common stock to himself. The following balance sheet for the new corporation was prepared:

Cornish Corporation
Balance Sheet
January 1, 1996

Cash	$ 10,000	Accounts payable—suppliers	$ 45,000
Accounts receivable	75,000	Capital stock, $10 par	100,000
Inventory	75,000	Additional paid-in capital	130,000
Equipment	115,000		
	$275,000		$275,000

During 1996, Cornish Corporation engaged in the following transactions:

(a) Cornish Corporation produced concrete costing $270,000. Concrete costs consisted of the following: $200,000, raw materials purchased; $25,000, labor; and $45,000, overhead. Cornish Corporation paid the $45,000 owed to suppliers as of January 1, and $130,000 of the $200,000 of raw materials purchased during the year. All labor, except for $1,500, and recorded overhead were paid in cash during the year. Other operating expenses of $15,000 were incurred and paid in 1996.
(b) Concrete costing $290,000 was sold during 1996 for $380,000. All sales were made on credit, and collections on receivables were $365,000.
(c) Cornish Corporation purchased machinery (fair market value = $190,000) by trading in old equipment costing $50,000 and paying $140,000 in cash. There is no accumulated depreciation on the old equipment as it was revalued when the new corporation was formed.
(d) Cornish Corporation issued an additional 4,000 shares of common stock for $25 per share and declared a dividend of $3 per share to all stockholders of record as of December 31, 1996, payable on January 15, 1997.
(e) Depreciation expense for 1996 was $27,000. The allowance for doubtful accounts after year-end adjustments is $2,500.

Instructions: Prepare a properly classified balance sheet in account form for the Cornish Corporation as of December 31, 1996.

CHAPTER 6

Statement of Cash Flows

CHAPTER TOPICS

- Historical Development of the Statement of Cash Flows
- Purposes of a Statement of Cash Flows
- Cash Equivalents
- Major Classifications of Cash Flows
- Cash Flows From Operating Activities—Indirect Method
- Cash Flows From Operating Activities—Direct Method
- Using Cash Flow Data to Assess Financial Strength
- Preparing a Statement of Cash Flows—T-Account Approach
- Preparing a Statement of Cash Flows—Work Sheet Approach (Appendix)

Karl Eller started out in the billboard business. After his company was acquired by Gannett, he sat on the firm's board and was one of a group of directors who opposed Gannett's risky plan to start up the first U.S. national daily newspaper, *USA Today.* He left Gannett and went to Columbia Pictures where he was one of the driving forces behind the sale of Columbia to Coca-Cola. (Columbia Pictures has since been sold again, this time to Sony.) In 1983, Mr. Eller went into the convenience store business and took on the challenge of transforming Circle K from a regional 1,200-store convenience store chain centered in Arizona into the second-largest chain in the United States (behind 7-Eleven). At its peak, Circle K operated 4,685 stores in 32 states.

Circle K's rapid expansion was financed through long-term borrowing. Circle K's long-term debt increased from $41 million in 1983 when Mr. Eller took over to $1.2 billion in 1990. The interest on this large debt, along with increased price competition from convenience stores operated by oil companies, combined to squeeze the profits of Circle K.[1] Net income dropped from a record high of $60 million in 1988 to $15 million in 1989. For the year ended April 30, 1990, Circle K reported a loss of $773 million. In May 1990, Circle K filed for Chapter 11 bankruptcy protection.

In 1990, at the same time it was reporting the disastrous $773 million loss, Circle K was reporting a record high positive cash flow from operations of $124 million. This compared to the previous high cash flow of $84 million in 1988. How could Circle K report positive cash flow at the same time it was reporting a record-breaking net loss? There are many causes for a difference between accrual net income and cash flow; these causes are introduced in this chapter. In Circle K's case, there were three primary contributing factors. First, much of the reported loss was due to a $639 million restructuring charge. This charge reduced reported income but did not involve an outflow of cash. It represented Circle K's estimate of the decline in value of various long-term assets. For example, because of the negative implications of the bankruptcy filing, goodwill previously recorded as a $371 million asset was written off by Circle K as being worthless. Second, Circle K added $75 million to its estimated liability for environmental cleanup charges resulting from leaky underground gasoline storage tanks. Again, this charge reduced income but did not involve an immediate cash outflow. Finally, the financial distress that resulted in the bankruptcy filing also forced Circle K to make its operations more efficient. One result of this was that Circle K reduced its amount of inventory by $65 million in 1990. This inventory reduction did not directly impact net income, but it did increase cash flow as $65 million in cash was liberated that otherwise would have been tied up in the form of gasoline, beer, and Twinkies.

In 1991, Circle K again showed positive cash flow from operations while reporting a large net loss. This positive cash flow was partially a result of the bankruptcy filing. When a company files for Chapter 11 bankruptcy protection, the courts allow the company to cease making interest payments on its old debts. During the fiscal year ended April 30, 1990, the year before the bankruptcy filing, Circle K paid $106 million in interest. In 1991, after the filing, Circle K paid a total of $6 million in interest, a cash savings of $100 million. In addition, in order to make it easier for financially distressed companies to get short-term loans, bankruptcy law offers incentives to new lenders. By law, these new, post-bankruptcy lenders are placed near the top of the creditor priority list, meaning that if the assets of the bankrupt company are ultimately liquidated and disbursed to the creditors, the post-bankruptcy creditors get paid back before the pre-bankruptcy creditors do. Accordingly, the bankruptcy filing strengthened the willingness of suppliers to sell to Circle K on credit, and, as a result, Circle K's accounts payable increased $80 million in 1991 (from $22 million to $102 million). This accounts payable increase freed up cash that otherwise would have been used to pay current bills.

Because of this positive cash flow from operations, Circle K was able to stay in business while its management devised a reorganization plan. As part of its bankruptcy restructuring, Circle K replaced Karl Eller as chief executive officer on May 8, 1990. Following a lengthy debate among the creditors, Circle K's bankruptcy reorganization plan was formally approved by a federal bankruptcy court judge on June 17, 1993. The plan calls for the acquisition of Circle K for $400 million by a diverse group of investors from Barcelona, Kuwait, and Pittsburgh.

Assessing the amounts, timing, and uncertainty of future cash flows is one of the primary objectives of financial reporting.[2] The statement that provides information needed to meet

1. Roy J. Harris Jr. "Karl Eller of Circle K, Always Pushing Luck, Now Lives to Regret It." *The Wall Street Journal,* March 28, 1990, p. A1.

2. *Statement of Financial Accounting Concepts No. 1,* "Objectives of Financial Reporting by Business Enterprises" (Stamford: Financial Accounting Standards Board, 1978), par. 37.

this objective is a **statement of cash flows.** This chapter provides an overview of reporting cash flows and outlines the techniques for preparing and analyzing a cash flow statement.

HISTORICAL PERSPECTIVE

As discussed in Chapters 4 and 5, the primary financial statements for a business enterprise include the balance sheet, the income statement, and the statement of cash flows. The balance sheet reports the financial position of a business at a given time. The income statement reports the operating results for the period and may be accompanied by a statement summarizing the changes in retained earnings or stockholders' equity in successive periods. The statement of cash flows provides information about the cash receipts and cash payments of an entity during a period of time. It has replaced the previously required **statement of changes in financial position** or **funds statement.**

The funds statement went through several years of development in becoming one of the primary financial statements. In 1961, Accounting Research Study No. 2, sponsored by the AICPA, recommended that a funds statement be prepared and included with the income statement and balance sheet in annual reports to shareholders.[3] Two years later, APB Opinion No. 3 was issued to provide guidelines for the preparation of the funds statement.[4] Even though Opinion No. 3 did not require a funds statement, most businesses recognized the value of the funds statement and included it in their annual reports. Thus, it was somewhat anticlimactic when, in 1971, the APB issued Opinion No. 19 officially requiring that a funds statement be included as one of the three primary financial statements in annual reports to shareholders and that it be covered by the auditor's report.[5]

Opinion No. 19 did not specify a single definition or concept of funds to be used in preparing the funds statement or a required format for the statement. Companies were allowed considerable flexibility in the reporting of funds flow information. In late 1987, the FASB issued Statement No. 95, which superseded APB Opinion No. 19. Instead of allowing various definitions of funds, such as cash or working capital, and a variety of formats, the FASB called for a statement of cash flows to replace the more general statement of changes in financial position. In addition, the FASB specified a format that highlights cash flows from operating, investing, and financing activities.[6] A major reason for the FASB's actions was the desire to help investors and creditors better predict future cash flows.

PURPOSES OF A STATEMENT OF CASH FLOWS

One of the questions asked most often about a company is where the cash came from and where it went. Cash is the lifeblood of a business organization. Knowing the major sources and uses of cash is extremely important. It is not surprising, therefore, that the major purpose of a statement of cash flows is to provide information about the cash receipts and cash payments of an entity for a period of time.

3. Perry Mason, *Accounting Research Study No. 2,* "Cash Flow Analysis and the Funds Statement" (New York: American Institute of Certified Public Accountants, 1961).

4. *Opinions of the Accounting Principles Board, No. 3,* "The Statement of Source and Application of Funds" (New York: American Institute of Certified Public Accountants, 1963).

5. *Opinions of the Accounting Principles Board, No. 19,* "Reporting Changes in Financial Position" (New York: American Institute of Certified Public Accountants, 1971).

6. *Statement of Financial Accounting Standards No. 95,* "Statement of Cash Flows" (Stamford: Financial Accounting Standards Board, November 1987).

Cash flow information should help investors and creditors assess an entity's ability to generate positive future net cash flows and to meet its current and long-term obligations, including possible future dividend payments. In addition, the statement of cash flows should help users assess the reasons for the differences between net income and the related cash receipts and payments. Finally, the statement of cash flows should help to determine the effects of both cash and noncash investing and financing transactions on an entity's financial position.[7]

To achieve these objectives, the FASB concluded that a statement of cash flows should report the cash effects of an entity's operations, its investing transactions, and its financial transactions. Additional disclosures should be made of any significant investing or financing transactions that affect an enterprise's financial position but do not directly affect cash flows during the period. Finally, a reconciliation of accrual net income and net cash flow from operating activities also should be provided.

The practical value of the cash flow statement becomes more apparent when one attempts to answer specific questions relative to a company's financial strength and profitability. And the answers to many of these questions are not readily available by analyzing just an income statement or balance sheet. For example, is there adequate cash to meet current and future debt obligations? Why are dividend payments not larger? How will the plant expansion be financed? Does the company have the financial strength for the planned acquisition? Can the company declare a dividend when it is reporting a net loss for the year?

The information provided by the cash flow statement helps answer these and other similar questions. It helps managers, investors, creditors and others predict such important variables as bankruptcy, loan defaults, and stock prices. The information also helps evaluate relative performance; for example, how a company is doing this period versus past periods or in relation to other companies in an industry. In a later section of the chapter, we describe the meaning of different cash flow patterns and selected cash flow ratios.

Cash Equivalents

A statement of cash flows explains the change during the period in cash and **cash equivalents**—short-term, highly liquid investments that can be converted easily into cash. To qualify as a cash equivalent, an item must be:[8]

1. Readily convertible to cash, and
2. So near its maturity that there is insignificant risk of changes in value due to changes in interest rates.

Generally, only investments with original maturities of three months or less qualify as cash equivalents. **Original maturity** in this case is determined from the date an investment was acquired by the reporting entity, which may not coincide with the date of issuance of the security. For example, both a three-month U.S. Treasury bill and a three-year Treasury note purchased three months prior to maturity qualify as cash equivalents. However, if the Treasury note were purchased three years ago, it would not qualify as a cash equivalent during the last three months prior to its maturity.[9] In addition to U.S. Treasury obligations, cash equivalents can include such items as money market funds and commercial paper. Investments in marketable *equity* securities (common and preferred stock) normally would not be classified as cash equivalents, because such securities have no definite maturity date and are subject to fluctuations in value.

7. *Ibid.*, par. 5.
8. *Ibid.*, par. 8.
9. *Ibid.*

Not all investments qualifying as cash equivalents need be reported as such. Management is required to establish a policy concerning which short-term, highly liquid investments are to be treated as cash equivalents. Once a policy is established, management should disclose which items are being treated as cash equivalents in presenting its cash flow statement. Any change in the established policy would be considered a change in accounting principle.

Major Classifications of Cash Flows

The funds statement required by APB Opinion No. 19 classified the flow of resources simply as sources and uses of funds. In the statement of cash flows, cash receipts and payments are classified according to three main categories: **operating activities, investing activities,** and **financing activities.** Exhibit 6—1 summarizes the major types of cash receipts and cash payments included in each category. Note that these are general classifications. Specific items might be classified differently for certain types of businesses.[10] Also note that the cash flows from purchases, sales, and maturities of certain securities are to be treated differently according to their classification. Thus, cash flows associated with securities that are intended to be "held-to-maturity" and those that are "available-for-sale" are to be classified as cash flows from investing activities. Cash flows involving "trading" securities, on the other hand, are to be classified as operating activities.[11]

Operating Activities. **Operating activities** include those transactions and events that normally enter into the determination of operating income. Cash receipts from selling goods or from providing services would be the major cash inflow for most businesses. Other cash receipts might come from interest, dividends, and similar items. Major cash outflows would include payments to purchase inventory and to pay wages, taxes, interest, utilities, rent, and similar expenses. The net amount of cash provided or used by operating activities is a key figure that should be highlighted on a statement of cash flows.

While cash inflows from interest or dividends logically might be classified as investing or financing activities, the FASB decided to classify them as operating activities, which conforms to their presentation on the income statement.

Investing Activities. Transactions and events involving the purchase and sale of securities (excluding cash equivalents), land, buildings, equipment, and other assets not generally held for resale, and the making and collecting of loans are classified as **investing activities.** These activities occur regularly and result in cash receipts and payments. They are not classified as operating activities, since they relate only indirectly to the central, ongoing operation of an entity, which is usually the sale of goods or services.

Financing Activities. **Financing activities** include transactions and events whereby cash is obtained from or repaid to owners (equity financing) and creditors (debt financing). For

10. With the issuance of Statement No. 102, the FASB has specifically modified Statement No. 95 with respect to the classification of certain securities or debt instruments held in a trading portfolio of a financial institution. Thus, the cash receipts or cash payments from acquisitions or sales of securities or other assets that are acquired specifically for resale and that are carried at market values in trading accounts should be classified as operating cash flows instead of investing cash flows. A similar reclassification should be made for loans that are acquired specifically for resale and that are carried at market or lower-of-cost-or-market values. See *Statement of Financial Accounting Standards No. 102,* "Statement of Cash Flows—Exemption of Certain Enterprises and Classification of Cash Flows From Certain Securities Acquired for Resale," (Norwalk: Financial Accounting Standards Board, February 1989), pars. 8-9.

11. FASB Statement No. 115 requires a classification of debt and equity securities into one of three categories: held-to-maturity, available-for-sale, or trading. (See *Statement of Financial Accounting Standards No. 115,* "Accounting for Certain Investments in Debt and Equity Securities," Financial Accounting Standards Board, May 1993.) The treatment of investments, including these securities, is covered in a later chapter in the book.

Exhibit 6—1
Major Classifications of Cash Flows

Operating Activities
Cash receipts from:
- Sale of goods or services
- Sale of trading securities
- Interest revenue
- Dividend revenue

Cash payments to:
- Suppliers for inventory purchases
- Employees for services
- Governments for taxes
- Lenders for interest expense
- Others for other expenses (e.g., utilities, rent)
- Purchase trading securities

Investing Activities
Cash receipts from:
- Sale of plant assets
- Sale of a business segment
- Sale of securities classified as either available-for-sale or held-to-maturity
- Collection of principal on loans made to other entities

Cash payments to:
- Purchase plant assets
- Purchase securities classified as either available-for-sale or held-to-maturity
- Make loans to other entities

Financing Activities
Cash receipts from:
- Issuance of own stock
- Borrowing (e.g., bonds, notes, mortgages)

Cash payments to:
- Stockholders as dividends
- Repay principal amounts borrowed
- Repurchase an entity's own stock (treasury stock)

example, the cash proceeds from issuing capital stock or bonds would be classified under financing activities. Similarly, payments to reacquire stock (treasury stock) or to retire bonds and the payment of dividends are considered financing activities.

Noncash Investing and Financing Activities

Some investing and financing activities affect an entity's financial position but not the entity's cash flows during the period. For example, equipment may be purchased with a note payable, or land may be acquired by issuing stock. Such **noncash investing and financing activities** were previously reported in a funds statement under the "all-financial-resources concept" as both a source and a use of funds. Now, according to FASB Statement No. 95, significant noncash investing and financing activities should be disclosed separately, either in the notes to the financial statements or in an accompanying schedule, not in the statement itself.[12] The statement of cash flows reports only operating, investing, and financing activities involving cash.

12. *FASB Statement No. 95*, par. 32.

REPORTING CASH FLOWS

Exhibit 6—2 illustrates the general format, with details and amounts omitted, for a statement of cash flows. The statement should report the net cash provided by, or used in, operating, investing, and financing activities and the net effect of total cash flows on cash and cash equivalents during the period. While the exact format of the statement is not specified by the FASB, the information is to be presented in a manner that reconciles beginning and ending cash and cash equivalent amounts.[13]

The preparation of the investing and financing activities sections of the statement of cash flows is straightforward. The operating activities section, however, is more complex, because it requires analysis of operating accounts to convert them from an accrual to a cash basis. In Chapter 4, the wide use of the accrual concept in recognizing revenues and expenses was discussed. Net income as defined by GAAP is an accrual concept. The statement of cash flows, on the other hand, is designed to report the cash effects of these same revenue and expense items.

There are two methods that may be used in calculating and reporting the amount of net cash flow from operating activities: the indirect method and the direct method. The most popular method used in reported financial statements is the indirect method. A survey of 600 companies providing a statement of cash flows for 1992 revealed that 585 of the companies used the indirect method.[14]

The **indirect method** begins with net income as reported on the income statement and adjusts this accrual amount for any items that do not affect cash flows. The adjustments are of three basic types: (1) revenues and expenses that do not involve cash inflows or outflows, e.g., cost allocations such as depreciation and amortization, (2) gains and losses on events reported in other sections of the statement of cash flows, and (3) conversions of current operating assets and liabilities from the accrual to the cash basis. The operating activities section of the statement of cash flows for Sears Roebuck & Company in Exhibit 6—3 illustrates the indirect method of reporting net cash flow from operations. Microsoft Corporation's statement of cash flows in Appendix A provides another illustration of the indirect method.

The **direct method** does not begin with reported net income, but instead analyzes the cash effects of operating activities and reports the total cash paid or received for each major type of activity. Because recorded accounting information normally reflects the accrual basis, a conversion of accounts, such as Sales, from the accrual basis to a cash basis is required. The direct method of reporting net cash flow from operating activities is illustrated by the partial statement of cash flows for American Building Maintenance Industries, Inc. in Exhibit 6—4.

Exhibit 6—2
General Format for a Statement of Cash Flows

Cash provided by (or used in):	
Operating activities	$XXX
Investing activities	XXX
Financing activities	XXX
Net increase (decrease) in cash and cash equivalents	$XXX
Cash and cash equivalents at beginning of year	XXX
Cash and cash equivalents at end of year	$XXX

13. Additional disclosures are required in reconciling the change in cash and cash equivalents for a company that has foreign currency transactions. Such entities must report the equivalent of foreign currency cash flows and should show the effect of any exchange rate fluctuations on the cash balances as a separate item in the cash flow statement. The complexities involved in reporting these foreign currency cash flows are considered beyond the scope of this text.

14. *Accounting Trends & Techniques*—1993 (New York: American Institute of Certified Public Accountants, 1993), p. 392.

■ **Exhibit 6—3**
Sears Roebuck & Company — Indirect Method of Reporting Cash Flow From Operating Activities

SEARS ROEBUCK & COMPANY
CONSOLIDATED STATEMENT OF CASH FLOWS

	Year ended December 31		
In millions of dollars	1992	1991	1990
Cash flow from operating activities:			
Net income (loss)	$(3,932.3)	$1,278.9	$ 902.2
Adjustments to reconcile net income (loss) to net cash provided by operating activities:			
Depreciation, amortization, and other noncash items	934.9	892.1	786.8
Cumulative effect of accounting changes	2,936.6	—	—
Restructuring charges	3,108.4	—	264.4
Provisions for uncollectible accounts	912.6	850.5	623.7
Gains on sales of property and investments	(248.8)	(218.6)	(393.3)
Increase in insurance reserves	3,891.6	4,414.5	4,903.0
Change in deferred taxes	(2,889.8)	(424.4)	(783.6)
Decrease (increase) in retail customer receivables	(1,325.4)	846.8	(284.7)
Decrease (increase) in merchandise inventories	357.4	(386.4)	278.1
Increase in other operating assets	(928.4)	(231.1)	(323.7)
Increase in other operating liabilities	808.6	742.8	221.6
Net cash provided by operating activities	3,625.4	7,765.1	6,194.5

■ **Exhibit 6—4**
American Building Maintenance Industries, Inc.—Direct Method of Reporting Cash Flow From Operating Activities

AMERICAN BUILDING MAINTENANCE INDUSTRIES, INC.
CONSOLIDATED STATEMENTS OF CASH FLOWS

	Year ended October 31		
	1992	1991	1990
In thousands of dollars			
Cash flows from operating activities:			
Cash received from customers	$ 745,223	$ 728,034	$ 668,986
Other operating cash receipts	693	457	901
Interest received	637	353	369
Cash paid to suppliers and employees	(730,708)	(706,619)	(652,785)
Interest paid	(2,060)	(3,106)	(2,634)
Income taxes paid	(8,853)	(13,077)	(11,796)
Net cash provided by operating activities	4,932	6,042	3,041

Both methods produce identical results—that is, the same amount of net cash flow provided by (or used in) operations. The indirect method is favored and used by most companies, because it is relatively easy to apply and it reconciles the difference between net income and the net cash flow provided by operations. The direct method is favored by many users of financial statements, because it reports directly the sources of cash inflows and outflows without the potentially confusing adjustments to net income. The FASB considered the arguments for both methods, and although the Board favored the clarity of the direct method, they finally permitted either method to be used.[15]

Because the indirect method is so widely used, it will be explained first, and the preparation of a statement of cash flows using the indirect method will be illustrated. The acceptable alternative —the direct method—will then be explained, and the reporting differences between the two methods will be highlighted.

The Indirect Method of Reporting Cash Flow From Operations

The adjustments to net income required to compute cash flow from operations using the indirect method can be determined by careful analysis of the income statement and balance sheet. The three basic types of adjustments identified previously (noncash items, gains and losses, and current operating accounts) are explained in the following sections. It is important to recognize that these adjustments are not entered in the accounting records. They are simply additions to, and subtractions from, net income on the statement of cash flows in order to convert from an accrual to a cash basis.

Adjustments for Noncash Income Statement Items. Some items reported in the income statement do not affect cash, although they are properly recognized as revenues or expenses. These items must be removed from net income to determine the cash flow from operations. Examples of **noncash items** include depreciation on buildings and equipment, amortization of intangible assets such as goodwill, and revenues realized in the form of noncash assets. The most common adjustment to net income is for depreciation. Because the journal entry to record periodic depreciation involves an expense account and a contra asset account (Accumulated Depreciation), but no cash, depreciation expense is a noncash item and must be added to reported net income to compute cash flows from operating activities.

This adjustment is sometimes misinterpreted by financial statement users as indicating that depreciation expense is an important source of cash inflows. Only revenue produces cash inflows from operating activities. The depreciation adjustment recognizes that reported net income includes expenses that do not require cash outflows, and these types of expenses must be eliminated (added back) to determine net cash flow from operations.

Adjustments for Gains and Losses From Sale of Assets. The net income amount used as a starting point with the indirect method also may include gains or losses from the sale of assets, such as investments in securities or property, plant, and equipment. The sale of assets, other than inventory, is an incidental or peripheral activity and not part of the central operations of a business. Such transactions are therefore properly classified as investing activities rather than operating activities. The proceeds from the sale of an asset include any gain or loss; thus, if the cash inflows are reported in the investing section and no adjustment is made to net income in the operating section, a double counting of the gain or loss will occur. This is corrected by deducting the gain or adding the loss to net income in computing operating cash flow.

To illustrate, assume that Halifax Corporation sold for $75,000 land that cost $50,000. This land had been held for possible expansion, but was no longer needed. The entry for the sale would be:

	Debit	Credit
Cash	75,000	
Land		50,000
Gain on Sale of Land		25,000

15. *Statement of Financial Accounting Standards No. 95* pars. 27-28.

Reporting Cash Flows in the United Kingdom

The first financial reporting standard issued by the Accounting Standards Board (ASB) in the United Kingdom deals with cash flow statements. Then chairman, David Tweedie, stated, "recent experience has demonstrated all too clearly that adequate information on cash is an essential element of a company's financial statements."

The UK standard is very similar to the FASB No. 95 standard, but there are some interesting differences. The UK standard requires information to be presented under the headings of "operating activities," "returns on investments and servicing of finance," "taxation," "investing activities," and "financing." The following is an illustrative example of a cash flow statement that complies with the UK Financial Reporting Standard 1 (FRS 1).*

XYZ Limited: Cash Flow Statement for the year ended 31 March 1996

Net cash inflow from operating activities		6,889
Returns on investments and servicing of finance		
Interest received	3,011	
Interest paid	(12)	
Dividends	(2,417)	
Net cash inflow from returns on investments and servicing of finance		582
Taxation		
Corporation tax paid (including advance corporation tax)	(2,922)	
Tax paid		(2,922)
Investing activities		
Payments to acquire intangible assets	(71)	
Payments to acquire fixed assets	(1,496)	
Receipts from sales of fixed assets	42	
Net cash outflow from Investing activities		(1,525)
Net cash inflow before financing		3,024
Financing		
Issue of ordinary share capital	211	
Repurchase of debenture loan	(149)	
Expenses paid in connection with share issues	(5)	
Net cash inflow from financing		57
Increase in cash and cash equivalents		3,081

Questions

1. What are the main similarities and differences in format between FASB No. 95 and FRS 1?
2. What advantages do you see, if any, to the format required by the UK standard for cash flow statements?

*Source:
Accounting Standards Board, Financial Reporting Standard No. 1, "Cash Flow Statements," September 1991. Reprinted in *Accountancy,* November 1991, pp. 129-140. The illustration is adapted from Illustrative Example 1 on page 134.

Since the $25,000 gain was included in net income, that amount would be subtracted in deriving cash flows from operating activities using the indirect method. The entire $75,000 is reported on the statement of cash flows under investing activities as cash received from the sale of land.

Adjustments for Changes in Current Operating Accounts. Net income under generally accepted accounting principles is reported on the accrual basis. This means that all revenues, expenses, current operating assets, and current operating liabilities are also recorded on an accrual basis. To convert net income from an accrual to a cash basis, adjustments must be made to net income for the increases or decreases in the balances of the current operating assets and liabilities.

Changes in Current Operating Asset Accounts. In general, increases in current operating assets are subtracted from net income and decreases in current operating assets are added to net income to adjust net income to net cash flow from operations. To illustrate, assume the ending balance in Accounts Receivable was $20,000 more than the beginning balance. This indicates that the amount of cash collected during the period was $20,000 less than the sales revenue reported in the income statement on an accrual basis. Thus, the $20,000 increase in accounts receivable would be subtracted from net income to reflect the cash received for the period on the cash flow statement. If a receivable balance decreases, the opposite would be true; the decrease would be added to net income because more cash was collected than is reflected in the revenue reported in the income statement.[16]

As with receivables, an increase in inventory is subtracted from net income, because more cash was used for purchases than is reflected in cost of goods sold on the income statement. A decrease in inventory is added to net income, because less cash was used to acquire goods than is reflected in the income statement.

Adjustments also must be made for changes in prepaid asset accounts. An increase in a prepaid asset, such as Prepaid Insurance, is subtracted from net income to reflect the amount of cash paid for insurance. A decrease in a prepaid account is added to net income.

The changes in most current asset accounts affect operating income and require adjustment as described above. As noted earlier, purchases and sales of trading securities also affect operating activities. Purchases and sales of other securities classified as either available-for-sale or held-to-maturity are considered investing activities. Those short-term investments that qualify as cash equivalents would be included with cash.

Changes in Current Operating Liability Accounts. Adjustments to reflect changes in current operating liabilities are just the opposite of the adjustments for changes in current operating assets. Increases in current operating liabilities are added to net income, and decreases in current operating liabilities are subtracted from net income to convert accrual net income to the cash basis. To illustrate, an increase in accounts payable means less cash was used than the amount of purchases or cost of goods sold recorded on an accrual basis. Thus, an increase in accounts payable is added to net income in deriving cash flow from operations. A decrease in accounts payable is deducted from net income, because more cash was paid than is reflected in accrual net income.

Similar adjustments for other current payables that affect income would be required. For example, the amount of wages expense, interest expense, and taxes expense reported on the income statement would have to be adjusted for increases and decreases in related payable balances to report the net cash flow provided by (used in) operating activities. Adjustments for increases or decreases in other current payables that do not affect income (e.g., dividends payable) would also have to be made. These adjustments would be reflected in the investing and financing activities sections of the cash flow statement rather than in the operating section.

Adjustments also must be made for changes in unearned revenue accounts, such as Advances From Customers or Unearned Rent Revenue. An increase in an unearned revenue account is added to net income, while a decrease is subtracted to adjust the revenue reported on the income statement to a cash basis.

Exhibit 6—5 summarizes the procedures for determining net cash flow from operating activities using the indirect method.

Preparing a Statement of Cash Flows

Four steps are generally required in preparing a statement of cash flows:

1. *Determine the change in cash* (including cash equivalents). This is simply the difference between beginning and ending cash balances for the period being analyzed. The change in cash is the "target figure"—the amount that will be explained by the statement of cash flows.

16. In this chapter, unless otherwise noted, it will be assumed that all accounts receivable amounts (as well as accounts payable amounts) are related to operations. Nontrade receivables and payables would be reported as investing and financing activities.

■ Exhibit 6—5
Cash Flows From Operating Activities—Indirect Method

Net income reported on the income statement		$XXX
Adjustments for noncash items:		
+ Depreciation	$XXX	
+ Amortization of intangible assets	XXX	
+/– Other noncash items included in net income	XXX	XXX
Adjustments for gains and losses:		
– Gains on sales of assets	$XXX	
+ Losses on sales of assets	XXX	XXX
Adjustments for changes in current operating accounts:		
– Increases in current operating asset accounts (except cash and cash equivalents)	$XXX	
+ Decreases in current operating asset accounts (except cash and cash equivalents)	XXX	
+ Increases in current operating liability accounts	XXX	
– Decreases in current operating liability accounts	XXX	XXX
Net cash provided by (used in) operating activities		$XXX

2. *Determine the net cash provided by (used in) operating activities.* This step requires analysis of comparative balance sheet amounts, income statement data, and specific transactions that relate to company operations.
3. *Determine the net cash provided by (used in) investing and financing activities.* This step requires analysis of the cash flow impact of all accounts and transactions relating to investing and financing activities.
4. *Prepare a formal statement of cash flows,* classified according to operating, investing, and financing activities. Note that the amount determined in Step 1 should equal the total net increase (decrease) in cash reported on the statement of cash flows and will, therefore, reconcile the beginning and ending cash balances for the period. Any significant noncash investing or financing transactions should be reported separately, not on the statement of cash flows.

Illustration—Indirect Method

To illustrate the process of analyzing accounts and preparing a statement of cash flows, a simple example will be considered. The balance sheets, income statement, and additional information for the Taylor Company provide the necessary data for the illustration. To emphasize the nature of the account analysis required in preparing a statement of cash flows, it is assumed that no other information is available. In practice, however, the data for preparing a cash flow statement can be taken directly from the accounting records.

Taylor Company
Comparative Balance Sheet
December 31, 1996 and 1995

	1996	**1995**
Assets		
Cash and cash equivalents	$ 82,000	$ 40,000
Accounts receivable	180,000	150,000
Inventory	170,000	200,000
Equipment	200,000	140,000
Accumulated depreciation	(72,000)	(60,000)
Total assets	$560,000	$470,000

	1996	1995
Liabilities and Stockholders' Equity		
Accounts payable	$100,000	$ 80,000
Long-term notes payable	100,000	50,000
Common stock	250,000	250,000
Retained earnings	110,000	90,000
Total liabilities and stockholders' equity	$560,000	$470,000

Taylor Company
Income Statement
For the Year Ended December 31, 1996

Sales revenue		$345,000
Cost of goods sold		120,000
Gross margin		$225,000
Expenses:		
Selling and general expenses	$58,000	
Depreciation	40,000	
Interest expense	2,000	100,000
Operating income		$125,000
Gain from sale of equipment		5,000
Income before income taxes		$130,000
Income tax expense		30,000
Net income		$100,000

Additional information:

1. Equipment costing $30,000, with a book value of $2,000, was sold for $7,000 during the year.
2. Retained Earnings was affected only by net income and cash dividends paid during the year.

Determining the change in cash and cash equivalents[17] is the first step in preparing a statement of cash flows. For Taylor Company, the cash balance has increased $42,000.

Since the primary purpose of the statement is to identify the cash receipts and payments for the period, and thus explain the change in the cash balance, the statement can be prepared by analyzing all noncash balance sheet accounts to determine what operating, investing, and financing transactions took place and what effect they had on cash flow.

To assist in the analysis of accounts, it is often helpful to use T-accounts, especially for certain accounts such as Retained Earnings, where the net change in the balance does not clearly show the total picture of the inflows and outflows of cash. To illustrate, the balance sheet shows that the December 31, 1995, balance in Retained Earnings for the Taylor Company was $90,000. It has increased $20,000 during 1996 to $110,000. Since the reported net income was $100,000 for 1996, there must have been reductions in Retained Earnings totaling $80,000. An analysis of the retained earnings account indicates a reduction of $80,000 for dividends.

Retained Earnings

Dividends	80,000	Beginning balance	90,000
		Net income	100,000
		Ending balance	110,000

17. Throughout the remainder of the chapter, the term "cash" includes cash equivalents where appropriate.

Based on this analysis, the $100,000 of net income, prior to any adjustments, would be shown as an operating source of cash and the $80,000 of dividends as a use of cash for financing activities. These items would appear on a partially completed cash flow statement as shown below:

Cash flows from operating activities:	
Net income	$100,000
Cash flows from financing activities:	
Payment of dividends	$ (80,000)

Continuing the example, Taylor Company's net income of $100,000 must be adjusted for any noncash items and for any gains or losses. The entry to record depreciation has no effect on cash, so the depreciation expense for the period must be added to net income to arrive at cash provided by (used in) operations.

The amount of depreciation expense for the period for Taylor Company can be determined from the income statement. If limited information were available (e.g., if depreciation were included with other operating expenses in the income statement), an analysis of Accumulated Depreciation and the related equipment account would be necessary. The following T-accounts facilitate the analysis.

Equipment

Beginning balance	140,000	Sale of equipment	30,000
Purchase of equipment	90,000		
Ending balance	200,000		

Accumulated Depreciation

Sale of equipment	28,000	Beginning balance	60,000
		Depreciation expense	40,000
		Ending balance	72,000

As illustrated, the net change in the equipment account is $60,000. Since $30,000 of equipment was sold, $90,000 of equipment must have been purchased, and this should be reflected on the cash flow statement as an investing activity. Similarly, the net change in Accumulated Depreciation is $12,000. The account was decreased by $28,000 due to the sale of equipment. The $40,000 of depreciation expense, a noncash item, should be added to net income as an adjustment to derive cash flow from operations.

In addition to adjustments for noncash items, net income must also be adjusted for gains and losses reported in the income statement. For Taylor Company, the $5,000 gain from the sale of equipment (selling price of $7,000 less book value of $2,000) must be subtracted from net income. The proceeds from the sale of equipment, $7,000 in this illustration, provide the cash, and this amount should be included in the cash flow statement as part of cash flows from investing activities. Because the $5,000 gain on the sale is included in net income, it must be subtracted from net income to avoid counting the gain twice.

The adjustments for Taylor Company for depreciation, to eliminate the gain on sale of equipment, and to record the increase and decrease in cash from the sale and purchase of equipment are illustrated in the developing statement of cash flows as follows:

Cash flows from operating activities:	
Net income	$100,000
Adjustments:	
Depreciation expense	40,000
Gain on sale of equipment	(5,000)
Cash flows from investing activities:	
Sale of equipment	$ 7,000
Purchase of equipment	(90,000)
Cash flows from financing activities:	
Payment of dividends	$ (80,000)

In the Taylor Company example, the amount of net income adjusted for items not requiring cash is $135,000 ($100,000 net income + $40,000 depreciation – $5,000 gain). When preparing a cash flow statement, this amount must be further adjusted to reflect net income measured on a cash basis. As discussed previously in the chapter, with the indirect method, changes in current operating accounts are recognized as adjustments to accrual net income in deriving net cash flow from operations.

T-accounts for the current operating asset and liability accounts of Taylor Company are presented below:

Accounts Receivable

Beginning balance	150,000		
Net increase	30,000		
Ending balance	180,000		

Inventory

Beginning balance	200,000	Net decrease	30,000
Ending balance	170,000		

Accounts Payable

		Beginning balance	80,000
		Net increase	20,000
		Ending balance	100,000

The $30,000 increase in receivables is deducted from net income, since cash receipts for goods and services sold were less than the revenue recognized in arriving at accrual net income. The $30,000 decrease in inventory is added to net income, since purchases were less than the charge made against revenue for cost of sales in arriving at net income. The $20,000 increase in accounts payable requires an addition to net income, since the cash disbursements for goods and services purchased were less than the charges made for these items in arriving at net income. These adjustments would result in the following presentation of cash flows from operating activities for Taylor Company:

Cash flows from operating activities:		
Net income	$100,000	
Adjustments:		
Depreciation expense	40,000	
Gain on sale of equipment	(5,000)	
Increase in accounts receivable	(30,000)	
Decrease in inventory	30,000	
Increase in accounts payable	20,000	
Net cash provided by operating activities		$155,000

At this point, all noncash accounts have been analyzed except Long-Term Notes Payable and Common Stock. In the Taylor Company example, there is no change in the common stock account, but there is an increase of $50,000 in the long-term notes payable account. Unless there is contrary information, it is reasonable to assume that this increase resulted from additional borrowing, a financing activity. Thus, the complete statement of cash flows, using the indirect method for operating activities, would appear as follows.

Taylor Company
Statement of Cash Flows (Indirect Method)
For the Year Ended December 31, 1996

Cash flows from operating activities:		
Net income	$100,000	
Adjustments:		
Depreciation expense	40,000	
Gain on sale of equipment	(5,000)	
Increase in accounts receivable	(30,000)	
Decrease in inventory	30,000	
Increase in accounts payable	20,000	
Net cash provided by operating activities		$155,000
Cash flows from investing activities:		
Sale of equipment	$ 7,000	
Purchase of equipment	(90,000)	
Net cash used in investing activities		(83,000)
Cash flows from financing activities:		
Payment of dividends	$ (80,000)	
Increase in long-term notes payable	50,000	
Net cash used in financing activities		(30,000)
Net increase in cash and cash equivalents		$ 42,000
Cash and cash equivalents at beginning of year		40,000
Cash and cash equivalents at end of year		$ 82,000

Supplemental Disclosure:

Cash payments for:	
Interest	$ 2,000
Income taxes	30,000

The completed statement highlights the major categories of inflows and outflows of cash. Taylor Company generated $155,000 from its operations. It used $83,000 for investments and another $30,000 for financing activities. The remaining $42,000 represents an increase in the cash balance and is the amount needed to reconcile the beginning-of-year and end-of-year cash and cash equivalent balances.

FASB Statement No. 95 requires disclosure of the amounts paid for interest expense and income taxes during the year. This supplemental disclosure can be presented with the statement of cash flows, as illustrated for Taylor Company, or in the notes to the financial statements. In the Taylor example, the amounts paid for interest and taxes are taken directly from the income statement. If the balance sheet had reported any beginning or ending payable balances for interest or taxes, the accrual-basis income statement amounts would have to be converted to a cash basis.

The Direct Method of Reporting Cash Flow From Operations

Unlike the indirect method, the direct method of determining cash flow from operations does not begin with net income, but reports *directly* the total cash inflows and outflows for each major category of operating activities. The inflows usually include cash receipts from (1) the sale of goods or services and (2) some peripheral activities, such as dividend and interest revenue. The outflows usually include cash payments made to (1) suppliers for inventory purchases, (2) employees for services, (3) governmental bodies for taxes, (4) lenders for interest expense, and (5) service providers for such items as rent and utilities. To determine these amounts, each cash transaction could be analyzed separately to derive the total cash receipts and payments for each category. Usually, however, summarized data provided in the financial statements can be analyzed to convert accrual-basis revenues and expenses to cash receipts and payments. No adjustment for noncash items, such as depreciation, is required under the direct method, since only cash events are reported.

To illustrate the analytical process that is used in preparing a cash flow statement with the direct method, consider sales revenue as an example. The amount of sales reported on the income statement must be adjusted for changes in accounts receivable balances to determine the cash collected during the period. The beginning receivables balance represents sales from the previous period. These receivables are assumed to have been collected in cash during the current period. The ending receivables represent sales of the current period that will be collected in a future period. Thus, to determine the cash collected from customers during the current period, the beginning receivables must be added to, and the ending receivables subtracted from, the accrual sales figure. If we assume reported sales of $500,000 and beginning and ending accounts receivable balances of $125,000 and $110,000 respectively, the computation would be:

Sales (reported on income statement)	$500,000
+ Beginning accounts receivable	125,000
– Ending accounts receivable	(110,000)
= Cash receipts from customers	$515,000

Rather than using the beginning and ending receivable balances, it is equally acceptable, and sometimes easier, to make the conversion using the increase or decrease in the accounts receivable balance. This method was illustrated when converting current operating assets and liabilities under the indirect method. Thus, a decrease in the accounts receivable balance would be added to the reported sales amount and an increase in receivables would be deducted. In the above example, accounts receivable decreased by $15,000 during the year ($125,000 – $110,000). The cash receipts from customers would be $515,000 ($500,000 + $15,000), the same amount derived by using beginning and ending balances.

An assumption made in the above example (and throughout this chapter) is that all accounts receivable are collectible. The complications associated with uncollectible accounts, including the estimated expense for bad debts, will be addressed in Chapter 8, which covers receivables.

The conversion process applicable to sales also is required for other revenues and their related receivable balances. Revenues collected in advance require further explanation. For example, when rent revenue is collected in advance, the cash is received before it is earned. For these types of revenue items, the ending unearned rent balance is added to and the beginning unearned rent balance is subtracted from the reported rent revenue amount to compute the cash received for rent during the period.

A similar process and rationale are applicable for converting expenses reported on an accrual basis to the amount of cash paid during the period. To illustrate, if $150,000 of wages expense is reported on the income statement and the beginning and ending wages payable amounts are $40,000 and $45,000 respectively, the amount of cash paid for wages would be as follows:

Wages expense (reported on income statement)	$150,000
+ Beginning wages payable	40,000
− Ending wages payable	(45,000)
= Cash paid for wages during the period	$145,000

The conversion process would be the same for all expenses that are incurred prior to being paid, e.g., utilities, interest, property taxes, and income taxes. Prepaid expenses, however, are paid and recorded as assets prior to becoming an expense. An example would be prepaid insurance. For these types of expenses, the following calculation is required. Assume that insurance expense reported for the current period is $4,000 and the beginning and ending balances in Prepaid Insurance are $1,000 and $500, respectively. The amount of cash paid for insurance would be:

Insurance expense (reported on income statement)	$4,000
+ Ending prepaid insurance	500
− Beginning prepaid insurance	(1,000)
= Cash paid for insurance	$3,500

The amount of cash paid for inventory also must be calculated. If a company is using a periodic inventory system, the amount of purchases can be determined directly from the purchases accounts. That amount would then be adjusted by adding the beginning accounts payable balance and subtracting the ending accounts payable balance to determine the cash paid for inventory. If a perpetual inventory system is used, the cost of goods sold is known, but the amount of purchases would have to be calculated by adding the ending inventory and subtracting the beginning inventory amounts. Then, purchases would be adjusted to a cash basis by considering the beginning and ending accounts payable balances. The following calculations, with assumed numbers, illustrate this point:

Cost of goods sold (from perpetual inventory records)	$240,000
+ Ending inventory	43,000
− Beginning inventory	(38,000)
= Purchases	$245,000
+ Beginning accounts payable	27,000
− Ending accounts payable	(30,000)
= Cash paid for inventory	$242,000

Exhibit 6—6 summarizes the adjusting procedures used to convert accrual amounts to the cash basis when using the direct method. The exhibit includes an example of each basic type of revenue and expense adjustment. If a company earns dividend revenue or incurs interest expense, FASB Statement No. 95 requires that those items be reported under operating activities. Dividend revenue is adjusted in the same manner as interest revenue. Interest expense is converted using the approach illustrated for wages expense.

Illustration—Direct Method

To illustrate the preparation of the operating activities section of a statement of cash flows prepared using the direct method, an analysis will be made of the Taylor Company information presented on pages 202 and 203.

■ Exhibit 6—6
Cash Flows From Operating Activities—Direct Method

Accrual Basis	Adjustment Required	= Cash Basis
Net sales	+ Beginning accounts receivable – Ending accounts receivable	= Cash receipts from customers
Other revenues (e.g., rent and interest):		
Rent revenue	+ Ending unearned rent – Beginning unearned rent	= Cash received for rent
Interest revenue	+ Beginning interest receivable – Ending interest receivable	= Cash received for interest
Cost of goods sold	+ Ending inventory – Beginning inventory + Beginning accounts payable – Ending accounts payable	= Cash paid for inventory
Operating expenses (e.g.) insurance and wages; excludes depreciation and other noncash items):		
Insurance expense	+ Ending prepaid insurance – Beginning prepaid insurance	= Cash paid for insurance
Wages expense	+ Beginning wages payable – Ending wages payable	= Cash paid for wages
Income tax expense	+ Beginning income taxes payable – Ending income taxes payable	= Cash paid for income taxes
		Net cash provided by (used in) operating activities

To determine the amount of cash collected from customers for Taylor Company, the $345,000 of sales revenue reported on the income statement must be converted to a cash basis. Following the analytical approach described above, the computation is as follows:

Sales revenue	$345,000
+ Beginning accounts receivable	150,000
– Ending accounts receivable	(180,000)
= Cash receipts from customers	$315,000

Similar adjustments must be made to determine the cash paid for inventory purchases.

Cost of goods sold	$120,000
+ Ending inventory	170,000
– Beginning inventory	(200,000)
= Goods purchased during year	$ 90,000
+ Beginning accounts payable	80,000
– Ending accounts payable	(100,000)
= Cash paid for inventory purchases	$ 70,000

For Taylor Company, the $58,000 of operating expenses (excluding depreciation and interest) does not require adjustment, since no related current asset or current liability balances changed during this period. The same is true for Taylor Company's interest expense and income tax expense. Thus, the cash paid for operating expenses was $58,000; for interest, $2,000; for income taxes, $30,000. Note also that no adjustments are needed for noncash items, such as the $40,000 depreciation expense and the $5,000 gain, when using the direct method.

Based on the preceding analysis, the operating activities section of the statement of cash flows for Taylor Company, using the direct method, would be as follows:

Taylor Company
Partial Statement of Cash Flows (Direct Method)
For the Year Ended December 31, 1996

Cash flows from operating activities:		
Cash receipts from customers		$315,000
Cash payments for:		
Inventory	$70,000	
Operating expenses	58,000	
Interest	2,000	
Income taxes	30,000	160,000
Net cash provided by operating activities		$155,000

Note that the amount of cash provided by operations, $155,000, is the same as the amount determined using the indirect method. The investing and financing sections of the statements would be identical. If the direct approach is used, the FASB requires that a schedule be included that reconciles net income to net cash provided by (used in) operations. A schedule to accompany Taylor Company's cash flow statement prepared using the direct method is provided below. If the indirect approach is used, this reconciliation is already part of the statement.

Taylor Company
Schedule Reconciling Net Income to Net Cash
Provided by Operating Activities
For the Year Ended December 31, 1996

Net income		$100,000
Adjustments to reconcile net income to net cash provided by operating activities:		
Depreciation expense	$40,000	
Gain on sale of equipment	(5,000)	
Increase in accounts receivable	(30,000)	
Decrease in inventory	30,000	
Increase in accounts payable	20,000	55,000
Net cash provided by operating activities		$155,000

USING CASH FLOW DATA TO ASSESS FINANCIAL STRENGTH

Various analytical techniques are used to assess a company's financial strength. Key variables are liquidity, profitability, growth potential, and overall risk. Traditionally, analysts have concentrated on the relationships captured in the income statement and the balance sheet. But more and more emphasis is now placed on cash flows and the relationships of data reported on the cash flow statement in conjunction with the income statement and the balance sheet.

Background of FASB Statement No. 95

Although Statement No. 95 has been around only since 1987, cash flow statements have a long history in the United States. In 1863, The Northern Central Railroad issued a summary of its financial transactions that included an outline of its cash receipts and cash disbursements for the year. Later, emphasis shifted away from cash flow and toward a broader definition of "funds." In 1902, United States Steel Corporation produced a report that listed the major causes of the change in "funds" during the year—funds being defined as current assets minus accounts payable. A working capital funds statement—reporting causes of changes in funds defined as current assets minus current liabilities—became increasingly popular after 1920. A funds statement was made mandatory in 1971 by APB Opinion No. 19. The definition of funds was left to the provider, with both a cash emphasis and a working capital emphasis being permissible.

During the early 1980s, the Financial Executives Institute (FEI) encouraged its members to adopt a cash emphasis in their funds statements. In 1980, only 10 percent of the Fortune 500 used a cash focus. By 1985, 70 percent used a cash focus. During this same period, the FASB issued *Statement of Financial Accounting Concepts No. 5,* which suggested that, conceptually, a cash flow statement should be part of a full set of financial statements. In April 1985 the FASB added a cash flow reporting project to its agenda.

The FASB cash flow pronouncement, *Statement of Financial Accounting Standards No. 95,* illustrates that the setting of accounting standards is not a science, but is a "balancing act" with the differing opinions of users and preparers being weighed against one another and the considerations of cost of implementation being weighed against the potential benefits. Since standard setting is a balancing act, not all interested parties will agree on the final outcome. In fact, three of the seven FASB members dissented to the final version of Statement No. 95.

One area of disagreement was in relation to the categorization of interest and dividend cash flows. Three of the Board members felt that interest and dividends paid are a cost of obtaining financing and should both be classified as cash outflows from financing activities. But, in Statement No. 95, dividend payments are included in the financing activities section, while interest payments are classified as cash outflows from operating activities. Similarly, the three Board members felt that interest and dividends received are returns on investments and therefore should be classified as cash inflows from investing activities. Statement No. 95 includes both these items in the operating activities section.

A more significant disagreement related to the permissibility of both the indirect and the direct methods of reporting cash flow from operations. Before the issuance of the Statement, a majority of the outside comments to the Board advocated requiring use of the direct method. Most of these comments were from commercial lenders who indicated that detailed cash flow information by category would help them to better assess a firm's ability to repay borrowing. Those opposed to this direct method requirement, and who instead advocated the permissibility of both methods, were mainly preparers and providers of financial statements. They argued that requiring use of the direct method would impose excessive implementation costs on some firms. They also argued that the indirect method provides more meaningful information because it is more similar to what has been used in the past. The final Statement allows both methods, but does "encourage" use of the direct method.

Statement No. 95 describes major change in financial reporting as "an evolutionary process." Conceptual purity is balanced against feasibility and cost of implementation. While it is likely that the standards of cash flow reporting will be further improved in the future, Statement No. 95 represents a significant incremental improvement over prior practice.

Questions:

1. Interest and dividends paid are both costs of obtaining financing—interest is the cost of obtaining debt financing, and dividends are the cost of obtaining equity financing. Accordingly, some have advocated classifying both interest and dividends paid as cash outflows from financing activities. What arguments can you think of to support classifying interest paid as an operating cash outflow, as required by Statement No. 95?
2. Assume that 10 years have passed since the issuance of Statement No. 95 and that you are a member of the FASB. The Board is reconsidering the issue of whether both the direct and indirect methods should be allowed, or whether use of the direct method should be made mandatory. What evidence would you look at to help you make your decision?

Sources:

James H. Thompson and Thomas E. Buttross, "Return to Cash Flow," *The CPA Journal,* March 1988: pp. 30-40.

Dennis R. Beresford, "The `Balancing Act' in Setting Accounting Standards," *Accounting Horizons,* March 1988: pp. 1-7.

Statement of Financial Accounting Standards No. 95, "Statement of Cash Flows" (1987), pars. 88-90 and 106-121.

One significant use of cash flow data is to provide a sense of the overall capital structure and philosophical direction of management. Companies can acquire cash internally through successful operating and investing performance or externally through debt or equity financing. In the long run, however, a company must generate positive cash flows through operations. Neither lenders nor stockholders will sustain cash needs over time unless a company is successful in generating positive internal cash flows.

It is possible to gain useful insights about a company by analyzing the relationships among cash flows by major category as reported in a cash flow statement. Exhibit 6-7 shows eight different patterns. Patterns 1 and 8 are unusual. Pattern 1 might exist where a firm is experiencing positive cash flows from all three activities and is seeking to significantly increase its cash position for some strategic reason, while at the same time selling some of its long-term assets. Pattern 8 shows negative cash flows from all activities and could only exist, even in the short-term, if a company had existing cash reserves to draw upon. In the long-term, this situation would lead to bankruptcy. Patterns 2-4 show positive operating cash flows that are sufficient by themselves (pattern 2) or are supplemented by investing (pattern 3) or financing (pattern 4) activities to settle debt, pay owners, or expand the business. Patterns 5-7 are not healthy over the long-term since operating cash short-falls have to be covered by selling long-term assets and/or by securing external financing. Reference to Appendix A at the end of the book will reveal that Microsoft's cash pattern is like #4. Microsoft is using its positive operating cash flows, with some help from financing cash flows, to increase its investments (primarily property, plant, and equipment and short-term investments) and bolster its cash balances.

Exhibit 6-7 Analysis of cash flow statement: Patterns

	#1	#2	#3	#4	#5	#6	#7	#8
CF from Operating	+	+	+	+	–	–	–	–
CF from Investing	+	–	+	–	+	–	+	–
CF from Financing	+	–	–	+	+	+	–	–
General Explanation	Company using cash generated from operations and from sale of assets and from financing to build up pile of cash—very liquid company—possibly looking for acquisition	Company using cash-flow generated from operations to buy fixed assets and to pay down debt or pay owners	Company using cash from operations and from sale of fixed assets to pay down debt or pay owners	Company using cash from operations and from borrowing (or from owner investment) to expand	Company's operating cash flow problems covered by sale of fixed assets and by borrowing or shareholder contributions	Company is growing rapidly but shortfalls in cash flow from operations and and from purchase of fixed assets financed by long-term debt or new investment	Company is financing operating cash flow shortages and payment to debt and/or stockholders via sale of fixed assets	Company is using cash reserve to finance operation shortfall and pay long-term creditors and/or investors

Source: Michael T. Dugan, Benton E. Gup, and William D. Samson. "Teaching the Statement of Cash Flows." *Journal of Accounting Education* Vol. 9, 1991, p. 36.

These cash flow patterns stress the importance of operating cash flows. Positive operating cash flows allow a company to pay its bills, its creditors, its shareholders, and to grow and expand. Negative operating cash flows mean a company has to look at other sources of cash, which eventually dry up if operations are not successful.

The data from a cash flow statement also can be used to compute selected ratios that help determine a company's financial strength. If such ratios are compared for the same company over a period of time or with other companies in the same industry, they also can be helpful in evaluating relative performance. Exhibit 6-8 provides several selected ratios.[18] None of these ratios by itself is going to tell the full story of a company's financial strength. But data from the cash flow statement, when analyzed carefully and in relation with other useful data, can help investors, creditors, and others better assess the overall risk and financial strength of a company and its potential for survival and growth in the future.

Exhibit 6-8 Cash Flow Ratios

1. Cash flow adequacy	$\frac{\text{Cash from operations}}{\text{Long-term debt paid + purchases of assets + dividends paid}}$
2. Long-term debt payment	$\frac{\text{Long-term debt payments}}{\text{Cash from operations}}$
3. Dividend payout	$\frac{\text{Dividends}}{\text{Cash from operations}}$
4. Reinvestment	$\frac{\text{Purchase of assets}}{\text{Cash from operations}}$
5. Total debt coverage	$\frac{\text{Total liabilities}}{\text{Cash from operations}}$
6. Depreciation—amortization impact	$\frac{\text{Depreciation + amortization}}{\text{Cash from operations}}$
7. Cash flow to sales	$\frac{\text{Cash from operations}}{\text{Sales}}$
8. Cash flow to net income	$\frac{\text{Cash from operations}}{\text{Income from continuing operations}}$
9. Cash flow return on assets	$\frac{\text{Cash from operations}}{\text{Total assets}}$

COMPREHENSIVE ILLUSTRATION OF STATEMENT OF CASH FLOWS

Examples in the preceding sections involved only a few accounts and were thus relatively simple. Ordinarily, however, more complex circumstances are encountered, and a more systematic approach is required in preparing a statement of cash flows. In the pages that follow, a comprehensive T-account approach for use with the indirect method is described first. The adjustments needed to prepare the operating activities section with the direct method are then discussed. The appendix to this chapter describes and illustrates a work sheet approach to preparing a statement of cash flows with the indirect method.

The illustrations and analysis that follow are based on the comparative balance sheets and combined income and retained earnings statement for Western Resources, Inc., on page 214, and the additional information on page 215.

18. Don E. Giacomino and David E. Mielke. "Cash Flows: Another Approach to Ratio Analysis." *Journal of Accountancy*, March, 1993, p. 57.

Western Resources, Inc.
Statement of Income and Retained Earnings
For the Year Ended December 31, 1996

Sales		$753,800
Cost of goods sold		524,100
Gross margin		$229,700
Expenses:		
Selling and general expenses	$146,400	
Depreciation and amortization expense	25,900	
Interest expense	3,600	175,900
Operating income		$ 53,800
Gain on sale of long-term investment		6,500
Income before income taxes		$ 60,300
Income tax expense		24,000
Net income		$ 36,300
Retained earnings, December 31, 1995		234,300
		$270,600
Cash dividends		25,100
Retained earnings, December 31, 1996		$245,500

Western Resources, Inc.
Comparative Balance Sheets
December 31, 1996 and 1995

	1996		1995	
Assets				
Current assets:				
Cash and cash equivalents	$ 46,300		$ 55,000	
Available-for-sale securities	12,000		10,000	
Accounts receivable	60,000		70,500	
Inventories	75,000		76,500	
Prepaid operating expenses	16,500	$209,800	12,000	$224,000
Investments (at cost)		10,000		106,000
Land, buildings, and equipment:				
Land	$183,500		$ 75,000	
Buildings	290,000		225,000	
Less accumulated depreciation	(130,600)		(155,000)	
Machinery and equipment	132,000		120,000	
Less accumulated depreciation	(58,800)	416,100	(43,500)	221,500
Patents		35,000		40,000
Total assets		$670,900		$591,500
Liabilities				
Current liabilities:				
Accounts payable	$ 91,000		$ 97,700	
Income taxes payable	10,000		9,500	
Dividends payable	4,400	$105,400	—	$107,200
Bonds payable		30,000		—
Total liabilities		$135,400		$107,200
Stockholders' Equity				
Common stock	$290,000		$250,000	
Retained earnings	245,500	535,500	234,300	484,300
Total liabilities and stockholders' equity		$670,900		$591,500

Additional information:

- Securities that are classified as available-for-sale were purchased during the year at a cost of $2,000.
- A tornado totally destroyed a building costing $40,000 with a book value of $10,000. The insurance company paid $10,000 cash; a new building was then constructed at a cost of $105,000. Payment was made in cash.
- Long-term investments costing $96,000 were sold for $102,500.
- Land was acquired for $108,500, the seller accepting in payment $40,000 of common stock and $68,500 in cash.
- New machinery was purchased for $12,000 cash.
- The amortization of patent cost and depreciation expense on buildings and equipment were recorded as follows:

Depreciation—buildings	$ 5,600
Depreciation—machinery and equipment	15,300
Amortization—patents	5,000
Total depreciation and amortization	$25,900

- Ten-year bonds were sold at their face value of $30,000 at the beginning of the year.

Indirect Method—T-Account Approach to Preparing a Statement of Cash Flows

With a comprehensive T-account approach, special "cash flows" T-accounts are established. These accounts are used to summarize cash flows from operations and from investing and financing activities during the period. They provide the basis for preparing the formal cash flow statement. Individual T-accounts are also established for Cash and all other balance sheet accounts.

During the process of analysis, the change in each account is explained as providing or using cash. In the three T-accounts summarizing cash flows from operating, investing, and financing activities, a debit represents an increase in cash, while a credit reflects a decrease. Once the changes in all balance sheet accounts have been reconciled and the cash flows T-accounts balanced, the formal cash flow statement can be prepared.

In preparing a cash flow statement for Western Resources, Inc., we begin by determining the change in cash balance, in this case an $8,700 decrease. All noncash accounts may now be analyzed using the T-accounts illustrated on the following pages. As noted, the cash flow statement is prepared directly from the cash flows T-accounts and is illustrated following those T-accounts.

Generally, the most efficient approach to developing T-accounts for a statement of cash flows is to begin with an analysis of the change in Retained Earnings. After the change in Retained Earnings has been accounted for, the remaining noncash accounts should be reviewed in conjunction with the income statement and supplementary information to determine what additional adjustments are required. Operating income should be adjusted to determine the actual amount of cash provided or used by operations [items (e), (i), (j), and (l)-(p)]. Analysis must also be made to determine all other cash flows from investing and financing activities [items (b), (c), (d), (e), (f), (h), (k), and (q)], and to reflect significant investing and financing activities that have no effect on cash [item (g)].

Explanations for individual adjustments for Western Resources, Inc., follow. The letter preceding each explanation corresponds with that used in the T-accounts, which are presented on later pages. Entries are presented to help explain the preparation of a statement of cash flows. They are not journal entries that would be recorded in the accounting records.

(a) Net income is recorded in the T-accounts as follows:

Cash Flows—Operating	36,300	
Retained Earnings		36,300

(b) The cash dividends declared and deducted from retained earnings are adjusted for the change in the dividends payable balance in arriving at the amount of dividends actually paid during the year. The entry would be:

Retained Earnings	25,100	
Dividends Payable		4,400
Cash Flows—Financing		20,700

(c) The destruction of the building and the subsequent insurance reimbursement have the effect of providing cash of $10,000, the proceeds from the insurance company. The entry would be:

Accumulated Depreciation—Buildings	30,000	
Cash Flows—Investing	10,000	
Buildings		40,000

(d) The buildings account was increased by the cost of constructing a new building, $105,000. The cost of the new building is reported separately as an investment of cash by the following entry:

Buildings	105,000	
Cash Flows—Investing		105,000

(e) The sale of long-term investments was recorded by a credit to the asset account at cost, $96,000, and a credit to a gain on sale of investment account. At the end of the period, the gain account was closed to retained earnings as part of income from continuing operations. Since the effect of the sale was to provide cash of $102,500, this amount is reported as cash provided by investing activities. The investments account balance is reduced, and cash provided by operations is decreased by the amount of the gain. The following adjustment is made:

Cash Flows—Investing	102,500	
Investments		96,000
Cash Flows—Operating		6,500

(f) and (g) Land was acquired at a price of $108,500; payment was made in common stock valued at $40,000 and cash of $68,500. Two separate entries are made to segregate the cash and noncash components of this transaction:

(f) Land	68,500	
Cash Flows—Investing		68,500
(g) Land	40,000	
Common Stock		40,000

The issuance of common stock for land has no effect on cash, but it is a significant transaction that should be disclosed separately. Recall that the body of the cash flow statement reports only transactions affecting cash, in accordance with FASB Statement No. 95.

(h) Machinery costing $12,000 was acquired during the year. Payment was made in cash and is reported as cash used for investing purposes. The adjustment for the acquisition of machinery is:

Machinery and Equipment	12,000	
Cash Flows—Investing		12,000

(i) and (j) The changes in the accumulated depreciation accounts and in the patents account result from the recognition of depreciation and amortization expense for the period. These noncash expenses are added in computing cash flows from operations by the following adjustments:

(i)	Cash Flows—Operating	20,900	
	Accumulated Depreciation—Buildings		5,600
	Accumulated Depreciation—Machinery and Equipment		15,300
(j)	Cash Flows—Operating	5,000	
	Patents		5,000

(k) During the year, bonds were issued at their face value of $30,000. The entry is:

Cash Flows—Financing	30,000	
Bonds Payable		30,000

(l)-(p) In preparing a cash flow statement, operating income must be adjusted from an accrual basis to a cash basis, as explained earlier in the chapter. The entries (l) through (p) reflect that analysis for Western Resources, Inc.

(l)	Cash Flows—Operating	10,500	
	Accounts Receivable		10,500
(m)	Cash Flows—Operating	1,500	
	Inventories		1,500
(n)	Prepaid Operating Expenses	4,500	
	Cash Flows—Operating		4,500
(o)	Accounts Payable	6,700	
	Cash Flows—Operating		6,700
(p)	Cash Flows—Operating	500	
	Income Taxes Payable		500

(q) As noted earlier in the chapter, available-for-sale securities are treated differently from other current assets in preparing a cash flow statement. The adjustment to reflect the purchase of $2,000 of available-for-sale securities would be:

Available-for-Sale Securities	2,000	
Cash Flows—Investing		2,000

(r) After all changes in account balances have been reconciled and the effects of the changes on cash flow have been recorded in the cash flow T-accounts, the balances of those T-accounts are determined and transferred to a Cash Flows Summary T-account as shown on page 218. The excess of credits (decreases in cash) over debits (increases in cash) is equal to the net change in the cash balance for the period of $8,700. The following entry is made to reflect the net decrease in cash:

Net Decrease in Cash	8,700	
Cash		8,700

Cash Flows—Operating

	(a)	36,300	(e)	6,500
	(i)	20,900	(n)	4,500
	(j)	5,000	(o)	6,700
	(l)	10,500		
	(m)	1,500		
	(p)	500		
Net cash provided by operating activities		57,000		

Cash Flows—Investing

	(c)	10,000	(d)	105,000
	(e)	102,500	(f)	68,500
			(h)	12,000
			(q)	2,000
Net cash used in investing activities				75,000

Cash Flows—Financing

	(k)	30,000	(b)	20,700
Net cash provided by financing activities		9,300		

Cash Flows Summary

Net cash provided—operating		57,000		
Net cash used—investing				75,000
Net cash provided—financing		9,300		
Net decrease in cash	(r)	8,700		
		75,000		75,000

Cash and Cash Equivalents

Beginning bal.	55,000	(r)	8,700
Ending bal.	46,300		

Available-for-Sale Securities

Beginning bal.	10,000		
(q)	2,000		
Ending bal.	12,000		

Accounts Receivable

Beginning bal.	70,500	(l)	10,500
Ending bal.	60,000		

Inventories

Beginning bal.	76,500	(m)	1,500
Ending bal.	75,000		

Prepaid Operating Expenses

Beginning bal.	12,000		
(n)	4,500		
Ending bal.	16,500		

Investments

Beginning bal.	106,000	(e)	96,000
Ending bal.	10,000		

Land

Beginning bal.	75,000		
(f)	68,500		
(g)	40,000		
Ending bal.	183,500		

Buildings

Beginning bal.	225,000	(c)	40,000
(d)	105,000		
Ending bal.	290,000		

Accumulated Depreciation—Buildings

(c)	30,000	Beginning bal.	155,000
		(i)	5,600
		Ending bal.	130,600

Machinery and Equipment

Beginning bal.	120,000		
(h)	12,000		
Ending bal.	132,000		

Accumulated Depreciation—Machinery and Equipment

		Beginning bal.	43,500
		(i)	15,300
		Ending bal.	58,800

Patents

Beginning bal.	40,000	(j)	5,000
Ending bal.	35,000		

Accounts Payable

(o)	6,700	Beginning bal.	97,700
		Ending bal.	91,000

Income Taxes Payable

		Beginning bal.	9,500
		(p)	500
		Ending bal.	10,000

Dividends Payable

		Beginning bal.	0
		(b)	4,400
		Ending bal.	4,400

Bonds Payable

		Beginning bal.	0
		(k)	30,000
		Ending bal.	30,000

Common Stock

		Beginning bal.	250,000
		(g)	40,000
		Ending bal.	290,000

Retained Earnings

(b)	25,100	Beginning bal.	234,300
		(a)	36,300
		Ending bal.	245,500

All T-accounts are now complete, and a statement of cash flows for Western Resources, Inc., can be prepared in an appropriate format, such as the one on page 220.

A reader analyzing the cash flow statement for Western Resources, Inc., can readily see that $57,000 cash was provided internally from operating activities. This amount was not sufficient to satisfy the investment needs of the company, and so additional cash was generated from external financing activities involving the issuance of bonds. The cash generated from operations clearly met the need for payment of cash dividends, but when other cash needs are considered, the total cash outflow exceeded the total inflow of cash for the period, causing the cash balance to decrease by $8,700, or 15.8%.

In addition to the formal statement of cash flows, supplemental disclosure is required for significant noncash investing and financing transactions. Thus, Western Resources would report the acquisition of land valued at $40,000 in exchange for common stock. When the indirect method is used to report operating activities, the amount of cash paid for interest and income taxes also must be disclosed. For Western Resources, the amount paid for interest, $3,600, is taken directly from the income statement, because there is no interest payable at the beginning or end of the year. The amount paid for taxes is determined as follows:

Income tax expense (reported in the income statement)	$24,000
Deduct increase in income taxes payable	(500)
Amount of cash paid for income taxes	$23,500

In the Western Resources illustration, the supplemental disclosures are presented in a schedule accompanying the statement of cash flows. Alternatively, the information could be presented in the notes to the financial statements.

Western Resources, Inc.
Statement of Cash Flows
For the Year Ended December 31, 1996

Cash flows from operating activities:		
Income from continuing operations	$ 36,300	
Adjustments:		
Depreciation expense	20,900	
Amortization of patents	5,000	
Gain on sale of investments	(6,500)	
Decrease in accounts receivable	10,500	
Decrease in inventories	1,500	
Increase in prepaid operating expenses	(4,500)	
Decrease in accounts payable	(6,700)	
Increase in income taxes payable	500	
Net cash provided by operating activities		$ 57,000
Cash flows from investing activities:		
Involuntary conversion of building	$ 10,000	
Construction of building	(105,000)	
Sale of long-term investments	102,500	
Purchase of land	(68,500)	
Purchase of machinery and equipment	(12,000)	
Purchase of available-for-sale securities	(2,000)	
Net cash used in investing activities		(75,000)
Cash flows from financing activities:		
Issuance of bonds	$ 30,000	
Payment of cash dividends	(20,700)	
Net cash provided by financing activities		9,300
Net decrease in cash and cash equivalents		$ (8,700)
Cash and cash equivalents at beginning of year		55,000
Cash and cash equivalents at end of year		$ 46,300
Supplemental Disclosure:		
Cash payments for:		
Interest	$ 3,600	
Income taxes	23,500	
Noncash transaction:		
Land acquired by issuing common stock	40,000	

Direct Method—Adjustments Required to Prepare the Operating Activities Section of a Statement of Cash Flows

As noted earlier, the direct and indirect methods differ only in their impact on the operating activities section of the statement of cash flows. When using the direct method, individual operating revenue and expense items reported on the income statement are converted from an accrual to a cash basis. The conversion procedures are summarized in Exhibit 6—6 on page 209.

The adjustments required to convert operating revenues and expenses for Western Resources, Inc., to a cash basis are presented at the top of the next page. In this illustration, net increases or decreases in the current operating accounts are used to make the conversion from accrual to cash rather than the beginning and ending balances as illustrated earlier in the chapter.

Sales	$753,800
Decrease in accounts receivable	10,500[1]
Cash receipts from customers	$764,300
Cost of goods sold	$524,100
Decrease in inventory	(1,500)[2]
Decrease in accounts payable	6,700[3]
Cash paid for inventory	$529,300
Selling and general expenses	$146,400
Increase in prepaid operating expenses	4,500[4]
Cash paid for selling and general expenses	$150,900
Interest expense	$ 3,600
Adjustment required	-0-[5]
Cash paid for interest	$ 3,600
Income tax expense	$ 24,000
Increase in income taxes payable	(500)[6]
Cash paid for income taxes	$ 23,500

Key to adjustments
[1]Decrease in accounts receivable (previous sales collected this period).
[2]Decrease in inventories (inventory sold this period but purchased last period).
[3]Decrease in accounts payable (purchases made last period but paid for this period).
[4]Increase in prepaid operating expenses (additional prepaid expenses paid for this period).
[5]No change in interest payable; therefore, no adjustment required.
[6]Increase in income taxes payable (income taxes of this period not yet paid).

With the direct method, only operating revenues and expenses involving cash are included in the conversion process. Noncash items, such as the depreciation and amortization expense of $25,900, are not relevant. Also, the $6,500 gain from the sale of an investment is ignored in the analysis, because it is an investing not an operating activity.

Cash flows from operating activities are presented on the statement of cash flows using the direct method as shown below. The rest of the statement is identical to the one presented on the previous page.

Western Resources, Inc.
Statement of Cash Flows
For the Year Ended December 31, 1996

Cash flows from operating activities:		
Cash receipts from customers		$764,300
Cash payments for:		
Inventory	$529,300	
Selling and general expenses	150,900	
Interest expense	3,600	
Income taxes	23,500	707,300
Net cash provided by operating activities		$ 57,000

A reconciliation of net income to net cash flow from operations, similar to that illustrated for Taylor Company on page 210, would be presented along with the statement of cash flows prepared using the direct method. Supplemental disclosure of the noncash transaction (exchange of stock for land) would be presented separately. When the direct method is used, cash paid for interest and taxes is included in the operating activities section of the statement.

Cash Flow Versus Earnings

Picking stocks based on price-earnings (PE) ratios is a strategy that has been used for over 50 years. (As explained in Chapter 4, a company's PE ratio equals stock price per share divided by earnings per share.) In general, the strategy involves buying stocks of firms with low PE ratios—low compared to the market average or low compared to the firm's average PE ratio in the past. This strategy places much emphasis on the usefulness of traditional reported net income based on accrual accounting.

Many analysts are now using cash flow as the basis for picking stocks. Operating cash flow is seen as a good indicator of how much money a company would have to respond to new expansion opportunities or to sustain itself in a crisis. Corporate raiders are attracted to firms with strong cash flow, because that cash can be used to pay interest on any debt used in an acquisition.

Cash flow analysis is sometimes hampered by inconsistency in the definition of "cash flow." Cash flow sometimes means: net income + depreciation + amortization. Increasingly, cash flow means the cash flow from operations reported in the statement of cash flows, which takes into account the changes in levels of operating receivables, inventories, and operating payables. Another measure of cash flow is sometimes called "free cash flow" and is defined as: operating cash flow + interest expense + income tax expense – capital expenditures – dividends. Free cash flow for a business has been compared to discretionary income for a family—that is, funds available for optional uses.

Real estate investments have long been evaluated based on cash flow. This same approach is increasingly being applied to all types of ventures. While Time Inc. and Warner Communications were negotiating their merger, J. Richard Munro, Chairman of Time Inc., told shareholders at the annual meeting: "When it comes to valuing media and entertainment companies like ours, what matters is not profits but cash flow."

Questions:

1. Having learned about the advantages of accrual accounting, what warnings would you give to someone using cash flow analysis to pick attractive investments?
2. What do you think makes cash flow analysis particularly useful for evaluating real estate investments?

Sources:

John R. Dorfman. "Two Money Managers Duke It Out in Debate on Stock-Value Theories." *The Wall Street Journal*, July 17, 1989: p. C1.

Jeffrey M. Laderman. "Earnings, Schmernings—Look at the Cash." *Business Week*, July 24, 1989: p. 56.

SUMMARY

The FASB's conceptual framework suggests that a statement of cash flows is essential in meeting the informational needs of investors and creditors. Statement No. 95 now requires that such a statement be presented as one of the three primary financial statements prepared for external users. The cash flows for the period are to be classified according to three main categories: operating activities, investing activities, and financing activities. The statement reports the net cash provided by or used in each category and explains the net increase or decrease in cash and cash equivalents. Significant financing and investing transactions not involving cash are to be reported in notes to the financial statements or in separate schedules, not in the statement of cash flows.

Companies may use either the indirect or the direct method in presenting cash flows from operating activities. The indirect method, which is used by a vast majority of companies, begins with net income for the period and adjusts this amount to net cash provided by (used in) operating activities. In contrast, the direct method does not begin with net income, but reports directly the amount of cash received or paid for each major type of operating activity, e.g., cash received from customers and cash paid to suppliers. A separate schedule reconciling net income to net cash provided by (used in) operating activities is required when the statement of cash flows is prepared using the direct method. If the indirect method is used, supplemental disclosures of cash paid for interest and income taxes are required. With the direct method, these amounts are included in the operating activities section of the statement of cash flows.

As a result of the specific reporting guidelines in FASB Statement No. 95, external users can expect a considerable degree of uniformity and comparability in the presentation of the statement of cash flows. Microsoft Corporation's 1993 statement of cash flows, included in Appendix A at the end of the text, illustrates how this company is complying with Statement No. 95.

All the basic aspects of cash flow reporting and disclosure have been covered in this chapter. Additional complexities are introduced in later chapters as appropriate. An expanded illustration, incorporating these complexities, is provided in the last chapter of the text.

APPENDIX

Work Sheet Approach to Preparing a Statement of Cash Flows — Indirect Method

This appendix illustrates a work sheet approach to preparing a statement of cash flows using the indirect method. As shown, this approach produces the same results as the T-account approach illustrated in the chapter; only the format is different. To highlight the similarities in the two approaches, the information and account analysis used in the T-account illustration for Western Resources, Inc., will also be used for the work sheet illustration.

Using a work sheet, such as the one following, facilitates the analysis of account changes when using the indirect method. The format of the work sheet is straightforward. The first amount column contains the beginning balances, then there are two columns for analysis of transactions to arrive at the ending balances in the fourth column.

In preparing a work sheet, accumulated depreciation balances, instead of being reported as credit balances in the debit (asset) section, may be more conveniently listed with liability and owners' equity balances in the credit section. Similarly, contra liability accounts and contra owners' equity balances may be separately recognized and more conveniently listed with assets in the debit section.

The lower portion of the work sheet shows the major categories of cash flows: operating, investing, and financing. A debit in the lower section means an increase in cash, while a credit is a decrease in cash. It is from the lower section of the work sheet that the formal statement of cash flows is prepared. In following the illustration, it may be helpful to refer to the detailed explanations for individual adjustments described on pages 216-217 of the chapter. Once the changes in all accounts have been reconciled and the work sheet is complete, the formal cash flow statement can be prepared, as illustrated on page 220.

Western Resources, Inc.
Work Sheet for Statement of Cash Flows—Indirect Method
For the Year Ended December 31, 1996

Accounts	Balance Dec. 31, 1995	Adjustments Debit	Adjustments Credit	Balance Dec. 31, 1996
Debits				
Cash and Cash Equivalents	55,000		(r) 8,700	46,300
Available-for-Sale Securities	10,000	(q) 2,000		12,000
Accounts Receivable	70,500		(l) 10,500	60,000
Inventories	76,500		(m) 1,500	75,000
Prepaid Operating Expenses	12,000	(n) 4,500		16,500
Investments	106,000		(e) 96,000	10,000
Land	75,000	(f) 68,500		
		(g) 40,000		183,500
Buildings	225,000	(d) 105,000	(c) 40,000	290,000
Machinery and Equipment	120,000	(h) 12,000		132,000
Patents	40,000		(j) 5,000	35,000
	790,000			860,300
Credits				
Accum. Depr.—Buildings	155,000	(c) 30,000	(i) 5,600	130,600
Accum. Depr.—Mach. and Equip.	43,500		(i) 15,300	58,800
Accounts Payable	97,700	(o) 6,700		91,000
Income Taxes Payable	9,500		(p) 500	10,000
Dividends Payable	-0-		(b) 4,400	4,400
Bonds Payable	-0-		(k) 30,000	30,000
Common Stock	250,000		(g) 40,000	290,000
Retained Earnings	234,300	(b) 25,100	(a) 36,300	245,500
	790,000	293,800	293,800	860,300

	Adjustments Debit	Adjustments Credit
Cash flows from operating activities:		
Net income	(a) 36,300	
Adjustments:		
Depreciation expense	(i) 20,900	
Amortization of patents	(j) 5,000	
Gain on sale of investments		(e) 6,500
Decrease in accounts receivable	(l) 10,500	
Decrease in inventories	(m) 1,500	
Increase in prepaid operating expenses		(n) 4,500
Decrease in accounts payable		(o) 6,700
Increase in income taxes payable	(p) 500	
Cash flows from investing activities:		
Involuntary conversion of building	(c) 10,000	
Construction of building		(d)105,000
Sale of long-term investments	(e) 102,500	
Purchase of land		(f) 68,500
Purchase of machinery and equipment		(h) 12,000
Purchase of available-for-sale securities		(q) 2,000
Cash flows from financing activities:		
Issuance of bonds	(k) 30,000	
Payment of cash dividends		(b) 20,700
	217,200	225,900
Net decrease in cash	(r) 8,700	
	225,900	225,900

KEY TERMS

Cash equivalents 194
Direct method 197
Financing activities 195
Indirect method 197
Investing activities 195
Noncash items 199
Noncash investing and financing activities 196
Operating activities 195
Statement of cash flows 193

QUESTIONS

1. (a) Why is the statement of cash flows one of three primary financial statements required to be presented to external users?
   (b) What is the major purpose of a cash flow statement?
2. What information does the cash flow statement provide that is not provided by an income statement or by comparative balance sheets?
3. Why has the statement of cash flows replaced the funds statement previously required by generally accepted accounting principles?
4. What uses might each of the following find for a cash flow statement?
   (a) Manager of a small laundry.
   (b) Stockholder interested in regular dividends.
   (c) Bank granting short-term loans.
   (d) Officer of a labor union.
5. What criteria must be met for an item to be considered a cash equivalent in preparing a statement of cash flows?
6. Why does the FASB in Statement No. 95 treat dividend payments as a financing activity but treat the receipt of dividends as an operating activity?
7. Either the direct method or the indirect method may be used to report cash flows from operating activities. What is the difference in approach for the two methods?
8. Why do many users prefer the direct method? Why do the majority of preparers prefer the indirect method?
9. What supplemental disclosures are required by FASB Statement No. 95 if a company elects to use the direct method in preparing its statement of cash flows? What disclosures are required if the indirect method is used?
10. (a) Why is it important to report cash flows from operating activities separately from investing and financing activities in the statement of cash flows?
    (b) To compute net cash provided by (used in) operating activities, what adjustments are applied to net income when using the indirect method?
11. How are significant noncash investing and financing transactions reported in connection with a statement of cash flows?
12. What alternatives are there for developing the information needed for the statement of cash flows?

DISCUSSION CASES

Case 6—1 (Is depreciation a source of cash?)

Brad Berrett and Jim Wong are roommates in college. Berrett is an accounting major while Wong is a finance major. Both have recently studied the statement of cash flows in their classes. Wong's finance professor stated that depreciation is a major source of cash for some companies. Berrett's accounting professor indicated in class that depreciation cannot be a source of cash because cash is not affected by the recording of depreciation.

Berrett and Wong wonder which professor is correct. Explain the positions taken by both professors and indicate which viewpoint you support and why.

Case 6—2 (Where does all the money go?)

Price Brothers Auto Parts has hired you as a consultant to analyze the company's financial position. One of the owners, David Price, is in charge of the financial affairs of the company. He makes all the deposits and pays the bills, but has an accountant prepare a balance sheet and an income statement once a year. The business has been quite profitable over the years. In fact, two years ago Price Brothers opened a second store and is now considering a third outlet. However, the economy has slowed and the cash position has become very tight. The company is having an increasingly difficult time paying its bills. David has not been able to satisfactorily explain to his brothers what is happening. What factors should you consider and what recommendations might you make to Price Brothers?

Case 6—3 **(Why do we have more cash?)**

Hot Lunch Delivery Service has always had a policy to pay stockholders annual dividends in an amount exactly equal to net income for the year. Joe Alberg, the company's president, is confused because the cash balance has been consistently increasing ever since Hot Lunch began operations 5 years ago, in spite of their faithful adherence to the dividend policy. Assuming no errors have been made in the bookkeeping process, explain why this situation might occur.

Case 6—4 **(But where is your statement of cash flows?)**

As controller of Moran Auto Sales, you have been asked to submit historical financial statements to the Far West Bank in order to obtain a loan. You send your banker a current balance sheet and income statement. Your company has had moderate income over the past three years, but has found itself short of cash and, therefore, in need of the loan.

After receiving the statements, the banker calls you and indicates that the financial statements are not complete; he needs to see a statement of cash flows. You argue that since your company is a private company, there is no need to submit such a statement; indeed, you haven't prepared one since college. Besides, everything on a statement of cash flows comes from the other two statements. Why do the additional work? Just analyze it from what we sent.

As a banker, why would you want the third statement? Is the controller correct in indicating that everything an analyst needs is in the balance sheet and income statements?

Case 6—5 **(Which method should we use: the direct or the indirect method?)**

As the assistant controller of Do-It-Right Company, you have been given the assignment to study FASB Statement No. 95 and make recommendations on how the company should prepare its statement of cash flows. Specifically, you are to indicate which method should be used in reporting cash flows from operating activities: the direct method or the indirect method. Which method do you recommend and why?

Case 6—6 **(Some kind of accountant you are!)**

Early in 1997, Laura Dennis, a recent graduate of Southeast State College, delivers the following financial statements to John Roberts of Roberts, Inc. After a quick review, Roberts exclaims, "What do you mean I had net income of $20,000? I borrowed $40,000 from the bank and my cash balance decreased by $2,000. I must have had a loss! Some kind of accountant you are!" How should Ms. Dennis answer Mr. Roberts?

Roberts, Inc.
Comparative Balance Sheet
December 31, 1996 and 1995

	1996	1995
Assets		
Cash	$ 3,000	$ 5,000
Accounts receivable	18,000	8,000
Inventory	20,000	15,000
Equipment (at cost)	52,000	20,000
Accumulated depreciation	(10,000)	(5,000)
Total assets	$83,000	$43,000
Liabilities and Stockholders' Equity		
Accounts payable	$ 4,000	$ 9,000
Notes payable—long-term	40,000	—
Common stock, $10 par	20,000	20,000
Retained earnings	19,000	14,000
Total liabilities and stockholders' equity	$83,000	$43,000

Roberts, Inc.
Combined Statement of Income and Retained Earnings
For the Year Ended December 31, 1996

Sales		$240,000
Cost of goods sold	$150,000	
Operating expenses (including depreciation of $5,000)	70,000	220,000
Net income		$ 20,000
Add retained earnings, January 1, 1996		14,000
Deduct dividends paid		(15,000)
Retained earnings, December 31, 1996		$ 19,000

Case 6—7 (How to generate cash)

Assume that you own and operate a small business. You have just completed your forecasts and budgets for next year and realize that you will need an infusion of $30,000 cash to get you through the year. You are reluctant to seek a partner because you do not want to dilute your control of the business. Preliminary talks with several lenders convince you that you probably won't be able to get a loan. What can you do to raise the $30,000 cash necessary to get you through the year?

Case 6—8 (Cash flow per share)

In Statement No. 95, the FASB explicitly prohibited the reporting of "cash flow per share" in the financial statements. Cash flow per share is an amount often reported by firms outside the financial statements and also often included in financial analyses prepared by investment advisory services. Why do you think the FASB explicitly prohibited the inclusion of cash flow per share in the financial statements?

Case 6—9 (The secret of cash flow patterns)

James Nemrow, a security analyst for Primer Mead & Co., asserts that he can tell more about a company's financial condition by looking at the trends of the negative or positive cash flows in the three categories than from other information found in the financial statements. He illustrates his theory with the following pattern of cash flows for Atlas Security over the past three years.

	1996	1995	1994
Net income	negative	positive	positive
Cash flows from operating activities	negative	negative	positive
Cash flows from financing activities	positive	positive	positive
Cash flows from investing activities	positive	positive	positive

How do you think James would analyze this pattern? Do you agree that analyzing cash flow patterns provides superior analytical information?

Case 6—10 (W.T. Grant: What Is "Cash Flow"?)

The case of W.T. Grant is a classic in cash flow analysis. During the 1960s and 1970s, Grant was one of the largest retailers in the United States, with over 1,200 stores nationwide. Grant was a stable New York Stock Exchange firm that had paid cash dividends every year since 1907. However, the inability of Grant's operations to generate positive cash flow indicated the existence of serious problems. From 1966 through 1973, while Grant's net income was steady at about $35 million per year, cash flow from operations was negative in every year except 1968 and 1969, and even in those years the positive cash flow generated was insignificant in amount. The results for the fiscal year ended January 31, 1973, are the most striking. Net income for the year was $38 million. A frequently used measure of "cash flow" (net income and depreciation) suggested that W. T. Grant's operations generated $48 million in cash. However, actual cash flow generated by operations for the year was *negative* $120 million. In October 1975, Grant filed for bankruptcy, and by early 1976, the company was liquidated and ceased to exist.

What might have caused the (net income + depreciation) measure of cash flow to be positive when in fact actual cash flow from operations was negative? Under what circumstances is the (net income + depreciation) measure of cash flow a good estimate of actual cash flow from operations? When is it a bad measure?

Source: James A. Largay, III and Clyde P. Stickney. "Cash Flows, Ratio Analysis and the W.T. Grant Company Bankruptcy." *Financial Analysts Journal*, July/August 1980, pp. 51-54; and *Moody's Handbook of Common Stocks*, Second Quarterly 1973 Edition.

Case 6—11 (Analysis of financial statements—Microsoft)

Refer to the financial statements of Microsoft Corporation in Appendix A in answering the following:

1. Analyze Microsoft's overall cash flow picture in light of the positive or negative flows for the three categories of its cash flows statement.
2. What is the composition of "cash and cash equivalents" at June 30, 1993?
3. The changes in several current asset and current liability accounts in the cash flows statement do not agree with the changes as reported on the balance sheet. Through analysis of other items on the cash flows statement, what is the probable cause of the differences?
4. Based on analysis of all three years, what general conclusion can you make about the cash liquidity of Microsoft?

EXERCISES

Exercise 6—12 (Classification of cash flows)

Indicate whether each of the following items would be classified as (1) an operating activity, an investing activity, or a financing activity, or (2) as a noncash transaction or noncash item.

(a) Cash collected from customers.
(b) Cash paid to suppliers for inventory.
(c) Cash received for interest on a nontrade note receivable.
(d) Cash received from issuance of stock.
(e) Cash paid for dividends.
(f) Cash received from bank on a loan.
(g) Cash paid for interest on a loan.
(h) Cash paid to retire bonds.
(i) Cash paid to purchase stock of another company as a long-term investment.
(j) Cash received from the sale of a business segment.
(k) Cash paid for property taxes.
(l) Cash received for dividend revenue.
(m) Cash paid for wages.
(n) Cash paid for insurance.
(o) Preferred stock retired by issuing common stock.
(p) Depreciation expense for the year.
(q) Cash paid to purchase machinery.
(r) Cash received from the sale of land.

Exercise 6—13 (Cash flow analysis)

State how each of the following items would be reflected on a statement of cash flows.

(a) Securities classified as available-for-sale were purchased for $5,000.
(b) Buildings were acquired for $187,500, the company paying $50,000 cash and signing a 12% mortgage note, payable in 5 years, for the balance.

(c) Cash of $62,500 was paid to purchase business assets consisting of: merchandise, $22,500; furniture and fixtures, $7,500; land and buildings, $23,750; and goodwill, $8,750.

(d) A cash dividend of $1,250 was declared in the current period, payable at the beginning of the next period.

(e) Accounts Payable shows a decrease for the period of $3,750.

Exercise 6—14 (Cash receipts and cash payments)

The accountant for Alpine Hobby Stores prepared the following selected information for the year ended December 31, 1996.

	Dec. 31, 1996	Dec. 31, 1995
(a) Equipment	$25,000	$30,000
(b) Accumulated depreciation	11,000	9,500
(c) Long-term debt	11,000	20,000
(d) Common stock	20,000	15,000

Equipment with a book value of $20,000 was sold for $17,000 cash. The original cost of the equipment was $25,000.

Determine the cash inflows and outflows during 1996 associated with each of the accounts listed. Indicate how the cash flows for each item would be presented on the statement of cash flows.

Exercise 6—15 (Format of statement of cash flows with indirect method)

From the following information for the Carter Corporation, prepare a statement of cash flows for the year ended December 31, 1996, using the indirect method.

Amortization of patent	$ 4,000
Depreciation expense	7,000
Issuance of common stock	25,000
Issuance of new bonds payable	30,000
Net income	55,000
Payment of dividends	22,500
Purchase of equipment	33,200
Retirement of long-term debt	40,000
Sale of land (includes $6,000 gain)	35,000
Decrease in accounts receivable	2,100
Increase in inventory	1,200
Increase in accounts payable	1,500
Increase in cash	56,700
Cash balance, January 1, 1996	62,800

Exercise 6—16 (Cash flow from operations—indirect method)

The following information was taken from the books of Tapwater Company. Compute the amount of net cash provided by (used in) operating activities during 1996 using the indirect method.

	Dec. 31, 1996	Dec. 31, 1995
Accounts receivable	$18,900	$16,750
Accounts payable	11,500	14,000
Accumulated depreciation (no plant assets were retired during the year)	26,000	22,000
Inventories	24,500	20,000
Other current liabilities	5,000	3,000
Prepaid insurance	1,200	2,000
Net income	35,500	

Exercise 6—17 (Cash flow from operations—direct method)
A summary of revenues and expenses for Stanton Company for 1996 follows:

Sales	$6,000,000
Cost of goods manufactured and sold	2,800,000
Gross profit	$3,200,000
Selling, general, and administrative expenses	2,000,000
Income before income tax	$1,200,000
Income tax	520,000
Net income	$ 680,000

Net changes in working capital accounts for 1996 were as follows:

	Debit	Credit
Cash	$104,000	
Trade accounts receivable	400,000	
Inventories		$ 60,000
Prepaid expenses (selling and general)	10,000	
Accrued expenses (75% of increase related to manufacturing activities and 25% to general operating activities)		32,000
Income taxes payable		48,000
Trade accounts payable		140,000

Depreciation on plant and equipment for the year totaled $600,000; 70% was related to manufacturing activities and 30% to general and administrative activities.

Prepare a schedule of net cash provided by (used in) operating activities for the year using the direct method.

Exercise 6—18 (Cash flow from operations—indirect method)
The following information was taken from the comparative financial statements of Buttercup Corporation:

Net income for year	$ 90,000
Sales revenue	500,000
Cost of goods sold (except depreciation)	300,000
Depreciation expense for year	60,000
Amortization of goodwill for year	10,000
Interest expense on short-term debt for year	3,500
Dividends declared and paid during year	65,000

Selected account balances:

	Beginning of Year	End of Year
Accounts Receivable	$43,000	$30,000
Inventory	42,000	50,000
Accounts Payable	59,400	56,000
Interest Payable	1,000	—

Using the indirect method, compute the net amount of cash provided by (used in) operating activities for the year.

Exercise 6—19 (Cash flow from operations—direct method)

Based on the information given in Exercise 6—18 and using the direct method, compute the net amount of cash provided by (used in) operating activities for the year.

Exercise 6—20 (Cash computations)

A comparative balance sheet and income statement data for the Xavier Metals Company are presented below and on the next page.

Xavier Metals Company
Comparative Balance Sheet
December 31, 1996 and 1995

	1996	1995
Assets		
Current assets:		
Cash	$ 119,000	$ 98,000
Available-for-sale securities	59,000	—
Accounts receivable	312,000	254,000
Inventory	278,000	239,000
Prepaid expenses	35,000	21,000
Total current assets	$ 803,000	$612,000
Property, plant, and equipment	$ 536,000	$409,000
Accumulated depreciation	76,000	53,000
	$ 460,000	$356,000
Total assets	$1,263,000	$968,000
Liabilities and Stockholders' Equity		
Current liabilities:		
Accounts payable	$ 212,000	$198,000
Accrued expenses	98,000	76,000
Dividends payable	40,000	—
Total current liabilities	$ 350,000	$274,000
Notes payable—due 1998	125,000	—
Total liabilities	$ 475,000	$274,000
Stockholders' equity:		
Common stock	$ 600,000	$550,000
Retained earnings	188,000	144,000
Total stockholders' equity	$ 788,000	$694,000
Total liabilities and stockholders' equity	$1,263,000	$968,000

Xavier Metals Company
Condensed Comparative Income Statement
For the Years Ended December 31, 1996 and 1995

	1996	1995
Net sales	$3,561,000	$3,254,000
Cost of goods sold	2,789,000	2,568,000
Gross profit	$ 772,000	$ 686,000
Expenses	521,000	486,000
Net income	$ 251,000	$ 200,000

Additional information for Xavier:

(a) All accounts receivable and accounts payable relate to trade merchandise.

(b) The proceeds from the notes payable were used to finance plant expansion.
(c) Capital stock was sold to provide additional working capital.

Compute the following for 1996:

1. Cash collected from accounts receivable, assuming all sales are on account.
2. Cash payments made on accounts payable to suppliers, assuming that all purchases of inventory are on account.
3. Cash payments for dividends.
4. Cash receipts that were not provided by operations.
5. Cash payments for assets that were not reflected in operations.

Exercise 6—21 (Statement of cash flows—indirect method)
Below is information for Boswell Manufacturing Company:

(a) Long-term debt of $450,000 was retired at face value.
(b) New machinery was purchased for $48,000.
(c) Common stock with a par value of $120,000 was issued for $150,000.
(d) Dividends of $18,000 declared in 1995 were paid in January 1996, and dividends of $27,000 were declared in December 1996, to be paid in 1997.
(e) Net income was $280,800. Included in the computation were depreciation expense of $60,000 and goodwill amortization of $30,000.

	Dec. 31, 1996	Dec. 31, 1995
Current assets:		
Cash and cash equivalents	$147,100	$140,000
Accounts receivable	213,000	200,000
Inventory	192,000	162,000
Current liabilities:		
Accounts payable	51,000	85,800
Dividends payable	27,000	18,000
Interest payable	11,100	3,000
Wages payable	84,000	12,000

Prepare a statement of cash flows for the year ended December 31, 1996, using the indirect method.

Exercise 6—22 (Cash flow from operations—comparison of indirect and direct methods)
The statement of cash flows for Riker Company (prepared using the indirect method) is shown below.

Riker Company
Statement of Cash Flows
For the Year Ended December 31, 1996

Cash flows from operating activities:		
Net income		$ 68,850
Adjustments:		
Depreciation	$ 65,000	
Amortization	10,000	
Loss on sale of machine	7,400	
Gain on retirement of long-term debt	(2,330)	
Increase in accounts receivable	(8,600)	
Decrease in inventory	12,430	
Decrease in prepaid operating expenses	1,680	
Decrease in accounts payable	(2,400)	
Increase in interest payable	500	
Increase in income taxes payable	2,500	86,180
Net cash provided by operating activities		$155,030

Cash flows from investing activities:		
Sale of machine	$ 12,000	
Purchase of fixed assets	(78,000)	
Net cash used in investing activities		(66,000)
Cash flows from financing activities:		
Retirement of long-term debt	$(65,000)	
Payment of dividends	(27,000)	
Net cash used in financing activities		(92,000)
Net decrease in cash		$ (2,970)
Cash at beginning of year		5,320
Cash at end of year		$ 2,350

Consider the following additional information:

(a) Sales for the year totaled $812,350. Cost of goods sold was $500,000. Operating expenses were $100,000. Interest expense was $23,000. Income tax expense was $40,430.

(b) 80% of the decrease in accounts payable related to inventory purchases; the remaining 20% related to operating expenses.

(c) Depreciation and amortization are period costs; they do not enter into the computation of cost of goods sold.

Prepare the operating activities section of the statement of cash flows for Riker Company using the direct method.

Exercise 6—23 (Statement of cash flows—indirect method)

The Sunnyvale Corporation prepared for 1996 and 1995 the following balance sheet data:

	Dec. 31, 1996	Dec. 31, 1995
Cash and cash equivalents	$ 418,500	$ 675,000
Accounts receivable	360,000	345,000
Merchandise inventory	750,000	654,000
Prepaid insurance	4,500	6,000
Buildings and equipment	5,515,500	4,350,000
Accumulated depreciation—buildings and equipment	(2,235,000)	(1,995,000)
Total	$4,813,500	$4,035,000
Accounts payable	$ 613,500	$ 945,000
Salaries payable	75,000	105,000
Notes payable—bank (current)	150,000	600,000
Notes payable—bank (long-term)	1,500,000	—
Capital stock, $5 par	2,400,000	2,400,000
Retained earnings (deficit)	75,000	(15,000)
Total	$4,813,500	$4,035,000

Cash needed to purchase new equipment and to improve the company's working capital position was raised by borrowing from the bank with a long-term note. Equipment costing $75,000 with a book value of $15,000 was sold for $18,000; the gain on sale was included in net income. The company paid cash dividends of $90,000 during the year and reported earnings of $180,000 for 1996. There were no entries in the retained earnings account other than to record the dividend and the net income for the year.

Prepare a statement of cash flows using the indirect method.

Exercise 6—24 (Statement of cash flows—indirect method)

The following are financial statements for LaForge Company:

LaForge Company
Comparative Balance Sheet
December 31, 1996 and 1995
(Dollars in thousands)

	1996	1995
Assets		
Cash	$ 22	$ 16
Accounts receivable	200	250
Inventory	125	95
Prepaid general expenses	18	10
Plant assets	1,019	1,000
Accumulated depreciation—plant assets	(527)	(597)
Total assets	$ 857	$ 774
Liabilities and Stockholders' Equity		
Accounts payable	$ 75	$ 50
Interest payable	10	8
Income taxes payable	90	107
Bonds payable	117	77
Common stock	338	300
Retained earnings	227	232
Total liabilities and stockholders' equity	$ 857	$ 774

LaForge Company
Condensed Income Statement
For the Year Ended December 31, 1996
(Dollars in thousands)

Sales		$1,300
Cost of goods sold		880
Gross profit		$ 420
Operating expenses:		
General expenses	$240	
Interest expense	15	
Income tax expense	35	
Depreciation expense	60	350
Net income		$ 70

The following information is also available for 1996:

(a) Plant assets were sold for their book value of $200 during the year. The assets had an original cost of $330.
(b) Cash dividends totaling $75 were paid during the year.
(c) All accounts payable relate to inventory purchases.
(d) All purchases of plant assets were cash transactions.

Prepare a statement of cash flows for 1996 for LaForge Company using the indirect method.

Exercise 6—25 (Statement of cash flows—direct method)

Using the information given in Exercise 6-24, prepare a statement of cash flows for 1996 for LaForge Company using the direct method.

Exercise 6—26 (Preparation of income statement using balance sheet and cash flow data)

The following are financial statements for Troi Company:

Troi Company
Comparative Balance Sheet
December 31, 1996 and December 31, 1995

	1996	1995
Assets		
Cash	$ 4,000	$ 3,400
Accounts receivable	25,000	18,000
Inventory	30,000	34,000
Prepaid general expenses	5,700	5,000
Property, plant, and equipment	305,000	320,000
Accumulated depreciation	(103,500)	(128,900)
Goodwill	36,000	40,000
Total assets	$302,200	$291,500
Liabilities and Stockholders' Equity		
Accounts payable	$ 25,000	$ 22,000
Wages payable	12,000	10,300
Interest payable	2,800	4,000
Dividends payable	14,000	—
Income taxes payable	1,600	1,200
Bonds payable	100,000	120,000
Common stock	50,000	50,000
Retained earnings	96,800	84,000
Total liabilities and stockholders' equity	$302,200	$291,500

Troi Company
Statement of Cash Flows
For the Year Ended December 31, 1996

Cash flows from operating activities:		
Cash receipts from customers		$685,300
Cash payments for:		
Purchases of inventory	$300,000	
General expenses	102,000	
Wage expense	150,000	
Interest expense	11,000	
Income tax expense	23,900	586,900
Net cash provided by operating activities		$ 98,400
Cash flows from investing activities:		
Sale of property, plant, and equipment	$ 27,200	
Purchase of property, plant, and equipment	(60,000)	
Net cash used in investing activities		(32,800)
Cash flows from financing activities:		
Retirement of bonds payable	$(23,000)	
Payment of dividends	(42,000)	
Net cash used in financing activities		(65,000)
Net increase in cash		$ 600
Cash at beginning of year		3,400
Cash at end of year		$ 4,000

Consider the following additional information:

(a) All the accounts payable relate to inventory purchases.
(b) Property, plant, and equipment sold had an original cost of $75,000 and a book value of $22,000.

Prepare the income statement for Troi Company for the year ended December 31, 1996.

Exercise 6-27

Using the statement of cash flows for Microsoft, as reproduced in Appendix A, compute Microsoft's 1993 cash flow ratios as described in Exhibit 6-8. What do these ratios indicate about Microsoft's financial strength?

PROBLEMS

Problem 6—28 **(Statement of cash flows—indirect method)**
Comparative balance sheet data for the Amber Company are presented below.

	Dec. 31, 1996	Dec. 31, 1995
Cash and cash equivalents	$ 11,000	$ 28,000
Accounts receivable	94,000	86,000
Inventory	110,000	100,000
Property, plant, and equipment	550,000	500,000
Accumulated depreciation—property, plant, and equipment	(277,500)	(250,000)
Total	$487,500	$464,000
Short-term notes payable	$ —	$ 20,000
Accounts payable	105,000	80,000
Long-term notes payable	100,000	75,000
Bonds payable	50,000	100,000
Common stock, $5 par	100,000	100,000
Additional paid-in capital	75,000	75,000
Retained earnings	57,500	14,000
Total	$487,500	$464,000

New equipment was purchased for $50,000, payment consisting of $25,000 cash and a long-term note for $25,000. Proceeds from the short-term notes payable were used for operating purposes. Cash dividends of $10,000 were paid in 1996; all other changes to retained earnings were caused by the net income for 1996, which amounted to $53,500.

Instructions: Prepare a statement of cash flows for the year ended December 31, 1996, using the indirect method.

Problem 6—29 **(Statement of cash flows—indirect method)**
The following information was taken from the records of Alderman Produce Company for the year ended June 30, 1996:

Borrowed on long-term notes	$20,000
Issued capital stock	50,000
Purchased equipment	27,000
Net income	47,000
Purchased treasury stock	1,500
Paid dividends	30,000
Depreciation expense	12,000
Retired bonds payable	70,000

Goodwill amortization	2,000
Sold long-term investment (at cost)	5,000
Increase in cash	11,000
Decrease in inventories	8,000
Increase in accounts receivable	8,500
Increase in accounts payable	4,000
Cash balance, July 1, 1995	20,000

Instructions:

1. From the information given, prepare a statement of cash flows using the indirect method.
2. Briefly explain what an interested party would learn from studying the cash flow statement for Alderman Produce Company.

Problem 6—30 (Statement of cash flows—indirect method)

The following information was obtained from analysis of selected accounts of Orlando Co. for the year ended December 31, 1996:

Increase in long-term debt	$ 57,000
Purchase of treasury stock	52,000
Depreciation and amortization	197,000
Gain on sale of equipment (included in net income)	6,000
Proceeds from issuance of common stock	184,000
Purchase of equipment	434,000
Proceeds from sale of equipment	20,000
Payment of dividends	49,000
Net income	375,000
Increase (decrease) in working capital accounts:	
Cash	45,000
Accounts receivable	229,000
Inventories	275,000
Trade notes payable	167,000
Accounts payable	124,000
Taxes payable	(34,000)
Cash balance, January 1, 1996	120,000

Instructions: From the information given, prepare a statement of cash flows using the indirect method.

Problem 6—31 (Statement of cash flows—direct method)

Based on an analysis of Cash and other accounts, the following information was provided by the controller of Lumbercamp, Inc., a manufacturer of wood burning stoves, for the year 1996.

(a) Cash sales for the year were $150,000; sales on account totaled $180,000.
(b) Cost of goods sold was 50 percent of total sales.
(c) All inventory is purchased on account.
(d) Depreciation on equipment was $93,000 for the year.
(e) Amortization of goodwill was $6,000.
(f) Collection of accounts receivable was $114,000.
(g) Payments on accounts payable for inventory equaled $117,000.
(h) Rent expense paid in cash was $33,000.
(i) 60,000 shares of $10 par stock were issued for $720,000.
(j) Land was acquired by issuance of a $300,000 bond that sold for $318,000.
(k) Equipment was purchased for cash at a cost of $252,000.
(l) Dividends of $138,000 were declared.
(m) $45,000 of dividends that had been declared the previous year were paid.
(n) A machine used on the assembly line was sold for $36,000. The machine had a book value of $21,000.

(o) Another machine with a book value of $1,500 was scrapped and was reported as an ordinary loss. No cash was received on this transaction.
(p) The cash account had a balance of $62,000 on January 1, 1996.

Instructions: Use the direct method to prepare a statement of cash flows for Lumbercamp, Inc., for the year ending December 31, 1996.

Problem 6—32 **(Statement of cash flows—indirect method)**
Comparative balance sheet data for the partnership of Young and Jones are as follows:

	Dec. 31, 1996	Dec. 31, 1995
Cash	$ 14,000	$ 10,500
Accounts receivable	22,000	25,500
Inventory	112,500	85,000
Prepaid expenses	3,500	4,250
Furniture and fixtures	64,500	42,000
Accumulated depreciation	(33,875)	(25,425)
Total	$182,625	$141,825
Accrued expenses	$ 7,000	$ 5,200
Accounts payable	19,425	28,875
Long-term note	17,700	—
Donna Young, capital	51,375	50,875
Diane Jones, capital	87,125	56,875
Total	$182,625	$141,825

Net income for the year was $43,000, and this was transferred in equal amounts to the partners' capital accounts. Further changes in the capital accounts arose from additional investments and withdrawals by the partners. The change in the furniture and fixtures account arose from a purchase of additional furniture; part of the purchase price was paid in cash and a long-term note was issued for the balance.

Instructions: Using the indirect method, prepare a statement of cash flows for 1996.

Problem 6—33 **(Statement of cash flows—indirect method)**
Berclay Tile Co. reported net income of $6,160 for 1996 but has been showing an overdraft in its bank account in recent months. The manager has contacted you as the auditor for an explanation. The comparative balance sheet was given to you for examination, along with the following information:

(a) Equipment was sold for $1,500, its cost was $2,500 and its book value was $500. The gain was reported as Other Revenue.
(b) Cash dividends of $4,500 were paid.

Berclay Tile Co.
Comparative Balance Sheet
December 31, 1996 and 1995

	1996	1995
Assets		
Current assets:		
Cash	$ (960)	$ 4,780
Accounts receivable	4,000	1,000
Inventory	2,350	750
Prepaid insurance	70	195
Total current assets	$ 5,460	$ 6,725

	1996		1995	
Land, buildings, and equipment:				
Land		$12,500		$12,500
Buildings	$25,000		$25,000	
Less: Accumulated depreciation	(15,000)	10,000	(14,000)	11,000
Equipment	$37,250		$30,850	
Less: Accumulated depreciation	(22,500)	14,750	(18,400)	12,450
Total land, buildings, and equipment		$37,250		$35,950
Total assets		$42,710		$42,675
Liabilities and Stockholders' Equity				
Current liabilities:				
Accounts payable		$ 4,250		$ 3,500
Taxes payable		1,400		2,350
Wages payable		750		1,675
Notes payable—current portion		1,500		3,500
Total current liabilities		$ 7,900		$11,025
Long-term liabilities:				
Notes payable		10,500		11,500
Stockholders' equity:				
Capital stock	$17,500		$15,000	
Retained earnings	6,810		5,150	
Total stockholders' equity		24,310		20,150
Total liabilities and stockholders' equity		$42,710		$42,675

Instructions: Prepare a statement of cash flows using the indirect method.

Problem 6—34 **(Statement of cash flows—direct method)**

The following data show the account balances of Novations, Inc., at the beginning and end of the company's accounting period:

Debits	**Dec. 31, 1996**	**Jan. 1, 1996**
Cash and Cash Equivalents	$176,400	$ 58,000
Accounts Receivable	32,000	26,600
Inventory	21,000	25,400
Prepaid Insurance	5,600	4,000
Long-Term Investments (at cost)	6,000	16,800
Equipment	80,000	66,000
Treasury Stock (at cost)	10,000	20,000
Cost of Goods Sold	368,000	
Operating Expenses	185,000	
Income Tax Expense	37,600	
Loss on Sale of Equipment	1,000	
Total debits	$922,600	$216,800
Credits		
Accumulated Depreciation—Equipment	$ 19,000	$ 18,000
Accounts Payable	7,000	11,200
Interest Payable	1,000	2,000
Income Taxes Payable	12,000	8,000
Notes Payable—Long-Term	16,000	24,000
Common Stock	110,000	100,000

Credits	Dec. 31, 1996	Jan. 1, 1996
Paid-In Capital in Excess of Par	32,000	30,000
Retained Earnings	19,600*	23,600
Sales	704,000	
Gain on Sale of Long-Term Investments	2,000	
Total credits	$922,600	$216,800

*Preclosing balance

The following information was also available:

(a) All purchases and sales were on account.
(b) Equipment costing $10,000 was sold for $3,000; a loss of $1,000 was recognized on the sale.
(c) Among other items, the operating expenses included depreciation expense of $7,000; interest expense of $2,800; and insurance expense of $2,400.
(d) Equipment was purchased during the year by issuing common stock and by paying the balance ($12,000) in cash.
(e) Treasury stock was sold for $4,000 less than it cost; the decrease in owners' equity was recorded by reducing retained earnings. No dividends were paid during the year.

Instructions:

1. Prepare a statement of cash flows for the year ended December 31, 1996, using the direct method of reporting cash flows from operating activities.
2. Comment on the lack of dividend payment. Does a "no dividend" policy seem appropriate under the current circumstances for Novations, Inc.?
3. Compute cash flow ratios for Novations, Inc. Comment on the financial strength of Novations based on your analysis of the cash flow ratios.

Problem 6—35 (Income statement and statement of cash flows—indirect method)
Refer to the data for Novations, Inc., in Problem 6—34.

Instructions:

1. Prepare an income statement for Novations, Inc., for the year ended December 31, 1996.
2. Prepare a statement of cash flows for the year ended December 31, 1996, using the indirect method.

Problem 6—36 (Analysis of cash flow data)
The following summary data are for Queue Company:

	1996	1995	1994
Cash	$ 75,000	$ 70,000	$ 60,000
Other current assets	450,000	400,000	370,000
Current liabilities	335,000	240,000	250,000
Depreciation expense	50,000	48,000	41,000
Net income	65,000	57,000	54,000

All current assets and current liabilities relate to operations.

Instructions:

1. Compute net cash provided by (used in) operating activities for 1995 and 1996.
2. How would the numbers you computed in (1) change if Queue had decided to delay payment of $50,000 in accounts payable from late 1995 to early 1996? This will increase both cash and accounts payable as of December 31, 1995; the December 31, 1996, amounts will be unaffected.

3. Ignore the change described in (2). How would the numbers you computed in (1) change if Queue had decided to delay purchase of $50,000 of inventory for cash from late 1995 to early 1996? This will increase cash but decrease inventory as of December 31, 1995; the December 31, 1996, amounts will be unaffected.
4. Can net cash from operations be manipulated? Explain your answer.

Problem 6—37 (Definitions of cash flow)

The following summary information is for Data Company:

	1996	1995	1994	1993
Net income	$ 50	$ 50	$ 50	$ 50
Depreciation expense	30	30	30	30
Change in accounts receivable	+10	0	+20	+15
Change in inventory	+15	−30	0	−5
Change in accounts payable	+20	+25	−15	+10

Instructions:

1. Compute net cash provided by (used in) operating activities for Data Company for the years 1993 through 1996.
2. One definition of "cash flow" often used in financial analysis is: net income + depreciation. Use this definition to compute "cash flow" for Data Company for the years 1993 through 1996.
3. Under what circumstances is the "net income + depreciation" measure of cash flow a good estimate of actual cash flow from operations? Under what circumstances is it a particularly misleading measure?

Problem 6—38 (Cash flow from operations—direct method)

The following combined income and retained earnings statement, along with selected balance sheet data, are provided for the Timberdale Company.

Timberdale Company
Combined Income and Retained Earnings Statement
For the Year Ended December 31, 1996

Revenues:		
Net sales revenue		$170,000
Other revenues		9,000*
Total revenues		$179,000
Expenses:		
Cost of goods sold	$102,000	
Selling and administrative expenses	29,400	
Depreciation expense	6,400	
Interest expense	2,800	
Total expenses		140,600
Income before taxes		$ 38,400
Income taxes		(11,520)
Net income		$ 26,880
Retained earnings, January 1, 1996		67,000
		$ 93,880
Dividends declared and paid		(5,000)
Retained earnings, December 31, 1996		$ 88,880

*Gain on sale of equipment (cost, $19,000; book value, $12,000; sales price, $21,000).

Balance Sheet Amounts

	Beginning of Year	End of Year
Accounts receivable	$21,000	$22,000
Inventory	38,600	36,000
Prepaid expenses	1,900	1,400
Accounts payable	14,400	16,000
Interest payable	3,000	2,000
Income taxes payable	1,000	5,000

Instructions:

1. Using the direct method, compute the amount of net cash provided by (used in) operating activities for Timberdale Company for 1996.
2. What is the impact of dividends paid on net cash from operations? Explain.

Problem 6—39 **(Statement of cash flows using T-accounts and indirect method)**
The post-closing trial balances are provided for the Dallas Department Store.

	Debit (Credit)	
	Trial Balance Dec. 31, 1996	Trial Balance Dec. 31, 1995
Cash and Cash Equivalents	$ 28,800	$ 12,000
Accounts Receivable	24,000	36,000
Inventory	144,000	96,000
Prepaid Expenses	7,200	6,000
Plant Assets	624,000	480,000
Accumulated Depreciation—Plant Assets	(122,400)	(48,000)
Accounts Payable	(30,000)	(24,000)
Accrued Liabilities	(12,000)	(9,600)
Mortgage Payable	(84,000)	(60,000)
Bonds Payable	(240,000)	(240,000)
Common Stock	(210,000)	(180,000)
Capital in Excess of Par	(36,000)	(30,000)
Retained Earnings	(93,600)	(38,400)
Total	$ -0-	$ -0-

The following additional information was obtained from Dallas Department Store's accounting records:

- All accounts receivable were from sales to customers.
- The inventory and accounts payable were for merchandise purchased for resale.
- The prepaid expenses and accrued liabilities were for operating expenses.
- During the year, plant assets were purchased by paying $180,000 cash and signing a $24,000 mortgage.
- Plant assets with a cost of $60,000 and accumulated depreciation of $24,000 were sold for $48,000 cash.
- Depreciation expense for the year was included in operating expenses.
- Common stock was sold for $36,000 cash.
- Cash dividends of $12,000 were paid during the year.

Instructions: Using T-accounts, prepare a statement of cash flows for Dallas Department Store for the year ended December 31, 1996, using the indirect method.

***Problem 6—40** **(Statement of cash flows using a work sheet and indirect method)**
Refer to the information for Dallas Department Store in Problem 6—39.

Instructions: Using a work sheet, prepare a statement of cash flows (indirect method) for the year ended December 31, 1996.

*Relates to Appendix

CHAPTER 7

The Time Value of Money: Accounting Applications

CHAPTER TOPICS

- The Time-Value-of-Money Concept
- Simple and Compound Interest
- Future- and Present-Value Techniques
- Business Applications
- Converting to Annuity-Due Factor Values
- Interpolation
- Computers and the Time Value of Money (Appendix)

Since the 1983 introduction of NBA salary caps, compensation for professional basketball players has grown increasingly creative. In 1993, the Charlotte Hornets signed Larry Johnson to a 12-year, $84 million contract—at that time the largest team-sport contract ever negotiated. Under the terms of the agreement, Johnson will continue to be paid his current salary, which increases from $3.1 million in 1993–94 to $4.4 million in 1996–97. In the summer of '97, he receives a signing bonus of $6 million. The contract peaks at $10 million in 2000–01 and then falls to $6 million in 2004–05—the final year of the contract. Since the contract is guaranteed, the Hornets must pay Johnson even if he dies, is disabled, or merely fizzles. However, if Johnson suffers a career-ending injury, the schedule of payments is revised. If he is hurt in the first four years of the contract, the remaining balance will be paid over 25 years; in the next four years, over 15 years; and in the final four years, over 10 years.[1]

On the day Larry Johnson signed the long-term contract, what was its value? $84 million? Does the fact that he does not receive more than 50% of his contract until the next century affect its valuation?

1. Andrew E. Serwer, *Sports Illustrated*, "How High?" November 8, 1993, p. 88.

THE TIME-VALUE-OF-MONEY CONCEPT

As illustrated by the Johnson contract, the concept of the **time value of money** is becoming increasingly important in today's business world. Decision makers, whether professional basketball players, business executives, or individual citizens, must try to adjust for the impact of interest and changing economic prices. Consider the following illustrative situations:

- You are in the market for a new car. A newspaper advertisement offers the vehicle you want with two payment options. You can choose between an immediate cash price of $12,500 or a 6% financing option with payments over two years of $532 at the end of each month. Which alternative purchase plan should you choose?
- You intend to provide income for your retirement. If you are 20 years old, how much must you invest now in order to establish a fund large enough to pay for your retirement in 45 years?
- Every month, millions of individuals make mortgage payments on their homes. Because part of each payment is interest, and therefore tax-deductible, a method is needed for calculating the interest portion of each payment. What are the procedures for determining the interest and principal portions of each payment over the life of the mortgage?

In each of the preceding situations, decisions must be made regarding inflows and outflows of money over an extended period of time. Making correct financial decisions requires that the time value of money be taken into account. This means that dollars to be received or paid in the future must be "discounted" or adjusted to their **present value.** Alternatively, current dollars may be "accumulated" or adjusted to their **future values** so that comparisons of dollar amounts at different time periods can be meaningful.

In the first example, you must decide whether to pay $12,500 cash now or make 24 monthly payments of $532. Assuming you have sufficient cash, wouldn't it be better to pay $12,500 for the car now instead of $12,768 (24 payments of $532) under the time-payment plan? The answer to that question is, "Not necessarily." This decision requires that the alternatives be made comparable in terms of the time value of money, that is, the two alternatives must be stated at their respective present values.

The present value of the first alternative, the cash purchase, is simply the amount of cash to be paid currently, or $12,500. The present value of the second alternative is equal to the present value of each of the 24 payments, as illustrated below.

The total present value of the 24 payments of $532 each discounted to the date of purchase at 6% interest is approximately $12,003.[2] This amount is less than the $12,500 cash price the dealer is willing to accept. Therefore, assuming no other factors are relevant to your decision, you should purchase the car on the time-payment plan. This conclusion and the other examples in the chapter ignore any tax implications, which may modify the decision in actual practice.

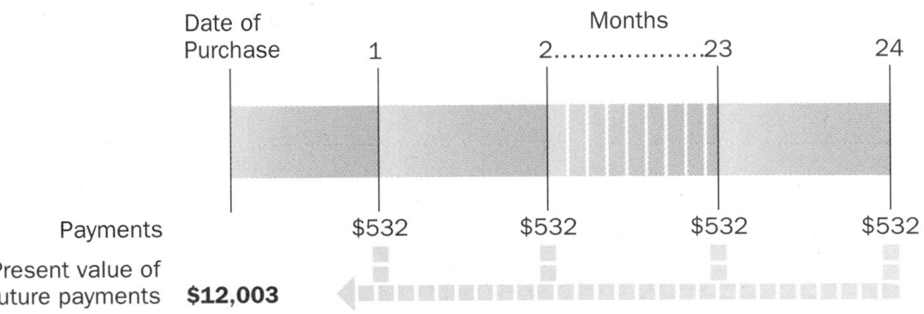

2. As will be explained later, the $12,003 is determined by discounting an annuity of $532 for 24 months at an annual interest rate of 6%.

There are many business situations where present or future value techniques must be used in making financial decisions. Common applications in accounting include the following categories:

1. Valuing long-term notes receivable and payable where there is no stated rate of interest or where the stated rate does not reflect existing economic conditions.
2. Determining bond prices and using the effective-interest method for amortizing bond premiums or discounts.
3. Determining appropriate values for long-term capital leases and measuring the amount of interest expense and principal applicable to the periodic lease payments.
4. Accounting for pension funds, including interest accruals and amortization entries.
5. Accounting for sinking funds, for example, when a fund is established to retire long-term debts.
6. Analyzing investment alternatives.
7. Establishing amortization schedules for mortgages and measuring periodic payments on long-term purchase contracts.
8. Determining appropriate asset, liability, and equity values in mergers and business combinations.

Since future and present value techniques are commonly used in business and have become increasingly important for accountants, this chapter explains these techniques and provides several illustrations of their use. The emphasis in the chapter is on present value techniques, since most applications in accounting require future amounts to be discounted to the present. The material presented may be a review for some students; for others, it will add to the theoretical foundation underlying current accounting practice. The techniques explained will be used throughout the text, especially in the chapters dealing with long-term investments and long-term liabilities. Before future and present value techniques can be explained, however, the concept of interest must first be defined.

COMPUTING THE AMOUNT OF INTEREST

Money, like other commodities, is a scarce resource and a payment for its use is generally required. This payment (cost) for the use of money is **interest.** For example, if $100 is borrowed, whether from an individual, a business, or a bank, and $110 is paid back, $10 in interest has been paid for the use of the $100. Thus, interest represents the excess cash paid or received over the amount of cash borrowed or loaned.

Simple Interest

Generally, interest is specified in terms of a percentage rate for a period of time, usually a year. For example, interest at 8% means the annual cost of borrowing an amount of money, called the **principal,** is equal to 8% of that amount. If $100 is borrowed for a period of one year at 8% annual interest, the total to be repaid is $108—the amount of the principal, $100, and the interest for a year, $8 ($100 × .08 × 1). Interest on a $1,000 note for 6 months at an annual rate of 8% is $40 ($1,000 × .08 × 6/12). In this case, the annual rate of 8% is multipled by 6/12 (or 1/2 year) because interest is being computed for less than one year. Thus, the formula for computing **simple interest** is:

$$i = p \times r \times t,$$

where:

i = Amount of simple interest
p = Principal amount
r = Interest rate (per period)
t = Time (number of periods)

The Difference Between Simple and Compound Interest

The preceding formula applies to the computation of simple interest. Most transactions, however, involve **compound interest.** This means that the amount of interest earned for a certain period is added to the principal for the next period. Interest for the subsequent period is computed on the new amount, which includes both principal and accumulated interest.

The difference between simple and compound interest can be quite significant, particularly over a long period of time. Consider, for example, the case of Christopher Columbus. On October 12, 1492, Columbus landed in the Americas and (although this is not well known) his first action was to deposit $100 in the First Bank of the Americas. The annual interest rate was 5%. On October 12, 1992, Columbus' heirs went to the bank to check the status of their ancestor's account. The bank manager informed them that certain records had been lost, and it was unknown whether Mr. Columbus had selected a simple or compound interest account. The heirs were given the option of making that choice now. After a few calculations, the heirs elected compound interest. Why? Using simple interest, the balance in Columbus' account had increased by $5 per year ($100 x .05) to a current total of $2,600 ($100 principal + $2,500 interest). Using compound interest, the money in Columbus' account (which had been earning interest on the interest) totaled $3,932,000,000,000, or approximately $4 trillion.

Computing Compound Interest. To illustrate the computation of compound interest, assume $100 is deposited in a bank and left for two years at 6% annual interest. At the end of the first year, the $100 has earned $6 interest ($100 × .06 × 1). At the end of the second year, $6 has been earned for the first year, plus another $6.36 interest (6% on the $106 balance at the beginning of the second year). Thus, the total interest earned is $12.36 rather than $12 because of the compounding effect. The table below, based on the foregoing example, illustrates the computation of simple and compound interest for four years.

	Simple Interest			Compound Interest		
Year	*Computation*	*Interest*	*Total*	*Computation*	*Interest*	*Total*
1	($100 × .06)	$6	$106	($100.00 × .06)	$6.00	$106.00
2	(100 × .06)	6	112	(106.00 × .06)	6.36	112.36
3	(100 × .06)	6	118	(112.36 × .06)	6.74	119.10
4	(100 × .06)	6	124	(119.10 × .06)	7.15	126.25

The Effect of Compounding Periods. The interest rate used in compound interest problems is the **effective rate of interest** and is generally stated as an annual rate, sometimes called "per annum." However, if the compounding of interest is for periods other than a year, the stated rate of interest must be adjusted. A comparable adjustment must be made to the number of periods. The adjustments required to the interest rate (i) and to the number of periods (n) for semiannual, quarterly, and monthly compounding of interest are as follows:

Example	Annual Compounding	Semiannual Compounding	Quarterly Compounding	Monthly Compounding
1.	i = 6%, n = 10	i = 3%, n = 20	i = 1.5%, n = 40	i =.5%, n = 120
2.	i = 12%, n = 5	i = 6%, n = 10	i = 3%, n = 20	i = 1%, n = 60
3.	i = 24%, n = 3	i = 12%, n = 6	i = 6%, n = 12	i = 2%, n = 36

As shown in the table, the semiannual compounding of interest requires the annual interest rate to be reduced by half and the number of periods to be doubled. Quarterly compounding of interest requires use of one-fourth the annual rate and 4 times the number of periods, and so forth. Because of this compounding effect, more interest is earned by an investor with semiannual interest than with annual interest, and more is earned with quarterly compounding than with semiannual compounding. Monthly compounding of interest is even better than quarterly compounding, from an investor's perspective.

FUTURE- AND PRESENT-VALUE TECHNIQUES

Since money earns interest over time, $100 received today is more valuable than $100 received one year from today. Future and present value analysis is a method of comparing the value of money received or expected to be received at different time periods.

Analyses requiring comparisons of present dollars and future dollars may be viewed from one of two perspectives, the future or the present. If a future time frame is chosen, all cash flows must be **accumulated** to that future point. In this instance, the effect of interest is to increase the amounts or values over time so that the future amount is greater than the present amount. For example, $500 invested today will accumulate to a future value of $1,079 (rounded) in 10 years if 8% annually compounded interest is paid on the investment.

If, on the other hand, the present is chosen as the point in time at which to evaluate alternatives, all cash flows must be **discounted** from the future to the present. In this instance, the discounting effect reduces the amounts or values. To illustrate, if an investor is earning 10% annual interest on a note receivable that will pay $10,000 in 3 years, what might the investor accept today in full payment, i.e., what is the present value of that note? The amount the investor should be willing to accept, assuming a 10% interest rate is satisfactory and that other considerations are held constant, is $7,513 (rounded), which is the discounted present value of the note. The rationale for the investor is that if the $7,513 could be invested at 10%, compounded annually, it would accumulate to $10,000 in 3 years.

As just illustrated, the future and present value situations involving single payments are essentially reciprocal relationships, and both future and present values are based on the concept of interest. Thus, if interest can be earned at 8% per year, the future value of $100 one year from now is $108 . Conversely, assuming the same rate of interest, the present value of a $108 payment due in one year is $100 [$108 ÷ (1 + .08)]. Similarly, $100 to be received in one year, at an 8% annual interest rate, is worth $92.59 today ($100 ÷ 1.08), because $92.59 invested at 8% will grow to $100 in one year.

Use of Formulas

There are four common future and present value situations, each with a corresponding formula. Two of the situations deal with one-time, single payments or receipts[3] (either future or present values), and the other two involve annuities (either future or present values). An **annuity** consists of a **series of equal payments** over a specified number of **equal time periods.** For example, a contract calling for three annual payments of $3,000 each would be an annuity. However, a similar contract requiring three annual payments of $2,000, $3,000, and $4,000, respectively, would not be an annuity since the payments are not equal.

Without going into the derivation of the formulas, the four common situations are as follows:

3. Hereafter in this chapter, the terms *payments* and *receipts* will be used interchangeably. A payment by one party in a transaction becomes a receipt to the other party and vice versa.

1. Future Value of a Single Payment: $FV = P(1 + i)^n$ where:

FV = Future value
P = Principal amount to be accumulated
i = Interest rate per period
n = Number of periods

Example. Future value of $1,500 to be accumulated at 10% annual interest for 5 years.

$FV = \$1,500\ (1 + .10)^5$
$FV = \underline{\underline{\$2,416}}$ (rounded)

2. Present Value of a Single Payment: $PV = A\left[\frac{1}{(1 + i)^n}\right]$ where:

PV = Present value
A = Accumulated amount to be discounted
i = Interest rate per period
n = Number of periods

Example. Present value of $2,416 to be discounted at 10% annual interest for 5 years.

$$PV = \$2,416\left[\frac{1}{(1 + .10)^5}\right]$$

$PV = \underline{\underline{\$1,500}}$ (rounded)

3. Future Value of an Annuity: $FV_n = R\left[\frac{(1 + i)^n - 1}{i}\right]$ where:

FV_n = Future value of an annuity
R = Annuity payment to be accumulated
i = Interest rate per period
n = Number of periods

Example. Future value of annuity of $2,000 for 10 years to be accumulated at 12% annual interest.

$$FV_n = \$2,000\left[\frac{(1 + .12)^{10} - 1}{.12}\right]$$

$FV_n = \underline{\underline{\$35,097}}$ (rounded)

4. Present Value of an Annuity: $PV_n = R\left[\frac{1 - \frac{1}{(1 + i)^n}}{i}\right]$ where:

PV_n = Present value of an annuity
R = Annuity payment to be discounted
i = Interest rate per period
n = Number of periods

Example. Present value of an annuity of $5,000 for 3 years to be discounted at 11% annual interest.

$$PV_n = \$5,000\left[\frac{1 - \frac{1}{(1 + .11)^3}}{.11}\right]$$

$PV_n = \underline{\underline{\$12,219}}$ (rounded)

Use of Tables

In the previous examples, formulas were used to make the computations. This is easily accomplished with most modern-day calculators or with microcomputers. Without such tools, however, use of the formulas is time-consuming. Because of this, future and present value tables have been developed for each of the four situations. These tables, such as those provided on pages 267–272, are based on computing the value of $1 for various interest rates and periods of time. Consequently, future and present value computations can be made by multiplying the appropriate table value factor for $1 by the applicable single payment or annuity amount involved in the particular situation. Thus, the formulas for the four situations may be rewritten as follows:

1. Future Value of a Single Payment:

$FV = P(1 + i)^n$ or $FV = P(FVF_{\overline{n|}i})$ or simply
$FV = P(\text{Table I factor})$

where:

$FVF_{\overline{n|}i}$ = Future value factor for a particular interest rate (i) and for a certain number of periods (n) from Table I.

Example (from example 1, previously illustrated)

FV = $1,500 (1.6105 = Factor from Table I; n = 5; i = 10%)
FV = $2,416 (rounded)

2. Present Value of a Single Payment:

$PV = A\left[\frac{1}{(1 + i)^n}\right]$ *or* $PV = A(PVF_{\overline{n|}i})$ *or* simply

$PV = A(\text{Table II factor})$

where:

$PVF_{\overline{n|}i}$ = Present value factor for a particular interest rate (i) and for a certain number of periods (n) from Table II.

Example (from example 2, previously illustrated):

PV = $2,416 (0.6209 = Factor from Table II; n = 5; i = 10%)
PV = $1,500 (rounded)

3. Future Value of an Annuity:

$FV_n = R\left[\frac{(1 + i)^n - 1}{i}\right]$ *or* $FV_n = R(FVAF_{\overline{n|}i})$ *or* simply

$FV_n = R(\text{Table III factor})$

where:

$FVAF_{\overline{n|}i}$ = Future value annuity factor for a particular interest rate (i) and for a certain number of periods (n) from Table III.

Example (from example 3; previously illustrated)

FV_n = $2,000 (17.5487 = Factor from Table III; n = 10; i = 12%)
FV_n = $35,097 (rounded)

4. Present Value of an Annuity:

$$PV_n = R\left[\frac{1 - \frac{1}{(1+i)^n}}{i}\right] \text{ or } PV_n = R(PVAF_{\overline{n|}i}) \text{ or simply}$$

PV_n = R (Table IV factor)

where:

$PVAF_{\overline{n|}i}$ = Present value annuity factor for a particular interest rate (i) and for a certain number of periods (n) from Table IV.

Example (from example 4, illustrated previously)

PV_n = $5,000 (2.4437 = Factor from Table IV; n = 3; i = 11%)
PV_n = $12,219 (rounded)

Note that the answers obtained in the examples by using the tables are the same as those obtained using the formulas with a calculator or microcomputer.

Business Applications

The following examples demonstrate the application of future and present value computations in solving business problems. Additional applications are provided in later sections as well as in the cases, exercises, and problems at the end of the chapter.

Example 1—Future Value of a Single Payment

Marywhether Company loans its president, Celia Phillips, $15,000 to purchase a car. Marywhether accepts a note due in 4 years with interest at 10% compounded semiannually. How much cash does Marywhether expect to receive from Phillips when the note is paid at maturity?

Solution: This problem involves a single payment to be accumulated 4 years into the future. In many present and future value problems, a time line is helpful in visualizing the problem:

Compensation for Loss of Income

In courts of law, attorneys commonly call on CPAs to assist in computing damages. For example, in cases where an individual is wrongly discharged and is prevented from continuing in a chosen profession, lost income must be computed and a settlement made.

Consider the case of Ann Hopkins. She was nominated for partnership at Price Waterhouse, an international CPA firm, in 1982. At the time, she was bringing more business into the firm than any of the other 87 partner candidates, who were all men. She was denied partnership and she subsequently resigned and sued the firm. A U.S. district judge ruled in 1990 that Hopkins was to be made a partner in Price Waterhouse and awarded back pay.

Questions:

1. How should the amount of back pay be computed? Should raises that might have been received be included? Should cost of living adjustments be factored in?
2. What assumptions should be made regarding the interest rate used in computing damages? Should the market rate of interest be used? Should the real interest rate be used (i.e., the market rate less the rate of inflation)?
3. If you were Ms. Hopkins, which interest rate would you argue for and why?
4. If you were Price Waterhouse, which interest rate would you argue for and why?

Source: *Public Accounting Report,* June 15, 1990, pp. 1–2.

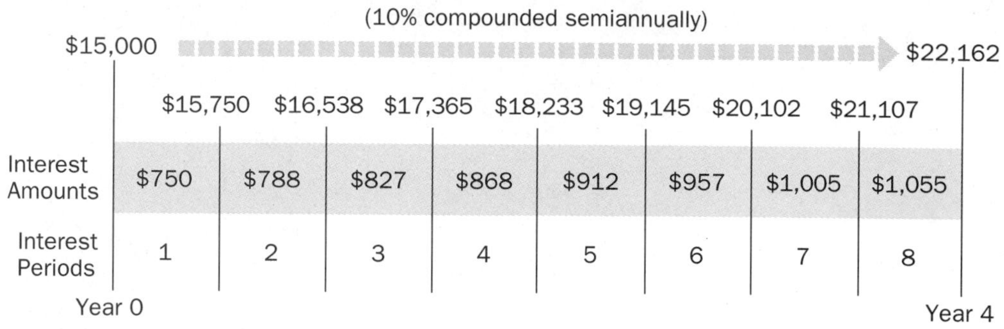

(10% compounded semiannually)

	$15,000 →							$22,162
	$15,750	$16,538	$17,365	$18,233	$19,145	$20,102	$21,107	
Interest Amounts	$750	$788	$827	$868	$912	$957	$1,005	$1,055
Interest Periods	1	2	3	4	5	6	7	8
Year 0								Year 4

The $15,000 must be accumulated for 4 years at 10% compounded semiannually. Table I may be used, and the applicable formula is:

$FV = P(FVF_{\overline{n}|i})$

where:

FV = The future value of a single payment
P = $15,000
n = 8 periods (4 years x 2)
i = 5% effective interest rate per period (10% ÷ 2)

$FV = \$15,000\ (\text{Table I}_{\overline{8}|5\%})$
FV = $15,000 (1.4775)
FV = $22,162 (rounded)

In 4 years, Marywhether will expect to receive $22,162, consisting of $15,000 principal repayment and $7,162 interest.

Example 2—Present Value of a Single Payment

Edgemont Enterprises holds a note receivable from a regular customer. The note is for $22,000, which includes principal and interest, and is due to be paid in exactly 2 years. The customer wants to pay the note now, and both parties agree that 10% is a reasonable annual interest rate to use in discounting the note. How much will the customer pay Edgemont Enterprises today to settle the obligation?

Solution: The single future payment must be discounted to the present value at the agreed upon annual rate of interest of 10%. Since this involves a present-value computation of a single payment, Table II is used, and the applicable formula is:

$PV = A(PVF_{\overline{n}|i})$

where:

PV = The present value of a single payment
A = $22,000
n = 2 periods
i = 10% effective interest rate per period

$PV = \$22,000\ (\text{Table II}_{\overline{2}|10\%})$
PV = $22,000 (0.8264)
PV = $18,181 (rounded)

The customer will pay approximately $18,181 today to settle the obligation.

Example 3—Present Value of Series of Unequal Payments

Casper Sporting Goods Co. is considering a $1 million capital investment that will provide the following expected net receipts at the *end* of each of the next six years.

Year	Expected Net Receipts
1	$195,000
2	457,000
3	593,000
4	421,000
5	95,000
6	5,000

Casper will make the investment only if the rate of return is greater than 12%. Will Casper make the investment?

Solution: A series of unequal future receipts must be compared with a present single-payment investment. For such a comparison to be made, all future cash flows must be discounted to the present.

If the rate of return on the investment is greater than 12%, then the total of all yearly net receipts discounted to the present at 12% will be greater than the amount invested. Since the future receipts are not equal, this situation does not involve an annuity. Each receipt must be discounted individually. Table II is used, and the applicable formula is: $PV = A(PVF_{\overline{n}|i})$ where:

(1) Year = n	(2) A (Net Receipts)	(3) Table II $_{\overline{n}|\,12\%}$	(2) x (3) = (4) PV (Discounted Amount)
1	$195,000	.8929	$ 174,116
2	457,000	.7972	364,320
3	593,000	.7118	422,097
4	421,000	.6355	267,546
5	95,000	.5674	53,903
6	5,000	.5066	2,533
			Total $1,284,515 (Rounded)

The total discounted receipts are greater than the $1 million investment; thus, the rate of return is more than 12%. Therefore, other things being equal, Casper will invest.

Example 4—Future Value of an Annuity

Boswell Co. owes an installment debt of $1,000 per quarter for 5 years. The creditor has indicated a willingness to accept an equivalent single payment at the end of the 5-year period instead of the series of equal payments made at the end of each quarter. If the money is worth 16% compounded quarterly, what is the equivalent single payment at the end of the contract period?

Solution: The equivalent single payment can be found by accumulating the quarterly $1,000 payments to the end of the contract period. Since the payments are equal, this is an annuity. Table III is used, and the applicable formula is:

$FV_n = R(FVAF_{\overline{n|}i})$

where:

FV_n = The unknown equivalent lump-sum payment
R = \$1,000 quarterly installment to be accumulated
n = 20 periods (5 years x 4 quarters)
i = 4% effective interest rate per period (16% ÷ 4)

FV_n = \$1,000 (Table III $_{\overline{20|}4\%}$)
FV_n = \$1,000 (29.7781)
FV_n = \$29,778 (rounded)

The \$29,778 paid at the end of 5 years is approximately equivalent to the 20 quarterly payments of \$1,000 each plus interest.

Example 5—Present Value of an Annuity

Mary Sabin, proprietor of Sabin Appliance, received two offers for her last deluxe-model refrigerator. Jerry Sloan will pay \$650 in cash. Elise Jensen will pay \$700 consisting of a down payment of \$100 and 12 monthly payments of \$50. If the installment interest rate is 24% compounded monthly, which offer should Sabin accept?

Solution: In order to compare the two alternative methods of payment, all cash flows must be accumulated or discounted to one point in time. As illustrated by the time line, the present is selected as the point of comparison.

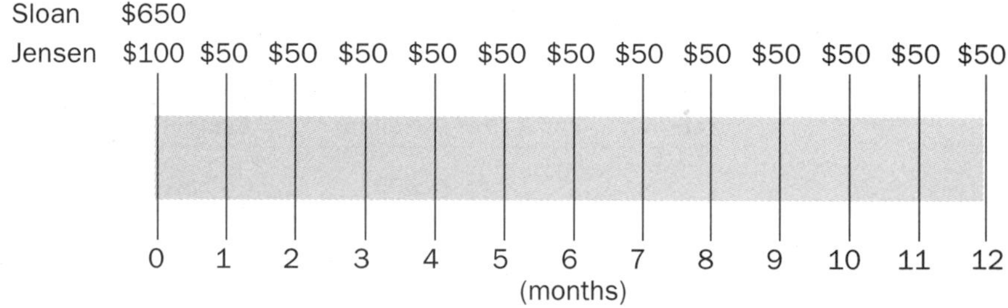

Sloan's offer is \$650 today. The present value of \$650 today is \$650. Jensen's offer consists of an annuity of 12 payments, plus \$100 paid today, which is not part of the annuity. The annuity may be discounted to the present by using Table IV and the applicable formula:

$PV_n = R(PVAF_{\overline{n|}i})$

where:

PV_n = Unknown present value of 12 payments
R = \$50 monthly payment to be discounted
n = 12 periods (1 year × 12 months)
i = 2% effective interest rate per period (24% ÷ 12)

PV_n = \$50 (Table IV $_{\overline{12|}2\%}$)
PV_n = \$50 (10.5753)
PV_n = \$529

Present value of Jensen's payments	\$529
Present value of Jensen's \$100 down payment	100
Total present value of Jensen's offer	\$629

Therefore, Sloan's offer of $650 cash is more desirable than Jensen's offer.

Determining the Number of Periods, the Interest Rate, or the Amount of Payment

So far, the examples and illustrations have required solutions for the future or present values, with the other three variables in the formulas being given. Sometimes business problems require solving for the number of periods, the interest rate,[4] or the amount of payment instead of the future or present value amounts. In each of the formulas, there are four variables. If information is known about any three of the variables, the fourth (unknown) value can be determined. The following examples illustrate how to solve for these other variables.

Example 6—Determining the Number of Periods

Rocky Mountain Survey Company wants to purchase new equipment at a cost of $100,000. The company has $88,850 available in cash but does not want to borrow the other $11,150 for the purchase. If the company can invest the $88,850 today at an interest rate of 12% compounded quarterly, how many years will it be before Rocky Mountain will have the $100,000 it needs to buy the equipment?

Solution: As illustrated below, Rocky Mountain Survey Company can invest $88,850 now at 12% interest compounded quarterly and needs to know how long it will take for this amount to accumulate to $100,000.

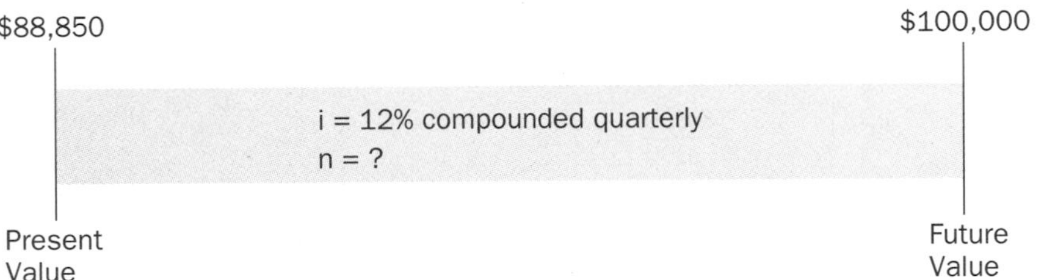

In this situation, involving both present values and future values, either Table I or Table II may be used. If Table I is used, the applicable formula is:

$$FV = P(FVF_{\overline{n|}\,i})$$
$$FV = P\text{ (Table I factor)}$$

The problem would be solved as follows:

$$\frac{FV}{P} = \text{Table I factor}$$

$$\frac{\$100{,}000}{\$88{,}850} = 1.1255$$

Reading down the 3% column (12% ÷ 4) in Table I, the factor value of 1.1255 is shown for n = 4. Therefore, it would take 4 periods (quarters) or 1 year for Rocky Mountain to earn enough interest to have $88,850 accumulate to a future value of $100,000.

4. When the interest rate is not known, it is properly called the **implicit rate of interest**, that is, the rate of interest implied by the terms of a contract or situation. (See Examples 7 and 10 in this chapter.)

If Table II is used, the applicable formula is:

$$PV = A\,(PVF_{\overline{n|}\,i})$$
$$PV = A\text{ (Table II factor)}$$

Solving,

$$\frac{PV}{A} = \text{Table II factor}$$

$$\frac{\$88{,}850}{\$100{,}000} = .8885$$

Reading down the 3% column in Table II, the factor of 0.8885 corresponds with n = 4 (quarters) or 1 year. This illustrates again the reciprocal nature of future and present values for single payments.

Example 7—Determining the Interest Rate

The Hughes family wishes to purchase a baby grand piano. The cost of the piano one year from now will be $5,800. If the family can invest $5,000 now, what annual interest rate must they earn on their investment to have $5,800 at the end of one year?

Solution: The Hughes family can invest $5,000 now and needs it to accumulate to $5,800 in one year. The rate of annual interest they need to earn can be computed as shown below.

If Table I is used, the applicable formula is:

$$FV = P\,(FVF_{\overline{n|}\,i})$$
$$FV = P\text{ (Table I factor)}$$

$$\frac{FV}{P} = \text{Table I factor}$$

$$\frac{\$5{,}800}{\$5{,}000} = 1.1600$$

Reading across the n = 1 row, the factor value 1.1600 corresponds to an annual effective interest rate of 16%. Therefore, the Hughes family would have to earn 16% annual interest to accomplish their goal. The same result is obtained if Table II is used to solve this problem.

Example 8—Determining the Amount of Payment

Provo 1st National Bank is willing to lend a customer $75,000 to buy a warehouse. The note will be secured by a 5-year mortgage and carry an annual interest rate of 12%. Equal payments are to be made at the end of each year over the 5-year period. How much will the yearly payment be?

Solution: This is an example of an unknown annuity payment. Since the present value ($75,000) is known, as well as the interest rate (12%) and the number of periods (5), the annuity payment can be determined using Table IV. The applicable formula is:

$$PV_n = R\,(PVAF_{\overline{n|}\,i})$$
$$PV_n = R\text{ (Table IV factor)}$$
$$\$75{,}000 = R\,(3.6048)\text{ (for n = 5 and i = 12\%)}$$

$$\frac{\$75{,}000}{3.6048} = R$$

$$\underline{\underline{\$20{,}806}}\text{ (rounded)} = R$$

The payment on this 5-year mortgage would be approximately $20,806 each year.

ADDITIONAL COMPLEXITIES

The illustrations up to this point have been fairly straightforward. In practice, however, complexities can arise that make it somewhat more difficult to use the future and present value tables. Two of these complexities involve: (1) converting ordinary annuity tables to annuity-due factor values, and (2) interpolation.

Ordinary Annuity Vs. Annuity Due

Annuities are of two types: ordinary annuities (annuities in arrears) and annuities due (annuities in advance). The periodic receipts or payments for an **ordinary annuity** are made at the *end of each period,* and the last payment coincides with the end of the annuity term. The periodic receipts or payments for an **annuity due** are made at the *beginning of the period,* and one period of the annuity term remains after the last payment. These differences are illustrated below.

Ordinary Annuity of $1 for 3 Years (10% annual interest)

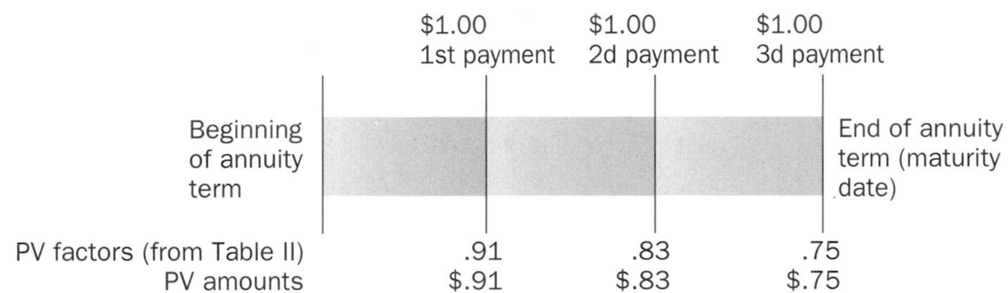

Therefore, assuming a 10% annual interest rate, the present value of an annuity of $1 per year to be received at the *end* of each of the next 3 years is $2.49 ($.91 + $.83 + $.75). Notice that the last $1 is received on the maturity date, or the end of the annuity term.

Again assuming a 10% annual interest rate, the present value of an annuity of $1 per year to be received at the *beginning* of each of the next 3 years is $2.74 ($1.00 + $.91 + $.83). Notice here that the last payment is received 1 year prior to the maturity date.

Annuity Due of $1 for 3 Years (10% annual interest)

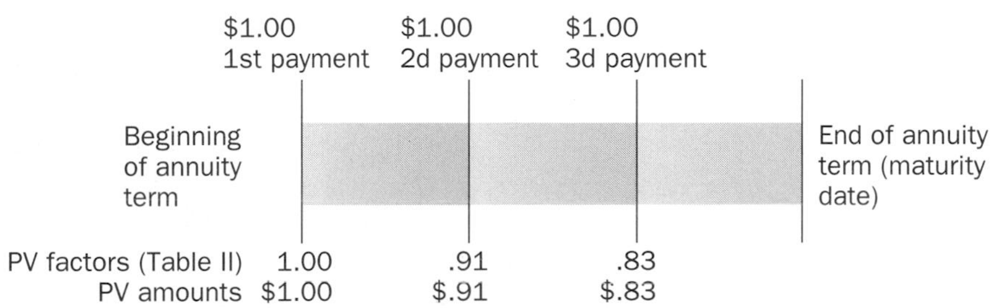

The difference in the two annuities is in the timing of the payments, and, therefore, how many interest periods are involved. As shown on page 258, both annuities require 3 payments. However, the ordinary annuity payments are at the end of each period, so there are only 2 periods of interest accumulation; the annuity-due payments are in advance or at the beginning of the period, so there are 3 periods of interest accumulation.

Accumulation of Ordinary Annuity for 3 Years

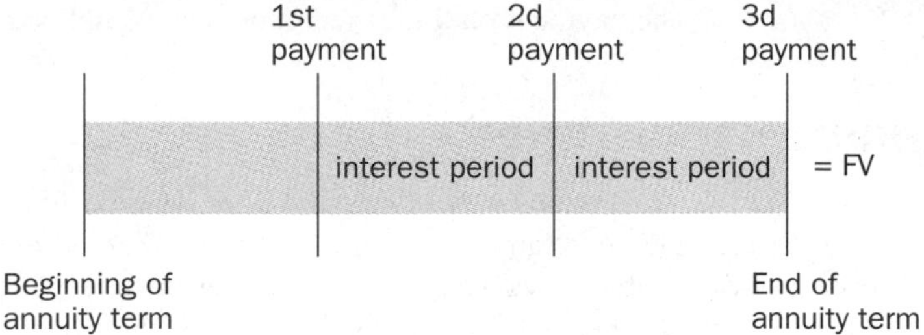

Accumulation of Annuity Due for 3 Years

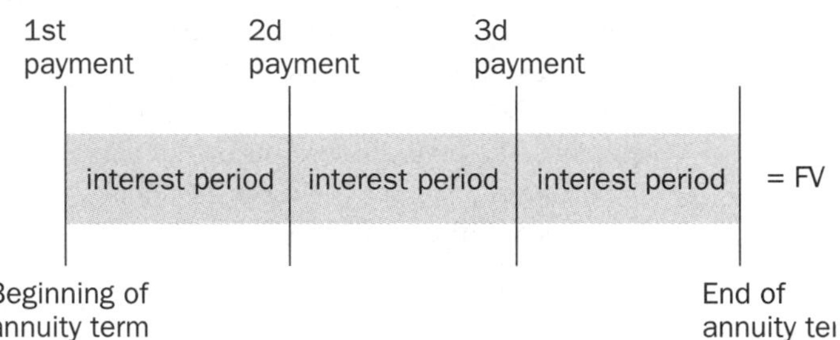

The preceding situation is exactly reversed when viewed from a present-value standpoint. The ordinary annuity has 3 interest or discount periods, while the annuity due has only 2 periods, as shown below.

Present Value of Ordinary Annuity for 3 Years

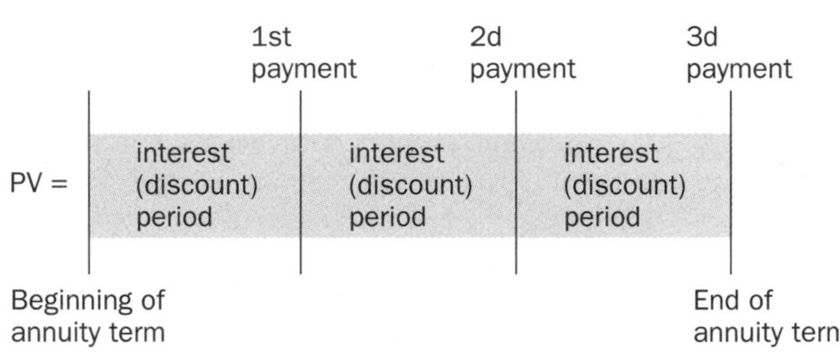

Present Value of Annuity Due for 3 Years

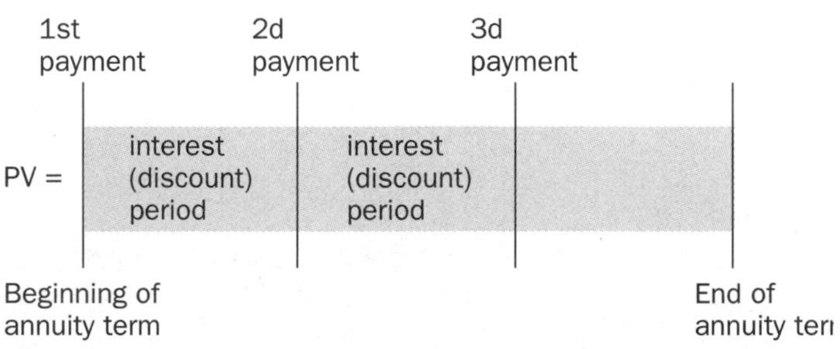

Even though most future- and present-value annuity tables are computed for ordinary annuities (payments at the end of the periods), these tables can be used for solving annuity-due problems where the payments are in advance. However, the following adjustments would be required:

1. To find the **future value of an annuity due** using ordinary annuity table values (Table III), select the appropriate table value for an ordinary annuity for one additional period (n + 1) and subtract the extra payment (which is 1.0000 in terms of the table value for rents of $1.00). The formula is:

$$FV_n = R(FVAF_{\overline{n+1}|\, i} - 1)$$

2. To find the **present value of an annuity due** using ordinary annuity table values (Table IV), select the appropriate table value for an ordinary annuity for one less period (n – 1) and add the extra payment (1.0000). The formula is:

$$PV_n = R(PVAF_{\overline{n-1}|\, i} + 1)$$

By making the above adjustments, when payments are in advance, ordinary annuity tables may be used for all annuity situations. For example, the table value (Table III) for the future amount of an annuity due for 3 periods at 10% is:

(1) Factor for future value of an ordinary annuity of $1 for 4 periods (n + 1) at 10%	4.6410
(2) Less one payment	1.0000
(3) Factor for future value of an annuity due of $1 for 3 periods at 10%	3.6410

The table value (Table IV) for the present value of an annuity due for 3 periods at 10% is:

(1) Factor for present value of an ordinary annuity of $1 for 2 periods (n – 1) at 10%	1.7355
(2) Plus one payment	1.0000
(3) Factor for present value of an annuity due of $1 for 3 periods at 10%	2.7355

As noted, ordinary annuity tables can be converted for use with annuity-due situations. There are annuity-due tables available, however, that make these conversions unnecessary. Table V and Table VI are provided for annuity-due factor values. Note that these table values are the same as those for Tables III and IV if annuity-due adjustments are made, as previously described.

The following examples illustrate the application of annuity-due table values.

Example 9—Using Annuity-Due Table Values for Future Amounts

The Porter Corporation desires to accumulate funds to retire a $200,000 bond issue at the end of 15 years. Funds set aside for this purpose can be invested to yield 8%. What annual payment, starting immediately, would provide the needed funds?

Solution: Annuity payments of an unknown amount, to be paid in advance, are to be accumulated toward a specific dollar amount at a known interest rate. Because the first payment is to be made immediately, all payments will fall due at the beginning of each period and an annuity due is used. Therefore, Table V is used. The appropriate formula is the same as that presented previously for an ordinary annuity, the only difference being the table in which the annuity factor is found.

$FV_n = R(FVAF_{\overline{n}|i})$

where:

FV_n = $200,000
R = Unknown annual payment
n = 15 periods
i = 8% annual interest
$200,000 = R(Table $V_{\overline{15}|8\%}$)
$200,000 = R(29.3243)

$\frac{\$200{,}000}{29.3243} = R$

$6,820 = R

Porter Corporation must deposit $6,820 annually, starting immediately, to accumulate $200,000 in 15 years at 8% annual interest.

Example 10—Using Annuity-Due Table Values for Present Values

Utah Corporation has completed negotiations to lease equipment with a fair market value of $45,897. The lease contract specifies semiannual payments of $3,775 for 10 years beginning immediately. At the end of the lease, Utah Corporation may purchase the equipment for a nominal amount. What is the implicit annual rate of interest on the lease purchase?

Solution: This is a common application of an annuity-due situation in accounting since most lease contracts require payments in advance, i.e., at the beginning of the period rather than at the end of the period. The implicit interest rate must be computed for the present value of an annuity due. The present value is the fair market value of the equipment, and the payment is the lease payment. Table VI is used, and the applicable formula is:

$PV_n = R(PVAF_{\overline{n}|i})$

where:

PV_n = $45,897
R = $3,775
n = 20 periods (10 years x 2 payments per year)
i = The unknown semiannual interest rate
$45,897 = $3,775 (Table $VI_{\overline{20}|i}$)

$\frac{\$45{,}897}{\$3{,}775} = 12.1581 = \text{Table } VI_{\overline{20}|i}$

i = 6%

Examination of Table VI for 20 periods and a factor of 12.1581 shows i = 6%. The implicit annual interest rate is twice the semiannual rate, or 2 × 6% = 12%.

Interpolation

Difficulty in using future- and present-value tables arises when the exact factor does not appear in the table. One solution is to use the applicable formula. **Interpolation** is another solution. Interpolation assumes the change between two table values is linear. Although such an assumption is not totally correct, the margin of error is often insignificant, especially if the table value ranges are not too wide.

For example, determine the table value for the present value of $1 due in 9 periods at 4 1/2%. The appropriate factor does not appear in Table II. However, the two closest values from Table II are .7026 and .6446. Interpolation relates the unknown value to the change in the known values. This relationship may be shown as a proportion:

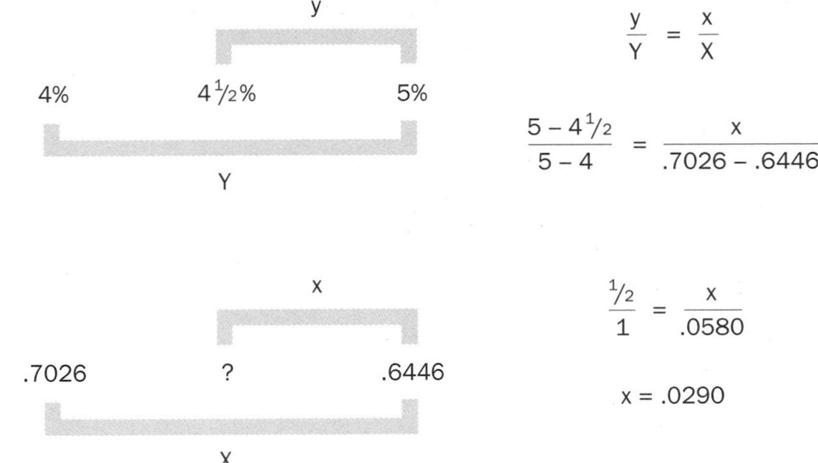

$$\frac{y}{Y} = \frac{x}{X}$$

$$\frac{5 - 4\frac{1}{2}}{5 - 4} = \frac{x}{.7026 - .6446}$$

$$\frac{\frac{1}{2}}{1} = \frac{x}{.0580}$$

$$x = .0290$$

The .0290 is the difference between the value for 5% and the value for 4 1/2%. Therefore, the value needed is .0290 + .6446 = .6736. Using the mathematical formula for Table II,

$$\left\{ PV = A \left[\frac{1}{(1 + i)^n} \right] \right\},$$

the present value of $1 at 4 1/2% interest for 9 periods is .6729.

$$\left\{ PV = 1 \left[\frac{1}{(1 + .045)^9} \right] \right\}.$$

The difference (.6736 – .6729 = .0007) is insignificant for most business purposes.

Interpolation is useful in finding a particular unknown table value that lies between two given values. This procedure is also used in approximating the number of periods or unknown interest rates when the table value is known. The following examples illustrate the determination of these two variables.

Example 11—Interpolation: Unknown Number of Periods

The Newbold Foundation contributes $600,000 to a university for a new building on the condition that construction will not begin until the gift, invested at 10% per year, amounts to $1,500,000. How long before construction may begin?

Solution: This problem involves finding the time (number of periods) required for a lump-sum payment to accumulate to a specified future amount. Table I is used and the applicable formula is:

$$FV = P(FVF_{\overline{n|}\,i})$$

where:

FV	= $1,500,000
P	= $600,000
n	= Unknown number of periods
i	= 10% effective interest rate per year

$$\$1{,}500{,}000 = \$600{,}000(\text{Table I}_{\overline{n|}\,10\%})$$

$$\frac{\$1{,}500{,}000}{\$600{,}000} = \text{Table I}_{\overline{n|}\,10\%}$$

$$\underline{\underline{2.5000}} = \text{Table I}_{\overline{n|}\,10\%}$$

Referring to Table I, reading down the $i = 10\%$ column:

n	Table Factor
9 =	2.3579
10 =	2.5937

Interpolating:

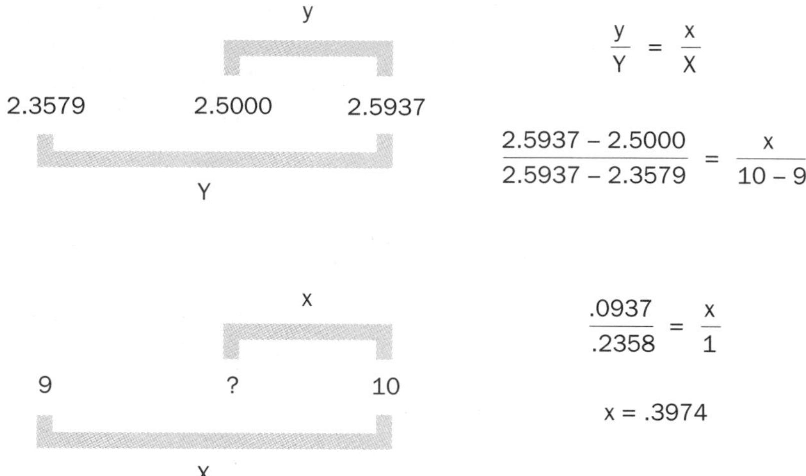

The .3974 is the difference between the number of periods at table factor 2.5937 and the number of periods at table factor 2.5000. Therefore, the number of periods needed is 10.0000 – .3974 = 9.6026. In other words, about 9.6 periods (in this case, years) are required for $600,000 to amount to $1,500,000 at 10% annual interest.

Example 12—Interpolation: Implicit Rate of Interest

Fellmar, Inc., has entered into an automobile lease arrangement. The fair market value of the leased automobile is $15,815, and the contract calls for quarterly payments of $1,525 due at the end of each quarter for 3 years. What is the implicit rate of interest on the lease arrangement?

Solution: The implicit interest rate must be computed for the present value of an ordinary annuity. The present value is the fair market value of the automobile, and the payment is the lease payment. Table IV is used, and the appropriate formula is given below.

$PV_n = R(PVAF_{\overline{n|}\,i})$

where:

PV_n = \$15,815
R = \$1,525
n = 12 (3 years × 4 payments per year)
i = The unknown quarterly interest rate

$\$15,815 = \$1,525\ (\text{Table IV}_{\overline{12|}\,i})$

$\frac{\$15,815}{\$1,525} = \text{Table IV}_{\overline{12|}\,i}$

$\underline{\underline{10.3705}} = \text{Table IV}_{\overline{12|}\,i}$

Reading across the $n = 12$ row of Table IV:

i	Table Factor
2% =	10.5753
3% =	9.9540

Interpolating:

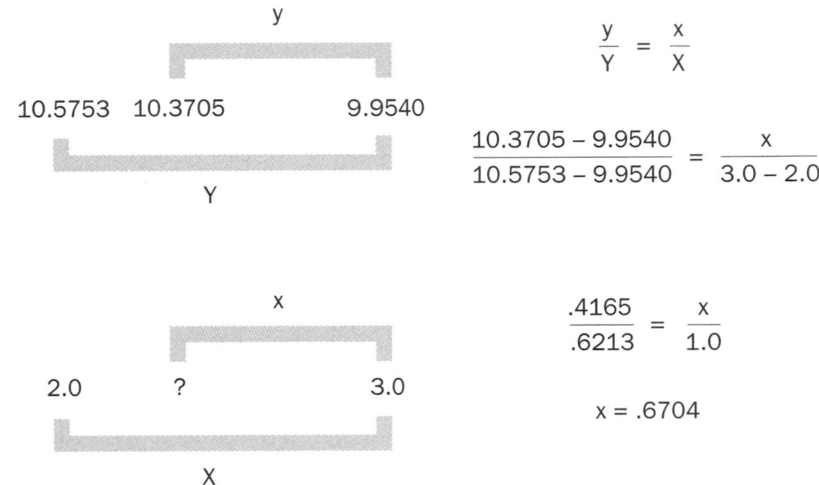

The .6704 is the difference between the interest rate at the table factor 9.9540 and the interest rate at the table factor 10.3705. Therefore, the quarterly implicit interest rate is 3.0000 – .6704 = 2.33%; and the annual implicit interest rate is 9.32% (2.33% × 4).

CONCLUDING COMMENT

As noted in Chapter 2, the FASB's conceptual framework allows for various measurement attributes, one of which is discounted present values. This measurement attribute is receiving additional attention from the FASB. In October 1988, the FASB added to its agenda a project that is considering the use of present values and interest in accounting measurements. In December 1990 the FASB issued a Discussion Memorandum entitled, "Present-Value-Based Measurements in Accounting."

The work of the FASB on this topic is in response to the need for a comprehensive study of present-value-based measurements. The FASB is addressing: (1) under what circumstances an amount should be recognized in financial statements based on the present value of estimated future cash flows; (2) when is it appropriate to use the effective interest method in accounting allocations over the life of an asset or liability; and (3) when the interest element involved with present-value-based measurements should be recognized as interest revenue or expense. The project will also explore related implementation issues.

This chapter has illustrated a few of the many business applications of present- and future-value measurement techniques. As the FASB continues to debate issues with long-term financial impact, e.g., deferred income taxes and postretirement employment benefits, the importance of the time-value-of-money concept will increase. In the remaining chapters of this text, additional illustrations of this important concept will be presented.

APPENDIX

Computers and the Time Value of Money

Computers have made present and future value calculations much easier. Software programs such as Lotus 1-2-3, Excel, and Quattro Pro have built-in financial functions that immediately provide the user with results without the user having to memorize formulas and access tables. In this appendix, we illustrate how one common software package, Lotus 1-2-3, can be used to compute present and future values. While spreadsheet packages differ slightly in the wording of commands, the concepts associated with the Lotus calculations illustrated here apply to other spreadsheets as well. Consult the help manual of your software program for the specific wording of a particular command.

LOTUS COMMANDS

Lotus provides a variety of commands to aid in the calculation of present and future values. Each of the computations illustrated in the text has a Lotus counterpart. Lotus has the ability to compute the present or future value of lump sums, annuities, and annuity dues. It can also determine appropriate interest rates, time periods, and payment amounts. The general format for computing either present or future values is as follows:

Present value of single payment or annuity:

@PVAL (payment, interest rate, time period, type, future value)

Future value of single payment or annuity:

@FVAL (payment, interest rate, time period, type, present value)

For each Lotus command, the user must input certain information. For the above commands, the elements of each command are defined as follows:

Payment	=	the amount of the periodic payment. (In the case of a lump sum, the periodic payment would be 0.)
Interest rate	=	the appropriate interest rate. (Remember that the interest rate and the time period must be adjusted if the compounding period is not yearly.)
Time period	=	the number of time periods over which interest is being compounded.
Type	=	If the payment is made at the end of the period, i.e., an ordinary annuity, type = 0. If payment is made at the beginning of the period, i.e., an annuity due, type = 1.
Future value	=	When computing the present value of a single payment, input the future value of the payment.
Present value	=	When computing the future value of a single payment, input the present value of the payment.

USING LOTUS FUNCTIONS TO COMPUTE SINGLE PAYMENT AMOUNTS

To illustrate how these formulas are used in computing present and future values, consider Examples 1 and 2 from pages 251 and 252 of the chapter.

Future Value of a Single Payment

In Example 1, an individual is borrowing $15,000 due in a single payment in 4 years with interest at 10% compounded semiannually. We are asked to compute the amount of the single payment to be repaid at the end of four years. Using the Lotus function, @FVAL, we input the following information:

@FVAL(0, .05, 8, 0, 15000) = $22,162 (rounded)

Note that since this is a single payment calculation, the first-term, payments, is set equal to 0. The interest rate and time period were adjusted to reflect that interest is compounded semiannually. Since the single payment will be made at the end of the fourth year, type is coded as a 0. The amount being borrowed today, $15,000, is input as the present value. The resulting answer is the same as was obtained when using the formulas or the tables.

Present Value of a Single Payment

In the case of Example 2, a company is going to receive $22,000 at the end of two years. The interest rate is 10%. Our objective is to compute the present value of the amount of the loan. Using the @PVAL function, we input the following formula:

@PVAL (0, .10, 2, 0, 22000) = $18,182 (rounded)

Again, since this is a single payment computation, the payment amount is $0. The interest rate and time periods do not need to be adjusted since they are both stated on an annual basis. The payment is made at the end of the period so type is set equal to 0. The future value of the obligation is input as $22,000.

USING LOTUS FUNCTIONS TO COMPUTE ANNUITY AMOUNTS

When computing the value of annuities, the same formulas are used except the payment field is input and the present and future value fields are omitted. Consider Examples 4 and 5 from pages 253 and 254 of the chapter.

Future Value of an Annuity

Example 4 presents the case of $1,000 payments made at the end of each quarter for five years, with an annual interest rate of 16% compounded quarterly. The @FVAL function would appear as follows:

@FVAL (1000, .04, 20, 0) = $29,778 (rounded)

Note that the interest rate and time period fields have been adjusted to reflect the fact that interest is compounded quarterly in this example. Also note, that the type field has been coded with a 0 to reflect that this is an ordinary annuity. If this had been an annuity due, the type field would have been coded with a 1. The present value field is omitted when computing annuities.

Present Value of an Annuity

In Example 5, we are trying to compute the present value of a series of $50 monthly payments made over a 12 month period. The relevant interest rate is 24% compounded monthly. Using the @PVAL function:

@PVAL (50, .02, 12, 0) = $529 (rounded)

The amount of the payment is input along with the adjusted interest rate and time periods. Again, if payments were being made at the beginning of each month instead of at the end, the type field would have been coded with a 1.

SUMMARY

The purpose of this appendix has been to introduce the reader to the use of spreadsheets to compute present and future value amounts. All of the computations made using the present and future value tables can also be made using a computer spreadsheet software package. While we have only reviewed the basic computations associated with lump sums and annuities, spreadsheets are available that compute interest rates, time periods, and other important financial factors. For those with an interest in investigating these more advanced functions, we suggest you consult the owner's manual of the software you are using.

Table I Future Value of a Single Payment

	1%	2%	3%	4%	5%	6%	7%	8%	9%	10%	11%	12%	14%	16%	20%
1	1.0100	1.0200	1.0300	1.0400	1.0500	1.0600	1.0700	1.0800	1.0900	1.1000	1.1100	1.1200	1.1400	1.1600	1.2000
2	1.0201	1.0404	1.0609	1.0816	1.1025	1.1236	1.1449	1.1664	1.1881	1.2100	1.2321	1.2544	1.2996	1.3456	1.4400
3	1.0303	1.0612	1.0927	1.1249	1.1576	1.1910	1.2250	1.2597	1.2950	1.3310	1.3676	1.4049	1.4815	1.5609	1.7280
4	1.0406	1.0824	1.1255	1.1699	1.2155	1.2625	1.3108	1.3605	1.4116	1.4641	1.5181	1.5735	1.6890	1.8106	2.0736
5	1.0510	1.1041	1.1593	1.2167	1.2763	1.3382	1.4026	1.4693	1.5386	1.6105	1.6851	1.7623	1.9254	2.1003	2.4883
6	1.0615	1.1262	1.1941	1.2653	1.3401	1.4185	1.5007	1.5869	1.6771	1.7716	1.8704	1.9738	2.1950	2.4364	2.9860
7	1.0721	1.1487	1.2299	1.3159	1.4071	1.5036	1.6058	1.7138	1.8280	1.9487	2.0762	2.2107	2.5023	2.8262	3.5832
8	1.0829	1.1717	1.2668	1.3686	1.4775	1.5938	1.7182	1.8509	1.9926	2.1436	2.3045	2.4760	2.8526	3.2784	4.2998
9	1.0937	1.1951	1.3048	1.4233	1.5513	1.6895	1.8385	1.9990	2.1719	2.3579	2.5580	2.7731	3.2519	3.8030	5.1598
10	1.1046	1.2190	1.3439	1.4802	1.6289	1.7908	1.9672	2.1589	2.3674	2.5937	2.8394	3.1058	3.7072	4.4114	6.1917
11	1.1157	1.2434	1.3842	1.5395	1.7103	1.8983	2.1049	2.3316	2.5804	2.8531	3.1518	3.4785	4.2262	5.1173	7.4301
12	1.1268	1.2682	1.4258	1.6010	1.7959	2.0122	2.2522	2.5182	2.8127	3.1384	3.4985	3.8960	4.8179	5.9360	8.9161
13	1.1381	1.2936	1.4685	1.6651	1.8856	2.1329	2.4098	2.7196	3.0658	3.4523	3.8833	4.3635	5.4924	6.8858	10.6993
14	1.1495	1.3195	1.5126	1.7317	1.9799	2.2609	2.5785	2.9372	3.3417	3.7975	4.3104	4.8871	6.2613	7.9875	12.8392
15	1.1610	1.3459	1.5580	1.8009	2.0789	2.3966	2.7590	3.1722	3.6425	4.1772	4.7846	5.4736	7.1379	9.2655	15.4070
16	1.1726	1.3728	1.6047	1.8730	2.1829	2.5404	2.9522	3.4259	3.9703	4.5950	5.3109	6.1304	8.1372	10.7480	18.4884
17	1.1843	1.4002	1.6528	1.9479	2.2920	2.6928	3.1588	3.7000	4.3276	5.0545	5.8951	6.8660	9.2765	12.4677	22.1861
18	1.1961	1.4282	1.7024	2.0258	2.4066	2.8543	3.3799	3.9960	4.7171	5.5599	6.5436	7.6900	10.5752	14.4625	26.6233
19	1.2081	1.4568	1.7535	2.1068	2.5270	3.0256	3.6165	4.3157	5.1417	6.1159	7.2633	8.6128	12.0557	16.7765	31.9480
20	1.2202	1.4859	1.8061	2.1911	2.6533	3.2071	3.8697	4.6610	5.6044	6.7275	8.0623	9.6463	13.7435	19.4608	38.3376
21	1.2324	1.5157	1.8603	2.2788	2.7860	3.3996	4.1406	5.0338	6.1088	7.4002	8.9492	10.8038	15.6676	22.5745	46.0051
22	1.2447	1.5460	1.9161	2.3699	2.9253	3.6035	4.4304	5.4365	6.6586	8.1403	9.9336	12.1003	17.8610	26.1864	55.2061
23	1.2572	1.5769	1.9736	2.4647	3.0715	3.8197	4.7405	5.8715	7.2579	8.9543	11.0263	13.5523	20.3616	30.3762	66.2474
24	1.2697	1.6084	2.0328	2.5633	3.2251	4.0489	5.0724	6.3412	7.9111	9.8497	12.2392	15.1786	23.2122	35.2364	79.4968
25	1.2824	1.6406	2.0938	2.6658	3.3864	4.2919	5.4274	6.8485	8.6231	10.8347	13.5855	17.0001	26.4619	40.8742	95.3962
26	1.2953	1.6734	2.1566	2.7725	3.5557	4.5494	5.8074	7.3964	9.3992	11.9182	15.0799	19.0401	30.1666	47.4141	114.4755
27	1.3082	1.7069	2.2213	2.8834	3.7335	4.8223	6.2139	7.9881	10.2451	13.1100	16.7386	21.3249	34.3899	55.0004	137.3706
28	1.3213	1.7410	2.2879	2.9987	3.9201	5.1117	6.6488	8.6271	11.1671	14.4210	18.5799	23.8839	39.2045	63.8004	164.8447
29	1.3345	1.7758	2.3566	3.1187	4.1161	5.4184	7.1143	9.3173	12.1722	15.8631	20.6237	26.7499	44.6931	74.0085	197.8136
30	1.3478	1.8114	2.4273	3.2434	4.3219	5.7435	7.6123	10.0627	13.2677	17.4494	22.8923	29.9599	50.9502	85.8499	237.3763
35	1.4166	1.9999	2.8139	3.9461	5.5160	7.6861	10.6766	14.7853	20.4140	28.1024	38.5749	52.7996	98.1002	180.3141	590.6682
40	1.4889	2.2080	3.2620	4.8010	7.0400	10.2857	14.9745	21.7245	31.4094	45.2593	65.0009	93.0510	188.8835	378.7212	1469.7716

Table II Present Value of a Single Payment

	1%	2%	3%	4%	5%	6%	7%	8%	9%	10%	11%	12%	14%	16%	20%
1	0.9901	0.9804	0.9709	0.9615	0.9524	0.9434	0.9346	0.9259	0.9174	0.9091	0.9009	0.8929	0.8772	0.8621	0.8333
2	0.9803	0.9612	0.9426	0.9246	0.9070	0.8900	0.8734	0.8573	0.8417	0.8264	0.8116	0.7972	0.7695	0.7432	0.6944
3	0.9706	0.9423	0.9151	0.8890	0.8638	0.8396	0.8163	0.7938	0.7722	0.7513	0.7312	0.7118	0.6750	0.6407	0.5787
4	0.9610	0.9238	0.8885	0.8548	0.8227	0.7921	0.7629	0.7350	0.7084	0.6830	0.6587	0.6355	0.5921	0.5523	0.4823
5	0.9515	0.9057	0.8626	0.8219	0.7835	0.7473	0.7130	0.6806	0.6499	0.6209	0.5935	0.5674	0.5194	0.4761	0.4019
6	0.9420	0.8880	0.8375	0.7903	0.7462	0.7050	0.6663	0.6302	0.5963	0.5645	0.5346	0.5066	0.4556	0.4104	0.3349
7	0.9327	0.8706	0.8131	0.7599	0.7107	0.6651	0.6227	0.5835	0.5470	0.5132	0.4817	0.4523	0.3996	0.3538	0.2791
8	0.9235	0.8535	0.7894	0.7307	0.6768	0.6274	0.5820	0.5403	0.5019	0.4665	0.4339	0.4039	0.3506	0.3050	0.2326
9	0.9143	0.8368	0.7664	0.7026	0.6446	0.5919	0.5439	0.5002	0.4604	0.4241	0.3909	0.3606	0.3075	0.2630	0.1938
10	0.9053	0.8203	0.7441	0.6756	0.6139	0.5584	0.5083	0.4632	0.4224	0.3855	0.3522	0.3220	0.2697	0.2267	0.1615
11	0.8963	0.8043	0.7224	0.6496	0.5847	0.5268	0.4751	0.4289	0.3875	0.3505	0.3173	0.2875	0.2366	0.1954	0.1346
12	0.8874	0.7885	0.7014	0.6246	0.5568	0.4970	0.4440	0.3971	0.3555	0.3186	0.2858	0.2567	0.2076	0.1685	0.1122
13	0.8787	0.7730	0.6810	0.6006	0.5303	0.4688	0.4150	0.3677	0.3262	0.2897	0.2575	0.2292	0.1821	0.1452	0.0935
14	0.8700	0.7579	0.6611	0.5775	0.5051	0.4423	0.3878	0.3405	0.2992	0.2633	0.2320	0.2046	0.1597	0.1252	0.0779
15	0.8613	0.7430	0.6419	0.5553	0.4810	0.4173	0.3624	0.3152	0.2745	0.2394	0.2090	0.1827	0.1401	0.1079	0.0649
16	0.8528	0.7284	0.6232	0.5339	0.4581	0.3936	0.3387	0.2919	0.2519	0.2176	0.1883	0.1631	0.1229	0.0930	0.0541
17	0.8444	0.7142	0.6050	0.5134	0.4363	0.3714	0.3166	0.2703	0.2311	0.1978	0.1696	0.1456	0.1078	0.0802	0.0451
18	0.8360	0.7002	0.5874	0.4936	0.4155	0.3503	0.2959	0.2502	0.2120	0.1799	0.1528	0.1300	0.0946	0.0691	0.0376
19	0.8277	0.6864	0.5703	0.4746	0.3957	0.3305	0.2765	0.2317	0.1945	0.1635	0.1377	0.1161	0.0829	0.0596	0.0313
20	0.8195	0.6730	0.5537	0.4564	0.3769	0.3118	0.2584	0.2145	0.1784	0.1486	0.1240	0.1037	0.0728	0.0514	0.0261
21	0.8114	0.6598	0.5375	0.4388	0.3589	0.2942	0.2415	0.1987	0.1637	0.1351	0.1117	0.0926	0.0638	0.0443	0.0217
22	0.8034	0.6468	0.5219	0.4220	0.3418	0.2775	0.2257	0.1839	0.1502	0.1228	0.1007	0.0826	0.0560	0.0382	0.0181
23	0.7954	0.6342	0.5067	0.4057	0.3256	0.2618	0.2109	0.1703	0.1378	0.1117	0.0907	0.0738	0.0491	0.0329	0.0151
24	0.7876	0.6217	0.4919	0.3901	0.3101	0.2470	0.1971	0.1577	0.1264	0.1015	0.0817	0.0659	0.0431	0.0284	0.0126
25	0.7798	0.6095	0.4776	0.3751	0.2953	0.2330	0.1842	0.1460	0.1160	0.0923	0.0736	0.0588	0.0378	0.0245	0.0105
26	0.7720	0.5976	0.4637	0.3607	0.2812	0.2198	0.1722	0.1352	0.1064	0.0839	0.0663	0.0525	0.0331	0.0211	0.0087
27	0.7644	0.5859	0.4502	0.3468	0.2678	0.2074	0.1609	0.1252	0.0976	0.0763	0.0597	0.0469	0.0291	0.0182	0.0073
28	0.7568	0.5744	0.4371	0.3335	0.2551	0.1956	0.1504	0.1159	0.0895	0.0693	0.0538	0.0419	0.0255	0.0157	0.0061
29	0.7493	0.5631	0.4243	0.3207	0.2429	0.1846	0.1406	0.1073	0.0822	0.0630	0.0485	0.0374	0.0224	0.0135	0.0051
30	0.7419	0.5521	0.4120	0.3083	0.2314	0.1741	0.1314	0.0994	0.0754	0.0573	0.0437	0.0334	0.0196	0.0116	0.0042
35	0.7059	0.5000	0.3554	0.2534	0.1813	0.1301	0.0937	0.0676	0.0490	0.0356	0.0259	0.0189	0.0102	0.0055	0.0017
40	0.6717	0.4529	0.3066	0.2083	0.1420	0.0972	0.0668	0.0460	0.0318	0.0221	0.0154	0.0107	0.0053	0.0026	0.0007

Table III Future Value of an Ordinary Annuity

	1%	2%	3%	4%	5%	6%	7%	8%	9%	10%	11%	12%	14%	16%	20%
1	1.0000	1.0000	1.0000	1.0000	1.0000	1.0000	1.0000	1.0000	1.0000	1.0000	1.0000	1.0000	1.0000	1.0000	1.0000
2	2.0100	2.0200	2.0300	2.0400	2.0500	2.0600	2.0700	2.0800	2.0900	2.1000	2.1100	2.1200	2.1400	2.1600	2.2000
3	3.0301	3.0604	3.0909	3.1216	3.1525	3.1836	3.2149	3.2464	3.2781	3.3100	3.3421	3.3744	3.4396	3.5056	3.6400
4	4.0604	4.1216	4.1836	4.2465	4.3101	4.3746	4.4399	4.5061	4.5731	4.6410	4.7097	4.7793	4.9211	5.0665	5.3680
5	5.1010	5.2040	5.3091	5.4163	5.5256	5.6371	5.7507	5.8666	5.9847	6.1051	6.2278	6.3528	6.6101	6.8771	7.4416
6	6.1520	6.3081	6.4684	6.6330	6.8019	6.9753	7.1533	7.3359	7.5233	7.7156	7.9129	8.1152	8.5355	8.9775	9.9299
7	7.2135	7.4343	7.6625	7.8983	8.1420	8.3938	8.6540	8.9228	9.2004	9.4872	9.7833	10.0890	10.7305	11.4139	12.9159
8	8.2857	8.5830	8.8923	9.2142	9.5491	9.8975	10.2598	10.6366	11.0285	11.4359	11.8594	12.2997	13.2328	14.2401	16.4991
9	9.3685	9.7546	10.1591	10.5828	11.0266	11.4913	11.9780	12.4876	13.0210	13.5795	14.1640	14.7757	16.0853	17.5185	20.7989
10	10.4622	10.9497	11.4639	12.0061	12.5779	13.1808	13.8164	14.4866	15.1929	15.9374	16.7220	17.5487	19.3373	21.3215	25.9587
11	11.5668	12.1687	12.8078	13.4864	14.2068	14.9716	15.7836	16.6455	17.5603	18.5312	19.5614	20.6546	23.0445	25.7329	32.1504
12	12.6825	13.4121	14.1920	15.0258	15.9171	16.8699	17.8885	18.9771	20.1407	21.3843	22.7132	24.1331	27.2707	30.8502	39.5805
13	13.8093	14.6803	15.6178	16.6268	17.7130	18.8821	20.1406	21.4953	22.9534	24.5227	26.2116	28.0291	32.0887	36.7862	48.4966
14	14.9474	15.9739	17.0863	18.2919	19.5986	21.0151	22.5505	24.2149	26.0192	27.9750	30.0949	32.3926	37.5811	43.6720	59.1959
15	16.0969	17.2934	18.5989	20.0236	21.5786	23.2760	25.1290	27.1521	29.3609	31.7725	34.4054	37.2797	43.8424	51.6595	72.0351
16	17.2579	18.6393	20.1569	21.8245	23.6575	25.6725	27.8881	30.3243	33.0034	35.9497	39.1899	42.7533	50.9804	60.9250	87.4421
17	18.4304	20.0121	21.7616	23.6975	25.8404	28.2129	30.8402	33.7502	36.9737	40.5447	44.5008	48.8837	59.1176	71.6730	105.9306
18	19.6147	21.4123	23.4144	25.6454	28.1324	30.9057	33.9990	37.4502	41.3013	45.5992	50.3959	55.7497	68.3941	84.1407	128.1167
19	20.8109	22.8406	25.1169	27.6712	30.5390	33.7600	37.3790	41.4463	46.0185	51.1591	56.9395	63.4397	78.9692	98.6032	154.7400
20	22.0190	24.2974	26.8704	29.7781	33.0660	36.7856	40.9955	45.7620	51.1601	57.2750	64.2028	72.0524	91.0249	115.3797	186.6880
21	23.2392	25.7833	28.6765	31.9692	35.7193	39.9927	44.8652	50.4229	56.7645	64.0025	72.2651	81.6987	104.7684	134.8405	225.0256
22	24.4716	27.2990	30.5368	34.2480	38.5052	43.3923	49.0057	55.4568	62.8733	71.4027	81.2143	92.5026	120.4360	157.4150	271.0307
23	25.7163	28.8450	32.4529	36.6179	41.4305	46.9958	53.4361	60.8933	69.5319	79.5430	91.1479	104.6029	138.2970	183.6014	326.2369
24	26.9735	30.4219	34.4265	39.0826	44.5020	50.8156	58.1767	66.7648	76.7898	88.4973	102.1742	118.1552	158.6586	213.9776	392.4842
25	28.2432	32.0303	36.4593	41.6459	47.7271	54.8645	63.2490	73.1059	84.7009	98.3471	114.4133	133.3339	181.8708	249.2140	471.9811
26	29.5256	33.6709	38.5530	44.3117	51.1135	59.1564	68.6765	79.9544	93.3240	109.1818	127.9988	150.3339	208.3327	290.0883	567.3773
27	30.8209	35.3443	40.7096	47.0842	54.6691	63.7058	74.4838	87.3508	102.7231	121.0999	143.0786	169.3740	238.4993	337.5024	681.8528
28	32.1291	37.0512	42.9309	49.9676	58.4026	68.5281	80.6977	95.3388	112.9682	134.2099	159.8173	190.6989	272.8892	392.5028	819.2233
29	33.4504	38.7922	45.2189	52.9663	62.3227	73.6398	87.3465	103.9659	124.1354	148.6309	178.3972	214.5828	312.0937	456.3032	984.0680
30	34.7849	40.5681	47.5754	56.0849	66.4388	79.0582	94.4608	113.2832	136.3075	164.4940	199.0209	241.3327	356.7868	530.3117	1181.8816
35	41.6603	49.9945	60.4621	73.6522	90.3203	111.4348	138.2369	172.3168	215.7108	271.0244	341.5896	431.6635	693.5727	1120.7130	2948.3411
40	48.8864	60.4020	75.4013	95.0255	120.7998	154.7620	199.6351	259.0565	337.8824	442.5926	581.8261	767.0914	1342.0251	2360.7572	7343.8578

Table IV Present Value of an Ordinary Annuity

	1%	2%	3%	4%	5%	6%	7%	8%	9%	10%	11%	12%	14%	16%	20%
1	0.9901	0.9804	0.9709	0.9615	0.9524	0.9434	0.9346	0.9259	0.9174	0.9091	0.9009	0.8929	0.8772	0.8621	0.8333
2	1.9704	1.9416	1.9135	1.8861	1.8594	1.8334	1.8080	1.7833	1.7591	1.7355	1.7125	1.6901	1.6467	1.6052	1.5278
3	2.9410	2.8839	2.8286	2.7751	2.7232	2.6730	2.6243	2.5771	2.5313	2.4869	2.4437	2.4018	2.3216	2.2459	2.1065
4	3.9020	3.8077	3.7171	3.6299	3.5460	3.4651	3.3872	3.3121	3.2397	3.1699	3.1024	3.0373	2.9137	2.7982	2.5887
5	4.8534	4.7135	4.5797	4.4518	4.3295	4.2124	4.1002	3.9927	3.8897	3.7908	3.6959	3.6048	3.4331	3.2743	2.9906
6	5.7955	5.6014	5.4172	5.2421	5.0757	4.9173	4.7665	4.6229	4.4859	4.3553	4.2305	4.1114	3.8887	3.6847	3.3255
7	6.7282	6.4720	6.2303	6.0021	5.7864	5.5824	5.3893	5.2064	5.0330	4.8684	4.7122	4.5638	4.2883	4.0386	3.6046
8	7.6517	7.3255	7.0197	6.7327	6.4632	6.2098	5.9713	5.7466	5.5348	5.3349	5.1461	4.9676	4.6389	4.3436	3.8372
9	8.5660	8.1622	7.7861	7.4353	7.1078	6.8017	6.5152	6.2469	5.9952	5.7590	5.5370	5.3282	4.9464	4.6065	4.0310
10	9.4713	8.9826	8.5302	8.1109	7.7217	7.3601	7.0236	6.7101	6.4177	6.1446	5.8892	5.6502	5.2161	4.8332	4.1925
11	10.3676	9.7868	9.2526	8.7605	8.3064	7.8869	7.4987	7.1390	6.8052	6.4951	6.2065	5.9377	5.4527	5.0286	4.3271
12	11.2551	10.5753	9.9540	9.3851	8.8633	8.3838	7.9427	7.5361	7.1607	6.8137	6.4924	6.1944	5.6603	5.1971	4.4392
13	12.1337	11.3484	10.6350	9.9856	9.3936	8.8527	8.3577	7.9038	7.4869	7.1034	6.7499	6.4235	5.8424	5.3423	4.5327
14	13.0037	12.1062	11.2961	10.5631	9.8986	9.2950	8.7455	8.2442	7.7862	7.3667	6.9819	6.6282	6.0021	5.4675	4.6106
15	13.8651	12.8493	11.9379	11.1184	10.3797	9.7122	9.1079	8.5595	8.0607	7.6061	7.1909	6.8109	6.1422	5.5755	4.6755
16	14.7179	13.5777	12.5611	11.6523	10.8378	10.1059	9.4466	8.8514	8.3126	7.8237	7.3792	6.9740	6.2651	5.6685	4.7296
17	15.5623	14.2919	13.1661	12.1657	11.2741	10.4773	9.7632	9.1216	8.5436	8.0216	7.5488	7.1196	6.3729	5.7487	4.7746
18	16.3983	14.9920	13.7535	12.6593	11.6896	10.8276	10.0591	9.3719	8.7556	8.2014	7.7016	7.2497	6.4674	5.8178	4.8122
19	17.2260	15.6785	14.3238	13.1339	12.0853	11.1581	10.3356	9.6036	8.9501	8.3649	7.8393	7.3658	6.5504	5.8775	4.8435
20	18.0456	16.3514	14.8775	13.5903	12.4622	11.4699	10.5940	9.8181	9.1285	8.5136	7.9633	7.4694	6.6231	5.9288	4.8696
21	18.8570	17.0112	15.4150	14.0292	12.8212	11.7641	10.8355	10.0168	9.2922	8.6487	8.0751	7.5620	6.6870	5.9731	4.8913
22	19.6604	17.6580	15.9369	14.4511	13.1630	12.0416	11.0612	10.2007	9.4424	8.7715	8.1757	7.6446	6.7429	6.0113	4.9094
23	20.4558	18.2922	16.4436	14.8568	13.4886	12.3034	11.2722	10.3711	9.5802	8.8832	8.2664	7.7184	6.7921	6.0442	4.9245
24	21.2434	18.9139	16.9355	15.2470	13.7986	12.5504	11.4693	10.5288	9.7066	8.9847	8.3481	7.7843	6.8351	6.0726	4.9371
25	22.0232	19.5235	17.4131	15.6221	14.0939	12.7834	11.6536	10.6748	9.8226	9.0770	8.4217	7.8431	6.8729	6.0971	4.9476
26	22.7952	20.1210	17.8768	15.9828	14.3752	13.0032	11.8258	10.8100	9.9290	9.1609	8.4881	7.8957	6.9061	6.1182	4.9563
27	23.5596	20.7069	18.3270	16.3296	14.6430	13.2105	11.9867	10.9352	10.0266	9.2372	8.5478	7.9426	6.9352	6.1364	4.9636
28	24.3164	21.2813	18.7641	16.6631	14.8981	13.4062	12.1371	11.0511	10.1161	9.3066	8.6016	7.9844	6.9607	6.1520	4.9697
29	25.0658	21.8444	19.1885	16.9837	15.1411	13.5907	12.2777	11.1584	10.1983	9.3696	8.6501	8.0218	6.9830	6.1656	4.9747
30	25.8077	22.3965	19.6004	17.2920	15.3725	13.7648	12.4090	11.2578	10.2737	9.4269	8.6938	8.0552	7.0027	6.1772	4.9789
35	29.4086	24.9986	21.4872	18.6646	16.3742	14.4982	12.9477	11.6546	10.5668	9.6442	8.8552	8.1755	7.0700	6.2153	4.9915
40	32.8347	27.3555	23.1148	19.7928	17.1591	15.0463	13.3317	11.9246	10.7574	9.7791	8.9511	8.2438	7.1050	6.2335	4.9966

Table V Future Value of an Annuity Due

	1%	2%	3%	4%	5%	6%	7%	8%	9%	10%	11%	12%	14%	16%	20%
1	1.0100	1.0200	1.0300	1.0400	1.0500	1.0600	1.0700	1.0800	1.0900	1.1000	1.1100	1.1200	1.1400	1.1600	1.2000
2	2.0301	2.0604	2.0909	2.1216	2.1525	2.1836	2.2149	2.2464	2.2781	2.3100	2.3421	2.3744	2.4396	2.5056	2.6400
3	3.0604	3.1216	3.1836	3.2465	3.3101	3.3746	3.4399	3.5061	3.5731	3.6410	3.7097	3.7793	3.9211	4.0665	4.3680
4	4.1010	4.2040	4.3091	4.4163	4.5256	4.6371	4.7507	4.8666	4.9847	5.1051	5.2278	5.3528	5.6101	5.8771	6.4416
5	5.1520	5.3081	5.4684	5.6330	5.8019	5.9753	6.1533	6.3359	6.5233	6.7156	6.9129	7.1152	7.5355	7.9775	8.9299
6	6.2135	6.4343	6.6625	6.8983	7.1420	7.3938	7.6540	7.9228	8.2004	8.4872	8.7833	9.0890	9.7305	10.4139	11.9159
7	7.2857	7.5830	7.8923	8.2142	8.5491	8.8975	9.2598	9.6366	10.0285	10.4359	10.8594	11.2997	12.2328	13.2401	15.4991
8	8.3685	8.7546	9.1591	9.5828	10.0266	10.4913	10.9780	11.4876	12.0210	12.5795	13.1640	13.7757	15.0853	16.5185	19.7989
9	9.4622	9.9497	10.4639	11.0061	11.5779	12.1808	12.8164	13.4866	14.1929	14.9374	15.7220	16.5487	18.3373	20.3215	24.9587
10	10.5668	11.1687	11.8078	12.4864	13.2068	13.9716	14.7836	15.6455	16.5603	17.5312	18.5614	19.6546	22.0445	24.7329	31.1504
11	11.6825	12.4121	13.1920	14.0258	14.9171	15.8699	16.8885	17.9771	19.1407	20.3843	21.7132	23.1331	26.2707	29.8502	38.5805
12	12.8093	13.6803	14.6178	15.6268	16.7130	17.8821	19.1406	20.4953	21.9534	23.5227	25.2116	27.0291	31.0887	35.7862	47.4966
13	13.9474	14.9739	16.0863	17.2919	18.5986	20.0151	21.5505	23.2149	25.0192	26.9750	29.0949	31.3926	36.5811	42.6720	58.1959
14	15.0969	16.2934	17.5989	19.0236	20.5786	22.2760	24.1290	26.1521	28.3609	30.7725	33.4054	36.2797	42.8424	50.6595	71.0351
15	16.2579	17.6393	19.1569	20.8245	22.6575	24.6725	26.8881	29.3243	32.0034	34.9497	38.1899	41.7533	49.9804	59.9250	86.4421
16	17.4304	19.0121	20.7616	22.6975	24.8404	27.2129	29.8402	32.7502	35.9737	39.5447	43.5008	47.8837	58.1176	70.6730	104.9306
17	18.6147	20.4123	22.4144	24.6454	27.1324	29.9057	32.9990	36.4502	40.3013	44.5992	49.3959	54.7497	67.3941	83.1407	127.1167
18	19.8109	21.8406	24.1169	26.6712	29.5390	32.7600	36.3790	40.4463	45.0185	50.1591	55.9395	62.4397	77.9692	97.6032	153.7400
19	21.0190	23.2974	25.8704	28.7781	32.0660	35.7856	39.9955	44.7620	50.1601	56.2750	63.2028	71.0524	90.0249	114.3797	185.6880
20	22.2392	24.7833	27.6765	30.9692	34.7193	38.9927	43.8652	49.4229	55.7645	63.0025	71.2651	80.6987	103.7684	133.8405	224.0256
21	23.4716	26.2990	29.5368	33.2480	37.5052	42.3923	48.0057	54.4568	61.8733	70.4027	80.2143	91.5026	119.4360	156.4150	270.0307
22	24.7163	27.8450	31.4529	35.6179	40.4305	45.9958	52.4361	59.8933	68.5319	78.5430	90.1479	103.6029	137.2970	182.6014	325.2369
23	25.9735	29.4219	33.4265	38.0826	43.5020	49.8156	57.1767	65.7648	75.7898	87.4973	101.1742	117.1552	157.6586	212.9776	391.4842
24	27.2432	31.0303	35.4593	40.6459	46.7271	53.8645	62.2490	72.1059	83.7009	97.3471	113.4133	132.3339	180.8708	248.2140	470.9811
25	28.5256	32.6709	37.5530	43.3117	50.1135	58.1564	67.6765	78.9544	92.3240	108.1818	126.9988	149.3339	207.3327	289.0883	566.3773
26	29.8209	34.3443	39.7096	46.0842	53.6691	62.7058	73.4838	86.3508	101.7231	120.0999	142.0786	168.3740	237.4993	336.5024	680.8528
27	31.1291	36.0512	41.9309	48.9676	57.4026	67.5281	79.6977	94.3388	111.9682	133.2099	158.8173	189.6989	271.8892	391.5028	818.2233
28	32.4504	37.7922	44.2189	51.9663	61.3227	72.6398	86.3465	102.9659	123.1354	147.6309	177.3972	213.5828	311.0937	455.3032	983.0680
29	33.7849	39.5681	46.5754	55.0849	65.4388	78.0582	93.4608	112.2832	135.3075	163.4940	198.0209	240.3327	355.7868	529.3117	1180.8816
30	35.1327	41.3794	49.0027	58.3283	69.7608	83.8017	101.0730	122.3459	148.5752	180.9434	220.9132	270.2926	406.7370	615.1616	1418.2579
35	42.0769	50.9944	62.2759	76.5983	94.8363	118.1209	147.9135	186.1021	235.1247	298.1268	379.1644	483.4631	790.6729	1300.0270	3538.0094
40	49.3752	61.6100	77.6633	98.8265	126.8398	164.0477	213.6096	279.7810	368.2919	486.8518	645.8269	859.1424	1529.9086	2738.4784	8812.6294

Table VI Present Value of an Annuity Due

	1%	2%	3%	4%	5%	6%	7%	8%	9%	10%	11%	12%	14%	16%	20%
1	1.0000	1.0000	1.0000	1.0000	1.0000	1.0000	1.0000	1.0000	1.0000	1.0000	1.0000	1.0000	1.0000	1.0000	1.0000
2	1.9901	1.9804	1.9709	1.9615	1.9524	1.9434	1.9346	1.9259	1.9174	1.9091	1.9009	1.8929	1.8772	1.8621	1.8333
3	2.9704	2.9416	2.9135	2.8861	2.8594	2.8334	2.8080	2.7833	2.7591	2.7355	2.7125	2.6901	2.6467	2.6052	2.5278
4	3.9410	3.8839	3.8286	3.7751	3.7232	3.6730	3.6243	3.5771	3.5313	3.4869	3.4437	3.4018	3.3216	3.2459	3.1065
5	4.9020	4.8077	4.7171	4.6299	4.5460	4.4651	4.3872	4.3121	4.2397	4.1699	4.1024	4.0373	3.9137	3.7982	3.5887
6	5.8534	5.7135	5.5797	5.4518	5.3295	5.2124	5.1002	4.9927	4.8897	4.7908	4.6959	4.6048	4.4331	4.2743	3.9906
7	6.7955	6.6014	6.4172	6.2421	6.0757	5.9173	5.7665	5.6229	5.4859	5.3553	5.2305	5.1114	4.8887	4.6847	4.3255
8	7.7282	7.4720	7.2303	7.0021	6.7864	6.5824	6.3893	6.2064	6.0330	5.8684	5.7122	5.5638	5.2883	5.0386	4.6046
9	8.6517	8.3255	8.0197	7.7327	7.4632	7.2098	6.9713	6.7466	6.5348	6.3349	6.1461	5.9676	5.6389	5.3436	4.8372
10	9.5660	9.1622	8.7861	8.4353	8.1078	7.8017	7.5152	7.2469	6.9952	6.7590	6.5370	6.3282	5.9464	5.6065	5.0310
11	10.4713	9.9826	9.5302	9.1109	8.7217	8.3601	8.0236	7.7101	7.4177	7.1446	6.8892	6.6502	6.2161	5.8332	5.1925
12	11.3676	10.7868	10.2526	9.7605	9.3064	8.8869	8.4987	8.1390	7.8052	7.4951	7.2065	6.9377	6.4527	6.0286	5.3271
13	12.2551	11.5753	10.9540	10.3851	9.8633	9.3838	8.9427	8.5361	8.1607	7.8137	7.4924	7.1944	6.6603	6.1971	5.4392
14	13.1337	12.3484	11.6350	10.9856	10.3936	9.8527	9.3577	8.9038	8.4869	8.1034	7.7499	7.4235	6.8424	6.3423	5.5327
15	14.0037	13.1062	12.2961	11.5631	10.8986	10.2950	9.7455	9.2442	8.7862	8.3667	7.9819	7.6282	7.0021	6.4675	5.6106
16	14.8651	13.8493	12.9379	12.1184	11.3797	10.7122	10.1079	9.5595	9.0607	8.6061	8.1909	7.8109	7.1422	6.5755	5.6755
17	15.7179	14.5777	13.5611	12.6523	11.8378	11.1059	10.4466	9.8514	9.3126	8.8237	8.3792	7.9740	7.2651	6.6685	5.7296
18	16.5623	15.2919	14.1661	13.1657	12.2741	11.4773	10.7632	10.1216	9.5436	9.0216	8.5488	8.1196	7.3729	6.7487	5.7746
19	17.3983	15.9920	14.7535	13.6593	12.6896	11.8276	11.0591	10.3719	9.7556	9.2014	8.7016	8.2497	7.4674	6.8178	5.8122
20	18.2260	16.6785	15.3238	14.1339	13.0853	12.1581	11.3356	10.6036	9.9501	9.3649	8.8393	8.3658	7.5504	6.8775	5.8435
21	19.0456	17.3514	15.8775	14.5903	13.4622	12.4699	11.5940	10.8181	10.1285	9.5136	8.9633	8.4694	7.6231	6.9288	5.8696
22	19.8570	18.0112	16.4150	15.0292	13.8212	12.7641	11.8355	11.0168	10.2922	9.6487	9.0751	8.5620	7.6870	6.9731	5.8913
23	20.6604	18.6580	16.9369	15.4511	14.1630	13.0416	12.0612	11.2007	10.4424	9.7715	9.1757	8.6446	7.7429	7.0113	5.9094
24	21.4558	19.2922	17.4436	15.8568	14.4886	13.3034	12.2722	11.3711	10.5802	9.8832	9.2664	8.7184	7.7921	7.0442	5.9245
25	22.2434	19.9139	17.9355	16.2470	14.7986	13.5504	12.4693	11.5288	10.7066	9.9847	9.3481	8.7843	7.8351	7.0726	5.9371
26	23.0232	20.5235	18.4131	16.6221	15.0939	13.7834	12.6536	11.6748	10.8226	10.0770	9.4217	8.8431	7.8729	7.0971	5.9476
27	23.7952	21.1210	18.8768	16.9828	15.3752	14.0032	12.8258	11.8100	10.9290	10.1609	9.4881	8.8957	7.9061	7.1182	5.9563
28	24.5596	21.7069	19.3270	17.3296	15.6430	14.2105	12.9867	11.9352	11.0266	10.2372	9.5478	8.9426	7.9352	7.1364	5.9636
29	25.3164	22.2813	19.7641	17.6631	15.8981	14.4062	13.1371	12.0511	11.1161	10.3066	9.6016	8.9844	7.9607	7.1520	5.9697
30	26.0658	22.8444	20.1885	17.9837	16.1411	14.5907	13.2777	12.1584	11.1983	10.3696	9.6501	9.0218	7.9830	7.1656	5.9747
35	29.7027	25.4986	22.1318	19.4112	17.1929	15.3681	13.8540	12.5869	11.5178	10.6086	9.8293	9.1566	8.0599	7.2098	5.9898
40	33.1630	27.9026	23.8082	20.5845	18.0170	15.9491	14.2649	12.8786	11.7255	10.7570	9.9357	9.2330	8.0997	7.2309	5.9959

KEY TERMS

Annuity 248
Annuity due 257
Compound interest 247
Effective rate of interest 247
Future value 245
Interest 246
Interpolation 260
Ordinary annuity 257
Present value 245
Principal 246
Simple interest 246

QUESTIONS

1. Explain what is meant by the time-value-of-money concept and describe its impact on business decisions.
2. Identify some common accounting applications of the time-value-of-money concept.
3. Explain the difference between simple interest and compound interest.
4. Determine the amount of interest earned on the following:
   (a) $9,000 borrowed from a bank at 10% simple annual interest for 8 months.
   (b) $15,000 invested for 2 years at 15% simple annual interest.
   (c) $1,500 invested for 26 days at 12% simple annual interest.
5. Indicate the rate per period and the number of periods for each of the following:
   (a) 10% per year for 3 years, compounded annually.
   (b) 10% per year for 3 years, compounded semiannually.
   (c) 10% per year for 3 years, compounded quarterly.
   (d) 10% per year for 3 years, compounded monthly.
6. What is meant by *discounting* cash flows?
7. Indicate the table and the table value that would be used in calculating the following:
   (a) The value today of $5,000 due in 3 years at 16% interest per year, compounded semiannually.
   (b) The value today of 5 future annual payments of $4,000 at 12% interest per year, compounded annually.
   (c) The value in 10 years of $6,000 deposited today at 10% interest per year, compounded semiannually.
   (d) The value in 5 years of quarterly payments of $1,500 for 5 years at 16% interest per year, compounded quarterly.
8. Determine how much interest is earned on the following (round to nearest dollar):
   (a) $10,500 invested for 5 years at 8% per year, compounded annually.
   (b) $7,500 invested for 10 years at 20% per year, compounded semiannually.
   (c) $12,000 invested for 4 years at 16% per year, compounded quarterly.
   (d) $1,750 invested for 1 year at 24% per year, compounded monthly.
9. Determine the table values that would be used for the following:
   (a) Present value of a single payment to be received at the end of 2 years at 10% interest compounded annually.
   (b) Present value of 14 semiannual payments made at the end of the period at 10% interest compounded semiannually.
   (c) Future value of a single payment invested for 5 years at 12% interest compounded annually.
   (d) Future value of 6 equal quarterly payments made at the end of the period at 16% interest compounded quarterly.
10. An accounting student bought an inexpensive computer for $260 to assist in homework assignments. The student financed the computer, agreeing to pay $26.12 at the end of each month for 12 months. What approximate monthly interest rate did the student pay?
11. Define an annuity. What is the difference between an "ordinary annuity" and an "annuity due"?
12. Explain how the table values for the future-value ordinary annuity table are converted to annuity-due values.
13. Explain how the table values for the present-value ordinary annuity table are converted to annuity-due values.
14. For each of the following, compute the future amount of an ordinary annuity (round to nearest dollar):
    (a) 12 annual payments of $100 at 6% per annum, compounded annually.
    (b) 8 semiannual payments of $50 at 8% per annum, compounded semiannually.
    (c) 19 quarterly payments of $125 at 12% per annum, compounded quarterly.
15. What are the future amounts in Question 14 if the annuities are annuities due?
16. For each of the following, compute the present value of an ordinary annuity:
    (a) $1,000 annually for 10 years at 8% per annum, compounded annually.
    (b) $2,050 semiannually for 6 years at 6% per annum, compounded semiannually.
    (c) $5,600 quarterly for 3 years at 8% per annum, compounded quarterly.
17. What are the present values in Question 16 if the annuities are annuities due?
18. What is interpolation, when is it used, and is it 100% accurate? Explain.

19. Determine by interpolation the table value that would be used for the following:
    (a) Future value of $1 in 6 years at 13% interest per year, compounded semiannually.
    (b) Future value of $1 paid annually for 10 years at 13% interest per year, compounded annually.
    (c) Present value of $1 due in 10 years at 9% interest per year, compounded quarterly.
    (d) Present value of semiannual payments of $1 for 10 years at 9% interest per year, compounded semiannually.
20. At what annual rate of interest would an investment of $20,000 accumulate to $38,000 at the end of 5 years? (Hint: Interpolation is needed.)

DISCUSSION CASES

Case 7—1 (But present value is a finance topic!)

James Rodham, a new accounting major, is surprised to learn that his accounting courses will discuss the mathematics of present value. "I thought that was a finance topic," he replied to his accounting professor's introduction to the topic. Professor Wyman used this response to ask the class to explain why present values are used in accounting and to provide examples of where it is successfully being used. He also wanted the class to identify additional areas in accounting where the use of present values might be beneficial. How would you respond to Professor Wyman's request?

Case 7—2 (Can we make present value measurements more reliable?)

In the summary of the FASB Discussion Memorandum, *Present Value-Based Measurements in Accounting,* the FASB Staff stated, "Almost 25 years have passed since the Accounting Principles Board first mentioned a potential project on discounting." Even for the APB and FASB, that seems like a long time. One possible explanation for the lengthy delay in studying this area is that present value accounting is not reliable enough to meet the qualitative characteristics identified in the conceptual framework. What information (variables) is needed to perform present value computations? Which of these variables is difficult to estimate and measure? How might accountants overcome this difficulty so present value measurements may be more universally used by accountants?

EXERCISES

Exercise 7—3 (Simple and compound interest)

Dietrick Corporation borrowed $30,000 from its major shareholder, the president of the company, at an annual interest rate of 12%.

1. Assuming simple interest,
    (a) How much will Dietrick have to pay to settle its obligation if the loan is to be repaid in 12 months?
    (b) How much of the payment is interest?
    (c) How much will Dietrick have to pay if the loan is due in 18 months?
2. If the loan is paid off in 18 months and interest is compounded annually, how much will the company have to pay?
3. Compare the answers for (1c) and (2) and explain why they differ.

Exercise 7—4 (Reciprocal relationships: future and present values)

Determine the amount that would accumulate for the following investments:

(a) $10,050 at 10% per annum, compounded annually for 6 years.
(b) $650 at 12% per annum, compounded quarterly for 10 years.
(c) $5,000 at 16% per annum, compounded annually for 4 years, and then reinvested at 16% per annum, compounded semiannually for 4 more years.
(d) $1,000 at 8% per annum, compounded semiannually for 5 years, an additional $1,000 added and then the entire amount reinvested at 12% per annum, compounded quarterly for 3 more years.

Exercise 7—5 **(Reciprocal relationships: future and present values)**

Determine the amount that must be deposited now at compound interest to provide the desired sum for each of the following:

(a) Amount to be invested for 10 years at 6% per annum, compounded semiannually, to equal $17,000.
(b) Amount to be invested for 2 1/2 years at 8% per annum, compounded quarterly, to equal $5,000.
(c) Amount to be invested for 15 years at 12% per annum, compounded semiannually, then reinvested at 16% per annum, compounded quarterly, for 5 more years to equal $25,000.
(d) Amount to be invested at 8% per annum, compounded semiannually for 3 years, then $5,000 more added and the entire amount reinvested at the same rate for another 3 years, compounded semiannually, to equal $12,500.

Exercise 7—6 **(Choosing between alternative investments)**

Heather Company has $10,000 to invest. One alternative will yield 10% per year, compounded annually for 4 years. A second alternative is to deposit the $10,000 in a bank that will pay 8% per year, compounded quarterly. Which alternative should Heather select?

Exercise 7—7 **(Future values of ordinary annuity payments)**

Compute the future values of the following periodic investments:

(a) $1,500 semiannual payments for 6 years at 10% per annum, compounded semiannually.
(b) $800 monthly payments for 1 year at 24% interest per annum, compounded monthly.
(c) $1,705 quarterly payments for 4 years at 16% per annum, compounded quarterly.

Exercise 7—8 **(Determining ordinary annuity deposits)**

Determine the amount of the periodic deposit for the following. Assume deposits are made at the end of the period.

(a) The monthly deposit invested at 24% per annum, compounded monthly, that will accumulate to $500,000 at the end of 1 year.
(b) The quarterly deposit invested at 8% per annum, compounded quarterly, that will accumulate to $1,050 at the end of 2 years.
(c) The annual deposit invested at 6% per annum, compounded annually, that will accumulate to $50,500 at the end of 4 years.

Exercise 7—9 **(Unknown annuity amount)**

Ryan Henry wants to buy his son a car for his 21st birthday. If Ryan's son is turning 16 today, and interest is 8% per annum, compounded semiannually, what would Ryan's semiannual investment need to be if the car will cost $26,000 and the first payment is made six months from today?

Exercise 7—10 **(Unequal payments)**

Joe Sluggo signed a contract to play baseball for the Rocky Mountain Whirlwinds. His 5-year contract calls for annual payments at the end of each year as shown below:

Year	Payment
1	$100,000
2	150,000
3	200,000
4	250,000
5	300,000

If interest is compounded at 12% annually, what is the present value of Mr. Sluggo's contract?

Exercise 7—11 **(Unknown investment periods)**

Determine the number of periods for which the following amounts would have to be invested, under the terms specified, to accumulate to $10,000. Convert the number of periods to years.

(a) $5,051 at 10% per annum, compounded semiannually.
(b) $5,002 at 8% per annum, compounded annually.
(c) $5,134 at 16% per annum, compounded quarterly.

Exercise 7—12 (Unknown interest rates)

Determine the annual interest rate that is needed for the following investments to accumulate to $50,000.

(a) $10,414 for 20 years, interest compounded semiannually.
(b) $7,102 for 10 years, interest compounded quarterly.
(c) $33,778 for 10 years, interest compounded annually.

Exercise 7—13 (Unknown investment periods—annuities)

Determine the number of periods for which the following annuity payments would have to be invested to accumulate to $20,000. Assume payments are made at the end of each period. Convert the number of periods to years.

(a) Annual payments of $5,927 at 12% per annum, compounded annually.
(b) Semiannual payments of $3,409 at 16% per annum, compounded semiannually.
(c) Quarterly payments of $4,640 at 20% per annum, compounded quarterly.

Exercise 7—14 (Unknown interest rates—annuities)

Determine the annual interest rate that is needed for the following annuities to accumulate to $25,000. Assume payments are made at the end of each period.

(a) Annual payments of $4,095 for 5 years, interest compounded annually.
(b) Semiannual payments of $5,715 for 2 years, interest compounded semiannually.
(c) Quarterly payments of $1,864 for 3 years, interest compounded quarterly

Exercise 7—15 (Determining ordinary annuity payments)

Determine the amount of the periodic payments needed to pay off the following purchases. Payments are made at the end of the period.

(a) Purchase of a waterbed for $1,205. Monthly payments are to be made for 1 year with interest at 24% per annum, compounded monthly.
(b) Purchase of a motor boat for $26,565. Quarterly payments are to be made for 4 years with interest at 8% per annum, compounded quarterly.
(c) Purchase of a condominium for $65,500. Semiannual payments are to be made for 10 years with interest at 10% per annum, compounded semiannually.

Exercise 7—16 (Determining annuity-due payments)

Compute the amount of the periodic payments for Exercise 7—15 if the payments are made at the beginning of the period.

Exercise 7—17 (Unknown purchase price for ordinary annuity payments)

Determine the purchase price for the different payment plans. Payments are at the end of the period.

(a) $25.12 monthly payments for 1 year, with 36% interest per annum, compounded monthly.
(b) $1,010.75 semiannual payments for 8 years, with 8% interest per annum, compounded semiannually.
(c) $5,801.69 annual payments for 20 years with 12% interest per annum, compounded annually.

Exercise 7—18 (Unknown purchase price for annuity-due payments)

Determine the purchase price for the payment plans in Exercise 7—17 if payments are made at the beginning of the period.

Exercise 7—19 **(Interpolation—unknown interest rate)**
On July 17, 1995, Jerry Sloan borrowed $40,000 from his rich Uncle George to open a sporting goods store. Starting July 17, 1996, Jerry has to make 5 equal annual payments of $10,500 each to repay the loan. What interest rate is Jerry paying?

Exercise 7—20 **(Interpolation—unknown interest rate)**
Demo Company has decided to purchase a new office building. Management signs a bank note to pay the Second State Bank $10,000 every 6 months for 10 years. At the date of purchase, the office building costs $120,000. The first payment is 6 months later. What is the approximate annual rate of interest on the note?

Exercise 7—21 **(Interpolation—unknown interest rate)**
If the payments in Exercise 7—20 began on the date the papers were signed, what would the annual interest rate be?

PROBLEMS

Problem 7—22 **(Determining unknown quantities)**
Determine the unknown quantity for each of the following independent situations using the appropriate interest tables:

1. Jeff and Nancy want to start a trust fund for their newborn son, Mark. They have decided to invest $5,000 today. If interest is 8% compounded semiannually, how much will be in the fund when Mark turns 20?
2. Nixon Corporation wants to establish a retirement fund. Management wants to have $1,000,000 in the fund at the end of 40 years. If fund assets will earn 12%, compounded annually, how much will need to be invested now?
3. How many payments would Star, Inc., need to make if it purchases a new building for $100,000 with annual payments made at the end of each year of $16,401.24 and interest of 16%, compounded annually?
4. An investment broker indicates that an investment of $10,000 in a CD for 10 years at the current interest rate will accumulate to $21,589. What is the current annual rate of interest if interest is compounded annually?

Problem 7—23 **(Determining unknown quantities)**
Determine the unknown quantity for each of the following independent situations using the appropriate interest tables:

1. Sue wants to have $10,000 saved when she begins college. If Sue enters college in 4 years and interest is 8% compounded annually, how much will Sue need to save each year assuming equal deposits at the end of each year?
2. XYZ Company has obtained a bank loan to finance the purchase of an automobile for one of its executives. The terms of the loan require monthly payments at the end of each month of $585. If the interest rate is 18% compounded monthly and the car costs $15,850, for how many months will XYZ have to make payments?
3. Diaz Company is offering the following investment plan. If deposits of $250 are made semiannually for the next 9 years, $7,726 will accrue. If interest is compounded semiannually, what is the approximate annual rate of interest on the investment?
4. Jack wants to buy a rental unit. For how many periods will he have to make annual deposits of $5,000 in order to accumulate $50,445, the price of the rental unit, if interest is 12% compounded annually? Assume deposits are made at the end of each year.

Problem 7—24 **(Comparing the value of two contracts)**
John Jock and Sam Sport, world famous football players, signed multi-year contracts with their respective teams. Now they are in a dispute over who is getting paid the most. John signed a 5-

year, $15 million contract, while Sam's 5-year contract totals only $14 million but includes a signing bonus paid at the beginning of the 5-year contract term. The annual salary payments and the signing bonus are as follows:

		John Jock	Sam Sport
Signing bonus		$ -0-	$ 1,000,000
Salaries:	Year 1	1,500,000	2,600,000
	Year 2.	2,000,000	2,600,000
	Year 3	2,750,000	2,600,000
	Year 4	3,750,000	2,600,000
	Year 5	5,000,000	2,600,000
Totals		$15,000,000	$14,000,000

1. If salaries are paid at the end of each year and interest is 12% annually, which player received the larger contract in terms of present value?
2. If salaries are paid at the end of each year and interest is 8% annually, which player received the larger contract in terms of present value?
3. What factors affect the present values of the above contracts?

Problem 7—25 (Determining the implicit interest rate)

Valley Technical College needs to purchase some computers. Because the college is short of cash, Computer Sales Company has agreed to let Valley have the computers now and pay $2,500 per computer 6 months from now. If the current cash price is $2,404, what is the rate of interest Valley would be paying?

Problem 7—26 (Choosing between purchase alternatives)

Foot Loose, Inc., needs to purchase a new shoelace-making machine. Machines Ready has agreed to sell them the machine for $22,000 down and 4 payments of $5,700 to be paid in semiannual installments for the next 2 years. Do-It-Yourself Machines has offered to sell Foot Loose a comparable machine for $10,000 down and 4 semiannual payments of $9,000. If the current interest rate is 16%, compounded semiannually, which machine should Foot Loose purchase?

Problem 7—27 (Choosing between rent payment alternatives)

Park City Construction is building a new office building, and management is trying to decide how rent payments for the office space should be structured. The alternatives are:

(a) Annual payment of $15,000 at the end of each year.
(b) Monthly payments of $1,200 at the end of each month.

Assuming an interest rate of 12% compounded monthly, which payment schedule should Park City use?

Problem 7—28 (Computing mortgage payments with the use of formulas)

George and Barbara Shrub would like to purchase a large white house and are evaluating their financing options. Bank A offers a 10-year mortgage at 12% annual interest, compounded monthly, with payments made at the end of each month. Bank B is offering a 10-year mortgage at 13% annual interest, compounded annually, with payments made at the end of each year. The purchase price of the white house is $250,000.

1. Use formulas to compute the following amounts:
   (a) The monthly payment for the Bank A mortgage.
   (b) The annual payment for the Bank B mortgage.
2. Which financing alternative would you advise the Shrubs to select?

Problem 7—29 (Future value of annuity-due deposits)

Rose Sanchez plans to save $1,000 each year to pay for a 2-week trip to Mexico. If Rose makes her first deposit on July 1, 1995, and her last deposit on July 1, 1997, how much will she have for her trip on July 1, 1998? Assume that the annual interest rate is 8%.

Problem 7—30 **(Determining number and amount of payments on retirement plan)**

Ed Anderson has $250,000 accumulated in a retirement account and plans to receive annual payments of $40,360 at the end of each year.

(a) If interest is 12% annually, how many payments will Ed receive?
(b) If payments are made at the beginning of the year, how many full payments would he receive, and how much would the last payment be?
(c) What would the payments have to be if Ed wants to receive 20 payments, each at the end of the year?
(d) What would the payments have to be if Ed wants to receive 20 payments, each at the beginning of the year?

Problem 7—31 **(Planning for the future)**

John Seymor turned 20 years old today and is trying to plan for his future. He would like to ensure that he has enough money to care for himself when he retires. If John plans on retiring when he turns 60 years old, and interest is 10%:

1. How much money would he need to invest at the end of every year in order to have $1,000,000 on his 60th birthday?
2. How much money would he need to invest at the end of every year in order to be able to withdraw $100,000 at the end of each year for 10 years, with the first withdrawal being on his 61st birthday?
3. In both of the above scenarios, John wants to have $1,000,000 available for his retirement. Why aren't the answers to (1) and (2) identical?

Problem 7—32 **(Choosing among alternative payment plans)**

The following payment plans are offered on the purchase of a new freezer:

(a) $375 cash.
(b) 8 monthly payments of $55.
(c) $100 cash down and 6 monthly payments of $50.

Which payment plan would you choose if interest is 24% annually, compounded monthly, if you are the purchaser? if you are the seller? (Assume ordinary annuities where applicable.)

Problem 7—33 **(Determining sinking fund payments)**

Payback Company wants to start a sinking fund to cover the retirement of a serial bond issuance. The bonds begin maturing in 15 years at a rate of $30,000 per year for 15 years. Payback Company can earn annual interest of 6% for the first 15 years and 10% for the remaining years. How much will Payback Company have to deposit annually under the following assumptions?

(a) Payments into the fund are made at the end of the year, and bonds are retired at the end of the year.
(b) Payments into the fund are made at the beginning of the year, and bonds are retired at the beginning of the year.
(c) Payments into the fund are made at the beginning of the year, and bonds are retired at the end of the year.

Problem 7—34 **(Determining amount of annuity-due payments and interest)**

Briercliff Inc. borrowed $4,000 on a 10%, 1-year note due on August 1, 1996. On that date, Briercliff was unable to pay the obligation but arranged for Western Loan Company to pay the holder $4,400. Briercliff agreed to pay Western Loan Company a series of 5 equal annual payments beginning August 1, 1996. Each payment is in part a reduction of principal and in part a payment of interest at 12% annually. (a) What is the amount of each payment? (b) What is the total amount of interest on the obligation?

Problem 7—35 **(Determining purchase price)**

Big Company purchased a machine on February 1, 1996, and will make 7 semiannual payments of $14,000 beginning 5 years from the date of purchase. The interest rate will be 12%, compounded semiannually. Determine the purchase price of the machine.

PART 2

Components of Financial Statements

CHAPTER 8

Cash and Receivables

CHAPTER TOPICS

- Composition of Cash
- Management and Control of Cash
- Petty Cash Fund
- Bank Reconciliations
- Classification of Receivables
- Recognition and Valuation of Accounts Receivable
- Accounts Receivable as a Source of Cash
- Recognition and Valuation of Notes Receivable
- Notes Receivable as a Source of Cash
- Presentation of Cash and Receivables on the Balance Sheet
- Four-Column Bank Reconciliation (Appendix)

In 64 minutes on Friday, May 13, 1988, an employee of First Chicago, a large bank holding company, transferred $70 million from the accounts of three major customers—Merrill Lynch, United Airlines, and Brown-Forman. Far from being a high-tech operation, the unauthorized transfers were accomplished by fake phone confirmations of the requested electronic transfers of funds. The First Chicago employee, while pretending to follow the required procedure of calling the customers to confirm the transfer requests, instead called his accomplices who were waiting at a south side Chicago home. Because the confirmation calls were often monitored, the accomplices had been coached on the correct coded responses. The confirmations were unquestioned and the electronic transfers were approved and made. The embezzlement was discovered later that day when First Chicago informed Merrill Lynch of an overdraft in its account. Merrill Lynch disagreed, an investigation ensued, the scheme was uncovered, and the funds were returned. Officials speculated at the time that the scheme might have gone uncovered longer if the schemers had not tried to take "a jillion dollars" in one bite.[1]

As the First Chicago example illustrates, liquid assets must be managed carefully. The first part of this book has established a perspective of accounting and its theoretical foundation. Part II explores the components of financial statements, beginning with cash and receivables.

CASH

Cash is perhaps the single most important item on a balance sheet. Since it serves as the medium of exchange in our economy, cash is involved directly or indirectly in almost all business transactions. Even when cash is not involved directly in a transaction, it provides the basis for measurement and accounting for all other items.

Another reason why cash is so important is that individuals, businesses, and even governments must maintain an adequate liquidity position; that is, they must have a sufficient amount of cash on hand to pay obligations as they come due if they are to remain viable operating entities. In the early stages of its conceptual framework project, the FASB identified the need to report information on cash and liquidity as one of the key objectives of financial reporting. This emphasis eventually led to the requirement of providing a statement of cash flows as one of the primary financial statements.

In striking contrast to the importance of cash as a key element in the liquidity position of an entity is its unproductive nature. Since cash is the measure of value, it cannot expand or grow unless it is converted into other properties. Cash kept under a mattress, for example, will not grow or appreciate, whereas land may increase in value if held. Excessive balances of cash on hand are often referred to as **idle cash**. Efficient cash management requires available cash to be continuously working in one of several ways as part of the operating cycle or as a short-term or long-term investment. The management of cash is therefore a critical business function.

Composition of Cash

Cash is the most liquid of current assets and consists of those items that serve as a medium of exchange and provide a basis for accounting measurement. To be reported as "cash," an item must be readily available and not restricted for use in the payment of current obligations. A general guideline is whether an item is *acceptable for deposit at face value* by a bank or other financial institution.

Items that are classified as cash include coin and currency on hand and unrestricted funds available on deposit in a bank, which are often called **demand deposits** since they can be withdrawn upon demand. Demand deposits would include amounts in checking, savings, and money market deposit accounts. Petty cash funds or change funds and negotiable instruments, such as personal checks, travelers' checks, cashiers' checks, bank drafts, and money orders are also items commonly reported as cash. The total of these items plus undeposited coin and currency is sometimes called **cash on hand**. Also included as cash would be any company checks that have been written but that have not been mailed or delivered. Deposits that are not immediately available due to withdrawal or other restrictions are sometimes referred to as **time deposits.** These deposits are often separately classified as "restricted cash" or "temporary investments." Examples of time

1. Jeff Bailey. "U.S. Charges Seven in 'No-Tech' Attempt to Steal $70 Million From First Chicago." *The Wall Street Journal,* May 19, 1988, p. 2.

deposits include certificates of deposit (CDs) and money market savings certificates. CDs, for example, generally may be withdrawn without penalty only at specified maturity dates.

Deposits in foreign banks that are subject to immediate and unrestricted withdrawal generally qualify as cash and are reported at their U.S. dollar equivalents as of the date of the balance sheet. However, cash in foreign banks that is restricted as to use or withdrawal should be designated as receivables of a current or noncurrent character and reported subject to appropriate allowances for estimated uncollectibles.

Some items do not meet the "acceptance at face value on deposit" test and should not be reported as cash. Examples include postage stamps (which are office supplies) and postdated checks, IOUs, and not-sufficient-funds (NSF) checks (all of which are in effect receivables).

Cash balances specifically designated by management for special purposes should be reported separately. Those cash balances to be applied to some current purpose or current obligation are properly reported in the current asset section on the balance sheet. For example, cash funds for employees' travel may be reported separately from cash but still be classified as a current asset. However, restricted cash should be reported as a current item only if it is to be applied to some current purpose or obligation. Classification of the cash balance as current or noncurrent should parallel the classification applied to the liability. Cash balances not available for current purposes require separate designation and classification under a noncurrent heading on the balance sheet.

A credit balance in the cash account resulting from the issuance of checks in excess of the amount on deposit is known as a **cash overdraft** and should be reported as a current liability. When a company has two or more accounts with a single bank, an overdraft can be offset against an account with a positive balance. If the depositor fails to cover the overdraft, the bank has the legal right to apply funds from one account to cover the overdraft in another. However, when a company has accounts with two different banks and there is a positive balance in one account and an overdraft in the other, both an asset balance and a liability balance should be recognized in view of the claim against one bank and the obligation to the other; if recognition of an overdraft is to be avoided, cash should be transferred to cover the deficiency, because the legal right of offset does not exist between two banks.

In summary, cash is a current asset comprised of coin, currency, and other items that (1) serve as a medium of exchange and (2) provide the basis for measurement in accounting. Most negotiable instruments (e.g., checks, bank drafts, and money orders) qualify as cash because they can be converted to currency on demand or are acceptable for deposit at face value by a bank. Components of cash restricted as to use or withdrawal should be disclosed or reported separately and classified as an investment, a receivable, or other asset. Exhibit 8—1 summarizes the classification of various items that have been discussed. The objective of disclosure is to provide the user of financial statements with information to assist in evaluating the entity's ability to meet obligations (i.e., its liquidity and solvency) and in assessing the effectiveness of cash management.

Compensating Balances

In connection with financing arrangements, it is common practice for a company to agree to maintain a minimum or average balance on deposit with a bank or other lending institution. These **compensating balances** are defined by the SEC as ". . . that portion of any demand deposit (or any time deposit or certificate of deposit) maintained by a corporation . . . which constitutes support for existing borrowing arrangements of the corporation . . . with a lending institution. Such arrangements would include both outstanding borrowings and the assurance of future credit availability."[2]

2. Securities and Exchange Commission, *Accounting Series Release No. 148,* "Disclosure of Compensating Balances and Short-Term Borrowing Arrangements" (Washington: U.S. Government Printing Office, 1973).

Exhibit 8—1
Classification of Cash and Noncash Items

Item	Classification
Undeposited coin and currency	Cash
Unrestricted funds on deposit at bank (demand deposits)	Cash
Petty cash & change funds	Cash
Negotiable instruments, such as checks, bank drafts, and money orders	Cash
Company checks written but not yet mailed or delivered	Cash
Restricted deposits, such as CDs and money market savings certificates (time deposits)	Temporary Investments
Deposits in foreign banks:	
Unrestricted	Cash
Restricted	Receivables
Postage stamps	Office Supplies
IOUs, postdated checks, and not-sufficient-funds (NSF) checks	Receivables
Cash restricted for special purposes	Restricted Cash*
Cash overdraft	Current Liability

*Separately reported as current or noncurrent asset depending on the purpose for which it is restricted.

Compensating balances provide a source of funds to the lender as partial compensation for credit extended. In effect, such arrangements raise the interest rate of the borrower because a portion of the amount on deposit with the lending institution cannot be used. These balances present an accounting problem from the standpoint of disclosure. Readers of financial statements are likely to assume the entire cash balance is available to meet current obligations, when, in fact, part of the balance is restricted.

The solution to this problem is to disclose the amount of compensating balances. The SEC recommends that any "legally restricted" deposits held as compensating balances be segregated and reported separately. If the balances are the result of short-term financing arrangements, they should be shown separately among the "cash items" in the current asset section; if the compensating balances are in connection with long-term agreements, they should be classified as noncurrent, either as investments or "other assets." In many instances, deposits are not legally restricted, but compensating balance agreements still exist as business commitments in connection with lines of credit. In these situations, the amounts and nature of the arrangements should be disclosed in the notes to the financial statements, as illustrated in Exhibit 8—2 for General Host Corporation.

Exhibit 8—2
General Host Corporation—Disclosure of Compensating Balances

The following disclosure was made by General Host Corporation in the notes to the financial statements of its 1992 annual report. The applicable portion of the note explaining notes payable and lines of credit reads as follows:

The Company also has available unsecured short-term lines of credit under which $15,000,000 may be borrowed at the prime rate or at other rates as offered by various banks. *These agreements require the Company maintain average compensating balances of up to 4% of the credit line. During 1992 no amounts were borrowed under these agreements.*

Management and Control of Cash

As noted earlier, a business enterprise must maintain sufficient cash for current operations and for paying obligations as they come due. Any excess cash should be invested temporarily to earn an additional return for the shareholders. Effective cash management also requires controls to protect cash from loss by theft or fraud. Since cash is the most liquid asset, it is particularly susceptible to misappropriation unless properly safeguarded. When computerized accounting systems are used, controls are still necessary, and are perhaps even more important than with a strictly manual system, in properly accounting for all inflows, outflows, and balances of cash.

The system for controlling cash must be adapted to a particular business. It is not feasible to describe all the features and techniques employed in businesses of various kinds and sizes. In general, however, systems of cash control deny access to the accounting records to those who handle cash. This reduces the possibility of improper entries to conceal the misuse of cash receipts and cash payments. The probability of misappropriation of cash is greatly reduced if two or more employees must conspire in an embezzlement. Further, systems normally provide for separation of the receiving and paying functions. The basic characteristics of a system of cash control are:

1. Specifically assigned responsibility for handling cash receipts.
2. Separation of handling and recording cash receipts.
3. Daily deposit of all cash received.
4. Voucher system to control cash payments.
5. Internal audits at irregular intervals.
6. Double record of cash—bank and books, with reconciliations performed by someone outside the accounting function.

These controls are more likely to be found in large companies with many employees. Small companies with few employees generally have difficulty in totally segregating accounting and cash-handling duties. Even small companies, however, should incorporate as many control features as possible.

To the extent that a company can incorporate effective internal controls, it can reduce significantly the chances of theft, loss, or inadvertent errors in accounting for and controlling cash. Even the most elaborate control system, however, cannot totally eliminate the possibilities of misappropriations or errors. The use of a petty cash fund can facilitate control over small cash payments, and periodic bank reconciliations can help identify any cash shortages or errors that may have been made in accounting for cash.

Petty Cash Fund

Immediate cash payments and payments too small to be made by check may be made from a **petty cash fund.** Under an **imprest petty cash system,** the petty cash fund is created by cashing a check for the amount of the fund. In recording the establishment of the fund, Petty Cash is debited and Cash is credited. The cash is then turned over to a cashier or some person who is solely responsible for payments made out of the fund. The cashier should require a signed receipt for all payments made. These receipts may be printed in prenumbered form. Frequently, a bill or other memorandum is submitted when a payment is requested. A record of petty cash payments may be kept in a *petty cash journal.*

Whenever the amount of cash in the fund runs low and also at the end of each fiscal period, the fund is replenished by writing a check equal to the payments made. In recording replenishment, expenses and other appropriate accounts are debited for petty cash disbursements and Cash is credited. When the fund fails to balance, an adjustment is usually made to a miscellaneous expense or revenue account, sometimes called "Cash Short and Over." Unless theft is involved, this will usually involve only a nominal amount arising, for example, from errors in making change.

As noted above, a petty cash fund is usually replenished at the end of each fiscal period. If replenishment does not occur at year-end, however, an adjustment to Petty Cash is required to properly record all expenditures from the fund during the period. The debit entries would be the same as those to record replenishment; the credit entry would be to Petty Cash, reflecting a reduction in that account.

Electronic Funds Transfer

For years it has been forecast that we would soon be living in a cashless, paperless society with all transfers of funds being done electronically. Although banks and financial institutions routinely use electronic funds transfer (EFT), most consumers still make all their payments with cash, check, or credit card. The most recent innovation for consumers is called EFT/POS (electronic funds transfer at the point of sale). Typically this involves the use of a debit card, which is similar to a credit card, except that at the time of sale the funds are immediately transferred from the purchaser's bank account to the seller's account.

In 1989, only two percent of customers expressed a preference for electronic payment systems, like debit cards, over paying by cash, check, or credit card. However, the benefits of electronic payment have led to forecasts of rapid growth, as much as a 50 percent increase by 1995. Debit card transactions cost less for retailers to process than credit card transactions, the retailer receives the cash instantly, and the number of bad debts is greatly reduced. For customers, debit cards reduce delays and uncertainties at the point of sale.

The effects of debit card transactions are not uniformly positive. Some users complain that the use of debit cards eliminates "float," the extra use of funds during the interval between when a person writes a check or makes a charge and when the amount is actually subtracted from that person's bank account. With a debit card, there is no interval and thus there is no float. Also, most of the benefits of debit card use accrue to the receiver (prompt receipt, low bad debts, etc.), leaving users with little incentive to use the cards. Some retailers are beginning to extend cash discounts to debit card users.

Banks are not completely in favor of debit cards either. Some fear that use of debit cards will reduce banks' lucrative credit card business. Also, as individuals become more comfortable with electronic banking in general, banks fear that they will make fewer visits to the banks themselves, thereby decreasing the amount of "cross-services," like consumer loans, safety-deposit boxes, and savings plans.

Widespread electronic payments have also been met with some resistance by civil libertarians. With computerized registers already tabulating everything a customer purchases, payment by debit card completes the database by supplying the name and address of the purchaser. Use of this database makes possible the study of individual consumers' spending habits. Marketers are already talking about targeting product promotions at those customers who have demonstrated an interest in similar products.

In spite of these difficulties, debit card usage is fast catching on in some market segments. Rapid growth in use is expected in gasoline sales. And, among demographic groups, college students are the most frequent users. In fact, some college bookstores are rapidly approaching a cashless state. One cash customer at a college bookstore, in a long line with debit and credit card users who experienced no difficulty in making their purchases, was surprised when the beleaguered cashier asked for a picture ID before he would accept a $20 bill as payment.

Questions:

1. What obstacles must be overcome before electronic funds transfers become widespread among consumers?
2. How would bank reconciliations differ if most transactions were made electronically?
3. Why might debit cards reduce the use of credit cards?

Sources:

Lauren Lekoski, "Is EFT Finally Ready to Lift Off?" *Supermarket Business,* October 1989, p. 38.

"Debit Cards, EFT Still Grasping for Toehold," *Chain Store Age Executive,* February 1989, p. 67.

"Cashless Buying Creeps Ahead," *Fortune,* September 21, 1992, p. 14.

To illustrate the appropriate entries in accounting for petty cash, assume that Keat Company establishes a petty cash fund on January 1 in the amount of $500. The following entry would be made.

Petty Cash	500	
Cash		500
To establish a $500 petty cash fund.		

During the next six months, the person responsible for the fund made payments for office supplies ($245), postage ($110), and office equipment repairs ($25). Receipts for these items are maintained as evidence supporting the petty cash disbursements. On July 1 the fund is replenished. At that time the coin and currency in the fund totaled $115. The entry to record the expenses and replenish the fund would be:

Office Supplies Expense	245	
Postage Expense	110	
Repair Expense	25	
Cash Short and Over (or Misc. Expense)	5	
Cash		385
To record expenses and replenish the petty cash fund.		

After this entry, the fund would be restored to its original amount, $500. If Keat Company decided to reduce the fund to $400, an entry would be required as follows:

Cash	100	
Petty Cash		100
To reduce the petty cash fund from $500 to $400.		

Assume further that during the next six months, Keat Company used its petty cash fund to purchase additional office supplies ($136), purchase decorations and refreshments for an office party ($89), and pay freight charges ($55). Even though the fund was not replenished on December 31, an entry would be required to properly record the expenditures from the fund for that period, as follows:

Office Supplies Expense	136	
Misc. Expenses	89	
Freight	55	
Petty Cash		280
To record expenses paid from the petty cash fund.		

The entry to increase a petty cash fund is the same as to establish the fund initially—a debit to Petty Cash and a credit to Cash. However, petty cash funds should only be large enough to cover small expenditures. Large amounts should be disbursed through an authorized voucher system.

Bank Reconciliations

When daily receipts are deposited and payments other than those from petty cash are made by check, the bank's statement of its transactions with the depositor can be compared with the record of cash as reported on the depositor's books. A comparison of the bank balance with the balance reported on the books is usually made monthly by means of a summary known as a **bank reconciliation.** A bank reconciliation is prepared to disclose any errors or irregularities in either the records of the bank or those of the business unit. It is developed in a form that points out the reasons for discrepancies in the two balances. It should be prepared by an individual who neither handles nor records cash. Any discrepancies should be brought to the immediate attention of appropriate company officials.

When the bank statement and the depositor's records are compared, certain items may appear on one and not the other, resulting in a difference in the two balances. Most of these differences result from temporary timing lags and are thus normal. Four common types of differences arise in the following situations:

1. A deposit made near the end of the month and recorded on the depositor's books is not received by the bank in time to be reflected on the bank statement. This amount, referred to as a **deposit in transit,** has to be added to the bank statement balance to make it agree with the balance on the depositor's books.
2. Checks written near the end of the month have reduced the depositor's cash balance, but have not cleared the bank as of the bank statement date. These **outstanding checks** must be subtracted from the bank statement balance to make it agree with the depositor's records.
3. The bank normally charges a monthly fee for servicing an account. The bank automatically reduces the depositor's account balance for this **bank service charge** and notes the amount on the bank statement. The depositor must deduct this amount from

the recorded cash balance to make it agree with the bank statement balance. The return of a customer's check for which insufficient funds are available, known as a **not-sufficient-funds (NSF) check**, is handled in a similar manner.

4. An amount owed to the depositor is paid directly to the bank by a third party and added to the depositor's account. Upon receipt of the bank statement (assuming prior notification has not been received from the bank), this amount must be added to the cash balance on the depositor's books. Examples include a direct payroll deposit by an individual's employer and interest added by the bank on a savings account.

If, after considering the items mentioned above, the bank statement and the book balances cannot be reconciled, a detailed analysis of both the bank's records and the depositor's books may be necessary to determine whether errors or irregularities exist on the records of either party.

Preparing a Bank Reconciliation. A common form of bank reconciliation is illustrated below. This form is prepared in two sections, the bank statement balance being adjusted to the corrected cash balance in the first section, and the book balance being adjusted to the same corrected cash balance in the second section. Any items not yet recognized by the bank (e.g., deposits in transit or outstanding checks) as well as any errors made by the bank are recorded in the first section. The second section contains any items the depositor has not yet recognized (e.g., direct deposits, NSF checks, or bank service charges) and any corrections for errors made on the depositor's books.

The reconciliation of bank and book balances to a corrected balance has two important advantages: it develops a corrected cash figure, and it shows separately all items requiring adjustment on the depositor's books.

An alternative form of reconciliation would be to reconcile the bank statement balance to the book balance. This form would not develop a corrected cash figure, however, and would make it more difficult to determine the adjustments needed on the depositor's books.

Svendsen, Inc.
Bank Reconciliation
November 30, 1996

Balance per bank statement, November 30, 1996			$2,979.72
Add:	Deposits in transit	$658.50	
	Charge for interest made to depositor's account by bank in error	12.50	671.00
			$3,650.72
Deduct outstanding checks:			
No. 1125		$ 58.16	
No. 1138		100.00	
No. 1152		98.60	
No. 1154		255.00	
No. 1155		192.07	703.83
Corrected bank balance			$2,946.89
Balance per books, November 30, 1996			$2,952.49
Add:	Interest earned during November	$ 98.50	
	Check No. 1116 to Ace Advertising for $46 recorded by depositor as $64 in error	18.00	116.50
			$3,068.99
Deduct:	Bank service charges	$ 3.16	
	Customer's check deposited November 25 and returned marked NSF	118.94	122.10
Corrected book balance			$2,946.89

After preparing the reconciliation, the depositor should record any items appearing on the bank statement and requiring recognition on the company's books as well as any corrections for errors discovered on its own books. The bank should be notified immediately of any bank errors. The following entries would be required on the books of Svendsen, Inc., as a result of the November 30 reconciliation:

Cash	98.50	
Interest Revenue		98.50
To record interest earned during November.		
Cash	18.00	
Advertising Expense		18.00
To record correction for check in payment of advertising recorded as $64 instead of the actual amount, $46.		
Accounts Receivable	118.94	
Miscellaneous General Expense	3.16	
Cash		122.10
To record customer's uncollectible check and bank charges for November.		

Bank Account Manipulation

From July 1980 through February 1982, E. F. Hutton was able to create an extra $1 billion in available funds by aggressively manipulating and shuffling $10 billion in branch office bank accounts. These extra funds provided considerable interest revenue (or interest expense savings), because during that time period, short-term interest rates were often in the 18 to 20 percent range.

One technique used involved the intentional overdrafting of accounts held at small local banks. Large withdrawals, sometimes ten times as much as the account balance, were made from small local banks, with the funds being deposited in Hutton's central bank account. The funds would earn interest in the central account until the local bank required the overdraft to be covered, a period often extending for several days.

Another abuse involved the overaggressive use of float in the local bank accounts. Float is extra money in a bank account, money that has already been spent by check, but that the bank has not yet deducted from the account because the check has yet to be presented at the bank for payment. For example, when a bank reconciliation is done, the total of the outstanding checks represents the amount of the float. Hutton intentionally opened accounts in small, rural banks because the collection process of such banks is typically slower, allowing for more float. Hutton reportedly particularly liked doing business with banks in Watertown, New York on the eastern shore of Lake Ontario, where heavy winter snowstorms could be expected to delay the mails and thus slow down the check clearing process. Taking advantage of checking account float is not illegal, or even unethical; it is good business practice. However, Hutton misused the process by creating chains of bank accounts and transferring funds from one to another by writing a check on one bank and depositing the check in another. During the check clearing interval, the funds would be earning interest in both banks.

This wasn't the first instance of overaggressive use of float. In October 1978, the SEC warned brokers to stop trying to extend the check clearing period and thus increase the float by paying East Coast customers with checks drawn on West Coast banks, and vice versa. And, in October 1979, a New York state judge assessed damages to Merrill Lynch for paying New York customers with California checks.

In May 1985, Hutton pleaded guilty to 2,000 counts of mail and wire fraud and agreed to pay approximately $10 million in fines and restitution.

Questions:

1. What ethical issues are involved in using float as E. F. Hutton did?
2. How can manipulation, as described in this case, be controlled?

Sources:

Andy Pasztor, Bruce Ingersoll, and Daniel Hertzberg. "Hutton Unit Pleads Guilty in Fraud Case." *The Wall Street Journal,* May 3, 1985, p. 3.

Andy Pasztor and Scott McMurray. "E. F. Hutton Scheme Involved More Cash Than Disclosed, U.S. Prosecutor Says." *The Wall Street Journal,* May 6, 1985, p. 3

Anthony Bianco and G. David Wallace. "What Did Hutton's Managers Know—And When Did They Know It?" *Business Week,* May 20, 1985, p. 110.

After these entries are posted, the cash account will show a balance of $2,946.89. If financial statements were prepared at November 30, this is the amount that would be reported as cash on the balance sheet. It should be noted that the bank reconciliation is not presented to external users. It is used as a control procedure and as an accounting tool to determine the adjustments required to bring the cash account and related account balances up to date.

RECEIVABLES

For most businesses, receivables are a significant item, often representing a major portion of the liquid assets of a company. Retail and merchandising companies, such as Sears, Roebuck and Co. or J. C. Penney Company, Inc., typically have 50 to 70 percent of total current assets tied up in receivables. For some service-type businesses, the percentage is even higher. Receivables also can provide a significant source of revenues from finance charges. For example, at December 31, 1992, Sears had approximately $7.1 billion of domestic accounts receivable. These receivables were expected to earn finance charge revenues at annual percentage rates ranging from 8 to 20 percent. On the other hand, a lack of control of receivables can result in substantial losses from uncollectible accounts. Even with good credit policies and collection procedures, bad debt losses often range from one to five percent of total credit sales. Finally, receivables can be used as collateral for a loan or sold to generate funds for operating purposes. During 1992, for example, Texaco Inc. sold $1.4 billion of receivables.

As the above examples illustrate, receivables can affect the profitability of company operations in a number of ways. This makes the management, control, and accounting for receivables important tasks. The major considerations in accounting for receivables involve their recognition, classification, valuation, and reporting. Collection of receivables and the use of receivables in financing company operations are also important considerations. These issues are addressed in the remaining sections of this chapter.

Classification of Receivables

In its broadest sense, the term **receivables** is applicable to all claims against others for money, goods, or services. For accounting purposes, however, the term is generally employed in a narrower sense to designate claims expected to be settled by the receipt of cash.

In classifying receivables, an important distinction is made between trade and nontrade receivables. **Trade receivables,** generally the most significant category of receivables, result from the normal operating activities of a business, i.e., credit sales of goods or services to customers. Trade receivables may be evidenced by a formal written promise to pay and classified as **notes receivable.** In most cases, however, trade receivables are unsecured "open accounts," often referred to simply as **accounts receivable.**

Accounts receivable represent an extension of short-term credit to customers. Payments are generally due within 30 to 90 days. The credit arrangements are typically informal agreements between seller and buyer supported by such business documents as invoices, sales orders, and delivery contracts. Normally trade receivables do not involve interest, although an interest or service charge may be added if payments are not made within a specified period. Trade receivables are the most common type of receivable and are generally the most significant in total dollar amount.

Nontrade receivables include all other types of receivables. They arise from a variety of transactions, such as: (1) the sale of securities or property other than inventory; (2) advances to stockholders, directors, officers, employees, and affiliated companies; (3) deposits with creditors, utilities, and other agencies; (4) purchase prepayments; (5) deposits to guarantee contract performance or expense payment; (6) claims for losses or damages; (7) claims for rebates and tax refunds; and (8) dividends and interest receivable.

Nontrade receivables should be summarized in appropriately titled accounts and reported separately in the financial statements.

Another way of classifying receivables relates to the **current** or short-term versus **noncurrent** or long-term nature of receivables. As indicated in Chapter 5, the "Current assets" classification, as broadly conceived, includes all receivables identified as collectible within one year or the normal operating cycle, whichever is longer. Thus, for classification purposes, all trade receivables are considered **current receivables;** each nontrade item requires separate analysis to determine whether it is reasonable to assume that it will be collected within one year. **Noncurrent receivables** are reported under the "Investments" or "Other noncurrent assets" caption, or as a separate item with an appropriate description.

In summary, receivables are classified in various ways, e.g., as accounts or notes receivable, as trade or nontrade receivables, and as current or noncurrent receivables. These categories are not mutually exclusive. For example, accounts receivable are trade receivables and are current; notes receivable may be trade receivables and therefore current in some circumstances, but may be nontrade receivables, either current or noncurrent, in other situations. The classifications used most often in practice and throughout this book will be simply *accounts receivable, notes receivable,* and *other receivables.*

ACCOUNTS RECEIVABLE

As indicated earlier, accounts receivable include all trade receivables not supported by a written agreement or "note." The following sections discuss the major accounting problems associated with accounts receivable: (1) when they are to be recognized; (2) how they are to be valued and reported; and (3) how they may be used as a source of cash in financing company operations.

Recognition of Accounts Receivable

The recognition of accounts receivable is related to the recognition of revenue. Since revenues are generally recorded when the earning process is complete and cash is realized or realizable, it follows that a receivable arising from the sale of goods is generally recognized when title to the goods passes to the buyer. Because the point at which title passes may vary with the terms of the sale, it is normal practice to recognize the receivable when goods are shipped to the customer. It is at this point in time that the revenue recognition criteria are normally satisfied. Receivables should not be recognized for goods shipped on approval, where the shipper retains title until there is a formal acceptance, or for goods shipped on consignment, where the shipper retains title until the goods are sold by the consignee. Receivables for service to customers are properly recognized when the services are performed. The entry for recognizing a receivable from the sale of goods or services is:

Accounts Receivable	XXX	
Sales		XXX

When the account is collected, Accounts Receivable is credited and Cash is debited.

For department stores and major oil and gas companies, a significant portion of receivables arise from *credit card sales.* The recognition of such receivables is similar to recognition of other trade receivables.

The treatment of credit card sales for other companies, such as American Express or banks that handle VISA or MasterCard, is somewhat different. These companies are generally responsible for approving customers' credit and collecting the receivables. Consequently, they usually charge a service fee, normally 2% to 5% of net credit card sales. These companies generally follow one of two procedures in reimbursing the retail companies that accept their cards: (1) the retailer must submit the credit card receipts in order to receive payments, or (2) they allow retailers to deposit the receipts directly into a checking account. American Express, Diners Club, Carte Blanche, and other travel and entertainment card companies generally follow the first procedure; bank cards are accounted for with the second method.[3]

As an example of how a retail company would account for credit card sales under these two approaches, assume that Little Italy Pizza Parlor has American Express drafts that total $1,200 on November 20. The entry to record the sales would be:

Accounts Receivable—American Express	1,200	
Sales		1,200
To record American Express credit card sales for November 20.		

Little Italy would then send the receipts to American Express, which would send a check to Little Italy for $1,200 less its service fees. Assuming a 5% service charge, which Little Italy would recognize as a selling expense, the entry to record the payment from American Express would be:

Cash	1,140	
Credit Card Service Charge	60	
Accounts Receivable		1,200
To record payment from American Express on credit card sales.		

Continuing the example, assume Little Italy also had VISA charge sales of $2,000. These sales are handled under the second method and are treated like a cash sale. In effect, bank credit card sales, such as VISA and MasterCard, are a form of factoring receivables, which is discussed later in the chapter. The retail company makes out a regular, but separate, bank deposit slip and deposits the credit card receipts as though they were cash. The bank receives the deposit slip and credit card receipts and increases the retailer's checking account balance for the total amount less the bank credit card service charge. Assuming a 4% bank service charge, in our example Little Italy would make the following entry:

Cash	1,920	
Credit Card Service Charge	80	
Sales		2,000
To record VISA credit card sales for November 20.		

Note that under this method a receivable is never established by the retail companies. The receivables from the customers are the responsibility of the bank that issued the credit card. The customers pay the bank directly and any uncollectibles are losses for the bank.

Valuation of Accounts Receivable

Theoretically, all receivables should be valued at an amount representing the present value of the expected future cash receipts. As explained in Chapter 7, the present value of a $1,000 receivable due in 1 year at a 10% interest rate is $909.10 ($1,000 × the present value factor of .9091 from Table II in Chapter 7). The difference in the present value and the amount to be received in the future ($90.90 in the example) is the implicit interest. Since accounts receivable are short-term, usually being collected within 30 to 90 days, the amount of interest is small relative to the amount of the receivable. Consequently, the accounting profession has chosen to ignore the interest element for these trade receivables.[4]

3. The total number of credit cards in the U.S. exceeds one billion. Consumers currently use plastic to pay for $28 out of every $100 spent on consumable goods and services. (Reported in *The Wall Street Journal,* July 26, 1990, p. A. 1 in "Business Bulletin" by Pamela Sabastian.)

4. See *Opinions of the Accounting Principles Board No. 21,* "Interest on Receivables and Payables, (New York: American Institute of Certified Public Accountants, 1971), par. 3(a).

Instead of valuing accounts receivable at a discounted present value, they are reported at their **net realizable value,** i.e., their expected cash value. This means that accounts receivable should be recorded net of estimated uncollectible items and trade discounts. The objective is to report the receivables at the amount of claims from customers actually expected to be collected in cash.

Uncollectible Accounts Receivable. Invariably, some receivables will prove uncollectible. The simplest method for recognizing the loss from these uncollectible accounts is to debit an expense account, such as Bad Debt Expense or Uncollectible Accounts Expense, and credit Accounts Receivable at the time it is determined that an account cannot be collected. This approach is called the **direct write-off method** and is often used by small businesses because of its simplicity. While the recognition of uncollectibles in the period of their discovery is simple and convenient, this method does not provide for the matching of current revenues with related expenses and does not report receivables at their net realizable value. Therefore, use of the direct write-off method is considered a departure from generally accepted accounting principles. The following sections describe the procedures used in estimating uncollectibles with the **allowance method,** which is required by GAAP.[5]

Establishing an Allowance for Doubtful Accounts. When using the allowance method, the amount of receivables estimated to be uncollectible is recorded by a debit to Doubtful Accounts Expense and a credit to Allowance for Doubtful Accounts. The terminology for these account titles may vary somewhat. Other possibilities, besides Allowance for Doubtful Accounts, include Allowance for Uncollectible Accounts and Allowance for Bad Debts. The expense account title usually is consistent with that of the allowance account. A typical entry, normally made as an end-of-the-period adjustment, would be as follows:

Doubtful Accounts Expense	XXX	
Allowance for Doubtful Accounts		XXX
To record estimated uncollectible accounts receivable for the period.		

The expense would be reported as a selling or general and administrative expense, and the allowance account would be shown as a deduction from Accounts Receivable, thereby reporting the net realizable amount of the receivables.

Writing Off an Uncollectible Account Under the Allowance Method. When positive evidence is available concerning the partial or complete worthlessness of an account, the account is written off by a debit to the allowance account, which was previously established, and a credit to Accounts Receivable. Positive evidence of a reduction in value is found in the bankruptcy, death, or disappearance of a debtor, failure to enforce collection legally, or barring of collection by the statute of limitations. Write-offs should be supported by evidence of the uncollectibility of the accounts from appropriate parties, such as courts, lawyers, or credit agencies, and should be authorized in writing by appropriate company officers. The entry to write off an uncollectible receivable would be:

Allowance for Doubtful Accounts	XXX	
Accounts Receivable		XXX
To record the write-off of an uncollectible account.		

Note that no entry is made to Doubtful Accounts Expense at this time. That entry was made when the allowance was established. The expense was thus recorded in the period

5. As a result of the Tax Reform Act of 1986, the direct write-off method of determining bad debt expense is required for income tax purposes. Prior to the Act, taxpayers could use either the direct write-off or the allowance method.

when the sale was made, not necessarily in the period when the account became uncollectible, as with the direct write-off method.

Occasionally, an account that has been written off as uncollectible is unexpectedly collected. Entries are required to reverse the write-off entry and to record the collection. Assuming an account of $1,500 was written off as uncollectible but was subsequently collected, the following entries would be made at the time of collection:

Accounts Receivable	1,500	
Allowance for Doubtful Accounts		1,500
To reverse the entry made to write off the account.		
Cash	1,500	
Accounts Receivable		1,500
To record collection of the account.		

Estimating Uncollectibles Based on Sales Percentage. The estimate for uncollectible accounts may be based on sales for the period or the amount of receivables outstanding at the end of the period. When a sales basis is used, the amount of uncollectible accounts in past years relative to total sales provides a percentage of estimated uncollectibles. This percentage may be modified by expectations based on current experience. Since doubtful accounts occur only with credit sales, it would seem logical to develop a percentage of doubtful accounts to credit sales of past periods. This percentage is then applied to credit sales of the current period. However, since extra work may be required in maintaining separate records of cash and credit sales or in analyzing sales data, the percentage is frequently developed in terms of total sales. Unless there is considerable periodic fluctuation in the proportion of cash and credit sales, the **percentage-of-total-sales method** will normally give satisfactory results.

To illustrate, if 2% of sales are considered doubtful in terms of collection and sales for the period are $100,000, the charge for Doubtful Accounts Expense would be 2% of the current period's sales, or $2,000. Note that any existing balance in the allowance account resulting from past-period charges to Doubtful Accounts Expense is ignored. The entry for this period would be simply:

Doubtful Accounts Expense	2,000	
Allowance for Doubtful Accounts		2,000
($100,000 × .02 = $2,000)		

The sales percentage method for estimating doubtful accounts is widely used in practice because it is simple to apply. Companies often use this method to estimate doubtful accounts periodically during the year and then adjust the allowance account at year-end in relationship to the accounts receivable balance, as explained in the next section.

Estimating Uncollectibles Based on Accounts Receivable Balance. Instead of using a percentage of sales to estimate uncollectible accounts, companies may base their estimates on a **percentage of total accounts receivable outstanding.** This method emphasizes the relationship between the accounts receivable balance and the allowance for doubtful accounts. For example, if total accounts receivable are $50,000 and it is estimated that 3% of those accounts will be uncollectible, then the allowance account should have a balance of $1,500 ($50,000 × .03). If the allowance account already has a $600 credit balance from prior periods, then the current-period adjusting entry would be:

Doubtful Accounts Expense	900	
Allowance for Doubtful Accounts		900

After posting the preceding entry, the balance in the allowance account would be $1,500, or 3% of total accounts receivable. Note that this method adjusts the existing balance to the desired balance based on a percentage of total receivables outstanding. If, in the example, the allowance account had a $200 debit balance caused by writing off more bad debts than had been estimated previously, the adjusting entry would be for $1,700 in order to bring the allowance account to the desired credit balance of $1,500, or 3% of total receivables.

The most commonly used method for establishing an allowance based on outstanding receivables involves **aging receivables.** Individual accounts are analyzed to determine those not yet due and those past due. Past-due accounts are classified in terms of the length of the period past due. An analysis sheet used in aging accounts receivable is shown below.

ICO Products, Inc.
Analysis of Receivables
December 31, 1996

Customer	Amount	Not Yet Due	Not More Than 30 days Past Due	31-60 Days Past Due	61-90 Days Past Due	91-180 Days Past Due	181-365 Days Past Due	More Than One Year Past Due
A.B. Andrews	$ 450			$ 450				
B.T. Brooks...........	300				$100	$200		
B. Bryant	200		$ 200					
L.B. Devine	2,100	$ 2,100						
K. Martinez	200							$ 200
M.A. Young	1,400	1,000		100	300			
Total.....................	$47,550	$40,000	$3,000	$1,200	$650	$500	$800	$1,400

Overdue balances can be evaluated individually to estimate the collectibility of each item as a basis for developing an overall estimate. An alternative procedure is to develop a series of estimated loss percentages and apply these to the different receivables classifications. The calculation of the allowance on the latter basis is illustrated below.

Just as with the previous method based on a percentage of total receivables outstanding, Doubtful Accounts Expense is debited and Allowance for Doubtful Accounts is credited for an amount bringing the allowance account to the required balance. Assuming

ICO Products, Inc.
Estimated Amount of Uncollectible Accounts
December 31, 1996

Classification	Balances	Uncollectible Accounts Experience Percentage	Estimated Amount of Uncollectible Accounts
Not yet due..	$40,000	2%	$ 800
Not more than 30 days past due	3,000	5%	150
31-60 days past due	1,200	10%	120
61-90 days past due	650	20%	130
91-180 days past due	500	30%	150
181-365 days past due	800	50%	400
More than one year past due	1,400	80%	1,120
	$47,550		$2,870

uncollectibles estimated at $2,870 as shown in the schedule above and a credit balance of $620 in the allowance account before adjustment, the following entry would be made:

Doubtful Accounts Expense	2,250	
Allowance for Doubtful Accounts		2,250

The aging method provides the most satisfactory approach to the valuation of receivables at their net realizable amounts. Furthermore, data developed through aging receivables may be quite useful to management for purposes of credit analysis and control. On the other hand, application of this method may involve considerable time and cost. This method still involves estimates, and the added refinement achieved by the aging process may not warrant the additional cost. With computer programs, however, the time and cost factors are not as significant as they once were.

Corrections to Allowance for Doubtful Accounts. As previously indicated, the allowance for doubtful accounts balance is established and maintained by means of adjusting entries at the close of each accounting period. If the allowance provisions are too large, the allowance account balance will be unnecessarily inflated and earnings will be understated; if the allowance provisions are too small, the allowance account balance will be inadequate and earnings will be overstated.

Care must be taken to see that the allowance balance follows the credit experience of the particular business. The process of aging receivables at different intervals may be employed as a means of checking the allowance balance to be certain that it is being maintained satisfactorily. Such periodic reviews may indicate a need for a correction in the allowance as well as a change in the rate or in the method employed.

When the uncollectible accounts experience approximates the estimated losses, the allowance procedure may be considered satisfactory, and no adjustment is required. When it appears that there has been a failure to estimate uncollectible accounts accurately, resulting in an allowance balance that is clearly inadequate or excessive, an adjustment is in order. Such an adjustment would be considered a change in accounting estimate under APB Opinion No. 20, and the effect would be reported in the current and future periods as an ordinary item on the income statement, usually as an addition to or subtraction from Doubtful Accounts Expense.

The actual write-off of receivables as uncollectible by debits to the allowance account and credits to the receivables account may result temporarily in a debit balance in the allowance account. A debit balance arising in this manner does not mean necessarily that the allowance is inadequate; debits to the allowance account simply predate the end-of-period adjustment for uncollectible accounts. The adjustment, when recorded, should cover uncollectibles already determined as well as those yet to be identified.

Impact of Uncollectible Accounts on the Statement of Cash Flows. As noted in Chapter 6, the amount of reported sales or net income on an accrual basis must be adjusted for the change in accounts receivable balances to derive the corresponding amount of cash flow from operations. The establishment of a provision for bad debts with a corresponding allowance for doubtful accounts and the subsequent write-off of uncollectible accounts may impact the reporting of cash flows, depending on whether the direct or indirect method is used and whether the analysis considers *gross* or *net* accounts receivable balances.

Since working with *net* accounts receivable changes is much easier for the indirect method and at least as good for the direct method, that is the approach used in this text. The amount of net change in receivables will always be determinable, either because that is how the receivables are reported in the financial statements or by simply subtracting the appropriate allowance accounts from the *gross* accounts receivable balances.

If the indirect method is used and the receivable balances are reported *net* of the allowance for doubtful accounts, which is the most common situation, any bad debt expense and any write-offs of uncollectible accounts may be ignored. Both the write-off and the estimated bad debt expense have already been netted against the receivable balances.

Similarly, if the direct method is used to compute cash flow from operations and the receivable balances are considered "net," any write-offs of uncollectible accounts can be ignored. The write-off reduces both the allowance account and the receivable account and thus leaves the net balance unchanged. However, with the direct method, sales would have to be reduced by the amount of the bad debt expense for the period to determine cash collected from customers. This is because the bad debt provision reduces the net receivable balance but does not generate any cash.

To illustrate, assume the following data:

	Beginning Balances	Ending Balances
Accounts receivable	$20,000	$25,000
Allowance for doubtful accounts	4,000	5,000
Net accounts receivable	$16,000	$20,000

Sales for the year	$1,000,000
Net income for the year	100,000
Bad debt expense for the year	2,000
Write-off of uncollectible amounts for the year	1,000
Cash expenses for the year	898,000

In order to focus on the impact of uncollectible accounts, the illustration assumes that all operating expenses other than bad debt expense were paid in cash. Also, it is assumed that, with the exception of accounts receivable, there were no changes in the levels of current assets and current liabilities.

Using the above data, the net cash flow provided by operations during the period would be computed as follows:

Direct Method

Sales	$1,000,000
Less: Net increase in accounts receivable	(4,000)
Bad debt expense	(2,000)
Cash collected from customers	$ 994,000
Cash expenses	(898,000)
Net cash flow provided by operations	$ 96,000

Indirect Method

Net income	$ 100,000
Less net increase in accounts receivable	(4,000)
Net cash flow provided by operations	$ 96,000

The above discussion is summarized in Exhibit 8—3.

Discounts. Many companies bill their customers at a gross sales price less an amount designated as a **trade discount.** The discount may vary by customer depending on the volume of business or size of order from the customer. In effect, the trade discount reduces the "list" sales price to the "net" sales price actually charged the customer. This net price is the amount at which the receivable and corresponding revenue should be recorded.

■ Exhibit 8—3
Guidelines for Considering the Impact of Uncollectible Accounts on the Statement of Cash Flows

Adjustments with *net* receivable balances:

Direct Approach	**Indirect Approach**
—Adjust for bad debt expense	—Ignore bad debt expense
—Ignore write-offs of uncollectible accounts	—Ignore write-offs of uncollectible accounts

Another type of discount is a **cash discount** or **sales discount** offered to customers by some companies to encourage prompt payment of bills. Cash discounts may be taken by the customer only if payment is made within a specified period of time, generally thirty days or less. Receivables are generally recorded at their gross amounts, without regard to any cash discount offered. If payment is received within the discount period, Sales Discounts (a contra account to Sales) is debited for the difference between the recorded amount of the receivable and the total cash collected. This method, which is simple and widely used, is illustrated below with credit terms of "2/10, n/30" (2% discount if paid within 10 days, net amount due in 30 days).

Cash Discounts—Gross Method

Sales of $1,000; terms 2/10, n/30:

Accounts Receivable	1,000	
Sales		1,000

Payments of $300 received within discount period:

Cash	294	
Sales Discounts	6	
Accounts Receivable		300

Payments of $700 received after discount period:

Cash	700	
Accounts Receivable		700

Sales Returns and Allowances. In the normal course of business, some goods will be returned by customers and some allowances will have to be made for such factors as goods damaged during shipment, spoiled or otherwise defective goods, or shipment of an incorrect quantity or type of goods. When goods are returned or an allowance is necessary, net sales and accounts receivable are reduced. To illustrate, assume merchandise costing $1,000 is sold and later returned. The return would be recorded in the following manner:

Sales Returns and Allowances	1,000	
Accounts Receivable		1,000

While the charge could be made directly to Sales, the use of a separate contra account preserves information that may be useful to management.

Monitoring Accounts Receivable

Managers as well as external users of financial information need to measure how efficiently a firm is utilizing its operating assets, particularly significant working capital elements such as receivables, inventories, and accounts payable. The two most common relationships used to monitor receivables are: (1) accounts receivable turnover, and (2) number of days' sales in receivables.

Accounts Receivable Turnover. The amount of receivables usually bears a close relationship to the volume of credit sales. The receivable position and approximate collection time may be evaluated by computing the **accounts receivable turnover.** This rate is determined by dividing net credit sales (or total net sales if credit sales are unknown) by the average trade accounts receivable outstanding during the year. In developing an average receivables amount, monthly balances should be used if available.

Assume for the WS Corporation that all sales are made on credit, that receivables arise only from sales, and that receivables totals for only the beginning and the end of the year are available. Receivables turnover rates for 1997 and 1996 are computed as follows:

	1997	**1996**
Net credit sales	$1,425,000	$1,650,000
Net receivables:		
Beginning of year	$ 375,000	$ 333,500
End of year	$ 420,000	$ 375,000
Average receivables [(beginning balance + ending balance) ÷ 2]	$ 397,500	$ 354,250
Receivables turnover for year	3.6 times	4.7 times

The value computed for receivables turnover represents the average number of sale/collection cycles completed by the firm during the year.

Number of Days' Sales in Receivables. Average receivables are sometimes expressed in terms of the **number of days' sales in receivables,** which shows the average time required to collect receivables. Average receivables outstanding divided by average daily credit sales gives the number of days' sales in average receivables. This measure is computed for the WS Corporation as illustrated below.

	1997	**1996**
Average receivables	$ 397,500	$ 354,250
Net credit sales	$1,425,000	$1,650,000
Average daily credit sales (net credit sales ÷ 365)	$ 3,904	$ 4,521
Number of days' sales in average receivables (average receivables ÷ average daily credit sales)	102 days	78 days

This same measurement can be obtained by dividing the number of days in the year by the receivables turnover.[6]

In some cases, instead of developing the number of days' sales in average receivables, it may be more useful to report the number of days' credit sales in receivables at the end of the period. This information would be significant in evaluating current position, and particularly the receivable position as of a given date. This information for the WS Corporation is presented below.

	1997	**1996**
Receivables at end of year	$420,000	$375,000
Average daily credit sales	$ 3,904	$ 4,521
Number of days' sales in receivables at end of year	108 days	83 days

6. A 365-day year is used in this chapter because most banks and other financial institutions use 365 days. For simplicity, ratios are sometimes calculated using a 360-day year.

What constitutes a reasonable number of days in receivables varies with individual businesses. For example, if merchandise is sold on terms of net 60 days, 40 days' sales in receivables would be reasonable, but if terms are net 30 days, a receivable balance equal to 40 days' sales would indicate slow collections. Typical levels for number of days' sales in receivables for several industries are presented below.

Industry (number of firms included)	Median Number of Days' Sales in Receivables
Dairy Farms (226)	22.9 days
Blast Furnaces and Steel Mills (274)	42.3 days
Electric Utilities (1,068)	33.2 days
Grocery Stores (1,424)	2.6 days
Jewelry Stores (2,244)	22.6 days
Personal Credit Institutions (573)	214.5 days
Legal Services (1,060)	47.5 days

Source: *Key Business Ratios* (New York: Dun & Bradstreet, Inc., 1993).

Sales activity just before the close of a period should be considered when interpreting accounts receivable measurements. If sales are unusually light or heavy just before the end of the fiscal period, this affects total receivables as well as the related measurements. When such unevenness prevails, it may be better to analyze accounts receivable according to their due dates, as was illustrated earlier in the chapter.

The problem of minimizing accounts receivable without losing desirable business is important. Receivables often do not earn interest revenue, and the cost of carrying them must be covered by the profit margin. The longer accounts are carried, the smaller will be the percentage return realized on invested capital. In addition, heavier bookkeeping and collection charges and increased bad debts must be considered.

To attract business, credit frequently is granted for relatively long periods. The cost of granting long-term credit should be considered. Assume that a business has average daily credit sales of $5,000 and average accounts receivable of $250,000, which represents 50 days' credit sales. If collections and the credit period can be improved so that accounts receivable represent only 30 days' sales, then accounts receivable will be reduced to $150,000. Assuming a total cost of 10% to carry and service the accounts, the $100,000 decrease would yield annual savings of $10,000.

Accounts Receivable as a Source of Cash

Accounts receivable are a part of the normal operating cycle of a business. Cash is used to purchase inventory, which in turn is often sold on account. The receivables are then collected, providing cash to start the cycle over. Frequently the operating cycle takes several months to complete. Sometimes companies need immediate cash and cannot wait for completion of the normal cycle. At other times companies are not in financial stress but want to accelerate the receivable collection process, shift the risk of credit and the effort of collection to someone else, or merely use receivables from customers as a source of financing.

Receivables financing was once looked upon as a desperate measure. In recent years, however, receivables financing has become quite popular for financing leveraged buyouts and for business expansion. As one executive put it, "receivables financing is no longer viewed as last-resort financing but as a legitimate business tool."[7]

7. See "Factoring: A Flexible Borrowing Tool," *Small Business Report* (March 1987), p. 50. Also, Charles Batchelor. "Lenders of Last Resort." *Accountancy*, September 1992, p. 76.

Accounts receivable may be converted to cash in one of three ways: (1) **assignment of receivables,** which is a borrowing arrangement with receivables pledged as security on the loan; (2) **factoring receivables,** which is a sale of receivables without recourse for cash to a third party, usually a bank or other financial institution; and (3) the **transfer of receivables with recourse,** which is a hybrid of the other two forms of receivables financing.

Assignment of Accounts Receivable. Loans are frequently obtained from banks or other lending institutions by assigning or pledging accounts receivable as security. The loan is evidenced by a written promissory note that provides for either a general assignment of receivables or an assignment of specific receivables.

With a **general assignment,** all accounts receivable serve as collateral on the note. There are no special accounting problems involved. The books simply report the loan (a debit to Cash and a credit to Notes Payable) and subsequent settlement of the obligation (a debit to Notes Payable and a credit to Cash). However, disclosure should be made on the balance sheet, by a parenthetical comment or a note, of the amount and nature of receivables pledged to secure the obligation to the lender.

When there is an **assignment of specific receivables** to a lender, the borrower should transfer the balance of those accounts to a special general ledger control account and clearly identify and account for the individually assigned accounts in the subsidiary ledger. The procedures involved are illustrated in the following example. It is assumed that the assignor (the borrower) collects the receivables, which is often the case.

On July 1, 1996, Provo Mercantile Co. assigns specific receivables totaling $300,000 to Salem Bank as collateral on a $200,000, 12% note. Provo Mercantile does not notify its account debtors and will continue to collect the assigned receivables. Salem assesses a 1% finance charge on assigned receivables in addition to the interest on the note. Provo is to make monthly payments to Salem with cash collected on assigned receivables. The entries on the following page would be made.

If in the preceding example Salem Bank assumes responsibility for collecting the assigned receivables, the account debtors would have to be notified to make their payments to the bank. Salem would then use a liability account (e.g., Payable to Provo Mercantile) to account for cash collections during the period. Since the receivables are still owned by Provo Mercantile, the bank would not record them as assets. Upon full payment of the note plus interest, the bank would remit to Provo Mercantile any cash collections in excess of the note along with any uncollected accounts.

In disclosing the specifically assigned accounts receivable, Provo Mercantile should report them separately as a current asset if they are material. In addition, the equity in assigned accounts should be disclosed parenthetically or in a note. For example, on July 1, Provo Mercantile had $100,000 equity in its assigned receivables ($300,000 – $200,000).

Factoring Accounts Receivable. Certain banks, dealers, and finance companies purchase accounts receivable outright on a nonrecourse basis. A **sale of accounts receivable without recourse**[8] is commonly referred to as accounts receivable **factoring,** and the buyer is referred to as a "factor." Customers are usually notified that their bills are payable to the factor, and this party assumes the burden of billing and collecting accounts. The flow of activities involved in factoring is presented in Exhibit 8—4.

8. Recourse is defined by the FASB as "the right of a transferee of receivables to receive payment from the transferor of those receivables for (a) failure of the debtors to pay when due, (b) the effects of prepayments, or (c) adjustments resulting from defects in the eligibility of the transferred receivables." *Statement of Financial Accounting Standards No. 77,* "Reporting by Transferors for Transfers of Receivables with Recourse" (December 1983), p. 7.

Illustrative Entries for Assignment of Specific Receivables

Provo Mercantile Co.			Salem Bank		
Issuance of note and assignment of specific receivables on July 1, 1996:					
Cash	197,000		Notes Receivable	200,000	
Finance Charge*	3,000		Finance Revenue*		3,000
Accounts Receivable—Assigned	300,000		Cash		197,000
Notes Payable		200,000			
Accounts Receivable		300,000			

*(1% × $300,000)

Collections of assigned accounts during July, $180,000 less cash discounts of $1,000; sales returns in July, $2,000:

Provo Mercantile Co.			Salem Bank		
Cash	179,000				
Sales Discounts	1,000		(No Entry)		
Sales Returns	2,000				
Accounts Receivable—Assigned		182,000			

Paid Salem bank amounts owed for July collections plus accrued interest on note to August 1:

Provo Mercantile Co.			Salem Bank		
Interest Expense*	2,000		Cash	181,000	
Notes Payable	179,000		Interest Revenue		2,000
Cash		181,000	Notes Receivable		179,000

*($200,000 × .12 × 1/12)

Collections of remaining assigned accounts during August less $800 written off as uncollectible:

Provo Mercantile Co.			Salem Bank		
Cash	117,200		(No Entry)		
Allowance for Doubtful Accounts	800				
Accounts Receivable—Assigned*		118,000			

*($300,000 – $182,000)

Paid Salem Bank remaining balance owed plus accrued interest on note to September 1:

Provo Mercantile Co.			Salem Bank		
Interest Expense*	210		Cash	21,210	
Notes Payable**	21,000		Interest Revenue*		210
Cash		21,210	Notes Receivable**		21,000

*($21,000 × .12 × 1/12)
**($200,000 – $179,000)

Exhibit 8—4
Flow of Activities Involved in Factoring

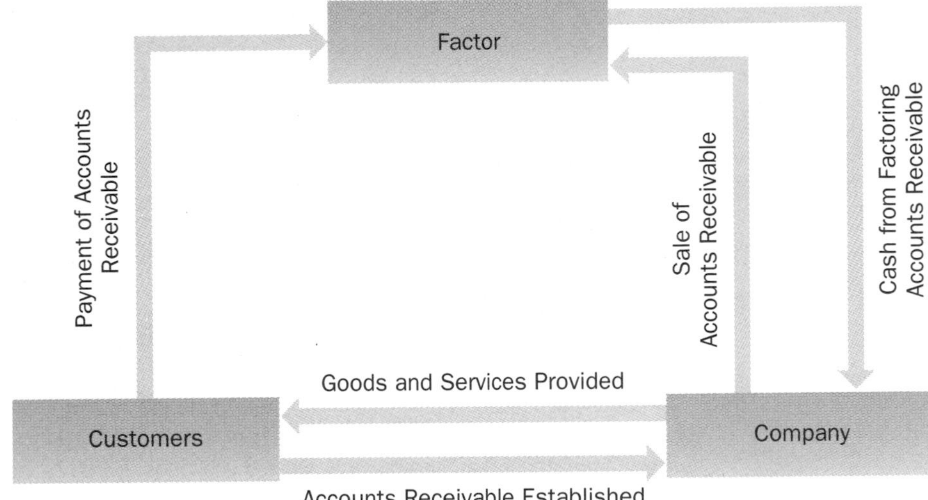

In many cases, factoring involves more than the purchase and collection of accounts receivable. Factoring frequently involves a continuing agreement whereby a financing institution assumes the credit function as well as the collection function. Under such an arrangement, the factor grants or denies credit, handles the accounts receivable records, bills customers, and makes collections. The business unit is relieved of all these activities, and the sale of goods provides immediate cash for business use. Because the factor absorbs the losses from bad accounts and frequently assumes credit and collection responsibilities, the charges associated with factoring generally exceed the interest charges on a loan with an assignment of receivables. Typically the factor will charge a fee of 10% to 30% of the net amount of receivables purchased, except for credit card factoring where the rate is 3% to 5%. The factor may withhold a portion of the purchase price for possible future charges for customer returns and allowances or other special adjustments. Final settlement is made after receivables have been collected.

When receivables are sold outright, without recourse, Cash is debited, receivables and related allowance balances are closed, and an expense account is debited for factoring charges. When part of the purchase price is withheld by the factor, a receivable from the factor is established pending final settlement. Upon receipt of the total purchase price from the bank or finance company, the factor receivable account is eliminated. To illustrate, assume that $10,000 of receivables are factored, i.e., sold without recourse, to a finance company for $8,500. An allowance for doubtful accounts equal to $300 was previously established for these accounts. This amount will need to be written off along with the accounts receivable being sold. The finance company withheld 5% of the purchase price as protection against sales returns and allowances. The entry to record the sale of the accounts would be:

Cash	8,075	
Receivable From Factor	425	
Allowance for Doubtful Accounts	300	
Loss From Factoring Receivables	1,200	
Accounts Receivable		10,000

Computations:
Cash = $8,500 – $425 = $8,075;
Factor receivable = $8,500 × 5% = $425;
Factoring loss = ($10,000 – $300) – $8,500 = $1,200

Assuming there were no returns or allowances, the final settlement would be recorded as follows:

Cash	425	
Receivable From Factor		425

Transfer of Accounts Receivable With Recourse. The third way that cash can be obtained from accounts receivable financing is by **transferring accounts receivable with recourse.** This is different from factoring, which generally is on a nonrecourse basis. Transferring with recourse means that a transferee (bank or finance company) advances cash in return for accounts receivable, but retains the right to collect from the transferor if debtors (transferor's customers) fail to make payments when due. An important accounting question is whether this type of transaction is a **borrowing transaction** (like an assignment with the receivables as collateral) or a **sale transaction** (like a factoring arrangement). If viewed as a borrowing transaction, a liability should be reported and the difference between the proceeds received and the net receivables transferred is a financing cost (interest). If viewed as a sale, the difference between the amount received from the finance company (the transfer price) and the net amount of the receivables transferred (the gross amount of the receivables adjusted for allowance for doubtful accounts and any finance and service charges) is to be recognized as a gain or loss on the sale, as illustrated previously in the factoring example.

The FASB in Statement No. 77 has concluded that a transfer of receivables with recourse should be accounted for and reported as a sale if all the following conditions are met:

1. The transferor surrenders control of the future economic benefit embodied in the receivables.
2. The transferor's obligation under the recourse provisions can be reasonably estimated.
3. The transferee cannot require the transferor to repurchase the receivables except pursuant to the recourse provisions.[9]

If these conditions are not met, the transfer is reported as a secured loan, i.e., in the same manner as an assignment of receivables discussed previously.

In summary, accounts receivable provide an important source of cash for many companies. The transfer of receivables to third parties in return for cash generally takes the form of an assignment (borrowing with the receivables pledged as collateral) or factoring (a sale without recourse). The financing arrangements are often complex and may involve a transfer of receivables on a recourse basis. Each transaction must be analyzed carefully to see if in form and substance it is a borrowing transaction or a sale transaction, and treated accordingly.

NOTES RECEIVABLE

A **promissory note** is an unconditional written promise to pay a certain sum of money at a specified time. The note is signed by the **maker** and is payable to the order of a specified payee or to bearer. Notes usually involve interest, stated at an annual rate and charged on the face amount of the note. Most notes are **negotiable notes** that are legally transferable by endorsement and delivery.

For reporting purposes, **trade notes receivable** should include only negotiable short-term instruments acquired from trade debtors and not yet due. Trade notes generally arise from sales involving relatively high dollar amounts where the buyer wants to extend payment beyond the usual trade credit period of 30 to 90 days. Also, sellers sometimes request notes from customers whose accounts receivable are past due. Most companies, however, have relatively few trade notes receivable.

9. *Statement of Financial Accounting Standards No. 77,* "Reporting by Transferors of Transfers of Receivables with Recourse" (December 1983), par. 5.

Nontrade notes receivable should be separately designated on the balance sheet under an appropriate title. For example, notes arising from loans to customers, officers, employees, and affiliated companies should be reported separately from trade notes.

Valuation of Notes Receivable

Notes receivable are initially recorded at their **present value,** which may be defined as the sum of future receipts discounted to the present date at an appropriate rate of interest.[10] In a lending transaction, the present value is the amount of cash received by the borrower. When a note is exchanged for property, goods, or services, the present value equals the current cash selling price of the items exchanged. The difference between the present value and the amount to be collected at the due date or maturity date is a charge for interest.

All notes arising in arm's-length transactions between unrelated parties involve an element of interest. However, a distinction as to form is made between interest-bearing and non-interest-bearing notes. An **interest-bearing note** is written as a promise to pay **principal** (or **face amount)** plus interest at a specified rate. In the absence of special valuation problems discussed in the next section, the face amount of an interest-bearing note is the present value upon issuance of the note.

A **non-interest-bearing note** does not specify an interest rate, but the face amount includes the interest charge. Thus, the present value is the difference between the face amount and the interest included in that amount, sometimes called the **implicit** (or **effective) interest.**

In recording receipt of a note, Notes Receivable is debited for the face amount of the note. When the face amount differs from the present value, as is the case with non-interest-bearing notes, the difference is recorded as a premium or discount and amortized over the life of the note. In the example to follow, a note receivable is established with credits to Sales and a discount on notes receivable account. The amount of discount is the implicit interest on the note and will be recognized as interest revenue as the note matures.

To illustrate, assume that High Value Corporation sells goods on January 1, 1996, with a price of $1,000. The buyer gives High Value a promissory note due December 31, 1997. The maturity value of the note includes interest at 10%. Thus, High Value will receive $1,210 ($1,000 × 1.21)[11] when the note is paid. The entries on page 306 show the accounting procedures for an interest-bearing note and one written in a non-interest-bearing form.

At December 31, 1996, the unamortized discount of $110 on the non-interest-bearing note would be deducted from notes receivable on the balance sheet. If the non-interest-bearing note were recorded at face value with no recognition of the interest included therein, the sales price and profit to the seller would be overstated. In subsequent periods interest revenue would be understated. Failure to record the discount would also result in an overstatement of assets.

Although the proper valuation of receivables calls for the amortization procedure just described, exceptions may be appropriate in some situations due to special limitations or practical considerations. The Accounting Principles Board in Opinion No. 21 provided guidelines for the recognition of interest on receivables and payables and the accounting subsequently to be employed. However, the board indicated that this process is not to be regarded as applicable under all circumstances. Among the exceptions are the following:

> *. . . receivables and payables arising from transactions with customers or suppliers in the normal course of business which are due in customary trade terms not exceeding approximately one year.*[12]

10. See Chapter 7 for a discussion of present-value concepts and applications.
11. The amount of $1 due in two years at an annual rate of 10% is $1.21. See Table I, Chapter 7.
12. *Opinions of the Accounting Principles Board, No 21,* "Interest on Receivables and Payables" (New York: American Institute of Certified Public Accountants, 1971), par. 3(a).

Illustrative Entries for Notes

	Interest-Bearing Note **Face Amount = Present Value = $1,000** **Stated Interest Rate = 10%**			**Non-Interest-Bearing Note** **Face Amount = Maturity = $1,210** **No Stated Interest Rate**		

To record note received in exchange for goods selling for $1,000:

1996						
Jan. 1	Notes Receivable	1,000		Notes Receivable	1,210	
	Sales		1,000	Sales		1,000
				Discount on Notes Receivable		210

To recognize interest earned for one year, $1,000 × .10:

Dec. 31	Interest Receivable	100		Discount on Notes Receivable	100	
	Interest Revenue		100	Interest Revenue		100

To record settlement of note at maturity and recognize interest earned for one year; ($1,000 + $100) × .10:

1997						
Dec. 31	Cash	1,210		Cash	1,210	
	Notes Receivable		1,000	Discount on Notes Receivable	110	
	Interest Receivable		100	Notes Receivable		1,210
	Interest Revenue		110	Interest Revenue		110

Accordingly, as mentioned earlier, short-term notes and accounts receivable arising from trade sales may be properly recorded at the amounts collectible in the customary sales terms.

Notes, like accounts receivable, are not always collectible. If notes receivable comprise a significant portion of regular trade receivables, a provision should be made for uncollectible amounts and an allowance account established using procedures similar to those for accounts receivable already discussed.

Special Valuation Problems. APB Opinion No. 21 was issued to clarify and refine existing accounting practice with respect to receivables and payables. The opinion is especially applicable to nontrade, long-term notes, such as secured and unsecured notes, debentures (bonds), equipment obligations, and mortgage notes. Examples are provided for notes exchanged for cash and for property, goods, or services.

Notes Exchanged for Cash. When a note is exchanged for cash, and there are no other rights or privileges involved, the present value of the note is presumed to be the amount of the cash proceeds. The note should be recorded at its face amount and any difference between the face amount and the cash proceeds should be recorded as a premium or discount on the note. The premium or discount should be amortized over the life of the note as illustrated previously for High Value Corporation. The total interest is measured by the difference in actual cash received by the borrower and the total amount to be received in the future by the lender. Any unamortized premium or discount on notes is reported on the balance sheet as a direct addition to or deduction from the face amount of the receivables, thus showing their net present value.

Notes Exchanged for Property, Goods, or Services. When a note is exchanged for property, goods, or services in an arm's-length transaction, the present value of the note is usually evidenced by the terms of the note or supporting documents. There is a general presumption that the interest specified by the parties to a transaction represents fair and adequate compensation for the use of borrowed funds.[13] Valuation problems arise, however, when one of the following conditions exists:[14]

1. No interest rate is stated.
2. The stated rate does not seem reasonable, given the nature of the transaction and surrounding circumstances.
3. The stated face amount of the note is significantly different from the current cash equivalent sales price of similar property, goods, or services, or from the current market value of similar notes at the date of the transaction.

Under any of the preceding conditions, APB No. 21 requires accounting recognition of the economic substance of the transaction rather than the form of the note. The note should be recorded at (1) the fair market value of the property, goods, or services exchanged or (2) the current market value of the note, whichever is more clearly determinable. The difference between the face amount of the note and the present value is recognized as a discount or premium and amortized over the life of the note.

To illustrate, assume that on July 1, 1996, Timberline Corporation sells a tract of land purchased three years ago at a cost of $250,000. The buyer gives Timberline a 1-year note with a face amount of $310,000 bearing interest at a stated rate of 8%. An appraisal of the land prior to the sale indicated a market value of $300,000, which in this example is considered to be the appropriate basis for recording the sale as follows:

1996			
July 1	Notes Receivable	310,000	
	Discount on Notes Receivable		10,000
	Land		250,000
	Gain on Sale of Land		50,000

When the note is paid at maturity, Timberline will receive the face value ($310,000) plus stated interest of $24,800 ($310,000 × .08), or a total of $334,800. The interest to be recognized, however, is $34,800—the difference between the maturity value of the note and the market value of the land at the date of the exchange. Thus the effective rate of interest on the note is 11.6% ($34,800 ÷ $300,000).

Assuming straight-line amortization of the discount and that Timberline's year-end is December 31, the following entries would be made to recognize interest revenue and to record payment of the note at maturity:

1996			
Dec. 31	Interest Receivable	12,400*	
	Discount on Notes Receivable	5,000	
	Interest Revenue		17,400

*$310,000 × .08 × 6/12 = $12,400

1997			
June 30	Cash	334,800	
	Discount on Notes Receivable	5,000	
	Notes Receivable		310,000
	Interest Receivable		12,400
	Interest Revenue		17,400

13. *Ibid.*, par. 12
14. *Ibid.*

The unamortized discount balance of $5,000 would be subtracted from Notes Receivable on the December 31, 1996, balance sheet.

Imputing an Interest Rate. If there is no current market price for either the property, goods or services, or the note, then the present value of the note must be determined by selecting an appropriate interest rate and using that rate to discount future receipts to the present. The **imputed interest rate** is determined at the date of the exchange and is not altered thereafter.

The selection of an appropriate rate is influenced by many factors, including the credit standing of the issuer of the note and prevailing interest rates for debt instruments of similar quality and length of time to maturity. APB Opinion No. 21 states:

In any event, the rate used for valuation purposes will normally be at least equal to the rate at which the debtor can obtain financing of a similar nature from other sources at the date of the transaction. The objective is to approximate the rate which would have resulted if an independent borrower and an independent lender had negotiated a similar transaction under comparable terms and conditions with the option to pay the cash price upon purchase or to give a note for the amount of the purchase which bears the prevailing rate of interest to maturity.[15]

To illustrate the process of imputing interest rates, assume that Horrocks & Associates surveyed 800,000 acres of mountain property for the Mountain Meadow Ranch. On December 31, 1996, Horrocks accepted a $45,000 note as payment for services. The note is non-interest-bearing and comes due in three yearly installments of $15,000 each beginning December 31, 1997. Assume there is no market for the note and no basis for estimating objectively the fair market value of the services rendered. After considering the current prime interest rate, the credit standing of the ranch, the collateral available, the terms for repayment, and the prevailing rates of interest for the issuer's other debt, a 10% imputed interest rate is considered appropriate. The note should be recorded at its present value and a discount recognized. The computation is based on Present Value Table IV, Chapter 7, as follows:

Face amount of note	$45,000
Less present value of note:	
$PV_n = R(PVAF_{\overline{3}\rceil 10\%})$	
$PV_n = \$15,000(2.4869)$	37,303*
Discount on note	$ 7,697

*Rounded to nearest dollar.

The entry to record the receipt of the note would be:

1996			
Dec. 31	Notes Receivable	45,000	
	Discount on Notes Receivable		7,697
	Service Revenue		37,303
	To record a non-interest-bearing note receivable at its present value based on an imputed interest rate of 10% per year.		

A schedule showing the amortization of the discount on the note is presented. This type of computation is commonly referred to as the effective interest amortization method.

15. *Ibid,* par. 13.

	(1) Face Amount Before Current Installment	(2) Unamortized Discount	(3) Net Amount (1) – (2)	(4) Discount Amortization 10% × (3)	(5) Payment Received
Dec. 31, 1997	$45,000	$7,697	$37,303	$3,730	$15,000
Dec. 31, 1998	30,000	3,967*	26,033	2,603	15,000
Dec. 31, 1999	15,000	1,364**	13,636	1,364	15,000
				$7,697	$45,000

*$7,697 – $3,730 – $3,967
**$3,967 – $2,603 = $1,364

At the end of each year, an entry similar to the following would be made:

1997			
Dec. 31	Cash	15,000	
	Discount on Notes Receivable	3,730	
	Interest Revenue		3,730
	Notes Receivable		15,000
	To record the first year's installment on notes receivable and recognize interest earned during the period.		

By using these procedures, at the end of the three years the discount will be completely amortized to interest revenue, the face amount of the note receivable will have been collected, and the appropriate amount of service revenue will have been recognized in the year it was earned. At the end of each year, the balance sheet will reflect the net present value of the receivable by subtracting the unamortized discount balance from the outstanding balance in Notes Receivable.

It is necessary to impute an interest rate only when the present value of the receivable cannot be determined through evaluation of existing market values of the elements of the transaction. The valuation and income measurement objectives remain the same regardless of the specific circumstances—to report notes receivable at their net present values and to record appropriate amounts of interest revenue during the collection period of the receivables.

Notes Receivable as a Source of Cash

As discussed earlier in the chapter, accounts receivable can be a source of immediate cash. A company can also obtain cash by "discounting" notes receivable. The discounting of notes receivable, sometimes called bank discounting, is not to be confused with the discounting of future cash receipts to arrive at present value or with the discount deducted from Notes Receivable on the balance sheet as discussed previously. **Bank discounting** involves the transfer of negotiable notes to a bank or other financial institution willing to exchange such instruments for cash.

When discounting an interest-bearing note, which is the usual situation, the following steps are taken to determine the amount to be received from the bank (the proceeds):[16]

1. Determine the maturity value of the note:

Maturity value = Face amount + Interest
Interest = Face amount × Interest rate × Interest period
Interest period = Date of note to date of maturity

16. The same procedures apply to the discounting of a non-interest-bearing note, except that the maturity value does not have to be computed (Step 1), since the face amount equals the maturity value.

2. Determine the amount of discount:

   Discount = Maturity value × Discount rate × Discount period
   Discount period = Date of discount to date of maturity

3. Determine the proceeds:

   Proceeds = Maturity value − Discount

Once the proceeds are determined, the transaction can be recorded, recognizing the applicable liability and net interest revenue or expense (if a borrowing transaction) or the gain or loss (if a sale transaction).

If a note is transferred **without recourse,** i.e., the bank assumes the risk of uncollectibility, the transaction should be recorded as a sale, much like the factoring of accounts receivable discussed earlier. If the note is transferred **with recourse,** which is the usual case, the discounting transaction may be recorded as a sale or a borrowing transaction, depending on the terms and conditions. The criteria for classifying a transfer of accounts receivable with recourse, set forth in FASB Statement No. 77 and presented on page 304, also apply to transfers of notes receivable with recourse.

To illustrate the recording of a transfer (discounting) of notes receivable with recourse, assume that Meeker Corporation received a 90-day, $5,000, 10% note from a customer on September 1 to settle a past-due account receivable. The note is discounted at a bank after 10 days at a discount rate of 15%. The transaction would be treated as a sale only if the FASB Statement No. 77 criteria are met. Otherwise, the transfer is recorded as a borrowing transaction. In this example (and in the end-of-chapter material), a 365-day year is assumed, because that is what most financial institutions use. In some applications and in some textbooks, a 360-day year is assumed in order to simplify the computations. Journal entries for both a sale and borrowing transaction are shown on page 311.

Several important points can be observed in the example. First, the loss or net interest expense recognized at the date of discounting ($45) is the difference between the amount charged by the bank to discount the note (in effect, interest expense of $168) and the amount of interest revenue the company would have earned if it had held the note to maturity ($123). Alternatively, the loss or net interest expense is the difference between the face amount of the note ($5,000) and the proceeds received from the bank ($4,955). Depending on how long the note is held prior to discounting and on the difference between the interest rate on the note and the discount rate charged by the bank, it is possible for the proceeds to be greater than the face amount of the note, which would result in a gain or net interest revenue being recorded. For example, if the Meeker Corporation had held the note for 60 days prior to discounting, the entries to record the discounting would be:

Transaction Recorded as Sale			**Transaction Recorded as Borrowing**		
Cash	5,060		Cash	5,060	
Gain on Sale of Note		60	Interest Revenue		60
Notes Receivable		5,000	Obligation on Discounted Notes Receivable		5,000

Computations (rounded to nearest dollar):
Maturity value (same) = $5,123
Discount = $5,123 × .15 x 30/365 = $63
Proceeds = $5,123 − $63 = $5,060
Gain/Interest Revenue = $123 − $63 = $60

Discounting Notes Receivable With Recourse

Transaction Recorded as Sale			Transaction Recorded as Borrowing		
Received a 90-day, $5,000, 10% note from a customer on September 1:					
Notes Receivable	5,000		Notes Receivable	5,000	
Accounts Receivable		5,000	Accounts Receivable		5,000
Discounted customer's note at bank on September 11 at a discount rate of 15%:					
Cash	4,955		Cash	4,955	
Loss on Sale of Note	45		Interest Expense	45	
Notes Receivable		5,000	Obligation on Discounted Notes Receivable		5,000

Computations (rounded to nearest dollar):
Maturity value = $5,000 + Interest ($5,000 × .10 × 90/365 = $123)= $5,123
Discount = $5,123 × .15 × 80/365 = $168
Proceeds = $5,123 – $168 = $4,955
Loss/Interest Expense = $168 – $123 = $45

Transaction Recorded as Sale			Transaction Recorded as Borrowing		
If maturity value of note paid to bank by customer on due date, November 30:					
(No Entry)			Obligation on Discounted Notes Receivable	5,000	
			Notes Receivable		5,000
If customer defaults and bank collects from Meeker Corporation on November 30 the maturity value ($5,123) plus a $25 protest fee:					
Notes Receivable—Past Due	5,148		Notes Receivable—Past Due	5,148	
Cash		5,148	Cash		5,148
			Obligation on Discounted Notes Receivable	5,000	
			Notes Receivable		5,000

As indicated in the Meeker example, when a note is discounted with recourse, the bank will require payment from the company that discounted the note if the maker of the note defaults on payment at maturity (often referred to as **dishonoring** the note). In addition, the bank generally will charge a protest fee, which in the example is $25. Subsequently, the company will attempt to collect from the customer and, if unsuccessful, will eventually write off the note as uncollectible.

If the note had been discounted without recourse, the transaction would have been recorded in exactly the same manner as shown for a sale in the example. However, no entries would be required after the discounting transaction is recorded on September 11, since the company has no liability with regard to the note after the transfer.

PRESENTATION OF CASH AND RECEIVABLES ON THE BALANCE SHEET

Since the concept of cash embodies the standard of value, few valuation problems are encountered in reporting those items qualifying as cash. When cash is comprised solely of cash on hand and unrestricted demand deposits, the total generally appears on the balance sheet as a single item — cash. When cash and certain types of temporary investments are

ZZZZ Best

Barry Minkow started operating his carpet-cleaning business out of the Minkow family garage when he was 15. At its peak six years later, the company, called ZZZZ Best, had a market value of $211 million. On paper, Minkow himself was worth $109 million. Minkow was a celebrity. In February 1987, he was selected as one of the top 100 young entrepreneurs in the United States. He spoke of making ZZZZ Best the General Motors of carpet cleaning. He talked of running for president one day. But, in a press release dated July 3, 1987, ZZZZ Best announced that Minkow had resigned as chief executive officer because of a "severe medical problem." Shortly thereafter, ZZZZ Best filed for Chapter 11 bankruptcy. The rapid growth of ZZZZ Best had been a fraud, and Barry Minkow was eventually sentenced to 25 years in prison.

The major aspect of the fraud involved reporting fictitious receivables and revenue from fire damage restoration jobs. For example, ZZZZ Best filed a registration statement with the SEC in 1985 in which it claimed to have a contract for a $2.3 million restoration job on an eight-story building in Arroyo Grande, California. Unfortunately, Arroyo Grande, a town of 13,000 people and five traffic lights, had no buildings over three stories. On May 19, 1987, *The Wall Street Journal* reported that ZZZZ Best had received a $13.8 million restoration contract for a Dallas job. Again, the job was nonexistent. With bogus revenue and receivables like this, ZZZZ Best was able to report net income for the year ended April 30, 1987, of $5 million on revenue of $50 million, up from $900,000 net income on $4.8 million revenue the year before.

Why didn't the auditor uncover these irregularities? Larry Gray, the partner in charge of auditing ZZZZ Best, did what he was supposed to, but in this case he didn't do it well enough. When ZZZZ Best reported a $7 million contract to restore a building in Sacramento, Gray demanded to see the building. This was difficult since neither the building nor the job existed. However, officials of ZZZZ Best managed to get access to a large office building in Sacramento for a weekend, and Gray was allowed to tour the building to inspect the "finished work." On another occasion, ZZZZ Best reported an $8.2 million restoration contract in San Diego. Again, Gray demanded to see the job site. This time he was led through an unfinished building and told that the work was still ongoing. Things got very complicated for ZZZZ Best when Gray later requested to see the finished job. ZZZZ Best had to spend $1 million to lease the building and hire contractors to finish six of the eight floors in ten days. Gray was led on another tour and wrote a memo saying, "Job looks very good." Gray has subsequently been faulted for looking only at what ZZZZ Best officials chose to show him without making independent inquiries.

Questions:

1. ZZZZ Best grossly inflated its operating results by reporting bogus revenue and receivables. What factors prevent a company from continuing to report fraudulent results indefinitely?
2. What could the auditor have done to uncover the ZZZZ Best fraud?

Sources

Daniel Akst, "How Whiz-Kid Chief of ZZZZ Best Had, and Lost, It All," *The Wall Street Journal,* July 9, 1987: p. 1.

Daniel Akst, "How Barry Minkow Fooled the Auditors," *Forbes,* October 2, 1989: p. 126.

combined, an increasingly popular title is Cash and Cash Equivalents.[17] **Cash equivalents,** as defined in Chapter 6, include time deposits and highly liquid debt instruments, usually having maturities of three months or less.

Some companies (like IBM in Exhibit 8-5) report cash separately from cash equivalents; other companies (like Ford Motor Company in Exhibit 8-6) combine cash with time deposits or other cash equivalent items. All companies generally report receivables separate from cash. Another example of the varying methods of reporting cash is provided in Appendix A at the end of the text for Microsoft Corporation.

Receivables qualifying as current items may be grouped for presentation on the balance sheet in the following classes: (1) notes receivable—trade debtors, (2) accounts receivable—trade debtors, and (3) other receivables. Alternatively, trade notes and accounts receivable can be reported as a single amount. The detail reported for other receivables depends on the relative significance of the various items included. Valuation accounts are deducted from the individual receivable balances or combined balances to

17. Use of this term as a balance sheet caption has become increasingly common due to FASB Statement No. 95, "Statement of Cash Flows," which requires that the cash flow statement report changes in cash and cash equivalents.

■ Exhibit 8—5
Separate Reporting of Cash and Cash Equivalents

CONSOLIDATED STATEMENT OF FINANCIAL POSITION
INTERNATIONAL BUSINESS MACHINES CORPORATION AND SUBSIDIARY COMPANIES

(Dollars in millions) At December 31:	1992	1991*
Assets		
Current Assets:		
Cash	$ 1,090	$ 1,171
Cash equivalents	3,356	2,774
Marketable securities at cost, which approximates market	1,203	1,206
Notes and accounts receivable—trade, net of allowances	12,829	15,391
Sales-type leases receivable	7,405	7,435
Other accounts receivable	1,370	1,491
Inventories	8,385	9,844
Prepaid expenses and other current assets	4,054	1,657
	$39,692	$40,969

■ Exhibit 8—6
Combined Reporting of Cash and Cash Equivalents

CONSOLIDATED BALANCE SHEET
FORD MOTOR COMPANY AND SUBSIDIARIES
December 31, 1992 and 1991 (in millions)

	1992	1991
ASSETS		
Automotive		
Cash and cash equivalents	$ 3,504.0	$ 4,958.0
Marketable securities, at cost and accrued interest (approximates market, Note 19)	5,530.9	4,794.5
Total cash, cash equivalents, and marketable securities	$ 9,034.9	$ 9,752.5
Receivables	2,883.6	3,150.6
Inventories (Note 4)	5,451.3	6,215.3
Deferred income taxes	2,479.7	2,112.0
Other current assets	618.6	529.4
Net current receivable from Financial Services (Note 15)	1,368.0	92.1
Total current assets	$21,836.1	$21,851.9

which they relate. Any long-term trade and nontrade receivables would be reported as "Other noncurrent assets" on the balance sheet.

When notes receivable have been discounted with recourse, a liability (e.g., Obligation on Discounted Notes Receivable) is reported in the balance sheet if the discounting is treated as borrowing. If treated as a sale, no liability is recognized, but a contingent liability should be disclosed in the notes to the financial statements or parenthetically on the balance sheet with notes receivable. If notes are discounted without recourse, there is no contingent liability. If notes or accounts receivable have been pledged to secure a loan, the amount should be disclosed.

Accounts and notes receivable as presented by GTE Corporation in its 1992 annual report are shown in Exhibit 8—7. An alternative disclosure method would be to show net trade receivables on the balance sheet and present the detailed information in a note to the financial statements. This latter approach is illustrated in Exhibit 8—8 for Cincinnati Milacron Inc.

■ Exhibit 8—7
Reporting Receivables—Allowance Amounts Shown in Balance Sheet

CONSOLIDATED BALANCE SHEETS
GTE Corporation and Subsidiaries

	December 31	
	1992	1991
	(Millions of Dollars)	
Assets		
Current Assets:		
Cash and temporary cash investments	$ 354	$ 517
Receivables, less allowance for $154 and $115	3,565	3,663
Inventories	814	910
Deferred income tax benefits	111	206
Net assets of discontinued operations	1,114	1,299
Other	338	971
Total current assets	$6,296	$7,566

■ Exhibit 8—8
Reporting Receivables—Allowance Amounts Disclosed in Note

CONSOLIDATED BALANCE SHEET
CINCINNATI MILACRON INC. AND SUBSIDIARIES
Fiscal year ends on Saturday closest to December 31

(In millions)	1992	1991
Assets		
Current assets		
Cash and cash equivalents	$ 14.9	$ 16.2
Notes and accounts receivable less allowances	177.0	194.7

Notes to Financial Statements (in part)

Receivables

The components of notes and accounts receivable less allowances are shown in the following table.

Notes and Accounts Receivable Less Allowances

(In millions)	1992	1991
Notes receivable	$ 8.8	$ 16.3
Accounts receivable	174.1	184.2
	$182.9	$200.5
Less allowances for doubtful accounts	5.9	5.8
	$177.0	$194.7

Notes receivable include amounts not due within one year of $2.2 million and $4.1 million in 1992 and 1991, respectively.

APPENDIX

Four Column Bank Reconciliation

A bank reconciliation is sometimes expanded to incorporate a proof of both receipts and disbursements as separate steps in the reconciliation process. This is often referred to as a **four-column bank reconciliation** or a **proof of cash.**

In a four-column reconciliation, columns are provided for the beginning reconciliation, deposits or receipts, withdrawals or disbursements, and the ending reconciliation. Thus, the four-column approach is really two reconciliations in one. The first column contains a reconciliation as of the end of the preceding period. The deposits per bank statement or receipts per books for the period are added to the beginning balances, and the withdrawals per bank statement or disbursements per books are subtracted to arrive at the ending balances. Deposits/receipts are reconciled in the second column and withdrawals/disbursements in the third column. The amounts must reconcile both vertically and horizontally for the ending bank and book balances to agree.

In order to complete this type of reconciliation, each adjustment must be carefully analyzed. Note that two columns are always affected for each adjustment. For example, a deposit of $425.40 on October 31, 1996, was recorded by the bank in November and is included in the total bank deposits of $21,312.40 for November. However, the deposit was properly recorded on the books as a receipt in October; thus the $425.40 is not included in the book receipts of $21,457 for November, but is included in the beginning book balance of $5,406.22. The reconciliation accounts for this by deducting the in-transit deposit from the total bank deposits for November and by adding the deposit to the beginning October 31 bank statement balance. This is the same type of analysis that would have been made on October 31 for a regular bank reconciliation on that date. Similarly, the $658.50 deposit in transit at the end of November is already recorded in the book receipts and ending cash balance as of November 30, but must be added to the bank deposits and ending balance to reconcile to the correct balances as of November 30.

A similar analysis is needed for reconciling the timing differences for outstanding checks. Checks totaling $810.50 were outstanding (had not cleared the bank) on October 31 and therefore should be deducted from the October 31 bank balance. The bank records include those checks as withdrawals for November (that is, the $810.50 is included in the total bank withdrawals of $24,228.10), and so the $810.50 must be subtracted from the November withdrawals to reconcile with the corrected balances. On the other hand, the outstanding checks at the end of November are valid withdrawals for November, and so the $703.83 must be added to the bank withdrawals for November and subtracted from the bank cash balance as of November 30.

The adjustment for a "not-sufficient-funds" (NSF) check depends on how the company and bank records are kept. Typically, a company will periodically deposit its checks, recording them as receipts and additions to the cash balance. The bank will similarly record the deposits as increases in cash for the company. However, when the bank determines that a particular check is not collectible from the maker (an NSF check), it usually will show the check as a withdrawal and thus a reduction in the company's cash balance. If, after checking with the customer, the company determines the check is now good, it may merely redeposit the check without making any entries on the books for the bank's return of the check or the redeposit. The bank, however, will again show the check as a deposit and an increase in the cash balance. After the redeposit, the bank will show the correct cash balance. However, the bank deposits included the check twice, once when originally deposited and a second time upon redeposit, and the bank withdrawals included the check once, when it became an NSF check. Therefore, to reconcile the bank and book deposits/receipts and withdrawals/disbursements, the NSF check ($100 in the example) is subtracted from both the bank deposits and withdrawals. (Alternatively, the $100 NSF check could be added to the book receipts and disbursements to make the books reconcile with the bank records.) The preceding discussion is illustrated in Exhibit 8—9 using (+) and (–) designations to reinforce this point.

Svendsen, Inc.
Proof of Cash
November 30, 1996

	Beginning Reconciliation October 31	**Deposits/ Receipts**	**Withdrawals/ Disbursements**	**Ending Reconciliation November 30**
Balance per bank statement	$5,895.42	$21,312.40	$24,228.10	$2,979.72
Deposits in transit:				
October 31	425.40	(425.40)		
November 30		658.50		658.50
Outstanding checks:				
October 31	(810.50)		(810.50)	
November 30			703.83	(703.83)
NSF check redeposited during November; no entry made on books for return or redeposit		(100.00)	(100.00)	
Charge for interest made by bank in error			(12.50)	12.50
Corrected bank balance	$5,510.32	$21,445.50	$24,008.93	$2,946.89
Balance per books	$5,406.22	$21,457.00	$23,910.73	$2,952.49
Bank service charges:				
October	(5.90)		(5.90)	
November			3.16	(3.16)
Customer's check deposited November 25 found to be uncollectible (NSF)			118.94	(118.94)
Interest earned:				
October	110.00	(110.00)		
November		98.50		98.50
Check No. 1116 for $46 recorded by depositor as $64 in error			(18.00)	18.00
Corrected book balance	$5,510.32	$21,445.50	$24,008.93	$2,946.89

■ Exhibit 8—9
Typical Treatment in Reconciling NSF Check

Bank	Balance (Oct. 31)	Deposits/ Receipts	Withdrawals/ Disbursements	Balance (Nov. 30)
1. Original deposit.		+		+
2. Check becomes NSF			+	−
3. Check redeposited		+		+
4. Adjustment to reconcile		−	−	
Correct balance		+		+
Books				
1. Original deposit		+		+
2. Check returned by bank (no book entry)				
3. Check redeposited (no book entry)				
Correct balance		+		+

If a company finds that an NSF check cannot be collected immediately, then instead of redepositing the check, it must record the check amount in accounts receivable on the books. Such is the case for the $118.94 check for Svendsen, Inc., in the illustration. Since the bank will have already shown the check as a withdrawal and a reduction in the cash balance, a similar adjustment must be made to the company records.

Another common type of adjustment may be required for errors made either on the bank or book records. These have to be corrected as illustrated for Svendsen, Inc. Once all adjustments are made, the total corrected balances will be the same for both the bank and book records for all four columns.

The illustrations for Svendsen, Inc., assume adjustments of the book amounts are made in the month subsequent to their discovery. If the adjustments were made in the same month, as might be true at year-end, there would be no adjustments in the first column for the book amounts. For example, the $5.90 October bank service charge in the illustration is recognized on the books in November. If the adjustment had been made at the end of October, the beginning book balance would have already shown $5,400.32 ($5,406.22 - $5.90), and the total book disbursements for November would have been $5.90 less. A similar rationale exists for the $110 interest recorded by the bank for Svendsen in October.

The expanded proof of cash or four-column reconciliation procedure normally reduces the time and effort required to find errors made by either the bank or the depositor. In developing comparisons of both receipts and disbursements, the areas in which errors have been made, as well as the amounts of the discrepancies within each area, are immediately identified. This procedure is frequently used by auditors when there is any question of possible discrepancies in the handling of cash.

KEY TERMS

Accounts receivable 290
Accounts receivable turnover 299
Aging receivables 295
Allowance method 293
Assignment of receivables 301
Bank discounting 309
Bank reconciliation 287
Bank service charge 287
Cash 282
Cash discount 298
Cash equivalents 312
Cash overdraft 283
Compensating balances 283
Demand deposits 282
Deposit in transit 287
Direct write-off method 293
Factoring receivables 301
Implicit or effective interest 305
Imprest petty cash system 285
Imputed interest rate 308
Interest-bearing note 305
Negotiable notes 304
Net realizable value 293
Non-interest-bearing note 305
Nontrade receivables 290
Notes receivable 290
Not-sufficient-funds (NSF) check 288
Outstanding checks 287
Petty cash fund 285
Present value 305
Principal or face amount 305
Promissory note 304
Receivables 290
Sales discount 298
Time deposits 282
Trade discount 297
Trade receivables 290
Transfer of receivables with recourse 301

QUESTIONS

1. Why is cash on hand both necessary and yet potentially unproductive?
2. The following items were included as cash on the balance sheet for the Lawson Co. How should each of the items have been reported?
   (a) Demand deposits with bank
   (b) Restricted cash deposits in foreign banks
   (c) Bank account used for payment of salaries and wages
   (d) Cash in a special cash account to be used currently for the construction of a new building
   (e) Customers' checks returned by the bank marked "Not Sufficient Funds"
   (f) Customers' postdated checks
   (g) IOUs from employees
   (h) Postage stamps received in the mail for merchandise
   (i) Postal money orders received from customers and not yet deposited
   (j) Notes receivable in the hands of the bank for collection
   (k) Special bank account in which sales tax collections are deposited
   (l) Customers' checks not yet deposited
3. On reconciling the cash account with the bank statement, it is found that the general cash fund is overdrawn $436 but the bond redemption account has a balance of $5,400. The treasurer wishes to show cash as a current asset at $4,964. Discuss.
4. The Melvin Company shows in its accounts a cash balance of $66,500 with Bank A and an overdraft of $1,500 with Bank B on December 31. Bank B regards the overdraft as, in effect, a loan to the Melvin Company and charges interest on the overdraft balance. How would you report the balances with Banks A and B? Would your answer be any different if the overdraft arose as a result of certain checks that had been deposited and proved to be uncollectible and if the overdraft was cleared promptly by the Melvin Company at the beginning of January?
5. Mills Manufacturing is required to maintain a compensating balance of $15,000 with its bank to maintain a line of open credit. The compensating balance is legally restricted as to its use. How should the compensating balance be reported on the balance sheet and why?
6. (a) What are the major advantages in using imprest petty cash funds?
   (b) What dangers must be guarded against when petty cash funds are used?
7. (a) Give at least four common sources of differences between depositor and bank balances. (b) Which of the differences in (a) require an adjusting entry on the books of the depositor?
8. Explain how each of the following factors affects the classification of a receivable: (a) the form of a receivable, (b) the source of a receivable, and (c) the expected length of time to maturity or collection.
9. (a) Describe the methods for establishing and maintaining an allowance for doubtful accounts.
   (b) How would the percentages used in estimating uncollectible accounts be determined under each of the methods?

10. In accounting for uncollectible accounts receivable, why is the allowance method, rather than the direct write-off method, required by generally accepted accounting principles?
11. An analysis of the accounts receivable balance of $8,702 on the records of Jorgenson, Inc., on December 31 reveals the following:

Accounts from sales of last three months (appear to be fully collectible)......	$7,460
Accounts from sales prior to October 1 (of doubtful value).................................	1,312
Accounts known to be worthless................	320
Dishonored notes charged back to customer accounts.	800
Credit balances in customer accounts..........	1,190

(a) What adjustments are required?
(b) How should the various balances be shown on the balance sheet?
12. In what section of the income statement would you report (a) doubtful accounts expense, and (b) sales discounts?
13. (a) How is accounts receivable turnover computed?
(b) How is the number of days' sales in receivables computed?
(c) What do these two measurements show?
14. How are attitudes regarding the financing of accounts receivable changing? Why do you think this is so?
15. Explain the difference between the general assignment of accounts receivable and specific assignment of accounts receivable with regard to (a) collateral and (b) disclosure on financial statements.
16. (a) Distinguish among the practices of (1) assignment of accounts receivable, (2) factoring accounts receivable, and (3) transfer of accounts receivable with recourse. (b) Describe the accounting procedures to be followed in each case.
17. According to FASB Statement No. 77, what three conditions must be met to record the transfer of receivables with recourse as a sale?
18. The Bockweg Co. enters into a continuing agreement with Goessling Financial Services, whereby the latter company buys without recourse all of the trade receivables as they arise and assumes all credit and collection functions. (a) Describe the advantages that may accrue to Bockweg Co. as a result of the factoring agreement. (b) Are there any disadvantages? Explain.
19. Comment on the statement, "There is no such thing as a non-interest-bearing note."
20. (a) When should a note receivable be recorded at an amount different from its face amount? (b) Describe the procedures employed in accounting for the difference between a note's face amount and its recorded value.
21. What is meant by imputing a rate of interest? How is such a rate determined?
22. The Lambert Optical Co. discounts at 20% the following three notes at the Security First Bank on July 1 of the current year. Compute the proceeds on each note, rounding amounts to the nearest dollar.
(a) A 90-day, 13% note receivable for $24,000 dated June 1.
(b) A 6-month, 11% note receivable for $16,000 dated May 13 and coming due on November 13.
(c) Its own 4-month note payable dated July 1 with face value of $8,000 and no stated interest rate.
23. Distinguish between accounting procedures for (a) a note receivable discounted with recourse that is subsequently dishonored, and (b) a note receivable discounted without recourse that is subsequently dishonored.
24. Identify alternative methods for presenting information on the balance sheet relating to (a) notes receivable discounted, and (b) assigned accounts receivable.

DISCUSSION CASES

Case 8—1 (Cash management)

Jack Wilson, manager of Expert Building Company, is a valued and trusted employee. He has been with the company from its start two years ago. Because of the demands of his job, he has not taken a vacation since he began working. He is in charge of recording collections on account, making the daily bank deposits, and reconciling the bank statement.

Early this year, clients began complaining to you, the president, about incorrect statements. As president, you check into this matter. Wilson tells you there is nothing to worry about. He attests, "The problem is due to the slow mail; customers' payments and statements are crossing in the mail." However, because clients were not complaining last year, you doubt that the mail is the primary reason for the problem.

What might be some of the reasons for the delay? What are some other problems that might begin to occur? What can be done to remedy the problem? What should be done to make sure the problems are avoided in the future?

Case 8—2 (Float management)

Bunsen Company's cash collections average $10,000 per day. Because Bunsen's customers are scattered across the country, the average interval between when a customer writes a check and when the check clears and the amount is credited to Bunsen's account is 7 days. Bunsen could reduce this to 3 days by implementing a lockbox system. With a lockbox system, a company makes arrangements with a bank to retrieve customer checks from a post office box and deposit them directly into the company's account.

Bunsen's cash payments also average $10,000 per day. Bunsen's checks are drawn on a bank located in a major metropolitan area so the check-clearing time is very short—2 days. If Bunsen were to use a checking account in a small rural bank, the average check-clearing time would increase to 5 days.

1. How much would Bunsen's net interest income increase if it were to implement the lockbox system and switch its checking account to a small rural bank? Assume that the interest rate on checking accounts is 6% per annum based on the average daily balance.
2. What if the banking fee for operating the lockbox system were $4,000 per year—should the lockbox system be implemented?

Case 8—3 (Allocation of Cash and Near-Cash Assets)

Bruno Johnson, Chief Financial Officer of Tollerud Company, has determined that Tollerud should keep on hand $35 million in cash or near-cash assets in order to maintain proper liquidity. Bruno is now trying to determine how to allocate the $35 million among the checking account, certificates of deposit, and treasury notes. What factors should influence Bruno's decision?

Case 8—4 (Accounting for petty cash)

You have just accepted a job with Philodendron Co. Your duties include being cashier of the petty cash fund. Upon inspection of the fund, you find that it includes $143 in currency, $5 in postage stamps, $21 in IOUs, and $37 in various receipts. Since no written records are kept of the petty cash fund, you had to find out from the previous cashier that the approved amount of the fund is $215.

1. Discuss the elements of control necessary for effective maintenance of a petty cash fund.
2. Suggest changes that Philodendron Co. can make to improve the effectiveness of its petty cash fund.

Case 8—5* (Did I hide it well enough?)

Jonathan Mitchell is the accountant for the Mantua Service Company. Due to heavy investments in lottery tickets, Jonathan found himself short of cash and decided to "borrow" funds from Mantua. Jonathan received and deposited cash receipts, recorded the checks written in the cash disbursements journal, and reconciled the bank account. He made the reconciliation balance by manipulating outstanding checks in the bank reconciliation. Would this type of embezzlement be detected with a four-column reconciliation? Justify your answer.

*Relates to Appendix

Case 8—6 (Should a company sell on credit?)

Olin Company currently makes only cash sales. Given the number of potential customers who have requested to buy on credit, Olin is considering allowing credit sales. What factors should Olin consider in making the decision whether to allow credit sales?

Case 8—7 (Accounting for uncollectibles)

During the audit of accounts receivable of Montana Company, the new CEO, Joe Frisco, asked why the company had debited the current year's expense for doubtful accounts on the assumption that some accounts will become uncollectible next year. Frisco believes that the financial statements should be based on verifiable, objective evidence. In his opinion it would be more objective to wait until specific accounts become uncollectible before the expense is recorded. What accounting issues are involved? Which method of accounting for uncollectible accounts would you recommend and why?

Case 8—8 **(Accounting for potential sales returns)**

Ultimate Corporation is a computer products supplier. Ultimate sells products to dealers who then sell the products to the end users. Most of the company's competitors require dealers to pay for shipments within 45 to 60 days. Ultimate has followed a more relaxed policy; in 1996 the average length of time it took the company to collect its receivables was 158 days. (This average collection period can be computed as Average Accounts Receivable Balance/Average Daily Credit Sales). It has been suggested that in return for this lax collection policy, dealers allowed Ultimate to ship more product than the dealers needed, allowing Ultimate to recognize the excess shipments as sales. In 1997, Ultimate attempted to reduce the level of its accounts receivable by stepping up collection efforts. As a result, product returns from dealers increased significantly.

1. Assume that Ultimate's sales for the year were $1,000 with cost of sales being $600. For simplicity, also assume that all of the sales occurred on December 31, and that on average, Ultimate expects about 15 percent of products sold to be returned by dissatisfied dealers or dealers who are unable to sell the products. What adjusting entry, if any, should be made at year-end to reflect the likelihood of future sales returns?
2. An allowance for sales returns is analogous to an allowance for doubtful accounts. Most companies disclose an allowance for doubtful accounts but very few disclose an allowance for sales returns. Why not?
3. What other, more conservative accounting treatment is possible in regard to the potential sales returns?

Case 8—9 **(Foreign loan write-offs)**

In July 1990, U.S. federal regulators ordered U.S. banks to write off 20% of their $11.1 billion in loans to Brazil and also 20% of their $2.9 billion in loans to Argentina. The action significantly affected the loan loss reserves of the banks. For example, Citicorp was ordered to write off loans totaling $780 million, compared to Citicorp's total loan loss reserve of $3.3 billion. However, it was reported that "the action won't automatically have any impact on bank earnings."

1. Why won't the ordered write-offs automatically impact bank earnings?
2. Might the ordered write-offs have an indirect impact on future bank earnings?
3. What effect would you expect to see on bank stock prices in response to this announcement?

Source: Robert Guenther. "Federal Regulators Order Banks to Take Write-Offs on Loans to Brazil, Argentina." *The Wall Street Journal,* July 12, 1990: p. A3.

Case 8—10 **(Accounts receivable as a source of cash)**

Assume you are the treasurer for Fullmer Products Inc. and one of your responsibilities is to ensure that the company always takes available cash discounts on purchases. The corporation needs $150,000 within one week in order to take advantage of current cash discounts. The lending officer at the bank insists on adequate collateral for a $150,000 loan. For various reasons, your plant assets are not available as collateral, but your accounts receivable balance is $205,000. What alternatives would you consider for obtaining the necessary cash?

Case 8—11 **(Is it a sale or a borrowing?)**

Columbine Enterprises decides to finance its operations by transferring its receivables with recourse to Larsen Financial, Inc. The provisions of the agreement provide for Columbine to transfer its ownership rights in the receivables to Larsen. Columbine guarantees collection of 80% of the receivable balance to Larsen Financial. James McCabe, Columbine's accountant, is not sure whether this arrangement should be recorded as a sale or as a borrowing. He is aware that the FASB has issued a standard covering this situation, but isn't sure how this arrangement fits the standard. He approaches you, the company auditor, and asks for your opinion as to how the transaction should be recorded. He also asks you to describe how these two approaches would affect the basic financial statements.

EXERCISES

Exercise 8—12 (Reporting cash on the balance sheet)

1. Indicate how each of the items below should be reported using the following classifications: (a) cash, (b) restricted cash, (c) temporary investment, (d) receivable, (e) liability, or (f) office supplies.

1. Checking account at First Security	$(20)
2. Checking account at Second Security	350
3. U.S. savings bonds	650
4. Payroll account	100
5. Sales tax account	150
6. Foreign bank account—restricted (in equivalent U.S. dollars)	750
7. Postage stamps	22
8. Employee's postdated check	30
9. IOU from president's brother	75
10. Credit memo from a vendor for a purchase return	87
11. Traveler's check.	50
12. Not-sufficient-funds check	18
13. Petty cash fund ($16 in currency and expense receipts for $84)	100
14. Money order	36

2. What amount would be reported as unrestricted cash on the balance sheet?

Exercise 8—13 (Restricted cash)

Club Med, Inc., operates Club Med resorts in the United States, Mexico, the Caribbean, Asia, the South Pacific, and the Indian Ocean Basin. Club Med routinely receives payment in advance from vacationers. In some countries, Club Med is required by law to deposit cash received as payment for future vacations in special accounts. Cash in these accounts is restricted as to its use.

Assume that on December 31 Club Med received cash totaling $6,000,000 as payment in advance for vacations at one of its resorts. The resort is in a country that requires the cash be deposited in a special account.

1. Prepare the journal entry necessary to record receipt of the $6,000,000.
2. Explain how the $6,000,000 would be disclosed in the December 31 balance sheet.

Exercise 8—14 (Accounting for petty cash)

An examination on the morning of January 2 by the auditor for the Santiago Appliance Company discloses the following items in the petty cash drawer.

Item		
Stamps		$ 43.00
Currency and coin		115.66
IOUs from members of the office staff		121.00
An envelope containing collections for a football pool, with office staff names attached		35.00
Petty cash vouchers for:		
Typewriter repairs	$13.00	
Stamps	70.00	
Telegram charges	28.50	
Delivery fees	12.00	123.50
Employee's check postdated January 15		225.00
Employee's check marked "NSF"		189.00
Check drawn by Santiago Appliance Company to Petty Cash		345.00
		$1,197.16

The ledger account discloses a $1,125 balance for Petty Cash. (1) What adjusting entries should be made so that petty cash is correctly stated on the balance sheet? (2) What is the correct amount of petty cash for the balance sheet? (3) How could the practice of borrowing by employees from the fund be discouraged?

Exercise 8—15 (Cash and internal control)

Explain why each of the following pairs of duties should *not* be performed by the same person:

(a) Receiving cash payments from customers.
Recording charges to customer accounts.
(b) Replenishing cash in the petty cash fund.
Controlling and recording payments from the petty cash fund.
(c) Preparing the bank reconciliation.
Recording daily cash receipt totals.
(d) Daily depositing of cash in the bank.
Preparing the bank reconciliation.
(e) Mailing of computer-generated checks.
Accessing the check-writing computer program.

Exercise 8—16 (Composition of cash)

Warfield Company had the following cash balances at December 31, 1996:

Undeposited coin and currency	$ 35,000
Unrestricted demand deposits	1,450,000
Company checks written (and deducted from the demand deposits amount) but not scheduled to be mailed until January 2	180,000
Time deposits restricted for use (expected use in 1997)	3,000,000

In exchange for a guaranteed line of credit, Warfield has agreed to maintain a minimum balance of $150,000 in its unrestricted demand deposits account. How much should Warfield report as "Cash" in its December 31, 1996, balance sheet?

Exercise 8—17 (Correct cash balance)

Sterling Company's bank statement for the month of March included the following information:

Ending balance, March 31	$28,046
Bank service charge for March	130
Interest paid by bank to Sterling for March	107

In comparing the bank statement to its own cash records, Sterling found the following:

Deposits made but not yet recorded by the bank	$3,689
Checks written and mailed but not yet recorded by the bank	4,786

In addition, Sterling discovered that it had erroneously recorded a check for $46 that should have been recorded for $64. What is Sterling's correct cash balance at March 31?

Exercise 8—18 (Correct cash balance)

Letterman Corporation's bank statement for the month of April included the following information:

Bank service charge for April	$130
Check deposited by Letterman during April was not collectible and has been marked "NSF" by the bank and returned	400

In comparing the bank statement to its own cash records, Letterman found the following:

Deposits made but not yet recorded by the bank	$1,324
Checks written and mailed but not yet recorded by the bank	987

All the deposits in transit and outstanding checks have been properly recorded in Letterman's books. Letterman also found a check for $350, payable to Letterman Corporation, that had not yet been deposited and had not been recorded in Letterman's books. Letterman's books show a bank account balance of $4,112 (before any adjustments or corrections). What is Letterman Corporation's correct cash balance at April 30?

Exercise 8—19 (Bank reconciliation and adjusting entries)

The accounting department supplied the following data in reconciling the September 30 bank statement for Thalman Auto:

Ending cash balance per bank	$15,496.91
Ending cash balance per books	14,692.71
Deposits in transit	2,615.23
Bank service charge	25.00
Outstanding checks	3,079.51
Note collected by bank including $45 interest (Thalman not yet notified)	1,045.00
Error by bank—check drawn by Thalerman Corp. was charged to Thalman's account.	617.08
Sale and deposit of $1,729.00 was entered in the sales journal and cash receipts journal as $1,792.00	

1. Prepare the September 30 bank reconciliation.
2. Give the journal entries required on the books to adjust the cash account.

Exercise 8—20 (Bank reconciliation)

On July 2, the Minnesota Manufacturing Co. received its bank statement for the month ending June 30. The bank statement indicates a balance of $5,680. The cash account as of the close of business on June 30 has a balance of $3,275. In reconciling the balances, the auditor discovers the following:

(a) Receipts on June 30 of $9,500 were not deposited until July 1.
(b) Checks outstanding on June 30 were $12,310.
(c) Collection by the bank of a note for $150 less collection fees of $25 was not recorded on the books.
(d) The bank charged the depositor for overdrafts, $80.
(e) A canceled check to W. E. Lee for $9,618 was entered in cash payments incorrectly as $9,168.

Prepare the June 30 bank reconciliation.

Exercise 8—21 (Bank reconciliation—analysis of outstanding checks)

The following information was included in the bank reconciliation for Rytton, Inc., for June. What was the total of outstanding checks at the beginning of June? Assume all other reconciling items are listed.

Checks and charges recorded by bank in June, including a June service charge of $30	$17,210
Service charge made by bank in May and recorded on the books in June	20

Total of credits to Cash in all journals during June	19,802
Customer's NSF check returned as a bank charge in June (no entry made on books)	100
Customer's NSF check returned in May and redeposited in June (no entry made on books in either May or June)	250
Outstanding checks at June 30	8,060
Deposit in transit at June 30	600

Exercise 8—22 (Classifying receivables)

Classify each of the items listed below as: (A) Accounts Receivable, (B) Notes Receivable, (C) Trade Receivable, (D) Nontrade Receivable, or (E) Other (indicate nature of item). Since the classifications are not mutually exclusive, more than one classification may be appropriate. Also indicate whether the item would normally be reported as a current or noncurrent asset assuming a 6-month operating cycle.

1. MasterCard or VISA credit card sale of merchandise to customer.
2. Overpayment to supplier for inventory purchased on account.
3. Insurance claim on automobile accident.
4. Charge sale to regular customer.
5. Advance to sales manager.
6. Interest due on 5-year note from company president, interest payable annually.
7. Acceptance of 3-year note on sale of land held as investment.
8. Acceptance of 6-month note for past-due account arising from the sale of inventory.
9. Claim for a tax refund from last year.
10. Prepaid insurance—four months remaining in the policy period.
11. Overpayment by customer of an account receivable.

Exercise 8—23 (Computing the accounts receivable balance)

The following information from Jumbo Company's first year of operations is to be used in testing the accuracy of Accounts Receivable. The December 31, 1996, balance is $36,000.

(a) Collections from customers, $72,000.
(b) Merchandise purchased, $98,000.
(c) Ending merchandise inventory, $23,500.
(d) Goods sell at 50% above cost.
(e) All sales are on account.

Compute the balance that Accounts Receivable should show and determine the amount of any shortage or overage.

Exercise 8—24 (Recording credit card sales)

Sue Milano owns a gift shop at the airport. She accepts only cash or VISA and MasterCard credit cards. During the last month, the gift shop had a total of $76,000 in sales. Of this amount, 75% were credit card sales. The bank charges a 3% fee on net credit card sales. Make the monthly summary entry to reflect the above transactions.

Exercise 8—25 (Recording credit card sales)

Greystone Inn is a fine restaurant specializing in French cuisine. The inn is situated on a picturesque location overlooking Dryden Lake. Greystone Inn accepts only two forms of payment: cash and American Express. The American Express receipts cannot be deposited directly in a checking account but must be submitted to American Express in order to receive payment. During April, sales totaled $90,000; cash sales accounted for only 15% of the total.

1. Make the monthly summary entry to record sales for April.
2. Make the summary entry to record receipt of payment from American Express. The service charge is 4%.

Exercise 8—26 (Estimating doubtful accounts)

Accounts Receivable of the Drummond Manufacturing Co. on December 31, 1996, had a balance of $300,000. Allowance for Doubtful Accounts had a $4,200 debit balance. Sales in 1996 were $1,690,000 less sales discounts of $14,000. Give the adjusting entry for estimated doubtful accounts expense under each of the following independent assumptions:

1. One-half of 1% of 1996 net sales will probably never be collected.
2. Three percent of outstanding accounts receivable are doubtful.
3. An aging schedule shows that $11,000 of the outstanding accounts receivable are doubtful.

Exercise 8—27 (Journal entries for doubtful accounts)

Health Care Inc. had gross sales of $155,000 during 1996, 30% of which were on credit. Accounts receivable outstanding at December 31, 1996, totaled $2,800, and the allowance for doubtful accounts had a $200 debit balance. Merchandise sold on account for $2,000 was returned by customers. Give the adjusting entry for doubtful accounts expense, assuming:

1. 1% of net credit sales will be uncollectible.
2. 2 1/2% of current accounts receivable are doubtful.

Exercise 8—28 (Journal entries for receivable write-offs)

McGraw Medical Center has received a bankruptcy notice for Phillip Hollister. Hollister owes the medical center $650. The bankruptcy notice indicates that the medical center can't expect to receive payment of any of the $650.

1. Make the journal entry necessitated by receipt of the bankruptcy notice.
2. Six months after the medical center received the bankruptcy notice, Hollister appeared requesting medical treatment. He agreed to pay his old bill in its entirety. Make the journal entry or entries necessary to record receipt of the $650 payment from Hollister.

Exercise 8—29 (Aging accounts receivable)

Blanchard Company's accounts receivable subsidiary ledger reveals the following information:

Customer	Account Balance Dec. 31, 1996	Invoice Amounts	and Dates
Allison, Inc.	$ 8,795	$3,500	12/6/96
		5,295	11/29/96
Banks Bros	5,230	3,000	9/27/96
		2,230	8/20/96
Barker & Co	7,650	5,000	12/8/96
		2,650	10/25/96
Marrin Co.	11,285	5,785	11/17/96
		5,500	10/9/96
Ring, Inc.	7,900	4,800	12/12/96
		3,100	12/2/96
West Corp.	4,350	4,350	9/12/96

Blanchard Company's receivable collection experience indicates that, on the average, losses have occurred as follows:

Age of Accounts	Uncollectible Percentage
0-30 days	.7%
31-60 days	1.4%
61-90 days	3.5%
91-120 days	10.2%
121 days and over	60.0%

The allowance for doubtful accounts credit balance on December 31, 1996, was $2,245 before adjustment.

1. Prepare an accounts receivable aging schedule.
2. Using the aging schedule from part (1), compute the allowance for doubtful accounts balance as of December 31, 1996.
3. Prepare the end-of-year adjusting entry.
4. (a) Where accounts receivable are few in number, such as in this exercise, what are some possible weaknesses in estimating doubtful accounts by the aging method?
   (b) Would the other methods of estimating doubtful accounts be subject to these same weaknesses? Explain.

Exercise 8—30 (Analysis of allowance for doubtful accounts)

The Transtech Publishing Company follows the procedure of debiting Doubtful Accounts Expense for 2% of all new sales. Sales for four consecutive years and year-end allowance account balances were as follows:

Year	Sales	Allowance for Doubtful Accounts End-of-Year Credit Balance
1993	$2,100,000	$21,500
1994	1,975,000	35,500
1995	2,500,000	50,000
1996	2,350,000	66,000

1. Compute the amount of accounts written off for the years 1994, 1995, and 1996.
2. The external auditors are concerned with the growing amount in the allowance account. What action do you recommend the auditors take?

Exercise 8—31 (Receivables and the statement of cash flows)

The following selected information is provided for Lynez Company. All sales are credit sales and all receivables are trade receivables.

Accounts receivable, Jan. 1 net balance	$150,000
Accounts receivable, Dec. 31 net balance	165,000
Sales for the year	800,000
Uncollectible accounts written off during the year	14,000
Bad debt expense for the year	24,000
Cash expenses for the year	681,000
Net income for the year	95,000

Based on the above information, answer the following independent questions:

1. Using the *direct* method, compute the net cash flow from operations that Lynez Company would report in its statement of cash flows.
2. Assuming use of the *indirect* method, what adjustments to net income would be required in reporting net cash flow from operations?

Exercise 8—32 (Cost to customers of missing cash discounts)

Duane Kennedy, the chief financial officer for Malott Company, is perplexed about the small number of customers who take the cash discount offered by Malott. The credit terms offered by Malott are 1/10, n/70.

1. Explain why so few customers take the cash discount offered by Malott. Hint: One way to view Malott's credit terms is that a customer is paying an extra 1% (the missed cash discount) for the privilege of keeping his or her money for an extra 60 days (the difference between the 10-day period and the 70-day extended period).

2. Assume that the interest rate on short-term borrowing is 15%. Determine which of the following credit terms might induce customers to take cash discounts.
   (a) 2/10, n/30 (c) 3/10, n/100
   (b) 2/15, n/55 (d) 1/10, n/30

Exercise 8—33 **(Analyzing accounts receivable)**

Trend Industries Company reported the following amounts on its 1995 and 1996 financial statements.

	1996	1995
Accounts receivable	$ 235,000	$ 210,000
Allowance for doubtful accounts	12,000	8,000
Net sales—credit	1,430,000	1,260,000
Net sales—cash	215,000	179,000
Cost of sales	1,067,000	856,000

(1) Compute the accounts receivable turnover for 1996.
(2) What is the number of days' sales in average accounts receivable during 1996? (Use 365 days.)

Exercise 8—34 **(Accounting for accounts receivable factoring)**

On July 15, Mann Company factored $600,000 in accounts receivable for cash of $550,000. The factor withheld 10% of the cash proceeds to allow for possible customer returns or account adjustments. An allowance for doubtful accounts of $80,000 had previously been established by Mann in relation to these accounts.

1. Make the journal entry necessary on Mann's books to record the factoring of the accounts.
2. Make the journal entry necessary on Mann's books to record final settlement of the factoring arrangement. No customer returns or account adjustments occurred in relation to the factored accounts.

Exercise 8—35 **(Accounting for a non-interest-bearing note)**

Zobell Corporation sells equipment with a book value of $8,000, receiving a non-interest-bearing note due in three years with a face amount of $10,000. There is no established market value for the equipment. The interest rate on similar obligations is estimated at 12%. Compute the gain or loss on the sale and the discount on notes receivable, and make the necessary entry to record the sale. Also, make the entries to record the amortization of the discount at the end of the first, second, and third year using effective-interest amortization. (Round to the nearest dollar.)

Exercise 8—36 **(Accounting for an interest-bearing note)**

High Country, Inc., purchased inventory costing $50,000. Terms of the purchase were 5/10, n/30. In order to take advantage of the cash discount, High Country borrowed $45,000 from Downtown 1st National, signing a 2-month, 12% note. The bank requires monthly interest payments. Make the entries to record the following:

1. Initial purchase of inventory on account
2. Payment to the supplier within the discount period
3. Loan from the bank
4. First month's payment to the bank
5. Second and final payment to the bank

Exercise 8—37 **(Discounting notes—computations)**

On December 21, the following notes are discounted by the bank at 15%. Determine the cash proceeds, rounded to the nearest dollar, from discounting each note.

1. 30-day, $4,500, non-interest-bearing note dated December 15.
2. 60-day, $3,380, 9% note dated December 1.
3. 60-day, $15,000, 13% note dated November 6.
4. 90-day, $6,775, 10% note dated November 24.

Exercise 8—38 (Accounting for notes receivable discounted)

Tandy Company accepted a $20,000, 90-day, 12% interest-bearing note dated September 1, 1996, from a customer for the sale of a piece of machinery. The machinery cost $25,000 and was 50% depreciated. On October 15, 1996, Tandy discounted the note, with recourse, at First National Bank at a 15% discount rate. The customer paid the note at maturity. Make the entries necessary to record the above transactions on Tandy Company's books. Assume the transfer of the note to the bank does not meet FASB criteria for recording as a sale. (Round amounts to the nearest dollar.)

Exercise 8—39 (Accounting for notes receivable discounted)

S. Atwater received from K. Rogers, on account, a 90-day, 12% note for $8,000, dated June 6, 1996. On July 6, Atwater discounted the note, with recourse, at 15% and recorded the discounting as a sale in accordance with FASB Statement No. 77. The note was not paid at maturity, and the bank charged Atwater protest fees of $25 in addition to the maturity value of the note. On September 28, 1996, the note was collected by Atwater with interest at 15% from the maturity date to the date of collection. What entries would appear on Atwater's books as a result of the foregoing? (Round amounts to the nearest dollar.)

Exercise 8—40 (Discounting a note receivable)

On June 1, 1996, Flint Company received a $5,200, 90-day, 11% interest-bearing note from a customer on an overdue account receivable. Flint discounted the note, with recourse, immediately at State Bank at a discount rate of 15%. The discounting transaction did not meet FASB criteria for recording as a sale. At the date of maturity, the bank notified Flint that the note had not been paid and that the amount of the note plus a $25 protest fee had been charged to its account. Flint is unable to collect from the customer. (Round amounts to the nearest dollar.)

1. How much money will Flint receive upon discounting the note?
2. What is the effective rate of interest the bank will earn on the note?
3. Prepare the journal entries to record the events described above.

Exercise 8—41* (Four-column bank reconciliation)

Tyler Corporation began doing business with Security Bank on October 1. On that date the correct cash balance was $4,000. All cash transactions are cleared through the bank account. Subsequent transactions during October and November relating to the records of Tyler and Security are summarized below.

	Tyler Corporation Books	Security Bank Books
October deposits	$7,360	$7,110
October checks	6,290	6,130
October service charge	—	10
October 31 balance	5,070	4,970
November deposits	8,220	8,280
November checks	9,410	9,220
November service charge	—	15
Note collected by bank in November (included $15 interest)	—	1,015
October service charge recorded in November	10	—
November 30 balance	3,870	5,030

On the basis of the foregoing data: (1) prepare a four-column reconciliation for the month ended November 30, reconciling both bank and book balances to a corrected balance, and (2) give entries that would be required on Tyler's books to adjust the cash account as of November 30.

*Relates to Appendix

PROBLEMS

Problem 8—42 **(Compensating balance and effective interest rates)**

Krebsbach Company is negotiating a loan with FIS Bank. Krebsbach needs $900,000. As part of the loan agreement, FIS Bank will require Krebsbach to maintain a compensating balance of 15% of the loan amount on deposit in a checking account at the bank. Krebsbach currently maintains a balance of $50,000 in the checking account. The interest rate Krebsbach is required to pay on the loan is 12%; the interest rate FIS pays on checking accounts is 4%.

Instructions:

1. Compute the amount of the loan.
2. Determine the effective interest rate on the loan. (Hint: Compute the net interest paid on the loan per year and the "take-home" amount of the loan.)

Problem 8—43 **(Accounting for petty cash)**

On December 1, 1996, LGA Corporation established an imprest petty cash fund. The operations of the fund for the last month of 1996 and the first month of 1997 are summarized as follows:

Dec. 1 The petty cash fund was established by cashing a company check for $2,000 and delivering the proceeds to the fund cashier.

21 A request for replenishment of the petty cash fund was received by the accounts payable department, supported by appropriate signed vouchers, summarized as follows:

Selling expenses	$ 324
Administrative expenses	513
Special equipment	176
Telephone, telegraph, and postage	48
Miscellaneous expenses	260
Total	$1,321

A check for $1,356 was drawn payable to the petty cash cashier.

31 The company's independent certified public accountant counted the fund in connection with the year-end audit work and found the following:

Cash in petty cash fund		$1,066
Employees' checks with January dates (postdated)		85
Expense vouchers properly approved as follows:		
Selling expenses	$146	
Administrative expenses	512	
Office supplies	28	
Telephone, telegraph, and postage	48	
Miscellaneous expenses	100	834
Total		$1,985

The petty cash fund was not replenished at December 31, 1996.

Jan. 15 The employees' checks held in the petty cash fund at December 31 were cashed and the proceeds retained in the fund.

31 A request for replenishment was made and a check was drawn to restore the fund to its original balance of $2,000. The support vouchers for January expenditures are summarized below.

Selling expenses	$ 85
Administrative expenses	406
Telephone, telegraph, and postage	35
Miscellaneous expenses	220
Total	$746

Instructions: Record the transactions in general journal form.

Problem 8—44 **(Bank reconciliation)**

The cash account of Delta, Inc., disclosed a balance of $17,056.48 on October 31. The bank statement as of October 31 showed a balance of $21,209.45. Upon comparing the statement with the cash records, the following facts were developed:

(a) Delta's account was charged on October 26 for a customer's uncollectible check amounting to $1,143.
(b) A 2-month, 9%, $3,000 customer's note dated August 25, discounted on October 12, was dishonored October 26 and the bank charged Delta $3,050.83, which included a protest fee of $5.83.
(c) A customer's check for $725 was entered as $625 by both the depositor and the bank but was later corrected by the bank.
(d) Check No. 661 for $1,242.50 was entered in the cash disbursements journal at $1,224.50 and Check No. 652 for $32.90 was entered as $329.00. The company uses the voucher system.
(e) Bank service charges of $39.43 for October were not yet recorded on the books.
(f) A bank memo stated that M. Sear's note for $2,500 and interest of $62.50 had been collected on October 29; and the bank charged $12.50. (No entry was made on the books when the note was sent to the bank for collection.)
(g) Receipts of October 29 for $6,850 were deposited November 1.
The following checks were outstanding on October 31:

No. 620	$1,250.00	No. 671	$ 732.50
No. 621	3,448.23	No. 673	187.90
No. 632	2,405.25	No. 675	275.72
No. 670	1,775.38	No. 676	2,233.15

Instructions:

1. Prepare a bank reconciliation as of October 31.
2. Give the journal entries required as a result of the preceding information.

Problem 8—45 **(Bank reconciliation)**

The books of Hawkins Company show a cash balance of $23,383 as of July 31. Hawkins' bank statement shows a cash balance for the company of $21,432. Additional information that might be useful in reconciling the disparity between the two balances follows:

(a) A deposit of $800 was recorded by the bank on July 3, but it should have been recorded for Hawker Company rather than Hawkins Company.
(b) Petty cash of $425 was included in the cash balance, but an actual count reveals $516 on hand.
(c) Check No. 315 in payment of electric bill for $125 was correctly recorded by the bank but was recorded in the cash disbursements journal of Hawkins as $215.
(d) The bank statement does not show receipts of $1,250 that were deposited on July 31.
(e) The bank statement indicated a monthly service charge of $35.
(f) A check for $372 was returned marked NSF. The check had been included in the July 24 deposit. As of July 31, the check had not been redeposited.
(g) Proceeds from cash sales of $1,530 for July 19 were stolen. The company expects to recover this amount from the insurance company. The cash receipts were recorded in the books, but no entry was made for the loss.
(h) Interest of $56 accrued on funds the bank had invested for Hawkins for the month of July.
(i) Outstanding checks totaled $1,420 as of July 31.
(j) The July 22 deposit included a check for $705 that had been returned on July 15 marked NSF. Hawkins Company had made no entry upon return of the check. The redeposit of the check on July 22 was recorded in the cash receipts journal of Hawkins as a collection on account.

Instructions:

1. Prepare a bank reconciliation as of July 31.
2. Make the necessary journal entries for Hawkins Company with the information provided on the bank reconciliation.

Problem 8—46 **(Reconciliation of an individual's bank account)**

The following data was taken from Sylvester Krueger's check register for the month of April. Sylvester's bank reconciliation for March showed one outstanding check, Check #78 for $43.00 (written on March 23), and one deposit in transit, Deposit #10499 for $87.00 (made on March 30).

Date		Item	Checks	Deposits	Balance
19—					
April	1	Beginning Balance			$123.00
	1	Deposit #10500		$523.34	646.34
	1	Check #79	$ 5.00		651.34
	4	Check #80	213.47		437.97
	27	Deposit #10501		235.48	673.45
	29	Check #81	264.35		409.80

The following is from Sylvester's bank statement for April:

Date		Item	Checks	Deposits	Balance
April	1	Beginning Balance			$ 79.00
	3	Check #79	$ 5.00		74.00
	3	Deposit #10499		$ 87.00	161.00
	5	Check #80	213.47		(52.47)
	5	Automatic Loan		163.00	110.53
	8	Deposit #10500		528.34	638.87
	20	NSF Check	20.00		618.87
	20	Service Charge	12.00		606.87
	30	Interest		1.65	608.52

Instructions: Prepare a reconciliation of Sylvester's bank account as of April 30. Show both a corrected balance per bank and a corrected balance per books. Assume that any errors or discrepancies you find are Sylvester's fault, not the bank's.

Problem 8—47 **(Accounting for receivables—journal entries)**

The following transactions affecting the accounts receivable of Wonderland Corporation took place during the year ended January 31, 1996:

Sales (cash and credit)	$591,050
Cash received from credit customers all of whom took advantage of the discount feature of the corporation's credit terms 2/10, n/30	303,800
Cash received from cash customers	210,270
Accounts receivable written off as worthless	5,250
Credit memoranda issued to credit customers for sales returns and allowances	63,800
Cash refunds given to cash customers for sales returns and allowances	13,318
Recoveries on accounts receivable written off as uncollectible in prior periods (not included in cash amount stated above)	8,290

The following two balances were taken from the January 31, 1995 balance sheet:

Accounts receivable	$95,842
Allowance for doubtful accounts	9,740 (credit)

The corporation provides for its net uncollectible account losses by crediting Allowance for Doubtful Accounts for 1 1/2% of net credit sales for the fiscal period.

Instructions:

1. Prepare the journal entries to record the transactions for the year ended January 31, 1996.
2. Prepare the adjusting journal entry for estimated uncollectible accounts on January 31, 1996.

Problem 8—48 **(Accounting for cash discounts)**

Beebe Company sold goods on account with a sales price of $50,000 on August 17. The terms of the sale were 2/10, n/30.

Instructions:

1. Record the sale using the gross method of accounting for cash discounts as illustrated in the text.
2. Record the sale using the net method of accounting for cash discounts. The net method differs from the gross method in that the original sale is recorded at the net amount (gross price minus cash discount). In essence, the net method assumes that the customer will take the cash discount.
3. Assume that the payment is received on August 25. Record receipt of the payment using both the gross method and the net method.
4. Assume that payment is received on September 15. Record receipt of the payment using both the gross method and the net method. In making the entry for the net method, you will need to use the account "Sales Discounts Not Taken." Is this account an asset, liability, revenue, or expense?
5. Which method makes more theoretical sense—the gross method or the net method? Why? Why don't more firms use the net method?

Problem 8—49 **(Estimating doubtful accounts expense; sales method vs. receivables method)**

During 1996, Lacee Enterprises had gross sales of $247,000. At the end of 1996, Lacee had accounts receivable of $83,000, and a credit balance of $5,600 in Allowance for Doubtful Accounts. Lacee has used the percent-of-gross-sales method to estimate the Allowance for Doubtful Accounts Expense. For the past several years, the amount estimated to be uncollectible has been 3%.

1. Using the percent-of-gross-sales method, estimate the doubtful accounts expense and make any necessary adjusting entries.
2. Assuming that 6% of receivables are estimated to be uncollectible and that Lacee decides to use the percent-of-receivables method to estimate doubtful accounts expense, estimate the doubtful accounts expense and make any adjusting entries.
3. Which of the two methods more accurately reflects the net realizable value of receivables? Explain.

Problem 8—50 **(Estimating uncollectible accounts by aging receivables)**

Rainy Day Company, a wholesaler, uses the aging method to estimate bad debt losses. The following schedule of aged accounts receivable was prepared at December 31, 1996.

Age of Accounts	Amount
0-30 days	$561,600
31-60 days	196,100
61-90 days	88,400
91-120 days	18,500
More than 120 days	9,600
	$874,200

The following schedule shows the year-end receivables balances and uncollectible accounts experience for the previous five years:

Loss Experience—Percent of Uncollectible Accounts

Year	Year-End Receivables	0-30 days	31-60 days	61-90 days	91-120 days	Over 120 days
1995	$780,700	0.5%	1.0%	10.2%	49.1%	78.2%
1994	750,400	0.4	1.1	10.0	51.2	77.3
1993	681,400	0.6	1.2	11.0	51.7	79.0
1992	698,200	0.5	0.9	10.1	52.3	78.5
1991	723,600	0.4	1.0	8.9	49.2	77.6

The unadjusted allowance for doubtful accounts balance on December 31, 1996, is $32,796.

Instructions: Compute the correct balance for the allowance account based on the average loss experience for the last five years and prepare the appropriate end-of-year adjusting entry.

Problem 8—51 (Bad debts and the statement of cash flows)

Sage Company had a $300,000 balance in Accounts Receivable on January 1. The balance in Allowance for Doubtful Accounts on January 1 was $36,000. Sales for the year totaled $1,700,000. All sales were credit sales. Bad debt expense is estimated to be 2% of sales. Write-offs of uncollectible accounts for the year were $28,000. The balance in Accounts Receivable on December 31 was $345,000. All receivables are trade receivables. Sage uses the direct method in preparing its statement of cash flows.

Instructions: What is the amount of cash collected from customers?

Problem 8—52 (Accounting for assignment of specific accounts receivable)

On July 1, 1996, Balmforth Company assigns specific receivables totaling $200,000 to Rocky Mountain Bank as collateral on a $150,000, 16% note. Balmforth will continue to collect the assigned receivables. In addition to the interest on the note, Rocky Mountain also receives a 2% finance charge, deducted in advance on the $150,000 value of the note. Additional information for Balmforth Company is as follows:

(a) July collections amounted to $145,000, less cash discounts of $750.
(b) On August 1, paid the bank the amount owed for July collections plus accrued interest on note to August 1.
(c) Balmforth collected the remaining assigned accounts during August except for $550 written off as uncollectible.
(d) On September 1, paid bank the remaining amount owed plus accrued interest.

Instructions: Prepare the journal entries necessary to record the above information on the books of both Balmforth Company and Rocky Mountain Bank.

Problem 8—53 (Assigning and factoring accounts receivable)

During its second year of operations, Shank Corporation found itself in financial difficulties. Shank decided to use its accounts receivable as a means of obtaining cash to continue operations. On July 1, 1996, Shank factored $75,000 of accounts receivable for cash proceeds of $69,500. No bad debt allowance was associated with these accounts. On December 17, 1996, Shank assigned the remainder of its accounts receivable, $250,000 as of that date, as collateral on a $125,000, 12% annual interest rate loan from Sandy Finance Company. Shank received $125,000 less a 2% finance charge. Additional information is as follows:

Allowance for Doubtful Accounts, 12/31/96	$3,200 (credit)
Estimated uncollectibles, 12/31/96	3% of Accounts Receivable
Accounts Receivable (not including factored and assigned accounts), 12/31/96	$50,000

None of the assigned accounts had been collected by the end of the year.

Instructions:

1. Prepare the journal entries to record the receipt of cash from (a) factoring and (b) general assignment of the accounts receivable.
2. Prepare the journal entry necessary to record the adjustment to Allowance for Doubtful Accounts.
3. Prepare the accounts receivable section of Shank's balance sheet as it would appear after the above transactions.
4. What entry would be made on Shank's books when the factored accounts have been collected?

Problem 8—54 (Discounting notes)

Dival Marketing Corporation completed the following transactions, among others:

May	5	Received a $5,000, 60-day, 10% note dated May 5 from R.D. Spears, on account.
	24	Received an $1,800, 90-day, non-interest-bearing-note dated May 23 from B. Collins as settlement for unpaid balance of $1,752.
	25	Had Spears' note discounted at the bank at 13%.
June	8	Had Collins' note discounted at the bank at 15%.
	25	Received from J.L. Smith, a customer, a $7,000, 90-day, 12% note dated June 5, payable to J.L. Smith and signed by the Racine Corp. Upon endorsement, gave the customer credit for the maturity value of the note less discount at 13%.
	29	Received a $3,500, 60-day, 9% note dated June 29 from B. Grady, on account.
July	5	Received notice from the bank that Spears' note was not paid at maturity. Bank charged protest fees of $15.
	21	Received payment from Spears on the dishonored note, including interest at 16% on the balance from maturity date to payment date.

Instructions:

1. Give the journal entries to record the above transactions. Assume notes are discounted with recourse and do not meet the FASB criteria for recording as a sale. (Show data used in calculations with each entry; round to the nearest dollar.)
2. Give the adjusting entries required on July 31.

Problem 8—55 (Accounting for discounted notes)

The following transactions were completed by M.D. Ellis over a three-month period:

Nov.	10	Received from G.R. Kack, on account, a $5,000, 60-day, 9% note dated Nov. 9.
	11	Received from M.C. Leckner on account, a $2,100, 60-day, 12% note dated Nov. 10.
	20	Discounted Leckner's note, without recourse, at the bank at 11%.
	24	Discounted Kack's note, with recourse, at the bank at 10%.
Dec.	3	Received a $2,950, 30-day, non-interest-bearing note dated Dec. 1 from M. Ichtemple, crediting Ichtemple's account at face value.
	7	Discounted Ichtemple's note, with recourse, at the bank at 12%.
	28	Received from S.E. Dillhunt, a $500, 90-day, 12% note dated Dec. 13 and made by Bell Realty Inc. Gave the customer credit for the maturity value of the note less discount at 10%.
	29	Received a $4,000, 10-day, 8% note dated Dec. 29 from M.L. Reinhard, on account.
Jan.	10	Received notice from the bank that Kack's note was not paid at maturity. A protest fee of $15 was charged by the bank.
	22	Received a $25,000, 120-day, 9% note dated Jan. 22 from V.M. Cherry, on account.
	28	Received payment on Reinhard's note, including interest at 10%, the legal rate, on the face value from the maturity date.

Instructions:

1. Give the entries to record the preceding transactions. Assume that notes discounted with recourse do not meet FASB criteria for recording as a sale. (Show data used in calculations with each entry; round amounts to nearest dollar.)
2. Give the necessary adjusting entries on January 31. Assume all notes discounted are paid when due unless otherwise indicated.

Problem 8—56 **(Discounting notes with and without recourse)**

Ladd, Inc., has $162,000 of accounts receivable on July 1, 1995. On that date, Ladd accepts a one-year, $27,000, 11% note from Travis Corporation in settlement of Travis' $27,000 accounts receivable balance. The note and interest are due June 30, 1996. Additional information:

(a) On November 30, 1995, Ladd discounts the note with First Valley National Bank at 12% interest.
(b) On June 30, 1996, Travis Corporation dishonors the note and the bank collects the maturity value plus a $150 protest fee from Ladd.
(c) On August 31, 1996, Travis pays the amount outstanding, including interest since the dishonor date at 11%.

Instructions:

1. Prepare the necessary journal entries on Ladd's books assuming the note is considered a borrowing with recourse. (Round to the nearest dollar and compute interest using months rather than days.)
2. Prepare the necessary journal entries assuming the note is discounted without recourse (Round to the nearest dollar and compute interest using months rather than days.)

Problem 8—57 **(Accounting for a non-interest-bearing note)**

On January 1, 1996, Lost Valley Realty sold a tract of land to three doctors as an investment. The land, purchased ten years ago, was carried on Lost Valley's books at a value of $125,000. Lost Valley received a non-interest-bearing note for $220,000 from the doctors. The note is due December 31, 1997. There is no readily available market value for the land, but the current market rate of interest for comparable notes is 10%.

Instructions:

1. Give the journal entry to record the sale of land on Lost Valley's books.
2. Prepare a schedule of discount amortization for the note with amounts rounded to the nearest dollar.
3. Give the adjusting entries to be made at the end of 1996 and 1997 to record the effective interest earned.

Problem 8—58 **(Note with below-market interest rate)**

On January 1, 1996, the Denver Company sold land that originally cost $400,000 to the Boise Company. As payment, Boise gave Denver a $600,000 note. The note bears an interest rate of 4% and is to be repaid in three annual installments of $200,000 (plus interest on the outstanding balance). The first payment is due on December 31, 1996. The market price of the land is not reliably determinable. The prevailing rate of interest for notes of this type is 14%.

Instructions: Prepare the entries required on Denver's books to record the land sale and the receipt of each of the three payments. Use the effective-interest method of amortizing any premium or discount on the note.

Problem 8—59 **(Factoring receivables)**

Freemont Factors provides financing to other companies by purchasing their accounts receivable on a nonrecourse basis. Freemont charges a commission to its clients of 15% of all receivables factored. In addition, Freemont withholds 10% of receivables factored as protection against sales returns or other adjustments. Freemont credits the 10% withheld to Client Retainer and makes payments to clients at the end of each month so that the balance in the retainer is equal to 10% of unpaid receivables at the end of the month. Freemont recognizes its 15%

commissions as revenue at the time the receivables are factored. Also, experience has led Freemont to establish an Allowance for Doubtful Accounts of 4% of all receivables purchased.

On January 4, 1996, Freemont purchased receivables from Detmer Company totaling $1,500,000. Detmer had previously established an allowance for doubtful accounts for these receivables of $35,000. By January 31, Freemont had collected $1,200,000 on these receivables.

Instructions:

1. Prepare the entries necessary on Freemont's books to record the above information. Freemont makes adjusting entries at the end of every month.
2. Prepare the entries on Detmer's books to record the above information.

Problem 8—60 **(Journal entries and balance sheet presentation)**

The balance sheet for the Itex Corporation on December 31, 1995, includes the following cash and receivables balances:

Cash—First Security Bank		$45,000
Currency on hand		16,000
Petty cash fund		1,000
Cash in bond sinking fund		15,000
Notes receivable (including notes discounted with recourse, $15,500)		36,500
Accounts receivable	$85,600	
Less allowance for doubtful accounts	4,150	81,450
Interest receivable		525

Current liabilities reported in the December 31, 1995, balance sheet included:

Obligation on discounted notes receivable	$15,500

Transactions during 1996 included the following:

(a) Sales on account were $767,000.

(b) Cash collected on accounts totaled $576,500, including accounts of $93,000 with cash discounts of 2%.

(c) Notes received in settlement of accounts totaled $82,500.

(d) Notes receivable discounted as of December 31, 1995, were paid at maturity with the exception of one $3,000 note on which the company had to pay the bank $3,090, that included interest and protest fees. It is expected that recovery will be made on this note early in 1997.

(e) Customer notes of $60,000 were discounted with recourse during the year, proceeds from their transfer being $58,500. (All discounting transactions were recorded as loans.) Of this total, $48,000 matured during the year without notice of protest.

(f) Customer accounts of $8,720 were written off during the year as worthless.

(g) Recoveries of doubtful accounts written off in prior years were $2,020.

(h) Notes receivable collected during the year totaled $27,000 and interest collected was $2,450.

(i) On December 31, accrued interest on notes receivable was $630.

(j) Uncollectible accounts are estimated to be 5% of the December 31, 1996, accounts receivable balance.

(k) Cash of $35,000 was borrowed from First Security Bank, accounts receivable of $40,000 being pledged on the loan. Collections of $19,500 had been made on these receivables [included in the total given in transaction (b)] and this amount was applied on December 31, 1996, to payment of accrued interest on the loan of $600, and the balance to partial payment of the loan.

(l) Petty cash fund was reimbursed based on the following analysis of expenditure vouchers:

Travel expense	$112
Entertainment expense	78
Postage	93
Office supplies	173
Cash over	6

(m) $3,000 cash was added to the bond sinking fund.
(n) Currency on hand at December 31, 1996, was $12,000.
(o) Total cash payments for all expenses during the year were $680,000. Charge to General Expenses.

Instructions:
1. Prepare journal entries summarizing the transactions and information given above.
2. Prepare a summary of current cash and receivables for balance sheet presentation.

Problem 8—61* (Four-column bank reconciliation)

The following data are applicable to the Morgan Building Co.:

(a) The July 31 bank statement balance of $74,875 included a bank service charge of $235 not previously reported to the company but recorded on the company's books in August.
(b) The cash account balance in the general ledger on July 31 was $66,715.
(c) Outstanding checks at July 31 totaled $13,475. Deposits in transit on July 31 were $5,080.
(d) The bank statement on August 31 had a balance of $78,265, recognizing deposits of $105,360 and withdrawals of $101,970. The withdrawals included a service charge for August of $270 not yet reported to Morgan Building Co.
(e) The cash account balance in the general ledger on August 31 was $80,435, recognizing receipts of $104,405 for August and checks written during August of $90,450. Deposits in transit on August 31 were $4,125, and checks of $2,225 were outstanding as of that date.

Instructions:
1. Prepare a four-column bank reconciliation as of August 31.
2. Give any entries at August 31 that may be required on the company's books.

*Relates to Appendix

Problem 8—62* (Four-column bank reconciliation)

The following information is related to Downtown Company:

	August	September
Bank statement balance—at month end	$ 2,412	$ 2,782
Cash account balance—at month end	1,975	2,296
Bank charges for NSF check returned (normally written off in month following return)	38	80
Outstanding checks—at month end	600	865
Deposits in transit—at month end	300	470
Bank service charges (normally recorded in month following bank charge)	25	29
Drafts collected by bank (not recorded by company until month following collection)	200	150
Total credits to cash account	14,853	17,979
Total deposits on bank statement	?	18,080

Check #411 was erroneously recorded in the company checkbook and journal as $286; the correct amount is $236. (This check was not outstanding on September 30.) All disbursements were made by check.

Instructions: Prepare a four-column bank reconciliation for the month of September.

*Relates to Appendix

CHAPTER 9

Inventories: Cost Allocation and Valuation

CHAPTER TOPICS

- Nature and Classification of Inventory
- Periodic and Perpetual Basis
- Determination of Inventory Cost
- Historical Cost Allocation Methods
    - Specific Identification
    - First-In, First-Out (FIFO)
    - Average Cost
    - Last-In, First-Out (LIFO)
    - Dollar Value
- Comparison and Evaluation of Allocation Methods
- Determination of Price Indexes (Appendix)

Regina, Inc. was a fast-growing floor-care company that went public in 1985 and went bankrupt in 1988. Regina went from a one-product company with $60 million in sales in 1985 to a four-product company with $181 million in sales in 1988. Reported earnings climbed from $1.1 million in 1985 to $10.9 million in 1988.

Following the bankruptcy, investigations revealed a massive management fraud. It seems that in an effort to boost sales, sound business practices were changed and the accounting records were modified accordingly. For example, product quality testing was reduced or, in some cases, eliminated. As a result, Regina had many returned products. In fact, in one quarter more than 40,000 Housekeeper vacuum cleaners were returned. This volume of returns was so unexpected that a separate building had to be leased to store the defective products. These returns were not recorded on Regina's books. In addition, revenues were recorded when orders were received rather than when goods were shipped. This practice accelerated recognition of revenue beyond accepted norms. Finally, Regina modified its computer system to generate fictitious invoices. Approximately 200 invoices worth $5.4 million in sales were created during the last three business days of the fiscal year ended June 30, 1988.

Uncovering the combined effect of these fraudulent activities led to restating 1988 income of $10.9 million to a loss of $16.8 million. Dan Sheelan, the president of Regina and the driving force behind these activities, was required to pay substantial fines and was eventually sentenced to serve time in prison.

The primary source of revenue for a nonservice enterprise is from the sale of inventory. Because there is normally a period of time that elapses between the purchase and sale of inventory, unsold inventory is frequently a significant element on the balance sheet. Sold inventory, on the other hand, is reported as cost of goods sold on the income statement. As illustrated by the Regina example, the valuation and allocation of inventory can have a material effect on these two primary financial statements.

The principal valuation problems for inventory relate to deciding which costs should be included in inventory and under what circumstances a deviation from historical cost should be used for balance sheet valuation. Typically, until revenue is recognized, usually at time of sale, inventory is valued at cost. When a sale occurs, the inventory cost is allocated to cost of sales. If the inventory cost is the same for all units, the allocation presents no problems. However, if the inventory units were acquired or produced at different costs, a decision must be made as to which costs are charged to cost of goods sold and which costs remain as the valuation of the asset. In addition, if there has been a reduction in the costs of inventory, the use of a valuation method other than historical cost may be required.

This chapter focuses on the various components of cost that are assigned to inventory and also on the cost allocation methods that are employed in practice. Some of these are unique to the United States and they have developed under economic circumstances of changing prices and income tax laws. Chapter 10 presents some additional valuation issues relating to inventory, including the lower-of-cost-or-market rule for adjusting cost valuation downward.

NATURE OF INVENTORY

The term **inventory** designates goods held for sale in the normal course of business and, in the case of a manufacturer, goods in production or to be placed in production. The nature of goods classified as inventory varies widely with the nature of business activities, and in some cases includes assets not normally thought of as inventory. For example, land and buildings held for resale by a real estate firm, partially completed buildings to be sold in the future by a construction firm, and marketable securities held for resale by a stockbroker are all properly classified as inventory by the respective firms.

Inventory represents one of the most active elements in business operations, being continuously acquired or produced and resold. A large part of a company's resources is frequently invested in goods purchased or manufactured.

The term **inventory** (or *merchandise inventory*) is generally applied to goods held by a merchandising firm, either wholesale or retail, when such goods have been acquired in a condition for resale. The terms **raw materials, goods in process,** and **finished goods** refer to the inventories of a manufacturing enterprise.

Raw Materials

Raw materials are goods acquired for use in the production process. Some raw materials are obtained directly from natural sources. More often, however, raw materials are purchased from other companies and represent the finished products of the suppliers. For example, newsprint is the finished product of the paper mill but represents raw material to the printer who acquires it.

Although the term raw materials can be used broadly to cover all materials used in manufacturing, this designation is usually restricted to materials that will be physically incorporated in the products being manufactured. Because these materials are used directly in the production of goods, they are frequently referred to as **direct materials.** The term **factory supplies,** or **indirect materials,** is then used to refer to auxiliary materials, i.e., materials that are necessary in the production process but are not directly incorporated in the products. Oils and fuels for factory equipment, cleaning supplies, and similar items fall into this grouping since these items are not incorporated in a product but simply facilitate production as a whole.

Although factory supplies may be summarized separately, they should be reported as a part of a company's inventories since they ultimately will be consumed in the production process. Supplies purchased for use in the delivery, sales, and general administrative functions of the enterprise should not be reported as part of the inventories, but as prepaid expenses.

Goods in Process

Goods in process, alternately referred to as **work in process,** consist of materials partly processed and requiring further work before they can be sold. This inventory includes three cost elements: (1) **raw materials,** (2) **direct labor,** and (3) **factory overhead** or **manufacturing overhead.** The cost of materials directly identified with the goods in production is included under (1). The cost of labor directly identified with goods in production is included under (2). The portion of factory overhead assignable to goods still in production forms the third element of cost.

Factory overhead consists of all manufacturing costs other than direct materials and direct labor. It includes factory supplies used and labor not directly identified with the production of specific products. It also includes general manufacturing costs such as depreciation, maintenance, repairs, property taxes, insurance, and light, heat, and power, as well as a reasonable share of the managerial costs other than those relating solely to the selling and administrative functions of the business.

Finished Goods

Finished goods are the manufactured products awaiting sale. As products are completed, the costs accumulated in the production process are transferred from Goods in Process to the finished goods inventory account. The diagram below illustrates the basic flow of product costs through the inventory accounts of a manufacturer.

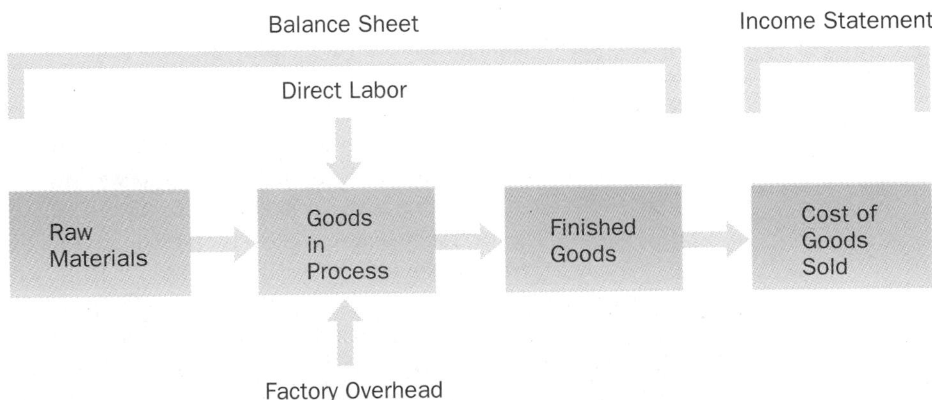

INVENTORY SYSTEMS

Inventory records may be maintained on either a periodic or a perpetual basis. A **periodic inventory system** requires a physical inventory, i.e., a counting, measuring, or weighing of goods, at the end of the accounting period to determine the quantities on hand. Values are then assigned to the quantities to determine the portion of the recorded costs to be carried forward on the balance sheet as inventory.

The **perpetual inventory system** requires the maintenance of records that provide a continuous summary of inventory items on hand. Individual accounts are kept for each class of goods. Inventory increases and decreases are recorded in the individual accounts, the resulting balances representing the amounts on hand. Perpetual records may be kept in terms of quantities only or in terms of both quantities and costs.

To illustrate the differences between the periodic and perpetual inventory systems, assume the following transactions occurred during the period for CyBorg Incorporated:

Beginning inventory	50 units @ $10	$ 500
Purchases during the period	300 units @ $10	$3,000
Sales during the period	275 units @ $15	$4,125

The journal entries to record these events for periodic and perpetual inventory systems are as follows:

Periodic Inventory System			**Perpetual Inventory System**		
Purchases during the period			**Purchases during the period**		
Purchases	3,000		Inventory	3,000	
Accounts Payable		3,000	Accounts Payable		3,000
Sales during the period			**Sales during the period**		
Accounts Receivable	4,125		Accounts Receivable	4,125	
Sales		4,125	Sales		4,125
			Cost of Goods Sold	2,750	
			Inventory		2,750
Adjusting entry			**Adjusting entry**		
Inventory	250		(no entry)		
Cost of Goods Sold	2,750				
Purchases		3,000			

Note that under the periodic inventory system, inventory that is not on hand at the end of the period is assumed to have been sold during the period. Purchases during the period ($3,000) are added to beginning inventory ($500) to arrive at goods available for sale ($3,500). A physical count of inventory is conducted at the end of the period and it is determined that 75 units are on hand at a cost of $750. Inventory that is not on hand is assumed to be sold. Thus, cost of goods sold is equal to goods available for sale ($3,500) less ending inventory ($750), or $2,750.

Suppose a physical count of inventory had revealed only 68 units on hand at the end of the period. Ending inventory would have then been valued at $680 and cost of goods sold would have been $2,820 ($3,500 - $680). Under the periodic inventory system, it is difficult to track inventory that may have been recorded incorrectly, lost, or stolen.

When a perpetual inventory system is employed, the company knows how much inventory should be on hand at any point in time. Comparing the inventory records to the result of a physical count allows the company to track discrepancies in inventory totals. Thus, even when a perpetual system is employed, physical counts of units on hand should be made at least once a year to confirm the balances on the books. The frequency of physical inventories varies depending on the nature of the goods, their rate of turnover, and the degree of internal control. A plan for continuous counting of inventory items on a rotation basis is frequently employed. Variations may be found between the recorded amounts and the amounts actually on hand as a result of recording errors, shrinkage, breakage, theft, and other causes. The inventory accounts should be adjusted to agree with the physical count when a discrepancy exists. To illustrate, in the CyBorg example ending inventory, according to records, should have been $750. The physical count indicates inventory valued at only $680. The entry to adjust the inventory account would be:

Loss Due to Inventory Adjustment	70	
Inventory		70

Normal inventory adjustments for shrinkage and breakage are reported on the income statement as adjustments to cost of goods sold. Abnormal shortages or thefts may be reported separately as operating expenses.

Practically all large trading and manufacturing enterprises and many relatively small organizations have adopted the perpetual inventory system as an integral part of their record keeping and internal control. With the costs of computers and point-of-sale systems so low, perpetual inventory systems are now more economical, and in today's fast moving world, almost a necessity. These systems offer a continuous check and control over inventories. Purchasing and production planning are facilitated, adequate inventories on hand are assured, and losses incurred through damage and theft are fully disclosed. The additional costs of maintaining such a system are usually well repaid by the benefits provided to management.

ITEMS TO BE INCLUDED IN INVENTORY

As a general rule, goods should be included in the inventory of the party holding title. The passing of title is a legal term designating the point at which ownership changes. In some situations, the legal rule may be waived for practical reasons or because of certain limitations in its application. When the rule of passing title is not observed, statements should include appropriate disclosure of the special practice followed and the factors supporting such practice. Application of the legal test under a number of special circumstances is described in the following paragraphs.

Goods in Transit

When terms of sale are **FOB (free on board) shipping point,** title passes to the buyer with the loading of goods at the point of shipment. Under these terms, application of the legal rule to a year-end shipment calls for recognition of a sale and an accompanying decrease in goods on hand on the books of the seller. Since title passes at the shipping point, goods in transit at year-end should be included in the inventory of the buyer despite the lack of physical possession. A determination of the goods in transit at year-end is made by a review of the incoming orders during the early part of the new period. The purchase records may be kept open beyond the fiscal period to permit the recognition of goods in transit as of the end of the period, or goods in transit may be recorded by means of an adjusting entry.

When terms of a sale are **FOB destination,** application of the legal test calls for no recognition of the transaction until goods are received by the buyer. In this case, because of the difficulties involved in ascertaining whether goods have reached their destination at year-end, the seller may prefer to ignore the legal rule and employ shipment as a basis for recognizing a sale and the accompanying inventory decrease.

In some cases, title to goods may pass before shipment takes place. For example, if goods are produced on special customer order, they may be recorded as a sale as soon as they are completed and segregated from the regular inventory. If the sale is recognized upon segregation by the seller, care must be taken to exclude such goods from the seller's inventory. The buyer, on the other hand, could recognize the in-transit goods as a purchase and thus as part of his inventory.

Goods on Consignment

Goods are frequently transferred to a dealer (**consignee**) on a consignment basis. The shipper (**consignor**) retains title and includes the goods in inventory until their sale by the consignee. For example, Caterpillar Tractor Co. often consigns heavy equipment to its dealers. The cost of these items is such that many dealers could not afford to stock an entire inventory line. By consigning the inventory, Caterpillar is increasing its opportunities for generating revenue. **Consigned goods** are properly reported at the sum of their costs and the handling and shipping costs incurred in their transfer to the consignee. The goods may be separately designated on the balance sheet as merchandise on consignment. The consignee does not own the consigned goods; hence, neither consigned goods nor obligations for such goods are reported on the consignee's financial statements. Accounting for consignments is discussed in a later chapter.

Other merchandise owned by a business but in the possession of others, such as goods in the hands of salespersons and agents, goods held by customers on approval, and goods held by others for storage, processing, or shipment, should also be shown as a part of that business' ending inventory.

Auditing consigned inventory presents the auditor with a special set of problems. Inventory that is on the premises may not belong to the company because the company is holding it on consignment while inventory that is located with a vendor on consignment, hundreds of miles away, still belongs to the company. Imagine an auditor walking out into a warehouse and seeing row upon row of inventory. "That's not ours," quips the warehouse manager. Then the warehouse manager leads the auditor to the shipping platform. "See that truck just leaving the gate? That truck and hundreds more just like it contain inventory that is still ours but has been shipped on consignment. Audit that!"

Conditional and Installment Sales

Conditional sales and installment sales contracts may provide for a retention of title by the seller until the sales price is fully recovered. Under these circumstances, the seller, who retains title, may continue to show the goods, reduced by the buyer's equity in such goods as established by collections; the buyer, in turn, can report an equity in the goods accruing through payments made. However, in the usual case when the possibilities of returns and defaults are very low, title to the goods should be relinquished and the transaction recorded in terms of the expected outcome. The seller, anticipating completion of the contract and the ultimate passing of title, recognizes the transaction as a regular sale involving deferred collections; the buyer, intending to comply with the contract and acquire title, recognizes the transaction as a regular purchase. Installment sales are discussed in detail in a later chapter.

DETERMINATION OF INVENTORY COST

After the goods to be included as inventory have been identified, the accountant must assign a dollar value to the physical units. As indicated earlier, the profession has historically favored retention of some measure of cost, generally historical cost for this purpose. Attention is directed in this chapter to identifying the elements that comprise cost, and to a consideration of how to determine the portion of historical costs to be retained as the inventory amount reported on the balance sheet and the amount to be charged against current revenues.

Items Included in Cost

Inventory costs consist of all expenditures, both direct and indirect, relating to inventory acquisition, preparation, and placement for sale. In the case of raw materials or goods acquired for resale, cost includes the purchase price, freight, receiving, storage, and all other costs incurred to the time goods are ready for sale. Certain expenditures can be traced to specific acquisitions or can be allocated to inventory items in some equitable manner. Other expenditures may be relatively small and difficult to allocate. Such items are normally excluded in the calculation of inventory cost and are thus charged in full against current revenue as **period costs.**

The charges to be included in the cost of manufactured products have already been mentioned. Proper accounting for materials, labor, and factory overhead items and their identification with goods in process and finished goods inventories are best achieved through adoption of a cost accounting system designed to meet the needs of a particular business unit. Certain costs relating to the acquisition or the manufacture of goods may be considered abnormal and may be excluded in arriving at inventory cost. For example, costs arising from idle capacity, excessive spoilage, and reprocessing are usually considered abnormal items chargeable to current revenue. Only those portions of general and administrative costs that are clearly related to procurement or production should be included in inventory cost.

A schedule of cost of goods manufactured is often prepared by manufacturing companies to illustrate how various costs affect inventories and, ultimately, cost of goods sold. An illustration of this schedule is presented below:

Bartlett Corporation
Schedule of Cost of Goods Manufactured
For the Year Ended December 31, 1996

Direct materials:		
Raw materials inventory, January 1, 1996	$ 21,350	
Purchases	107,500	
Cost of raw materials available for use	$128,850	
Less raw materials inventory, December 31, 1996	22,350	
Raw materials used in production		$106,500
Direct labor		96,850
Factory overhead:		
Indirect labor	$ 40,000	
Factory supervision	29,000	
Depreciation expense—factory buildings and equipment	20,000	
Light, heat, and power	18,000	
Factory supplies expense	15,000	
Miscellaneous factory overhead	12,055	134,055
Total manufacturing costs		$337,405
Add goods in process inventory, January 1, 1996		29,400
		$366,805
Less goods in process inventory, December 31, 1996		26,500
Cost of goods manufactured		$340,305

In practice, companies take different positions in classifying certain costs. For example, costs of the purchasing department, costs of accounting for manufacturing activities, and costs of pensions for production personnel may be treated as inventoriable costs by some companies and period costs by others.

Discounts as Reductions in Cost

Discounts treated as a reduction of cost in recording the acquisition of goods should similarly be treated as a reduction in the cost assigned to the inventory. **Trade discounts** are discounts converting a catalog price list to the prices actually charged to a buyer. The discount available may vary with such factors as the quantity purchased. Thus, trade discounts are frequently stated in a series. For example, given trade discount terms based on the quantity ordered of 30/20/10, a customer would be entitled to a discount of either 30%, 30% and 20%, or 30% and 20% and 10%, depending on the size of the order. Each successive discount is applied to the net invoice cost after deducting any earlier discounts. To illustrate, assume that an inventory item is listed in a catalog for $5,000 and a buyer is given terms of 20/10/5. The net invoice price is calculated as follows:

Discount	Net Invoice Amount
$5,000 × 20% = $1,000	$5,000 – $1,000 = $4,000
$4,000 × 10% = $ 400	$4,000 – $ 400 = $3,600
$3,600 × 5% = $ 180	$3,600 – $ 180 = $3,420

An alternative approach to the preceding computation is to compute a composite discount rate that can be applied to the initial gross amount. The following computation could be made for the above invoice:

Discount Rate	×	Percentage of Original Invoice Cost	=	Composite Discount Rate
20%		100%		20.00%
10%		80%(100% – 20%)		8.00
5%		72%(80% – 8%)		3.60
				31.60%

Computation of discount: $5,000 × 31.6% = $1,580 discount
Net price = $5,000 – $1,580 = $3,420

The advantage of the composite approach is that once a composite rate is computed, it can be used directly for all purchases that have the same trade discount terms.

Cost is defined as the list price less the trade discount. No record needs to be made of the discount, and the purchases should be recorded at the net price of $3,420 as follows:

Inventory	3,420	
Accounts Payable		3,420

Cash discounts are discounts granted for payment of invoices within a limited time period. Business use of such discounts has declined in popularity over the past years, although they are still found in some industries. Cash discounts are usually stated as a certain percentage to be allowed if the invoice is paid within a certain number of days, with the full amount due within another time period. For example, 2/10, n/30 (two ten, net thirty) means that 2% is allowed as a cash discount if the invoice is paid within 10 days after the invoice date, but that the full or "net" amount is due within 30 days. Terms of 3/10 eom mean a 3% discount is allowed if the invoice is paid within 10 days after the end of the month in which the invoice is written.

Theoretically, inventory should be recorded at the discounted amount, i.e., the gross invoice price less the allowable discount. This **net method** reflects the fact that discounts not taken are in effect credit-related expenditures incurred for failure to pay within the discount period. They are recorded in the discounts lost account and reported as a separate item on the income statement. Discounts lost usually represent a relatively high rate of interest. To illustrate, assume a purchase of $10,000 provides for payment on a 2/10, n/30 basis. This means that if the buyer pays for the purchase by the tenth day, only $9,800 must be paid. Twenty days later the full $10,000 is due. Thus, a discount of $200 is earned for 20 days advance payment. If the liability is not paid within the discount period, the difference between the recorded liability ($9,800) and the amount of cash paid ($10,000) would be debited to "Discounts Lost" and disclosed on the income statement as an expense. The implicit annual interest rate in this arrangement is 36%,[1] clearly a desirable rate even if a loan is necessary to obtain the cash for the advance payment. Failure on the part of management to take a cash discount usually represents carelessness in considering payment alternatives.

Under the **gross method** of recording discounts, cash discounts are booked only when they are taken. While the net method tracks discounts not taken, the gross method provides no such information and inventory records are maintained at the gross unit price. When a periodic system is used, cash discounts taken are reflected through a contra purchases account, Purchase Discounts. With a perpetual inventory system, discounts are credited directly to Inventory.

Because of its control features, the net method of accounting for purchases is strongly preferred; however, many companies still follow the historical practice of recognizing cash discounts only as payments are made. If the payment is made in the same period the inventory is purchased, use of either method will result in the same net income. However, if inventory is purchased in one period and payment is made in a subsequent period, net income is affected and a proper matching of costs against revenue will not take place. If the net method is used, an adjusting entry should be made at the end of each period to record the discounts lost on unpaid invoices for which the discount period has passed.

The entries required for both the gross and net methods are illustrated in the following table. A perpetual inventory method is assumed.

Transaction	**Purchases Reported Net**			**Purchases Reported Gross**		
Purchase of merchandise priced at $10,000 along with a cash discount of 2%.	Inventory	9,800		Inventory	10,000	
	Accounts Payable		9,800	Accounts Payable		10,000
(a) Assuming payment of the invoice within discount period.	Accounts Payable	9,800		Accounts Payable	10,000	
	Cash		9,800	Inventory		200
				Cash		9,800
(b) Assuming payment of the invoice after discount period.	Accounts Payable	9,800		Accounts Payable	10,000	
	Discounts Lost	200		Cash		10,000
	Cash		10,000			
(c) Required adjustment at the end of the period assuming that the invoice has not been paid and the discount period has lapsed.	Discounts Lost	200		No entry required		
	Accounts Payable		200			

1. $I = P \times R \times T$
$\$200 = \$10,000 \times R \times 20/360$
$\$200 = \$556 \times R$
$R = 200/556$
$R = 36\%$

Purchase Returns and Allowances

Adjustments to invoice cost are also made when merchandise either is damaged or is of a lesser quality than ordered. Sometimes the merchandise is physically returned to the supplier. In other instances, a credit is allowed to the buyer by the supplier to compensate for the damage or the inferior quality of the merchandise. In either case, the liability is reduced and a credit is made directly to the inventory account under a perpetual inventory system, or to a contra purchases account, Purchase Returns and Allowances, under a periodic inventory system.

TRADITIONAL HISTORICAL COST ALLOCATION METHODS

One of the more difficult issues facing the user of financial statements is understanding the effect of the allocation of specific unit prices, measured at the unit's historical cost at the time of purchase, to cost of goods sold and to inventory. Several methods have evolved to make this allocation between expense and inventory. The methods discussed in this section of the chapter are (1) **specific identification** (2) **first-in, first-out (FIFO),** (3) **average cost,** and (4) **last-in, first-out (LIFO).** Each has certain characteristics that make it preferable under certain conditions. One of them, the last-in, first-out method, was specifically developed as an attempt to reduce the impact of changing prices on net income. All four methods have in common the fact that inventory cost, as defined in this chapter, is allocated between the income statement and the balance sheet. Only the specific identification method determines the cost allocation according to the physical inventory flow. Unless individual inventory items, such as automobiles, are clearly definable, inventory items are exchangeable. Thus, the emphasis in inventory valuation is on the accounting cost allocation, not the physical flow. No adjustment for price changes is made to the total amount to be allocated.

Except for specific identification, all the cost methods are frequently encountered in practice. Many companies use more than one method, applying different methods to different classes of inventory. *Accounting Trends & Techniques* reported the following data regarding the inventory methods used by the 600 companies surveyed.[2] Note that many companies use more than one inventory method, applying different methods to different classes of inventory.

Method	Number Using Identified Method—1992
Last-in, first-out (LIFO)	358
First-in, first-out (FIFO)	415
Average cost	193
Other	45

There have been few guidelines developed by the profession to assist companies in choosing among these alternative cost allocation methods. Some accountants have suggested that, conceptually, costs attach to the inventory as they are incurred and thus should follow the inventory to its disposition. This argument suggests that methods that allocate the cost of inventory sold according to the physical flow of goods would be preferred. Other writers have emphasized capital maintenance concepts and suggest the use of methods that provide for maintenance of a physical quantity of inventory before recognizing income from its sale. The following discussion of the allocation methods demonstrates how each method relates to these different viewpoints.

2. *Accounting Trends & Techniques*—1993 (New York: American Institute of Certified Public Accountants, 1993), p. 145.

Inventory Fraud and Instant Profits

The Wall Street Journal frequently reports on companies whose financial statements have been misstated via the inventory account. Phar-Mor, Laribee Wire, Digital Equipment, ZZZZ Best, and Comptronix are a few examples that have made the headlines because of alleged inventory fraud. Why is inventory such a common area for manipulation? The primary reason: Inventory is often very difficult to audit and therefore management can often hide the fraud.

For large companies, inventory can be spread all across the United States. For example, Phar-Mor had over 300 stores in 30 states, yet the auditor visited only five stores. In the case of Laribee Wire Manufacturing Company, inventory was often transferred between plants — and recorded as inventory at each plant. The audit firm did not inventory the plants simultaneously and as a result did not detect the fraud.

In the case of Digital Equipment Corporation, the company was accused of not valuing obsolete inventory appropriately and the auditor, it is alleged, should have been aware of this. In the up-and-down world of computers, it would be difficult to know from one day to the next what was and was not obsolete. For ZZZZ Best, company officials spent millions of dollars creating actual restoration job sites for fictitious contracts so the auditor could conduct on-site reviews.

For almost every case of inventory fraud, the audit firm responds by saying "the audit was conducted in accordance with professional standards" and that "a well-concealed fraud being directed by top management would be difficult to detect."

Questions:

1. How can inventory fraud create "instant profits"?
2. Why do historical cost valuation methods make it easier to perpetuate an inventory fraud?
3. In your opinion, what responsibilities should an auditor have for detecting inventory fraud?

Sources:

"Convenient Fiction: Inventory Chicanery Tempts More Firms, Fools More Auditors." *The Wall Street Journal*, December 12, 1992, pg. A1, A5.

Specific Identification

Costs may be allocated between goods sold during the period and goods on hand at the end of the period according to the actual cost of specific units. This **specific identification method** requires a means of identifying the historical cost of each unit of inventory up to the time of sale. With specific identification, the flow of recorded costs matches the physical flow of goods.

The specific identification method is a highly objective approach to matching historical costs with revenues. As stated in Accounting Research Study No. 13, "There appears to be little theoretical argument against the use of specific identification of cost with units of product if that method of determining inventory cost is practicable."[3] Application of this method, however, is often difficult or impossible. When inventory is composed of a great many items or identical items acquired at different times and at different prices, cost identification procedures are likely to be slow, burdensome, and costly. Furthermore, when units are identical and interchangeable, this method opens the doors to possible profit manipulation through the selection of particular units for delivery. Finally, significant changes in costs during a period may warrant charges to expense on a basis other than past identifiable costs.

First-in, First-Out Method

The **first-in, first-out (FIFO) method** is based on the assumption that costs should be charged to expense (cost of goods sold) in the order in which the costs are incurred. Inventories are thus stated in terms of the most recent costs. To illustrate the application of this method, assume the following data:

3. Horace G. Barden. *Accounting Research Study No. 13*, "The Accounting Basis of Inventories." (New York: American Institute of Certified Public Accountants, 1973) p. 83.

Jan.						
Jan.	1	Inventory	200 units at $10	=	$ 2,000
	12	Purchase	400 units at 12	=	4,800
	26	Purchase	300 units at 11	=	3,300
	30	Purchase	100 units at 12	=	1,200
		Total	1,000 units		$11,300

A physical inventory on January 31 shows 300 units on hand. The most recent costs would be assigned to the units as follows:

Most recent purchase, Jan. 30	100 units at $12	=	$1,200
Next most recent purchase, Jan. 26	200 units at 11	=	2,200
Total	300 units		$3,400

If the ending inventory is $3,400, cost of goods sold is $7,900 ($11,300 – $3,400). Thus, the earliest costs incurred are charged to expense and the most recent costs are allocated to inventory. In a periodic inventory system, the following adjusting entry (similar to that on page 342) would be made:

Inventory	1,400*	
Cost of Goods Sold	7,900	
Purchases		9,300

**$3,400 – $2,000 beginning inventory balance*

In the above example, ending inventory was computed and the cost of goods sold was inferred. A similar procedure can be used to compute cost of goods sold and then infer ending inventory. If 300 units are in ending inventory, then 700 units can be assumed sold. Under the FIFO method, cost of goods sold is computed as follows:

Jan.	1	Inventory	200 units at $10	=	$2,000
	12	Purchase	400 units at 12	=	4,800
	26	Purchase	100 units at 11	=	1,100
		Total	700 units		$7,900

If cost of goods sold is $7,900, ending inventory is $3,400 ($11,300 – $7,900). Because the number of units in ending inventory is typically less than the number of units sold, computing ending inventory first requires fewer computations. However, the resulting cost of goods sold and ending inventory figures are the same regardless of which is computed first.

When perpetual inventory accounts are maintained, a form similar to that illustrated on the next page is used to record the cost assigned to units issued and the cost relating to the goods on hand. The columns show the quantities and values of goods acquired, goods issued, and balances on hand. Recall that when a perpetual system is used, no journal entry is required to adjust ending inventory at the end of the period because inventory records are continuously updated. The only exception to this, as discussed earlier, is when a physical count indicates a difference between inventory on hand and the inventory records. It should be observed that identical values for periodic and perpetual inventories are obtained when FIFO is applied.

FIFO can be supported as a logical and realistic approach to the flow of costs when it is impractical or impossible to achieve specific cost identification. FIFO assumes a cost flow closely paralleling the usual physical flow of goods sold. Expense is charged with costs considered applicable to the goods actually sold; ending inventories are reported in terms of most recent costs—costs closely approximating the current value of inventories at the balance sheet date. FIFO affords little opportunity for profit manipulation because the assignment of costs is determined by the order in which costs are incurred.

COMMODITY: X (FIFO)

	RECEIVED			ISSUED			BALANCE		
DATE	*Quantity*	*Unit Cost*	*Total Cost*	*Quantity*	*Unit Cost*	*Total Cost*	*Quantity*	*Unit Cost*	*Total Cost*
Jan. 1							200	$10	$2,000
12	400	$12	$4,800				200 400	10 12	2,000 4,800
16				200 300	$10 12	$2,000 3,600	100	12	1,200
26	300	11	3,300				100 300	12 11	1,200 3,300
29				100 100	12 11	1,200 1,100	200	11	2,200
30	100	12	1,200				200 100	11 12	2,200 1,200

Average Cost Method

Some companies value inventories using an **average cost method** that assigns the same average cost to each unit. This cost is computed using a weighted average technique for a periodic system or a moving average technique for a perpetual system.

The **weighted average technique** is based on the assumption that goods sold should be charged at an average cost, such average being influenced or weighted by the number of units acquired at each price. Inventories are stated at the same weighted average cost per unit. Using the cost data in the preceding section, the weighted average cost of a physical inventory of 300 units on January 31 would be as follows:

Jan. 1	Inventory	200 units at $10	=	$ 2,000
12	Purchase	400 units at 12	=	4,800
26	Purchase	300 units at 11	=	3,300
30	Purchase	100 units at 12	=	1,200
	Total	1,000 units		$11,300

Weighted average cost .... $11,300 ÷ 1,000 = $11.30
Ending inventory...................... 300 units at $11.30 = $3,390

The ending inventory is assigned a cost of $3,390; cost of goods sold is $7,910 ($11,300 - $3,390), thus charging cost of goods sold, in the following journal entry, with a weighted average cost.

Inventory	1,390*	
Cost of Goods Sold	7,910	
Purchases		9,300

**$3,390 – $2,000 beginning inventory balance*

These calculations were made for costs of one month. Similar calculations could be developed for a periodic inventory system for a quarter or for a year.

When a perpetual inventory system that records both quantities and amounts is used, a variation of the weighted average technique is required. A new weighted average amount is calculated after each purchase, and this amount is used to cost each subsequent sale until another purchase is made. Because this method results in continuous updating of the average, it is referred to as the **moving average technique.** The use of this approach is illustrated on the next page.

COMMODITY: X (moving average)

		RECEIVED			ISSUED			BALANCE		
DATE		Quantity	Unit Cost	Total Cost	Quantity	Unit Cost	Total Cost	Quantity	Unit Cost	Total Cost
Jan.	1							200	$10.00	$2,000
	12	400	$12	$4,800				600	11.33	6,800
	16				500	$11.33	$5,665	100	*11.35	1,135
	26	300	11	3,300				400	11.09	4,435
	29				200	11.09	2,218	200	11.09	2,217
	30	100	12	1,200				300	11.39	3,417

*Increase in unit cost due to rounding.

On January 12 the new unit cost of $11.33 was found by dividing $6,800, the total cost, by 600, the number of units on hand. Then on January 16, the balance of $1,135 represented the previous balance of $6,800 less $5,665, the cost assigned to the 500 units issued on this date. New unit costs were calculated on January 26 and 30 when additional units were acquired.

With successive recalculations of cost and the use of such different costs during the period, the cost identified with the ending inventory differs from that determined when cost is assigned to the ending inventory in terms of average cost for all goods available during the period. A periodic inventory system and use of the weighted average method resulted in a value for the ending inventory of $3,390; a perpetual inventory system and use of the moving average method resulted in a value for the ending inventory of $3,417.

The average cost method can be supported as realistic and as paralleling the physical flow of goods, particularly where there is an intermingling of identical inventory units. Unlike the other inventory methods, the average approach provides the same cost for similar items of equal utility. The method does not permit profit manipulation. Limitations of the average method are that inventory values perpetually contain some degree of influence of earliest costs and that inventory values may lag significantly behind current prices in periods of rapidly rising or falling prices.

Last-In, First-Out Method—Specific Goods

The **last-in, first-out (LIFO) method** is based on the assumption that the latest costs of a specific item should be charged to cost of goods sold. Inventories are thus stated at earliest costs. Using the cost data in the preceding section, a physical inventory of 300 units on January 31 would have a cost as follows:

Earliest costs relating to goods, Jan. 1	200 units at $10	$2,000
Next earliest cost, Jan. 12	100 units at 12	1,200
Total	300 units	$3,200

The ending inventory is assigned a cost of $3,200 and cost of goods sold is $8,100 ($11,300 – $3,200). Thus, cost of goods sold is charged with the most recently incurred costs, shown in the following journal entry.

Inventory	1,200*	
Cost of Goods Sold	8,100	
Purchases		9,300

**$3,200 – $2,000 beginning inventory balance*

When perpetual inventories are maintained, it is necessary to calculate costs on a last-in, first-out basis using the cost data on the date of each issue as illustrated below.

COMMODITY: X (moving average)

	RECEIVED			ISSUED			BALANCE		
DATE	*Quantity*	*Unit Cost*	*Total Cost*	*Quantity*	*Unit Cost*	*Total Cost*	*Quantity*	*Unit Cost*	*Total Cost*
Jan. 1							200	$10	$2,000
12	400	$12	$4,800				200 400	10 12	2,000 4,800
16				400 100	$12 10	$4,800 1,000	100	10	1,000
26	300	11	3,300				100 300	10 11	1,000 3,300
29				200	11	2,200	100 100	10 11	1,000 1,100
30	100	12	1,200				100 100 100	10 11 12	1,000 1,100 1,200

It should be noted that LIFO values obtained under a periodic system usually differ from those determined on a perpetual basis. In the example, a cost of $3,200 was obtained for the periodic inventory, whereas $3,300 was obtained when costs were calculated as goods were issued. This difference results because it was necessary to "dip into" the beginning inventory layer and charge 100 units of the beginning inventory at $10 to the issue of January 16. The ending inventory thus reflects only 100 units at the beginning unit cost.

These temporary liquidations of inventory frequently occur during the year, especially for companies with seasonal business. These liquidations cause monthly reports prepared on the LIFO basis to be unrealistic and meaningless. Because of this, most companies using LIFO maintain their internal records using other inventory methods, such as FIFO or weighted average, and adjust the statements to LIFO at the end of the year with a **LIFO allowance** account. Burlington Holdings, Inc. (Exhibit 9-1) includes a note to its balance sheet that itemizes its inventories at average cost, and then includes a separate allowance account, identified as "excess of average cost over LIFO," to reduce the inventory to LIFO cost.

Assuming the allowance was used by Burlington Holdings for the first time in 1990, the entry to record the allowance would be as follows:

Cost of Goods Sold	42,391	
Allowance for Excess of Average Cost Over LIFO		42,391

In 1991 the difference was less, therefore, the adjusting entry would decrease the allowance account to its new difference.

Allowance for Excess of Average Cost Over LIFO	17,327	
Cost of Goods Sold		17,327

Each year, the allowance would be adjusted in this manner to properly record the LIFO inventory on the financial statements.

LIFO Conformity Rule. The LIFO inventory method was developed in the United States during the late 1930s as a method of permitting deferral of illusory inventory profits during

Exhibit 9—1
Burlington Holdings, Inc.—Dollar-Value LIFO Inventory Disclosure

Inventories: Inventories are valued at the lower of cost or market. Cost of substantially all components of textile inventories in the United States is determined using the dollar-value last-in, first-out (LIFO) method. All other inventories are valued principally at average cost.

Note D—Inventories

Inventories are summarized as follows (in thousands):

	1991	1990
Inventories at average cost:		
Raw materials	$ 37,970	$ 48,453
Stock in process	100,786	109,346
Produced goods	159,642	195,569
Dyes, chemicals, and supplies	17,919	20,151
	$316,317	$373,519
Less excess of average cost over LIFO	25,064	42,391
Total	$291,253	$331,128

periods of rising prices. Petition was made to Congress by companies desiring to use this method for tax purposes, and in the Revenue Act of 1938, it became an acceptable tax method. There was, however, a unique provision attached to the use of the LIFO inventory method. It has become known as the **LIFO conformity rule** and specifies that only those taxpayers who use LIFO for financial reporting purposes may use it for tax purposes. LIFO inventory is the only accounting method that must be reported the same way for tax and book purposes. In the early years, the rule was strictly applied. Companies were not permitted to report inventory values using any other method either in the body of the financial statements or in the attached notes. This provision was to avoid the implication that some value other than LIFO was really a better one. Over time, the IRS has gradually relaxed the conformity rule. In 1981, the IRS regulations were further relaxed by (1) permitting companies to provide non-LIFO disclosures such as those presented by Burlington as long as they are not presented on the face of the income statement, and (2) allowing companies to apply LIFO differently for book purposes than for tax purposes as long as they use some acceptable form of LIFO.[4] Differences between book and tax LIFO inventories arise from different definitions of "LIFO pools" or from different application of market values that are lower than LIFO cost.

Prior to the relaxation of the LIFO conformity rule, the income tax regulations became the governing rules for book purposes. The accounting standards bodies elected not to address the method except to recognize that LIFO was an acceptable inventory method.[5] Now that companies may apply LIFO differently for book and tax purposes, both the SEC and the AICPA have addressed the LIFO issue for financial statement reporting purposes. In July 1981, the SEC issued ASR No. 293 which provided guidelines for companies to follow in making supplemental non-LIFO income disclosures. They also included several examples of what they labeled inappropriate use of the LIFO method. Their concern with LIFO as applied was stated as follows:

For too long, the application of the LIFO method for financial accounting and reporting has been unduly influenced by the tax application. Most explanations or analysis of LIFO in textbooks and articles have been oriented toward tax implications, rather than financial accounting and reporting.

4. Treasury Decision 7756, Title 26 CFR 1.472-2(e), (Washington, D.C.: U.S. Government Printing Office, 1981).
5. *Accounting Research Bulletin No. 43,* "Restatement and Revision of Accounting Research Bulletins" (New York: American Institute of Certified Public Accountants, 1953), Chapter 4, par. 6.

Inventory Around the World

In the United States a variety of methods are available to account for inventory. One of the most common of these methods is LIFO. However, an accountant who steps out of this country quickly finds that LIFO seems to be an American creation associated with tax laws that require companies who adopt LIFO for tax purposes to use LIFO for financial accounting purposes as well.

In the United Kingdom LIFO is not permitted for tax purposes. Thus, companies have little incentive to incur the costs associated with using LIFO for financial purposes and another method for tax purposes. In France LIFO is not allowed when valuing individual inventory items. The most common inventory method used in that country is average cost. Turkey places severe restrictions on the use of LIFO, and in Russia the concept of both LIFO and FIFO are foreign. Only in Germany, where the tax laws were changed to allow the use of LIFO for tax purposes, can one see the LIFO method to any great degree.

Questions:

1. Does using LIFO, FIFO, or average cost affect the amount of cash that a company pays when it purchases inventory?
2. What is the major advantage of using LIFO?
3. Why would taxing authorities around the world be reluctant to allow the use of LIFO for tax purposes?
4. In terms of the financial statements and their users, how will using LIFO affect these statements and the decisions made with them?
5. What problems are encountered by multinational corporations because of different levels of LIFO acceptability? Should LIFO be disallowed in the United States?

Source: *European Accounting Guide, U.S. Edition*, HBJ Professional Publishing, 1991.

With few exceptions, the accounting profession has deferred to the IRS in this area; indeed many accountants appear to view IRS LIFO regulations as if they were generally accepted accounting principles ("GAAP"). The Commission disagrees with this approach and believes that since LIFO may now be applied differently for book accounting and tax accounting, it is appropriate for the current practices used in the application of LIFO to be examined.[6]

The AICPA responded to this request, and under the direction of the Accounting Standards Executive Committee, appointed a nine-person Task Force on LIFO Inventory Problems to study the area. Their study resulted in the publication in November 1984 of an Issues Paper, "Identification and Discussion of Certain Financial Accounting and Reporting Issues Concerning LIFO Inventories." The task force addressed over fifty separate issues and reported by vote their views on the topic. Although the task force did not have the power to establish definitive accounting standards, the SEC has accepted their report as authoritative pending review of this area by the FASB. Where applicable, the views of the task force will be referenced in the detailed discussion of LIFO that follows.

Specific-Goods LIFO Pools. With large and diversified inventories, application of the LIFO procedures to specific goods is extremely burdensome. Because of the complexity and cost involved, companies frequently selected only a few very important inventory items, usually raw materials, for application of the LIFO method. As a means of simplifying the valuation process and extending its applicability to more items, an adaptation of LIFO applied to specific goods was developed and approved by the IRS. This adaptation permitted the establishment of **LIFO inventory pools** of substantially identical goods. At the end of a period, the quantity of items in the pool is determined, and costs are assigned to those items. Units equal to the beginning quantity in the pool are assigned the beginning unit costs. If the number of units in ending inventory exceeds the

6. *Accounting Series Release No. 293*, "The Last-In, First-Out Method of Accounting for Inventories" (Washington, D.C.: U.S. Government Printing Office, 1981), section II.

number of beginning units, the additional units are regarded as an incremental layer within the pool.

The unit cost assigned to the items in the new layer may be based on any one of the following measurements:

1. Actual costs of earliest acquisitions within the period (LIFO)
2. The weighted average cost of acquisitions within the period
3. Actual costs of the latest acquisitions within the period (FIFO)

Increments in subsequent periods form successive inventory layers. A decrease in the number of units in an inventory pool during a period is regarded as a reduction in the most recently added layer, then in successively lower layers, and finally in the original or base quantity. Once a specific layer is reduced or eliminated, it is not restored.

To illustrate the LIFO valuation process, assume that a company uses three inventory pools. The changes in the pools are as listed below. The inventory calculations that follow the listing are based on the assumption that weighted average costs are used in valuing annual incremental layers.

Inventory Pool Increments and Liquidations

	Inventory Pool A	Inventory Pool B	Inventory Pool C
Inv., Dec. 31, 1995	3,000 @ $6	3,000 @ $5	2,000 @ $10
Purchases—1996	3,000 @ $7	2,000 @ $6	3,000 @ $11
	1,000 @ $9		
Total available for sale	7,000	5,000	5,000
Sales—1996	3,000	1,000	3,500
Inv., Dec. 31, 1996	4,000	4,000	1,500
Purchases—1997	1,000 @ $8	2,000 @ $6	3,000 @ $11
	3,000 @ $10		
Total available for sale	8,000	6,000	4,500
Sales—1997	3,500	2,500	2,000
Inv., Dec. 31, 1997	4,500	3,500	2,500

Inventory Valuation Using Specific-Goods LIFO Pools

	Inventory Pool A		Inventory Pool B		Inventory Pool C	
Inv., Dec. 31, 1995	3,000 @ $6	$18,000	3,000 @ $5	$15,000	2,000 @ $10	$20,000
Inv., Dec. 31, 1996	3,000 @ $6	$18,000	3,000 @ $5	$15,000	1,500 @ $10	$15,000
	1,000 @ $7.50[1]	7,500	1,000 @ $6	6,000		
	4,000	$25,500	4,000	$21,000	1,500	$15,000
Inv., Dec. 31, 1997	3,000 @ $6	$18,000	3,000 @ $5	$15,000	1,500 @ $10	$15,000
	1,000 @ $7.50	7,500	500 @ $6	3,000	1,000 @ $11	11,000
	500 @ $9.50[2]	4,750				
	4,500	$30,250	3,500	$18,000	2,500	$26,000

[1]Cost of units acquired in 1996, $30,000, divided by number of units acquired, 4,000, or $7.50.
[2]Cost of units acquired in 1997, $38,000, divided by number of units acquired, 4,000, or $9.50.

The layer process for LIFO inventories is further illustrated as follows.

	Inventory Pool A		Inventory Pool B		Inventory Pool C	
Inventory Dec. 31, 1995	3,000 @ $6 = $18,000		3,000 @ $5 = $15,000		2,000 @ $10 = $20,000	
Inventory Dec. 31, 1996	1,000 @ $7.50 = $7,500 3,000 @ $6 = $18,000	$25,500	1,000 @ $6= $6,000 3,000 @ $5 = $15,000	$21,000	1,500 @ $10 = $15,000	
Inventory Dec. 31, 1997	500 @ $9.50 = $4,750 1,000 @ $7.50 = $7,500 3,000 @ $6 = $18,000	$30,250	500 @ $6 = $3,000 3,000 @ $5 = $15,000	$18,000	1,000 @ $11 = $11,000 1,500 @ $10 = $15,000	$26,000

A new layer was added to Inventory Pool A each year. Previously established layers were reduced in 1997 for Inventory Pool B and in 1996 for Inventory Pool C.

Last-In, First-Out Method—Dollar Value

Even the grouping of substantially identical items into quantity pools does not produce all the benefits desired from the use of the LIFO method. Technological changes sometimes introduce new products thus requiring the elimination of inventory in old pools, and requiring the establishment of new pools for the new product that does not qualify as being substantially identical to the old product. For example, the introduction of synthetic fabrics to replace cotton meant that "cotton" pools were eliminated and new "synthetic fabric" pools established. This change resulted in the loss of lower LIFO bases by companies changing the type of fabrics they used. To overcome this type of problem and to further simplify the clerical work involved, the **dollar-value LIFO inventory method** was developed.[7] Under this method, the unit of measurement is the dollar rather than the quantity of goods. All similar items, such as all raw materials for a given line of business, are grouped into a pool, and layers are determined based on total dollar changes. The dollar-value method has become the most widely used adaptation of the LIFO concept. In a survey of LIFO users, Reeve and Stanga found that 95% of the 206 companies responding to their survey used some version of the dollar-value method.[8]

General Procedures—Dollar-Value LIFO.

All goods in the inventory pool to which dollar-value LIFO is to be applied are viewed as though they are identical items. To determine if the dollar quantity of inventory has increased during the year, it is necessary to value the ending inventory in a pool at the base-year[9] prices and compare the total with that at the beginning of the year, also valued at base-year prices. If the end-of-year inventory at base-year prices exceeds the beginning-of-year inventory at base-year prices, a new LIFO layer is created. If there has been a decrease, the most recent LIFO layer (or layers) is reduced.

7. When new items are introduced, the dollar-value LIFO method does not give the same result as the specific-goods LIFO method. See D. R. Bainbridge, "Is Dollar-Value LIFO Consistent with Authoritative GAAP?" *Journal of Accounting, Auditing, and Finance* (Summer 1984), pp. 334-346, for a discussion as to why dollar-value LIFO may violate the historical cost principle and the concept of financial capital maintenance.

8. James M. Reeve and Keith G. Stanga. "The LIFO Pooling Decision: Some Empirical Results from Accounting Practice." *Accounting Horizons*, June 1987, p. 27.

9. Base-year prices are the prices in effect at the date the LIFO inventory method is adopted by a company. Thus, if a company adopted the LIFO inventory method in 1990, the base year for LIFO computations would be 1990.

The following four techniques are applied in practice to determine the ending inventory at base-year prices:

1. Double extension (100% of inventory)
2. Double extension index (sample of inventory)
3. Link-chain index (sample of inventory)
4. Externally published index

The income tax regulations specify that the preferred technique is **double extension.** This technique results in a direct computation of the ending inventory at base-year prices because it requires extending all items in the ending inventory at both the base-year and the end-of-year prices. Because the double extension technique is time-consuming when there are many inventory items, the IRS has permitted the use of an index approach to compute the ending inventory at base-year prices. The IRS has ruled that the preferred index is an internal one developed from a sample of items from the company inventory. Under certain conditions, the IRS has permitted the use of an externally published index.

In practice, most companies have adopted some form of an index method, therefore, the examples and discussion that follow are based on the use of indexes. Indexes are typically computed by comparing one year's inventory costs with another year's costs. To illustrate, assume a company has in its 1994 ending inventory 20 items at a cost of $1,000 each. If, at the end of 1995, those same 20 items would cost $1,200 each, then the index for 1995 would be computed as follows:

$$\text{Index} = \frac{\text{Inventory cost in 1995 dollars}}{\text{Inventory cost in 1994 dollars}} = \frac{\$24{,}000}{\$20{,}000} = 1.20$$

A further discussion of different types of indexes is included in the Appendix to this chapter.

Assume the index numbers and inventories at end-of-year prices for Ahlander Wholesale Co. are as follows:

Date	Year-End Price Index*	Inventory at End-of-Year Prices
December 31, 1993	1.00	$38,000
December 31, 1994	1.20	54,000
December 31, 1995	1.32	66,000
December 31, 1996	1.40	56,000
December 31, 1997	1.25	55,000

*Many published indexes appear as percentages without decimals, e.g., 100, 120, 132, 140, 125.

The effects of adding or deleting inventory layers in this situation can be most easily observed by preparing a work sheet that includes the following steps:

1. Determine the ending inventory in the pool at year-end prices.
2. Convert the ending inventory to base-year prices using the year-end price index.
3. Determine the inventory layers in base-year dollars.
4. Adjust the inventory to dollar-value LIFO layers by applying appropriate indexes to each base-year layer.

The work sheet on page 359 follows these steps and is based on the assumed data for Ahlander.

Date	Inventory at End-of-Year Prices		Year-End Price Index		Inventory at Base-Year Prices	Layers in Base-Year Prices		Incremental Layer Index		Dollar-Value LIFO Cost
December 31, 1993	$38,000	÷	1.00	=	$38,000	$38,000	×	1.00	=	$38,000
December 31, 1994	$54,000	÷	1.20	=	$45,000	$38,000	×	1.00	=	$38,000
						7,000	×	1.20	=	8,400
						$45,000				$46,400
December 31, 1995	$66,000	÷	1.32	=	$50,000	$38,000	×	1.00	=	$38,000
						7,000	×	1.20	=	8,400
						5,000	×	1.32	=	6,600
						$50,000				$53,000
December 31, 1996	$56,000	÷	1.40	=	$40,000	$38,000	×	1.00	=	$38,000
						2,000	×	1.20	=	2,400
						$40,000				$40,400
December 31, 1997	$55,000	÷	1.25	=	$44,000	$38,000	×	1.00	=	$38,000
						2,000	×	1.20	=	2,400
						4,000	×	1.25	=	5,000
						$44,000				$45,400

The following items should be observed in the example:

December 31, 1994—With an ending inventory of $45,000 in terms of base prices, the inventory has increased in 1994 by $7,000; however, the $7,000 increase is stated in terms of base-year prices and needs to be restated in terms of 1994 year-end prices which are 120% of the base level.

December 31, 1995—With an ending inventory of $50,000 in terms of base prices, the inventory has increased in 1995 by another $5,000; however, the $5,000 increase is stated in terms of base-year prices and needs to be restated in terms of 1995 year-end costs which are 132% of the base level.

December 31, 1996—When the ending inventory of $40,000 (expressed in base-year dollars) is compared to the beginning inventory of $50,000 (also expressed in base-year dollars), it is apparent that the inventory has been decreased by $10,000, in base-year terms. Under LIFO procedures, the decrease is assumed to take place in the most recently added layers, reducing or eliminating them. As a result, the 1995 layer, priced at $5,000 in base-year terms, is completely eliminated, and $5,000 of the $7,000 layer from 1994 is eliminated. This leaves only $2,000 of the 1994 layer, plus the base-year amount. The remaining $2,000 of the 1994 layer is multiplied by 1.20 to restate it to 1994 dollars, and is added to the base-year amount to arrive at the ending inventory amount of $40,400.

December 31, 1997—The ending inventory of $44,000 in terms of the base prices indicates an inventory increase for 1997 of $4,000; this increase requires restatement in terms of 1997 year-end prices which are 125% of the base level.

As discussed earlier, the Internal Revenue Service allows the incremental LIFO layer to be valued using FIFO, average, or LIFO costing. Thus the incremental index used to compute the new layer may be (1) a beginning-of-year index representing costs in the order of acquisition during the year (LIFO costing); (2) an average index, based on an average purchase price during the year (average costing); or (3) a year-end index, based on the latest acquisition price (FIFO costing).[10]

When FIFO costing is used to value the incremental layer, as in the previous example, the incremental index is the same as the year-end index used to determine if a new layer exists. However, if average or LIFO costing is used to compute the new layer, the incremental index will differ from the year-end index. To illustrate, using data from the preceding example, assume that LIFO costing is used to value incremental inventory layers. The beginning-of-year indexes, representing the earliest purchases in each year, are as follows:

Date	Price Index Beginning-of-Year Purchases
December 31, 1994	1.02
December 31, 1995	1.21
December 31, 1996	1.35
December 31, 1997	1.38

The computation of year-end inventories would then be made as follows:

Date	Inventory at End-of-Year Prices		Year-End Price Index		Inventory at Base-Year Prices	Layers in Base-Year Prices		Incremental Layer Index		Dollar-Value LIFO Cost
December 31, 1993	$38,000	÷	1.00	=	$38,000	$38,000	×	1.00	=	$38,000
December 31, 1994	$54,000	÷	1.20	=	$45,000	$38,000	×	1.00	=	$38,000
						7,000	×	1.02	=	7,140
						$45,000				$45,140
December 31, 1995	$66,000	÷	1.32	=	$50,000	$38,000	×	1.00	=	$38,000
						7,000	×	1.02	=	7,140
						5,000	×	1.21	=	6,050
						$50,000				$51,190
December 31, 1996	$56,000	÷	1.40	=	$40,000	$38,000	×	1.00	=	$38,000
						2,000	×	1.02	=	2,040
						$40,000				$40,040
December 31, 1997	$55,000	÷	1.25	=	$44,000	$38,000	×	1.00	=	$38,000
						2,000	×	1.02	=	2,040
						4,000	×	1.38	=	5,520
						$44,000				$45,560

In some cases, the index for the first year of the LIFO layers is not 1.00. This is especially true when an externally generated index is used. When this occurs, it is simpler to convert all inventories to a base of 1.00 rather than to use the index for the initial year of the LIFO layers. The computations are done in the same manner as in the previous example except the inventory is stated in terms of the base year of the index, not the first year of the inventory

10. The Task Force on LIFO Inventory Problems considered this issue from an accounting principles standpoint and unanimously agreed that "the order of acquisition approach (LIFO costing) generally is most compatible with the LIFO objective, but as a practical matter, any of the three pricing approaches consistently applied may be used for financial reporting purposes." *Issues Paper,* "Identification and Discussion of Certain Financial Accounting and Reporting Issues Concerning LIFO Inventories," (New York: American Institute of Certified Public Accountants, 1984), p. 9.

layers. To illustrate, assume the same facts as stated for the example on page 358 except that the base year of the external index is 1989; in 1993, the index is 1.20; and, in 1994, it is 1.44. The schedule showing the LIFO inventory computations would be modified as follows for the first two years. Note that the inventory cost is the same under either situation.

Date	Inventory at End-of-Year Prices		Year-End Price Index		Inventory at Base = 1.00 (1989 Prices)	Layers in Base = 1.00 (1989 Prices)		Incremental Layer Index		Dollar-Value LIFO Cost
December 31, 1993	$38,000	÷	1.20	=	$31,667	$31,667	×	1.20	=	$38,000
December 31, 1994	$54,000	÷	1.44	=	$37,500	$31,667	×	1.20	=	$38,000
						5,833	×	1.44	=	8,400
						$37,500				$46,400

Selection of Pools. The selection of inventory pools is critical in dollar-value LIFO. A company should have a minimum number of pools to benefit most from the use of the LIFO method. For manufacturers and processors, **natural business unit pools** are recommended. If it can be shown that a business has only one natural business unit, one pool may be used for all its inventory, including raw materials, goods in process, and finished goods. If, however, a business enterprise is composed of more than one natural business unit, more than one pool will be required. If the company maintains separate divisions for internal management purposes, has distinct production facilities and processes, or maintains separate income records for different units, more than one business unit pool is inferred. The Income Tax Regulations give the following example of a company with more than one natural business unit pool:

A corporation manufactures, in one division, automatic clothes washers and driers of both commercial and domestic grade as well as electric ranges, mangles, and dishwashers. The corporation manufactures, in another division, radios and television sets. The manufacturing facilities and processes used in manufacturing the radios and television sets are distinct from those used in manufacturing the automatic clothes washers, etc. Under these circumstances, the enterprise would consist of two business units and two pools would be appropriate, one consisting of all of the LIFO inventories entering into the manufacture of clothes washers and driers, electric ranges, mangles, and dishwashers and the other consisting of all of the LIFO inventories entering into the production of radios and television sets.[11]

A manufacturer or processor may choose to use **multiple pools** rather than include all inventory in natural business units. Each pool should consist of inventory items that are substantially similar, including raw materials.

Pools for wholesalers, retailers, etc., are usually defined by major lines, types, or classes of goods. The departments of a retail store are examples of separate pools for these entities. The number and propriety of inventory pools are reviewed periodically by the IRS, and continued use of established pools is subject to the results of the evaluation.

Although it is not necessary for companies to use the same pools for tax and accounting purposes, Reeve and Stanga found that most companies do, even when the IRS regulations require more pools than might be necessary for accounting purposes.[12] In some cases, companies have increased the number of pools to increase income. For example, in 1982 Stauffer Chemical Co. increased its number of LIFO pools for accounting purposes from 8 to 280. In

11. *Treasury Regulations,* Sec. 1.472.8(b) (2) (ii).

12. For additional insight into how the selection of pools can be used for tax planning and income determination, see Reeve and Stanga, *op. cit.,* pp. 25-33, and Crom, William R. & Randall B. Hayes. "The Dollar-Value LIFO Pooling Decision: The Conventional Wisdom is Too General." *Accounting Horizons,* December 1989, pp. 57-64.

general, the fewer the pools, the lower the ending inventory due to the ability to retain older costs in inventory layers through substitution of decreased inventory for one product with an increase in another. As the number of pools increases, more dipping into layers occurs with a resulting increase in income. In Stauffer's case, the increase in pools resulted in an increase of $16,515,000 in net income, or 13% of earnings.[13] The SEC objected to the change and, in 1984, required Stauffer to restate its financial statements using fewer pools.

The Economic Recovery Tax Act of 1981, and later the Tax Reform Act of 1986, simplified the selection and use of pools for smaller businesses. Any business with average gross receipts not in excess of $5 million for the three most recent taxable years may group their pools in accordance with the 11 general categories of the Consumer Price Index (CPI) or the 15 general categories of the Producer Price Indexes. The company may then use the published index for the category into which its goods are classified to determine its LIFO inventory values.

COMPARISON OF COST ALLOCATION METHODS

In using first-in, first-out, inventories are reported on the balance sheet at or near current costs. With last-in, first-out, inventories not changing significantly in quantity are reported at more or less fixed amounts relating back to the earliest purchases. Use of the average method generally provides inventory values closely paralleling first-in, first-out values, since purchases during a period are normally several times the opening inventory balance and average costs are thus heavily influenced by current costs. Specific identification can produce any variety of results depending on the desires of management. When the prices paid for merchandise do not fluctuate significantly, alternative inventory methods may provide only minor differences on the financial statements. However, in periods of steadily rising or falling prices, the alternative methods may produce material differences.

Differences in inventory valuations on the balance sheet are accompanied by differences in earnings on the income statement for the period. Use of first-in, first-out in a period of rising prices matches oldest low-cost inventory with rising sales prices, thus expanding the gross profit margin. In a period of declining prices, oldest high-cost inventory is matched with declining sales prices, thus narrowing the gross profit margin. Using an average method, the gross profit margin tends to follow a similar pattern in response to changing prices. On the other hand, use of last-in, first-out in a period of rising prices relates current high costs of acquiring goods with rising sales prices. Thus LIFO tends to have a stabilizing effect on gross profit margins.

The application of the different methods, excluding specific identification, in periods of rising and falling prices is illustrated in the following example. Assume that the Wisconsin Sales Co. sells its goods at 50% over prevailing costs from 1994 to 1997. The company sells its inventories and terminates activities at the end of 1997. Sales, costs, and gross profits using each of the three methods are shown in the tabulation on page 363.

Although the different methods give the same total gross profit on sales for the four-year period, use of first-in, first-out resulted in increased gross profit percentages in periods of rising prices and a contraction of gross profit percentages in periods of falling prices, while last-in, first-out resulted in relatively steady gross profit percentages in spite of fluctuating prices. The weighted average method offered results closely comparable to those obtained by first-in, first-out. Assuming operating expenses at 30% of sales, use of last-in, first-out would result in a net income for each of the four years; first-in, first-out would result in larger net incomes in 1994 and 1995, but net losses in 1996 and 1997. Inventory valuation on the last-in, first-out basis tends to smooth the peaks and fill the troughs of business fluctuations.

13. Stauffer Chemical Company, *1982 annual report*.

	FIFO			Weighted Average*			LIFO		
1994:									
Sales, 500 units @ $9			$4,500			$4,500			$4,500
Inventory, 200 units	@ $5	$1,000		200 @ $5	$1,000		200 @ $5	$1,000	
Purchases, 500 units	@ $6	3,000		500 @ $6	3,000		500 @ $6	3,000	
Goods available for sale		$4,000			$4,000			$4,000	
				200 @ $5.71					
1994:									
Ending Inv., 200 units	@ $6	1,200		($4,000 ÷ 700)	1,142		200 @ $5	1,000	
Cost of goods sold			2,800			2,858			3,000
Gross profit on sales			$1,700			$1,642			$1,500
1995:									
Sales, 450 units @ $12			$5,400			$5,400			$5,400
Inventory, 200 units	@ $6	$1,200		200 @ $5.71	$1,142		200 @ $5	$1,000	
Purchases, 500 units	@ $8	4,000		500 @ $8	4,000		500 @ $8	4,000	
Goods available for sale		$5,200			$5,142			$5,000	
Ending Inv., 250 units	@ $8	2,000		250 @ $7.35 ($5,142 ÷ 700)	1,838		200 @ $5 50 @ $8	1,400	
Cost of goods sold			3,200			3,304			3,600
Gross profit on sales			$2,200			$2,096			$1,800
1996:									
Sales, 475 units @ $10.50			$4,988			$4,988			$4,988
Inventory, 250 units	@ $8	$2,000		250 @ $7.35	$1,838		200 @ $5 50 @ $8	$1,400	
Purchases, 450 units	@ $7	3,150		450 @ $7	3,150		450 @ $7	3,150	
Goods available for sale		$5,150			$4,988			$4,550	
Ending Inv., 225 units	@ $7	1,575		225 @ $7.13 ($4,988 ÷ 700)	1,604		200 @ $5 25 @ $8	1,200	
Cost of goods sold			3,575			3,384			3,350
Gross profit on sales			$1,413			$1,604			$1,638
1997:									
Sales, 625 units @ $7.50			$4,688			$4,688			$4,688
Inventory, 225 units	@ $7	$1,575		225 @ $7.13	$1,604		200 @ $5 25 @ $8	$1,200	
Purchases, 400 units	@ $5	2,000		400 @ $5	2,000		400 @ $5	2,000	
Cost of goods sold			3,575			3,604			3,200
Gross profit on sales			$1,113			$1,084			$1,488

*Totals in the illustration are calculated to the nearest dollar.

The foregoing transactions are summarized in the table below.

		FIFO			Weighted Average			LIFO		
Year	*Sales*	*Cost of Goods Sold*	*Gross Profit on Sales*	*Gross Profit % to Sales*	*Cost of Goods Sold*	*Gross Profit on Sales*	*Gross Profit % to Sales*	*Cost of Goods Sold*	*Gross Profit on Sales*	*Gross Profit % to Sales*
1994	$ 4,500	$ 2,800	$1,700	37.8%	$ 2,858	$1,642	36.5%	$ 3,000	$1,500	33.3%
1995	5,400	3,200	2,200	40.7	3,304	2,096	38.8	3,600	1,800	33.3
1996	4,988	3,575	1,413	28.3	3,384	1,604	32.2	3,350	1,638	32.8
1997	4,688	3,575	1,113	23.7	3,604	1,084	23.1	3,200	1,488	31.7
	$19,576	$13,150	$6,426	32.8%	$13,150	$6,426	32.8%	$13,150	$6,426	32.8%

Income Tax Considerations

The preceding comparison of cost methods was made without considering the income tax impact of the method used. As indicated earlier, if a company elects to use LIFO for tax purposes, it must also use some form of LIFO in its financial reports. In a period of inflation, the lower reported profit using LIFO results in lower income taxes. Thus the tax liability on gross profit, assuming a 35% tax rate, for the three illustrated methods over the four-year period would be as follows:

Tax Liability

	FIFO	*Weighted Average*	*LIFO*
1994	$ 595	$ 575	$ 525
1995	770	734	630
1996	494	561	573
1997	390	379	521
Totals	$2,249	$2,249	$2,249

In this example, a complete cycle of price increases and decreases occurred over the four-year period; thus the total income tax liability for the four years was the same under each method. However, by using LIFO to defer part of the tax during 1994 and 1995, more cash was available to the company for operating purposes. In periods of constantly increasing inflation, the deferral tends to become permanent and is a condition sought by many companies. Whenever inflation starts to accelerate in the United States, many companies begin to report larger net incomes primarily caused by the illusory influence of holding gains. To protect their cash flows, a significant number of companies change to LIFO inventory to reduce their present and future tax liabilities. These changes have to be approved by the Internal Revenue Service and are subject to specific rules governing adoption of the LIFO method. The complexity of some of these rules has deterred other companies from making the change even though the tax consequences promised to be favorable.[14]

When a company changes its method of valuing inventory, the change is accounted for as a change in accounting principle. If the change is to average cost or FIFO, both the beginning and ending inventories can usually be computed on the new basis. Thus the effect of changing inventory methods can be determined and reported in the financial statements as explained in a later chapter. If the change is *to* LIFO from another method, however, a company's records are generally not complete enough to reconstruct the prior years' inventory layers. Therefore, the base-year layer for the new LIFO inventory is the opening inventory for the year in which LIFO is adopted (also the ending inventory for the year *before* LIFO is adopted). There is no adjustment to the financial statements to reflect the change to LIFO. However, the impact of the change on income for the current year must be disclosed in a note to the statements. In addition, the note should explain why there is no effect on the financial statements. Required disclosures for a change to LIFO are illustrated in the following note from the 1991 annual report of Sun Company, Inc.

14. A survey in 1980 of 213 companies who were not using LIFO indicated many different reasons for their decision. Principal among them were (1) the company had no tax libility, (2) prices were declining in their industry, and (3) the change to LIFO would have an immaterial impact because of rapid inventory turnover. Micheal H. Granof and Daniel G. Short. "Why Do Companies Reject Lifo?" *Journal of Accounting, Auditing, and Finance* (Summer 1984), pp. 323-333.

Exhibit 9—2
Sun Company, Inc—Disclosure of Change to LIFO Method

Effective January 1, 1991, Sun changed its method of accounting for the cost of crude oil and refined product inventories at Suncor from the FIFO method to the LIFO method. Sun believes that the use of the LIFO method better matches current costs with current revenues. The cumulative effect of this accounting change for years prior to 1991 is not determinable, nor are the pro forma effects of retroactive application of the LIFO method to prior years. This change decreased the 1991 net loss and net loss per share of common stock by $3 million and $.03, respectively.

EVALUATION OF LIFO AS A COST ALLOCATION METHOD

Because so many companies have resorted to LIFO as a means of reducing reported income and, consequently, their income tax liability, it is important to identify the advantages and disadvantages of this unique inventory method. It should be noted once again that LIFO is a historical cost allocation method; it assigns the most recent historical cost to expense (cost of goods sold) and the oldest relevant historical cost to inventory. Its ability to match recent historical cost, which approximates current cost, to revenue depends upon the rate of price change, inventory turnover, and frequency of purchase. Because LIFO allocates only historical cost between the balance sheet and income statement, it cannot adjust for changes in the general price level and in specific prices since the acquisition date.

Major Advantages of LIFO

The advantages of LIFO may be summarized as follows:

Tax Benefits. Temporary or permanent deferrals of income taxes can be achieved with LIFO, resulting in current cash savings. These deferrals continue as long as the price level is increasing and inventory quantities do not decline. The improved cash flow enables a company to either decrease its borrowing and reduce interest cost, or invest the savings to produce revenue.

Better Measurement of Income. Because LIFO allocates the most recently incurred costs to cost of sales, this method produces an income figure that tends to report only the operating income and defers recognition of the holding gain until prices or quantities decline. The illusory inflation profits discussed earlier tend not to appear as part of net income when LIFO inventory is used.

Major Disadvantages of LIFO

The disadvantages of LIFO are more subtle than the advantages. Companies adopting LIFO sometimes realize too late that LIFO can produce some severe side effects.

Reduced Income. The application of the most recent prices against current revenue produces a decrease in net income in an inflationary period. If management's goal is to maximize reported income, the adoption of LIFO will produce results that are in opposition to that goal.

Investors and other users of financial statements frequently base their evaluations of a company's performance on the "bottom line" or net income. Failure on the part of users to recognize that a lower net income is due to the use of LIFO rather than a decline in operating proficiency may have a depressing effect on the market price of a company's stock. The reduced income may be perceived as a failure on the part of management. Further, the use of LIFO will reduce employee bonus payments that are based on net income and could reduce the amount of dividends distributed to shareholders.

Unrealistic Inventory Balances on the Balance Sheet. The allocation of older inventory costs to the balance sheet can cause a serious understatement of inventory values. Depending on the length of time the LIFO layers have been developing and the severity of the price increase, the reported inventory values can be substantially lower than current replacement values. For example, General Motors provided the following disclosure in the notes to their 1991 financial statements.

Exhibit 9—3
General Motors Corporation — Disclosure of Inventory Valuation

Inventories are stated generally at cost, which is not in excess of market. The cost of substantially all domestic inventories other than the inventories of GM Hughes Electronics Corporation (GMHE) is determined by the last-in, first-out (LIFO) method. If the first-in, first-out (FIFO) method of inventory valuation had been used for inventories valued at LIFO cost, such inventories would have been $2,862.7 million higher at December 31, 1991 and $2,598.8 million higher at December 31, 1990.

General Motors reported LIFO inventories of $10,066,000,000 on December 31, 1991. Thus, valuing their inventory using FIFO would have increased the inventory account by approximately 28%.

Because inventory costs enter into the determination of working capital, the current ratio can be seriously distorted under a LIFO inventory system. Although this discussion of LIFO assumes an inflationary economy, if prices were to decrease, LIFO would produce inventory values higher than current replacement costs. It is fair to assume that should this occur, there would be strong pressure for special action to permit the write-down of inventory balances to replacement cost.

Unanticipated Profits Created by Failing to Maintain Inventory Quantities. The income advantages summarized previously will be realized only if inventory quantity levels are maintained. If the ending inventory quantities decline, the old layers of cost eliminated are charged against current revenue. If the inventory costs of these layers are significantly less than the current replacement costs, the reported profit will be artificially increased by the failure to maintain inventory levels.

To avoid the distortion caused by a temporary reduction of LIFO layers at the end of a year, some accountants advocate establishing a replacement allowance that charges the current period for the extra replacement cost expected to be incurred in the subsequent period when the inventory is replenished. However, the use of an allowance for temporary liquidation of LIFO layers, sometimes referred to as the **base-stock method,** is not currently acceptable for financial reporting or tax purposes. The use of this type of allowance on the books could disqualify a company from filing its tax returns on the LIFO basis, and therefore, it is seldom used in practice.

Unrealistic Flow Assumptions The cost assignment resulting from the application of LIFO does not normally approximate the physical movement of goods through the business. One would seldom encounter in practice the actual use or transfer of goods on a last-in, first-out basis.

SELECTION OF AN INVENTORY METHOD

As indicated in this chapter, companies have many alternative ways to value inventories. Guidelines for the selection of a proper method are very broad, and a company may justify almost any accepted method. After a lengthy study of inventory practices, Horace Barden, retired partner of Ernst and Whinney, concluded his research study by stating:

. . . one must recognize that no neat package of principles or other criteria exists to substitute for the professional judgment of the responsible accountant. The need for the exercise of judgment in accounting for inventories is so great that I recommend to authoritative bodies that they refrain from establishing rules that, in isolation from the conditions and circumstances that may exist in practice, attempt to determine the accounting treatment to be applied under any and all circumstances.[15]

Many companies use more than one inventory costing method. For example, The Quaker Oats Company uses three different methods and includes the following disclosure in its financial statements:

Exhibit 9—4
The Quaker Oats Company—Disclosure of Inventory Methods

Inventories. Inventories are valued at the lower of cost or market, using various cost methods, and include the cost of raw materials, labor and overhead. The percentage of fiscal year-end inventories valued using each of the methods is as follows:

	1992	1991	1990
Last-in, first-out (LIFO)	57%	61%	62%
Average quarterly cost	31%	27%	27%
First-in, first-out (FIFO)	12%	12%	11%

The decision as to which method to use depends on not only the tax consequences but also the nature of the inventories themselves. For inventories other than those valued using LIFO, a company may use a different method for tax purposes than it uses for financial reporting purposes. This creates a temporary difference with respect to cost of goods sold and the resulting net income, which leads to a need for interperiod income tax allocation.

Companies sometimes change their inventory methods, especially as economic conditions change. For instance, several research studies have shown that the stock market reacts favorably to companies that elect to adopt the LIFO method.[16] When inventories are a material item, a change in the inventory method by a company may impair comparability of that company's financial statements with prior years' statements and with the financial statements of other entities. Such changes require careful consideration and should be made only when management can clearly demonstrate the preferability of the alternative method. This position was emphasized by the Accounting Principles Board in Opinion No. 20 with the statement, "The burden of justifying other changes rests with the entity proposing the change."[17] If a change is made, complete disclosure of the impact of the change is encouraged by the FASB.

USING INVENTORY INFORMATION FOR FINANCIAL ANALYSIS

The inventory balances contained in the financial statements are often used to measure how efficiently the company is utilizing its inventory. The amount of inventory carried frequently relates closely to sales volume. The inventory position and the appropriateness of its size may be evaluated by computing the **inventory turnover.** The inventory turnover is measured by dividing cost of goods sold by average inventory.

15. Horace G. Barden. *Accounting Research Study No. 13*, "The Accounting Basis of Inventories" (New York: American Institute of Certified Public Accountants, 1973), p. 141.

16. For an example, see Francis L. Stevenson. "New Evidence on LIFO Adoption: The Effects of More Precise Event Dates." *Journal of Accounting Research*, Autumn 1987, pp. 306-316.

17. *Opinions of the Accounting Principles Board, No. 20*, "Accounting Changes" (New York: American Institute of Certified Public Accountants, 1971), par. 16.

Consider the financial information relating to inventories for General Motors provided in Exhibit 9—5.

Exhibit 9—5
General Motors Corporation — Inventory Disclosure

Major Classes of Inventories (Dollars in Millions)	**1991**	**1990**	**1989**
Productive material, work in process, and supplies	$ 4,854.1	$ 4,098.0	$3,816.9
Finished product, service parts, etc.	5,211.9	5,233.3	4,174.8
Total	$10,066.0	$ 9,331.3	$7,991.7
Cost of goods sold	$97,550.7	$96,155.7	

Inventory turnover rates for General Motors would be computed as follows:

	1991	**1990**
Cost of Goods Sold / Average Inventory*	$97,550.7 / $ 9,698.65 = 10.06 times	$96,155.7 / $ 8,661.5 = 11.10 times

*Average inventory [(beginning balance + ending balance) / 2]
1991: ($9,331.3 + $10,066.0) / 2 = $9,698.65
1990: ($7,991.7 + $9,331.3) / 2 = $8,661.5

This example has been simplified using total inventory. If separate turnovers were computed for raw materials, work in process, and finished goods, different denominators would be needed for each computation. Care must be exercised when using inventory turnover information for comparison purposes. For example, had General Motors used FIFO instead of LIFO (as disclosed in the note in Exhibit 9-3), inventory turnover for 1991 would have been 7.67 computed as follows:

$$\frac{\text{Cost of goods sold}}{\text{Average inventory}} \quad \frac{\$97{,}550.7}{\dfrac{(\$9{,}331.3 + \$2{,}598.8) + (\$10{,}066.0 + \$2{,}862.7)}{2}} = 7.85 \text{ times}$$

If, for example, Ford Motor were to use FIFO and General Motors were to use LIFO, an adjustment to the inventory figure would be necessary before any useful comparisons between the two companies could be made.

Average inventories are sometimes expressed as number of days' sales in inventories. Information is thus afforded concerning the average time it takes to turn over the inventory. The number of days' sales in inventory is calculated by dividing average inventory by average daily cost of goods sold. The number of days' sales in inventory also can be obtained by dividing the number of days in the year by the inventory turnover rate. The latter procedure for General Motors is illustrated below:

	1991	**1990**
Inventory turnover for year	10.06 times	11.10 times
Number of days' sales in average inventory (365 / inventory turnover)	36.3 days	32.9 days

With an increased inventory turnover, the investment necessary for a given volume of business is smaller, and consequently the return on invested capital is higher. This conclusion assumes an enterprise can acquire goods in smaller quantities sufficiently often at no price disadvantage. If merchandise must be bought in very large quantities to get favorable prices, then the savings on quantity purchases must be weighed against the additional investment, increased costs of storage, and other carrying charges.

Inventory investments and turnover rates vary among businesses, and each business must be judged in terms of its financial structure and operations. Management must establish an inventory policy that avoids the extremes of a dangerously low stock, which may impair sales, and an overstocking of goods, which involves a heavy capital investment along with risks of spoilage and obsolescence, price declines, and difficulties in meeting purchase obligations. The following table lists the average number of days' sales in inventory for several industries:[18]

Industry (Number of firms included)	Average Number of Days' Sales in Inventory
Dairy (303)	103.0
Blast Furnace and Steel Mills (550)	48.5
Grocery Stores (2,183)	26.8
Jewelry Stores (2,319)	259.8

18. "Industry Norms and Key Business Ratios," Dun and Bradstreet, Inc., 1990.

APPENDIX

Determination of Price Indexes

The chapter illustrated the use of an index method to compute the ending inventory at base-year prices. There are two common approaches for determining price indexes for a particular inventory: (1) developing a specific internal index from the company's inventory records; or (2) using a published external index relating to the inventory.

Internal Indexes. A widely used technique for developing internal indexes for dollar-value LIFO is double extension. A **double extension index** is computed by extending a representative sample of a specific ending inventory pool at both base-year and year-end prices. An index can then be computed applying the following formula:

$$\text{Double extension index} = \frac{\text{Inventory extended at year-end prices}}{\text{Inventory extended at base-year prices}}$$

To illustrate, assume an inventory pool contained seven items. The following sample of four items was drawn to compute a double extension index.

Item	Ending Quantity	Year-End Price	Base-Year Price	Extended Year-End	Extended Base-Year
A	200	$ 50	$30	$10,000	$ 6,000
B	500	70	40	35,000	20,000
C	150	30	25	4,500	3,750
D	200	100	60	20,000	12,000
			Total	$69,500	$41,750

$$\text{Double extension index} = \frac{\$69{,}500}{\$41{,}750} = 1.66$$

The Internal Revenue Service has stated that a nonstatistical sample must include at least 50% of the items and represent 70% or more of the dollar value. Fewer items are necessary if a carefully constructed random sample is used.

The double extension index has two principal disadvantages: (1) it is time-consuming and costly for companies having a large number of different inventory items; and (2) if new inventory items are being added, it may be difficult to determine base-year prices for them. This latter disadvantage is overcome with the **link-chain index.** This modification of the double extension index requires extending a statistically representative portion of the ending inventory at year-end prices and at beginning-of-year, rather than base-year, prices. The index computed from this valuation is then multiplied by a cumulative index carried forward from previous years to determine the current index.

Using the inventory data above, assume that the cumulative link-chain index at the beginning of the current year was 1.51. The following illustrates the computation of the yearly index, i.e., the new "link," and a new cumulative index to use for dollar-value LIFO purposes.

Item	Ending Quantity	Year-End Price	Beginning-of-Year Price	Extended Year-End	Extended Beginning-of-Year
A	200	$ 50	$46	$10,000	$ 9,200
B	500	70	65	35,000	32,500
C	150	30	30	4,500	4,500
D	200	100	85	20,000	17,000
			Total	$69,500	$63,200

$$\text{Yearly index} = \frac{\$69{,}500}{\$63{,}200} = 1.10 \text{ (new link)}$$

$$\text{Link-chain index} = 1.51 \times 1.10 = 1.66$$

This approach has the advantage of simplicity because historical records of base-year costs are not necessary. It permits adding new inventory items without causing difficulty in computing base-year prices for the new items. A company may change from the double extension index method to the link-chain index if it has had at least a 90% turnover of inventory items in the preceding five-year period.

External Indexes. Although many price-level indexes are published by governmental and private agencies, only the Bureau of Labor Statistics' (BLS) department store indexes were automatically acceptable for income tax purposes until the Economic Recovery Tax Act of 1981 was passed. This Act directed the IRS to prescribe regulations providing for an expansion of external indexes for use by LIFO companies. As a result, regulations were issued permitting small businesses with annual sales of $5 million or less to use either monthly consumer price indexes (CPIs) or monthly producer price indexes (PPIs).[19] Companies that do not qualify as small businesses may use these same indexes, but they may only incorporate in their inventory calculations 80 percent of the reported change in the index being used. A separate index must be used for each inventory item that comprises more than 10 percent of the total inventory value. However, aggregation is permitted of each item comprising less than 10 percent of the total inventory value.

The BLS department store indexes that are still acceptable for retail department stores are divided into twenty groups, and each group becomes a separate dollar-value pool.

The increased number of external indexes available was intended to make the LIFO method more feasible for smaller companies by reducing the cost of implementation required if an internal index must be developed. For this reason, the use of the additional external indexes is referred to as "simplified LIFO." The IRS has decided that adoption of these external indexes in place of internal indexes is a change in accounting method. Except for limited situations, companies making the change must obtain prior approval from the Commissioner of Internal Revenue.

The AICPA Task Force on LIFO Inventory considered the use of external indexes and recommended that the IRS regulations concerning their use be accepted for financial reporting except for the limitation on companies that do not qualify as small businesses and thus can incorporate only 80 percent of the index change in the inventory. By a vote of 5 to 3, the Task Force did not accept the limitation on the use of the external index for reporting purposes.[20]

19. *IRS Income Tax Regulations*, Section 1.472-8(e)(3).

20. Issues Paper, Task Force on LIFO Inventory, Accounting Standards Division, AICPA, "The Acceptability of 'Simplified LIFO' for Financial Reporting Purposes" (New York: American Institute of Certified Public Accountants, 1982), p. 9.

KEY TERMS

QUESTIONS

1. What economic conditions make the allocation of inventory costs most difficult?
2. (a) What are the three cost elements entering into goods in process and finished goods? (b) What items enter into factory overhead?
3. Distinguish between raw materials and factory supplies. Why are the terms "direct" and "indirect materials" often used to refer to raw materials and factory supplies, respectively?
4. Would you expect to find a perpetual or a periodic inventory system used in each of the following situations?
   (a) Diamond ring department of a jewelry store.
   (b) Computer department of a college bookstore.
   (c) Candy department of a college bookstore.
   (d) Automobile dealership—new car department.
   (e) Automobile dealership—parts department.
   (f) Wholesale dealer of small tools.
   (g) A plumbing supply house—brass fittings department.
5. Under what conditions is merchandise-in-transit legally reported as inventory by the (a) seller? (b) buyer?
6. How should the following items be treated in computing year-end inventory costs: (a) segregated goods? (b) conditional sales?
7. State how you would report each of the following items on the financial statements:
   (a) Manufacturing supplies.
   (b) Goods on hand received on a consignment basis.
   (c) Goods received without an accompanying invoice.
   (d) Goods in stock to be delivered to customers in subsequent periods.
   (e) Goods in hands of agents and consignees.
   (f) Deposits with vendors for merchandise to be delivered next period.
   (g) Goods in hands of customers on approval.
   (h) Defective goods requiring reprocessing.
8. (a) What are the two methods of accounting for cash discounts? (b) Which method is generally preferred? Why?
9. Theoretically, there is little wrong with inventory costing by the specific cost identification method. What objections can be raised to the use of this method?
10. Would you expect to find the specific identification method or some other historical cost flow assumption, such as average cost or LIFO, used for the items noted in Question 4?
11. What advantages are there to using the average cost method of inventory pricing?
12. The Wallace Co. decides to adopt specific goods LIFO as of January 1, 1996, and determines the cost of the different kinds of merchandise carried as of this date. (a) What three different methods may be employed at the end of a period in assigning costs to quantity increases in specific pools? (b) What procedure is employed at the end of each period for quantity decreases of specific items?
13. (a) What is the LIFO conformity rule? (b) How has the rule changed since it was first adopted? (c) How might the changes in the conformity rule affect LIFO inventories reported on the financial statements?
14. Assume a car manufacturer and a discounting retail firm have identical sales and income and that price changes affecting the various factors of production increase at the same rate. The car manufacturer has an inventory turnover rate of 2 times a year and the discounting firm an inventory turnover of 15 times per year. Assume that each firm wants to match a historical cost that approximates current cost against revenue. Which firm will benefit more by changing from FIFO to LIFO?
15. Assume there is no change in the physical quantity of inventory for the current accounting period. During a period of rising prices, which historical cost flow (LIFO or FIFO) will result in the greater dollar value of ending inventory and the greater dollar value of cost of goods sold? Will the beginning and ending inventory value under LIFO and FIFO be equal? Why or why not?
16. What are the major advantages of dollar-value LIFO over specific goods LIFO?

17. Indexes are used for two different purposes in computing the layers of a dollar-value LIFO pool. Clearly distinguish between these uses and describe how the indexes are applied.
18. The selection of inventory pools is very important in using the dollar-value LIFO method of inventory costing. What factors should be considered in identifying the pools for a specific company?
19. Discuss the advantages and disadvantages of LIFO as a cost allocation method.
*20. Identify the three different types of indexes that can be used in applying dollar-value LIFO. What are the advantages and disadvantages of each?

*Relates to Appendix

DISCUSSION CASES

Case 9—1 (Should we adopt LIFO?)

You are the controller of the Ford Steel Co. Assume the economy enters a period of rapidly increasing inflation. The turnover of inventory in your company occurs about once every nine months. The inflation is causing revenue to rise more rapidly than the historical cost of the goods sold. Although profits are higher this year than last, you realize that the cost to replace the sold inventory is also higher. You are aware that many companies are changing to the LIFO inventory method, but you are concerned that what goes up will eventually come down, and when prices decline, the LIFO method will result in high profits and taxes. Since declining prices are usually equated with economic recession, it is likely that the higher taxes will have to be paid at a time when revenues are declining.

What factors should you consider before making a change to LIFO? Based on the above considerations, what would you recommend?

Case 9—2 (What is an inventoriable cost?)

You have been hired by Midwestern Products Co. to work in its accounting department. As part of your assignment, you have been asked to review the inventory costing procedures. In the past, the company has attempted to keep its inventory as low as possible to hedge against future declines in demand. One way of doing this has been to charge off as many costs as can be justified as expenses of the current period. Sales have declined, however, and the controller wants to include as high an ending inventory valuation as possible to show the stockholders a better income figure for the current year. Your study shows the following costs have been consistently treated as period costs for financial reporting purposes:

Depreciation of plant
Fringe payroll benefits for factory personnel
Repairs of equipment
Salaries of foremen
Warehouse rental for storage of finished products
Pension costs for factory personnel
Training program—all employees
Cafeteria costs—all employees
Interest expense
Depreciation and maintenance of fleet of delivery trucks

Which items do you suggest could be deferred by including them as inventoriable costs? Evaluate the wisdom and propriety of making the suggested changes.

Case 9—3 (Which method shall we use?)

The White Wove Corporation began operations in 1996. A summary of the first quarter appears below.

	Purchases	
	Units	*Total Cost*
January 2	250	$23,250
February 11	100	9,500
February 20	400	38,400
March 21	200	19,600
March 27	225	22,275

	Other Data		
	Sales in Units	*Sales Price Per Unit*	*Operating Expenses*
January	200	$140	$9,575
February	225	142	7,820
March	350	145	7,905

The White Wove Corporation used the LIFO perpetual inventory method and computed an inventory value of $38,300 at the end of the first quarter. Management is considering changing to a FIFO costing method. They have also considered using a periodic system instead of the perpetual system presently being used. You have been hired to assist management in making the decision. What would you advise?

Case 9—4 ("Just in time" may not be for us!)

One management technique to improve efficiency in operations is to adopt a "just in time" (JIT) inventory method. This approach reduces inventory carrying costs by having arrangements with suppliers to deliver inventory just as it is needed for production or sale. As financial officer of Duo-Therm, you are excited with the carrying cost savings JIT offers, but because Duo-Therm uses the LIFO inventory method, you are concerned about losing LIFO layers through reduced inventory levels. What will be the impact on Duo-Therm's income statement of adopting the JIT inventory concept? Why would you be concerned about these results if you were Duo-Therm's financial officer?

Case 9—5 (Should we switch to dollar-value LIFO?)

The Innovative Production Co. has used the LIFO method of valuing its inventories for several years. Layers for some of the inventory items are valued at amounts 1/3 to 1/2 of the current market price. The products manufactured and marketed by the company are subject to rapid technological obsolescence, and the company is continually developing new products and phasing out old ones. As items are discontinued, the company finds its income and taxes increasing as old costs are matched against current revenues. However, since new products must be produced at higher costs, it has been difficult to maintain a positive cash flow for the company. The president of Innovative Production, having heard a competitor mention dollar-value LIFO, approaches you, the chief accountant, with the following questions: "Would this help us?" "What differences are there between our LIFO system and dollar-value LIFO?"

Case 9—6 (A new use for bricks)

In 1989 an investigation by the United States Department of Justice Criminal Division uncovered a massive fraud perpetrated by top management of Miniscribe Corporation. Miniscribe manufactured and sold computer disk drives. The investigation revealed such practices as shipping bricks in place of disk drives to boost sales and inventory figures. How would shipping bricks boost sales? If sales are inflated this year by selling bricks, what must happen next year to maintain the sales trend?

Case 9—7 (But we do have inventory, and it does have problems)

The Mountain-Top Realty Company has decided to develop the mountain area around Hitown and has purchased several plats of mountainside property. In addition, the company acts as a realtor for existing homes in the area. Greg Hatch has recently graduated from school with an accounting degree and has been hired to work as Mountain-Top's accountant. Greg's favorite topic in Intermediate Accounting was inventory, and he's disappointed that he works for a firm without any inventory and its related problems. Mark Bowman, sales manager, overhears Greg mentioning this to a friend at lunch. "But we do have inventory, Greg, and I think you might be surprised at how many accounting problems a realtor can have with the inventory." (1) What is the nature of Mountain-Top's inventory? (2) What problems do you think Mark was referring to? (3) What other types of companies have "different" kinds of inventory?

Case 9—8 (Should we accept the base-stock inventory method?)

John Marshall, an accounting student at Rider College, is writing a research paper on inventories. He discovers that Accounting Research Study No. 13 on inventories was issued in the 1970s by the Accounting Principles Board. As he scans the report, he is surprised to find an inventory method referred to as the "base-stock" method. He had not encountered this method in his intermediate accounting textbook. The research study identifies this method as one that defines a base quantity of inventory that is carried forward from year to year at its original cost. Deficiencies in quantity at year-end are considered temporary and replacement of the deficiency in the next period is permitted. The method was used in the late 1800s and in the first part of the twentieth century. When LIFO was accepted for income tax purposes, the base stock method was specifically disallowed for income tax use because LIFO was viewed as a substitute for base stock. Similarly, it was disallowed for financial statement purposes by the Committee on Accounting Procedures.

The author of the research study concludes the discussion of the base-stock method by recognizing its appropriateness to some industries and urging steps to remove the prohibitions against its use. Assume you are John Marshall and wish to include in your report a support of the base-stock method. Identify the principal positive arguments for recognizing the base-stock method as a legitimate cost flow assumption. What are its advantages over the LIFO method?

Case 9—9 (How well am I really doing?)

Fay Stocks sells oriental rugs. She uses the FIFO method of inventory costing and maintains perpetual inventory records. The inventory available for sale for a particular style of rug is as follows:

Invoice date	Current Inventory	Cost
June 14, 1996	4 @	$1,200 each
June 21, 1996	3 @	$1,500 each
July 5, 1996	6 @	$1,700 each

A wealthy customer purchases 3 rugs paying $2,600 for each. Fay immediately replaces those rugs with 3 new rugs at a cost of $1,900 apiece. What is Fay's gross margin from the sale of the rugs? What is Fay's net cash flow from the sale of the rugs and the subsequent purchase of 3 new rugs? Why is there a substantial difference between gross margin and cash flow? What circumstances lead to differences like those illustrated in this case?

Case 9—10 (Are inventory summaries enough?)

John Craston is presenting information to the audit committee relating to this year's annual financial statements. In discussing inventory, Mr. Craston argues, "There is no need to provide detail as to the components of inventory. A summary figure is all that investors and creditors require. Why should they care if inventory is in the form of raw materials, goods in process, or finished goods?" Information relating to inventory is as follows:

(in thousands)	1996	1995
Raw Materials	$162	$ 92
Goods in Process	60	65
Finished Goods.................	53	93
Total	$275	$250

As an owner of 10% of the company's stock, which type of disclosure would you prefer? Why? What information is contained in the detailed inventory figures that cannot be inferred from the summary inventory figure?

Case 9—11 (The war in the Gulf)

In August of 1990, Iraq invaded Kuwait. For gasoline distributors, this meant that the price they paid for oil in the future could increase dramatically. For consumers, the effect was more immediate. Within a week, gasoline prices had jumped by as much as 20 cents per gallon. The American public accused gasoline distributors of ripping off consumers by raising the price on gas that was purchased prior to the Gulf Crisis. Distributors countered by stating that it is replacement cost, not historical cost, that dictates selling price. Assuming FIFO costing of inventory, what would be the effect of an increased selling price on the income statement of a gasoline distributor? What would be the effect on the distributor's statement of cash flows as the firm replaced the inventory with more expensive petroleum products? Was the American public correct in claiming that gasoline distributors used the Gulf Crisis as an opportunity to increase profits?

Case 9—12 (The steel industry's LIFO problem)

In the early 1980s, the American steel industry was experiencing severe financial troubles. An increase in foreign competition as well as advancing technology combined to contribute to the decline of industry profits. The demand for domestic steel was down, and, as a result, many firms laid off workers. However, the use of the LIFO method of accounting for inventory distorted the actual financial position of many firms as illustrated by the following simple example:

USA Steel Co. has the following LIFO inventory layers on January 1, 1982:

Layer 1	6,000 tons @ $10 per ton
Layer 2	5,000 tons @ $15 per ton
Layer 3	8,000 tons @ $25 per ton

Assume steel is selling for $50 per ton in 1983 and it costs $35 per ton to produce. Because of a decrease in demand for domestic steel, USA Steel shuts down its production facilities and elects to sell the inventory that is on hand rather than produce additional inventory. If USA Steel Co. sells 15,000 tons of steel during 1983, what is the gross margin in this simplified example using LIFO? What is USA Steel's gross margin if the 15,000 tons of steel had been costed at the current cost of $35 per ton? Does the LIFO gross margin accurately depict the financial situation of USA Steel Co.? In order for the LIFO inventory method to accurately match current costs with current revenues, what sort of inventory policy must a company have regarding its LIFO layers?

EXERCISES

Exercise 9—13 (Computing cash expenditure for inventory)

Using the following data, compute the total cash expended for inventory in 1996:

Accounts payable:	
January 1, 1996	$200,000
December 31, 1996	240,000
Cost of goods sold—1996	900,000
Inventory balance:	
January 1, 1996	300,000
December 31, 1996	200,000

Exercise 9—14 (Passage of title)

The management of Kauer Company has engaged you to assist in the preparation of year-end (December 31) financial statements. You are told that on November 30, the correct inventory level was 150,000 units. During the month of December, sales totaled 50,000 units including 25,000 units shipped on consignment to Towsey Company. A letter received from Towsey indicates that as of December 31, it had sold 12,000 units and was still trying to sell the remainder. A review of the December purchase orders, to various suppliers, shows the following:

Date of Purchase Order	Invoice Date	Quantity in Units	Date Shipped	Date Received	Terms
12-2-96	1-3-97	10,000	1-2-97	1-3-97	FOB shipping point
12-11-96	1-3-97	8,000	12-22-96	12-24-96	FOB destination
12-13-96	1-2-97	13,000	12-28-96	1-2-97	FOB shipping point
12-23-96	12-26-96	12,000	1-2-97	1-3-97	FOB shipping point
12-28-96	1-10-97	10,000	12-31-96	1-5-97	FOB destination
12-31-96	1-10-97	15,000	1-3-97	1-6-97	FOB destination

Kauer Company uses the "passing of legal title" for inventory recognition. Compute the number of units that should be included in the year-end inventory.

Exercise 9—15 (Passage of title)

The Joliet Manufacturing Company reviewed its in-transit inventory and found the following items. Indicate which items should be included in the inventory balance at December 31, 1996. Give your reasons for the treatment you suggest.

(a) A packing case containing a product costing $816 was standing in the shipping room when the physical inventory was taken. It was not included in the inventory because it was marked "Hold for shipping instructions." The customer's order was dated December 18, but the case was shipped and the customer billed on January 10, 1997.

(b) Merchandise costing $625 was received on December 28, 1996, and the invoice was recorded. The invoice was in the hands of the purchasing agent; it was marked "On consignment."

(c) Merchandise received on January 6, 1997, costing $720 was entered in the purchase register on January 7. The invoice showed shipment was made FOB shipping point on December 31, 1996. Since it was not on hand during the inventory count, it was not included.

(d) A special machine, fabricated to order for a particular customer, was finished and in the shipping room on December 30. The customer was billed on that date and the machine was excluded from inventory although it was shipped January 4, 1997.

(e) Merchandise costing $2,350 was received on January 3, 1997, and the related purchase invoice was recorded January 5. The invoice showed the shipment was made on December 29, 1996, FOB destination.

Exercise 9—16 (Trade and cash discounts)

Olavssen Hardware regularly buys merchandise from Dawson Suppliers and is allowed a trade discount of 20/10/10 from the list price. Olavssen uses the net method to record purchases and discounts. On August 15, Olavssen Hardware purchased material from Dawson Suppliers. The invoice received from Dawson showed a list price of $7,000, and terms of 2/10, n/30. Payment was sent to Dawson Suppliers on August 28. Prepare entries to record the purchase and subsequent payment assuming a periodic inventory system. (Round to nearest dollar.)

Exercise 9—17 (Net and gross methods—entries)

On December 3, Hakan Photography purchased inventory listed at $8,600 from Mark Photo Supply. Terms of the purchase were 3/10, n/20. Hakan Photography also purchased inventory from Erickson Wholesale on December 10, for a list price of $7,500. Terms of the purchase were 3/10 eom. On December 16, Hakan paid both suppliers for these purchases. Hakan does not use a perpetual inventory system.

1. Give the entries to record the purchases and invoice payments assuming that (a) the net method is used, (b) the gross method is used.
2. Assume that Hakan has not paid either of the invoices at December 31. Give the year-end adjusting entry, if the net method is being used.

Exercise 9—18 (Cost of goods manufactured schedule)
The following quarterly cost data has been accumulated for Garrison Mfg. Inc.:

Raw Materials—Beginning Inventory (Jan. 1, 1996)................	100 units @ $ 6.00
Purchases	85 units @ $ 7.00
	110 units @ $ 7.50
Transferred 215 units to Goods in Process	
Goods in Process—Beginning Inventory (Jan. 1, 1996)...........	56 units @ $13.50
Direct Labor..	$2,500
Factory Overhead	$3,250
Goods in Process—Ending Inventory (Mar. 1, 1996)..............	68 units @ $13.75

Garrison uses the FIFO method for valuing raw materials inventories. Prepare a cost of goods manufactured schedule for Garrison Mfg. Inc. the quarter ended March 31, 1996.

Exercise 9—19 (Inventory computation using different cost flows)
The Webster Store shows the following information relating to one of its products.

Inventory, January 1	300 units @ $17.50
Sales, January 8	200 units
Purchases, January 10	900 units @ $18.00
Sales, January 18	800 units
Purchases, January 20	1,200 units @ $18.25
Sales, January 25	1,000 units

What are the values of ending inventory under (1) perpetual and (2) periodic methods assuming the cost flows below? (Round unit costs to three decimal places.)

(a) FIFO
(b) LIFO
(c) Average

Exercise 9—20 (Inventory computation using different cost flows)
Richmond Corporation had the following transactions relating to Product AB during September.

Date		Units	Unit Cost
September 1	Balance on hand	500 units	$5.00
6	Purchase	100 units	4.50
12	Sale	300 units	
13	Sale	200 units	
18	Purchase	200 units	6.00
20	Purchase	200 units	4.00
25	Sale	200 units	

Determine the ending inventory value under each of the following costing methods:

1. FIFO (perpetual)
2. FIFO (periodic)
3. LIFO (perpetual)
4. LIFO (periodic)

Exercise 9—21 (Comparison of inventory methods)

Spearman Truck Sales sells semitrailers. The current inventory includes the following five semitrailers (identical except for paint color) along with purchase dates and costs:

Semitrailer #	Purchase Date	Cost
1	April 4, 1996	$64,000
2	April 12, 1996	60,000
3	April 12, 1996	60,000
4	May 3, 1996	68,000
5	May 12, 1996	68,500

On May 20, 1996, a trucking firm purchases semitrailer #3 from Spearman for $75,000.

1. Compute the gross margin on this sale assuming Spearman uses:
   (a) FIFO inventory method.
   (b) LIFO inventory method.
   (c) Specific identification method.
2. Which inventory method do you think Spearman should use? Why?

Exercise 9—22 (LIFO inventory computation)

White Farm Supply's records for the first three months of its existence show purchases of Commodity Y2 as follows:

	Number of Units	Cost
August	5,500	$28,050
September	8,000	41,600
October	5,100	27,030

The inventory of Commodity Y2 at the end of October using FIFO is valued at $36,390.

1. Assuming that none of Commodity Y2 was sold during August and September, what value would be shown at the end of October if LIFO cost was assumed?
2. Prepare the journal entry to value the inventory at LIFO assuming a LIFO allowance account is used for the first time on October 31.

Exercise 9—23 (Inventory computation from incomplete records)

A flood recently destroyed many of the financial records of Riboldi Manufacturing Company. Management has hired you to recreate as much financial information as possible for the month of July. You are able to find out that the company uses a weighted average inventory costing system. You also learn that Riboldi makes a physical count at the end of each month in order to determine monthly ending inventory values. By examining various documents you are able to gather the following information:

Ending inventory at July 31	50,000 units
Total cost of units available for sale in July	$118,800
Cost of goods sold during July	$99,000
Cost of beginning inventory, July 1	$0.35 per unit
Gross margin on sales for July	$101,000

July Purchases

Date	*Units*	*Unit Cost*
July 4	60,000	$0.40
July 11	50,000	0.41
July 15	40,000	0.42
July 16	50,000	0.45

You are asked to provide the following information:

1. Number of units on hand, July 1.
2. Units sold during July.
3. Unit cost of inventory at July 31.
4. Value of inventory at July 31.

Exercise 9—24 **(Computation of beginning inventory)**

A note to the financial statements of Alpine Inc. at December 31, 1996, reads as follows:

Because of the manufacturer's production problems for our Widget Limited line, our inventories were unavoidably reduced. Under the LIFO inventory accounting method currently being used for tax and financial accounting purposes, the net effect of all the inventory changes was to increase pretax income by $1,200,000 over what it would have been had the inventory of Widget Limited been maintained at the normal physical levels on hand at the start of the year.

The unit purchase price of the merchandise was $20 per unit during the year. Alpine Inc. uses the periodic inventory system. Additional data concerning Alpine's inventory was as follows:

Date	Physical Count of Inventory	LIFO Cost of Inventory
January 1, 1996	400,000 units	$?
December 31, 1996	300,000 units	$2,900,000

1. What was the unit average cost for the 100,000 units sold from the beginning inventory?
2. What was the reported value for the January 1, 1996, inventory?

Exercise 9—25 **(Computation of beginning inventory from ending inventory)**

The Killpack Company sells Product N. During a move to a new location, the inventory records for Product N were misplaced. The bookkeeper has been able to gather some information from the sales records, and gives you the data shown below.

July sales: 57,200 units at $10.00

July Purchases

Date	*Quantity*	*Unit Cost*
July 5	10,000	$6.50
July 9	12,500	6.25
July 12	15,000	6.00
July 25	14,000	6.20

On July 31, 16,000 units were on hand with a total value of $98,800. Killpack has always used a periodic FIFO inventory costing system. Gross profit on sales for July was $205,875. Reconstruct the beginning inventory (quantity and dollar value) for the month of July.

Exercise 9—26 **(Computing inventory using LIFO pools)**

Miller Mfg. applies the LIFO method to specific inventory pools. Information relating to Product OU812 is as follows:

Beginning inventory, January 1	60 units @ $10 each
Purchase, February 12	45 units @ $12 each
Purchase, February 28	75 units @ $13 each
Purchase, March 15	65 units @ $12.50 each
Sales for the first quarter	135 units

Compute the ending LIFO inventory value for the first quarter assuming new layers are computed based on:

1. FIFO
2. LIFO
3. Average cost

Exercise 9—27 (Dollar-value LIFO inventory method)

The Johnson Manufacturing Company manufactures a single product. The managers, Ron and Ken Johnson, decided on December 31, 1994, to adopt the dollar-value LIFO inventory method. The inventory value on that date using the newly adopted dollar-value LIFO method was $500,000. Additional information follows:

Date	Inventory at Year-End Prices	Year-End Price Index
Dec. 31, 1995	$605,000	1.10
Dec. 31, 1996	597,360	1.14
Dec. 31, 1997	700,000	1.25

Compute the inventory value at December 31 of each year using the dollar-value method, assuming incremental layers are costed at year-end prices.

Exercise 9—28 (Dollar-value LIFO inventory method)

Jennifer Inc. adopted dollar-value LIFO on December 31, 1994. Data for 1994-1997 follows:

Inventory and index on the adoption date, December 31, 1994:

Dollar-value LIFO inventory	$250,000
Price index at year-end (the base year)	1.00

Inventory information in succeeding years:

Date	Inventory at Year-End Prices	Year-End Price Index	Incremental Layer Index
Dec. 31, 1995	$314,720	1.12	1.04
Dec. 31, 1996	361,800	1.20	1.14
Dec. 31, 1997	353,822	1.27	1.20

1. Compute the inventory value at December 31 of each year under the dollar-value method, assuming new layers are costed at the incremental layer index.
2. Compute the inventory value at December 31, 1997, assuming that dollar-value procedures were adopted at December 31, 1995, rather than in 1994. The beginning layer is the December 31, 1995 balance.

Exercise 9—29 (Impact on profit of failure to replace LIFO layers)

Harrison Lumber Company uses a periodic LIFO method for inventory costing. The following information relates to the plywood inventory carried by Harrison Lumber.

Plywood Inventory

Date	*Quantity*	*LIFO Costing Layers*
May 1	600 sheets	300 sheets at $ 8.00
		225 sheets at $11.00
		75 sheets at $13.00

Plywood Purchases

May 8	115 sheets at $14.00
May 17	95 sheets at $15.00
May 29	200 sheets at $14.50

All sales of plywood during May were at $20 per sheet. On May 31, there were 360 sheets of plywood in the storeroom.

1. Compute the gross profit on sales for May, as a dollar value and as a percent of sales.
2. Assume that because of a lumber strike, Harrison Lumber is not able to purchase the May 29 order of lumber until June 10. Assuming sales remained the same, recompute the gross profit on sales for May, as a dollar value and as a percent of sales.
3. Compare the results of part (1) and part (2) and explain the difference.

Exercise 9—30 (Gross margin differences—FIFO vs. LIFO)

Assume the Bullock Corporation had the following purchases and sales of its single product during its first 3 years of operation.

	Purchases		Sales	
Year	*Units*	*Unit Cost*	*Units*	*Unit Price*
1	10,000	$10	8,000	$14
2	9,000	$12	9,000	$17
3	8,000	$15	10,000	$18
	27,000		27,000	

1. Determine the gross margin for each of the three years assuming FIFO historical cost flow.
2. Determine the gross margin for each of the three years assuming LIFO historical cost flow.
3. Compare the total gross margin over the life of the business. How do the different cost flow assumptions affect the gross margin and cash flows over the life of the business? Does it matter which assumption of cash flow is used?

Exercise 9—31 (Income differences—FIFO vs. LIFO)

First-in, first-out has been used for inventory valuation by the Atwood Co. since it was organized in 1994. Using the data that follows, redetermine the net incomes for each year on the assumption of inventory valuation on the last-in, first-out basis:

	1994	1995	1996	1997
Reported net income—FIFO basis.	$15,500	$ 40,000	$ 34,250	$ 44,000
Reported ending inventories—				
FIFO basis	61,500	102,000	126,000	120,000
Inventories—LIFO basis	56,500	75,100	95,000	105,000

Exercise 9—32 (Inventory turnover)

The Boise Implement Company showed the following data in its financial statements.

	1997	1996
Cost of goods sold	$1,400,000	$1,200,000
Beginning inventory.............	200,000	150,000
Ending inventory	300,000	200,000

1. Compute the number of days' sales in inventory for both 1996 and 1997. What can you infer from these numbers?
2. How would you interpret the answer to part (1) if this company were in the business of selling fresh fruit and vegetables? What if this company sold real estate?

***Exercise 9—33 (Double extension and link-chain indexes)**

On December 31, 1996, the controller of Hardman Enterprises selected six items to use as a representative sample of the company's inventory. Information relative to these products was compiled and summarized in the following schedule:

Base year	1991
January 1, 1996, cumulative index	1.15

	Products in Sample Inventory					
	1	*2*	*3*	*4*	*5*	*6*
Historical cost	$ 20	$ 45	$10	$ 60	$100	$85
January 1, 1991, price	20	50	8	50	92	60
January 1, 1996, price	24	51	13	60	102	71
December 31, 1996, price	26	55	17	62	111	78
December 31, 1996, quantity	300	530	60	180	780	30

1. Compute a price index for use in determining the December 31, 1996, inventory at:
   (a) base-year prices assuming the use of double extension.
   (b) beginning-of-year prices assuming the use of link-chain.
2. Compute the link-chain index at January 1, 1997.

*Relates to Appendix

*Exercise 9—34 (Link-chain indexes)

On December 31, 1996, Kristen's Toy Store took a statistical sample of its inventory. The inventory revealed the following information:

	Quantity		Cost	
	Dec. 31, 1995	*Dec. 31, 1996*	*Dec. 31, 1995*	*Dec. 31, 1996*
Electronic games	600	750	$20.00	$22.60
Dolls	290	250	4.50	5.75
Stuffed animals	260	140	7.10	7.80
Puzzles	440	376	3.50	3.90

The link-chain cumulative price index at December 31, 1995, was 1.51. Compute the cumulative index at December 31, 1996.

*Relates to Appendix

*Exercise 9—35 (Dollar-value LIFO inventory; link-chain indexes)

LaRae's Fashion Clothing Store has hired you to assist with some year-end financial data preparation. The company's accountant quit three weeks ago and left many items incomplete. Information for computation of yearly price indexes and the inventory summary is in the table below. LaRae's uses the link-chain index for LIFO inventory valuation.

	1995	1996	1997
Ending inventory (Dec. 31) at beginning-of-year prices	$155,000	?	$191,500
Ending inventory at end-of-year prices	?	$188,600	?
Beginning cumulative index at January 1	?	?	1.775
Yearly price index	1.100	1.060	?
Cumulative index at end of current year	?	1.775	1.955

Determine the inventory data that are missing from the table. Carry each index to three decimal places.

*Relates to Appendix

PROBLEMS

Problem 9—36 (Computing cost of goods sold for a manufacturing firm)

The following information is available for Woodfield Inc.

	1997	1996	1995
Raw materials:			
Beginning inventory	$ 117	$?	$ 100
Purchases	391	382	?
Material available to use	$?	$?	$ 450
Ending inventory	121	?	?
Raw materials used	$?	$ 390	$ 325
Direct labor	325	?	300
Factory overhead	405	411	?
Total manufacturing costs	$?	$1,118	$1,025
Goods in process, January 1	85	?	55
	$1,202	$?	$?
Goods in process, December 31	?	85	?
Cost of goods manufactured	$?	$?	$1,005
Finished goods, January 1	?	92	87
	$1,212	$?	$?
Finished goods, December 31	?	105	?
Cost of goods sold	$1,122	$1,095	$?

Instructions: Compute the missing amounts.

Problem 9—37 (Whose inventory is it?)

Streuling Inc. is preparing its 1996 year-end financial statements. Prior to any adjustments, inventory is valued at $76,050. The following information has been found relating to certain inventory transactions.

(a) Goods valued at $11,000 are on consignment with a customer. These goods are not included in the $76,050 inventory figure.

(b) Goods costing $2,700 were received from a vendor on January 5, 1997. The related invoice was received and recorded on January 12, 1997. The goods were shipped on December 31, 1996, terms FOB shipping point.

(c) Goods costing $8,500 were shipped on December 31, 1996, and were delivered to the customer on January 2, 1997. The terms of the invoice were FOB shipping point. The goods were included in ending inventory for 1996 even though the sale was recorded in 1996.

(d) A $3,500 shipment of goods to a customer on December 31, terms FOB destination was not included in the year-end inventory. The goods cost $2,600 and were delivered to the customer on January 8, 1997. The sale was properly recorded in 1997.

(e) An invoice for goods costing $3,500 was received and recorded as a purchase on December 31, 1996. The related goods, shipped FOB destination, were received on January 2, 1997, and thus were not included in the physical inventory.

(f) Goods valued at $6,500 are on consignment from a vendor. These goods are not included in the year-end inventory figure.

(g) A $6,000 shipment of goods to a customer on December 30, 1996, terms FOB destination, was recorded as a sale in 1996. The goods, costing $3,700 and delivered to the customer on January 6, 1997, were not included in 1996 ending inventory.

Instructions:

1. Determine the appropriate accounting treatment for each of the above items. Justify your answers.

2. Compute the proper inventory amount to be reported on Streuling Inc.'s balance sheet for the year ended December 31, 1996.
3. By how much would the income statement have been misstated if no adjustments were made for the above transactions?

Problem 9—38 **(Inventory computation using different cost flows)**
The Gidewall Corporation uses Part 210 in a manufacturing process. Information as to balances on hand, purchases, and requisitions of Part 210 is given in the following table:

	Quantities			
Date	*Received*	*Issued*	*Balance*	*Unit Purchase Price*
January 8		—	200	$1.55
January 29	200	—	400	1.70
February 8	—	80	320	—
March 20	—	160	160	—
July 10	150	—	310	1.75
August 18	—	110	200	—
September 6	—	75	125	—
November 14	250	—	375	2.00
December 29	—	100	275	—

Instructions: What is the closing inventory under each of the following pricing methods? (Round unit costs to three decimal places.)

1. Perpetual FIFO
2. Periodic FIFO
3. Perpetual LIFO
4. Periodic LIFO
5. Moving average
6. Weighted average

Problem 9—39 **(Inventory computation using different cost flows)**

Records of the Schwab New Products Co. show the following data relative to Product C:

March	2	Inventory	325 units at $25.50
	3	Sale	300 units at $37.50
	6	Purchase	300 units at $26.00
	13	Purchase	350 units at $27.00
	20	Sale	200 units at $35.70
	25	Purchase	50 units at $27.50
	28	Sale	125 units at $36.00

Instructions: Calculate the inventory balance and the gross profit on sales for the month on each of the following bases:

1. Perpetual FIFO
2. Periodic FIFO
3. Perpetual LIFO
4. Periodic LIFO
5. Moving average (Carry calculations to four decimal places and round to three.)
6. Weighted average

Problem 9—40 **(Inventory calculations—LIFO and FIFO)**
The Zerbel Manufacturing Co. was organized in 1995 to produce a single product. The company's production and sales records for the period 1995-1997 are summarized on the next page.

	Units Produced		Sales	
	No. of Units	*Production Costs*	*No. of Units*	*Sales Revenue*
1995	340,000	$153,000	200,000	$187,000
1996	310,000	161,200	290,000	230,000
1997	270,000	153,900	260,000	221,000

Instructions: Calculate the gross profit for each of the three years assuming that inventory values are calculated in terms of:

1. LIFO (average cost used for incremental layers)
2. FIFO

Problem 9—41 (Computation of LIFO inventory with LIFO pools)

The Bergman Company sells three different products. Five years ago, management adopted the LIFO inventory method and established three specific pools of goods. Bergman values all incremental layers of inventory at the average cost of purchases within the period. Information relating to the three products for the first quarter of 1997 is given below.

	Product 400	Product 401	Product 402
Purchases:			
January	1,000 @ $12.00	500 @ $25	5,000 @ $5.30
February	1,500 @ $12.50	250 @ $26	4,850 @ $5.38
March	1,200 @ $12.25	—	3,500 @ $5.45
First quarter sales (units)	2,850	775	10,750
January 1, 1997, inventory	950 @ $11.50	155 @ $24	3,760 @ $5.00

Instructions: Compute the ending inventory value for the first quarter of 1997. (Round unit inventory values to the nearest cent and final inventory values to the nearest dollar.)

Problem 9—42 (Computation of inventory from balance sheet and transaction data)

A portion of the Stark Company's balance sheet appears as follows:

	December 31, 1997	December 31, 1996
Assets:		
Cash	$353,300	$100,000
Notes receivable	-0-	25,000
Inventory	?	199,875
Liabilities:		
Accounts payable	?	75,000

Stark Company pays for all operating expenses with cash and purchases all inventory on credit. During 1997, cash totaling $471,700 was paid on accounts payable. Operating expenses for 1997 totaled $220,000. All sales are cash sales. The inventory was restocked by purchasing 1,500 units per month and valued by using periodic FIFO. The unit cost of inventory was $32.60 during January 1997 and increased $0.10 per month during the year. Stark sells only one product. All sales are made for $50 per unit. The ending inventory for 1996 was valued at $32.50 per unit.

Instructions:

1. Compute the number of units sold during 1997.
2. Compute the December 31, 1997, accounts payable balance.
3. Compute the beginning inventory quantity.
4. Compute the ending inventory quantity and value.
5. Prepare an income statement for 1997 (including a detailed cost of goods sold section and ignoring income taxes).

Problem 9—43 **(Impact of LIFO inventory system)**

The Manuel Corporation sells household appliances and uses LIFO for inventory costing. The inventory contains ten different products, and historical LIFO layers are maintained for each of them. The LIFO layers for one of the products, Easy Chef, were as follows at December 31, 1996:

1995 layer.............	4,000 @ $90
1990 layer.............	3,500 @ $85
1986 layer.............	1,000 @ $75
1984 layer.............	3,000 @ $52

Instructions:

1. What was the value of the ending inventory of Easy Chefs at December 31, 1996?
2. How did the December 31, 1996, quantity of Easy Chefs compare with the December 31, 1995, quantity?
3. What was the value of the ending inventory of Easy Chefs at December 31, 1997, assuming that there were 11,200 units on hand?
4. How would income in part (3) be affected if, in addition to the quantity on hand, 1,250 units were in transit to Manuel Corporation at December 31, 1997? The shipment was made on December 26, 1997, terms FOB shipping point. Total invoice cost was $131,250.

Problem 9—44 **(Dollar-value LIFO inventory method)**

Steve's Repair Shop began operations on January 1, 1992. After discussing the matter with his accountant, Steve decided dollar-value LIFO should be used for inventory costing. Information concerning the inventory of Steve's Repair Shop is shown below.

Date	Inventory at Year-End Prices	Year-End Index
Dec. 31, 1992	$20,500	1.00
Dec. 31, 1993	34,000	1.18
Dec. 31, 1994	55,600	1.36
Dec. 31, 1995	37,800	1.14
Dec. 31, 1996	72,250	1.72
Dec. 31, 1997	53,900	2.05

Instructions: Compute the inventory value at December 31 of each year under the dollar-value LIFO inventory method, assuming incremental layers are costed at year-end prices.

Problem 9—45 **(Dollar-value LIFO inventory method)**

The Mietus Company manufactures a single product. The company adopted the dollar-value LIFO inventory method on December 31, 1992. More information concerning Mietus Company is shown below.

Inventory and index on the adoption date, December 31, 1992:

Dollar-value LIFO inventory..........	$300,900
Price index at year-end (the base year)..........	1.18

Inventory information in succeeding years:

Date	Inventory at Year-End Prices	Year-End Price Index	Incremental Layer Index
Dec. 31, 1993	$369,600	1.320	1.240
Dec. 31, 1994	420,206	1.420	1.368
Dec. 31, 1995	435,095	1.505	1.452
Dec. 31, 1996	417,073	1.543	1.515
Dec. 31, 1997	451,627	1.588	1.552

Instructions: Compute the inventory value at December 31 of each year under the dollar-value LIFO inventory method.

Problem 9—46 **(LIFO inventory pools—unit LIFO)**

On January 1, 1993, Nolder Company changed its inventory cost flow method from FIFO to LIFO for its raw material inventory. The change was made for both financial statement and income tax reporting purposes. Nolder uses the multiple-pools approach under which substantially identical raw materials are grouped into LIFO inventory pools; weighted average costs are used in valuing annual incremental layers. The composition of the December 31, 1995, inventory for the Class F inventory pool is as follows:

	Units	Weighted Average Unit Cost	Total Cost
Base year inventory—1993	9,000	$10.00	$ 90,000
Incremental layer—1994	3,000	11.00	33,000
Incremental layer—1995	2,000	12.50	25,000
Inventory, December 31, 1995	14,000		$148,000

Inventory transactions for the Class F inventory pool during 1996 and 1997 were as follows:

1996
Mar. 1 4,800 units were purchased at a unit cost of $13.50 for $64,800.
Sept. 1 7,200 units were purchased at a unit cost of $14.00 for $100,800.

A total of 15,000 units were used for production during 1996.

1997
Jan. 10 7,500 units were purchased at a unit cost of $14.50 for $108,750.
May 15 5,500 units were purchased at a unit cost of $15.50 for $85,250.
Dec. 29 7,000 units were purchased at a unit cost of $16.00 for $112,000.

A total of 16,000 units were used for production during 1997.

Instructions:

1. Prepare a schedule to compute the inventory (unit and dollar amounts) of the Class F inventory pool at December 31, 1996. Show supporting computations in good form.
2. Prepare a schedule to compute the cost of Class F raw materials used in production for the year ended December 31, 1996.
3. Prepare a schedule to compute the inventory (unit and dollar amounts) of the Class F inventory pool at December 31, 1997. Show supporting computations in good form.

(AICPA adapted)

Problem 9—47 **(Change from FIFO to LIFO inventory)**

The Greenriver Manufacturing Company manufactures two products: Raft and Float. At December 31, 1996, Greenriver used the FIFO inventory method. Effective January 1, 1997, Greenriver changed to the LIFO inventory method. The cumulative effect of this change is not determinable and, as a result, the ending inventory for 1996 for which the FIFO method was used, is also the beginning inventory for 1997 for the LIFO method. Any layers added during 1997 should be costed by reference to the first acquisitions of 1997.

The following information was available from Greenriver inventory records for the two most recent years:

	Raft		**Float**	
	Units	*Unit Cost*	*Units*	*Unit Cost*
1996 purchases:				
January 7	5,000	$4.00	22,000	$2.00
April 16	12,000	4.50		
November 8	17,000	5.00	18,500	2.50
December 13	10,000	6.00		

1997 purchases:				
February 11	3,000	7.00	23,000	3.00
May 20	8,000	7.50		
October 15	20,000	8.00		
December 23			15,500	3.50
Units on hand:				
December 31, 1996	15,000		14,500	
December 31, 1997	16,000		13,000	

Instructions: Compute the effect on income before income taxes for the year ended December 31, 1997, resulting from the change from the FIFO to the LIFO inventory method.

(AICPA adapted)

Problem 9—48 (Inventory turnover analysis)

The following information for Valdez Industries was taken from the company's financial statements (amounts in thousands).

	1996	1995	1994	1993
Sales	$24,000	$18,000	$15,000	$12,000
Cost of goods sold	19,600	13,900	10,200	7,200
Inventory	1,400	1,200	910	890
Accounts receivable	3,900	3,600	4,100	3,200
Accounts payable	2,300	1,200	1,500	1,800
Net income	560	320	510	430

Instructions:

1. Compute the inventory turnover and the number of days in inventory for the years 1994-1996.
2. Evaluate Valdez's inventory turnover trend.

***Problem 9—49 (Link-chain index)**

On December 31, 1997, Lelegren Architectural Supply took a statistical inventory of items for the sample of its inventory. The inventory revealed the following information:

	Dec. 31, 1995		Dec. 31, 1996		Dec. 31, 1997	
	Quantity	*Cost*	*Quantity*	*Cost*	*Quantity*	*Cost*
Pencil leads	2,000	$ 5.00	2,000	$ 5.50	2,200	$ 5.40
Masking tape	1,000	3.00	1,000	3.30	800	3.50
Pink erasers	5,000	4.00	5,000	4.40	5,500	4.75
Vellum paper	3,000	12.00	3,000	13.20	3,200	14.00
Sketch pads	6,000	8.00	6,000	8.80	5,000	9.00
Triangles	1,000	8.00	1,000	8.80	1,000	8.50
Cost of total inventory at year-end prices		$750,000		$950,000		$1,020,000

Instructions:

1. Compute the cumulative index for Lelegren Architectural Supply at December 31, 1996 and 1997, using the link-chain method. Assume the cumulative index at December 31, 1995, was 1.5.
2. Compute the LIFO inventory at December 31, 1997. Assume the December 1995 LIFO inventory at base-year prices was $500,000 and the balance reported on the balance sheet was $625,000.

*Relates to Appendix

*Problem 9—50 (Double extension index)

Kristy's Cosmetics Supply is interested in generating price indexes for inventory. To aid in accomplishing this task, on December 31, 1996, the controller assembled information on various inventory items.

	Dec. 31, 1993	Dec. 31, 1994		Dec. 31, 1995		Dec. 31, 1996	
	Cost	*Quantity*	*Cost*	*Quantity*	*Cost*	*Quantity*	*Cost*
Bath oil	$ 8.00	2,000	$ 8.80				
Body lotion	4.50	1,000	4.80	1,500	$ 5.25		
Eye shadow	6.00	5,000	6.15	5,025	6.35		
Base makeup	5.50	3,000	5.70	3,200	5.90	3,500	$ 5.85
Blush	8.50	6,000	8.55	6,600	8.80	6,200	9.00
Facial cream	6.20	1,000	6.60	1,200	6.80	1,600	7.40
Carrying cases	14.00			2,000	14.80	2,200	15.75
Compacts	17.50					3,100	19.00
Mascara	3.25					5,500	3.95

The controller indicated that 1993 is the base year.

Instructions: Using the double extension method, compute the year-end price indexes at December 31, 1994, 1995, and 1996.

*Relates to Appendix

CHAPTER 10

Inventories: Estimation and Noncost Valuation Procedures

CHAPTER TOPICS

- Gross Profit Method
- Retail Inventory Method
- Dollar-Value LIFO Retail Method
- Valuation at Lower of Cost or Market
- Purchase Commitments, Trade-Ins, and Repossessions
- Effects of Errors in Recording Inventory
- Foreign Currency Inventory Transactions
- Inventories on the Balance Sheet

Combine cool air from Canada with moist air from the Gulf of Mexico — throw in a stalled high-pressure system called a Bermuda high — and the result is the Great Flood of 1993. The Bermuda high prevented thunderstorms from moving across the country. Three rivers — the Illinois, the Missouri, and the Mississippi — reached record levels as a result of the rainfall, causing flooding from Minnesota to Missouri. Cedar Rapids, Iowa, for example, received three feet of rain from April through July.

Levees, man-made dams designed to direct the flow of water along riverbanks, failed at record rates. Of the 1,576 public and private levees in the affected area, 70 percent failed in the summer of 1993. The resulting damage was portrayed on televisions around the country: an estimated 50 people dead, 72,000 homes and 36,000 square miles affected, and more than ten billion dollars in damage.

In some areas as much as 15 feet of water flooded homes and businesses. In Missouri alone, an estimated 3,200 businesses were flooded. Billions of dollars of inventory was ruined, some of it unrecoverable as it floated downstream. In situations such as this, how can a firm value inventory that may no longer exist? How would an insurance company estimate the amount to pay in claims?

This chapter introduces two inventory estimation techniques—the gross profit and the retail inventory methods. Inventory estimation may be necessary whenever it is too costly or it is not possible to physically count the inventory. This may occur when there is a natural disaster, a fire, or a theft, or when monthly financial statements are prepared. The valuation of inventory at the lower of cost or market and foreign currency inventory transactions are also discussed.

GROSS PROFIT METHOD

The **gross profit method** of estimating inventory costs is based on an assumed relationship between gross profit and sales. A gross profit percentage is applied to sales to determine cost of goods sold; then, cost of goods sold is subtracted from the cost of goods available for sale to arrive at an estimated inventory balance.

The gross profit method is useful when:

1. A periodic system is in use and inventories are required for interim statements or for the determination of the week-to-week or month-to-month inventory position, and the cost of taking physical inventories would be excessive for such purposes.
2. Inventories have been destroyed or lost by fire, theft, or other casualties, and the specific data required for inventory valuation is not available.
3. It is desired to test or check the validity of inventory figures determined by other means. Such application is referred to as the **gross profit test.**

To be useful, the gross profit percentage used must be a reliable measure of current experience. In developing a reliable rate, reference is made to past rates and these are adjusted for variations considered to exist currently. Past gross profit rates, for example, may require adjustment when inventories are valued at last-in, first-out and significant fluctuations in inventory position and/or prices have occurred. Current changes in cost-price relationships or in the sales mix of specific products also create a need for modifying past rates.

The calculations of cost of goods sold and inventory depend on whether the gross profit percentage is developed and stated in terms of sales or in terms of cost. The procedures to be followed in each case are shown below.

Example 1—Gross Profit as a Percentage of Sales

Assume sales are $100,000 and goods are sold at a gross profit of 40% of sales. If gross profit is 40% of sales, then cost of goods sold must be 60% of sales.

Sales	100%		Sales	100%
Cost of goods sold	?	=	Cost of goods sold	60%
Gross profit	40%		Gross profit	40%

Cost of goods sold, then, is 60% of $100,000, or $60,000. Goods available for sale less the estimated cost of goods sold gives the estimated cost of the remaining inventory. Assuming the cost of goods available for sale is $85,000, this balance less the estimated cost of goods sold, $60,000, gives an estimated inventory of $25,000.

Example 2—Gross Profit as a Percentage of Cost (or Markup on Cost)
Assume sales are $100,000 and goods are sold at a gross profit that is 60% of their cost. If sales are made at a gross profit that is 60% of cost, then sales must be equal to the sum of cost, considered 100%, and the gross profit on cost, 60%. Sales, then, are 160% of cost:

Sales	?	} =	Sales	160%
Cost of goods sold	100%		Cost of goods sold	100%
Gross profit	60%		Gross profit	60%

To find cost, or 100%, sales may be divided by 160 and multiplied by 100, or sales may simply be divided by 1.60. Cost of goods sold, then, is $100,000 ÷ 1.60 = $62,500. This amount is subtracted from the cost of goods available for sale to determine the estimated inventory. If goods available for sale is $85,000, then ending inventory is estimated to be $22,500 ($85,000 – $62,500).

When various lines of merchandise are sold at different gross profit rates and the product mix is unstable, it may be possible to develop a reliable inventory value only by making separate calculations for each line. Under such circumstances, it is necessary to develop summaries of sales, goods available for sale, and gross profit data for the different merchandise lines.

In order to use the gross profit method, four elements must be determinable: (1) cost of the beginning inventory, (2) cost of net purchases for the period, (3) sales, and (4) a gross profit percentage. Given these four elements, an estimate of the ending inventory can be made. A common application of the gross profit method is the estimation of inventory when a physical count is impossible because of the loss or destruction of goods.

For example, assume that on October 31, 1996, a fire in the warehouse of a wholesale distributing company totally destroyed the contents, including many accounting records. Remaining records indicated that the last physical inventory was taken on December 31, 1995, and that the inventory at that date was $329,500. Microfilm bank records of canceled checks disclosed that during 1996, payments to suppliers for inventory items were $1,015,000. Unpaid invoices at the beginning of 1996 amounted to $260,000, and communication with suppliers indicated a balance due at the time of the fire of $315,000. Bank deposits for the ten months amounted to $1,505,000. All deposits came from customers for goods purchased. Accounts receivable at the beginning of the year were $328,000, and an analysis of the available records indicated that accounts receivable on October 31 totaled $275,000. Gross profit percentages on sales for the preceding four years were:

1992	28%	1994	23%
1993	25%	1995	24%

From these facts, the inventory in the warehouse at the time of the fire could be estimated as shown below.

Estimate of sales January 1 to October 31, 1996

Collection of accounts receivable	$1,505,000
Add accounts receivable balance at October 31, 1996	275,000
	$1,780,000
Deduct accounts receivable balance at January 1, 1996	328,000
Estimate of sales January 1 to October 31, 1996	$1,452,000
Average gross profit percentage on sales for past 4 years: (.28 + .25 + .23 + .24) ÷ 4	25%
Average cost percentage on sales for past 4 years	75%
Estimate of cost of goods sold to October 31, 1996 ($1,452,000 × 75%)	$1,089,000

Estimate of inventory on October 31, 1996

Inventory, December 31, 1995		$ 329,500
Add: Payments to suppliers—1996	$1,015,000	
Accounts payable to suppliers, October 31, 1996	315,000	
	$1,330,000	
Deduct accounts payable to suppliers, January 1, 1996	260,000	
Estimate of purchases January 1 to October 31, 1996		1,070,000
Goods available for sale		$1,399,500
Estimate of cost of goods sold for 1996 (from previous page)		1,089,000
Estimated inventory, October 31, 1996		$ 310,500

RETAIL INVENTORY METHOD

The **retail inventory method** is widely employed by retail concerns, particularly department stores, to arrive at reliable estimates of inventory position whenever desired. This method, like the gross profit method, permits the calculation of an inventory amount without the time and expense of taking a physical inventory or maintaining a detailed perpetual inventory record for each of the thousands of items normally included in a retail inventory. When this method is used, records of goods purchased are maintained at two amounts—cost and retail. The computer has now made it feasible to maintain cost records for the thousands of items normally included in a retail inventory. A **cost percentage** is computed by dividing the goods available for sale at cost by the goods available for sale at retail. This cost percentage can then be applied to the ending inventory at retail, an amount that can be readily calculated by subtracting sales for the period from the total goods available for sale at retail.

The computation of retail inventory at the end of a month is illustrated by the following example:

	Cost	Retail
Inventory, January 1	$30,000	$45,000
Purchases in January	20,000	35,000
Goods available for sale	$50,000	$80,000
Cost percentage ($50,000 ÷ $80,000) = 62.5%		
Deduct sales for January		25,000
Inventory, January 31, at retail		$55,000
Inventory, January 31, at estimated cost ($55,000 x 62.5%)	$34,375	

The effect of the above procedure is to provide an inventory valuation in terms of average cost. No cost sequence, such as LIFO or FIFO, is recognized in the preceding computation; the percentage of cost to retail for the ending inventory is the same as the percentage of cost to retail for goods sold.

Use of the retail inventory method offers the following advantages:

1. Estimated interim inventories can be obtained without a physical count.
2. When a physical inventory is actually taken for financial statement purposes, it can be taken at retail and then converted to cost without reference to individual costs and invoices, thus saving time and expense.
3. Significant shoplifting losses can be determined and monitored. Since physical counts of inventory costed at retail should agree with the calculated retail inventory, any material difference not accounted for by clerical errors in the company records must be attributable to actual physical loss by shoplifting or employee theft.

Remnants of a Riot

The verdict in the trial of the police officers involved in the beating of Rodney King resulted in riots throughout various cities. However, South Central Los Angeles was the center of the worst of the rioting. Entire city blocks went up in flames, stores were looted, cars were ignited, and people were hurt. More than 50 people were killed in the several days of rioting in the South Central region. Once the situation was brought under control and business owners were able to sift through the remains of their once thriving operations, insurance companies were inundated with claims. One insurer, Los Angeles-based Farmers Group Inc. estimated that it would eventually pay about $70 million to policyholders for losses associated with the Los Angeles riots.

Questions:

1. If you were an insurance agent called in to estimate the value of inventory that had been completely destroyed during the riots, what procedures would you employ? Where would you start?
2. Assume that all of that business' accounting records had been destroyed during the riots, how would you proceed in estimating the value of its inventory?

Source:
Frederick Rose, "Adjusters Fan Out to Tackle Riot Claims," *Wall Street Journal*, May 15, 1992, p. B1.

Although this method permits the estimation of a value for inventory, errors can occur in accounting for the dual prices and in applying the retail method. Thus a physical count of the inventory to be reported on the annual financial statements is required at least once a year. Retail inventory records should be adjusted for variations shown by the physical count so that records reflect the actual status of the inventory for purposes of future estimates and control.

The accounting entries for the retail inventory method are similar to those made using a periodic inventory system. The retail figures are part of the analysis necessary to compute the cost of the inventory; however, they do not actually appear in the accounts. Thus the following entries would be made to record the inventory data included in the preceding example.

Purchases	20,000	
Accounts Payable		20,000
Accounts Receivable	25,000	
Sales		25,000
Inventory	4,375	
Cost of Goods Sold	15,625	
Purchases		20,000
To adjust inventory, cost of goods sold, and related accounts.		

Markups and Markdowns—Conventional Retail

In the earlier inventory calculations, it was assumed that there were no changes in retail prices after the goods were originally recorded. Frequently, however, retail prices do change because of changes in the price level, shifts in consumer demand, or other factors. The following terms are used in discussing the retail method:

1. **Original retail**—the initial sales price, including the original increase over cost referred to as the **initial markup.**
2. **Additional markups**—increases that raise sales prices above original retail.
3. **Markup cancellations**—decreases in additional markups that do not reduce sales prices below original retail.
4. **Net markups**—Additional markups less markup cancellations.
5. **Markdowns**—decreases that reduce sales prices below original retail.
6. **Markdown cancellations**—decreases in the markdowns that do not raise the sales prices above original retail.
7. **Net markdowns**—markdowns less markdown cancellations.

To illustrate the use of these terms, assume that goods originally placed for sale are marked at 50% above cost. Merchandise costing $4 a unit, then, is marked at $6, which is the **original retail.** The **initial markup** of $2 is referred to as a "50% markup on cost" or a "33 1/3% markup on sales price." In anticipation of a heavy demand for the article, the retail price is subsequently increased to $7.50. This represents an **additional markup** of $1.50. At a later date, the price is reduced to $7. This is a **markup cancellation** of 50 cents and not a markdown since the retail price has not been reduced below the original sales price. But assume that goods originally marked to sell at $6 are subsequently reduced to a sales price of $5. This represents a **markdown** of $1. At a later date, the goods are marked to sell at $5.25. This is a **markdown cancellation** of 25 cents and not a markup, since sales price does not exceed the original retail.

Retail inventory results will vary depending on whether net markdowns are used in computing the cost percentage. When applying the most commonly used retail method, net markups are added to goods available for sale at retail before calculating the cost percentage; net markdowns, however, are not deducted in arriving at the percentage. This method, sometimes referred to as the **conventional retail inventory method,** is illustrated in the following example:

Net markdowns not deducted to calculate cost percentage (conventional retail)

	Cost	Retail
Beginning inventory	$ 8,600	$ 14,000
Purchases	72,100	110,000
Additional markups		13,000
Markup cancellations		(2,500)
Goods available for sale	$80,700	$134,500
Cost percentage ($80,700 ÷ $134,500) = 60%		
Deduct: Sales		$108,000
Markdowns		4,800
Markdown cancellations		(800)
		$112,000
Ending inventory at retail		$ 22,500
Ending inventory at estimated cost ($22,500 × 60%)	$13,500	

Once these computations are made, the inventory account could then be adjusted with the following journal entry:

Inventory	4,900	
Cost of Goods Sold	67,200	
Purchases		72,100

The conventional retail method results in a lower cost percentage and, correspondingly, a lower inventory amount and a higher cost of goods sold than would be obtained if net markdowns were deducted before calculating the cost percentage. This latter approach, the **average cost retail inventory method,** is illustrated below.

Net markdowns deducted to calculate cost percentage (average cost retail):

	Cost	Retail
Goods available for sale (conventional retail)	$80,700	$134,500
Deduct net markdowns.		4,000
Goods available for sale (average cost retail)		$130,500
Cost percentage ($80,700 ÷ $130,500) = 61.84%		
Deduct sales		108,000
Ending inventory at retail		$ 22,500
Ending inventory at estimated cost ($22,500 × 61.84%)	$13,914	

The lower inventory obtained with the conventional retail method approximates a **lower-of-average-cost-or-market** valuation. The lower-of-cost-or-market concept, discussed in detail later in this chapter, requires recognition of declines in the value of inventory in the period such declines occur. Under the conventional retail method, markdowns are viewed as indicating a decline in the value of inventory and are deducted as a current cost of sales. When markdowns are included in the cost percentage computation, the result is an average cost allocated proportionately between cost of sales and ending inventory. Thus only a portion of the decline in value is charged to the current period. The remainder is carried forward in ending inventory to be charged against future sales.

Markdowns may be made for special sales or clearance purposes, or they may be made as a result of market fluctuations and a decline in the replacement cost of goods. In either case, their omission in calculating the cost percentage is necessary if the objective is to value the inventory at the lower of cost or market. This is illustrated in the two examples that follow.

Example 1—Markdowns for Special Sales Purposes

Assume that merchandise costing $50,000 is marked to sell for $100,000. To dispose of part of the goods immediately, one-fourth of the stock is marked down $5,000 and is sold. The cost of the ending inventory is calculated as follows:

	Cost	Retail
Purchases	$50,000	$100,000
Cost percentage ($50,000 ÷ $100,000) = 50%		
Deduct: Sales		$ 20,000
Markdowns		5,000
		$ 25,000
Ending inventory at retail		$ 75,000
Ending inventory at estimated cost ($75,000 × 50%)	$37,500	

If cost, $50,000, had been related to sales price after markdowns, $95,000, a cost percentage of 52.6% would have been obtained, and the inventory, which is three-fourths of the merchandise originally acquired, would have been reported at 52.6% of $75,000, or $39,450. The inventory would thus be stated above the $37,500 cost of the remaining inventory and cost of goods sold would be understated by $1,950. A markdown relating to goods no longer on hand would have been recognized in the development of a cost percentage to be applied to the entire inventory. Reductions in the goods available at sales prices resulting from shortages or damaged goods should likewise be disregarded in calculating the cost percentage.

Example 2—Markdowns as a Result of Market Declines

Assume that merchandise costing $50,000 is marked to sell for $100,000. With a drop in replacement cost of merchandise to $40,000, sales prices are marked down to $80,000. Three-fourths of the merchandise is sold. The cost of the ending inventory is calculated as follows:

	Cost	Retail
Purchases	$50,000	$100,000
Cost percentage ($50,000 ÷ $100,000) = 50%		
Deduct: Sales		$ 60,000
Markdowns		20,000
		$ 80,000
Ending inventory at retail		$ 20,000
Ending inventory at estimated cost ($20,000 × 50%)	$10,000	

If cost, $50,000, had been related to sales price after markdowns, $80,000, a cost percentage of 62.5% would have been obtained, and the inventory would have been reported at 62.5% of $20,000, or $12,500. The use of the 50% cost percentage in the example reduces the inventory to $10,000 ($^1/_4$ × $40,000), a balance providing the usual gross profit in subsequent periods if current prices and relationships between cost and retail prices prevail.

Freight, Discounts, Returns, and Allowances

In calculating the cost percentage, **freight-in** should be added to the cost of the purchase; purchase discounts and returns and allowances should be deducted. A purchase return affects both the cost and the retail computations, while a purchase allowance affects only the cost total unless a change in retail price is made as a result of the allowance. Sales returns are proper adjustments to gross sales since the inventory is returned; however, sales discounts and sales allowances are not deducted to determine the estimated ending retail inventory. The deduction is not made because the sales price of an item is added into the computation of the retail inventory when it is purchased and deducted when it is sold, all at the gross sales price. Subsequent price adjustments included in the computation would leave a balance in the inventory account with no inventory on hand to represent it.

To illustrate the complexities associated with sales discounts and allowances, consider the following example. Docutron, Inc. had net purchases for the period as disclosed. All inventory was sold with the exception of $4,000 in goods that were returned by the customer and subsequently returned by Docutron to the original supplier. In addition, sales discounts totaling $1,000 were taken by customers during the period. The cost percentage is determined as follows:

	Cost	Retail
Purchases	$50,000	$100,000
Freight-in	1,000	
Purchase Discounts	(500)	
Purchase Returns	(2,000)	(4,000)
Purchase Allowances	(1,340)	
Goods Available for Sale	$47,160	$ 96,000
Cost percentage ($47,160 ÷ $96,000) = 49%		
Deduct: Sales		100,000
Sales Returns		(4,000)
Ending Inventory at Retail		$ 0

Since all inventory was sold during the period, ending inventory at retail is $0, as is ending inventory at cost. However, if sales discounts of $1,000 had been deducted, ending inventory at retail would have been $1,000 even though no inventory was on hand. Thus, use caution when dealing with returns, discounts, and allowances.

Retail Method With Varying Profit Margin Inventories

The calculation of a cost percentage for all goods carried in inventory is valid only when goods on hand can be regarded as representative of the total goods handled. Varying markup percentages and sales of high-margin and low-margin items in proportions that differ from purchases will require separate records and the development of separate cost percentages for different classes of goods. For example, assume that a store operates three departments and that for July the following information pertains to these departments:

	Department A		Department B		Department C		Total	
	Cost	*Retail*	*Cost*	*Retail*	*Cost*	*Retail*	*Cost*	*Retail*
Beginning inventory	$20,000	$ 28,000	$10,000	$15,000	$16,000	$ 40,000	$ 46,000	$ 83,000
Net purchases	57,000	82,000	20,000	35,000	20,000	60,000	97,000	177,000
Goods available for sale	$77,000	$110,000	$30,000	$50,000	$36,000	$100,000	$143,000	$260,000
Cost percentage	70%		60%		36%		55%	
Sales		80,000		30,000		40,000		150,000
Inventory at retail		$ 30,000		$20,000		$ 60,000		$110,000
Inventory at cost		$ 21,000		$12,000		$ 21,600		$ 60,500

$54,600

Because of the range in cost percentages from 36% to 70% and the difference in mix of the purchases and ending inventory, the ending inventory balance, using an overall cost percentage, is $5,900 higher ($60,500 – $54,600) than when the departmental rates are used. When material variations exist in the cost percentages by departments, separate departmental rates should be computed and applied.

The retail method is acceptable for income tax purposes, provided the taxpayer maintains adequate and satisfactory records supporting inventory calculations and applies the method consistently on successive tax returns.

DOLLAR-VALUE LIFO RETAIL METHOD

The dollar-value LIFO procedures described in Chapter 9 can be applied to the retail inventory method in developing inventory values reflecting a last-in, first-out valuation approach.[1] The **dollar-value LIFO retail method** requires that index numbers be applied to inventories stated at retail in arriving at the quantitative changes in inventories. After the LIFO retail layers have been identified and priced at the incremental price index, a further adjustment is needed to state the inventory at cost. This is done by multiplying the retail inventory of each layer by the incremental cost percentage.

The incremental cost percentages for the dollar-value LIFO retail method are computed in a slightly different manner from that done for the conventional retail method. The two principal differences are:

1. Beginning inventory values are disregarded. The LIFO inventory is composed of a base cost and subsequent cost layers that have not been assigned to revenues. Because costs for prior periods remain unchanged, only the cost of a current incremental layer requires calculation.
2. Markdowns, as well as markups, are recognized in calculating the cost percentage applicable to goods stated at retail. Markdowns were not recognized in arriving at the cost percentage when the objective was to arrive at a lower-of-cost-or-market valuation. However, because LIFO measurements require inventory valuation in terms of cost, the recognition of both markups and markdowns is appropriate.

1. Reeve and Stanga found that 195 retail companies in the U.S. used LIFO and that over 95% of those used the dollar-value LIFO retail method. James M. Reeve and Keith G. Stanga, "The LIFO Pooling Decision: Some Empirical Results from Accounting Practice," *Accounting Horizons* (June 1987), p. 27.

Even though the beginning inventories are not included in the computation of the cost percentage, they are used to determine the amount of retail inventory that should be on hand at the end of the period. Because the retail inventory is adjusted for markups and markdowns, the ending inventory is automatically stated at year-end retail prices.

To illustrate the computation of the LIFO retail incremental cost percentage, the ending inventory at year-end retail prices, and the inventory at dollar-value LIFO retail, assume that the following LIFO retail layer data applies to Morris Department Stores Inc. as of December 31, 1996.

Layer Year	Year-End and Incremental Price Index	Incremental Cost Percentage	Inventory at End-of-Year Retail Prices
1993	1.00	.60	$60,000
1994	1.05	.62	69,300
1995	1.10	.64	77,000
1996	1.12	.65	71,120

Assume that the 1997 year-end price index is 1.08. The incremental cost percentage and 1997 ending inventory at end-of-year retail prices are computed as follows.

	Cost	Retail
Beginning inventory—December 31, 1996		$ 71,120
Purchases	$63,000	$ 98,000
Purchase returns	(2,000)	(3,000)
Purchase discounts	(1,000)	
Freight-in	2,220	
Markups, net of cancellations		8,000
Markdowns, net of cancellations		(1,000)
Totals to determine incremental cost percentage—retail-LIFO	$62,220	$102,000
Incremental cost percentage ($62,220 ÷ $102,000) = 61%		
Goods available for sale		$173,120
Deduct: Sales		94,820
Ending inventory at retail (year-end prices)		$ 78,300

From this data, a work sheet similar to that illustrated in Chapter 9 for dollar-value LIFO can be constructed to determine the LIFO retail inventory layers. One additional column is necessary to record the incremental cost percentage that will reduce the retail inventory to cost. It is important to note that the incremental cost percentage is used only if an incremental layer is added to the inventory in the current period. In the example, this situation occurred in 1996 when no layer was added. If the inventory level has declined, previous inventory layers will be reduced using the respective years' incremental layer index and incremental cost percentage. Note that when an inventory layer is eliminated, it is not reintroduced in subsequent years when layers are added. This is illustrated in the example when, in 1996, the $4,000 layer formed in 1995 is eliminated. In 1997, that $4,000 layer is not included when a new layer is added. Instead, the new layer is comprised of 1997 percentages.

Dollar-Value LIFO Retail

Date	Inventory at End-of-Year Retail Prices		Year-End Price Index		Inventory at Base-Year Retail Prices	Layers		Incremental Layer Index		Incremental Cost Percentage		Dollar-Value LIFO Retail Cost
December 31, 1993	$60,000	÷	1.00	=	$60,000	$60,000	×	1.00	×	.60	=	$36,000
December 31, 1994	$69,300	÷	1.05	=	$66,000	$60,000	×	1.00	×	.60	=	$36,000
						6,000	×	1.05	×	.62	=	3,906
						$66,000						$39,906
December 31, 1995	$77,000	÷	1.10	=	$70,000	$60,000	×	1.00	×	.60	=	$36,000
						6,000	×	1.05	×	.62	=	3,906
						4,000	×	1.10	×	.64	=	2,816
						$70,000						$42,722
December 31, 1996	$71,120	÷	1.12	=	$63,500	$60,000	×	1.00	×	.60	=	$36,000
						3,500	×	1.05	×	.62	=	2,279*
						$63,500						$38,279
December 31, 1997	$78,300	÷	1.08	=	$72,500	$60,000	×	1.00	×	.60	=	$36,000
						3,500	×	1.05	×	.62	=	2,279*
						9,000	×	1.08	×	.61	=	5,929*
						$72,500						$44,208

*Rounded to nearest dollar

To adjust the inventory balance from its beginning balance at January 1, 1997, of $38,279 to the ending balance of $44,208 would then require the following journal entry:

Inventory	5,929	
Cost of Goods Sold	56,291	
Purchase Returns	2,000	
Purchase Discounts	1,000	
Purchases		63,000
Freight-in		2,220

INVENTORY VALUATIONS AT OTHER THAN COST

The basic cost procedures for determining inventory values have been discussed in this and the previous chapter. In some cases, generally accepted accounting principles permit deviations from cost, especially if a write-down of inventory values is warranted. The following sections of this chapter discuss some of these departures from historical cost and the circumstances under which they are appropriate.

Inventory Valuation at Lower of Cost or Market

The conceptual framework establishes and defines recognition criteria for the elements of the financial statements. The definition of an asset requires that it produce future benefits to the owner. If at any time the monetary value assigned to an asset overstates these future benefits, an adjustment should be made to reflect a loss. Recognition criteria limit the adjustment to situations where the asset value can be estimated and a probable loss exists. The application of these accounting concepts to inventory is known as valuation at the **lower of cost or market (LCM).**

Currently, generally accepted accounting principles permit recognition of increases in the value of inventory above cost only after the increase is realized and/or earned.

The current practice of recognizing inventory write-downs before realization but not inventory write-ups until after realization results in inconsistent treatment of value changes.

The American Institute of Certified Public Accountants (AICPA) sanctioned lower-of-cost-or-market valuation in the following statement:

A departure from the cost basis of pricing the inventory is required when the utility of the goods is no longer as great as its cost. Where there is evidence that the utility of goods, in their disposal in the ordinary course of business, will be less than cost, whether due to physical deterioration, obsolescence, changes in price levels, or other causes, the difference should be recognized as a loss of the current period. This is generally accomplished by stating such goods at a lower level commonly designated as market.[2]

In applying the lower-of-cost-or-market rule, the cost of the ending inventory, as determined under an appropriate cost allocation method, is compared with market value at the end of the period. If market is less than cost, an adjusting entry is made to record the loss and restate ending inventory at the lower value. It should be noted that no adjustment to LIFO cost is permitted for tax purposes; however, for financial reporting purposes, the lower-of-cost-or-market rule applies to all inventories. Application of LCM to LIFO inventories for financial reporting purposes does not violate the "LIFO conformity" rules if IRS approval is obtained.

Definition of Market. The term **market** in "lower of cost or market" is interpreted as replacement cost with upper and lower limits that reflect estimated realizable values. This concept of market was stated by the AICPA as follows:

As used in the phrase lower of cost or market, the term market means current replacement cost (by purchase or by reproduction, as the case may be) except that:

1. *Market should not exceed the net realizable value (i.e., estimated selling price in the ordinary course of business less reasonably predictable costs of completion and disposal); and*
2. *Market should not be less than net realizable value reduced by an allowance for an approximately normal profit margin.*[3]

Replacement cost, sometimes referred to as **entry cost,** includes the purchase price of the product or raw materials plus all other costs incurred in the acquisition or manufacture of goods. Because wholesale and retail prices are generally related, declines in entry costs usually indicate declines in selling prices or **exit values.** However, exit values do not always respond immediately and in proportion to changes in entry costs. If selling price does not decline, there is no loss in utility and a write-down of inventory values would not be warranted. On the other hand, selling prices may decline in response to factors unrelated to replacement costs. Perhaps an inventory item has been used as a demonstrator which reduces its marketability as a new product. Or perhaps an item is damaged in storage or becomes shopworn from excessive handling.

The AICPA definition considers exit values as well as entry costs by establishing a ceiling for the market value at sales price less costs of completion and disposal and a floor for market at sales price less both the costs of completion and disposal and the normal profit margin. The **ceiling limitation** is applied so the inventory is not valued at more than its net realizable value (NRV). Failure to observe this limitation would result in charges to future revenue that exceed the utility carried forward and an ultimate loss on the sale of the inventory. The **floor limitation** is applied so the inventory is not valued at less than its

2. *Accounting Research and Terminology Bulletins—Final Edition,* No. 43, "Restatement and Revision of Accounting Research Bulletins" (New York: American Institute of Certified Public Accountants, 1961), Ch. 4, Statement 5.
3. *Ibid* Statement 6.

net realizable value minus a **normal profit.** The concept of normal profit is a difficult one to measure objectively. Profits vary by item and over time. Records are seldom accurate enough to determine a normal profit by individual inventory item. Despite these difficulties, however, the use of a floor prevents a definition of market that would result in a write-down of inventory values in one period to create an abnormally high profit in future periods.

Applying Lower-of-Cost-or-Market Method. Application of the LCM rule to determine the appropriate inventory valuation may be summarized in the following steps:

1. Define pertinent values: cost, lower limit (NRV—normal profit), replacement cost, upper limit (NRV).
2. Determine "market" (replacement cost as modified by upper or lower limits).
3. Compare cost with market (as defined in 2 above), and select the lower amount.

To illustrate these steps, assume that a certain commodity sells for $1; selling expenses are $.20; the normal profit is 25% of sales or $.25. The lower of cost or market as modified by the upper and lower limits is developed in each case as shown in the illustration below.

Case	Cost	Lower Limit—Floor (estimated sales price less selling expenses and normal profits)	Replacement Cost	Upper Limit—Ceiling (estimated sales price less selling expenses)	Market (limited by floor and ceiling values)	Lower of Cost or Market
A	$.65	$.55	$ .70	$.80	$.70	$.65
B	.65	.55	.60	.80	.60	.60
C	.65	.55	.50	.80	.55	.55
D	.50	.55	.45	.80	.55	.50
E	.75	.55	.85	.80	.80	.75
F	.90	.55	1.00	.80	.80	.80

A: Market is not limited by floor or ceiling; cost is less than market.
B: Market is not limited by floor or ceiling; market is less than cost.
C: Market is limited to floor; market is less than cost.
D: Market is limited to floor; cost is less than market.
E: Market is limited to ceiling; cost is less than market.
F: Market is limited to ceiling; market is less than cost.

The following dollar line graphically illustrates the floor and ceiling range. B and A replacement costs clearly are within bounds and therefore are defined as market. D and C replacement costs are below the floor and thus the market is the floor; E and F replacement costs are above the ceiling and market therefore is the ceiling.

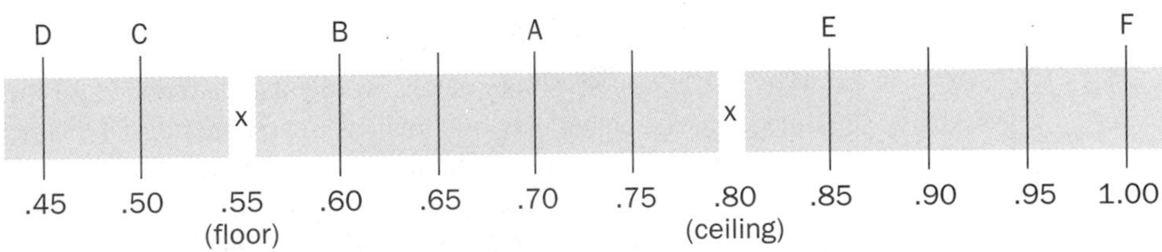

Note that the market value is always the middle value of three amounts: replacement cost, floor, and ceiling.

The lower-of-cost-or-market method may be applied to each inventory item, to the major classes or categories of inventory items, or to the inventory as a whole. Application of this procedure to the individual inventory items will result in the lowest inventory value and is the most commonly used application because it is required for income tax purposes. Once an individual item is reduced to a lower market price, the new market price is considered to be the item's cost for future inventory valuations; cost reductions once made are not restored. Thus detailed inventory records must be adjusted to reflect the new values.

To illustrate the difference in valuation applications, assume Clarks Men's Store classifies its inventories into three categories: (1) formal wear, (2) casual wear, and (3) sportswear. As shown below, the inventory, on an individual item basis, would be valued at $360,300, a reduction from cost of $29,500. The valuation based on categories and on the total inventory would be $371,300 and $377,300 respectively.

Clarks Men's Store Applications of Lower of Cost or Market

			Cost or Market Whichever is Lower		
Classes and Items	*Cost*	*Market*	*Individual Items*	*Inventory Categories*	*Total Inventory*
Formal wear:					
Tuxedos	$ 75,000	$ 70,000	$ 70,000		
Suits	120,000	130,000	120,000		
Dress shirts	30,000	28,000	28,000		
Dress shoes	18,000	21,000	18,000		
Total formal wear	$243,000	$249,000	$236,000	$243,000	
Casual wear:					
Slacks	$ 39,500	$ 32,000	$ 32,000		
Casual shirts	26,000	23,000	23,000		
Sweaters	15,000	17,000	15,000		
Total casual wear	$ 80,500	$ 72,000	$ 70,000	$ 72,000	
Sportswear:					
Sport shirts	$ 39,000	$ 29,000	$ 29,000		
Swimming wear	10,000	8,000	8,000		
Warm-ups	17,300	19,300	17,300		
Total sportswear	$ 66,300	$ 56,300	$ 54,300	$ 56,300	
Total inventory	$389,800	$377,300			$377,300
			$360,300	$371,300	$377,300

The entry to record the write-down of the inventory on an individual item basis is usually made directly to the inventory control account as follows:

Loss From Decline in Value of Inventory	29,500	
Inventory		29,500
Write-down of inventory to market.		

Any subsidiary inventory record would also be reduced for the decline. The loss on the decline in market value may be shown as a separate item in the income statement after cost of goods sold. Alternatively, the loss may be reflected directly in the cost of goods sold section by reporting the ending inventory at market rather than cost. To illustrate the following two reporting alternatives, assume that sales for the period totaled $1.2 million and beginning inventory and net purchases were $280,000 and $855,000, respectively. Separate reporting of the loss has the advantage of providing readers with increased information to forecast operations and cash flows.

Inventory Loss Reported Separately

Sales		$1,200,000
Cost of goods sold:		
Beginning inventory	$ 280,000	
Purchases	855,000	
Cost of goods available for sale	$1,135,000	
Ending inventory (at cost)	389,800	745,200
Gross profit		$ 454,800
Inventory loss due to write-down of cost to market		29,500
		$ 425,300

Inventory Loss Included in Cost of Goods Sold

Sales		$1,200,000
Cost of goods sold:		
Beginning inventory	$ 280,000	
Purchases	855,000	
Cost of goods available for sale	$1,135,000	
Ending inventory (at market, which is lower than cost)	360,300	774,700
Gross profit		$ 425,300

Rather than reducing the inventory directly, the inventory control account could be maintained at cost, and an allowance for inventory decline used to record the decline in value. This method would generally be used when inventory is valued on a category or entire inventory basis. The entry to record the write-down using an allowance for the categories of Clarks Men's Store would be as follows:

Loss From Decline in Value of Inventory	18,500	
Allowance for Decline in Value of Inventory		18,500

The allowance account would be reported as an offset to the inventory account on the balance sheet. In subsequent years, it will be adjusted upward or downward depending on the amount required to adjust cost to market. If the required allowance declines, a recovery or gain entry would be recorded. The recovery is limited by the amount in the allowance account. Assume the difference between cost and market for the three categories in the next year is only $5,500. The adjusting entry to record this information in the next year would be as follows:

Allowance for Decline in Value of Inventory	13,000	
Recovery of Decline in Value of Inventory		13,000

Application of the lower-of-cost-or-market method to inventory classes or to the inventory as a whole produces a more representative valuation and avoids the necessity of adjusting individual inventory items. Because declines in the value of some items are offset by increases in value of other items, the value of the items in the detailed inventory records are not adjusted. The category and total inventory applications are not acceptable for income tax purposes.[4]

Evaluation of Lower-of-Cost-or-Market Rule. As mentioned earlier, the lower-of-cost-or-market rule is evidence of the concept of accounting conservatism. Its strict application

4. Many disputes have arisen through the years between taxpayers and the IRS as to what constitutes a recognizable decline in inventory value. An important tax case in this area was settled by the U.S. Supreme Court in 1979. The taxpayer, Thor Power Tool Co., had followed the practice of writing down the value of spare parts inventories that were being held to cover future warranty requirements. Although the sales prices did not decline, the probability of the parts being sold, and thus their net realizable value, decreased as time passed. The write-down to reflect the current decline in value is consistent with the accounting principle of recognizing declines in value as they occur. The Supreme Court, however, ruled that for tax purposes the reduction must await the actual decline in the sales price for the parts in question.

has been applied to avoid valuing inventory on the balance sheet at more than replacement cost. Also as discussed earlier, the AICPA replaced a strict entry valuation with a utility measure that relies partially upon exit prices. If selling prices for the inventory have declined and the decline is expected to hold until the inventory is sold, the adjustment of income in the period of the decline seems justified. The value of the inventory has been impaired, which requires current adjustment. However, care must be taken in using this method not to manipulate income by allowing excessive charges against income in one period to be offset by excessive income in the next period.

Some accountants have argued against the use of lower of cost or market because it violates the cost concept. Market valuations are often subjective and based on expectations. To the extent these expectations are not realized, misleading financial statements will be produced. To illustrate, assume that activities summarized in terms of cost provide the following results over a three-year period:

	1995		1996		1997	
Sales		$200,000		$225,000		$250,000
Cost of goods sold:						
Beginning inventory	$ 60,000		$ 80,000		$127,500	
Purchases	120,000		160,000		90,000	
Goods available for sale	$180,000		$240,000		$217,500	
Less ending inventory	80,000	100,000	127,500	112,500	92,500	125,000
Gross profit on sales		$100,000		$112,500		$125,000
Operating expenses		80,000		90,000		100,000
Net income		$ 20,000		$ 22,500		$ 25,000
Rate of income to sales		10%		10%		10%

Assume estimates as to the future utility of ending inventories indicated market values as follows:

1995	1996	1997
$75,000	$110,000	$92,500

If the expected decline in selling prices did not occur, inventory valuation at the lower of cost or market would provide the following results.

	1995		1996		1997	
Sales		$200,000		$225,000		$250,000
Cost of goods sold:						
Beginning inventory	$ 60,000		$ 75,000		$110,000	
Purchases	120,000		160,000		90,000	
Goods available for sale	$180,000		$235,000		$200,000	
Less ending inventory	75,000	105,000	110,000	125,000	92,500	107,500
Gross profit on sales		$ 95,000		$100,000		$142,500
Operating expenses		80,000		90,000		100,000
Net income		$ 15,000		$ 10,000		$ 42,500
Rate of income to sales		7.5%		4.4%		17.0%

Reduction of an inventory below cost reduces the net income of the period in which the reduction is made and increases the net income of a subsequent period over what it would have been. In the example just given, total net income for the three-year period is the same under either set of calculations. But the reduction of inventories to lower market values reduced the net income for 1995 and for 1996 and increased the net income for 1997. The fact that inventory reductions were not followed by decreases in the sales prices resulted in net income determinations that varied considerably from those that might reasonably have been expected from increasing sales and costs that normally vary with sales volume.

Objection to valuation at the lower of cost or market is also raised on the grounds that it produces inconsistencies in the measurements of both the financial position and the operations of the enterprise. Market decreases are recognized, but increases are not. Although this system does produce some inconsistent application to the upward and downward movement of market, the authors feel that the lower-of-cost-or-market concept is preferable to a strict cost measurement. A loss in the utility of any asset should be reflected in the period the impairment is first recognized and a reasonable estimate of its significance can be determined.

Valuation of Trade-Ins and Repossessions

When goods are acquired in secondhand condition as a result of repossessions and trade-ins, they should be recorded at their estimated cash purchase prices. In some industries, these prices are defined and made available to dealers. One of the more organized used markets is that for automobiles. A book, published frequently in the various geographical markets of the country, lists low, medium, and high market values for the different models and makes of cars. It also distinguishes between retail and wholesale values. Similar lists are provided for machinery and equipment in some lines. When these publications exist, the prices listed may be used to value repossessed or trade-in inventory.

When published prices are not available, it is more difficult to measure the equivalent cash purchase price of the inventory. Under these conditions, the consistent use of **floor values**—amounts that, after adding reconditioning charges and selling expenses, will permit the recognition of normal profits—would be appropriate.

Accounting for trade-ins is illustrated by the following example: Christensen Department Store sells a new washing machine to a customer for $350 cash and a trade-in of an old washer. It is estimated that a realistic floor value for the trade-in is $50. Reconditioning costs of $30 are incurred after which the trade-in washer is sold for $120, an amount that provides a normal profit. Perpetual inventory records are maintained for trade-ins but not for the regular inventory. The following entries reflect these transactions.

Cash	350	
Trade-In Inventory	50	
Sales		400
To record sale of new washer and receipt of old washer as trade-in.		
Trade-In Inventory	30	
Cash		30
To record cost to recondition trade-in.		
Cash	120	
Sales—Trade-Ins		120
To record sale of trade-in washing machine.		
Cost of Trade-Ins Sold	80	
Trade In Inventory		80
To record cost of trade-in washing machine.		

Another approach to valuing trade-in inventories is to establish clearly the sales price of the new inventory being sold, and charge the trade-in inventory for the difference between a cash sales price and the cash required with the trade-in. Assume in the case of the washing machine that the regular cash sales price without a trade-in could be established at $390. The value assigned to the trade-in would thus be $40, the difference between $390 and $350.

Accounting for repossessions requires a slightly different approach. Assume Christensen Department Store sold another washing machine on account for $350 plus interest on the unpaid balance. The customer made principal payments of $200 on the machine and then defaulted on the contract. The machine was repossessed and overhauled at a cost of $40. It was then sold for $150, a price that provided a normal profit of 50% on cost.

The following entries reflect the repossession and subsequent resale:

Allowance for Doubtful Accounts	90	
Repossessed Inventory	60	
Accounts Receivable		150

Computation:
Value of repossession established to permit 50% normal profit on cost (33 1/3% on selling price).

Selling price	$150
Less profit at 33 1/3% of $150	50
Cost of repossessed goods sold	$100
Less cost of overhaul	40
Value of repossessed inventory	$ 60

Repossessed Inventory	40	
Cash		40
To record cost to overhaul repossessed washing machine.		
Cash	150	
Sales—Repossessed Inventory		150
To record sale of repossessed washing machine.		
Cost of Repossessed Goods Sold	100	
Repossessed Inventory		100
To record cost of repossessed washing machine ($60 + $40).		

Losses on Purchase Commitments

Purchase commitments are contracts made for the future purchase of goods at fixed prices. No entry is required to record the purchase prior to delivery of the goods. However, when price declines take place subsequent to such commitments and they are outstanding at the end of an accounting period, it is considered appropriate to measure and recognize these losses on the books just as losses on goods on hand are recognized. A decline is recorded by a debit to a special loss account and a credit to either a contra asset account or an accrued liability account, such as Estimated Loss on Purchase Commitments. Acquisition of the goods in a subsequent period is recorded by a credit to Accounts Payable, a debit canceling the credit balance in the contra asset or accrued liability account, and a debit to Purchases for the difference.

For example, assume that Rollins Oat Company entered into a purchase contract on November 1, 1996, for 100,000 bushels of wheat at $3.40 per bushel to be delivered in March of 1997. At the end of 1996, the market price for wheat had dropped to $3.20 per bushel. The entries to record this decline in value and the subsequent delivery of the wheat would be as follows:

1996			
Dec. 31	Loss on Purchase Commitments	20,000	
	Estimated Loss on Purchase Commitments		20,000
1997			
Mar. 31	Estimated Loss on Purchase Commitments	20,000	
	Purchases	320,000	
	Accounts Payable		340,000

The loss is thus assigned to the period in which the decline took place, and a subsequent period is charged for no more than the economic utility of the goods it receives. Current loss recognition would not be appropriate when commitments can be canceled, when commitments provide for price adjustment, when hedging transactions[5] prevent losses, or when declines do not suggest reductions in sale prices. No adjustments are customarily made if a recovery occurs prior to delivery.

EFFECTS OF ERRORS IN RECORDING INVENTORY POSITION

Failures to report the inventory position accurately result in misstatements on both the balance sheet and the income statement. The effect on the income statement is sometimes difficult to evaluate because of the different amounts that can be affected by an error. Analysis of the impact is aided by recalling the structure of the cost of goods sold section of the income statement:

Beginning Inventory
+
Purchases
=
Goods Available for Sale
–
Ending Inventory
=
Cost of Goods Sold

An overstatement of the beginning inventory will thus result in an overstatement of goods available for sale and cost of goods sold. Because the cost of goods sold is deducted from sales to determine the gross profit, the overstated cost of goods sold results in an understated gross profit and finally an understated net income. Sometimes an error may affect two of the amounts in such a way that they offset each other. For example, if a purchase in transit under the FIFO method is neither recorded as a purchase nor included in the ending inventory, the understatement of purchases results in an understatement of goods available for sale; however, the understatement of ending inventory subtracted from goods available for sale offsets the error and creates a correct cost of goods sold, gross profit, and net income. Inventory and accounts payable, however, will be understated on the balance sheet.

Because the ending inventory of one period becomes the beginning inventory of the next period, undetected accounting errors affect two accounting periods. If left undetected, the errors will offset each other under a FIFO or average method. Errors in LIFO layers, however, may perpetuate themselves until the layer is eliminated.

This type of analysis is required for all inventory errors. It is unwise to try to memorize the impact an error has on the financial statements. It is preferable to analyze each situation. The following analysis of four typical inventory errors, with their impact on both the current and succeeding years, provide additional examples of the above type of analysis.

5. Purchases or sales entered into for the purpose of balancing, respectively, sales or purchases already made or under contract in order to offset the effects of price fluctuations.

1. Overstatement of the ending inventory through errors in the count of goods on hand, pricing, or the inclusion in inventory of goods not owned or goods already sold:

   Current year:

   Income statement—overstatement of the ending inventory will cause the cost of goods sold to be understated and the net income to be overstated.
   Balance sheet—the inventory will be overstated and the owners' equity will be overstated.

   Succeeding year:

   Income statement—overstatement of the beginning inventory will cause the cost of goods sold to be overstated and the net income to be understated.
   Balance sheet—the error of the previous year will have been counter-balanced on the succeeding income statement and the balance sheet will be correctly stated.

2. Understatement of ending inventory through errors in the count of goods on hand, pricing, or the failure to include in inventory goods purchased or goods transferred but not yet sold:

   Misstatements indicated in (1) above are reversed. The succeeding year's balance sheet will be correctly stated because the error of the previous year will have been counterbalanced on the succeeding income statement.

3. Overstatement of ending inventory accompanied by failure to recognize sales and corresponding receivables at end of period:

   Current year:

   Income statement—sales are understated by the sales price of the goods and cost of goods sold is understated by the cost of the goods relating to the sales; gross profit and net income are thus understated by the gross profit on the sales.
   Balance sheet—receivables are understated by the sales price of the goods and the inventory is overstated by the cost of goods that were sold; current assets and owners' equity are thus understated by the gross profit on the sales.

   Succeeding year:

   Income statement—sales of the preceding year are recognized in this year in sales and cost of sales; gross profit and net income, therefore, are overstated by the gross profit on such sales.
   Balance sheet—the error of the previous year is counterbalanced on the succeeding income statement and the balance sheet will be correctly stated.

4. Understatement of ending inventory accompanied by failure to recognize purchases and corresponding payables at end of period:

   Current year:

   Income statement—purchases are understated, but this is counterbalanced by the understatement of the ending inventory; gross profit and net income are correctly stated as a result of the counterbalancing effect of the error.
   Balance sheet—although owners' equity is reported correctly, both current assets and current liabilities are understated.

   Succeeding year:

   Income statement—the beginning inventory is understated, but this is counterbalanced by an overstatement of purchases, as purchases at the end of the prior year are recognized currently; gross profit and net income are correctly stated as a result of the counterbalancing effect of the error.
   Balance sheet—the error of the previous year no longer affects balance sheet data.

This analysis can be summarized in tabular form as shown below; (+) indicates overstatement, (–) indicates understatement, and (0) indicates no effect.

Summary of Impact on Inventory Errors on Financial Statements

	Current Year						Subsequent Year					
	Income Statement			Balance Sheet			Income Statement			Balance Sheet		
	Sales	*Cost of Goods Sold*	*Net Income*	*Assets*	*Lia-bilities*	*Equity*	*Sales*	*Cost of Goods Sold*	*Net Income*	*Assets*	*Lia-bilities*	*Equity*
(1) Overstatement of ending inventory	0	–	+	+	0	+	0	+	–	0	0	0
(2) Understatement of ending inventory	0	+	–	–	0	–	0	–	+	0	0	0
(3) Overstatement of ending inventory and understatement of sales	–	–	–	–	0	–	+	+	+	0	0	0
(4) Understatement of ending inventory and understatement of purchases	0	0	0	–	–	0	0	0	0	0	0	0

The correcting entry for each of these errors depends on when the error is discovered. If it is discovered in the current year, adjustments can be made to current accounts, and the reported net income and balance sheet amounts will be correct. If the error is not discovered until the subsequent period, the correcting entry qualifies as a prior period adjustment if the net income of the prior period was misstated. The error to a prior year's income is corrected through retained earnings. To illustrate these entries, assume that error number three has occurred. The correcting entries required, depending on when the error is discovered, would be as follows. Assume the use of a perpetual inventory system.

Error discovered in current year (cost of inventory $1,000; sales price of inventory, $1,500).

Accounts Receivable	1,500	
Cost of Goods Sold	1,000	
Inventory		1,000
Sales		1,500

Error discovered in subsequent year (sale has been recorded in subsequent year).

Sales	1,500	
Cost of Goods Sold		1,000
Retained Earnings		500

If trend statistics are included in the annual reports, prior years' balances should be adjusted to reflect the correction of the error. Present-day audit techniques can substantially reduce the probability of material inventory errors.

FOREIGN CURRENCY INVENTORY TRANSACTIONS

The discussion of inventories thus far has centered around the purchase and valuation of inventories in a domestic environment, that is, within the United States. As noted in

Chapter 1, business has become increasingly global in perspective. Exports and imports of materials and finished goods are a significant part of many companies' purchases and sales. Depending on how a purchase or sale transaction is structured, additional gains or losses may occur in foreign inventory transactions because of fluctuations in the currency exchange rates between two countries. This section of the chapter addresses issues associated with foreign currency inventory transactions.

Foreign currency transactions are those transactions that involve a buyer and a seller whose financial reporting currencies are different. If a Japanese company sells goods to an American company and the American company is expected to pay for those goods in yen, the result is a foreign currency transaction for the American company. These types of transactions are becoming more commonplace as business activity becomes more global. Consider, for example, the impact of international operations on IBM Corporation. In 1992, IBM reported a net loss before changes in accounting principles of $6,865 million—including a loss of $1,320 million from foreign operations and a loss of $5,545 million from domestic operations. Even if one never leaves the United States, students of accounting must be prepared to deal with the intricacies associated with international business operations.

To illustrate the complexities associated with foreign transactions, we will first consider a simple domestic transaction involving the purchase of inventory on account. Suppose that Washington, Inc., purchases $10,000 worth of inventory from California Co. on November 1, 1995, and payment is due on February 1, 1996. The journal entry made by Washington, Inc., on the date of purchase would be:

Inventory	10,000	
Accounts Payable		10,000

When the account is paid on February 1, 1996, Washington, Inc., would make the following journal entry:

Accounts Payable	10,000	
Cash		10,000

If Washington, Inc., had purchased the inventory from a foreign company, the purchase transaction could be structured to require payment for the purchase either in dollars or in the foreign currency. **Denominated currency** is the term used to designate the currency to be used for payment. The denomination agreement determines who will bear the risk associated with foreign currency rate changes. If the U.S. dollar is the designated denomination currency for the foreign inventory purchase, Washington, Inc., would treat the purchase as a domestic transaction, and the journal entries for the purchase and the payment would be the same as above. Washington, Inc., would not bear the risk for any exchange rate changes. However, if the invoice had been denominated in a foreign currency, the amount of the invoice would have to be converted from the foreign currency into dollars before a purchase entry could be made. In order to do this, the exchange rate at the date of the transaction must be determined.

Exchange Rates

As the business environment has become more international, companies have required access to various foreign currencies. As a result, foreign currency markets have developed where currencies of different countries can be bought or sold. *The Wall Street Journal* quotes foreign exchange rates on a daily basis. For example, on January 31, 1994, one French franc was worth $.170. This rate is termed a **direct quote** in that the foreign currency is stated in terms of how many dollars one unit of foreign currency can purchase. An **indirect quote** is stated as the number of foreign currency units required to purchase one dollar. The indirect quote on January 31, 1994, was 5.881, i.e., 5.881 francs could be purchased for $1. Note the following relationship between a direct and indirect quote:

$$\text{Direct quote} = \frac{1}{\text{Indirect quote}}$$

or

$$\$.170 = \frac{\$1}{5.881 \text{ francs}}$$

The direct quote will be used throughout this chapter. For accounting purposes, three different terms are used to designate exchange rates as of particular points in time. The first is the **spot rate,** that is, the rate at which currencies can be traded immediately. The second exchange rate is the historical rate. The **historical rate** is the exchange rate in effect on the date of a specific transaction. The third rate, the **current rate,** is the exchange rate in effect on the date the balance sheet is prepared.

The Financial Accounting Standards Board has dealt with foreign currency issues throughout its existence. Currently, the standard that determines the accounting for foreign transactions is FASB Statement No. 52, "Foreign Currency Translation." This standard requires the use of the historical rate in recording a purchase or sale of inventory if the transaction is denominated in a foreign currency. The standard requires that any subsequent changes in the exchange rate, as measured by the spot rate and the current rate, be recorded as transaction gains and losses and be reflected in income in the period in which exchange rates change.

Measurement of a Purchase Transaction

Assume that Washington, Inc., had purchased the inventory from France Co. and the invoice was denominated in francs with a purchase price of 50,000 francs. Using the exchange rate in effect on the transaction date (assume the direct quote is $.200), Washington, Inc., would make the following journal entry to record the purchase:

1995			
Nov. 1	Inventory	10,000	
	Accounts Payable (fc)		10,000
	Purchased inventory from France Co. for 50,000 francs (50,000 × $.200 = $10,000).		

The (fc) designation is used for convenience to indicate those items that are denominated in a foreign currency. It is important to recognize, however, that the amounts in the journal entry represent the domestic currency—in this case, dollars.

The impact of a foreign currency inventory purchase is recognized when the liability is paid. If the terms call for payment of the liability on February 1, 1996, Washington, Inc., will have to credit cash on that date, but for how much? Recall that the invoice requires payment in francs—not dollars. Washington, Inc., will have to purchase 50,000 francs from a foreign currency broker. How much will the company be required to pay the broker? The answer depends on the spot rate on that date. If the spot rate is $.215 on February 1, 1996, then Washington, Inc., will have to pay $10,750 to purchase 50,000 francs. The journal entry to record the payment of the liability to France Co. would then be:

1996			
Feb. 1	Accounts Payable (fc)	10,000	
	Exchange Loss	750	
	Cash		10,750
	Purchased 50,000 francs from broker and paid France Co. (50,000 × $.215 = $10,750).		

Washington, Inc., incurs a loss in this situation because the exchange rate, and thus the number of dollars required to purchase francs, has increased since the initial purchase transaction. On November 1, 1995, Washington, Inc., would have had to pay only $10,000 to purchase 50,000 francs. However, to purchase the same number of francs on February 1, 1996, requires $10,750. The exchange loss would appear on the income statement in the period incurred and is typically classified as "other income or expenses."

This situation could just as easily have resulted in an exchange gain for Washington, Inc. If the exchange rate had declined, then fewer dollars would have been required to purchase 50,000 francs. Suppose the exchange rate for French francs had been $.195 on February 1, 1996. Washington, Inc., would have recorded the following journal entry and recognized an exchange gain:

1996			
Feb. 1	Accounts Payable (fc)	10,000	
	Exchange Gain		250
	Cash		9,750
	Purchased 50,000 francs from broker and paid France Co. (50,000 × $.195 = $9,750).		

A second requirement of FASB Statement No. 52 relates to balance sheet adjustments. The pronouncement states that balances denominated in a foreign currency be adjusted to the exchange rate as of the balance sheet date, i.e., the current rate. This requirement is consistent with the matching principle, which states that increases and decreases in assets and liabilities should be recorded in the period in which those increases and decreases occur rather than when cash is paid or received. Continuing the initial example, suppose that Washington, Inc.'s, accounting year ends on December 31 and the exchange rate on December 31, 1995, was $.208. On that date, Washington, Inc., would make the following adjusting entry to record the change in the amount of cash required to pay the liability:

1995			
Dec. 31	Exchange Loss	400	
	Accounts Payable (fc)		400
	Recognized loss from increase in exchange rate. [(50,000 francs × $.208) − $10,000 = $400].		

This journal entry adjusts the liability to its value of $10,400 given the current exchange rate ($.208) and allocates the exchange rate loss to the period in which the change in exchange rates occurred. When the liability is subsequently paid on February 1, 1996, when the exchange rate for francs is $.215, the journal entry would be:

1996			
Feb. 1	Accounts Payable (fc)	10,400	
	Exchange Loss	350	
	Cash		10,750
	Purchased 50,000 francs from broker and paid France Co. (50,000 × $.215 = $10,750).		

Note that the exchange losses of $400 and $350 recorded on December 31 and February 1, respectively, total $750—the same amount that is obtained if no adjusting entry were made. The adjusting entry simply allocates the exchange loss to the appropriate accounting periods.

An obvious question at this point is, Why didn't Washington, Inc., avoid the exchange loss and pay the liability early? If Washington, Inc., knew that exchange rates were going to rise, they probably would have. However, predicting the direction and amount of change in the exchange rate for a particular currency is as difficult as predicting whether the price of a specific stock on the New York Stock Exchange is going to rise or fall, and by how much.

Measurement of a Sales Transaction

The accounting treatment for sales transactions is similar to that discussed for purchase transactions. The only major difference is that a receivable is denominated in a foreign currency instead of a payable. In the example of a purchase transaction, if exchange rates increased, Washington, Inc., recorded an exchange loss, and if exchange rates decreased, the company recorded a gain. The reverse is true with a sales transaction. If a firm is expecting to receive 10,000 foreign currency units and the value of those units declines, the firm will incur an exchange loss. If the exchange rate should rise, then the value of the foreign currency units will increase and a gain will result.

Consider the following example: On December 1, 1995, American Co. sold inventory to German Inc. for 22,000 German marks. Assume that the exchange rate for marks on that day was $.595, and the exchange rate on December 31, 1995, was $.600. American Co. received a check in full payment of German Inc.'s account on January 15, 1996, when the exchange rate was $.613. American Co. would make the following journal entries to record the above events:

1995			
Dec. 1	Accounts Receivable (fc)	13,090	
	Sales		13,090
	Sold inventory to German Inc. for 22,000 marks (22,000 × $.595 = $13,090).		
31	Accounts Receivable (fc)	110	
	Exchange Gain		110
	Recognized gain from increase in exchange rate.		
1996			
Jan. 15	Cash (fc)	13,486	
	Exchange Gain		286
	Accounts Receivable (fc)		13,200
	Collected 22,000 marks from German Inc. (22,000 × $.613 = $13,486).		
15	Cash	13,486	
	Cash (fc)		13,486
	Converted the 22,000 marks received from German Inc. into dollars.		

The entry on December 1 records the account receivable at its value given the exchange rate on the day of the transaction. On December 31, an adjusting entry is made to recognize that the value of the 22,000 marks that American Co. is entitled to receive has increased. The adjustment increases the receivable balance to $13,200 ($13,090 + $110). When the account is collected on January 15, American Co. receives 22,000 marks, and their value on the date of receipt is $13,486. Because the exchange rate on January 15 is higher than the December 31 rate, an additional gain of $286 is recognized when American Co. records receipt of the marks. The 22,000 marks are converted immediately into dollars, and a second entry is made on January 15 to record the conversion. If American Co. had not converted the marks into dollars on the day of their receipt, the company would have been exposing itself to additional risk associated with exchange rate changes.

INVENTORIES ON THE BALANCE SHEET

It is customary to report both merchandise and manufacturing inventories as current assets even though in some situations, considerable time will elapse before portions of such inventories are realized in cash. Among the items that are generally reported separately under the inventories heading are merchandise inventory or finished goods, goods in process, raw materials, factory supplies, goods and materials in transit, goods on consignment, and goods in the hands of agents and salespersons. Inventories are normally listed in the order of their liquidity. Any advance payments on purchase commitments should be reported separately and should not be included with inventories. Such advances are preferably listed after inventories in the current asset section since they have not entered the inventory phase of the operating cycle.

The inventory valuation procedures used must be disclosed in a note to the financial statements outlining all significant accounting policies followed.[6] The basis of valuation (such as cost or lower of cost or market), together with the method of arriving at cost (LIFO, FIFO, average, or other method), should be indicated. The reader of a statement may assume that the valuation procedures indicated have been consistently applied and financial statements are comparable with those of past periods. If this is not the case, a special note should be provided stating the change in the method and the effects of the change upon the financial statements.

If significant inventory price declines take place between the balance sheet date and the date the financial statements are issued, such declines should be disclosed by parenthetical remark or note. When relatively large orders for merchandise have been placed by the reporting company in a period of widely fluctuating prices, but the title to such goods has not yet passed, such commitments should be described by special note. Information should also be provided concerning possible losses on purchase commitments. Similar information may be appropriate for possible losses on sales commitments.

Replacement costs of inventories may be disclosed in a note to the financial statements. Until such time as market valuation of inventories becomes generally acceptable for reporting purposes, only supplemental disclosure of current values is permitted.

When inventories have been pledged as security on loans from banks, finance companies, or factors, the amounts pledged should be disclosed either parenthetically in the inventory section of the balance sheet or in the notes.

6. *Opinions of the Accounting Principles Board, No. 22,* "Disclosure of Accounting Policies" (New York: American Institute of Certified Public Accountants, 1972), par. 12.

KEY TERMS

Additional markups 395
Average cost retail inventory method 396
Ceiling limitation 402
Conventional retail inventory method 396
Cost percentage 394
Current rate 413
Denominated currency 412
Direct quote 412
Dollar-value LIFO retail method 399
Entry cost 402
Exit values 402
Floor limitation 402
Foreign currency transactions 412
Freight-in 398
Gross profit method 392
Historical rate 413
Indirect quote 412
Initial markup 396
Lower of cost or market (LCM) 401
Markdown cancellations 395
Markdowns 395
Market (in "lower of cost or market") 402
Markup cancellations 395
Net markdowns 395
Net markups 395
Original retail 395
Replacement cost 402
Retail inventory method 394
Spot rate 413

QUESTIONS

1. What is meant by the term "gross profit test"?
2. Distinguish between: (a) gross profit as a percentage of cost and gross profit as a percentage of sales; (b) the gross profit method of calculating estimated inventory cost and the retail inventory method of calculating estimated inventory cost.
3. What effect would the use of the LIFO inventory method have upon the applicability of the gross profit method of valuing inventory?
4. (a) How are markdowns treated under the conventional retail method? (b) What costing method is approximated by this approach?
5. How does the conventional retail inventory method differ from the average cost retail inventory method?
6. How are purchase discounts and sales discounts treated when using the retail inventory method?
7. (a) Describe dollar-value LIFO retail. (b) How does the LIFO retail cost percentage differ from the conventional retail cost percentage?
8. Under what circumstances would a decline in replacement cost of an item not justify a departure from the cost basis of valuing an inventory?
9. The use of lower of cost or market is an archaic continuation of conservative accounting. Comment on this view.
10. Why are ceiling and floor limitations on replacement cost considered necessary by the AICPA?
11. The Muhlstein Corporation began business on January 1, 1995. Shown below is information about inventories, as of December 31 for three consecutive years, under different valuation methods. Using this information and assuming that the same method is used each year, you are to choose the phrase which best answers each of the following questions:

	LIFO Cost	FIFO Cost	Market	Lower of Cost or Market*
1995	$10,200	$10,000	$ 9,600	$ 8,900
1996	9,100	9,000	8,800	8,500
1997	10,300	11,000	12,000	10,900

*FIFO Cost, item-by-item valuation.

    (a) The inventory basis that would result in the highest net income for 1995 is: (1) LIFO cost, (2) FIFO cost, (3) Market, (4) Lower of cost or market.
    (b) The inventory basis that would result in the highest net income for 1996 is: (1) LIFO cost, (2) FIFO cost, (3) Market, (4) Lower of cost or market.
    (c) The inventory basis that would result in the lowest net income for the three years combined is: (1) LIFO cost, (2) FIFO cost, (3) Market, (4) Lower of cost or market.
    (d) For the year 1996, how much higher or lower would net income be on the FIFO cost basis than on the lower-of-cost-or-market basis? (1) $400 higher, (2) $400 lower, (3) $600 higher, (4) $600 lower, (5) $1,000 higher, (6) $1,000 lower, (7) $1,400 higher, (8) $1,400 lower.
12. How does the accounting treatment for losses on purchase commitments differ between actual losses which have already occurred and losses which may occur in the future?
13. What is the justification for valuing trade-ins or repossessions so that a normal profit can be realized upon their sale?
14. How should repossessed goods be valued for inventory purposes? Give reasons for your answers.

15. State the effect of each of the following errors made by Clawson Inc. upon the balance sheet and the income statement (1) of the current period and (2) of the succeeding period:
    (a) The company fails to record a sale of merchandise on account; goods sold are excluded in recording the ending inventory.
    (b) The company fails to record a sale of merchandise on account; the goods sold are included, however, in recording the ending inventory.
    (c) The company fails to record a purchase of merchandise on account; goods purchased are included in recording the ending inventory.
    (d) The company fails to record a purchase of merchandise on account; goods purchased are not recognized in recording the ending inventory.
    (e) The ending inventory is understated as the result of a miscount of goods on hand.
16. Are all transactions with foreign companies classified as foreign currency transactions? If not, what determines if a transaction is a foreign currency transaction?
17. Why does a seller recognize a gain on a foreign currency transaction when exchange rates go up?
18. Why does the FASB require an adjustment to be made on the balance sheet date to reflect exchange rate changes?
19. How would you recommend that the following items be reported on the balance sheet?
    (a) Unsold goods in the hands of consignees.
    (b) Purchase orders outstanding.
    (c) Advance payments on purchase commitments.
    (d) Raw materials pledged as security on notes payable to bank.
    (e) Raw materials in transit from suppliers, FOB shipping point.
    (f) Goods produced by special order and set aside to be picked up by customer.
    (g) Finished parts to be used in the assembly of final products.
    (h) Office supplies.

DISCUSSION CASES

Case 10—1 (Where has the inventory gone?)

Main Street Department Store uses the retail inventory method. Periodically, a physical count is made of the inventory and compared with the book figure computed from the company sales and purchase records. This year the extended valuation of the physical count resulted in a total inventory value 10% lower than the book figure. Jennifer Strack, the controller, is concerned by the variance. A 2% to 3% loss from shoplifting has been tolerated through the years. But 10% is too much. The branch manager, Bryan Smith, who is summoned to account for the discrepancy, insists that the book figures must be wrong. He is confident that the shortage could not be that high but that bookkeeping errors must be at fault. Strack, however, is not satisfied with the explanation and asks Smith to outline specifically what types of errors could have caused such a variance. Prepare Smith's outline for Strack.

Case 10—2 (Inventory valuation without records)

The Ma & Pa Grocery Store has never kept many records. The proceeds from sales are used to pay suppliers for goods delivered. When the owners, Donald and Alicia Wride, need some cash, they withdraw it from the till without any record being made of it. The Wrides realize that eventually tax returns must be filed, but for three years, "they just haven't got around to it." Finally, the Internal Revenue Service catches up with the Wrides, and an audit of the company records is conducted. The auditor requests the general ledger, special journals, inventory counts, and supporting documentation—very little of which is available. Records of expenditures are extremely sketchy because most expenses are paid in cash. If you were the IRS auditor, what might you do to make a reasonable estimate of income for the company?

Case 10—3 (What really is the difference between retail methods?)

Karen Stewart, president of Laronco, Inc., recently attended a seminar on effectively managing a business. One session of the seminar that particularly impressed Karen was the discussion of inventory management and the various types of inventory estimation methods available for producing interim financial statements. While the seminar only highlighted the characteristics of the various methods, Karen has come to you, the company's chief financial officer, and asked you to detail the similarities and differences between the retail inventory method and the dollar-value LIFO retail method. Under what circumstances would the dollar-value LIFO retail method result in a higher ending inventory figure?

Case 10—4 **(Have we really had a loss?)**

The Destro Company is experiencing an unusual inventory situation. The replacement cost of its principal product has been declining, but because of a unique market condition, Destro has not had to reduce the selling price of the item. Eric Dona, company controller, is aware that GAAP requires the valuation of inventory at the lower of cost or market. He considers market to be replacement cost, and he is concerned that to reduce the ending inventory to replacement cost will improperly reduce net income for the current period. Has an inventory loss occurred? Discuss.

Case 10—5 **(What value should we place on the clunker?)**

The Ritchie Automobile Agency is an exclusive agency for the sales of foreign sports cars. As part of its sales strategy, Ritchie allows liberal trade-in allowances on the sale of its new cars. A used car division of the company sells these trade-ins at a separate location, usually at an amount significantly lower than the trade-in allowance. This division is continually showing large losses because the cars are charged to the division at their trade-in values. John Lund, manager of the used car division, has requested that the costing procedure be changed and that trade-ins be recorded at a price sufficiently below expected retail to allow a reasonable profit to his division. Janet Perry, controller of the agency, acknowledges that some adjustment needs to be made to the inflated trade-in values, but feels that expected retail value should be used without allowance for a profit. What value should be used on the financial statements for the ending inventory of trade-ins? Discuss the reasonableness of this method for internal management evaluations.

Case 10—6 **(Silver's ups and downs)**

In 1979 and 1980, the Hunt brothers from Texas attempted to corner the world's silver market. Their hope was to own enough silver to be able to dictate world prices. They made purchase commitments, which locked in the price they would pay for silver, and for a while, their plan worked. The price of silver rose, and the Hunt brothers used the silver they owned as collateral to purchase more silver.

Their plans were shattered when the price of silver started to decline. From a high in January 1980 of $50.35 an ounce, silver fell to $10.80 in just two months. The silver they were using as collateral decreased in value, requiring the Hunt brothers to provide additional collateral. This collateral was in the form of oil, sugar, and real estate, each of which was faring poorly at the time of the silver crash. At the same time, the purchase commitments they had made required them to buy silver at prices higher than the current market value of silver. The Hunt brothers sought protection in bankruptcy court and the scheme eventually cost them approximately $4 billion. What are the risks associated with making purchase commitments? Why do accounting standards require that price declines subsequent to the purchase commitment but prior to the actual purchase be recorded immediately? Can firms take any action to reduce their exposure to changing prices?

Case 10—7 **(Can we avoid losses from exchange rate changes?)**

Smith & Sons routinely purchases inventory from Mistuhaki Corp. Because of unpredictability in the foreign currency markets, transactions denominated in yen leave Smith & Sons exposed to the risks associated with exchange rate changes. Identify and discuss methods by which Smith & Sons can reduce its exposure to foreign currency losses.

Case 10—8 **(But they won't buy ducks anymore!)**

The Bright-Lite Shirt Company buys wholesale sweat shirts, night shirts, t-shirts, and other clothing items and, using a novel four-color processing system, imprints hundreds of designs on the items. The printed shirts are marketed widely to sports stores, department stores, college campus outlets, variety stores, vacation shops, etc. Gordon Smith, marketing manager, likes to have a wide variety of products on hand so orders can be promptly met. As the number of designs has grown, so has the inventory. However, the designs often exhibit "fad" characteristics, and ducks, bears, flowers, or sports heroes can change fairly rapidly. Beverly Patton, the controller, has expressed dismay at the growing inventory, and especially the issue of inventory obsolescence. She sends a report to Gordon urging him to reduce his inventory and change his production concept. Gordon is reluctant to change because Bright-Lite has developed an excellent reputation for meeting emergency requests for inventory. How might obsolescence be controlled in a fashion company such as Bright-Lite? How should the inventory be valued on the financial statements?

Case 10—9 (Sales are still increasing—or are they?)

Nu-Ware, Inc. sells cookware with a specialized coating that protects the product and prevents sticking better than other coatings on the market. The design of the cookware is also unique, and during the first two years of operations, Nu-Ware's sales increased dramatically. Inventory production increased continuously to meet the expanding demand. When the economy softened and sales started to level and even decline, Nu-Ware was caught with excessive inventory.

Shirley Morris, president of Nu-Ware, was concerned about the company's image. Stock had been sold with the representation of continuing growth increases. She contacted several customers, and persuaded them to accept merchandise shipments that had not been ordered in case their needs were higher than anticipated. She assumed the risk for her customers by deferring payment for 6 months, and agreeing to allow a 40% return on goods shipped in this manner. As a result of this arrangement, the company continued to show growth and the inventory levels were reduced. As the new year passed, the recession stubbornly held on, and customers either returned excess stock or held it for the busy Christmas season.

Assume you are assigned to audit Nu-Ware and know nothing of the above arrangements with customers. What analytical measures could suggest to you that the shipping and billing procedures had changed?

EXERCISES

Exercise 10—10 (Inventory loss—gross profit method)

On August 15, 1996, a hurricane damaged a warehouse of Rheinhart Merchandise Company. The entire inventory and many accounting records stored in the warehouse were completely destroyed. Although the inventory was not insured, a portion could be sold for scrap. Through the use of microfilmed records, the following data is assembled:

Inventory, January 1	$ 375,000
Purchases, January 1-August 15	1,385,000
Cash sales, January 1-August 15	225,000
Collection of accounts receivable, January 1-August 15	2,115,000
Accounts receivable, January 1	175,000
Accounts receivable, August 15	265,000
Salvage value of inventory	5,000
Gross profit percentage on sales	32%

Compute the inventory loss as a result of the hurricane.

Exercise 10—11 (Inventory loss—gross profit method)

On June 30, 1996, a flash flood damaged the warehouse and factory of Bend Corporation, completely destroying the work-in-process inventory. There was no damage to either the raw materials or finished goods inventories. A physical inventory taken after the flood revealed the following valuations:

Finished goods	$112,000
Work in process	-0-
Raw materials	52,000

The inventory on January 1, 1996, consisted of the following:

Finished goods	$120,000
Work in process	115,000
Raw materials	42,500
	$277,500

A review of the books and records disclosed that the gross profit margin historically approximated 34% of sales. The sales for the first six months of 1996 were $428,000. Raw materials purchases were $96,000. Direct labor costs for this period were $90,000, and factory overhead has historically been applied at 60% of direct labor.

Compute the value of the work-in-process inventory lost at June 30, 1996. Show supporting computations in good form.

Exercise 10—12 (Retail inventory method)

Carmel Department Store uses the retail inventory method. On December 31, 1996, the following information relating to the inventory was gathered:

	Cost	Retail
Inventory, January 1, 1996	$ 26,550	$ 45,000
Sales		430,000
Purchases	309,000	435,000
Purchase discounts	4,200	
Freight-in	5,250	
Net markups		30,000
Net markdowns		10,000
Sales discounts		5,000

Compute the ending inventory value at December 31, 1996, using the conventional retail inventory method.

Exercise 10—13 (Retail inventory method)

The Evening Out Clothing Store values its inventory under the retail inventory method at the lower of cost or market. The following data is available for the month of November 1996:

	Cost	Selling Price
Inventory, November 1	$ 53,800	$ 76,000
Markdowns		5,700
Markups		11,200
Markdown cancellations		2,200
Markup cancellations		5,600
Purchases	157,304	223,600
Sales		244,000
Purchase returns	3,000	3,600
Sales returns		12,000
Sales allowances		6,000

Based upon the data presented above, prepare a schedule in good form to compute the estimated inventory at November 30, 1996, at the lower of cost or market under the retail inventory method.

(AICPA adapted)

Exercise 10—14 (Retail inventory method)

The Ivory Tower Bookstore recently received a shipment of accounting textbooks from the publisher. Following the receipt of the shipment, the FASB issued a major new accounting standard that related directly to the contents of one chapter of the text. Portions of this chapter became "obsolete" immediately as a result of the FASB's action. In order to sell the books, the bookstore marked down the selling price and offered a separate supplement covering the new standard, which was provided at no cost by the publisher. Information relating to the cost and selling price of the text for the month of September is given below:

	Cost	Retail
Beginning inventory	$ 1,500	$ 1,800
Purchases	24,000	29,760
Freight-in	1,100	
Markdowns		2,100
Sales		27,500

Based on the data given, compute the estimated inventory at the end of the month using the retail inventory method and assuming:

1. lower-of-cost-or-market valuation (conventional retail)
2. average cost valuation

Exercise 10—15 (Dollar-value LIFO retail method)

The Paradise Hardware Store began using the dollar-value LIFO retail method in 1995 for determining inventory values. In 1995, the cost percentage was computed at 62%. Information relating to the inventory for 1996 is given below:

		Cost	Retail
Inventory, January 1		$ 39,680	$ 64,000
Purchases		165,000	270,600
Purchase returns		11,200	18,368
Freight-in		26,000	
Sales			269,000
Net markups			26,000
Net markdowns			8,000
Price index:			
1995—All year	1.00		
1996—December 31	1.08		

1. Compute the cost percentage for 1996. (Round percentage to two decimal places.)
2. Compute the inventory value to be reported at December 31, 1996, assuming incremental layers are costed at end-of-year prices.

Exercise 10—16 (Dollar-value LIFO retail method)

On July 31, 1997, Rooker, Madras & Associates compiled the following information concerning inventory for five years. They used the dollar-value LIFO retail inventory method.

Date	Year-End Price Index	Incremental Layer Index	Incremental Cost Percentage	Inventory at Retail
Dec. 31, 1992	1.00	1.00	71%	$155,000
Dec. 31, 1993	1.04	1.02	72%	188,600
Dec. 31, 1994	1.14	1.09	64%	192,500
Dec. 31, 1995	1.12	1.11	63%	194,200
Dec. 31, 1996	1.16	1.12	67%	195,800

Compute the inventory cost at the end of each year under the dollar-value LIFO retail method. (Round all dollar amounts to the nearest dollar.)

Exercise 10—17 (Lower-of-cost-or-market valuation)

Determine the proper carrying value of the following inventory items if priced in accordance with the recommendations of the AICPA:

Item	Cost	Replacement Cost	Sales Price	Selling Expenses	Normal Profit
Product 561	$1.85	$1.82	$2.30	$.35	$.20
Product 562	.69	.72	1.00	.30	.04
Product 563	.31	.24	.43	.15	.07
Product 564	.92	.70	1.05	.27	.05
Product 565	.84	.82	1.00	.19	.09
Product 566	1.19	1.25	1.43	.13	.09

Exercise 10—18 (Lower-of-cost-or-market valuation)

The following inventory data is available for Alpine Ski Shop at December 31:

	Cost	Market
Skis	$60,000	$65,000
Boots	37,500	35,000
Ski Equipment	15,000	14,000
Ski Apparel	12,000	13,500

1. Determine the value of ending inventory using the lower-of-cost-or-market method applied to (a) individual items and (b) total inventory.
2. Prepare any journal entries required to adjust the ending inventory if lower of cost or market is applied to (a) individual items and (b) total inventory.

Exercise 10—19 (Lower-of-cost-or-market valuation)

Newcomer, Inc., values inventories at the lower-of-cost-or-market method applied to total inventory. Inventory values at the end of the company's first and second years of operation are presented below.

	Ending Inventory	
	Cost	*Market*
Year 1	$58,000	$53,000
Year 2	75,000	73,800

1. Prepare the journal entries necessary to reflect the proper inventory valuation at the end of each year. (Assume Newcomer uses an inventory allowance account.)
2. For Year 1, assume sales were $390,000 and purchases were $320,000. What amount would be reported as cost of goods sold on the income statement for Year 1 if: (a) the inventory decline is reported separately? and (b) the inventory decline is not reported separately?

Exercise 10—20 (Loss on purchase commitments)

On October 1, 1996, Gore Electronics Inc. entered into a six-month, $520,000 purchase commitment for a supply of Product A. On December 31, 1996, the market value of this material has fallen so that current acquisition of the ordered quantity would cost $441,500. It is anticipated that a further decline will occur during the next three months and that market at date of delivery will be approximately $390,000. What entries would you make on December 31, 1996, and on March 31, 1997, assuming the expected decline in prices does occur?

Exercise 10—21 (Valuation of trade-in)

Wailea Inc. sells new equipment with a $28,000 list price. Assume that Wailea sells one unit of equipment and accepts a trade-in plus $24,100 in cash. The expected sales price of the reconditioned equipment is $3,500; the reconditioning expenses are estimated to be $500; and normal profit is 30% of the sales price.

1. Prepare the journal entry to record the sale assuming that floor values are used.
2. Prepare the journal entry to record the sale assuming that the sale of new equipment is recorded at its normal list price.
3. Evaluate the entries.

Exercise 10—22 (Repossessed inventory)

Prawitt Equipment Inc. sells its inventory on a time basis. In about 5% of the sales, the customer defaults in the payments and the equipment must be repossessed. Assume that equipment was sold for $21,000 which included interest of $2,250 (the company uses an allowance for unearned finance charges account). The customer defaulted after making payments of $10,350, which included $1,425 interest. The equipment was repossessed and overhauled at a cost of $2,900. It was then sold on a thirty-day account for $17,000, a price that provided a normal profit of 25% on cost. What journal entries would be required to record the repossession and subsequent resale of the equipment?

Exercise 10—23 (Correction of inventory errors)

Annual income for the Stoker Co. for the period 1992-1996 appears below. However, a review of the records for the company reveals inventory misstatements as listed. Calculate corrected net income for each year.

	1992	1993	1994	1995	1996
Reported net income (loss)	$18,000	$13,000	$2,000	$(5,800)	$16,000
Inventory overstatement, end of year		5,500			3,600
Inventory understatement, end of year	2,800			10,500	

Exercise 10—24 (Effect on net income of inventory errors)

The Martin Company reported income before taxes of $370,000 for 1995, and $526,000 for 1996. A later audit produced the following information:

(a) The ending inventory for 1995 included 2,000 units erroneously priced at $5.90 per unit. The correct cost was $9.50 per unit.

(b) Merchandise costing $17,500 was shipped to the Martin Company, FOB shipping point, on December 26, 1995. The purchase was recorded in 1995, but the merchandise was excluded from the ending inventory since it was not received until January 4, 1996.

(c) On December 28, 1995, merchandise costing $2,900 was sold to Deluxe Paint Shop. Deluxe had asked Martin to keep the merchandise for them until January 2, when they would come and pick it up. Because the merchandise was still in the store at year-end, the merchandise was included in the inventory count. The sale was correctly recorded in December 1995.

(d) Craft Company sold merchandise costing $1,500 to Martin Company. The purchase was made on December 29, 1995, and the merchandise was shipped on December 30. Terms were FOB shipping point. Because the Martin Co. bookkeeper was on vacation, neither the purchase nor the receipt of goods was recorded on the books until January 1996.

Assuming all amounts are material and a physical count of inventory was taken every December 31,

(1) Compute the corrected income before taxes for each year.
(2) By what amount did the total net income change for the two years combined?
(3) Assume all errors were found in January 1997, before the books were closed for 1996; what journal entry would be made?

Exercise 10—25 (Correction of LIFO inventory)

The Cardoza Products Company's inventory record appears below:

	Purchases		Sales
	Quantity	*Unit Cost*	*Quantity*
1994	9,000	$5.60	6,500
1995	9,500	5.75	10,000
1996	7,200	5.82	6,000

The company uses a LIFO cost flow assumption. It reported ending inventories as follows for its first 3 years of operations:

1994	$14,000
1995	11,600
1996	18,600

Determine if the Cardoza Products Company has reported its inventory correctly. Assuming that 1996 accounts are not yet closed, make any necessary correcting entries.

Exercise 10—26 (Foreign transaction—purchase)

Guenther's, a German company that supplies your firm with a necessary raw material, recently shipped 10,000 units of the material to your production facility.

1. Prepare the necessary journal entries to record the purchase of the goods and the subsequent payment 30 days later if the selling price on the invoice is $6 per unit.
2. Prepare the necessary journal entries to record the purchase of the goods and the subsequent payment 30 days later if the selling price on the invoice is 4 German marks per unit. The spot rate for German marks on the date of purchase is $1.50, and the rate on the date of payment is $1.60.

Exercise 10—27 (Foreign transaction—sale)

Meny Yawnas Inc., a Japanese firm, regularly purchases semiconductors from your company, Semiconductors, Inc. An order for 1,000 semiconductors was recently shipped to Meny Yawnas.

1. Prepare the necessary journal entries to record the sale of the semiconductors and the subsequent receipt of payment if the denominated selling price for the goods was $12 per unit.
2. Prepare the necessary journal entries to record the sale of the semiconductors and the subsequent receipt of payment if the denominated selling price for the goods was 120 yen per unit. The spot rate for Japanese yen on the date of sale is $.10, and the rate on the date of payment is $.11.

Exercise 10—28 (Foreign transaction—purchase)

Koreaco produces automobile transmissions which are then sent to the United States where they are installed in domestically built cars. CarCo, an American auto company, received a shipment of transmissions on December 15, 1995. The transmissions were subsequently paid for on January 30, 1996. The invoice was denominated in Korean won and totaled 5,000,000 won. The relevant exchange rates are as follows:

	Exchange Rates
December 15, 1995	$.055
December 31, 1995	.057
January 30, 1996	.060

Provide the necessary journal entries to record the above transactions assuming CarCo's fiscal year-end is December 31.

PROBLEMS

Problem 10—29 (Inventory fire loss)

Kimbell Manufacturing began operations five years ago. On August 13, 1996, a fire broke out in the warehouse destroying all inventory and many accounting records relating to the inventory. The information available is presented below. All sales and purchases are on account.

	January 1, 1996	August 13, 1996
Inventory	$143,850	
Accounts receivable	130,590	$128,890
Accounts payable	88,140	122,850
Collection on accounts receivable, January 1-August 13		753,800
Payments to suppliers, January 1-August 13		487,500
Goods out on consignment at August 13, at cost		32,500

Summary of previous years sales:

	1993	1994	1995
Sales	$626,000	$705,000	$680,000
Gross profit on sales	187,800	183,300	231,200

Instructions: Determine the inventory loss suffered as a result of the fire.

Problem 10—30 (Interim inventory computation—gross profit method)

The following information was taken from the records of the Prairie Company.

	Jan. 1, 1995-Dec. 31, 1995	Jan. 1, 1996-Sept. 30, 1996
Sales (net of returns)	$2,500,000	$1,500,000
Beginning inventory	420,000	785,000
Purchases	2,152,000	1,061,000
Freight-in	116,000	72,000
Purchase discounts	30,000	15,000
Purchase returns	40,000	13,000
Purchase allowances	8,000	5,000
Ending inventory	785,000	
Selling and general expenses	450,000	320,000

Instructions: Compute by the gross profit method the value to be assigned to the inventory as of September 30, 1996, and prepare an income statement for the nine-month period ending on this date.

Problem 10—31 (Inventory theft loss)

In December 1996, Bullseye Merchandise Inc. had a significant portion of its inventory stolen. The company determined the cost of inventory remaining to be $35,300. The following information was taken from the records of the company:

	January 1, 1996 to Date of Theft	1995
Purchases	$154,854	$185,375
Purchase returns and allowances	7,225	8,420
Sales	254,300	261,800
Sales returns and allowances	3,300	2,600
Salaries	9,600	10,800
Rent	6,480	6,480
Insurance	1,160	1,178
Light, heat, and water	1,361	1,525
Advertising	5,100	3,216
Depreciation expense	1,506	1,536
Beginning inventory	69,923	64,040

Instructions: Estimate the cost of the stolen inventory.

Problem 10—32 (Retail inventory method)

Soho Clothing Store values its inventory under the retail inventory method. The following data is available for 1996:

	Cost	Selling Price
Inventory, January 1	$ 46,053	$ 79,100
Additional markdowns.		21,000
Additional markups		40,600
Markdown cancellations		6,000
Markup cancellations		9,000
Purchases	142,390	221,600
Sales		251,500
Purchase returns	4,000	6,000
Sales allowances		12,000
Freight-in	14,600	

Instructions:

1. Prepare a schedule to compute the estimated inventory at December 31, 1996, at the lower of average cost or market under the retail method.
2. Prepare the summary accounting journal entries to record the above inventory data (include entries to record the purchases, sales, and closing of inventory to cost of goods sold).
3. What gross profit on sales would be reported on the income statement for 1996?

Problem 10—33 (Retail inventory method)

The following information was taken from the records of Trump Inc. for the years 1995 and 1996.

	1996	1995
Sales	$138,600	$135,600
Sales discounts	1,840	1,200
Sales returns	2,100	1,600
Freight-in	4,000	3,640
Purchases (at cost)	78,000	68,560
Purchases (at retail)	100,500	92,480
Purchase discounts	4,155	1,000
Beginning inventory (at cost)		65,600
Beginning inventory (at retail)		87,520

Instructions: Compute the value of the inventory at the end of 1995 and 1996 using the conventional retail inventory method.

Problem 10—34 (Retail inventory method)

Johnson & Jones, a pharmaceutical company, has used the retail method for several years. The following limited information is available for the past three years:

	1997		1996		1995	
	Cost	*Retail*	*Cost*	*Retail*	*Cost*	*Retail*
Inventory, Jan. 1	$ 5,536	$?	$?	$?	$ 8,255	$ 14,000
Purchases	77,809	114,750	84,500	?	71,000	105,000
Net markups		?		13,000		?
Goods available	$?	133,780	$?	$?	$?	$?
Cost percentage	?		64.9%		?	
Deduct: Net markdowns		7,750		?		?
Sales		?		132,450		110,000
Inventory, Dec. 31	$ 9,255	$?	$?	$ 8,530	$ 10,890	$ 18,000

Instructions: Compute the missing amounts from the information given.

Problem 10—35 (Dollar-value LIFO retail inventory method)

In 1994, Van Hover Inc. adopted the dollar-value LIFO retail inventory method. The January 1, 1994 price index was 1.00. The following data is available for a four-year period ending December 31, 1997.

		Cost	Retail
1994	Inventory, January 1	$148,050	$235,000
	Purchases	393,700	635,000
	Sales		590,000
	Year-end price index		1.12
1995	Purchases	363,000	550,000
	Sales		579,170
	Year-end price index		1.08
1996	Purchases	377,000	650,000
	Sales		641,955
	Year-end price index		1.09
1997	Purchases	504,000	800,000
	Sales		762,500
	Year-end price index		1.12

Instructions: Calculate the inventories to be reported at the end of 1994, 1995, 1996, and 1997. Incremental layers are costed at end-of-year prices.

Problem 10—36 (Dollar-value LIFO retail inventory method)

The St. George Sports Shop values its inventory on the dollar-value LIFO retail basis. Incremental inventory layers are costed at end-of-year prices. At December 31, 1995, the inventory was valued as follows:

LIFO Layer Year	Cost	Year-End Retail	Year-End Price Index	Retail at Base of 1.00
1989	$14,760	$24,600	1.00	$24,600
1991	9,482	13,545	1.05	12,900
1993	13,442	26,884	1.03	26,100
1994	4,500	6,000	1.10	5,454
	$42,184	$71,029		$69,054

The December 31, 1995, inventory at 1995 retail prices was $77,340. Information relating to 1996 transactions follows:

Purchases—cost	$476,100
Purchases—selling price	673,845
Freight-in	9,900
Sales returns	11,220
Sales discounts	1,950
Markups	4,740
Markup cancellations	1,080
Markdowns	2,505
Gross sales	702,000
Year-end price index for 1996	1.08

Instructions: Based on the above information, compute the following:

1. 1996 cost ratio.
2. Inventory amount that would be reported on the balance sheet at December 31, 1996.

Problem 10—37 (Lower-of-cost-or-market valuation)

Witte Inc. carries four items in inventory. The following data is relative to such goods at the end of 1996:

		Per Unit				
	Units	*Cost*	*Replacement Cost*	*Estimated Sales Price*	*Selling Cost*	*Normal Profit*
Category 1:						
Commodity A	3,000	$5.50	$5.25	$8.00	$ .90	$2.00
Commodity B	1,650	6.00	6.00	9.25	.80	1.25
Category 2:						
Commodity C	5,000	2.50	2.00	4.20	.95	.50
Commodity D	3,250	7.00	7.50	7.50	1.20	1.75

Instructions:

1. Calculate the value of the inventory under each of the following methods:
   (a) cost
   (b) the lower of cost or market applied to the individual inventory items
   (c) the lower of cost or market applied to the inventory categories
   (d) the lower of cost or market applied to the inventory as a whole
2. Prepare any journal entries necessary to reflect the proper inventory valuation assuming inventory is valued at:
   (a) cost
   (b) the lower of cost or market applied to the individual inventory items
   (c) the lower of cost or market applied to the inventory categories (Use valuation allowance.)
   (d) the lower of cost or market applied to the inventory as a whole

Problem 10—38 (Lower-of-cost-or-market valuation)

Oriental Sales Co. uses the first-in, first-out method in calculating cost of goods sold for three of the products that Oriental handles. Inventories and purchase information concerning these three products are given for the month of August.

			Product A	Product B	Product C
Aug.	1	Inventory	5,000 units at $6.00	3,000 units at $10.00	6,500 units at $.90
Aug.	1-15	Purchases	7,000 units at $6.50	4,500 units at $10.50	3,000 units at $1.25
Aug.	16-31	Purchases	3,000 units at $8.00		
Aug.	1-31	Sales	10,500 units	5,000 units	4,500 units
Aug.	31	Sales Price	$8.00 per unit	$11.00 per unit	$2.00 per unit

On August 31, Oriental's suppliers reduced their prices from the most recent purchase prices by the following percentages: Product A, 20%; Product B, 10%; Product C, 8%. Accordingly, Oriental decided to reduce its sales prices on all items by 10% effective September 1. Oriental's selling cost is 10% of sales price. Products A and B have a normal profit (after selling costs) of 30% on sales prices, while the normal profit on Product C (after selling costs) is 15% of sales prices.

Instructions:

1. Calculate the value of the inventory at August 31, using the lower-of-cost-or-market method (applied to individual items).
2. Calculate the FIFO cost of goods sold for August and the amount of inventory write-off due to the market decline.

Problem 10—39 (Trade-ins and repossessed inventory)

The Jamison Appliance Company began business on January 1, 1995. The company decided from the beginning to grant allowances on merchandise traded in as partial payment on new sales. During 1996 the company granted trade-in allowances of $64,035. The wholesale value of merchandise traded in was $40,875. Trade-ins recorded at $39,000 were sold for their wholesale value of $27,000 during the year. The following summary entries were made to record annual sales of new merchandise and trade-in sales for 1996:

Accounts Receivable	439,890	
Trade-In Inventory	64,035	
Sales		503,925
Cash	27,000	
Loss on Trade-In Inventory	12,000	
Trade-In Inventory		39,000

When a customer defaults on the accounts receivable contract, the appliance is repossessed. During 1996 the following repossessions occurred:

	Original Sales Price	Unpaid Contract Balance
On 1995 contracts	$37,500	$15,600
On 1996 contracts	24,000	17,800

The wholesale value of these goods is estimated by the trade as follows:

(a) Goods repossessed during year of sale are valued at 50% of original sales price.
(b) Goods repossessed in later years are valued at 20% of original sales price.

Instructions:

1. At what values should Jamison Appliance report the trade-in and repossessed inventory at December 31, 1996?
2. Give the entry that should have been made to record the repossessions of 1996.
3. Give the entry that is required to correct the trade-in summary entries.

Problem 10—40 (Inventory transactions—journal entries)

The Olsen Company values its perpetual inventory at the lower of FIFO cost or market. The inventory accounts at December 31, 1995, had the following balances:

Raw Materials	$ 81,000
Allowance to Reduce Raw Materials Inventory From Cost to Market	4,200
Work in Process	131,520
Finished Goods	205,200

The following are some of the transactions that affected the inventory of the Olsen Company during 1996:

Feb. 10 Olsen Company purchases raw materials at an invoice price of $25,000; terms 3/15, n/30. Olsen Company uses the net method of valuing inventories.

Mar. 15 Olsen Company repossesses an inventory item from a customer who was overdue in making payment. The unpaid balance on the sale is $190. The repossessed merchandise is to be refinished and placed on sale. It is expected that the item can be sold for $300 after estimated refinishing costs of $85. The normal profit for this item is considered to be $40.

Apr. 1 Refinishing costs of $80 are incurred on the repossessed item.

10 The repossessed item is resold for $300 on account, 20% down.

May 30 A sale on account is made of finished goods that have a list price of $740 and a cost of $480. A reduction of $100 off the list price is granted as a trade-in allowance. The trade-in item is to be priced to sell at $80 as is. The normal profit on this type of inventory is 25% of the sales price.

Nov. 30 Olsen Company orders materials to be delivered January 31, 1997, at a cost of $21,600. No discount terms are included.

Dec. 31 The following information is available to adjust the accounts for the annual statements:

(a) The market value of the items ordered on November 30 has declined to $18,000.

(b) The raw materials inventory account has a cost balance of $110,400. Current market value is $101,400.

(c) The finished goods inventory account has a cost balance of $177,600. Current market value is $189,000.

Instructions: Record this information in journal entry form, including any required adjusting entries at December 31, 1996.

Problem 10—41 (Trade-ins and repossessed inventory)

Good Buy Auto Sales buys and sells automobiles. They deal in both new and used cars and often accept trade-ins, which they recondition and sell. Recently, a young couple traded in their 1971 Mustang convertible for a more conservative 1985 Caprice station wagon. The Caprice had a cash price of $3,500. The couple paid $2,400 in cash plus their Mustang. The Mustang was reconditioned by Good Buy at a cost of $250 and sold for $1,150 to be paid in monthly payments to Good Buy. After three months, the new owner failed to make the monthly payment and the Mustang was repossessed. The defaulted receivable amounted to $1,000. After additional reconditioning of $100, the Mustang was sold for a cash price of $900, yielding a 20 percent profit on cost.

Instructions:

1. Prepare the journal entries to record the trade-in of the Mustang and the purchase of the station wagon.
2. Prepare the journal entries to record the reconditioning and sale of the Mustang.
3. Prepare the journal entries to record the repossession of the Mustang and its subsequent reconditioning and resale.

Problem 10—42 (Inventory error correction)

The Sonntag Corporation has adjusted and closed its books at the end of 1995. The company arrives at its inventory position by a physical count taken on December 31 of each year. In March of 1996, the following errors were discovered.

(a) Merchandise which cost $2,500 was sold for $3,400 on December 29, 1995. The order was shipped December 31, 1995, with terms of FOB shipping point. The merchandise was not included in the ending inventory. The sale was recorded on January 12, 1996, when the customer made payment on the sale.

(b) On January 3, 1996, Sonntag Corporation received merchandise which had been shipped to them on December 30, 1995. The terms of the purchase were FOB shipping point. Cost of the merchandise was $1,750. The purchase was recorded and the goods included in the inventory when payment was made in January 1996.

(c) On January 8, 1996, merchandise that had been included in the ending inventory was returned to Sonntag because the consignee had not been able to sell it. The cost of this merchandise was $1,200 with a selling price of $1,800.
(d) Merchandise costing $750, located in a separate warehouse, was overlooked and excluded from the 1995 inventory count.
(e) On December 26, 1995, Sonntag Corporation purchased merchandise costing $1,175 from a supplier. The order was shipped December 28 (terms FOB destination) and was still "in-transit" on December 31. Since the invoice was received on December 31, the purchase was recorded in 1995. The merchandise was not included in the inventory count.
(f) The corporation failed to make an entry for a purchase on account of $835 at the end of 1995, although it included this merchandise in the inventory count. The purchase was recorded when payment was made to the supplier in 1996.
(g) The corporation included in its 1995 ending inventory merchandise with a cost of $1,350. This merchandise had been custom-built and was being held until the customer could come and pick up the merchandise. The sale, for $1,825, was recorded in 1996.

Instructions: Give the entry in 1996 (1995 books are closed) to correct each error. Assume that the errors were made during 1995 and all amounts are material.

Problem 10—43 (Foreign transactions)

Charles & Sons, a U.S. computer supplies firm, had the following transactions with foreign companies during December of 1995:

(a) Goldstar Co., Ltd., a Korea-based firm, sold 5,000 computer hard drives to Charles & Sons for 1,000 won per drive on December 12, 1995. Charles & Sons paid the bill on January 13, 1996.
(b) Charles & Sons sold 2,000 computer hard drives to a Swiss firm, Lockner Inc., on December 21, 1995. Lockner Inc. agreed to pay $135 per hard drive. Payment was received by Charles & Sons on February 4, 1996.
(c) Charles & Sons sold 2,400 computer hard drives to Geopacific, Inc., a company with headquarters in Canada, on December 28, 1995. Geopacific was billed 148 Canadian dollars per drive. Payment was received on January 10, 1996.
(d) Charles & Sons received 1,000 printers from Printco, a Japanese company, on December 28, 1995. Printco billed Charles & Sons 4,500 yen per printer. Charles & Sons paid the liability on January 14, 1996.

Relevant exchange rates for the above transactions are as follows:

	Exchange Rates		
	As of Date of Sale or Purchase	*As of Balance Sheet Date*	*As of Date of Payment or Receipt*
Korean won	$ .103	$ .112	$ .115
Swiss franc	1.670	1.632	1.655
Canadian dollar	.910	.935	.905
Japanese yen	.075	.069	.073

Instructions Prepare the journal entries necessary to record each of the above transactions for the following: (1) date of the original transaction, (2) balance sheet date, and (3) date of payment or receipt of cash.

CHAPTER 11

Noncurrent Operating Assets: Acquisition

CHAPTER TOPICS

- Classification of Noncurrent Operating Assets
- Valuation of Noncurrent Operating Assets at Acquisition
- Recognition of Goodwill
- Recording Noncurrent Operating Assets Under Various Methods of Acquisition
- Classifying Expenditures as Assets or Expenses
    - Research and Development Expenditures
    - Computer Software Development Expenditures
    - Post-Acquisition Expenditures
- Goodwill Estimation (Appendix)

Jerry Jones didn't win many friends in Texas when one of his first acts after buying the Dallas Cowboys in 1989 was to fire Tom Landry, the only head coach the Cowboys ever had. Jones was even less popular when the Cowboys lost 15 out of 16 games in their first year under new head coach Jimmy Johnson.[1] In those days, the Cowboys stunk as a football team but looked like a pretty shrewd business investment. When Jones, an Arkansas oil man, purchased the Cowboys for $140 million, he acquired a diverse array of assets. These assets included miscellaneous football equipment, stadium leases, radio and TV broadcast rights, cable TV rights, luxury stadium suites, player contracts, a lease on the Cowboys' luxurious Valley Ranch training facility, and the Cowboys' NFL franchise rights. Allocation of the purchase price among these assets and defining their useful lives was a difficult and strategic task. When H.R. "Bum" Bright, Jones' predecessor, bought the

1. William P. Barrett. "Maybe They Should Let Jerry Play." *Forbes*, (February 19, 1990); p. 140.

Dallas Cowboys for $85 million in 1984, he was able to allocate half the purchase price to Players' Contracts, an amortizable asset that, for tax purposes, was written off over four years.[2] Jones received a similar tax break when he acquired the Cowboys.

Gradually, the on-field performance of the Cowboys began to match the success of Jerry Jones' energy, real estate, and banking investments. In 1990, the Cowboys improved their record to 7 and 9, and in 1991 they made the playoffs, advancing to the second round. The Cowboys' return to glory was capped in January 1993 when they returned to the Super Bowl for the first time since 1978 and routed the Buffalo Bills, 52-17.

Many billions of dollars are invested each year in new property, plant, equipment, and intangible assets. Enterprises must continually make choices as to how they will invest their limited resources to acquire the operating assets needed to reach their goals and objectives. Capital budgets are prepared by management to help evaluate the available alternatives and to identify the priorities for implementation.

Many accounting questions are introduced with the acquisition of assets whose lives and economic benefits extend beyond one year, including:

1. How should the various categories of noncurrent operating assets be recorded on the balance sheet?
2. Which costs should be capitalized as assets and which ones should be recognized as expenses in the period of disbursement?
3. At what amounts should the assets be recorded under various methods of purchase?
4. How should expenditures made subsequent to acquisition be recorded?
5. What recognition should be given to changes in either the value of the dollar or the replacement cost of new assets?

These are the central issues concerning the acquisition of noncurrent operating assets that will be explored in this chapter.

CLASSIFICATION OF NONCURRENT OPERATING ASSETS

Assets are probable future economic benefits that are controlled by an economic entity and are the result of past events. While the actual form of an asset is not an essential characteristic, it is common to group noncurrent operating assets according to whether they are tangible or intangible.

Tangible noncurrent operating assets include land, buildings, and equipment used in revenue-producing activities. Specific categories of equipment include automobiles and trucks, machinery, patterns and dies, furniture and fixtures, and returnable containers.

Intangible noncurrent operating assets include patents, copyrights, franchises, trademarks, trade names, organization costs, software development costs, and goodwill. While these assets cannot be directly observed, they usually are identified by agreements, contracts, or other documentation.

VALUATION OF NONCURRENT OPERATING ASSETS AT ACQUISITION

Noncurrent operating assets are recorded initially at cost—the original bargained or cash sales price. In theory, the maximum price an entity should be willing to pay for an operating asset is the present value of the net benefit the entity expects to obtain from the use and final disposition of the asset. In a competitive economy, the market value, or cost, of an asset at acquisition is assumed to reflect the present value of its future benefits.

2. Hal Lancaster. "Football Team's Sale Is Strictly Business." *The Wall Street Journal*, April 18, 1989: p. B1.

The cost of property includes not only the original purchase price or equivalent value, but also any other expenditures required in obtaining and preparing the asset for its intended use. Any taxes, freight, installation, and other expenditures related to the acquisition should be included in the asset's cost. Post-acquisition costs, costs incurred *after* the asset is placed into service, are usually expensed rather than added to the acquisition cost. Exceptions to this general rule apply to some major replacements or improvements and will be discussed later in the chapter.

Although most noncurrent operating asset categories have similar acquisition costs, over time accounting practice has identified some specific costs that are included for different asset categories. Exhibits 11—1 and 11—2 summarize the types of costs normally included as acquisition cost for each major noncurrent asset category.

Because land is a nondepreciable asset, costs assigned to land should be those costs that directly relate to land's unlimited life. Together with clearing and grading costs, costs of removing unwanted structures from newly acquired land are considered part of the cost to prepare the land for its intended use and are added to the purchase price of the land. Government assessments for water lines, sewers, roads, and other such items are considered part of the land's cost since maintenance of these items is the responsibility of the government; thus, to the landowner, they have unlimited life. These types of improvements are distinguished from similar costs for landscaping, parking lots, and interior sidewalks that are installed by the owner and must be replaced over time. These owner-responsible improvements are generally classified as land improvements and are depreciated.

The cost of purchased buildings includes any reconditioning costs necessary before occupancy. Because self-constructed buildings have many unique costs, a separate discussion of self-constructed assets is included later in this chapter.

Equipment costs include freight and insurance charges while the equipment is in transit and any expenditures for testing and installation. Costs for reconditioning purchased used equipment are also part of the asset cost.

Intangible assets also are generally recorded at cost; however, acquisition costs differ between externally purchased intangibles and those that are internally developed. Intangible assets arising from exclusive rights granted by the U.S. Government, such as copyrights, patents, and trademarks, are recorded at their purchase price if externally obtained. Internal research and development costs incurred to generate the items subject to government license are generally expensed as incurred because of the uncertainty as to whether the work will result in a successful product. Only the actual legal and filing costs are included as part of the intangible asset cost for these internally developed items. Any cost to defend the rights in court are added to the intangible asset cost if successful. If not successful, all asset costs related to the rights would be written off as an expense.

Exhibit 11—1 Acquisition Cost of Tangible Noncurrent Operating Assets

Asset	Description	Examples of Acquisition Costs
Land	Realty used for business purposes.	Purchase price, commissions, legal fees, escrow fees, surveying fees, clearing and grading costs, street and water line assessments.
Land Improvements	Items such as landscaping, paving, fencing that improve the usefulness of property.	Cost of improvements, including expenditures for materials, labor, and overhead.
Buildings	A structure used to house a business operation.	Purchase price, commissions, reconditioning costs.
Equipment	Assets used in the production of goods or in providing services. Examples include automobiles, trucks, machinery, patterns and dies, and furniture and fixtures.	Purchase price, taxes, freight, insurance, installation, and any expenditures incurred in preparing the asset for its intended use, e.g., reconditioning and testing costs.

Exhibit 11—2 Acquisition Cost of Intangible Noncurrent Operating Assets

Asset	Description	Examples of Acquisition Costs
Copyright	An exclusive right granted by the U.S. government that permits an author to sell, license, or control his/her work. Copyright expires 50 years after the death of the author.	Purchase price, filing and registry fees, cost of subsequent litigation to protect right. Does not include internal research and development costs. (Applies to Copyright, Patent, and Trademark and Trade Name)
Patent	An exclusive right granted by the U.S. government that enables an inventor to control the manufacture, sale, or use of an invention. Legal life is 17 years.	
Trademark and Trade Name	An exclusive right granted by the U.S. government that permits the use of distinctive symbols, labels, and designs, e.g., McDonald's golden arches, Levi's pocket patch, Chrysler's star. Legal life is virtually unlimited.	
Franchise	An exclusive right or privilege received by a business or individual to perform certain functions or sell certain products or services.	Expenditures made to purchase the franchise. Legal fees and other costs incurred in obtaining the franchise.
Organization Costs	Costs incurred in forming a corporation.	Expenditures to organize the corporation: cost of stock certificates, underwriting costs, state incorporation fees.
Software Development Costs	Costs incurred in the development of computer software.	Expenditures made after software is determined to be technologically feasible but before it is ready for commercial production.
Goodwill	Miscellaneous intangible resources,factors, and conditions that allow a company to earn above-normal income with its identifiable net assets. Goodwill is recorded only when a business entity is acquired by a purchase.	Portion of purchase price that exceeds the sum of the current market value for all identifiable net assets.

Franchise operations have become so common in our everyday life that we often don't realize we are dealing with them. The cost of a franchise includes any sum paid specifically for the franchise right as well as legal fees and other costs incurred in obtaining it. Although the value of a franchise at the time of its acquisition may be substantially in excess of its cost, the amount recorded should be limited to actual outlays. When a franchise is purchased from another company, the amount paid is recorded as the franchise cost.

In forming a corporation, certain organization costs are incurred, including legal fees, promotional costs, stock certificate costs, underwriting costs, and state incorporation fees. The benefits to be derived from these expenditures normally extend beyond the first fiscal period. Because the primary benefits of these start-up costs relate to the first few years of operation, they are usually written off to expense fairly rapidly. Some development stage companies have included such costs as interest, administrative salaries, and taxes as part of organization costs. The Financial Accounting Standards Board concluded that these administrative costs should not be classified as an intangible asset. The same accounting principles should apply to development-stage companies as for mature companies. Only the costs related to the actual formation of the company, as mentioned above, should be included as part of organization costs.[3]

3. *Statement of Financial Accounting Standards No. 7,* "Accounting and Reporting by Development Stage Enterprises" (Stamford: Financial Accounting Standards Board, 1975), par. 10.

In recent years, the tremendous growth in the computer industry, particularly in microcomputers, has raised some significant accounting issues relating to expenditures for the development and production of computer software. Because these costs have been addressed separately by the FASB, the accounting and reporting issues relating to software development expenditures are discussed in detail later in the chapter.

The most frequently reported intangible asset is goodwill. In the 1993 edition of *Accounting Trends & Techniques,* 383 of the 600 surveyed companies reported goodwill. The next most frequent intangible asset was patents, reported by 62 companies. Goodwill is reported only when it arises from the purchase of another entity for more than the market value of the identifiable net assets. Because of its unique character, it will be discussed in more depth than the other intangibles summarized in Exhibit 11—2.

Goodwill

Of all the intangible assets, goodwill is perhaps the most controversial. In a general sense, **goodwill** is often referred to as that intangible something that makes the whole company worth more than its individual parts. In general, goodwill represents all the special advantages, not otherwise identifiable, enjoyed by an enterprise, such as a good name, capable staff and personnel, high credit standing, reputation for superior products and services, and favorable location. From an accounting point of view, goodwill is recognized as the intangible resources, factors, and conditions that allow a business to earn above-normal income with the identifiable assets employed in the business. Above-normal income means a rate of return greater than that normally required to attract investors into a particular type of business.

Goodwill differs from most other assets in that it cannot be exchanged or sold separately from the entity itself. Because goodwill is recorded on the books only as part of an entity acquisition, it is difficult to compare a company that has recorded goodwill with one that hasn't. Merely because a company has not purchased another company does not mean it does not have goodwill as defined above. Thus, current accounting principles may result in misleading users of financial statements as far as goodwill is concerned. On the other hand, to allow companies to place a value on their own goodwill would introduce a significant amount of added subjectivity to the financial statements. These difficulties have led some accountants to suggest that all purchased goodwill should be written off to expense as soon as it is acquired. Advocates of this position include the authors of Accounting Research Study No. 10, "Accounting for Goodwill," whose justification for immediate write-off was given as follows:

1. Goodwill is not a resource or property right that is consumed or utilized in the production of earnings. It is the result of expectations of future earnings by investors and thus is not subject to normal amortization procedures.
2. Goodwill is subject to sudden and wide fluctuations. The value has no reliable or continuing relation to costs incurred in its creation.
3. Under existing practices of accounting, neither the cost nor the value of nonpurchased goodwill is reported in the balance sheet. Purchased goodwill has no continuing, separately measurable existence after the combination and is merged with the total goodwill value of the continuing business entity. As such, its write-off cannot be measured with any validity.
4. Goodwill as an asset account is not relevant to an investor. Most analysts ignore any reported goodwill when analyzing a company's status and operations.[4]

4. George R. Catlett and Norman O. Olson, "Accounting for Goodwill," *Accounting Research Study No. 10* (New York: American Institute of Certified Public Accountants, 1968).

Accounting for Goodwill: The United States Against the World

Sanford Pensler, a mergers-and-acquisitions investment banker writing on the editorial page of the *The Wall Street Journal,* said: "Would-be U.S. purchasers of U.S. firms are burdened by accounting rules that favor foreign buyers." Mr. Pensler was referring to the requirement that U.S. companies record goodwill acquired in a purchase as an asset and amortize the goodwill against earnings over a period not to exceed 40 years. This goodwill amortization can result in a very significant earnings reduction. Consider the case of the acquisition of Kraft by Philip Morris. The purchase price was $12.9 billion, $11.6 billion of which was recorded as goodwill on Philip Morris' books. These numbers suggest a minimum annual goodwill amortization expense amount of $290 million; for comparison, Kraft's net income in 1987, the year before the purchase, was $489 million. One Arthur Andersen partner was quoted as saying: "Chief executives are compensated based on earnings per share. That makes them very wary about taking a big bite of goodwill."

In contrast, in the United Kingdom goodwill is usually recorded as a direct, one-time reduction in equity with no subsequent amortization and thus no effect on earnings. In Japan firms can choose to expense the entire amount of goodwill in the current period, or they can capitalize the goodwill and amortize it over a period not exceeding five years.

In addition to these financial statement differences, there are also differences in the international treatment of goodwill for income tax purposes. In Canada, Japan, and Germany, goodwill amortized or written off is deductible for tax purposes. In the United Kingdom, only the portion of goodwill attributable to "know-how" is deductible. Historically, no tax deduction for goodwill amortization was allowed in the U.S. Of the major industrial countries, only the United States required goodwill to be charged against earnings for financial reporting purposes but allowed no write-off for tax purposes. In 1993, as part of the Clinton tax package, Congress authorized tax deductions for amortization of goodwill acquired in certain types of transactions. The specified amortization period is 15 years.

Questions:

1. Examples such as these are cited as justification for working to arrive at a "harmonization" between the standards of different countries. How might representatives of different countries go about resolving such wide differences in practice?
2. "Resolution of accounting standard differences must consider cultural, legal, and business differences among countries." Do you agree with this statement? Can these differences justify different accounting standards in various countries?
3. How do the rules for accounting for goodwill give foreign firms an advantage over U.S. firms?

Sources:

Jeannie D. Johnson and Michael G. Tearney. "Goodwill: An Eternal Controversy." *The CPA Journal,* (April 1993), p. 58.

Penelope Wang. "The Unlevel Accounting Field." *Forbes,* November 28, 1988, p. 170.

Sanford Pensler. "Accounting Rules Favor Foreign Bidders." *The Wall Street Journal,* March 24, 1988, p. 30.

1988 Annual Report of Philip Morris Companies Inc.

This position has been consistently rejected by the accounting principles-setting bodies, and the immediate write-off of purchased goodwill is not permitted under GAAP. They maintain that a price has been paid for the excess earnings power, and it should be recognized as an asset. Because of the poor connotative image the term *goodwill* has acquired, some companies use more descriptive titles for reporting purposes, such as "Excess of Cost Over Net Assets of Acquired Companies."

In the purchase of a going business, the actual price paid for goodwill usually results from bargaining and compromises between the parties concerned. A basis for negotiation in arriving at a price for goodwill involves many variables, including:

1. The level of projected future income.
2. An appropriate rate of return.
3. Current valuation of the net business assets other than goodwill.

A brief discussion of how these variables might affect a firm's value is presented in the Appendix to this chapter. A complete treatment of business valuation would involve the introduction of valuation models and capital structure theories that are outside the scope of this text.

When a lump-sum amount is paid for an established business and no explicit evaluation is made of goodwill, goodwill may still be recognized. In this case the identifiable net assets require appraisal, and the difference between the full purchase price and the value of identifiable net assets can be attributed to the purchase of goodwill. In appraising properties for this purpose, current market values should be sought rather than the values reported in the accounts. Receivables should be stated at amounts estimated to be realized. Inventories and securities should be restated in terms of current market values. Land, buildings, and equipment may require special appraisals in arriving at their present replacement or reproduction values. Intangible assets, such as patents and franchises, should be included at their current values even though, originally, expenditures were reported as expenses or were reported as assets and amortized against revenue. Care should be taken to determine that liabilities are fully recognized. Assets at their current fair market values less the liabilities to be assumed provide the net assets total that together with estimated future earnings are used in arriving at a purchase price.

To the extent possible, the amount paid for any existing company should be related to identifiable assets. If an excess does exist, the use of a term other than goodwill can avoid the implication that only companies that purchase other companies have goodwill.

To illustrate the purchase and recording of an ongoing business, assume that Airnational Corporation purchases the net assets of Speedy Freight Airlines for $675,000 cash. A schedule of net assets for Speedy Freight at the time of acquisition is presented below.

Speedy Freight Airlines
Schedule of Net Assets
December 31, 1996

Assets		
Cash and temporary investments	$ 21,000	
Receivables	146,000	
Inventory	292,000	
Long-term investments	72,000	
Land, buildings, and equipment (net)	489,200	
Patents, trademarks, and trade names	16,500	$1,036,700
Liabilities		
Current liabilities	$286,000	
Long-term debt	183,500	469,500
Net assets		$ 567,200

Analysis of the $107,800 difference between the purchase price ($675,000) and the net asset book value ($567,200) reveals the following differences between the recorded costs and market values of the assets:

	Cost	Market
Inventory	$292,000	$327,000
Long-term investments	72,000	85,000
Land, buildings, and equipment	489,200	504,500
Patents	7,000	12,000
Trademarks and trade names	9,500	10,000
Franchises		5,000
Totals	$869,700	$943,500

The identifiable portion of the $107,800 difference amounts to $73,800 ($943,500 – $869,700) and is allocated to the respective assets. The remaining difference of $34,000 is recorded as an intangible asset, Goodwill.

The entry to record the purchase is as follows:

Cash and Temporary Investments	21,000	
Receivables	146,000	
Inventory	327,000	
Long-Term Investments	85,000	
Land, Buildings, and Equipment	504,500	
Patents	12,000	
Trademarks and Trade Names	10,000	
Franchises	5,000	
Goodwill (excess of market value over cost paid for net assets)	34,000	
Current Liabilities		286,000
Long-Term Debt		183,500
Cash		675,000

Negative Goodwill. Occasionally, the amount paid for another company is less than the fair market value of the net assets of the acquired company. This condition can arise when economic conditions are depressed and where bargain purchases are possible. The accounting profession has discussed from time to time how such **negative goodwill** should be recorded. Some accountants have suggested that it should be recorded as part of owners' equity.

The APB, however, did not want the total assets to be recorded at an aggregate amount that exceeded cost. The Board decided, therefore, to require the allocation of the excess against all acquired noncurrent assets, except for noncurrent marketable equity securities. If this allocation reduces the noncurrent assets to a zero balance, any remaining excess is credited to a deferred credit account and amortized against revenue over the period benefited.[5]

For example, assume Goodtime, Inc., purchases the net assets of Funtime, Inc., for $500,000. The fair market values of Funtime's assets are as follows:

Cash and temporary investments	$ 75,000
Receivables	125,000
Inventories	160,000
Property and equipment	250,000
Investment in noncurrent marketable equity securities	75,000
Other noncurrent investments	50,000
	$735,000

Offsetting the above assets are the following liabilities:

Current liabilities	$ 50,000
Noncurrent liabilities	125,000
	$175,000

The market value of net assets for Funtime is thus $560,000 ($735,000 – $175,000), and the indicated negative goodwill is $60,000 ($560,000 – $500,000). The only noncurrent assets that would meet the Board's criteria for adjustment would be property and equipment and other noncurrent investments. The allocation of the $60,000 would be performed as follows:

5. *Opinions of the Accounting Principles Board No. 16,* "Business Combinations" (New York: American Institute of Certified Public Accountants, 1970), par. 91. Some accountants have suggested that in a negative goodwill transaction all acquired assets and liabilities should be recorded at their fair market values and that the entire excess of purchase price over net assets acquired be recorded as a one-time increase to stockholders' equity. See Wig De Moville and A. George Petrie, "Accounting for a Bargain Purchase in a Business Combination." *Accounting Horizons* (September 1989), pp. 38-43.

	Book Value	Allocation of Negative Goodwill According to Relative Book Values	Negative Goodwill Assigned to Individual Assets
Property and equipment	$250,000	250,000/300,000 × $60,000	$50,000
Other noncurrent investments	50,000	50,000/300,000 × $60,000	10,000
	$300,000		$60,000

The $60,000 negative goodwill is thus allocated $50,000 against property and equipment and $10,000 against other investments. The acquisition is then recorded as follows:

Cash and Temporary Investments	75,000	
Receivables	125,000	
Inventories	160,000	
Property and Equipment	200,000	
Investment in Noncurrent Marketable Equity Securities.	75,000	
Other Noncurrent Investments	40,000	
Cash		500,000
Current Liabilities		50,000
Noncurrent Liabilities		125,000
To record acquisition of Funtime, Inc.		

Exhibit 11—3 illustrates a note included in Centura Bank's 1991 annual report describing a negative goodwill transaction.

Exhibit 11—3
Centura Bank—Disclosure of Negative Goodwill Transaction

On December 31, 1991, the Corporation acquired Citizens Federal Savings and Loan Association. . . The acquisition was accounted for as a purchase and, accordingly, negative goodwill of $8,863,000 was recorded to represent the excess of the fair value of net assets acquired over the purchase price after. . . reducing the adjusted basis in Citizens' premises and equipment of $334,157 to zero. The amount of negative goodwill is being accreted into earnings over a period of approximately ten years.

RECORDING ACQUISITION OF NONCURRENT OPERATING ASSETS

When an asset is purchased for cash, the acquisition is simply recorded at the amount of cash paid, including all outlays relating to its purchase and preparation for intended use. Assets can be acquired under a number of other arrangements, however, some of which present special problems relating to the cost to be recorded. The acquisition of assets is discussed under the following headings:

1. Assets acquired for a lump-sum purchase price
2. Purchase on deferred payment contract
3. Acquisition under capital lease
4. Acquisition by exchange of nonmonetary assets
5. Acquisition by issuance of securities
6. Acquisition by self-construction
7. Acquisition by donation or discovery

Assets Acquired for a Lump-Sum Purchase Price

In some purchases, a number of assets may be acquired for one lump sum. Some of the assets in the group may be depreciable, others nondepreciable. Depreciable assets may have different useful lives. If there is to be accountability for the assets on an individual basis, the total purchase price must be allocated among the individual assets. When part of a purchase price can be clearly identified with specific assets, such a cost assignment should be made and the balance of the purchase price allocated among the remaining assets. When no part of the purchase price can be related to specific assets, the entire amount must be allocated among the different assets acquired. Appraisal values or similar evidence provided by a competent independent authority should be sought to support such allocation.

To illustrate the allocation of a joint asset cost, assume that land, buildings, and equipment are acquired for $160,000. Assume further that assessed values for the individual assets as reported on the property tax bill are considered to provide an equitable basis for cost allocation. The allocation is made as shown below.

	Assessed Values	Cost Allocation According to Relative Assessed Values	Cost Assigned to Individual Assets
Land	$ 28,000	28,000/100,000 × $160,000	$ 44,800
Buildings	60,000	60,000/100,000 × $160,000	96,000
Equipment	12,000	12,000/100,000 × $160,000	19,200
	$100,000		$160,000

The entry to record this acquisition, assuming a cash purchase, would be as follows:

Land	44,800	
Buildings	96,000	
Equipment	19,200	
Cash		160,000

Purchase on Deferred Payment Contract

The acquisition of real estate or other property frequently involves deferred payment of all or part of the purchase price. The indebtedness of the buyer is usually evidenced by a note, debenture, mortgage, or other contract that specifies the terms of settlement of the obligation. The debt instrument may call for one payment at a given future date or a series of payments at specified intervals. Interest charged on the unpaid balance of the contract should be recognized as an expense.

To illustrate the accounting for a deferred payment purchase contract, assume that land is acquired for $100,000; $35,000 is paid at the time of purchase, and the balance is to be paid in semiannual installments of $5,000 plus interest on the unpaid principal at an annual rate of 10%. Entries for the purchase and for the first payment on the contract are shown below.

Transaction	Entry		
January 2, 1996			
Purchased land for $100,000 paying $35,000 down, the balance to be paid in semiannual payments of $5,000 plus interest at 10%.	Land	100,000	
	Cash		35,000
	Note Payable		65,000
June 30, 1996			
Made first payment.	Interest Expense	3,250	
Amount of payment:	Note Payable	5,000	
$5,000 + $3,250 (5% of $65,000) = $8,250	Cash		8,250

In the preceding example, the contract specified both a purchase price and interest at a stated rate on the unpaid balance. Sometimes, however, a contract may simply provide for a payment or series of payments without reference to interest, or may provide for a stated interest rate that is unreasonable in relation to the market. As indicated in Chapter 8, APB Opinion No. 21, "Interest on Receivables and Payables," requires that in these circumstances, the note, sales price, and cost of the property, goods, or services exchanged for the note should be recorded at the fair market value of the property, goods, or services or at the current market value of the note, whichever value is more clearly determinable.[6] Application of Opinion No. 21 with respect to the seller was illustrated in Chapter 8. The following example illustrates the accounting by the purchaser.

Assume that certain equipment, which has a cash price of $50,000, is acquired under a deferred payment contract. The contract specifies a down payment of $15,000 plus seven annual payments of $7,189 each, or a total price, including interest, of $65,323. Although not stated, the effective interest rate implicit in this contract is 10%, the rate that discounts the annual payments of $7,189 to a present value of $35,000, the cash price less the down payment.[7] As specified in APB Opinion No. 21, if the cash equivalent price, that is, the fair market value of the asset, varies from the contract price because of delayed payments, the difference should be recorded as a discount (contra liability) and amortized over the life of the contract using the implicit or effective interest rate. The entries to record the purchase, the amortization of the discount for the first two years, and the first two payments would be as follows.

Transaction	**Entry**		
January 2, 1996 Purchased equipment with a cash price of $50,000 for $15,000 down plus seven annual payments of $7,189 each, or a total contract price of $65,323.	Equipment Discount on Note Payable Note Payable Cash	50,000 15,323	 50,323 15,000
December 31, 1996 Made first payment of $7,189. Amortization of debt discount: 10% × $35,000 = $3,500 ($50,323 − $15,323 = $35,000)	Note Payable Cash Interest Expense Discount on Note Payable	7,189 3,500	 7,189 3,500
December 31, 1997 Made second payment of $7,189. Amortization of debt discount: 10% × $31,311* = $3,131	Note Payable Cash Interest Expense Discount on Note Payable	7,189 3,131	 7,189 3,131

*$50,323 − $7,189 = $43,134 Note payable
$15,323 − $3,500 = 11,823 Discount on note payable
$31,311 Present value of note payable at end of first year

6. The term *notes* was used by the APB in Opinion No. 21 as a general term for contractual rights to receive money or contractual obligations to pay money at specified or determinable dates.

7. As illustrated in Chapter 7, the effective or implicit interest rate is computed as follows:

$$PV_n = R(PVAF_{\overline{n|}i})$$
$$\$50{,}000 - \$15{,}000 = \$7{,}189\,(PVAF_{\overline{n|}i})$$
$$PVAF_{\overline{n|}i} = \frac{\$35{,}000}{\$7{,}189}$$
$$PVAF_{\overline{n|}i} = 4.8685$$

From Table IV, Chapter 7, the interest rate for the present value of 4.8684 when $n = 7$ is 10%. Additional examples of computing an implicit rate of interest are presented in Chapter 7.

When there is no established cash price for the property, goods, or services, and there is no stated rate of interest on the contract, or the stated rate is unreasonable under the circumstances, an imputed interest rate must be used. A discussion of the determination and application of imputed interest rates was included in Chapter 8.

Property is often acquired under a conditional sales contract whereby legal title to the asset is retained by the seller until payments are completed. The failure to acquire legal title may be disregarded by the buyer and the transaction recognized in terms of its substance—the acquisition of an asset and assumption of a liability. The buyer has the possession and use of the asset and must absorb any decline in its value; title to the asset is retained by the seller simply as a means of assuring payment on the purchase contract.

Acquisition Under Capital Lease

A **lease** is a contractual agreement whereby a **lessee** is granted a right to use property owned by the **lessor** for a specified period of time for a specified periodic cost. Many leases, referred to as **capital leases,** are in effect purchases of property. In such cases, the property should be recorded on the lessee's books as an asset at the present value of the future lease payments. Because lease accounting is a complex area, an entire chapter is devoted to accounting for leases. Even when a lease is not considered to be the same as a purchase and the periodic payments are recorded as rental expense, certain lease prepayments or improvements to the property by the lessee may be treated as capital expenditures. Since leasehold improvements, such as partitions in a building, additions, and attached equipment, revert to the owner at the expiration of the lease, they are properly capitalized on the books of the lessee and amortized over the remaining life of the lease. Some lease costs are really expenses of the period and should not be capitalized. These include improvements that are made in lieu of rent, e.g., a lessee builds partitions in a leased warehouse for storage of its product, and the lessor allows the lessee to offset the cost against rental expense for the period. These costs should be expensed by the lessee.

Acquisition by Exchange of Nonmonetary Assets

In some cases, an enterprise acquires a new asset by exchanging or trading existing nonmonetary assets.[8] Generally, the new asset should be valued at its fair market value or at the fair market value of the asset given up, whichever is more clearly determinable.[9] If the nonmonetary asset is used equipment, the fair market value of the new asset is generally more clearly determinable, and therefore used to record the exchange. It should be observed that determining the fair market value of a new asset can sometimes be difficult.

The quoted or list price for an asset is not always a good indicator of the market value and is often higher than the actual cash price for the asset. An inflated list price permits the seller to increase the indicated trade-in allowance for a used asset. The price for which the asset could be acquired in a cash transaction is the fair market value that should be used to record the acquisition.

To illustrate, assume the sticker on the window of a new car sitting in a dealer's showroom lists a total selling price of $13,500. The sticker includes a base price plus an itemized listing of all the options that have been added. If you, as a buyer, approached the dealer with your old clunker as a trade-in, you might be surprised to be offered $2,000 for a car you know is worth no more than $1,000. If you offered to pay cash for the new car

8. Monetary assets are those assets whose amounts are fixed in terms of currency, by contract, or otherwise. Examples include cash and short- or long-term accounts receivable. Nonmonetary assets include all other assets, such as inventories, land, buildings, and equipment.

9. *Opinions of the Accounting Principles Board No. 29,* "Accounting for Nonmonetary Transactions" (New York: American Institute of Certified Public Accountants, 1973), par. 18.

with no trade-in, however, you could probably buy it for approximately $12,500, or the list price reduced by the inflated amount of allowance offered for the trade-in. The fair market value of the new asset is thus not the list price of $13,500 but the true cash price of $12,500.

If the nonmonetary asset given up to acquire the new asset is also property or equipment, a disposition of property occurs simultaneously with the acquisition. Because of the need to first discuss depreciation methods and practices before presenting the disposition of assets, the full discussion of acquisition and disposition by exchange is covered in Chapter 12.

Acquisition by Issuance of Securities

A company may acquire certain property by issuing its own bonds or stocks. When a market value for the securities can be determined, that value is assigned to the asset; in the absence of a market value for the securities, the fair market value of the asset acquired would be used. If bonds or stocks are selling at more or less than par value, Bonds Payable or Capital Stock should be credited at par and the difference recorded as a premium or discount. To illustrate, assume that a company issues 1,000 shares of $25 par stock in acquiring land; the stock is currently selling on the market at $45. An entry should be made as follows:

Land	45,000	
Capital Stock		25,000
Paid-In Capital in Excess of Par		20,000

When securities do not have an established market value, appraisal of the acquired assets by an independent authority may be required to arrive at an objective determination of their fair market value. If satisfactory market values cannot be obtained for either the securities issued or the assets acquired, values may have to be established by the board of directors for accounting purposes. The source of the valuation should be disclosed on the balance sheet. Assignment of values by the board of directors is normally not subject to challenge unless it can be shown that the board has acted fraudulently. Nevertheless, evidence should be sought to validate the fairness of original valuations, and if, within a short time after an acquisition, the sale of stock or other information indicates that original valuations were erroneous, the affected asset and owners' equity accounts should be adjusted.

Property is frequently acquired in exchange for securities in conjunction with a corporate merger or consolidation. When such combination represents the transfer of properties to a new owner, the combination is designated a *purchase* and the acquired assets are reported at their cost to the new owner. But when such combination represents essentially no more than a continuation of the original ownership in the enlarged entity, the combination is designated a *pooling of interests,* and accounting authorities have approved the practice of recording properties at the original book values as shown on the books of the acquired company. Specific guidelines for distinguishing between a purchase and a pooling of interests are included in APB Opinion No. 16 and are discussed in detail in advanced accounting texts.[10]

Acquisition by Self-Construction

Sometimes buildings or equipment are constructed by a company for its own use. This may be done to save on construction costs, to utilize idle facilities, or to achieve a higher quality of construction.

10. See, for example, Paul M. Fischer, William James Taylor, and J. Arthur Leer. *Advanced Accounting* (Cincinnati: South-Western Publishing Co., 1993).

Self-constructed assets, like purchased assets, are recorded at cost, including all expenditures incurred to build the asset and make it ready for its intended use. Some considerations in determining the cost of self-constructed assets are discussed in the following sections.

Overhead Chargeable to Self-Construction. All costs that can be related to construction should be charged to the assets under construction. There is no question about the inclusion of charges for material and labor directly attributable to the new construction. However, there is a difference of opinion regarding the amount of overhead properly assignable to the construction activity. Some accountants take the position that assets under construction should be charged with no more than the incremental overhead—the increase in a company's total overhead resulting from the special construction activity. Others maintain that overhead should be assigned to construction just as it is assigned to normal operations. This would call for the inclusion of not only the increase in overhead resulting from construction activities but also a pro rata share of the company's fixed overhead.

The argument for limiting overhead charges to incremental amounts is that the cost of construction is actually no more than the extra costs incurred. Charges should not be shifted from normal operations to construction activities. Management is aware of the cost of normal operations and decides to undertake a project on the basis of the anticipated added costs. The position that construction should carry a fair share of the fixed overhead if the full cost of the asset is to be reported is based on the premise that overhead has served a dual purpose during the construction period and this is properly reflected in reduced operating costs. The latter argument may be particularly persuasive if construction takes place during a period of subnormal operations and utilizes what would otherwise represent idle capacity cost, or if construction restricts production or other regular business activities.

The assignment to construction of normal overhead otherwise chargeable to current operations will increase net income during the construction period. The recognition of a portion of overhead is postponed and related to subsequent periods through depreciation expense.

The accounting profession has not been successful in coming to an agreement on this issue. Authors of a research study for the AICPA have suggested the following criterion to help resolve the issue:

. . . in the absence of compelling evidence to the contrary, overhead costs considered to have "discernible future benefits" for the purpose of determining the cost of inventory should be presumed to have "discernible future benefits" for the purpose of determining the cost of a self-constructed depreciable asset.[11]

This criterion would charge both normal and incremental overhead costs to self-constructed fixed assets and has the advantage of providing consistency within a company in the treatment of overhead costs.

Saving or Loss on Self-Construction. When the cost of self-construction of an asset is less than the cost to acquire it through purchase or construction by outsiders, the difference for accounting purposes is not a profit but a savings. The construction is properly reported at its actual cost. The savings will emerge as income over the life of the asset as lower depreciation is charged against periodic revenue. Assume, on the other hand, the cost of self-construction is greater than bids originally received for the construction. There

11. Charles Lamden, Dale L. Gerboth, and Thomas McRae. "Accounting for Depreciable Assets." *Accounting Research Monograph No. 1* (New York: American Institute of Certified Public Accountants, 1975), p. 57.

is generally no assurance that the asset under alternative arrangements might have been equal in quality to that which was self-constructed. In recording this transaction, just as in recording others, accounts should reflect those courses of action taken, not the alternatives that might have been selected. However, if there is evidence indicating cost has been materially excessive because of certain construction inefficiencies or failures, and the cost exceeds the fair market value of the asset, the excess is properly recognized as a loss; subsequent periods should not be burdened with charges for depreciation arising from costs that could have been avoided.

Interest During Period of Construction. In public utility accounting, interest during a period of construction has long been recognized as a part of asset cost. This practice applies both to interest actually paid and to an implicit interest charge if the public utility uses its own funds. Interest costs, then, are charged to expense through depreciation over the useful life of the asset. Service rates established by regulatory bodies are based on current charges, including depreciation, and thus provide for a recovery of past interest costs.

Generally accepted accounting principles also permit the deferral of certain construction-period interest by nonutility companies. Deferred interest is often referred to as **capitalized interest.** Only interest costs actually incurred are capitalized, and no implicit interest on internal funds is recognized. The practice of capitalizing interest as part of asset cost is supported on the grounds that interest is a legitimate cost of construction, and the proper matching of revenues and expenses suggests that interest be deferred and charged over the life of the constructed asset. It can also be argued that if buildings or equipment were acquired by purchase rather than by self-construction, a charge for interest during the construction period would be implicit in the purchase price.

Arguments advanced against this practice are:

1. It is difficult to follow cash once it is invested in a firm. Is the interest charge really related to the constructed asset, or is it a payment made to meet general financial needs? Even when a loan is made for specific purposes, it frees cash raised by other means to be used for other projects.
2. To be consistent, implicit interest on all funds used, not just borrowed funds, should be charged to the asset cost. This practice is followed in utility accounting and requires determining a cost of capital for internal funds used, a very difficult task.

Historically, interest capitalization was not a common practice outside the public utility industry. Beginning in the mid-1970s, however, an increasing number of nonutility companies changed their accounting method to a policy of capitalizing interest, an action that tended to increase net income. In 1979, FASB Statement No. 34 was issued recommending limited capitalization of interest cost. If the development of an asset for use or in limited cases, for sale or lease, requires a significant period of time between the initial expenditure related to its development and its readiness for intended use, interest cost on borrowed funds should be capitalized as part of the asset cost.

The amount of interest to be capitalized is:

. . . that portion of the interest cost incurred during the assets' acquisition periods that theoretically could have been avoided (for example, by avoiding additional borrowings or by using the funds expended for the assets to repay existing borrowings) if expenditures for the assets had not been made.[12]

Capitalization of interest is permitted for assets, such as buildings and equipment, that are being self-constructed for an enterprise's own use and assets that are intended to be

12. *Statement of Financial Accounting Standards No. 34,* "Capitalization of Interest Cost" (Stamford: Financial Accounting Standards Board, 1979), par. 12.

leased or sold to others that can be identified as **discrete projects,** that is, projects that can be clearly identified as to the assets involved. The construction project should have the following characteristics before interest charges are capitalized:[13]

1. Costs are separately accumulated.
2. Construction covers an extended period of time.
3. Construction costs are substantial.

Interest should not be capitalized for inventories manufactured or produced on a repetitive basis, for assets that are currently being used, or for assets that are idle and are not undergoing activities to prepare them for use. Thus, real property that is being held for future development does not qualify for interest capitalization.[14]

Once it is determined that the construction project qualifies for interest capitalization, the amount of interest to be capitalized must be determined. The following basic principles govern the computation of capitalized interest:[15]

1. Only **interest expense actually incurred** can be capitalized. There is no provision for including an interest cost on equity capital.
2. The **maximum interest** that can be capitalized is the **total interest expense paid or accrued** for the year. In consolidated companies, this includes all interest paid by the parent and subsidiaries.
3. Interest charges begin when the first expenditures are made on the project and continue as long as the activities to get the asset ready for its intended use are in progress, and until the asset is completed and actually ready for use.
4. The **average amount of accumulated expenditures** is used as the cost on which to compute the interest charge. This can be computed for each expenditure or can be estimated using the assumption that costs are being incurred evenly over the construction period. Expenditures mean cash disbursements, not accruals.
5. If the construction period covers more than one fiscal period, accumulated expenditures include prior years' capitalized interest.
6. The **interest rates** to be applied to the average accumulated expenditures are applied in a priority order as follows:
   (a) Rate incurred for any debt specifically incurred for funds used on the project.
   (b) **Weighted average interest rate** from all other enterprise borrowings regardless of the use of funds.
7. If borrowed funds are invested awaiting expenditure on the project, revenue from the investment is not offset against the interest expense in determining the actual interest expense incurred, unless the funds came from tax-exempt borrowings.[16]
8. Disclosure must be made of the total interest expense incurred for the period and the portion that was included as a capitalized cost.

The following illustration demonstrates the application of these guidelines. Cutler Industries, Inc., has decided to construct a new computerized assembly plant. It is estimated that the construction period will be two years and that the cost of construction will be $6.4 million. A 12% construction loan for $2 million is obtained at the beginning of construction.

In addition to the construction loan, Cutler has the following outstanding debt during the construction period:

13. Alex T. Arcady and Charles Baker. "Interest Cost Accounting: Some Practical Guidance." *The Journal of Accountancy* (March 1981), p. 64.

14. *Statement of Financial Accounting Standards No. 34,* par. 10.

15. All items in the list are included in FASB Statement No. 34 except as otherwise noted.

16. *FASB Technical Bulletin 81-5,* "Offsetting Interest to Be Capitalized with Interest Income" (Stamford: Financial Accounting Standards Board, 1981) as amended by *Statement of Financial Accounting Standards No. 62,* "Capitalization of Interest Cost in Situations Involving Certain Tax-Exempt Borrowings and Certain Gifts and Grants" (Stamford: Financial Accounting Standards Board, 1982).

5-year notes payable, 11% interest	$ 750,000
Mortgage on other plant, 9% interest	1,200,000

Expenditures on the project are incurred evenly during each year, beginning January 1, 1996, and ending on December 31, 1997. The expenditures incurred during 1996 amounted to $3,000,000.

The first step in determining the portion of interest expense to capitalize for Cutler Industries is to determine the total interest paid during the year. This amount becomes the maximum interest that can be capitalized. In the example, the debt described below is assumed to be outstanding during all of 1996 and 1997. The interest paid is computed as follows:

Computation of Maximum Interest That Can Be Capitalized Each Year

Debt	Amount	Interest Rate	Annual Interest
Construction Loan	$2,000,000	12%	$240,000
Notes Payable	750,000	11%	82,500
Mortgage Payable	1,200,000	9%	108,000
Maximum Capitalizable Interest			$430,500

The next step is to compute a weighted average interest rate on outstanding debt not directly obtained for construction. For Cutler Industries, this rate is computed as follows:

Computation of Weighted Average Interest Rate

Non-Construction Debt	Principal	Rate	Interest Cost
Notes Payable	$ 750,000	11%	$ 82,500
Mortgage	1,200,000	9%	108,000
	$1,950,000	9.8%*	$190,500

*Weighted average rate = $190,500 ÷ $1,950,000 = 9.8% (rounded)

The computation of the average accumulated expenditures must be made for each year. This is done by weighting each expenditure by the number of months left in the year after the expenditure is made. If the $3,000,000 in construction expenditures for 1996 all occurred on May 1, the average accumulated expenditures for the year would be $2,000,000 ($3,000,000 × $^8/_{12}$), since there were eight months left in the year when the expenditures were made. If $1,200,000 of the expenditures occurred on May 1 and the remaining $1,800,000 occurred on October 1, the average accumulated expenditures for the year would be $1,250,000 [($1,200,000 × $^8/_{12}$) + ($1,800,000 × $^3/_{12}$)].

Since it is assumed that Cutler Industries incurred its expenditures evenly throughout the year, a simplifying method may be used to compute the average accumulated expenditures; simply average the beginning and ending total accumulated expenditures. The average for Cutler Industries for 1996 and 1997 would be computed as follows. Note that the beginning balance in 1996 is $0, but in 1997, it is $3,180,000, the total expenditures for 1996 plus the capitalized 1996 interest.

Computation of Weighted Average Accumulated Expenditures—1996

Accumulated expenditures, Jan. 1, 1996	$ -0-
Expenditures incurred during 1996	3,000,000
Accumulated expenditures, Dec. 31, 1996	$3,000,000
Average accumulated expenditures—1996 ($3,000,000 ÷ 2)	$1,500,000

Computation of Interest Eligible for Capitalization—1996

$1,500,000 × 12% (rate on construction loan) = $180,000

Since $180,000 is less than the actual interest expense, the $180,000 is capitalized as interest cost.

Assume that the project was completed at the end of 1997 and that expenditures during 1997 totaled $3.2 million, bringing the actual total cost of construction (excluding interest) to $6.2 million.

Computation of Weighted Average Accumulated Expenditures—1997

Accumulated expenditures, Dec. 31, 1996	$3,000,000
Interest capitalized—1996	180,000
Adjusted accumulated expenditures, Dec. 31, 1996*	$3,180,000
Expenditures incurred during 1997	3,200,000
Accumulated expenditures, Dec. 31, 1997	$6,380,000
Average accumulated expenditures—1997 [($3,180,000 + $6,380,000)÷ 2]	$4,780,000

*1996 expenditures are considered incurred for all of 1997.

Computation of Interest Eligible for Capitalization—1997

$2,000,000*	×	12%	$240,000
2,780,000**	×	9.8%	272,440
			$512,440

*Amount of construction loan

**$4,780,000 – $2,000,000

Since $512,440 is more than the actual annual interest of $430,500, the actual interest expense is capitalized for 1997.

There are several important observations about this example. In 1996, the interest expense actually incurred exceeded the amount of interest computed on the average accumulated expenditures. The computed interest amount, therefore, was capitalized. In 1997, however, more of the company's internal funds were used for the construction, and the computation of interest that could have been capitalized exceeded the interest actually paid. The interest actually paid, therefore, was capitalized.

The example assumed no new loans were obtained during 1997. If additional monies were borrowed specifically for the project, the rate on the new borrowings would have been applied to expended funds before applying the weighted average rate on all other borrowings. If additional general borrowings were made, a new computation of the weighted average rate would have been necessary. The example also assumed that all loans were outstanding for the entire two-year construction period. The computation of interest eligible for capitalization is a bit more complex if new borrowing occurs during construction.[17] For example, assume that the $2,000,000 12% construction loan was obtained on July 1, 1996, rather than on January 1, 1996. Just as expenditures during the year are weighted to determine the average accumulated expenditures, loans obtained during the year can be weighted to compute a weighted average loan amount. The 1996 weighted average loan amount for the July 1 $2,000,000 construction loan is $1,000,000 ($2,000,000 × 6/12). The computation of interest eligible for capitalization for 1996 is as follows:

17. FASB Statement No. 34 is unclear whether the interest rate on specific borrowing is applied to the full amount of the loan or to a weighted average of the loan reflecting the period it was outstanding. For a discussion of the implications of these two alternatives, see Kathryn M. Means and Paul M. Karenski, "SFAS 34: A Recipe for Diversity." *Accounting Horizons*, (September 1988), pp. 62-67.

Computation of Interest Eligible for Capitalization — 1996
Construction Loan Obtained on July 1, 1996

$1,000,000* × 12%	$120,000
$ 500,000** × 9.8%	49,000
	$169,000

*Weighted average amount for the July 1 construction loan: $2,000,000 × 6/12.
**$1,500,000 – $1,000,000. Recall that the average accumulated expenditures for 1996 was $1,500,000.

If the construction loan had been obtained on July 1, total interest for 1996 would have been $310,500 [($750,000 × .11) + ($1,200,000 × .09) + ($2,000,000 × .12 × 6/12)]. Since the $169,000 is less than the actual interest that would have been incurred, capitalized interest for the year would be $169,000. The reason only $169,000 would be capitalized in this example while $180,000 was capitalized in the original example is because, in the second example, the construction loan was not needed until six months after the beginning of the project. Predictably, with lower interest costs traceable to the project, the amount of interest capitalized is lower.

FASB Statement No. 34 requires disclosure of the total interest expense for the year and the amount capitalized. This disclosure can be made either in the body of the income statement or in a note to the statements.

To illustrate these two methods, assume that Cutler Industries reported the 1996 interest information in the income statement and the 1997 information in a note as shown following.

Cutler Industries, Inc.
Income Statement
For the Year Ended December 31, 1996

Operating income		$ XXX,XXX
Other expenses and losses:		
Interest expense	$430,500	
Less capitalized interest	180,000	250,500
Income before income taxes		$ XXX,XXX
Income taxes		XXX,XXX
Net income		$ XXX,XXX

Cutler Industries Notes—1997

Note X—Interest expense

Total interest of $430,500 was capitalized in 1997 as part of the cost of construction for the computerized assembly line building in accordance with the requirements of FASB Statement No. 34.

The capitalization of interest costs as part of the cost of self-constructed assets has been subject to much criticism. The initial acceptance vote of the FASB was by a 4-3 margin, the minimum acceptable. It is interesting to note that, since January 1, 1991, the rules governing the FASB have required a minimum of five votes for passage of a standard. Under these rules, the interest capitalization standard would not have been adopted. The conceptual question that still remains is whether the interest added to asset cost truly adds to the expected future benefit of the constructed asset. For now, the profession has specified the conditions where the answer is yes.

Acquisition by Donation or Discovery

When property is received through donation, there is no cost that can be used as a basis for its valuation. This type of transaction is classified as a **nonreciprocal transfer of a**

nonmonetary asset.[18] Even though certain expenditures may have to be made incident to the gift, these expenditures are generally considerably less than the value of the property. Here cost obviously fails to provide a satisfactory basis for asset valuation.

Property acquired through donation should be appraised and recorded at its fair market value. A donation is recognized as a revenue or gain in the period in which it is received.[19] To illustrate, if the Beverly Hills Chamber of Commerce donates land and buildings appraised at $400,000 and $1,500,000 respectively, the entry on the books of the donee would be:

Land	400,000	
Buildings	1,500,000	
Revenue or Gain		1,900,000

Depreciation of an asset acquired by gift should be recorded in the usual manner, the value assigned to the asset providing the basis for the depreciation charge.

If a gift is contingent upon some act to be performed by the donee, no asset should be reported until the conditions of the gift have been met. At that time, both the increase in assets and the revenue or gain should be recognized in the accounts and on the financial statements.[20]

Occasionally, valuable resources are discovered on land already owned. The discovery greatly increases the value of the property. However, because the cost of the land is not affected by the discovery, it is common practice to ignore this increase in value. Similarly, the increase in value for assets that change over time, such as growing timber or aging wine, is ignored in common practice. Failure to recognize these discovery or accretion values ignores the economic reality of the situation and tends to materially understate the assets of the entity. More meaningful decisions probably could be made if the users of the statements were made aware of these changes in value.

CLASSIFYING EXPENDITURES AS ASSETS OR EXPENSES

The decision whether a given expenditure is an asset or an expense is one of the many areas in which an accountant must exercise judgment. If the expenditure is expected to benefit future periods, it is by definition an asset. If the expenditure benefits the current period only, it is an expense.

Income cannot be measured fairly unless expenditures are properly classified. For example, an incorrect charge to an equipment account instead of an expense account results in the overstatement of current earnings on the income statement and the overstatement of assets and owners' equity on the balance sheet. As the charge is assigned to operations in subsequent periods, earnings of such periods will be understated; assets and equity on the successive balance sheets will continue to be overstated, although by lesser amounts each year, until the asset is written off and the original error is fully counterbalanced. On the other hand, an incorrect charge to an expense instead of an equipment account results in the understatement of current earnings and the understatement of assets and equity. Earnings of subsequent periods will be overstated in the absence of debits for depreciation or amortization; assets and equity will continue to be understated, although by lesser amounts each year, until the original error is completely offset.

In many companies, not all expenditures for assets that have future benefits are recorded in the noncurrent asset accounts. A lower limit to the definition of an asset expen-

18. *Statement of Financial Accounting Standards No. 116,* "Accounting for Contributions Received and Contributions Made" (Norwalk: Financial Accounting Standards Board, 1993), par. 5.
19. *Ibid.*, par. 8.
20. *Ibid.*, par. 22.

diture is established to avoid the excessive costs of accounting for relatively small deferred costs. Thus, any expenditure under the established limit is always expensed currently even though future benefits are expected from that expenditure. This practice is justified on the grounds of expediency and materiality. The amount of the limit varies with the size of the company. Limits of $100, $500, and $1,000 are not unusual. This treatment is acceptable as long as it is consistently applied and no material misstatements arise due to unusual expenditure patterns or other causes.

Previous sections of the chapter have described the types of expenditures that typically are recorded as assets and under various types of acquisition arrangements. The remainder of the chapter focuses on areas where some special problems and considerations arise in determining whether an expenditure is an asset or an expense. These areas are: research and development expenditures, computer software development expenditures, and post-acquisition expenditures.

Research and Development Expenditures

Historically, expenditures for **research and development (R&D)** purposes were reported sometimes as assets and sometimes as expenses. The FASB inherited this problem from the Accounting Principles Board and made this area the subject of its first definitive standard.[21] The Board defined **research activities** as those undertaken to discover new knowledge that will be useful in developing new products, services, or processes or that will result in significant improvements of existing products or processes. **Development activities** involve the application of research findings to develop a plan or design for new or improved products and processes. Development activities include the formulation, design, and testing of products, construction of prototypes, and operation of pilot plants.

In general, the FASB concluded that research and development expenditures should be expensed in the period incurred.[22] This decision was reached after much analysis and after many attempts to establish criteria for selectively recording some research and development expenditures as assets and expensing others. Among the arguments for expensing these costs is the frequent inability to find a definite causal relationship between the expenditures and future revenues. Sometimes very large expenditures do not generate any future revenue, while relatively small expenditures lead to significant discoveries that generate large revenues. The Board found it difficult to establish criteria that would distinguish between those research and development expenditures that would most likely benefit future periods and those that would not.

As defined by the FASB in Statement No. 2, research and development costs include those costs of materials, equipment, facilities, personnel, purchased intangibles, contract services, and a reasonable allocation of indirect costs that are related specifically to research and development activities and that have no alternative future uses.[23] Such activities include:

1. Laboratory research aimed at discovery of new knowledge.
2. Searching for applications of new research findings or other knowledge.
3. Conceptual formulation and design of possible product or process alternatives.
4. Testing in search for or evaluation of product or process alternatives.
5. Modification of the formulation or design of a product or process.
6. Design, construction, and testing of preproduction prototypes and models.
7. Design of tools, jigs, molds, and dies involving new technology.

21. *Statement of Financial Accounting Standards No. 2,* "Accounting for Research and Development Costs" (Stamford: Financial Accounting Standards Board, 1974).

22. *Ibid.,* par. 12.

23. *Ibid.,* par. 11.

8. Design, construction, and operation of a pilot plant that is not of a scale economically feasible to the enterprise for commercial production.
9. Engineering activity required to advance the design of a product to the point that it meets specific functional and economic requirements and is ready for manufacture.[24]

The Board stipulated, however, that expenditures for certain items having alternative future uses, either in additional research projects or for productive purposes, can be recorded as an asset and allocated against future projects or periods as research and development expenses. This exception permits the deferral of costs incurred for materials, equipment, facilities, and purchased intangibles, but only if an alternative use can be identified.

The Board was very careful to distinguish between research and development expenses and other expenditures that are related to research activities but classified in other categories. These other expenditures are also usually regarded as expenses in the period incurred, but not as research and development expenses. To illustrate how research-related expenditures are recorded under current GAAP, assume the Robotics Corporation made the expenditures listed during 1996 related to the development of robots for commercial and productive use.

Robotics Corporation

Description of Expenditure	Accounting Treatment Per GAAP
1. Purchase of land to construct research facility.	1. Record as land.
2. Self-construction of building to use in all robotic research.	2. Record as building and depreciate as R&D expense.
3. Purchase of special equipment to be used solely for the development of a robot for the space program. The equipment is not expected to have any use beyond this project.	3. Expense immediately as R&D.
4. Purchase of more generalized equipment that can be used for a wide variety of robotic projects.	4. Record as equipment and depreciate as R&D expense.
5. Research salaries dedicated to improvement of general robotic technology.	5. Expense immediately as R&D.
6. Purchase of patent for innovative construction of arm and hand segments.	6. Record as patent and amortize as cost of production.
7. Labor and material costs incurred in building a prototype model of a robot for space travel.	7. Expense immediately as R&D.
8. Costs to produce ten robots to specified design.	8. Include in cost of goods manufactured. Report robots as inventory on balance sheet until sold.
9. Salary of marketing executive assigned to find customers for the space robot.	9. Expense immediately as marketing expense.
10. Costs of testing the prototype robot under simulated space travel conditions.	10. Expense immediately as R&D.
11. Legal costs to protect patents purchased.	11. Record as patent and amortize as cost of production.
12. Legal costs of filing for patent on space robot.	12. Record as patent and amortize as cost of production.
13. Research costs for Japanese manufacturer who has contracted with Robotics Corporation for research technology.	13. Record as receivable for contracted amount.

24. *Ibid.*, par. 9.

Evaluation of FASB Position. Research and development costs vary widely among companies. Many expenditures do have future worth, while others are so highly uncertain as to future worth that recording them as assets is clearly improper. For the FASB to ignore these differences and issue a blanket rule that all research and development expenditures should be handled the same seems arbitrary and without theoretical support. In studying this area, the International Accounting Standards Committee disagreed with the FASB and identified general situations in which they felt deferral of development costs would be justified. Development costs of a project may be deferred to future periods if the five criteria are satisfied.

1. The product or process is clearly defined and the costs attributable to the product or process can be separately identified.
2. The technical feasibility of the product or process has been demonstrated.
3. The management of the enterprise has indicated its intention to produce and market, or use, the product or process.
4. There is a clear indication of a future market for the product or process or, if it is to be used internally rather than sold, its usefulness to the enterprise can be demonstrated.
5. Adequate resources exist, or are reasonably expected to be available, to complete the project and market the product or process.[25]

The FASB recently has shown more flexibility in this area, as evidenced by its standard on accounting for computer software development, discussed on following pages.

Computer Software Development Expenditures

When the use of personal computers first became widespread, the development of computer software required little in the way of initial capital investment, and thus led to the formation of hundreds of small software companies, each developing its own special software programs. Scores of computer magazines advertising these programs emerged in the last decade as businesses and households have purchased their own micros. Software programs such as *Lotus 1-2-3, Excel, Word Perfect, Paradox,* and *Peachtree* have magnified the power of the computer for everyday use. Specialized accounting, tax, architectural, library, medical, educational, and recreational software packages have been developed by these hundreds of companies and marketed throughout the world.

A major accounting question related to the development of computer software has been how to account for the costs of development and production of the finished product. Many companies considered the development costs as research and development and expensed them in the period incurred as required by FASB Statement No. 2, discussed in the previous section. Other companies argued that these costs should be deferred and written off against future revenues. Since these costs were a very significant part of the total expenditures of a software company, the alternate methods used to account for them created considerable differences among the financial statements of the various companies. The FASB, with strong support from the SEC, addressed this issue and in 1985 issued FASB Statement No. 86, "Accounting for the Costs of Computer Software to Be Sold, Leased, or Otherwise Marketed."

The Board's conclusions concerning computer software costs are summarized in Exhibit 11—4.

As demonstrated by Exhibit 11—4, all costs incurred up to the point where technological feasibility is established are to be expensed as research and development. They include costs incurred for planning, designing, and testing activities. Costs incurred after this point up until the product is ready for commercial production, such as further

25. *International Accounting Standard No. 9,* "Accounting for Research and Development Activities" (London, England: International Accounting Standards Committee, 1978), par. 17.

Exhibit 11—4
Development of Successful Software

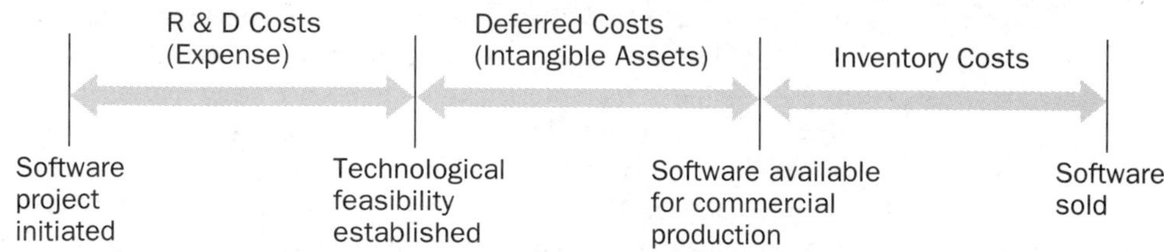

coding, testing, and production of masters, are to be recorded as an intangible asset. Additional costs to actually produce software from the masters and package the software for distribution are inventoriable costs and will be charged against revenue as the product is sold.

Considerable judgment is required to determine when technological feasibility has been established. The Board attempted to assist in the judgment with specific definitions and examples. At a minimum, **technological feasibility** shall be attained when an enterprise has produced either:[26]

1. A **detail program design** of the software establishing that the necessary skills, hardware, and software technology are available to the enterprise to produce the product (includes coding and testing necessary to resolve uncertainties for high-risk development issues), or
2. A **working model** of the software has been completed and tested.

If an enterprise purchases computer software externally for further development and resale, it should be accounted for in the same manner as described above for internally developed software. While Statement No. 86 does not directly address accounting for costs of computer software that is to be *used* internally by an enterprise as opposed to being *sold* externally, the Board indicated that the limited deferral of software costs would "likely be applied to costs incurred in developing software for internal use as well as for sale or lease to others."[27]

The treatment of computer software development costs by the FASB demonstrates how the more general research and development guidelines of FASB Statement No. 2 may be applied in future specific situations. By establishing two transitional points (technological feasibility and availability for general release to customers), the Board has recognized a separation between costs that are identified as being expenses and those that are assets to be deferred and amortized against future revenues. This treatment seems more in keeping with the approach used by the International Accounting Standards Committee for all research and development costs as described earlier.

Post-Acquisition Expenditures

Over the useful lives of plant assets, regular as well as special expenditures are incurred. Certain expenditures are required to maintain and repair assets; others are incurred to increase their capacity or efficiency or to extend their useful lives. Each expenditure requires careful analysis to determine whether it should be charged to an expense account, or whether it should be assigned to revenue of more than one period, which requires a charge to an asset account or to an accumulated depreciation account. In many cases the answer may not be clear, and the procedure chosen may be a matter of judgment.

26. *Statement of Financial Accounting Standards No. 86*, "Accounting for the Costs of Computer Software to Be Sold, Leased, or Otherwise Marketed" (Stamford: Financial Accounting Standards Board, 1985), par. 4.
27. *Ibid.*, par. 26.

The terms maintenance, repairs, betterments, improvements, additions, and rearrangements are used in describing expenditures made in the course of asset use. These are described in the following sections. Exhibit 11—5 summarizes the accounting for these subsequent expenditures.

Maintenance and Repairs. Expenditures to maintain plant assets in good operating condition are referred to as **maintenance.** Among these are expenditures for painting, lubricating, and adjusting equipment. Maintenance expenditures are ordinary and recurring and do not improve the asset or add to its life; therefore, they are recorded as expenses when they are incurred.

Expenditures to restore assets to good operating condition upon their breakdown or to restore and replace broken parts are referred to as **repairs.** These are ordinary and recurring expenditures that benefit only current operations; thus, they also are debited to expense immediately.

Renewals and Replacements. Expenditures for overhauling plant assets are frequently referred to as **renewals.** Substitutions of parts or entire units are referred to as **replacements.** If these expenditures are necessary to achieve the original plans and do not change the original estimates of useful life or cash flows, they should be expensed. If, however, these expenditures extend the life of the asset or increase the cash flows generated by the asset, they should be capitalized by either adding them to the asset value or deducting them from accumulated depreciation.

Theoretically, if a part is removed and replaced with a superior part, the cost and accumulated depreciation related to the replaced part should be removed from the accounts, a loss recognized for the undepreciated book value, and the expenditure for the replacement added to the asset value. Often it is not possible to identify the cost related to a specific

Exhibit 11—5 Summary of Expenditures Subsequent to Acquisition

Type of Expenditure	Definition	Accounting Treatment
Maintenance and repairs	Normal cost of keeping property in operating condition.	Expense as incurred.
Renewals and replacements:		
1. No extension of useful life or increase in future cash flows.	Unplanned replacement. Expenditure needed to fulfill original plans.	Expense as incurred.
2. Extends useful life or increases future cash flows.	Improvement resulting from replacement with better component.	Record as an asset by one of two methods: 1. If cost of old component is known: Remove cost of old part and its accumulated depreciation, recognizing gain or loss. Defer cost of new component. 2. If cost of old component is not known: Deduct cost of new component from accumulated depreciation.
Additions and betterments	Expenditures that add to asset usefulness by either extending life or increasing future cash flows. No replacement of component involved.	Add to the cost of an asset.

part of an asset. In these instances, by debiting Accumulated Depreciation, the undepreciated book value is increased without creating a buildup of the gross asset values. When this entry is made, no immediate loss related to the removal of the old asset is recognized.

To illustrate replacements, assume the Mendon Fireworks Company replaces the roof of its manufacturing plant for $40,000 and extends the estimated life of the building by five years. Assume that the original cost of the building was $1,600,000 and it is 3/4 depreciated. If the original roof cost $20,000, the following entry could be made to remove the undepreciated book value of the old roof and record the expenditure for the new one.

Buildings (new roof)	40,000	
Accumulated Depreciation (old roof)	15,000	
Loss From Replacement of Roof	5,000	
Buildings (old roof)		20,000
Cash		40,000

If Mendon could not identify the cost of the old roof, the following entry would be made:

Accumulated Depreciation	40,000	
Cash		40,000

The book value of the building after the first entry is $435,000 ($1,600,000 – $1,200,000 + $40,000 – $5,000). Assuming the second entry is made, the book value would be $440,000 ($1,600,000 – $1,200,000 + $40,000). The $5,000 additional cost would be reflected in higher depreciation charges over the remaining life of the building.

Additions and Betterments. Enlargements and extensions of existing facilities are referred to as **additions.** Changes in assets designed to provide increased or improved services are referred to as **betterments.** If the addition or betterment does not involve a replacement of component parts of an existing asset, the expenditure should be deferred by adding it to the cost of the asset. If a replacement is involved, it is accounted for as discussed in the previous section.

VALUATION OF ASSETS AT CURRENT VALUES

Throughout this chapter, the valuation of assets has been based on historical costs. As discussed in Chapter 2, FASB Concepts Statement No. 5 identified other measurement attributes that might be used if they were more relevant than historical cost and if their reliability could be improved.[28]

The discussion of current values in accounting ebbs and flows with the economic environment. In the late 1980s, the dramatic bail-out of the savings and loan industry by the federal government highlighted the excesses that can occur when current market values are not reported. Reexamination of the accounting for financial institutions led to FASB Statement No. 115, which requires most marketable securities to be reported at their current market values. It is likely that the continuing call by financial statement users for current value information will result in a reconsideration of the appropriateness of historical cost accounting for noncurrent operating assets. This is especially true given that many countries around the world already employ current value accounting for noncurrent operating assets (see the boxed item on page 459).

28. *Statement of Financial Accounting Concepts No. 5,* "Recognition and Measurement in Financial Statements of Business Enterprises" (Stamford: Financial Accounting Standards Board, 1984), par. 30.

Asset Write-Ups

The Rouse Company, a real estate developer, is well-known as one of the few U.S. companies to report the current value of property and equipment in its financial statements. Before the formation of the SEC in 1934, it was common for U.S. companies to report the upward revaluation of property and equipment. However, by 1940 the SEC had effectively eliminated this practice, not by explicitly banning it, but through informal administrative pressure. Much of the suspicion about asset revaluations stemmed from a Federal Trade Commission investigation, completed in 1935, that uncovered a number of cases in the public utility industry in which a utility had improperly revalued assets upward to boost its rate base.

Statement No. 16 of the International Accounting Standards Committee permits the inclusion of upward asset revaluations in the financial statements. However, rules enacted by national accounting standard-setting authorities vary greatly around the world. In France, companies are allowed to write up property and equipment, but such write-ups are not common since the company is taxed on the amount of the write-up. In Germany, as in the U.S., upward revaluations are not allowed. In fact, German rules are seen as encouraging write-downs, resulting in the creation of so-called "hidden reserves" which constitute a systematic understatement of assets. In March 1993, Daimler-Benz, the largest industrial firm, disclosed that it had hidden reserves of $2.45 billion.

Asset revaluations occur quite frequently in the United Kingdom. One example can be found in the financial statements of Grand Metropolitan, the consumer products firm and parent of Pillsbury, Green Giant, and Burger King. As of September 30, 1992, the reported gross amount for land and buildings was 1.848 billion British pounds. This number is a mix of historical cost numbers and amounts obtained from professional revaluations. Without the revaluations, the gross amount of land and buildings would have been 1.34 billion British pounds.

Questions:

1. Why might real estate companies be among the leaders in encouraging the disclosure of the current value of property and equipment?
2. If German companies have "hidden" reserves, why do you think Daimler-Benz chose to reveal the magnitude of their hidden reserves in March 1993? What is the advantage to a company of having hidden reserves in the first place?
3. As an auditor, how would you feel about auditing the financial statements of a company that uses appraisal values instead of historical cost?

Sources:

Timothy Aeppel. "Daimler-Benz Discloses Hidden Reserves of $2.45 Billion, Seeks Big Board Listing." *The Wall Street Journal*, March 25, 1993, p.A10.

David Alexander and Simon Archer. *HBJ Miller Comprehensive European Accounting Guide* (Harcourt Brace Jovanovich, San Diego: 1991).

R.G. Walker. "The SEC's Ban on Upward Asset Revaluations and the Disclosure of Current Values." *Abacus* (March 1992), p.3.

Henry Schwarzbach and Richard Vangermeersch. "The Current Value Experiences of The Rouse Company, 1973-1989." *Accounting Horizons* (June 1991), p. 45.

SUMMARY

The most challenging issue facing accountants in the area of asset acquisitions is deciding which costs should be deferred and matched against future revenue and which should be expensed immediately. Costs to acquire new property items with lives in excess of one fiscal period clearly should be charged against future periods. Accounting for repairs, additions, and similar costs incurred subsequent to the initial acquisition is less clear, and such expenditures must be individually evaluated in light of existing conditions. The historical acquisition cost of an asset is widely accepted as the basis for the gross investment, whether for tangible or intangible assets. Methods for matching these costs against future revenues will be discussed in the next chapter, as well as accounting for the retirement of assets.

APPENDIX
Goodwill Estimation

As indicated previously, there are many factors that can be considered in determining the purchase price for a business. In deciding whether more than the current value of identifiable net assets should be paid, management may utilize one or more of the following goodwill valuation methods:

1. Capitalization of average income
2. Capitalization of average excess income
3. Number of years' excess income
4. Present value of future excess income

It should be remembered that business valuation is a very complex process, and this appendix is intended to be only an introduction.

VARIABLES USED IN GOODWILL VALUATION

Before discussing the methods identified above, two variables that are used in all methods are discussed: (1) an estimate of future income and (2) an appropriate rate of return.

Estimating the Level of Future Income

Past earnings ordinarily offer the best basis on which to develop an estimate of the level of future income. In considering past income as a basis for projection into the future, reference should be made to income most recently experienced. A sufficient number of periods should be included in the analysis so a representative measurement of business performance is available and significant trends are observable. In certain instances, it may be considered necessary to restate revenue and expense balances to give effect to alternative depreciation or amortization methods, inventory methods, or other measurement processes considered desirable in summarizing past operations. Irregular or extraordinary gains and losses that cannot be considered a part of regular activities would be excluded from past operating results. Depending on the circumstances, these items may include gains and losses from the sale of investments and land, buildings, and equipment, gains and losses from the retirement of debt, and losses from casualties.

Regular earnings from operations should be analyzed to determine their trend and stability. If earnings over a period of years show a tendency to decline, careful analysis is necessary to determine whether this decline may be expected to continue. There may be greater confidence in possible future income when past income has been relatively stable rather than widely fluctuating.

Any changes in the operations of the business that may be anticipated after the transfer of ownership should also be considered. The elimination of a division, the disposal of substantial property items, or the retirement of long-term debt, for example, could materially affect future income.

The regular income of the past is used as a basis for estimating income of the future. Business conditions, the business cycle, sources of supply, demand for the company's products or services, price structure, competition, and other significant factors must be studied in developing data making it possible to convert past income into estimated future income.

Determining the Appropriate Rate of Return

The existence of above-normal income, if any, can be determined only by reference to a normal rate of return. The **normal income rate** is that which would ordinarily be required to attract investors in the particular type of business being acquired. In judging this rate, consideration must be given to such factors as money market rates, business conditions at the time of the purchase, competitive factors, risks involved, entrepreneurial abilities required, and alternative investment opportunities.

In general, the greater the risk entailed in an investment, the higher the rate of return required. Because most business enterprises are subject to a considerable amount of risk, investors generally expect a relatively high rate of return to justify their investment. A long history of stable income or the existence of certain tangible assets that can be easily sold reduce the degree of risk in acquiring a business and thus reduce the rate of return required by a potential investor.

If goodwill is to be purchased, it should be looked upon as an investment and must offer the prospect of sufficient return to justify the commitment. Special risks are associated with goodwill. The value of goodwill is uncertain and fluctuating. It cannot be separated from the business as a whole and sold, as can most other business properties. Furthermore, it is subject to rapid deterioration and may be totally lost in the event of business sale or liquidation. As a result of the greater risk, a higher rate of return normally would be required on the purchase of goodwill than on the purchase of other business properties.

METHODS OF VALUING GOODWILL

Assume that the following information is available for Company A:

Income after adjustment and elimination of unusual and extraordinary items

1993	$120,000
1994	80,000
1995	110,000
1996	75,000
1997	115,000
Total	$500,000

Average income 1993-1997: $500,000 ÷ 5 = $100,000. Net assets as appraised on January 2, 1998, before recognizing goodwill, $1,000,000. (Land, buildings, equipment, inventories, and receivables, $1,200,000; liabilities to be assumed by purchaser, $200,000.)

The average income figure of $100,000 for the five-year period 1993-1997 was used in arriving at an estimate of the probable future income. Different goodwill amounts may be computed using this data depending on which of the four valuation methods listed at the beginning of this appendix is used. Each of these methods will be described and illustrated with examples.

Capitalization of Average Income

The amount to be paid for a business may be determined by capitalizing expected future income at a rate representing the required return on the investment. Capitalization of income, as used in this sense, means calculation of the principal value that will yield the stated income at the specified rate indefinitely or in perpetuity. This is accomplished by dividing the income by the specified rate.[29] The difference between the amount to be paid for the business as thus obtained and the appraised values of the individual property items may be considered the price paid for goodwill.

If, in the example, a return of 8% were required on the investment and income were estimated at $100,000 per year, the business would be valued at $1,250,000 ($100,000 ÷ .08). Since net assets, with the exception of goodwill, were appraised at $1,000,000, goodwill would be valued at $250,000. If a 10% return were required on the investment, the business would be worth only $1,000,000. In acquiring the business for $1,000,000, there would be no payment for goodwill.

Capitalization of Average Excess Income

In the above method, a single rate of return was applied to the estimated annual income in arriving at the value of the business. No consideration was given to what extent the income was attributable to net identifiable assets and to what extent the income was attributable to goodwill. It would seem reasonable, however, to expect a higher return on an investment in goodwill than on the other assets acquired. To illustrate, assume the following facts:

	Company A	Company B
Net assets as appraised	$1,000,000	$500,000
Estimated future income	100,000	100,000

If the estimated income is capitalized at a uniform rate of 8%, the value of each company is found to be $1,250,000. The goodwill for Company A is then $250,000, and for Company B, $750,000 as shown:

	Company A	Company B
Total net asset valuation (income capitalized at 8%)	$1,250,000	$1,250,000
Deduct net assets as appraised	1,000,000	500,000
Goodwill	$ 250,000	$ 750,000

These calculations ignore the fact that the appraised value of the net assets identified with Company A exceed those of Company B. Company A, whose income of $100,000 is accompanied by net assets valued at $1,000,000, would certainly command a higher price than Company B, whose income of $100,000 is accompanied by net assets valued at only $500,000.

Satisfactory recognition of both earnings and asset contributions is generally effected by (1) requiring a fair return on identifiable net assets, and (2) viewing any excess income as attributable to goodwill and capitalizing the excess at a higher rate in recognition of the degree of risk that characterizes goodwill. To illustrate, assume in the previous cases that 8% is considered a normal return on identifiable net assets and that excess income is capitalized at 20% in determining the amount to be paid for goodwill. Amounts to be paid for Companies A and B would be calculated as follows:

	Company A	Company B
Estimated income	$100,000	$100,000
Normal return on net assets:		
Company A—8% of $1,000,000	80,000	
Company B—8% of $500,000		40,000
Excess income	$20,000	$60,000
Excess income capitalized at 20%	÷ .20	÷ .20
Value of goodwill	$100,000	$300,000

29. This may be shown as follows: P = principal amount or the capitalized income to be computed; r = the specified rate of return; E = expected annual income. Then, $E = P \times r$, and $P = E \div r$.

	Company A	Company B
Value of net assets offering normal return of 8%	$1,000,000	$500,000
Value of goodwill, excess income capitalized at 20%	100,000	300,000
Total net asset valuation	$1,100,000	$800,000

Number of Years' Excess Income

Behind each of the capitalization methods just described, there is an implicit assumption that the superior earning power attributed to the existence of goodwill will continue indefinitely. The very nature of goodwill, however, makes it subject to rapid decline. A business with unusually high income may expect the competition from other companies to reduce income over a period of years. Furthermore, the high levels of income frequently may be maintained only by special efforts on the part of the new owners, and they cannot be expected to pay for something they themselves must achieve.

As the goodwill being purchased cannot be expected to last beyond a specific number of years, one frequently finds payment for excess income stated in terms of years of excess income rather than capitalization in perpetuity.[30] For example, if excess annual income of $20,000 is expected and payment is to be made for excess income for a five-year period, the purchase price for goodwill would be $100,000. If the excess annual income is expected to be $60,000 and the payment is to be made for four years' excess income, the price for goodwill would be $240,000.

The years-of-excess earnings method has the advantage of conceptual simplicity. It is related to the common business practice of evaluating investment opportunities in terms of their payback period—the number of years expected for recovery of the initial investment.

Present Value of Future Excess Income

The concept of number-of-years' excess income can be combined with the concept of a rate of return on investment. Excess income can be expected to continue for only a limited number of years, but an investment in this income should provide an adequate return, considering the risks involved. The amount to be paid for goodwill, then, is the discounted or present value of the excess income expected to become available in future periods.

To illustrate the calculation of goodwill by the present-value method, assume the income of Company A exceeds a normal return on the net identifiable assets used in the business by $20,000 per year. This excess income is expected to continue for a period of five years, and a return of 12% is considered necessary to attract investors in this industry. The amount to be paid for goodwill, then, may be regarded as the discounted value at 12% of five installments of $20,000 to be received at annual intervals. Present-value tables may be used in determining the present value of the series of payments. The present value of 5 annual payments of $1 each, to provide a return of 12%, is found to be 3.6048.[31] Goodwill would be computed as the present value of five payments of $20,000 each, or $20,000 × 3.6048 = $72,096.

The principal advantage of the present-value method is the explicit recognition of the anticipated duration of excess income together with the use of a realistic rate of return. Thus, this method focuses on the factors most relevant to the goodwill evaluation.

30. Calculation of goodwill in terms of number of years of excess income will yield results identical to the capitalization method when the number of years used is equal to the reciprocal of the capitalization rate. Payment for the five years' income, for example, is equivalent to capitalizing earnings at a 20% rate (1 ÷ 0.20 = 5). Payment of four years' income is equivalent to capitalization at a 25% rate (1 ÷ 0.25 = 4).

31. See Table IV, Chapter 7.

KEY TERMS

QUESTIONS

1. In the balance sheet of many companies, the largest classification of assets in amount is noncurrent operating assets. Name the items, in addition to the amount paid to the former owner or contractor, that may be properly included as part of the acquisition cost of the following property items: (a) land, (b) buildings, and (c) equipment.
2. What acquisition costs are included in (a) copyrights, (b) franchises, and (c) trademarks?
3. How would a trademark worth $5,000,000 be reported on the balance sheet if (a) the trademark were purchased for $5,000,000 or (b) the trademark gradually became identified over the years as a company symbol?
4. How should development stage enterprises report their (a) organization costs and (b) net operating losses?
5. (a) Under what conditions may goodwill be reported as an asset? (b) The Roper Company engages in a widespread advertising campaign on behalf of new products, charging above-normal expenditures to goodwill. Do you approve of this practice? Why or why not?
6. How should negative goodwill be reported in the financial statements?
7. What procedure should be followed to allocate the cost of a lump-sum purchase of assets among specific accounts?
8. What special accounting problems are introduced when a company purchases equipment on a deferred payment contract rather than with cash?
9. (a) Why is the "list price" of an asset often not representative of its fair market value? (b) Under these conditions, how should a fair market value be determined?
10. Gaylen Corp. decides to construct a building for itself and plans to use whatever plant facilities it has to further such construction. (a) What costs will enter into the cost of construction? (b) What two positions can the company take with respect to general overhead allocation during the period of construction? Evaluate each position and indicate your preference.
11. What characteristics must a construction project have before interest can be capitalized as part of the project cost?
12. What are the general guidelines for determining the amount of interest that can be capitalized?
13. What are the principal arguments against capitalizing interest as presently mandated by the FASB?
14. The Parkhurst Corporation acquires land and buildings valued at $250,000 as a gift from Industrial City. The president of the company maintains that since there was no cost for the acquisition, neither cost of the facilities nor depreciation needs to be recognized for financial statement purposes. Evaluate the president's position assuming (a) the donation is unconditional, (b) the donation is contingent upon the employment by the company of a certain number of employees for a ten-year period.
15. Why do some companies expense asset expenditures that are under an established monetary amount?
16. Indicate the effects of the following errors on the balance sheet and the income statement in the current year and succeeding years:
    (a) The cost of a depreciable asset is incorrectly recorded as an expense.
    (b) An expense expenditure is incorrectly recorded as an addition to the cost of a depreciable asset.
17. (a) What type of activities are considered to be research and development activities? (b) Under what conditions, if any, are research and development costs deferred?
18. What conceptual modification to the FASB standard on research and development costs is apparent in the later standard on accounting for computer software development costs?
19. Which of the following items would be recorded as expenses and which would be recorded as assets?
    (a) Cost of installing machinery
    (b) Cost of unsuccessful litigation to protect patent
    (c) Extensive repairs as a result of a fire
    (d) Cost of grading land

(e) Insurance on machinery in transit
(f) Bond discount amortization during construction period
(g) Cost of major unexpected overhaul on machinery
(h) New safety guards on machinery
(i) Commission on purchase of real estate
(j) Special tax assessment for street improvements
(k) Cost of repainting offices

20. Why are some asset expenditures made subsequent to acquisition recorded as an increase in an asset account and others recorded as a decrease in Accumulated Depreciation?

*21. What factors should be considered in estimating the future income of a business in order to develop a fair valuation of goodwill?

*22. (a) Identify and discuss four methods for arriving at a goodwill valuation using estimated future income as a basis for these calculations. (b) Which method do you think would give the most relevant valuation of goodwill?

*Relates to Appendix

DISCUSSION CASES

Case 11—1 (Where should we charge it?)

Fugate Energy Corp. has recently purchased the assets of a small local company, Gleave Inc., for $556,950 cash. The chief accountant of Fugate has been given the assignment of preparing the journal entry to record the purchase. An investigation disclosed the following information about the assets of Gleave Inc.:

(a) Gleave owned land and a small manufacturing building. The book value of the property on Gleave's records was $115,000. An appraisal for fire insurance purposes had been made during the year. The building was appraised by the insurance company at $175,000. Property tax assessment notices showed that the building's worth was five times the worth of the land.
(b) Gleave's equipment had a book value of $75,000. It is estimated by Gleave that it would take six times the amount of book value to replace the old equipment with new. The old equipment is, on the average, 50% depreciated.
(c) Gleave had a franchise to produce and sell solar energy units from another company in a set geographic area. The franchise was transferred to Fugate as part of the purchase. Gleave carried the asset on its books at $40,000, the unamortized balance of the original cost of $90,000. The franchise is for an unlimited time. Similar franchises are now being sold by the company for $120,000 per geographic area.
(d) Gleave had two excellent research scientists who were responsible for much of the company's innovation in product development. They are each paid $50,000 per year by Gleave. They have agreed to work for Fugate Energy at the same salary.
(e) Gleave held two patents on its products. Both had been fully amortized and were not carried as assets on Gleave's books. Gleave feels they could have been sold separately for $75,000 each.

Evaluate each of the above items and prepare the journal entry that should be made to record the purchase on Fugate's books.

Case 11—2 (How much does it cost?)

The Bakeman Co. decides to construct a piece of specialized machinery using personnel from the maintenance department. This is the first time the maintenance personnel have been used for this purpose, and the cost accountant for the factory is concerned as to the accounting for costs of the machine. Some of the issues raised by the maintenance department management are highlighted.

(a) The supervisor of the maintenance department has instructed the workers to schedule work so all the overtime hours are charged to the machinery. Overtime is paid at 150% of the regular rate, or at a 50% premium.
(b) Material used in the production of the machine is charged out from the materials storeroom at 125% of cost, the same markup used when material is furnished to subsidiary companies.

(c) The maintenance department overhead rate is applied on maintenance hours. No extra overhead is anticipated as a result of constructing the machine.
(d) The maintenance department personnel are not qualified to test the machine on the production line. This will be done by production employees.
(e) Although the machine will take about one year to build, no extra borrowing of funds will be necessary to finance its construction. The company does, however, have outstanding bonds from earlier financing.
(f) It is expected that the self-construction of the machinery will save the company at least $20,000.

What advice can you give the cost accountant to help in the determination of a proper cost for the machine?

Case 11—3 **(But computer software is my inventory!)**

Strategy, Inc., was organized by Elizabeth Durrant and Ramona Morales, two students working their way through college. Both Elizabeth and Ramona had played with computers while in high school and had become very proficient users. Elizabeth had a special ability for designing computer software games that challenged the reasoning power of players. Ramona could see great potential in marketing Elizabeth's products to other computer buffs, and so the two began Strategy. Sales have exceeded expectations, and they have added ten employees to their company to design additional products, debug new programs, and produce and distribute the final software products.

Because of its growing size, increased capital is needed for the company. The partners decide to apply for a $100,000 loan to support the growing cost of research. As part of the documentation to obtain the loan, the bank asks for audited financial statements for the past year. After some negotiation, Mark Dawson, CPA, is hired. Strategy had produced a preliminary income statement that reported net income of $35,000. After reviewing the statements, Dawson indicates that the company actually had a $10,000 loss for the year. The major difference relates to $45,000 of wage and material costs that Strategy had capitalized as an intangible asset but that Dawson determined should be expensed.

"It's all research and development," Dawson insisted.

"But we'll easily recoup it in sales next year," countered Ramona. "I thought you accountants believed in the matching principle. Why do you permit us to capitalize the equipment we're using, but not our software development costs? We'll never look profitable under your requirements."

What major issues are involved in this case? Which position best reflects the FASB Statement relating to software development costs?

Case 11—4 **(Why can't I include the value of that gold on my balance sheet?)**

The Ling Company owns several mining claims in Nevada and California. The claims are carried on the books at the cost paid to acquire them ten years ago. At that time, it was estimated that the claims represented ore reserves valued at $250,000, and the price paid for the properties reflected this value. Subsequent mining and exploration activities have indicated values up to four times the original estimate. Additional capital is needed to pursue the claims, and Ling has decided to issue new shares of common stock. The company wants to report the true value of the claims in the financial statements in order to make the stock more attractive to potential investors. The accountant, Jennifer Harrison, realizes that the cost basis of accounting does not permit the recording of discovery values. On the other hand, she believes that to ignore the greatly increased value of the claims would be misleading to users. Isn't there some way the asset values can be increased to better reflect future cash flows arising from the claims?

You are hired as an accounting consultant to assist Ling in its fund raising. What recommendations can you make?

Case 11—5 **(Is it an asset or not?)**

The Hunter Company has developed a computerized machine to assist in the production of appliances. It is anticipated that the machine will do well in the marketplace; however, the company lacks the necessary capital to produce the machine. Rosalyn Finch, the secretary-treasurer of the Hunter Company, has offered to transfer land to the company to be used as collateral for a bank loan. Consideration for the transfer is an employment contract for five years and a percentage of any profits earned from sales of the new machine. The title to the land is to be transferred unconditionally. In the event Hunter defaults on the employment contract, a lump-sum cash settlement for lost wages will be paid to Finch.

What are the arguments for and against recording the land as an asset on Hunter's books? Is it a contingent asset? What effect does the provision for a cash settlement in the event of default have on your decision?

Case 11—6 (Why is my ROA lower than yours?)

Terri Morton has been recently hired as a financial analyst. Terri's first assignment is to analyze why the reported ROA (return on assets) for Arnold Company is so much different than that of Baker Company. Arnold Company develops and markets innovative consumer products. Baker Company is a fabricator of heavy steel products. Both companies have net incomes of $1 million, but Arnold has reported total assets of only $3 million, compared to $6 million for Baker. Terri suspects her new boss is using this assignment to test her understanding of financial statements. Terri's boss did give her one cryptic clue: unrecorded assets. Prepare Terri's analysis.

Case 11—7 (The asbestos must go, but where do we charge it?)

The FASB's Emerging Issues Task Force (EITF) considered the question of how the costs incurred in removing asbestos from buildings should be treated (Issue 89-13). This is a widespread issue since studies indicate that some 20% of buildings in the U.S. contain asbestos. The EITF considered the following specific questions:

1. If a company purchases a building with a known asbestos problem, should the removal costs be expensed or capitalized?
2. If a company discovers an asbestos problem in a building it already owns, should the removal costs be expensed or capitalized?

If you had been on the Task Force, how would you have ruled on these two questions?

Case 11—8 (Why are the costs of buildings different?)

In FASB Statement No. 34, the FASB called for the capitalization of interest costs associated with projects involving the construction or development of assets extending over a significant time period. Interest capitalized is restricted to the amount of interest actually incurred.

Consider the case of the following two companies that each constructed a building with a total construction cost of $20 million (the costs were incurred evenly over the course of a year) but that chose to finance the construction differently. (See details in the accompanying table.)

	Company A	Company B
Weighted average accumulated expenditures on building project during the year	$10,000,000	$10,000,000
Total construction cost of building (excluding interest)	20,000,000	20,000,000
Company financing (outstanding at year-end):		
Construction loan (14%)	20,000,000	-0-
Common stock issue	-0-	20,000,000
Total construction loan interest during the year (based on average outstanding loan balance)	1,400,000	-0-

As the auditor for both companies, you are asked by your supervisor to prepare a report that calculates the total cost for each building that would be included in each company's financial statements. Because both companies had the option of purchasing the buildings from a contractor rather than constructing them, your report should include your estimate of the price the contractor would have charged and how you explain the discrepancy in the way cost was determined for the two buildings. Conclude your report by proposing a change in the accounting standards that could eliminate this discrepancy.

Case 11—9 (Expensing R&D: Will it kill me?)

In 1974, as the FASB considered requiring the expensing of all in-house research and development expenditures, the Board received many comments predicting that if firms were required to expense R&D, they would significantly cut back on research expenditures to avoid hurting reported earnings. Subsequent to the adoption of FASB Statement No. 2, such an impact proved to be difficult to document. Elliott, et. al. summarized and extended conflicting prior research and concluded that R&D expenditures did decrease after the adoption of FASB Statement No. 2, but that the decrease may have been a function of the generally unfavorable economic conditions in the U.S. in the mid-1970s.

Would you expect that a rule requiring all firms to expense R&D outlays would cause R&D expenditures to decrease? Why or why not?

Source: John Elliott, Gordon Richardson, Thomas Dyckman, and Roland Dukes. "The Impact of SFAS No. 2 on Firm Expenditures on Research and Development: Replications and Extensions." *Journal of Accounting Research* 22 (Spring 1984), pp. 85-102.

EXERCISES

Exercise 11—10 (Cost of specific plant items)

The following expenditures were incurred by the Lyon Enterprises Co. in 1996:

Purchase of land	$ 390,000
Land survey	5,200
Fees for search of title for land	600
Building permit	3,500
Temporary quarters for construction crews	10,750
Payment to tenants of old building for vacating premises	4,600
Razing of old building	30,000
Excavation of basement	10,000
Special assessment tax for street project	2,000
Dividends	5,000
Damages awarded for injuries sustained in construction (no insurance was carried; the cost of insurance would have been $1,000)	8,400
Costs of construction	1,900,000
Cost of paving parking lot adjoining building	40,000
Cost of shrubs, trees, and other landscaping	29,000

What is the cost of the land, land improvements, and building?

Exercise 11—11 (Determining cost of patent)

Chen King Enterprises Inc. developed a new machine that reduces the time required to insert the fortunes into their fortune cookies. Because the process is considered very valuable to the fortune cookie industry, Chen King had the machine patented. The following expenses were incurred in developing and patenting the machine:

Research and development laboratory expenses	$25,000
Metal used in construction of the machine	8,000
Blueprints used to design the machine	3,200
Legal expenses to obtain patent	12,000
Wages paid for employees' work on the research, development, and building of the machine (60% of the time was spent in actually building the machine)	30,000
Expense of drawings required by the patent office to be submitted with the patent application	900
Fees paid to government patent office to process application	2,500

One year later, Chen King Enterprises Inc. paid $14,000 in legal fees to successfully defend the patent against an infringement suit by Dragon Cookie Co.

Give the entries on Chen King's books indicated by the above events. Ignore any amortization of the patent or depreciation of the machine.

Exercise 11—12 (Correcting organization costs account)

The Delta Products Co. was incorporated on January 1, 1996. In reviewing the accounts in 1997, you find the organization costs account in the general ledger appears as follows:

Account: ORGANIZATION COSTS

			Balance	
Item	**Debit**	**Credit**	**Debit**	**Credit**
Incorporation fees	3,750		3,750	
Legal fees relative to organization	21,150		24,900	
Stock certificate cost	6,000		30,900	
Cost of rehabilitating building acquired at end of 1996	165,600		196,500	
Advertising expenditures to promote company products in 1996	29,000		225,500	
Net loss for 1996	40,000		265,500	

Give the entry or entries required to correct the account.

Exercise 11—13 (Purchase of a company)

Hull Company purchased Heaston Company for $750,000 cash. A schedule of the market values of Heaston's assets and liabilities as of the purchase date is given below.

Heaston Company
Schedule of Asset and Liability Market Values

Assets		
Cash and temporary investments	$ 5,000	
Receivables	78,000	
Inventory	136,000	
Land, buildings, and equipment	436,000	$655,000
Liabilities		
Current liabilities	$ 80,000	
Long-term debt	120,000	200,000
Net asset market value		$455,000

1. Make the journal entry necessary for Hull Company to record the purchase.
2. Assume that the purchase price is $400,000 cash. Make the journal entry necessary to record the purchase.

Exercise 11—14 (Lump-sum acquisition)

The Allred Shipping Co. acquired land, buildings, and equipment at a lump-sum price of $920,000. An appraisal of the assets at the time of acquisition disclosed the following values:

Land	$150,000
Buildings	600,000
Equipment	250,000

What cost should be assigned to each asset?

Exercise 11—15 (Lump-sum acquisition)

The Boswell Corporation purchased land, a building, a patent, and a franchise for the lump sum of $975,000. A real estate appraiser estimated the building to have a resale value of $400,000 ($2/3$ of the total worth of land and building). The franchise had no established resale value. The patent was valued by management at $250,000. Give the journal entry to record the acquisition of the assets.

Exercise 11—16 (Equipment purchase on deferred payment contract)

Foley Industries purchases new specialized manufacturing equipment on July 1, 1996. The equipment cash price is $79,000, however, Foley signs a deferred purchase contract that provides for a down payment of $10,000 and an eight-year note for $103,472. The note is to be paid in eight equal annual payments of $12,934. The payments include 10% interest and are made on June 30 of each year beginning June 30, 1997. Prepare the journal entries for 1996, 1997, and 1998 related to the equipment purchase and the contract. Foley's fiscal year ends on June 30.

Exercise 11—17 (Purchase on deferred payment contract)

HiTech Industries purchases new electronic equipment for its telecommunication system. The contractual arrangement specifies ten payments of $8,600 each to be made over a ten year period. If HiTech had borrowed money to buy the equipment, they would have paid interest at 9%. HiTech's accountant recorded the purchase as follows:

Equipment	86,000	
Notes Payable		86,000

Prepare the correcting acquisition entry, taking into consideration the implicit interest in the purchase.

Exercise 11—18 (Lump-sum acquisition with stock)

On January 31, 1996, Cesarino Corp. exchanged 10,000 shares of its $25 par common stock for the following assets:

(a) A trademark valued at $120,000.
(b) A building, including land, valued at $650,000 (20% of the value is for the land).
(c) A franchise right. No estimate of value at time of exchange.

Cesarino Corp. stock is selling at $91 per share on the date of the exchange. Give the entries to record the exchange on Cesarino's books.

Exercise 11—19 (Purchase of building with bonds and stock)

The Fellingham Co. enters into a contract with the Dice Construction Co. for construction of an office building at a cost of $710,000. Upon completion of construction, the Dice Construction Co. agrees to accept in full payment of the contract price Fellingham Co. 10% bonds with a face value of $300,000 and common stock with a par value of $300,000 and no established fair market value. Fellingham Co. bonds are selling on the market at this time at 104. How would you recommend the building acquisition be recorded?

Exercise 11—20 (Acquisition of land and building for stock and cash)

Valdilla's Music Store acquired land and an old building in exchange for 50,000 shares of its common stock, par $10, and cash of $80,000. The auditor ascertains that the company's stock was selling on the market at $15 when the purchase was made. The following additional costs were incurred to complete the transaction:

Legal cost to complete transaction	$10,000
Property tax for previous year	30,000
Cost of building demolition	13,000
Salvage value of demolished building	(6,000)

What entry should be made to record the acquisition of the property?

Exercise 11—21 (Cost of self-constructed asset)

The Brodhead Manufacturing Company has constructed its own special equipment to produce a newly developed product. A bid to construct the equipment by an outside company was received for $1,200,000. The actual costs incurred by Brodhead to construct the equipment were as follows:

Direct material	$320,000
Direct labor	200,000

It is estimated that incremental overhead costs for construction amount to 140% of direct labor costs. In addition, fixed costs (exclusive of interest) of $700,000 were incurred during the construction period and allocated to production on the basis of total prime costs (direct labor plus direct material). The prime costs incurred to build the new equipment amounted to 30% of the total prime costs incurred for the period. The company follows the policy of capitalizing all possible costs on self-construction projects.

In order to assist in financing the construction of the equipment, a $500,000, 10% loan was acquired at the beginning of the six-month construction period. The company carries no other debt except for trade accounts payable. Assume expenditures were incurred evenly over the six-month period. Compute the cost to be assigned to the new equipment.

Exercise 11—22 (Capitalization of interest)

Lodi Department Stores, Inc., constructs its own stores. In the past, no cost has been added to the asset value for interest on funds borrowed for construction. Management has decided to change its policy and desires to include interest as part of the cost of a new store just being completed. (a) Based on the following information, how much interest would be added to the cost of the store in 1996? (b) In 1997?

Total construction expenditures:		
January 2, 1996	$600,000	
May 1, 1996	600,000	
November 1, 1996	500,000	
March 1, 1997	700,000	
September 15, 1997	400,000	
December 31, 1997	500,000	
		$3,300,000
Outstanding company debt:		
Mortgage related directly to new store; interest rate 12%; term, five years from beginning of construction		$1,000,000
General bond liability:		
Bonds issued just prior to construction of store; interest rate 10% for ten years		$ 500,000
Bonds issued June 30, 1996—8%, mature in five years		$1,000,000
Estimated cost of equity capital		14%

Exercise 11—23 (Interest capitalization decision)

For each of the situations described below, indicate when interest should be capitalized (C) and when it should not be capitalized (NC).

1. King Company is constructing a piece of equipment for its own use. Total construction costs are expected to be $5 million, and the construction period will be 3 months.
2. Ortegren Company is constructing a piece of equipment for sale. Total construction costs are expected to exceed $8 million and the construction period will be about 10 months. This is a special order—Ortegren has never produced a piece of equipment like this before.
3. Lowe Company is constructing a piece of equipment for sale. Total construction costs are expected to exceed $8 million and the construction period will be about 10 months. This particular piece of equipment is Lowe's best seller.

4. Nair Company is constructing a piece of equipment for its own use. Total construction costs are expected to be $6,000, and the construction period will be 10 months.
5. Rittenberg Company is constructing a piece of equipment for its own use. Total construction costs are expected to be $11 million and the construction period will be about 2 years. The forecasted total construction cost is only a very rough estimate because Rittenberg has no system in place to accumulate separately the costs associated with this project.
6. LeClair Company is in the process of renovating its corporate office building. The project will cost $13 million and will take about 15 months. The building will remain in use throughout the project.
7. Ricketts Company owns a piece of undeveloped land. The land originally cost $27 million. Ricketts plans to hold onto the land for 3 to 4 years and then develop it into a vacation resort.

Exercise 11—24 (Research and development costs)

In 1996 the Juarez Corporation incurred research and development costs as follows:

Materials and equipment	$130,000
Personnel	100,000
Indirect costs	50,000
	$280,000

These costs relate to a product that will be marketed in 1997. It is estimated that these costs will be recouped by December 31, 2000.

1. What is the amount of research and development costs that should be charged to income in 1996?
2. Assume that of the above costs, equipment of $110,000 can be used on other research projects. Estimated useful life of the equipment is five years with no salvage value, and it was acquired at the beginning of 1996. What is the amount of research and development costs that should be charged to income in 1996 under these conditions? Assume depreciation on all equipment is computed on a straight-line basis.

Exercise 11—25 (What are the R&D costs?)

Pringle Company has a substantial research department. Below are listed, in chronological order, some of the major activities associated with one of Pringle's research projects.

Project Started

(a) Purchased special equipment to be used solely for this project.
(b) Purchased general equipment that will be usable in Pringle's normal operations.
(c) Allocated overhead to the project.

Technological Feasibility Established

(d) Purchased more special equipment to be used solely for this project.
(e) Performed tests on an early model of the product.
(f) Allocated overhead to the project.

Product Becomes Ready for Production

(g) Incurred direct production costs.
(h) Allocated overhead to the products.

1. For each activity (a) through (h), indicate whether the cost should be capitalized (C), expensed (E), or included in cost of inventory (I).
2. Follow the instructions in (1) assuming that Pringle is a computer software development company.

Exercise 11—26 (Classifying expenditures as assets or expenses)

One of the most difficult problems facing an accountant is the determination of which expenditures should be deferred as assets and which should be immediately charged off as expenses. What position would you take in each of the following instances?

(a) Painting of partitions in a large room recently divided into four sections.
(b) Labor cost of tearing down a wall to permit extension of assembly line.

(c) Replacement of motor on a machine. Life used to depreciate the machine is 8 years. The machine is 4 years old. Replacement of the motor was anticipated when the machine was purchased.
(d) Cost of grading land prior to construction.
(e) Assessment for street paving.
(f) Cost of tearing down a previously occupied old building in preparation for new construction; old building is fully depreciated.

*Exercise 11—27 (Calculation of normal pretax income)

In analyzing the accounts of Dahlstrom in an attempt to value goodwill, you find pretax income of $675,000 for 1996 after debits and credits for the items listed below. Land, buildings, and equipment are appraised at 40% above cost for purposes of the sale. What is the normal pretax income for purposes of your calculations?

Depreciation of land, buildings, and equipment (at cost)	$ 75,000
Special year-end bonus to president of company	40,000
Gain on sale of securities	45,000
Gain on revaluation of securities	25,000
Write-off of goodwill	115,000
Amortization of patents and leaseholds	62,500
Income tax refund for 1995	20,000

*Relates to Appendix

*Exercise 11—28 (Calculation of goodwill—various methods)

The appraised value of net assets of the Hillery Co. on December 31, 1996, was $800,000. Average income for the past 5 years after elimination of unusual or extraordinary gains and losses was $135,000. Calculate the amount to be paid for goodwill under each of the following assumptions.

(a) Income is capitalized at 15% in arriving at the business's worth.
(b) A return of 9% is considered normal on net assets at their appraised value; excess income is to be capitalized at 15% in arriving at the value of goodwill.
(c) A return of 10% is considered normal on net assets at their appraised value; goodwill is to be valued at 5 years' excess income.
(d) A return of 10% is considered normal on net identifiable assets at their appraised value. Excess income is expected to continue for six years. Goodwill is to be valued by the present-value method using a rate of 12%. (Use the present-value table in Chapter 7.)

*Relates to Appendix

*Exercise 11—29 (Computation of goodwill—decision)

Because of superior earning power, Caruthers Inc. is considering paying $609,416 for K&M Properties with the following assets and liabilities:

	Cost	Fair Market Value
Accounts receivable	$240,000	$220,000
Inventory	140,000	150,000
Prepaid insurance	10,000	10,000
Buildings and equipment (net)	170,000	300,000
Accounts payable	(160,000)	(160,000)
Net assets	$400,000	$520,000

Estimated future income is expected to exceed normal income by $27,600 for four years. Caruthers Inc. uses the present-value method of valuing goodwill. Caruthers is willing to purchase K&M if the rate of return on excess income for K&M exceeds 10%. Should Caruthers purchase K&M Properties? (Use the present-value table in Chapter 7.)

*Relates to Appendix

***Exercise 11—30 (Computation of goodwill)**

The owners of the Summers Clothing Store are contemplating selling the business to new interests. The cumulative income for the past 5 years amounted to $600,000 including extraordinary gains of $40,000. The annual income based on an average rate of return on investment for this industry would have been $76,000. Excess income is to be capitalized at 25%. What is the amount of implied goodwill using the capitalization of excess income method?

*Relates to Appendix

PROBLEMS

Problem 11—31 (Correcting noncurrent operating asset valuation)

On December 31, 1996, the Lakeside Co. shows the following account for machinery it had assembled for its own use during 1996:

Account: MACHINERY (Job Order #1329)

Item	Debit	Credit	Balance Debit	Balance Credit
Cost of dismantling old machine	14,480		14,480	
Cash proceeds from sale of old machine		12,000	2,480	
Raw materials used in construction of new machine	76,000		78,480	
Labor in construction of new machine	49,000		127,480	
Cost of installation	11,200		138,680	
Materials spoiled in machine trial runs	2,400		141,080	
Profit on construction	24,000		165,080	
Purchase of machine tools	13,000		178,080	

An analysis of the detail in the account disclosed the following:

(a) The old machine, which was removed in the installation of the new one, had been fully depreciated.
(b) Cash discounts received on the payments for materials used in construction totaled $3,000 and these were reported in the purchase discounts account.
(c) The factory overhead account shows a balance of $292,000 for the year ended December 31, 1996; this balance exceeds normal overhead on regular plan activities by approximately $16,900 and is attributable to machine construction.
(d) A profit was recognized on construction for the difference between costs incurred and the price at which the machine could have been purchased.

Instructions:

1. Determine the machinery and machine tools balances as of December 31, 1996.
2. Give individual journal entries necessary to correct the accounts as of December 31, 1996, assuming that the nominal accounts are still open.

Problem 11—32 (Cost classification for a golf course)

The accountant for Stansbury Development Company is uncertain how to record the following costs associated with the construction of a golf course:

(a) Building man-made lakes.
(b) Moving earth around to enhance the "hilliness" of the course.
(c) Planting fairway grass.
(d) Planting trees and shrubs.
(e) Installing an automatic sprinkler system.
(f) Installing golf cart paths.
(g) 50 wooden sandtrap rakes (at $1 each).

(h) Paying attorneys' fees to prepare and file the land title.
(i) Demolishing an old house situated on the site planned for the clubhouse.

Instructions: Indicate which costs should be expensed (E), which should be capitalized and considered to be nondepreciable (CN), and which should be capitalized and depreciated (CD). Include explanations for each classification.

Problem 11—33 (Acquisition of land and buildings)

The Manheim Corporation has decided to expand its operations and has purchased land in Carterville for construction of a new manufacturing plant. The following costs were incurred in purchasing the property and constructing the building:

Land purchase price	$ 120,000
Payment of delinquent property taxes	35,000
Title search and insurance	6,500
City improvements for water and sewer	18,000
Building permit	8,000
Cost to destroy existing building on land ($9,000 worth of salvaged material used in new building)	20,000
Contract cost of new building	1,800,000
Land improvements—landscaping	82,000
Sidewalks and parking lot	32,000
Fire insurance on building—1 year	18,000

The depreciated value of the old building on the books of the company from which the land was purchased was $26,000. The old building was never used by Manheim.

Instructions:

1. Determine the cost of the land and land improvements. Show clearly the elements included in the totals.
2. Determine the cost of the new building. Show clearly the elements included in the total.

Problem 11—34 (Transactions involving property)

The following transactions were completed by the Space Age Toy Co. during 1996:

Mar. 1 Purchased real property for $628,250, which included a charge of $18,250 representing property tax for March 1-June 30 that had been prepaid by the vendor; 20% of the purchase price is deemed applicable to land, and the balance to buildings. A mortgage of $375,000 was assumed by the Space Age Toy Co. on the purchase. Cash was paid for the balance.

2-30 Previous owners had failed to take care of normal maintenance and repair requirements on the building, necessitating current reconditioning at a cost of $29,600.

May 15 Garages in the rear of the building were demolished, $4,500 being recovered on the lumber salvage. The company proceeded to construct a warehouse. The cost of such construction was $67,600, which was almost exactly the same as bids made on the construction by independent contractors. Upon completion of construction, city inspectors ordered extensive modifications in the buildings as a result of failure on the part of the company to comply with the building safety code. Such modifications, which could have been avoided, cost $9,600.

June 1 The company exchanged its own stock with a fair market value of $40,000 (par $30,000) for a patent and a new toy-making machine. The machine has a market value of $25,000.

July 1 The new machinery for the new building arrived. In addition to the machinery, a new franchise was acquired from the manufacturer of the machinery to produce toy robots. Payment was made by issuing bonds with a face value of $50,000 and by paying cash of $18,000. The value of the franchise is set at $20,000 while the fair market value of the machine is $45,000.

Nov. 20 The company contracted for parking lots and landscaping at a cost of $45,000 and $9,600 respectively. The work was completed and paid for on November 20.

Dec. 31 The business was closed to permit taking the year-end inventory. During this time, required redecorating and repairs were completed at a cost of $7,500.

Instructions: Give the journal entries to record each of the preceding transactions. (Disregard depreciation.)

Problem 11—35 (Acquisition of land and construction of plant)

The Crawford Corporation was organized in June 1996. In auditing the books of the company, you find the land, buildings, and equipment account below.

Account: LAND, BUILDINGS, AND EQUIPMENT

Date		Item	Debit	Credit	Balance Debit	Balance Credit
1996						
June	8	Organization fees paid to the state	20,000		20,000	
	16	Land site and old building	315,000		335,000	
	30	Corporate organization costs	30,000		365,000	
July	2	Title clearance fees	18,400		383,400	
Aug.	28	Cost of razing old building	20,000		403,400	
Sept.	1	Salaries of Crawford Corporation executives	60,000		463,400	
	1	Cost to acquire patent for special equipment	60,000		523,400	
Dec.	12	Stock bonus to corporate promoters, 2,000 shares of common stock, $50 market value	100,000		623,400	
	15	County real estate tax	14,400		637,800	
	15	Cost of new building completed and occupied on this date	1,750,000		2,387,800	

An analysis of this account and of other accounts disclosed the following additional information:

(a) The building acquired on June 16, 1996, was valued at $35,000.
(b) The corporation paid $20,000 for the demolition of the old building, then sold the scrap for $12,000 and credited the proceeds to Miscellaneous Revenue.
(c) The corporation executives did not participate in the construction of the new building.
(d) The county real estate tax was for the six-month period ended December 31, 1996, and was assessed by the county on the land.

Instructions: Prepare journal entries to correct the books of the Crawford Corporation. Each entry should include an explanation.

Problem 11—36 (Acquisition of intangible assets)

In your audit of the books of Dyer Corporation for the year ending September 30, 1996, you found the following items in connection with the company's patents account:

(a) The company had spent $120,000 during its fiscal year ended September 30, 1995, for research and development costs and debited this amount to its patents account. Your review of the company's cost records indicated the company had spent a total of $141,500 for the research and development of its patents, of which $21,500 spent in its fiscal year ended September 30, 1995, had been debited to Research and Development Expense.

(b) The patents were issued on April 1, 1995. Legal expenses in connection with the issuance of the patents of $14,280 were debited to Legal and Professional Fees.
(c) The company paid a retainer of $15,000 on October 5, 1995, for legal services in connection with a patent infringement suit brought against it. This amount was debited to Deferred Costs.
(d) A letter dated October 15, 1996, from the company's attorneys in reply to your inquiry as to liabilities of the company existing at September 30, 1996, indicated that a settlement of the patent infringement suit had been arranged. The other party had agreed to drop the suit and to release the company from all future liabilities in exchange for $20,000. Additional fees due to the attorneys amounted to $1,260.

Instructions: From the information given, prepare correcting journal entries as of September 30, 1996.

Problem 11—37 (Acquisition of intangible assets)

Transactions during 1996 of the newly organized Menlove Corporation included the following:

Jan. 2 Paid legal fees of $15,000 and stock certificate costs of $8,300 to complete organization of the corporation.

15 Hired a clown to stand in front of the corporate office for two weeks and hand out pamphlets and candy to create goodwill for the new enterprise. Clown cost $1,000; pamphlets and candy, $500.

Apr. 1 Patented a newly developed process with the following costs:

Legal fees to obtain patent	$42,900
Patent application and licensing fees	6,350
Total	$49,250

It is estimated that in six years other companies will have developed improved processes making the Menlove Corporation process obsolete.

May 1 Acquired both a license to use a special type of container and a distinctive trademark to be printed on the container in exchange for 600 shares of Menlove Corporation no-par common stock selling for $50 per share. The license is worth twice as much as the trademark, both of which may be used for 6 years.

July 1 Constructed a shed for $131,000 to house prototypes of experimental models to be developed in future research projects.

Dec. 31 Salaries for an engineer and a chemist involved in product development totaled $175,000 in 1996.

Instructions:

1. Give journal entries to record the foregoing transactions. Give explanations in support of your entries. (Ignore amortization of intangible assets.)
2. Present in good form the "Intangible assets" section of the Menlove Corporation balance sheet at December 31, 1996.

Problem 11—38 (Lump-sum acquisition of noncurrent operating assets)

The Wenatcher Wholesale Company incurred the following expenses in 1996 for a warehouse acquired on July 1, 1996, the beginning of its fiscal year:

Cost of land	$ 90,000
Cost of building	510,000
Remodeling and repairs prior to occupancy	67,500
Escrow fee	10,000
Landscaping	25,000
Property tax for period prior to acquisition	15,000
Real estate commission	30,000

The company signed a non-interest-bearing note for $500,000 on July 1, 1996. The implicit interest rate is 10%. Payments of $25,000 are to be made semiannually beginning December 31, 1996, for 10 years.

Instructions: Give the required journal entries to record (1) the acquisition of the land and building (assume that cash is paid to equalize the cost of the assets and the present value of the note), and (2) the first two semiannual payments, including amortization of note discount.

Problem 11—39 (Income statement for computer software company)

The Betterword Company is engaged in developing computer software for the small business and home computer market. Most of the computer programmers are involved in developmental work designed to produce software that will perform fairly specific tasks in a user-friendly manner. Extensive testing of the working model is performed before it is released to production for preparation of masters and further testing. As a result of careful preparation, Betterword has produced several products that have been very successful in the marketplace. The following costs were incurred during 1996:

Salaries and wages of programmers doing research	$235,000
Expenses related to projects prior to establishment of technological feasibility	78,400
Expenses related to projects after technological feasibility has been established but before software is available for production	49,500
Amortization of capitalized software development costs from current and prior years	26,750
Costs to produce and prepare software for sale	56,300

Additional data for 1996 includes:

Sales of products for the year	$515,000
Beginning inventory	142,000
Portion of goods available for sale sold during year	60%

Instructions: Prepare an income statement for Betterword for the year 1996. Income tax rate is 35%.

Problem 11—40 (Valuation of property)

At December 31, 1995, certain accounts included in the noncurrent operating assets section of the Salvino Company's balance sheet had the following balances:

Land	$150,000
Buildings	910,000
Leasehold improvements	500,000
Machinery and equipment	600,000

During 1996 the following transactions occurred:

(a) Land site #653 was acquired for $1,600,000. Additionally, to acquire the land, Salvino paid a $90,000 commission fee to a real estate agent. Costs of $25,000 were incurred to clear the land. During the course of clearing the land, timber and gravel were recovered and sold for $20,000.

(b) A second tract of land (site #654) with a building was acquired for $700,000. The closing statement indicated that the land value was $510,000 and the building value was $215,000. Shortly after acquisition, the building was demolished at a cost of $30,000. A new building was constructed for $600,000 plus the following costs:

Excavation fees	$35,000
Architectural design fees	19,000
Building permit fee	15,000
Imputed interest on funds used during construction	60,000

The building was completed and occupied on September 30, 1996.

(c) A third tract of land (site #655) was acquired for $600,000 and was put on the market for resale.

(d) Extensive work was done to a building occupied by Salvino under a lease agreement that expires on December 31, 2005. The total cost of work was $150,000, which consisted of the following:

Painting of ceilings	$ 10,000	(estimated useful life is one year)
Electrical work......................................	60,000	(estimated useful life is ten years)
Construction of extension to current working area.	80,000	(estimated useful life is thirty years)
	$150,000	

The lessor paid half of the costs incurred in connection with the extension to the current working area.

(e) During December 1996, costs of $70,000 were incurred to improve leased office space. The related lease will terminate on December 31, 1998, and is not expected to be renewed.

(f) A group of new machines was purchased under a royalty agreement that provides for payment of royalties based on units of production for the machines. The invoice price of the machines was $90,000, freight costs were $2,000, unloading charges were $2,500, and royalty payments for 1996 were $13,000.

Instructions:

1. Prepare a detailed analysis of the changes in each of the following balance sheet accounts for 1996:

   Land
   Buildings
   Leasehold improvements
   Machinery and equipment
   (Disregard the related accumulated depreciation accounts.)

2. List the items in the foregoing information that were not used to determine the answer to (1), and indicate where, if at all, these items should be included in Salvino's financial statements.

(AICPA adapted)

Problem 11—41 (Acquisition of noncurrent operating assets)

At December 31, 1996, Arnold Company's noncurrent operating asset accounts had the following balances:

Category	Cost
Land	$ 175,000
Buildings	1,500,000
Machinery and equipment..........................	1,125,000
Automobiles	172,000
Leasehold improvements...........................	216,000
Land improvements..................................	—

Transactions for 1997 included the following:

Jan. 6 A plant facility consisting of land and a building was acquired from Jesco Corp. in exchange for 25,000 shares of Arnold's common stock. On this date, Arnold's stock had a market price of $50 a share. Current assessed values of land and building for property tax purposes are $187,500 and $562,500, respectively.

Mar. 25 New parking lots, streets, and sidewalks at the acquired plant facility were completed at a total cost of $192,000.

July 1 Machinery and equipment were purchased at a total invoice cost of $325,000, which included $14,000 of sales tax. Additional costs of $10,000 for delivery and $50,000 for installation were incurred.

Aug.	30	Arnold purchased a new automobile for $12,500.
Nov.	4	Arnold purchased for $350,000 a tract of land as a potential future building site.
Dec.	20	A machine with a cost of $17,000 and a remaining book value of $2,975 at date of disposition was scrapped without cash recovery.

Instructions: Prepare a schedule analyzing the changes in each of the noncurrent operating asset accounts during 1997. This schedule should include columns for beginning balance, increase, decrease, and ending balance for each of the noncurrent operating asset accounts.

(AICPA adapted)

Problem 11—42 (Capitalization of interest)

Oceanwide Enterprises, Inc., is involved in building and operating cruise ships. Each ship is identified as a separate discrete job in the accounting records, and costs are incurred evenly during the construction period. At the end of 1996, Oceanwide correctly reported $5,400,000 as Construction in Progress on the following jobs:

Ship	Completion Date (end of month)	Accumulated Costs (including 1996 interest) December 31, 1996
#340	October 31, 1996*	$2,300,000
#341	June 30, 1997	1,150,000
#342	September 30, 1997	1,200,000
#343	January 31, 1998	750,000

*Ship #340 was completed and ready for use in October 1996 and will be placed in service May 1, 1997.

Labor, material, and overhead costs for 1997 were as follows:

Ship	Costs
#341	$1,200,000
#342	1,600,000
#343	2,200,000
#344	810,000 (construction began May 1)
#345	360,000 (construction began Nov. 1)

Oceanwide had the following general liabilities at December 31, 1997:

12%, 5-year note (maturity date—1999)	$1,000,000
10%, 10-year bonds (maturity date—2002)...........................	4,000,000

On January 1, 1997, Oceanwide borrowed $1,000,000 specifically for the construction projects. The loan was for 3 years with interest at 13%.

Instructions:

1. Compute the maximum interest that can be capitalized in 1997.
2. Compute the weighted average interest rate for the general liabilities for 1997.
3. Compute the weighted average accumulated expenditures for 1997.
4. Compute the interest that Oceanwide should capitalize during 1997.

Problem 11—43 (Interest capitalization—varied loan dates)

Assume the following information for Company A and Company B:

A) Average accumulated expenditures for self-constructed asset, 1996—$1,050,000
   Interest bearing instruments:
   Construction loan:
   $500,000 10% loan issued on April 1, 1996

General debt:
$500,000 8% bonds issued on June 30, 1995
$1,200,000 12% note issued October 1, 1996

B) Average accumulated expenditures for self-constructed asset, 1996—$3,400,000
Interest bearing instruments:
Construction loan:
$2,400,000 11% loan issued on March 1, 1996

General debt:
$1,500,000 10% bonds issued on July 1, 1996
$500,000 9% note issued January 1, 1996

Instructions: Compute the amount of interest that should be capitalized in 1996 for (1) Company A and (2) Company B.

Problem 11—44 (Self-construction of equipment)

American Corporation received a $400,000 low bid from a reputable manufacturer for the construction of special production equipment needed by American in an expansion program. Because its own plant was not operating at capacity, American decided to construct the equipment itself and recorded the following production costs related to the construction:

Services of consulting engineer	$ 10,000
Work subcontracted	20,000
Materials	200,000
Plant labor normally assigned to production	65,000
Plant labor normally assigned to maintenance	100,000
Total	$395,000

Management prefers to record the cost of the equipment under the incremental cost method. Approximately 40% of the corporation's production is devoted to government supply contracts, which are all based in some way on cost. The contracts require that any self-constructed equipment be allocated its full share of all costs related to the construction.

The following information also is available:

(a) The above production labor was for partial fabrication of the equipment in the plant. Skilled personnel were required and were assigned from other projects. The maintenance labor amount ($100,000) represents the cost of nonproduction plant employees assigned to the construction project. Had these workers not been assigned to construction, the $100,000 cost would still have been incurred for their idle time.

(b) Payroll taxes and employee fringe benefits are approximately 30% of labor cost and are included in manufacturing overhead cost. Total manufacturing overhead for the year was $5,630,000 including the $100,000 maintenance labor used to construct the equipment.

(c) Manufacturing overhead is approximately 50% variable and is applied on the basis of production labor cost. Production labor cost for the year for the corporation's normal products totaled $6,810,000.

(d) General and administrative expenses include $22,500 of executive salary cost and $10,500 of postage, telephone, supplies, and miscellaneous expenses identifiable with this equipment construction.

Instructions:

1. Prepare a schedule computing the amount that should be reported as the full cost of the constructed equipment to meet the requirements of the government contracts. Any supporting computations should be in good form.
2. Prepare a schedule computing the incremental cost of the constructed equipment.
3. What is the greatest amount that should be capitalized as the cost of the equipment? Why?

Problem 11—45 (Summary entries for interest payments)

Clarksville Company reported interest expense in 1996 and 1995 of $350,000 and $300,000, respectively. The balance in Accrued Interest Payable at the end of 1996, 1995, and 1994 was $30,000, $47,000, and $23,000, respectively. In addition, a note to Clarksville's 1996 financial statements included the following:

Interest costs related to construction in progress are capitalized as incurred. The company capitalized $500,000 and $200,000 of interest costs during the years 1996 and 1995, respectively.

Instructions:

1. What summary journal entries would be needed to record all information related to interest in 1996 and 1995?
2. How would interest paid be disclosed in Clarksville's statement of cash flows for 1996 and 1995? Clarksville uses the indirect method in reporting cash flow from operating activities.

Problem 11—46 (Classifying expenditures as assets or expenses)

As of December 31, 1996, W. W. Cole Company's total assets were $325 million and total liabilities were $180 million. Net income for 1996 was $38 million. During 1996, W. W. Cole's chief executive officer had put extreme pressure on employees to meet the profitability goal the CEO had set for them. The goal was to achieve a return on stockholders' equity in 1996 of 25 percent (Net income ÷ Stockholders' equity). The rumor among Cole's employees is that, in order to meet this goal, the accounting for some items may have been overly "aggressive." The following items are of concern:

(a) Research and development costs totaling $18 million were capitalized. None of these costs related to items with alternative uses. The capitalized R&D was assigned a useful life of 6 years; $3 million was written off during 1996.
(b) During the year, a building was acquired in exchange for 5 million shares of Cole common stock. The building was assigned a value of $27 million by the board of directors. At the time of the exchange, Cole common stock was trading on the New York Stock Exchange for $3 per share.
(c) On December 31, equipment was purchased for $1 million in cash and an agreement to pay $3 million per year for the next 8 years—the first payment to be made in one year. The cost of the equipment was recorded at $25 million. The interest rate implicit in the contract was 12%. (Use Present-Value Table IV in Chapter 7.)
(d) Interest of $7 million was capitalized during the year. The only items produced during the year by Cole were routine inventory items.

Instructions:

1. Ignoring any concerns raised by items (a) through (d), did W. W. Cole Company meet its profitability goal for the year?
2. After making any adjustments suggested by items (a) through (d), did W. W. Cole meet its profitability goal? (Ignore income taxes.)
3. What should prevent accounting abuses like those described above?

Problem 11—47 (Classifying expenditures as assets or expenses)

The Rolitz Company completed a program of expansion and improvement of its plant during 1996. You are provided with the following information concerning its buildings account:

(a) On October 31, 1996, a 30-foot extension to the present factory building was completed at a contract cost of $329,000.
(b) During the course of construction, the following costs were incurred for the removal of the end wall of the building where the extension was to be constructed:
    (1) Payroll costs during the month of April arising from employees' time spent in removing the wall, $12,360.
    (2) Payments to a salvage company for removing unusual debris, $1,520.

(c) The cost of the original structure allocable to the end wall was estimated to be $26,400 with accumulated depreciation thereon of $11,100. Rolitz Company received $5,930 from the construction company for windows and other assorted materials salvaged from the old wall.
(d) The old floor covering was replaced with a new type of long-lasting floor covering at a cost of $5,290. Cost of old floor covering was not available.
(e) The interior of the plant was repainted in new bright colors for a contract price of $8,290.
(f) New and improved shelving was installed at a cost of $3,620. Cost of old shelving was not determinable.
(g) Old electrical wiring was replaced at a cost of $10,218. Cost of the old wiring was determined to be $4,650 with accumulated depreciation to date of $2,055.
(h) New electrical fixtures using fluorescent bulbs were installed. The new fixtures were purchased on the installment plan; the schedule of monthly payments showed total payments of $9,300, which included interest and carrying charges of $720. The old fixtures were carried at a cost of $2,790 with accumulated depreciation to date of $1,200. The old fixtures have no scrap value.

Instructions: Prepare journal entries including explanations for the above information. Briefly justify the asset-vs.-expense decision for each item.

*Problem 11—48 (Computation of goodwill)

The Aurora Corp. in considering acquisition of the Payette Company assembles the information following.

Payette Company
Balance Sheet
December 31, 1997

Assets	Per Company's Books	As Adjusted by Appraisal and Audit
Current assets	$ 96,000	$ 87,000
Investments	32,000	28,000
Land, buildings, and equipment (net)	279,200	260,000
Goodwill	79,000	79,000
	$486,200	$454,000
Liabilities and Stockholders' Equity		
Current liabilities	$ 15,000	$ 25,000
Long-term liabilities	160,000	160,000
Capital stock	160,000	160,000
Retained earnings	151,200	109,000
	$486,200	$454,000

An analysis of retained earnings discloses the following information:

	Per Company's Books	As Adjusted by Appraisal and Audit
Retained earnings, January 1, 1995	$130,560	$ 73,600
Add net income, 1995-1997	49,440	64,200
Deduct dividends, 1995-1997	(28,800)	(28,800)
Retained earnings, December 31, 1997	$151,200	$109,000
Loss on sale of plant assets in 1997, included in net income	$ 48,960	$ 52,800

Instructions:

1. Calculate the amount to be paid for goodwill, assuming that income of the future is expected to be the same as average normal income of the past three years, 10% is accepted as a reasonable return on net assets other than goodwill as of December 31, 1997, and average income in excess of 10% is capitalized at 16% in determining goodwill. Use capitalization of average excess income method.
2. Give the entry on the books of the Aurora Corp., assuming purchase of the assets of the Payette Company and assumption of its liabilities on the basis as indicated in (1). Cash is paid for net assets acquired.

*Relates to Appendix

*Problem 11—49 (Computation of goodwill)

Southern Industries Inc. assembles the following data relative to the Mendoza Corp. in determining the amount to be paid for the net assets and goodwill of the latter company:

Assets at appraised value (before goodwill)	$1,900,000
Liabilities	825,000
Stockholders' equity	$1,075,000

Income (after elimination of extraordinary items):

1993	$180,000
1994	149,000
1995	194,000
1996	155,000
1997	222,000

Instructions: Calculate the amount to be paid for goodwill under each of the following assumptions:

1. Average income is capitalized at 16% in arriving at the business's worth.
2. A return of 12% is considered normal on net assets at appraised values. Goodwill is valued at 5 years' excess income.
3. A return of 14% is considered normal on net assets at appraised values; excess income is to be capitalized at 20%.
4. Goodwill is valued at the sum of the income of the last 3 years in excess of a 10% annual yield on net assets at appraised values. (Assume that net assets are the same for the 3-year period.)
5. A return of 10% is considered normal on net identifiable assets at their appraised values. Excess income is expected to continue for 10 years. Goodwill is to be valued by the present-value method using a 20% rate. (Use the present-value table in Chapter 7.)

*Relates to Appendix

CHAPTER 12

Noncurrent Operating Assets: Utilization and Retirement

CHAPTER TOPICS

- Depreciation of Tangible Noncurrent Operating Assets
- Amortization of Intangible Noncurrent Operating Assets
- Depletion of Natural Resources
- Changes in Estimates of Cost Allocation Variables
- Asset Retirements
- Balance Sheet Presentation and Disclosure

Garbage — that's how H. Wayne Huizenga made his first splash on the national scene. He built a conglomeration of local garbage companies into Waste Management Inc., the largest trash hauler in the country. After his retirement from the trash business in 1984, Huizenga's eye fell on a small, 20-store video chain in Dallas called Blockbuster Video.[1] By the end of 1987, Huizenga had acquired control of Blockbuster and had increased the number of stores to 130. Through a combination of aggressive expansion and the acquisition of existing video chains, Blockbuster soon became the nation's largest video chain. By the end of 1992, there were 3,127 Blockbuster Video stores, primarily located in the U.S. and Canada.

Of these 3,127 stores, 1,125 are owned and operated by franchisees. In its 1992 Form 10-K, Blockbuster outlined its agreement with these franchise operators. In exchange for an upfront fee, the franchisees are given the exclusive right to develop a specified number of stores in a defined geographic area. The typical agreement is for 20 years and entitles Blockbuster to receive from three to eight percent of the franchisee's gross revenue. In addition, franchisees must pay Blockbuster a monthly software maintenance fee and must contribute funds for national advertising campaigns.

1. Eric Calonius. "Meet the King of Video." *Fortune*, June 4, 1990, p. 208.

On May 8, 1989, a Bear, Stearns investment report was released that was critical of some of Blockbuster's accounting practices, particularly its depreciation policies. The report suggested that the 40-year life Blockbuster used for goodwill was much too long; to quote from the report: "Have you ever seen a 40-year old video tape store?" Five years was suggested as a more reasonable amortization period. The report also criticized Blockbuster for increasing the depreciation period for video tapes from 9 months to 36 months.[2] Revising both these items to use the shorter amortization periods would have cut Blockbuster's 1988 net income almost in half — from $.57 per share to $.32 per share. Release of the Bear, Stearns report caused Blockbuster's stock price to drop from $33.50 to $26.25 in two days, a 22 percent drop. This represented a total decline in market value of approximately $200 million. Blockbuster's management was understandably upset with the report. The report wasn't "worth the powder to blow it to hell," according to one Blockbuster official.[3] Blockbuster's management pointed out that estimates of asset useful lives are necessarily a matter of judgment and the estimates Blockbuster used were reasonable. This view was at least partially vindicated when, within six weeks, Blockbuster's stock regained the 22 percent loss.

A fundamental characteristic of noncurrent operating assets is that they are used to produce revenues over more than one accounting period. Another characteristic common to these assets is that they have limited economic or useful lives. A notable exception to this generalization is land—even farm land can be kept productive indefinitely with proper fertilization and care. All other noncurrent operating assets, however, have limited lives. The economic benefits provided by intangible assets are, in some cases, limited to a period of time specified by law or contract. Other intangible assets tend to decline in usefulness with the passage of time.

In order to match costs with related revenues, the cost of an operating asset (other than land) must be allocated in some manner over the estimated useful life of the asset. In practice, three different terms have evolved to describe this cost allocation process depending on the type of asset involved. The allocation of tangible property costs is referred to as depreciation. For mineral and other natural resources, the cost allocation process is appropriately called **depletion.** For intangible assets, such as patents, copyrights, and goodwill, the process is referred to as **amortization.** Sometimes the latter term is used generically to encompass all the other terms. Because the principles underlying each of these terms are similar, they are discussed together in this chapter.

DEPRECIATION OF NONCURRENT OPERATING ASSETS

Depreciation is the systematic and rational allocation of tangible asset cost over the periods benefited by the use of the asset. There has been a tendency, however, on the part of many readers of financial statements to interpret depreciation accounting as somehow related to the accumulation of a fund for asset replacement. Terminology used in the past, such as "provision for depreciation" and "reserve for depreciation" has contributed toward this misinterpretation. These terms have been replaced by more descriptive terms, e.g., "depreciation expense" and "accumulated depreciation."

The charge for depreciation is the recognition of the declining service potential of an asset. The nature of this charge is no different from those made to recognize the expiration of insurance premiums or patent rights. It is true that revenues equal to or in excess of expenses for a period result in a recovery of these expenses; salary expense is thus recovered by revenues, as is insurance expense, patent amortization, and charges for depreciation. But this does not mean that cash equal to the recorded depreciation will be segregated

2. Dana Wechsler. "Earnings Helper." *Forbes* (June 12, 1989), p. 150.
3. Eric Savitz. "An End to Fast Forward?" *Barron's* (December 11, 1989), p. 13.

for property replacement. Revenues may be applied to many uses: to the increase in receivables, inventories, or other working capital items; to the acquisition of new property or other noncurrent items; to the retirement of debt or the redemption of stock; or to the payment of dividends. If a special fund is to be established for the replacement of property, specific authorization by management would be required. Such a fund is seldom found, however, because fund earnings would usually be less than the return from alternative uses of the resources.

Depreciation is also not a technique of asset valuation. The notion of depreciation frequently is motivated by speaking of it as "the decrease in asset value during the year as a consequence of business use of the asset." Thinking of depreciation in this way is not correct. The book value of an asset (historical cost less accumulated depreciation) is the asset cost remaining to be allocated to future periods, and not an estimate of the asset's current value.

Factors Affecting the Periodic Depreciation Charge

Four factors must be recognized in determining the periodic charge for depreciation: (1) **asset cost**, (2) **residual or salvage value**, (3) **useful life**, and (4) **pattern of use**.

Asset Cost. The cost of an asset includes all the expenditures relating to its acquisition and preparation for use as described in Chapter 11. The cost of property less the expected residual value, if any, is the depreciable cost or depreciation base, i.e., the portion of asset cost to be charged against future revenues.

Residual or Salvage Value. The **residual (salvage) value** of property is an estimate of the amount that can be realized upon retirement of the asset. This depends on the retirement policy of the company as well as market conditions and other factors. If, for example, the company normally uses equipment until it is physically exhausted and no longer serviceable, the residual value, represented by the scrap or junk that can be salvaged, may be nominal. But if the company normally replaces its equipment after a relatively short period of use, the residual value, represented by the selling price or trade-in value, may be relatively high. From a theoretical point of view, any estimated residual value should be subtracted from cost in arriving at the portion of asset cost to be charged to depreciation.

In practice, however, residual values are frequently ignored in determining periodic depreciation charges. This practice is not objectionable when residual values are relatively small or are not subject to reasonable estimation, and when it is doubtful more useful information will be provided through such refinement.

Useful Life. Noncurrent operating assets other than land have a limited **useful life** as a result of certain physical and functional factors. The **physical factors** that limit the service life of an asset are (1) wear and tear, (2) deterioration and decay, and (3) damage or destruction. Everyone is familiar with the processes of wear and tear that render an automobile, a typewriter, or furniture no longer usable. A tangible asset, whether used or not, also is subject to deterioration and decay through aging. Finally, fire, flood, earthquake, or accident may reduce or terminate the useful life of an asset.

The **functional factors** limiting the lives of these assets are (1) inadequacy and (2) obsolescence. An asset may lose its usefulness when, as a result of altered business requirements or technical progress, it no longer can produce sufficient revenue to justify its continued use. Although the asset is still usable, its inability to produce sufficient revenue has cut short its service life. An example of rapid obsolescence can be observed in the computer industry. The rapid technological changes in this field have rendered perfectly good electronic equipment obsolete for efficient continued use long before the physical asset itself has worn out.

Both physical and functional factors must be considered in estimating the useful life of a depreciable asset. This recognition requires estimating what events will take place in the future and requires careful judgment on the part of the accountant.[4] Physical factors are more readily apparent than functional factors in predicting asset life. But when functional factors are expected to hasten the retirement of an asset, these also must be recognized.

In practice, many companies as a matter of policy dispose of certain classes of assets after a predetermined period, without regard to the serviceability of individual assets within a class. Company automobiles, for example, may be replaced routinely every two or three years.

The useful life of a depreciable plant asset may be expressed in terms of either an estimated time factor or an estimated use factor. The **time factor** may be a period of months or years; the **use factor** may be a number of hours of service or a number of units of output. The cost of the asset is allocated in accordance with the lapse of time or extent of use. The rate of cost allocation may be modified by other factors, but basically depreciation must be recognized on a time or use basis.

Pattern of Use. In order to match asset cost against revenues, periodic depreciation charges should reflect as closely as possible the pattern of use. If the asset produces a varying revenue pattern, then the depreciation charges should vary in a corresponding manner. When depreciation is measured in terms of a time factor, the pattern of use must be estimated. Because of the difficulty in identifying a pattern of use, several somewhat arbitrary methods have come into common practice. Each method represents a different pattern and is designed to make the time basis approximate the use basis. The time factor is employed in two general classes of methods: **straight-line depreciation** and **decreasing-charge depreciation.** When depreciation is measured in terms of a use factor, the units of use must be estimated. The depreciation charge varies periodically in accordance with the services provided by the asset. The use factor is employed in **service-hours depreciation** and in **productive-output depreciation.**

Recording Periodic Depreciation

The periodic allocation of property costs is made by debiting either a production overhead cost account or a selling or administrative expense account, and crediting an allowance or contra asset account. If the charge is made to a production overhead account, it becomes part of the cost of the finished and unfinished goods inventories and is deferred to the extent inventory has not been sold or completed. If the charge is made to selling or administrative expenses, it is considered a period cost and is written off against revenue as an operating expense of the current period.

The valuation or allowance account that is credited in recording periodic depreciation is commonly titled Accumulated Depreciation. The accumulation of expired cost in a separate account rather than crediting the asset account directly permits identification of the original cost of the asset and the accumulated depreciation. The FASB requires disclosure of both cost and accumulated depreciation for property on the balance sheet or notes to the financial statements. This enables the user to estimate the relative age of all assets and provides some basis for predicting future cash outflows for the replacement of assets.

4. Although the concept of useful life is generally recognized to be difficult to apply, there has been relatively little written on it in accounting literature. For a thorough discussion of the topic, see Charles Lamden, Dale L. Gerboth, and Thomas McRae, "Accounting for Depreciable Assets," *Accounting Research Monograph No. 1* (New York: American Institute of Certified Public Accountants, 1975), Ch. 5.

Methods of Depreciation

There are a number of different methods for allocating the costs of depreciable assets. The depreciation method used in any specific instance is a matter of judgment and, conceptually, should be selected to most closely approximate the actual pattern of use expected from the asset. In practice, most firms select one depreciation method, such as straight-line, and use it for substantially all their assets. The following methods are described in this chapter:

Time-Factor Methods

1. Straight-line depreciation
2. Decreasing-charge (accelerated) methods
   (a) Sum-of-the-years-digits depreciation
   (b) Declining-balance depreciation
3. Accelerated cost recovery system (ACRS) and modified accelerated cost recovery system (MACRS)

Use-Factor Methods

1. Service-hours depreciation
2. Productive-output depreciation

Group-Rate and Composite-Rate Methods

1. Group depreciation
2. Composite depreciation

The examples that follow assume the acquisition of a polyurethane plastic molding machine at the beginning of 1996 by Schuss Boom Ski Manufacturing, Inc., at a cost of $100,000 with an estimated residual value of $5,000. The following symbols are used in the formulas for the development of depreciation rates and charges:

C = Asset cost
R = Estimated residual value
n = Estimated life in years, hours of service, or units of output
r = Depreciation rate per period, per hour of service, or per unit of output
D = Periodic depreciation charge

Time-Factor Methods. The most common methods of cost allocation are related to the passage of time. In general, a productive asset is used up over time. Possible obsolescence due to technological changes is also a function of time. Of the **time-factor depreciation methods,** straight-line depreciation has been by far the most popular. *Accounting Trends & Techniques* reported that 564 of the 600 companies surveyed used the straight-line method in their 1992 financial statements.[5]

The use of **decreasing-charge depreciation methods,** sometimes referred to as "accelerated depreciation" methods, is based largely on the assumption that there will be rapid reductions in asset efficiency, output, or other benefits in the early years of an asset's life. As assets age they often require increased charges for maintenance and repairs. Charges for depreciation decline, then, as the economic advantages afforded through ownership of the asset decline. The most commonly used decreasing-charge methods are sum-of-the-years-digits and some variation of a declining-balance method.

Straight-Line Depreciation. Straight-line depreciation relates cost allocation to the passage of time and recognizes equal periodic charges over the life of the asset. The allocation

5. *Accounting Trends & Techniques* (New York: American Institute of Certified Public Accountants, 1993), p. 341.

assumes equal usefulness per time period, and in applying this assumption, the charge is not affected by asset productivity or efficiency variations. In developing the periodic charge, an estimate is made of the useful life of the asset in terms of months or years. The difference between the asset cost and residual value is divided by the useful life of the asset in arriving at the cost assigned to each time unit.

Using data for the machine acquired by Schuss Boom Ski Manufacturing (see the preceding page) and assuming a 5-year life, annual depreciation is determined as follows:

$$D = \frac{C - R}{n}, \text{ or } \frac{\$100{,}000 - \$5{,}000}{5 \text{ years}} = \$19{,}000 \text{ per year}$$

Annual depreciation also can be computed by applying a percentage, or **depreciation rate,** to depreciable cost. The rate is the reciprocal value of the useful life expressed in periods, or r (per period) = 1 ÷ n. In the example, the depreciation rate would be 1 ÷ 5 = 20%, and annual depreciation can be computed as follows:

$$\$95{,}000 \times 20\% = \$19{,}000$$

A table summarizing the cost allocation process for the asset in the example, using the straight-line method, follows:

Asset Cost Allocation—Straight-Line Method

End of Year	Depreciation Computation		Depreciation Amount	Accumulated Depreciation	Asset Book Value
					$100,000
1996	$95,000 ÷ 5	=	$19,000	$19,000	81,000
1997	95,000 ÷ 5	=	19,000	38,000	62,000
1998	95,000 ÷ 5	=	19,000	57,000	43,000
1999	95,000 ÷ 5	=	19,000	76,000	24,000
2000	95,000 ÷ 5	=	19,000	95,000	5,000
		Total	$95,000		

It was indicated earlier that residual value is frequently ignored when it is a relatively minor amount. If this were done in the example, depreciation would be recognized at $20,000 per year instead of $19,000.

Sum-of-the-Years-Digits Depreciation. The **sum-of-the-years-digits depreciation method** provides decreasing charges by applying a series of fractions, each of a smaller value, to depreciable asset cost. Fractions are developed in terms of the sum of the asset life periods. The numerators are the years-digits listed in reverse order. The denominator for the fraction is obtained by adding these digits.

For example, given an asset with a 3-year life, the denominator, which is the same each year, would be 6, the "sum-of-the-years-digits" (1 + 2 + 3). Since the numerators, which decrease each year, are the years-digits in reverse order (3, 2, 1), the fractions would be: 3/6 for the first year; 2/6 for the second year; and 1/6 for the third year. The total of these fractions is 6/6; thus 100% of the depreciable cost is charged to expense at the end of 3 years. The following formula can be used to facilitate computation of the denominator:

$$[(n + 1) \div 2] \times n$$

If useful life is 15 years, the denominator, determined by the formula, is: [(15 + 1) ÷ 2] × 15 = 120. The fraction applied to depreciable cost in the first year would be 15/120, in the second year, 14/120, and so on.

In the Schuss Boom example, useful life is 5 years, and the denominator of the fraction is: [(5 + 1) ÷ 2] × 5 = 15. Alternatively, the denominator can be found by adding the years-digits (1 + 2 + 3 + 4 + 5 = 15). Depreciation using the sum-of-the-years-digits method is summarized in the following table:

Asset Cost Allocation—Sum-of-the-Years-Digits Method

End of Year	Depreciation Computation		Depreciation Amount	Accumulated Depreciation	Asset Book Value
					$100,000
1996	$95,000 × $5/15$	=	$31,667	$31,667	68,333
1997	95,000 × $4/15$	=	25,333	57,000	43,000
1998	95,000 × $3/15$	=	19,000	76,000	24,000
1999	95,000 × $2/15$	=	12,667	88,667	11,333
2000	95,000 × $1/15$	=	6,333	95,000	5,000
		Total	$95,000		

Note that under this method, the annual charge to depreciation expense declines by $1/15$ of the depreciation asset base each year, or by $6,333.

Declining-Balance Depreciation. The **declining-balance depreciation methods** provide decreasing charges by applying a constant percentage rate to a declining asset book value. The most popular rates are 1.5 times the straight-line rate, often referred to as "150% declining balance," and 2 times the straight-line rate, often referred to as **double-declining-balance depreciation.**[6] Residual value is not used in the computations under this method; however, it is generally recognized that depreciation should not continue once the book value is equal to the residual value. The percentage to be used is a multiple of the straight-line rate, calculated for various useful lives as follows:

Estimated Useful Life in Years	Straight-Line Rate	1.5 times Straight-Line Rate	2.0 times Straight-Line Rate
3	33 $1/3$%	50%	66 $2/3$%
5	20	30	40
7	14 $2/7$	21 $3/7$	28 $4/7$
8	12 $1/2$	18 $3/4$	25
10	10	15	20
20	5	7 $1/2$	10

Depreciation using the double-declining-balance method for the asset described earlier is summarized in the following table.

Asset Cost Allocation—Double-Declining Balance Method

End of Year	Depreciation Computation		Depreciation Amount	Accumulated Depreciation	Asset Book Value
					$100,000
1996	$100,000 × 40%	=	$40,000	$40,000	60,000
1997	60,000 × 40	=	24,000	64,000	36,000
1998	36,000 × 40	=	14,400	78,400	21,600
1999	21,600 × 40	=	8,640	87,040	12,960
2000	12,960 × 40	=	5,184	92,224	7,776
		Total	$92,224		

It should be noted that the rate of 40% is applied to the decreasing book value of the asset each year. This results in a declining amount of depreciation expense. In applying this rate, the book value after 5 years exceeds the residual value by $2,776

6. The pure declining-balance method computes a constant rate that, when applied to a declining book value, will cause the book value to equal the estimated residual value at the end of the estimated useful life. The formula to arrive at this rate is $1 - \sqrt[n]{R \div C}$, where R is the residual value, C is cost of the asset, and n is the life of the asset. This method is seldom used in practice because it often exceeds the double-declining-balance rate, a limit imposed in the past through the tax code.

($7,776 – $5,000). This condition arises whenever residual values are relatively low in amount. Since it is impossible to bring a value to zero by using a constant multiplier, most adopters of this method switch to the straight-line method when the remaining annual depreciation computed using straight-line exceeds the depreciation computed by continuing to apply the declining-balance rate. In this example, the depreciation expense for the year 2000 would be $7,960 if a switch were made from double-declining balance to straight-line. This would reduce the book value of the asset to its $5,000 residual value. In this example, the switch was made in the last year of the asset's life, and the depreciation expense was simply the amount necessary to reduce the asset's book value to its residual value. However, if the asset in the example had a lower residual value, the switch could have been made in the fourth year. For example, assume the asset is expected to have no residual value. The book value under the double-declining-balance method at the end of the third year as shown above is $21,600, thus the straight-line depreciation for Years 4 and 5 would be $10,800 ($21,600 ÷ 2). Since the straight-line depreciation of $10,800 exceeds the double-declining depreciation of $8,640, the straight-line amount would be used for Years 4 and 5.

Accelerated Cost Recovery System (ACRS). The Economic Recovery Tax Act (ERTA) of 1981 introduced an adaptation of the declining-balance depreciation method to be used for income tax purposes. It is referred to as the **accelerated cost recovery system (ACRS).** Subsequent revisions to the income tax laws have altered the original provisions. Because the Tax Reform Act of 1986 made several significant changes to ACRS, the new system is now referred to as the **modified accelerated cost recovery system (MACRS).**

The term "cost recovery" was used in the tax regulations to emphasize that ACRS is not a standard depreciation method since the system is not based strictly on asset life or pattern of use. ACRS has largely replaced traditional depreciation accounting for income tax purposes. Its original purpose was to both simplify the computation of tax depreciation and provide for a more rapid write-off of asset cost to reduce income taxes and thus stimulate investment in noncurrent operating assets. Simplification was to be achieved by using one of three **cost recovery periods** for all assets rather than a specific useful life for each class of asset as previously prescribed by the income tax regulations. In addition, salvage values were to be ignored. A more rapid write-off was achieved by allowing companies to write off most machinery and equipment over 3 to 5 years, and all real estate over 15 years, even though previously prescribed income tax class lives were for much longer periods. The class lives prescribed by the IRS were based on estimates of actual useful lives for specific assets in specific industries.

The subsequent modifications to ACRS by Congress have tended to dampen both of its original objectives, primarily because Congress has become more concerned with increasing tax revenues to offset the rapidly growing federal deficit without increasing income tax rates than with simplification or stimulating growth in the economy.[7] The original three recovery periods have been replaced with six recovery periods for personal property,[8] such as equipment, automobiles, and furniture, and two periods for real property, or buildings. At the same time, the recovery periods for most assets have been extended so that less rapid write-off of asset cost is permitted.

Exhibit 12—1 illustrates the cost recovery periods and depreciation methods under

7. The Revenue Reconciliation Act of 1993 increased the recovery period for nonresidential real property from 31.5 years to 39 years. In addition, the Act allows the amortization of acquired intangibles over 15 years. *RIA United States Tax Reporter, Tax Bulletin* (August 12, 1993), No. 33.

8. Personal property is a general term that encompasses all property other than real property (land and buildings).

MACRS. The exhibit applies to assets purchased after December 31, 1986, the date MACRS became effective. For personal property, the appropriate cost recovery period is determined by reference to the IRS class lives defined in the tax regulations. The real property recovery periods relate to the type of real property involved rather than class lives. ACRS initially provided for a 150% declining-balance depreciation. The 1986 Reform Act increased the number of asset recovery periods and extended the recovery periods for most assets. The effects of these changes were partially offset by changing the method of depreciation for most personal property to the 200% declining-balance method.

Exhibit 12—1 MACRS Cost Recovery Periods and Depreciation Methods

	IRS-Defined Class Lives	MACRS Cost Recovery Period	Depreciation Method	Examples of Business Assets
Personal Property	Less than 4 years	3 years	200% declining-balance	Small tools
	4 to < 10 years	5 years	200% declining-balance	Cars, trucks, office machinery
	10 to < 16 years	7 years	200% declining-balance	Office furniture, most factory machinery
	16 to < 20 years	10 years	200% declining-balance	Land improvements
	20 to < 25 years	15 years	150% declining-balance	Communication equipment
	More than 25 years	20 years	150% declining-balance	Farm buildings
	Type of Property			
Real Property—Buildings	Residential rental	27.5 years	Straight-line	
	Nonresidential	39 years	Straight-line	

Both the AICPA and FASB expressed opposition to the use of ACRS for financial reporting purposes because of the wide disparity between the recovery periods permitted for income tax purposes and the actual useful lives of the assets. The 1986 Reform Act modifications have reduced this disparity, and in many cases, the MACRS recovery periods may represent reasonable estimates of useful life for financial reporting purposes. However, companies should exercise caution in adopting MACRS rules for financial reporting purposes because of the volatility of income tax laws and regulations.

Comparison of Time-Factor Methods. Exhibit 12—2 illustrates the pattern of depreciation expense for the time-factor methods discussed in the preceding sections. Note that when the straight-line method is used, depreciation is a constant or fixed charge each period. When the life of an asset is affected primarily by the lapse of time rather than by the degree of use, recognition of depreciation as a constant charge is generally appropriate. However, net income measurements become particularly sensitive to changes in the volume of business activity. With above-normal activity, there is no increase in the depreciation charge; with below-normal activity, there is no decrease in the depreciation charge.

Straight-line depreciation is a widely used procedure for financial reporting purposes. It is readily understood and frequently parallels asset use. It has the advantage of simplicity and under normal conditions offers a satisfactory means of cost allocation. Normal asset conditions exist when (1) assets have been accumulated over a period of years so that the total of depreciation plus maintenance is comparatively even from period to period,

■ Exhibit 12—2
Time-Factor Methods: Depreciation Patterns Compared

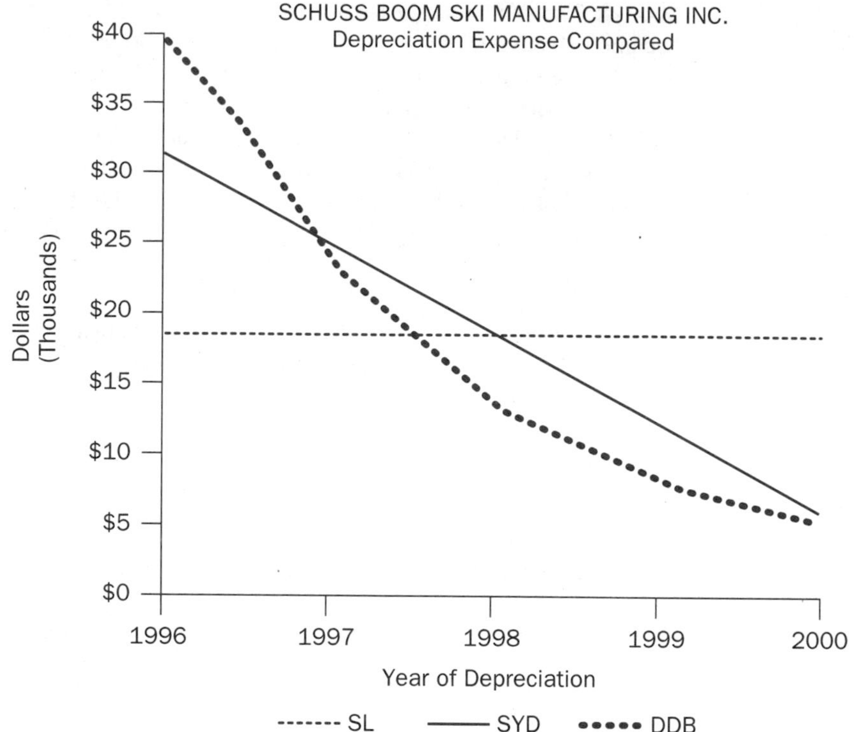

and (2) service potentials of assets are being steadily reduced by functional as well as physical factors. The absence of either of these conditions may suggest the use of some depreciation method other than straight line.

Decreasing-charge methods can be supported as reasonable approaches to cost allocation when the annual benefits provided by an asset decline as it grows older. These methods, too, are suggested when an asset requires increasing maintenance and repairs over its useful life.[9] When straight-line depreciation is employed, the combined charges for depreciation, maintenance, and repairs will increase over the life of the asset; when the decreasing-charge methods are used, the combined charges will tend to be equalized. Exhibit 12—3 illustrates this relationship.

Other factors suggesting the use of a decreasing-charge method include: (1) the anticipation of a significant contribution in early periods with the extent of the contribution to be realized in later periods being less definite; (2) the possibility that inadequacy or obsolescence may result in premature retirement of the asset.

Depreciation for Partial Periods. The discussion thus far has assumed that assets were purchased on the first day of a company's fiscal period. In reality, of course, asset transactions occur throughout the year. When a time-factor method is used, depreciation on assets acquired or disposed of during the year may be based on the number of

9. The AICPA Committee on Accounting Procedure has stated, "The declining-balance method is one of those which meets the requirements of being 'systematic and rational.' In those cases where the expected productivity or revenue-earning power of the asset is relatively greater during the earlier years of its life, or where maintenance charges tend to increase during the later years, the declining-balance method may well provide the most satisfactory allocation of cost." These conclusions apply to other decreasing-charge methods, including the sum-of-the-years-digits method, that produce substantially similar results. See *Accounting Research and Terminology Bulletins—Final Edition,* "No. 44 (Revised), Declining-Balance Depreciation" (New York: American Institute of Certified Public Accountants, 1961), par. 2.

■ Exhibit 12—3 Decreasing-Charge Depreciation and Repairs and Maintenance Expense

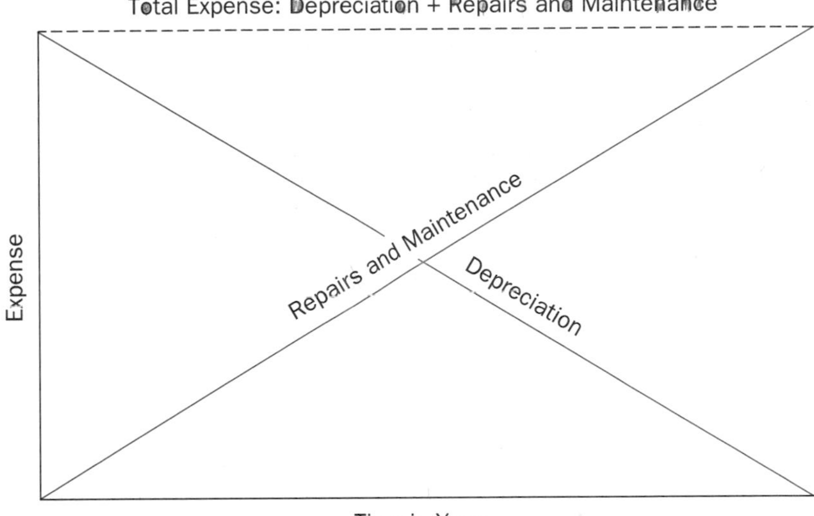

days the asset was held during the period. When the level of acquisitions and retirements is significant, however, companies often adopt a less burdensome policy for recognizing depreciation for partial periods. Some alternatives found in practice include the following:

1. Depreciation is recognized to the nearest whole month. Assets acquired on or before the 15th of the month are considered owned for the entire month; assets acquired after the 15th are not considered owned for any part of the month. Conversely, assets sold on or before the 15th of the month are not considered owned for any part of the month; assets sold after the 15th are considered owned for the entire month.
2. Depreciation is recognized to the nearest whole year. Assets acquired during the first six months are considered held for the entire year; assets acquired during the last six months are not considered in the depreciation computation. Conversely, no depreciation is recorded on assets sold during the first six months, and a full year's depreciation is recorded on assets sold during the last six months.
3. One-half year's depreciation is recognized on all assets purchased or sold during the year. A full year's depreciation is taken on all other assets. This approach is required for tax purposes (ACRS and MACRS).
4. No depreciation is recognized on acquisitions during the year, but depreciation for a full year is recognized on retirements.
5. Depreciation is recognized for a full year on acquisitions during the year, but no depreciation is recognized on retirements.

Alternatives 2 through 5 are attractive because of their simplicity. However, alternative 1 provides greater accuracy, and its use is assumed in the examples and problems in the text except for MACRS problems that require alternative 3.

If a company uses the sum-of-the-years-digits method of depreciation and recognizes partial year's depreciation on assets in the year purchased, the depreciation expense for the second year must be determined by the following allocation procedure. Assume that the asset acquired by Schuss Boom Ski Manufacturing (see page 489) was purchased 3/4 of the way through the fiscal year. The computation of depreciation expense for the first two years would be as follows:

First year:		
Depreciation for full year (See page 491)	$31,667	
One-fourth year's depreciation ($31,667 ÷ 4)		$ 7,917
Second year:		
Depreciation for balance of first year ($31,667 – 7,917)		$23,750
Depreciation for second full year (See page 491)	$25,333	
One-fourth year's depreciation ($25,333 ÷ 4)]		6,333
Total depreciation—second year		$30,083

From this point, each year's depreciation will be $6,333 less than the previous year's depreciation. This difference equals 1/15 of the original depreciable asset base of $95,000. A summary of the depreciation charges for the five-year period is as follows:

	Depreciation	Asset Book Value
Year 1	$ 7,917	$92,083
Year 2	30,083	62,000
Year 3	23,750	38,250
Year 4	17,417	20,833
Year 5	11,083	9,750
Year 6	4,750	5,000
Total	$95,000	

Year 5 depreciation is $6,334 less than previous year due to effects of rounding.

Alternatively, depreciation for Years 2 through 6 can be computed using the standard sum-of-the-years-digits computation with the numerator being the number of years remaining in the asset's useful life as of the beginning of the year. For the second year, the number of years remaining in the asset's useful life at the beginning of the year is 4.75. The depreciation for Year 2 is: $95,000 × 4.75/15 = $30,083.

If a company uses a declining-balance method of depreciation, the computation of depreciation when partial years are involved is relatively straightforward. After the first year's depreciation is computed, the remaining years are calculated in the same manner as illustrated on page 491; a constant percentage is multiplied by a declining book value. Again assuming a purchase 3/4 of the way through the fiscal year and the use of alternative 1, the double-declining-balance depreciation expense for the asset described on page 489 would be as follows, assuming a switch to straight-line depreciation in Year 5.

		Depreciation	Asset Book Value
Year 1	($100,000 × .40 × 1/4)	$10,000	$90,000
Year 2	($90,000 × .40)	36,000	54,000
Year 3	($54,000 × .40)	21,600	32,400
Year 4	($32,400 × .40)	12,960	19,440
Year 5	($19,440 – $5,000) ÷ 1 3/4	8,251*	11,189
Year 6	($11,189 – $5,000)	6,189	5,000
	Total	$95,000	

*rounded

In contrast, the MACRS method for personal property requires use of alternative 3, the half-year convention, and ignores residual value. The cost recovery amounts for the same asset would be as follows:

		Cost Recovery Amount	Asset Book Value
Year 1	($100,000 × .40 × 1/2)	$ 20,000	$80,000
Year 2	($80,000 × .40)	32,000	48,000
Year 3	($48,000 × .40)	19,200	28,800
Year 4	($28,800 × .40)	11,520	17,280
Year 5	($17,280 ÷ 1.5)	11,520	5,760
Year 6	(Remaining book value)	5,760	-0-
		Total $100,000	

Even though the asset was purchased 3/4 of the way through the year, for tax purposes $20,000 is reported as the cost recovery in the first year rather than $10,000 determined by computing depreciation to the nearest month. Note that a switch to the straight-line method was made in Year 5. If the double-declining-balance method had been applied to this year, only $6,912 ($17,280 × .40) would have been reported rather than $11,520 using straight-line for the remaining 1.5 years.

Use-Factor Method. **Use-factor depreciation methods** view asset exhaustion as related primarily to asset use or output and provide periodic charges varying with the degree of such service. Service life for certain assets can best be expressed in terms of hours of service; for others, in terms of units of production.

Service-Hours Method. **Service-hours depreciation** is based on the theory that purchase of an asset represents the purchase of a number of hours of direct service. This method requires an estimate of the life of the asset in terms of service hours. Depreciable cost is divided by total service hours in arriving at the depreciation rate to be assigned for each hour of asset use. The use of the asset during the period is measured, and the number of service hours is multiplied by the depreciation rate in arriving at the periodic depreciation charge. Depreciation charges against revenue fluctuate periodically according to the contribution the asset makes in service hours.

Using asset data previously given and an estimated service life of 20,000 hours, the rate to be applied for each service hour is determined as follows:

$$r \text{ (per hour)} = \frac{C - R}{n}, \text{ or } \frac{\$100{,}000 - \$5{,}000}{20{,}000 \text{ hours}} = \$4.75 \text{ per hour}$$

Allocation of asset cost in terms of service hours is summarized in the following table.

Asset Cost Allocation—Service-Hours Method

End of Year	Service Hours	Depreciation: Computation	Depreciation: Amount	Accumulated Depreciation	Asset Book Value
					$100,000
1996	3,000	3,000 × $4.75 =	$14,250	$14,250	85,750
1997	5,000	5,000 × $4.75 =	23,750	38,000	62,000
1998	5,000	5,000 × $4.75 =	23,750	61,750	38,250
1999	4,000	4,000 × $4.75 =	19,000	80,750	19,250
2000	3,000	3,000 × $4.75 =	14,250	95,000	5,000
	20,000		$95,000		

It is assumed that the original estimate of service hours is confirmed and the asset is retired after 20,000 hours are reached in the fifth year. Such precise confirmation would seldom be found in practice. Procedures for handling changes in estimates are discussed later in the chapter.

It should be observed that straight-line depreciation resulted in an annual charge of $19,000 regardless of fluctuations in productive activity. When asset life is affected directly by the degree of use, and when there are significant fluctuations in such use in successive periods, the service-hours method, which recognizes hours used instead of hours available for use, normally provides the more equitable charges to operations.

Productive-Output Method. **Productive-output depreciation** is based on the theory that an asset is acquired for the service it can provide in the form of production output. This method requires an estimate of the total unit output of the asset. Depreciable cost divided by the total estimated output gives the equal charge to be assigned for each unit of output. The measured production for a period multiplied by the charge per unit gives the charge to be made against revenue. Depreciation charges fluctuate periodically according to the contribution the asset makes in unit output.

Using the previous asset data and an estimated productive life of 25,000 units, the rate to be applied for each unit produced is determined as follows:

$$r = \frac{C - R}{n}, \text{ or } \frac{\$100{,}000 - \$5{,}000}{25{,}000 \text{ units}} = \$3.80 \text{ per unit}$$

A table for the productive-output method would be similar to that prepared for the service-hours method.

Evaluation of Use-Factor Methods. When quantitative measures of asset use can be reasonably estimated, the use-factor methods provide highly satisfactory approaches to asset cost allocation. Depreciation as a fluctuating charge tends to follow the revenue curve: high depreciation charges are assigned to periods of high activity; low charges are assigned to periods of low activity. When the useful life of an asset is affected primarily by the degree of its use, recognition of depreciation as a variable charge is particularly appropriate.

However, certain limitations in applying the use-factor methods need to be pointed out. Asset performance in terms of service hours or productive output is often difficult to estimate. Measurement solely in terms of these factors could fail to recognize special conditions, such as increasing maintenance and repair costs, as well as possible inadequacy and obsolescence. Furthermore, when service life expires even in the absence of use, a use-factor method may conceal actual fluctuations in earnings; by relating periodic depreciation charges to the volume of operations, periodic operating results may be smoothed out, thus creating a false appearance of stability.

Group and Composite Methods. It was assumed in preceding discussions that depreciation expense is associated with individual assets and is applied to each separate unit. This practice is commonly referred to as **unit depreciation.** There may be certain advantages in associating depreciation with a group of assets and applying a single rate to the collective cost of the group at any given time. Group cost allocation procedures are referred to as **group depreciation** and **composite depreciation.**[10]

Group Depreciation. When useful life is affected primarily by physical factors, a group of similar items purchased at one time should have the same expected life, but in fact some will probably remain useful longer than others. In recording depreciation on a unit basis, the sale or retirement of an asset before or after its anticipated lifetime requires recognition of a gain or loss. Such gains and losses, however, can usually be attributed to normal variations in useful life rather than to unforeseen disasters and windfalls.

10. These methods are sometimes referred to as multiple-asset methods of depreciation. See Stephen T. Limberg and Bill N. Schwartz. "Should You Use Multiple Asset Accounts?" *The CPA Journal* (October 1981), pp. 25-31.

The **group-depreciation** procedure treats a collection of similar assets as a single group. Depreciation is accumulated in a single account, and the depreciation rate is based on the average life of assets in the group. Because the accumulated depreciation account under the group procedure applies to the entire group of assets, it is not related to any specific asset. Thus, no book value can be calculated for any specific asset and there are no fully depreciated assets. To arrive at the periodic depreciation charge, the depreciation rate is applied to the recorded cost of all assets remaining in service, regardless of age.

When an item in the group is retired, no gain or loss is recognized; the asset account is credited with the cost of the item and the accumulated depreciation account is debited for the difference between cost and any salvage. With normal variations in asset lives, the losses not recognized on early retirements are offset by the continued depreciation charges on those assets still in service after the average life has elapsed. Group depreciation is generally computed as an adaptation of the straight-line method, and the illustrations in this chapter assume this approach.[11]

To illustrate, assume that 100 similar machines having an average expected useful life of 5 years are purchased at the beginning of 1996 at a total cost of $2,000,000. Of this group, 30 machines are retired at the end of 1999, 40 at the end of 2000, and the remaining 30 at the end of 2001. Based on the average expected useful life of 5 years, a depreciation charge of 20% is reported on those assets in service each year. The charges for depreciation and the changes in the group asset and accumulated depreciation accounts are summarized below, assuming there was no salvage value at retirement.

Asset Cost Allocation—Group Depreciation

		Asset			Accumulated Depreciation			
End of Year	**Depreciation Expense (20% of cost)**	**Debit**	**Credit**	**Balance**	**Debit**	**Credit**	**Balance**	**Asset Book Value**
		$2,000,000		$2,000,000				$2,000,000
1996	$ 400,000			2,000,000		$ 400,000	$ 400,000	1,600,000
1997	400,000			2,000,000		400,000	800,000	1,200,000
1998	400,000			2,000,000		400,000	1,200,000	800,000
1999	400,000		$ 600,000	1,400,000	$ 600,000	400,000	1,000,000	400,000
2000	280,000		800,000	600,000	800,000	280,000	480,000	120,000
2001	120,000		600,000	—	600,000	120,000	—	—
	$2,000,000	$2,000,000	$2,000,000		$2,000,000	$2,000,000		

It should be noted that the depreciation charge is exactly $4,000 per machine-year. In each of the first four years, 100 machine-years of service[12] are utilized, and the annual depreciation charge is $400,000. In the fifth year, when only 70 machines are in operation, the charge is $280,000 (20% of $1,400,000). In the sixth year, when 30 units are still in service, a proportionate charge for such use of $120,000 (20% of $600,000) is made.

If the 30 machines retired in 1999 had been sold for $50,000, the entry to record the sale using the group-depreciation method would have been as follows:

Cash	50,000	
Accumulated Depreciation—Equipment	550,000	
Equipment		600,000

11. The multiple-asset approach may be modified for unusual retirements. In order to preserve the average-life computations, retirements arising from involuntary conversion or other such unusual causes may be recorded at a loss. In order to do this, however, there must be enough detail in the records to approximate the book value of the item at the date of the loss.

12. It should be observed that in the example the original estimate of an average useful life of 5 years is confirmed in the use of the assets. Such precise confirmation would seldom be the case. In instances where assets in a group are continued in use after their cost has been assigned to operations, no further depreciation charges would be recognized. On the other hand, where all of the assets in a group are retired before their costs have been assigned to operations, a special charge related to such retirement would have to be recognized.

Because no gain or loss is recognized, the debit to Accumulated Depreciation is the difference between the cost of the equipment and the cash received.

The preceding example assumed that no new assets were added to the group. This is referred to as a "closed" group. Companies may create such a group, for example, for all furniture acquired in a given year. The group method may also be applied to an "open-ended" group. In this case, additions are made to the group, and thus the accounts are never "closed." Assume the previous example is changed to include additions of 20 machines at the end of 1997 at a cost of $425,000, 30 machines at the end of 2000 at a cost of $650,000, and 50 machines at the end of 2001 at a cost of $1,100,000. Assume that all retired machines are from the initial purchase. The charges for the first 6 years under these assumptions are summarized below. Application of the group-depreciation procedure under circumstances such as these provides an annual charge that is more closely related to the quantity of productive facilities being used. Gains and losses due solely to normal variations in asset lives are not recognized, and operating results are stated more meaningfully. The convenience of applying a uniform depreciation rate to a number of similar items also may represent a substantial advantage.

Asset Cost Allocation—Open-Ended Group Depreciation

End of Year	Depreciation Expense (20% of cost)	Asset			Accumulated Depreciation			Asset Book Value
		Debit	Credit	Balance	Debit	Credit	Balance	
		$2,000,000		$2,000,000				$2,000,000
1996	$400,000			2,000,000		$400,000	$ 400,000	1,600,000
1997	400,000	425,000		2,425,000		400,000	800,000	1,625,000
1998	485,000			2,425,000		485,000	1,285,000	1,140,000
1999	485,000		$600,000	1,825,000	$ 600,000	485,000	1,170,000	655,000
2000	365,000	650,000	800,000	1,675,000	800,000	365,000	735,000	940,000
2001	335,000	1,100,000	600,000	2,175,000	600,000	335,000	470,000	1,705,000

Composite Depreciation. The basic procedures employed under the group method for allocating the cost of substantially identical assets may be extended to include dissimilar assets. This special application of the group procedure is known as **composite depreciation.** The composite method retains the convenience of the group method, but because assets with varying service lives are aggregated to determine an average life, it is unlikely to provide all the reporting advantages of the group method.

A composite rate is established by analyzing the various assets or classes of assets in use and computing the depreciation as an average of the straight-line annual depreciation as follows:

Asset	Cost	Residual Value	Depreciable Cost	Estimated Life in Years	Annual Depreciation Expense (Straight-Line)
A	$ 2,000	$ 120	$ 1,880	4	$ 470
B	6,000	300	5,700	6	950
C	12,000	1,200	10,800	10	1,080
	$20,000	$1,620	$18,380		$2,500

Composite depreciation rate to be applied to cost: $2,500 ÷ $20,000 = 12.5%
Composite or average life of assets: $18,380 ÷ $2,500 = 7.35 years

It will be observed that a rate of 12.5% applied to the cost of the assets, $20,000, results in annual depreciation of $2,500. Annual depreciation of $2,500 will accumulate to a total of $18,380 in 7.35 years; hence 7.35 years may be considered the composite or average life of the assets. Composite depreciation would be reported in a single accumulated depreciation account. Upon the retirement of an individual asset, the asset account is credited and Accumulated Depreciation is debited with the difference between cost and residual value. As with the group procedure, no gains or losses are recognized at the time individual assets are retired.

After a composite rate has been set, it is ordinarily continued in the absence of significant changes in the lives of assets or asset additions and retirements having a material effect upon the rate. It is assumed in the preceding example that the assets are replaced with similar assets when retired. If they are not replaced, continuation of the 12.5% rate will misstate depreciation charges.

Historical Cost Versus Current Cost Allocation

A difficult problem in accounting for property utilization arises in determining the periodic charges to revenues in periods of changing prices. In accounting practice, depreciation,

College Depreciation: FASB vs. GASB

In August 1987, the FASB issued Statement No. 93 that required all not-for-profit organizations, including public and private colleges and universities, to recognize depreciation in their external financial statements. Prior to the issuance of the statement, more than 90% of colleges and universities had not reported depreciation and many questioned its usefulness. However, the FASB adopted Statement No. 93 with a unanimous vote.

Soon after Statement No. 93 was adopted, the GASB (Governmental Accounting Standards Board), which has responsibility for setting accounting standards for governmental bodies, issued Statement No. 8 that exempted public colleges and universities from the FASB's depreciation rule. A significant issue of comparability arose since public universities would now be reporting under a different set of standards from that of private universities. Some private universities threatened to openly disregard the rule. Others declared their intention to ask Congress to force the FASB to back down. Bond-rating agencies promised not to lower the bond ratings of any institutions that refused to comply with the rule. In the face of all this opposition, the FASB issued Statement No. 99, delaying the effective date of the depreciation standard until January 1990.

The Financial Accounting Foundation (FAF), which oversees both the FASB and the GASB, was faced with a critical jurisdictional dispute. Clearly, the FASB had authority to set accounting standards for business entities. Clearly, the GASB had authority to set accounting standards for governmental entities. However, who had authority to set the standards for those special entities whose ownership could be either public or private, such as hospitals and universities? The FAF originally considered giving jurisdiction over all these special entities to the FASB. This was deemed unacceptable by many governmental officials and they threatened to withdraw their support from the FAF and establish their own independent body for setting governmental accounting standards. In late 1989, the FAF altered its position and gave the GASB authority over financial reporting by all governmental entities. For now, the comparability issue for special entities remains something that will have to be ironed out by the FASB and the GASB on a case-by-case basis.

This case illustrates how jurisdictional issues can significantly impact the setting of accounting standards. As the world community attempts to harmonize international accounting standards in the near future, this type of jurisdictional issue may be the most difficult problem addressed.

Questions:

1. What reasons are there for requiring colleges and universities to report depreciation? What arguments could be made against the requirement?
2. What dangers are there in jurisdictional disputes of this kind?

Sources:

Dennis M. Patten. "Battle of the Boards: Identifying the Political Nature of the Standard-Setting Controversies." *Government Accountants Journal* (Fall 1989), p. 3.

News Report, "FAF Alters Position on FASB-GASB Jurisdiction," Journal of *Accountancy* (January 1990), p. 13.

Lee Berton. "Several Private Colleges May Ignore New Accounting Rule on Depreciation." *The Wall Street Journal* (February 4, 1988), p. 24.

depletion, and amortization have traditionally been viewed as an allocation of the acquisition cost over the life of the asset. This meaning can be observed in the definition of depreciation accounting adopted by the Committee on Terminology in the 1940s and still accepted today:

> ***Depreciation accounting*** *is a system of accounting which aims to distribute the cost or other basic value of tangible capital assets, less salvage (if any), over the estimated useful life of the unit (which may be a group of assets) in a systematic and rational manner. It is a process of allocation, not of valuation.* ***Depreciation for the year*** *is the portion of the total charge under such a system that is allocated to the year. Although the allocation may properly take into account occurrences during the year, it is not intended to be a measurement of the effect of all such occurrences.*[13]

Under this allocation view, the total amount charged against revenue is fixed by the acquisition cost less any estimated residual value. While the pattern of charges may vary with the allocation method used, the total amount charged against revenue cannot exceed the historical cost of the asset. For any group of assets at any given time, the cumulative amount charged against past revenues plus the remaining asset carrying or book value will equal the original acquisition cost adjusted by any additions or betterments.

There are many accountants who advocate a charge against revenue based on a current asset value, i.e., the **replacement cost** or **current cost.** This allocation approach matches current rather than past costs against current revenues, resulting in a net income figure that better reflects income available for dividends and that is more useful for estimating future cash flows of a business entity. Noncurrent operating assets must be replaced, and that portion of current and future earnings needed for replacement will not be available for distribution to owners or for payments to creditors.

In the United States, enthusiasm for reporting depreciation based on replacement costs or on inflation-adjusted numbers has ebbed and flowed, primarily in concert with rising and falling inflation rates. Double-digit inflation in the late 1970s and early 1980s coincided with the release of SEC Accounting Series Release No. 190, "Notice of Adoption of Amendments to Regulation S-X Requiring Disclosure of Certain Replacement Cost Data," and FASB Statement No. 33, "Financial Reporting and Changing Prices," in 1976 and 1979, respectively. These pronouncements, although differing in their details, had the common purpose of requiring supplemental disclosure of, among other things, depreciation expense based on the increased values of assets stemming from the high inflation rate. These pronouncements are no longer in effect, Statement No. 33 having been rescinded by Statement No. 89, "Financial Reporting and Changing Prices," which was issued in 1986. The demise of current value depreciation in the United States resulted primarily from the drop of inflation rates (averaging less than three percent in the latter half of the 1980s and early 1990s), which reduced the difference between current value and historical cost financial statements. In addition, the Statement No. 33 supplemental disclosures were not widely used by investors and creditors even when inflation was high. This is another illustration of the relevance vs. reliability trade-off — financial statement users felt that the increased relevance (in theory) of the current value numbers did not compensate for the reliability lost when departing from historical cost.

AMORTIZATION OF INTANGIBLE NONCURRENT OPERATING ASSETS

The life of an intangible asset is usually limited by the effects of obsolescence, shifts in demand, competition, and other economic factors. Because of the difficulty in estimating

13. *Accounting Research and Terminology Bulletins*—Final Edition, "Accounting Terminology Bulletins, No. 1, Review and Resume" (New York: American Institute of Certified Public Accountants, 1961), par. 56.

such highly uncertain future events, in the past companies sometimes did not amortize the cost of intangible assets but assumed their value was never used up. This practice was frequently followed for trademarks, goodwill, and some franchises. The Accounting Principles Board, however, felt that eventually all intangible assets became of insignificant worth to the company. The Board, therefore, issued Opinion No. 17, requiring that the recorded costs of all intangible assets acquired after October 31, 1970—the effective date of the Opinion—be amortized over the estimated useful life.[14] Many companies do not amortize certain intangibles, notably goodwill, acquired prior to November 1, 1970, although amortization of these assets was encouraged by the Board.

The useful life of an intangible asset may be affected by a variety of factors, all of which should be considered in determining the amortization period. Useful life may be limited by legal, regulatory, or contractual provisions. These factors, including options for renewal or extension, should be evaluated in conjunction with the economic factors noted above and other pertinent information. A patent, for example, has a legal life of 17 years; but if the competitive advantages afforded by the patent are expected to terminate after 5 years, then the patent cost should be amortized over the shorter period.

Although the life of an intangible asset is to be estimated by careful analysis of the surrounding circumstances, a maximum life of 40 years was established for amortization purposes. APB Opinion No. 17 included this limitation as follows:

The cost of each type of intangible asset should be amortized on the basis of the estimated life of that specific asset and should not be written off in the period of acquisition. . . .

The period of amortization should not, however, exceed forty years. Analysis at the time of acquisition may indicate that the indeterminate lives of some intangible assets are likely to exceed forty years and the cost of those assets should be amortized over the maximum period of forty years, not an arbitrary shorter period.[15]

The requirement that the recorded cost of all intangible assets be amortized and the arbitrary selection of a 40-year life are of questionable theoretical merit. An analysis of the expected future benefits to be derived from a particular asset should be the basis for capitalizing and amortizing the cost of any asset, whether tangible or intangible. However, the very nature of intangible assets makes estimating their useful lives a difficult problem in practice.

The establishment by the APB of a 40-year maximum period for the amortization of intangible assets was not intended to determine the normal write-off period as 40 years. However, for some assets, such as goodwill and franchise costs, 40 years has become the most popular period to use. While it is difficult to determine exactly how long goodwill benefits a company, the amortization period should be established based on sound reasoning, not some arbitrary period of time. Some accountants feel that a five- to ten-year period should be used, because after that period, a company has probably built its own goodwill based on expenditures and actions during that period. Others feel that goodwill should be written off immediately against equity because of the lack of comparability among companies, some of whom report purchased goodwill and others who do not. The degree of diversity in the amortization of intangible assets, especially goodwill, suggests that further guidelines may be forthcoming in this area.

Amortization, like depreciation, may be charged as an operating expense of the period or allocated to production overhead if the asset is related directly to the manufacture of goods. In practice, the credit entry is often made directly to the asset account rather than to a separate allowance account. This practice is arbitrary, and there is no reason why

14. *Opinions of the Accounting Principles Board, No. 17,* "Intangible Assets" (New York: American Institute of Certified Public Accountants, 1970).

15. *Ibid.,* pars. 28-29.

Baseball Accounting

In May 1985, George Sorter, a professor of accounting at New York University, was asked by the major league baseball team owners to estimate the aggregate profit or loss for the 26 major league teams for 1984. Baseball's profitability (or lack thereof) was a major point of contention in the labor negotiations between the owners and the players. Professor Sorter was called in as an outside expert (his credentials included a long-time devotion to the hapless Chicago Cubs). Professor Sorter identified the following three areas as being the most contentious from an accounting standpoint.

Deferred Compensation. A standard player's contract might state that a player is to receive $500,000 for a season, $300,000 to be paid during the year and $200,000 to be deferred for ten years. Most of the baseball teams failed to use the present value of the $200,000 deferred compensation when computing salary expense. Professor Sorter estimated that this error had caused the owners to overstate their losses by $700,000.

Related Party Transactions. Professional sports teams are often owned as an integrated array of assets and it is difficult, and sometimes misleading, to carve out and report the results of the sports operations separately. For example, the Atlanta Braves and the Chicago Cubs are owned by companies that also operate television "superstations" (WTBS in Atlanta and WGN in Chicago) which broadcast Braves and Cubs games nationwide. It isn't clear that the fees "paid" by the superstations to the baseball teams reflect the value that those broadcast rights would command in an arm's-length transaction. Professor Sorter was unable to come to a definite conclusion, but it is possible that related party transactions allow team owners to shift reported profits away from baseball operations.

Initial Roster Depreciation. When a team changes hands, up to 50% of the purchase price is allocated to an asset called Initial Roster. This asset represents the value of the team, over and above the value of the individual players. The owners included $12 million of initial roster depreciation expense in their 1984 results. The troubling thing about this expense is that it is recorded only for teams that have changed hands recently. If a team is still owned by the original owner, the Initial Roster asset would still exist in an economic sense, but it would not be recognized in the accounting records. In addition, the reported profits of teams recognizing initial roster depreciation are hit twice for player development costs — player development expenditures for the current period are expensed along with initial roster depreciation that represents the expensing of the capitalized value of past player development expenditures. Professor Sorter concluded that initial roster depreciation was a result of recent owner changes in major league baseball and should not be included in evaluating the profitability of baseball operations.

Professor Sorter's final estimate was that the 26 major league baseball teams lost a total of $27 million in 1984 — a diplomatic finding almost exactly halfway between the owners' claim of a $65 million loss and the players' claim of a $9 million profit. Armed with these diverse profitability estimates, the players and owners went to the negotiating table. Who won the negotiations? The increased freedom to move from team to team acquired by the players has resulted in significantly escalated salaries. In 1984, only a few star players made more than $1 million. In 1993, the *average* baseball salary exceeded $1 million. In 1984, *Sports Illustrated* reported that Ryne Sandberg, star second baseman for the Chicago Cubs, had signed a lucrative six-year contract in 1984 paying him $660,000 a year. In 1993, Sandberg was the highest paid player in baseball, making $6,475,000.

Questions:

1. All teams have an Initial Roster asset; however, the asset is recorded and depreciated only by those teams that have recently changed hands. Do other types of businesses (i.e., manufacturers, retailers, etc.) have assets similar in nature to baseball's Initial Roster asset? Explain.
2. The accounting treatment of the Initial Roster asset makes it difficult to compare the financial statements of a team that has never been sold to those of a team that has recently changed hands. Make a suggestion for a solution to this problem.

Sources:

George H. Sorter. "Accounting for Baseball." *Journal of Accountancy,* June 1986, p. 126.

Daniel Seligman. "Computers, Baseball, and Guys Named Mike." *Fortune,* May 17, 1993, p. 139.

charges for amortization cannot be accumulated in a separate account in the same manner as depreciation. The FASB requires disclosure of both cost and accumulated depreciation for tangible assets, but does not require similar disclosure for intangible assets. When amortization is recorded in a separate account, such an account is typically called Accumulated Amortization.

Amortization of intangible assets is made evenly in most instances, or on a straight-line allocation basis. APB Opinion No. 17 states:

The Board concludes that the straight-line method of amortization—equal annual amounts—should be applied unless a company demonstrates that another systematic method is more appropriate.[16]

Although practice favors straight-line amortization, analysis of many intangibles such as patents, franchises, and even goodwill suggests that greater benefit is often realized in the early years of the asset's life than in the later years. In those instances, a decreasing-charge amortization seems justified.

DEPLETION OF NATURAL RESOURCES

Natural resources, also called **wasting assets,** move toward exhaustion as the physical units representing these resources are removed and sold. The withdrawal of oil or gas, the cutting of timber, and the mining of coal, sulfur, iron, copper, or silver ore are examples of processes leading to the exhaustion of natural resources. Depletion expense is a charge for the using-up of the resources.

Computing Periodic Depletion

The computation of depletion expense is an adaptation of the productive-output method of depreciation. Perhaps the most difficult problem in computing depletion expense is estimating the amount of resources available for economical removal from the land. Generally, a geologist, mining engineer, or other expert is called upon to make the estimate, and it is subject to continual revision as the resource is extracted or removed.

Developmental costs, such as costs of drilling, sinking mine shafts, and constructing roads should be capitalized and added to the original cost of the property in arriving at the total cost subject to depletion. These costs are often incurred before normal activities begin.

To illustrate the computation of depletion expense, assume the following facts: land containing mineral deposits is purchased at a cost of $5,500,000. The land has an estimated value after removal of the resources of $250,000; the natural resource supply is estimated at 1,000,000 tons. The unit-depletion charge and the total depletion charge for the first year, assuming the withdrawal of 80,000 tons are calculated as follows:

Depletion charge per ton = ($5,500,000 − $250,000) ÷ 1,000,000 = $5.25
Depletion charge for the first year = 80,000 tons × $5.25 = $420,000

The following entries should be made to record these events:

Land	250,000	
Mineral Deposits	5,250,000	
Cash		5,500,000
To purchase mineral rights.		
Depletion Expense	420,000	
Accumulated Depletion (or Mineral Deposits)		420,000
To record depletion expense.		

If the 80,000 tons are sold in the current year, the entire $420,000 would be included as part of the cost of goods sold. If only 60,000 tons are sold, $105,000 is reported as part of ending inventory on the balance sheet.

16. *Opinions of the Accounting Principles Board, No. 17,* par. 30.

When buildings and improvements are constructed in connection with the removal of natural resources and their usefulness is limited to the duration of the project, it is reasonable to recognize depreciation on such properties on an output basis consistent with the charges to be recognized for the natural resources themselves. For example, assume buildings are constructed at a cost of $250,000; the useful lives of the buildings are expected to terminate upon exhaustion of the natural resource consisting of 1,000,000 units. Under these circumstances, a depreciation charge of $.25 ($250,000 ÷ 1,000,000) should accompany the depletion charge recognized for each unit. When improvements provide benefits expected to terminate prior to the exhaustion of the natural resource, the cost of such improvements should be allocated on the basis of the units to be removed during the life of the improvements or on a time basis, whichever is considered more appropriate.

Special Problems—Oil and Gas Properties

The preceding discussion relates to depletion of all natural resources. Special problems exist in the oil and gas industry in the determination of the asset cost to be used in computing depletion. Even though apparently valuable property rights are acquired, no one can truly measure their value until exploratory activities have been completed. The nature of oil exploration generally results in several dry wells for each "gusher" that is discovered. The accounting question is, "How should these exploratory costs be recorded? Are they part of the asset cost regardless of their success, or are they a period expense?"

The brief history of accounting for oil and gas exploration outlined below illustrates that accounting standards are a compromise between proper theory and concerns about the economic consequences of the reported numbers.

Two methods of accounting have developed to account for exploratory costs. The first method is the full cost approach, and the second method is the successful efforts approach. Under the **full cost approach,** all exploratory costs are deferred and written off against revenues as depletion expense. Under the **successful efforts approach,** exploratory costs for unsuccessful projects are expensed, and only exploratory costs for successful projects are deferred as assets. Most large, successful oil companies follow the second approach. Adobe Resources Corporation included the following explanation of its depletion method in the notes to the 1991 financial statements:

Exhibit 12—4
Adobe Resources Corporation

Change to Successful Efforts Accounting Method. *During the quarter ended March 31, 1991, the Corporation changed the method of accounting for its oil and gas operations from the full cost method to the successful efforts method. Although the full cost method continues to be generally accepted, the Financial Accounting Standards Board has expressed a preference for the successful efforts method. Management believes the successful efforts method is a more appropriate measure of the results of the Corporation's oil and gas operations and enables investors and others to better compare the Corporation to other oil and gas companies.*

For smaller companies, the full cost approach has been popular. This method encourages such companies to continue exploration without the severe penalty of recognizing all costs of unsuccessful projects as immediate expenses. Proponents of the full cost approach argue that often valuable exploratory information is discovered even when a "dry hole" is drilled. The cost of a producing well, therefore, should include these unsuccessful costs. MDU Resources Group, Inc., explains its use of full cost in a note reproduced in Exhibit 12—5.

Exhibit 12—5
MDU Resources Group, Inc.

Oil and Natural Gas. *The company uses the full-cost method of accounting for its oil and natural gas production activities. Under this method, all costs incurred in the acquisition, exploration and development of oil and natural gas properties are capitalized and amortized on the units of production method based on total proved reserves. Cost centers for amortization purposes are determined on a country-by-country basis. Capitalized costs are subject to a "ceiling test" that limits such costs to the aggregate of the present value of future net revenues of proved reserves and the lower of cost or fair value of unproved properties.*

The issue of how to account for exploratory costs of the oil and gas industry has attracted the attention of the FASB, the SEC, and even the U.S. Congress. When an apparent oil shortage developed in the 1970s, there was strong pressure placed on oil companies to expand their exploration to discover new sources of oil and gas. The FASB was encouraged to identify one of the two alternatives for recording exploratory costs as preferred. In 1977, it selected a form of the successful efforts approach, and issued FASB Statement No. 19, "Financial Accounting and Reporting by Oil and Gas Producing Companies." The smaller companies objected to this standard, arguing that their exploration activities would be less vigorous if they had to immediately expense their drilling costs. In 1979, the SEC issued its own standard that rejected both alternatives, and suggested adoption of a new method it called **Reserve Recognition Accounting (RRA).** This method was, in reality, a form of **discovery accounting** that would recognize as an asset the value of the reserves rather than their cost. Under public and congressional pressure, the FASB issued its Statement No. 25 that suspended its earlier standard, and effectively permitted again the use of either the full cost or successful efforts approach.[17]

When oil and gas prices declined, the SEC withdrew its support of RRA. However, the commission still favored some form of current-value disclosure. As a result, the FASB issued Statement No. 69 in 1982 which requires oil and gas producing companies to provide supplemental current-value disclosures.

CHANGES IN ESTIMATES OF COST ALLOCATION VARIABLES

The allocation of asset costs benefiting more than one period cannot be precisely determined at acquisition because so many of the variables cannot be known with certainty until a future time. Only one factor in determining the periodic charge for depreciation, amortization, or depletion is based on historical information—asset cost. Other factors—residual value, useful life or output, and the pattern of use or benefit—must be estimated. The question frequently facing accountants is how adjustments to these estimates, which arise as time passes, should be reflected in the accounts. As indicated in Chapter 4, a change in estimate is normally reported in the current and future periods rather than as an adjustment of prior periods. This type of adjustment would be made for residual value and useful-life changes. However, a change in the cost allocation method based on a revised expected pattern of use is a change in accounting principle and is accounted for in a different manner. Changes in accounting principles are discussed in a later chapter.

Change in Estimated Life

To illustrate the procedure for a change in estimated life affecting allocation of asset cost, assume that a company purchased $50,000 of equipment and estimated a 10-year life for

17. *Statement of Financial Accounting Standards No. 25,* "Suspension of Certain Accounting Requirements for Oil and Gas Producing Companies," (Stamford: Financial Accounting Standards Board, 1979).

depreciation purposes. Using the straight-line method with no residual value, the annual depreciation would be $5,000. After four years, accumulated depreciation would amount to $20,000, and the remaining undepreciated book value would be $30,000. Early in the fifth year, a re-evaluation of the life indicates only four more years of service can be expected from the asset. An adjustment must therefore be made for the fifth and subsequent years to reflect the change. A new annual depreciation charge is calculated by dividing the remaining book value by the remaining life of four years. This would result in an annual charge of $7,500 for the fifth through eighth years ($30,000 ÷ 4 = $7,500).

A change in the estimated life of an intangible asset is accounted for in the same manner, i.e., the unamortized cost is allocated over the remaining life based on the revised estimate. Because of the uncertainties surrounding the estimation of the life of an intangible asset, frequent evaluation of the amortization period should be made to determine if a change in estimated life is warranted. For example, assume a patent costing $51,000 is being amortized over 17 years. Amortization per year would be $3,000 ($51,000 ÷ 17). If, at the end of 5 years, the patent is estimated to have a remaining life of 4 years, the book value of $36,000 [$51,000 – ($3,000 × 5)] will be amortized over 4 years at $9,000 per year.

Asset Cost Allocation—Change in Estimated Life (Straight-Line Method)

End of Year	Depreciation Computation	Depreciation Amount	Accumulated Depreciation
1996	$50,000 ÷ 10 =	$ 5,000	$ 5,000
1997	$50,000 ÷ 10 =	5,000	10,000
1998	$50,000 ÷ 10 =	5,000	15,000
1999	$50,000 ÷ 10 =	5,000	20,000
2000	($50,000 – $20,000) ÷ 4 =	7,500	27,500
2001	($50,000 – $20,000) ÷ 4 =	7,500	35,000
2002	($50,000 – $20,000) ÷ 4 =	7,500	42,500
2003	($50,000 – $20,000) ÷ 4 =	7,500	50,000
		$50,000	

Change in Estimated Units of Production

Another change in estimate occurs in accounting for natural resources when the estimate of the recoverable units changes as a result of further discoveries, improved extraction processes, or changes in sales prices that indicate changes in the number of units that can be extracted profitably. A revised depletion rate is established by dividing the remaining resource cost balance by the estimated remaining recoverable units.

To illustrate, assume the facts used in the example on page 505. Land is purchased at a cost of $5,500,000 with estimated residual value of $250,000. The original estimated supply of natural resources in the land is 1,000,000 tons. As indicated previously, the depletion rate under these conditions would be $5.25 per ton, and the depletion charge for the first year when 80,000 tons were mined would be $420,000. Assume that in the second year of operation, 100,000 tons of ore are withdrawn, but before the books are closed at the end of the second year, appraisal of the expected recoverable tons indicates a remaining tonnage of 950,000. The new depletion rate and the depletion charge for the second year would be computed as follows:

Cost assignable to recoverable tons as of the beginning of the second year:	
Original costs applicable to depletable resources	$5,250,000
Deduct depletion charge for the first year	420,000
Balance of cost subject to depletion	$4,830,000

Estimated recoverable tons as of the beginning of the second year:	
Number of tons withdrawn in the second year	100,000
Estimated recoverable tons as of the end of the second year	950,000
Total recoverable tons as of the beginning of the second year	1,050,000

Depletion charge per ton for the second year = $4,830,000 ÷ 1,050,000 = $4.60
Depletion charge for the second year = 100,000 × $4.60 = $460,000

Sometimes an increase in estimated recoverable units arises from additional expenditures for capital developments. When this occurs, the additional costs should be added to the remaining recoverable cost and divided by the number of tons remaining to be extracted. To illustrate this situation, assume in the preceding example that $525,000 of additional costs had been incurred at the beginning of the second year. The preceding computation of depletion rate and depletion expense would be changed as follows:

Cost assignable to recoverable tons as of the beginning of the second year:	
Original costs applicable to depletable resources	$5,250,000
Add additional costs incurred in the second year	525,000
	$5,775,000
Deduct depletion charge for the first year	420,000
Balance of cost subject to depletion	$5,355,000
Estimated recoverable tons as of the beginning of the second year (as above)	1,050,000

Depletion charge per ton for the second year = $5,355,000 ÷ 1,050,000 = $5.10
Depletion charge for the second year = 100,000 × $5.10 = $510,000

Accounting is made up of many estimates. The procedures outlined in this section are designed to prevent the continual restating of reported income from prior years. Adjustments to prior-period income figures are made only if actual errors have occurred, not when reasonable estimates have been made that later prove inaccurate.

Impairment of Asset Values

Events sometimes occur after the purchase of an asset and before the end of its estimated life that impair its value and require an immediate write-down of the asset rather than making a normal allocation of cost over a period of time. This type of **impairment** can occur with operating assets.

As an example, in 1990, MCI Communications Corp. accelerated the conversion of its long-distance telephone network from analog to digital technology to keep pace with US Sprint and AT&T. This action left MCI with a lot of obsolete analog equipment. Interviewed in August 1990, O. Gene Gabbard, chief financial officer of MCI, stated it was "highly likely" that the conversion would result in a write-down of the analog equipment but the write-down was "not a final decision at this point in time" and "the big question is the final amount."[18] In the notes to its 1990 financial statements, MCI disclosed that it had decided to record the write-down to recognize "the permanent impairment in the value of analog equipment caused by the acceleration of the company's digitization plan."

As illustrated by the comments from MCI's chief financial officer, whether to recognize the impairment of operating assets is not a simple decision. In addition, once the decision to recognize the impairment has been made, one is still faced with the question of the

18. Mary Lu Carnevale. "Technology: MCI Speeds Conversion to Digital." *The Wall Street Journal* (August 22, 1990), p. B1.

amount of the write-down. The authoritative accounting literature has not included a clear statement of accounting standards governing the recognition of asset impairment.

The Emerging Issues Task Force considered the issue of impairment several times in the mid-1980s but could come to no consensus on a standard. In November 1988, the FASB added the impairment project to its agenda and released an Exposure Draft in November 1993, "Accounting for the Impairment of Long-Lived Assets." The debate continues, but the Board has reached the following tentative conclusions:[19]

- A company should review its assets for possible impairment whenever the following types of events occur:
  - A significant decrease in the market value of an asset,
  - A significant change in the way an asset is used,
  - A significant adverse change in legal factors or in the business climate
  - Asset acquisition or construction cost significantly greater than expected, and
  - Forecast of continuing losses associated with an asset.
- An entity should recognize an impairment loss only when the undiscounted sum of estimated future cash flows from an asset is less than the carrying amount of the asset.
- The impairment loss should be measured based on the fair value of the asset, when reasonably estimatable, or based on the present value of estimated future cash flows from the asset.
- No restoration of a previously recognized impairment loss should be allowed.
- Disclosure should include a description of the impaired asset, reasons for the impairment, a description of the measurement assumptions, and, for public companies, the business segment or segment affected.

ASSET RETIREMENTS

Assets may be retired by sale, exchange, or abandonment. Generally, when an asset is disposed of, any unrecorded depreciation or amortization for the period is recorded to the date of disposition. A book value as of the date of disposition can then be computed as the difference between the cost of the asset and its accumulated depreciation. If the disposition price exceeds the book value, a **gain** is recognized. If the disposition price is less than the book value, a **loss** is recorded. The gain or loss is reported on the income statement as "Other revenues and gains" or "Other expenses and losses" in the year of asset disposition. As part of the disposition entry, the balances in the asset and accumulated depreciation accounts for the asset are canceled. The following sections illustrate the asset retirement process under varying conditions.

Asset Retirement by Sale

If the proceeds from the sale of an asset are in the form of cash or a receivable **(monetary asset),** the recording of the transaction follows the order outlined in the previous paragraph. For example, assume that on April 1, 1996, Firestone Supply Co. sells for $43,600 manufacturing equipment that is recorded on the books at cost of $83,600 and accumulated depreciation as of January 1, 1996, of $50,600. The company depreciates its manufacturing equipment on the books using a straight-line, 10% rate. It follows the policy of depreciating its assets to the nearest month.

19. *Proposed Statement of Financial Accounting Standards Board,*" Accounting for the Impairment of Long-Lived Assets" (Norwalk: Financial Accounting Standards Board, November, 1993).

The following entries would be made to record this transaction:

Depreciation Expense—Machinery	2,090	
Accumulated Depreciation—Machinery		2,090
To record depreciation for three months in 1996 ($83,600 × .10 × 3/12).		
Cash	43,600	
Accumulated Depreciation—Machinery	52,690	
Machinery		83,600
Gain on Sale of Machinery		12,690*
To record sale of machinery at a gain.		

*Computation of gain:

Sales price	$43,600
Book value ($83,600 – $52,690)	30,910
Gain on sale	$12,690

The preceding entries could be combined in the form of a single compound entry as follows:

Cash	43,600	
Depreciation Expense—Machinery	2,090	
Accumulated Depreciation—Machinery	50,600	
Machinery		83,600
Gain on Sale of Machinery		12,690

Asset Retirement by Exchange for Other Nonmonetary Assets

As indicated in Chapter 11, when operating assets are acquired in exchange for other nonmonetary assets, the new asset acquired is generally recorded at its fair market value or the fair market value of the nonmonetary asset given in exchange, whichever is more clearly determinable. This is referred to as the "general case" exchange transaction and is the more common exchange transaction.

When accounting for exchanges of property, two questions must be asked: (1) Are the assets being exchanged similar in nature? and (2) Are the parties involved in the exchange in the same line of business; i.e., are they both either dealers of the assets or nondealers? If the answers to both of these questions are affirmative, and if the transaction results in a gain, a "special case" approach may be used to record the exchange. The general case will be illustrated first.

The entries required to record the general case for an exchange involving nonmonetary assets are identical to those illustrated in the previous section except that a nonmonetary asset is increased rather than a monetary one. Gains and losses arising from the exchange are recognized when the exchange takes place.

To illustrate, assume in the previous example that the retirement of the described asset was effected by exchanging it for delivery equipment that had a market value of $43,600. The entries would be the same as illustrated except that instead of a debit to Cash, Delivery Equipment would be debited for $43,600. The gain would still be computed by comparing the book value of the machine and the market value of the asset acquired in the exchange.

Delivery Equipment	43,600	
Depreciation Expense—Machinery	2,090	
Accumulated Depreciation—Machinery	50,600	
Machinery		83,600
Gain on Exchange of Machinery		12,690

If the machinery's fair market value were more clearly determinable than the value of the delivery equipment, the value of the machinery would be used to compute the gain or loss and to determine the value for the delivery equipment. Assume the delivery equipment is used and has no readily available market price, but the machinery had a market value of $25,000. Under these circumstances, a loss of $5,910 ($30,910 – $25,000) would be indicated, and the combined entry to record the exchange would be as follows:

Delivery Equipment	25,000	
Depreciation Expense—Machinery	2,090	
Accumulated Depreciation—Machinery	50,600	
Loss on Exchange of Machinery	5,910	
Machinery		83,600

Often the exchange of nonmonetary assets includes a transfer of cash, since the nonmonetary assets in most exchange transactions do not have equivalent market values. The cash part of the transaction adjusts the market values of the assets received to those of the assets given up. Thus, if in the previous example the exchange of delivery equipment were accompanied by cash of $3,000, the loss would be reduced to $2,910 and the combined entry would be as follows:

Cash	3,000	
Delivery Equipment	25,000	
Depreciation Expense—Machinery	2,090	
Accumulated Depreciation—Machinery	50,600	
Loss on Exchange of Machinery	2,910	
Machinery		83,600

In this example, the exchange involved assets that were dissimilar in nature: delivery equipment and machinery. If the exchange involved similar assets, e.g., a used truck for a new one, the same accounting entries would be required unless the exchange is between two parties in the same line of business. This special case is discussed in the following section.

Asset Retirement by Exchange of Nonmonetary Assets—Special Case

Not all exchanges of nonmonetary assets have the features to justify the recognition of a gain. Sometimes an exchange of **similar assets** is made to facilitate one of the parties to the exchange in making a sale to an ultimate consumer. For example, the Tri-City Cadillac dealership has a buyer for a blue Eldorado but has only a red one in stock. Another dealership in a nearby town has a blue Eldorado and is willing to exchange its car for Tri-City's red one. This exchange of similar assets is not intended to be an earnings transaction for either party and, therefore, should not reflect any gain, even if the market values of the cars have increased since they were originally acquired from the manufacturer. Another example of such an exchange would occur if two manufacturing companies exchanged similar equipment that both companies used in the production process.

In both of these illustrations, similar assets were transferred between parties in the same line of business. In the first instance, both parties were dealers of automobiles. In the second example, both parties were nondealers of machines being used in the production process. In neither case was the earning process culminated.

When the Accounting Principles Board studied the exchange of non-monetary assets issue, it determined that an exception to the general rule was needed when the exchange did not culminate the earning process for either party and a gain was otherwise indicated.[21]

21. *Opinions of the Accounting Principles Board, No. 29,* "Accounting for Nonmonetary Transactions," (New York: American Institute of Certified Public Accountants, 1973), pars. 20-23. The "same line of business" test was added by the Emerging Issues Task Force in Issue No. 86-29, "Nonmonetary Transactions: Magnitude of Boot and the Exceptions to the Use of Fair Value," *EITF Abstracts,* October 1, 1987, pp. 275-277.

The exception provided that **no gain** is to be recognized for these special exchanges unless cash (boot) is received as part of the exchange. If a significant amount of cash is involved in the exchange, the transaction becomes a monetary exchange rather than a nonmonetary one. The Emerging Issues Task Force was asked to determine what is significant, and, in its *Issue No. 86-29,* it concluded that if the cash payment is 25% or more of the fair value of the exchange, the transaction should be considered a monetary exchange with the fair values used to determine a gain or loss. If the cash payment is less than 25%, the party paying the cash records no gain, but the party receiving the cash recognizes a proportionate share of the gain.[22] If the transaction indicates that a loss has occurred, the exception does not apply and the exchange is recorded as illustrated in the previous section. Thus, four conditions must exist for the special case to apply:

1. The assets must be similar in nature; i.e., they must be expected to fulfill similar functions in the entity.
2. The parties to the transaction must be in the same line of business, i.e., they must both be dealers or both be nondealers.
3. A gain must be indicated in the transaction; i.e., the market value of the assets surrendered must exceed their book value.
4. If cash is involved, it is less than 25% of the fair value of the exchange.

To illustrate the special case, three examples are included below. In the first example, no cash is involved in the exchange. In the second example, the exchange includes a transfer of cash. In the third example, cash makes up 25% or more of the value of the transaction.

Example 1—No Cash Involved

The Republic Manufacturing Company owns a special molding machine that it no longer uses because of a change in products being manufactured. The machine still has several years of service remaining. Through discussions with other companies in the industry, Republic has located a buyer, Logan Square Company. However, Logan Square is low on funds and suggests an exchange for one of its machines that could be used in Republic's packaging department. It is decided that both machines meet the definition of being similar in use and have the same market values. The following cost and market data relate to the two machines:

	Republic	Logan
Costs of machines to be exchanged	$46,000	$54,000
Book values of machines to be exchanged	14,000	18,000
Market values of machines to be exchanged	16,000	16,000

The entry on Republic's books to record the exchange is as follows:

Machinery (new)	14,000	
Accumulated Depreciation on Machinery ($46,000 – $14,000)	32,000	
Machinery (old)		46,000

The entry on Logan's books to record the exchange is as follows:

Machinery	16,000	
Accumulated Depreciation on Machinery ($54,000 – $18,000)	36,000	
Loss on Exchange of Machinery	2,000	
Machinery (old)		54,000

22. *EITF Issue No. 86-29,* "Nonmonetary Transactions: Magnitude of Boot and the Exceptions to the Use of Fair Value," *loc. cit.*

Note that in Republic's entry, the special case is used. All four conditions are present: the machines are similar, both parties are nondealers, the market value of the asset surrendered exceeds its book value (an indicated gain), and no cash is involved. Thus, the value assigned to Republic's newly acquired packaging machine is the book value of its old molding machine.

In Logan's entry, however, the general case is used. The market value of the asset exchanged is less than the book value, so a loss is indicated. The molding machine, therefore, is recorded on Logan's books at its market value, the general-case solution.

Example 2 Transfer of Cash

Assume the same facts as in Example 1, except that it is decided the molding machine has a market value of $16,000 and the packaging machine is worth $20,000. To make the exchange equal, Republic agrees to pay Logan Square $4,000 cash (20% of the fair value of the exchange) in addition to the molding machine. The entry on Republic's books for Example 2 is as follows:

Machinery (new)	18,000	
Accumulated Depreciation on Machinery ($46,000 – $14,000)	32,000	
Machinery (old)		46,000
Cash		4,000

As was true for Example 1, the facts of this case require Republic to use the special case. The market value of the assets surrendered ($16,000 + $4,000) exceeds their book values ($14,000 + $4,000). A $2,000 gain is thus indicated. The machines are similar in use and the parties are both nondealers. The gain, therefore, is deferred and not recognized. The new machine is recorded at $18,000, the market value of the asset received in the exchange ($20,000) less the deferred gain ($2,000).

In Example 2, the book value of the packaging machine on Logan Square's books is less than the market value, indicating a gain ($20,000 – $18,000, or $2,000). The similar assets and similar parties indicate the special case; however, because Logan Square received less than 25% cash as part of the transaction, generally accepted accounting principles specify that a portion of the $2,000 **indicated gain** should be recognized as having been earned. The amount to be recognized is computed using the following formula:

$$\text{Recognized gain} = \frac{\text{Cash received}}{\text{Cash received} + \text{Market value of acquired asset}} \times \text{Total indicated gain}$$

Using the figures from Example 2, Logan Square, therefore, would recognize $400 of the gain computed as follows:

$$\frac{\$4{,}000}{\$4{,}000 + \$16{,}000} \times \$2{,}000 = \$400$$

The recorded value of the molding machine on Logan's books is $14,400, the book value of the packaging machine exchanged less the cash received plus the gain recognized, ($18,000 – $4,000 + $400). Another way of computing the recorded value is by deducting the **deferred gain** from the market value of the asset received ($16,000 – $1,600, or $14,400).

The entry on Logan Square's books to record the exchange is as follows:

Cash	4,000	
Machinery (new)	14,400	
Accumulated Depreciation on Machinery ($54,000 – $18,000)	36,000	
Machinery (old)		54,000
Gain on Exchange of Machinery		400

While the exceptions to the general case seem complex, they occur in relatively rare instances. The general effect of the special case is to defer any indicated gain until the new asset is disposed of through sale, trade, or abandonment.[23]

Example 3 Transfer of Cash Exceeding 25% of the Fair Value of the Exchange

Assume the same facts as in Example 2, except that it is decided that the molding machine has a market value of $15,000 and that Republic agrees to pay $5,000 cash to make the exchange equal. In this case, the cash equals 25% of the fair value of the exchange ($20,000), so the transaction is considered to be a monetary exchange with recognition of gains and losses. The entry on Republic's books would be:

Machinery (new)	20,000	
Accumulated Depreciation—Machinery	32,000	
Machinery (old)		46,000
Cash		5,000
Gain on Exchange of Machinery		1,000

The entry on Logan Square's books would be:

Cash	5,000	
Machinery (new)	15,000	
Accumulated Depreciation—Machinery	36,000	
Machinery (old)		54,000
Gain on Exchange of Machinery		2,000

Exhibit 12—6 summarizes the accounting for exchanges under the various conditions.

Exhibit 12—6 Summary of Retirement or Exchange of Noncurrent Operating Assets

Retirement of Assets Exchange of Assets	Recognize All Loss	Recognize All Gain	Recognize No Gain	Recognize Part Gain
Market value of assets surrendered $<$ Book value of assets surrendered (loss condition)	×			
Market value of assets surrendered $>$ Book value of assets surrendered (gain condition):				
1. Dissimilar assets		×		
2. Similar assets:				
a. Earning culminated		×		
b. Earning not culminated:				
(1) No cash involved			×	
(2) Cash given			×	
(3) Cash received				×

Earnings process not culminated for similar assets if:
1. Cash involved $<$ 25% of market value of assets received, and
2. Parties to transaction are both in same line of business.

Effects of above rules on valuation of assets acquired in a retirement or an exchange:
1. If all losses and gains are recognized, the recorded value of all assets received is equal to the market value of the assets surrendered.
2. If no gains are recognized, the recorded value of any nonmonetary asset received is the book value of the asset surrendered plus any cash given.
3. If partial gains are recognized, the recorded value of any nonmonetary asset received is the book value of the asset surrendered less any cash received plus the portion of the gain recognized.

Assumption: Fair market value of assets received and of assets surrendered are equal. If not, use market value of asset that is more clearly evident.

23. For a further discussion of the special case, see James B. Hobbs and D. R. Bainbridge, "Nonmonetary Exchange Transactions: Clarification of APB Opinion No. 29," *Accounting Review* (January 1982), pp. 171-175. Also see David Marcinko and Enrico Petri, "A Clarification of Certain Issues Arising Out of Nonmonetary Exchanges, *Journal of Accounting Education* (1991), pp. 365-372.

Retirement by Involuntary Conversion

Sometimes retirement of noncurrent operating assets occurs because of extensive damage caused by such events as fire, earthquake, flood, or condemnation. Retirements caused by these types of uncontrollable events have been classified as **involuntary conversions.** Some of these events are insurable risks, and the occurrence of the event triggers reimbursement from an insurance company. If the proceeds exceed the book value of the destroyed assets, a gain is recognized on the books. If the proceeds are less than the book value, a loss is recorded.

If the loss was either not insurable or a company failed to carry insurance on the property, the remaining book value of the asset should be recorded as a loss. Because these types of events are unusual and infrequent, the gains and losses realized are often recorded as an extraordinary item. Of course, if the event has a high probability of recurrence, e.g., a factory built in a low area that frequently experiences flooding, the gain or loss may be classified as an ordinary item.

To illustrate the recording of an involuntary conversion, assume that a flood destroyed a factory building with a $1,200,000 cost and a book value of $350,000. If $400,000 was recovered from the flood insurance policy, the entry to record the gain would be as follows:

Receivable From Insurance Company	400,000	
Accumulated Depreciation—Building	850,000	
Building		1,200,000
Gain on Involuntary Conversion		50,000

In some cases, the involuntary conversion is caused by government condemnation of private property. Usually such proceedings require the condemning party to pay a fair market value for the assets seized. This generally results in a recognized gain. Some accountants have argued that since these proceeds are often reinvested in similar assets, the gain on such conversion should be deferred by reducing the cost of the new asset. The FASB, however, has indicated that the condemnation and the acquisition of new assets should be viewed as two separate transactions.[24] Thus, the gain is recognized on the condemnation, and the new assets are recorded at their acquisition cost.

For example, assume that the Valley Mining Company had land condemned by the state for a state park. The cost of the land to Valley was $50,000. The agreed-upon market value was $260,000. The entry to record the cash receipt would be as follows:

Cash	260,000	
Land		50,000
Gain on Condemnation		210,000

BALANCE SHEET PRESENTATION AND DISCLOSURE

Tangible noncurrent operating assets, natural resources, and intangible assets are usually shown separately on the balance sheet. As indicated earlier in this chapter, both the gross cost and accumulated depreciation must be disclosed for depreciable assets. Such disclosure is not required for intangible assets and natural resources, and many companies report only net values for these assets. Because of the alternative cost allocation methods available to compute the charges for depreciation, amortization, and depletion, the methods used must be disclosed in the financial statements. Without this information, a user of the statements might be misled in trying to compare the financial results of one company with another. Cost allocation methods are normally reported in the first note to the financial statements, "Significant Accounting Policies." For example, in the notes to its financial statements included in Appendix A at the end of this text, Microsoft discloses that it uses the straight-line method and has different estimated useful lives for its buildings, its leasehold improvements, and its computer equipment.

24. *FASB Interpretation No. 30,* "Accounting for Involuntary Conversions of Nonmonentary Assets to Monetary Assets," (Stamford: Financial Accounting Standards Board, 1979).

KEY TERMS

Accelerated cost recovery system (ACRS) 492
Amortization 486
Composite depreciation 498
Cost recovery periods 492
Current cost 502
Declining-balance depreciation methods 491
Decreasing-charge depreciation methods 489
Depletion 486
Depreciation 486
Double-declining-balance depreciation 491
Full cost approach 506
Group depreciation 498
Impairment 509
Involuntary conversions 516
Modified accelerated cost recovery system (MACRS) 492
Natural resources 505
Productive-output depreciation 498
Replacement cost 502
Reserve Recognition Accounting (RRA) 507
Residual (salvage) value 487
Service-hours depreciation 497
Similar assets 516
Straight-line depreciation 489
Successful efforts approach 506
Sum-of-the-years-digits depreciation method 490
Time-factor depreciation methods 489
Unit depreciation 498
Use-factor depreciation methods 497
Useful life 487

QUESTIONS

1. Distinguish among depreciation, depletion, and amortization expenses.
2. What factors must be considered in determining the periodic depreciation charges that should be made for a company's depreciable assets?
3. Distinguish between the functional and physical factors affecting the useful life of a tangible noncurrent operating asset.
4. What role does residual or salvage value play in the various methods of time-factor depreciation?
5. Distinguish between time-factor and use-factor methods of depreciation.
6. The accelerated cost recovery system of depreciation is used for income tax purposes but may not be acceptable for financial reporting. Why is this true?
7. The certified public accountant is frequently called on by management for advice regarding methods of computing depreciation. Although the question arises less frequently, of comparable importance is whether the depreciation method should be based on the consideration of the property items as units, as groups, or as having a composite life.
   (a) Briefly describe the depreciation methods based on recognizing property items as (1) units, (2) groups, or (3) having a composite life.
   (b) Present the arguments for and against the use of each of these methods.
   (c) Describe how retirements are recorded under each of these methods.
8. What arguments can be made for charging more than an asset's historical cost against revenue?
9. What factors determine the period and method for amortizing intangible assets?
10. What procedures must be followed when the estimate of recoverable natural resources is changed due to subsequent development work?
11. Under what circumstances should an asset's remaining book value be written off immediately as a loss?
12. Why is 40 years used as the maximum number of years for amortizing an intangible asset?
13. (a) Distinguish between the "full cost" and "successful efforts" approaches to recording exploratory costs for oil and gas properties. (b) The SEC recommended a third approach be followed. What were its distinguishing characteristics?
14. Under what circumstances is a gain or loss recognized when a productive asset is exchanged for a similar productive asset?
15. (a) What are some types of involuntary conversions that can take place with property? (b) What are the arguments for and against recognizing gains and losses on such conversions?
16. Machinery in the finishing department of Universal Co., although less than 50% depreciated, has been replaced by new machinery. The company expects to find a buyer for the old machinery, and on December 31 the machinery is in the yard and available for inspection. How should it be reported on the balance sheet?
17. How should property, wasting assets, and intangibles be reported on the balance sheet? What note disclosure should be made for these assets?

DISCUSSION CASES

Case 12—1 (We don't need no depreciation!)

The managements of two different companies argue that because of specific conditions in their companies, recording depreciation expense should be suspended for 1996. Evaluate carefully their arguments.

(1) The president of Guzman Co. recommends that no depreciation be recorded for 1996 since the depreciation rate is 5% per year, and price indexes show that prices during the year have risen by more than this figure.

(2) The policy of Liebnitz Co. is to recondition its building and equipment each year so that they are maintained in perfect repair. In view of the extensive periodic costs incurred in 1996, officials of the company feel that the need for recognizing depreciation is eliminated.

Case 12—2 (Why write off goodwill?)

The Nevada Corporation purchased the Stardust Club for $2,000,000, which included $500,000 for goodwill. Nevada Corporation incurs large promotional and advertising expenses to maintain Stardust Club's popularity. As the annual financial statements are being prepared, the CPA of the Nevada Corporation, Emily Teeson, insists that some of the goodwill be amortized against revenue. Teeson cites APB Opinion No. 17 that requires all intangible assets to be written off over a maximum life of 40 years. Mark Stevenson, the Nevada Corporation controller, feels that amortization of the purchased goodwill in the same periods as heavy expenses are incurred to maintain the goodwill in effect creates a double charge against income of the period. Stevenson argues that no write-off of goodwill is necessary. Indeed, goodwill has increased in value and should even be increased on the books to reflect this improvement. Evaluate the logic of these two positions.

Case 12—3 (Is it really worth that much?)

International Enterprises, Inc., owns a building in Des Moines, Iowa, that was built at a cost of $5,000,000 in 1985. The building was used as a manufacturing facility from 1986-1995. However, economic conditions have made it necessary to consolidate International's operations, and the building has been leased as of January 1, 1996, as a warehouse for ten years at an annual rental of $240,000. Taxes, insurance, and normal maintenance costs are to be paid by the lessee. At the end of the ten-year period, International may offer the lessee a renewal of the lease, or again use the building in its operations. The building is being depreciated on a straight-line basis over a forty-year life.

Petersen & Sons, a CPA firm, is completing the audit for 1996. Julie Ramos, a new staff auditor, has been assigned to review the building accounts and raises a question with Alison Crowther, the senior auditor on the job, concerning the carrying value of the Des Moines building. Julie had written a paper in school concerning accounting for the impairment of noncurrent operating assets. She feels the Des Moines building has been impaired and should be written down in value. Alison is unsure about the current position of the FASB on this issue, and invites Julie to prepare a memorandum recommending a specific write-down amount, with supporting justification. Prepare the memorandum, assuming current interest rates are 10%.

Case 12—4 (Should alternative methods of depreciation be eliminated?)

The FASB receives recommendations from its advisory board as to areas it should consider for study. Depreciation accounting has not been addressed as a separate topic by the FASB, and several alternative methods are used for recording this expense on the books. Recognizing this situation, assume that a recommendation is made to the Board that a study be made of depreciation accounting with the objective of selecting one method as the only acceptable one. Those making the recommendation reason that only then will comparability in financial statements be achieved. Present the arguments for and against the FASB following the recommendation. If you were a member of the FASB, what would be your position?

Case 12—5 (Which depreciation method should we use?)

The Atwater Manufacturing Company purchased a new machine especially built to perform one particular function on the assembly line. A difference of opinion has arisen as to the method of depreciation to be used in connection with this machine. Three methods are now being considered:

(a) The straight-line method
(b) The productive-output method
(c) The sum-of-the-years-digits method

List separately the arguments for and against each of the proposed methods from both the theoretical and practical viewpoints.

Case 12—6 (Should financial reporting follow tax legislation?)

During the 1960s and 1970s, the United States Congress used a tax measure known as the Investment Tax Credit to encourage companies to expand their investment base. Under these provisions, companies received reductions of their tax liabilities based on a percentage of new investments in noncurrent operating assets. This approach was used in lieu of reducing tax rates as a stimulus to expansion. In 1981, the adoption of the ACRS method of cost allocation for noncurrent operating assets added further stimulation to the economy by permitting companies to write off the cost of their property over a shorter than normal period.

In 1986, Congress passed a massive Tax Reform Act that significantly reduced tax rates for all taxpaying entities. At the same time, the Investment Tax Credit was eliminated and the ACRS legislation was replaced by a modified ACRS approach that lengthened the time period for the allocation. These latter provisions reduced the net impact of the reduced tax rates. Because elected government officials do not like to be identified with increased tax rates, there remains the possibility that further modifications to tax accounting for noncurrent operating assets will be made.

Should financial reporting for noncurrent operating assets be affected by tax legislation? Support your answer.

Case 12—7 (How do we charge that motion picture cost to revenue?)

In today's high tech, high cost entertainment industry, motion pictures often have costs in the tens of millions of dollars. Of course, it is hoped that these movies will be box office winners, and that the revenues will exceed the cost outlay. With first runs, reruns, video reprints, video rentals, etc., it has become increasingly difficult to determine how the initial cost should be amortized against the revenue. Considering this industry and its characteristics, what amortization method would you suggest for these movie production costs?

Case 12—8 (Is nothing sacred?)

FASB Statement No. 93 required all not-for-profit organizations to compute and report depreciation expense in their external financial statements. Previously, many not-for-profits, including many religious institutions, did not report depreciation expense. Many users and preparers of financial statements for religious institutions are upset about the idea of depreciating churches. Robert Anthony, a well-known professor of accounting at Harvard University was quoted as saying, "Depreciating cathedrals and churches is stupid." Monsignor Austin Bennett of Brooklyn claimed that the rule would cause "more trouble for American churches than all the sinners in their congregations." Robert K. Mautz in an article "Monuments, Mistakes and Opportunities," *Accounting Horizons*, June 1988, argues that buildings and monuments owned by governments and not-for-profit institutions may be more liabilities than assets because no revenue is generated from them, but they must be maintained. In considering this issue, the following questions and comments were raised in an accounting class:

1. Why do churches prepare external financial statements?
2. It is claimed that requiring churches to record depreciation expense will increase the cost of a church's annual audit. How?
3. One person was quoted in *The Wall Street Journal* as saying, "As some . . . communities change in character, so does the value of the churches. Our depreciation values would have to change every year."

How would you respond to these questions and comments in the class discussion?

Source: Lee Berton. "Is Nothing Sacred? Churches Fight Plan to Alter Accounting." *The Wall Street Journal* (April 16, 1987), p. 1.

Case 12—9 (Let's take a bath!)

DeAngelo (1988) finds evidence suggesting that when the management of a company is ousted under fire, the new management tends to take an earnings "bath" after gaining control. A "bath" is a large reduction in earnings due to asset write-downs, reorganization charges, discontinuance of segments, and other extraordinary charges.

As an example, The Circle K Corporation declared Chapter 11 bankruptcy and also changed management during fiscal 1990. For the year, Circle K reported a reorganization and restructuring charge of $639 million, consisting primarily of write-downs of long-term assets. This contributed to a net loss for the year of $773 million, compared to average net income for the previous 4 years of about $40 million per year. Why might the new management of a company want to "take a bath" in its first year?

Sources:
Linda DeAngelo. "Managerial Compensation, Information Costs, and Corporate Governance." *Journal of Accounting and Economics* 10 (January 1988), pp. 3-36.
1990 Annual Report of The Circle K Corporation.

Case 12—10 (But what is a reasonable life for my airplane?)

Airlines are often used as illustrations of firms depreciating the same assets but using different useful life and residual value assumptions. As an example, Continental Airlines depreciates its aircraft over a period of 28 years while Delta Airlines has a policy of depreciating its aircraft, many of which are the same Boeing aircraft Continental uses, over a period of 15 years. What might cause a firm to decide to increase the estimated useful life of a depreciable asset?

EXERCISES

Exercise 12—11 (Computation of asset cost and depreciation expense)

A machine is purchased at the beginning of 1996 for $36,000. Its estimated life is 6 years. Freight-in on the machine is $2,000. Installation costs are $1,200. The machine is estimated to have a residual value of $2,000 and a useful life of 40,000 hours. It was used 6,000 hours in 1996.

1. What is the cost of the machine for accounting purposes?
2. Compute the depreciation charge for 1996 using (a) the straight-line method and (b) the service-hours method.

Exercise 12—12 (Computation of depreciation expense)

The Feng Company purchased a machine for $180,000 on June 15, 1996. It is estimated that the machine will have a 10-year life and a salvage value of $18,000. Its working hours and production in units are estimated at 36,000 and 600,000, respectively. It is the company's policy to take a half-year's depreciation on all assets for which it used the straight-line or double-declining-balance depreciation method in the year of purchase. During 1996, the machine was operated 5,000 hours and produced 70,000 units. Which of the following methods will give the greatest depreciation expense for 1996? (1) double-declining balance; (2) productive-output; or (3) service-hours. (Show computations for all three methods.)

Exercise 12—13 (Service-hours depreciation)

Jen and Barry's Ice Milk Company used cash to purchase a new ice milk mixer on January 1, 1996. The new mixer is estimated to have a 20,000-hour service life. Jen and Barry's depreciates equipment on the service-hours method. The total price paid for the machine was $57,000. This price included $2,000 freight-in, $1,800 installation costs, and $3,000 for a two-year maintenance contract.

During 1996, Jen and Barry's used the machine for 2,500 hours and in 1997, 3,000 hours. Prepare all related journal entries for purchase of equipment, annual depreciation, and maintenance expense for 1996 and 1997.

Exercise 12—14 (Inferring useful lives)

The following information is from the balance sheet of Hampton Company for December 31, 1996, and December 31, 1995:

	Dec. 31, 1996	Dec. 31, 1995
Cost—Equipment	$ 980,000	$ 980,000
Accumulated Depreciation—Equipment	(550,000)	(330,000)
Cost—Buildings	2,450,000	2,450,000
Accumulated Depreciation—Buildings	(340,000)	(230,000)

Hampton did not acquire or dispose of any buildings or equipment during 1996. Hampton uses the straight-line method of depreciation. If residual values are assumed to be 10% of asset cost, what is the average useful life of Hampton's (a) equipment? (b) buildings?

Exercise 12—15 (Computation of depreciation expense)

Ray Construction purchased a concrete mixer on July 15, 1996. Company officials revealed the following information regarding this asset and its acquisition:

Purchase price	$125,000
Residual value	$ 18,000
Estimated useful life	10 years
Estimated service hours	38,000
Estimated production in units	500,000 yards

The concrete mixer was operated by construction crews in 1996 for a total of 5,225 hours and it produced 77,000 yards of concrete.

It is company policy to take a half-year's depreciation on all assets for which it used the straight-line or double-declining-balance depreciation method in the year of purchase.

Calculate the resulting depreciation expense for 1996 under each of the following methods and specify which method allows the greatest depreciation expense:

1. Double-declining balance
2. Productive-output
3. Service-hours
4. Straight-line

Exercise 12—16 (Computation of book and tax depreciation)

Midwest States Manufacturing purchased factory equipment on March 15, 1995. The equipment will be depreciated for financial purposes over its estimated useful life, counting the year of acquisition as one-half year. The company accountant revealed the following information regarding this machine:

Purchase price	$75,000
Residual value	$9,000
Estimated useful life (class life)	10 years

1. What amount should Midwest States Manufacturing record for depreciation expense for 1996 using the (a) double-declining-balance method? (b) sum-of-the-years-digits method?
2. Assuming the equipment is classified as 7-year property under the modified accelerated cost recovery system (MACRS), what amount should Midwest States Manufacturing deduct for depreciation on its tax return in 1996?

Exercise 12—17 (MACRS computation)

The Timpanogas Equipment Company purchases a new piece of factory equipment on May 1, 1996, for $26,500. For income tax purposes, the equipment is classified as a 7-year asset. Because this is similar to the economic life expected for the asset, Timpanogas decides to use the tax depreciation for financial reporting purposes. The equipment is not expected to have any residual value at the end of the seven years. Prepare a depreciation schedule for the life of the asset using the MACRS method of cost recovery.

Exercise 12—18 (Productive-output depreciation and asset retirement)

Equipment was purchased at the beginning of 1994 for $100,000 with an estimated product life of 300,000 units. The estimated salvage value was $4,000. During 1994, 1995, and 1996, the equipment produced 80,000 units, 120,000 units, and 40,000 units, respectively. The machine was damaged at the beginning of 1997, and the equipment was scrapped with no salvage value.

1. Determine depreciation using the productive-output method for 1994, 1995, and 1996.
2. Give the entry to write off the equipment at the beginning of 1997.

Exercise 12—19 (Composite depreciation)

Holdaway, Inc., a small furniture manufacturer, purchased the following assets at the end of 1995:

Description	Cost	Salvage	Life
Delivery truck	$24,000	$5,000	5 years
Circular Saws (2)	900	130	7 years
Workbench	320	—	8 years
Forklift	6,000	500	5 years

Compute the following amounts for 1996 using composite depreciation on a straight-line basis:

(a) depreciation expense
(b) composite depreciation rate
(c) composite life of the assets

Exercise 12—20 (Composite depreciation)

A schedule of machinery owned by Delgado Manufacturing Company is presented below:

	Total Cost	Estimated Salvage Value	Estimated Life in Years
Machine A	$700,000	$70,000	12
Machine B	200,000	20,000	8
Machine C	40,000	—	5

Delgado computes depreciation on the straight-line method. Based on the information presented, calculate (a) the composite depreciation rate and (b) the composite life of these assets.

Exercise 12—21 (Group depreciation—closed group)

The NLG International Co. maintains its tools and dies on a closed group basis. A new group is created for each year's purchase of tools and dies. The assets are depreciated at a 25% rate beginning in the year following the acquisition year. Any gain or loss is deferred until final disposition of the entire group of assets. Assume that for 1995, $150,000 was spent for tools and dies. Disposition of these tools and dies was made as follows (assume that disposals occurred at the beginning of each year):

Year	Cost	Disposition Cash Price
1996	$ 3,000	$ 1,500
1997	22,000	9,000
1998	53,000	22,000
1999	42,000	17,500
2000	10,000	3,000
2001	20,000	2,000

Prepare all journal entries required to account for tools and dies for the years 1996-2001. All tools and dies are disposed of by the beginning of 2001.

Exercise 12—22 (Group depreciation entries—open group)

Lundquist, Inc., uses the group-depreciation method for its furniture account. The depreciation rate used for furniture is 21%. The balance in the furniture account on December 31, 1995, was $125,000, and the balance in Accumulated Depreciation—Furniture was $61,000. The following purchases and dispositions of furniture occurred in the years 1996-1998 (assume that disposals occurred at the beginning of each year):

		Assets Sold	
Year	Assets Purchased—Cost (Cash)	Cost	Selling Price (Cash)
1996	$35,000	$27,000	$8,000
1997	27,600	15,000	6,000
1998	24,500	32,000	8,000

1. Prepare the summary journal entries Lundquist should make each year (1996-1998) for the purchase, disposition, and depreciation of furniture.
2. Prepare a summary of the furniture and accumulated depreciation accounts for the years 1996-1998.

Exercise 12—23 (Depreciation of special components)

Towsey Manufacturing acquired a new milling machine on April 1, 1991. The machine has a special component that requires replacement before the end of the useful life. The asset was originally recorded in two accounts, one representing the main unit and the other for the special component. Depreciation is recorded by the straight-line method to the nearest month, residual values being disregarded. On April 1, 1997, the special component is scrapped and is replaced with a similar component. This component is expected to have a residual value of approximately 25% of cost at the end of the useful life of the main unit and because of its materiality, the residual value will be considered in calculating depreciation. Specific asset information is as follows:

Main milling machine:	
Purchase price in 1991	$52,400
Residual value	$ 4,400
Estimated useful life	10 years
First special component:	
Purchase price	$10,000
Residual value	$ 250
Estimated useful life	6 years
Second special component:	
Purchase price	$15,250

What are the depreciation charges to be recognized for the years (a) 1991, (b) 1997, and (c) 1998?

Exercise 12—24 (Accounting for patents)

The Deep South Co. applied for and received numerous patents at a total cost of $30,345 at the beginning of 1991. It is assumed the patents will be useful evenly during their full legal life. At the beginning of 1993, the company paid $7,875 in successfully prosecuting an attempted infringement of these patent rights. At the beginning of 1996, $25,200 was paid to acquire patents that could make its own patents worthless; the patents acquired have a remaining life of 15 years but will not be used.

1. Give the entries to record the expenditures relative to patents.
2. Give the entries to record patent amortization for the years 1991, 1993, and 1996.

Exercise 12—25 (Depletion expense)

On January 2, 1995, Cynthia Foster purchased land with valuable natural ore deposits for $10 million. The estimated residual value of the land was $2 million. At the time of purchase, a geological survey estimated 2 million tons of removable ore was under the ground. During 1995, roads were constructed on the land to aid in the extraction and transportation of the mined ore at a cost of $550,000. In 1995, 50,000 tons were mined. In 1996, Cynthia fired her mining engineer and hired a new expert. A new survey made at the end of 1996 estimated 3 million tons of ore were available for mining. In 1996, 150,000 tons were mined. Assuming all the ore mined was sold, how much was the depletion expense for 1995 and 1996?

Exercise 12—26 (Computation and recording of depletion expense)

Rich Strike Mining sought to increase reserves of a special mineral resource. During 1994, the company purchased a piece of property that was expected to retain some value after removal of the mineral resources was complete. Company records reveal the following:

In the year 1994:	
Purchase price for property	$4,450,000
Estimated supply of mineral resource	3,640,000 tons
Estimated property value after removal of mineral resource	$650,000
Total resource removal this year	0 tons
In the year 1995:	
Developmental costs	$750,000
Total resource removal this year	0 tons
In the year 1996:	
Total resource removal this year	700,000 tons
In the year 1997:	
Estimated total resources to be recovered in future years (based on new discoveries)	3,660,000 tons
Additional developmental costs	$1,195,800
Total resource removal this year	850,000 tons

Show computations and entries made to recognize depletion for (a) 1996 and (b) 1997.

Exercise 12—27 (Full cost and successful efforts)

Playfair Company is an oil and gas exploration firm. During 1996, Playfair engaged in 67 different exploratory projects. Only 9 of these projects were successful. The total cost of this exploration effort was $12 million, $2 million of which was associated with the successful projects. As of the end of 1996, production had not yet begun at the successful sites.

1. Using the successful efforts method of accounting for oil and gas exploration costs, how much exploration expense would be shown in Playfair's income statement for 1996? How much of the exploration cost will be capitalized and shown as an asset on the company's balance sheet as of December 31, 1996?
2. What would be your answers if Playfair uses the full cost method?

Exercise 12—28 (Change in estimated useful life)

Zierbel Corporation purchased a machine on January 1, 1991, for $300,000. At the date of acquisition, the machine had an estimated useful life of 15 years with no salvage value. The machine is being depreciated on a straight-line basis. On January 1, 1996, as a result of Zierbel's experience with the machine, it was decided that the machine had an estimated useful life of 10 years from the date of acquisition. What is the amount of depreciation expense on this machine in 1996 using a new annual depreciation charge for the remaining 5 years?

Exercise 12—29 (Change in estimated useful life)

Pierce Corporation purchased a machine on July 1, 1993, for $180,000. The machine was estimated to have a useful life of 10 years with an estimated salvage value of $10,000. During 1996 it became apparent that the machine would become uneconomical after December 31, 2000, and that the machine would have no scrap value. Pierce uses the straight-line method of depreciation for all machinery. What should be the charge for depreciation in 1996 under a new annual depreciation charge for the remaining life?

Exercise 12—30 (Recording the sale of equipment with note)

On December 31, 1996, Beckham Corporation sold for $10,000 an old machine having an original cost of $50,000 and a book value of $6,000. The terms of the sale were as follows: $2,000 down payment, $4,000 payable on December 31 of the next two years. The agreement of sale made no mention of interest; however, 10% would be a fair rate for this type of transaction. Give the journal entries on Beckham's books to record the sale of the machine and receipt of the two subsequent payments. (Round to the nearest dollar.)

Exercise 12—31 (Recording the sale of equipment)

Schuthess, Inc., purchased equipment costing $220,000 on June 30, 1995, having an estimated life of 5 years and a residual value of $40,000. The company uses the sum-of-the-years-digits method of depreciation and takes one-half year's depreciation on assets in the year of purchase. The asset was sold on December 31, 1997, for $75,000. Give the entry to record the sale of the equipment.

Exercise 12—32 (Exchange of machinery)

Assume that Coaltown Corporation has a machine that cost $52,000, has a book value of $35,000, and has a market value of $40,000. The machine is used in Coaltown's manufacturing process. For each of the following situations, indicate the value at which the company should record the new asset and why it should be recorded at that value.

(a) Coaltown exchanged the machine for a truck with a list price of $43,000.
(b) Coaltown exchanged the machine with another manufacturing company for a similar machine with a list price of $41,000.
(c) Coaltown exchanged the machine for a newer model machine from another manufacturing company. The new machine had a list price of $60,000, and Coaltown paid cash of $15,000.
(d) Coaltown exchanged the machine plus $3,000 cash for a similar machine from Newton Inc., a manufacturing company. The newly acquired machine is carried on Newton's books at its cost of $55,000 with accumulated depreciation of $42,000; its fair market value is $43,000. In addition to determining the value, give the journal entries for both companies to record the exchange.

Exercise 12—33 (Exchange of truck)

On January 2, 1996, Bline Delivery Company traded with a dealer an old delivery truck for a newer model. Data relative to the old and new trucks follows:

Old truck:	
Original cost	$12,000
Accumulated depreciation as of January 2, 1996	9,000
Average published market price	1,700
New truck:	
List price	$15,000
Cash price without trade-in	14,000
Cash paid with trade-in	12,700

1. Give the journal entries on Bline's books to record the purchase of the new truck.
2. Give the journal entries on Bline's books if the cash paid was $10,700.

Exercise 12—34 (Exchange of assets)

The Maynard Equipment Company exchanged the following assets during 1996. Prepare the journal entries on Maynard's books for each exchange.

(a) Exchanged with Loeb Equipment Company (dealer to dealer) a similar machine. Cost of machine exchanged, $25,000; book value of machine exchanged, $13,000; market value of machine exchanged, $15,000. No cash received.
(b) Same as in (a), except received $3,000 cash and machine with market value of $12,000.
(c) Purchased from Baker Manufacturing Company (dealer to nondealer) a new machine with a $50,000 list price. Paid $35,000 cash and a similar used machine; cost of machine exchanged, $40,000; book value of machine exchanged, $12,000; market value of machine exchanged, $10,000.

PROBLEMS

Problem 12—35 (Time-factor methods of depreciation)

A delivery truck was acquired by Navarro Inc. for $20,000 on January 1, 1995. The truck was estimated to have a 3-year life and a trade-in value at the end of that time of $5,000. The following depreciation methods are being considered:

(a) Depreciation is to be calculated by the straight-line method.
(b) Depreciation is to be calculated by the sum-of-the-years-digits method.
(c) Depreciation is to be calculated by the 150% declining-balance method.
(d) Depreciation is to be calculated using the modified accelerated cost recovery system for 5-year recovery property.

Instructions: Prepare tables reporting periodic depreciation and asset book value over a 3-year period for each assumption listed.

Problem 12—36 (Depreciation under different methods)

On January 1, 1993, Ron Shelley purchased a new tractor to use on his farm. The tractor cost $100,000. Ron also had the dealer install a front-end loader on the tractor. The cost of the front-end loader was $7,000. The shipping charges were $600 and the cost to install the loader was $800. The estimated life of the tractor was 8 years and the estimated service-hour life of the tractor was 11,200 hours. Ron estimated that he could sell the tractor for $15,000 at the end of 8 years or 11,200 hours. The tractor was used for 1,725 hours in 1996. A full year's depreciation was taken in 1993, the year of acquisition.

Instructions: Compute depreciation expense for 1996 under each of the following methods:

1. Straight-line
2. Double-declining balance
3. Sum-of-the-years-digits
4. Service-hours

Problem 12—37 (Maintenance charges and depreciation of components)

A company buys a machine for $25,400 on January 1, 1994. The maintenance costs for the years 1994-1997 are as follows: 1994, $1,500; 1995, $1,200; 1996, $7,300 (includes $6,100 for cost of a new motor installed in December 1996); 1997, $2,100.

Instructions:

1. Assume the machine is recorded in a single account at a cost of $25,400. No record is kept of the cost of the component parts. Straight-line depreciation is used and the asset is estimated to have a useful life of 8 years. It is assumed there will be no residual value at the end of the useful life. What are the total expenses related to the machine for each of the first 4 years?
2. Assume the cost of the frame of the machine was recorded in one account at a cost of $19,600 and the motor was recorded in a second account at a cost of $5,800. Straight-line depreciation is used with a useful life of 10 years for the frame and 4 years for the motor. Neither item is assumed to have any residual value at the end of its useful life. What are the total expenses and losses related to the machine?
3. Evaluate the two methods.

Problem 12—38 (Depreciation and the steady state)

Lyell Company started a newspaper delivery business on January 1, 1996. On that date, the company purchased a small pickup truck for $7,000. Lyell planned to depreciate the truck over 3 years and assumed a $400 residual value. During 1996 and 1997, Lyell's business expanded. On January 1, 1997, Lyell purchased a second truck, identical to the first. On January 1, 1998, Lyell purchased a third truck, again identical to the first two. During 1998, Lyell's growth leveled off. However, on January 1, 1999, Lyell bought another truck to replace the one (purchased in 1996) that had just worn out. All trucks purchased cost the same amount as the first truck.

Instructions:

1. Compute depreciation expense for 1996, 1997, 1998, and 1999 using both of the following methods:
   (a) straight-line
   (b) sum-of-the-years-digits
2. What general conclusions can be drawn from your calculations in (1)?

Problem 12—39 (Group depreciation and asset retirement)

The Wright Manufacturing Co. acquired 20 similar machines at the beginning of 1992 for $75,000. The machines have an average life of 5 years and no residual value. The group-depreciation method is employed in writing off the cost of the machines. They were retired as follows:

2 machines at the end of 1994	8 machines at the end of 1996
4 machines at the end of 1995	6 machines at the end of 1997

Assume the machines were not replaced.

Instructions: Give the entries to record the retirement of the machines and the periodic depreciation for the years 1992-1997 inclusive.

Problem 12—40 (Composite depreciation)

Machines are acquired by Siegel Inc. on March 1, 1996, as follows:

Machines	Cost	Estimated Residual Value	Estimated Life in Years
#301	$46,000	$6,000	5
#302	20,000	2,000	6
#303	20,000	4,000	8
#304	18,000	1,500	6
#305	26,000	None	10

Instructions:

1. Calculate the composite-depreciation rate for this group.
2. Calculate the composite or average life in years for the group.
3. Give the entry to record the depreciation for the year ending December 31, 1996.

Problem 12—41 (Depreciation of racing bicycles)

The following independent cases describe facts concerning the ownership of racing bicycles.

(a) Maurizio Fondriest, winner of the 1993 Milan-San Remo cycling classic, purchased a new Colnago bicycle for $8,000 at the beginning of 1993. The bicycle was being depreciated using the straight-line method over an estimated useful life of seven years, with a $1,000 salvage value. At the beginning of 1995, the Italian superstar paid $1,600 to upgrade the bicycle. As a result, the useful life of the bicycle was extended by one year. The salvage value remained $1,000.

(b) John Museeuw, winner of his country's own Tour of Flanders cycling classic in 1993, purchased a new Bianchi bicycle for $6,000 at the beginning of 1992. The bicycle was being depreciated using the double-declining balance method over an estimated useful life of five years, with a $1,000 salvage value. At the beginning of 1993, when the Belgian superstar won at Flanders, the salvage value of his Bianchi (eventual selling price) jumped to $2,000.

(c) Gilbert Duclose-Lasalle, winner of the 1992 and 1993 Paris-Roubaix cycling classics, purchased a new Greg Lemond bicycle for $7,000 in 1991. The French superstar did not use his new bicycle during the 1991 season. However, in 1992 and 1993 Lasalle used his bicycle to win Paris-Roubaix and logged 6,000 and 8,000 kilometers respectively each year. Lasalle estimated that the bicycle had a productive life of 20,000 kilometers. He did not use the bike in 1994, but in 1995 he decided to upgrade the bike with $2,000 of new components giving the bicycle an additional 10,000 kilometers of productive use. During the 1995 season, he logged 12,000 kilometers on the bike. The estimated salvage value of the bicycle is $1,000.

Instructions: In each case, compute the depreciation for 1995.

Problem 12—42 (Accounting for patents)

On January 10, 1989, the Masterson Company spent $96,000 to apply for and obtain a patent on a newly developed product. The patent had an estimated useful life of 10 years. At the beginning of 1993, the company spent $18,000 in successfully prosecuting an attempted infringement of the patent. At the beginning of 1994, the company purchased for $40,000 a patent that was expected to prolong the life of its original patent by 5 years. On July 1, 1997, a competitor obtained rights to a patent which made the company's patent obsolete.

Instructions: Give all the entries that would be made relative to the patent for the period 1989-1997, including entries to record the purchase of the patent, annual patent amortization, and ultimate patent obsolescence. (Assume the company's accounting period is the calender year.)

Problem 12—43 (Financial statements for mining company)

The Roscoe Corp. was organized on January 2, 1996. It was authorized to issue 74,000 shares of common stock, par $50. On the date of organization, it sold 20,000 shares at par and gave the remaining shares in exchange for certain land bearing recoverable ore deposits estimated by geologists at 900,000 tons. The property is deemed to have a value of $2,700,000 with no residual value.

During 1996, purchases of mine buildings and equipment totaled $250,000. During the year, 75,000 tons were mined; 8,000 tons of this amount were on hand unsold on December 31, the balance of the tonnage being sold for cash at $17 per ton. Expenses incurred and paid for during the year, exclusive of depletion and depreciation, were as follows:

Mining	$173,500
Delivery	20,000
General and administrative	19,500

Cash dividends of $2 per share were declared on December 31, payable January 15, 1997.

It is believed that buildings and sheds will be useful only over the life of the mine; hence, depreciation is to be recognized in terms of mine output.

Instructions: Prepare an income statement and a balance sheet for 1996. Submit working papers showing the development of statement data. Ignore income taxes.

Problem 12—44 (Depletion expense)

In 1993, the Kilbourne Mining Co. purchased property with natural resources for $6,200,000. The property was relatively close to a large city and had an expected residual value of $1,500,000. However, $600,000 will have to be spent to restore the land for use.

The following information relates to the use of the property:

1. In 1993, Kilbourne spent $400,000 in development costs and $300,000 in buildings on the property. Kilbourne does not anticipate that the buildings will have any utility after the natural resources are depleted.
2. In 1994 and 1996, $300,000 and $800,000, respectively, was spent for additional developments on the mine.
3. The tonnage mined and estimated remaining tons for years 1993-1997 are as follows:

Year	Tons Extracted	Estimated Tons Remaining
1993		5,000,000
1994	1,500,000	3,500,000
1995	1,800,000	2,000,000
1996	1,700,000	900,000
1997	900,000	-0-

Instructions: Compute the depletion and depreciation expense for the years 1993-1997.

Problem 12—45 (Depletion and depreciation)

Sunbeam Corporation owns and operates three gold mines in Northern Zimbabwe. In 1992 Sunbeam acquired a silver mine in eastern Alaska. Because the mine is located deep in the Alaskan frontier, Sunbeam was able to acquire the mine for the low price of $50,000. In 1993 Sunbeam constructed a road from Nowhere to Somewhere costing $5,000,000. The road was built to facilitate the removal and transportation of the mined silver ore. Improvements to the mine made in 1993 cost $750,000. Because of the improvements to the mine and to the surrounding land, it is estimated that the mine can be sold for $600,000 when mining activities are complete.

During 1994, five buildings were constructed near the mine site to house the mine workers and their families. The total cost of the five buildings was $1,500,000. Estimated residual value is $250,000. In 1992, geologists estimated 4 million tons of silver ore could be removed from the mine for refining. During 1995, the first year of operations, only 5,000 tons of silver ore were removed from the mine. However, in 1996, workers mined one million tons of silver. During that same year, geologists discovered that the mine contained three million tons of silver ore in addition to the original four million tons. Improvements of $275,000 were made to the mine early in 1996 to facilitate the removal of the additional silver. Early in 1996, an additional building was constructed at a cost of $225,000 to house the additional workers needed to excavate the added silver. This building is not expected to have any residual value.

In 1997, 2.5 million tons of silver were mined and costs of $500,000 were incurred at the beginning of the year for improvements to the mine.

Instructions:

1. Compute the depreciation and depletion charges for 1995, 1996, and 1997.
2. Give the journal entries to record the depreciation and depletion charges for 1997.

Problem 12—46 (Computation of depreciation and depletion)

The following independent situations describe facts concerning the ownership of various assets.

(a) The Dewey Company purchased a tooling machine in 1986 for $60,000. The machine was being depreciated on the straight-line method over an estimated useful life of 20 years, with no salvage value. At the beginning of 1996, when the machine had been in use for 10 years, Dewey paid $12,000 to overhaul the machine. As a result of this improvement, Dewey estimated that the useful life of the machine would be extended an additional 5 years.

(b) Emerson Manufacturing Co., a calendar-year company, purchased a machine for $65,000 on January 1, 1994. At the date of purchase, Emerson incurred the following additional costs:

Loss on sale of old machinery	$1,500
Freight-in	500
Installation cost	2,000
Testing costs prior to regular operation	400

The estimated salvage value of the machine was $5,000 and Emerson estimated that the machine would have a useful life of 20 years, with depreciation being computed on the straight-line method. In January 1996, accessories costing $4,860 were added to the machine in order to reduce its operating costs. These accessories neither prolonged the machine's life nor did they provide any additional salvage value.

(c) On July 1, 1996, Lund Corporation purchased equipment at a cost of $34,000. The equipment has an estimated salvage value of $3,000 and is being depreciated over an estimated life of eight years under the double-declining-balance method of depreciation. For the six months ended December 31, 1996, Lund recorded one-half year's depreciation.

(d) The Aiken Company acquired a tract of land containing an extractable natural resource. Aiken is required by its purchase contract to restore the land to a condition suitable for recreational use after it has extracted the natural resource. Geological surveys estimate that the recoverable reserves will be 3,800,000 tons, and that the land will have a value of $500,000 after restoration. Relevant cost information follows:

Land	$9,000,000
Estimated restoration costs	$1,000,000
Tons mined and sold in 1996	700,000

(e) In January 1996, Marcus Corporation entered into a contract to acquire a new machine for its factory. The machine, which had a cash price of $200,000, was paid for as follows:

Down payment	$ 30,000
Notes payable in 10 equal monthly installments, including interest at 10%	150,000
500 shares of Marcus common stock with an agreed value of $50 per share	25,000
Total	$205,000

Prior to the machine's use, installation costs of $7,000 were incurred. The machine has an estimated useful life of 10 years and an estimated salvage value of $10,000. The straight-line method of depreciation is used.

Instructions: In each case, compute the amount of depreciation or depletion for 1996.

Problem 12—47 (Depreciation and the cash flow statement)

Hutton Company is a manufacturing firm. Work-in-process and finished goods inventories for December 31, 1996, and December 31, 1995, are listed below.

	Dec. 31, 1996	Dec. 31, 1995
Work-in-process inventory (including depreciation)	$ 60,000	$ 63,000
Finished goods inventory (including depreciation)	131,000	120,000

Depreciation is a major portion of Hutton's overhead, and the inventories listed above include depreciation in the following amounts:

	Dec. 31, 1996	Dec. 31, 1995
Depreciation included in work-in-process inventory	$14,000	$13,000
Depreciation included in finished goods inventory	30,000	32,000

Hutton's net income for 1996 was $50,000. General and administrative expenses for the year included $16,000 in depreciation related to non-manufacturing functions.

Instructions: Compute net cash flow from operating activities for Hutton Company for 1996. Assume that the levels of all current assets (except for inventories) and all current liabilities were unchanged from beginning of year to end of year.

Problem 12—48 (Tax depreciation methods and the time value of money)

The following two depreciation methods are acceptable for tax purposes:

(a) Straight-line with a half-year convention. The half-year convention is the assumption that all assets are acquired in the middle of the year. Therefore, a half-year's depreciation is allowed in the first year.

(b) 200% declining-balance with a half-year convention. There is a switchover to straight-line depreciation on the remaining cost when straight-line yields a larger amount than does 200% declining-balance.

On January 1, 1996, Burnet Company purchased a piece of equipment for $500,000. The equipment has an estimated useful life of 5 years and no estimated residual value.

Instructions:

1. For tax purposes, depreciation reduces taxes payable by reducing taxable income. If the tax rate is 40%, for example, a $100 depreciation deduction will reduce taxes by $40. Ignoring the time value of money, calculate the total reduction in taxes Burnet will realize through the recovery of the asset cost over the life of the equipment. Assume that the tax rate is 40%. Is the answer the same for each of the two acceptable depreciation methods?
2. For each of the acceptable methods, compute the present value (as of January 1, 1996) of the depreciation tax savings. Assume that the appropriate interest rate is 10% and that the tax savings occur at the end of the year. Use the present value tables in Chapter 7.
3. Should a company be required to use the same depreciation method in its financial statements as it uses for tax purposes?

Problem 12—49 (Exchange of assets)

A review of the books of Lakeshore Electric Co. disclosed that there were five transactions involving gains and losses on the exchange of fixed assets. The transactions were recorded as indicated in the following ledger accounts:

Cash

(b)	5,000	(e)	1,000
(c)	6,000		

Buildings and Equipment

(a)	10,000	(c)	118,000
(b)	25,000	(d)	850,000
(d)	550,000		

Accum. Depr.—Buildings and Equipment

(c)	110,000		
(d)	390,000		

Intangible Assets

(e)	1,000		

Gain on Exchange—Buildings and Equipment

		(a)	10,000
		(b)	30,000
		(d)	90,000

Loss on Exchange—Buildings and Equipment

(c)	2,000		

Investigation disclosed the following facts concerning these dealer-to-dealer transactions:

(a) Exchanged a piece of equipment with a $50,000 original cost, $20,000 book value, and $30,000 current market value for a piece of similar equipment owned by Highlite Electric that had a $60,000 original cost, $10,000 book value, and a $30,000 current market value.

(b) Exchanged a machine, cost $70,000, book value $10,000, current market value $40,000, for a similar machine, market value $35,000, and $5,000 in cash.

(c) Exchanged a building, cost $150,000, book value $40,000, current market value $30,000, for a building with market value of $24,000 plus cash of $6,000.

(d) Exchanged a factory building, cost $850,000, book value $460,000, current market value $550,000, for equipment owned by Romeo Inc. that had an original cost of $900,000, accumulated depreciation of $325,000, and current market value of $550,000.

(e) Exchanged a patent, cost $12,000, book value $6,000, current market value $3,000 and cash of $1,000 for another patent with market value of $4,000.

Instructions: Analyze each recorded transaction as to its compliance with generally accepted accounting principles. Prepare adjusting journal entries where required.

Problem 12—50 (Exchange of assets)

The Mutual Development Co. acquired the following assets in exchange for various nonmonetary assets:

1996

Mar. 15 Acquired from another company a computerized lathe in exchange for three old lathes. The old lathes had a total cost of $35,000 and had a remaining book value of $14,000. The new lathe had a market value of $22,000, approximately the same value as the three old lathes.

June 1 Acquired 200 acres of land by issuing 3,000 shares of common stock with par value of $10 and market value of $90. Market analysis reveals that the market value of the stock was a reasonable value for the land.

July 15 Acquired a used piece of heavy, earth-moving equipment, market value $120,000, by exchanging a used molding machine with a market value of $20,000 (book value $8,000; cost $40,000) and land with a market value of $110,000 (cost $40,000). Cash of $10,000 was received by Mutual Development Co. as part of the transaction.

Aug. 15 Acquired a patent, franchise, and copyright for two used milling machines. The book value of each milling machine was $1,500 and each had originally cost $10,000. The market value of each machine is $12,500. It is estimated that the patent and franchise have about the same market values, and the market value of the copyright is 50% of the market value of the patent.

Nov. 1 Acquired from a dealer a new packaging machine for four old packaging machines. The old machines had a total cost of $50,000 and a total remaining book value of $20,000. The new packaging machine has an indicated market value of $30,000, approximately the same value as the four machines.

Instructions: Prepare the journal entries required on Mutual Development Co.'s books to record the exchanges.

Problem 12—51 (Balance sheet presentation of noncurrent operating assets)

The following account balances pertain to the Liberty Company:

Account Title	Debit	Credit
Equipment	$ 675,000	
Goodwill	435,000	
Inventory	90,000	
Land	400,000	
Franchises	260,000	
Cash	65,000	
Accounts Receivable	137,000	
Buildings	1,400,000	
Patents	15,000	
Notes Receivable	456,000	
Accumulated Depreciation—Equipment		$ 365,000
Accounts Payable		147,000
Notes Payable		1,500,000
Accumulated Depreciation—Buildings		385,000

Additional information:

(a) Notes payable in the amount of $600,000 are secured by a direct lien on the building.
(b) The company uses the sum-of-the-years-digits method of cost allocation for buildings and equipment and uses straight-line for patents, franchises, and goodwill.
(c) Inventory valuation was made using the retail method.

Instructions: Prepare the land, buildings, and equipment section and the intangible asset section of the balance sheet.

Problem 12—52 (Computation of depreciation and amortization)

Information pertaining to Hedlund Corporation's property, plant, and equipment for 1996 is presented below.

Account balances at January 1, 1996:

	Debit	Credit
Land	$ 150,000	
Buildings	1,200,000	
Accumulated Depreciation—Buildings		$263,100
Machinery and Equipment	900,000	
Accumulated Depreciation—Machinery and Equipment		250,000
Automotive Equipment	115,000	
Accumulated Depreciation—Automotive Equipment		84,600

Depreciation data:

	Depreciation Method	Useful Life
Buildings	150% declining-balance	25 years
Machinery and Equipment	Straight-line	10 years
Automotive Equipment	Sum-of-the-years-digits	4 years
Leasehold Improvements	Straight-line	

The salvage values of the depreciable assets are immaterial. Depreciation is computed to the nearest month.

Transactions during 1996 and other information are as follows:

(a) On January 2, 1996, Hedlund purchased a new car for $10,000 cash and trade-in of a two-year-old car with a cost of $9,000 and a book value of $2,700. The new car has a cash price of $12,000; the market value of the trade-in is not known.

(b) On April 1, 1996, a machine purchased for $23,000 on April 1, 1991, was destroyed by fire. Hedlund recovered $15,500 from its insurance company.

(c) On May 1, 1996, costs of $168,000 were incurred to improve leased office premises. The leasehold improvements have a useful life of eight years. The related lease, which terminates on December 31, 2002, is renewable for an additional six-year term. The decision to renew will be made in 2002 based on office space needs at that time.

(d) On July 1, 1996, machinery and equipment were purchased at a total invoice cost of $280,000; additional costs of $5,000 for freight and $25,000 for installation were incurred.

(e) Hedlund determined that the automotive equipment comprising the $115,000 balance at January 1, 1996, would have been depreciated at a total amount of $18,000 for the year ended December 31, 1996.

Instructions:

1. For each asset classification prepare schedules showing depreciation and amortization expense, and accumulated depreciation and amortization that would appear on Hedlund's income statement for the year ended December 31, 1996, and balance sheet at December 31, 1996.
2. Prepare a schedule showing gain or loss from disposal of assets that would appear in Hedlund's income statement for the year ended December 31, 1996.
3. Prepare the noncurrent operating assets section of Hedlund's December 31, 1996, balance sheet.

(AICPA adapted)

Problem 12—53 (Comprehensive depreciation and amortization)

At December 31, 1996, Martin Company's noncurrent operating asset and accumulated depreciation and amortization accounts had balances as follows:

Category	Cost of Asset	Accumulated Depreciation and Amortization
Land	$ 130,000	
Buildings	1,200,000	$265,400
Machinery and Equipment	775,000	196,200
Automobiles and Trucks	132,000	86,200
Leasehold Improvements	221,000	110,500

Category	Depreciation Method	Useful Life
Buildings	150% declining-balance	25 years
Machinery and Equipment	Straight-line	10 years
Automobiles and Trucks	150% declining-balance	5 years
Leasehold Improvements	Straight-line	8 years
Land Improvements	Straight-line	12 years

Depreciation is computed to the nearest month. The salvage values of the depreciable assets are immaterial.

Transactions during 1997 and other information are as follows:

(a) On January 6, 1997, a plant facility consisting of land and a building was acquired from Atlas Corp. for $600,000. Of this amount, 20% was allocated to land.
(b) On April 6, 1997, new parking lots, streets, and sidewalks at the acquired plant facility were completed at a total cost of $192,000. These expenditures had an estimated useful life of 12 years.
(c) The leasehold improvements were completed on December 31, 1993, and had an estimated useful life of eight years. The related lease, which would have terminated on December 31, 1999, was renewable for an additional four-year term. On April 29, 1997, Martin exercised the renewal option.
(d) On July 1, 1997, machinery and equipment were purchased at a total invoice cost of $250,000. Additional costs of $10,000 for delivery and $30,000 for installation were incurred.
(e) On August 30, 1997, Martin purchased a new automobile for $15,000.
(f) On September 30, 1997, a truck with a cost of $24,000 and a carrying amount of $8,100 on the date of sale was sold for $11,500. Depreciation for the 9 months ended September 30, 1997, was $2,352.
(g) On December 20, 1997, a machine with a cost of $17,000 and a carrying amount of $2,975 at date of disposition was scrapped without cash recovery.

Instructions: For each category, prepare a schedule showing depreciation or amortization expense for the year ended December 31, 1997. Round computations to the nearest whole dollar.

(AICPA adapted)

CHAPTER 13

Liabilities: Current and Contingent

CHAPTER TOPICS

- Definition of Liabilities
- Classification and Measurement of Liabilities
- Accounting for Liabilities That Are Definite in Amount
- Accounting for Estimated Liabilities
- Accounting for Contingent Liabilities, Including Environmental Liabilities
- Presentation of Liabilities on the Balance Sheet

In early 1984, Pennzoil sued Texaco for $14 billion as a result of Texaco's interference in Pennzoil's attempted acquisition of Getty Oil. In December of 1985, a jury awarded $10.5 billion to Pennzoil. The case was appealed in both 1986 and 1987, with judgment in each instance against Texaco. In December of 1987, Pennzoil and Texaco agreed to settle the litigation by Texaco paying Pennzoil $3 billion in early 1988. At what point during this period did Texaco have a liability?

In the late 1980s, Du Pont acknowledged that one of its products, a fungicide called Benlate, seemed to be at fault for damage to millions of acres of nurseries and fruit plantations. In 1992, after paying approximately $510 million in claims, the company concluded its product was not responsible for the damage and halted further damage payments.[1] This set the stage for over 500 lawsuits. In 1993, Du Pont settled a $430 million case out of court for $4.25 million. In a second case, the jury awarded an orchid grower $3 million.[2] With hundreds of suits still pending, should Du Pont recognize any liability?

1. Peter Katel, "The Legacy of Dead Tomatoes," *Newsweek*, (August 9, 1993), p. 48.
2 Jerry Jackson, "Florida Growers Praise Verdict in Benlate Case," *The Orlando Sentinel*, (September 25, 1993), p. C1.

As these examples suggest, it is not always easy to identify and measure a company's liabilities. In this chapter, the general nature of liabilities is discussed as well as how to account for current and contingent liabilities. Subsequent chapters focus on noncurrent liabilities that are relatively complex in nature and, in some cases, directly related to asset accounts.

To illustrate the importance of accurately reporting the liabilities of a company, consider the following hypothetical, but realistic, situation. Judge E.J. Wright is currently deliberating over a type of case that is becoming increasingly common in our society. A suit has been filed by three stockholders against Transcontinental Corporation alleging that Transcontinental's year-end balance sheet was misleading because it did not accurately reflect the financial position of the company at that date. The stockholders relied on the published financial statements and subsequently lost money on their investments in Transcontinental. Two specific points are at issue. First, Transcontinental chose not to estimate its liability under certain warranty provisions, but instead accounted for warranty expenses on a cash basis. The plaintiffs contend that the warranties were in fact liabilities and should have been reported as such under accrual accounting procedures. Second, Transcontinental did not report a contingent liability relating to a significant, pending lawsuit with a supplier, which Transcontinental subsequently lost. Plaintiffs contend again that this information was material and relevant and should have been disclosed.

Although hypothetical, the above situation is typical of many lawsuits being filed against companies, accountants, underwriters, and financial analysts and advisers. With respect to liabilities, the basic questions are:

- What is a liability?
- When and how should liabilities be measured and disclosed?

These questions relate to definition, recognition, measurement, and reporting addressed by the FASB's conceptual framework, as discussed in Chapter 2.

DEFINITION OF LIABILITIES

Liabilities have been defined by the FASB as "probable future sacrifices of economic benefits arising from present obligations of a particular entity to transfer assets or provide services to other entities in the future as a result of past transactions or events."[3] This definition contains significant components that need to be explained before individual liability accounts are discussed.

A liability is a result of **past transactions or events.** Thus, a liability is not recognized until incurred. This part of the definition excludes contractual obligations from an exchange of promises if performance by both parties is still in the future. Such contracts are referred to as **executory contracts.** Determining when an executory contract qualifies as a liability is not always easy. For example, the signing of a labor contract that obligates both the employer and the employee does not give rise to a liability in current accounting practice, nor does the placing of an order for the purchase of merchandise. However, under some conditions, the signing of a lease is recognized as an event that requires the current recognition of a liability even though a lease is essentially an executory contract.

A liability must involve a **probable future transfer of assets or services.** Although liabilities result from past transactions or events, an obligation may be contingent upon the occurrence of another event sometime in the future. When occurrence of the future event seems probable, the obligation is defined as a liability. Although the majority of liabilities are satisfied by payment of cash, some obligations are satisfied by transferring other types

3. *Statement of Financial Accounting Concepts No. 6,* "Elements of Financial Statements" (Stamford: Financial Accounting Standards Board, December 1985), par. 35.

of assets or by providing services. For example, revenue received in advance requires recognition of an obligation to provide goods or services in the future. Usually, the time of payment is specified by a debt instrument, e.g., a note requiring payment of interest and principal on a given date or series of dates. Some obligations, however, require the transfer of assets or services over a period of time, but the exact dates cannot be determined when the liability is incurred, e.g., obligations to provide parts or service under a warranty agreement.

A liability is the **obligation of a particular entity,** i.e., the entity that has the responsibility to transfer assets or provide services. As long as the payment or transfer is probable, it is not necessary that the entity to whom the obligation is owed be identified. Thus, a warranty to make any repairs necessary to an item sold by an entity is an obligation of that entity even though it is not certain which customers will receive benefits. Generally, the obligation rests on a foundation of legal rights and duties. However, obligations created, inferred, or construed from the facts of a particular situation may also be recognized as liabilities. For example, if a company regularly pays vacation pay or year-end bonuses, accrual of these items as a liability is warranted even though no legal agreement exists to make these payments.

Although the FASB's definition is helpful, the question of when a liability exists is not always easy to answer. Examples of areas where there are continuing controversies include the problems associated with off-balance sheet financing, deferred income taxes, leases, pensions, and even some equity securities, such as redeemable preferred stock. Once an item is accepted as having met the definition of a liability, there is still the need to appropriately classify, measure, and report the liability.

CLASSIFICATION AND MEASUREMENT OF LIABILITIES

For reporting purposes, liabilities are usually classified as **current** or **noncurrent.** The distinction between current and noncurrent liabilities was introduced and explained in Chapter 5, where it was pointed out that the computation of working capital is considered by many to be a useful measure of the liquidity of an enterprise.

Current Versus Noncurrent Classification

As noted in Chapter 5, the same rules generally apply for the classification of liabilities as for assets. If a liability arises in the course of an entity's normal operating cycle, it is considered current if current assets will be used to satisfy the obligation within one year or one operating cycle, whichever period is longer. On the other hand, bank borrowings, notes, mortgages, and similar obligations are related to the general financial condition of the entity, rather than directly to the operating cycle, and are classified as current only if they are to be paid with current assets within one year.

When debt that has been classified as noncurrent will mature within the next year, the liability should be reported as a current liability in order to reflect the expected drain on current assets. However, if the liability is to be paid by transfer of noncurrent assets that have been accumulated for the purpose of liquidating the liability, the obligation continues to be classified as noncurrent.

The distinction between current and noncurrent liabilities is important because of the impact on a company's **current ratio,** also called the **working capital ratio.** This fundamental measurement of a company's liquidity is computed by dividing total current assets by total current liabilities.

The current ratio is a measure of an entity's ability to meet current obligations. Care must be taken to determine that proper items have been included in the current asset and current liability categories. A ratio of current assets to current liabilities of less than two for a trading or manufacturing company has frequently been considered unsatisfactory. However, because liquidity needs vary among different industries and companies, any such arbitrary guideline should not be viewed as appropriate in all cases. The table below presents median current ratios for a set of diverse industries.[4]

Industry (number of firms included)	Median Current Ratio
Blast Furnaces and Steel Mills (274)	1.8
Dairy Farms (138)	1.9
Electric Services (1068)	1.8
Family Clothing Stores (1464)	4.8
Grocery Stores (1424)	2.1
Jewelry Stores (2244)	3.3
Legal Services (1060)	1.9
Personal Credit Institutions (573)	1.8
Physical Fitness Facilities (179)	1.2
Video Tape Rental Stores (385)	1.7

A comfortable margin of current assets over current liabilities suggests that a company will be able to meet maturing obligations even in the event of unfavorable business conditions or losses on such assets as securities, receivables, and inventories. A current ratio of 2.1 means, for example, that a company could liquidate its total current liabilities 2.1 times using only its current assets.

Measurement of Liabilities

The distinction between current and noncurrent liabilities is also an important consideration in the measurement of liabilities. Obviously, before liabilities can be reported on the financial statements, they must be stated in monetary terms. The measurement used for liabilities is the **present value of the future cash outflows** to settle the obligation. Generally, this is the amount of cash required to liquidate the obligation if it were paid today.

If a claim isn't to be paid until sometime in the future, as is the case with noncurrent liabilities, the claim should either provide for interest to be paid on the debt, or the obligation should be reported at the discounted value of its maturity amount. Current obligations that arise in the course of normal business operations are generally due within a short period, e.g., 30-60 days, and normally are not discounted.[5] Thus, trade accounts payable are not discounted even though they carry no interest provision. However, this is an exception to the general rule; most nonoperating business transactions, such as the borrowing of money, purchase of assets over time, and long-term leases, do involve the discounting process. The obligation in these instances is the present value of the future resource outflows.

For measurement purposes, liabilities can be divided into three categories:

1. Liabilities that are definite in amount.
2. Estimated liabilities.
3. Contingent liabilities.

The measurement of liabilities always involves some uncertainty, since a liability, by definition, involves a *future* outflow of resources. However, for the first category above,

4. The industry ratios in this table are taken from *Industry Norms and Key Business Ratios: 1992-93 Edition*, Dun and Bradstreet, Inc. (1993).

5. *Opinions of the Accounting Principles Board No. 21*, "Interest on Receivables and Payables" (New York: American Institute of Certified Public Accountants, 1971), par. 3.

both the existence of the liability and the amount to be paid are determinable because of a contract, trade agreement, or general business practice. An example of a **liability that is definite in amount** is the principal payment on a note.

The second category includes items that are definitely liabilities, i.e., they involve a definite future resource outflow, but the actual amount of the obligation cannot be established currently. In this situation, the amount of the liability is estimated so that the obligation is reflected in the current period, even though at an approximated value. A warranty obligation that is recorded on an accrual basis is an example of an **estimated liability.**

Generally, liabilities from both of the first two categories are reported on a balance sheet as claims against recorded assets, either as current or noncurrent liabilities, whichever is appropriate. However, items that resemble liabilities but are contingent upon the occurrence of some future event are not recorded until it is probable that the event will occur. Even though the amount of the potential obligation may be known, the actual existence of a liability is questionable, since it is contingent upon a future event for which there is considerable uncertainty. An example of a **contingent liability** is a pending lawsuit. Only if the lawsuit is lost, or is settled out of court, will a liability be recorded. While not recorded in the accounts, some contingent liabilities should be disclosed in the notes to the financial statements, as discussed and illustrated later in the chapter.

LIABILITIES THAT ARE DEFINITE IN AMOUNT

Representative of liabilities that are definite in amount and reported on the balance sheet are accounts payable, notes payable, and miscellaneous operating payables including salaries, payroll taxes, property and sales taxes, and income taxes. Some liabilities accrue as time passes. Most notable in this category are interest and rent, although the latter is frequently paid in advance. Some of the problems that arise in determining the balances to be reported for liabilities definite in amount are described in the following sections.

Accounts Payable

Most goods and services in today's economic environment are purchased on credit. The term **accounts payable** usually refers to the amount due for the purchase of materials by a manufacturing company or merchandise by a wholesaler or retailer. Other obligations, such as salaries and wages, rent, interest, and utilities, are reported as separate liabilities in accounts descriptive of the nature of the obligation. Accounts payable are usually not recorded when purchase orders are placed but when legal title to the goods passes to the buyer. The rules for the customary recognition of legal passage of title were presented in Chapter 9. If goods are in transit at year-end, the purchase should be recorded if the shipment terms indicate that title has passed. This means that care must be exercised to review the purchase of goods and services near the end of an accounting period to assure a proper cutoff and reporting of liabilities and inventory.

It is customary to report accounts payable at the expected amount of the payment. Because the payment period is normally short, no recognition of interest is required. As indicated in Chapter 9, if cash discounts are available, the liability should be reported net of the expected cash discount. Failure to use the net method in recording purchases usually results in reported liabilities being in excess of the payment finally made, since most companies are careful to take advantage of available cash discounts.

Short-Term Debt

Companies often borrow money on a short-term basis for operating purposes other than for the purchase of materials or merchandise involving accounts payable. Collectively, these obligations may be referred to as **short-term debt.** In most cases, such debt is evidenced by a **promissory note,** a formal written promise to pay a sum of money in the future, and is usually reflected on the debtor's books as **Notes Payable.**

Notes issued to trade creditors for the purchase of goods or services are called **trade notes payable.** Notes issued to banks or to officers and stockholders for loans to the company, and those issued to others for the purchase of noncurrent operating assets, are called **nontrade notes payable.** It is normally desirable to classify current notes payable on the balance sheet as trade or nontrade, since such information would reveal to statement users the sources of indebtedness and the extent to which the company has relied on each source in financing its activities.

The problems encountered in the valuation of notes payable are the same as those discussed in Chapter 8 with respect to notes receivable. Thus, a short-term note payable is recorded and reported at its present value, which is normally the face value of the note. This presumes that the note bears a reasonable stated rate of interest. However, if a note has no stated rate of interest, or if the stated rate is unreasonable, then the face value of the note would need to be discounted to its present value to reflect the effective rate of interest implicit in the note. This is accomplished by debiting Discount on Notes Payable when the note is issued, and by writing off the discount to Interest Expense over the life of the note, in the same manner as was illustrated for the discount on notes receivable in Chapter 8.

Discount on Notes Payable is a contra account to Notes Payable and would be reported on the balance sheet as follows:

Current liabilities:		
Notes payable	$100,000	
Less discount on notes payable	10,000	$90,000

Short-Term Obligations Expected to Be Refinanced

As noted at the beginning of the chapter, omissions or misrepresentation in the reporting of liabilities can create serious problems for users of financial statements. A similar problem can result from the misclassification of liabilities. Since the "current" classification is reserved for those obligations that will be satisfied with current assets within a year, a short-term obligation that is expected to be refinanced on a long-term basis should not be reported as a current liability. This applies to the currently maturing portion of a long-term debt and to all other short-term obligations except those arising in the normal course of operations that are due in customary terms. Similarly, it should not be assumed that a short-term obligation will be refinanced, and therefore classified as a noncurrent liability, unless the refinancing arrangements are secure. Thus, to avoid potential manipulation, the refinancing expectation must be realistic and not just a mere possibility.

An example will illustrate this last point and show the importance of proper classification. Assume that a company borrows a substantial amount of money that it expects to pay back at the end of 5 years. The president of the company signs a 6-month note, which the loan officer at the bank verbally agrees will be renewed "automatically" until the actual maturity date in 5 years. The only current obligation expected is payment of the accrued interest each renewal period. Under these circumstances, the company reports the obligation as noncurrent, except for the accrued interest obligation. Assume further that the loan officer leaves the bank and that the new bank official will not allow the short-term note to be refinanced. The financial picture of the company is now dramatically changed. What was considered a long-term obligation because of refinancing expectations is suddenly a current liability requiring settlement with liquid assets in the near future. This hypothetical situation is similar to what actually happened to Penn Central Railroad before it went bankrupt.

To assist with this problem, the FASB in 1975 issued Statement No. 6, which contains the authoritative guideline for classifying short-term obligations expected to be refinanced. According to the FASB, *both* of the following conditions must be met before a short-term obligation may be properly excluded from the current liability classification.[6]

1. Management must *intend to refinance* the obligation on a long-term basis.
2. Management must *demonstrate an ability to refinance* the obligation.

Concerning the second point, an ability to refinance may be demonstrated by:

(a) Actually refinancing the obligation during the period between the balance sheet date and the date the statements are issued.
(b) Reaching a firm agreement that clearly provides for refinancing on a long-term basis.

The terms of the refinancing agreement should be noncancellable as to all parties and extend beyond the current year. In addition, the company should not be in violation of the agreement at the balance sheet date or the date of issuance, and the lender or investor should be financially capable of meeting the refinancing requirements.

If an actual refinancing does occur before the balance sheet is issued, the portion of the short-term obligation that is to be excluded from current liabilities cannot exceed the proceeds from the new debt or equity securities issued to retire the old debt. For example, if a $400,000 long-term note is issued to partially refinance $750,000 of short-term obligations, only $400,000 of the short-term debt can be excluded from current liabilities.

An additional question relates to the timing of the refinancing. If the obligation is paid prior to the actual refinancing, the obligation should be included in current liabilities on the balance sheet.[7] To illustrate, assume that the liabilities of CareFree Inc. at December 31, 1995, include a note payable for $200,000 due January 15, 1996. The management of CareFree intends to refinance the note by issuing 10-year bonds. The bonds are actually issued before the issuance of the December 31, 1995, balance sheet on February 15, 1996. If the bonds were issued prior to payment of the note, the note should be classified as noncurrent on the December 31, 1995, balance sheet. If payment of the note preceded the sale of the bonds, however, the note should be included in current liabilities.

Normally, classified balance sheets are presented that show a total for "current liabilities." If a short-term obligation is excluded from that category due to refinancing expectations, disclosure should be made in the notes to the financial statements. The note should include a general description of the refinancing agreement.

Miscellaneous Operating Payables

Many miscellaneous payables arise in the course of a company's operating activities. Three of these are specifically discussed in this section. They are indicative of other specific liabilities that could be reported by a given entity. In general, the points made in discussing the definition of liabilities in the opening section of this chapter apply to these miscellaneous operating liabilities.

Salaries and Wages. In an ongoing entity, salaries and wages of officers and other employees accrue daily. Normally, no entry is made for these expenses until payment is made. A liability for unpaid salaries and wages is recorded, however, at the end of an accounting period when a more precise matching of revenues and expenses is desired. An

6. *Statement of Financial Accounting Standards No. 6,* "Classification of Short-Term Obligations Expected to Be Refinanced" (Stamford: Financial Accounting Standards Board, 1975), pars. 10 and 11.

7. *FASB Interpretation No. 8,* "Classification of a Short-Term Obligation Repaid Prior to Being Replaced by a Long-Term Security" (Stamford: Financial Accounting Standards Board, 1976), par. 3.

estimate of the amount of unpaid wages and salaries is made, and an adjusting entry is prepared to recognize the amount due. Usually, the entire accrued amount is identified as salaries payable with no attempt to identify the withholdings associated with the accrual. When payment is made in the subsequent period, the amount is allocated between the employee and other entities such as government taxing units, unions, and insurance companies.

For example, assume that a company has 15 employees who are paid every two weeks. At December 31, four days of unpaid wages have accrued. Analysis reveals that the 15 employees earn a total of $1,000 a day. Thus the adjusting entry at December 31 would be:

Salaries and Wages Expense	4,000	
Salaries and Wages Payable		4,000

This entry may be reversed at the beginning of the next period or, when payment is made, Salaries and Wages Payable may be debited for $4,000.

Additional compensation in the form of accrued bonuses or commissions also should be recognized. Bonuses are often based on some measure of the employer's income. For example, assume that Photo Graphics, Inc. gives its store managers a 10 percent bonus based on individual store earnings. The bonus is to be based on income after deduction for the bonus but before deduction for income taxes. Assume further that income for a particular store is $100,000 before charging any bonus or income taxes. The bonus would be calculated as follows:

$$\begin{aligned} B &= .10\,(\$100{,}000 - B) \\ B &= \$10{,}000 - .10B \\ B + .10B &= \$10{,}000 \\ 1.10B &= \$10{,}000 \\ B &= \$9{,}091 \text{ (rounded)} \end{aligned}$$

The bonus would be reported on the income statement as an operating expense, and the bonus payable would be shown as a current liability on the balance sheet, unless the bonus was paid immediately in cash.

Payroll Taxes. Social security and income tax legislation impose four taxes based on payrolls:

1. Federal old-age, survivors', disability, and hospital insurance (tax to both employer and employee).
2. Federal unemployment insurance (tax to employer only).
3. State unemployment insurance (tax to employer only).
4. Individual income tax (tax to employee only, but withheld and paid by employer).

Federal Old-Age, Survivors', Disability, and Hospital Insurance. The Federal Insurance Contributions Act (FICA), generally referred to as social security legislation, provides for FICA taxes from both employers and employees to provide funds for federal old-age, survivors', disability, and hospital insurance benefits for certain individuals and members of their families. At one time, only employees were covered by this legislation; however, coverage now includes most individuals who are self-employed.

Provisions of the legislation require an employer of one or more employees, with certain exceptions, to withhold FICA taxes from each employee's wages. The amount of the tax is based on a tax rate and wage base as currently specified in the law. The tax rate and wage base both have increased dramatically since the inception of the social security program in the 1930s. The initial rate of FICA tax was 1% in 1937; the rate in effect for 1994 was 7.65%.[8] During that same period, the annual wages subject to FICA tax increased from $3,000 to $60,600 (and for part of the tax, an unlimited amount). The taxable wage base is subject to yearly increases based on cost-of-living adjustments in social security benefits.

The employer remits the amount of FICA tax withheld for all employees, along with a matching amount, to the federal government. The employer is required to maintain complete records and submit detailed support for the tax remittance. The employer is responsible for the full amount of the tax even if employee contributions are not withheld.

Federal Unemployment Insurance. The Federal Social Security Act and the Federal Unemployment Tax Act (FUTA) provide for the establishment of unemployment insurance plans. Employers with covered workers employed in each of 20 weeks during a calendar year or who pay $1,500 or more in wages during any calendar quarter are affected.

Under present provisions of the law, the federal government taxes eligible employers on the first $7,000 paid to every employee during the calendar year. The rate of tax in effect since 1985 is 6.2%, but the employer is allowed a tax credit limited to 5.4% for taxes paid under state unemployment compensation laws. No tax is levied on the employee. When an employer is subject to a tax of 5.4% or more as a result of state unemployment legislation, the federal unemployment tax, then, is 0.8% of the qualifying wages.

Payment to the federal government is required quarterly. Unemployment benefits are paid by the individual states. Revenues collected by the federal government under the acts are used to meet the cost of administering state and federal unemployment plans as well as to provide supplemental unemployment benefits.

State Unemployment Insurance. State unemployment compensation laws are not the same in all states. In most states, laws provide for tax only on employers; but in a few states, taxes are applicable to both employers and employees. Each state law specifies the classes of exempt employees, the number of employees required or the amount of wages paid before the tax is applicable, and the contributions that are to be made by employers and employees. Exemptions are frequently similar to those under the federal act. Tax payment is generally required on or before the last day of the month following each calendar quarter.

Although the normal tax on employers may be 5.4%, states have merit rating or experience plans providing for lower rates based on employers' individual employment experiences. Employers with stable employment records are taxed at a rate in keeping with the limited amount of benefits required for their former employees; employers with less satisfactory employment records contribute at a rate more nearly approaching 5.4% in view of the greater amount of benefits paid to their former employees. Savings under state merit systems are allowed as credits in the calculation of the federal contribution, so the federal tax does not exceed 0.8% even though payment of less than 5.4% is made by an employer entitled to a lower rate under the merit rating system.

Income Tax. Federal income tax on the wages of an individual are collected in the period in which the wages are paid. The "pay-as-you-go" plan requires employers to withhold income tax from wages paid to their employees. Most states and many local governments also impose income taxes on the earnings of employees that must be withheld and remitted by the employer. Withholding is required not only of employers engaged in a trade or business, but also of religious and charitable organizations, educational institutions, social organizations, and governments of the United States, the states, the territories, and their agencies, instrumentalities, and political subdivisions. Certain classes of wage payments are exempt from withholding although these are still subject to income tax.

8. For illustrative purposes and end-of-chapter exercises and problems, a rate of 7.65% will be used.

An employer must meet withholding requirements under the law even if wages of only one employee are subject to such withholdings. The amounts to be withheld by the employer are developed from formulas provided by the law or from tax withholding tables made available by the government. Withholding is based on the length of the payroll period, the amount earned, and the number of withholding exemptions claimed by the employee. Taxes required under the Federal Insurance Contributions Act (both employee and employer portions) and income tax that has been withheld by the employer are paid to the federal government at the same time. These combined taxes are deposited in an authorized bank quarterly, monthly, or several times each month depending on the amount of the liability. Quarterly and annual statements must also be filed providing a summary of all wages paid by the employer.

Accounting for Payroll Taxes To illustrate the accounting procedures for payroll taxes, assume that salaries for the month of January for a retail store with 15 employees are $16,000. The state unemployment compensation law provides for a tax on employers of 5.4%. Income tax withholdings for the month are $1,600. Assume FICA rates are 7.65% for employer and employee. Entries for the payroll and the employer's payroll taxes follow:

Salaries Expense	16,000	
FICA Taxes Payable		1,224
Employees Income Taxes Payable		1,600
Cash		13,176
To record payment of payroll and related employee withholdings.		
Payroll Tax Expense	2,216	
FICA Taxes Payable		1,224
State Unemployment Taxes Payable		864
Federal Unemployment Taxes Payable		128
To record the payroll tax liability of the employer.		

Computation:	
Tax under Federal Insurance Contributions Act (7.65% × $16,000)	$1,224
Tax under state unemployment insurance legislation (5.4% × $16,000)	864
Tax under Federal Unemployment Tax Act [0.8% (6.2% − credit of 5.4%) × $16,000]	128
Total payroll tax expense	$2,216

When tax payments are made to the proper agencies, the tax liability accounts are debited and Cash is credited.

The employer's payroll taxes, as well as the taxes withheld from employees, are based on amounts paid to employees during the period regardless of the basis employed for reporting income. When financial reports are prepared on the accrual basis, the employer will have to recognize both accrued payroll and the employer's payroll taxes relating thereto by adjustments at the end of the accounting period.

For example, assume that the salaries and wages accrued at December 31 were $9,500. Of this amount, $2,000 was subject to unemployment tax and $6,000 to FICA tax. Although the salaries and wages will not be paid until January of the following year, the concept of matching requires these costs to be allocated in the period in which they were incurred. This allocation is accomplished with an adjusting entry. The adjusting entry for the employer's payroll taxes would be as follows:

Payroll Tax Expense	583	
FICA Taxes Payable		459
State Unemployment Taxes Payable		108
Federal Unemployment Taxes Payable		16
To accrue the payroll tax liability of the employer.		

Computation:

Tax under Federal Insurance Contributions Act (7.65% × $6,000)	$459
Tax under state unemployment insurance legislation (5.4% × $2,000)	108
Tax under Federal Unemployment Tax Act (0.8% × $2,000)	16
Total payroll tax expense	$583

As was true with the adjusting entry for the salaries and wages discussed on page 542, the preceding entry may be reversed at the beginning of the new period, or the accrued liabilities may be debited when the payments are made to the taxing authorities.

Agreements with employees may provide for payroll deductions and employer contributions for other items, such as group insurance plans, pension plans, savings bonds purchases, or union dues. Such agreements call for accounting procedures similar to those described for payroll taxes.

Other Tax Liabilities. There are many different types of taxes imposed on business entities. In addition to the several payroll taxes discussed in the previous section, a company usually must pay property taxes, federal and state income taxes on their earnings, and serve as an agent for the collection of sales taxes. Each of these liabilities has some unusual features that can complicate accounting for them.

Property Taxes. Real and personal property taxes are based on the assessed valuation of properties as of a particular date. This has given rise to the view held by courts and others that taxes accrue as of a particular date. Generally, the date of accrual has been held to be the date of property assessment, or **lien date,** and a liability for the full year's property tax can be established at that date. The offset to the liability is a deferred expense, since the tax liability is being established in advance of payment and incurrence of the tax expense. The tax expense is generally recognized as a charge against revenue over the fiscal year of the taxing authority for which the taxes are levied. This procedure relates the tax charge to the period in which the taxes provide benefits through government service. The date for payment of the liability is determined by the taxing authority and is accounted for independently from the monthly recognition of property tax expense.

To illustrate accounting for property taxes, assume that the taxing authority is on a July 1 to June 30 fiscal year, but the entity paying the tax is on a calendar-year basis. Property taxes assessed for the period July 1, 1995, to June 30, 1996, are $60,000, and the full year's tax is to be paid on or before November 15, 1995. The following entry is made by the taxpaying entity at the lien date, July 1, 1995, to accrue property taxes for the year:

Deferred Property Taxes	60,000	
Property Taxes Payable		60,000

Each month, the following entry would be made to recognize the expense:

Property Tax Expense	5,000	
Deferred Property Taxes		5,000

The entry to record payment of the property taxes on November 15, 1995, would be:

Property Taxes Payable	60,000	
Cash		60,000

At December 31, 1995, the deferred property tax account would have a debit balance of $30,000, representing the property taxes to be recognized as expenses in 1996. If the tax were due in January 1996, and no payment had been made as of December 31, 1995, Property Taxes Payable would have a $60,000 credit balance, which would be reported as a current liability on the balance sheet.

Although the preceding approach seems to reflect the current definition of liabilities as established by the FASB, some companies recognize the liability ratably over the year rather than on the assessment or lien date. Under this latter approach, a prepaid property tax account is created when the full year's tax is paid before the end of the taxing authority's fiscal year. In the authors' opinion, this practice is not as informative and useful as that illustrated.

Income Taxes. Both federal and state governments raise a large portion of their revenue from income taxes assessed against both individuals and corporations. The taxable income of a business entity is determined by applying the tax rules and regulations to the operations of the business. As indicated in Chapter 4, the income tax rules do not always follow generally accepted accounting principles. Thus, the income reported for tax purposes may differ from that reported on the income statement. This difference can give rise to deferred income taxes. The actual amount payable for the current year must be determined after all adjusting entries are made at the close of a fiscal period. Federal and some state income tax regulations require companies to estimate their tax liability and make periodic payments during the year in advance of the final computation and submission of the tax returns. Thus, the amount of income tax liability at year-end is usually much lower than the total tax computed for the year. Because income tax returns are always subject to government audit, a contingent liability exists for any year within the statute of limitations not yet reviewed by the Internal Revenue Service. If an additional liability arises as a result of an audit, the additional assessment should be reported as a liability until the payment is made.

Sales and Use Taxes. With the passage of sales and use tax laws by state and local governments, additional duties are required of a business unit. Laws generally provide that the business unit must act as an agent for the governmental authority in the collection from customers of sales tax on the transfers of tangible personal properties. The buyer is responsible for the payment of sales tax to the seller when both buyer and seller are in the same tax jurisdiction; however, the buyer is responsible for the payment of use tax directly to the tax authority when the seller is outside the jurisdiction of such authority. Provision must be made in the accounts for the liability to the government for the tax collected from customers and the additional tax that the business must absorb.

The sales tax payable is generally a stated percentage of sales. The actual sales total and the sales tax collections are usually recorded separately at the time of sale. Cash or Accounts Receivable is debited; Sales and Sales Tax Payable are credited. The amount of sales tax to be paid to the taxing authority is computed on the recorded sales.

Unearned Revenues

Another category of liabilities that are definite in amount is referred to as **unearned revenues.** Frequently, these liabilities represent an obligation to provide services rather than tangible resources. Examples of unearned revenue include advances from customers, unearned rent, and unearned subscription revenue for publishing companies. Unearned revenue accounts are classified as current or noncurrent liabilities depending on when the revenue will be earned. When the revenue is earned, e.g., when services are performed, the unearned revenue account is debited and an appropriate revenue account is credited. If advances are refunded without providing goods or services, the liability is reduced by the payment, and no revenue is recognized.

ESTIMATED LIABILITIES

The amount of an obligation is generally established by contract or accrues at a specified rate. There are instances, however, when an obligation clearly exists on a balance sheet date but the amount ultimately to be paid cannot be definitely determined. Because the amount to be paid is not definite does not mean the liability can be ignored or given a contingent status. The claim must be estimated from whatever data are available. Obligations arising from current operations, for example, the cost of meeting warranties for service and repairs on goods sold, must be estimated when prior experience indicates there is a definite liability. Here, uncertainty as to the amount and timing of expenditures is accompanied by an inability to identify the payees; but the fact that there are charges yet to be absorbed is certain.

Liabilities that are estimated in amount and frequently found on financial statements include the following:

1. Refundable deposits, reporting the estimated amount to be refunded to depositors.
2. Warranties for service and replacements, reporting the estimated future claims by customers as a result of past guarantees of services or products or product part replacements.
3. Customer premium offers, reporting the estimated value of premiums or prizes to be distributed as a result of past sales or sales promotion activities.
4. Tickets, tokens, and gift certificates, reporting the estimated obligations in the form of services or merchandise arising from the receipt of cash in past periods.
5. Compensated absences, reporting the estimated future payments attributable to past services of employees.

Refundable Deposits

Liabilities of a company may include an obligation to refund amounts previously collected from customers as deposits. **Refundable deposits** may be classified as current or noncurrent liabilities depending on the purpose of the deposit. If deposits are made to protect the company against nonpayment for future services to be rendered, and the services are expected to be provided over a long period, the deposit should be reported as a noncurrent liability. Utility companies characteristically charge certain customers, such as those renting their homes, a deposit that is held until a customer discontinues the service, usually because of a move.

Another type of customer deposit is one made for reusable containers, such as bottles or drums, that hold the product being purchased. When a sale is recorded, a liability is recognized for the deposit. When a container is returned, a refund or credit is given for the deposit made. Periodically, an adjustment to recognize revenue is recorded for containers not expected to be returned. The asset "containers" and the related accumulated depreciation account should be reduced to eliminate the book value of containers not expected to be returned, and any gain or loss is recognized on the "sale" of the containers.

Warranties for Service and Replacements

Many companies agree to provide free service on units failing to perform satisfactorily or to replace defective goods. When these agreements, or **warranties,** involve only minor costs, such costs may be recognized in the periods incurred. When these agreements involve significant future costs and when experience indicates a definite future obligation exists, estimates of such costs should be made and matched against current revenues. Such estimates are usually recorded by a debit to an expense account and a credit to a liability account. Subsequent costs of fulfilling warranties are debited to the liability account and credited to an appropriate account, e.g., Cash or Inventory.

To illustrate accounting for warranties, consider the following example. MJW Video & Sound sells compact stereo systems with a two-year warranty. Past experience indicates that 10% of all sets sold will need repairs in the first year, and 20% will need repairs in the second year. The average repair cost is $50 per system. The number of systems sold in 1995 and 1996 was 5,000 and 6,000, respectively. Actual repair costs were $12,500 in 1995 and $55,000 in 1996; it is assumed that all repair costs involved cash expenditures.

1995	Warranty Expense	75,000	
	Estimated Liability Under Warranties		75,000
	Estimated warranty expense based on systems sold: 5,000 × .30 × $50 = $75,000.		
	Estimated Liability Under Warranties	12,500	
	Cash		12,500
	Cost of actual repairs in 1995.		
1996	Warranty Expense	90,000	
	Estimated Liability Under Warranties		90,000
	Estimated warranty expense based on systems sold: 6,000 × .30 × $50 = $90,000.		
	Estimated Liability Under Warranties	55,000	
	Cash		55,000
	Cost of actual repairs in 1996.		

Periodically, the warranty liability account should be analyzed to see if the actual repairs approximate the estimate. Adjustment to the percentages used in estimating future warranty obligations will be required if experience differs materially from the estimates. These adjustments are changes in estimates and are reported prospectively, i.e., in current and future periods. If sales and repairs in the preceding example are assumed to occur evenly through the year, analysis of the liability account at the end of 1996 shows the ending balance of $97,500 ($75,000 + $90,000 – $12,500 – $55,000) is reasonably close to the predicted amount of $100,000 based upon the 10% and 20% estimates.

Computation:

1995 sales still under warranty for 6 months:	
$50 × [5,000 (1/2 × .20)]	$ 25,000
1996 sales still under warranty for 18 months:	
$50 × [6,000 (1/2 × .10) + 6,000 (.20)]	75,000
Total	$100,000

On occasion, an estimate may differ from actual experience to this point. Misleading financial statements may result if an adjustment is not made. In those instances, an adjustment is made to the liability account in the current period. Continuing the previous example, assume that warranty costs incurred in 1996 were only $35,000. Then the ending balance of $117,500 would be much higher than the $100,000 estimate. If the $17,500 difference was considered to be material, an adjustment to warranty expense would be made in 1996 as follows:

Estimated Liability Under Warranties	17,500	
Warranty Expense		17,500
Adjustment of estimate for warranty repairs.		

In certain cases, customers are charged special fees for a service or replacement warranty covering a specific period. When fees are collected, an unearned revenue account is credited. The unearned revenue is then recognized as revenue over the warranty period. Costs incurred in meeting the contract requirements are debited to Expense; Cash, Inventory, or another appropriate account is credited. The **service contract** is in reality an insurance contract, and the amount charged for the contract is based on the past repair experience of the company for the item sold. The fee usually is set at a rate that will produce a profit margin on the contract if expectations are realized.

To illustrate accounting for service contracts, assume a company sells 3-year service contracts covering its product. During the first year, $50,000 was received on contracts, and expenses incurred for parts and labor in connection with these contracts totaled $5,000. It is estimated from past experience that the pattern of repairs, based on the total dollars spent for repairs, is 25% in the first year of the contract, 30% in the second year, and 45% in the third year. In addition, it is assumed that sales of the contracts are made evenly during the year. The following entries would be made in the first year:

Cash	50,000	
Unearned Revenue From Service Contracts		50,000
Sale of service contracts.		
Unearned Revenue From Service Contracts	6,250	
Revenue From Service Contracts		6,250
Estimated revenue earned from contracts, 12 $^1/_2$% ($^1/_2$ of 25%) of $50,000, or $6,250.		
Service Contract Expense	5,000	
Inventory		5,000
Cost of actual repairs made during the year.		

Based on the above entries, a profit of $1,250 on service contracts would be recognized in the first year. If future expectations change, adjustments will be necessary to the unearned revenue account to reflect the change in estimate.

The accounts Estimated Liability Under Warranties and Unearned Revenue From Service Contracts are classified as current or noncurrent liabilities depending on the period remaining on the warranty. Those warranty costs expected to be incurred within one year or unearned revenues expected to be earned within one year are classified as current; the balance as long-term. In the above illustration, the expected revenue percentage for the second year, assuming that sales of the contracts were made evenly during the first year, would be 27 $^1/_2$% of the contract price, i.e., 12 $^1/_2$% for balance of first year expectations and 15% ($^1/_2$ of 30%) for one-half of the second year expectations, or $13,750. This amount would be classified as current. The remaining 60%, or $30,000, of unearned revenue would be classified as noncurrent.

The method of accounting illustrated above does not recognize any income on the initial sale of the contract, but only as the period of the service contract passes and the actual costs are matched against an estimate of the earned revenue. Alternatively, a company could estimate in advance the cost of the repairs and recognize the difference between the amount of the service contract and the expected repair cost in the period of the contract sale. The choice of which method to use depends on the degree of confidence in the estimated repair cost. As discussed more fully in Chapter 18, revenue recognition varies with the facts involved. When collection is reasonably assured and future costs are known with a high degree of certainty, immediate income recognition is recommended. In the case of service contracts, the uncertainty of future expenses usually dictates use of the deferred revenue method.

Customer Premium Offers

Many companies offer special premiums to customers to stimulate the regular purchase of certain products. These offers may be open for a limited time or may be of a continuing nature. The premium is normally made available when the customer submits the required number of product labels or other evidence of purchase. In certain instances, the premium offer may provide for an optional cash payment.

If a premium offer expires on or before the end of the company's fiscal period, adjustments in the accounts are not required; premium obligations are fully met and the premium expense account summarizes the full charge for the period. However, when a premium offer is continuing, an adjustment must be made at the end of the period to recognize the liability for future redemptions—Premium Expense is debited and an appropriate liability account is credited. The expense is thus charged to the period benefiting from the premium plan, and current liabilities reflect the claim for premiums outstanding.

To illustrate the accounting for a premium offer, assume the following. Good Foods offers a set of breakfast bowls upon the receipt of 20 certificates, one certificate being included in each package of the cereal distributed by this company. The cost of each set of bowls to the company is $2. It is estimated that only 40% of the certificates will be redeemed. In 1995, the company purchased 10,000 sets of bowls at $2 per set; 400,000 packages of cereal containing certificates were sold at a price of $1.20 per package. By the end of 1995, 30% of the certificates had been redeemed. Entries for 1995 are as follows:

Transaction		**Entry**		
1995:				
Premium purchases:		Premiums—Bowl Sets	20,000	
10,000 sets × $2 = $20,000		Cash		20,000
Sales:		Cash	480,000	
400,000 packages × $1.20 = $480,000		Sales		480,000
Premium claim redemptions:		Premium Expense	12,000	
120,000 certificates, or		Premiums—Bowl Sets		12,000
6,000 sets × $2 = $12,000				
December 31, 1995:				
Coupons estimated redeemable in future periods:		Premium Expense	4,000	
Total estimated redemptions:		Estimated Premium Claims Outstanding		4,000
40% of 400,000	160,000			
Redemptions in 1995	120,000			
Estimated future redemptions	40,000			
Estimated claims outstanding: 40,000 certificates, or 2,000 sets @ $2	$ 4,000			

The balance sheet at the end of 1995 will show premiums of $8,000 as a current asset and estimated premium claims outstanding of $4,000 as a current liability; the income statement for 1995 will show premium expense of $16,000 as a selling expense.

Experience indicating a redemption percentage that differs from the assumed rate will call for an appropriate adjustment in the subsequent period and the revision of future redemption estimates.

The estimated cost of the premiums may be shown as a direct reduction of sales by recording the premium claim at the time of the sale. This requires an estimate of the premium cost at the time of the sale. For example, in the previous illustration, the summary entry for sales recorded during the year, employing the sales reduction approach, would be as follows:

Cash	480,000	
Sales		464,000
Estimated Premium Claims Outstanding		16,000

The redemption of premium claims would call for debits to the liability account. Either the expense method or the sales reduction method is acceptable, and both are found in practice. As an example, Chrysler Corporation changed its method of accounting for sales incentive programs in 1991. During 1989 and 1990, Chrysler accounted for the cost of special sales incentives using the expense method and recognized the cost when a retail sale was made. In 1991, Chrysler switched to the sales reduction method, recognizing the sales reduction at the time a vehicle was sold by Chrysler to a dealer. Chrysler reported that the change was adopted in response to the increased magnitude and frequency of its sales incentive programs. In essence, since car buyers have now come to routinely expect "cash back" and other sales incentives, these incentives have been transformed from a special promotional cost to a routine cut in the effective sales price.

Tickets, Tokens, and Gift Certificates Outstanding

Many companies sell tickets, tokens, and gift certificates that entitle the owner to services or merchandise; for example: airlines issue tickets used for travel, local transit companies issue tokens good for fares, and department stores sell gift certificates redeemable in merchandise.

When instruments redeemable in services or merchandise are outstanding at the end of the period, accounts should be adjusted to reflect the obligations under such arrangements. The nature of the adjustment will depend on the entries originally made in recording the sale of the instruments.

Ordinarily, the sale of instruments redeemable in services or merchandise is recorded by a debit to Cash and a credit to a liability account. As instruments are redeemed, the liability balance is debited and Sales or an appropriate revenue account is credited. Certain claims may be rendered void by lapse of time or for some other reason as defined by the sales agreement. In addition, experience may indicate that a certain percentage of outstanding claims will never be presented for redemption. These factors must be considered at the end of the period, when the liability balance is reduced to the balance of the claim estimated to be outstanding and a revenue account is credited for the gain indicated from forfeitures. If Sales or a special revenue account is originally credited on the sale of the redemption instrument, the adjustment at the end of the period calls for a debit to the revenue account and a credit to a liability account for the claim still outstanding.

Compensated Absences

Compensated absences include payments by employers for vacation, holiday, illness, or other personal activities. Employees often earn paid absences based on the time employed. Generally, the longer an employee works for a company, the longer the vacation allowed, or the more liberal the time allowed for illnesses. At the end of any given accounting period, a company has a liability for earned but unused compensated absences. The matching principle requires that the estimated amounts earned be charged against current revenue, and a liability established for that amount.[9] The difficult part of this accounting treatment is estimating how much should be accrued. In Statement No. 43, the FASB requires a liability to be recognized for compensated absences that (1) have been earned through services already rendered, (2) vest or can be carried forward to subsequent years, and (3) are estimable and probable.

For example, assume that a company has a vacation pay policy for all employees. If all employees had the same anniversary date for computing time in service, the computations would not be too difficult. However, most plans provide for a flexible employee starting date. In order to compute the liability, a careful inventory of all employees must be made that includes the number of years of service, rate of pay, carryover of unused vacation from prior periods, turnover, and the probability of taking the vacation.

9. *Statement of Financial Accounting Standards No. 43,* "Accounting for Compensated Absences" (Stamford: Financial Accounting Standards Board, 1980), par. 6.

To illustrate the accounting for compensated absences, assume that S&N Corporation has 20 employees who are paid an average of $350 per week. During 1995, a total of 40 vacation weeks were earned by all employees, but only 30 weeks of vacation were taken that year. The remaining 10 weeks of vacation were taken in 1996 when the average rate of pay was $400 per week. The entry to record the accrued vacation pay on December 31, 1995, would be:

Wages Expense	3,500	
Vacation Wages Payable		3,500
To record accrued vacation wages ($350 × 10 weeks).		

The above entry assumes that Wages Expense has already been recorded for the 30 weeks of vacation taken during 1995. Therefore, the income statement would reflect the total Wages Expense for the entire 40 weeks of vacation earned during the period. On its December 31, 1995, balance sheet, S&N would report a current liability of $3,500 to reflect the obligation for the 10 weeks of vacation pay that are owed. In 1996, when the additional vacation weeks are taken and the payroll is paid, S&N would make the following entry:

Wages Expense	500	
Vacation Wages Payable	3,500	
Cash		4,000
To record payment at current rates of previously earned vacation time ($400 × 10 weeks).		

Since the vacation weeks are now used, the above entry eliminates the liability. An adjustment to Wages Expense is required because the liability was recorded at the rates of pay in effect during the time the compensation (vacation pay) was earned. However, the cash is being paid at the current rate, which requires an adjustment to Wages Expense. If the rate of pay for the 10 weeks of vacation taken in 1996 had remained the same as the rate used to record the accrual on December 31, 1995, there would not have been an adjustment to Wages Expense. The entry to record payment in 1996 would simply be a debit to the payable and a credit to Cash for $3,500.

An exception to the requirement for accrual of compensated absences, such as vacation pay, is made for sick pay. The FASB decided that sick pay should be accrued only if it vests with the employee, i.e., the employee is entitled to compensation for a certain number of "sick days" regardless of whether the employee is actually absent for that period. Upon leaving the firm, the employee would be compensated for any unused sick time. If the sick pay does not vest, it is recorded as an expense only when actually paid.[10]

Although compensated absences are not deductible for income tax purposes until the vacation, holiday, or illness occurs and the payment is made, they are required by GAAP to be recognized as liabilities on the financial statements.

CONTINGENT LIABILITIES

A *contingency* is defined in FASB Statement No. 5 as:

> *. . . an existing condition, situation, or set of circumstances involving uncertainty as to possible gain . . . or loss . . . to an enterprise that will ultimately be resolved when one or more future events occur or fail to occur.*[11]

As defined, contingencies may relate to either assets or liabilities, and to either a gain or loss. In this chapter, attention is focused on **contingent losses** that might give rise to a liability.

10. *Ibid,* par. 7.

11. *Statement of Financial Accounting Standards No. 5,* "Accounting for Contingencies" (Stamford: Financial Accounting Standards Board, 1975), par. 1.

Frequent Flyer Miles

As individuals navigate the airways, they often earn frequent flyer miles that, once enough miles are accumulated, can be redeemed for free trips. Rather than account for these bonus miles as they accumulate, airlines typically book a liability only after enough mileage has been accumulated to claim a free ticket. Thus, while experts estimate there are 25 billion miles of free travel resulting from frequent flyer programs, airlines have recognized a liability for approximately only 30 percent, or 7.5 billion miles. During 1990 alone, nine U.S. airlines collectively gave 4.5 million free trips to members of frequent flier programs.

Some members of the accounting profession have argued that a portion of the revenue from each ticket should be deferred, as a "liability reserve," and matched against future periods when the bonus miles are redeemed. Following three years of debate within the accounting profession about whether and how airlines should account for this potential liability, the Financial Accounting Standards Board ultimately decided not to do anything. The Securities and Exchange Commission, however, is requiring airline companies to disclose information regarding frequent-flier programs in their 10-K reports.

The airline companies maintain that many of the free trips earned will not be taken. American Airlines estimates 20 percent of its free trips will not be used; similarly, United Airlines estimates 25 percent will go unused. Airlines are reducing their exposure to these liabilities by fixing deadlines to redeem miles for free trips and by raising the number of miles needed to qualify for certain trips. Nevertheless, the numbers are significant. In 1990, United owed 5.4 million trips worth $160.2 million; American owed 2.8 million free trips valued at $157.1 million.

Questions:

1. Do frequent flyer miles meet the definition of a liability?
2. If frequent flyer miles are a liability, can the liability be estimated at the time a ticket is sold?
3. When should frequent flyer miles be recorded on the books of the airlines: when tickets are sold or as bonus miles are redeemed?
4. If airlines are required to make a cumulative catch-up adjustment to account for their frequent flyer liabilities, the effects on the financial statements of many airlines could be catastrophic. Should this factor enter into the decision process of accounting rule makers?

Sources: Penelope Wang, *Forbes*, June 13, 1988, p. 62. "Accounting for Frequent Fliers," *USA Today*, May 22, 1991, p. 9B.

Historically, when liabilities were classified as contingent, they were not recorded on the books but were disclosed in notes to financial statements. The distinction between a recorded liability and a **contingent liability** was not always clear. If a legal liability existed and the amount of the obligation was either definite or could be estimated with reasonable certainty, the liability was recorded on the books. If the existence of the obligation depended on the happening of a future event, recording of the liability was deferred until the event occurred. In an attempt to make the distinction more precise, the FASB used three terms in FASB Statement No. 5 to identify the range of possibilities of the event occurring. Different accounting action was recommended for each term. The terms, their definitions, and the accounting actions recommended are as follows:[12]

Term	Definition	Accounting Action
Probable	The future event or events are likely to occur.	Record the probable event in the accounts if the amount can be reasonably estimated. If not estimable, disclose facts in a note.
Reasonably possible	The chance of the future event or events occurring is more than remote but less than likely.	Report the contingency in a note.
Remote	The chance of the future event or events occurring is slight.	No recording or reporting unless contingency represents a guarantee. Then note disclosure is required.

12. *Ibid.*, par. 3.

If the occurrence of an event that would create a liability is **probable,** and if the amount of the obligation can be **reasonably estimated,** the contingency should be recognized as a liability. Some of the liabilities already presented as estimated liabilities may be considered probable contingent liabilities because the existence of the obligation is dependent on some event occurring, e.g., warranties are dependent on the need to provide future repairs or service, gift certificates are dependent on the certificate being turned in for redemption, and vacation pay is dependent on a person taking a vacation. These liabilities are not included in this section, however, because historically they have been recognized as recorded liabilities. Other items, such as unsettled litigation claims, self-insurance, loan guarantees, and environmental liabilities are typically treated as unrecorded contingent liabilities and will be explored in the following pages.

If an event is **reasonably possible,** defined as more than remote but less than likely, the company should report the contingency in a note to the financial statements. If the event is **remote,** i.e., the chance of occurrence is slight, there is no requirement to report the possible liability. The FASB statement does not provide specific guidelines as to how these three terms should be interpreted in probability percentages. Surveys made of statement preparers and users disclosed a great diversity in the probability interpretations of the terms. It is unlikely, therefore, that FASB Statement No. 5 has significantly reduced the diversity in practice in recording some of these contingent items.

Litigation

An increasing number of lawsuits are being filed against companies and individuals. Lawsuits may result in substantial payments being made to successful plaintiffs. Typically, litigation takes a long time to conclude. Even after a decision has been rendered by a lower court, there are many appeal opportunities available. Thus, both the amount and timing of a loss arising from litigation are generally highly uncertain. Some companies carry insurance to protect them against these losses, so the impact of the losses on the financial statements is minimized. For uninsured risks, however, a decision must be made as to when the liability for litigation becomes probable, and thus a recorded loss. FASB Statement No. 5 identifies several key factors to consider in making the decision. These include:[13]

1. The nature of the litigation.
2. The period when the cause of action occurred. (Liability is not recognized in any period before the cause of action occurred.)
3. Progress of the case in court, including progress between date of the financial statements and their issuance date.
4. Views of legal counsel as to the probability of loss.
5. Prior experience with similar cases.
6. Management's intended response to the litigation.

If analysis of these and similar factors results in the judgment that a loss is probable, and the amount of the loss can be reasonably estimated, the liability should be recorded. A settlement after the balance sheet date but before the statements are issued would be evidence that the loss was probable at the year-end, and would result in a reporting of loss in the current financial statements.

Another area of potential liability involves unasserted claims, i.e., a cause of action has occurred but no claim has yet been asserted. For example, a person may be injured on the property of a company, but as of the date the financial statements are issued, no legal action has been taken; or a violation of a government regulation may occur, but no federal action has yet been taken. If it is probable that a substantiated claim will be filed, and the amount

13. *Ibid.*, par. 36.

of the claim can be reasonably estimated, accrual of the liability should be made. If the amount cannot be reasonably estimated, note disclosure is required. If assertion of the claim is judged not to be at least reasonably possible, no accrual or disclosure is necessary.

As a practical matter, it should be noted that a company would be very unlikely to record a loss from unasserted claims or from pending litigation unless negotiations for a settlement had been substantially completed. When that is the case, the loss is no longer a contingency, but an estimated loss.

Some companies do not disclose any information regarding potential liabilities from litigation. Others provide a brief, general description of pending litigation. Sometimes companies provide fairly specific information about pending actions and claims. However, companies must be careful not to increase their chances of losing pending lawsuits, and they generally do not disclose dollar amounts of potential losses, which might be interpreted as an admission of guilt and a willingness to pay a certain amount. As an illustration, Exxon Corporation disclosed the following information in its 1991 annual report in connection with lawsuits filed as a result of the Valdez oil spill.

Exhibit 13—1
Exxon Corporation—Disclosure of Litigation

LITIGATION (IN PART)

On March 24, 1989, the Exxon Valdez, a tanker owned by Exxon Shipping Company, a subsidiary of Exxon Corporation, ran aground on Bligh Reef in Prince William Sound off the port of Valdez, Alaska, and released approximately 260,000 barrels of crude oil. More than 315 lawsuits, including class actions, have been brought in various courts against Exxon Corporation and certain of its subsidiaries. Most of these lawsuits seek unspecified compensatory and punitive damages; several lawsuits seek damages in varying specified amounts. Certain of the lawsuits seek injunctive relief. Of these lawsuits, more than 55 have been dismissed or settled.

In August 1989, the State of Alaska filed a suit in Superior Court in Alaska against Exxon Shipping Company, Exxon Corporation, and others, seeking substantial civil penalties and unspecified damages arising from the oil spill. On February 27, 1990, an indictment was returned in the United States District Court in Anchorage, Alaska, charging Exxon Shipping Company and Exxon Corporation with violation of the Refuse Act, the Migratory Bird Treaty Act, the Clean Water Act, the Ports and Waterways Safety Act, and the Dangerous Cargo Act. In March 1991, the United States filed a civil suit against Exxon Shipping Company, Exxon Corporation, and others, and the State of Alaska filed a separate civil suit against Exxon Shipping Company and Exxon Corporation. These suits, seeking unspecified damages from the oil spill, were filed in the United States District Court for the District of Alaska.

On October 8, 1991, the United States District Court for the District of Alaska approved a civil agreement and consent decree executed by Exxon Corporation, Exxon Shipping Company, Exxon Pipeline Company, the United States, and the State of Alaska and accepted a plea agreement executed by Exxon Corporation, Exxon Shipping Company, and the United States. These agreements provided for guilty pleas to certain misdemeanors, the dismissal of all felony charges and the remaining misdemeanor charges by the United States, and the release of all civil claims against Exxon Corporation, Exxon Shipping Company, and Exxon Pipeline Company (except certain claims by the State under the Fisheries Business Act) by the United States and the State of Alaska. The agreements also released all claims related to or arising from the oil spill by Exxon Corporation, Exxon Shipping Company, and Exxon Pipeline Company against the governments.

Payments under the plea agreement totaled $125 million – $25 million in fines and $100 million in payments to the United States and Alaska for restoration projects in Alaska. Payments under the civil agreement and consent decree will total $900 million over a ten year period. The civil agreement also provides for the possible payment, between September 1, 2002, and September 1, 2006, of up to $100 million for substantial loss or decline in populations, habitats or species in areas affected by the oil spill which could not have been reasonably anticipated on September 25, 1991.

The remaining cost to the corporation from the Valdez accident is difficult to predict and cannot be determined at this time. It is believed the final outcome, net of reserves already provided, will not have a materially adverse effect upon the corporation's operations or financial condition.

Self-Insurance

Some large companies with widely distributed risks may decide not to purchase insurance for protection against the normal business risks of fire, explosion, flood, or damage to other persons or their property. These companies in effect insure themselves against these risks. An accounting question arises as to whether a liability should be accrued and a loss recognized for the possible occurrence of the uninsured risk. Sometimes companies have recorded as an expense an amount equal to the insurance premium that would have been paid had commercial insurance been carried. The FASB considered this specific subject in Statement No. 5, and concluded that no loss or liability should be recorded until the loss has occurred. Fires, explosions, or other casualties are random in occurrence and, as such, are not accruable. Further, they stated that:

> *. . . unlike an insurance company, which has a contractual obligation under policies in force to reimburse insurers for losses, an enterprise can have no such obligation to itself and, hence, no liability.*[14]

Thus, although an exposed condition does exist, it is a future period that must bear any loss that occurs, not a current period.

Loan Guarantees

Enterprises sometimes enter into a contract guaranteeing a loan for another enterprise, frequently a subsidiary company, a supplier, or even a favored customer. These guarantees obligate the entity to make the loan payment if the principal borrower fails to make the payment. A similar contingent obligation exists when the payee of a note receivable discounts the note at a bank, but is held contingently liable in the event the maker of the note defaults. Discounted notes receivable were discussed in Chapter 8. If the default on the loan or the note is judged to be probable based on the events that have occurred prior to the issuance date of the financial statements, the loss and liability should be accrued in accordance with the general guidelines discussed in this section. Otherwise, note disclosure is required even if the likelihood of making the payment is remote. This exception to not disclosing remote contingencies arose because companies have traditionally disclosed guarantees in notes to the financial statements, and the FASB did not want to reduce this disclosure practice.

Accounting for Environmental Liabilities

An area that is receiving increasing attention in our society, both politically and from an accounting perspective, is the environment. The need to protect our environment, and in many instances to recover from past environmental abuses, is recognized by most citizens. What is not so obvious are the staggering costs associated with environmental liabilities. As but one example, current legislation in the United States mandates the clean-up of existing toxic waste sites. The Environmental Protection Agency (EPA) is empowered to clean up waste sites and then can charge the clean-up costs to those parties the EPA deems responsible. This can cost companies $25-$100 million or more for each polluted site.

Even though environmental costs are one of the critical issues facing businesses today, many, if not most, companies do not reflect those costs in their financial statements. The primary reason is that these loss contingencies often cannot be reasonably estimated. For example, USX Corporation is one of 17 companies involved in ground-water pollution at a refinery site in Minnesota. The cost of cleanup is estimated at $55 million. USX estimates it was responsible for only 5 percent of the waste, and thus 5 percent of the cleanup. But one of the biggest dumpers is in Chapter 11 bankruptcy and those responsible for 50 percent

14. *Ibid.*, par. 28.

GERMAN LIABILITIES

BASF Aktiengesellschaft is a diversified German-based firm in the oil and gas and chemical industries. BASF is probably best known to consumers in the U.S. for its audio and video tapes. Sales in 1992 totaled 45 billion Deutsche marks and the firm's market value as of May 31, 1993, was $8.2 billion, making it the 10th largest public company in Germany.

In the liability and equity portion of its 1992 balance sheet, BASF included the following three major sections:

	(In millions of Deutsche marks)
Equity	14,483
Provisions	13,702
Liabilities	10,472

Examples of items included under the provision and liability headings are:

Provisions: Deferred taxes, estimated obligations for environmental cleanups, pension and other personnel obligations, and warranty obligations.

Liabilities: Bonds, taxes payable, accounts payable, and bank loans payable.

Questions:

1. Do you perceive a difference between a "provision" and a "liability"?
2. In the notes to its financial statements, BASF includes a discussion of "Other financial commitments." This discussion primarily describes the remaining cost of uncompleted construction projects. BASF does not recognize these commitments in the financial statements as liabilities. Would these commitments be accounted for as liabilities in the United States?

Sources: The Forbes International 500, *Forbes*, July 19, 1993, p. 136. BASF Group 1992 Annual Report.

of the waste cannot be found. Under the doctrine of joint and several liability, USX might have to pick up most of the tab. The result is that most companies provide only a brief description of the potential liability in the notes to the financial statements, if they report environmental liabilities at all. Exhibit 13-2 presents an example of reporting on environmental matters from Lockheed Corporation's notes to its financial statements for 1992.

Notwithstanding current practice, there is increasing pressure for additional disclosures relative to environmental liabilities. The Emerging Issues Task Force (EITF) recently reached consensus on several aspects of accounting for environmental liabilities (Issue 93-5). In addition, the SEC Staff has issued Staff Accounting Bulletin (SAB) No. 92, which sets forth the Staff's interpretation of GAAP regarding contingent liabilities, with particular applicability to companies having environmental liabilities. A general conclusion of these pronouncements is that an environmental liability should be evaluated independently from any potential claim for recovery. Also, presentation on the balance sheet should be at the gross, rather than net, amount of the liability. The discounting of an environmental liability for a specific clean-up site to reflect the time value of money is appropriate only if the total amounts and the timing of cash payments are fixed or reliably determinable to that site. If discounted, SAB 92 sets a maximum discount rate equal to the rate on risk-free monetary assets.

As evidence of the increased recognition of environmental liabilities and the need to account for them in the financial statements, several trends are noted. First, an increasing number of companies have established committees, often at the Board of Directors level, to oversee environmental compliance. Second, more companies now have written environmental accounting policies, which are disclosed in the accounting policies note to the financial statements. Finally, there is a heightened awareness of the need for improving environmental liability accounting. With the current regulatory environment and these trends, it is likely that there will be further accounting developments and increased financial disclosures of environmental liabilities in the future.

Exhibit 13—2
Lockheed Corporation - Environmental Disclosures

NOTE II — COMMITMENTS AND CONTINGENCIES

ENVIRONMENTAL MATTERS: In March 1991, the company entered into a consent decree with the U.S. Environmental Protection Agency (EPA) relating to certain property in Burbank, California which obligates the company to design and construct facilities to monitor, extract, and treat groundwater and operate and maintain such facilities for approximately eight years. The company currently estimates that expenditures required to comply with the terms of the consent decree over the term of the project, measured at the anticipated value of the expenditures when they are incurred, including estimated inflation, will approximate $139 million.

The company has also been operating under a cleanup and abatement order from the California Regional Water Quality Control Board affecting its facilities in Burbank, California. This order requires site assessment and action to abate groundwater contamination by a combination of groundwater and soil cleanup and treatment. Based on experience being derived from initial activities, the company currently estimates the anticipated costs of these actions in excess of the requirements under the EPA consent decree to approximate $124 million over the term of the project; however, this estimate will be subject to changes as work progresses and as additional experience is gained.

Under an agreement with the U.S. government, these remediation expenditures are being allocated to all of the company's operations as general and administrative costs (see Note I) and under existing governmental regulations, the expenditures are allowable in establishing the prices of the company's products and services. As a result, a substantial portion of the expenditures will be reflected in the company's sales and costs of sales as the expenditures are made. The liability for the remaining amount has been accrued.

The company is also involved in several other proceedings and potential proceedings relating to environmental matters, including disposal of hazardous wastes and soil and water contamination. The company has not incurred any material costs relating to these environmental matters. The extent of the company's financial exposure cannot be reliably estimated at this time. The company's financial exposure related to environmental matters will be decreased by the extent to which other parties are held to be responsible for the particular conditions and the extent to which the company obtains recovery under certain of its insurance policies. In addition, a substantial portion of any costs will be allowable under terms of existing U.S. government procurement regulations, in the establishment of prices of the company's products and services.

BALANCE SHEET PRESENTATION

The liability section of the balance sheet is usually divided between current and noncurrent liabilities as previously discussed. The nature of the detail to be presented for current liabilities depends on the use to be made of the financial statement. A balance sheet prepared for stockholders might report little detail; on the other hand, creditors may insist on full detail concerning current debts.

Assets are normally recorded in the order of their liquidity, and consistency would suggest that liabilities be reported in the order of their maturity. The latter practice may be followed only to the extent it is practical; observance of this procedure would require an analysis of the different classes of obligations and separate reporting for classes with varying maturity dates.

Liabilities should not be offset by assets to be applied to their liquidation. Disclosure as to future debt liquidation, however, may be provided by an appropriate parenthetical remark or note. Disclosure of liabilities secured by specific assets should also be made by a parenthetical remark or note.

The current liabilities section of a balance sheet prepared on December 31, 1996, might appear as follows.

Current liabilities:		
Notes payable:		
Trade creditors	$12,000	
Banks (secured by pledge of accounts receivable)	20,000	
Officers	12,500	$ 44,500
Accounts payable		35,250
Current portion of long-term debt		10,000
Salaries and wages payable		1,250
Income taxes payable		6,000
Real and personal property taxes payable		1,550
Dividends payable		4,500
Other current liabilities:		
Advances from customers	$ 7,500	
Estimated warranty costs	2,500	10,000
Total current liabilities		$113,050

For a further illustration of a liabilities section of a balance sheet, with related notes, see the Microsoft financial statements presented in Appendix A at the end of this book.

KEY TERMS

Compensated absences 551
Contingent liability 539
Current ratio 537
Liabilities 536
Nontrade notes payable 540
Promissory note 540
Refundable deposits 547
Trade notes payable 540
Unearned revenues 546
Warranties 547
Working Capital Ratio 537

QUESTIONS

1. Identify the major components included in the definition of liabilities established by the FASB.
2. (a) What is meant by an executory contract? (b) Do these contracts fit the definition of liabilities included in this chapter?
3. Distinguish between current and noncurrent liabilities.
4. At what amount should liabilities generally be reported?
5. Under what conditions would debt that will mature within the next year be reported as a noncurrent liability?
6. Distinguish between the following categories: (a) liabilities that are definite in amount, (b) estimated liabilities, and (c) contingent liabilities.
7. The sales manager for Off-Road Enterprises is entitled to a bonus equal to 12% of profits. What difficulties may arise in the interpretation of this profit-sharing agreement?
8. Gross payroll is taxed by both federal and state governments. Identify these taxes and indicate who bears the cost of the tax, the employer or the employee.
9. How should a company account for revenue received in advance for a service contract?
10. Why should a company normally account for product warranties on an accrual basis?
11. What information must a firm accumulate in order to adequately account for estimated liabilities on tickets, tokens, and gift certificates?
12. How should compensated absences be accounted for?
13. How should contingent liabilities that are reasonably possible of becoming liabilities be reported on the financial statements?
14. What factors are important in deciding whether a pending lawsuit should be reported as a liability on the balance sheet?
15. Why does accounting for self-insurance differ from accounting for insurance premiums with outside carriers?

DISCUSSION CASES

Case 13—1 (What is a liability?)

Professional athletes regularly sign long-term, multimillion dollar contracts in which they promise to play for a particular team for a specified time period. Owners of these teams often sign long-term leases for the use of playing facilities for a specified time period. GAAP requires the leases to be booked as liabilities but does not require the obligations associated with pro athletes' contracts to be recorded.

Discuss the reasons for the differing treatment of these two seemingly similar events. Do you think the disclosure currently required by GAAP in these instances satisfies the needs of investors and creditors?

Case 13—2 (Measuring liabilities)

Long term leases and long-term debt are typically disclosed on the financial statements at their discounted present values. This disclosure recognizes the time value of money. However, the standards related to accounting for deferred income taxes do not involve discounting expected future tax obligations.

Why do you suppose the FASB requires the use of discounting with some long-term liabilities and not with others? Should discounting be required for all long-term liabilities? Provide support for your answer.

Case 13—3 (Leave my current ratio alone!)

Soto Inc., a closely held corporation, has never been audited and is seeking a large bank loan for plant expansion. The bank has requested audited financial statements. In conference with the president and majority stockholder of Soto, the auditor is informed that the bank looks very closely at the current ratio. The auditor's proposed reclassifications and adjustments include the following:

(a) A note payable issued 4 1/2 years ago matures in six months from the balance sheet date. The auditor wants to reclassify it as a current liability. The controller says no, because "we are probably going to refinance this note with other long-term debt."

(b) An accrual for compensated absences. Again the controller objects because the amount of the pay for these absences cannot be estimated. "Some employees quit in the first year and don't get vacation, and it is impossible to predict which employees will be absent for illness or other causes. Without being able to identify the employees, we can't determine the rate of compensation."

How would you, if you were the auditor, respond to the controller?

Case 13—4 (When is a loss a loss?)

How should Newport Company report each of the following contingencies?

(a) A threat of expropriation exists for one of Newport's manufacturing plants located in a foreign country. Expropriation is deemed to be reasonably possible. Any compensation from the foreign government would be less than the carrying amount (book value) of the plant.

(b) Potential costs exist due to the discovery of a safety hazard related to one of Newport's products. These costs are probable and can be reasonably estimated.

(c) One of Newport's warehouses located at the base of a mountain could no longer be insured against rock-slide losses. No rock-slide losses have occurred.

Case 13—5 (Should a liability be recorded?)

Angela Company is a manufacturer of toys. During the year, the following situations arose:

(a) A safety hazard related to one of its toy products was discovered. It is considered probable that liabilities have been incurred. Based on past experience, a reasonable estimate of the amount of loss can be made.

(b) One of its small warehouses is located on the bank of a river and could no longer be insured against flood losses. No flood losses have occurred after the date that the insurance became unavailable.

(c) This year, Angela began promoting a new toy by including a coupon, redeemable for a movie ticket, in each toy's carton. The movie ticket, which cost Angela $2, is purchased in advance and then mailed to the customer when the coupon is received by Angela. Angela estimated, based on past experience, that sixty percent of the coupons would be redeemed. Forty percent of the coupons were actually redeemed this year, and the remaining twenty percent of the coupons are expected to be redeemed next year.

How should Angela Company account for each of these situations?

Case 13—6 (Is it really self-insurance?)

The auditors of Data Retrieval Systems are concerned with how to account for the insurance premiums on a liability policy carried with a large insurance company. Premiums on the policy are based on the average loss experience of Data Retrieval Systems over the past five years. In some years, no insured loss occurs; however, the company follows the practice of recognizing expenses for the premiums paid to the insurance company regardless of actual loss. The senior auditor, Gary Wells, has read FASB Statement No. 5 and argues that the premiums paid are really deposits with the insurance company. Since the premiums are based on the losses actually incurred, income should be charged only when the losses occur, not when the premiums are paid. By charging the premiums to expense, an artificial smoothing of income results, something FASB Statement No. 5 was designed to prevent. Barbara Orton, controller, argues that the premiums are arm's-length payments, that FASB Statement No. 5 applies only to self-insurance, and that the policy carried by Data Retrieval Systems is obviously with an outside carrier. Thus, Orton believes the premiums should be recognized as a valid period expense. As audit manager, you are asked to render your opinion on the matter.

Case 13—7 (Is "probable" enough?)

One of the most difficult estimation questions in accounting is when contingent liabilities need to be recognized in a company's financial statements. The FASB indicated in Statement No. 5

that a liability and loss should be reported in the financial statements if it is probable that a loss will be incurred and the amount of the loss can be estimated. But what is the meaning of probable? Some accountants have interpreted this as meaning near certainty; others as being at a lesser percentage of certainty such as above 90%, 85%, or some other number.

In 1992, the FASB issued Statement No. 109 that required reporting of deferred income tax assets if it is more likely than not that a company will have future income sufficient to realize the asset. The term "more likely than not" was defined as an amount slightly above 50%.

Because of the use of a new probability concept, some accountants have suggested that the definition of "probable" used in Statement No. 5 should be made more specific, perhaps even using the "more likely than not" criteria for contingent liabilities. What are the arguments for and against this suggestion?

Case 13—8 (Do we need standards for environmental and other contingent liabilities?)

Many state and federal laws place possible future liabilities on companies as a result of environmental pollution, sexual discrimination, safety requirements, and other social responsibilities. In general, these items are part of those potential losses and liabilities covered by FASB Statement No. 5. Some companies are reporting these items as liabilities while others are waiting for more specific guidelines by the FASB before reporting them. Should the FASB adopt specific guidelines for the reporting of these liabilities, or should the decision be left to companies to make based on the general conceptual guidelines of FASB Statement No. 5?

EXERCISES

Exercise 13—9 (Types of liabilities)

For each of the following scenarios, identify whether the event described is an actual liability, a contingent liability, or not a liability. If you conclude that the event involves an actual liability, determine if the liability is (1) current or noncurrent, and (2) definite in amount or involves an estimate.

(a) Apple Inc. purchased inventory on November 1. The invoice totaled $17,000 and payment is expected to be made within 30 days.
(b) Banana Corp. financed its warehouse facilities with a long-term mortgage that calls for semiannual payments of $7,000. The mortgage's current outstanding balance is $98,000.
(c) Orange Company sells computer systems and supplies. It offers its customers a 30-day, money-back guarantee. In the past, approximately 10% of customers have exercised this return privilege.
(d) Kiwi Industries manufactures and distributes outdoor recreational equipment. An individual recently filed a lawsuit as a result of injuries sustained while using Kiwi equipment. Attorneys for Kiwi feel the chance of losing the case is minimal.
(e) Berry Incorporated, a newly formed company, has an unfunded pension plan that calls for retirement benefits to be paid to employees who retire after a minimum of ten years of employment with the company.
(f) John Townson, a successful entrepreneur, has expressed a desire to establish university scholarships for disadvantaged youth in his community. He has been contacted by numerous universities, but as of yet, nothing firm has been established.

Exercise 13—10 (Purchase with non-interest-bearing note)

On September 1, 1995, Specialized Manufacturing Co. purchased two new company automobiles from Top Quality Auto Sales. The terms of the sale called for Specialized to pay $30,723 to Top Quality on September 1, 1996. Specialized gave the seller a non-interest-bearing note for that amount. At the date of purchase, the interest rate for short-term loans was 7.8%.

1. Prepare the journal entries necessary on September 1, 1995, December 31, 1995, (year-end adjusting), and September 1, 1996.
2. Show how notes payable would be presented in the December 31, 1995, balance sheet.

Exercise 13—11 (Recording payroll and payroll taxes)

The Express Company paid one week's wages of $10,600 in cash (net pay after all withholdings and deductions) to its employees. Income tax withholdings were equal to 17% of the gross payroll, and the only other deductions were 7.65% for FICA tax and $160 for union dues. Give the entries that should be made on the books of the company to record the payroll and the tax accruals to be recognized by the employer, assuming that the company is subject to unemployment taxes of 5.4% (state) and 0.8% (federal). Assume that all wages for the week are subject to FICA and unemployment taxes.

Exercise 13—12 (Monthly payroll entries)

Aggie Co. sells agricultural products. Aggie pays its salespeople a salary plus a commission. The salary is the same for each salesperson, $1,000 per month. The commission varies by length of time of employment, and is a percentage of the company's total gross sales. Each salesperson starts with a commission of 1.0%, which is increased an additional 0.5% for each full year of employment with Aggie, to a maximum of 5.0%. The total gross sales for the month of January were $120,000.

Aggie has six salespeople as follows:

	No. of Years
Frank	10
Sally	9
Tina	8
Barry	6
Mark	3
Lisa	9 mos.

Assume the FICA rate is 7.65%, the FUTA rate is 6.2%, and the state unemployment rate is 5.4%. (Assume the federal government allows the maximum credit for state unemployment tax paid.) The federal income tax withholding rate is 30%. Compute the January salaries and commissions expense and make any necessary entries to record the payroll transactions.

Exercise 13—13 (Calculation of bonus)

Illinois Wholesale Company has an agreement with its sales manager whereby that individual is entitled to 8% of company earnings as a bonus. Company income for a calendar year before bonus and income tax is $350,000. Income tax is 40% of income after bonus. Compute the amount of the bonus under each of the following conditions.

(a) The bonus is calculated on income before deductions for bonus and income tax.
(b) The bonus is calculated on income after deduction for bonus but before deduction for income tax.

Exercise 13—14 (Accounting for property taxes)

On November 20, 1995, Miranda Floral Shop received a property tax assessment of $14,400 for the taxing unit's fiscal year ending June 30, 1996. No entry was made to record the assessment. Later, Miranda's accountant was preparing the yearly financial statements (based on a February 1 to January 31 fiscal year) and came across the property tax assessment. Give the journal entries to record the tax payment (if any) and any adjusting entries necessary on January 31, 1996, assuming:

(a) The full tax of $14,400 had been paid on January 5, 1996, and charged to expense.
(b) None of the tax had been paid as of January 31, 1996.
(c) A portion of the tax ($9,050) had been paid on January 20, 1996, and charged to expense.

Exercise 13—15 (Warranty liability)

In 1995 Hampton Office Supply began selling a new computer that carried a two-year warranty against defects. Based on the manufacturer's recommendations, Hampton projects estimated warranty costs (as a percentage of dollar sales) as follows:

First year of warranty	3%
Second year of warranty	9%

Sales and actual warranty repairs for 1995 and 1996 are presented below.

	1995	1996
Sales	$500,000	$625,000
Actual warranty repairs	10,600	22,450

1. Give the necessary journal entries to record the liability at the end of 1995 and 1996.
2. Analyze the warranty liability account as of the year ending December 31, 1996, to see if the actual repairs approximate the estimate. Should Hampton revise the manufacturer's warranty estimate? (Assume sales and repairs occur evenly throughout the year.)

Exercise 13—16 (Warranty liability)

Modern Appliance Company's accountant has been reviewing the firm's past television sales. For the past two years, Modern has been offering a special service warranty on all televisions sold. With the purchase of a television, the customer has the right to purchase a three-year service contract for an extra $60. Information concerning past television and warranty contract sales is given below.

Color-All Model II Television

	1995	1996
Television sales in units	460	550
Sales price per unit	$400	$500
Number of service contracts sold	300	350
Expenses relating to television warranties	$3,350	$9,630

Modern's accountant has estimated from past records that the pattern of repairs has been 40% in the first year after sale, 36% in the second year, and 24% in the third year. Give the necessary journal entries related to the service contracts for 1995 and 1996. In addition, indicate how much profit on service contracts would be recognized in 1996. Assume sales of the contracts are made evenly during the year.

Exercise 13—17 (Premium liability)

Cipollini Cosmetics Company began a sales promotion campaign for a new shampoo on June 30, 1996. Part of this promotion included providing a coupon with each bottle of shampoo sold. Customers can redeem 10 coupons for a hand-held hairdryer. The shampoo is sold for $14.50 per bottle in department stores and beauty salons. Each hairdryer costs Cipollini $6.95. Cipollini estimated that 60% of the coupons issued would be redeemed. For the six months ended December 31, 1996, the following information is available:

Bottles of shampoo sold	260,000
Hairdryers purchased	19,500
Coupons redeemed	87,400

What is the estimated liability for premium claims outstanding at December 31, 1996?

Exercise 13—18 (Premium liability)

On June 1, 1996, the National Pet Company began marketing a new dog food created specifically to meet the nutritional requirements of puppies. As a promotion, National was offering a free doghouse to all customers returning the weight seals from the purchase of 1,000 pounds of the new dog food. National estimates that 30% of the weight seals will be returned. At December 31, 1996, the following information was available:

Sales (1,650,000 pounds × $.40)	$660,000
Doghouses purchased (495 × $30)	14,850
Doghouses distributed (265 × $30)	7,950

Give the journal entries to record the sales of dog food, purchase of doghouse premiums, redemption of weight seals, and the estimated liability for outstanding premium offers as of the end of the year.

Exercise 13—19 (Compensated absence—vacation pay)

The Merckx Company employs six people. Each employee is entitled to two weeks' paid vacation every year the employee works for the company. The conditions of the paid vacation are: (a) for each *full* year of work, an employee will receive two weeks of paid vacation (no vacation accrues for a portion of a year), (b) each employee will receive the same pay for vacation time as the regular pay in the year taken, and (c) unused vacation pay can be carried forward. The following data were taken from the firm's personnel records:

Employee	Starting Date	Cumulative Vacation Taken as of December 31, 1996	Weekly Salary
Andy Hampsten	December 21, 1989	11 weeks	$475
Phil Anderson	March 6, 1994	2 weeks	600
Lance Armstrong	August 13, 1995	none	450
Steve Bauer	December 17, 1994	3 weeks	400
Sean Yates	March 29, 1996	none	500
Michele Fellows	May 31, 1988	15 weeks	700

Compute the liability for vacation pay as of December 31, 1996.

Exercise 13—20 (Disclosure of contingencies)

Sound Wave, Inc., a manufacturer of electronic greeting cards, has had a lawsuit filed against it by Sounds Good, another manufacturer of electronic greeting cards. The suit alleges patent right infringements by Sound Wave and asks for compensatory damages.

For the following possible situations, determine whether Sound Wave should: (1) report as a liability on the balance sheet and if so, how much, (2) disclose in a note, or (3) do nothing. Give reasons for your answers.

(a) Sound Wave's legal counsel is convinced that the suit will result in a loss to Sound Wave but isn't sure how much.
(b) Sound Wave's legal counsel believes an out-of-court settlement is probable and will cost Sound Wave approximately $600,000.
(c) Sound Wave's legal counsel believes it is reasonably possible that the case will result in a $2,000,000 loss to Sound Wave.
(d) Sound Wave's legal counsel believes it is probable that the case will result in an undeterminable loss to Sound Wave.
(e) Sound Wave's legal counsel believes there is a remote chance for a loss to occur.
(f) The suit hasn't been filed, but Sound Wave's legal counsel has informed management that an unintentional patent infringement has occurred.

Exercise 13—21 (Contingent losses)

Conrad Corporation sells motorcycle helmets. In 1995, Conrad sold 4 million helmets before discovering a significant defect in the helmet's construction. By December 31, 1995, two lawsuits had been filed against Conrad. The first lawsuit, which Conrad has little chance of winning, is expected to settle out of court for $900,000 in January of 1996. Conrad's attorneys think the company has a fifty-fifty chance of winning the second lawsuit, which is for $400,000. What accounting treatment should Conrad give the pending lawsuits in the year-end financial statements? (Include any necessary journal entries.)

Exercise 13—22 (Contingent liabilities)

Bell Industries is a multinational company. In preparing the annual financial statements, the auditors met with Bell's attorneys to discuss various legal matters facing the firm. For each of the following independent items, determine the appropriate disclosure.

(a) Bell is being sued by a distributor for breach of contract. The attorneys feel there is a 30% chance of Bell's losing the suit.
(b) One of Bell's subsidiaries has been accused by a federal agency of violating numerous environmental laws. The company faces significant fines if found guilty. The attorneys feel that the subsidiary has complied with all applicable laws and therefore place the probability of incurring the fines at less than 10%.
(c) A subsidiary operating in a foreign country whose government is unstable was recently taken over by the government and nationalized. Bell is negotiating with representatives of that government but company attorneys feel the probability of the company losing possession of its assets is approximately 90%.

Exercise 13—23 (Balance sheet reporting of current liabilities)

1. Prepare the current liabilities section of the balance sheet for the Ilena Company on December 31, 1995, from the information below.
   (a) Short-term notes payable: arising from purchase of goods, $62,680; arising from loans from banks, $20,000, on which securities valued at $26,100 have been pledged as security; arising from short-term advances by officers, $22,600.
   (b) Accounts payable arising from purchase of goods, $59,300.
   (c) Employees' income taxes payable, $1,584.
   (d) First-mortgage serial bonds, $175,000, payable in semiannual installments of $7,000 due on March 1 and September 1 of each year.
   (e) Advances received from customers on purchase orders, $4,140.
   (f) Estimated expense of meeting warranty-for-service requirements on merchandise sold, $6,480.
2. Assuming Ilena reported current assets of $319,500, compute its current ratio.

Exercise 13—24 (Recording liabilities)

Bicknell Co. is a retail outlet selling lawn care equipment. During the month of April, the following events occurred:

(a) Sales totaled $60,000 net of sales tax (all on account). The state sales tax rate is 6%.
(b) The cost of inventory sold was $28,000.
(c) Salary expense was $12,000. The FICA rate is 7.65%; income taxes totaled 15% of the gross salary expense; and the state and federal unemployment tax rates are 5.4% and 0.8%, respectively. All salaries are subject to FICA and unemployment taxes.
(d) Inventory costing $35,000 was purchased on account.
(e) Other miscellaneous expenses totaled $15,000, of which $2,500 represents depreciation and $3,000 remained unpaid at the end of the month.
(f) The sales tax and the state unemployment tax were remitted on the last day of the month.

1. Prepare the journal entries to record each of the above events. (Omit explanations.)
2. Prepare a condensed income statement for the month ended April 30, 1996.

PROBLEMS

Problem 13—25 (Miscellaneous operating payables)

The Benesto Corporation closes its books and prepares financial statements on an annual basis. The following information is gathered by the chief accountant to assist in preparing the liability section of the balance sheet:

(a) Property taxes of $66,000 were assessed on the property in May 1995 for the subsequent period of July 1 to June 30. The payment of taxes is divided into three equal installments—November 1, February 1, and May 1. The November 1 payment was made and charged to Property Tax Expense. No other entries have been made for property taxes relative to the 1995-96 assessment.

(b) The estimated 1995 pretax income for Benesto is $754,000. The effective state income tax rate is 12% (applied to pretax income). The effective rate for federal income taxes is estimated at 30% (applied to income after deducting state income taxes). Income tax payments of $320,000 were made by Benesto during 1995, including $80,000 as the final payment on 1994 federal income taxes, $50,000 for 1995 estimated state taxes, the balance for 1995 estimated federal taxes.

(c) Taxable sales for 1995 were $8,250,000. The state sales tax rate is 6.25%. Quarterly statements have been filed, and the following tax payments were made with the return.

1st Quarter	$106,000
2nd Quarter	125,000
3rd Quarter	150,000

The balance in the sales tax payable account is $133,000 at December 31, 1995.

Instructions:

1. Based on the above data, what amounts should be reported on the balance sheet as liabilities at December 31, 1995?
2. Prepare the necessary adjusting entries to record the liabilities.

Problem 13—26 (Accrued payroll and payroll taxes)

Tomasso Clothiers' employees are paid on the 7th and 23rd of each month for the period ending the last day of the previous month and the 15th of the current month, respectively. An analysis of the payroll on Thursday, November 7, 1996, revealed the following data:

	Gross Pay	FICA	Federal Income Tax	State Income Tax	Insurance	Net Pay
Office staff salaries	$13,250	$ 624	$ 1,300	$ 550	$ 370	$10,406
Officers' salaries	27,000	324	5,000	1,200	400	20,076
Sales salaries	22,000	812	3,800	770	410	16,208
Totals	$62,250	$1,760	$10,100	$2,520	$1,180	$46,690

It is determined that for the October 31 pay period, no additional employees exceeded the wage base for FICA purposes than had done so in prior pay periods. All of the officers' salaries, 80% of the office staff salaries, and 45% of the sales salaries for the payroll period ending October 31 were paid to employees who had exceeded the wage base for unemployment taxes. Assume the unemployment tax rates in force are as follows: federal unemployment tax, 0.8%, and state unemployment tax, 5.4%.

Instructions: Prepare the adjusting entries that would be required at October 31, the end of Tomasso's fiscal year, to reflect the accrual of the payroll and any related payroll taxes. Separate salary and payroll taxes expense accounts are used for each of the three employee categories: office staff, officers', and sales salaries.

Problem 13—27 (Accounting for payroll)

Bags, Inc., a manufacturer of suitcases, has 10 employees. Five of the employees are paid on a salary basis, and five are hourly employees. The employees and their compensations are as follows:

	Annual Salary
Ken Scott (president)	$91,500
Tatia Furgins	57,000
Jennifer Poulins	48,750
Robyn Meek	23,800
Kyle Roberts	13,900
	Rate Per Hour
Richard Dean (50 hours per week)	$14.00
Denise Ray (40 hours per week)	11.50
Dale Frank (40 hours per week)	9.75
Bryan Leslie (30 hours per week)	4.50
Albert Lamb (20 hours per week)	3.65

The salaried employees are covered by a comprehensive medical and dental plan. The cost of the plan is $45 per employee and is deducted from each paycheck. The hourly employees are covered only by a medical plan. The cost is calculated at 3.5% of gross pay and is deducted from each check. The FICA rate is 7.65%, and FUTA is 6.2%, with the maximum credit for state unemployment allowed. The state unemployment tax is 5.4%. In addition, each of the hourly employees, except Albert, belongs to the Suitcase Workers of America Union. Union dues are $5.65 per month and are deducted and paid on behalf of the hourly employees. The income tax withholding rate is 28% for employees with annual incomes above $29,500 and 15% for employees with annual incomes of $29,500 or less.

Hourly employees are paid weekly on Friday, January 6, 13, 20, and 27. Salaried employees are paid twice a month, on January 13 and 27. Assume that payroll taxes and all employee withholdings and deductions are paid on the 15th and the last day of each month.

Instructions: Make all entries related to Bags, Inc.'s, payroll for January 6 and January 13.

Problem 13—28 (Tax liability)

Lucille's Cafe, a new business in town, has asked you for help in calculating and recording its property and sales tax liability. On July 1, 1995, Lucille's received notice that property taxes totaling $24,000 were to be paid by October 1, 1995. The property tax was for the period of July 1, 1995, to June 30, 1996. Lucille's Cafe had sales of $89,460 in 1995. This amount included sales tax collections. The sales tax rate in the area is 5%. Sales taxes are due on January 31, 1996.

Instructions:

1. Give the entries to record the accrual, monthly expensing, and payment of property taxes. (Give only one example of the monthly recognition of property tax.) What is the December 31, 1995, balance in the deferred property taxes account?
2. Calculate the amount of sales tax payable as of December 31, 1995. Make the entry needed to record this liability at year-end. Also give the entry to record payment of sales tax on January 31, 1996.

Problem 13—29 (Warranty liability)

High Fidelity Corporation sells stereos under a two-year warranty contract that requires High Fidelity to replace defective parts and provide free labor on all repairs. During 1995, 1,050 units were sold at $900 each. In 1996, High Fidelity sold an additional 900 units at $925. Based on past experience, the estimated two-year warranty costs are $20 for parts and $25 for labor per unit. It is also estimated that 40% of the warranty expenditures will occur in the first year and 60% in the second year.

Actual warranty expenditures were as follows:

	Warranty Costs	
	1996	1997
Stereos sold in 1995	$18,300	$26,500
Stereos sold in 1996	—	18,100

Instructions: Assuming sales occurred on the last day of the year for both 1995 and 1996, give the necessary journal entries for the years 1995 through 1997. Analyze the warranty liability account for the year ending December 31, 1997, to see if the actual repairs approximate the estimate. Should High Fidelity revise its warranty estimates?

Problem 13—30 (Warranty liability)

Monroe Corporation, a client, requests that you compute the appropriate balance of its estimated liability for the product warranty account for a statement as of June 30, 1996.

Monroe Corporation manufactures television tubes and sells them with a six-month warranty under which defective tubes will be replaced without charge. On December 31, 1995, Estimated Liability for Product Warranty had a balance of $510,000. By June 30, 1996, this balance had been reduced to $80,250 by debits for estimated net cost of tubes returned that had been sold in 1995.

The corporation started out in 1996 expecting 8% of the dollar volume of sales to be returned. However, due to the introduction of new models during the year, this estimated percentage of returns was increased to 10% on May 1. It is assumed that no tubes sold during a given month are returned in that month. Each tube is stamped with a date at time of sale so that the warranty may be properly administered. The following table of percentages indicates the likely pattern of sales returns during the six-month period of the warranty, starting with the month following the sale of tubes.

Month Following Sale	Percentage of Total Returns Expected
First	20%
Second	30
Third	20
Fourth through sixth—10% each month	30
	100%

Gross sales of tubes were as follows for the first six months of 1996:

Month	Amount	Month	Amount
January	$3,600,000	April	$2,850,000
February	3,300,000	May	2,000,000
March	4,100,000	June	1,800,000

The corporation's warranty also covers the payment of freight cost on defective tubes returned and on the new tubes sent out as replacements. This freight cost runs approximately 10% of the sales price of the tubes returned. The manufacturing cost of the tubes is roughly 80% of the sales price, and the salvage value of returned tubes averages 15% of their sales price. Returned tubes on hand at December 31, 1995, were thus valued in inventory at 15% of their original sales price.

Instructions: Using the data given, prepare a schedule for arriving at the balance of the estimated liability for the product warranty account as of June 30, 1996, and give the proposed adjusting entry.

Problem 13—31 (Premium liability)

The Village Corp. manufactures a special type of low-suds laundry soap. A dish towel is offered as a premium to customers who send in two proof-of-purchase seals from these soap boxes and a remittance of $2. Data for the premium offer are summarized below.

	1995	1996
Soap sales ($2.50 per package)	$2,500,000	$3,125,000
Dish towel purchases ($2.50 per towel)	$ 130,000	$ 176,250
Number of dish towels distributed as premiums	50,000	70,000
Number of dish towels expected to be distributed in subsequent periods	8,500	3,000

Mailing costs are $0.26 per package.

Instructions:

1. Give the entries for 1995 and 1996 to record product sales, premium purchases and redemptions, and year-end adjustments.
2. Present T-accounts with appropriate amounts as of the end of 1995 and 1996.

Problem 13—32 (Compensated absences)

Ludwig Electronics Inc. has a plan to compensate its employees for certain absences. Each employee can receive five days' sick leave each year plus 10 days' vacation. The benefits carry over for two additional years, after which the provision lapses on a FIFO flow basis. Thus, the maximum accumulation is 45 days. In some cases, the company permits vacations to be taken before they are earned. Payments are made based on current compensation levels, not on the level in effect when the absence time was earned.

Employee	Days Accrued Jan. 1, 1996	Daily Rate Jan. 1, 1996	Days Earned 1996	Days Taken 1996	Days Accrued Dec. 31, 1996	Daily Rate Dec. 31, 1996
A	20	$68	15	13	22	$70
B	15	74	15	15	15	76
C	25	62	7	32	0	Terminated June 15— Rate = $64
D	– 5	56	15	20	–10	$58
E	40	78	15	5	50	82
F	Hired July 1— Rate = $60	—	8	2	6	60

Instructions:

1. How much is the liability for compensated absences at December 31, 1996?
2. Prepare a summary journal entry to record compensation absence payments during the year and the accrual at the end of the year. Assume the payroll liability account is charged for all payments made during the year for both sickness and vacation leaves. The average rate of compensation for the year may be used to value the hours taken except for Employee C, who took leaves at the date of termination. The end-of-year rate should be used to establish the ending liability.

Problem 13—33 (Contingent liabilities)

The Western Supply Co. has several contingent liabilities at December 31, 1996. The following brief description of each liability is obtained by the auditor:

(a) In May 1995, Western Supply became involved in litigation. In December 1996, a judgment for $800,000 was assessed against Western by the court. Western is appealing the amount of the judgment. Attorneys for Western feel it is probable that they can reduce the assessment on appeal by 50%. No entries have been made by Western pending completion of the appeal process, which is expected to take at least a year.

(b) In July 1996, Morgan County brought action against Western for polluting the Jordan River with its waste products. It is reasonably possible that Morgan County will be successful, but the amount of damages Western might have to pay should not exceed $200,000. No entry has been made by Western to reflect the possible loss.

(c) Western Supply has elected to self-insure its fire and casualty risks. At the beginning of the year, the account Reserve for Insurance had a balance of $2,500,000. During 1996, $750,000 was debited to Insurance Expense and credited to the reserve account. After payment for losses actually sustained in 1996, the reserve account had a balance of $2,800,000 at December 31, 1996. The opening balance was a result of several years of activity similar to 1996.

(d) Western Supply has signed as guarantor for a $50,000 loan by Guaranty Bank to Midwest Parts Inc., a principal supplier to Western. Because of financial problems at Midwest, it is probable that Western Supply will have to pay the $50,000 with only a 40% recovery anticipated from Midwest. No entries have been made to reflect the liability.

Instructions:

1. What amount should be reported as a liability on the December 31, 1996, balance sheet?
2. What note disclosure should be included as part of the balance sheet for each of the above items?
3. Prepare the journal entries necessary to adjust Western's books to reflect your answers in (1) and (2).

Problem 13—34 (Contingencies)

In the introduction to this chapter, the legal history of the case between Pennzoil and Texaco was briefly outlined. Texaco was ordered to pay $10.5 billion to Pennzoil in 1985. Subsequent appeals in 1986 and 1987 affirmed the judgment against Texaco. The two companies agreed in late 1987 to a settlement of $3 billion, and in 1988 Texaco paid Pennzoil.

Instructions:

1. In 1984, when the lawsuit was initially filed, how should Texaco have disclosed the event? If a journal entry is required, prepare it.
2. In 1985 following the initial jury award, how should Texaco have disclosed the event? If a journal entry is required, prepare it.
3. In 1986 following the outcome of the appeal, how should Texaco have disclosed the event? If a journal entry is required, prepare it.
4. In 1987 following the $3 billion agreement between Texaco and Pennzoil, how should Texaco have disclosed the event? If a journal entry is required, prepare it.
5. Prepare the journal entry to record Texaco's settlement in 1988.
6. How should Pennzoil have disclosed this event during the years 1984 through 1987?

Problem 13—35 (Recording and reporting liabilities)

Landon Manufacturing pays its employees on the last day of each month. On December 31, 1996, Landon paid $19,450 in cash to its employees for December salaries and wages. Subject to FICA is $25,000 of the gross payroll for December, and $5,000 is subject to unemployment taxes. The FICA tax rate is 7.65%. The FUTA tax rate is 6.2% and the state unemployment tax rate is 5.7%. The federal government allows the maximum credit for state unemployment tax paid. Payroll and withholding taxes for December are to be paid to the taxing authorities in January 1997. The combined withholding rate for federal, state, and local income taxes is 30%.

Landon has a mortgage of $455,000 for a plant it constructed and completed on September 1, 1993. The entire mortgage balance has been classified as a long-term obligation on the balance sheet. Interest has been paid each September 1, beginning in 1994. The interest is 10% of the outstanding mortgage balance. Beginning September 1, 1997, Landon is required to make annual payments of $46,528, which include both principal and interest.

In addition, Landon has a $15,000, five-year note payable to First Thrift Bank that matures December 31, 1997. Interest is payable on the note at 12% each January 1. Landon management plans to refinance the note when it comes due. A refinancing agreement has been signed with the bank.

On October 1 of each year, Landon pays property taxes in advance and records the payment as an asset. On October 1, 1996, Landon paid property taxes of $13,500 for the 12-month period ending September 30, 1997. The balance in the asset account as of January 1, 1996, was $9,375.

In August of 1996, a lawsuit was filed against Landon. The plaintiff in the lawsuit has asked for $6 million in damages for injuries allegedly resulting from a defective product manufactured by Landon. Landon's legal counsel believes it is probable that the suit will result in a loss to Landon, but the amount of the potential loss cannot be reasonably estimated as of December 31, 1996.

Instructions:

1. Make all necessary entries at December 31, 1996, to reflect the above transactions and events.
2. Prepare the liabilities section of Landon's classified balance sheet.

Problem 13—36 (Accounting for environmental liabilities and other events)

Asbestos Inc. is a manufacturer of heat shields for use in oil refineries. Management has prepared financial statements for the year ended 1996 for review by the auditors. The audit team has questioned several items contained in the financial statements and has asked for your advice concerning the proper treatment of these items. Each of the items being questioned is listed below.

(a) In November of 1996, attorneys for current and former employees of Asbestos Inc. filed a class action lawsuit alleging that exposure to asbestos has caused significant medical problems. Attorneys for Asbestos Inc. are uncertain as to the outcome of the case. However, similar lawsuits against other firms in the asbestos industry have resulted in significant payments by the employer.

(b) On January 12, 1997, a fire at a production facility resulted in a number of adjacent buildings (owned by other businesses) being burned. Asbestos' insurance policy does not cover damage to the property of others. Insurance companies for those other businesses have billed Asbestos for the estimated cost of $2.4 million required to restore the damaged buildings.

(c) One of Asbestos' production plants is located on the shores of Lake Obewankanobe. The lake has been rising for a number of years and the company has installed dikes to prevent flooding. The dikes are currently operating at or near capacity. Weather forecasters have predicted that the lake will rise another 8 inches this coming summer. If this occurs, significant damage will likely result from the dikes being stressed beyond capacity.

(d) A national magazine printed an article regarding the dangers of asbestos and specifically named Asbestos Inc. as "a killer of innocent victims." Attorneys for Asbestos filed suit for libel and were awarded $1.3 million in damages on December 16, 1996. The newspaper has indicated it would appeal the verdict.

Instructions:

Determine how each of the above events should be disclosed on the financial statements of Asbestos Inc. for the year ended December 31, 1996. Provide support for your position.

Problem 13—37 (Adjusting entries and balance sheet presentation)

The unadjusted trial balance of Sunset Company at December 31, 1995, showed the following account balances:

Sales	$427,000
Mortgage Note Payable	80,000
Bank Notes Payable	10,000
Accounts Payable	19,400
Wages Payable	4,000

Additional information:

(a) The sales account included amounts collected from customers for a 5 percent sales tax. The tax was remitted to the state on January 31, 1996.
(b) The mortgage note is due on March 1, 1996. Interest at 12 percent has been paid through December 31. Sunset intended at December 31, 1995, to refinance the note on its due date with a new 5-year mortgage note. In fact, on March 1, 1996, Sunset paid $20,000 in cash on the principal balance and refinanced the remaining $60,000.
(c) The bank notes are due over the next four years. The current portion of the notes is $2,500 at December 31, 1995. Interest of $500 has not been accrued. It is to be paid during 1996.
(d) On October 1, 1995, a previous employee filed a suit against Sunset, alleging age discrimination and asking for damages of $500,000. At December 31, 1995, Sunset's attorney felt that the likelihood of losing the lawsuit was possible but not probable.
(e) During 1995, Sunset remitted to the federal government estimated income tax payments of $55,000. The actual taxes for 1995 amounted to $75,000. No accrual has been made as of December 31, 1995.

Instructions:

1. Prepare adjusting journal entries to correct the liability accounts at December 31, 1995. Assume the financial statements will be issued on April 1, 1996.
2. Prepare the current and noncurrent liability sections of the December 31, 1995, balance sheet.

CHAPTER 14

Long-Term Debt

CHAPTER TOPICS

- Nature and Characteristics of Bonds
- Issuance of Bonds
- Accounting for Bond Interest
- Retirement of Bonds at Maturity
- Early Extinguishment of Debt
- Troubled Debt Restructuring
- Off-Balance-Sheet Financing
- Analyzing a Firm's Debt Position
- Reporting Bonds and Long-Term Notes as Liabilities
- Accounting for Serial Bonds (Appendix)

Many corporations incurred large amounts of debt in financing expansion in the 1980s. By applying novel techniques, such as deferring interest payments, using gradually increasing interest rates, and making interest payments by issuing additional debt rather than by paying cash, corporations postponed having to service these large amounts of debt. In the 1990s, these strategies are coming back to haunt business executives. Western Union has seen the interest rate on its long-term debt increase to 19.25%. Dr. Pepper/Seven-Up must come up with $84 million in interest payments over and above the $75 million they currently pay annually. As a result of scenarios like these, experts estimate that over $69 billion in bond defaults will occur during the next few years.[1]

1. Fred R. Bleakley, "Many Firms Find Debt They Piled on in 1980's Is a Cruel Taskmaster," *The Wall Street Journal*, October 9, 1990.

The use of long-term debt securities to finance new products, to expand operations, to acquire other companies, or for a host of other reasons is common practice in today's business environment. This is especially true during periods of low interest rates, allowing companies to use relatively "cheap" money not only for business expansion but also to retire existing higher-cost debt or, in some cases, to retire equity securities. Large new issues of bonds in recent years have also occurred as a result of the significant increase in debt-financed corporate takeovers, or buy-outs.

In addition to bonds, the **long-term debt** classification includes mortgages, leases, pensions, and other types of long-term obligations. This chapter explains the relative advantages and disadvantages of debt and equity financing, and specifically focuses on how to account for bonds and long-term notes. In discussing issuance and retirement of bonds, both the liability of the issuer (bonds payable) and the asset of the investor (bond investment) are explained so that the total picture can be seen at one time. Issues related to valuation are discussed in the investments chapter.

FINANCING WITH LONG-TERM DEBT

The long-term financing of a corporation is accomplished either through the issuance of long-term debt instruments, usually bonds or notes, or through the sale of additional stock. The issuance of bonds or notes instead of stock may be preferred by management and stockholders for the following reasons:

1. Present owners continue in control of the corporation.
2. Interest is a deductible expense in arriving at taxable income, while dividends are not.
3. Current market rates of interest may be favorable relative to stock market prices.
4. The charge against earnings for interest may be less than the amount of dividends that might be expected by shareholders.

There are, however, certain limitations and disadvantages of financing with long-term debt securities. Debt financing is possible only when a company is in satisfactory financial condition and can offer adequate security to creditors. Furthermore, interest obligations must be paid regardless of the company's earnings and financial position. If a company has operating losses and is unable to raise sufficient cash to meet periodic interest payments, debt security holders may take legal action to assume control of company assets.

A complicating factor is that the distinction between debt and equity securities may become fuzzy. Usually, a debt instrument has a fixed interest rate and a definite maturity date when the principal must be repaid. Also, holders of debt instruments generally have no voting privileges. A traditional equity security, on the other hand, has no fixed repayment obligation or maturity date, and dividends on stock become obligations only after being formally declared by the board of directors of a corporation. In addition, common stockholders generally have voting and other ownership privileges. The problem is that certain convertible debt securities have many equity characteristics, and some preferred stocks have many of the characteristics of debt. This makes it important to recognize the distinction between debt and equity and to provide the accounting treatment that is most appropriate under the specific circumstances.

ACCOUNTING FOR BONDS

Conceptually, bonds and long-term notes are similar types of financial instruments. There are some technical differences, however. For example, the trust indenture associated with bonds generally provides more extensive detail than the contract terms of a note, often including restrictions on the payment of dividends or incurrence of additional debt. The length of time to maturity is also generally longer for bonds than for notes. Some bonds do not mature for twenty years or longer, while most notes mature in one to five years. Other characteristics of bonds and notes are similar. Therefore, although the discussion that follows deals specifically with bonds, the accounting principles and reporting practices related to bonds can also be applied to long-term notes.

There are three main considerations in accounting for bonds:

1. Recording the issuance or purchase.
2. Recognizing the applicable interest during the life of the bonds.
3. Accounting for the retirement of bonds, either at maturity or prior to the maturity date.

Before these considerations are discussed, the nature of bonds and the determination of bond market prices will be reviewed.

Nature of Bonds

The power of a corporation to create bond indebtedness is found in the corporation laws of a state and may be specifically granted by charter. In some cases, formal authorization by a majority of stockholders is required before a board of directors can approve a bond issue.

Borrowing by means of bonds involves the issuance of certificates of indebtedness. **Bond certificates,** commonly referred to simply as "bonds," are frequently issued in denominations of $1,000, referred to as the **face amount, par value,** or **maturity value** of the bond, although in some cases, bonds are issued in varying denominations.

The group contract between the corporation and the bondholders is known as the **bond indenture.** The indenture details the rights and obligations of the contracting parties, indicates the property pledged as well as the protection offered on the loan, and names the bank or trust company that is to represent the bondholders.

Bonds may be sold by the company directly to investors, or they may be underwritten by investment bankers or a syndicate. The underwriters may agree to purchase the entire bond issue or that part of the issue not sold by the company, or they may agree simply to manage the sale of the security on a commission basis, often referred to as a "best efforts" basis.

Most companies attempt to sell their bonds to underwriters to avoid incurring a loss after the bonds are placed on the market. An interesting example of this occurred several years ago when IBM Corporation went to the bond market for the first time and issued a record $1 billion worth of bonds and long-term notes. After the issue was released by IBM to the underwriters, interest rates soared as the Federal Reserve Bank sharply increased its discount rate. The market price of the IBM securities fell, and the brokerage houses and investment bankers participating in the underwriting incurred a loss in excess of $50 million on the sale of the securities to investors.

Issuers of Bonds. Bonds and similar debt instruments are issued by private corporations, the United States Government, state, county, and local governments, school districts, and government-sponsored organizations, such as the Federal Home Loan Bank and the Federal National Mortgage Association. The total amount of debt issued by these organizations is now well in excess of $1 trillion.

The U.S. debt includes not only Treasury bonds, but also Treasury bills, which are notes with less than one year to maturity date, and Treasury notes, which mature in one to seven years. Both Treasury bills and Treasury notes are in demand in the marketplace, perhaps even more so in recent years than Treasury bonds.

Debt securities issued by state, county, and local governments and their agencies are collectively referred to as **municipal debt.** A unique feature of municipal debt is that the interest received by investors from such securities is exempt from federal income tax. Because of this tax advantage, "municipals" generally carry lower interest rates than debt securities of other issuers, enabling these governmental units to borrow at favorable interest rates. The tax exemption is in reality a subsidy granted by the federal government to encourage capital investment in state and local governments.

Types of Bonds. Bonds may be categorized in many different ways, depending on the characteristics of a particular bond issue. The major distinguishing features of bonds are identified and discussed in the following sections.

Term Versus Serial Bonds. Bonds that mature on a single date are called **term bonds.** When bonds mature in installments, they are referred to as **serial bonds.** Serial bonds are much less common than term bonds, and the special considerations in accounting for serial bonds are covered in the appendix to this chapter.

Secured Versus Unsecured Bonds. Bonds issued by private corporations may be either secured or unsecured. **Secured bonds** offer protection to investors by providing some form of security, such as a mortgage on real estate or a pledge of other collateral. A **first-mortgage bond** represents a first claim against the property of a corporation in the event of the company's inability to meet bond interest and principal payments. A **second-mortgage bond** is a secondary claim ranking only after the claim of the first-mortgage bond or senior issue has been completely satisfied. A **collateral trust bond** is usually secured by stocks and bonds of other corporations owned by the issuing company. Such securities are generally transferred to a trustee, who holds them as collateral on behalf of the bondholders and, if necessary, will sell them to satisfy the bondholders' claim.

Unsecured bonds are not protected by the pledge of any specific assets and are frequently termed **debenture bonds,** or **debentures.** Holders of debenture bonds simply rank as general creditors along with other unsecured parties. The risk involved in these securities varies with the financial strength of the debtor. Debentures issued by a strong company may involve little risk; debentures issued by a weak company whose properties are already heavily mortgaged may involve considerable risk. Quality ratings for bonds are published by both Moody's and Standard and Poor's investment services companies. For example, Moody's bond ratings range from prime, or highest quality (AAA) to default (C) for a very high-risk bond. Standard and Poor's range is from AAA to D.

Registered Versus Bearer (Coupon) Bonds. Registered bonds call for the registry of the owner's name on the corporation books. Transfer of bond ownership is similar to that for stock. When a bond is sold, the corporate transfer agent cancels the bond certificate surrendered by the seller and issues a new certificate to the buyer. Interest checks are mailed periodically to the bondholders of record. **Bearer** or **coupon bonds** are not recorded in the name of the owner, title to such bonds passing with delivery. Each bond is accompanied by coupons for individual interest payments covering the life of the issue. Coupons are clipped by the owner of the bond and presented to a bank for deposit or collection. The issue of bearer bonds eliminates the need for recording bond ownership changes and preparing and mailing periodic interest checks. But coupon bonds fail to offer the bondholder the protection found in registered bonds in the event the bonds are lost or stolen. In some cases, bonds provide interest coupons but require registry as to principal. Here, ownership safeguards are provided, while the time-consuming routines involved in making interest payments are avoided. Bonds of recent issue are registered rather than coupon bonds.

Zero-Interest Bonds and Bonds With Variable Interest Rates. In recent years, some companies have issued long-term debt securities that do not bear interest. Instead, these securities sell at a significant discount that provides an investor with a total interest payoff at maturity. These bonds are known as **zero-interest bonds** or **deep-discount bonds.** Another type of zero-interest bond delays interest payments for a period of time.

Because of potentially wide fluctuations in interest rates, some bonds and long-term notes are issued with **variable (or floating) interest rates.** Over the life of these obligations, the interest rate changes as prevailing market interest rates increase or decrease. A variable interest rate security reduces the risk to the investor when interest rates are rising, and to the issuer when interest rates are falling.

Junk Bonds. High-risk, high-yield bonds issued by companies that are heavily in debt or otherwise in weak financial condition are often referred to as **junk bonds.** These bonds are rated Ba or lower by Moody's investment service and BB or lower by Standard and Poor's.[2] Junk bonds typically yield at least 12%, and some yield in excess of 20%. Some are zero-interest (deep discount) bonds that pay no interest until maturity or pay no interest for the first few years. While junk bonds are generally not an appropriate investment for individuals due to their high risk, they have been a significant segment of the corporate bond market in recent years.

Junk bonds are issued in at least three types of circumstances. First, they are issued by companies that once had high credit ratings but have fallen on hard times. Several companies in the steel industry are included in this category. Second, junk bonds are issued by emerging growth companies, such as Continental Cablevision, that lack adequate cash flow, credit history, or diversification to permit them to issue higher grade (i.e., lower risk) bonds. The third, and largest, category of junk bonds consists of those issued by companies undergoing restructuring, often in conjunction with a leveraged buyout (LBO), discussed later in the chapter. Metromedia Inc. is one of many examples of such companies. In 1990, the market for junk bonds was estimated to exceed $200 billion.

Convertible and Commodity-Backed Bonds. Bonds may provide for their conversion into some other security at the option of the bondholder. Such bonds are known as **convertible bonds.** The conversion feature generally permits the owner of bonds to exchange them for common stock. The bondholder is thus able to convert the claim into an ownership interest if corporate operations prove successful and conversion becomes attractive; in the meantime, the special rights of a creditor are maintained. Bonds may also be redeemable in terms of commodities, such as oil or precious metals. These types of bonds are sometimes referred to as **commodity-backed bonds** or **asset-linked bonds.**

Callable Bonds. Bond indentures frequently give the issuing company the right to call and retire the bonds prior to their maturity. Such bonds are termed **callable bonds.** When a corporation wishes to reduce its outstanding indebtedness, bondholders are notified of the portion of the issue to be surrendered, and they are paid in accordance with call provisions. Interest does not accrue after the call date.

Market Price of Bonds

The market price of bonds varies with the safety of the investment and the current market interest rate for similar instruments. When the financial condition and earnings of a corporation are such that payment of interest and principal on bond indebtedness is virtually

2. Ben Weberman, "High-Grade Junk," *Forbes,* August 21, 1989, p. 115.

assured, the interest rate a company must offer to sell a bond issue is relatively low. As the risk factor increases, a higher interest return is necessary to attract investors. The amount of interest paid on bonds is a specified percentage of the face value. This percentage is termed the **stated** or **contract rate.** This rate, however, may not be the same as the prevailing or **market rate** for bonds of similar quality and length of time to maturity at the time the issue is sold. Furthermore, the market rate constantly fluctuates. These factors often result in a difference between bond face values and the prices at which the bonds actually sell on the market.

The purchase of bonds at face value implies agreement between the bond stated rate of interest and the prevailing market rate of interest. If the stated rate exceeds the market rate, the bonds will sell at a **premium;** if the stated rate is less than the market rate, the bonds will sell at a **discount.** The **bond premium** or the **bond discount** is the amount needed to adjust the stated rate of interest to the actual market rate of interest for that particular bond. Thus, the stated rate adjusted for the premium or the discount on the purchase gives the actual rate of return on the bonds, known as the **market, yield,** or **effective interest rate.** A declining market rate of interest subsequent to issuance of the bonds results in an increase in the market value of the bonds; a rising market rate of interest results in a decrease in their market value.

Bonds are quoted on the market as a percentage of face value. For example, a bond quotation of 96.5 means the market price is 96.5% of face value; thus, the bond is trading at a discount. A bond quotation of 104 means the market price is 104% of face value; thus, the bond is trading at a premium. U.S. Government note and bond quotations are made in 32s rather than 100s. This means that a Government bond selling at 98.16 is selling at 98 $^{16}/_{32}$, or in terms of decimal equivalents, 98.5%.

The market price of a bond at any date can be determined by discounting the maturity value of the bond and each remaining interest payment at the market rate of interest for similar debt on that date. The present-value tables in Chapter 7 can be used for computing bond market prices.

To illustrate the computation of a bond market price from the tables, assume 10-year, 8% bonds of $100,000 are to be sold on the bond issue date. Further assume that the effective interest rate for bonds of similar quality and maturity is 10%, compounded semiannually.

The computation of the market price of the bonds may be divided into two parts:

Part 1 Present value of principal (maturity value)

Maturity value of bonds after 10 years, or 20 semiannual periods	$100,000	
Effective interest rate = 10% per year, or 5% per semiannual period; present value factor (PVF), Table II $\overline{20|}\,5$	× .3769	
Present value of $100,000 discounted at 5% for 20 periods		$37,690

Part 2 Present value of 20 interest payments

Semiannual payment, 4% of $100,000	$ 4,000	
Effective interest rate, 10% per year, or 5% per semiannual period; present value of annuity factor (PVAF), Table IV $\overline{20|}\,5$	×12.4622	
Present value of 20, $4,000 payments, discounted at 5%		49,849
Total present value (market price) of bond		$87,539

The market price for the bonds would be $87,539, the sum of the present values of the two parts. Because the effective interest rate is higher than the stated interest rate, the bonds would sell at a $12,461 discount at the issuance date. It should be noted that if the effective rate on these bonds were 8% instead of 10%, the sum of the present values of the two parts would be $100,000, meaning that the bonds would sell at their face amount, or at par. If the effective interest rate were less than 8%, the market price of the bonds would be more than $100,000, and the bonds would sell at a premium.

Specially adapted present-value tables are available to determine directly the price to be paid for bonds if they are to provide a certain return. A portion of such a bond table is illustrated below.

Note that the market price from the bond table for 8% bonds sold to yield 10% in 10 years is $87,539, the same amount as computed using present-value tables. Also, the bond table shows that if the effective interest rate were 8%, the bonds would sell at par, $100,000. If the effective rate were 7.5%, the market price would be $103,476.

The bond table can also be used to determine the effective rate of interest on a bond acquired at a certain price. To illustrate, assume that a $1,000, 8% bond due in 10 years is selling at $951. Reference to the column "10 years" for $95,070 shows an annual return of 8.75% is provided on an investment of $950.70.

Bond Table
Values to the Nearest Dollar of 8% Bond for $100,000
Interest Payable Semiannually

Yield or Effective Interest	8 years	8 1/2 years	9 years	9 1/2 years	10 years
7.00	$106,046	$106,325	$106,595	$106,855	$107,107
7.25	104,495	104,699	104,896	105,090	105,272
7.50	102,971	103,100	103,232	103,360	103,476
7.75	101,472	101,537	101,595	101,658	101,718
8.00	100,000	100,000	100,000	100,000	100,000
8.25	98,552	98,494	98,437	98,372	98,325
8.50	97,141	97,012	96,893	96,787	96,678
8.75	95,746	95,568	95,398	95,232	95,070
9.00	94,383	94,147	93,920	93,703	93,496
9.25	93,042	92,757	92,480	92,214	91,953
9.50	91,723	91,380	91,055	90,751	90,452
9.75	90,350	89,960	89,588	89,238	88,902
10.00	89,162	88,726	88,310	87,914	87,539

Issuance of Bonds

Bonds may be sold directly to investors by the issuer or they may be sold on the open market through securities exchanges or through investment bankers. Over 50% of bond issues are privately placed with large investors. Regardless of how placed, when bonds are issued (sold), the issuer must record the receipt of cash and recognize the long-term liability. The purchaser must record the payment of cash and the bond investment.

An issuer normally records the bond obligation at its face value—the amount that the company must pay at maturity. Hence, when bonds are issued at an amount other than face value, a bond discount or premium account is established for the difference between the cash received and the bond face value. The premium is added to or the discount is subtracted from the bond face value to report the bonds at their present value. Although an investor could also record the investment in bonds at their face value by using a premium or discount account, traditionally, investors record their bond investments at cost, that is, the face value net of any premium or discount. Cost includes brokerage fees and any other costs incident to the purchase.

Will Mickey Mouse Be Around in 100 Years?

In July of 1993, Walt Disney Company began marketing 100-year bonds yielding 7.5%. The bonds have a face amount of $150 million and will mature in 2093. Traditionally, bonds have had lives of 20 or 30 years but in 1992, one company sold 50-year bonds - the first such issue in over a decade. However, Disney's issue of 100-year bonds is the first such issue since 1954. In 1954, Chicago and Eastern Illinois, a railroad, issued 100-year bonds with a stated rate of 5%. For the Chicago and Eastern Illinois bonds, especially during the late 1970's and early 1980's with its double-digit inflation, investors have had marginal returns. An analysis of the Disney bonds prepared by Morgan Stanley indicates that even without factoring in the effects of inflation, if long-term yields were to rise by one point, the return for Disney bondholders would be -4.19% for the next year. However, if long term bond yields were to drop one point, the return would exceed 22%. Comments from securities brokers range from, "It's crazy" to the Disney issue will turn out to be a "historic artifact, a curiosity."

Questions

1. What are the advantages to the issuer of using longer term bonds?
2. What are the disadvantages to the issuer?
3. Why would investors purchase bonds with 100-year maturities?

Source: Thomas T. Vogel, Jr., "Disney Amazes Investors With Sale of 100-Year Bonds," *The Wall Street Journal*, July 21, 1993, p. C1.

Bonds issued or acquired in exchange for noncash assets or services are recorded at the fair market value of the bonds, unless the value of the exchanged assets or services is more clearly determinable. A difference between the face value of the bonds and the cash value of the bonds or the value of the property acquired is recognized as bond discount or bond premium. When bonds and other securities are acquired for a lump sum, an apportionment of such cost among the securities is required.

As indicated earlier, bonds may be issued at par, at a discount, or at a premium. They may be issued on an interest payment date or between interest dates, which calls for the recognition of accrued interest. Each of these situations will be illustrated using the following data: $100,000, 8%, 10-year bonds are issued. Semiannual interest of $4,000 ($\$100,000 \times .08 \times 6/12$) is payable on January 1 and July 1.

Bonds Issued at Par on Interest Date. When bonds are issued at par, or face value, on an interest date, there is no premium or discount to be recognized nor any accrued interest at the date of issuance. The appropriate entries for the first year, on the issuer's books and on the investor's books, assuming the data in the preceding paragraph and issuance on January 1 at par value, would be:

Issuer's Books				Investor's Books		
Jan. 1	Cash	100,000		Bond Investment	100,000	
	Bonds Payable		100,000	Cash		100,000
July 1	Interest Expense	4,000		Cash	4,000	
	Cash		4,000	Interest Revenue		4,000
Dec. 31	Interest Expense	4,000		Interest Receivable	4,000	
	Interest Payable		4,000	Interest Revenue		4,000

Bonds Issued at Discount on Interest Date. Now assume that the bonds were issued on January 1 but that the effective rate of interest was 10%, requiring recognition of a discount of $12,461 ($100,000 – $87,539). The appropriate entries on January 1 are shown on the next page. The interest entries on July 1 and December 31 are illustrated in a later section that discusses the amortization of discounts and premiums.

Issuer's Books				Investor's Books		
Jan. 1	Cash	87,539		Bond Investment	87,539	
	Discount on Bonds Payable	12,461		Cash		87,539
	Bonds Payable		100,000			

Bonds Issued at Premium on Interest Date. Again using the data above, assume that the bonds were sold at an effective interest rate of 7%, resulting in a premium of $7,107. In this case, the entries on January 1 would be:

Issuer's Books				Investor's Books		
Jan. 1	Cash	107,107		Bond Investment	107,107	
	Premium on Bonds Payable		7,107	Cash		107,107
	Bonds Payable		100,000			

Bonds Issued at Par Between Interest Dates. When bonds are issued between interest dates, an adjustment is made for the interest accrued between the last interest payment date and the date of the transaction. A buyer of the bonds pays the amount of accrued interest along with the purchase price and then receives the accrued interest plus interest earned subsequent to the purchase date when the next interest payment is made. This practice avoids the problem an issuer of bonds would have in trying to split interest payments for a given period between two or more owners of the securities. To illustrate, if the bonds in the previous example were issued at par on March 1, the appropriate entries would be:

Issuer's Books[3]				Investor's Books		
Mar. 1	Cash	101,333		Bond Investment	100,000	
	Bonds Payable		100,000	Interest Receivable	1,333	
	Interest Payable		1,333*	Cash		101,333
	*($100,000 x .08 x 2/12)					
July 1	Interest Expense	2,667*		Cash	4,000	
	Interest Payable	1,333		Interest Receivable		1,333
	Cash		4,000	Interest Revenue		2,667
	*($100,000 x .08 x 4/12)					

Bond Issuance Costs. The issuance of bonds normally involves costs to the issuer for legal services, printing and engraving, taxes, and underwriting. Traditionally, these costs have been either (1) summarized separately as **bond issuance costs,** classified as deferred charges, and charged to expense over the life of the bond issue, or (2) offset against any premium or added to any discount arising on the issuance and thus netted against the face value of the bonds. The Accounting Principles Board in Opinion No. 21 recommended that these costs be reported on the balance sheet as deferred charges.[4] However, in Statement of Financial Accounting Concepts No. 3, the FASB stated that such costs fail to meet the definition of assets adopted by the Board.[5] Concepts statements do not establish GAAP,

3. As an alternative, the accrued interest could be initially credited to Interest Expense by the issuer and debited to Interest Revenue by the investor. When the first interest payment is made, the debit to Interest Expense for the issuer, when combined with the initial entry, would result in the proper amount of interest expense being recognized. A similar procedure can be applied by the investor in determining interest revenue.

4. *Opinions of the Accounting Principles Board No. 21,* "Interest on Receivables and Payables" (New York: American Institute of Certified Public Accountants, 1971), par. 16.

5. *Statement of Financial Accounting Concepts No. 3,* "Elements of Financial Statements of Business Enterprises" (Stamford: Financial Accounting Standards Board, December 1980), par. 161.

however, and until such time as the FASB addresses this issue, the APB Opinion governs generally accepted practice.

Accounting for Bond Interest

With coupon bonds, cash is paid by the issuing company in exchange for interest coupons on the interest dates. Payments on coupons may be made by the company directly to bondholders, or payments may be cleared through a bank or other disbursing agent. Subsidiary records with bondholders are not maintained, since coupons are redeemable by bearers. In the case of registered bonds, interest checks are mailed either by the company or its agent. When bonds are registered, the bonds account requires subsidiary ledger support. The subsidiary ledger shows holdings by individuals and changes in such holdings. Checks are sent to bondholders of record as of the interest payment dates.

When bonds are issued at a premium or discount, the market acts to adjust the stated interest rate to a market or effective interest rate. Because of the initial premium or discount, the periodic interest payments made over the bond life by the issuer do not represent the total expense for the periods involved. An adjustment to the interest expense associated with the cash payment is necessary to reflect the effective interest being incurred on the bonds. This adjustment is referred to as bond **premium or discount amortization.** This periodic adjustment results in a gradual adjustment of the carrying value toward the bond's face value.

A premium on issued bonds recognizes that the stated interest rate is higher than the market interest rate. Amortization of the premium reduces the interest expense below the amount of cash paid. A discount on issued bonds recognizes that the stated interest rate is lower than the market interest rate. Amortization of the discount increases the amount of interest expense above the amount of cash paid.

Two main methods are used to amortize the premium or discount: (1) the straight-line method and (2) the effective-interest method. The straight-line method is explained first, because the computations are simpler. This method is acceptable, however, only when its application results in periodic interest expense that does not differ materially from the amounts that would be reported using the effective-interest method.[6]

Straight-Line Method. The **straight-line method** provides for the recognition of an equal amount of premium or discount amortization each period. The amount of monthly amortization is determined by dividing the premium or discount at purchase or issuance by the number of months remaining to the bond maturity date. For example, if a 10-year, 10% bond issue with a maturity value of $200,000 was sold on the issuance date at 103, the $6,000 premium would be amortized evenly over the 120 months until maturity, or at a rate of $50 per month ($6,000 ÷ 120). If the bonds were sold three months after the issuance date, the $6,000 premium would be amortized evenly over 117 months, or at a rate of $51.28 per month ($6,000 ÷ 117). The amortization period is always the time from original sale to maturity. The premium amortization would reduce both interest expense on the issuer's books and interest revenue on the investor's books. A discount amortization would have the opposite results: both accounts would be increased.

To illustrate the accounting for bond interest using straight-line amortization, consider again the earlier example of the $100,000, 8%, 10-year bonds issued on January 1. When sold at a $12,461 discount, the appropriate entries to record interest on July 1 and December 31 would be as follows:

6. *Opinions of the Accounting Principles Board No. 21*, par. 15.

Issuer's Books				Investor's Books		
July 1	Interest Expense	4,623		Cash	4,000	
	Discount on Bonds			Bond Investment	623	
	Payable		623	Interest Revenue		4,623
	Cash		4,000			
	[$100,000 x .08 x $^6/_{12}$ = $4,000 cash; $12,461 ÷ 120 x 6 months = $623 (rounded) discount amortization]					
Dec. 31	Interest Expense	4,623		Interest Receivable	4,000	
	Discount on Bonds			Bond Investment	623	
	Payable		623	Interest Revenue		4,623
	Interest Payable		4,000			

Note that the discount amortization has the effect of increasing the effective interest rate over the life of the bond from the 8% stated rate to the 10% market rate of interest that the bonds were sold to yield. Over the life of the bond, the $12,461 discount will be charged to interest expense for the issuer and recognized as interest revenue by the investor.[7]

To illustrate the entries that would be required to amortize a bond premium, consider again the situation where the 8% bonds were sold to yield 7%, or $107,107. The $7,107 premium would be amortized on a straight-line basis as follows:

Issuer's Books				Investor's Books		
July 1	Interest Expense	3,645		Cash	4,000	
	Premium on Bonds			Bond Investment		355
	Payable	355		Interest Revenue		3,645
	Cash		4,000			
	[$7,107 ÷ 120 x 6 months = $355 (rounded) premium amortization for 6-month period]					
Dec. 31	Interest Expense	3,645		Interest Receivable	4,000	
	Premium on Bonds			Bond Investment		355
	Payable	355		Interest Revenue		3,645
	Interest Payable		4,000			

The amortization of the premium has the effect of reducing the amount of interest expense or interest revenue over the life of the bond to the actual yield or market rate of the bonds, 7%.

Effective-Interest Method. The **effective-interest method** of amortization uses a uniform interest rate based on a changing investment balance and provides for an increasing premium or discount amortization each period. In order to use this method, the effective-interest rate for the bonds must be known. This is the rate of interest at bond issuance that discounts the maturity value of the bonds and the periodic interest payments to the market price of the bonds. This rate is used to determine the amount of revenue or expense to be recorded on the books.

To illustrate the amortization of a bond discount using the effective-interest method, consider once again the $100,000, 8%, 10-year bonds sold for $87,539, based on an effective-interest rate of 10%. The discount amortization for the first six months using the effective-interest method would be computed as follows:

7. Because the amount amortized for each six-month period is identical, many companies make the amortization entry only once a year.

Investment balance (carrying value) at beginning of first period	$87,539
Effective rate per semiannual period	5%
Stated rate per semiannual period	4%
Interest amount based on carrying value and effective rate ($87,539 × .05)	$ 4,377
Interest payment based on par value and stated rate ($100,000 × .04)	4,000
Discount amortization—difference between interest based on effective rate and stated rate	$ 377

This difference between the amount paid and the compound interest expense is the discount amortization for the first period using the effective-interest method. For the second semiannual period, the bond carrying value increases by the amount of discount amortized. The amortization for the second semiannual period would be computed as follows:

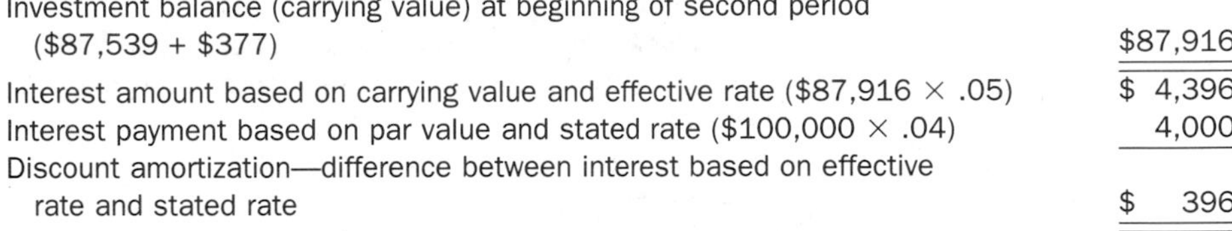

Investment balance (carrying value) at beginning of second period ($87,539 + $377)	$87,916
Interest amount based on carrying value and effective rate ($87,916 × .05)	$ 4,396
Interest payment based on par value and stated rate ($100,000 × .04)	4,000
Discount amortization—difference between interest based on effective rate and stated rate	$ 396

The amount of interest to be recognized each period is computed at a uniform rate on an increasing balance. This results in an increasing discount amortization over the life of the bonds, which is graphically demonstrated and compared with straight-line amortization below.

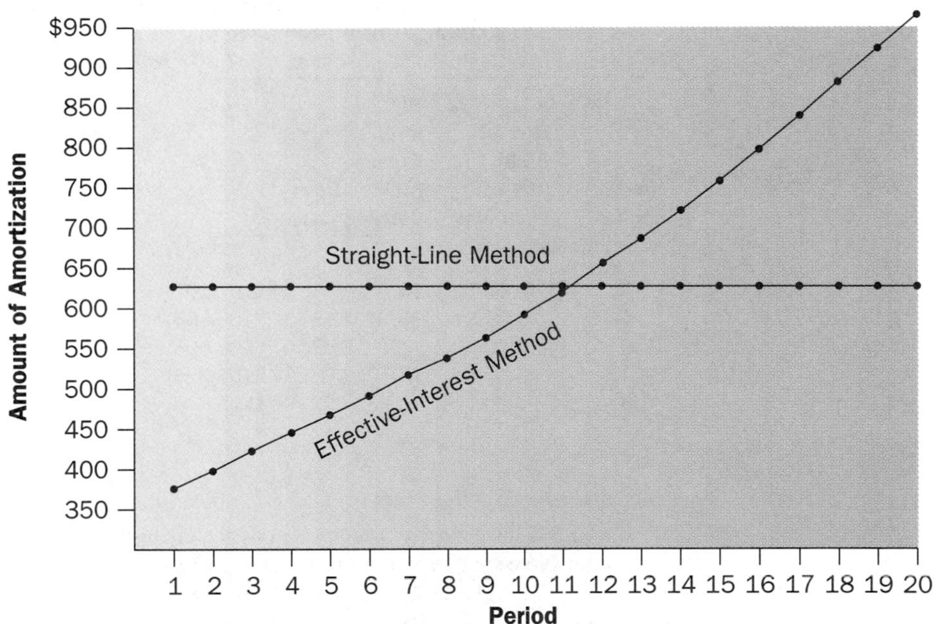

The entries for amortizing the discount would be the same as those shown for straight-line amortization; only the amounts would be different.

Premium amortization would be computed in a similar way except that the interest payment based on the stated interest rate would be higher than the interest amount based on the effective rate. For example, assume that the $100,000, 8%, 10-year bonds were sold on the issuance date for $107,107, thus providing an effective interest rate of 7%. The premium amortization for the first and second six-month periods would be computed as follows (amounts are rounded to the nearest dollar):

Investment balance (carrying value) at beginning of first period.	$107,107
Effective rate per semiannual period	3.5%
Stated rate per semiannual period	4.0%
Interest payment based on par value and stated rate ($100,000 × .04)	$ 4,000
Interest amount based on carrying value and effective rate ($107,107 × .035)	3,749
Premium amortization—difference between interest based on stated rate and effective rate	$ 251
Investment balance (carrying value) at beginning of second period ($107,107 – $251)	$106,856
Interest payment based on par value and stated rate ($100,000 × .04)	$ 4,000
Interest amount based on carrying value and effective rate ($106,856 × .035)	3,740
Premium amortization—difference between interest based on stated rate and effective rate	$ 260

As illustrated, as the investment or liability balance is reduced by the premium amortization, the interest, based on the effective rate, also decreases. The difference between the interest payment and the effective interest amount increases in a manner similar to discount amortization. Bond amortization tables may be prepared to determine the periodic adjustments to the bond carrying value, i.e., the present value of the bond. A partial bond amortization table is illustrated below.

Amortization of Bond Premium—Effective-Interest Method
$100,000, 10-Year Bonds, Interest at 8% Payable Semiannually,
Sold at $107,107 to Yield 7%

Interest Payment	A Interest Paid (.04 × $100,000	B Interest Expense (.035 × Bond Carrying Value)	C Premium Amortization (A – B)	D Unamortized Premium (D – C)	E Bond Carrying Value ($100,000 + D)
				$7,107	$107,107
1	$4,000	$3,749 (.035 × $107,107)	$251	6,856	106,856
2	4,000	3,740 (.035 × $106,856)	260	6,596	106,596
3	4,000	3,731 (.035 × $106,596)	269	6,327	106,327
4	4,000	3,721 (.035 × $106,327)	279	6,048	106,048
5	4,000	3,712 (.035 × $106,048)	288	5,760	105,760

Because the effective-interest method adjusts the stated interest rate to an effective-interest rate, it is theoretically more accurate as an amortization method than is the straight-line method. Note that the total amortization over the life of the bond is the same under either method; only the interim amounts differ. Since the issuance of APB Opinion No. 21, the effective-interest method is the recommended amortization method. However, as stated previously, the straight-line method may be used by a company if the interim results of using it do not differ materially from the amortization using the effective-interest method.

Cash Flow Effects of Amortizing Bond Premiums and Discounts

The amortization of a bond discount or premium does not involve the receipt or payment of cash and, like other noncash items, must be considered in preparing a statement of cash flows. Recall that when the indirect method is used to report cash flows from operating activities, net income is adjusted for noncash items. When a bond discount is amortized, interest expense reported on the income statement is higher than interest paid, and net income, on a cash basis, is understated. The appropriate adjustment is to add the amount of discount amortization back to net income. The reverse is true in the case of a bond premium. That is, the amount of bond premium amortization is subtracted from net income to arrive at cash flow from operations.

Using the direct method requires conversion of individual accrual-basis revenue and expense items to a cash basis. Thus, to convert interest expense to cash paid for interest, the expense reported on the income statement is decreased by the amount of discount amortization for the period or increased by the amount of premium amortization.

The following example illustrates the adjustments necessary when preparing a statement of cash flows. Consider the information used in the previous examples related to a bond discount—the company issues $100,000, 8%, 10-year bonds when the effective rate of interest is 10%. The bonds are issued at a price of $87,539. The calculations for the discount amortization during the first year are on page 585. The amount of discount amortized during the first year is $773 ($377 + $396). The amount of interest expense disclosed on the income statement for the year is $8,773 ($4,377 + $4,396) and the amount of cash paid to bondholders is $8,000. Assume that the company reported net income for the year of $90,000.

Using the indirect method, the amount of discount amortized ($773) is added back to net income. Under the direct method, the amount of the discount is subtracted from reported interest expense to convert that amount to a cash basis as follows: $8,773 interest expense – $773 discount amortization = $8,000 cash paid for interest. In this case, where only one bond issue is involved, cash paid for interest could instead be computed by multiplying the stated interest rate by the face amount of the bonds ($100,000 × .08). A partial statement of cash flows for each method appears below.

Indirect Method	
Cash flows from operating activities:	
Net income	$90,000
Adjustments:	
Add amortization of bond discount	773

Direct Method	
Cash flows from operating activities:	
Cash payments for interest	$ 8,000

Retirement of Bonds at Maturity

Bonds always include a specified termination or maturity date. At that time, the issuer must pay the current investors the maturity or face value of the bonds. When bond discount or premium and issuance costs have been properly amortized over the life of the bonds, bond retirement simply calls for elimination of the liability or the investment by a cash transaction, illustrated as follows assuming a $100,000 bond:

Issuer's Books			**Investor's Books**		
Bonds Payable	100,000		Cash	100,000	
Cash		100,000	Bond Investment		100,000

There is no recognition of any gain or loss on retirement, since the carrying value is equal to the maturity value, which is also equal to the market value of the bonds at that point in time.

The Largest Investment-Grade Domestic Bond Issue Ever

In the 1990's IBM has seen decreasing market share, lower profit margins, record losses, and high demand for their record-setting bond issue. In 1993, IBM issued $1.25 billion of seven-year notes and $550 million of 20-year debentures. The stated interest rate for the notes is 6.375% and 7.50% for the bonds. These two issues provide investors with a yield just 0.7 percent above that provided by comparable Treasury instruments—a spread much lower than anticipated. Because of IBM's recent financial woes, many thought that the spread would be much higher.

Evidence of IBM's spiral from being one of the top performers among the blue chips is found in the company's changing credit ratings. In January of 1993, Standard & Poors Corp. downgraded IBM's credit rating from the highest rating of AAA down to AA-. In March, Moody's Investor Service Inc. also lowered IBM from A-1 to AA-2. Prior to these downgrades, IBM was able to finance debt on the market at approximately 0.5 percent above the Treasury yield.

QUESTIONS

1. Why would the bond market be so anxious to purchase IBM's bonds given the company's recent financial performance?
2. What factors would prompt credit rating agencies such as Standard & Poors and Moody's to downgrade a company's credit rating?

SOURCE: Thomas T. Vogel, Jr. and Leslie Scism, "Investors Snap Up $1.8 Billion of IBM Securities As Corporations Scramble to Best Higher Interest Rates," *The Wall Street Journal,* June 9, 1993, p. C16.

Any bonds not presented for payment at their maturity date should be removed from the bonds payable balance on the issuer's books and reported separately as Matured Bonds Payable; these are reported as a current liability except when they are to be paid out of a bond retirement fund. Interest does not accrue on matured bonds not presented for payment. If a bond retirement fund is used to pay off a bond issue, any cash remaining in the fund may be returned to the cash account.

Extinguishment of Debt Prior to Maturity

When debt is retired or "extinguished" prior to the maturity date, a gain or loss must be recognized for the difference between the carrying value of the debt security and the amount paid to satisfy the obligation.[8] This gain or loss is classified as an **early extinguishment of debt** and, according to FASB Statement No. 4, is to be reported as an extraordinary item on the income statement.[9]

The problems that arise in retiring bonds or other forms of long-term debt prior to maturity are described in the following sections. Bonds may be retired prior to maturity in one of the following ways:

1. Bonds may be **redeemed** by the issuer by purchasing the bonds on the open market or by exercising the call provision that is frequently included in bond indentures;
2. Bonds may be **converted,** i.e., exchanged for other securities; or
3. Bonds may be **refinanced** (sometimes called "refunded") by using the proceeds from the sale of a new bond issue to retire outstanding bonds.

Another form of early extinguishment of debt, called **in-substance defeasance,** will also be discussed. Unlike redemption, conversion, and refinancing, in-substance defeasance does not involve the actual retirement of debt.

8. *Opinions of the Accounting Principles Board No. 26,* "Early Extinguishment of Debt" (New York: American Institute of Certified Public Accountants, 1972), par. 20.

9. *Statement of Financial Accounting Standards No. 4,* "Reporting Gains and Losses from Extinguishment of Debt" (Stamford: Financial Accounting Standards Board, 1975), par. 8. Note that an exception to the extraordinary classification is made if the early termination is necessary to satisfy bond retirement (sinking) fund requirements within a one-year period; see *Statement of Financial Accounting Standards No. 64,* "Extinguishment of Debt Made to Satisfy Sinking-Fund Requirements" (Stamford: Financial Accounting Standards Board, 1982), par. 3.

Redemption by Purchase of Bonds on the Market. Corporations frequently purchase their own bonds on the market when prices or other factors make such actions desirable. When bonds are purchased, amortization of bond premium or discount and issue costs should be brought up to date. Purchase by the issuer calls for the cancellation of the bond face value together with any related premium, discount, or issue costs as of the purchase date.

To illustrate a bond redemption prior to maturity, assume that $100,000, 8% bonds of Triad Inc. are not held until maturity but are redeemed by the issuer on February 1, 1996, at 97. The carrying value of the bonds on both the issuer's and investor's books is $97,700 as of February 1. Interest payment dates on the bonds are January 31 and July 31. Entries on both the issuer's and investor's books at the time of redemption would be as follows:

Issuer's Books

Feb. 1 Bonds Payable	100,000	
Discount on Bonds Payable		2,300
Cash		97,000
Gain on Bond Redemption		700
To record bond redemption.		

Computation:

Carrying value of bonds, February 1, 1996	$97,700
Purchase (redemption) price	97,000
Gain on redemption	$ 700

Investor's Books

Feb. 1 Cash	97,000	
Loss on Sale of Bonds	700	
Investment in Triad Inc. Bonds		97,700
To record sale of bonds.		

If the redemption had occurred between interest payment dates, adjusting entries would have to be made to recognize the accrued interest and to amortize the bond discount or premium.

Redemption by Exercise of Call Provision. A call provision gives the issuer the option of retiring bonds prior to maturity. Frequently the call must be made on an interest payment date, and no further interest accrues on the bonds not presented at this time. When only a part of an issue is to be redeemed, the bonds called may be determined by lot.

The inclusion of call provisions in a bond agreement is a feature favoring the issuer. The company is in a position to terminate the bond agreement and eliminate future interest charges whenever its financial position makes such action feasible. Furthermore, the company is protected in the event of a fall in the market interest rate by being able to retire the old issue from proceeds of a new issue paying a lower rate of interest. A bond contract normally requires payment of a premium if bonds are called. A bondholder is thus offered special compensation if the investment is terminated early.

When bonds are called, the difference between the amount paid and the bond carrying value is reported as a gain or a loss on both the issuer's and investor's books. Any interest paid at the time of the call is recorded as a debit to Interest Expense on the issuer's books and a credit to Interest Revenue on the investor's books. The entries to be made are the same as illustrated previously for the purchase of bonds by the issuer.

Convertible Bonds. The issuance of **convertible debt securities,** most frequently bonds, has become increasingly popular.[10] These securities raise specific questions as to the nature

10. Leslie Pittel, "Playing Safe—and Sporty, Too," *Forbes* (October 22, 1984), pp. 248-252.

of the securities, i.e., whether they should be considered debt or equity securities, the valuation of the conversion feature, and the treatment of any gain or loss on conversion.

Convertible debt securities usually have the following features:[11]

1. An interest rate lower than the issuer could establish for nonconvertible debt.
2. An initial conversion price higher than the market value of the common stock at time of issuance.
3. A call option retained by the issuer.

The popularity of these securities may be attributed to the advantages to both an issuer and a holder. An issuer is able to obtain financing at a lower interest rate because of the value of the conversion feature to the holder. Because of the call provision, an issuer is in a position to exert influence upon the holders to exchange the debt for equity securities if stock values increase; the issuer has had the use of relatively low interest rate financing if stock values do not increase. On the other hand, the holder has a debt instrument that, barring default, assures the return of investment plus a fixed return and, at the same time, offers an option to transfer his or her interest to equity capital should such transfer become attractive.

Many convertible bond issues place no restriction on when an issuer can call in bonds, and interest accrued on such bonds is sometimes absorbed in a conversion and not paid to the investor. Thus, a company can have the use of interest-free money as a result of calling in bonds prior to the first interest payment. Widespread use of early call provisions in the early 1980s led some investors to demand a provision restricting exercise of the call provision for a specified time period.[12]

Differences of opinion exist as to whether convertible debt securities should be treated by an issuer solely as debt, or whether part of the proceeds received from the issuance of debt should be recognized as equity capital. One view holds that the debt and the conversion privilege are inseparably connected, and therefore the debt and equity portions of a security should not be separately valued. A holder cannot sell part of the instrument and retain the other. An alternate view holds that there are two distinct elements in these securities and that each should be recognized in the accounts: that portion of the issuance price attributable to the conversion privilege should be recorded as a credit to Paid-In Capital; the balance of the issuance price should be assigned to the debt. This would decrease the premium otherwise recognized in the debt or perhaps result in a discount.

These views are compared in the illustration that follows. Assume that 500 ten-year bonds, face value $1,000, are sold at 105, or a total issue price of $525,000 (500 × $1,000 × 1.05). The bonds contain a conversion privilege that provides for exchange of a $1,000 bond for 20 shares of stock, par value $40. The interest rate on the bonds is 8%. It is estimated that without the conversion privilege, the bonds would sell at 96. The journal entries to record the issuance on the issuer's books under the two approaches are as follows.

Debt and Equity Not Separated

Cash	525,000	
Bonds Payable		500,000
Premium on Bonds Payable		25,000

11. *Opinions of the Accounting Principles Board No. 14,* "Accounting for Convertible Debt and Debt Issued with Stock Purchase Warrants" (New York: American Institute of Certified Public Accountants, 1969), par. 3.

12. Ben Weberman, "The Convertible Bond Scam," *Forbes* (January 19, 1981), p. 92.

Debt and Equity Separated

Cash	525,000	
Discount on Bonds Payable	20,000[1]	
Bonds Payable		500,000
Paid-In Capital Arising From Bond Conversion Feature		45,000[2]

Computations:

[1]Par value of bonds (500 × $1,000)	$500,000
Selling price of bonds without conversion feature ($500,000 × .96)	480,000
Discount on bonds without conversion feature	$ 20,000
[2]Total cash received on sale of bonds	$525,000
Selling price without conversion feature	480,000
Amount applicable to conversion feature (equity portion)	$ 45,000

The periodic charge for interest will differ depending on which method is employed. To illustrate the computation of interest charges, assume that the straight-line method is used to amortize bond premium or discount. Under the first approach, the annual interest charge would be $37,500 ($40,000 paid less $2,500 premium amortization). Under the second approach, the annual interest charge would be $42,000 ($40,000 paid plus $2,000 discount amortization).

The Accounting Principles Board stated that when convertible debt is sold at a price or with a value at issuance not significantly in excess of the face amount, ". . . no portion of the proceeds from the issuance . . . should be accounted for as attributable to the conversion feature."[13]

The APB stated that greater weight for this decision was placed on the inseparability of the debt and the conversion option than upon the practical problems of valuing the separate parts. However, the practical problems are considerable. Separate valuation requires asking the question: How much would the security sell for without the conversion feature? In many instances, this question would appear to be unanswerable. Investment bankers responsible for selling these issues are frequently unable to separate the two features for valuation purposes; they contend that the cash required simply could not be raised without the conversion privilege.

On the other hand, there would seem to be strong theoretical support for separating the debt and equity portions of the proceeds from the issuance of convertible debt on the issuer's books. Despite these theoretical arguments, current practice follows APB Opinion No. 14, and no separation is usually made between debt and equity. This is true even when separate values are determinable.

When conversion takes place, a special valuation question must be answered. Should the market value of the securities be used to compute a gain or loss on the transaction? If the convertible security is viewed as debt, then the conversion to equity would seem to be a significant economic transaction and a gain or loss would be recognized. If, however, the convertible security is viewed as equity, the conversion is really an exchange of one type of equity capital for another, and the historical cost principle would seem to indicate that no gain or loss would be recognized. In practice, the latter approach seems to be most commonly followed by both the issuer and investor of the bonds. No gain or loss is recognized either for book or tax purposes. The book value of the bonds is transferred to become the book value of the stock issued. However, this treatment seems inconsistent with APB Opinion No. 14, in which convertible debt is considered to be debt rather than equity.

If an investor views the security as debt, conversion of the debt could be viewed as an exchange of one asset for another. The general rule for the exchange of nonmonetary

13. *Opinions of the Accounting Principles Board No. 14*, par. 12.

assets is that the market value of the asset exchanged should be used to measure any gain or loss on the transaction.[14] If there is no market value of the asset surrendered or if its value is undeterminable, the market value of the asset received should be used. The market value of convertible bonds should reflect the market value of the stock to be issued on the conversion, and thus the market value of the two securities should be similar.

To illustrate bond conversion for the investor recognizing a gain or loss on conversion, assume HiTec Co. offers bondholders 40 shares of HiTec Co. common stock, $20 par, in exchange for each $1,000, 8% bond held. An investor exchanges bonds of $10,000 (carrying value as brought up to date for both investor and issuer, $9,850) for 400 shares of common stock having a market price at the time of the exchange of $26 per share. The exchange is completed at the interest payment date. The exchange is recorded on the books of the investor as follows:

Investment in HiTec Co. Common Stock	10,400	
Investment in HiTec Co. Bonds		9,850
Gain on Conversion of HiTec Co. Bonds		550

If the investor chose not to recognize a gain or loss, the journal entry would be as follows:

Investment in HiTec Co. Common Stock	9,850	
Investment in HiTec Co. Bonds		9,850

Similar differences would occur on the issuer's books depending on the viewpoint assumed. If the issuer desired to recognize the conversion of the convertible debt as a significant culminating transaction, the market value of the securities would be used to record the conversion. The HiTec example can be used to illustrate the journal entries for the issuer using this reasoning. The conversion would be recorded as follows:

Bonds Payable	10,000	
Loss on Conversion of Bonds	550	
Common Stock, $20 par		8,000
Paid-In Capital in Excess of Par		2,400
Discount on Bonds Payable		150
Computation:		
Market value of stock issued (400 shares at $26)		$10,400
Face value of bonds payable	$10,000	
Less unamortized discount	150	9,850
Loss to company on conversion of bonds		$ 550

If the issuer did not consider the conversion as a culminating transaction, no gain or loss would be recognized. The bond carrying value would be transferred to the capital stock account on the theory that the company upon issuing the bonds is aware of the fact that bond proceeds may ultimately represent the consideration identified with stock. Thus, when bondholders exercise their conversion privileges, the value identified with the obligation is transferred to the security that replaces it. Under this assumption, the conversion would be recorded as follows:

Bonds Payable	10,000	
Common Stock, $20 par		8,000
Paid-In Capital in Excess of Par		1,850
Discount on Bonds Payable		150

The profession has not resolved the accounting issues surrounding convertible debt. Although the practice of not recognizing gain or loss on either the issuer's or the investor's books is widespread, it seems inconsistent with the treatment of other items that are trans-

14. *Opinions of the Accounting Principles Board No. 29,* "Accounting for Nonmonetary Transactions" (New York: American Institute of Certified Public Accountants, 1973), par. 18.

ferred by an entity. The economic reality of the transaction would seem to require a recognition of the change in value at least at the time conversion takes place.

Bond Refinancing. Cash for the retirement of a bond issue is frequently raised through the sale of a new issue and is referred to as **bond refinancing,** or **refunding.** Bond refinancing may take place when an issue matures, or bonds may be refinanced prior to their maturity when the interest rate has dropped and the interest savings on a new issue will more than offset the cost of retiring the old issue. To illustrate, assume that a corporation has outstanding 12% bonds of $1,000,000 callable at 102 and with a remaining 10-year term, and similar 10-year bonds can be marketed currently at an interest rate of only 10%. Under these circumstances it would be advantageous to retire the old issue with the proceeds from a new 10% issue, since the future savings in interest will exceed by a considerable amount the premium to be paid on the call of the old issue.

The desirability of refinancing may not be so obvious as in the preceding example. In determining whether refinancing is warranted in marginal cases, careful consideration must be given to such factors as the different maturity dates of the two issues, possible future changes in interest rates, changed loan requirements, different indenture provisions, income tax effects of refinancing, and legal fees, printing costs, and marketing costs involved in refinancing.

When refinancing takes place before the maturity date of the old issue, the problem arises as to how to dispose of the call premium and unamortized discount and issue costs of the original bonds. Three positions have been taken with respect to disposition of these items:

1. Such charges are considered a loss on bond retirement.
2. Such charges are considered deferrable and to be amortized systematically over the remaining life of the original issue.
3. Such charges are considered deferrable and to be amortized systematically over the life of the new issue.

Although arguments can be presented supporting each of these alternatives, the APB concluded that "all extinguishments of debt before scheduled maturities are fundamentally alike. The accounting for such transactions should be the same regardless of the means used to achieve the extinguishment."[15] The first position, immediate recognition of the gain or loss, was selected by the Board for all early extinguishment of debt. The Financial Accounting Standards Board considered the nature of this gain or loss and defined it as being an extraordinary item requiring separate income statement disclosure, as indicated earlier.

In-Substance Defeasance. Another form of early extinguishment of debt is referred to as **in-substance defeasance,** or economic defeasance. This is a technique used by companies to reduce the amount of long-term debt reported on the balance sheet. In-substance defeasance is a process of transferring assets, generally cash and securities, to an irrevocable trust, and using the assets and earnings therefrom to satisfy the long-term obligations as they come due. The transfer of the assets is treated as an extinguishment of debt, and an extraordinary gain may be recognized on the early retirement, even though the debt has not actually been paid at that point. In some instances, the debt holders are not even aware of these transactions and continue to rely on the issuer of the debt for settlement of the obligation. In other words, there has been no "legal defeasance" or release of the debtor from the legal liability.

To illustrate the effects of in-substance defeasance and the practical problems associated with these arrangements, assume that Tenax Corporation transfers $350,000 cash to a trust estab-

15. *Opinions of the Accounting Principles Board No. 26,* par. 19.

lished solely for the retirement of $400,000 of Tenax bonds outstanding. The trust purchases government securities for $350,000. Interest and proceeds from the eventual sale or maturity of the government securities will be used to pay off the principal and interest of the bond indebtedness. Tenax removes the bonds from its balance sheet and recognizes an extraordinary gain of $50,000 on the extinguishment, i.e., the difference between the $400,000 liability to bondholders and the $350,000 cash transferred to the trust. The results of Tenax Corporation's in-substance defeasance are illustrated in the following condensed financial statements.

Before In-Substance Defeasance:

Tenax Corporation
Balance Sheet

Assets		Liabilities and Equity	
Cash	$ 400,000	Current liabilities	$ 200,000
Other assets	6,000,000	Bonds payable	400,000
		Other long-term liabilities	1,200,000
		Equity (400,000 common shares outstanding)	4,600,000
Total assets	$6,400,000	Total liabilities and equity	$6,400,000

Income Statement

Revenues	$ 8,000,000
Expenses	(6,000,000)
Net income	$ 2,000,000
Earnings per share ($2,000,000 ÷ 400,000 shares)	$5.00
Debt-to-equity ratio (total liabilities ÷ equity = $1,800,000 ÷ $4,600,000)	.39
Return on assets (net income ÷ total assets = $2,000,000 ÷ $6,400,000)	.31

After In-Substance Defeasance:

Tenax Corporation
Balance Sheet

Assets		Liabilities and Equity	
Cash	$ 50,000	Current liabilities	$ 200,000
Other assets	6,000,000	Other long-term liabilities	1,200,000
		Equity	4,650,000
Total assets	$6,050,000	Total liabilities and equity	$6,050,000

Income Statement

Revenues	$ 8,000,000
Extraordinary gain ($400,000 – $350,000)	50,000
Expenses	(6,000,000)
Net income	$ 2,050,000
Earnings per share ($2,050,000 ÷ 400,000 shares)	$5.13
Debt-to-equity ratio ($1,400,000 ÷ $4,650,000)	.30
Return on assets ($2,050,000 ÷ $6,050,000)	.34

As the statements show, the transaction improves both the earnings per share and key financial ratios of Tenax. Earnings are increased by the amount of gain recognized by Tenax, $50,000 or $.13 per share. The debt is removed from the balance sheet, without actually being retired, thereby decreasing the debt-to-equity ratio and increasing the return on assets. In many in-substance defeasance cases, the actual retirement of debt may not be desirable due to market conditions, or may be too costly due to significant call premiums.

To deal with the potential problems of overstating earnings or manipulating financial position, the FASB issued Statement No. 76 as a guideline for in-substance defeasance transactions. For a transaction to qualify as an extinguishment of debt, and therefore for removal of the debt from the balance sheet, the debtor must place cash or risk-free securities (those backed by the U.S. Government) in an irrevocable trust for the sole purpose of retiring the debt principal and interest obligations. In addition, the possibility that the debtor will be required to make further payments on that particular debt security must be remote.[16] Thus, in the Tenax example, the $350,000 placed in the trust must provide a return sufficient to make interest payments on the debt as well as to accumulate an additional $50,000 to be able to retire the face amount of the debt when it comes due.

Not all accountants agree with the conclusions of FASB Statement No. 76. Some argue that until a debt is actually retired, it should not be removed from the balance sheet under any conditions. Others are skeptical of recognizing a gain or loss on a transaction where the debtor is not legally released from the primary obligation of the debt. On the other hand, supporters of the FASB position claim that the economic reality of in-substance defeasance transactions is essentially the same as a cash settlement. They further maintain that the strict guidelines of having risk-free securities placed in an irrevocable trust and having the probability of additional payments being remote are sufficient to recognize the transaction as an extinguishment of debt. Regardless of individual viewpoints, since FASB Statement No. 76 is generally accepted, transactions that qualify as in-substance defeasance are treated in the same manner as other forms of early retirement. Regardless of the reasons for extinguishment or the means used to accomplish the early retirement, a gain or loss should be recognized as an extraordinary item of that period.

TROUBLED DEBT RESTRUCTURING

Another significant accounting problem is created when economic conditions make it difficult for an issuer of long-term debt to make the cash payments required under the terms of the debt instrument. These payments include interest payments, principal payments on installment obligations, periodic payments to bond retirement funds, or even payments to retire debt at maturity. To avoid bankruptcy proceedings or foreclosure on the debt, investors may agree to make concessions and revise the original terms of the debt to permit the issuer to recover from financial problems. The revision of debt terms in such situations, referred to as **troubled debt restructuring,** can take many different forms. For example, there may be a suspension of interest payments for a period of time, a reduction in the interest rate, an extension of the maturity date of the debt, or even an exchange of assets or equity securities for the debt. The primary accounting question in these cases, on both the books of the issuer and the investor, is whether a gain or loss should be recognized upon the restructuring of the debt.

The issue became critical in the mid-1970s when several issues of municipal bonds, notably New York City bonds, were restructured due to the financial difficulties of the issuing organizations. Investors in the bonds were faced with interest and fund payments in arrears and a near bankrupt situation for New York City. Most investors felt the decline was only temporary and did not recognize any loss on the books. After considerable negotiation,

16. *Statement of Financial Accounting Standards No. 76,* "Extinguishment of Debt" (Stamford: Financial Accounting Standards Board, 1983), p. 5. It should be noted that current accounting practice does not allow extinguishment of debt through *instantaneous* in-substance defeasance, which means newly issued debt is immediately "retired" by having assets placed in trust to meet the interest and principal obligations as they come due. Instantaneous defeasance must be accounted for as a borrowing and as an investment, not as an extinguishment. See also *FASB Technical Bulletin No. 84-4,* "In-Substance Defeasance of Debt" (Stamford: Financial Accounting Standards Board, 1984).

the terms of the bonds were restructured. Changes included a moratorium on interest and fund payments and extended maturity dates. Other municipalities and private companies such as Chrysler and Massey-Ferguson have experienced similar restructuring needs.

The FASB considered the area of debt restructuring carefully and issued Statement No. 15 in 1977. In this statement the Board defined **troubled debt restructuring** as a situation where "the creditor for economic or legal reasons related to the debtor's financial difficulties grants a concession to the debtor that it would not otherwise consider. That concession either stems from an agreement between the creditor and the debtor or is imposed by law or a court."[17] The key word in this definition is *concession*. If a concession is not made by creditors, accounting for the restructuring follows the procedures discussed for extinguishment of debt prior to maturity.

The major issue addressed by the FASB in Statement No. 15 is whether a troubled debt restructuring agreement should be viewed as a significant economic transaction. It was decided that if it is considered to be a significant economic transaction, entries should be made on the issuer's books to reflect any gain or loss. If the restructuring is not considered to be a significant economic transaction, no entries are required. The accounting treatment thus depends on the nature of the restructuring. The FASB conclusions are summarized in the following table:

Accounting for Different Types of Troubled Debt Restructuring

Type	Restructuring Considered Significant Economic Transaction: Gain or Loss Recognized	Restructuring Not Considered Significant Economic Transaction: No Gain or Loss Recognized
Transfer of assets in full settlement (asset swap)	×	
Grant of equity interest in full settlement (equity swap)	×	
Modification of terms: total payment under new structure exceeds debt carrying value		×
Modification of terms: total payment under new structure is less than debt carrying value	×	

For the issuer, each type of restructuring is discussed and illustrated in the following sections. For the investor, the procedures associated with an asset swap and an equity swap are discussed in this chapter. The complexities associated with a modification of terms from the point of view of the investor (or creditor) are discussed in Ch. 17 where we discuss the accounting for the impairment of a loan. Under FASB Statement No. 15, the accounting for troubled-debt restructuring was similar for both the issuer and the investor. In 1993, however, the FASB issued Statement No. 114, "Accounting by Creditors for Impairment of a Loan," which drastically changed how the investor accounts for a modification of terms.

Transfer of Assets in Full Settlement (Asset Swap)

A debtor that transfers assets, such as real estate, inventories, receivables, or investments, to a creditor to fully settle a payable usually will recognize two types of gains or losses:

17. *Statement of Financial Accounting Standards No. 15,* "Accounting by Debtors and Creditors for Troubled Debt Restructuring" (Stamford: Financial Accounting Standards Board, 1977), par. 2.

(1) **a gain or loss on disposal of the asset,** and (2) **a gain arising from the concession** granted in the restructuring of the debt. The computation of these gains and/or losses is made as follows:

Carrying value of assets being transferred	
	Difference represents gain or loss on disposal
Market value of asset being transferred	
	Difference represents gain on restructuring
Carrying value of debt being liquidated	

The gain or loss on disposal of an asset is usually reported as an ordinary income item unless it meets criteria for reporting it as an unusual or irregular item. However, the gain on restructuring is considered to arise from an early extinguishment of debt and must be reported as an extraordinary item.[18]

An investor always recognizes **a loss on the restructuring** due to the concession granted unless the investment has already been written down in anticipation of the loss. The computation of the loss is made as follows:

Carrying value of investment liquidated	
	Difference represents loss on restructuring
Market value of asset being transferred	

The classification of this loss depends on the criteria being used to recognize irregular or extraordinary items. However, usually the loss is anticipated as market values of the investment decline, and it is recognized as an ordinary loss, either prior to the restructuring or as part of the restructuring.

To illustrate these points, assume that Stanton Industries is behind in its interest payments on outstanding bonds of $500,000, and is threatened with bankruptcy proceedings. The carrying value of the bonds on Stanton's books is $545,000 after deducting the unamortized discount of $5,000 and adding unpaid interest of $50,000. To settle the debt, Stanton transfers long-term investments it holds in Worth common stock with a carrying value of $350,000 and a current market value of $400,000, to all investors on a pro rata basis.

Assume Realty Inc. holds $40,000 face value of bonds. Because of the troubled financial condition of Stanton Industries, Realty Inc. has previously recognized as a loss a $5,000 decline in the value of the debt and is carrying the investment at $35,000 on its books plus interest receivable of $4,000. The entries to record the asset transfer would be as follows:

Stanton Industries (Issuer)

Interest Payable	50,000	
Bonds Payable	500,000	
Discount on Bonds Payable		5,000
Long-Term Investments—Worth Common		350,000
Gain on Disposal of Worth Common		50,000
Gain on Restructuring of Debt		145,000

Computation:

Carrying value of Worth Common	$350,000	
		$50,000 gain on disposal
Market value of Worth Common	$400,000	
		$145,000 gain from restructuring
Carrying value of debt liquidated	$545,000	

18. *Ibid.*, par. 21.

Realty Inc. (Investor)

Long-Term Investments—Worth Common	32,000	
Loss on Restructuring of Debt	7,000	
Long-Term Investments—Stanton Bonds		35,000
Interest Receivable		4,000

Computation:
Percentage of debt held by Realty Inc.: $40,000/$500,000 = 8%
Market value of long-term investment received in settlement of debt:
8% × $400,000 = $32,000

If an active market does not exist for the assets being transferred, estimates of the value should be made based on transfer of similar assets or by analyzing future cash flows from the assets.[19]

Grant of Equity Interest (Equity Swap)

A debtor that grants an equity interest to the investor as a substitute for a liability must recognize an extraordinary gain equal to the difference between the fair market value of the equity interest and the carrying value of the liquidated liability. A creditor (investor) must recognize a loss equal to the difference between the same fair market value of the equity interest and the carrying value of the debt as an investment. For example, assume that Stanton Industries transferred 20,000 shares of common stock to satisfy the $500,000 face value of bonds. The par value of the common stock per share is $15, and the market value at the date of the restructuring is $20 per share. Assume the other facts described in the preceding illustration of an asset swap are unchanged. The entries to record the grant of the equity interest on both sets of books would be as follows:

Stanton Industries (Issuer)

Interest Payable	50,000	
Bonds Payable	500,000	
Discount on Bonds Payable		5,000
Common Stock		300,000
Paid-In Capital in Excess of Par		100,000
Gain on Restructuring of Debt		145,000

Computation:
Market value of common stock $400,000
Carrying value of debt liquidated $545,000
145,000 gain from restructuring

Realty Inc. (Investor)

Long-Term Investments—Stanton Common	32,000	
Loss on Restructuring of Debt	7,000	
Long-Term Investments—Stanton Bonds		35,000
Interest Receivable		4,000

The entry on Stanton's books for an equity swap differs from that made for the asset swap, because there can be no gain or loss on disposal of a company's own stock. However, the entry on Realty's books for an equity swap is identical with that for an asset swap except that the investment is in Stanton common stock.

Modification of Debt Terms

There are many ways debt terms may be modified to aid a troubled debtor. Modification may involve either the interest, the maturity value, or both. Interest concessions may involve a reduction of the interest rate, forgiveness of unpaid interest, or a moratorium on

19. *Ibid.*, par. 13.

interest payments for a period of time. Maturity value concessions may involve an extension of the maturity date or a reduction in the amount to be repaid at maturity. Basically, the FASB decided that most modifications of debt did not result in a significant economic transaction for the issuer of the debt and thus did not give rise to a gain or loss at the date of restructuring. It argued that the new terms were merely an extension of an existing debt and that the modifications should be reflected in future periods through modified interest charges based on computed implicit interest rates. The only exception to this general rule occurs if the total payments to be made under the new structure, including all future interest payments, are less than the carrying value of the debt or the investment at the time of restructuring. Under this exception, the difference between the total future cash payments required and the carrying value of the debt or investment is recognized immediately as a gain on the debtor's books.

To illustrate the accounting for this type of restructuring, assume the interest rate on the Stanton Industries bonds (see page 597) is reduced from 10% to 7%, the maturity date is extended from 3 to 5 years from the restructuring date, and the past interest due of $50,000 is forgiven. The total future payments to be made after this restructuring are as follows:

Maturity value of bonds	$500,000
Interest—7% × $500,000 × 5 years	175,000
Total payments to be made after restructuring	$675,000

Since the $675,000 exceeds the carrying value of $545,000, no gain is recognized on the books of Stanton Industries at the time of restructuring.

However, if in addition to the preceding changes, $200,000 of maturity value is forgiven, the future payments would be reduced as follows:

Maturity value of bonds	$300,000
Interest—7% × $300,000 × 5 years	105,000
Total payments to be made after restructuring	$405,000

Now the carrying value exceeds the future payments by $140,000, and this gain would be recognized by Stanton as follows:

Interest Payable	50,000	
Bonds Payable	500,000	
Discount on Bonds Payable		5,000
Restructured Debt		405,000
Gain on Restructuring of Debt		140,000
To reclassify restructured debt and recognize a gain of $140,000 on restructuring.		

When terms are modified, the amount recognized as interest expense or interest revenue in the remaining periods of the debt instrument's life is based on a computed implicit interest rate. The implicit interest rate is the rate that equates the present value of all future debt payments to the present carrying value of the debt or investment. The interest expense or interest revenue for each period is equal to the carrying value of the debt for the period involved times the implicit interest rate. The computation of the implicit interest rate can be complex and usually requires the use of a computer program. However, approximations can be made by using a trial-and-error approach from the present-value tables in Chapter 7.

To illustrate the computation of an implicit interest rate, the restructuring of Stanton Industries described on page 597 will be used. The question to be answered is what rate of interest will equate the total future payments of $675,000 to the present carrying value of $545,000. Trial-and-error use of Tables II and IV in Chapter 7 shows that the rate is between 4% and 6% per year. The computations are as follows:

	Interest Rate 6% (3% Per Semiannual Period)		Interest Rate 4% (2% Per Semiannual Period)	
Present value of maturity value due in 5 years (10 semiannual periods)	.7441 × $500,000 =	$372,050	.8203 × $500,000 =	$410,150
Present value of $17,500 interest payments for 10 semiannual periods	8.5302 × $ 17,500 =	149,279	8.9826 × $ 17,500 =	157,196
Total present value		$521,329		$567,346

Interpolation indicates that the present value of $545,000 lies almost exactly midway between the present values computed at 6% and 4%; therefore, the approximate interest rate is 5%. For purposes of the illustration, the 5% rate will be used, or 2 1/2% per semiannual payment period.

Using this rate, the recorded interest expense for the first six months would be $13,625, or 2 1/2% of $545,000. Since the actual cash payment for interest is $17,500, the carrying value of the debt will decline by $3,875 ($17,500 – $13,625). The interest expense for the second semiannual period will be less than for the first period because of the decrease in the carrying value of the debt [($545,000 – $3,875) × 2.5% = $13,528 interest expense]. These computations are the same as those required in applying the effective-interest method of amortization described on pages 584-586. If the exact implicit interest rate were used, continuation of the procedure for the 10 periods would leave a balance of $500,000, the maturity value, in the liability account of Stanton Industries. The entries to record the restructuring on Stanton's books and the first two interest payments would be as follows:

	Debit	Credit
Bonds Payable	500,000	
Interest Payable	50,000	
Discount on Bonds Payable		5,000
Restructured Debt		545,000
To reclassify debt into one account.		
Interest Expense	13,625	
Restructured Debt	3,875	
Cash		17,500
To record payment of first semiannual interest after restructuring.		
Interest Expense	13,528	
Restructured Debt	3,972	
Cash		17,500
To record payment of second semiannual interest after restructuring.		

The preceding discussion covers all situations when bond restructuring reflects a modification of terms except when the cash to be received after the restructuring is less than the carrying value of the debt. Under these conditions the implicit interest rate is negative. In order to raise the rate to zero, the carrying value must be reduced to the cash to be realized and a gain recognized for the difference. All interest payments in the future are offset directly to the debt account. No interest expense will be earned in the future because of the extreme concessions made in the restructuring. By charging all interest payments to the debt account, the balance remaining at the maturity date will be the maturity value of the debt.

Any combination of these methods of bond restructuring may be employed. Accounting for these multiple restructurings can become very complex and must be carefully evaluated. As stated previously, the accounting for a modification of terms by the creditor is discussed in Chapter 17.

OFF-BALANCE-SHEET FINANCING

A major issue facing the accounting profession today is how to deal with companies that do not disclose all their debt in order to make their financial position look stronger. This is often referred to as **off-balance-sheet financing.** Traditionally, leasing has been one of the most common forms of off-balance-sheet financing. (Accounting for leases is covered in detail in Chapter 19.) Other techniques that have been used to borrow money while keeping the debt off the balance sheet are:

1. Sale of receivables with recourse.
2. Unconsolidated entities.
3. Research and development arrangements.
4. Project financing arrangements.

Sale of Receivables With Recourse

In Chapter 8, the transfer of receivables was identified as a source of financing. It was noted that the transfer of receivables is no longer a "last-ditch" method to prevent bankruptcy, but is a method commonly used by companies to raise needed funds or to avoid the collection and management problems associated with receivables. When receivables are transferred with recourse, and the transaction qualifies as a sale under FASB Statement No. 77, no liability need be reported on the balance sheet. However, companies are required to disclose the sale of receivables with recourse in notes accompanying the statements. An example of such disclosure is presented in Exhibit 14-1 for Ralston Purina Company.

Unconsolidated Entities

In 1987, the FASB issued Statement No. 94 requiring all majority-owned subsidiaries to be consolidated.[20] Prior to the issuance of FASB Statement No. 94, subsidiaries involved in operations unrelated to the parent company's primary focus were not required to be consolidated. For example, IBM Credit Corporation, Chrysler Finance Corporation, General Motors Acceptance Corporation, and Sears Roebuck Acceptance Corporation are each financing subsidiaries of their respective parent companies. The tremendous debt associ-

20. *Statement of Financial Accounting Standards No. 94,* "Consolidation of all Majority-Owned Subsidiaries" (Stamford: Financial Accounting Standards Board, 1987).

Exhibit 14—1
Ralston Purina Company—Disclosure of Sale of Receivables With Recourse

(In millions of dollars)

The Company sells certain of its trade accounts receivable to others subject to defined limited recourse provisions. The Company is responsible for collection of the accounts and remits the proceeds to the purchaser on a monthly basis. During 1989, the Company sold, on average, accounts totaling $50.0 each month. At September 30, 1989, $.4 of transferred receivables were outstanding and subject to recourse provisions.

During 1986, the Company sold $47.7 of long-term notes receivable subject to defined recourse provisions which include the repurchase by the Company of delinquent notes. The Company is responsible for collection of the accounts and remits the principal amounts collected plus a floating rate of interest to the purchaser on a monthly basis. At September 30, 1989, $10.9 of the notes remain uncollected and subject to recourse provisions.

ated with these financing subsidiaries was not disclosed on the balance sheet of their parent companies, because the subsidiaries were involved in nonhomogeneous operations. However, with the issuance of Statement No. 94, even these subsidiaries are now consolidated. Thus, the FASB eliminated one opportunity that companies have used for off-balance-sheet financing.

However, companies are still able to avoid debt associated with unconsolidated subsidiaries. As an example, Coca-Cola Inc. sold 51% interest in a subsidiary that was loaded with $2.4 billion in debt. Coca-Cola still retained effective control of the subsidiary by having interlocking boards of directors and was able to influence pricing decisions. This example is another illustration of the extreme to which companies may go to comply with the accounting standards while ignoring a standard's intent. Unconsolidated subsidiaries still represent a potential use of off-balance-sheet financing although Statement No. 94 eliminated many of the opportunities for abuse.

Research and Development Arrangements

Another way a company may obtain off-balance-sheet financing is with **research and development arrangements.** These involve situations where an enterprise obtains the results of research and development activities funded partially or entirely by others. The main accounting issue is whether the arrangement is, in essence, a means of borrowing to fund research and development or if it is simply a contract to do research for others.[21] In deciding on the appropriate accounting treatment, a major consideration is whether the enterprise is obligated to repay the funds provided by the other parties regardless of the outcome of the research and development activities. If there is an obligation to repay, then the enterprise should estimate and recognize that liability and record the research and development expenses in the current year in accordance with FASB Statement No. 2. If the financial risk associated with the research and development is transferred from the enterprise to other parties and there is no obligation to them, then a liability need not be reported by the enterprise.

Research and development arrangements may take a variety of forms, including a limited partnership. For example, assume Kincher Company formed a limited partnership for the purpose of conducting research and development. Kincher is the general partner and manages the activities of the partnership. The limited partners are strictly investors. The question is—Should Kincher record the research and development expenses and the obligation to the investors on its books? The answer depends on an assessment of who is at risk and if Kincher is obligated to repay the limited partners regardless of the results of the

21. *Statement of Financial Accounting Standards No. 68,* "Research and Development Arrangements" (Stamford: Financial Accounting Standards Board, 1982).

research and development. If the limited partners are at risk and have no guarantee or claim against Kincher Company for any of the funds contributed, the debt and related expenses need not be reported on Kincher's books.

Project Financing Arrangements

At times, companies become involved in long-term commitments that are related to **project financing arrangements.** As an example, assume that two oil- and gas-producing companies, Striker Corporation and Jetco, Inc., agree to a joint venture. They form a separate company to construct a refinery in Alaska that both will use. The new company borrows funds for the construction and plans to repay the debt from the proceeds of the project. Striker and Jetco guarantee the repayment of the debt by the new company. The advantage to Striker and Jetco under such an arrangement is that neither of them shows the liability from the borrowing on its balance sheet. Each would report a contingency related to the guarantee of debt repayment in a note to the financial statements. This type of arrangement is another form of off-balance-sheet financing.[22]

Reasons for Off-Balance-Sheet Financing

There are several reasons why companies might use one of the preceding or other techniques to avoid including debt on the balance sheet. It may allow a company to borrow more than it otherwise could due to debt-limit restrictions. Also, if a company's financial position looks stronger, it will usually be able to borrow at a lower cost. Another reason may be that inflation tends to understate assets, and so companies seek ways to understate liabilities.

Whatever the reasons, the problems of off-balance-sheet financing are serious. Many investors and lenders aren't sophisticated enough to see through the off-balance-sheet borrowing tactics, and so make ill-informed decisions. For example, in periods of economic downturn, a company with hidden debt may find it is not able to meet its obligations and, as a result, may suffer severe financial distress or, in extreme cases, business failure. In turn, unsuspecting creditors and investors may sustain substantial losses that could have been avoided had they known the true extent of the company's debt.

The explosion of new financial instruments in recent years has created many accounting issues. Some of these issues arise because the new financial products are not addressed in the accounting literature or because the literature provides conflicting guidance. To address these issues, in May 1986, the FASB added to its agenda a major project on financial instruments and off-balance-sheet financing. This project is expected to develop standards that will aid in resolving issues raised by inconsistent practices that have developed over the years for specialized financial transactions.

The FASB project is divided into phases and will address several separate, yet related, specific questions. The identified phases relate to:[23]

1. Disclosure—This phase of the project addresses the disclosure of information relating to financial instruments and the risks associated with those instruments. In March 1990, the FASB issued FASB Statement No. 105, "Disclosure of Information About Financial Instruments with Off-Balance-Sheet Risk and Financial Instruments with Concentrations of Credit Risk," and No. 107, "Disclosures About Fair Value of Financial Instruments."

22. *Statement of Financial Accounting Standards No. 47,* "Disclosure of Long-Term Obligations" (Stamford: Financial Accounting Standards Board, 1981).

23. *Status Report,* Financial Accounting Standards Board, October 18, 1990.

2. Recognition and Measurement—The FASB is working to develop standards in this area to resolve such issues as the accounting for the sale of receivables with recourse, the accounting for transactions that transfer market and credit risk, and the measurement of financial instruments, e.g., historical cost, market value, etc.

The FASB and the accounting profession will no doubt continue to deal with the potentially serious problems of off-balance-sheet financing.[24] As the techniques and financial instruments become more complex and widely used, there is growing concern that the amount of total corporate debt is reaching unhealthy proportions.

Company takeovers, especially debt-financed acquisitions called **leveraged buy-outs (LBOs),** and related financial instruments such as junk bonds are major contributors to the problem of increasing corporate debt. "Hostile" takeovers are sometimes initiated by outsiders (often referred to as corporate raiders) against the wishes of management. In other instances, management or a combination of management and outside investors become the new owners through a "friendly" takeover.

Traditionally, acquisitions of companies have been paid for mostly with cash or stock. With a leveraged buy-out, often 90 percent or more of the purchase price is debt financed. Thus, the acquiring company has to pay cash of only 10 percent or less of the total purchase price to gain control. After the purchase, the new owners usually sell off parts of the acquired business to raise the money necessary to reduce the company debt. In many cases, the acquired company is later resold, after the debt has been reduced, sometimes at a much higher price than that paid in the LBO. For example, Shearson Lehman Hutton invested $100,000 in Tiffany in 1984 and cashed out with $2.2 million in 1988.

While an LBO may offer advantages to its investors, it frequently is disadvantageous to the acquired company's existing bondholders. The significant amount of new debt created by the LBO often causes the value of existing bonds to fall. In 1988, for example, the $25 billion LBO of RJR Nabisco Inc. by Kohlberg Kravis Roberts & Co. caused the price of RJR bonds to drop over $150 for each $1,000 face amount. The significant decline in the price of RJR bonds led investing companies such as ITT Corporation's Hartford Insurance Division and Metropolitan Life Insurance Co. to sue RJR Nabisco.

ANALYZING A FIRM'S DEBT POSITION

Those parties considering investing in, or lending money to, a firm are particularly interested in that firm's obligations and capital structure. The term *leverage* refers to the relationship between a firm's debt and assets or its debt and stockholders' equity. A firm that is highly leveraged would have a large amount of debt relative to its assets or equity. A common measure of a firm's leverage is the **debt-to-equity ratio,** calculated by dividing total liabilities by total stockholders' equity. As an example, consider the following information from the 1993 annual report of Caesars World, owner of Caesars Palace in Las Vegas as well as numerous other casino and hotel properties:

(in millions)	1993	1992
Long-term debt	$243,024	$258,466
Total liabilities	482,829	517,621
Total stockholders' equity	472,890	384,648
Income before income taxes	113,976	117,360
Interest expense	26,883	43,518

24. John E. Stewart and Benjamin S. Neuhausen, "Financial Instruments and Transactions: The CPA's Newest Challenge," *Journal of Accountancy* (August 1986), pp. 102-110.

Caesars World's debt-to-equity ratios for 1993 and 1992 would be:

1993: $482,829/$472,890 = 1.021

1992: $517,621/$384,648 = 1.346

A debt-to-equity ratio exceeding 1.0 indicates that the firm has more liabilities than stockholders' equity. For Caesars World, the debt-to-equity ratio has dropped significantly from 1992 to 1993. Investors generally prefer a higher debt-to-equity ratio to obtain the advantages of financial leverage, while creditors favor a lower ratio to increase the safety of their debt. Median debt-to-equity ratios for a diverse group of industries are presented below:

Industry (number of firms included)	Median Debt-to-Equity Ratios
Dairy farms (303)	0.560
Blast Furnace and Steel Mills (550)	1.153
Electric Utilities (2,167)	1.592
Grocery Stores (2,183)	0.832
Jewelry Stores (2,319)	0.578
Personal Credit Institutions (2,463)	2.015
Legal Services (2,463)	0.708

As these data illustrate, what constitutes an acceptable debt-to-equity ratio depends to a great extent upon the industry in which a firm operates.

Because there is no hard and fast rule for what is included in the term "debt," alternative definitions and interpretations of the debt-to-equity ratio have developed. For example, the ratio is often varied to include only long-term debt. If this definition were used for Caesars World, the debt-to-equity ratio for the two-year period would be:

1993: $243,024/$472,890 = 0.514

1992: $258,466/$384,648 = 0.672

Note that, in this example, the trend in the debt-to-equity ratio is the same regardless of how the term debt is defined. Another common variation of the leverage measure is to compare total liabilities to total assets. This measure, frequently called the **debt ratio,** was introduced in Chapter 5 (see page 162).

Another measure of a firm's performance relating to debt is the number of times interest is earned. This measure compares a firm's interest obligations with its earnings ability. **Times interest earned** is calculated by dividing a firm's income before income taxes and interest expense by the interest expense for the period. In the case of Caesars World, times interest earned for 1993 and 1992 is computed as follows:

1993: ($113,976 + $26,883) / $26,883 = 5.24 times

1992: ($117,360 + $43,518) / $43,518 = 3.70 times

The number of times interest is earned reflects the company's ability to meet interest payments and the degree of safety afforded the creditors. Note that from 1992 to 1993, Caesars World has increased its ability to cover interest through its earnings process.

REPORTING BONDS AND LONG-TERM NOTES AS LIABILITIES

In reporting long-term debt on the balance sheet, the nature of the liabilities, maturity dates, interest rates, methods of liquidation, conversion privileges, sinking fund requirements, borrowing restrictions, assets pledged, dividend limitations, and other significant matters should be indicated. The portion of long-term debt coming due in the current period should also be disclosed.

Bond liabilities are often combined with other long-term debt for balance sheet presentation, with supporting detail disclosed in a note. An example of such a note taken from the 1992 annual report of Goodyear, is presented in Exhibit 14—2.

Exhibit 14—2
The Goodyear Tire and Rubber Company—Disclosure of Long-Term Debt

NOTES TO FINANCIAL STATEMENTS

Note 6 (In Part): Credit Arrangements
B. Long-Term Debt

(in Millions)	1992	1991
Promissory notes:		
12.15% due 1993-2000	$ 40.0	$ 45.0
10.26% due 1999	118.4	118.4
Sinking fund debentures:		
8.60% due 1993-1994	—	19.0
7.35% due 1993-1997	—	30.7
Swiss franc bonds:		
5.375% due 2000	136.8	175.9
5.375% due 2006	126.2	146.6
Yen bonds:		
6.875% due 1994	—	89.1
7.125% due 1995	—	194.4
6.625% due 1996	—	77.7
6.30% Yen bank term loan due 1994	40.2	39.8
6.875% Convertible Debentures due 2003	150.0	150.0
Bank term loans due 1995-2000	218.0	468.5
Revolving credit agreements	255.0	140.5
Other domestic debt	228.3	15.5
International subsidiary debt	178.7	333.7
	$1,491.6	$2,044.8

At December 31, 1992, the fair value of the Company's long-term debt amounted to $1,475.2 million compared to the carrying amount of $1,491.6 million. The difference was attributable primarily to the Swiss franc bonds. The fair value was estimated using quoted market prices or discounted future cash flows.

At December 31, 1992, the Company had available long-term credit sources totaling $3,662.5 million, of which $2,320.0 million were unused.

During 1992, the Company retired, ahead of scheduled maturities, long-term debt totaling $809.4 million. Included in these retirements were all of the sinking fund debentures totaling $49.7 million, a portion of the Swiss franc bond issues totaling $36.3 million, all of the Yen bond issues totaling $358.4 million and various bank term loans totaling $365.0 million. Certain Swiss franc and Yen currency hedges were also liquidated in conjunction with the Swiss franc and Yen bond retirements.

APPENDIX
Accounting for Serial Bonds

As noted in the chapter, serial bonds mature in installments at various dates. Usually, each bond indicates when it will mature. Because of the difference in time and maturity, the interest rate often varies depending on the due date. In some instances, the stated interest rate remains constant for all maturity dates, but the effective interest rate differs as the selling prices for the different maturity dates vary to reflect the changing risk. When serial bonds are issued at other than par, the premium or discount could be related to the bonds maturing on each specific date, and the amortization of the premium or discount could be made as though each maturity date were a separate bond issue. No new problems related to accounting for interest arise under this approach.

However, an entire serial bond issue is sometimes sold directly to underwriters at a lump-sum price that differs from the total face value of the issue. When this occurs, the issue price usually cannot be identified with each maturity date. Under these circumstances, the premium or discount on the entire serial bond issue must be amortized as a unit. This requires that either an average effective rate be determined for the entire issue, and the effective-interest method used to determine the amortization, or that a variation of the straight-line method known as the **bonds-outstanding method** be applied. Both methods provide for decreases in the amortization schedule as the principal amounts of the serial bonds mature.

Bonds-Outstanding Method

Amortization by the bonds-outstanding method is illustrated in the example that follows. Assume that bonds with a face value of $100,000, dated January 1, 1995, are issued on this date for a lump-sum price of $101,260. Bonds of $20,000 mature at the end of each year starting on December 31, 1995. The bonds pay interest of 8% annually. The company's accounting period ends on December 31; the accounting period and the bond year thus coincide. A table showing the premium to be amortized each year is developed as shown in the schedule at the top of page 608.

The annual premium amortization is found by multiplying the premium by a fraction whose numerator is the number of bond dollars outstanding in that year and whose denominator is the total number of bond dollars outstanding for the life of bond issue. As bonds are retired, the amounts of premium amortization decline accordingly.

Amortization Schedule—Bonds-Outstanding Method

Year	Bonds Outstanding	Fraction of Premium to Be Amortized	Annual Premium Amortization (Fraction × $1,260)
1995	$100,000	100,000/300,000 (or 10/30)	$ 420
1996	80,000	80,000/300,000 (or 8/30)	336
1997	60,000	60,000/300,000 (or 6/30)	252
1998	40,000	40,000/300,000 (or 4/30)	168
1999	20,000	20,000/300,000 (or 2/30)	84
	$300,000	300,000/300,000 (or 30/30)	$1,260

An alternative computation can be made by computing the amount of amortization related to each $1,000 of outstanding bonds. In the preceding example, this would be $4.20 per $1,000 bond ($1,260 ÷ 300). Applying this amount to the number of $1,000 bonds outstanding each year would result in the same amortization shown in the table, e.g., for 1996, 80 x $4.20, or $336. The use of this alternative method of computing the amortization is especially useful when computing the unamortized premium or discount on serial bonds retired early.

Periodic amortization may be incorporated in a table summarizing the interest charges and changes in bond carrying values as follows:

Amortization of Premium—Serial Bonds
Bonds-Outstanding Method

Date	A Interest Payment (8% of Face Value)	B Premium Amortization	C Interest Expense (A – B)	D Principal Payment	E Bond Carrying Value Decrease (B + D)	F Bond Carrying Value (F – E)
Jan. 1, 1995						$101,260
Dec. 31, 1995	$8,000	$420	$7,580	$20,000	$20,420	80,840
Dec. 31, 1996	6,400	336	6,064	20,000	20,336	60,504
Dec. 31, 1997	4,800	252	4,548	20,000	20,252	40,252
Dec. 31, 1998	3,200	168	3,032	20,000	20,168	20,084
Dec. 31, 1999	1,600	84	1,516	20,000	20,084	—

Effective-Interest Method

Present-value tables show that the bonds in the preceding example were sold to return approximately 7 1/2%. Use of this rate results in the following interest charges and premium amortization using the effective-interest method.

Amortization of Premium—Serial Bonds
Effective-Interest Method

	A	B	C	D	E	F
Date	**Interest Payment (8% of Face Value)**	**Interest Expense ($7\frac{1}{2}$% of Bond Carrying Value)**	**Premium Amortization (A – B)**	**Principal Payment**	**Bond Carrying Value Decrease (C + D)**	**Bond Carrying Value (F – E)**
Jan. 1, 1995						$101,260
Dec. 31, 1995	$8,000	$7,595	$405	$20,000	$20,405	80,855
Dec. 31, 1996	6,400	6,064	336	20,000	20,336	60,519
Dec. 31, 1997	4,800	4,539	261	20,000	20,261	40,258
Dec. 31, 1998	3,200	3,019	181	20,000	20,181	20,077
Dec. 31, 1999	1,600	1,523*	77*	20,000	20,077	—

*The last payment is adjusted because the effective rate was not exactly $7\frac{1}{2}$%. On the final payment, the premium balance is closed and interest expense is reduced by this amount.

The bonds-outstanding method of amortization provides for the recognition of uniform amounts of amortization in terms of the par value of bonds outstanding. The effective-interest method provides for the recognition of interest at a uniform rate on the declining debt balance.

KEY TERMS

QUESTIONS

1. What factors should be considered in determining whether cash should be raised by the issuance of bonds or by the sale of additional stock?
2. Distinguish between (a) secured and unsecured bonds, (b) collateral trust and debenture bonds, (c) convertible and callable bonds, (d) coupon and registered bonds, (e) municipal and corporate bonds, and (f) term and serial bonds.
3. What is meant by market rate of interest, stated or contract rate, and effective or yield rate? Which of these rates changes during the lifetime of the bond issue?
4. An investor purchases bonds with a face value of $100,000. Payment for the bonds includes (a) a premium, (b) accrued interest, and (c) brokerage fees. How would each of these charges be recorded and what disposition would ultimately be made of each of these charges?
5. How should bond issuance costs be accounted for on the issuer's books?
6. What amortization method for premiums and discounts on bonds is recommended by APB Opinion No. 21? Why? When can the alternative method be used?
7. Under what conditions would the following statement be true? "The effective-interest method of bond premium or discount amortization for the issuer results in higher net income than would be reported using straight-line amortization."
8. List three ways that bonds are commonly retired prior to maturity. How should the early extinguishment of debt be presented on the income statement?
9. What purpose is served by issuing callable bonds?
10. What are the distinguishing features of convertible debt securities? What questions relate to the nature of this type of security?
11. The conversion of convertible bonds to common stock by an investor may be viewed as an exchange involving no gain or loss, or as a transaction for which market values should be recognized and a gain or loss reported. What arguments support each of these views for the investor and for the issuer?
12. Why do companies find the issuance of convertible bonds a desirable method of financing?
13. What is meant by refinancing or refunding a bond issue? When may refinancing be advisable?
14. What is in-substance defeasance, and what action must the debtor take for it to qualify as an early extinguishment of debt?
15. What distinguishes a troubled debt restructuring from other debt restructurings?
16. What is the recommended accounting treatment for bond restructurings effected as:
    (a) asset swap?
    (b) An equity swap?
    (c) A modification of terms?
17. Why is off-balance-sheet financing popular with many companies? What problems are associated with the use of this method of financing?
18. What is a leveraged buy-out? Why have LBOs become popular? What is the risk to bondholders if a leveraged buy-out occurs?

*19. Describe the bonds-outstanding method for premium or discount amortization for serial bonds. How does this method differ from the effective-interest method of amortization?

*Relates to Appendix

DISCUSSION CASES

Case 14—1 (Accounting for bonds)

Startup Company decided to issue $100,000 worth of 10%, 5-year bonds dated January 1, 1995, with interest payable semiannually on January 1 and July 1 of each year. Due to printing and other delays, Startup was not able to sell the bonds until July 1, 1995. The bonds were sold to yield 12% interest, and they are callable at 102 after January 1, 1997. The company expects interest rates to fall during the next few years and is planning to retire this bond issue and to replace it with a less costly one if the expected decline occurs.

Assume that you have just been hired as the accountant for Startup Company. The financial vice president would like you to identify the accounting issues involved with the bond transaction. You are also asked to explain why the company received less than $100,000 on the sale of the bonds, and to compute the anticipated gain or loss on retirement of the bonds, assuming retirement on July 1, 1997, and use of straight-line amortization.

Case 14—2 (Is there a loss on conversion?)

Holton Co. recently issued $1,000,000 face value, 8%, 30-year subordinated debentures at 97. The debentures are callable at 103 upon 30 days' notice by the issuer at any time beginning 10 years after the date of issue. The debentures are convertible into $10 par value common stock of the company at the conversion price of $12.50 per share for each $500 or multiple thereof of the principal amount of the debentures ($500 ÷ $12.50 = 40 shares for each $500 of face value).

Assume that no value is assigned to the conversion feature at the date of issue of the debentures. Assume further that 5 years after issue, debentures with a face value of $100,000 and book value of $97,500 are tendered for conversion on an interest payment date when the market price of the debentures is 104 and the common stock is selling at $14 per share. J. K. Biggs, the company accountant, records the conversion as follows:

Bonds Payable	100,000	
Discount on Bonds Payable		2,500
Common Stock		80,000
Paid-In Capital in Excess of Par		17,500

Julie Robinson, staff auditor for the company's CPA firm, reviews the transaction and feels the conversion entry should reflect the market value of the stock. According to Robinson's analysis, a loss on the bond conversion of $14,500 should be recognized. Biggs objects to recognizing a loss, so Robinson discusses the problem with the audit manager, K. Ashworth. Ashworth has a different view and recommends using the market value of the debentures as a basis for recording the conversion and recognizing a loss of only $6,500.

Evaluate the various positions. Include in your evaluation the substitute entries that would be made under both Robinson's and Ashworth's proposals.

Case 14—3 (Do we really have income?)

The Jefferson Corporation has $20,000,000 of 10% bonds outstanding. Because of cash flow problems, the company is behind in interest payments and in contributions to its bonds retirement fund. The market value of the bonds has declined until it is currently only 50% of the face value of the bonds. After lengthy negotiations, the principal bondholders have agreed to exchange their bonds for preferred stock that has a current market value of $10,000,000. The accountant for Jefferson Corporation recorded the transaction by charging the bond liability for the entire $20,000,000, and crediting Preferred Stock for the same amount. This entry thus transfers the amount received by the company from debt to equity.

The CPA firm performing the annual audit, however, does not agree with this treatment. The auditors argue that this transfer represents a troubled debt restructuring due to the significant concessions made by the bondholders, and under these conditions, the FASB requires Jefferson to use the market value of the preferred stock as its recorded value. The difference between the $20,000,000 face value of the bonds and the $10,000,000 market value of the preferred stock is a reportable gain.

The controller of Jefferson, L. Rogers, is flabbergasted, "Here we are, almost bankrupt, and you tell us we must report the $10,000,000 as a gain. I don't care what the FASB says; that's a ridiculous situation. You can't be serious."

But the auditor in charge of the engagements is adamant, "We really have no choice. You have had a forgiveness of debt for $10,000,000. You had use of the money, and based on current conditions, you won't have to pay it back. That situation looks like a gain to me."

What position do you think should be taken? Consider the external users of the statement and their needs in your discussion.

Case 14—4 (I like these "no interest" bonds.)

J. R. Chump, president of ProKeeper Industries, is contemplating the issuance of long-term debt to finance plant expansion and renovation. In the past, his company has issued traditional debt instruments that require regular interest payments and a retirement of the principal on the maturity date. However, he has noticed that several competitors have recently issued bonds that either do not require interest payments or defer interest payments for several years. He has asked you, as his chief financial officer, to prepare a summary addressing the following questions:

1. Why would a company issue bonds that require interest payments if bonds that do not require interest payments are being sold in the open market?
2. If the company were to issue 10-year bonds with a face value of $100,000 and the market rate of interest is 10%, what would be the proceeds from the sale if the bonds were zero-coupon bonds? What would be the proceeds if the annual interest payments did not begin for 5 years and the stated rate of interest were 10%? What would be the proceeds if the bonds paid interest annually for 10 years at 10%?
3. What factors must a business consider when determining the interest terms associated with long-term debt?

Case 14—5 (Deferred interest and interest rate resets)

Corporations commonly incur debt in financing the acquisition of other companies or in fighting takeover attacks by competitors. Two strategies often employed involve deferring interest payments and incorporating interest rate resets. For example, Interco Inc. incurred large amounts of debt in 1989 to make itself unattractive as a takeover target. The debt postponed interest payments until 1991 at which time interest was to be paid at 14%. Interco's strategy was to sell a portion of its business, Ethan Allen Inc., to redeem the debt. However, the sale netted $120 million less than expected.

Western Union incurred $500 million in debt that carried with it a reset provision. The provision called for increased interest rates if the bonds were not trading at a specified price. Western Union's reset provision increased interest rates from 16.5% to 19.25% in 1990. While interest expense rose, revenues dropped 28% from 1988 to 1989 as a result of the fax machine's making Western Union's telex service obsolete.

1. What is the significance of debt with respect to company acquisitions?
2. Why would corporations use deferred interest features and interest rate resets?
3. In the case of Interco, how would incurring large amounts of debt be an effective method for fighting a takeover?

Case 14—6 (Circle K Corporation and its Debt Covenants)

When companies raise money through the issuance of bonds or other long-term debt instruments, debt holders typically require the company to comply with certain conditions, or covenants. The notes to Circle K's 1989 financial statements provide an example of debt covenants:

The notes (Senior Secured Notes) required the Company to observe certain financial covenants, including covenants relating to maintenance of a minimum consolidated net worth, a fixed charge coverage ratio, limitations on dividends, purchases of capital stock and a requirement that any successor by merger or similar transaction to the Company have a comparable net worth and assume all the obligations under the Notes.

In addition to using debt to finance expansion, Circle K finances many of its stores through sales and leaseback transactions. These types of transactions represent a form of long-term debt financing and often involve covenants as well. The notes to the 1989 financial statements detail the results of a violation of covenants.

As of April 30, 1989, the Company was not in compliance with the fixed charge ratio of one of its sale and leaseback transactions involving 250 stores. Because of its non-compliance with such ratio, the Company is required to place $5 million per year into escrow.

1. What is the purpose of debt covenants?
2. What is the purpose of requiring an annual $5 million payment into escrow?
3. If Circle's financial condition is such that it violates its financing covenants, will requiring the company to place $5 million in escrow help to ease the financial strains?

Case 14—7 (What is meant by valuing liabilities at current values?)
John Jex, CPA, had just delivered a keynote address to a banker's organization on the merits of valuing loan portfolio assets at market values that reflected changing interest rates. During the question and answer period, he was asked why bank liabilities should not be valued using current interest rates if assets are to be revalued for interest rate changes. His answer did not seem to satisfy the banker and the meeting soon adjourned. After the meeting, John is asked by a listener to explain the impact changing interest rates would have on liabilities if a revaluation were to occur. How would you respond to such a request?

Case 14—8 (Let's get that debt off the balance sheet)
Both Coca-Cola Co. and Marriott Corporation recently improved the appearance of their parent company balance sheets by organizing separate companies and transferring significant amounts of debt to these newly organized entities. To avoid including these new companies in their consolidated financial statements, they retained less than 50% of the outstanding common stock in them. Andrea and Rick, students in intermediate accounting, have the assignment to evaluate this action and consider its appropriateness in light of current GAAP. If GAAP is deficient , they are to suggest changes that will make the reporting more representative of economic reality. Prepare the report you would submit to fulfill the assignment.

EXERCISES

Exercise 14—9 (Computation of market values of bond issues)
What is the market value of each of the following bond issues? (Round to the nearest dollar.)

(a) 10% bonds of $100,000 sold on bond issue date; 10-year life; interest payable semiannually; effective rate, 12%.
(b) 9% bonds of $200,000 sold on bond issue date; 5-year life; interest payable semiannually; effective rate, 8%.
(c) 8% bonds of $150,000 sold 30 months after bond issue date; 15-year life; interest payable semiannually; effective rate, 10%.

Exercise 14—10 (Selling bonds at par, premium, or discount)
In each of the following independent cases, state whether the bonds were issued at par, a premium, or a discount. Explain your answers.

(a) Pop-up Manufacturing sold 1,500 of its $1,000, 8% stated-rate bonds when the market rate was 9%.
(b) Splendor, Inc., sold 500 of its $2,000, 8 3/4% bonds to yield 9%.
(c) Cards Corporation issued 1,000 of its 9%, $100 face-amount bonds at an effective rate of 8 1/2%.
(d) Floppy, Inc., sold 3,000 of its 10% bonds with a face value of $2,500 at a time when the market rate was 9%.
(e) Cintron Co. sold 5,000 of its 12% contract-rate bonds with stated value of $1,000 at an effective rate of 12%.

Exercise 14—11 (Zero-coupon bonds)

Allrite Inc. is considering issuing bonds to finance the acquisition of a nationwide chain of distributors of Allrite's products. Allrite is contemplating two different types of bonds to raise the required $30 million purchase price. The first is a traditional 10-year, 10% bond with semiannual interest payments. The second is a 10-year, zero-coupon bond.

Assuming the market rate of interest is 10%, compute the face amount of the bond issuance and the journal entries to record the issuance if (a) a traditional bond is issued, and (b) a zero-coupon bond is issued.

Exercise 14—12 (Issuance and reacquisition of bonds)

On January 1, 1995, the Housen Company issued 10-year bonds of $500,000 at 102. Interest is payable on January 1 and July 1 at 10%. On April 1, 1996, the Housen Company reacquires and retires 50 of its own $1,000 bonds at 98 plus accrued interest. The fiscal period for the Housen Company is the calendar year.

Prepare entries to record (a) the issuance of the bonds, (b) the interest payments and adjustments relating to the debt in 1995, (c) the reacquisition and retirement of bonds in 1996, and (d) the interest payments and adjustments relating to the debt in 1996. Assume the premium or discount is amortized on a straight-line basis. (Round to the nearest dollar.)

Exercise 14—13 (Amortization of bond premium or discount)

On January 1, 1995, Terrel Company sold $100,000 of 10-year, 8% bonds at 93.5, an effective rate of 9%. Interest is to be paid on July 1 and December 31. Compute the premium or discount to be amortized in 1995 and 1996 using (a) the straight-line method and (b) the effective-interest method. Make the journal entries to record the amortization when the effective-interest method is used.

Exercise 14—14 (Bond interest and premium or discount amortization)

Assume that $200,000, Baker School District 6% bonds are sold on the bond issue date for $185,788. Interest is payable semiannually, and the bonds mature in 10 years. The purchase price provides a return of 7% on the investment.

1. What entries would be made on the investor's books for the receipt of the first two interest payments, assuming premium or discount amortization on each interest date by (a) the straight-line method and (b) the effective-interest method? (Round to the nearest dollar.)
2. What entries would be made on Baker School District's books to record the first two interest payments, assuming premium or discount amortization on each interest date by (a) the straight-line method and (b) the effective-interest method? (Round to the nearest dollar.)

Exercise 14—15 (Discount and premium amortization)

The Rolstone Corporation issued $200,000 of 8% debenture bonds to yield 10%, receiving $184,556. Interest is payable semiannually and the bonds mature in 5 years.

1. What entries would be made by Rolstone for the first two interest payments, assuming premium or discount amortization on interest dates by (a) the straight-line method and (b) the effective-interest method? (Round to nearest dollar.)
2. Assuming the situation in (1) above, what entries would be made on the books of the investor for the first two interest receipts assuming one party obtained all the bonds and the straight-line method of amortization was used? (Round to the nearest dollar.)
3. If the sale is made to yield 6%, $217,062 being received, what entries would be made by Rolstone for the first two interest payments, assuming premium or discount amortization on interest dates by (a) the straight-line method and (b) the effective-interest method? (Round to nearest dollar.)

Exercise 14—16 (Sale of bond investment)

Jennifer Stack acquired $50,000 of Oldtown Corp. 9% bonds on July 1, 1993. The bonds were acquired at 92; interest is paid semiannually on March 1 and September 1. The bonds mature September 1, 2000. Stack's books are kept on a calendar-year basis. On February 1, 1996, Stack sold the bonds for 97 plus accrued interest. Assuming straight-line amortization and no reversing entry at January 1, 1996, give the entry to record the sale of the bonds on February 1. (Round to the nearest dollar.)

Exercise 14—17 (Retirement of debt before maturity)

The long-term debt section of Starr Company's balance sheet as of December 31, 1995, included 9% bonds payable of $200,000 less unamortized discount of $16,000. Further examination revealed that these bonds were issued to yield 10%. The amortization of the bond discount was recorded using the effective-interest method. Interest was paid on January 1 and July 1 of each year. On July 1, 1996, Starr retired the bonds at 102 before maturity.

Prepare the journal entries to record the July 1, 1996, payment of interest, the amortization of the discount since December 31, 1995, and the early retirement on the books of Starr Company.

Exercise 14—18 (Retirement of bonds)

The December 31, 1995, balance sheet of Worsham Company includes the following items:

9% bonds payable due December 31, 2004	$400,000
Premium on bonds payable	10,800

The bonds were issued on December 31, 1994, at 103, with interest payable on June 30 and December 31 of each year. The straight-line method is used for premium amortization.

On March 1, 1996, Worsham retired $100,000 of these bonds at 98, plus accrued interest. Prepare the journal entries to record retirement of the bonds, including accrual of interest since the last payment and amortization of the premium.

Exercise 14—19 (Retirement and refinancing of bonds)

Chiam Corporation has $300,000 of 12% bonds, callable at 102, with a remaining 10-year term, and interest payable semiannually. The bonds are currently valued on the books at $290,000 and the company has just made the interest payment and adjustments for amortization of any premium or discount. Similar bonds can be marketed currently at 10% and would sell at par.

1. Give the journal entries to retire the old debt and issue $300,000 of new 10% bonds at par.
2. In what year will the reduction in interest offset the cost of refinancing the bond issue?

Exercise 14—20 (Issuance of convertible bonds)

Ricardo Insurance decides to finance expansion of its physical facilities by issuing convertible debenture bonds. The terms of the bonds are: maturity date 20 years after May 1, 1995, the date of issuance; conversion at option of holder after 2 years; 40 shares of $30 par value stock for each $1,000 bond held; interest rate of 12% and call provision on the bonds of 104. The bonds were sold at 101.

1. Give the entry on Ricardo's books to record the sale of $1,000,000 of bonds on July 1, 1995; interest payment dates are May 1 and November 1.
2. Assume the same condition as in (1) except that the sale of the bonds is to be recorded in a manner that will recognize a value related to the conversion privilege. The estimated sales price of the bonds without the conversion privilege is 98.

Exercise 14—21 (Convertible bonds)

Clarkston Inc. issued $1,000,000 of convertible 10-year, 11% bonds on July 1, 1995. The interest is payable semiannually on January 1 and July 1. The discount in connection with the issue was $8,500, which is amortized monthly using the straight-line basis. The debentures are convertible after 1 year into 5 shares of the company's $50 par common stock for each $1,000 of bonds.

On August 1, 1996, $100,000 of the bonds were converted. Interest has been accrued monthly and paid as due. Any interest accrued at the time of conversion of the bonds is paid in cash.

Prepare the journal entries on Clarkston's books to record the conversion, amortization, and interest on the bonds as of August 1 and August 31, 1996. (Round to the nearest dollar.)

Exercise 14—22 (Troubled debt restructuring—asset swap)

The Buck Machine Company has outstanding a $150,000 note payable to the Ontario Investment Corporation. Because of financial difficulties, Buck negotiates with Ontario to exchange inventory of machine parts to satisfy the debt. The cost of the inventory transferred is carried on Buck's books at $90,000. The estimated retail value of the inventory is $120,000. Buck uses a perpetual inventory system. Prepare journal entries for the exchange on the books of both Buck Machine Company and Ontario Investment Corporation according to the requirements of FASB Statement No. 15.

Exercise 14—23 (Troubled debt restructuring—equity swap)

Southwest Enterprises is threatened with bankruptcy due to its inability to meet interest payments and fund requirements to retire $5,000,000 of long-term notes. The notes are all held by Imperial Insurance Company. In order to prevent bankruptcy, Southwest has entered into an agreement with Imperial to exchange equity securities for the debt. The terms of the exchange are as follows: 250,000 shares of $5 par common stock, current market value $8 per share, and 20,000 shares of $10 par preferred stock, current market value $70 per share. Prepare journal entries for the exchange on the books of both Imperial Insurance Company and Southwest Enterprises according to the requirements of FASB Statement No. 15.

Exercise 14—24 (Modification of debt terms)

Moriarty Co. is experiencing financial difficulties. Income has exhibited a downward trend, and the company reported its first loss in company history this past year. The firm has been unable to service its debt and, as a result, has missed two semiannual interest payments. In an attempt to turn the company around, management has negotiated a modification of its debt terms with bondholders. These modified terms are effective January 1, 1998. The bonds are $10,000,000, 10-year, 10% bonds that were issued on January 2, 1993, and currently have an unamortized premium of $210,000. Prepare the necessary journal entries on Moriarty's books for each of the following independent situations:

(a) Bondholders agree to forgive past-due interest and reduce the interest rate on the debt from 10% to 5%.
(b) Bondholders agree to forgive past-due interest and forgive $3,000,000 of the face amount of the debt.
(c) Bondholders agree to forgive past-due interest, reduce the interest rate on the debt from 10% to 6%, and forgive $2,000,000 of the face amount of the debt.

***Exercise 14—25 (Issuance of serial bonds)**

On January 1, 1994, JVJ Corporation issued and sold $1,000,000 in 5-year, 10% serial bonds to be repaid in the amount of $200,000 on January 1 of 1995, 1996, 1997, 1998, and 1999. Interest is payable at the end of each year. The bonds were sold to yield a rate of 12%. Prepare the entry to record the issuance of the serial bonds on the books of JVJ Corporation.

*Relates to Appendix

***Exercise 14—26 (Bonds-outstanding table)**

Rafael Corporation purchased 9% serial bonds on April 1, 1995, face value $2,000,000. The bonds mature in $400,000 lots on April 1 of each of the following years. Interest is payable semiannually; the issue has an overall discount of $50,000. Assuming that Rafael reports on a calendar year, prepare a table summarizing interest charges and bond carrying values by the bonds-outstanding method.

*Relates to Appendix

PROBLEMS

Problem 14—27 (Bond issuance and adjusting entries)

On January 1, 1996, Bel Air Company issued bonds with a face value of $1,000,000 and a maturity date of December 31, 2005. The bonds have a stated interest rate of 10%, payable on January 1 and July 1. They were sold to Mercur Company for $885,300, a yield of 12%. It cost Bel Air $30,000 to issue the bonds. This amount was deferred and amortized over the life of the issue using the straight-line method. Assume that both companies have December 31 year-ends and that Bel Air uses the effective-interest method to amortize any premium or discount and Mercur uses the straight-line method.

Instructions:

1. Make all entries necessary to record the sale and purchase of the bonds on the two companies' books.
2. Prepare the adjusting entries as of December 31, 1996, for both companies. Assume Mercur is carrying the bonds as a long-term investment.

Problem 14—28 (Computation of bond market price and amortization of premium or discount)

Signal Enterprises decided to issue $800,000 of 10-year bonds. The interest rate on the bonds is stated at 7%, payable semiannually. At the time the bonds were sold, the market rate had increased to 8%.

Instructions:

1. Determine the maximum amount an investor should pay for these bonds. (Round to the nearest dollar.)
2. Assuming that the amount in (1) is paid, compute the amount at which the bonds would be reported after being held for one year. Use two recognized methods of handling amortization of the difference in cost and maturity value of the bonds, and give support to the method you prefer. (Round to the nearest dollar.)

Problem 14—29 (Premium or discount amortization table)

The Allen Co. acquired $20,000 of Locust Sales Co. 7% bonds, interest payable semiannually, bonds maturing in 5 years. The bonds were acquired at $20,850, a price to return approximately 6%.

Instructions:

1. Prepare tables to show the periodic adjustments to the investment account and the annual bond earnings, assuming adjustment by each of the following methods: (a) the straight-line method, and (b) the effective-interest method. (Round to the nearest dollar.)
2. Assuming use of the effective-interest method, give entries for the first year on the books of both companies.

Problem 14—30 (Amortizing deferred interest bonds)

R. J. Winter Co. recently issued $100,000, 10-year deferred interest bonds. The bonds have a stated rate of 10% and interest is to be paid in 10 semiannual payments beginning 5 1/2 years after the date of issuance. The market rate of interest on the date of issuance was 8%.

Instructions:

1. Compute the maximum amount an investor should pay for these bonds. (Round to the nearest dollar.)
2. Prepare a bond amortization schedule for Winter assuming the effective-interest method is used. (Round to the nearest dollar.)

Problem 14—31 (Cash flow effects of a bond premium)

On January 3, 1996, Datalink Inc. issued $100,000, 10%, 10-year bonds when the market rate of interest was 8%. The following financial information is available:

Sales	$300,000
Cost of sales	180,000
Gross profit	$120,000
Interest expense	?
Depreciation expense	14,500
Other expenses	82,000
Net income	$?

	Dec. 31, 1996	Jan. 1, 1996
Accounts receivable	$55,000	$48,000
Inventory	87,000	93,000
Accounts payable	60,000	58,000

All purchases of inventory are on account. Other expenses are paid for in cash.

Instructions:

1. Prepare the journal entry to record the issuance of the bonds on January 3, 1996.
2. Compute (a) the amount of cash paid to bondholders for interest during 1996, (b) the amount of premium amortized during 1996 assuming Datalink uses the straight-line method for amortizing bond premiums and discounts, and (c) the amount of interest expense for 1996.
3. Prepare the "Cash flows from operating activities" section of Datalink's statement of cash flows using (a) the direct method, and (b) the indirect method.

Problem 14—32 (Bond entries—issuer)

On April 1, 1985, the Miromar Tool Company issued $8 million of 7% convertible bonds with interest payment dates of April 1 and October 1. The bonds were sold on July 1, 1985, and mature on April 1, 2005. The bond discount totaled $426,600. The bond contract entitles the bondholders to receive 25 shares of $15 par value common stock in exchange for each $1,000 bond. On April 1, 1995, the holders of bonds with total face value of $1,000,000 exercised their conversion privilege. On July 1, 1995, the Miromar Tool Company reacquired bonds, face value $500,000, on the open market. The balances in the capital accounts as of December 31, 1994, were:

Common stock, $15 par, authorized 3 million shares, issued and outstanding, 250,000 shares	$3,750,000
Paid-in capital in excess of par	2,500,000

Market values of the common stock and bonds were as follows:

Date	Bonds (per $1,000)	Common Stock (per share)
April 1, 1995	$1,220	$47
July 1, 1995	1,250	51

Instructions: Prepare journal entries on the issuer's books for each of the following transactions. (Use the straight-line amortization method for the bond discount.)

1. Sale of the bonds on July 1, 1985.
2. Interest payment on October 1, 1985.
3. Interest accrual on December 31, 1985, including bond discount amortization.
4. Conversion of bonds on April 1, 1995. (Assume that interest and discount amortization are correctly shown as of April 1, 1995. No gain or loss on conversion is recognized.)
5. Reacquisition and retirement of bonds on July 1, 1995. (Assume that interest and discount amortization are correctly reported as of July 1, 1995.)

Problem 14—33 (Bond entries—issuer)

The Decker Company sold $3,000,000 of 9% first-mortgage bonds on October 1, 1988, at $2,873,640 plus accrued interest. The bonds were dated July 1, 1988; interest payable semiannually on January 1 and July 1; redeemable after June 30, 1993, to June 30, 1996, at 101, and thereafter until maturity at 100; and convertible into $100 par value common stock as follows:

Until June 30, 1993, at the rate of 6 shares for each $1,000 bond.
From July 1, 1993, to June 30, 1996, at the rate of 5 shares for each $1,000 bond.
After June 30, 1996, at the rate of 4 shares for each $1,000 bond.

The bonds mature 10 years from their issue date. The company adjusts its books monthly and closes its books as of December 31 each year.

The following transactions occur in connection with the bonds:

1994
July 1 $1,000,000 of bonds were converted into stock, with no gain or loss recognized.
1995
Dec. 31 $500,000 face amount of bonds were reacquired at 99 1/4 plus accrued interest. These were immediately retired.
1996
July 1 The remaining bonds were called for redemption and accrued interest was paid. For purposes of obtaining funds for redemption and business expansion, a $4,000,000 issue of 7% bonds was sold at 97. These bonds are dated July 1, 1996, and are due in 20 years.

Instructions: Prepare in journal form the entries necessary for Decker Company in connection with the preceding transactions, including monthly adjustments where appropriate, as of the following dates. Assume bond discount amortization is made using the straight-line method. (Round to nearest dollar.)

(1) October 1, 1988
(2) December 31, 1988
(3) July 1, 1994
(4) December 31, 1995
(5) July 1, 1996

(AICPA adapted)

Problem 14—34 (Bond entries—investor)

On June 1, 1995, Sunderland Inc. purchased, as a long-term investment, 400 of the $1,000 face value, 8% bonds of Stateline Corporation for $369,150. The bonds were purchased to yield 10% interest. Interest is payable semiannually on December 1 and June 1. The bonds mature on June 1, 2000. Sunderland uses the effective-interest method of amortization. On November 1, 1996, Sunderland sold the bonds for $392,500. This amount includes the appropriate accrued interest.

Instructions: Prepare a schedule showing the income or loss before income taxes from the bond investment that Sunderland should record for the years ended December 31, 1995, and 1996.

(AICPA adapted)

Problem 14—35 (Bond entries—investor)

On May 1, 1993, Desert Co. acquired $40,000 of Extel Corp. 9% bonds at 97 plus accrued interest. Interest on bonds is payable semiannually on March 1 and September 1, and bonds mature on September 1, 1996.

On May 1, 1994, Desert Co. sold bonds of $12,000 for 103 plus accrued interest. On July 1, 1995, bonds of $16,000 were exchanged for 2,250 shares of Extel Corp. no-par common, quoted on the market on this date at $8. Interest was received on bonds to date of exchange.

On September 1, 1996, remaining bonds were redeemed and accrued interest was received.

Instructions: Give journal entries for 1993-1996 to record the foregoing transactions on the books for Desert Co., including any adjustments that are required at the end of each fiscal year ending on December 31. Assume bond premium or discount amortization by the straight-line method.

Problem 14—36 (Note payable entries—investor and issuer)

Fitzgerald Inc. issued $750,000 of 8-year, 11% notes payable dated April 1, 1992. Interest on the notes is payable semiannually on April 1 and October 1. The notes were sold on April 1, 1992, to an underwriter for $720,000 net of issuance costs. The notes were then offered for sale by the underwriter, and on July 1, 1992, L. Baum purchased the entire issue as a long-term investment. Baum paid 101 plus accrued interest for the notes. On June 1, 1995, Baum sold the investment in Fitzgerald notes to J. Gott as a short-term investment. Gott paid 96 plus accrued interest for the notes as well as $1,500 for brokerage fees. Baum paid $1,000 brokerage fees to sell the notes. Gott held the investment until April 1, 1996, when the notes were called at 104 by Fitzgerald.

Instructions: Prepare all journal entries required: on the books of Fitzgerald Inc. for 1992 and 1996; on the books of Baum for 1992 and 1995; and on the books of Gott for 1995 and 1996. Assume each entity uses the calendar year for reporting purposes and that issue costs are netted against the note proceeds by Fitzgerald. Any required amortization is made using the straight-line method.

Problem 14—37 (Adjustment of bond investment account)

In auditing the books for the Carmicheal Corporation as of December 31, 1996, before the accounts are closed, you find the following long-term investment account balance:

Account: INVESTMENT IN BIG OIL 9% BONDS (MATURITY DATE, JUNE 1, 2000)

Date		Item	Debit	Credit	Balance Debit	Balance Credit
1996						
Jan.	21	Bonds, $200,000 par, acquired at 102 plus accrued interest	206,550		206,550	
Mar.	1	Proceeds from sale of bonds, $100,000 par and accrued interest		106,000	100,550	
June	1	Interest received		4,500	96,050	
Nov.	1	Amount received on call of bonds, $40,000 par, at 101 and accrued interest		41,900	54,150	
Dec.	1	Interest received		2,700	51,450	

Instructions:

1. Give the entries that should have been made relative to the investment in bonds, including any adjusting entries that would be made on December 31, the end of the fiscal year. (Assume bond premium or discount amortization by the straight-line method.)
2. Give the journal entries required at the end of 1996 to correct and bring the accounts up to date in view of the entries actually made.

Problem 14—38 (Reacquisition of bonds)

Guerra Company issued $500,000 of 12%, 10-year debentures on January 1, 1991. Interest is payable on January 1 and July 1. The entire issue was sold on April 1, 1991, at 102 plus accrued interest. On April 1, 1996, $250,000 of the bond issue was reacquired and retired at 99 plus accrued interest. On June 30, 1996, the remaining bonds were reacquired at 97 plus accrued interest and refunded with $400,000, 9% bonds issue sold at 100.

Instructions: Give the journal entries for 1991 and 1996 (through June 30) on the Guerra Company books. The company's books are kept on a calendar-year basis. (Round to nearest dollar. Assume straight-line amortization of premium or discount.)

Problem 14—39 (Deferred interest bonds and the selling of assets)

At the beginning of 1994, Wheel R. Dealer purchased the net assets of Consolidated Corp. by issuing 10-year, 10% bonds with a face amount of $100,000,000, with semiannual interest payments made on June 30 and December 31 and no interest payments made until 1999. Dealer hopes to sell off assets of Consolidated and realize enough cash to buy back the bonds on the open market prior to interest payments becoming due in 1999. At the end of 1996, Dealer sold net assets with a carrying value of $85,000,000 for $70,000,000 and used the proceeds to retire the bonds issue.

Instructions:

1. Prepare the journal entry to record the issuance of the bonds on January 2, 1994, assuming a market rate of 8%.
2. Prepare the journal entry to record the sale of assets.
3. Compute the market value of the bonds on January 3, 1997, the day of retirement, assuming a market rate of 14%.
4. Prepare the journal entry to record the retirement of the bond issue on January 3, 1997, assuming a carrying value of $96,000,000 and the market value as computed in (3) above.
5. Explain how Mr. Dealer can buy his bonds back three years after their initial sale for less than he originally sold them for and without ever having made an interest payment.

6. Should Mr. Dealer be able to reduce the liability to market value even if he does not retire the bonds?

Problem 14—40 (Convertible bonds)

The Robison Co. issued $1,000,000 of convertible 10-year debentures on July 1, 1995. The debentures provide for 9% interest payable semiannually on January 1 and July 1. The discount in connection with the issue was $12,000, which is being amortized monthly on a straight-line basis.

The debentures are convertible after 1 year into 7 shares of the Robison Co.'s $100 par value common stock for each $1,000 of debentures.

On August 1, 1996, $100,000 of debentures were turned in for conversion into common stock. Interest has been accrued monthly and paid as due. Accrued interest on debentures is paid in cash upon conversion.

Instructions: Prepare the journal entries to record the conversion, amortization, and interest in connection with the debentures as of: August 1, 1996, August 31, 1996, and December 31, 1996—including closing entries for end of year. No gain or loss is to be recognized on the conversion. (Round to nearest dollar.)

(AICPA adapted)

Problem 14—41 (Early extinguishment and conversion of bonds)

On January 1, 1995, Brewster Company issued 2,000 of its 5-year, $1,000 face value, 11% bonds dated January 1 at an effective annual interest rate (yield) of 9%. Interest is payable each December 31. Brewster uses the effective-interest method of amortization. On December 31, 1996, the 2,000 bonds were extinguished early through acquisition in the open market by Brewster for $1,980,000.

On July 1, 1995, Brewster issued 5,000 of its 6-year, $1,000 face value, 10% convertible bonds dated July 1 at an effective annual interest rate (yield) of 12%. Interest is payable every June 30 and December 31. The bonds are convertible at the investor's option into Brewster's common stock at a ratio of 10 shares of common stock for each bond. On July 1, 1996, an investor in Brewster's convertible bonds tendered 1,500 bonds for conversion into 15,000 shares of Brewster's common stock, which had a fair market value of $105 and a par value of $90 at the date of conversion.

Instructions:

1. Make all necessary journal entries for the issuer and the investor to record the issuance of both the 11% and the 10% bonds.
2. Make all necessary journal entries to record the early extinguishment of both debt instruments assuming:
   (a) Brewster considered the conversion to be a significant culminating event, and the investors considered their investment in convertible bonds to be debt rather than equity.
   (b) Brewster considered the conversion to be a nonculminating event, and the investors considered their investment in convertible bonds to be equity rather than debt.

Problem 14—42 (Troubled debt restructuring—modification of terms)

Risky Company, after having experienced financial difficulties in 1994, negotiated with two major creditors and arrived at an agreement to restructure their debts on December 31, 1994. The two creditors were M. Barboza and R. Janeiro. Barboza was owed principal of $300,000 and interest of $60,000 but agreed to accept equipment worth $60,000 and notes receivable from Risky Company's customers worth $250,000. The equipment had an original cost of $80,000 and accumulated depreciation of $30,000. Janeiro was owed $500,000 and agreed to extend the terms and to accept immediate payment of $100,000 and the remaining agreed on balance of $424,360 to be paid on December 31, 1996. All payments were made according to schedule.

Instructions: Prepare Risky's journal entries to record the restructuring on December 31, 1994, and the entries necessary to make the adjustments and record payments on December 31, 1995, and 1996.

Problem 14—43 (Troubled debt restructuring—modification of terms)

In the latter part of 1995, Caltex Company experienced severe financial pressure and is in default of meeting interest payments on long-term notes of $6,000,000 due on December 31, 2000. The interest rate on the debt is 11%, payable semiannually on June 30 and December 31. In an agreement with Modern Investment Corporation, Caltex obtained acceptance of a change in principal and interest terms for the remaining 5-year life of the notes. The changes in terms are as follows:

(a) A reduction of principal of $600,000.
(b) A reduction in the interest rate to 8%.
(c) Caltex agreed to pay on December 31, 1995, both the $660,000 of interest in arrears and the normal interest payment under the old terms.

Instructions:

1. What is the total dollar difference in cash payments by Caltex over the 5-year period as a result of the restatement of terms?
2. What journal entries for the restructuring of the debt, payment of interest under the old terms, and the first two interest payments under the new terms would Caltex make? (Assume an implicit interest rate of 6%.)

*Problem 14—44 (Serial bonds—amortization of premium or discount)

A serial bond issue in the amount of $2,000,000, dated January 1, 1994, bearing 8% interest payable at December 31 each year, is sold by Rural Farm Co. to yield 9% per year. The bonds mature in the amount of $400,000 on January 1 of each year starting in 1995.

Instructions:

1. Compute the bond price and any premium or discount.
2. Prepare an amortization schedule using the bonds outstanding method.

*Relates to Appendix

*Problem 14—45 (Bonds-outstanding tables)

The Hanifer Manufacturing Company issued $2,000,000 of 8% serial bonds on January 1, 1988, at 98. The bonds mature in units of $250,000 beginning January 1, 1993, with interest payable semiannually on January 1 and July 1. On June 1, 1996, Hanifer reacquired, at 101 plus accrued interest, $200,000 of the bonds due January 1, 1998, and $100,000 due January 1, 1999.

Instructions:

1. Assuming premium or discount amortization by the bonds-outstanding method and bond retirements as scheduled, prepare a table summarizing interest charges and bond carrying values for the bond life, supported by a schedule showing the calculation of amortization amounts. (Round to the nearest dollar.)
2. Prepare a similar table summarizing interest charges and bond carrying values for the bond life, taking into consideration bond redemptions in advance of maturity dates as indicated. (Round to nearest dollar.)
3. Record in general journal form the retirement of bonds on June 1, 1996.

*Relates to Appendix

CHAPTER 15

Owners' Equity: Contributed Capital

CHAPTER TOPICS

- Nature and Classifications of Capital Stock
- Preferred and Common Stock Features
- Issuance of Capital Stock
- Accounting for Treasury Stock
- Accounting for Stock Rights, Warrants, and Options
- Stock Conversions and Stock Splits
- Balance Sheet Disclosure of Contributed Capital

Microsoft, founded in 1975 by Bill Gates and Paul Allen, was originally best known for developing the operating system used with IBM personal computers and their clones. Microsoft subsequently developed a variety of popular software packages, such as Word, Excel, and Windows. In 1985, Microsoft decided to issue its stock publicly for the first time. Before this time, Microsoft had stock outstanding, but the stock was held by company officials and employees and was not publicly traded. Goldman Sachs, a Wall Street investment banking firm, was selected to be the lead underwriter on the issue. The underwriters provided technical advice as the issue was prepared, bought the shares from the firm, and then resold the shares to the public. For their services, the underwriters on the Microsoft issue received 6.24% of the proceeds.

A key consideration, of course, was what price to charge when issuing the shares. An initial price range of $16 to $19 per share was set, based on Microsoft's earnings per share and the price/earnings ratios for similar firms that already had publicly traded stock. A prospectus describing the company was filed with the SEC (with care taken not to exaggerate, since the SEC is particularly concerned that investors be fully informed of significant risks associated with new issues). Copies of the prospectus were sent to 38,000 brokers and potential investors. The large amount of interest in the Microsoft stock issue resulted in the final offering price being raised to $21 per share. On March 13, 1986, Microsoft shares were first publicly traded, on the over-the-counter market, at $25.75 per share. By the end of the first day of trading, the shares were at $27.75.[1] In February 1994, the stock was trading for a split-adjusted $756 per share.

As the Microsoft example illustrates, firms often seek to raise funds by selling stock to investors. Alternatively, companies may raise capital by generating income and investing those profits back into the business, or they may borrow funds from creditors. The basic accounting equation—**Assets = Liabilities + Owners' Equity**—shows this key relationship. Thus, the assets of an enterprise are provided by creditors and by owners. Assets represent entity resources, while liabilities reflect the creditor claims against those resources. Since the difference between assets and liabilities is owners' equity, the **owners' equity** of an entity represents the residual interest of the owners in the net assets (total assets less total liabilities) of the enterprise.

Reductions in capital result primarily from distributions to owners and business losses. In a **proprietorship,** the entire owner's equity resulting from investments, withdrawals, and earnings or losses is reflected in a single capital account. Similarly, in a **partnership**, a single capital account for each partner reports the partner's equity resulting from investments, withdrawals, and earnings or losses. In reporting **corporate capital,** however, a distinction is made between (1) investments by owners, called **contributed (paid-in) capital** and (2) increases in net assets arising from earnings, designated as **retained earnings.**

The issues surrounding contributed capital are discussed in this chapter, while those relating to retained earnings are addressed in Chapter 16. Accounting for corporations is emphasized because they are the dominant form of organization in today's economy. Not only are corporations the major source of our national output, but they also provide the majority of employment opportunities. Millions of people hold equity securities (capital stock) in corporations throughout the world.

NATURE AND CLASSIFICATIONS OF CAPITAL STOCK

A **corporation** is an artificial entity created by law that has an existence separate from its owners and may engage in business within prescribed limits just as a natural person. Unless the life of a corporation is limited by law, it has perpetual existence. The modern corporation makes it possible for large amounts of resources to be assembled under one management. These resources are transferred to the corporation by individual owners, because they believe they can earn a greater rate of return through the corporation's efficient use of the resources than would be possible from alternative investments. In exchange for these resources, the corporation issues **stock certificates** evidencing ownership interests. Directors elected by stockholders delegate to management responsibility for supervising the use, operation, and disposition of corporate resources.

Business corporations may be created under the incorporating laws of any one of the fifty states or of the federal government. Since the states do not follow a uniform incorporating act, the conditions under which corporations may be created and under which they may operate are somewhat varied.

In most states at least three individuals must join in applying for a corporate charter. Application is made by submitting **articles of incorporation** to the secretary of state or other appropriate official. The articles must set forth the name of the corporation, its pur-

1. Bro Uttal, "Inside the Deal That Made Bill Gates $350,000,000," *Fortune*, July 21, 1986, p. 23.

pose and nature, the stock to be issued, those persons who are to act as first directors, and other data required by law. If the articles conform to the state's laws governing corporate formation, they are approved and are recognized as the **charter** for the new corporate entity. When stock of a corporation is to be offered or distributed outside the state in which it is incorporated, registration with the Securities and Exchange Commission may be required. The objective of such registration is to ensure that all facts relative to the business and its securities will be adequately and honestly disclosed. A stockholders' meeting is called at which a code of rules or **bylaws** governing meetings, voting procedures, and other internal operations are adopted; a **board of directors** is elected; and the board appoints company administrative officers. Corporate activities may now proceed in conformance with laws of the state of incorporation and charter authorization. A complete record of the proceedings of both the stockholders' and the directors' meetings should be maintained in a minutes book.

When a corporation is formed, a single class of stock, known as **common stock,** is usually issued. Corporations may later find that there are advantages to issuing one or more additional classes of stock with varying rights and priorities. Stock with certain preferences (rights) over the common stock is called **preferred stock.** All shares within a particular class of stock are identical in terms of ownership rights represented.

Rights of Ownership

Unless restricted or withheld by terms of the articles of incorporation or bylaws, certain basic rights are held by each stockholder. These rights are as follows:

1. To share in distributions of corporate earnings.
2. To vote in the election of directors and in the determination of certain corporate policies.
3. To maintain one's proportional interest in the corporation through purchase of additional capital stock if issued, known as the *preemptive right* (In recent years, some states have eliminated this right.)
4. To share in distributions of cash or other properties upon liquidation of the corporation.

If both preferred and common stock are issued, the special features of each class of stock are stated in the articles of incorporation or in the corporation bylaws and become a part of the contract between the corporation and its stockholders. One must be familiar with the overall capital structure to understand fully the nature of the equity found in any single class of stock. Frequently, the stock certificate describes the rights and restrictions relative to the ownership interest it represents together with those pertaining to other securities issued. Shares of stock represent personal property and may be freely transferred by their owners in the absence of special restrictions.

Par or Stated Value of Stock

As indicated, the capital of a corporation is divided between contributed capital and retained earnings. This is an important distinction because readers of financial statements need to know the portion of equity derived from investments by owners as contrasted with the portion of equity that has been earned and retained by the business. The invested or contributed capital may be further classified into (a) an amount forming the corporate **legal capital,** and (b) the balance, if any, in excess of legal capital. The amount of the investment representing the legal capital is reported as **capital stock.** The remaining balance is recognized as **additional paid-in capital.** As discussed in this chapter, additional paid-in capital may arise from several sources, including the sale of stock at more than par or stated value, and treasury stock transactions. Additional paid-in capital includes all sources of contributed capital other than, or in excess of, legal capital.

The major components of owners' equity for a corporation are shown below. It should be recognized, however, that the definitions and classifications of legal and other capital categories may vary according to state statutes.

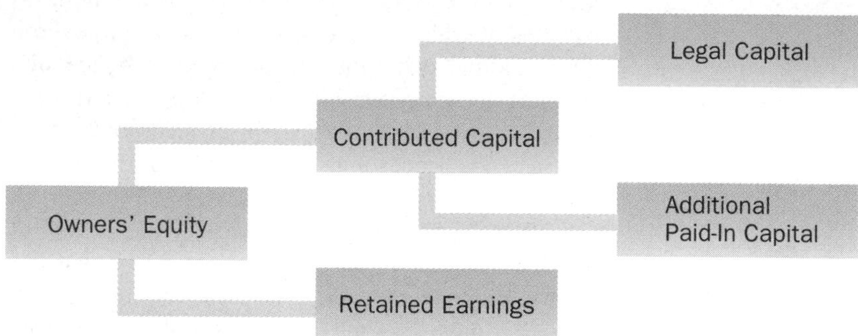

The significance of legal capital is that most state incorporation laws provide that dividends cannot reduce corporate capital below an amount designated as legal capital. Modern corporation laws normally go beyond these limitations and add that legal capital cannot be impaired by the reacquisition of capital stock. Creditors of a corporation cannot hold individual stockholders liable for claims against the company. But with a portion of the corporate capital restricted as to distribution, creditors can rely on the absorption by the ownership group of losses equal to the legal capital before losses are applied to the creditors' equity. As a practical matter, the legal capital of a corporation is generally small in comparison to total capital and does not strongly influence dividend policy nor provide significant creditor protection.

When a value is assigned to each share of stock, whether common or preferred, and is reported on the stock certificate, the stock is said to have a **par value;** stock without such an assigned value is called **no-par** stock. When shares have a par value, the legal capital is normally the aggregate par value of all shares issued and subscribed. When a corporation is authorized to issue stock with a par value, the incorporation laws of most states permit such issue only for an amount equal to or in excess of par. Par value may be any amount, for example, $100, $5, or 25 cents. An amount received on the sale of stock in excess of its par value is recorded in a separate account, such as Paid-In Capital in Excess of Par. The balance in this account is added to capital stock at par in reporting total contributed capital.

From a financial reporting perspective, the concept of par value has little significance. Par value also has virtually no economic significance. Originally, the par value of stock was equal to the market value of the stock at the date of issue. Today, however, most par value stock has only a nominal value; that is, the par value is significantly below its issue or market price. Par value does have legal significance in the historical development of common law and statutory law. But the modern trend is away from par value.[2]

When shares are no-par, laws of certain states require that the total consideration received for the shares, even when they are sold at different prices, be recognized as legal capital. Laws of a number of states, however, permit the corporate directors to establish legal capital by assigning an arbitrary value to each share regardless of issue price,

2. For a more complete discussion of the legal significance of par value, see Philip McGough, "The Legal Significance of the Par Value of Common Stock: What Accounting Educators Should Know," *Issues in Accounting Education,* Fall 1988, pp. 330-350.

although in some instances the value cannot be less than a certain minimum amount. The value fixed by the board of directors or the minimum value required by law is known as the share's **stated value,** and an amount received in excess of stated value is reported in the same manner as an excess over par value, using an appropriate account title, e.g., Paid-In Capital in Excess of Stated Value.

Prior to 1912, corporations were permitted to issue only stock with a par value. In 1912, however, New York State changed its corporation laws to permit the issuance of stock without a par value, and since that time, all other states have followed with similar statutory provisions. Today, a number of stocks listed on the major securities exchanges are no-par. Of 656 common stock issues surveyed in *Accounting Trends & Techniques*, 594 had a par value. Of 172 preferred stock issues, 114 had a par value.[3] Often, no-par stock has a stated value for reporting purposes. This makes it very similar to par stock and defines a separation of the stock proceeds between stated value and additional paid-in capital.

Preferred Stock

When a corporation issues both preferred and common stock, the preference rights attached to preferred stock normally consist of prior claims to dividends. A dividend preference does not assure stockholders of dividends on the preferred issue but simply means that dividend requirements must be met on preferred stock before anything may be paid on common stock. Dividends do not legally accrue; a dividend on preferred stock, as on common stock, requires the ability on the part of the company to make such a distribution as well as appropriate action by the board of directors. When the board of directors fails to declare a dividend on preferred stock at the time such action would be called for, the dividend is said to be "passed." Although preferred stockholders have a prior claim on dividends, such preference is usually accompanied by limitations on the amount of dividends they may receive.

Preferred stock is generally issued with a par value. When preferred stock has a par value, the dividend is stated in terms of a percentage of par value. When preferred stock is no-par, the dividend must be stated in terms of dollars and cents. Thus, holders of 5% preferred stock with a $50 par value are entitled to an annual dividend of $2.50 per share before any distribution is made to common stockholders; holders of $5 no-par preferred stock are entitled to an annual dividend of $5 per share before dividends are paid to common stockholders.

A corporation may issue more than one class of preferred stock. For example, preferred issues may be designated "first preferred" or "second preferred" with the first preferred issue having a first claim on earnings and the second preferred having a second claim on earnings. In other instances, the claim to earnings on the part of several preferred issues may have equal priority, but dividend rates or other preferences may vary. Holders of the common stock may receive dividends only after the satisfaction of all preferred dividend requirements.

Other characteristics and conditions are frequently added to preferred stock in the extension of certain advantages or in the limitation of certain rights. For example, preferred stock may be cumulative, participating, convertible, callable, or redeemable. More than one of these characteristics may be applicable to a specific issue of preferred stock. As an illustration of the extent to which firms can create stock with varying preferences, General Motors describes 13 classes of preferred stock in the notes to its 1992 financial statements. The classes vary in terms of dividend rates, redemption requirements, convertibility, and other features.

3. *Accounting Trends & Techniques—1993* (New York: AICPA, 1993), pp. 246-247.

Cumulative and Noncumulative Preferred Stock. When a corporation fails to declare dividends on **cumulative preferred stock,** such dividends accumulate and require payment in the future before any dividends may be paid to common stockholders.

For example, assume that Good Time Corporation has outstanding 100,000 shares of 9% cumulative preferred stock, $10 par. Dividends were last paid in 1993. Total dividends of $300,000 are declared in 1996 by the board of directors. The majority of this amount will be paid to the preferred shareholders as follows:

	Dividends to Preferred Shareholders	Dividends to Common Shareholders	Total Dividends
Cumulative dividend for 1994	$ 90,000	—	$ 90,000
Cumulative dividend for 1995	90,000	—	90,000
Dividends for 1996	90,000	$30,000	120,000
Totals	$270,000	$30,000	$300,000

Dividends on cumulative preferred stock that are passed are referred to as **dividends in arrears.** Although these dividends are not a liability until declared by the board of directors, this information is of importance to stockholders and other users of the financial statements. Disclosure of the amount of dividends in arrears is made by special note on the balance sheet.

With **noncumulative preferred stock,** it is not necessary to provide for passed dividends. A dividend omission on preferred stock in any one year means it is irretrievably lost. Dividends may be declared on common stock as long as the preferred stock receives the preferred rate for the current period. Thus, in the previous example, if the preferred stock were noncumulative, the 1996 dividends would be distributed as follows:

	Dividends to Preferred Shareholders	Dividends to Common Shareholders	Total Dividends
Dividend passed in 1994	—	—	—
Dividend passed in 1995	—	—	—
Dividends for 1996	$90,000	$210,000	$300,000
Totals	$90,000	$210,000	$300,000

Preferred stock contracts normally provide for cumulative dividends. Also, courts have generally held that dividend rights on preferred stock are cumulative in the absence of specific provisions to the contrary.

Participating Preferred Stock. Dividends on preferred stock are generally of a fixed amount. However, **participating preferred stock** issues provide for additional dividends to be paid to preferred stockholders after dividends of a specified amount are paid to the common stockholders. For example, additional dividends would be paid to holders of a 6% participating preferred stock after dividends totaling 6% of the par value of the common stock were also paid. Fully participating preferred stock shares equally with common stock in the excess dividends; partially participating preferred stock dividends are capped at some limit. Clearly, a participative provision makes preferred stock less like debt and more like equity. Although once quite common, participating preferred stocks are now relatively rare.

Convertible Preferred Stock. Preferred stock is **convertible** when terms of the issue provide that it can be exchanged by its owner for some other security of the issuing corporation.

Conversion rights generally provide for the exchange of preferred stock into common stock. Since preferred stock normally has a prior but limited right to earnings, large earnings resulting from successful operations accrue to the common stockholders. The conversion privilege gives the preferred stockholders the opportunity to exchange their holdings for stock in which the rights to earnings are not limited. In some instances, preferred stock may be convertible into bonds, thus allowing investors the option of changing their positions from stockholders to creditors. Convertible preferred issues have become popular with some companies. The journal entries required for stock conversions are illustrated later in the chapter.

Callable Preferred Stock. Preferred stock is **callable** when it can be called or redeemed at the option of the corporation. Many preferred issues are callable. The **call price** is usually specified in the original agreement and provides for payment of dividends in arrears as part of the repurchase price. When convertible stock has a call provision, the holders of the stock, at the time of the call, are frequently given the option of converting their holdings into common stock rather than accepting the call price. The decision made by the investor will be based on the market price of the common stock.

Redeemable Preferred Stock. Preferred stock is sometimes subject to mandatory redemption requirements or other redemption provisions that give the security overlapping debt and equity characteristics. This type of stock is referred to as **redeemable preferred stock** and is defined as preferred stock that is redeemable at the option of the holder, or at a fixed or determinable price on a specific date, or upon other conditions not solely within the control of the issuer (e.g., redemption upon reaching a certain level of earnings). The FASB currently requires disclosure of long-term obligations, including the extent of redemption requirements for all issues of capital stock that are redeemable at fixed or determinable prices on fixed or determinable dates. Redemption requirements may be disclosed separately for each issue or for all issues combined.[4] The SEC has ruled (in Accounting Series Release No. 268) that firms with publicly traded securities must not include mandatory redeemable preferred stock under the "Stockholders' Equity" heading. Instead, mandatory redeemable preferred is listed above the equity section in a "gray area" between the liabilities and equities. The entries for reacquiring stock by exercising a call or redemption feature are discussed later in the chapter.

Asset and Dividend Preferences Upon Corporation Liquidation. Preferred stock generally takes priority over common stock as to assets distributed upon corporate liquidation. Such a preference, however, cannot be assumed but must be specifically stated in the preferred stock contract. The asset preference for stock with a par value is an amount equal to par, or par plus any amount paid in excess of par; in the absence of a par value, the preference is a stated amount. Terms of the preferred contract may also provide for the full payment of any dividends in arrears upon liquidation, regardless of the retained earnings balance reported by the company. When this is the case and there are insufficient retained earnings, i.e., a deficit, such dividend priorities must be met from paid-in capital of the common stock; the common stockholders receive whatever assets remain after settlement with the preferred group.

Common Stock

Strictly speaking, there should be but one kind of common stock, representing the residual ownership equity of a company. In recent years, however, a few companies have begun

4. *Statement of Financial Accounting Standards No. 47,* "Disclosure of Long-Term Obligations" (Stamford: Financial Accounting Standards Board, 1981), par. 10c.

to issue different classes of common stock with different ownership rights. For example, Ben & Jerry's, the premium ice cream company, has two classes of common stock. For most companies, there is but one class of common stock.

Common stock carries the greatest risk, since common shareholders receive dividends only after preferred dividends are paid. In return for this risk, common stock ordinarily shares in earnings to the greatest extent if the corporation is successful. There is no inherent distinction in voting rights between preferred and common stocks; however, voting rights are frequently given exclusively to common stockholders as long as dividends are paid regularly on preferred stock. Upon failure to meet preferred dividend requirements, special voting rights may be granted to preferred stockholders, thus affording this group a more prominent rôle in the management. In some states, voting rights cannot be withheld on any class of stock.

Is It Equity or Is It Debt?

In the field of finance, a debt claim is viewed as one that entitles the debt holders to a fixed payment when company assets are sufficient to meet that payment; if company assets are below that amount, the debt holders get all the assets. An equity claim is viewed as one that entitles the equity holders to all company assets in excess of the debt holders' portion. The definitions of liabilities and equities given by the FASB in its *Statement of Accounting Concepts No. 6* embody similar notions—equity is defined as the residual amount of assets left after deducting the liability claims.

Although examples of pure equity (common stock) and pure debt (a bank loan) are easy to distinguish, many securities are in a middle ground and have characteristics of both debt and equity. For example, preferred stock is like debt in that the payments (both dividend and liquidation amounts) are typically capped, but it is also like equity since the payments aren't guaranteed and have lower priority than debt claims. As another example, convertible debt may be exchanged for equity if the issuing firm performs well, and thus as the performance of the issuing firm improves, the convertible debt gradually changes in nature from debt to equity. And finally, although employee stock options are currently accounted for as equity, some have suggested that they have some characteristics of a liability since they obligate a company to issue its own stock at a specified price in the future.

These examples illustrate that the line between a liability and an equity can be very unclear. The FASB is currently engaged in a fundamental review of the accounting distinction between debt and equity. One suggestion for improved disclosure is to have a third category on the right side of the balance sheet where items with elements of both debt and equity would be reported. Mandatory redeemable preferred stock is already treated essentially this way. Another possibility is to have no artificial division between liabilities and equities, but instead list long-term sources of capital according to their mix of debt and equity characteristics—pure long-term debt could be listed first, common stock listed last, and the intermediate items listed in between. A committee of the American Accounting Association has recommended retaining the balance sheet distinction between debt and equity and using financial models to allocate the proceeds from the issuance of complex securities into their debt and equity components. One thing is certain—as innovative securities continue to be introduced, drawing the accounting boundary between debt and equity will only become more difficult.

Questions:

1. As described above, it has been suggested that the artificial division between liabilities and equities be removed from the balance sheet. What implications would this have for the income statement?
2. Imagine two companies, A and B. Forty percent of A's financing comes from debt, the remainder comes from equity. B's financing is 99 percent debt and one percent equity. How does the debt of B differ from the debt of A?

Sources:

Clifford C. Woods III and Halsey G. Bullen, "An Overview of the FASB's Financial Instruments Project," *Journal of Accountancy* (November 1989), p. 42.

"Distinguishing Between Liability and Equity Instruments and Accounting for Instruments With Characteristics of Both," FASB Discussion Memorandum (August 21, 1990).

American Accounting Association's Financial Accounting Standards Committee. "Response to the FASB Discussion Memorandum 'Distinguishing Between Liability and Equity Instruments and Accounting for Instruments with Characteristics of Both.' *Accounting Horizons*, September 1993, p. 105.

ISSUANCE OF CAPITAL STOCK

In accounting for capital stock, it should be recognized that stock may be:

1. Authorized but unissued.
2. Subscribed for and held for issuance pending receipt of cash for the full amount of the subscription price.
3. Outstanding in the hands of stockholders.
4. Reacquired and held by the corporation for subsequent reissuance.
5. Canceled by appropriate corporation action.

Thus, an accurate record of all transactions involving capital stock must be maintained by a corporation. Separate general ledger accounts are required for each source of capital including each class of stock. In addition, subsidiary records are needed to keep track of individual stockholders and stock certificates.

Capital Stock Issued for Cash

The issuance of stock for cash is recorded by a debit to Cash and a credit to Capital Stock for the par or stated value.[5] When the amount of cash received from the sale of stock is greater than the par or stated value, the excess is recorded separately as a credit to an additional paid-in capital account. This account is carried on the books as long as the stock to which it relates is outstanding. When stock is retired, the capital stock balance as well as any related additional paid-in-capital balance is generally canceled.

To illustrate, assume the Goode Corporation is authorized to issue 10,000 shares of $10 par common stock. On April 1, 1996, 4,000 shares are sold for $45,000 cash. The entry to record the transaction is:

1996			
April 1	Cash	45,000	
	Common Stock		40,000
	Paid-In Capital in Excess of Par		5,000
	To record the issuance of 4,000 shares of $10 par common stock for $45,000.		

If, in the example, the common stock were no-par stock but with a $10 stated value, the entry would be the same except that the $5,000 would be designated Paid-In Capital in Excess of Stated Value. Generally, stock is assigned a par or a stated value. However, if there is no such value assigned, the entire amount of cash received on the sale of stock is credited to the capital stock account and there is no additional paid-in capital account associated with the stock. Assuming Goode Corporation's stock were no-par common without a stated value, the entry to record the sale of 4,000 shares for $45,000 would be:

1996			
April 1	Cash	45,000	
	Common Stock		45,000
	To record the issuance of 4,000 shares of no-par, no-stated-value common stock for $45,000.		

Capital Stock Sold on Subscription

Capital stock may be issued on a subscription basis. A **subscription** is a legally binding contract between the subscriber (purchaser of stock) and the corporation (issuer of stock). The contract states the number of shares subscribed, the subscription price, the terms of payment, and other conditions of the transaction. A subscription, while giving the corpo-

5. The term *Capital Stock* is used in account titles in the text when the class of stock is not specifically designated. When preferred and common designations are given, these are used in the account titles.

ration a legal claim for the contract price, also gives the subscriber the legal status of a stockholder unless certain rights as a stockholder are specifically withheld by law or by terms of the contract. Ordinarily, stock certificates evidencing share ownership are not issued until the full subscription price has been received by the corporation.

When stock is subscribed for, Capital Stock Subscriptions Receivable is debited for the subscription price, Capital Stock Subscribed is credited for the amount to be recognized as capital stock when subscriptions have been collected, and a paid-in capital account is credited for the amount of the subscription price in excess of par or stated value. Subscriptions may be collected in cash or in other assets accepted by the corporation. When collections are made, the appropriate asset account is debited and the receivable account is credited.

Capital Stock Subscriptions Receivable should normally not be shown as an asset but instead as an offset to equity.[6] This treatment is deemed appropriate because the legal penalty against subscribers who don't fully pay the contract price is often minimal, increasing the probability that the issuer of the stock may not fully collect on the Subscriptions Receivable. SEC rules allow subscription amounts receivable as of the balance sheet date to be shown as a current asset if the full contract price is collected prior to the date the financial statements are actually issued.

Recording and Issuance of Capital Stock Sold on Subscription. The actual issuance of stock is recorded by a debit to Capital Stock Subscribed and a credit to Capital Stock. The following entries illustrate the recording and issuance of capital stock sold on subscription. It is assumed that the Feitz Corporation is authorized to issue 10,000 shares of $10 par value common stock.

November 1-30: Received subscriptions for 5,000 shares of $10 par common at $12.50 per share with 50% down, balance due in 60 days.

Common Stock Subscriptions Receivable	62,500	
Common Stock Subscribed		50,000
Paid-in Capital in Excess of Par		12,500
Cash	31,250	
Common Stock Subscriptions Receivable		31,250

December 1-31: Received balance due on one-half of subscriptions and issued stock to the fully paid subscribers, 2,500 shares.

Cash	15,625	
Common Stock Subscriptions Receivable		15,625
Common Stock Subscribed	25,000	
Common Stock		25,000

Contributed capital would be reported in the stockholders' equity section of the December 31 balance sheet as follows:

Stockholders' Equity

Contributed capital:	
Common stock, $10 par, 10,000 shares authorized, 2,500 shares issued and outstanding	$25,000
Common stock subscribed, 2,500 shares	25,000
Paid-in capital in excess of par	12,500
	62,500
Less Common Stock subscriptions receivable	(15,625)
Total contributed capital	$46,875

6. Emerging Issues Task Force, *EITF Abstract 85-1*, "Classifying Notes Received for Capital Stock."

Subscription Defaults. If a subscriber defaults on a subscription by failing to make a payment when it is due, a corporation may (1) return to the subscriber the amount paid, (2) return to the subscriber the amount paid less any reduction in price or expense incurred on the resale of the stock, (3) declare the amount paid by the subscriber as forfeited, or (4) issue to the subscriber shares equal to the number paid for in full. The practice followed will depend on the policy adopted by the corporation within the legal limitations set by the state in which it is incorporated.

The issuing corporation sometimes chooses to terminate a subscription issue when investor interest is insufficient. For example, the following note was included in the 1992 financial statements of Alleco, Inc., a printer of fabric designs and manufacturer of lightweight rivets:

"To permanently fund its operating activities, Apparel Funding [a business unit of Alleco] plans to offer, through a private placement which management plans to have completed by September 1993, a maximum of 50 Investment Units . . . In the event that the minimum number of Investment Units (25 or $2,500,000) are not sold . . ., all subscription funds will be returned to investors with interest."

Capital Stock Issued for Consideration Other Than Cash

When capital stock is issued for consideration in the form of property other than cash or for services received, the fair market value of the stock or the fair market value of the property or services, whichever is more objectively determinable, is used to record the transaction. If a quoted market price for the stock is available, that amount should be used as a basis for recording the exchange. Otherwise, it may be possible to determine the fair market value of the property or services received, e.g., through appraisal by a competent outside party.

To illustrate, assume that AC Company issues 200 shares of $100 par value common stock in return for land. The company's stock is currently selling for $150 per share. The entry on AC Company's books would be:

Land	30,000	
Common Stock		20,000
Paid-In Capital in Excess of Par		10,000

If, on the other hand, the land has a readily determinable market price of $25,000 but AC Company's common stock has no established fair market value, the transaction would be recorded as follows:

Land	25,000	
Common Stock		20,000
Paid-In Capital in Excess of Par		5,000

If an objective value cannot be established for either the stock or the property or services received, the board of directors normally has the right to assign values to the securities issued and the assets or services received. These values will stand for all legal purposes in the absence of proof that fraud was involved. However, the assignment of values by the board of directors should be subject to careful scrutiny, because assigning excessive values to the consideration received for stock falsely improves the company's reported financial position. When the value of the consideration cannot be clearly established and the directors' valuations are used in reporting assets and invested capital, the source of the valuations should be disclosed on the balance sheet. When there is evidence that improper values have been assigned to the consideration received for stock, such values should be restated.

Issuance of Capital Stock in Exchange for a Business

A corporation, upon its formation or at some later date, may be combined with another ongoing business, issuing capital stock in exchange for the net assets acquired. This is referred to as a **business combination.** In determining the amount of stock to be issued, the fair market value of the stock, as well as the values of the net assets acquired, must be considered.

Frequently the value of the stock transferred by a corporation will exceed the value of the identifiable assets acquired because of a favorable earnings record of the business acquired. If the exchange is accounted for as a **purchase,** the value of the stock in excess of the values assigned to identifiable assets is recognized as goodwill (see Chapter 12). Under this approach, the retained earnings of the company acquired *do not* become part of the combined retained earnings. On the other hand, if the exchange is treated as a **pooling of interests,** neither the revaluation of assets nor the recognition of goodwill is recorded. Assets are stated at the amounts previously reported; the retained earnings accounts of the two companies are added together and become the amount of retained earnings for the combined entity. The purchase method assumes that one of the companies is dominant and is acquiring the other company. The pooling-of-interests method assumes equal status and continuity of common ownership. Accounting for business combinations is dealt with in APB Opinion No. 16 and is discussed in detail in advanced accounting texts.

CAPITAL STOCK REACQUISITION

For a variety of reasons, a company may find it desirable to reacquire shares of its own stock. For example, in January 1994, Toys "R" Us Inc., the large U.S. toy retailer, announced plans to spend up to $1 billion over several years in buying back its own shares. The buyback was announced because Toys "R" Us was generating substantial excess cash flow even after internally funding its aggressive expansion plans. In general, companies acquire their own stock to:

1. Finance acquisitions.
2. Provide for incentive compensation and employee savings plans.
3. Improve per-share earnings by reducing the number of shares outstanding.
4. Support the market price of the stock.
5. Increase the ratio of debt to equity.
6. Obtain shares for conversion to other securities.
7. Invest excess cash temporarily.

Whatever the reason, a company's stock may be reacquired by exercise of call or redemption provisions, by repurchase of the stock in the open market, or by donation from stockholders. In reacquiring stock, a company must comply with applicable state laws, which can have a significant impact on transactions involving a company's stock. For example, state laws normally provide that the reacquisition of stock must serve a legitimate corporate purpose and must be made without injury or prejudice to the creditors or to the remaining stockholders. Another general restriction relates to the preserving of sufficient legal capital of the corporation.

In accounting for the reacquisition of stock, it should be emphasized that *reacquisitions do not give rise to income or loss.* A company issues stock to raise capital, which it intends to employ profitably; in reacquiring shares of its stock, the company reduces the capital to be employed in subsequent operations. Gains or losses arise from the operating and investing activities of the business, not from transactions with its shareholders.

A company's stock may be reacquired for immediate retirement or be reacquired and held as treasury stock for subsequent disposition, either eventual retirement or reissuance. Accounting for immediate retirements will be discussed first, followed by accounting for treasury stock transactions.

Stock Reacquired for Immediate Retirement

If shares of stock are reacquired at par or stated value and then retired, the capital stock account is debited and Cash is credited. However, if the purchase price of the stock exceeds the par or stated value, the excess amount may be: (1) charged to any paid-in capital balances applicable to that class of stock, (2) allocated between paid-in capital and retained earnings, or (3) charged entirely to retained earnings.[7] The alternative used depends on the existence of previously established paid-in capital amounts and on management's preference. To illustrate the application of the alternatives, assume that Interwest Corporation reports the following balances related to an issue of preferred stock:

Preferred Stock ($10 par, 10,000 shares outstanding)	$100,000
Paid-In Capital in Excess of Par	10,000

Assume Interwest redeems and retires 2,000 shares, or 20%, of the preferred stock at $12.50 per share, or a total purchase price of $25,000. Reductions are made in the preferred stock account for $20,000 (2,000 shares at par of $10) and in the related paid-in capital account for a pro rata share, 20% of $10,000, or $2,000. The remainder of the purchase price, $3,000, is charged to Retained Earnings. The journal entry would be:

Preferred Stock	20,000	
Paid-In Capital in Excess of Par	2,000	
Retained Earnings	3,000	
Cash		25,000

Alternatively, the entire amount paid over par or stated value of the retired shares can be debited to Retained Earnings. In the above example, the entry would be:

Preferred Stock	20,000	
Retained Earnings	5,000	
Cash		25,000

When a corporation reacquires stock at a price that is less than par or stated value, the difference is credited to a paid-in capital account, not to Retained Earnings. To illustrate, assume Interwest Corporation redeems the 2,000 shares of preferred stock at only $9 per share, or a total of $18,000. The preferred stock account is reduced by the par value of the shares, $20,000, and the difference between the debit to Preferred Stock and the amount paid is credited to a paid-in capital account, as illustrated in the following entry:

Preferred Stock	20,000	
Cash		18,000
Paid-In Capital From Preferred Stock Reacquisition		2,000

If additional shares of preferred stock are subsequently reacquired at amounts in excess of par, the excess can be debited to Paid-In Capital in Excess of Par, Paid-In Capital From Preferred Stock Reacquisition, and/or Retained Earnings.

The preceding discussion and illustrations dealt only with the corporation's books. From the investor's perspective, a stock redemption is recorded by a debit to Cash for the call price received and a credit to the investment account at cost; the difference, if any, is recorded as a gain or loss. Generally, a gain is recognized, since the call price is usually higher than the cost of the investment. Using the first example given for the Interwest Corporation (reacquisition price of $12.50 per share) and assuming only one investor held the 2,000 shares of preferred stock at a cost of $22,000, the entry for the stockholder would be:

Cash	25,000	
Gain on Redemption of Interwest Corporation Preferred Stock		3,000
Investment in Interwest Corporation Preferred Stock		22,000

7. *Opinions of the Accounting Principles Board No. 6,* "Status of Accounting Research Bulletins" (New York: American Institute of Certified Public Accountants, 1965), par. 12a.

Treasury Stock

When a company's own stock is reacquired and held in the name of the company rather than formally retired, it is referred to as **treasury stock.** Treasury shares may subsequently be reissued or formally retired. Before discussing how to account for treasury stock, several important features should be noted.

First, treasury stock should not be viewed as an asset; instead, it should be reported as a reduction in total owners' equity.[8] A company cannot have an ownership interest in itself. Furthermore, treasury stock does not confer upon the corporation stockholder rights, e.g., cash dividends or voting rights. Treasury shares may or may not participate in stock dividends or stock splits, depending on the circumstances. The distribution of stock dividends on treasury stock is specifically prohibited by law in some states. In states where such distributions are permitted, stock dividends generally would be distributed on treasury shares only in certain situations, for example when the treasury shares are intended for distribution to employees under a stock option plan. When a stock split alters the par or stated value of all the shares of a particular class of stock, treasury shares would participate in the split.

Second, legal capital is not affected by the acquisition or reissuance of treasury stock. The acquisition of treasury stock decreases the number of shares outstanding, while reissuance increases the number of shares outstanding, but the legal capital is not changed by either the reacquisition or the subsequent reissuance. Third, as noted earlier, there is no income or loss on the reacquisition, reissuance, or retirement of treasury stock. Finally, as illustrated in the next section, Retained Earnings can be decreased by treasury stock transactions, but is never increased by such transactions.

Two methods for recording treasury stock transactions are generally accepted: (1) the **cost method,** where the purchase of treasury stock is viewed as giving rise to a capital element whose ultimate disposition remains to be determined; and (2) the **par (or stated) value method,** where the purchase of treasury stock is viewed as effective or "constructive" retirement of outstanding stock.

Cost Method of Accounting for Treasury Stock. Under the cost method, the purchase of treasury stock is recorded by debiting a treasury stock account for the cost of the purchase and crediting Cash. The cost is determined by the current market price of the stock and is not necessarily tied to the original stock issue price. The balance in the treasury stock account is reported as a deduction from total stockholders' equity on the balance sheet. If treasury stock is subsequently retired, the debit balance in the treasury stock account is eliminated by allocating proportionate amounts to the appropriate capital stock, paid-in capital, and retained earnings accounts, as noted previously. If treasury stock is subsequently sold, the difference between the acquisition cost and the selling price is reported as an increase or decrease in stockholders' equity. If stockholders' equity is increased by the sale of treasury stock, a paid-in capital account, such as Paid-In Capital From Treasury Stock, is credited. If stockholders' equity is decreased, paid-in capital accounts established from previous treasury stock transactions may be debited, or the entire amount may be debited to Retained Earnings.

The cost method of accounting for treasury stock transactions is illustrated in the following example:

1995 Newly organized corporation issued 10,000 shares of common stock, $10 par, at $15:

8. Occasionally, however, treasury stock is shown as an asset when shares are acquired in connection with an employee stock option plan. However, such instances are rare. *Accounting Trends & Techniques—1993* (p. 260) reports two occurrences in 1989, one in 1990, and none in 1991 and 1992.

Cash	150,000	
Common Stock		100,000
Paid-In Capital in Excess of Par		50,000

Net income for first year of business, $30,000:

Income Summary	30,000	
Retained Earnings		30,000

1996 Reacquired 1,000 shares of common stock at $16 per share:

Treasury Stock	16,000	
Cash		16,000

Sold 200 shares of treasury stock at $20 per share:

Cash	4,000	
Treasury Stock		3,200
Paid-In Capital From Treasury Stock		800

Sold 500 shares of treasury stock at $14 per share:

Cash	7,000	
Paid-In Capital From Treasury Stock	800	
Retained Earnings	200	
Treasury Stock		8,000

Retired 300 shares of treasury stock (3% of original issue of 10,000 shares):

Common Stock	3,000	
Paid-In Capital in Excess of Par	1,500*	
Retained Earnings	300*	
Treasury Stock (300 × $16)		4,800

*As indicated earlier, the entire $1,800 difference between the debit to Common Stock and the cost to acquire the treasury stock may be debited to Retained Earnings.

In the preceding example, if a balance sheet were prepared after the acquisition of the treasury stock but prior to the reissuance and retirement of the stock, the stockholders' equity section would appear as follows:

Stockholders' Equity

Contributed capital:	
Common stock	$100,000
Paid-in capital in excess of par	50,000
Total contributed capital	$150,000
Retained earnings	30,000
Total contributed capital and retained earnings	$180,000
Less treasury stock at cost	16,000
Total stockholders' equity	$164,000

It should be noted that in the example, all treasury stock was acquired at $16 per share. If several acquisitions of treasury stock are made at different prices, the resale or retirement of treasury shares must be recorded using the actual cost to reacquire the shares being sold or retired (specific identification) or on the basis of a cost-flow assumption, such as FIFO or average cost.

Par (or Stated) Value Method of Accounting for Treasury Stock. If the par (or stated) value method is used, the purchase of treasury stock is regarded as a withdrawal of a group of stockholders. Similarly, the sale or reissuance of treasury stock, under this approach, is viewed as the admission of a new group of stockholders, requiring entries giving effect to the investment by this group. Thus, the purchase and sale are viewed as two separate and unrelated transactions.

Using the data given for the cost method illustration, the following entries would be made for 1996 under the par value method:

1996 Reacquired 1,000 shares of common stock at $16 per share:

Treasury Stock	10,000	
Paid-In Capital in Excess of Par	5,000	
Retained Earnings	1,000	
Cash		16,000

Sold 200 shares of treasury stock at $20 per share:

Cash	4,000	
Treasury Stock		2,000
Paid-In Capital in Excess of Par		2,000

Sold 500 shares of treasury stock at $14 per share:

Cash	7,000	
Treasury Stock		5,000
Paid-In Capital in Excess of Par		2,000

Retired 300 shares of treasury stock:

Common Stock	3,000	
Treasury Stock		3,000

Prior to the reissuance or retirement of treasury stock in the example using the par value method, the stockholders' equity section would show:

Stockholders' Equity	
Contributed capital:	
Common stock	$100,000
Less treasury stock at par value	10,000
Common stock outstanding	$ 90,000
Paid-in capital in excess of par	45,000
Total contributed capital	$135,000
Retained earnings	29,000
Total stockholders' equity	$164,000

Evaluating the Cost and Par Value Methods. Neither the AICPA, through the Accounting Principles Board, nor the FASB has expressed a preference between the two methods of accounting for treasury stock transactions. Although there is theoretical support for each approach, in practice, the cost method is strongly favored because of its simplicity. As noted in the 1993 *Accounting Trends & Techniques,* only 24 of 382 companies that reported treasury stock used some form of par or stated value method.[9]

The following comparison shows the impact on stockholders' equity of the two approaches after all treasury stock transactions have occurred in the illustrative example. Note that total stockholders' equity is the same regardless of which method is used. As shown by the example, however, there may be differences in the relative amounts of contributed capital and retained earnings reported. Note again that Retained Earnings may be

9. *Accounting Trends & Techniques—1993* (New York: American Institute of Certified Public Accountants, 1993), p. 260.

decreased by treasury stock transactions, but can never be increased by buying or selling treasury stock.

Comparison of Stockholders' Equity

	Cost Method	Par Value Method
Contributed capital:		
Common stock	$ 97,000	$ 97,000
Paid-in capital in excess of par	48,500	49,000
Total contributed capital	$145,500	$146,000
Retained earnings	29,500	29,000
Total contributed capital and retained earnings	$175,000	$175,000
Less treasury stock	-0-	-0-
Total stockholders' equity	$175,000	$175,000

STOCK RIGHTS, WARRANTS, AND OPTIONS

A corporation may issue rights, warrants, or options that permit the purchase of the company's stock for a specified period (the **exercise period**) at a certain price (the **exercise**

Stock Buybacks in the 1980s

The most significant trend in corporate capital structures during the 1980s was the increasing amount of debt and the decreasing amount of equity. In fact, the combination of takeovers and stock buybacks decreased the amount of New York Stock Exchange-traded stocks by an average of 6.5% per year from 1984 through 1989. This continued the trend of increasing debt ratios (total liabilities/total assets) in the post-World War II period.

Some of the buybacks announced were very large indeed. For example, in November 1989, General Electric announced its intention to spend $10 billion to buy back its own shares. This buyback announcement followed a decade in which GE had spent $19 billion making some significant acquisitions, including the high-profile purchase of RCA. The change in strategy came about because "we don't see value out there to make acquisitions. . . the best bet is our own stock." GE claimed that 60% of the cash needed for the buyback would come from free cash flow (cash flow from operations less capital expenditures and dividend payments), with the rest coming from borrowing.

The most controversial buybacks of the 80s came in the wake of the 508-point stock market crash on October 19, 1987. According to an SEC study, after the crash, 645 companies announced open-market buyback plans totaling $77 billion. These buyback announcements were intended to inspire investor confidence and stop the slide in stock prices. Typical quotes from company executives were:

"It is an acknowledgement of confidence in our current and future value."

"It just underscores our financial stability and sends a signal that we believe in ourselves."

The controversy about these post-crash buyback announcements is that it subsequently became clear that at least some of the announcements had been made purely for their psychological effect and that the actual buybacks were not going to take place. One credit analyst characterized the buyback plans as representing "only a statement of faith, intended to bolster shareholder confidence, rather than a plan of action."

Questions:

1. When it announced its stock buyback program in November 1989, General Electric claimed that it would be able to implement the buybacks without raising its debt-to-equity ratio (total liabilities/total equity). Is this possible?
2. Many claim that a stock buyback will increase earnings per share. Do you agree?

Sources:

Christopher Winans, "Stock Market Loses Vital Corporate Crutch," *The Wall Street Journal* (July 23, 1990), p. C1.

Amal Kumar Naj, "General Electric Buy-Back Plan Signals New Tack, Reflects Earnings Optimism," *The Wall Street Journal* (November 20, 1989), p. A3.

Jay Palmer, "Promises, Promises: Or What Happened to All Those Post-Crash Buybacks?" *Barron's* (April 25, 1988), p. 13.

price). Although the terms *rights, warrants,* and *options* are sometimes used interchangeably, a distinction may be made as follows:

1. **Stock rights**—issued to existing shareholders to permit them to maintain their proportionate ownership interests when new shares are to be issued. (Some state laws require this preemptive right.)
2. **Stock warrants**—sold by the corporation for cash, generally in conjunction with another security.
3. **Stock options**—granted to officers or employees, sometimes as part of a compensation plan.

A company may offer rights, warrants, or options: (1) to raise additional capital, (2) to encourage the sale of a particular class of securities, or (3) as compensation for services received. The exercise period is generally longer for warrants and options than for rights. Warrants and rights may be traded independently among investors, whereas options generally are restricted to a particular person or specified group to whom the options are granted. The accounting considerations relating to stock rights, warrants, and options are described in the following sections.

Stock Rights

When announcing rights to purchase additional shares of stock, the directors of a corporation specify a date on which the rights will be issued. All stockholders of record on the issue date are entitled to receive the rights. Thus, between the announcement date and the issue date, the stock is said to sell *rights-on.* After the rights are issued, the stock sells *ex-rights,* and the rights may be sold separately by those receiving them from the corporation. An expiration date is also designated when the rights are announced, and rights not exercised by this date are worthless.

Accounting for Stock Rights by the Issuer. When rights are issued to stockholders, only a memorandum entry is made on the issuing company's books stating the number of shares that may be claimed under the outstanding rights. This information is required so the corporation may retain sufficient unissued or reacquired stock to meet the exercise of the rights. Upon surrender of the rights and the receipt of payments as specified by the rights, the stock is issued. At this time, a memorandum entry is made to record the decrease in the number of rights outstanding accompanied by an entry to record the stock sale. The entry for the sale is recorded the same as any other issue of stock, with appropriate recognition of the cash received, the par or stated value of the stock issued, and any additional paid-in capital.

Information concerning outstanding rights should be reported with the corporation's balance sheet so that the effects of the future exercise of remaining rights may be determined.

Accounting for Stock Rights by the Investor. The receipt of stock rights by a stockholder is comparable to the receipt of a stock dividend (to be discussed fully in Chapter 16). The corporation has made no asset distribution, and stockholders' equity remains unchanged. However, a stockholders' investment is now evidenced by shares of stock previously acquired and by rights that have a value of their own when they permit the purchase of shares at less than the market price. These circumstances call for an **allocation of cost** between the shares of stock and the rights. Since the shares and the rights have different values, an apportionment should be made in terms of the relative market values as of the date the rights are issued. Subsequently, the stock and the rights are accounted for separately. Accounting for stock rights by the shareholder is illustrated in the following example.

Assume that in 1995, Northern Supply Co. acquired 100 shares of Telstar Inc.'s common stock at $180 per share. In 1996, Telstar issues rights to purchase 1 share of common at $110 for every 5 shares owned. Northern thus receives 100 rights—1 right for each share owned. However, since 5 rights are required for the acquisition of a single share, the 100 rights enable Northern to subscribe for only 20 new shares. Northern's original investment cost of $18,000 now applies to 2 assets, the shares and the rights. This cost is apportioned on the basis of the relative market values of each security as of the date that the rights are issued to the stockholders.[10] The cost allocation may be expressed as follows:

$$\text{Cost assigned to rights} = \text{Original cost of stock} \times \frac{\text{Market value of rights}}{\text{Market value of stock ex-rights} + \text{Market value of rights}}$$

$$\text{Cost assigned to stock} = \text{Original cost of stock} \times \frac{\text{Market value of stock ex-rights}}{\text{Market value of stock ex-rights} + \text{Market value of rights}}$$

Assume that Telstar Inc.'s common stock is selling ex-rights at $129 per share, and rights are selling at $4 each. The cost allocation would be made as follows:

To rights:

$$\$18{,}000 \times \frac{\$4}{\$129 + \$4} = \$541 \text{ (rounded); } \$541 \div 100 = \$5.41 \text{ cost per right}$$

To stock:

$$\$18{,}000 \times \frac{\$129}{\$129 + \$4} = \$17{,}459 \text{ (rounded); } \$17{,}459 \div 100 = \$174.59 \text{ cost per share}$$

The following entry may be made to record the allocation:

Investment in Telstar Inc. Stock Rights	541	
Investment in Telstar Inc. Common Stock		541
Received 100 rights permitting the purchase of 20 shares at $110.		

The cost apportioned to the rights is used in determining any gain or loss arising from the sale of rights. Assume that the rights in the preceding example are sold for $4.50 each. The following entry would be made:

Cash	450	
Loss on Sale of Telstar Inc. Stock Rights	91	
Investment in Telstar Inc. Stock Rights		541
Sold 100 rights at $4.50.		

If the rights are exercised rather than sold, the cost of the new shares acquired consists of the cost assigned to the rights plus the cash that is paid on the exercise of rights. Assume that, instead of selling the rights, Northern Supply Co. exercises its rights to purchase 20 additional shares at $110. The following entry would be made:

Investment in Telstar Inc. Common Stock	2,741	
Investment in Telstar Inc. Stock Rights		541
Cash		2,200
Exercised rights, acquiring 20 shares at $110.		

10. If the market value of the rights or of the stock is not readily determinable, the market value of the known quantity is used, and the residual purchase price is allocated to the security with the unknown market value.

Upon exercising the rights, Northern's records show an investment balance of $20,200 consisting of two lots of stock as follows:

Lot 1 (1995 acquisition) 100 shares: ($17,459 ÷ 100 = $174.59 cost per share, adjusted for stock rights)	$17,459
Lot 2 (1996 acquisition) 20 shares: ($2,741 ÷ 20 = $137.05 cost per share, acquired through stock rights)	2,741
Total	$20,200

These costs provide the basis for calculating gain or loss on subsequent sale of the stock.

Frequently the receipt of rights includes 1 or more rights that cannot be used in the purchase of a whole share. For example, assume that the owner of 100 shares receives 100 rights; 6 rights are required for the purchase of 1 share. Here the holder uses 96 rights in purchasing 16 shares. Several alternatives are available to the holder: allow the remaining 4 rights to lapse; sell the rights and report a gain or a loss on such sale; or supplement the rights held by the purchase of 2 more rights making possible the purchase of an additional share of stock.

If the owner of valuable rights allows them to lapse, it would appear that the cost assigned to such rights should be written off as a loss. This can be supported on the theory that the issuance of stock by the corporation at less than current market price results in a dilution in the equities identified with original holdings. However, when changes in the market price of the stock make the exercise of rights unattractive to all investors and none of the rights can be sold, no dilution has occurred and any cost of rights reported separately should be returned to the investment account.

Stock Warrants

As noted previously, warrants may be sold in conjunction with other securities as a "sweetener" to make the purchase of the securities more attractive. For example, warrants to purchase shares of a corporation's common stock may be issued with bonds to encourage investors to purchase the bonds. A warrant has value when the exercise price is less than the market value, either present or potential, of the security that can be purchased with the warrants. Warrants issued with other securities may be detachable or nondetachable. **Detachable warrants** are similar to stock rights because they can be traded separately from the security with which they were originally issued. **Nondetachable warrants** cannot be separated from the security they were issued with.

As described in Chapter 14, the Accounting Principles Board in Opinion No. 14 recommended assigning part of the issuance price of debt securities to any detachable stock warrants and classifying it as part of owners' equity.[11] The value assigned to the warrant is determined by a procedure similar to that described for stock rights and is expressed in the following equation:

$$\text{Value assigned to warrants} = \text{Total issue price} \times \frac{\text{Market value of warrant}}{\text{Market value of security without warrant} + \text{Market value of warrant}}$$

Although Opinion No. 14 is directed only to warrants attached to debt, it appears logical to extend the conclusions of that Opinion to warrants attached to preferred stock. Thus, if a

11. *Opinions of the Accounting Principles Board No. 14,* "Accounting for Convertible Debt and Debt Issued with Stock Purchase Warrants" (New York: American Institute of Certified Public Accountants, 1969), par. 16.

market value exists for the warrants at the issuance date, a separate equity account is credited with that portion of the issuance price assigned to the warrants. If the warrants are exercised, the value assigned to the common stock is the value allocated to the warrants plus the cash proceeds from the issuance of the common stock. If the warrants are allowed to expire, the value assigned to the warrants may be transferred to a permanent paid-in capital account.

Accounting for detachable warrants attached to a preferred stock issue is illustrated as follows. Assume the Stewart Co. sells 1,000 shares of $50 par preferred stock for $58 per share. As an incentive to purchase the stock, Stewart Co. gives the purchaser detachable warrants enabling holders to subscribe to 1,000 shares of $20 par common stock for $25 per share. The warrants expire after one year. Immediately following the issuance of the preferred stock, the warrants are selling at $3, and the fair market value of the preferred stock without the warrant attached is $57. The proceeds of $58,000 should be allocated by the Stewart Co. as follows:

$$\text{Value assigned to the warrants} = \$58{,}000 \times \frac{\$3}{\$57 + \$3} = \$2{,}900$$

A similar allocation would be made by the investor, and the warrants would subsequently be accounted for in the same manner as stock rights.

The entry on Stewart's books to record the sale of the preferred stock with detachable warrants is:

Cash	58,000	
Preferred Stock, $50 par		50,000
Paid-In Capital in Excess of Par—Preferred Stock		5,100
Common Stock Warrants		2,900

If the warrants are exercised, the entry to record the issuance of common stock would be:

Common Stock Warrants	2,900	
Cash	25,000	
Common Stock, $20 par		20,000
Paid-In Capital in Excess of Par—Common Stock		7,900

This entry would be the same regardless of the market price of the common stock at the issuance date.

If the warrants in the example were allowed to expire, the following entry would be made:

Common Stock Warrants	2,900	
Paid-In Capital From Expired Warrants		2,900

If warrants are nondetachable, the securities are considered inseparable, and no allocation is made to recognize the value of the warrant. The entire proceeds are assigned to the security to which the warrant is attached. Thus, for nondetachable warrants, the accounting treatment is similar to that for convertible securities, such as convertible bonds. Some accountants feel this inconsistency is not justified, since the economic value of a warrant exists, even if the warrant cannot be traded separately or "detached." This is essentially the same argument made for recognizing the conversion feature of a convertible security. Notwithstanding this argument, a separate instrument does not exist for a nondetachable warrant, and current practice does not require a separate value to be assigned to these warrants.

Accounting for Stock-Based Compensation

During the first half of 1993, many high-technology and start-up companies, along with the venture capitalists who typically provide the seed money for such companies, were anxiously awaiting an Exposure Draft from the FASB on accounting for stock-based compensation. Estimates published in *The Wall Street Journal* suggested that the rules being contemplated by the FASB could lower profits at some companies by as much as 50%.[12] The following decreases were forecast for the major software companies: Microsoft, –18.9%, Novell, –15.0%, Lotus Development, –49.6%. After release of the Exposure Draft in June 1993, vociferous complaints arose from financial executives, auditors, and politicians. The following quotes appeared in the *Harvard Business Reveiw*[13]:

- *"U.S. entrepreneurial stalwarts, in this era of rapidly shrinking employment, are to be sacrificed on the altar of accounting principles by the high priests of the double-entry ledger."—T.J. Rodgers, President, Cypress Semiconductor.*
- *"The FASB has attempted to use a political tailwind and its position of unfettered power to fix a problem that doesn't exist in the view of financial statement issuers, auditors, and users." —James F. Morgan, Chairman, Morgan Holland Ventures Corporation.*

The FASB received this onslaught of criticism because it proposed to supersede APB Opinion No. 25, which has governed the accounting for employee stock options since 1972.[14] In particular, the FASB sought to eliminate the inconsistency between the accounting for fixed stock option plans and performance-based option plans. A **fixed stock option plan** is one in which the plan terms (i.e., the option exercise price and the number of options granted) are fixed as of the date the options are granted. In a **performance-based stock option plan,** the plan terms are dependent on how well the individual or company performs after the date the options are granted. The provisions of APB Opinion No. 25 typically result in no compensation expense being recorded in connection with fixed stock option plans, whereas expense is usually recorded with performance-based plans. As a result, most U.S. companies have structured their stock compensation programs as fixed stock option plans. This result has been particularly disturbing since a fixed stock option plan in some ways is more valuable to employees because the receipt of options under a fixed stock option plan is not contingent on the company or the employee meeting additional financial targets.

The major accounting questions associated with stock-based compensation are:

1. How should stock options and similar instruments be valued?
2. What amount of compensation expense should be recognized in each period?
3. What information should be disclosed relative to stock-based compensation plans?

The accounting for fixed stock option and performance-based stock option plans as stipulated in the provisions of APB Opinion No. 25 is illustrated below. The discussion also includes consideration of possible revisions to this standard, as outlined in the FASB's June 1993 Exposure Draft on accounting for stock-based compensation.

Fixed Stock Option Plans. On January 1, 1994, the board of directors of the Neff Company authorized the grant of 10,000 stock options to supplement the salaries of certain employees. Each stock option permits the purchase of one share of Neff common stock at a price of $50 per share; the market price of the stock on January 1, 1994 is $55 per share. The options vest, or become exercisable, beginning on January 1, 1997 and only if the employees stay with the company for the entire three-year vesting period. The options expire on December 31, 1997.

12. Lee Berton, "New Payroll Rule May Eat Into 1997 Profits," *The Wall Street Journal*, June 3, 1993, p. C1.
13. "Taking Account of Stock Options," *Harvard Business Review*, January-February 1994, p. 27.
14. *Opinions of the Accounting Principles Board No. 25*, "Accounting for Stock Issued to Employees" (New York: American Institute of Certified Public Accountants, 1972).

Conceptually, the recording of the grant of the stock options at January 1, 1994 is relatively straightforward: the valuable options are granted to the employees in advance to compensate them for work to be performed over the following three years. The journal entry to record the grant is as follows (the amounts are omitted):

Prepaid Compensation	×××	
Options Outstanding		×××

Prepaid Compensation is an asset just like any other payment for services in advance. Options Outstanding is an equity account. The difficult accounting issue is how to compute a value for the options. Under APB Opinion No. 25, the value of a fixed stock option is equal to the difference between the option exercise price and the market price at the grant date. In the Neff example, each option has a value of $5 ($55 market price at grant date – $50 exercise price). Since the plan grants 10,000 options, prepaid compensation expense related to the three-year vesting period is $50,000 (10,000 options × $5). The journal entry required on the grant date is as follows:

January 1, 1994		
Prepaid Compensation (10,000 × $5)	50,000	
Options Outstanding		50,000
To recognize the value of options granted on January 1, 1994: 10,000 options; market value of underlying stock, $55; option exercise price, $50.		

This valuation issue is precisely the aspect of APB Opinion No. 25 that led to the reexamination of stock option accounting by the FASB. Clearly, each option has value above $5 because there is a chance that the stock price may increase during the three-year period and the options give the employees the right to buy the stock at the lower option price of $50. Under the provisions of the June 1993 Exposure Draft, Neff would be required to compute the fair value of the options as of the grant date. Computation of the fair value involves consideration of factors like the expected volatility of the stock price and the length of time the options are valid.[15] For example, the higher the volatility of the stock price, the higher the value of the option because there is a bigger chance that the stock price will increase significantly. Of course, increased volatility also means that there is an increased probability that the stock price will decrease, but this doesn't negatively impact the option value since the employees can choose not to exercise the option if the share price drops below the option price of $50. Also, an option with a longer term has increased value because there is more chance of a significant stock price increase over a long time period than there is over a short one. Exact computation of option values involves use of mathematical models that are beyond the scope of this book, but, as stated by the FASB, "software available for personal computers reduces the application of those models to a fill-in-the-blank exercise."[16]

Once the options granted have been valued and Prepaid Compensation recorded, the remaining accounting problem is determining when the compensation expense should be recognized. Generally, the compensation should be charged to the current and future periods in which the employees perform the services for which the options were granted.[17] In the Neff example, no specific service period is mentioned so compensation cost is allocated over the three-year period between the January 1, 1994 grant date and the January 1, 1997 vesting date. The journal entries to record the recognition of compensation expense for 1994 and 1995 are as follows:

15. *Proposed Statement of Financial Accounting Standards*, "Accounting for Stock-based Compensation," (Financial Accounting Standards Board, Norwalk, June 30, 1993), para. 16.

16. *Ibid.*, para. 47.

17. The June 1993 Exposure Draft stipulates that "if an award is for past services, the related compensation cost shall be recognized in the period in which it is granted." See para. 20.

December 31, 1994		
Compensation Expense ($50,000 / 3 years)	16,667	
Prepaid Compensation		16,667
To recognize compensation expense for 1994. (Total compensation cost is allocated evenly over the three-year vesting period.)		
December 31, 1995		
Compensation Expense ($50,000 / 3 years)	16,667	
Prepaid Compensation		16,667
To recognize compensation expense for 1995.		

In 1996, several employees left Neff and forfeited their rights to a total of 500 stock options. Under the provisions of APB Opinion No. 25, option forfeitures should be accounted for by decreasing compensation expense in the period of the forfeiture.[18] A journal entry is made in 1996 to adjust the original valuation estimate for the occurrence of the forfeitures:

December 31, 1996		
Options Outstanding	2,500	
Prepaid Compensation (500 × $5)		2,500
Decrease in estimated value of options resulting from the forfeiture of 500 options.		

The journal entry to record compensation expense for 1996 is as follows:

December 31, 1996		
Compensation Expense	14,166	
Prepaid Compensation		14,166
To recognize compensation expense for 1996. (Since 1996 is the last year of the vesting period, the total remaining amount of prepaid compensation is recognized as expense: $50,000 – $16,667 – $16,667 – $2,500 = $14,166.)		

The following journal entry records the exercise of all 9,500 of the nonforfeited options on December 31, 1997 to purchase shares of Neff's no-par common stock:

December 31, 1997		
Cash (9,500 × $50)	475,000	
Options Outstanding ($50,000 – $2,500)	47,500	
Common Stock (no par)		522,500
To recognize the issuance of Neff no-par common stock upon exercise of 9,500 employee stock options at an exercise price of $50 per share.		

If the options had been allowed to expire unexercised, the following journal entry would have been necessary on December 31, 1997, the end of the exercise period:

December 31, 1997		
Options Outstanding	47,500	
Paid-In Capital from Expired Options		47,500
To record the expiration of unexercised options.[19]		

Performance-Based Stock Option Plan. In the fixed stock option plan of Neff Company that was illustrated above, Neff's employees needed only to stay with the company for the entire three-year vesting period in order to receive the full value of the options. Another type of stock-based compensation plan is one in which the terms of the

18. APB Opinion No. 25, para 15. Under the provisions of the June 1993 Exposure Draft, estimates of expected forfeitures are incorporated into the original valuation of the options at the grant date. Deviations from these estimates are accounted for in the same way as is shown for forfeitures under APB Opinion No. 25.

19. Under APB Opinion No. 25, the value of options forfeited through the actions of an employee (i.e., leaving the company before the end of the vesting period) is expensed in the period of the forfeiture. The value of options voluntarily allowed to expire unexercised is transferred to an appropriately named paid-in capital account.

option depend on how well an employee performs or how well the company performs during the vesting period. As noted previously, this type of plan is called a performance-based stock option plan. For example, assume that the terms of the Neff Company stock-based compensation plan are as follows. The number of options granted, instead of being fixed at 10,000, is contingent on Neff's level of sales for 1996. If Neff's sales for 1996 are less than $50 million, only the 10,000 options will vest. If Neff's 1996 sales are between $50 million and $80 million, an additional 2,000 options will vest, making a total of 12,000. Finally, if Neff's 1996 sales exceed $80 million, a total of 15,000 options will vest.

For the Neff performance-based stock option plan, the valuation of prepaid compensation on the grant date is done using the number of options that are probable to vest. This depends, of course, on the probable level of 1996 sales. As of January 1, 1994, Neff forecasts that 1996 sales will be around $60 million, indicating that 12,000 options will vest. Under APB Opinion No. 25, each option is valued at $5, the difference between the option exercise price of $50 and the January 1, 1994 market price of $55. The journal entry to record the grant of the options is as follows:

January 1, 1994		
Prepaid Compensation (12,000 × $5)	60,000	
Options Outstanding		60,000
To recognize the value of options granted on January 1, 1994: 12,000 options expected to vest with a value of $5 each ($55 market price – $50 exercise price).		

Under APB Opinion No. 25, the Options Outstanding equity account recorded in connection with a performance-based plan is remeasured at the end of each period in response to changes in the variables used to compute the initial value. In the Neff example, the initial valuation was based on a forecast of 1996 sales and the January 1, 1994 stock price of $55 per share. At December 31, 1994, Options Outstanding is remeasured using an updated forecast of 1996 sales and the December 31, 1994 stock price. This process differs substantially from the accounting for fixed stock option plans that was illustrated previously. With fixed stock options, changes in stock price occurring after the grant date are ignored — the Options Outstanding equity account is remeasured only when options are forfeited by employees. This difference in accounting stems from a difference in measurement date as defined in APB Opinion No. 25. The Opinion states that the measurement date is the first date on which both of the following are known: (1) the number of shares that an individual employee is entitled to receive, and (2) the exercise price.[20] For fixed stock options, both quantities are known at the grant date; for performance-based plans, one or both of the quantities can only be estimated at the grant date. These estimates are revised at the end of each period.

As of December 31, 1994, the forecast of 1996 sales is unchanged at $60 million, suggesting that 12,000 options will be granted. The stock price on December 31, 1994 is $56 per share. The journal entries to record the remeasurement of Options Outstanding and to record compensation expense for the year are as follows:

December 31, 1994		
Prepaid Compensation	12,000	
Options Outstanding [12,000 × ($56 – $55)]		12,000
Increase in estimated value of options resulting from a change in stock price during the year. This increases total options outstanding to $72,000 ($60,000 + $12,000).		
December 31, 1994		
Compensation Expense ($72,000 / 3 years)	24,000	
Prepaid Compensation		24,000
To recognize compensation expense for 1994. Total compensation cost is allocated over the three-year vesting period.		

20. APB Opinion No. 25, para. 10b.

Events in 1995 lead Neff to lower its forecast of 1996 sales. As of December 31, 1995, Neff expects 1996 sales to be only $40 million. Accordingly, it is probable that only 10,000 options will vest on January 1, 1997. In addition, the stock price on December 31, 1995 is $57 per share. The journal entry necessary to adjust the original valuation estimate for this updated information is as follows:

December 31, 1995		
Options Outstanding	2,000	
Prepaid Compensation ($72,000 – $70,000)		2,000

Decrease in estimated value of options resulting from a change in stock price and a change in 1996 forecasted sales. [12,000 × ($56 – $50)] – [10,000 × ($57 – $50)] = $2,000. This decreases total options outstanding to $70,000 ($60,000 + $12,000 – $2,000).

December 31, 1995		
Compensation Expense	22,667	
Prepaid Compensation		22,667

To recognize compensation expense for 1995. With two-thirds of the vesting period elapsed, the remaining balance in Prepaid Compensation should represent just one-third of the total amount of Options Outstanding, $23,333 ($70,000 / 3). The indicated amount for 1995 compensation expense is thus $22,667. See the T-account below.

Prepaid Compensation

	Debit	Credit
Grant Date	60,000	
1994 Revision	12,000	
1994 Expense		24,000
1995 Revision		2,000
1995 Expense		22,667
December 31, 1995 Balance	23,333	

Upon close examination, it can be seen that this computation of compensation expense differs from that typically encountered in situations with changing accounting estimates. Usually, the effects of changes in estimates are spread over current and future periods. In this case, such a procedure would result in 1995 compensation expense of $23,000, an allocation of the remaining Prepaid Compensation of $46,000 ($60,000 + $12,000 – $24,000 – $2,000) evenly over the remaining two years of the service period, 1995 and 1996. However, FASB Interpretation No. 28 requires a "catch-up" adjustment when recognizing compensation expense related to performance-based option plans.[21] The catch-up adjustment reduces the amount of Prepaid Compensation to the level it would have been had the updated information for stock price and 1996 sales been used when originally recording the stock options on January 1, 1994.

Actual sales for 1996 are $85 million (Neff had a pretty good year). As a result, according to the terms of the performance-based plan, 15,000 options will vest as of January 1, 1997. In addition, Neff's stock price is $60 per share on December 31, 1996. The entries to adjust the original valuation for this new information and to record compensation expense for 1996 are as follows:

December 31, 1996		
Prepaid Compensation	80,000	
Options Outstanding		80,000

Increase in estimated value of options resulting from a change in stock price and actual 1996 sales different from forecast. [15,000 × ($60 – $50)] – [10,000 × $57–$50)] = $80,000. This increases total options outstanding to $150,000 ($60,000 + $12,000 – $2,000 + $80,000).

21. *FASB Interpretation No. 28*, "Accounting for Stock Appreciation Rights and Other Variable Stock Option or Award Plans" (Stamford: Financial Accounting Standards Board, 1978).

December 31, 1996

Compensation Expense	103,333	
Prepaid Compensation		103,333

To recognize compensation expense for 1996. The Prepaid Compensation remaining before 1996 expense recognition was $103,333 ($23,333 + $80,000).

The Neff example illustrates why very few stock-based compensation plans in the United States are structured as performance-based plans. In the example, compensation expense in each year of the three-year vesting period was as follows:

1994	$ 24,000
1995	22,667
1996	103,333

With a fixed stock option plan, total compensation expense for the vesting period is known as of the grant date (except for possible reductions stemming from option forfeitures). With Neff's performance-based plan, total compensation expense for the vesting period was not known until the end of the vesting period. Also, with the performance-based plan, Neff's compensation expense varied significantly among periods because of changes in the stock price and the forecasted level of the performance target. The provisions of APB Opinion No. 25 cause performance-based plans to yield more volatile amounts for compensation expense than do fixed option plans. Managers and investors have long shown a preference for smooth earnings. Consequently, the provisions of APB Opinion No. 25 have seriously hindered the adoption of performance-based stock option plans in the United States.

The June 1993 Exposure Draft seeks to reduce the difference in the accounting treatment of fixed option and performance-based plans. Under the provisions of the Exposure Draft, options under both types of plans would be valued at the grant date and those values would *not* be changed in response to subsequent changes in stock prices. An accounting difference that the Exposure Draft preserves is that the valuation of options under performance-based plans would still be adjusted at the end of each period to reflect changes in the forecasted levels of any performance targets included in the plan.

Awards That Call for Settlement in Cash. Neff Company's stock-based compensation plans discussed above stipulated that the compensation would be paid in the form of stock options. Since settlement of these stock options requires Neff to issue its own stock and does not require any transfer of assets, the stock options are considered to be equity instruments. When a stock-based compensation plan calls for a cash settlement or gives the employee the option of choosing a cash settlement instead of receiving stock options, the transaction at the grant date is viewed as the creation of a liability since the grant obligates the firm to transfer assets in the future. Under the provisions of APB Opinion No. 25, the accounting treatment for plans that call for settlement in cash is very similar to that used for performance-based plans.

To illustrate the accounting for awards that call for settlement in cash, assume that Neff Company has decided that, instead of granting its employees 10,000 stock options, it will grant an equal number of cash **stock appreciation rights (SAR).** A cash SAR awards an employee a cash amount equal to the market value of the issuing firm's shares above a specified threshold price. Neff Company promises that, after January 1, 1997, it will pay the exerciser of each cash SAR an amount equal to the excess of the share price on the exercise date over the $50 threshold price. As in the fixed stock option illustration, the cash SARs vest beginning on January 1, 1997 only for the employees who stay with the company for the entire three-year vesting period. The cash SARs expire on December 31, 1997. From an employee's standpoint, this cash SAR plan is economically equivalent to the fixed option plan illustrated previously.

However, since the plan obligates Neff to transfer cash, APB Opinion No. 25 dictates that the cash SARs be accounted for in a manner similar to that used for a performance-based plan.

All journal entries for 1994, 1995, and 1996 and for the redemption of the cash SARs on December 31, 1997 are given below. Assume the following information:

Neff Share Price	
January 1, 1994	$55
December 31, 1994	56
December 31, 1995	57
December 31, 1996	60
December 31, 1997	61

January 1, 1994		
Prepaid Compensation (10,000 × $5)	50,000	
Cash SAR Payable		50,000

To recognize the value of SARs granted on January 1, 1994: 10,000 SARs; market value of underlying stock, $55; SAR threshold price, $50.

Note that this entry is almost the same as that made at the grant date in the Neff fixed stock option example illustrated on page 645. The difference is that, with a fixed stock option plan in which options to purchase equity shares are granted, the credit is to an equity account. When the plan allows employees to choose a cash settlement, the grant is considered to entail the creation of a liability.

Just as with performance-based plans, the forecast of the cash settlement amount is updated at the end of each period using current stock price information. Recall that, in the fixed stock option example, no adjustments were made for subsequent changes in stock price. This is the primary difference under APB Opinion No. 25 between the accounting for fixed stock options and the accounting for performance-based plans and plans allowing for cash settlements.

December 31, 1994		
Prepaid Compensation	10,000	
Cash SAR Payable [($56–$55) × 10,000]		10,000

To update the recorded value of the cash SAR liability based on information available on December 31, 1994. Neff's share price on December 31, 1994 is $56. This increases the cash SAR liability to $60,000 [($56 – $50) × $10,000].

December 31, 1994		
Compensation Expense ($60,000 / 3 years)	20,000	
Prepaid Compensation		20,000

To recognize compensation expense for 1994. Total compensation cost is allocated evenly over the three-year vesting period.

December 31, 1995		
Prepaid Compensation	10,000	
Cash SAR Payable [($57–$56) × 10,000]		10,000

To recognize the increase in the estimated liability resulting from an increase in Neff's share price to $57. The estimated liability as of December 31, 1995 is $70,000 [($57–$50) × 10,000].

December 31, 1995		
Compensation Expense	26,667	
Prepaid Compensation		26,667

To recognize compensation expense for 1995. With two-thirds of the vesting period elapsed, the remaining balance in Prepaid Compensation should represent just one-third of the total cash SAR liability, $23,333 ($70,000 / 3). The indicated amount for 1995 compensation expense is thus $26,667. See the following T-account.

Prepaid Compensation

	Debit	Credit
Grant Date	50,000	
1994 Revision	10,000	
1994 Expense		20,000
1995 Revision	10,000	
1995 Expense		26,667
December 31, 1995 Balance	23,333	

Note that, as with performance-based plans, accounting for the SAR plan requires a catch-up adjustment when a change in stock price results in a revaluation of the estimated SAR liability.

December 31, 1996		
Prepaid Compensation	30,000	
Cash SAR Payable [$60–$57) × 10,000]		30,000
To recognize the increase in the estimated liability resulting from an increase in Neff's share price. The estimated liability as of December 31, 1996 is $100,000 [$60–$50) × 10,000].		
December 31, 1996		
Compensation Expense	53,333	
Prepaid Compensation		53,333
To recognize compensation expense for 1996. Since the entire vesting period has elapsed, the remaining balance in Prepaid Compensation is expensed. Beginning balance ($23,333) + revision ($30,000) = Remaining balance ($53,333).		
December 31, 1997		
Compensation Expense	10,000	
Cash SAR Payable [($61–$60) × 10,000]		10,000
To recognize the increase in the estimated liability resulting from an increase in Neff's share price. The estimated liability as of December 31, 1997 is $110,000 [($61–$50) × 10,000].		

If the exercise period extended beyond 1997 and if cash SARs remained outstanding, an entry would be made at the end of each year to revise the estimated amount of the cash SAR liability. These revisions are recognized as part of compensation expense for the period.

December 31, 1997		
Cash SAR Payable	110,000	
Cash [10,000 × ($61 – $50)]		110,000
To record the cash payments made to holders of the 10,000 cash SARs that vested on January 1, 1997 and were exercised on December 31, 1997.		

Broad-Based Plans

Some employers grant employee stock options and employee stock purchase rights to substantially all employees. For example, the notes to Microsoft's 1993 financial statements included in Appendix A indicate that all Microsoft employees are enrolled in an incentive stock option plan that grants 10-year options with the option price being not greater than the market price on the date of grant. In addition, all eligible Microsoft employees can spend up to 10% of their gross salaries to buy shares of Microsoft stock, at a 15% discount from the prevailing market price. Under APB Opinion No. 25, neither of these plans results in recorded compensation expense for Microsoft: the stock option plan results in no expense because it is a fixed option plan with an option price less than or equal to the market price on the grant date; the stock purchase plan produces no expense because APB Opinion No. 25 explicitly excludes broad-based plans allowing employees to purchase stock at a reasonable discount (usually taken to be 15%).

The June 1993 Exposure Draft provides for the recognition of compensation expense for all stock-based compensation plans, broad-based or otherwise.[22] As stated in the Exposure Draft, "The Board sees no reason. . . for the value of stock options granted to an entity's chief executive officer (CEO) to be charged to expense while the value of similar options granted to the CEO's administrative assistant are not."

Disclosure

Under APB Opinion NO. 25, firms are required to disclose the status of all stock-based compensation plans as of the end of the period, including the number of options granted, the option price, and the number of options that are exercisable. In addition, disclosure should be made of the number of shares issued during the period as a result of the exercise of options, along with the exercise price.

The proposed disclosure requirements in the June 1993 Exposure Draft are more extensive and are as follows:[23]

- Description of all stock-based compensation plans, including the general terms of the plans, vesting requirements, maximum term of options granted, and number of shares authorized for grants of options.
- Number and weighted-average exercise price of options outstanding at the beginning and the end of the year.
- Number of options granted, exercised, forfeited, and expired during the year.
- Weighted-average fair value of options granted during the year.
- Description of the method and assumptions used in calculating option values.
- Total compensation cost recognized during the year for stock-based compensation awards.
- Terms of any significant modifications made during the year to outstanding option grants.

A group of preparers and users of financial statements, backed by the large public accounting firms, has opposed the FASB's project to replace the provisions of APB Opinion No. 25 and has instead suggested that more useful information can be conveyed to users through increased financial statement note disclosure than through changing the rules for compensation expense recognition. The FASB has thus far rejected this approach, contending that the granting of stock options is a form of employee compensation that should be recognized as an expense and that disclosure is not a substitute for recognition.[24] However, it is possible, given the large outcry against the provisions of the June 1993 Exposure Draft, that the FASB may revise its position and adopt the disclosure-only proposal. At a minimum, the FASB has proposed an extended phase-in period for any new stock-based compensation accounting standard in order to allow preparers to get familiar with the valuation models needed to implement the standard, to allow users to develop techniques for analyzing the new disclosures, and to give the FASB time to work out any bugs in the standard before the recognition provisions become mandatory.[25]

The Securities and Exchange Commission has also recently shown an increased interest in disclosures related to stock-based compensation, particularly the compensation for top executives. In October 1992, the SEC mandated increased executive compensation disclosures in proxy statements with tables detailing cash compensation values of stock options and stock appreciation rights.

STOCK CONVERSIONS

As noted earlier, stockholders may be permitted by the terms of their stock agreement or by special action of the corporation to exchange their holdings for stock of other classes.

22. Exposure Draft, para. 155.
23. Exposure Draft, para. 30.
24. Exposure Draft, para. 74.
25. Exposure Draft, para. 33-34.

No gain or loss is recognized by the issuer on these conversions, because it is an exchange of one form of equity for another. In certain instances, the exchanges may affect only corporate contributed capital accounts; in other instances, the exchanges may affect both capital and retained earnings accounts.

To illustrate the different conditions, assume that the capital of the Sorensen Corporation on December 31, 1996, is as follows:

Preferred stock, $100 par, 10,000 shares	$1,000,000
Paid-in capital in excess of par	100,000
Common stock, $25 stated value, 100,000 shares	2,500,000
Paid-in capital in excess of stated value	500,000
Retained earnings	1,000,000

Preferred shares are convertible into common shares at any time at the option of the shareholder.

Case 1 Converting One Share of Preferred for Four Shares of Common

Assume the terms of conversion permit the exchange of one share of preferred for four shares of common. On December 31, 1996, 1,000 shares of preferred stock are exchanged for 4,000 shares of common. The amount originally paid for the preferred, $110,000, is now the consideration identified with 4,000 shares of common stock with a total stated value of $100,000. The conversion is recorded by the issuer as follows:

Preferred Stock, $100 par	100,000	
Paid-In Capital in Excess of Par	10,000	
Common Stock, $25 Stated Value		100,000
Paid-In Capital in Excess of Stated Value		10,000

Case 2 Converting One Share of Preferred for Five Shares of Common

Assume terms of conversion permit the exchange of one share of preferred for five shares of common. In converting 1,000 shares of preferred for 5,000 shares of common, an increase in common stock of $125,000 must be recognized, although it is accompanied by a decrease in the preferred equity of only $110,000. The increase in the legal capital related to the issue of common stock is generally accomplished by a debit to Retained Earnings. The conversion on Sorensen's books, then, is recorded as follows:

Preferred Stock, $100 par	100,000	
Paid-In Capital in Excess of Par	10,000	
Retained Earnings	15,000	
Common Stock, $25 stated value		125,000

On the investor's books at the conversion date, an entry would be required to eliminate the cost of the investment in preferred stock and to establish the investment in common stock of Sorensen Corporation. The accounting issue here is similar to the one discussed for convertible bonds. That is, should a gain or loss be recognized on the conversion? If the transaction is viewed as a continuation of the previous investment, then it would be appropriate to record the investment in common stock at the same cost as the preferred stock investment. Since no additional cost has been incurred, this approach is consistent with the cost basis of accounting. Using Case 1 as an example, the entry on the investor's books would be:

Investment in Sorensen Corp. Common Stock	110,000	
Investment in Sorensen Corp. Preferred Stock		110,000

If, on the other hand, the transaction is viewed as a culminating event and if the market value of the common stock is known, then it would be appropriate to record the investment in the common stock at its current market price and recognize a gain or loss on the conversion. The gain or loss is the difference between the current market price of the common stock and the investment cost of the preferred stock. Assuming, for example, the situation for Case 2 and an objective market price of $24 per share for Sorensen Corp.'s common stock at the conversion date, the entry on the investor's books would be:

Investment in Sorensen Corp. Common Stock	120,000	
Investment in Sorensen Corp. Preferred Stock		110,000
Gain on Conversion		10,000

The problems relating to the conversion of bonds for capital stock were described in Chapter 14. When either stocks or bonds have conversion rights, the company must be in a position to issue securities of the required class. Unissued or reacquired securities may be maintained by the company for this purpose. Detailed information should be given on the balance sheet or in notes to the financial statements relative to security conversion features as well as the means for meeting conversion requirements.

STOCK SPLITS AND REVERSE STOCK SPLITS

When the market price of shares is relatively high and it is felt that a lower price will result in more active trading and a wider distribution of ownership, a corporation may authorize the shares outstanding to be replaced by a larger number of shares. For example, 100,000 shares of stock, par value $5, are exchanged for 500,000 shares of stock, par value $1. Each stockholder receives 5 new shares for each share owned. The increase in shares outstanding in this manner is known as a **stock split.** The reverse procedure, replacement of shares outstanding by a smaller number of shares, may be desirable when the price of shares is low and it is felt there may be certain advantages in having a higher price for shares. The reduction of shares outstanding by combining shares is referred to as a **reverse stock split.**

After a stock split or reverse stock split, the capital stock balance for the issue remains the same; however, the change in the number of shares of stock outstanding is accompanied by a change in the par or stated value of the stock. Similarly, the amount of recorded investment for the investor remains the same, but the number of shares and cost per share will be adjusted. The change in the number of shares outstanding, as well as the change in the par or stated value, may be recorded by means of a memorandum entry.

Stock splits are sometimes effected by issuing a large stock dividend. In this case, the par value of the stock is not changed, and an amount equal to the par value of the newly issued shares is transferred to the capital stock account from either additional paid-in capital or from retained earnings. A further discussion of this type of stock split is included in Chapter 16.

BALANCE SHEET DISCLOSURE OF CONTRIBUTED CAPITAL

Contributed capital and its components should be disclosed separately from Retained Earnings in the balance sheet. Within the contributed capital section, it is important to identify the major classes of stock and the additional paid-in capital. Although it is common practice to report a single amount for additional paid-in capital, separate accounts should be provided in the ledger to identify the individual sources of additional paid-in capital, e.g., paid-in capital in excess of par or stated value, paid-in capital from treasury stock, or from forfeited stock subscriptions.

For each class of stock, a description of the major features should be disclosed, such as par or stated value, dividend preference, or conversion terms. The number of shares authorized, issued, and outstanding should also be disclosed. For an example, see the balance sheet and accompanying notes for Microsoft in Appendix A.

KEY TERMS

Business combination 634
Common stock 625
Contributed (paid-in) capital 624
Corporation 624
Cumulative preferred stock 628
Dividends in arrears 628
Fixed stock option plan 644
Legal capital 625
Noncumulative preferred stock 628
Owners' equity 628
Par value 626
Participating preferred stock 628
Partnership 624
Performance-based stock option plan 644
Pooling of interests 634
Preferred stock 625
Proprietorship 624
Purchase 634
Redeemable preferred stock 629
Retained earnings 624
Reverse stock split 654
Stated value 627
Stock appreciation rights (SARs) 649
Stock options 640
Stock rights 640
Stock split 654
Stock warrants 640
Treasury stock 636

QUESTIONS

1. What are the basic rights inherent in the ownership of capital stock? What modifications of these basic rights are usually found in preferred stock?
2. What are the two major classifications of contributed capital?
3. Distinguish between cumulative preferred stock and noncumulative preferred stock. If a company with cumulative preferred stock outstanding fails to declare dividends during the year, what disclosure should be made in the financial statements?
4. What is callable preferred stock? Redeemable preferred stock? Convertible preferred stock?
5. Why are Capital Stock Subscriptions Receivable classified as equity offsets rather than assets?
6. The Merrill Co. treats proceeds from capital stock subscription defaults as miscellaneous revenue. (a) Do you approve of this practice? Explain. (b) What alternatives would the Merrill Co. have when dealing with subscription defaults? (c) What limits the choice among the alternatives in (b)?
7. Explain the accounting principle followed in recording the issuance of capital stock in exchange for nonmonetary assets or services.
8. Why might a company purchase its own stock?
9. The Daytime Co. reports treasury stock as a current asset, explaining that it intends to sell the stock soon to acquire working capital. Do you approve of this reporting?
10. (a) What is the basic difference between the cost method and the par value method of accounting for treasury stock? (b) How will total stockholders' equity differ, if at all, under the two methods?
11. There is frequently a difference between the purchase price and the selling price of treasury stock. Why isn't this difference properly shown as an income statement item, especially in view of accounting pronouncements that restrict entries to Retained Earnings?
12. (a) What entries should be made on both the issuer's books and the investor's books when stock rights are issued to stockholders? (b) What entries should be made by both issuer and investor when stock is issued on the exercise of rights? (c) What information, if any, should appear on the company's balance sheet relative to outstanding rights?
13. The FASB has recommended some significant changes to accounting for employee stock options. Describe the most significant changes and explain why they were recommended.
14. What determines the measurement date for purposes of a stock option plan valuation?
15. Distinguish between fixed stock options and performance-based stock options.
16. What is the appropriate accounting treatment for stock options that provide for a cash settlement equal to the difference between the option and market prices of the stock? How does this accounting treatment differ from that applied to traditional stock options that anticipate an actual transfer of company stock?
17. Preferred stockholders of the Lexus Corporation exchange their holdings for no-par common stock in accordance with terms of the preferred stock issue. How should this conversion be reported on the corporation books?
18. The controller of Williams Company contends that the redemption of preferred stock at less than its issuance price should be reported as an increase in Retained Earnings, since redemption at more than issuance price calls for a decrease in Retained Earnings. How would you answer the controller's argument?
19. Define a stock split and identify the major objectives of this corporate action.

DISCUSSION CASES

Case 15—1 (Should par value be used to determine the amount of contributed capital?)

The Raton Company, in payment for services, issues 5,000 shares of common stock to persons organizing and promoting the company and another 20,000 shares in exchange for properties believed to have valuable mineral rights. The par value of the stock, $10 per share, is used in recording the consideration for the shares. Shortly after organization, the company decides to sell the properties and use the proceeds for another venture. The properties are sold for $265,000. What accounting issues are involved? How would you record the sale of properties and why?

Case 15—2 (Is the sum of the parts worth more than the whole?)

In 1988, four companies offered investors the opportunity to purchase new securities called "unbundled stock units." These companies (American Express, Dow Chemical, Pfizer, and Sara Lee) argued that the common stock security is undervalued when sold as a single unit. So they proposed to "unbundle" the value represented by common stock and sell three new securities as an alternative to the common stock certificate. The new security package would contain a 30-year bond paying interest at the stock's current dividend rate; a preferred stock that initially would pay no dividends but would match any dividend increases on the company's common stock over the next 30 years; and a security closely resembling a stock warrant that would allow investors to profit from stock appreciation. In effect, the three new securities would provide a package allowing investors to profit explicitly in the same way that common stockholders do with a single security, i.e., from dividends, from dividend increases, and from capital appreciation in the value of common stock. What these companies were counting on is that the value of the three securities would be worth more to investors than common stock sold as a single security.

Why might investors be willing to pay a premium for such a package, i.e., pay more for the three securities than for the single common stock security? What disadvantages can you see for investors in exchanging their common stock for the unbundled stock units?

Source: "Package Deal," *The Wall Street Journal,* December 6, 1988.

Case 15—3 (Conversion of preferred stock)

Colter Corporation suspended dividend payments on all four classes of capital stock outstanding because of a downturn in the economy. The four classes of stock include: 7% preferred stock, cumulative, $50 par; 5% preferred stock, noncumulative, convertible, $35 par; 9% preferred stock, noncumulative, $80 par; and common stock. Fifteen thousand shares of each class of stock were outstanding. Dividends had been paid through 1993. Colter did not pay dividends in 1994 or 1995. In 1996, the economy improved and a proposal to pay a dividend of $1.50 per share of common stock was made.

You own 100 shares of the 5%, noncumulative, convertible preferred stock and have been thinking of converting those 100 shares to common stock at the existing conversion rate of 3 to 1 (3 shares of common for 1 share of preferred). The rate is scheduled to drop to 2 to 1 at the end of 1996. Because the price of common stock has been rising rapidly, you are trying to decide between retaining your preferred stock or converting to common stock before the price goes higher and the ratio is lowered.

Assuming there is no conversion of preferred stock, how much cash does Colter need to pay the proposed dividend? What are the merits of converting your stock at this time as opposed to waiting until after the dividend is paid and the conversion ratio decreases? Explain the issues involved.

Case 15—4 (Which kind of bonus would you prefer?)

Many companies have incentive compensation plans whereby executives receive bonuses based on the reported net income of the company. Another kind of incentive plan gives executives options on the company's stock. What are the advantages and disadvantages of an income-based incentive plan? of a stock option plan?

Case 15—5 (What is a stock warrant worth?)

A stock warrant entitles the owner to buy a specified number of shares of stock at a specified price. Suppose that a certain stock warrant entitled the owner to buy one share of common stock for $50, while the current market price of a share of common stock is $40. Does the warrant have any value? What factors would influence the value of the warrant?

Case 15—6 (Treasury stock transactions—You can't lose!)

The following is adapted from an article appearing in *Forbes:*

The board of Hospital Corp. of America authorized the buyback of 12 million of the firm's own shares at a total cost of $564 million. However, after the stock market crash of 1987, HCA's shares were trading at only 31 1/8. So, HCA was now out $190.5 million on its investment—right? Common sense would answer yes, but beyond common sense lurks the logic of accounting. According to generally accepted accounting principles, HCA didn't lose a penny on the buyback. Call it a no-risk investment. In this era of stock market volatility, stock buybacks offer firms the opportunity to tell shareholders that they have a terrific investment—without ever having to own up to the bad news if it turns sour.

Consider the criticism in the paragraph above and evaluate the reasonableness of the accounting for treasury stock transactions.

Source: Penelope Wang, "Losses? What Losses?" *Forbes* (February 8, 1988), p. 118.

Case 15—7 (Fiat's treatment of treasury stock)

The Fiat Group is the largest investor-owned industrial group in Italy. Fiat is known in the United States primarily for its Fiat, Ferrari, and Alfa Romeo automobiles.

A condensed version of Fiat's 1992 balance sheet is shown below. All amounts are in billions of lire. On December 31, 1992, lire were trading at 1,475 per 1 U.S. dollar.

ASSETS	(billions of lire)
Treasury stock	537
Other assets	11,046
LIABILITIES AND STOCKHOLDERS' EQUITY	
Total liabilities	2,566
Stockholders' equity and reserves	9,017

The notes to the financial statements read as follows (in part):

"Treasury stock is recorded among assets since such shares are stated at purchase cost."

Explain how Fiat's treatment of treasury stock differs from the treatment prescribed by U.S. generally accepted accounting principles (GAAP). Prepare a restated balance sheet (in lire) for Fiat that conforms with U.S. GAAP.

Case 15—8 (Debt-to-equity ratio and mandatory redeemable preferred stock)

Below is a summary of the liability and equity section of the balance sheet of The Circle K Corporation as of April 30, 1989. The amounts are in thousands.

Current liabilities	$ 350,445
Long-term debt	1,103,762
Deferred income taxes	93,045
Other liabilities	119,792
Mandatory redeemable preferred stock	47,500
Stockholders' equity	330,396

In the Management Discussion and Analysis portion of the annual report, Circle K reports a "debt-to-equity ratio" of 3.34. Show how Circle K computed this "debt-to-equity ratio." What might be a better name for the ratio? Mandatory redeemable preferred stock is preferred stock that must be redeemed by the issuing firm. What aspects of mandatory redeemable preferred stock are like debt? like equity?

Case 15—9 **(Equity section for Grand Metropolitan)**

Grand Metropolitan PLC is based in the United Kingdom. It sells food and dairy products and also operates 1,500 pubs and 450 restaurants in the United Kingdom and Ireland. Grand Metropolitan is best known in the United States for its food products (Pillsbury baked goods, Green Giant vegetables), pet foods (ALPO), wines and spirits (Smirnoff Vodka, Lancers, Cinzano), eyecare products (Pearle Vision), and fast food restaurant (Burger King).

The equity section from Grand Metropolitan's September 30, 1992, balance sheet is given below. All amounts are in millions of pounds.

Called-up share capital	526
Share premium account	599
Revaluation reserve	666
Goodwill reserve	(2,205)
Profit and loss account	4,173

The revaluation and goodwill reserve accounts included, among other things, the following items:

(a) Goodwill acquired.
(b) Surplus on revaluation of property. This item resulted from writing up assets to their estimated market values.
(c) Capitalization of brand names. This item resulted from recording as an asset the estimated value of brand names.

Refer to Grand Metropolitan's equity section and identify the comparable item to the following: common stock at par, additional paid-in capital, and retained earnings. Of the three items listed as appearing in the revaluation and goodwill reserves section, which, if any, would be acceptable under U.S. accounting principles?

Case 15—10 **(Microsoft's Stock Option Plans)**

One of the notes to Microsoft's 1993 financial statements is titled "Employee Stock and Savings Plans." (See Appendix A.) The note discloses that Microsoft's employee stock purchase plan allows eligible employees to purchase Microsoft common stock at 85% of its market price. The note also reveals that incentive options granted to directors, officers, and employees have an exercise price that is at least as great as the market price of the common stock on the date of grant. Why doesn't Microsoft's plan allow employees to purchase common stock at a lower percentage of market value, e.g., at 80% of market price? Why doesn't Microsoft set the incentive option exercise price at less than the stock price on the grant date?

Case 15—11 **(Understanding the Minimum Value Method)**

Derrald Han is considering buying an option to purchase a share of stock in Cheon Company. Derrald is trying to calculate the appropriate price to pay for the option. The option exercise price is equal to the current stock price of $50, and the option cannot be exercised until five years have elapsed. Cheon Company has historically paid an annual cash dividend of $2 per share. In valuing the option, Derrald has decided to view it in the following way: Buying the option allows a person to, in effect, buy the stock now but avoid paying for it until five years from now. However, in the interim, the person does not receive any cash dividends that are paid.

Derrald has prepared the following option value calculation (assuming a discount rate of 10%):

Current stock price	$50.00
Less: Present value of exercise price ($50 × .6209*)	31.05

Value of payment deferral	$18.95
Less: Present value of cash dividend lost ($2 × 3.7908**)	7.58
Value of option	$11.37

*Present value factor for 5 periods at 10% (Table II, page 268)
**Present value annuity factor, 5 periods at 10% (Table IV, page 270)

Derrald's option valuation technique has been called the "minimum value method" by the FASB. Why do you think $11.37 is the *minimum* value of the option?

EXERCISES

Exercise 15—12 (Issuance of common stock)

The Verdero Company is authorized to issue 100,000 shares of $30 par value common stock. Verdero has the following transactions:

(a) Issued 20,000 shares at par value; received cash.
(b) Issued 250 shares to attorneys for services in securing the corporate charter and for preliminary legal costs of organizing the corporation. The value of the services was $9,000.
(c) Issued 300 shares, valued objectively at $10,000, to the corporate promoters.
(d) Issued 12,500 shares of stock in exchange for buildings valued at $295,000 and land valued at $80,000. (The building was originally acquired by the investor for $250,000 and has $100,000 of accumulated depreciation; the land was acquired for $30,000.)
(e) Received cash for 6,500 shares of stock sold at $38 per share.
(f) Issued 8,000 shares at $45 per share; received cash.

1. Record the above transactions in journal entry form for Verdero Company.
2. Record the above transactions in journal entry form for the investors.

Exercise 15—13 (Par and stated values)

At the time of formation, the Olmstead Corporation was authorized to issue 100,000 shares of common stock. Olmstead later received cash from the issuance of 25,000 shares at $24.50 per share. Record the entries for the issuance of the common stock under each of the following independent assumptions.

(a) Stock has a par value of $22 per share.
(b) Stock has a stated value of $20 per share.
(c) Stock has no par or stated value.

Exercise 15—14 (Dividends per share; cumulative and noncumulative features)

The Anderson Company paid dividends at the end of each year as follows: 1994, $150,000; 1995, $240,000; 1996, $560,000. Determine the amount of dividends per share paid on common and preferred stock for each year, assuming independent capital structures as follows:

(a) 300,000 shares of no-par common; 10,000 shares of $100 par, 9% noncumulative preferred.
(b) 250,000 shares of no-par common; 20,000 shares of $100 par, 9% noncumulative preferred.
(c) 250,000 shares of no-par common; 20,000 shares of $100 par, 9% cumulative preferred.
(d) 250,000 shares of $10 par common; 30,000 shares of $100 par, 9% cumulative preferred.

Exercise 15—15 (Dividends—different classes of stock)

Sun Spot Inc. began operations on June 30, 1994, and issued 40,000 shares of $10 par common stock on that date. On December 31, 1994, Sun Spot declared and paid $25,600 in dividends. After a vote of the board of directors, Sun Spot issued 24,000 shares of 6% cumulative, $12 par, preferred stock on January 1, 1996. On December 31, 1996, Sun Spot declared and paid $15,500 in dividends and again on December 31, 1997, Sun Spot declared and paid $28,660 in dividends. Determine the amount of dividends to be distributed to each class of stock for each of Sun Spot's dividend payments.

Exercise 15—16 (Computing liquidation amounts)

The stockholders' equity for the Baum Company on July 1, 1996, is given below.

Contributed capital:	
Preferred stock, cumulative, $10 stated value, 37,000 shares outstanding, entitled upon involuntary liquidation to $12 per share plus dividends in arrears amounting to $4 per share on July 1, 1996	$370,000
Common stock, $2 stated value, 90,000 shares outstanding	180,000
Paid-in capital from sale of common stock at more than stated value	200,000
Retained earnings	56,000
Total stockholders' equity	$806,000

Determine the amounts that would be paid to each class of stockholders if the company is liquidated on this date, assuming cash available for stockholders after meeting all of the creditors' claims is (a) $300,000; (b) $500,000; (c) $640,000.

Exercise 15—17 (Issuance of capital stock with subscriptions)

The Timpview Company was incorporated on January 1, 1996, with the following authorized capitalization:

20,000 shares of common stock, stated value $50 per share.
5,000 shares of 7% cumulative preferred stock, par value $15 per share.

Give the entries required for each of the following transactions:

(a) Issued 12,000 shares of common stock for a total of $672,000 and 3,000 shares of preferred stock at $20 per share.
(b) Subscriptions were received for 2,500 shares of common stock at a price of $52. A 30% down payment is received.
(c) Collected the remaining amount owed on the stock subscriptions and issued the stock.
(d) The remaining authorized shares of common stock are sold at $57.50 per share.

Exercise 15—18 (Acquisition and retirement of stock)

The Steinbeck Company reported the following balances related to common stock as of December 31, 1995:

Common stock, $20 par, 100,000 shares issued and outstanding	$2,000,000
Paid-in capital in excess of par	100,000

The company purchased and immediately retired 5,000 shares at $26 on August 1, 1996, and 12,000 shares at $18 on December 31, 1996. Give the entries to record the acquisition and retirement of the common stock. (Assume all shares were originally sold at the same price.)

Exercise 15—19 (Treasury stock: par value and cost methods)

The stockholders' equity of the Thomas Company as of December 31, 1995, was as follows:

Common stock, $15 par, authorized 275,000 shares; 240,000 shares issued and outstanding	$3,600,000
Paid-in capital in excess of par	480,000
Retained earnings	900,000

On June 1, 1996, Thomas reacquired 15,000 shares of its common stock at $16. The following transactions occurred in 1996 with regard to these shares:

July 1	Sold 5,000 shares at $20.
Aug. 1	Sold 7,000 shares at $14.
Sep. 1	Retired 1,000 shares.

1. Using the *cost method* to account for treasury stock:
   (a) Prepare the journal entries to record all treasury stock transactions in 1996.
   (b) Prepare the stockholders' equity section of the balance sheet at December 31, 1996, assuming retained earnings of $1,005,000 (before the effects of treasury stock transactions).
2. Using the *par value method* to account for treasury stock:
   (a) Prepare the journal entries to record all treasury stock transactions in 1996.
   (b) Prepare the stockholders' equity section of the balance sheet at December 31, 1996, assuming retained earnings of $1,005,000 (before the effects of treasury stock transactions).

Exercise 15—20 (Stock rights)

J. Matson bought 2,000 shares of Layton Mining Co. common stock for $15 per share on April 3, 1995. On June 22, 1996, Layton Mining Co. issued stock rights to its holders of common stock, one right for each share owned. The terms of the exercise required 5 rights plus $15 for each share purchased. Layton stock was selling ex-rights for $19 per share, and the rights have a market value of $1 each. On September 1, 1996, Matson exercised 1,000 rights, and on October 15, 1996, sold the remaining rights at $1.40 each.

What entries would be required to reflect the stock rights transactions in Matson's accounting records?

Exercise 15—21 (Stock rights)

The Jordan Co. holds stock of Caltex Inc. acquired as follows:

	Shares	Total Cost
Lot A, 1994	75	$ 6,000
Lot B, 1995	125	11,000

In 1996, Jordan Co. receives 200 rights to purchase Caltex Inc. stock at $75 per share. The shares have a par value of $70. Six rights are required to purchase one share. At issue date, rights had a market value of $4 each and stock was selling ex-rights at $96. Jordan Co. used rights to purchase 30 additional shares of Caltex Inc. Subsequently, the market price of the stock fell to $92, and Jordan Co. allowed the unexercised rights to lapse. Both companies use the first-in, first-out method of identifying stock rights exercised.

1. What entries are required to record the preceding events in Jordan's accounting records?
2. What entries are required to record the preceding events in Caltex's accounting records?

Exercise 15—22 (Accounting for stock warrants)

The Western Company wants to raise additional equity capital. After analysis of the available options, the company decides to issue 1,000 shares of $20 par preferred stock with detachable warrants. The package of the stock and warrants sells for $90. The warrants enable the holder to purchase 1,000 shares of $25 par common stock at $30 per share. Immediately following the issuance of the stock, the stock warrants are selling at $9 per share. The market value of the preferred stock without the warrants is $85.

1. Prepare a journal entry for Western Company to record the issuance of the preferred stock and the attached warrants.
2. Assuming that all the warrants are exercised, prepare a journal entry for Western to record the exercise of the warrants.
3. Assuming that only 80% of the warrants are exercised, prepare a journal entry for Western to record the exercise and expiration of the warrants.

Exercise 15—23 (Fixed stock options)

On January 1, 1995, the Layton Hardware Company established a fixed stock option plan for its senior employees. A total of 60,000 options were issued that permitted employees to purchase 60,000 shares of $20 par common stock at $48 per share. Options were exercisable on January

1, 1998 and could be exercised anytime during 1998. Market prices for Layton common stock for 1995-1998 were as follows:

January 1, 1995	$55
December 31, 1995	58
December 31, 1996	65
December 31, 1997	70
December 31, 1998	66

Assume that all options were exercised on December 31, 1998. Prepare all entries required under APB Opinion No. 25 for the years 1995-1998.

Exercise 15—24 (Accounting for compensatory stock options)

The stockholders of the Zollinger Co. on December 24, 1989, approved a plan granting certain officers of the company nontransferable fixed options to buy 100,000 shares of no-par common stock at $32 per share. Stock was selling at this time at $40 per share. The option plan provides that the officers must be employed by the company for the next five years, that options can be exercised after January 1, 1995, and that options will expire at the end of 1996. One of the officers who had been granted options for 20,000 shares left the company at the beginning of 1993; remaining officers exercised their rights under the option plan at the end of 1996.

Give the entries that should be made on the books of the corporation at the end of each year for 1989-1996 inclusive. The market price of the stock at January 1, 1995, was $60 per share.

Exercise 15—25 (Accounting for performance-based stock option plan-APB Opinion No. 25)

The Rhiener Corporation initiated a performance-based employee stock option plan on January 1, 1995. The performance base for the plan is 1997 net sales. The plan provides for stock options to be awarded to the employees as a group on the following basis:

Level	Net Sales Range	Options Granted
1	< $250,000	10,000
2	$250,000 – $499,999	20,000
3	$500,000 – $1,000,000	30,000
4	> $1,000,000	40,000

The options become exercisable on January 1, 1998. The option price established for the stock is $20 per share. The market prices of Rhiener stock on selected dates in 1995 – 1997 were as follows:

January 1, 1995	$25
December 31, 1995	30
December 31, 1996	35
December 31, 1997	32

1997 sales estimates as of selected dates were as follows:

January 1, 1995	$400,000
December 31, 1995	450,000
December 31, 1996	550,000

Actual sales for 1997 were $700,000. What compensation expense should Rhiener report for the years 1995, 1996, and 1997 related to the stock option plan under the provisions of APB Opinion No. 25?

Exercise 15—26 (Performance-based stock option plan—1993 FASB exposure draft)

Assume the same facts as in Exercise 15-25, but assume the FASB exposure draft relating to stock options is in effect. Assume that application of an option valuation technique yields $9

as the estimated value of the option at the grant date. Under these conditions, what compensation expense should Rhiener report for 1995, 1996, and 1997?

Exercise 15—27 (Performance-based stock option plan — variable exercise price)

On March 31, 1993, the board of directors of Allied Industries approved a stock option plan for its twenty executives to purchase 500 shares of $25 par common stock each. The plan further indicated that the executives must remain with the company until March 31, 1996, at which time they could exercise their options. The exercise price is 90% of the market price of the stock on December 31, 1995. All outstanding options expire on December 31, 1997.

Assuming the following stock prices and that all options are exercised on June 27, 1996, give the journal entries for the company for its calendar years 1993, 1994, 1995, and 1996 under APB Opinion No. 25. Note: On any given date the stock price on that date is viewed as the best estimate of what the stock price will be on December 31, 1995.

Date	Stock Price
March 31, 1993	$30
December 31, 1993	35
December 31, 1994	45
December 31, 1995	42
March 31, 1996	45
June 27, 1996	46

Exercise 15—28 (Stock appreciation rights)

San Juan Corporation established a stock option plan that provides for cash payment to employees based on the appreciation of stock prices from an established option price. The plan was instituted on January 1, 1996 and provides benefits to employees who work for the following three years. Cash payments to employees will be made on January 1, 1999, and will equal the excess of the stock price over the option price on that date. Each employee received 500 options. Twenty employees were eligible for the plan, but two of them quit during the third year of service, so only 18 employees were given the cash payment.

The option price established for the stock is $10 per share. The market price of San Juan stock on selected dates in 1996-1998 was as follows:

January 1, 1996	$15
December 31, 1996	16
December 31, 1997	20
December 31, 1998	18

Prepare the journal entries on San Juan's books for the years 1996, 1997, 1998, and 1999 related to this plan under the provisions of APB Opinion No. 25.

Exercise 15—29 (Convertible preferred stock)

Stockholders' equity for the Yuri Co. on December 31 was as follows:

Preferred stock, $15 par, 30,000 shares issued and outstanding	$ 450,000
Paid-in capital in excess of par—preferred stock	90,000
Common stock, $10 par, 150,000 shares issued and outstanding	1,500,000
Paid-in capital in excess of par—common stock	750,000
Retained earnings	1,450,000

Preferred stock is convertible into common stock.

1. Give the entry made on Yuri Co.'s books assuming 2,000 shares of preferred are converted under each assumption listed:
   (a) Preferred shares are convertible into common on a share-for-share basis.
   (b) Each share of preferred stock is convertible into 4 shares of common.
   (c) Each share of preferred stock is convertible into 1.5 shares of common.

2. Assuming that all 30,000 shares of the preferred stock are converted into common stock under the conditions in 1a, 1b, and 1c above and that Stadium Inc. owns 45% of Yuri Co.'s preferred stock, give the entry made on the books of Stadium Inc. given the following:
   (a) The stock conversion is recorded at the cost of the preferred stock.
   (b) The stock conversion is recorded at the current market price of the common stock. The common stock was selling at $21 per share on the date of conversion.
   (c) The stock conversion is recorded at the current market price of the common stock. The common stock was selling at $11 per share on the date of the conversion.

(Assume all of Yuri Co.'s preferred shares were originally acquired by Stadium Inc. at the same price.)

Exercise 15—30 (Analysis of owners' equity)

From the following information, reconstruct the journal entries that were made by the Rivers Corporation during 1996.

	December 31, 1996		December 31, 1995	
	Amount	Shares	Amount	Shares
Common stock	$175,000	—	—	6,000
Paid-in capital in excess of par	54,250	—	36,000	
Paid-in capital from treasury stock	1,000	200	—	—
Retained earnings	76,500*	—	49,000	—
Treasury stock	15,000	300	—	—

*Includes net income for 1996 of $40,000. There were no dividends.

2,500 shares of common stock (issued when the company was formed) were purchased at the beginning of 1996 and were retired later in the year. The cost method is used to record treasury stock transactions.

PROBLEMS

Problem 15—31 (Journalizing stock transactions)

Vicars Company began operations on January 1. Authorized were 20,000 shares of $10 par value common stock and 4,000 shares of $100 par value convertible preferred stock. The following transactions involving stockholders' equity occurred during the first year of operations:

Jan.	1	Issued 500 shares of common stock to the corporation promoters in exchange for property valued at $17,000 and services valued at $7,000. The property had cost the promoters $9,000 three years before and was carried on the promoters' books at $5,000.
Feb.	23	Issued 1,000 shares of convertible preferred stock with a par value of $100 per share. Each share can be converted to 5 shares of common stock. The stock was issued at a price of $150 per share, and the company paid $7,500 to an agent for selling the shares.
Mar.	10	Sold 3,000 shares of the common stock for $39 per share. Issue costs were $2,500.
Apr.	10	4,000 shares of common stock were sold under stock subscriptions at $45 per share. No shares are issued until a subscription contract is paid in full. No cash was received.
July	14	Exchanged 700 shares of common stock and 140 shares of preferred stock for a building with a fair market value of $51,000. The building was originally purchased for $38,000 by the investors and has a book value of $22,000. In addition, 600 shares of common stock were sold for $24,000 in cash.

Aug. 3 Received payments in full for half of the stock subscriptions and payments on account on the rest of the subscriptions. Total cash received was $140,000. Shares of stock were issued for the subscriptions paid in full.

Dec. 1 Declared a cash dividend of $10 per share on preferred stock, payable on December 31 to stockholders of record on December 15, and a $2-per-share cash dividend on common stock, payable on January 5 of the following year to stockholders of record on December 15. (No dividends are paid on unissued subscribed stock.)

Dec. 31 Received notice from holders of stock subscriptions for 800 shares that they would not pay further on the subscriptions since the price of the stock had fallen to $25 per share. The amount still due on those contracts was $30,000. Amounts previously paid on the contracts are forfeited according to the agreements.

Net income for the first year of operations was $60,000. Vicars uses an income summary account.

Instructions:

1. Prepare journal entries to record the preceding transactions on Vicars' books.
2. Prepare the stockholders' equity section of the balance sheet at December 31 for Vicars.

Problem 15—32 (Stockholders' equity transactions and balance sheet presentation)

The Pacific Basin Corporation was organized on September 1, 1996, with authorized capital stock of 200,000 shares of 9% cumulative preferred with a $40 par value and 1,000,000 shares of no-par common stock with a $30 stated value. During the balance of the year, the following transactions relating to capital stock were completed:

Oct. 1 Subscriptions were received for 300,000 shares of common stock at $42, payable $22 down and the balance in two equal installments due November 1 and December 1. On the same date, 16,500 shares of common stock were issued to Jan Smoot in exchange for her business. Assets transferred to the corporation were valued as follows: land, $210,000; buildings, $250,000; equipment, $50,000; merchandise, $110,000. Liabilities of the business assumed by the corporation were: mortgage payable, $41,000; accounts payable, $11,000; accrued interest on mortgage, $550. No goodwill is recognized in recording the issuance of the stock for net assets.

3 Subscriptions were received for 120,000 shares of preferred stock at $45, payable $15 down and the balance in two equal installments due November 1 and December 1.

Nov. 1 Amounts due on this date were collected from all common and preferred stock subscribers.

12 Subscriptions were received for 480,000 shares of common stock at $44, payable $22 down and the balance in two equal installments due December 1 and January 1.

Dec. 1 Amounts due on this date were collected from all common stock and preferred stock subscribers and stock fully paid for was issued.

Instructions:

1. Prepare journal entries to record the foregoing transactions.
2. Prepare the contributed capital section of stockholders' equity for the corporation as of December 31, including any equity offsets.

Problem 15—33 (Reconstruction of equity transactions)

The Manti Company had the following account balances on its balance sheet at December 31, 1996, the end of its first year of operations. All stock was issued on a subscription basis.

Common Stock Subscriptions Receivable	$150,000
Common Stock, $25 par	75,000
Common Stock Subscribed	225,000
Paid-In Capital in Excess of Par—Common Stock	60,000
8% Preferred Stock, $100 par	120,000
Paid-In Capital in Excess of Par—8% Preferred Stock	60,000
10% Preferred Stock, $50 par	25,000
Retained Earnings	10,000

The reported net income for 1996 was $55,000. Manti uses an income summary account.

Instructions: From the data given, reconstruct in summary form the journal entries to record all transactions involving the company's stockholders. Indicate the amount of dividends distributed on each class of stock.

Problem 15—34 (Comprehensive analysis and reporting of stockholders' equity)

The Lasser Company has two classes of capital stock outstanding: 9%, $20 par preferred and $70 par common. During the fiscal year ending November 30, 1996, the company was active in transactions affecting the stockholders' equity. The following summarizes these transactions:

Type of Transaction	Number of Shares	Price Per Share
(a) Issue of preferred stock	10,000	$28
(b) Issue of common stock	35,000	70
(c) Reacquisition and retirement of preferred stock	2,000	30
(d) Purchase of treasury stock—common (reported at cost)	5,000	80
(e) Stock split—common (par value reduced to $35)	2 for 1	
(f) Reissue of treasury stock—common (after stock split)	5,000	52

Balances of the accounts in the stockholders' equity section of the November 30, 1995, balance sheet were:

Preferred Stock, 50,000 shares	$1,000,000
Common Stock, 100,000 shares	7,000,000
Paid-In Capital in Excess of Par—Preferred	400,000
Paid-In Capital in Excess of Par—Common	1,200,000
Retained Earnings	550,000

Dividends were paid at the end of the fiscal year on the common stock at $1.20 per share and on the preferred stock at the preferred rate. Net income for the year was $850,000.

Instructions: Based on the preceding data, prepare the stockholders' equity section of the balance sheet as of November 30, 1996. (Note: A work sheet beginning with November 30, 1995, balances and providing for transactions for the current year will facilitate the preparation of this section of the balance sheet.)

Problem 15—35 (Accounting for various capital stock transactions)

The stockholders' equity section of Webster Inc. showed the following data on December 31, 1995: common stock, $30 par, 300,000 shares authorized, 250,000 shares issued and outstanding, $7,500,000; paid-in capital in excess of par $300,000; options outstanding, $150,000;

retained earnings, $480,000. The stock options were granted to key executives and provided them the right to acquire 30,000 shares of common stock at $35 per share. The stock was selling at $40 at the time the options were granted.

The following transactions occurred during 1996:

Mar.	31	Exercised 4,500 options outstanding at December 31, 1995. The market price per share was $44 at this time.
Apr.	1	The company issued bonds of $2,000,000 at par, giving each $1,000 bond a detachable warrant enabling the holder to purchase 2 shares of stock at $40 for a 1-year period. Market values immediately following issuance of the bonds were: $4 per warrant and $998 per $1,000 bond without the warrant.
June	30	The company issued rights to stockholders (1 right on each share, exercisable within a 30-day period) permitting holders to acquire 1 share at $40 with every 10 rights submitted. Shares were selling for $43 at this time. All but 6,000 rights were exercised on July 31, and the additional stock was issued.
Sep.	30	All warrants issued with the bonds on April 1 were exercised.
Nov.	30	The market price per share dropped to $33 and options came due. Since the market price was below the option price, no remaining options were exercised.

Instructions:

1. Give entries to record the foregoing transactions.
2. Prepare the stockholders' equity section of the balance sheet as of December 31, 1996 (assume net income of $210,000 for 1996).

Problem 15—36 (Accounting for various capital stock transactions)

Pineview Co., organized on June 1, 1995, was authorized to issue stock as follows:

80,000 shares of preferred 9% stock, convertible, $100 par
250,000 shares of common stock, $25 stated value

During the remainder of the Pineview Co.'s fiscal year ending May 31, 1996, the following transactions were completed in the order given.

(a) 30,000 shares of preferred stock were subscribed for at $105 and 90,000 shares of common stock were subscribed for at $26. Both subscriptions were payable 30% upon subscription, the balance in one payment.
(b) The second subscription payment was received, except one subscriber for 6,000 shares of common stock defaulted on payment. The full amount paid by this subscriber was returned, and all the fully paid stock was issued.
(c) 15,000 shares of common stock were reacquired by purchase at $28. (Treasury stock is recorded at cost.)
(d) Each share of preferred stock was converted into 4 shares of common stock.
(e) The treasury stock was exchanged for machinery with a fair market value of $430,000.
(f) There was a 2-for-1 stock split, and the stated value of the new common stock is $12.50.
(g) Net income was $83,000. Pineview uses an income summary account.

Instructions:

1. Give the journal entries to record the foregoing transactions. (For net income, give the entry to close the income summary account to Retained Earnings.)
2. Prepare the stockholders' equity section as of May 31, 1996.

Problem 15—37 (Issuance, reacquisition, and resale of capital stock)

Tucker Company had the following transactions occur during 1996:

(a) Issued 8,000 shares of common stock to the founders for land valued at $450,000. Par value of the common stock is $30 per share.
(b) Issued 5,000 shares of $100 par preferred stock for cash at $110.
(c) Sold 1,000 shares of common stock to the company president for $60 per share.

(d) Purchased 400 shares of outstanding preferred stock issued in (b) for cash at par.
(e) Purchased 500 shares of the outstanding common stock issued in (a) for $55 per share.
(f) Reissued 150 shares of repurchased preferred stock at $102.
(g) Reissued 300 shares of reacquired common stock for $58 per share.
(h) Repurchased 100 shares of the common stock sold in (g) for $53 per share. These same 100 shares were later reissued for $50 per share.

Instructions:

1. Prepare the necessary entries to record the preceding transactions involving Tucker preferred stock. Assume that the par value method is used for recording treasury stock.
2. Prepare the necessary entries for the common stock transactions assuming that the cost method is used for recording treasury stock.

Problem 15—38 (Treasury stock transactions)

Transactions that affected Barter Company's stockholders' equity during 1996, the first year of operations, are given below.

(a) Issued 30,000 shares of 9% preferred stock, $20 par, at $26.
(b) Issued 50,000 shares of $30 par common stock at $33.
(c) Purchased and immediately retired 4,000 shares of preferred stock at $28.
(d) Purchased 6,000 shares of its own common stock at $35.
(e) Reissued 1,000 shares of treasury stock at $37.

No dividends were declared in 1996, and net income for 1996 was $185,000.

Instructions:

1. Record each of the transactions. Assume treasury stock acquisitions are recorded at cost.
2. Prepare the stockholders' equity section of the balance sheet at December 31, 1996.

Problem 15—39 (Accounting for stock options)

The board of directors of the Mellencamp Company adopted a fixed stock option plan to supplement the salaries of certain executives of the company. Options to buy common stock were granted as follows:

Date	Employee	Number of Shares	Option Price	Price of Shares at Date of Grant
Jan. 10, 1993	Q. L. Peck	75,000	$20	$21
June 30, 1993	A. G. Byrd	50,000	25	26
June 30, 1993	K. C. Nelson	20,000	25	26

Options are nontransferable and can be exercised 3 years after date of grant providing the executive is still in the employ of the company. Options expire 2 years after the date they can first be exercised. Nelson left the employ of the company at the beginning of 1995. Stock options were exercised as follows:

Date	Employee	Number of Shares	Price of Shares at Date of Exercise
Jan. 15, 1996	Q. L. Peck	60,000	$45
Dec. 20, 1996	Q. L. Peck	15,000	36
Dec. 22, 1996	A. G. Byrd	50,000	32

Stock of the company has a $14 par value. The accounting period for the company is the calendar year.

Instructions: Give all entries that would be made on the books of the company relative to the stock option agreement for the period 1993 to 1996 inclusive.

Problem 15—40 (Performance-based stock options)

Bauil Corporation, a new environmental control company, initiated a performance-based stock option plan for its management on January 1, 1995. The plan provided for the granting of a variable number of stock options to management personnel who worked for the entire four-year period ending December 31, 1998, depending on the net income earned by the company in 1998. No options were granted for the first $50,000 of net income. Thereafter, the following options were available based on the performance measure of net income.

$50,000–$99,999	5,000 Stock options
$100,000–$124,999	10,000 Stock options
$125,000–$149,999	15,000 Stock options
$150,000 or more	25,000 Stock options

The option price for the $5 par common stock was $25 per share.

Assume the market price for the Bauil stock and Bauil's forecasted 1998 net income were as follows at each of the following dates:

	Stock Price	Forecasted 1998 Income
January 1, 1995	$27	$110,000
December 31,1995	30	130,000
December 31,1996	29	160,000
December 31,1997	35	140,000
December 31,1998	36	130,000 (actual)

Instructions:

(a) Prepare journal entries related to the stock options of Bauil for the period 1995-1998 assuming that all available options are exercised on December 31, 1998. Use the provisions of APB Opinion No. 25.

(b) Prepare journal entries related to the stock options of Bauil for the period 1995-1998 using the provisions of the FASB 1993 exposure draft. Assume that an option valuation technique was used on the grant date to compute a value of $7 for each option.

Problem 15—41 (Performance-based stock options — variable exercise price)

The Ruez Manufacturing Company adopted an executive stock option plan on January 1, 1993. The plan states that all executives remaining with the firm until the exercisable date would be eligible for the stock. The options are exercisable beginning January 1, 1996, and will expire on December 31, 1996. The option price is to be 75% of the market price on January 1, 1995. The stock price on December 31, 1993, was $90 and on December 31, 1995, was $120. The following information was given for 1996:

Change in common stock (par $30) from options exercised	$180,000
Change in paid-in capital on common stock from options exercised	450,000
Balance remaining in options outstanding	78,750

Instructions:

1. Compute the following:
   (a) The stock price at January 1, 1995.
   (b) Cash received on options exercised.
   (c) The total number of shares optioned to the executives.
   (d) The executive compensation expense for 1993, 1994, and 1995.
2. Give the journal entries for 1996.

Problem 15—42 (Analysis of stock transactions)

You have been asked to audit the Greystone Company. During the course of your audit, you are asked to prepare comparative data from the company's inception to the present. You have determined the following:

(a) Greystone Company's charter became effective on January 2, 1992, when 2,000 shares of no-par common and 1,000 shares of 7% cumulative, nonparticipating, preferred stock were issued. The no-par common stock had no stated value and was sold at $120 per share, and the preferred stock was sold at its par value of $100 per share.

(b) Greystone was unable to pay preferred dividends at the end of its first year. The owners of the preferred stock agreed to accept 2 shares of common stock for every 50 shares of preferred stock owned in discharge of the preferred dividends due on December 31, 1992. The shares were issued on January 2, 1993. The fair market value was $100 per share for common on the date of issue.

(c) Greystone Company acquired all the outstanding stock of Booth Corporation on May 1, 1994, in exchange for 1,000 shares of Greystone common stock.

(d) Greystone split its common stock 3 for 2 on January 1, 1995, and 2 for 1 on January 1, 1996.

(e) Greystone offered to convert 20% of the preferred stock to common stock on the basis of 2 shares of common for 1 share of preferred. The offer was accepted, and the conversion was made on July 1, 1996.

(f) No cash dividends were declared on common stock until December 31, 1994. Cash dividends per share of common stock were declared as follows:

	June 30	Dec. 31
1994		$3.19
1995	$1.75	2.75
1996	1.25	1.25

Instructions: Prepare schedules that show the computation of:

1. The number of shares of each class of stock outstanding on the last day of each year from 1992 through 1996.
2. Total cash dividends applicable to common stock for each year from 1994 through 1996.

Problem 15—43 (Auditing stockholders' equity)

You have been assigned to the audit of Belcore Inc., a manufacturing company. You have been asked to summarize the transactions for the year ended December 31, 1996, affecting stockholders' equity and other related accounts. The stockholders' equity section of Belcore's December 31, 1995, balance sheet follows:

Stockholders' Equity

Contributed capital:	
Common stock, $20 par value, 500,000 shares authorized, 90,000 shares issued	$1,800,000
Paid-in capital from treasury stock	22,500
Paid-in capital in excess of par	200,000
Total contributed capital	$2,022,500
Retained earnings	324,689
Total contributed capital and retained earnings	$2,347,189
Less cost of 1,210 shares of treasury stock	72,600
Total stockholders' equity	$2,274,589

You have extracted the following information from the accounting records and audit working papers:

1996

Jan. 15 Belcore reissued 650 shares of treasury stock for $40 per share. The 1,210 shares of treasury stock on hand at December 31, 1995, were purchased in one block in 1995. Belcore used the cost method for recording the treasury shares purchased.

Feb. 2 Sold 90 $1,000, 9% bonds due February 1, 1999, at 103 with one detachable stock purchase warrant attached to each bond. Interest is payable annually on February 1. The fair market value of the bonds without the stock warrants is 97. The detached warrants have a fair value of $60 each and expire on February 1, 1997. Each warrant entitles the holder to purchase 10 shares of common stock at $40 per share.

Mar. 6 Subscriptions for 1,400 shares of common stock were issued at $44 per share, payable 40% down and the balance by March 20.

Mar. 20 The balance due on 1,200 shares was received and those shares were issued. The subscriber who defaulted on the 200 remaining shares forfeited the down payment in accordance with the subscription agreement.

Nov. 1 55 stock warrants detached from the bonds were exercised.

Instructions: Give journal entries required to summarize the preceding transactions.

CHAPTER 16

Owners' Equity: Retained Earnings

CHAPTER TOPICS

- Factors Affecting Retained Earnings
- Prior-Period Adjustments
- Restrictions on Retained Earnings
- Accounting for Dividends
- Stock Dividends Versus Stock Splits
- Quasi-Reorganizations
- Reporting Stockholders Equity

Many companies are proud of their record of consecutive years of cash dividend payments. For example, General Electric reports that it has paid cash dividends each year since 1899. Chase Manhattan has a continuous cash dividend stream dating back to 1848. Chemical Bank's record goes back to 1827. TNP Enterprises, the parent company of Texas-New Mexico Power Company, even went so far as buying advertising space in *The Wall Street Journal* in November 1993 to proudly declare its "232nd consecutive quarterly cash dividend."

Berkshire Hathaway is one of the few companies that unhesitatingly reports that it does *not* pay cash dividends and has not paid them since 1967. The company prefers to reinvest profits. Berkshire Hathaway is involved in a number of diverse lines of business. Its largest operations are in property and casualty insurance.[1] However, it also produces and sells

1. 1992 Annual Report of Berkshire Hathaway Inc.

Kirby vacuums, See's chocolates, and World Book encyclopedias. In addition, Berkshire Hathaway has a substantial investment portfolio: it owns 18% of the stock of Capital Cities/ABC, 11% of Gillette, 7% of Coca Cola, 15% of the Washington Post, 11% of Wells Fargo, 14% of General Dynamics, 14% of Salomon, and 48% of GEICO (a large insurance company). As might be expected of a company that retains all profits, Berkshire Hathaway has grown rapidly. From 1964 to 1992, its increase in equity value averaged 24% per year. During 1993, the company's common stock traded for as high as $17,800 per share—the highest per-share price on the New York Stock Exchange. In 1993, ownership of $8.3 billion in Berkshire Hathaway stock vaulted the company's chairman, Warren Buffett, over Microsoft's Bill Gates to the top of the *Forbes* list of the 400 richest Americans.[2]

Evaluating growth by increase in share price can be misleading. Berkshire Hathaway's share price is high because of real growth, but also because of the absence of stock dividends and stock splits. Most firms use stock dividends or splits to maintain their per-share price in the range that is considered normal, usually between $20 and $80 per share in the United States. For example, IBM common stock traded for $56 per share in February 1994. However, if it hadn't been for a long history of stock dividends (26 stock dividends since 1925, the last being in 1967) and stock splits (13 stock splits since 1926, the latest being a 4-for-1 split in 1979),[3] the per-share price of IBM stock would have been $170,000!

In the previous chapter, **owners' equity** was defined as the residual ownership interest in the net assets (total assets minus total liabilities) of a business. Owners' equity was further classified into that portion of capital that is contributed by owners and the amount of earnings generated and retained by the enterprise. Chapter 15 discussed the accounting issues associated with contributed capital. The purpose of this chapter is to identify and explain the different types of transactions and events that directly affect **retained earnings.**

A company's retained earnings balance has historically served as a constraint on the payment of cash dividends and on the repurchase of treasury shares. For example, the General Corporation Law of the state of California states that:

"Neither a corporation nor any of its subsidiaries shall make any distribution to the corporation's shareholders [unless]... the amount of the retained earnings of the corporation immediately prior thereto equals or exceeds the amount of the proposed distribution." (Division 1, Chapter 5, Section 500)

However, in most states this constraint is no longer absolute. California law allows the payment of cash dividends even if the above retained earnings provision is not satisfied, as long as the total equity and working capital of the corporation are at specified levels. Other states, with Delaware often being viewed as the leader, have even less restrictive laws.

This flexibility in state laws doesn't mean that the level of retained earnings is not important. Banks and other lenders often place retained earnings restrictions in their loan contracts. This is illustrated in a note from the 1992 financial statements of Appalachian Power Company:

"Covenants in mortgage indentures, debenture and bank loan agreements, charter provisions and orders of regulatory authorities place various restrictions on the use of retained earnings of the Company to pay dividends (other than stock dividends) on its common stock and for other purposes. At December 31, 1992, approximately $43.8 million of retained earnings were restricted."

In summary, a firm with a low or restricted retained earnings balance can be constrained from paying cash dividends. As a result, accountants and financial managers alike are interested in the factors that affect retained earnings.

2. "The Forbes Four Hundred," *Forbes*, October 18, 1993, p. 112.
3. *Moody's Industrial Manual*, 1993, Vol. 1, p. 289.

FACTORS AFFECTING RETAINED EARNINGS

The nature of retained earnings is frequently misunderstood, and this misunderstanding may lead to incorrect impressions in reading and interpreting financial statements. The retained earnings account is essentially the meeting place of balance sheet and income statement accounts. In successive periods, retained earnings are increased by income and decreased by losses and dividends. As a result, the retained earnings balance represents the net accumulated earnings of a corporation. If the retained earnings account were affected *only* by income (losses) and dividends, there would be little confusion in its interpretation. A number of other factors, however, can affect retained earnings.

In addition to earnings or losses and cash dividends, factors that affect retained earnings include prior-period adjustments for corrections of errors, quasi-reorganizations, stock dividends, and treasury stock transactions (discussed in Chapter 15). The transactions and events that increase or decrease retained earnings may be summarized as follows:

Retained Earnings

Decreases	Increases
Prior-period adjustments for overstatements of past earnings	Prior-period adjustments for understatements of past earnings
Certain changes in accounting principle	Certain changes in accounting principle
Current net loss	Current net income
Cash dividends	Quasi-reorganizations
Stock dividends	
Treasury stock transactions	

Prior-Period Adjustments

In some situations, errors made in past years are discovered and corrected in the current year by an adjustment to the retained earnings account, referred to as a **prior-period adjustment.** There are several types of errors that may occur in measuring the results of operations and the financial status of an enterprise. Accounting errors can result from mathematical mistakes, a failure to apply appropriate accounting procedures, or a misstatement or omission of certain information. For example, First Financial Shares, a savings and loan holding company, reported in its 1992 annual report that it was recording a prior period adjustment to reduce retained earnings by $148,134 because it had erroneously reported interest revenue on loans that were no longer outstanding. In addition, a change from an accounting principle that is not generally accepted to one that is accepted is considered a correction of an error.[4]

Fortunately, most errors are discovered during the accounting period, prior to closing the books. When this is the case, corrections can be made by making adjusting entries directly to the accounts. The corrected balances are then shown on the balance sheet and on the income statement.

Sometimes errors go undetected during the current period, but they are offset by an equal misstatement in the subsequent period; that is, they are **counterbalanced.** When this happens, the under- or overstatement of income in one period is counterbalanced by an equal over- or understatement of income in the next period, and after the closing process is completed for the second year, the retained earnings account is correctly stated. If a counterbalancing error is discovered during the second year, however, it should be corrected at that time.

4. *Opinions of the Accounting Principles Board No. 20,* "Accounting Changes" (New York: American Institute of Certified Public Accountants, 1971) par. 13.

When errors of past periods are not counterbalancing, retained earnings will be misstated until a correction is made in the accounting records. If the error is material, a prior-period adjustment should be made directly to the retained earnings account.[5] If an error resulted in an understatement of income in previous periods, a correcting entry would be needed to increase retained earnings; if an error overstated income in prior periods, then retained earnings would have to be decreased. These adjustments for corrections in net income of prior periods would typically be shown as a part of the total change in retained earnings as follows:

Retained Earnings, unadjusted beginning balance	$XXX
Add or deduct prior-period adjustments	XX
Retained Earnings, adjusted beginning balance	$XXX
Add current year's net income or deduct current year's net loss	XX
	$XXX
Deduct dividends	XX
Retained Earnings, ending balance	$XXX

When errors are discovered, the accountant must be able to analyze the situation and determine what action is appropriate under the circumstances. This calls for an understanding of accounting standards as well as good judgment. Techniques for analyzing and correcting errors are covered in detail in a later chapter.

Earnings

The primary source of retained earnings is the net income generated by a business. The retained earnings account is increased by net income and is reduced by net losses from business activities. When operating losses or other debits to Retained Earnings produce a debit balance in this account, the debit balance is referred to as a **deficit.**

Corporate earnings originate from transactions with individuals or businesses outside the company. No earnings are recognized for the construction of buildings or other plant assets for a company's own use, even though the cost of such construction is below the market price for similar assets; self-construction at less than the asset purchase price is regarded simply as a savings in cost. No increases in retained earnings are recognized from transactions with stockholders involving treasury stock; however, as indicated in Chapter 15, decreases may be recognized. The earnings of a corporation may be distributed to the stockholders or retained to provide for expanding operations.

Dividends

Dividends are distributions to the stockholders of a corporation in proportion to the number of shares held by the respective owners. Distributions may take the form of (1) cash, (2) other assets, (3) notes or other evidence of corporate indebtedness, in effect, deferred cash dividends, and (4) stock dividends, i.e., shares of a company's own stock. Most dividends involve reductions in retained earnings. Exceptions include (1) some stock dividends issued in the form of stock splits, which involve a transfer from additional paid-in capital to legal capital, and (2) dividends in corporate liquidation, which represent a return to stockholders of a portion or all of their investment and call for reductions in contributed capital.

Use of the term *dividend* without qualification normally implies the distribution of cash. Dividends in a form other than cash, such as property or stock dividends, should be designated by their special form. Distributions from a capital source other than retained

5. *Ibid.*, par. 36.

earnings should carry a description of their special origin, e.g., *liquidating dividend* or *dividend distribution of paid-in capital*.

"Dividends paid out of retained earnings" is an expression frequently encountered. Accuracy, however, requires recognition that dividends are paid out of cash, which serves to reduce retained earnings. Earnings of the corporation increase net assets or stockholders' equity. Dividend distributions represent no more than asset withdrawals that reduce net assets. The nature and types of dividends are covered in depth later in the chapter.

Other Changes in Retained Earnings

The most common changes in retained earnings result from earnings (or losses) and dividends. Other changes may occur, however, resulting from treasury stock transactions or from a quasi-reorganization, which is effected only under special circumstances in which a business seeks a "fresh start."

The remainder of this chapter focuses on accounting for dividends, followed by a discussion of quasi-reorganizations.

ACCOUNTING FOR DIVIDENDS

Among the powers delegated by the stockholders to the board of directors is the power to control the dividend policy. Whether dividends shall or shall not be paid, as well as the nature and the amount of dividends, are matters that the board determines. In setting dividend policy, the board of directors must answer two questions:

1. Do we have the legal right to declare a dividend?
2. Is a dividend distribution financially advisable?

In answering the first question, the board of directors must observe the legal requirements governing the maintenance of legal capital. The laws of different states range from those making any part of capital other than legal capital available for dividends to those permitting dividends only to the extent of retained earnings and under specified conditions. In most states, dividends cannot be declared in the event of a deficit; in a few states, however, dividends equal to current earnings may be distributed despite a previously accumulated deficit. The availability of capital as a basis for dividends is a determination to be made by the legal counsel and not by the accountant. The accountant must report accurately the sources of each capital increase or decrease; the legal counsel investigates the availability of such sources as bases for dividend distributions.

The board of directors must also consider the second question, i.e., the financial aspect of dividend distributions. The company's cash position relative to present and future cash requirements is a key factor. For example, a corporation may have retained earnings of \$500,000. If it has cash of only \$150,000, however, cash dividends must be limited to this amount unless it converts certain assets into cash or borrows cash. If the cash required for regular operations is \$100,000, the cash available for dividends is then only \$50,000. Although legally able to declare dividends of \$500,000, the company would be able to distribute no more than one tenth of that amount at this time. Generally, companies pay dividends that are significantly less than the legal amount allowed or the amount of cash on hand.

When a dividend is legally declared and announced, it cannot be revoked. In the event of corporate insolvency after a dividend declaration but prior to payment of the dividend, stockholders have claims as a creditor group to the dividend, and as an ownership group to any assets remaining after all corporate liabilities have been paid. A dividend that was illegally declared, however, is revocable; in the event of insolvency at the time of declaration, such action is nullified and stockholders participate in asset distributions only after creditors have been paid in full.

Restrictions on Retained Earnings

Although state laws generally permit the distribution of dividends to the extent of retained earnings, other factors may limit the amount of dividends that can be declared. As noted earlier in the chapter, a portion of retained earnings may be restricted as a result of contractual requirements, such as an agreement with creditors that provides for the retention of earnings to ensure repayment of debt at maturity. Retained earnings may also be restricted at the discretion of the board of directors. For example, the board may designate a portion of retained earnings as restricted for a particular purpose, such as expansion of plant facilities.

If restrictions on retained earnings are material, they are generally disclosed in a note to the financial statements. Sometimes, however, the restricted portion of retained earnings is reported on the balance sheet separately from the unrestricted amount that is available for dividends. The restricted portion may be designated as **appropriated retained earnings** and the unrestricted portion as **unappropriated (or free) retained earnings.** When the restrictions are recognized in the accounts, the entry is a debit to the regular retained earnings account and a credit to a special appropriated retained earnings account.

As an example, assume Silverstein Company restricted $100,000 of its $600,000 retained earnings balance for possible plant expansion by making the following entry on January 1, 1996:

1996			
Jan. 1	Retained Earnings	100,000	
	Appropriated Retained Earnings		100,000
	To restrict retained earnings for possible plant expansion.		

The balance sheet subsequent to this entry would reflect both retained earnings accounts.

Appropriated retained earnings	$100,000	
Unappropriated retained earnings	500,000	
Total retained earnings		$600,000

Once the purpose of the appropriation has been served, the original entry creating the appropriated retained earnings balance is reversed. To illustrate, assume that on June 15, the Silverstein Company decided not to expand its plant and to eliminate the appropriated retained earnings balance. The applicable entry would be:

June 15	Appropriated Retained Earnings	100,000	
	Retained Earnings		100,000
	To discontinue the appropriation of retained earnings for plant expansion.		

Note that there is no segregation of funds and no gain or loss involved in the restriction of retained earnings. Whatever the form of disclosure, the main idea behind restrictions on retained earnings is to notify stockholders that some of the assets that might otherwise be available for dividend distribution are being retained within the business for specific purposes. Because the amount of dividends actually paid is usually much less than the retained earnings balance, this is generally not a significant issue.

Recognition and Payment of Dividends

Three dates are essential in the recognition and payment of dividends: (1) **date of declaration,** (2) **date of record,** and (3) **date of payment.** Dividends are made payable to stockholders of record as of a date following the date of declaration and preceding the date of payment. The liability for dividends payable is recorded on the declaration date and is canceled on the payment date. No entry is required on the record date, but a list of the stockholders is made as of the close of business on this date. These are the persons who receive dividends on the payment date. For example, on November 28, 1990, *The Wall Street Journal* published an announcement that Walt Disney Company had declared a quarterly cash dividend of 14 1/2 cents per share, payable on February 20, 1991, to shareholders of record on January 18, 1991.

Stockholders become aware of a forthcoming dividend upon its declaration and announcement. If stock is sold and a new owner is recognized by the corporation prior to the record date, the dividend is paid to the new owner. If a stock transfer is not recognized by the corporation until after the record date, the dividend will be paid to the former owner, i.e., the shareholder of record. After the record date, stock no longer carries a right to dividends and sells at a lower price or **ex-dividend.**[6] Accordingly, a stockholder is justified in recognizing the corporate dividend action on the record date by debiting a receivable and crediting Dividend Revenue. Upon receipt of the dividend, Cash is debited and the receivable is eliminated. In practice, however, the accrual is frequently omitted, and dividend revenue is recognized when the cash is received.

Cash Dividends

The most common type of dividend is a **cash dividend.** For the corporation, these dividends involve a reduction in retained earnings and in cash. For the investor, a cash dividend generates cash and is recognized as dividend revenue. Entries to record the declaration and payment of a $100,000 cash dividend by a corporation follow:

Declaration of Dividend

Dividends (or Retained Earnings)	100,000	
Dividends Payable		100,000

Payment of Dividend

Dividends Payable	100,000	
Cash		100,000

An investor owning five percent of the outstanding stock would record the dividend as follows:

Receipt of Dividend

Cash	5,000	
Dividend Revenue		5,000

Computation:
$100,000 (total dividends) × .05 (investor's share) = $5,000

As noted previously, the investor could recognize dividend revenue and the corresponding receivable at the date of record. In practice, however, investors typically recognize dividend revenue at the time of receipt.

Property Dividends

A distribution to stockholders that is payable in some asset other than cash is generally referred to as a **property dividend.** Frequently the assets to be distributed are securities of other companies owned by the corporation. The corporation thus transfers to its stockholders its ownership interest in such securities. Property dividends occur most frequently in closely held corporations.

This type of transfer is sometimes referred to as a **nonreciprocal transfer to owners,** inasmuch as nothing is received by the company in return for its distribution to the stockholders.

6. Stock on the New York Stock Exchange is normally quoted ex-dividend (or ex-rights) four full trading days prior to the record date because of the time required to deliver the stock and to record the stock transfers.

These transfers should be recorded using the fair market value (as of the day of declaration) of the assets distributed, and a gain or loss recognized for the difference between the carrying value on the books of the issuing company and the fair market value of the assets.[7] Property dividends are valued at carrying value if the fair market value is not determinable.

To illustrate the entries for a property dividend, assume that the Bigler Corporation owns 100,000 shares in the Tri-State Oil Co., cost $2,000,000, fair market value $3,000,000, or $30 per share, which it wishes to distribute to its stockholders. There are 1,000,000 shares of Bigler Corporation stock outstanding. Accordingly, a dividend of $^1/_{10}$ of a share of Tri-State Oil Co. stock is declared on each share of Bigler Corporation stock outstanding. The entries for Bigler for the dividend declaration and payment are:

Declaration of Dividend		
Dividends (or Retained Earnings)	3,000,000	
Property Dividends Payable		2,000,000
Gain on Distribution of Property Dividends		1,000,000
Payment of Dividend		
Property Dividends Payable	2,000,000	
Investment in Tri-State Oil Co. Stock		2,000,000

An investor owning 5,000 shares of Bigler stock would make the following entry to record the receipt of the property (Tri-State Oil stock) dividend:

Receipt of Dividend		
Investment in Tri-State Oil Co. Stock	15,000	
Dividend Revenue		15,000

Computation:
5,000 shares × $^1/_{10}$ = 500 shares
500 shares × $30 per share = $15,000

Stock Dividends

A corporation may distribute to stockholders additional shares of the company's own stock as a **stock dividend.** A stock dividend permits the corporation to retain within the business net assets produced by earnings while at the same time offering stockholders additional ownership shares.

Accounting for Stock Dividends by the Investor. From the shareholders' point of view, a stock dividend does not change the proportional ownership interests. Although the number of shares held by each individual stockholder has gone up, there are now a greater total number of shares outstanding, and proportionate interests remain unchanged. This division of equities into a greater number of parts does not provide income to the investor. To illustrate, assume the following information for Jeff's Corporation and a shareholder owning 10 shares of stock:

	Prior to 10% Stock Dividend	After 10% Stock Dividend
Common stock outstanding	10,000 shares	11,000 shares
Total stockholders' equity	$330,000	$330,000
Company book value per share	$33	$30
Individual stockholder book value	$330 ($33 × 10 shares)	$330 ($30 × 11 shares)

7. *Opinions of the Accounting Principles Board No. 29,* "Accounting for Nonmonetary Transactions" (New York: American Institute of Certified Public Accountants, 1973), par. 18.

As indicated in this example, the book value per share would decrease, but total book value would not change. Theoretically, the same relative decrease should occur in the market price as occurred in the book value. In any event, since there is no effect on the underlying book value of the investment, the investor need only make a memorandum entry noting the receipt of additional shares and the new, lower per-share cost basis of the investment.

An important point to remember is that receipt of a stock dividend is an economic non-event as far as a shareholder is concerned. Fear that investors were being deceived into thinking that receipt of a stock dividend actually represented income led to development of the rules governing how the issuing company must account for stock dividends.

Accounting for Stock Dividends by the Issuer. As described by Professor James Tucker[8], stock dividends acquired a shady reputation in the late 1800s because they were viewed as being similar to "stock watering." Stock watering is the practice of issuing stock without receiving adequate compensation in return, thus diluting the value of the shares. In addition, in the 1920s and 1930s, accountants and regulatory authorities became concerned that companies issuing stock dividends were wrongly leading investors to believe that receiving a stock dividend was equivalent to receiving a cash dividend. This impression was particularly easy to convey when a company had a practice of issuing small, regular stock dividends (i.e., a 2.5% annual stock dividend). And, from the issuing company's standpoint, a stock dividend involved no cash outlay, and the standard accounting treatment required only a small reduction in retained earnings equal to the par value of the newly issued shares. The Committee on Accounting Procedure (CAP) issued Accounting Research Bulletin (ARB) No. 11 in September 1941 which made it considerably more difficult for firms to issue small stock dividends by requiring a reduction in retained earnings equal to the market value of the newly issued shares. To see what a difference this makes, recall that par values are typically around $1 per share, whereas market values usually range between $20 and $80 per share. Professor Stephen Zeff cites ARB No. 11 as one of the earliest examples of the economic consequences of accounting standards — in this case, the use of an accounting standard to reduce the incidence of small, regular stock dividends.[9]

When distributing stock as a dividend, the issuing corporation must meet legal requirements relative to the minimum amounts to be capitalized (i.e., transferred to the capital stock account). If stock has a par or a stated value, an amount equal to the par or stated value of the shares issued will have to be transferred to capital stock; if stock has no par value and no stated value, the laws of the state of incorporation may provide specific requirements as to the amounts to be transferred, or they may leave such determinations to the corporate directors.

Small Versus Large Stock Dividends. In accounting for stock dividends, a distinction is made between a small and a large stock dividend.[10] Recall that the specific objective of the Committee on Accounting Procedure was to discourage regularly recurring small stock dividends. As a general guideline, a stock dividend of less than 20%-25% of the number of shares previously outstanding is considered a **small stock dividend.** Stock dividends involving the issuance of more than 20%-25% are considered **large stock dividends.**[11]

8. James J. Tucker III, "The Role of Stock Dividends in Defining Income, Developing Capital Market Research and Exploring the Economic Consequences of Accounting Policy Decisions," *The Accounting Historians Journal,* Fall 1985, pp. 73-94.

9. Stephen A. Zeff, "Towards a Fundamental Rethinking of the Role of the 'Intermediate' Course in the Accounting Curriculum," The Impact of Rule-Making on Intermediate Financial Accounting Textbooks (Daniel J. Jensen, ed.), Columbus, Ohio: 1982, pp. 33-51.

10. See *Accounting Research and Terminology Bulletins—Final Edition, No. 43,* "Restatement and Revision of Accounting Research Bulletins," (New York: American Institute of Certified Public Accountants, 1961), Ch. 7, Sec. B.

11. In *Accounting Series Release No. 124,* the SEC specified that for publicly traded companies, stock dividends of 25% or more should be accounted for as large stock dividends and those of less than 25% as small stock dividends.

With a small stock dividend, companies must transfer from Retained Earnings to capital stock and additional paid-in capital an amount equal to the fair market value of the additional shares at the declaration date. Such a transfer is consistent with the general public's view of a stock dividend as a distribution of corporate earnings at an amount equivalent to the fair market value of the shares received. The following example illustrates the entries for the declaration and issuance of a small stock dividend.

Assume that stockholders' equity for the Fuji Company on July 1 is as follows:

Common stock, $1 par, 100,000 shares outstanding	$ 100,000
Paid-in capital in excess of par	1,100,000
Retained earnings	750,000

The company declares a 10% stock dividend, or a dividend of 1 share of common for every 10 shares held. The stock is selling on the market on this date at $16 per share. The stock dividend is to be recorded at the market value of the shares issued, or $160,000 (10,000 shares at $16). The entries to record the declaration of the dividend and the issuance of stock by Fuji Company are:

Declaration of Dividend		
Retained Earnings	160,000	
Stock Dividends Distributable		10,000
Paid-In Capital in Excess of Par		150,000
Issuance of Dividend		
Stock Dividends Distributable	10,000	
Common Stock		10,000

Because the focus of the CAP was on reducing the number of small stock dividends, the accounting requirements governing large stock dividends are less specific than those for small stock dividends. Accounting Research Bulletin No. 43, which summarizes all the preceding standards issued by the CAP, states the following about the accounting for large stock dividends:

"... no transfer from earned surplus [i.e., Retained Earnings] to capital surplus or capital stock account is called for, other than to the extent occasioned by legal requirements." (Chapter 7B, para. 15)

In practice, this standard results in the par or stated value of the newly issued shares being transferred to the capital stock account from either retained earnings or paid-in capital in excess of par[12]. To illustrate, assume that Fuji company declares a large stock dividend of 50%, or a dividend of 1 share for every 2 held. Legal requirements call for the transfer to capital stock of an amount equal to the par value of the shares issued. Entries for the declaration of the dividend and the issuance of stock follow:

Declaration of Dividend		
Retained Earnings	50,000	
Stock Dividends Distributable		50,000
OR		
Paid in Capital in Excess of Par	50,000	
Stock Dividends Distributable		50,000
Issuance of Dividend		
Stock Dividends Distributable	50,000	
Common Stock, $1 par		50,000

Fractional Share Warrants. When stock dividends are issued by a company, it may be necessary to issue **fractional share warrants** to certain stockholders. For example, when

12. Some large stock dividends are effected by reducing both paid-in-capital in excess of par and retained earnings by a total of the par value of the newly issued shares.

a 10% stock dividend is issued, a stockholder owning 25 shares can be given no more than 2 full shares; however, the holdings in excess of an even multiple of 10 shares are recognized by issuing a fractional share warrant for one-half share. The warrant for one-half share may be sold, or a warrant for an additional half share may be purchased so that a full share may be claimed from the company. In some instances, the corporation may arrange for the payment of cash in lieu of fractional warrants or it may issue a full share of stock in exchange for warrants accompanied by cash for the fractional share deficiency.

Assume that the Fuji Company in distributing a stock dividend issues fractional share warrants equivalent to 500 shares of $1 par common. The entry for the fractional share warrants issued would be as follows:

Stock Dividends Distributable	500	
Fractional Share Warrants Issued		500

Assuming 80% of the warrants are ultimately turned in for shares and the remaining warrants expire, the following entry would be made:

Fractional Share Warrants Issued	500	
Common Stock, $1 par		400
Paid-In Capital From Forfeitures of Fractional Share Warrants		100

Stock Dividends Versus Stock Splits. As noted in Chapter 15, a corporation may effect a **stock split** by reducing the par or stated value of capital stock and increasing accordingly the number of shares outstanding. For example, a corporation with 1,000,000 shares outstanding may split the stock on a 3-for-1 basis. After the split, the corporation will have 3,000,000 total shares outstanding and each stockholder will have 3 shares for every 1 previously held. However, each share now represents only one-third of the capital interest it previously represented; furthermore, each share of stock can be expected to sell for approximately one-third of its previous market price. From an investor's perspective, therefore, a stock split can be viewed the same as a stock dividend. In fact, the accounting for the investor is the same for stock splits as for stock dividends. With an increase in the number of shares, each new share is assigned a portion of the original cost.

Although a stock dividend can be compared to a stock split from the investor's point of view, its effects on corporate capital differ from those of a stock split. A stock dividend results in not only an increase in the number of shares outstanding, but also an increase in the capital stock balance, with no change in the value assigned to each share of stock on the company records; the increase in capital stock outstanding is effected by a transfer from the retained earnings balance, retained earnings available for dividends being permanently reduced by this transfer. A stock split merely divides the existing capital stock balance into more parts, with a reduction in the stated or legal value related to each share; there is no change in the retained earnings balance or the capital stock balance.

Exhibit 16—1 provides a comparative example of the effects of a 100% stock dividend and a 2-for-1 stock split, both from the issuing company's perspective and from an investor's perspective.

The simple example in the exhibit illustrates that, from an accounting perspective, the effects of a large stock dividend can be very different from the effects of a stock split even though both result in the creation of the same number of new shares. The required transfer from retained earnings (or paid-in capital in excess of par) can significantly impact the shareholders' equity section of the balance sheet. For example, in the illustration in Exhibit 16-1, the 100% stock dividend may hinder the issuing firm's ability to pay future *cash* dividends since the retained earnings balance is so drastically reduced; no such constraint arises when the issuance of the new shares is accounted for as a 2-for-1 stock split.

Exhibit 16—1 Comparative Example—Stock Dividend Versus Stock Split

Stockholders' Equity (Prior to Stock Dividend or Stock Split)

Common stock, 200,000 shares authorized, $5 par, 50,000 shares outstanding	$250,000
Paid-in capital in excess of par	400,000
Retained earnings	300,000
Total stockholders' equity	$950,000

Issuing Company's Perspective

Stockholders' Equity *After* 100% Stock Dividend	
Common stock, 200,000 shares authorized, $5 par, 100,000 shares outstanding	$500,000
Paid-in capital in excess of par*	400,000
Retained earnings	50,000
Total stockholders' equity	$950,000

Stockholders' Equity *After* 2-for-1 Stock Split	
Common stock, 400,000 shares authorized, $2.50 par, 100,000 shares outstanding	$250,000
Paid-in capital in excess of par	400,000
Retained earnings	300,000
Total stockholders' equity	$950,000

*Some or all of the $250,000 transfer to common stock at par could have been made from paid-in capital in excess of par.

Investor's Perspective**

Effect of 100% Stock Dividend	
Original investment (1,000 × $15)	$15,000
Investment after 100% stock dividend (2,000 × $7.50)	$15,000

Effect of 2-for-1 Stock Split	
Original investment (1,000 × $15)	$15,000
Investment after 2-for-1 stock split (2,000 × $7.50)	$15,000

**Assume an original investment of 1,000 shares at $15 cost per share.

Although stock splits and stock dividends are distinctly different in an accounting sense, the terms "stock split" and "stock dividend" are used interchangeably in the financial press and sometimes even in the issuing company's annual report. For example, *The Wall Street Journal* description of a distribution as a split or dividend agrees with the actual accounting for the distribution only about 25% of the time.[13] And, the issuing firm's own description of the distribution in the narrative portion of the annual report matches the actual accounting treatment only 67% of the time.

Stock Dividends on the Balance Sheet. Special disclosure should be provided on the balance sheet when retained earnings have been reclassified as paid-in capital as a result of stock dividends, recapitalizations, or other actions. Information concerning the amount of retained earnings transferred to paid-in capital will contribute to an understanding of the extent to which business growth has been financed through corporate earnings. For example, assume the information for the Fuji Company on page 681 and that Fuji chose to transfer paid-in capital of $50,000 as a result of a 50% stock dividend entirely from retained earnings. The stockholders' equity may be presented as illustrated below.

Contributed capital:		
Common stock, $1 par, 150,000 shares	$ 150,000	
Paid-in capital in excess of par	1,100,000	$1,250,000
Retained earnings	$ 750,000	
Less amount transferred to paid-in capital by stock dividend	50,000	700,000
Total stockholders' equity		$1,950,000

13. See Graeme Rankine and Earl K. Stice, "Stock Splits and Large Stock Dividends: Security Return Impact of an Accounting Choice," working paper, Rice University, June 1994.

If a balance sheet is prepared after the declaration of a stock dividend but before issue of the shares, Stock Dividends Distributable is reported in the stockholders' equity section as an addition to capital stock outstanding. Through stock dividends, the corporation reduces its retained earnings or paid-in capital in excess of par balances and increases its capital stock.

Liquidating Dividends

A **liquidating dividend** is a distribution representing a return to stockholders of a portion of contributed capital. Whereas a normal cash dividend provides a return on investment and is accounted for by reducing Retained Earnings, a liquidating dividend provides a return of investment. A liquidating dividend is accounted for by reducing paid-in capital.

To illustrate, assume the Stubbs Corporation declared and paid a cash dividend and a partial liquidating dividend amounting to $150,000. Of this amount, $100,000 represents a regular $10 cash dividend on 10,000 shares of common stock. The remaining $50,000 represents a $5-per-share liquidating dividend, which is recorded as a reduction to Paid-In Capital in Excess of Par. The entries would be:

Declaration of Dividend		
Dividends (or Retained Earnings)	100,000	
Paid-In Capital in Excess of Par	50,000	
Dividends Payable		150,000

Stock Dividends—Why Do They Exist?

Viewed very simply, stock dividends are purely cosmetic. They should have no effect on the total value of a company, since they involve no inflow or outflow of assets. A stock dividend merely causes the value of the declaring company to be sliced into smaller pieces. For example, a firm with a total market value of $1,000 with 10 shares of stock outstanding (market value of $100 per share) would, after a 100% stock dividend, still have a total market value of $1,000, but now would have 20 shares of stock outstanding (market value of $50 per share).

This cosmetic view of stock dividends makes theoretical sense, but the fact that real companies spend real money (in the form of administrative costs) to enact stock dividends suggests that there must be something more to them. It has been suggested that the accounting treatment of stock dividends makes their declaration a credible way of sending a signal to the market that the firm has favorable future prospects. The reasoning goes like this: A declaration of a stock dividend requires that an amount be transferred from retained earnings to paid-in capital. Since *cash* dividend payments are often restricted to the amount of retained earnings, the reduction in retained earnings occasioned by a *stock* dividend might make it more difficult to declare *cash* dividends in the future. Only firms with favorable future prospects would be likely to declare stock dividends, since they are confident that future earnings will bolster the retained earnings balance, making up for the reduction required by the stock dividend declaration. So, according to this reasoning, a stock dividend declaration is a signal from management that they expect future earnings to be adequate to cover future cash dividend declarations. This view of stock dividends is supported by the fact that, on average, firms' stock prices increase 5% in the days following the announcement of a stock dividend.

Questions:

Assume that there is validity to this signaling theory of stock dividends. Which would be a stronger signal:

1. A 20% stock dividend or a 30% stock dividend?
2. A 100% stock dividend or a 2-for-1 stock split?

Sources:

Graeme Rankine and Earl K. Stice, "Accounting Rules and the Signaling Properties of Stock Dividends and Stock Splits," working paper, Rice University, September 1993.

Graeme Rankine and Earl K. Stice, "Stock Splits and Large Stock Dividends: Security Return Impact of an Accounting Choice," working paper, Rice University, June 1994.

Payment of Dividend

Dividends Payable	150,000	
Cash		150,000

Stockholders should be notified as to the allocation of the total dividend payment, so they can determine the amount that represents revenue and the amount that represents a return of investment. An investor owning 500 shares of Schwab Corporation common stock would record receipt of the dividend as follows:

Cash	7,500	
Dividend Revenue (500 shares × $10)		5,000
Investment in Stubbs Corp. Common Stock (500 shares × $5)		2,500

QUASI-REORGANIZATIONS

As noted earlier, a debit balance in the retained earnings account is called a deficit. It may be the result of accumulated losses over a number of years or other significant debits to Retained Earnings. Sometimes a company with a large deficit is forced to discontinue operations and/or enter into bankruptcy proceedings. In some cases, however, where state laws permit, a company may eliminate a deficit through a restatement of invested capital balances. This provides, in effect, a fresh start for the company with a zero retained earnings balance. This is known as a **quasi-reorganization.** The advantage of a quasi-reorganization is that the procedure does not require recourse to the courts as in a formal reorganization or bankruptcy, and there is no change in the legal corporate entity or interruption of business activity.

Quasi-reorganizations are not common, but may be appropriate for a company operating under circumstances that are quite different from those of the past, e.g., a company with new management. Even if operated profitably, the company may take years to eliminate the deficit that was created under a prior management. In the meantime, the corporation generally cannot pay dividends to stockholders. With a quasi-reorganization, however, the accumulated deficit is eliminated. Performance from the reorganization date forward can then be measured and reported without having past mistakes and negative results reflecting unfavorably on the "new" company.

Normally in a quasi-reorganization, assets are revalued to reflect their current market values. This may require significant write-downs of assets against Retained Earnings, thus increasing the deficit. The total deficit is then written off (Retained Earnings is adjusted to a zero balance) against paid-in capital balances, giving the company a new capital structure. The Securities and Exchange Commission provides that any deficit reclassification is to be considered a quasi-reorganization and can only be made if all requisite conditions for a quasi-reorganization are met. Furthermore, the SEC requires that any anticipated accounting changes should be an integral part of the quasi-reorganization, and that the reorganization should not result in a write-up of net assets of the company.[14]

To illustrate the nature of a quasi-reorganization, assume TSS Corporation has suffered operating losses for some time, but is now operating profitably and expects to continue to do so. Current and projected income, however, will not be sufficient to eliminate the deficit in the near term. It also appears that plant assets are overstated considering current prices and economic conditions. After receiving permission from state authorities and approval from the shareholders, the board of directors of TSS Corporation decides to restate company assets and paid-in capital balances in order to remove the deficit and make possible the declaration of dividends from profitable operations. A balance sheet for the company just prior to this action is presented on the next page.

14. *Staff Accounting Bulletin No. 78,* "Quasi-Reorganizations" (Washington: SEC, August 25, 1988).

TSS Corporation
Balance Sheet
June 30, 1996

Current assets		$ 250,000	Liabilities		$300,000
Land, buildings, and equipment	$1,500,000		Common stock, $10 par, 100,000 shares	$1,000,000	
Less accumulated depreciation	600,000	900,000	Less deficit	150,000	850,000
Total assets		$1,150,000	Total liabilities and stockholders' equity		$1,150,000

The quasi-reorganization is to be accomplished as follows:

1. Land, buildings, and equipment are to be reduced to their present fair market value of $600,000 by reducing the asset and accumulated depreciation balances by 33 1/3%.
2. Common stock is to be reduced to a par value of $5, $500,000 in capital stock thus being converted into "additional paid-in capital."
3. The deficit of $450,000 ($150,000 as reported on the balance sheet increased by $300,000 arising from the write-down of land, buildings, and equipment) is to be applied against the capital from the reduction of the par value of stock.

Entries to record the changes follow:

Transaction	Entry		
(1) To write down land, buildings, and equipment and accumulated depreciation balances by 33 1/3%.	Retained Earnings	300,000	
	Accumulated Depreciation	200,000	
	Land, Buildings, and Equipment		500,000
(2) To reduce the common stock balance from $10 par to $5 par and to establish paid-in capital from reduction in stock par value.	Common Stock, $10 par	1,000,000	
	Common Stock, $5 par		500,000
	Paid-In Capital From Reduction in Stock Par Value		500,000
(3) To apply the deficit after asset devaluation against paid-in capital from reduction in stock par value.	Paid-In Capital From Reduction in Stock Par Value	450,000	
	Retained Earnings		450,000

The balance sheet after the quasi-reorganization is shown below.

TSS Corporation
Balance Sheet
June 30, 1996

Assets			Liabilities and Stockholders' Equity	
Current assets		$250,000	Liabilities	$300,000
Land, buildings, and equipment	$1,000,000		Common stock, $5 par, 100,000 shares	500,000
Less accumulated depreciation	400,000	600,000	Paid-in capital from reduction in stock par value	50,000
Total assets		$850,000	Total liabilities and stockholders' equity	$850,000

After the quasi-reorganization, the accounting for the company's operations is similar to that for a new company. Earnings subsequent to the quasi-reorganization, however, should be accumulated in a **dated retained earnings account.** On future balance sheets, retained earnings dated as of the time of account readjustment will inform readers of the date of such action and of the fresh start in earnings accumulation.

Exhibit 16—2 describes the quasi-reorganization undertaken by Genentech Inc., a firm engaged in the development, manufacture, and marketing of genetically engineered products.

Exhibit 16—2
Genentech Inc.—Note Disclosure of Quasi-Reorganization

On February 19, 1988, the Company's Board of Directors approved the elimination of the Company's accumulated deficit through an accounting reorganization of its stockholders' equity accounts (quasi-reorganization) effective October 1, 1987. The quasi-reorganization did not involve any revaluation of assets or liabilities, because for similar classes of assets, their fair values were no less than their book values, and for similar classes of liabilities, their book values were no less than their fair values. The effective date of the quasi-reorganization reflected the beginning of the quarter in which the Company received approval for and commenced marketing of its second major product, and as such, marked a turning point in the Company's operations. The accumulated deficit was eliminated by a transfer from additional paid-in capital in an amount equal to the accumulated deficit.

REPORTING STOCKHOLDERS' EQUITY

In reporting stockholders' equity, it is important to provide readers with information concerning:

1. The sources of stockholders' equity, especially the amount paid in by stockholders (contributed capital) and the amount representing earnings retained in the business (retained earnings).
2. The classes of capital stock, including par or stated values; number of shares authorized, issued, and outstanding; number of shares of treasury stock.
3. Any restrictions on retained earnings.

In addition to the preceding information, the cost (or par value) of treasury stock should be deducted from stockholders' equity. Similarly, as explained in Chapter 17, any unrealized gains or losses on investment securities classified as "available for sale" are disclosed in a separate account in the stockholders' equity section of the balance sheet.

As an illustration, the stockholders' equity section of the balance sheet of Hypothetical Corporation as of December 31, 1996, is presented. Many companies do not provide as much detail in the balance sheet as is illustrated for Hypothetical Corporation. A typical presentation is made in the actual financial statements of Microsoft Corporation in Appendix A.

Stockholders' Equity

Contributed capital:		
6% preferred stock, $100 par, cumulative, callable, 5,000 shares authorized and issued	$500,000	
Common stock, $5 stated value, 100,000 shares authorized, 60,000 shares issued; treasury stock, 5,000 shares—deducted below	300,000	$ 800,000
Paid-in capital in excess of stated value	$260,000	
Paid-in capital from treasury stock	16,000	276,000
Total contributed capital		$1,076,000
Retained earnings:		
Appropriated for contingencies (Note X)	$125,000	
Unappropriated	225,000	
Total retained earnings		350,000
Total contributed capital and retained earnings		$1,426,000
Deduct: Common treasury stock, at cost (5,000 shares acquired at $8)	$ 40,000	
Unrealized loss on available-for-sale securities	24,000	64,000
Total stockholders' equity		$1,362,000

Readers of financial statements should be provided with an explanation of the changes in individual equity balances during the period. Frequently, such explanation is provided in notes to the financial statements. When stockholders' equity is composed of numerous accounts, as in the preceding example, a **statement of changes in stockholders' equity** is frequently presented. An illustrative statement for the Hypothetical Corporation is shown below.

Hypothetical Corporation
Statement of Changes in Stockholders' Equity
For the Year Ended December 31, 1996

	Preferred Stock	Common Stock	Paid-In Capital	Appropriated Retained Earnings for Contingencies	Unappropriated Retained Earnings	Contra Equity Balances	Total
Balances, December 31, 1995	$300,000	$300,000	$260,000*	$ 90,000	$222,500	$(20,000)	$1,152,500
Prior-period adjustment—correction of 1994 error, net of tax					(25,000)		(25,000)
Adjusted balances, December 31, 1995	$300,000	$300,000	$260,000	$ 90,000	$197,500	$(20,000)	$1,127,500
Sale of 2,000 shares of preferred stock in January 1996, at par value	200,000						200,000
Sale of 2,500 shares of treasury stock, common, in January 1996, cost $20,000, for $36,000			16,000			20,000	36,000
Net income for 1996					120,000		120,000
Cash dividends:							
Preferred stock, $6 on 5,000 shares, $30,000 Common stock, 50¢ on 55,000 shares, $27,500					(57,500)		(57,500)
Retained earnings appropriated for contingencies				35,000	(35,000)		
Purchase of 5,000 shares of common treasury stock @ cost, $8						(40,000)	(40,000)
Net unrealized loss on available-for-sale securities						(24,000)	(24,000)
Balances, December 31, 1996	$500,000	$300,000	$276,000	$125,000	$225,000	$(64,000)	$1,362,000

*From sale of common stock at more than stated value

The net ownership equity of a business is an important element. Analysis of the amounts and sources of contributed capital compared to those generated and retained by the company provide useful information for assessing the long-term profitability and solvency of a business. The techniques for analyzing financial statements are discussed in the last chapter of the text.

KEY TERMS

Appropriated retained earnings 677
Cash dividend 678
Deficit 675
Dividends 675
Liquidating dividend 684
Owners' Equity 673
Prior-period adjustment 674
Property dividend 678
Quasi-reorganization 685
Retained earnings 673
Statement of changes in stockholders' equity 688
Stock dividend 679
Stock split 682
Unappropriated (free) retained earnings 677

QUESTIONS

1. What is the impact of each of the following transactions or events on retained earnings or total stockholders' equity?
   (a) Operating profits.
   (b) Discovery of an understatement of income in a previous period.
   (c) Release of Retained Earnings Appropriated for Purchase of Treasury Stock upon the sale of treasury stock.
   (d) Issuance of bonds at a premium.
   (e) Purchase of a corporation's own capital stock.
   (f) Increase in a company's earning capacity, assumed to be evidence of considerable goodwill.
   (g) Construction of equipment for a company's own use at a cost less than the prevailing market price of identical equipment.
   (h) Sale of land, buildings, and equipment at a gain.
   (i) Gain on bond retirement.
   (j) Conversion of bonds into common stock.
   (k) Conversion of preferred stock into common stock.
2. What are the two major considerations of a board of directors in making decisions involving dividend declarations?
3. Very few companies pay dividends in amounts equal to their retained earnings. Why?
4. The following announcement appeared on the financial page of a newspaper:
   The Board of Directors of Benton Co., at their meeting on June 15, 1996, declared the regular quarterly dividend on outstanding common stock of $1.40 per share, payable on July 10, 1996, to the stockholders of record at the close of business June 30, 1996.
   (a) What is the purpose of each of the three dates given in the announcement?
   (b) When would the common stock of Benton Co. normally trade "ex-dividend"?
5. Dividends are sometimes said to have been paid "out of retained earnings." What is wrong with such a statement?
6. The directors of The Dress Shoppe are considering issuance of a stock dividend. They have asked you to answer the following questions regarding the proposed action: (a) How are stock dividends accounted for by the issuing corporation? (b) By the stockholder?
7. Often, when a company declares a stock dividend, fractional share warrants are issued to certain stockholders. (a) What is a fractional share warrant? (b) What can the stockholder do with fractional share warrants? (c) If the company does not want to issue fractional share warrants, what alternatives are available?
8. At a regular meeting of the board of directors of the Greenwood Corporation, a property dividend payable in the stock of the Mossey Corporation is to be declared. The stock of Mossey Corporation is recorded on the books of the Greenwood Corporation at $190,000; the market value of the stock is $230,000. The question is raised whether the amount to be recorded for the dividend payable should be the book value or the market value. What is the proper accounting treatment?
9. (a) What is a liquidating dividend? (b) Under what circumstances are such distributions made?
10. (a) Why might a company seek a quasi-reorganization? (b) What are the steps in a quasi-reorganization?
11. In reviewing the financial statements of Farmer Inc., a stockholder does not understand the purpose of Appropriation of Retained Earnings for Bond Redemption Fund that has been set up by periodic debits to Retained Earnings. The stockholder is told that this balance will not be used to redeem the bonds at their maturity. (a) What account will be reduced by the payment of the bonds? (b) What purpose is accomplished by the Appropriation of Retained Earnings for Bond Redemption Fund? (c) What disposition is made of the appropriation after the bonds are retired?

DISCUSSION CASES

Case 16—1 (Small stock dividends)

The president of Info Company suggests including the following statements in this year's annual report:

On December 18, a 10% common stock dividend was distributed to stockholders, resulting in a transfer of $1,536,000 from Retained Earnings to Common Stock and Capital in Excess of Par. While the percentage of the stock dividend was the same as the previous year, the sum transferred to stockholders' equity was nearly $80,000 less.

The seeming inconsistency is the result of the requirement of regulatory authorities that the value of stock dividends on the company's books be related to the market value of the stock. As a result, the present year's dividend was valued at $65 per share as compared to $74 per share for last year's stock dividend.

The president feels that this statement would help clarify the apparent inconsistency in the company's dividend policy. As partner for the accounting firm that is performing the annual audit of Info Company, you feel that the president's statement may mislead the readers of the report even though the figures are correct.

State how the stock dividends should be accounted for in a situation such as this one, explaining your reasoning. What criticism, if any, do you have of the terminology used by the president? Explain.

Case 16—2 (How much should our dividend be?)

Largo Corp. has paid quarterly dividends of $0.70 per share for the last three years and is trying to continue this tradition. Largo's balance sheet is as follows:

Largo Corp.
Balance Sheet
December 31, 1996

Assets		Liabilities	
Current assets:		Current liabilities:	
Cash	$ 50,000	Accounts payable	$ 520,000
Accounts receivable	450,000	Taxes payable	100,000
Inventory	1,200,000	Accrued liabilities	90,000
Total current assets	$1,700,000	Total current liabilities	$ 710,000
Investments	500,000	Bonds payable	1,500,000
Land, buildings and equipment (net)	1,600,000	Total liabilities	$2,210,000
		Stockholders' Equity	
		Common stock ($10 par, 69,000 shares outstanding)	$690,000
		Retained earnings	900,000
		Total stockholders' equity	$1,590,000
Total assets	$3,800,000	Total liabilities and stockholders' equity	$3,800,000

Discuss Largo's possibilities concerning the issuance of dividends.

Case 16—3 (Cash or stock dividend?)

Best Ski Manufacturer is considering offering a 10% stock dividend rather than its normal cash dividend of $1 per share in the first quarter of 1996. However, some of Best's stockholders have expressed displeasure at the idea and say they strongly prefer cash dividends.

Discuss the issue of a stock dividend as opposed to a cash dividend from the points of view of (a) a stockholder and (b) the board of directors.

Case 16—4 **(Stock splits and stock dividends)**

Assume Union and Eastern Corporation has been one of the more popular growth stocks during the past several years. In 1996, its $20 par common stock was selling in the range of $200-$230, with 146,000 shares outstanding. On May 1, 1996, Union and Eastern announced that, effective May 10, 1996, its stock would be split 4-for-1 and the par value decreased proportionately. This was the first time since 1976 that Union and Eastern's stock had been split, although several stock dividends had been issued during the past 20 years. (a) What are the differences between a stock dividend and a stock split with reduction in par value both from the standpoint of the investor and the company? (b) What are some possible reasons for Union and Eastern issuing stock dividends prior to 1996?

Case 16—5 **(Are cash dividends relevant?)**

On March 23, 1996, the board of directors of Mycroft Company declared a quarterly cash dividend on its $1 par common stock of $0.50 per share, payable on May 10, 1996, to the shareholders of record on April 14, 1996. Before April 9, Mycroft's shares traded in the stock market "with dividend," meaning that the quoted stock price included the right to receive the dividend. After April 9, the shares traded "ex-dividend," meaning that the quoted price did not include the right to receive the dividend. Before April 9, Mycroft's shares were selling for $30 per share. What should happen to Mycroft's stock price on April 9, the ex-dividend date? What should happen to Mycroft's stock price on March 23, the dividend declaration date?

Case 16—6 **(Out of sight, out of mind)**

Accounting standards vary significantly among countries throughout the world. In Japan, for example, payments of bonuses to directors may be deducted from retained earnings rather than being charged to income of the year. How does this standard affect the economic decision of paying such bonuses to directors? Can accounting standards be neutral in their impact on economic decision making by companies? Should they be neutral?

Case 16—7 **(Sending a signal)**

You are the controller of a company that has decided to double its number of shares outstanding. The board of directors has asked you to decide whether this should be done through a 100% stock dividend or a 2-for-1 stock split. Draft a memo to the board explaining your recommended accounting treatment.

Case 16—8 **(What shall we do with these restructuring charges?)**

Restructuring of a company's operations can lead to significant layoffs of employees resulting in severance, retraining, and relocation costs. Companies often estimate the costs of restructuring and recognize these costs on the financial statements before any funds have been expended. How should these restructuring charges be recognized? Under what circumstances, if any, might they be charged directly to Retained Earnings?

EXERCISES

Exercise 16—9 **(Reporting errors from previous periods)**

Endicott Company's December 31, 1995, balance sheet reported retained earnings of $86,500, and net income of $124,000 was reported in the 1995 income statement. While preparing financial statements for the year ending December 31, 1996, Tom Dryden, accountant for Endicott Company, discovered that net income for 1995 had been overstated by $22,000 due to an error in recording depreciation expense for 1995. Net income for 1996 was $106,000, and dividends of $30,000 were declared and paid in 1996.

1. What effect, if any, would the $22,000 error made in 1995 have on the company's 1996 financial statements?
2. Compute the amount of retained earnings to be reported in Endicott Company's December 31, 1996, balance sheet.

Exercise 16—10 (Cash and stock dividends)

On September 30, 1996, Lomax Company issued 4,000 shares of its $5 par common stock in connection with a stock dividend. No entry was made on the stock dividend declaration date. The market value of the stock on the date of declaration was $10 per share. The stockholders' equity accounts of Lomax Company immediately before issuance of the stock dividend shares were as follows:

Common stock, $5 par; 100,000 shares authorized; 40,000 shares outstanding	$200,000
Additional paid-in capital	300,000
Retained earnings	350,000

On December 30, 1996, Lomax Company declared a cash dividend of $3.50 per share payable January 5, 1997. Give the necessary entries to record the declaration and payment or issuance of the dividends.

Exercise 16—11 (Property dividends)

Bradley Company distributed the following dividends to its stockholders:

(a) 400,000 shares of Shell Corporation stock, carrying value of investment $1,200,000, fair market value $2,300,000.

(b) 230,000 shares of Evans Company stock, a closely held corporation. The shares were purchased by Bradley three years ago at $5.60 per share, but no current market price is available.

Give the journal entries to account for the declaration and the payment of the dividends.

Exercise 16—12 (Accounting for property dividends)

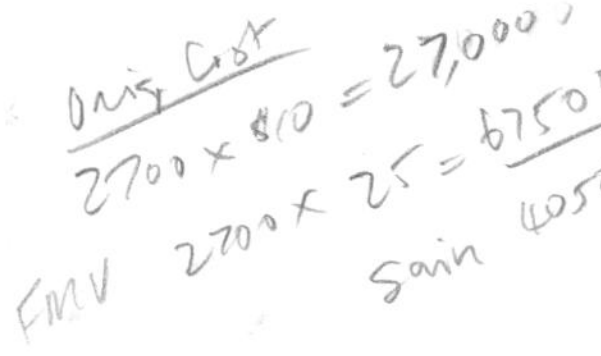

Hartz Corporation owned 2,700 shares of Finch Corporation common stock that it had purchased in 1993 for $10 per share. On August 15, 1996, when the value of Finch stock was $25 per share, Hartz declared a property dividend of 1 share of Finch for every 15 shares of Hartz common stock held by stockholders on October 15, 1996. Hartz had 40,500 shares of common outstanding. The Finch shares were distributed on December 15, 1996.

1. Prepare the journal entries on Hartz's books to record the property dividend.
2. Prepare the journal entry to record the property dividend on the books of an investor who owns 900 shares of Hartz Corporation common stock.

Exercise 16—13 (Dividend computations)

Consistent Company has been paying regular quarterly dividends of $1.50 and wants to pay the same amount in the third quarter of 1996. Given the following information, (1) what is the total amount that Consistent will have to pay in dividends in the third quarter in order to pay $1.50 per share, and (2) what is the total amount of dividends to be distributed during the year assuming no equity transactions occur after June 30?

1996		
Jan.	1	Shares outstanding, 800,000; $8 par (1,500,000 shares authorized).
Feb.	15	Issued 50,000 new shares at $10.50.
Mar.	31	Paid quarterly dividends of $1.50 per share.
May	12	$1,000,000 of $1,000 bonds were converted to common stock at the rate of 100 shares of stock per $1,000 bond.
June	15	Issued a 15% stock dividend.
	30	Paid quarterly dividends of $1.50 per share.

Exercise 16—14 (Stock dividends)

The balance sheet of the Carmen Corporation shows the following:

Common stock, $5 stated value, 80,000 shares issued and outstanding	$400,000
Paid-in capital in excess of stated value	800,000
Retained earnings	350,000

A 25% stock dividend is declared, the board of directors authorizing a transfer from Retained Earnings to Common Stock at the stated value of the shares.

1. Give entries to record the declaration and issuance of the stock dividend.
2. What was the effect of the issuance of the stock dividend on the ownership equity of each stockholder in the corporation?
3. Give entries to record the declaration and issuance of the dividend if the board of directors had elected to transfer an amount from Retained Earnings equal to the market value of the stock ($10 per share).

Exercise 16—15 (Stock dividends and stock splits)

The capital accounts for Shop Right Market on June 30, 1996, are as follows:

Common stock, $15 par, 40,000 shares	$ 600,000
Paid-in capital in excess of par	435,000
Retained earnings	2,160,000

Shares of the company's stock are selling at this time at $25. What entries would you make in each of the following cases?

(a) A 10% stock dividend is declared and issued.
(b) A 50% stock dividend is declared and issued.
(c) A 3-for-1 stock split is declared and issued. Shop Right records this split in the form of a stock dividend, with no change in par value.

Exercise 16—16 (Accounting for stock splits)

Effective December 31, 1996, the stockholders of Cushion Corp. approved a 2-for-1 split of the company's common stock and an increase in authorized common shares from 200,000 (par value $10 per share) to 400,000 shares (par value $5 per share). Cushion's stockholders' equity accounts immediately before these events are summarized as follows:

Common stock ($10 par, 200,000 shares authorized, 100,000 issued and outstanding)	$1,000,000
Additional paid-in capital—common stock	150,000
Total contributed capital	$1,150,000
Retained earnings	1,350,000
Total stockholders' equity	$2,500,000

1. Make the necessary entries to record the stock split for both Cushion and the investors.
2. Prepare the stockholders' equity section of Cushion's December 31, 1996, balance sheet.

Exercise 16—17 (Stock dividend computation)

The directors of Warehouser Inc., whose $80 par value common stock is currently selling at $100 per share, have decided to issue a stock dividend. Warehouser has authorization for 400,000 shares of common, has issued 220,000 shares, all of which are currently outstanding, and desires to capitalize $2,400,000 of the retained earnings account balance. What percent stock dividend should be issued to accomplish this goal?

Exercise 16—18 (Stock split recorded as a large stock dividend)

Gabetzco, Inc. issued a 3-for-1 stock split but decided to retain the same $10 par value the stock had before the split. The number of issued common shares increased from 200,000 shares to 600,000 shares. The following balances existed in Gabetzco's stockholders' equity accounts prior to recording the stock split.

Common Stock, 200,000 shares at $10	$ 2,000,000
Additional Paid-In Capital	700,000
Retained Earnings	10,000,000

Prepare journal entries to record the split under the following situations:

a. Gabetzco desires to transfer amounts to Common Stock from Additional Paid-In Capital rather than from Retained Earnings.
b. Gabetzco wants to reduce Retained Earnings as much as possible to relieve pressure from stockholders to pay more cash dividends.

Exercise 16—19 (Accounting for dividends)

The following information has been taken from the balance sheet of Kain Company:

Current assets	$371,250
Investments	431,400
Common stock (par value $20)	337,000
Paid-in capital in excess of par	200,000
Retained earnings	385,000

Prepare the journal entries for the following unrelated transactions:

(a) A 30% stock dividend is declared and distributed when the market value of the stock is $23 per share.
(b) Par value of the common stock is reduced to $5, and the stock is split 4-for-1.
(c) A dividend of 1 share Northern Co. common stock for every share of Kain Company stock is declared and distributed. Northern Co. common stock is carried on the books of Kain Company at a cost of $0.80 per share, and the market value is $1.10 per share.

Exercise 16—20 (Fractional share warrants)

Groton Company has 500,000 shares of $1 par common stock outstanding. The market price of the shares is $25 per share. In declaring and distributing a 10% stock dividend, Groton initially issued only 46,000 new shares; the other stock dividend shares were not issued, because some investors did not own Groton shares in even multiples of ten. To these stockholders Groton issued fractional share warrants. Prepare all journal entries necessary to record the declaration and distribution of the stock dividend assuming that 90% of the fractional share warrants were ultimately turned in for shares.

Exercise 16—21 (Restricting retained earnings)

On January 1, 1994, Northwest Manufacturing Corporation issued $20,000,000 of bonds payable. The bond issue agreement with the underwriters required Northwest Manufacturing to appropriate earnings of $1,250,000 at the end of each year until the bonds are retired. During their June 1996 board meeting, the directors decided to change the company's financial structure to include only short-term debt and to drop their present insurance policy in favor of a self-insurance plan. On July 1, 1996, the company retired the bond issue and set up the first annual appropriation for self-insurance for $28,000.

1. Give the entries to record the periodic appropriations under the bond issue agreement for 1994 and 1995 and their cancellation in 1996.
2. Give the entry to record the appropriation for self-insurance.

Exercise 16—22 (Computation of retained earnings)

The following information has been taken from the accounts of Oviatt Corporation:

Total net income reported since incorporation	$300,000
Total cash dividends paid	80,000
Capitalized value of stock dividends distributed	70,000
Paid-in capital from treasury stock	35,000
Bond discount	75,000
Appropriation for plant expansion	100,000

Determine the current balance of unappropriated retained earnings.

Exercise 16—23 (Correcting the retained earnings account)

The retained earnings account for Gotfried Corp. shows the following debits and credits. Give all entries required to correct the account. What is the corrected amount of retained earnings?

Account: RETAINED EARNINGS

Date		Item	Debit	Credit	Balance Debit	Balance Credit
Jan.	1	Balance				263,200
(a)		Loss from fire	2,625			260,575
(b)		Write-off of goodwill	26,250			234,325
(c)		Stock dividend	70,000			164,325
(d)		Loss on sale of equipment	24,150			140,175
(e)		Officers' compensation related to income of prior periods—accrual overlooked	162,750		22,575	
(f)		Loss on retirement of preferred shares at more than issuance price	35,000		57,575	
(g)		Paid-in capital in excess of par		64,750		7,175
(h)		Stock subscription defaults		4,235		11,410
(i)		Gain on retirement of preferred stock at less than issuance price		12,950		24,360
(j)		Gain on early retirement of bonds at less than book value		7,525		31,885
(k)		Gain on life insurance policy settlement		5,250		37,135
(l)		Correction of prior-period error		25,025		62,160

Exercise 16—24 (Liquidating dividend)

Van Etten Company declared and paid a cash dividend of $4.50 per share on its $1 par common stock. Van Etten has 100,000 shares of common stock outstanding and total paid-in capital from common stock of $800,000. As part of the dividend announcement, Van Etten stated that retained earnings served as the basis for only $0.50 of the dividend; investors should consider the remainder to be a return of investment. Prepare the journal entries necessary on Van Etten's books to record the declaration and distribution of this dividend.

Exercise 16—25 (Quasi-reorganization)

Hard Luck Corporation has incurred losses from operations for many years. At the recommendation of the newly hired president, the board of directors voted to implement a quasi-reorganization, subject to stockholders' approval. Immediately prior to the quasi-reorganization, on June 30, 1996, Hard Luck's balance sheet was as follows:

Current assets	$ 275,000
Property, plant, and equipment (net)	675,000
Other assets	100,000
	$1,050,000
Total liabilities	$ 300,000
Common stock	800,000
Additional paid-in capital	150,000
Retained earnings	(200,000)
	$1,050,000

The stockholders approved the quasi-reorganization effective July 1, 1996, to be accomplished by a reduction in property, plant, and equipment (net) of $175,000, a reduction in other assets of $75,000, and appropriate adjustment to the capital structure.

1. Prepare the journal entries to record the quasi-reorganization on July 1, 1996.
2. Prepare a new balance sheet after the quasi-reorganization.

(AICPA adapted)

Exercise 16—26 (Reporting stockholders' equity)

Kenny Co. began operations on January 1, 1995, by issuing at $15 per share one-half of the 950,000 shares of $10 par value common stock that had been authorized for sale. In addition, Kenny has 500,000 shares of $5 par value, 6% preferred shares authorized. During 1995, Kenny had $1,025,000 of net income and declared $237,500 of dividends.

During 1996 Kenny had the following transactions:

Jan.	10	Issued an additional 100,000 shares of common stock for $17 per share.
Apr.	1	Issued 150,000 shares of the preferred stock for $8 per share.
July	19	Authorized the purchase of a custom-made machine to be delivered in January of 1997. Kenny restricted $295,000 of retained earnings for the purchase of the machine.
Oct.	23	Sold an additional 50,000 shares of the preferred stock for $9 per share.
Dec.	31	Reported $1,215,000 of net income and declared a dividend of $645,000 to stockholders of record on January 15, 1997, to be paid on February 1, 1997.

Prepare the stockholders' equity section of Kenny's balance sheet for December 31, 1995, and December 31, 1996.

PROBLEMS

Problem 16—27 (Accounting for stock transactions)

Morris Corporation is publicly owned, and its shares are traded on a national stock exchange. Morris has 16,000 shares of $25 stated value common stock authorized. Only 75% of these shares have been issued, and of the shares issued, only 11,000 are outstanding. On December 31, 1995, the stockholders' equity section revealed that the balance in Paid-In Capital in Excess of Stated Value was $140,000, and the retained earnings balance was $110,000. Treasury stock was purchased at an average cost of $37.50 per share.

During 1996, Morris had the following transactions:

Jan.	15	Morris issued, at $55 per share, 800 shares of $50 par, 5% cumulative preferred stock; 2,000 shares are authorized.
Feb.	1	Morris sold 1,500 shares of newly issued $25 stated value common stock at $42 per share.
Mar.	15	Morris declared a cash dividend on common stock of $0.15 per share, payable on April 30 to all stockholders of record on April 1.
Apr.	15	Morris reacquired 200 shares of its common stock for $43 per share. Morris uses the cost method to account for treasury stock.
	30	Employees exercised 1,000 options granted in 1991 under a fixed stock option plan. When the options were granted, each option entitled the employee to purchase 1 share of common stock for $50 per share. The share price on the grant date was also $50 per share. On April 30, when the market price was $55 per share, Morris issued new shares to the employees.
May	1	Morris declared a 10% stock dividend to be distributed on June 1 to stockholders of record on May 7. The market price of the common stock was $50 per share on May 1. (Assume treasury shares do not participate in stock dividends.)

	31	Morris sold 150 treasury shares reacquired on April 15 and an additional 200 shares costing $7,500 that had been on hand since the beginning of the year. The selling price was $57 per share.
Sep.	15	The semiannual cash dividend on common stock was declared, amounting to $0.15 per share. Morris also declared the yearly dividend on preferred stock. Both are payable on October 15 to stockholders of record on October 1.

Net income for 1996 was $50,000.

Instructions:

1. Compute the number of shares and dollar amount of treasury stock at the beginning of 1996.
2. Make the necessary journal entries to record the transactions in 1996 relating to stockholders' equity.
3. Prepare the stockholders' equity section of Morris Corporation's December 31, 1996, balance sheet.

Problem 16—28 (Accounting for stock transactions)

Brady Company has 30,000 shares of $10 par value common stock authorized and 20,000 shares issued and outstanding. On August 15, 1996, Brady purchased 1,500 shares of treasury stock for $12 per share. (All outstanding shares were issued for $11 per share.) Brady uses the cost method to account for treasury stock. On September 14, 1996, Brady sold 500 shares of the treasury stock for $14 per share.

On October 30, 1996, when the market value of the common stock was $16 per share, Brady declared and distributed 2,000 shares as a "small" stock dividend, 1,500 from unissued shares and 500 from treasury shares. (Assume treasury shares do not participate in stock dividends.)

On December 20, 1996, Brady declared a $1-per-share cash dividend, payable on January 10, 1997, to shareholders of record on December 31, 1996.

Instructions:

1. Make the entries necessary for Brady to record the above transactions.
2. Assuming that Brady's stockholders' equity consists of only the above mentioned items and that retained earnings was $375,000 as of December 31, 1995 (net income for 1996 was $56,000), prepare the stockholders' equity section of Brady's balance sheet as of December 31, 1996.

(AICPA adapted)

Problem 16—29 (Accounting for stock transactions)

Ellis Corporation was organized on June 30, 1993. After two and one-half years of profitable operations, the equity section of Ellis's balance sheet was as follows:

Contributed capital:	
Common stock, $30 par, 600,000 shares authorized, 200,000 shares issued and outstanding	$6,000,000
Paid-in capital in excess of par	600,000
Retained earnings	2,800,000
Total stockholders' equity	$9,400,000

During 1996, the following transactions affected the stockholders' equity:

Jan.	31	10,000 shares of common stock were reacquired at $32; treasury stock is recorded at cost.
Apr.	1	The company declared a 30% stock dividend. (Applies to all issued stock.)
	30	The company declared a $0.75 cash dividend. (Applies only to outstanding stock.)

June	1	The stock dividend was issued, and the cash dividend was paid.
Aug.	31	All treasury stock was sold at $35.

Instructions: Give journal entries to record the stock transactions.

Problem 16—30 (Stock dividend and cash dividend)

On January 1, 1996, Homer Company has 100,000 shares of $0.50 par common stock outstanding. The market value of Homer's common stock is $20 per share. Homer's retained earnings balance on January 1 was $580,000. During 1995, Homer declared and paid cash dividends of $0.70 per share. Net income for 1996 is expected to be $110,000. Homer has a large loan from Garth Bank; part of the loan agreement stipulates that Homer must maintain a minimum retained earnings balance of $400,000.

Homer's board of directors is debating whether to declare a stock dividend. Three proposals have been presented: (1) no stock dividend, (2) a 10% stock dividend, and (3) a 25% stock dividend.

Instructions: As a shareholder in Homer Company, which of the three proposals do you favor? Support your answer.

Problem 16—31 (Stockholders' equity transactions)

The stockholders' equity of the Seasoned Lumber Co. on June 30, 1996, was as follows:

Contributed capital:	
5% preferred stock, $50 par, cumulative, 30,000 shares issued, dividends 5 years in arrears	$1,500,000
Common stock, $30 par, 100,000 shares issued	3,000,000
	$4,500,000
Deficit from operations	(600,000)
Total stockholders' equity	$3,900,000

On July 1 the following actions were taken:

(a) Common stockholders turned in their old common stock and received in exchange new common stock, 1 share of the new stock being exchanged for every 4 shares of the old. New common stock was given a stated value of $60 per share.
(b) One-half share of the new common stock was issued on each share of preferred stock outstanding in liquidation of dividends in arrears on preferred stock.
(c) The deficit from operations was applied against the paid-in capital arising from the common stock restatement.

Transactions for the remainder of 1996 affecting the stockholders' equity were as follows:

Oct.	1	10,000 shares of preferred stock were called at $55 plus dividends for 3 months at 5%. Stock was formally retired.
Nov.	10	60,000 shares of new common stock were sold at $65.
Dec.	31	Net income for the 6 months ended on this date was $400,000. (Debit Income Summary.) The semiannual dividend was declared on preferred shares, and a $0.75 dividend was declared on common shares, dividends being payable January 20, 1997.

Instructions:

1. Record in journal form the foregoing transactions.
2. Prepare the stockholders' equity section of the balance sheet as of December 31, 1996.

Problem 16—32 (Stockholders' equity transactions)

Seneca Inc. was organized on January 2, 1995, with authorized capital stock consisting of 50,000 shares of 10%, $200 par preferred, and 200,000 shares of no-par, no-stated-value common. During the first 2 years of the company's existence, the following selected transactions took place:

1995		
Jan.	2	Sold 10,000 shares of common stock at $16.
	2	Sold 3,000 shares of preferred stock at $216.
Mar.	2	Sold common stock as follows: 10,800 shares at $22; 2,700 shares at $25.
July	10	A nearby piece of land, appraised at $400,000, was acquired for 600 shares of preferred stock and 27,000 shares of common. (Preferred stock was recorded at $216, the balance being assigned to common.)
Dec.	16	The regular preferred and a $1.50 common dividend were declared.
	28	Dividends declared on December 16 were paid.
	31	The income summary account showed a credit balance of $450,000, which was transferred to Retained Earnings.
1996		
Feb.	27	The corporation reacquired 12,000 shares of common stock at $19. The treasury stock is carried at cost. (State law required that an appropriation of retained earnings be made for the purchase price of treasury stock. Appropriations are to be returned to Retained Earnings upon resale of the stock.)
June	17	Resold 10,000 shares of the treasury stock at $23.
July	31	Resold all of the remaining treasury stock at $18.
Sep.	30	The corporation sold 11,000 additional shares of common stock at $21.
Dec.	16	The regular preferred dividend and an $0.80 common dividend were declared.
	28	Dividends declared on December 16 were paid.
	31	The income summary account showed a credit balance of $425,000, which was transferred to Retained Earnings.

Instructions:

1. Give the journal entries to record the foregoing transactions.
2. Prepare the stockholders' equity section of the balance sheet as of December 31, 1996.

Problem 16—33 (Accounting for stockholders' equity)

A condensed balance sheet for Sharp Tax Inc. as of December 31, 1993, appears below.

Sharp Tax Inc.
Condensed Balance Sheet
December 31, 1993

Assets		Liabilities and Stockholders' Equity	
Assets	$525,000	Liabilities	$120,000
		8% preferred stock, $100 par	75,000
		Common stock, $50 par	150,000
		Paid-in capital in excess of par	30,000
		Retained earnings	150,000
Total assets	$525,000	Total liabilities and stockholders' equity	$525,000

Capital stock authorized consists of 750 shares of 8%, cumulative preferred stock, and 15,000 shares of common stock.

Information relating to operations of the succeeding 3 years follows:

	1994	1995	1996
Dividends declared on Dec. 20, payable on Jan. 10 of the following year:			
Preferred stock	8% cash	8% cash	8% cash
Common stock	$1.00 cash	$1.25 cash	$1.00 cash
	50% stock		
Net income for year	$67,500	$39,000	$51,000

1995

Feb. 12 Accumulated depreciation was reduced by $72,000 following an income tax investigation. (Assume that this was an error that qualified as a prior-period adjustment.) Additional income tax of $22,500 for prior years was paid.

Mar. 3 Purchased 300 shares of common stock at $54 per share; treasury stock is recorded at cost, and retained earnings are appropriated equal to such costs.

1996

Aug. 10 All the treasury stock was resold at $59 per share and the retained earnings appropriation was canceled.

Sep. 12 By vote of the stockholders, each share of the common stock was exchanged by the corporation for 4 shares of no-par common stock with a stated value of $15.

Instructions:

1. Give the journal entries to record the foregoing transactions for the 3-year period ended December 31, 1996.
2. Prepare the stockholders' equity section of the balance sheet as it would appear at the end of 1994, 1995, and 1996.

Problem 16—34 (Adjustments to retained earnings)

On March 31, 1996, the retained earnings account of Universal Services showed a balance of $19,000,000. The board of directors of Universal made the following decisions during the remainder of 1996 that possibly affect the retained earnings account.

Apr. 1 Universal decided to assume the risk for workers' compensation insurance. The estimated liability for 1996 was $120,000. Also, a fund was set up to cover the estimated liability.

30 Universal has not experienced even a small fire since 1949; therefore, the board of directors decided to start a self-insurance plan. They decided to start with a $400,000 appropriation.

May 15 A fire did considerable damage to the outside warehouse. It cost $360,000 to repair the warehouse.

Aug. 20 The board of directors received a report from the plant engineer indicating that the company is possibly in violation of pollution control standards. The fine for such a violation is $800,000. As a result of the engineer's report, the board decided to set up a general contingency appropriation for $800,000.

Sep. 1 The company reacquired 80,000 shares of its own stock at $29; treasury stock is recorded at cost. Due to legal restrictions, Universal has to set up an appropriation to cover the cost of the treasury stock.

Dec. 31 The company had to pay an $800,000 fine for pollution control violations and the treasury stock was sold at $31. No workers' compensation was paid during the year.

Instructions: Prepare all the necessary entries to record the transactions.

Problem 16—35 (Reporting stockholders' equity)

The following data (presented in alphabetical order) were derived from the accounts of High Country Ranch as of December 31, 1996:

	Debits	Credits
Accumulated depreciation—buildings		$ 255,000
Bonds payable		325,000
Bond retirement fund	$ 138,000	
Buildings	1,150,000	
Common stock, $10 par (89,000 shares authorized, 63,200 shares issued		632,000
Common stock subscribed (4,000 shares)		40,000
Common stock subscriptions receivable	25,000	
Current assets	790,200	
Current liabilities—other		270,000
Customer deposits		17,000
Dividends payable—cash		16,000
Income taxes payable		43,000
Paid-in capital from treasury stock		32,000
Paid-in capital in excess of par		49,000
Retained earnings appropriated for contingencies		100,000
Retained earnings appropriated for bond retirement fund		138,000
Retained earnings appropriated for purchase of treasury stock		56,000
Stock dividends distributable (5,040 shares)		50,400
Treasury stock (4,800 shares at cost)	56,000	
Unappropriated retained earnings		135,800
	$2,159,200	$2,159,200

Instructions: From these data, prepare the stockholders' equity section as it would appear on the balance sheet.

Problem 16—36 (Retained earnings and the statement of cash flows)

The following items relate to the activities of Cortland Company for 1996:

(a) Cash dividends declared and paid on common stock during the year totaled $80,000. In addition, on January 15, 1996, dividends of $15,000 that were declared in 1995 were paid.
(b) Retained earnings of $130,000 were appropriated during the year in anticipation of a major capital expansion in future years.
(c) Depreciation expense was $50,000.
(d) Equipment was purchased for $250,000 in cash.
(e) Early in the year, a 10% stock dividend was declared and distributed. This stock dividend resulted in the distribution of 50,000 new shares of $1 par common stock. The market value per share before the stock dividend was $40.
(f) Cash revenues for the year totaled $600,000.
(g) Cash expenses for the year totaled $320,000.
(h) Old machinery was sold for its book value of $10,000.
(i) Near the end of the year, a 2-for-1 stock split was declared. The 550,000 shares of $1 par common stock outstanding at the time were exchanged for 1,100,000 shares with a par value of $0.50.
(j) Cash dividends totaling $35,000 were declared and paid on preferred stock.
(k) Land was acquired in exchange for 6,000 shares of $0.50 par common stock. The land had a fair market value of $130,000.
(l) Assume no changes in current operating receivable and payable balances during the year.

Instructions: Prepare a statement of cash flows for Cortland Company for the year ended December 31, 1996. Use the indirect method for reporting cash flow from operating activities.

Problem 16—37 (Quasi-reorganization)

Kennington Copper has experienced several loss years and has plant assets on its books that are overvalued. Kennington plans to revalue its assets downward and eliminate the deficit. At December 31, 1996, the company owns the following plant assets:

	Cost	Accumulated Depreciation	Book Value	Market Value
Land	$ 600,000	—	$ 600,000	$300,000
Buildings	850,000	$350,000	500,000	250,000
Machinery and Equipment	450,000	250,000	200,000	150,000
	$1,900,000	$600,000	$1,300,000	$700,000

The balance sheet on December 31, 1996, reported the following balances in the stockholders' equity section:

Common stock, $25 par, 70,000 shares	$1,750,000
Paid-in capital in excess of par	300,000
Retained earnings (deficit)	(350,000)
Total	$1,700,000

As part of the reorganization, the common stock is to be canceled and reissued at $10 par.

Instructions:

1. Prepare the journal entries to record the quasi-reorganization.
2. Give the plant asset section and stockholders' equity section of the company's balance sheet as they would appear after the entries are posted.

Problem 16—38 (Balance sheet preparation)

The following trial balance was taken from the books of Alvarez Manufacturing, a calendar-year corporation, as of April 30, 1996:

Alvarez Manufacturing
Trial Balance
April 30, 1996

	Debit	Credit
Cash	$ 310,000	
Accounts Receivable	800,000	
Finished Goods	500,000	
Goods in Process	100,000	
Raw Materials	750,000	
Land, Buildings, and Equipment	1,460,000	
Prepaid Expenses	5,400	
Sales Returns and Allowances	25,000	
Administrative Salaries	65,000	
Cost of Goods Sold	2,350,000	
Travel Expense	30,030	
Interest Expense	10,570	
Accounts Payable		$ 175,000
Notes Payable		100,000
Payroll Payable		6,000
Interest Payable on 6% Bonds		10,000
6% Preferred Stock, $50 par		1,000,000
Common Stock, $100 par		1,416,000
6% Bonds Payable (due June 30, 2004)		500,000
Sales		2,500,000
Retained Earnings, December 31, 1995		520
Additional Paid-In Capital		698,480
	$6,406,000	$6,406,000

The following transactions have been completed by the company:

(a) The company has purchased various lots of its $100 par value common stock, totaling 840 shares, at an average price of $65.50 per share, for $55,020. In recording these transactions, the company has canceled the stock certificates and debited the common stock account with the par value of $84,000 and credited the paid-in capital account with the $28,980 difference between par and the cash paid.
(b) Additional Paid-In Capital was previously credited for $20 per share on the sale of 15,000 shares of common stock at $120.
(c) 6% bonds with a total face amount of $250,000 falling due on December 31, 2002, were issued on January 1, 1978, at a 10% discount. To June 30, 1994, $16,500 of this discount had been charged against revenues, and as of this date, the entire issue of these bonds was retired at par and the unamortized discount debited to Additional Paid-In Capital.
(d) A new issue of $500,000, 6%, 10-year bonds was sold at par on July 1, 1994. Expenses incurred with respect to this issue in the amount of $20,000 were debited to Additional Paid-In Capital.

Instructions: Prepare a balance sheet as of April 30, 1996, making any corrections necessary in view of the company's treatment of the preceding transactions.

(AICPA adapted)

Problem 16—39 (Dividends and stock rights—entries for company and investor)

On April 1, 1995, Estancia Co. purchased 1,000 shares of Cooper Co. common stock, par $10, at $20. On June 1, when the stock was selling for $22 on the open market, Estancia Co. received a 10% stock dividend from Cooper Co. On October 26, Cooper Co. paid Estancia Co. a dividend of $0.75 on the stock and granted a stock right to purchase 1 share at $15 for every 5 shares held. On this date, the stock had a market value ex-rights of $22.50, and each right had a value of $1.70; the stock cost was allocated on this basis. On November 15, Estancia Co. sold 120 rights at $1.25 and exercised the remaining rights. On March 3, 1996, Estancia Co. received a cash dividend from Cooper Co. of $1.50 per share. On October 13, Cooper Co. declared a 2-for-1 stock split recorded as a 100% stock dividend and, on October 31, declared dividends of $0.40 per share. On December 31, Estancia Co. sold all of its shares in Cooper Co. for $11.50.

Instructions: Prepare all entries for the preceding transactions on the books of (a) Estancia Co. and (b) Cooper Co. (Omit explanations but show computations. Assume these are the only equity transactions for Cooper Co.)

Problem 16—40 (Reporting stockholders' equity)

The stockholders' equity section of Nilsson Corporation's balance sheet as of December 31, 1995, is as follows:

Common stock ($5 par, 500,000 shares authorized, 275,000 issued and outstanding)	$1,375,000	
Additional paid-in capital—common stock	550,000	
Total paid-in capital		$1,925,000
Unappropriated retained earnings	$1,335,000	
Appropriated retained earnings	500,000	
Total retained earnings		1,835,000
Total stockholders' equity		$3,760,000

Nilsson Co. had the following stockholders' equity transactions during 1996:

Jan.	15	Completed the building renovation for which $500,000 of retained earnings had been restricted. Paid the contractor $485,000, all of which is capitalized.
Mar.	3	Issued 100,000 additional shares of the common stock for $8 per share.
May	18	Declared a dividend of $1.50 per share to be paid on July 31, 1996, to stockholders of record on June 30, 1996.
June	19	Approved additional building renovation to be funded internally. The estimated cost of the project is $400,000, and Retained Earnings are to be restricted for that amount.

July	31	Paid the dividend.
Nov.	12	Declared a property dividend to be paid on December 31, 1996, to stockholders of record on November 30, 1996. The dividend is to consist of 35,000 shares of Hampton Inc. stock that Nilsson purchased for $9 per share. The fair market value of the stock on November 12 is $13 per share.
Dec.	31	Reported $885,000 of net income on the December 31, 1996, income statement. In addition, the stock was distributed in satisfaction of the property dividend. The Hampton stock closed at $14 per share at the end of the day's trading.

Instructions:

1. Make all necessary journal entries for Nilsson to account for the transactions affecting stockholders' equity.
2. Prepare the December 31, 1996, stockholders' equity section of the balance sheet for Nilsson.

CHAPTER 17

Investments in Debt and Equity Securities

CHAPTER TOPICS

- Accounting for the Purchase of Debt and Equity Securities
- Recognition of Revenue From Investments in Securities
- Accounting for Changes in Value of Securities
- Accounting for Sales of Securities
- Recording Transfers of Securities Between Categories
- Classification and Disclosure of Investment in Securities
- Long-Term Investments in Funds (Appendix 17—1)
- Cash Surrender Value of Life Insurance (Appendix 17—2)
- Accounting by Creditors for Impairment of a Loan (Appendix 17—3)

Which company is the soft drink leader—Pepsi or Coke? A look at each company's 1993 income statement would indicate that Pepsi, with reported revenues of over $25 billion, outsells Coke which has reported revenues of almost $14 billion. However, a closer look at each company's financial statements reveals a strategic level of ownership in subsidiaries for one company and an interesting conglomeration of products for the other. Without a knowledge of how these factors are reflected in the financial statements, a user could reach misleading conclusions by focusing only on the income statements for the two firms.

Consider the 1993 financial statements of Coke. The reported revenues of $14 billion do not reflect any of the sales reported by two large bottling operations—Coca-Cola Enterprises, Inc. and Coca-Cola Amatil Ltd. Co.—even though Coke has a 44% ownership in the former and a 51% ownership in the latter. Sales for these two bottlers exceeded

$13.5 billion in 1993. On the other hand, Pepsi's revenues of $25 billion consist of revenues from three major business segments: the Snack Foods segment (accounting for 28% of Pepsi's revenues) with products like Doritos, Ruffles, Cheetos, and Fritos; the Restaurants segment (37% of revenues) with such chains as Taco Bell, KFC, and Pizza Hut; and the Beverages segment (35% of revenues) with the well-known brands of Pepsi (in all its varieties), Mountain Dew, and Slice. In a direct comparison of soft drink revenues, Coke outsells Pepsi $12.2 billion to $8.6 billion.

In this chapter, we will discuss why and how companies invest in other companies. Available excess cash is often invested to generate revenue that would not be available if cash were left idle. Companies generally make investments to receive a return of their investment as well as a return on the investment in the form of dividends, interest, or gains from appreciation upon sale or maturity of the investment. However, a company may invest in another company as a means of diversifying its products or services. This is precisely what Pepsi has done—it is no longer just a soft drink company. Companies also invest in other companies to exercise significant influence over them. Coke has a significant investment in its largest bottlers to ensure that production facilities are available.

Investments in debt and equity securities may be temporary or long-term in nature. Temporary investments can include such items as stocks and bonds and such investments as CDs, money market certificates, commercial paper (high-yield notes issued by corporations and generally maturing within 30 days to nine months) or Treasury Bills (U.S. government obligations that are sold at a weekly auction and have maturities ranging from 13 weeks to one year). Examples of securities classified as long-term include securities acquired to gain control of a company and securities held to maintain a business relationship with a company.

The topic of accounting for investments in debt and equity securities has generated a great deal of interest over the past several years. The primary area of concern is the disclosure of changes in market value. Because the value of investment securities can change dramatically in a short period of time, accounting information that reflects this change in value would be useful to businesses and financial statement users. To address the issue of valuation, the FASB issued Statement of Financial Accounting Standards No. 115, "Accounting for Certain Investments in Debt and Equity Securities." The major effect of this standard, issued in May of 1993, is to require businesses to record many of their investment securities at fair market value. This position differs from previous standards in that increases, as well as decreases, in the value of certain securities are reported in the financial statements.

In this chapter, we will address issues associated with investments in both debt and equity securities. Accounting for these investments involves four primary recording activities: (1) the initial purchase of securities, (2) the recognition of interest or dividend revenue, (3) changes in value (both temporary and permanent) of securities while they are held, and (4) the subsequent sale of securities. Each of these issues will be addressed in turn. Following the discussion of these issues, the accounting issues related to transferring investments from one classification to another are discussed. Two other common types of investments, special-purpose funds and cash surrender value of life insurance, are covered in Appendices 17-1 and 17-2, respectively. Appendix 17-3 addresses valuation issues associated with investments for which a readily determinable fair market value is not available.

PURCHASE OF SECURITIES

One of the characteristics of a free enterprise economy is the considerable level of intercorporate investment. An investment in equity securities reflects an ownership interest in the company whose stock is being purchased, while an investment in debt securities[1] reflects a creditor relationship. As indicated previously, a corporation may acquire securities of another established corporation for a variety of reasons. Whatever the specific objective, an investment in the securities of another corporate entity is expected to enhance the economic well-being of the acquiring company. Sophisticated markets have developed for the sale and purchase of both debt and equity securities.

As mentioned previously, FASB Statement No. 115 was issued to address the valuation of securities. The statement applies to all debt securities and to equity securities for which a readily determinable fair value is available.[2] If, however, the investment in equity securities of a company is large enough, i.e., ownership of more than 20% of the outstanding voting stock of the investee, other methods of accounting for equity securities are applied. Those other methods, the equity method and consolidation, are introduced later in this chapter. When the securities purchased fall within the scope of FASB Statement No. 115, the investing company is required to classify the securities into one of three categories. Each of these categories is introduced and defined below:

1. **Trading Securities**—Debt and equity securities purchased with the intent of selling them in the near future. Trading involves frequent buying and selling of securities, generally for the purpose of "generating profits on short-term differences in price."[3]
2. **Held-to-Maturity Securities**—Debt securities purchased by a company with the intent and ability to hold those securities until they mature.[4] Note that this category includes *only debt securities* because equity securities typically do not mature. Note also that the company must have the intention of holding the security until it matures. Simply intending to hold a security for a long period of time does not qualify for inclusion in this category.
3. **Available-for-Sale Securities**—Debt and equity securities that are not being held to maturity and are not classified as trading securities are, by default, considered "available-for-sale securities."[5]

The reason for these three distinctions is that the FASB requires different accounting and disclosure depending on the classification of the security. Securities classified as trading securities are reported at their fair market value on the balance sheet with any unrealized holding gains or losses being reported on the income statement as part of net income. Securities classified as available-for-sale securities are also reported on the balance sheet at fair market value. However, any unrealized holding gains and losses associated with these securities are reported as a separate component of stockholders' equity and thus do not affect income for the period. Held-to-maturity securities are reported on the balance sheet at their amortized cost and are not reported at fair value. The accounting for held-to-maturity securities is discussed in Chapter 14. The accounting for these securities remains relatively unchanged by FASB Statement No. 115.

Purchase of Debt Securities

The purchase of debt securities is recorded at cost, which includes brokerage fees, taxes, and other charges incurred in their acquisition. When debt securities are acquired between

1. Many of the accounting issues associated with investing in debt securities were addressed in Chapter 14. In that chapter, transactions involving debt securities were detailed from the point of view of both the creditor and the investor and it was noted that many aspects of accounting for debt securities are the same for both the issuer and the investor. In this section, we will often reference the material discussed in Chapter 14.
2. *Statement of Financial Accounting Standards No. 115,* "Accounting for Certain Investments in Debt and Equity Securities" (Norwalk: Financial Accounting Standards Board, 1993), par. 3.
3. *Ibid.,* par. 12a.
4. *Ibid.,* par. 7.
5. *Ibid.,* par. 12b.

interest payment dates, the amount paid for the security is increased by a charge for accrued interest to the date of purchase. This charge should not be reported as part of the investment cost. Two assets have been acquired—the security and the accrued interest receivable—and should be reported in two separate asset accounts. Upon receipt of the interest, the accrued interest account is closed and Interest Revenue is credited for the amount of interest earned since the purchase date. Instead of recording the interest as a receivable (asset approach), Interest Revenue may be debited for the accrued interest paid at the time of purchase. The subsequent collection of interest would then be credited in full to Interest Revenue. The latter procedure (revenue approach) is usually more convenient.

To illustrate the entries for the acquisition of debt securities, assume that $100,000 in U.S. Treasury notes are purchased at 104 1/4 (debt securities are normally quoted at a price per $100 face value), including brokerage fees, on May 1. Interest is 9% payable semiannually on January 1 and July 1. Accrued interest of $3,000 would thus be added to the purchase price. The debt securities are classified by the purchaser as trading securities because management will sell the securities if a change in the price will result in a profit. The entries to record the purchase of the treasury notes and the subsequent collection of interest under the alternate procedures would be as follows:

Asset Approach:			
May 1	Investment in Trading Securities	104,250	
	Interest Receivable	3,000	
	Cash		107,250
July 1	Cash	4,500	
	Interest Receivable		3,000
	Interest Revenue		1,500
Revenue Approach:			
May 1	Investment in Trading Securities	104,250	
	Interest Revenue	3,000	
	Cash		107,250
July 1	Cash	4,500	
	Interest Revenue		4,500

The important point is that under either approach, the interest revenue recognized for the period is equal to the interest earned, not the amount received. In this case, the company earned $1,500, representing interest for the period May 1 to June 30.

Purchase of Equity Securities

Shares of stock are usually purchased for cash through stock exchanges (e.g., New York, American, or regional exchanges) and from individuals and institutional investors rather than from the corporations themselves. The investment is recorded at the amount paid, including brokers' commissions, taxes, and other fees incidental to the purchase price. Even when part of the purchase price is deferred, the full cost should be recorded as the investment in stock, with a liability account established for the amount yet to be paid. If stock is acquired in exchange for properties or services instead of cash, the fair market value of the consideration given or the value at which the stock is currently selling, whichever is more clearly determinable, should be used as the basis for recording the investment. If two or more securities are acquired for a lump-sum price, the cost should be allocated to each security in an equitable manner, as illustrated in earlier chapters.

To illustrate the accounting for the purchase of equity securities, assume Gondor Enterprises purchased 300 shares of Boromir Co. stock at $75 per share plus brokerage fees of $800 and 500 shares of Faramir Inc. stock at $50 per share plus brokerage fees of $300. Gondor classifies the Boromir stock as a trading security because management has no intention of holding these securities for a long period of time and will sell them as soon as it is economically advantageous for the company. The Faramir stock is classified as available-for-sale. The journal entry to record the purchase would be as follows:

Investment in Trading Securities—Boromir Co.	23,300	
Investment in Available-for-Sale Securities—Faramir Inc.	25,300	
Cash		48,600

RECOGNITION OF REVENUE FROM INVESTMENTS

A primary reason that companies invest in the debt or equity securities of other companies is to earn a return in the form of either interest or dividends. In the case of debt securities, the computation of that return is complicated because a difference often exists between the purchase price and the maturity value of the debt instrument. The resulting premium or discount affects the amount of interest revenue recognized in each future period. For equity securities, the recognition of revenue from an investment depends on the level of ownership in the investee. Each of these issues is discussed in the following sections.

Recognition of Interest Revenue

Recall from Chapter 14 that debt securities carry with them a stated rate of interest which, when multiplied by the maturity value of the securities, indicates the amount of cash to be received in interest each year. Often, interest is received on a semiannual basis. When interest is received, cash is debited and interest revenue is credited. However, when debt securities are acquired at a higher or lower price than their maturity value, periodic amortization of the premium or accumulation of the discount with corresponding adjustments to interest revenue is required. As explained in Chapter 14, a premium or discount results when the stated rate of interest and the market rate of interest on the date of acquisition of the debt security are different. If the stated rate of interest is higher than the prevailing market rate, investors will pay a higher price for the debt security in order to receive the higher interest payments. When the market rate of interest is higher than the stated rate, investors will pay less than the face amount of the debt security, resulting in a discount.

The present value computations associated with computing the value of a debt security were illustrated in Chapter 14 and an example is included here. Assume that on January 1, 1995, Silmaril Technologies purchased 5-year, 10% bonds with a face value of $100,000 and interest payable semiannually on January 1 and July 1. Silmaril intends, and has the ability, to hold the bonds until they mature. The market rate on bonds of similar quality and maturity is 8%. Silmaril computes the market price of the bonds as follows:

Present value of principal:		
Maturity value of bonds after 5 years	$100,000	
Present value factor, 10 periods, 4% semiannual market rate	× .6756	
Present value of $100,000 discounted at 4% for 10 periods		$ 67,560
Present value of interest payments:		
Semiannual payment, 5% of $100,000	$ 5,000	
Present value of annuity factor, 10 periods, 4%	× 8.1109	
Present value of 10 payments of $5,000 discounted at 4%		40,555
Total present value (market price) of the bonds		$108,115

Silmaril would make the following journal entry to record the initial purchase of the bonds (the amount is rounded):

Investment in Held-to-Maturity Securities	108,115	
Cash		108,115

Recall from Chapter 14 that the investor typically does not use a premium or discount account but instead records the investment at cost and nets the face value and any premium or discount.

To determine the amount of premium to amortize each period, Silmaril would prepare an amortization table, as illustrated below. This table is based on the effective-interest method of amortization.[6]

Amortization of Bond Premium – Effective-Interest Method
$100,000, 5-year bonds, Interest at 10% Payable Semiannually,
Sold at $108,115 to Yield 8%

Interest Payment	A Interest Received (.05 × $100,000)	B Interest Revenue (.04 × Bond Carrying Value)	C Premium Amortization (A-B)	D Unamortized Premium (D-C)	Bond Carrying Value ($100,000 + D)
				$8,115	$108,115
1	$5,000	$4,325	$675	7,440	107,440
2	$5,000	4,298	702	6,738	106,738
3	$5,000	4,270	730	6,008	106,008
4	$5,000	4,240	760	5,248	105,248
5	$5,000	4,210	790	4,458	104,458
6	$5,000	4,178	822	3,636	103,636
7	$5,000	4,145	855	2,781	102,781
8	$5,000	4,111	889	1,892	101,892
9	$5,000	4,076	924	968	100,968
10	$5,000	4,032*	968	0	100,000

*rounding differences are adjusted with last entry

When the first interest payment of $5,000 is received from the bond issuer, Silmaril would make the following journal entry:

Cash	5,000	
Interest Revenue		4,325
Investment in Held-to-Maturity Securities		675

Subsequent receipts of interest would be recorded with a similar journal entry, the only difference being that the amount amortized would differ depending on which interest payment was received.

Recognition of Revenue From Investment in Equity Securities

Once an equity security is purchased, one of three basic methods must be used to account for the revenue earned on that investment: consolidation, cost, or equity. Which method is appropriate depends on the control or degree of influence exercised by the acquiring company (investor) over the acquired company (investee).

6. As explained in Chapter 14, the straight-line method of interest amortization can be used when the results do not differ materially from effective-interest amortization. However, in all the examples that follow as well as in the end-of-chapter material, we will use the effective-interest method.

Choosing Among Consolidation, Cost, and Equity Methods. When one company acquires a majority voting interest in another company through the acquisition of **more than 50 percent** of its voting common stock, the acquiring company has control over the acquired company. The investor and investee are referred to respectively as the **parent company** and the **subsidiary company.** Where control exists, the **consolidation method** is required. This means that the financial statement balances of the parent and subsidiary companies are combined or consolidated for financial reporting purposes even though the companies continue to operate as separate entities. In the consolidation process, any intercompany transactions are eliminated, e.g., any sales and purchases between the parent and subsidiary companies. By eliminating all intercompany transactions, the combined balances or consolidated totals appropriately reflect the financial position and results of operation of the total economic unit. This treatment reflects the fact that majority ownership of common stock assures control by the parent over the decision-making processes of the subsidiary.

Previous accounting standards allowed separate reporting for certain majority-owned subsidiaries if those subsidiaries had "nonhomogeneous" operations, a large minority interest, or a foreign location. Separate reporting by subsidiaries occurred most often when the operations of the subsidiary and parent were significantly different (i.e., nonhomogeneous). Typically, the subsidiary was engaged in finance, insurance, leasing, or real estate, while the parent company was a manufacturer or merchandiser. Examples include General Motors Acceptance Corporation (GMAC) and IBM Credit Corporation, which are finance companies that are wholly owned by General Motors Corp. and IBM Corp., respectively. Traditionally, the financial statements of these subsidiaries were not consolidated with those of their respective parent companies.

With the issuance of Statement of Financial Accounting Standards No. 94, the FASB now requires the consolidation of all majority-owned subsidiaries unless control is temporary or does not rest with the majority owner (as, for instance, where the subsidiary is in legal reorganization or in bankruptcy).[7] Thus, even though a subsidiary has nonhomogeneous operations, a large minority interest, or a foreign location, it should be consolidated. The reporting entity is to be the total economic unit consisting of the parent and all its subsidiaries. Accounting for consolidated entities is covered in advanced accounting texts.[8]

Consolidated financial statements are appropriate only when the investor holds a majority voting interest (more than 50 percent) in the investee. When an investor owns **50 percent or less** of the investee company, the investor may or may not exercise significant influence over the financial and operating decisions of the other company. If conditions indicate that the acquiring company **does exercise significant influence,** the **equity method** of accounting should be used. This method closely parallels the accounting followed when actual control exists, which requires consolidated statements. The equity method is sometimes referred to as a "one-line consolidation."

When the acquiring company **does not exercise significant influence** over the investee, the **cost method** of accounting should be used. This method recognizes the separate identities of the companies. Since preferred stock is generally nonvoting stock and does not provide for significant influence, the cost method is always used for investments in preferred stock. If the cost method is used, then the procedures outlined in FASB Statement No. 115 are applied.

The ability of the investor to exercise significant influence over such decisions as dividend distribution and operational and financial administration may be indicated in several

7. *Statement of Financial Accounting Standards No. 94,* "Consolidation of All Majority-Owned Subsidiaries," (Stamford: Financial Accounting Standards Board, 1987).

8. See, for example, Paul M. Fisher et al., *Advanced Accounting* (Cincinnati: South-Western Publishing Co., 1993).

ways: e.g., representation on the investee's board of directors, participation in policy-making processes, material intercompany transactions, interchange of managerial personnel, or technological dependency of investee on investor. Another important consideration is the **extent of ownership** by an investor in relation to the concentration of other stockholdings. While it is clear that ownership of over 50 percent of common stock virtually assures control by the acquiring company, ownership of 50 percent or less may give effective control if the remaining shares of the stock are widely held, and no significant blocks of stockholders are consistently united in their ownership.

The Accounting Principles Board, in Opinion No. 18, recognized that the degree of influence and control will not always be clear and that judgment will be required in assessing the status of each investment. To achieve a reasonable degree of uniformity in the application of its position, the Board set 20 percent as an ownership standard; the ownership of **20 percent or more** of the voting stock of the company carries the presumption, in the absence of evidence to the contrary, that an investor has the ability to exercise significant influence over that company. Conversely, ownership of **less than 20 percent** leads to the presumption that the investor does not have the ability to exercise significant influence unless such ability can be demonstrated.[9]

In May 1981, the FASB issued Interpretation No. 35 to emphasize that the 20 percent criterion is only a guideline and that judgment is required in determining the appropriate accounting method in cases where ownership is 50 percent or less. Interpretation No. 35 lists five illustrative examples of circumstances that might indicate that the investor does not have significant influence, regardless of the percentage of ownership:[10]

1. Opposition by the investee, such as litigation or complaints to governmental regulatory authorities.
2. An agreement between the investor and investee under which the investor surrenders significant rights as a shareholder.
3. Majority ownership of the investee is concentrated among a small group of shareholders who operate the investee without regard to the views of the investor.
4. The investor needs or wants more financial information to apply the equity method than is available to the investee's other shareholders (for example, the investor wants quarterly financial information from an investee who publicly reports only annually), tries to obtain the information, and fails.
5. The investor tries and fails to obtain representation on the investee's board of directors.

While the FASB examples may be helpful in some cases, evaluating the degree of investor influence is often a very subjective process. As a result, the percentage-of-ownership criterion set forth in APB Opinion No. 18 has been widely accepted as the basis for determining the appropriate method of accounting for long-term investments in equity securities when the investor does not possess absolute voting control.

To summarize, in the absence of persuasive evidence to the contrary, the **cost method** is used when ownership is **less than 20 percent**; the **equity method** is used when ownership is 20 to 50 percent; the **consolidation method** is used when ownership is **over 50 percent**. These relationships dealing with the effect of ownership interest and control or influence and the proper accounting method to be used are summarized in Exhibit 17—1.[11]

9. *Opinions of the Accounting Principles Board No. 18,* "The Equity Method of Accounting for Investments in Common Stock" (New York: American Institute of Certified Public Accountants, 1971).

10. *FASB Interpretation No. 35,* "Criteria for Applying the Equity Method of Accounting for Investments in Common Stock" (Stamford: Financial Accounting Standards Board, 1981), par. 4.

11. It should be noted that the FASB has a project on its agenda to consider the reporting entity. This project will review accounting for consolidations and the equity method.

Exhibit 17—1
Effect of Ownership Interest and Control or Influence on Accounting for Long-Term Investments in Common Stocks

Ownership Interest	Control or Degree of Influence	Accounting Method
More than 50%	Control	Consolidated statements
20% to 50%	Significant influence	Equity method
Less than 20%	No significant influence	Cost method

This chapter discusses and illustrates the accounting and reporting issues encountered with the cost and equity methods. The cost method is presented first, followed by the more complex equity method.

The Cost Method. When an investment in another company's stock does not involve either a controlling interest or significant influence, the investment should be accounted for using the cost method. FASB Statement No. 115 applies to equity securities purchased using the cost method. Revenue is recognized when dividends are received from the investee. Continuing a previous example, assume that Gondor Enterprises receives the following dividends from its investees:

Company	Classification	Number of Shares Held	Dividends Received Per Share
Boromir Co.	Trading security	300	$2.00
Faramir Inc.	Available-for-sale security	500	3.75

The journal entry to record receipt of the dividends would be:

Cash	2,475	
Dividend Revenue		2,475

The Equity Method. The equity method of accounting for long-term investments in common stock reflects the economic substance of the relationship between the investor and investee rather than the legal distinction of the separate entities. The objective of this method is to reflect the underlying claim by the investor on the net assets of the investee company.

Under the equity method, just as under the cost method, the investment is initially recorded at cost. However, with the equity method, the investment account is periodically adjusted to reflect changes in the underlying net assets of the investee. The investment balance is increased to reflect a proportionate share of the earnings of the investee company, or decreased to reflect a share of any losses reported. If preferred stock dividends have been declared by the investee, they must be deducted from income reported by the investee before computing the investor's share of investee earnings or losses. When dividends are received by the investor, the investment account is reduced. Thus, the equity method results in an increase in the investment account when the investee's net assets increase; similarly, the investment account decreases when the investee records a loss or pays out dividends.

Cost and Equity Methods Compared. To contrast and illustrate the accounting entries under the cost and equity methods, assume that Powell Corporation purchases 5,000 shares of San Juan Company common stock on January 2 at $20 per share, including commissions and other costs. San Juan has a total of 25,000 shares outstanding; thus, the 5,000 shares represent a 20 percent ownership interest. As discussed earlier in the chapter, the equity method is used when ownership is 20 to 50 percent unless there is persuasive evidence that the investor does not have significant influence over the investee. Under the cost method, assume the securities are accounted for as available-for-sale securities. The appropriate entries under both the cost and equity methods are shown in Exhibit 17—2. The actual method used would depend on the degree of influence exercised by the investor as indicated by a consideration of all relevant factors, as well as the percentage owned. Exhibit 17—2 highlights the basic differences in accounting for long-term investments under the cost and equity methods. Under both methods, the investment is originally recorded at cost. Dividends received are recognized as Dividend Revenue under the cost method and as a reduction in the investment account under the equity method. The investor's percentage of the earnings of the investee company are recorded as income and as an increase to the investment account under the equity method, while no entry is required for this event under the cost method.

Exhibit 17—2
Comparison of Cost and Equity Methods

Cost Method			Equity Method		
Jan. 2 Purchased 5,000 shares of San Juan Company common stock at $20 per share					
Investment in Available-for-Sale Securities	100,000		Investment in San Juan Company Stock	100,000	
Cash		100,000	Cash		100,000
Oct. 31 Received dividend of $.80 per share from San Juan Company ($.80 × 5,000 shares):					
Cash	4,000		Cash	4,000	
Dividend Revenue		4,000	Investment in San Juan Company Stock		4,000
Dec. 31 San Juan Company announced earnings for the year of $60,000:					
No Entry			Investment in San Juan Company Stock	12,000	
			Income From Investment in San Juan Company Stock (.20 × $60,000)		12,000

Complexities Under the Equity Method. When a company is purchased by another company, the purchase price usually differs from the recorded book value of the underlying net assets of the acquired company. For example, assume Snowbird Company purchased 100 percent of the common stock of Ski Resorts International for $8 million, although the book value of Ski Resorts' net assets is only $6.5 million. In effect, Snowbird is purchasing some undervalued assets, above-normal earnings potential, or both.

As explained in Chapter 11, if the purchase price of an ongoing business exceeds the recorded value, the acquiring company must allocate this purchase price among the assets acquired using their current market values as opposed to the amounts carried on the books of the acquired company. If part of the purchase price cannot be allocated to specific assets, that amount is recorded as goodwill. If the purchase price is less than recorded net asset value, the assets acquired must be recorded at an amount less than their carrying value on the books of the acquired company. Whether assets are increased or decreased as a result of the purchase, future income determination will use the new (adjusted) values to determine the depreciation and amortization charges.

When only a portion of a company's stock is purchased and the equity method is used to reflect the income of the partially owned company, an adjustment to the investee's reported income, similar to that just described, may be required. In order to determine whether such an adjustment is necessary, the acquiring company must compare the purchase price of the common stock with the recorded net asset value of the acquired company at the date of purchase. If the purchase price exceeds the investor's share of book value, the computed excess must be analyzed in the same way as described above for a 100 percent purchase. Although no entries to adjust asset values are made on the books of either company, an adjustment to the investee's reported income is required under the equity method for the investor to reflect the economic reality of paying more for the investment than the underlying net book value. If depreciable assets had been adjusted to higher market values on the books of the investee to reflect the price paid by the investor, additional depreciation would have been taken by the investee company. Similarly, if the purchase price reflected goodwill, additional amortization would have been required. These adjustments would have reduced the reported income of the investee. To reflect this condition, an adjustment is made by the investor to the income reported by the investee in applying the equity method. This adjustment serves to meet the objective of computing the income reported using the equity method in the same manner as would be done if the company were 100 percent purchased and consolidated financial statements were prepared.

To illustrate, assume that the book value of common stockholders' equity (net assets) of Stewart Inc. was $500,000 at the time Phillips Manufacturing Co. purchased 40% of its common shares for $250,000. Based on a 40% ownership interest, the market value of the net assets of Stewart Inc. would be $625,000 ($250,000 ÷ .40), or $125,000 more than the book value. Assume that a review of the asset values discloses that the market value of depreciable properties exceeds the carrying value of these assets by $50,000. The remaining $75,000 difference ($125,000 – $50,000) is attributed to goodwill. Assume further that the average remaining life of the depreciable assets is 10 years and that goodwill is amortized over 40 years. Phillips Manufacturing Co. would adjust its share of the annual income reported by Stewart Inc. to reflect the additional depreciation and the amortization of goodwill as follows:

Additional depreciation	($50,000 × 40%) ÷ 10 years =	$2,000
Goodwill amortization	($75,000 × 40%) ÷ 40 years =	750
		$2,750

Each year for the first 10 years, Phillips would make the following entry in addition to entries made to recognize its share of Stewart Inc.'s income and dividends:

Income From Investment in Stewart Inc. Stock	2,750	
Investment in Stewart Inc. Stock		2,750
To adjust share of income on Stewart Inc. common stock for proportionate depreciation on excess market value of depreciable property, $2,000, and for amortization of goodwill from acquisition of the stock, $750.		

After the tenth year, the adjustment would be for $750 until the goodwill amount is fully amortized.

To complete the illustration, assume that the purchase was made on January 2, 1996; Stewart Inc. declared and paid dividends of $70,000 to common stockholders during 1996, and Stewart Inc. reported net income of $150,000 for the year ended December 31, 1996. At the end of 1996, the investment in Stewart Inc. common stock would be reported on the balance sheet of Phillips Manufacturing Co. at $279,250, computed as shown on the next page.

This illustration assumes that the fiscal years of the two companies coincide and that the purchase of the stock is made at the first of the year. If a purchase is made at a time other than the beginning of the year, the income earned up to the date of the purchase is assumed to be included in the cost of purchase. Only income earned by the investee subsequent to acquisition should be recognized by the investor.

Investment in Stewart Inc. Common Stock

Acquisition cost	$250,000	
Add: Share of 1996 earnings of investee company ($150,000 × .40)	60,000	$310,000
Less: Dividends received from investee ($70,000 × .40)	$ 28,000	
Additional depreciation of undervalued assets	2,000	
Amortization of unrecorded goodwill	750	30,750
Year-end carrying value of investment (equity in investee company)		$279,250

The adjustment for additional depreciation and goodwill amortization is needed only when the purchase price is greater than the underlying book value at the date of acquisition. If the purchase price is less than the underlying book value at the time of acquisition, it is assumed that specific assets of the investee are overvalued or that there is negative goodwill as discussed in Chapter 11, and an adjustment is necessary to reduce the depreciation or amortization included in the reported income of the investee. The journal entry to reflect this adjustment is the reverse of the one illustrated previously. The computations would also be similar except that the adjustments for overvalued assets would be added to (instead of subtracted from) the carrying value of the investment.

CHANGE IN VALUE OF SECURITIES

The value of debt and equity securities can rise and fall on a daily basis. Some of these changes in value can be considered temporary while others might be of a more permanent nature. Prior to FASB Statement No. 115, if temporary price changes occurred, only declines (and their subsequent recovery) in value of securities were recognized in the financial statements. The new standard requires, for many types of debt and equity securities, both increases and decreases in value to be reflected in the financial statements. For equity securities accounted for using the equity method or consolidation, only permanent declines in value are recognized. This section of the chapter deals with accounting for temporary changes in a security's value followed by a discussion of the accounting for permanent declines in value.

Accounting for Temporary Changes in the Value of Securities

Recall from our previous discussion that all debt securities and those equity securities accounted for using the cost method are to be classified into one of three categories. Those categories and their required disclosure are summarized in Exhibit 17—3.

Exhibit 17—3
Summary of Classification and Disclosure Under FASB Statement No. 115

Classification of Securities	Types of Securities	Disclosed at	Reporting of Changes in Fair Value
Trading	Debt and Equity	Fair Value	Income Statement
Available-for-Sale	Debt and Equity	Fair Value	Stockholders' Equity
Held-to-Maturity	Debt	Amortized Cost	Not Recognized

The following example will be used throughout this section to illustrate accounting for changes in fair value. Eastwood Incorporated purchased five different securities on March 1, 1996. The type and cost of each security, along with its fair value on December 31, 1996, is as follows:

Security	Classified as	Cost	Fair Value Dec. 31, 1996
1	Trading Security	$ 8,000	$ 7,000
2	Trading Security	3,000	3,500
3	Available-for-Sale Security	5,000	6,100
4	Available-for-Sale Security	12,000	11,500
5	Held-to-Maturity Security	20,000[12]	19,000

The entries to record the initial purchase would be as follows:

Investment in Trading Securities	11,000	
Investment in Available-for-Sale Securities	17,000	
Investment in Held-to-Maturity Securities	20,000	
Cash		48,000

Securities 1 and 2 are classified by management as trading securities because management has no intention of holding these securities for a long period of time and will sell them as soon as it is economically advantageous for the company. Securities 3 and 4 are deemed by management to be available-for-sale securities. Management purchased Security 5 at face value and intends to hold it until it matures.

During an accounting period, the fair value of securities will rise and fall. Only at the end of the period, when financial statements are prepared, is a company required to account for any change in market value. At the end of the accounting period, the fair value of the portfolio of securities for certain categories is compared with the historical cost and an adjustment is made for the difference.

Trading Securities. At the end of 1996, the value of the trading securities portfolio has decreased by $500. As a result, the following journal entry would be made:

Unrealized Loss on Trading Securities—Income	500	
Market Adjustment—Trading Securities		500

The loss of $500 ($11,000 cost less $10,500 fair value) reflects the fact that the value of the trading securities portfolio has declined during the period. The loss is classified as unrealized as these securities have not been sold. This entry introduces a valuation account, "Market Adjustment—Trading Securities." This account is combined with the account, "Investment in Trading Securities," and reported on the balance sheet. The use of a valuation account allows the company to maintain a record of historical cost. To determine realized and unrealized holding gains and losses, a record of historical cost is necessary. The account "Unrealized Loss on Trading Securities" would be disclosed on the income statement under "Other Expenses and Losses."

Available-for-Sale Securities. For available-for-sale securities, similar adjustments to those illustrated for trading securities would be made with the only difference being that instead of any unrealized gain or loss being disclosed on the income statement, it would be reported directly in stockholders' equity. Continuing the Eastwood example, at the end of 1996, their available-for-sale portfolio had increased from $17,000 to $17,600. This $600 increase in fair value of the securities above their cost would be recorded with the following journal entry:

Market Adjustment—Available-for-Sale Securities	600	
Unrealized Increase/Decrease in Value of Available-for-Sale Securities—Equity		600

12. Security 5 was purchased at face value. If the security were purchased at a price other than face value, then the amortization procedures described previously would be employed.

Note that the account Unrealized Increase/Decrease in Value of Available-for-Sale Securities would serve to increase the amount of stockholders' equity, which is consistent with the fact that an asset has increased in value.

Held-to-Maturity Securities. Security 5 has decreased in value from $20,000 to $19,000. However, because this security is classified as held-to-maturity, no adjustment is made for differences between carrying value and fair market value. Exhibit 17—4 summarizes how the securities and the resulting increases and decreases in value would be disclosed in the financial statements for 1996.

Exhibit 17—4
Financial Statement Disclosure of Securities

Eastwood Inc.
Balance Sheet (partial)
December 31, 1996

Assets:		
Investment in trading securities, at cost	$11,000	
Less: Market adjustment—trading securities	(500)	$10,500
Investment in available-for-sale securities, at cost	$17,000	
Add: Market adjustment—available-for-sale securities	600	17,600
Investment in held-to-maturity securities, at amortized cost		20,000
Stockholder's Equity:		
Add: Unrealized increase in value of available-for-sale securities		$ 600

Eastwood Inc.
Income Statement (partial)
For the Year Ended December 31, 1996

Other Expenses and Losses:	
Unrealized loss on trading securities	$500

At the end of 1997, similar adjustments must be made to reflect changes in fair value. Assume the following fair market values at the end of 1997:

Security	Classified as	Cost	Fair Value Dec. 31, 1997
1	Trading Security	$ 8,000	$ 7,700
2	Trading Security	3,000	3,600
3	Available-for-Sale Security	5,000	6,500
4	Available-for-Sale Security	12,000	10,700
5	Held-to-Maturity Security	20,000	20,700

By the end of 1997, the **trading securities** portfolio had increased to a value of $11,300 ($7,700 plus $3,600). Comparing this amount to the historical cost of $11,000 indicates that the account Market Adjustment—Trading Securities should have a debit balance of $300. Since its current balance is a $500 credit (carried over from 1996), an adjusting entry must be made. The adjusting entry would be as follows:

Market Adjustment—Trading Securities	800	
Unrealized Gain on Trading Securities—Income		800

The balance in the account Market Adjustment—Trading Securities, which appears on the next page in t-account form, would be added to the account Investment in Trading Securities and disclosed on the balance sheet.

Market Adjustment—Trading Securities

		12/31/96 Bal.	500
12/31/97 Adj.	800		
12/31/97 Bal.	300		

At the end of 1997, the value of the **available-for-sale securities** has decreased from $17,600 to $17,200. Since fair value now exceeds historical cost by $200, the market adjustment account should have a $200 debit balance. Its current balance, carried over from 1996, is $600 (debit). The journal entry made at the end of 1997 to adjust the account is as follows:

Unrealized Increase/Decrease in Value of Available-for-Sale Securities—Equity	400	
Market Adjustment—Available-for-Sale Securities		400

The effect on the account Market Adjustment—Available-for-Sale Securities is reflected in the following t-account. Again, no adjustment is made for changes in value of **held-to-maturity securities.**

Market Adjustment—Available-for-Sale Securities

12/31/96 Bal.	600		
		12/31/97 Adj.	400
12/31/97 Bal.	200		

The financial statements for Eastwood Inc. at the end of 1997 would include the effects of each of the above adjusting entries as shown in Exhibit 17—5.

Exhibit 17—5
Financial Statement Disclosure of Securities

Eastwood Inc.
Balance Sheet (Partial)
December 31, 1997

Assets:		
Investment in trading securities, at cost	$11,000	
Add: Market adjustment—trading securities	300	$11,300
Investment in available-for-sale securities, at cost	$17,000	
Add: Market adjustment—available-for-sale securities	200	17,200
Investment in held-to-maturity securities, at amortized cost		20,000
Stockholder's Equity:		
Add: Unrealized increase in value of available-for-sale securities		$ 200

Eastwood Inc.
Income Statement (partial)
For the Year Ended December 31, 1997

Other Revenues and Gains:	
Unrealized gain on trading securities	$800

Accounting for Permanent Changes in the Value of Securities

Sometimes the fair value of investments declines due to economic circumstances that are unlikely to improve. For example, in the late 1980s the value of numerous savings and loan stocks decreased significantly without much expectation that they would recover.

If a decline in the market value of an individual security is judged to be permanent, regardless of whether the security is debt or equity and regardless of whether the cost method, equity method, or consolidation is being used, the cost basis of that security should be reduced by crediting the investment account rather than a market adjustment account. In addition, the write-down should be recognized as a loss and charged against current income. The new cost basis for the security may not be adjusted upward to its original cost for any subsequent increases in market value. If, however, the security is classified as a trading security or an available-for-sale security, a market adjustment account may be used to record future increases and decreases in value.

SALE OF SECURITIES

When securities are sold, an entry must be made to remove the carrying value of the security from the investor's books and to record the receipt of cash. The difference between the cost and the cash received is a realized gain or loss. Note the difference between an unrealized gain or loss (as discussed in the previous section) and a realized gain or loss. An unrealized gain or loss results when the value of a security changes but the security is still being held by the investor. A realized gain or loss arises when the value of a security has changed while being held and the security is subsequently sold. Any market adjustment account associated with the security being sold will be adjusted at year end. In the case of a debt security, an entry must be made prior to recording the sale to record any interest earned to the date of the sale and to amortize any premium or discount. For example, continuing the Silmaril example from page 709, assume that the debt securities are sold on April 1, 1997 for $103,000, which includes accrued interest of $2,500. The carrying value of the debt securities on April 1, 1997 is $105,248. Interest revenue of $2,015 ($105,248 × .08 × 3/12) would be recorded and a receivable relating to interest of $2,500 would be established. The investment account would be reduced by $485 to reflect the amortization of the premium for the three-month period between January 1 and April 1.

Interest Receivable	2,500	
Investment in Held-to-Maturity Securities		485
Interest Revenue		2,015

A second entry would remove the book value of the investment from Silmaril's books, record the receipt of cash of $103,000, eliminate the Interest Receivable balance, and record a loss equal to the difference between the investment's carrying value and the amount of cash received (net of interest).

Cash	103,000	
Realized Loss on Sale of Securities	4,263	
Interest Receivable		2,500
Investment in Held-to-Maturity Securities		104,763

These two entries could easily be combined into the following journal entry:

Cash	103,000	
Realized Loss on Sale of Securities	4,263	
Investment in Held-to-Maturity Securities		105,248
Interest Revenue		2,015

TRANSFERRING SECURITIES BETWEEN CATEGORIES

On occasion, management will change its intentions with respect to holding certain securities. For example, a company may originally purchase securities for the purpose of making effective use of excess cash and subsequently the company may decide to pursue a long-term business relationship with the investee. As a result, the company may reclassify the security from a trading security to an available-for-sale security. In addition, a company may initially purchase an equity security as a short-term investment and subsequently elect to increase its ownership interest to the point where the equity method is appropriate. This section of the chapter first discusses the procedures employed when a security is transferred between categories as described in FASB Statement No. 115. This section concludes by illustrating the accounting for changes between the cost and equity method of accounting for equity securities.

Transferring Debt and Equity Securities Between Categories

Under the provisions of FASB Statement No. 115, if a company reclassifies a security, the security is accounted for at the fair value at the time of the transfer.[13] Since these securities are maintained on the books at their historical cost, the historical cost of the security must be removed from the "old" category and the security is recorded in the "new" category at its current fair value. The change in value that has occurred is accounted for differently depending on the category being transferred to and the category being transferred from. Exhibit 17—6 summarizes how these unrealized gains and losses are accounted for in each category.

Exhibit 17—6
Accounting for Transfers of Securities Between Categories

Transferred	Treatment of the Change in Value
From "Trading"	Any unrealized change in value not previously recognized will be recognized in net income in the current period. Previously recognized changes in value are not to be reversed.
To "Trading"	Any unrealized change in value not previously recognized will be recognized in net income in the current period.
From "Held-to-Maturiy" to "Available-for-Sale"	Recognize any unrealized change in value in a stockholders' equity account.
From "Available-for-Sale" to "Held-to-Maturity"	Any unrealized change in value recorded in a stockholders' equity account is to be amortized over the security's remaining life using the effective interest method.[14]

To illustrate each type of transfer, we will use the Eastwood Inc. example (page 718) as of December 31, 1997. Recall that on that date Eastwood Inc. has the following securities:

Security	Classified as	Cost	Fair Value Dec. 31, 1997
1	Trading Security	$ 8,000	$ 7,700
2	Trading Security	3,000	3,600
3	Available-for-Sale Security	5,000	6,500
4	Available-for-Sale Security	12,000	10,700
5	Held-to-Maturity Security	20,000	20,700

During 1998, Eastwood Inc. elects to reclassify certain of its securities. The category being transferred from and to along with the fair value for each security on the date of the transfer is as follows:

13. *Statement of Financial Accounting Standards No. 115*, par. 15.
14. *Ibid.*, par. 15d.

Security	Transferring From	Transferring To	Fair Value at Date of Transfer
2	Trading	Available-for-Sale	$ 3,800
3	Available-for-Sale	Held-to-Maturity	5,900
4	Available-for-Sale	Trading	10,300
5	Held-to-Maturity	Available-for-Sale	20,400

The different types of reclassifications are illustrated below.

From the "Trading Security" Category. Assume that Eastwood elects to reclassify Security 2 from a trading security to an available-for-sale security. The security's historical cost is removed from the trading security classification, along with the associated $600 market adjustment (as of December 31, 1997), and the security is recorded at its current fair market value as an available-for-sale security. The $200 difference between the fair value as of December 31, 1997, and the fair value at the date of transfer is recorded as an unrealized gain. The following journal entry illustrates this procedure:

Investment in Available-for-Sale Securities	3,800	
Market Adjustment—Trading Securities		600
Unrealized Gain on Transfer of Securities—Income		200
Investment in Trading Securities		3,000

Into the "Trading Security" Category. Suppose Eastwood Inc. elects to reclassify Security 4 from an available-for-sale security to a trading security. Recall that unrealized holding gains and losses associated with available-for-sale securities are recorded in the stockholders' equity account Unrealized Increase/Decrease in Value of Available-for-Sale Securities. The amount in this account associated with Security 4 is removed and the security recorded as a trading security at its current fair market value.

Investment in Trading Securities	10,300	
Market Adjustment—Available-for-Sale Securities	1,300	
Unrealized Loss on Transfer of Securities—Income	1,700	
Unrealized Increase/Decrease in Value of Available-for-Sale Securities—Equity		1,300
Investment in Available-for-Sale Securities		12,000

With this journal entry, Security 4 is recorded as a trading security at its current fair market value of $10,300. The carrying value of Security 4 (historical cost less market adjustment) as an available-for-sale security is eliminated from the company's books. Since the security is now classified as a trading security, all changes in fair value should be reflected in the income statement. Thus, this journal entry transfers the unrealized changes in value from the stockholders' equity account to the income statement and recognizes the additional $400 decline in value since the last balance sheet date. The amount of the unrealized increase/decrease is determined by comparing the security's historical cost, obtained from subsidiary records, with its carrying value as of December 31, 1997. In this example, the unrealized decrease is $1,300 ($12,000 less $10,700). The final result of this journal entry is to reclassify the security and to record, on the income statement, the decline in fair value since the purchase of the security.

From the "Held-to-Maturity" to the "Available-for-Sale" Category. While transfers of debt securities from the held-to-maturity category should not occur often, they will happen on occasion. FASB Statement No. 115 includes a number of circumstances that might lead a firm to reclassify a held-to-maturity security.[15] In this instance, Eastwood Inc. has elected to reclassify Security 5 from a security being held to maturity to one that is available for sale. Recall that Security 5's fair value on the date of the transfer is $20,400. The security is recorded as an available-for-sale security at its current fair value with any difference between its carrying cost and its fair value being recorded as an unrealized increase/decrease in value of available-for-sale securities. The following journal entry will accomplish these objectives:

Investment in Available-for-Sale Securities	20,400	
Unrealized Increase/Decrease in Value of Available-for-Sale Securities—Equity		400
Investment in Held-to-Maturity Securities		20,000

Since Security 5 was originally classified as being held to maturity, no adjustment has been made in prior periods to record any changes in value. Thus, there is no market adjustment account related to this transfer.

From the "Available-for-Sale" to the "Held-to-Maturity" Category. Eastwood Inc. elects to reclassify Security 3 from one that is available for sale to a security that will be held to maturity. Recall that Security 3 was originally purchased for $5,000, had a fair value on December 31, 1997, of $6,500, and has a fair value on the date of the transfer of $5,900.

Investment in Held-to-Maturity Securities	5,900	
Unrealized Increase/Decrease in Value of Available-for-Sale Securities—Equity	600	
Investment in Available-for-Sale Securities		5,000
Market Adjustment—Available-for-Sale Securities		1,500

The debit to Unrealized Increase/Decrease in Value of Available-for-Sale Securities reflects the fact that the security has declined in value by $600 since the last balance sheet date. The credit to the market adjustment account removes the previously recorded increase in value for this security ($6,500 – $5,000) while it was classified as being available for sale.

Once the security is classified as held-to-maturity, increases and decreases in its value will not be reflected in the financial statements. However, FASB Statement No. 115 states that those unrealized increases and decreases in value ($900 in this example) that have been recorded to date (while the security has been available for sale) must be amortized over the remaining life of the security using the effective interest method and offset against any interest revenue received on the debt security. As if this isn't complex enough, the company must also begin amortizing the held-to-maturity security down to its eventual maturity value. For example, if Security 2 has a maturity value of $4,500, then Eastwood Inc. must, in addition to amortizing the $900 in unrealized changes in value, amortize, similar to a premium, the $1,400 difference between the security's carrying value and its maturity value ($5,900 less $4,500) as discussed previously. Can we net these two figures and perform just one amortization? In many cases, combining the unrealized increase or decrease in value with the premium or discount or accounting for them separately would not result in a material difference. Thus, combining the amounts would seem appropriate. However, FASB Statement No. 115 specifically states that "the unrealized holding gain or loss at the date of the transfer shall continue to be reported in a separate component of shareholders' equity..." and the amortized amount "will offset or mitigate the effect on interest income of the amortization of the premium or discount."[16] We must wait and see how practitioners interpret this aspect of FASB Statement No. 115.

15. *Ibid.*, par. 8.
16. Ibid., par. 15d.

Changes Between Cost and Equity Methods

Variations in percentage of ownership caused by additional purchases or sales of stock by the investor or by the additional sale or retirement of stock by the investee may require a change in accounting method. For example, if the equity method has been used but subsequent events reduce the investment ownership below 20 percent, a change should be made to the cost method effective for the year when the reduced ownership occurs. Similarly, if the cost method has been used but subsequent acquisitions increase the investment ownership to 20 percent or more, a change should be made to the equity method. The required accounting is different depending on whether the change is from the equity method to the cost method or vice versa.

Change From Equity to Cost Method. If an investment in equity securities has been accounted for under the equity method, but circumstances dictate a change to the cost method, no adjustment to the investment account is needed. At the time of change, the carrying amount of the investment, as determined by the equity method for prior years, becomes the new basis for applying the cost method. From that time forward, the investment account would not be adjusted for a proportionate share of investee earnings, nor would any adjustments be made for additional depreciation or amortization of undervalued or unrecorded assets, and dividends received would be credited to a revenue account, not the investment account. Thus, once the equity method is no longer appropriate, the cost method is applied just as in any other situation where the cost method is used.

Change From Cost to Equity Method. Accounting for a change from the cost method to the equity method is more complex. A **retroactive adjustment** is required for prior years to reflect the income that would have been reported using the equity method. This adjustment modifies the carrying value of the investment, in effect restating it on an equity basis, as if the equity method had been used during the previous periods that the investment was held. The offsetting entry for the adjustment is to Retained Earnings. From the date of change forward, the equity method is applied normally.

To illustrate, assume that MTI Corporation acquired stock of Excellcior Inc. over the three-year period 1994-1996 and originally accounted for the stock as available-for-sale. Purchase, dividend, and income information for these years are as follows (the purchases were made on the first day of each year):

Year	Percentage Ownership Acquired	Purchase Price*	Excellcior Inc. Dividends Paid Dec. 31	Excellcior Inc. Income Earned
1994	10%	$ 50,000	$100,000	$200,000
1995	5	30,000	120,000	300,000
1996	15	117,000	180,000	400,000

*Purchase price equal to underlying book value at date of purchase.

The following entries would be made on the books of MTI Corporation to reflect the cost method for the years 1994 and 1995:

			Debit	Credit
1994				
Jan.	1	Investment in Available-for-Sale Securities	50,000	
		Cash		50,000
		To record purchase of 10% interest.		
Dec.	31	Cash	10,000	
		Dividend Revenue		10,000
		To record receipt of dividends from Excellcior Inc. (10% × $100,000).		

1995				
Jan.	1	Investment in Available-for-Sale Securities	30,000	
		Cash		30,000
		To record purchase of 5% interest. (Total ownership interest is now 15%.)		
Dec.	31	Cash	18,000	
		Dividend Revenue		18,000
		To record receipt of dividends from Excellcior Inc. (15% × $120,000).		

The additional acquisition of stock at the beginning of 1996 increases ownership to 30%, and a retroactive adjustment to change to the equity method must be made at the time of acquisition. The adjustment is for the difference between the revenue reported using the cost method and that which would have been reported if the equity method had been used. The adjustment would be computed as follows:

Year	Percentage Ownership	Revenue Recognized—Cost Method	Revenue Recognized—Equity Method	Required Retroactive Adjustment
1994	10%	$10,000	$20,000*	$10,000
1995	15%	18,000	45,000**	27,000
			Total adjustment	$37,000

*$200,000 × 10%
**$300,000 × 15%

The following entries would be made on the books of MTI Corporation to reflect the equity method for 1996:

1996				
Jan.	1	Investment in Excellcior Inc. Stock	197,000	
		Cash		117,000
		Investment in Available-for-Sale Securities		80,000
		To record purchase of 15% interest and reclassify securities. (Total ownership interest is now 30%.)		
	1	Investment in Excellcior Inc. Stock	37,000	
		Retained Earnings		37,000
		To retroactively reflect revenue for 1994 and 1995 for investment in Excellcior Inc. as if the equity method had been used.		
Dec.	31	Investment in Excellcior Inc. Stock	120,000	
		Income From Investment in Excellcior Inc. Stock		120,000
		To record 30% of income earned by Excellcior Inc. using equity method.		
	31	Cash	54,000	
		Investment in Excellcior Inc. Stock		54,000
		To record receipt of dividend from Excellcior Inc. using equity method (30% × $180,000).		

Note that in the previous example the retroactive adjustment restates the investment account to an equity basis. From that point on, the equity method is applied in a normal manner. For simplicity, the illustration assumed a purchase price equal to the underlying book value at date of purchase. If this were not the case, an adjustment to income for depreciation and amortization would be needed as discussed in an earlier section.

CLASSIFICATION AND DISCLOSURE

To this point, we have focused on the treatment of the gains and losses (both realized and unrealized) associated with selling and/or valuing securities. Gains and losses from the sale of securities and unrealized gains and losses from changes in value while holding trading securities are disclosed on the income statement as "Other Revenues and Expenses." Unrealized gains and losses on available-for-sale securities are disclosed in a separate account in stockholders' equity. As with any asset, significant permanent declines in the value of investments are recognized as a loss in the year they occur.

Appropriate presentation of individual securities on the balance sheet depends upon the intention of management. If management intends or is willing to sell the securities within one year or the current operating cycle, whichever is longer, the security would be classified as a current asset. Because trading securities are short-term by definition, they would always be classified as current. Held-to-maturity securities will always be classified as noncurrent unless they mature within a year. Available-for-sale securities could be classified as current or noncurrent depending on the intentions of management. Because banks and other financial institutions do not present classified balance sheets, determining the current and noncurrent status of investments would not be an issue.

Under previous accounting standards, the buying and selling of securities was classified as an investing activity on the statement of cash flows. However, with FASB Statement No. 115, cash flows associated with the purchase, sale, and redemption of trading securities are now reported as an operating activity.

In addition to the disclosure required in the income statement, balance sheet, and statement of cash flows, FASB Statement No. 115 requires disclosure in the notes to the financial statements. Specifically, FASB Statement No. 115 requires the following additional disclosure:

1. Trading securities
   - the change in net unrealized holding gain or loss that is included in the income statement
2. Available-for-sale securities
   - aggregate fair value, gross unrealized holding gains and gross unrealized holding losses, and amortized cost basis by major security type. For debt securities the company should disclose information about contractual maturities
   - the proceeds from sales of available-for-sale securities and the gross realized gains and losses on those sales and the basis on which cost was determined in computing realized gains and losses
   - the change in net unrealized holding gain or loss on available-for-sale securities that has been included in stockholders' equity during the period
3. Held-to-maturity securities
   - aggregate fair value, gross unrealized holding gains and gross unrealized holding losses, and amortized cost basis by major security type. In addition, the company should disclose information about contractual maturities
4. Transfers of securities between categories
   - gross gains and losses included in earnings from transfers of securities from available-for-sale into the trading category
   - for securities transferred from held-to-maturity, the company should disclose the amortized cost amount transferred, the related realized or unrealized gain or loss, and the reason for transferring the security

SUMMARY

Investments in debt and equity securities are always initially recorded at cost, which includes commissions and similar expenditures. With all debt securities and with those

The FASB Votes to Put a Stop to Cherry-Picking

It was no small feat when the FASB finally issued Statement No. 115, "Accounting for Certain Investments in Debt and Equity Securities." The standard was strongly opposed by banks and insurance companies because of the anticipated negative effects on profits. The banking and insurance industries also objected to having to value the asset side of the balance sheet at market value while not being allowed to value the liability side at market as well. These debates were not restricted to the business world. Even on the Board there was a great deal of disagreement regarding the issue of marking securities to market value. At one time, the FASB thought they had the issues worked out only to have one Board member surprise his colleagues by changing his vote at the last minute. The member stated the "FASB should go back to the drawing board and take another look at this proposal."

Meanwhile, the SEC continued to insist on a movement towards market value accounting. The SEC had desired market value disclosures as a means of providing financial statement users with more, and better, information regarding a firm's securities portfolio. The SEC was also concerned with a phenomenon known as "cherry-picking." Cherry-picking occurs when securities whose prices have increased are sold, resulting in realized gains, while securities whose prices have declined are maintained at their historical cost. The issuance of FASB Statement No. 115 directly addressed this issue by requiring many securities to be valued at market.

Finally, in September of 1993, the Board voted 5-2 to adopt Statement No. 115. The SEC quickly hailed the new standard saying that it would "clarify the rules of the road" and lessen "enforcement actions."

Questions:

1. Should intense lobbying by certain industry groups be allowed to influence the standard-setting process?
2. The SEC has long urged the FASB to issue standards relating to market value accounting. Should pressure from the SEC be allowed to significantly influence the standard-setting process?
3. What is wrong with "cherry-picking?" If an investment's value has increased, why shouldn't a firm be allowed to record that increase?

Sources:

Lee Berton, "FASB Balks on Current-Market Rules for Banks as Member Switches His Vote," *The Wall Street Journal,* January 16, 1992, p. A3.

Lee Berton, "FASB Votes to Make Banks and Insurers Value Certain Bonds at Current Price," *The Wall Street Journal,* September 19, 1993, p. A3.

equity securities accounted for using the cost method, revenue is recognized through the receipt of interest (in the case of debt securities) and dividends (in the case of equity securities). When securities are subsequently sold, a gain or loss is computed as the difference between the security's cost and its fair value.

FASB No. 115 has resulted in businesses being required to record on their books both increases and decreases in the value of their investment securities. This pronouncement applies to all debt securities and to equity securities where the degree of ownership does not allow for the exercise of significant influence on the investee by the investor. For those securities covered by FASB Statement No. 115, companies are required to classify their securities into one of three categories: (1) trading securities, (2) available-for-sale securities, and (3) held-to-maturity securities. Changes in market value are accounted for differently depending upon how the security is classified. Changes in the value of trading securities are included in the income statement, changes in the value of available-for-sale securities are reported separately in stockholders' equity, and temporary changes in the value of debt securities held-to-maturity are not reported in the body of the financial statements. For all types of investments, permanent declines in value are recognized as a loss and charged against income in the current period.

In those instances where an equity interest is held in an investee that allows for significant influence by the investor, the equity method is used to account for the investment. When the equity method is used, no valuation to market is needed. The investment account is increased to reflect a proportionate share of investee income and decreased to reflect investee losses and dividends received from the investee.

APPENDIX 17-1

Long-Term Investments in Funds

Cash and other assets set apart for certain designated purposes are called **funds.** Some funds are to be used for specific current obligations and are appropriately reported as current assets. Examples of these are petty cash funds, payroll funds, interest funds, dividend funds, and withholding, social security, and other tax funds. Other funds are accumulated over a long term for such purposes as the acquisition or replacement of properties, retirement of long-term debt, the redemption of capital stock, operation of a pension plan, or possible future contingencies. These funds are properly considered noncurrent and are reported under the long-term investment heading.

ESTABLISHMENT AND ACCUMULATION OF FUNDS

A fund may be established through the voluntary action of management, or it may be established as a result of contractual requirements. The fund may be used for a single purpose, such as the redemption of preferred stock, or it may be used for several related purposes, such as the periodic payment of interest on bonds, the retirement of bonds at various intervals, and the ultimate retirement of the remaining bond indebtedness.

When a fund is voluntarily created by management, control of the fund and its disposition are arbitrary matters depending on the wishes of management. When a fund is created through some legal requirement, it must be administered and applied in accordance therewith. Such a fund may be administered by one or more independent trustees under an agreement known as a **trust indenture.** If the trustee assumes responsibility for fulfillment of the requirement, as may be true for a bond retirement or pension program, neither the fund nor the related liability is carried on the company's books. However, if the indenture does not free the company from further obligation, the fund must be accounted for as if there were no trustee.

When a corporation is required by agreement to establish a fund for a certain purpose, such as the retirement of bonds or the redemption of stock, the agreement generally provides that fund deposits shall (1) be fixed amounts, (2) vary according to gross revenue, net income, or units of product sold, or (3) be equal periodic sums that, together with earnings, will produce a certain amount at some future date. The latter arrangement is based on compound-interest factors, and as noted in Chapter 7, compound interest or annuity tables may be used to determine the equal periodic deposits. For example, in order to accumulate a fund of $100,000 by a series of 5 equal annual deposits at 8% compounded annually, a periodic deposit of $17,045.65 is required.[17]

17. This amount can be determined from Table III in Chapter 7. The rent or annual payment for an annuity of $100,000 at 8% for 5 periods is computed as follows:

$$R = \frac{FV_n}{FVAF_n} = \frac{FV_n}{\text{Table III}_{\overline{5}|8\%}} = \frac{\$100{,}000}{5.8666} = \$17{,}045.65$$

A schedule can be developed to show the planned fund accumulation through deposits and earnings. Such a schedule is illustrated below.

Fund Accumulation Schedule

Year	Earnings on Fund Balance for Year	Amount Deposited in Fund	Total Increase in Fund for Year	Accumulated Fund Total
1	—	$17,045.65	$17,045.65	$ 17,045.65
2	$1,363.65	17,045.65	18,409.30	35,454.95
3	2,836.40	17,045.65	19,882.05	55,337.00
4	4,426.96	17,045.65	21,472.61	76,809.61
5	6,144.74	17,045.65	23,190.39	100,000.00

Assuming deposits at the end of each year, the table shows a fund balance at the end of the first year of $17,045.65 resulting from the first deposit. At the end of the second year, the fund is increased by (1) earnings at 8% on the investment in the fund during the year, $1,363.65, and (2) the second deposit to the fund, $17,045.65. The total in the fund at this time is $35,454.95. Fund earnings in the following year are based on a total investment of $35,454.95 as of the beginning of the year.

The schedule is developed on the assumption of annual earnings of 8%. However, various factors, such as fluctuations in the earnings rate and gains and losses on investments, may provide earnings that differ from the assumed amounts. If the fund is to be maintained in accordance with the accumulation schedule, deposits must be adjusted for earnings that differ from estimated amounts. Smaller deposits, then, can be made in periods when earnings exceed the assumed rate; larger deposits are necessary when earnings fail to meet the assumed rate.

ACCOUNTING FOR FUNDS

A fund is usually composed of cash and securities but could include other assets. The accounting for debt and equity securities held in a fund is the same as that described earlier in this chapter.

To illustrate the accounting for a fund, assume that a preferred stock redemption fund is established with annual payments to the fund of $20,000. The fund administrator invests 90% of its assets in stock and places the remainder in bank certificates of deposit paying 8% interest. Journal entries for the first year's transactions are as follows:

Account	Debit	Credit
Stock Redemption Fund Cash	20,000	
Cash		20,000
Annual fund contribution.		
Stock Redemption Fund Securities	18,000	
Stock Redemption Fund Cash		18,000
Investment of fund cash in securities.		
Stock Redemption Fund Certificates of Deposit	2,000	
Stock Redemption Fund Cash		2,000
Investment of fund cash in certificates of deposit.		
Stock Redemption Fund Cash	1,400	
Stock Redemption Fund Revenue		1,400
Dividends on fund securities.		
Stock Redemption Fund Cash	160	
Stock Redemption Fund Revenue		160
Interest on certificates of deposit.		
Stock Redemption Fund Expenses	200	
Stock Redemption Fund Cash		200
Expenses to operate fund.		

At the end of the year, the stock redemption fund assets are as follows:

Stock redemption fund cash ($1,400 + $160 – $200)	$ 1,360
Stock redemption fund certificates of deposit	2,000
Stock redemption fund securities	18,000
Total	$21,360

This total amount would be reported under the "investments" heading on the balance sheet.

Stock redemption fund revenue for the year is $1,560 and stock redemption fund expense is $200, resulting in income from the fund operation of $1,360. This amount is reported on the income statement as other revenue. When stock is redeemed, the payment is made from Stock Redemption Fund Cash after the securities are converted to cash.

APPENDIX 17-2
Cash Surrender Value of Life Insurance

Many business enterprises carry life insurance policies on the lives of their executives because the business has a definite stake in the continuing services of its officers. In some cases the insurance plan affords a financial cushion in the event of the loss of such personnel. In other instances the insurance offers a means of purchasing the deceased owner's interest in the business, thus avoiding a transfer of such interest to some outside party or the need to liquidate the business in effecting a settlement with the estate of the deceased. In these cases, the company is the beneficiary.

Insurance premiums normally consist of an amount for insurance protection and the balance for a form of investment. The investment portion is the **cash surrender value** available to the policyholder in the event of policy cancellation. If this cash surrender value belongs to the business, it should be reported as a long-term investment. Insurance expense for a fiscal period is the difference between the insurance premium paid and the increase in the cash surrender value of the policy.

An insurance policy with a cash surrender value also has a **loan value.** The amount an insurance company will lend on a policy is normally limited to the cash surrender value at the end of the policy year less discount from the loan date to the cash surrender value date. For example, assume a cash surrender value of $3,000 at the end of the fifth policy year. The maximum loan value on the policy at the beginning of the fifth year, assuming the insurance premium for the fifth year is paid, is $3,000 discounted for one year. If the discount rate applied by the insurance company is 5%, the policy loan value is calculated as follows: $3,000 ÷ 1.05 = $2,857 (rounded).[18]

When the policyholder uses the policy as a basis for a loan, such a loan may be liquidated by payments of principal and interest, or the loan may be continuing, to be applied against the insurance proceeds upon policy cancellation or ultimate settlement. Although it is possible for the policyholder to recognize policy loan values instead of cash surrender values, the latter values are generally used.

The policyholder may authorize the insurance company to apply any dividends declared on insurance policies to the reduction of the annual premium payment or to the increase in cash surrender value, or the dividends may be collected in cash. Dividends should be viewed as a reduction in the cost of carrying insurance rather than as a source of supplementary revenue. Hence, if dividends are applied to the reduction of the annual premium, Insurance Expense is simply debited for the net amount paid. If the dividend is applied to the increase in the policy cash surrender value or if it is collected in cash, it should still be treated as an offset to the periodic expense of carrying the policy; the cash surrender value or Cash is debited and Insurance Expense is credited. After a number of years, the periodic dividends plus increases in cash surrender value may exceed the premium payments, thus resulting in revenue rather than expense on policy holdings.

18. The discounted value can also be determined using Table I in Chapter 7 ($3,000 × .9524 = $2,857).

Collection of a policy upon death of the insured requires cancellation of any cash surrender balance. The difference between the insurance proceeds and the balances relating to the insurance policy is recognized as a gain in the period of death. The nature of the insurance policies carried and their coverage should be disclosed by appropriate comment on the balance sheet.

The entries to be made for an insurance contract are illustrated in the following example. The Pro Style Company insured the life of its president, Tom Jolly, on January 1, 1994. The amount of the policy was $50,000; the annual premiums were $2,100 to be paid in advance.

Policy Year	Gross Premium	Dividend	Net Premium	Increase in Cash Value	Insurance Expense
1	$2,100	—	$2,100	—	$2,100
2	2,100	—	2,100	$1,150	950
3	2,100	$272	1,828	1,300	528

The fiscal period for the company is the calendar year. Jolly died on July 1, 1996. The premium rebate for the period July 1 to December 31, 1996, is $1,050, and the dividend accrued as of July 1, 1996, is $210. The entries made in recording transactions relating to the insurance contract are shown below. The procedures illustrated use the asset approach for recording premium payments. The expense approach may be preferred if the entire premium is to be applied during the current year.

Transaction			Entry		
January 1, 1994			Prepaid Insurance	2,100	
Paid first annual premium, $2,100.			Cash		2,100
December 31, 1994			Life Insurance Expense	2,100	
To record insurance expense for 1994			Prepaid Insurance		2,100
January 1, 1995			Cash Surrender Value of Life		
Paid second annual premium, $2,100.			Insurance (as of 12/31/95)	1,150	
Premium		$2,100	Prepaid Insurance	950	
Less cash surrender value		1,150	Cash		2,100
Net insurance charge		$ 950			
December 31, 1995			Life Insurance Expense	950	
To record insurance expense for 1995.			Prepaid Insurance		950
January 1, 1996			Cash Surrender Value of Life		
Paid third annual premium, $2,100.			Insurance (as of 12/31/96)	1,300	
Premium		$2,100	Prepaid Insurance	528	
Less: Cash surrender value	$1,300		Cash		1,828
Dividend	272	1,572			
Net insurance charge		$ 528			
July 1, 1996			Life Insurance Expense	264	
To record insurance expense for Jan. 1-July 1:			Prepaid Insurance		264
1/2 × $528 = $264.					
July 1, 1996			Receivable From Insurance Co.	51,260	
To record cancellation of policy upon death of insured:			Cash Surrender Value of Life Insurance		2,450
Amount recoverable on policy:					
Face of policy		$50,000	Prepaid Insurance		264
Premium rebate for period July 1-Dec. 31 and current-year dividend		1,260	Gain on Settlement of Life Insurance		48,546
		$51,260			
Cancellation of asset values:					
Cash surrender values		$ 2,450			
Prepaid insurance		264			
		$ 2,714			
Gain on policy settlement		$48,546			

APPENDIX 17-3

Accounting by Creditors for Impairment of a Loan

The investments discussed in this chapter are classified as marketable debt and equity securities. A company may have other investments that do not have a market value. They include the cash surrender value of life insurance discussed in Appendix 17-2 and loan receivables discussed in this appendix.

Accounting for loan receivables is straightforward except for impairment.[19] Loans may arise by a company lending money to a borrower or by selling inventory and assets in return for a receivable. An entry to Loans Receivable is thus offset by a credit to Sales, Cash, or a surrendered asset. Financial institutions engage in such loans on a regular basis. A critical issue with these loans is when cost should be abandoned as the valuation basis. Many people in the financial community believe that a failure to abandon cost soon enough was a major contributor to the savings and loans crisis of the late 1980s and early 1990s.

The FASB addressed the valuation issues concerning investments in loan receivables in Statement No. 114, issued in May 1993. Because it is assumed that no market exists for these loans, the market valuations prescribed by FASB Statement No. 115 cannot apply. Loans receivable are thus carried at a cost valuation unless evidence exists of a probable impairment. Statement No. 114 defines impairment as follows:

A loan is impaired when, based on current information and events, it is probable that a creditor will be unable to collect all amounts due according to the contractual terms of the loan agreement.[20]

All amounts due according to contractual terms includes both interest and principal payments. The term "probable" is applied in accordance with FASB No. 5, an assessment that future collections will not be made. Troubled debt restructuring is direct evidence of impairment; however, impairment may occur even though a formal restructuring has not occurred. If sufficient writedown has not previously been made, the restructuring will give rise to an additional decrease in the value of the loan receivable. On the other hand, the restructuring might actually provide for a higher value than the impaired balance. Under these conditions, loan receivables will increase in value.

MEASUREMENT OF IMPAIRMENT

FASB Statement No. 114 specifies that a creditor shall measure impairment for loans with no market value at the present value of expected future cash flows discounted at the loan's effective interest rate, i.e., the rate implicit in the original loan contract. The impairment is recorded by creating a valuation allowance account and charging the estimated loss to bad debt expense. Thus, accounting for loans receivable is similar to accounting for accounts receivable except that the measurement method is more specifically defined by the FASB.

19. See Chapter 8 for discussion of notes receivable.

20. *Statement of Financial Accounting Standards No. 114,* "Accounting by Creditors for Impairment of a Loan" (Norwalk: Financial Accounting Standards Board, 1993), par. 8.

If a loan agreement is restructured in a troubled debt restructuring, the interest rate to be used to discount the new modified contract terms is based on the original contract rate, not the rate specified in the restructuring agreement. The selection of the discount rate to use was one of the difficult issues addressed by the FASB. The continued use of the original loan rate is consistent with the historic cost principle. The estimate of future cash flows is based on the creditor's best estimate based on reasonable and supportable assumptions and projections. Any future changes in the estimates or timing of future cash flows results in a recalculation of the impairment and an adjustment of the receivable and valuation allowance accounts with a charge or credit to bad debt expense. Income arising from the passage of time will be recognized as part of interest revenue in each respective reporting period.

Example of Accounting for Loan Impairment

Assume Malone Enterprises reports a loan receivable from Stockton Co. in the amount of $500,000. The initial loan's repayment terms include a 10% interest rate plus annual principal payments on January 1 each year of $100,000. The loan was made on January 1, 1993. Stockton made the $50,000 interest payment in 1993, but did not make the $100,000 1994 principal payment nor the $50,000 1994 interest payment. Malone is preparing its annual financial statements at December 31, 1994. The loan receivable has a carrying value of $550,000 including the $50,000 interest receivable for 1994. Stockton is having financial difficulty, and Malone has concluded that the loan is impaired. Analysis of Stockton's financial conditions indicates the principal and interest currently due can probably be collected, but it is probable that no further interest can be collected. The probable amount and timing of the collections is determined to be as follows:

December 31, 1995	$175,000
December 31, 1996	200,000
December 31, 1997	175,000
	$550,000

The present value at December 31, 1994 of the expected future cash flows discounted at 10% is $455,851, calculated as follows:

Date	Payment	Time of Discount	Table Value	Present Value @ 10%
December 31, 1995	$175,000	1 year	.9091	$159,093
December 31, 1996	200,000	2 years	.8264	165,280
December 31, 1997	175,000	3 years	.7513	131,478
Present Value at December 31, 1994				$455,851

The impairment loss to be reported for 1994 is $94,149 or the $550,000 carrying value less the present value of $455,851. The journal entry to record the impairment would be as follows:

1994				
Dec.	31	Bad Debt Expense	94,149	
		Allowance for Loan Impairment		94,149

The allowance would be reported as an offset to the account Loan Receivable.

If Stockton makes the payments as projected, the accounting for the cash received and the recognition of interest revenue is computed by constructing an amortization schedule similar to that illustrated below.

Interest Revenue from Loan Impairment

Date	(1) Loan Receivable Before Current Payment	(2) Allowance for Loan Impairment	(3) Net Receivable (1) – (2)	(4) Interest Revenue 10% × (3)	(5) Payment Received
Dec. 31, 1995	$550,000	$94,149	$455,851	$45,585	$175,000
Dec. 31, 1996	375,000	48,564*	326,436	32,644	200,000
Dec. 31, 1997	175,000	15,920**	159,080	15,920**	175,000
				$94,149	$550,000

*$94,149 – $45,585 = $48,564
**$48,564 – $32,644 = $15,920
***Rounded to close (2)

The entries at December 31, 1995 to record the receipt of the 1995 loan payment and recognize interest revenue for the year would be as follows:

1995			
Dec. 31	Cash	175,000	
	Loan Receivable		175,000
	Allowance for Loan Impairment	45,585	
	Interest Revenue*		45,585

*Alternatively, Statement No. 114 allows a company to show all changes in present value as an adjustment to Bad Debt Expense in the same manner in which impairment initially was recognized.[21]

The T-accounts for the loan receivable and allowance accounts for 1994 and 1995 would appear as follows:

Loan Receivable

Debit		Credit	
Beg. Bal.	550,000		
		12/31/95	175,000
Bal.	375,000		

Allowance for Loan Impairment

Debit		Credit	
		12/31/94	94,149
12/31/95	45,585		
		Bal.	48,564

Similar entries would be made at the end of 1996 and 1997 using the amounts included in the above amortization schedule. Note that computation of the amortization of the Allowance for Loan Impairment account is identical to the computation for the amortization of Discount on Notes Receivable account used in Chapter 8. If all payments are made as scheduled, the loan receivable and allowance accounts will both be closed out as of December 31, 1997.

Example of Loan Impairment Due to Troubled Debt Restructuring

If a further impairment is expected, and the timing of future cash flows are further changed due to a troubled debt restructuring in which concessions are made to the debtor in a

21. *FASB Statement No. 114*, par. 17b.

formal way, additional adjustments to bad debts will be necessary. Assume that Stockton does not make the planned December 31, 1996 payment and Malone agrees to restructure Stockton's debt. The modified terms of the original agreement include a reduced principal amount due of $300,000 (reduced from $375,000), a reduction in interest rate from 10% to 5% effective January 1, 1997, and a forgiveness of the 1996 interest. The new principal and interest payments schedule is as follows:

Date	Principal Payment	Interest Payment	Total Payment
December 31, 1997	$ 75,000	$15,000*	$ 90,000
December 31, 1998	125,000	11,250**	136,250
December 31, 1999	100,000	5,000	105,000
Totals			$331,250

*$300,000 @ 5% for one year
**$225,000 @ 5% for one year

As was true with the original estimate of impairment, the new carrying value of the investment at December 31, 1996 will be the present value of these future payments discounted at the original effective interest rate. This calculation is as follows:

Date	Payment	Time of Discount	Table Value	Present Value @10%
December 31, 1997	$ 90,000	1 year	.9091	$ 81,819
December 31, 1998	$136,250	2 years	.8264	112,597
December 31, 1999	$105,000	3 years	.7513	78,887
PV at January 1, 1996				$273,303

Since the carrying value of the loan before the restructuring, as shown in the amortization schedule and the T-accounts on the preceding page, is $326,436 ($375,000 – $48,564), a further reduction of $53,133 is necessary to reflect the newly computed present value of the loan ($326,436 – $273,303). Since the total undiscounted payments in the restructured loan, including interest, amounts to $331,250, the loan receivable account will be reduced by $43,750 ($375,000 – $331,250) and the allowance account will be increased by $9,383 ($53,133 – $43,750) to reflect the new present value of the loan. The further loan impairment from rescheduling is charged to 1996 Bad Debt Expense.

1996			
Dec. 31	Bad Debt Expense	53,133	
	Loan Receivable		43,750
	Allowance for Loan Impairment		9,383

The new amortization schedule for the restructured loan that reflects the new terms of the loan is shown below.

Interest Revenue from Troubled Debt Restructuring

Date	(1) Loan Receivable Before Current Payment	(2) Allowance for Loan Impairment	(3) Net Receivable (1) – (2)	(4) Interest Revenue 10% × (3)	(5) Payment Received
Dec. 31, 1997	$331,250	$57,947	$273,303	$27,330	$ 90,000
Dec. 31, 1998	241,250	30,617	210,633	21,063	136,250
Dec. 31, 1999	105,000	9,553	95,447	9,553	105,000
				$57,947	$331,250

*Rounded to close (2)

As schedule payments are received, they are credited to Loans Receivable and the interest revenue earned due to the passage of time is adjusted through the allowance account as illustrated earlier. Thus, entries at December 31, 1997 taken from the amortization schedule would be as follows:

1997				
Dec.	31	Cash	90,000	
		Loan Receivable		90,000
		Allowance for Loan Impairment	27,330	
		Interest Revenue		27,330

The creditor accounting when terms are modified in troubled debt restructuring for loans receivable without a market value differs from the debtor accounting for the same loan that was described in Chapter 14, pages 599 – 601.[22] Prior to FASB Statement No. 114, the FASB had prescribed a symmetrical treatment in FASB Statement No. 15 for both the debtor and the creditor in a troubled debt restructuring. However, this symmetry was abandoned in FASB Statement No. 114 when terms are modified. The Board recognized this and included the following explanation in the new statement:

The Board recognizes that this Statement introduces asymmetry between creditors' and debtors' accounting for troubled debt restructuring involving a modification of terms. However, the Board concluded that this Statement should address only creditors' accounting and that debtors' accounting should not be considered because expanding the scope of this Statement to address debtors' accounting likely would delay issuance of the final Statement.[23]

This explanation seems to leave the door open for the Board to later reconsider debtors' accounting still governed by FASB Statement No. 15.

Effective Date and Transition

Statement No. 114 is effective for all financial statements for fiscal years beginning after December 15, 1994. Because this statement deals with changing the way in which estimates of impairment are made, it is not to be considered as a change in accounting principle. No retroactive adjustment to prior years' statements are permitted, and the adjustment is made to bad debt expense rather than to a cumulative effect account.

22. According to FASB Statement No. 15, in this example Stockton, the debtor, would record its liability at the total of the undiscounted future payments, or $321,250, rather than at $265,039.

23. *FASB Statement No. 114*, par. 63

KEY TERMS

QUESTIONS

1. Identify the four major recording activities associated with investments in debt and equity securities.
2. What securities fall under the scope of FASB Statement No. 115?
3. Identify the alternative accounting methods for those equity securities not covered by FASB Statement No. 115.
4. What criteria must be met for a security to be classified as a trading security?
5. What criteria must be met for a security to be classified as held-to-maturity?
6. How are changes in value disclosed on the financial statements for trading securities? Available-for-sale securities? Held-to-maturity securities?
7. What two methods may be used to record the payment for accrued interest on interest-bearing securities? Which method is preferable?
8. When computing the price to be paid for a debt security, the stated rate of interest is used to determine what value? How does the market, or effective, rate affect a debt security's value?
9. What two methods may be used when amortizing the premium or discount on a debt security? Which method is preferable?
10. How does one compute the interest revenue to be recognized on a debt security if the effective interest method is being used?
11. Why might a company invest in the stock of another company?
12. What is the general rule used for determining the appropriate method of accounting for investments in equity securities when the investor does not possess absolute voting control?
13. (a) What factors may indicate the ability of an investor owning less than a majority voting interest to exercise significant influence on the investee's operating and financial policies?
    (b) What factors may indicate the investor's inability to exercise significant influence?
14. Distinguish between the method used to recognize revenue under the equity method and under the cost method.
15. What type of account is "Market Adjustment"? How is it disclosed on the financial statements?
16. How is a permanent decline in the value of investments recorded?
17. Where are the cash flow effects of purchases and sales of equity securities disclosed?
18. When transferring securities between categories under the provisions of FASB Statement No. 115, how is the transfer accounted for? At what value are the securities recorded?
19. What adjustment is needed when a company switches from (a) the equity method to the cost method and (b) the cost method to the equity method of valuing securities?
20. How are trading, available-for-sale, and held-to-maturity securities disclosed on the balance sheet—as current or long-term assets?
21. What additional disclosures are recommended under FASB Statement No. 115 for trading, available-for-sale, and held-to-maturity securities?

*22. Why is the impairment of a loan accounted for differently than the decline in value of a debt security?

*23. What does the balance in the account Allowance for Loan Impairment represent?

*Relates to Appendix 17-3

DISCUSSION CASES

Case 17—1 (But do we really have "mark to market" accounting now?)

The movement toward the use of market value for investments has been given the label "mark to market." Previously, marketable equity securities were valued at the lower of cost or market. The shift to market, whether higher or lower than cost, is a significant departure from the past. Even though all investments classified as trading or available-for-sale will now be valued at market values, only market changes for trading securities will affect the income statement. To many accounting theorists, this is indeed a cop-out on the part of the FASB. These accountants reason that if market changes are going to be recognized on the balance sheet, they should be recognized on the income statement as well. This position was held by two of the seven FASB members, who voted against the issuance of Statement No. 115.

Evaluate the rationale for this compromise position. What arguments for the two different approaches (income and equity) do you think are most persuasive and why? What future events could cause standard-setters to revise this approach?

Case 17—2 (Let's maximize profits through FASB Statement No. 115)

FASB Statement No. 115 is another example of the Board's emphasis on the balance sheet as contrasted with the income statement. As treasurer of Diamond Instrument, you desire to maximize income over the short-run. Diamond has had excess cash and you have chosen to invest it in both marketable debt and equity securities. What classification policy could you follow to maximize your investment's impact on net income? How would you justify this policy to your auditors?

Case 17—3 (I'm not a bank? Why must I worry about FASB Statement No. 115?)

Financial institutions, such as savings and loan companies and banks, were the major reasons the FASB studied the valuation issues relating to investments. FASB Statement No. 115, however, affects all companies that invest in marketable debt and equity securities. As controller of a retailing company, you are concerned with the classification of "trading security." How can you decide if the investments you have are trading or available-for-sale securities? In discussing this issue with other controllers, you are surprised to hear some of them indicate that Statement No. 115 really doesn't affect the reported income of nonfinancial institutions, and that all securities for these companies are considered available-for-sale securities. Other controllers were concerned by this statement because this reasoning would make accounting for investments less conservative than it was before FASB Statement No. 115. Do you agree with either of these points of view and why? In what way has FASB Statement No. 115 made accounting for investments less conservative?

Case 17—4 (Why is 49% ownership enough?)

In 1986, Coca-Cola Co. borrowed $2.4 billion to purchase several large soft drink bottling operations. Then a separate company, Coca-Cola Enterprises, was formed to bottle and distribute Coke throughout the country. Coca-Cola Co. sold 51 percent of Coca-Cola Enterprises to the public and retained a 49 percent ownership. The $2.4 billion in debt incurred to finance the purchase was transferred to the balance sheet of Coca-Cola Enterprises.

While 49 percent ownership does not guarantee control, it does give Coca-Cola Co. significant influence over the bottling company. For example, Coca-Cola Co. determines the price at which it will sell concentrate to Coca-Cola Enterprises and reviews Coca-Cola Enterprises' marketing plan. In addition, Coca-Cola Co.'s chief operating officer is chairman of Coca-Cola Enterprises, and six other current or former Coca-Cola Co. officials are serving on Coca-Cola Enterprises' board of directors.

1. From an accounting standpoint, what is the significance of owning more than 50 percent of a company's stock?
2. Why would the Coca-Cola Co. elect to own less than 50 percent of its distribution network?
3. In the consolidation process, the parent and the subsidiary's individual asset and liability account balances are added together and reported on the consolidated financial statements, whereas with the equity method, the net investment is reported as an asset on the investor company's balance sheet. Why would Coca-Cola Co. want to avoid consolidation?

Source: *The Wall Street Journal*, October 15, 1986, pp. 1 and 12.

Case 17—5 (Which method of accounting for investments is appropriate?)

International Inc. has ownership of companies in countries all over the world. International is reviewing its methods of accounting for those companies and has asked you to provide input as to whether the cost method, the equity method, or consolidation is appropriate for each of the following subsidiaries. Provide justification for your suggestions.

Subsidiary #1

This subsidiary, MEOil, is an oil company located in the Middle East. A growing anti-American sentiment in the country in which the company is located has led International to remove all non-native employees. There is a growing fear that the government may nationalize MEOil. International Inc. owns 75% of the oil company.

Subsidiary #2

Ecological Inc., a company that produces environmentally safe products, has production facilities in over 10 states. The ownership of the company is widely held, with International Inc. holding the largest block of stock. International has succeeded in placing its president and vice president in two of the five board of directors seats of Ecological Inc. International owns 15% of Ecological Inc.'s outstanding stock.

Subsidiary #3

International Inc. recently purchased 100% of the outstanding stock of Harmon National Bank. This subsidiary represents International's first purchase of a nonmanufacturing facility, and management has expressed concern about the comparability of the different accounting methods used by financial institutions.

Subsidiary #4

International has been involved in a takeover battle with Beatrix Inc. involving Campton Soups. Beatrix recently purchased 50% of the stock of Campton. International has owned 30% of Campton for five years.

Case 17—6 (What is the difference in accounting between the cost and equity methods?)

Analogic Corporation, a producer of medical products, disclosed the following investments in affiliates in the notes to its July 31, 1996, financial statements:

	1996	1995
Investments, at cost	$ 822,188	$ 50,000
Investments, at equity	1,677,181	2,009,647

Discuss the factors that determine whether Analogic uses the cost or the equity method in accounting for its investment in affiliates. What events are recorded when the cost method is used? What events are recorded when the equity method is used? What does the investment account summarize using the cost method? using the equity method?

Case 17—7 (How does increased ownership in another company affect our books?)

For the past three years Mapleton Corp. has maintained an investment (properly accounted for and reported upon) in Johnson Co. reflecting a 15% interest in the voting common stock of Johnson. The purchase price was $800,000, and the underlying net equity in Johnson at the date of purchase was $660,000. On January 2 of the current year, Mapleton purchased an additional 10% (total ownership interest is now 25%) of the voting common stock of Johnson for $1,100,000; the underlying net equity of the additional investment at January 2 was $1,000,000. Johnson has been profitable and has paid dividends annually since Mapleton's initial acquisition.

Discuss how this increase in ownership affects the accounting for and reporting on the investment in Johnson. Include in your discussion the adjustments, if any, that must be made to the amount shown prior to the increase in investment to bring the amount into conformity with generally accepted accounting principles. Also include how current and subsequent periods would be reported on.

***Case 17—8 (Cash surrender value)**

During your examination of the financial statements of Jones Paint, which has never before been audited, you discover that the cash surrender value of a $500,000 life insurance policy on the president, for which Jones is the beneficiary, has not been recorded in the accounting records. The president states that the total premium on the policy was charged to the insurance expense account each year because the company has no intention of "cashing in" the policy or of using the cash surrender value as collateral for a loan from the insurance company or a bank. Therefore, asserts the president, it would be misleading for the company to record as an asset an amount never expected to be realized or used by the company.

Evaluate the position of the president of Jones Paint.

*Relates to Appendix 17—2

*Case 17—9 (Now how do we account for troubled debt restructuring?)

The issuance of FASB Statements No. 114 and 115 concurrently has led to confusion as to their relationship to each other. Especially confusing is the accounting for troubled debt restructuring. These statements deal with creditor accounting for restructured debts while FASB Statement No. 15 still deals with debtor accounting for restructured debt. Assume you are asked to write a paper distinguishing between debtor and creditor accounting for restructured debt including a distinction between creditor accounting under FASB Statements No. 114 and 115. In outline form, indicate the major points you would include in your paper.

*Relates to Appendix 17—3

EXERCISES

Exercise 17—10 (Recording securities transactions)

Prepare the entries necessary to record the following transactions of Rexton, Inc. All transactions occurred within the same accounting period.

(a) Purchased $80,000 U.S. Treasury 8% bonds, paying 102.5 plus accrued interest of $1,500. In addition, Rexton paid brokerage fees of $590. Rexton uses the revenue approach to record accrued interest on purchased bonds. Rexton classified this security as a trading security.
(b) Purchased 1,000 shares of Agler Co. common stock at $175 per share plus brokerage fees of $1,200. Rexton classifies this stock as an available-for-sale security.
(c) Received semiannual interest on the U.S. Treasury bonds.
(d) Sold 150 shares of Agler at $185 per share.
(e) Sold $20,000 of U.S. Treasury 8% bonds at 103 plus accrued interest of $275.
(f) Purchased a $15,000, 6-month certificate of deposit. The certificate is classified as a trading security.

Exercise 17—11 (Accounting for the purchase and sale of securities)

During January 1996, Aragorn Inc. purchased the following securities:

Security	Classification	No. of Shares	Total Cost
Gimli Corporation stock	Trading	500	$ 9,000
Legolas International Inc. stock	Available-for-sale	1,000	22,000
Glorfindel Enterprises stock	Available-for-sale	2,500	42,500
Mirkwood Co. bonds	Held-to-maturity	—	24,000
U.S. Treasury bonds	Trading	—	11,000

During 1996, Aragorn received interest from Mirkwood and the U.S. Treasury totaling $3,630. Dividends received on the stock held amounted to $1,760. During November of 1996, Aragorn sold 300 shares of the Gimli stock at $17 per share and 500 shares of the Glorfindel stock at $19 per share.

Give the journal entries required by Aragorn to record the:

1. Purchase of the debt and equity securities
2. Receipt of interest and dividends during 1996.
3. Sale of the equity securities during November.

Exercise 17—12 (Accounting methods for equity securities)

For each of the following independent situations, determine the appropriate accounting method to be used: consolidation, cost, or equity. If you answer the cost method, determine whether the security should be classified as trading or available-for-sale. Explain the rationale for your decision.

1. ATV Company manufactures and sells four-wheel recreational vehicles. It also provides insurance on its products through its wholly-owned subsidiary, RV Insurance Company.
2. Buy Right Inc. purchased 20,000 shares of Big Supply Company common stock to be held as a long-term investment. Big Supply has 200,000 shares of common stock outstanding.
3. Super Tire Manufacturing Co. holds 5,000 shares of the 10,000 outstanding shares of non-voting preferred stock of Valley Corporation. Super Tire considers the investment as being long-term in nature.
4. Takeover Company owns 15,000 of the 50,000 shares of common stock of Western Supply Company. Takeover has tried and failed to obtain representation on Western's board of directors. Takeover intends to sell the securities if they cannot obtain board representation at the next stockholders' meeting, scheduled in 3 weeks.
5. Espino Inc. purchased 50,000 shares of Independent Mining Company common stock. Independent has a total of 125,000 common shares outstanding. Espino has no intention to sell the securities in the foreseeable future.

Exercise 17—13 (Investment in equity securities—cost and equity methods)

On January 10, 1996, Booker Corporation acquired 16,000 shares of the outstanding common stock of Atlanta Company for $800,000. At the time of purchase, Atlanta Company had outstanding 80,000 shares with a book value of $4 million. On December 31, 1996, the following events took place:

(a) Atlanta reported net income of $180,000 for the calendar year 1996.
(b) Booker received from Atlanta a dividend of $0.75 per share of common stock.
(c) The market value of Atlanta Company stock had temporarily declined to $45 per share.

Give the entries that would be required to reflect the purchase and subsequent events on the books of Booker Corporation, assuming:

1. The cost method is appropriate and the security is classified as available-for-sale.
2. The equity method is appropriate.

Exercise 17—14 (Investment in equity securities—unrecorded goodwill)

Alpha Co. acquired 20,000 shares of Beta Co. on January 1, 1995, at $12 per share. Beta Co. had 80,000 shares outstanding with a book value of $800,000. There were no identifiable undervalued assets at the time of purchase. Beta Co. recorded earnings of $260,000 and $290,000 for 1995 and 1996, respectively, and paid per-share dividends of $1.60 in 1995 and $2.00 in 1996. Assuming a 40-year straight-line amortization policy for goodwill, give the entries to record the purchase in 1995 and to reflect Alpha's share of Beta's earnings and the receipt of the dividends for 1995 and 1996.

Exercise 17—15 (Investment in equity securities—market value different from book value)

On January 3, 1996, McDonald Inc. purchased 40% of the outstanding common stock of Old Farms Co., paying $128,000 when the book value of the net assets of Old Farms equaled $250,000. The difference was attributed to equipment, which had a book value of $60,000 and a fair market value of $100,000, and to buildings, with a book value of $50,000 and a fair market value of $80,000. The remaining useful life of the equipment and buildings was 5 years and 10 years, respectively. During 1996, Old Farms reported net income of $80,000 and paid dividends of $50,000.

Prepare the journal entries made by McDonald Inc. during 1996 related to its investment in Old Farms.

Exercise 17—16 (Amortization of a discount on a debt security)

On January 1, 1996, Wilcox Incorporated purchased $500,000 of 10-year, 9% bonds when the market rate of interest was 8%. Interest is to be paid on June 30 and December 31 of each year.

1. Prepare the journal entry to record the purchase of the debt security.
2. Prepare the journal entry to record the receipt of the first two interest payments assuming that Wilcox accounts for the debt security as being available-for-sale and uses the effective-interest method.

Exercise 17—17 (Amortization of a premium on a debt security)
On January 1, 1996, Cougar Creations Inc. purchased $100,000 of 5-year, 8% bonds when the effective rate of interest was 10%, paying $92,277. Interest is to be paid on July 1 and December 31.

1. Prepare an interest amortization schedule for the bonds.
2. Prepare the journal entries made by Cougar Creations on July 1 and December 31 of 1996 to recognize the receipt of interest and to amortize the discount.

Exercise 17—18 (Valuation of a debt security)
Using the information from Exercise 17—17, provide the journal entry that would be necessary to properly value the debt security if, on December 31, 1996, the bond's fair value was $98,500. Assume the security was initially classified as:

1. A trading security.
2. An available-for-sale security.
3. A held-to-maturity security.

Exercise 17—19 (Trading Securities)
During 1996, Litten Company purchased trading securities as a short-term investment. The cost of the securities, and their market values on December 31, 1996, are listed below:

Security	Cost	Market Value Dec. 31, 1996
A	$ 65,000	$ 81,000
B	100,000	54,000
C	220,000	226,000

At the beginning of 1996, Litten had a zero balance in the account Market Adjustment—Trading Securities. Before any adjustments related to these trading securities, Litten had net income of $300,000.

1. What is net income after making any necessary trading security adjustments? (Ignore income taxes)
2. What would net income be if the market value of Security B were $95,000?

Exercise 17—20 (Accounting for trading securities)
During 1995, Sunshine Inc. purchased the following trading securities:

Security	Cost	Market Value Dec. 31, 1995
Wexler Co. Common	$12,000	$14,000
10% U.S. Treasury Notes	18,000	11,000
TexCo Bonds	25,000	27,000

At the beginning of 1995, Sunshine had a zero balance in the account Market Adjustment—Trading Securities.

1. What entry would be made at year-end assuming the above values?
2. What entry would be made during 1996 assuming one-half of the Wexler Co. common stock is sold for $7,000?
3. What entry would be made at the end of 1996 assuming: (a) the market value of remaining securities is $45,000? (b) the market value of remaining securities is $48,000? (c) The market value of remaining securities is $55,000?

Exercise 17—21 (Debt and equity securities)
American Steel Corp. acquired the following securities in 1996:

Security	Classification	Cost	Market Value Dec. 31, 1996
A	Trading	$10,000	$12,000
B	Trading	14,000	10,000
C	Available-for-sale	12,000	15,000
D	Available-for-sale	20,000	15,000
E	Held-to-maturity	20,000	22,000

At the beginning of 1996, American Steel had a zero balance in each of its market adjustment accounts.

1. What entry(ies) would be made at the end of 1996 assuming the above market values?
2. If net income before any adjustments related to marketable securities was $100,000, what would reported income be after adjustments? (Ignore income taxes.)

Exercise 17—22 (Temporary and permanent changes in value)
The securities portfolio for Hill Top Industries contained the trading securities listed below.

Securities (Common Stock)	Initial Cost	Market Value Dec. 31, 1995	Market Value Dec. 31, 1996
Randall Co.	$10,000	$12,000	$15,000
Streuling Co	7,000	3,000	2,000
Santana Co	21,000	18,000	22,000

1. Assuming all changes in fair value are considered temporary, what is the effect of the changes in value on the 1995 and 1996 financial statements? Give the valuation entries for these years.
2. Assume that at December 31, 1996, management believed that the market value of the Streuling Co. common stock reflected a permanent decline in the value of that stock. Give the entries to be made on December 31, 1996, under this assumption.

Exercise 17—23 (Reclassification of securities)
Surhako Inc. had the following portfolio of securities at the end of its first year of operations:

Security	Classification	Cost	Year-End Market Value
A	Trading	$15,000	$18,000
B	Trading	20,000	22,000

1. Provide the entry necessary to adjust the portfolio of securities to its market value.
2. After adjusting the securities to market, Surhako elects to reclassify Security B as an available-for-sale security. On the date of the transfer, Security B's market value is $21,500. Provide the journal entry to reclassify Security B.

Exercise 17—24 (Reclassification of securities)
Bicknel Technologies Inc. purchased the following securities during 1995:

Security	Classification	Cost	Market Value (12/31/95)
A	Trading	$ 2,000	$ 4,000
B	Trading	7,000	6,000
C	Available-for-sale	18,000	16,000
D	Available-for-sale	5,000	4,000
E	Held-to-maturity	14,000	15,000

At the beginning of 1995, Bicknel Technologies had a zero balance in each of its market adjustment accounts. During 1996, after the 1995 financial statements had been issued, Bicknel determined that Security B should be reclassified as an available-for-sale security and Security C should be reclassified as a trading security. The market values on the date of the transfer are $5,500 for Security B and $17,000 for Security C.

Prepare the journal entries to:

1. Adjust the portfolio of securities to its market value.
2. Reclassify Security B as an available-for-sale security.
3. Reclassify Security C as a trading security.

Exercise 17—25 (Accounting for securities)

During 1995, the first year of its operations, Soelberg Industries purchased the following securities:

Security	Classification	Cost	Market Value Dec. 31, 1995	Market Value Dec. 31, 1996
A	Trading	$22,000	$14,000	$ 9,000
B	Trading	7,000	10,000	11,000
C	Available-for-sale	16,000	15,000	16,000
D	Available-for-sale	20,000	25,000	12,000

During 1996, Soelberg sold one-half of Security A for $10,000 and one-half of Security D for $13,000.

Provide the journal entries required to:

1. Adjust the portfolio of securities to its market value at the end of 1995.
2. Record the sale of securities A and D.
3. Adjust the portfolio of securities to its market value at the end of 1996.

Exercise 17—26 (Valuation of securities)

Bridgeman Paper Co. reported the following selected balances on its financial statements for each of the four years 1994-1997:

	1994	1995	1996	1997
Market Adjustment—Trading Securities	$0	$5,500	$3,750	$ (700)
Market Adjustment—Available-for-Sale Securities	0	(1,300)	900	$1,150

Based on these balances, reconstruct the valuation entries that must have been made each year.

Exercise 17—27 (Investment in common stock—equity to cost method)

Porter Co. purchased 50,000 shares of Cannon Manufacturing Co. common stock on July 1, 1995, at $16.50 per share, which reflected book value as of that date. Cannon Manufacturing Co. had 200,000 common shares outstanding at the time of the purchase. Prior to this purchase, Porter Co. had no ownership interest in Cannon. In its second quarterly statement, Cannon

Manufacturing Co. reported net income of $168,000 for the six months ended June 30, 1995. Porter Co. received a dividend of $21,000 from Cannon on August 1, 1995. Cannon reported net income of $360,000 for the year ended December 31, 1995, and again paid Porter Co. dividends of $21,000. On January 1, 1996, Porter Co. sold 20,000 shares of Cannon Manufacturing Co. common stock for $17 per share. Cannon reported net income of $372,000 for the year ended December 31, 1996, and paid Porter Co. dividends of $12,000. Give all entries Porter Co. would make in 1995 and 1996 in regard to the Cannon Manufacturing Co. stock. Assume that the market price remained constant throughout the two-year period.

Exercise 17—28 (Investment in common stock—equity to cost method)

On January 1, 1995, Medproducts Inc. purchased 50% of Electronico, paying $600,000. On that date, Medproducts' net assets had a book value of $1,100,000. The difference between fair value and book value is attributed to goodwill and is amortized over 20 years. On January 1, 1996, Medproducts sold 80% of its ownership in Electronico (40% of the outstanding stock) for $575,000. Net income and dividends for 1995 and 1996 for Electronico are given below.

	1995	1996
Net income	$85,000	$100,000
Dividends	20,000	30,000

Give the required journal entries made by Medproducts relating to its investment in Electronico for the years 1995 and 1996 assuming no change in market value during the two-year period.

Exercise 17—29 (Investment in common stock—cost to equity method)

Peterson Inc. purchased 15% of the outstanding common stock of Sunspot Co. on January 1, 1996, when Sunspot's net assets had a book value and fair value of $400,000. Peterson Inc. paid $75,000. Any excess of fair value over cost is attributable to goodwill. Goodwill, when amortized, is amortized over a 40-year period. On January 1, 1997, Peterson purchased an additional 15% of the outstanding stock of Sunspot, paying another $75,000. (Assume net asset book and fair value is still $400,000.) Sunspot's reported income and dividends for 1996 and 1997 are given below.

	1996	1997
Net income	$30,000	$50,000
Dividends	30,000	40,000

Prepare the journal entries made by Peterson during 1996 and 1997 related to its investment in Sunspot Co., including the adjusting entries necessary to reflect the change from the cost to the equity method.

Exercise 17—30 (Investment in common stock—cost to equity method)

Devers Corporation purchased 5% of the 100,000 outstanding common shares of Milo Inc. on January 1, 1994, for a total purchase price of $7,500. Net assets of Milo Inc. at the time had a book and fair value of $150,000. Net income for Milo Inc. for the year ended December 31, 1994, was $50,000. Devers received dividends from Milo during the year of $1,500. There was no change of Devers' ownership of Milo Inc. during 1995, and Milo reported net income of $70,000 for the year ended December 31, 1995. Devers received dividends of $2,000 from Milo for that year. On January 1, 1996, Devers purchased an additional 20% of Milo Inc.'s common stock or 20,000 shares for a total price of $40,000. Milo Inc.'s net asset book and fair value at the time of the purchase was $200,000. For the year ended December 31, 1996, Milo Inc. reported net income of $100,000; Devers received dividends from Milo Inc. totaling $10,000 for the year ended December 31, 1996.

Prepare journal entries for Devers Corporation to reflect the preceding transactions, including adjusting entries necessary to reflect the change from the cost method to the equity method of accounting for Devers Corporation's investment in Milo Inc.

Exercise 17—31 (Securities and the statement of cash flows)

Indicate how each of the following transactions or events would be reflected in a statement of cash flows prepared using the indirect method. Each transaction or event is independent of the others. For items (a) and (d), assume that the balance in the market adjustment account was zero at the beginning of the year.

(a) At year-end, the trading securities portfolio has an aggregate cost of $170,000 and an aggregate fair value of $150,000.

(b) During the year, trading securities and available-for-sale securities were purchased for $50,000 and $70,000, respectively. The securities were paid for in cash.

(c) During the year, trading securities purchased at the beginning of the year at a cost of $40,000 were sold for $53,000 cash.

(d) At year-end, the trading securities portfolio has an aggregate cost of $170,000 and an aggregate fair value of $190,000.

*Exercise 17—32 (Fund investments)

On December 31, 1995, Haws Corporation set up a stock redemption fund, with an initial deposit of $150,000. On February 1, 1996, Haws Corporation invested $127,500 stock redemption fund cash in 10% preferred stock of Mackay Inc., par value of $75,000. Mackay normally declares and pays dividends on the preferred stock semiannually: March 1 and September 1. On April 1, 1996, Haws exchanged the stock with another investor for 4,000 shares of Lamas Corporation common stock. The market value of the common stock at the date of exchange was $35 per share. Give all the entries necessary to record the preceding transactions assuming semiannual dividends were paid.

*Relates to Appendix 17—1

*Exercise 17—33 (Fund accumulation schedule)

Fund tables show that 5 annual deposits of $16,379.75 accruing interest at 10% compounded annually will result in a total accumulation of $100,000 immediately after the fifth payment.

1. Prepare a fund accumulation schedule showing the theoretical growth of a property acquisition fund over the 5-year period.
2. Give all of the entries that would appear on the books for the increases in the property acquisition fund balance for the first 3 years.

*Relates to Appendix 17—1

*Exercise 17—34 (Cash surrender value)

Case Company follows the practice of taking out whole-life insurance policies on its key employees. The annual premium of $8,400 is paid on May 1. The cash surrender value at December 31, 1995, was $39,400. At the end of 1996, the cash surrender value had increased to $41,200. Give the journal entries for 1996.

*Relates to Appendix 17—2

*Exercise 17—35 (Accounting for the impairment of a loan)

Starship Enterprises loaned $100,000 to Pikkard Inc. on January 1, 1995. The terms of the loan require principal payments of $20,000 each year for five years plus interest at 8%. The first principal and interest payment is due on January 1, 1996. Pikkard made the required payments during 1996 and 1997. However, during 1997 Pikkard began to experience financial difficulties, requiring Starship to reassess the collectability of the loan. On December 31, 1997, Starship determines that the remaining principal payments will be collected but the collection of interest is unlikely.

1. Compute the present value of the expected future cash flows as of December 31, 1997.
2. Provide the journal entry to record the loan impairment as of December 31, 1997.
3. Provide the journal entries for 1998 to record the receipt of the principal payment on January 1 and the recognition of interest revenue as of December 31, assuming that Starship's assessment of the collectability of the loan has not changed.

*Relates to Appendix 17—3

***Exercise 17—36 (Accounting for troubled debt restructuring)**
In payment of an overdue account receivable, Robison Co. accepted, on January 1, 1995, a note from Harris Inc. in the amount of $250,000. The terms of the note require five annual principal payments with interest at a rate of 10%. The interest and principal payments are due on January 1. Harris made the first two principal and interest payments. During 1997, Harris experienced severe financial difficulties and, as a result, negotiated with Robison a restructuring of terms of the outstanding note. Robison agreed to forgive $30,000 of the remaining principal, requiring three remaining principal payments of $40,000, and to reduce the interest rate of the note from 10% to 4% effective January 2, 1997. Compute the present value of the future payments as of December 31, 1997. Provide the journal entry to record the loan impairment as of December 31, 1997. Provide the journal entries made during 1998 to record the receipt of the principal and interest payments and to recognize interest revenue on December 31.

*Relates to Appendix 17—3

PROBLEMS

Problem 17—37 (Accounting for trading securities)
Fox Company made the following transactions in the common stock of NOP Company:

July 10, 1994	Purchased 10,000 shares at $45 per share.
Sept. 29, 1995	Sold 2,000 shares for $51 per share.
Aug. 17, 1996	Sold 2,500 shares for $33 per share.

The end-of-year market prices for the shares were as follows:

December 31, 1994	$47 per share
December 31, 1995	$39 per share
December 31, 1996	$31 per share

Instructions: Prepare the necessary entries for 1994, 1995, and 1996 assuming the NOP stock is classified as a trading security.

Problem 17—38 (Recording and valuing trading securities)
Myers & Associates reports the following information on the December 31, 1994 balance sheet:

Trading Securities (at cost)	$225,850	
Less Market Adjustment—Trading Securities	2,260	$223,590

Supporting records of Myers' trading securities portfolio show the following debt and equity securities:

Security	Cost	Market Value
200 shares Conway Co. common	$ 25,450	$ 24,300
$80,000 U.S. Treasury 7% bonds	79,650	77,400
$120,000 U.S. Treasury 7 1/2% bonds	120,750	121,890
Total	$225,850	$223,590

Interest dates on the Treasury bonds are January 1 and July 1. Myers & Associates makes reversing entries and uses the revenue approach to record the purchase of bonds with accrued interest. During 1995 and 1996, Myers & Associates completed the following transactions related to trading securities:

1995

Jan.	1	Received semiannual interest on U.S. Treasury bonds. (The entry to reverse the interest accrual at the end of last year has already been made.)
Apr.	1	Sold \$60,000 of the 7 1/2% U.S. Treasury bonds at 102 plus accrued interest. Brokerage fees were \$200.
May	21	Received dividends of 25 cents per share on the Conway Co. common stock. The dividend had not been recorded on the declaration date.
July	1	Received semiannual interest on U.S. Treasury bonds, then sold the 7% treasury bonds at 97 1/2. Brokerage fees were \$250.
Aug.	15	Purchased 100 shares of Nieman Inc. common stock at 116 plus brokerage fees of \$50.
Nov.	1	Purchased \$50,000 of 8% U.S. Treasury bonds at 101 plus accrued interest. Brokerage fees were \$125. Interest dates are January 1 and July 1.
Dec.	31	Market prices of securities were: Conway Co. common, 110; 7 1/2 % U.S. Treasury bonds, 101 3/4; 8% U.S. Treasury bonds, 101; Nieman Inc. common, 116 3/4.

1996

Jan.	2	Recorded the receipt of semiannual interest on the U.S. Treasury bonds.
Feb.	1	Sold the remaining 7 1/2 % U.S. Treasury bonds at 101 plus accrued interest. Brokerage fees were \$300.

Instructions:

1. Prepare journal entries for the foregoing transactions and to accrue interest on December 31, 1995. Ignore any amortization of premium or discount on treasury bonds. Give computations in support of your entries.
2. Show how trading securities would be presented on the December 31, 1995 balance sheet.

Problem 17—39 (Accounting for debt and equity securities)

During 1996, Merz Company purchased 3,000 shares of Silko Company common stock for \$16 per share and 2,000 shares of Monroe Company common stock for \$33 per share. These investments are intended to be held as ready sources of cash and are classified as trading securities.

Also in 1996, Merz purchased 3,500 shares of Barclay Company common stock for \$29 per share and \$40,000 of treasury notes at 101. These securities are classified as available-for-sale.

During 1996, Merz received the following interest and dividend payments on its investments:

Silko Company	\$1 per share dividend
Monroe Company	\$3 per share dividend
Barclay Company	\$2 per share dividend
Treasury notes	6% annual interest earned for 6 months

Market values of the securities at December 31, 1996, were as follows:

Silko Company	\$20 per share
Monroe Company	\$22 per share
Barclay Company	\$27 per share
Treasury notes	102

On March 23, 1997, the 2,000 shares of Monroe common stock were sold for \$17 per share. On June 30, 1997, the treasury notes were sold at 100.5 plus accrued interest.

Market values of remaining securities at December 31, 1997, were as follows:

Silko Company	\$19 per share
Barclay Company	\$32 per share

Instructions:

1. Prepare all 1996 and 1997 journal entries related to these securities.
2. Describe how the following items would be treated on Merz Company's statement of cash flows for the year ended December 31, 1997. Merz uses the indirect method of reporting cash flows from operating activities.
   (a) Proceeds from the sale of Monroe shares and the treasury securities.
   (b) Any realized gain or loss on the sale of the above securities.
   (c) Any unrealized gain or loss on the remaining securities.

Problem 17—40 (Journal entries and balance sheet presentation for investments in securities)

On December 31, 1994, Durst Company's balance sheet showed the following balances related to its securities accounts:

Trading securities	$155,000	
Less: Market adjustment—trading securities	(7,250)	$147,750
Available-for-sale securities	$108,000	
Add: Market adjustment—available-for-sale securities	10,000	118,000
Interest receivable—NYC Water bonds		1,250

Durst's securities portfolio on December 31, 1994 was made up of the following securities:

Security	Classification	Cost	Market
1,000 shares Herzog Corp. stock	Trading	$75,000	$76,250
800 shares Taylor Inc. stock	Trading	55,000	52,825
10% New York City Water bonds (interest payable semiannually on January 1 and July 1)	Trading	25,000	18,675
1,000 shares Martin Inc. stock	Available-for-sale	59,000	65,000
2,000 shares Outdoors Unlimited Inc. stock	Available-for-sale	49,000	53,000

During 1995, the following transactions took place:

Jan.	3	Received interest on the New York City Water bonds.
Mar.	1	Purchased 300 additional shares of Herzog Corp. stock for $22,950; classified as a trading security.
Apr.	15	Sold 400 shares of the Taylor Inc. stock for $69 per share.
May	4	Sold 400 shares of the Martin Inc. stock for $62 per share.
July	1	Received interest on the New York City water bonds.
Oct.	30	Purchased 1,500 shares of Cook Co. stock for $83,250; classified as a trading security.

Durst makes reversing entries on January 1 for all year-end accrual entries. The market values of the stocks and bonds on December 31, 1995, are as follows:

Herzog Corp. stock	$76.60 per share
Taylor Inc. stock	$68.50 per share
Cook Co. stock	$55.25 per share
New York City Water bonds	$20,555
Martin Inc. stock	$61.00 per share
Outdoors Unlimited Inc. stock	$27.00 per share

Instructions:

1. Make all necessary journal entries for 1995, including any year-end accrual or adjusting entries.
2. Show how the marketable securities would be presented on the balance sheet at December 31, 1995. Assume that the available-for-sale securities are classified as current assets.

Problem 17—41 (Journal entries for trading securities)

During 1996 and 1997, the Kopson Co. made the following journal entries to account for transactions involving trading securities.

				Debit	Credit
1996					
(a)	Nov.	1	Investment in Trading Securities (10% U.S. Treasury Bonds)	106,883	
			Cash		106,883
			To record the purchase of $100,000 of U.S. Treasury bonds at 103 1/4. Brokerage fees were $300. Interest is payable semiannually on January 1 and July 1.		
(b)	Dec.	31	Unrealized Increase/Decrease in Value of Available-for-Sale Securities—Equity	4,283	
			Market Adjustment—Trading Securities		4,283
			To record the decrease in market value of the current marketable securities based on the following data:		

	Cost	Market	Market Adjustment
Fleming Co. stock	$ 25,250	$ 23,350	$1,900 cr
Dobson Co. stock	32,450	33,950	1,500 dr
10% U.S. Treasury bonds	106,883	103,000	3,883 cr
	$164,583	$160,300	$4,283 cr

The beginning balance in the account Market Adjustment—Trading Securities was a $500 credit. There were no other entries in 1996.

				Debit	Credit
1997					
(c)	Jan.	1	Cash	5,000	
			Interest Revenue		5,000
			To record interest revenue for six months.		
(d)	July	1	Cash	5,000	
			Interest Revenue		5,000
			To record interest revenue for six months.		
(e)	Dec.	6	Investment in Available-for-Sale Securities—Fleming Company	25,250	
			Investment in Trading Securities—Fleming Co.		25,250
			To reclassify Fleming Co. Stock from trading securities to available-for-sale securities. Market price was $24,500 at the date of reclassification.		
(f)	Dec.	31	Unrealized Increase/Decrease in Value of Available-for-Sale Securities—Equity	3,483	
			Market Adjustment—Available-for-Sale Securities		300
			Market Adjustment—Trading Securities		3,183
			To record the decrease in market value of available-for-sale securities based on the following data:		

	Cost	Market	Market Adjustment
Dobson Co. stock	$ 32,450	$ 32,650	$ 200 dr
10% U.S. Treasury bonds	106,883	103,500	3,383 cr
Fleming Co. stock	25,250	24,950	300 cr
	$164,583	$161,100	$3,483 cr

There were no other entries in 1997.

Instructions: For each incorrect entry, give the entry that *should have been made*. Assume the revenue approach is used. Ignore any premium or discount amortization on treasury bonds.

Problem 17—42 (Valuation of equity securities)

The investment portfolio of Morris Inc. at December 31, 1995, contains the following securities:

Opus Co. common, 3% ownership, 5,000 shares; cost, $100,000; market value, $95,000. Classified as a trading security.

Garrod Inc. preferred, 2,000 shares; cost, $40,000; market value, $43,000. Classified as a trading security.

Sherrill Inc. common, 30% ownership, 20,000 shares; cost, $1,140,000; market value, $1,130,000. Classified as controlling investment.

Jennings Co. common, 15% ownership, 25,000 shares; cost, $67,500; market value, $50,000. Classified as an available-for-sale security.

Instructions:

1. Give the valuation adjustment required at December 31, 1995, assuming all investments were purchased in 1995 and none of the indicated declines in market value are considered permanent.
2. Assume the Jennings Co. common stock market decline is considered permanent. Give the valuation entries required at December 31, 1995, under this change in assumption.
3. Assume the market values for the long-term investment portfolio at December 31, 1996, were as follows:

Opus Co. Common	$ 102,000
Garrod Inc. Preferred	43,000
Sherrill Inc. Common	1,115,000
Jennings Co. Common	45,000

Give the valuation entries at December 31, 1996, assuming all declines in 1995 and 1996 are temporary except for the 1995 decline in Jennings Co. stock and that the investment categories remain the same.

Problem 17—43 (Investments in common stock)

Arroyo Inc. and the Bell Corp. each have 100,000 shares of no-par common stock outstanding. Universal Inc. acquired 10,000 shares of Arroyo stock for $5 per share and 25,000 shares of Bell stock for $10 per share in 1993. Both securities are being held as long-term investments. Changes in retained earnings for Arroyo and Bell for 1995 and 1996 are as follows:

	Arroyo Inc.	Bell Corp.
Retained earnings (deficit), January 1, 1995	$200,000	$(35,000)
Cash dividends, 1995	(25,000)	—
	$175,000	$(35,000)
Net income, 1995	40,000	65,000
Retained earnings, December 31, 1995	$215,000	$ 30,000
Cash dividends, 1996	(30,000)	(10,000)
Net income, 1996	60,000	25,000
Retained earnings, December 31, 1996	$245,000	$ 45,000
Market value of stock: December 31, 1995	$7.00	$12.00
December 31, 1996	6.50	15.00

Instructions: Give the entries required on the books of Universal Inc. for 1995 and 1996 to account for its investments.

Problem 17—44 (Long-term investments in stock—equity method)

On January 1, 1996, Compustat Co. bought 30% of the outstanding common stock of Freelance Corp. for $258,000 cash. Compustat Co. accounts for this investment by the equity method. At the date of acquisition of the stock, Freelance Corp.'s net assets had a carrying value of $620,000. Assets with an average remaining life of five years have a current market value that is $130,000 in excess of their carrying values. The remaining difference between the purchase price and the value of the underlying stockholders' equity cannot be attributed to any tangible asset. Compustat Co. has a policy of amortizing goodwill over 40 years. At the end of 1996, Freelance Corp. reports net income of $180,000. During 1996, Freelance Corp. declared and paid cash dividends of $20,000.

Instructions: Give the entries necessary to reflect Compustat Co.'s investment in Freelance Corp. for 1996.

Problem 17—45 (Investment in common stock)

On July 1 of the current year, Melissa Co. acquired 25% of the outstanding shares of common stock of International Co. at a total cost of $700,000. The underlying equity (net assets) of the stock acquired by Melissa was only $600,000. Melissa was willing to pay more than book value for the International Co. stock for the following reasons:

(a) International owned depreciable plant assets (10-year remaining economic life) with a current fair value of $60,000 more than their carrying amount.
(b) International owned land with a current fair value of $300,000 more than its carrying amount.
(c) Melissa believed International possessed enough goodwill to justify the remainder of the cost. Melissa's accounting policy with respect to goodwill is to amortize it over 40 years.

International Co. earned net income of $540,000 evenly over the current year ended December 31. On December 31, International declared and paid a cash dividend of $105,000 to common stockholders. Market value of Melissa's share of the stock at December 31 is $750,000. Both companies close their accounting records on December 31.

Instructions:

1. Compute the total amount of goodwill of International Co. based on the price paid by Melissa Co.
2. Prepare all journal entries in Melissa's accounting records relating to the investment for the year ended December 31, under the cost method of accounting, classifying the securities as available-for-sale.
3. Prepare all journal entries in Melissa's accounting records relating to the investment for the year ended December 31, under the equity method of accounting.

Problem 17—46 (Investment in common stock—fair market value less than book value)

MMM Inc. purchased 40% of XYZ Co. on January 4, 1996, for $250,000 when XYZ's book value was $630,000. On that day, the market value of the net assets of XYZ equaled their book values with the following exceptions:

	Book	Market
Equipment	$185,000	$160,000
Buildings	30,000	50,000

The equipment has a remaining useful life of 10 years, and the building has a remaining useful life of 20 years. XYZ reported the following related to operations for 1996 and 1997:

	Net Income	Dividends
1996	$ 75,000	$10,000
1997	(15,000)	5,000

Instructions: Provide the entries made by MMM Inc. relating to its investment in XYZ for the years 1996 and 1997.

Problem 17—47 (Reclassification of securities)

One Tree Incorporated had the following portfolio of securities on December 31, 1995:

Security	Classification	Cost	Market Value Dec. 31, 1995
A	Trading	$14,000	$17,000
B	Trading	22,000	31,000
C	Available-for-sale	7,000	9,000
D	Available-for-sale	18,000	20,500
E	Available-for-sale	21,000	15,000
F	Held-to-maturity	50,000	51,000

The balances in the market adjustment accounts as of January 1, 1995 were as follows:

Market adjustment—trading securities	$8,000 debit
Market adjustment—available-for-sale securities	2,500 credit

During 1996, One Tree Inc. determined that certain securities should be reclassified. Those reclassifications are as follows:

Security	Reclassify FROM	TO	Market Value at Date of Reclassification
A	Trading	Available-for-sale	$18,000
C	Available-for-sale	Trading	8,500
D	Available-for-sale	Held-to-maturity	21,000
F	Held-to-maturity	Trading	48,000

Instructions:

1. Make the necessary journal entries to adjust One Tree's portfolio of securities to market value as of December 31, 1995.
2. Make the necessary journal entries to reclassify the securities in 1996.

Problem 17—48 (Accounting for marketable equity securities)

The Trans America Trust Co. owns both trading and available-for-sale securities. The following securities were owned on December 31, 1995:

Trading Securities

Security	Shares	Total Cost	Market Value Dec. 31, 1995	Market Adjustment
Albert Groceries, Inc.	600	$ 9,000	$11,500	$2,500 dr
West Data, Inc	1,000	27,000	18,000	9,000 cr
Steel Co.	450	9,900	10,215	315 dr
		$45,900	$39,715	$6,185 cr

Available-for-Sale Securities

Security	Shares	Total Cost	Market Value Dec. 31, 1995	Market Adjustment
Dairy Products	2,000	$ 86,000	$ 90,000	$ 4,000 dr
Vern Movies, Inc.	15,000	390,000	365,000	25,000 cr
Disks, Inc.	5,000	60,000	80,000	20,000 dr
		$536,000	$535,000	$ 1,000 cr

The following transactions occurred during 1996:

(a) Sold 500 shares of West Data for $9,500.
(b) Sold 200 shares of Disks, Inc., for $3,000.
(c) Transferred all of Albert Groceries to the available-for-sale portfolio when the total market value was $12,900.
(d) Transferred the remaining shares of Disks, Inc., to the trading securities portfolio when the market price was $20 per share. These shares were subsequently sold for $18 per share.

At December 31, 1996, market prices for the remaining securities were as follows:

Security	Market Price Per Share
Albert Groceries Inc.	$22
West Data, Inc.	15
Steel Co.	21
Dairy Products	42
Vern Movies, Inc.	28

Instructions: Prepare all journal entries necessary to record Trans America Trust Co.'s marketable equity securities transactions and year-end adjustments for 1996. Assume all declines in market value are temporary.

Problem 17—49 (Accounting for long-term investments—cost and equity methods)

On January 2, 1994, Brozo Company acquired 20% of the 200,000 shares of outstanding common stock of Newberry Corp. for $30 per share. The purchase price was equal to Newberry's underlying book value. Brozo plans to hold this stock to control the activities of Newberry.

The following data is applicable for 1994 and 1995:

	1994	1995
Newberry dividends (paid Oct. 31)	$20,000	$24,000
Newberry earnings	70,000	80,000
Newberry stock market price at year-end	32	31

On January 2, 1996, Brozo Company sold 10,000 shares of Newberry stock for $31 per share. During 1996, Newberry reported net income of $60,000, and on October 31, 1996, Newberry paid dividends of $10,000. At December 31, 1996, after a significant stock market decline, which is expected to be temporary, Newberry's stock was selling for $22 per share. After selling the 10,000 shares, Brozo does not expect to exercise significant influence over Newberry and the shares are classified as available-for-sale.

Instructions:

1. Make all journal entries for Brozo Company for 1994, 1995, and 1996 assuming the 20% original ownership interest allowed significant influence over Newberry.
2. Make the year-end valuation adjusting entries for Brozo Company for 1994, 1995, and 1996 assuming the 20% original ownership interest did not allow significant influence over Newberry.

Problem 17—50 (Accounting for cost to equity method)

On January 1, 1995, Beans Inc. paid $400,000 for 10,000 shares of Keller Company's voting common stock, which was a 15% interest in Keller. At this date, the net assets of Keller totaled $2 million. The fair values of all of Keller's identifiable assets and liabilities were equal to their book values. Beans did not have the ability to exercise significant influence over the operating and financial policies of Keller. Beans received dividends of $0.70 per share from Keller on October 1, 1995. Keller reported net income of $250,000 for the year ended December 31, 1995. The stock was classified as available-for-sale. Market price for the 10,000 shares was $450,000.

On July 1, 1996, Beans paid $1,500,000 for 30,000 additional shares of Keller Company's voting common stock, which represents a 25% interest in Keller. The fair value of all Keller's identifiable assets, net of liabilities, was equal to their book values of $4,600,000. As a result of this transaction, Beans has the ability to exercise significant influence over the operating and financial policies of Keller. Beans received a dividend of $0.80 per share from Keller on April 1, 1996, and $1.35 per share from Keller on October 1, 1996. Keller reported net income of $300,000 for the year ended December 31, 1996, and $100,000 for the six months ended December 31, 1996. Beans amortizes goodwill over a 40-year period.

Instructions:

1. Determine the amount of income from the investment in Keller Company common stock that should be reported in Beans' income statement for the year ended December 31, 1995.
2. Beans issues comparative financial statements for the years ended December 31, 1996 and 1995. Prepare schedules showing the income or loss that Beans should report from its investment in Keller Company for 1996 and 1995 (restated).

Problem 17—51 (Investment in common stock—cost to equity to cost method)

Cook Inc. wants to gain a controlling interest in Fox Chemical Co. in order to assure a steady source of a raw material manufactured by Fox. The following transactions occurred with respect to Cook and Fox. Both companies keep their books on a calendar-year basis. The stock is classified as available-for-sale when it is accounted for on the cost method.

1992

Jan. 2 Cook purchased 5,000 shares (5%) of Fox common stock for $10 per share. The assets of Fox had a net carrying value of $800,000. At that date, certain depreciable equipment owned by Fox had a fair market value $30,000 in excess of its carrying value, with an estimated remaining useful life of 10 years. Fox also carried land on its books that had a fair market value $70,000 in excess of its book value. The balance of the excess of the cost of the stock over the underlying equity in net assets was attributable to goodwill, which is amortized over 40 years. (Unless circumstances indicate otherwise, Cook's policy is to amortize any recognized goodwill evenly over a 40-year period from date of acquisition.)

Feb. 15 Cook received a dividend of $3,000 representing a distribution from income earned in 1991.

July 1 Cook purchased 10,000 additional shares of Fox stock for $11 per share. Fox's net income for the first six months of 1992 was $150,000. The net carrying value of Fox stockholders' equity at July 1, 1992, was $890,000. The difference between the fair market value of Fox's depreciable assets and their carrying value at this date was $30,000, and the equipment had an estimated remaining useful life of 9.5 years from the date of purchase. The market value of the land remained $70,000 over book value. Fox had not issued any new stock during the past six months.

Dec. 31 Fox reported net income for the year of $260,000, and the market value of Fox stock was $14 per share.

1993

Feb. 15 Cook received a cash dividend from Fox of $18,000.

Dec. 31 Fox reported net income for the year of $320,000. Market value of Fox stock was $11.50 per share.

1994

Jan. 2 Cook purchased 20,000 additional shares of Fox stock for $13 per share, which permitted Cook to exercise significant influence over Fox. At this time, Fox was experiencing a boycott of its products that was expected to last indefinitely. Although the difference between the fair market value of its assets and their carrying values remained the same, Fox's boycott problems detracted from the long-term attractiveness of its shares, and no implied goodwill was included in the purchase price. (There has been no change in the estimated useful lives of depreciable assets from the date of the original purchase on January 2, 1992.)

Feb. 15 Cook received a cash dividend of $49,000 from Fox.

1994

Dec. 31 Fox reported net income of $280,000. In view of Fox's boycott situation, Cook decided to write off remaining goodwill over a period of 10 years, beginning this year. The market value of the Fox stock was $15 per share.

1995

Feb. 15 Cook received a cash dividend of $39,200 from Fox.

Apr. 1 Cook, after experiencing a series of reversals in the marketplace, ceased manufacturing the product containing the raw material from Fox. On this date, Cook sold 20,000 shares of Fox stock for $12 per share. Cook used the average cost of its investment in Fox in calculating its cost basis per share in the investment. Assume Fox had no income for the first quarter of 1995.

Dec. 31 Fox reported net income of $295,000 for the year ended December 31, 1995. The market value of the Fox stock was $13 per share.

1996

Feb. 15 Cook received a dividend of $17,700 from Fox.

Mar. 20 Cook sold its remaining 15,000 shares of Fox stock for $11.50 per share.

Instructions: Give all the entries necessary to record these transactions on the books of Cook Inc. for all years. (Round computations to the nearest dollar.)

*Problem 17—52 (Fund accumulation)

On December 31, 1994, a fund is set up to redeem $50,000 of preferred stock. The fund is guaranteed to earn 8% compounded annually and must generate enough income to enable the company to retire the stock after four payments. The annual installments paid to the fund trustee are $11,096.07. The first deposit is made immediately.

Instructions:

1. Give the journal entries in connection with the fund for the years 1994 and 1995. (The company keeps its books on the calendar-year basis.)
2. Assume that on December 31, 1997, the fund balance of $50,000 consisted of $10,000 cash and $40,000 in securities that were purchased in 1996. The securities are sold at the end of 1997 for $48,000. Give all the journal entries that would be made to record the sale of the securities, retire the $50,000 of preferred stock, and liquidate any balance in the fund account. Ignore any valuation adjustments to the securities.

*Relates to Appendix 17—1

*Problem 17—53 (Establishing a fund for the retirement of bonds)

Starkson Inc. has elected to establish a bond redemption fund in order to have the necessary funds available to retire a bond that matures in five years. The bonds have a face value of $100,000. Management invests the annual payments into a fund that is guaranteed to return 8% compounded annually.

Instructions:

1. What is the amount of the annuity payment management must make each year in order to accumulate $100,000 at the end of five years if the first payment is made today?
2. Prepare a fund accumulation schedule in connection with the redemption fund, assuming the actual rates earned on the funds were 8%, 8.5%, 10%, 8%, and 9% in Years 1-5, respectively.
3. Provide the journal entry to retire the bond at the end of the fifth year. Why didn't the bond redemption fund have exactly $100,000 in it at the end of Year 5?

*Relates to Appendix 17—1

*Problem 17—54 (Cash surrender value)

During the course of the audit of Houston Company, which closes its accounts on December 31, you examine the life insurance policies, premium receipts, and confirmations returned by the insurance companies in response to your request for information. You find that in 1996 the company had paid premiums on the life insurance policy of the president, Bill Houston, as shown on the next page.

Sole Owner and Beneficiary	Face of Policy	Billed Premiun 1996	Dividend Used to Reduce Premium	Annnual Premium Date	Cash Surrender Value December 31 1995	1996
(1) Houston Company	$500,000	$5,000	$2,000	Aug. 30	$126,000	$130,000
(2) Sue Houston. Bill's wife	200,000	4,500	750	Sept. 30	50,000	53,000
(3) Houston Company	50,000	2,500	250	Mar. 1	15,000	16,500

Instructions:

1. Prepare all journal entries required for the year 1996.
2. What balances relating to these insurance policies would appear on the balance sheet prepared on December 31, 1996?

*Relates to Appendix 17—2

*Problem 17—55 (Accounting for the impairment of a loan)

Jayleen Associates loaned Norris Company $750,000 on January 1, 1994. The terms of the loan were payment in full on January 1, 1999, plus annual interest payments at 11%. The interest payment was made as scheduled on January 1, 1995; however, due to financial setbacks, Norris was unable to make its 1996 interest payment. Jayleen considers the loan impaired, and projects the following cash flows from the loan as of December 31, 1996 and 1997. Assume that Jayleen accrued the interest at January 1, 1996, but did not continue to accrue interest due to the impairment of the loan.

Projected Cash Flows:

Date of Flow	Amount Projected as of Dec. 31, 1996	Amount Projected as of Dec. 31, 1997
Dec. 31, 1997	$ 50,000	$ 50,000
Dec. 31, 1998	100,000	150,000
Dec. 31, 1999	200,000	300,000
Dec. 31, 2000	300,000	250,000
Dec. 31, 2001	100,000	

Instructions:

1. Prepare the valuation adjusting entry at December 31, 1996.
2. Prepare the journal entry to record the $50,000 receipt on December 31, 1997.
3. Prepare the valuation adjusting entry at December 31, 1997.
4. Prepare the 1998 journal entries assuming receipt of $150,000 as scheduled; also assume that estimates for future cash flows remain the same as they were at the end of 1997.

*Relates to Appendix 17—3

*Problem 17—56 (Troubled debt restructuring—loans receivable)

Guilder, Inc. reports a $650,000 loan receivable from Maxima Corporation on its December 31, 1995, balance sheet. This amount includes accrued unpaid interest of $75,000. The original interest rate was 9%. Guilder also reports an Allowance for Loan Impairment on this loan of $100,000. Guilder restructures the loan on this date and Maxima agrees to the following terms:

New interest rate of 5%; payments to be made annually.
Forgiveness of accrued unpaid interest.
New principal loan of $575,000 due December 31, 1999.

Instructions:

1. Prepare the journal entries on Guilder's books at December 31, 1995 to record the restructuring of the debt.
2. Prepare a schedule showing the interest receipts and the recognition of interest for the period 1996-1999.
3. Prepare journal entries based on the schedule including final receipt of the principal amount.
4. Describe how Maxima's accounting for the restructuring would differ from Guilder's.

*Relates to Appendix 17—3

PART 3

Special Problems in Income Determination

CHAPTER 18

Complexities of Revenue Recognition

CHAPTER TOPICS

- Revenue Recognition Prior to Delivery of Goods or Services
  - Accounting for Long-Term Construction-Type Contracts
  - Accounting for Long-Term Service Contracts
- Revenue Recognition After Delivery of Goods
  - Installment Sales Method
  - Cost Recovery Method
  - Cash Method
- Methods of Accounting for The Transfer of Assets Prior to the Recognition of Revenue
  - Deposit Method
  - Consignment Sales
- Recognition Issues Involving The Sale of Real Estate (Appendix)

Kendall Square Research Corporation produces and sells supercomputers, primarily to leading research universities around the world. In many cases, these supercomputers are shipped to universities with the anticipation that the university will pay for the computers once research grants and other outside sources of revenue are obtained. For example, the computer science department at the University of Washington has two KSR1 supercomputers with a total of 60 processors—price tag for the unit, $2 million; revenue recognized, $2 million; cash collected, $1 million. A physicist at the California Institute of Technology purchased a 32-processor unit in 1992. The following spring, the researcher wanted to double the size of the system and applied for a research grant to facilitate the upgrade. Kendall shipped the supercomputer immediately—revenue recognized, the entire amount; grant money received, $0.

Because of the competitive nature of the supercomputer industry, sales tactics like those employed by Kendall are not unusual. What is unusual is Kendall's revenue recognition methods. As this chapter will point out, revenue should be recognized when the earnings process is substantially complete and payment or a valid promise to pay has been received. In the case of Kendall Square Research Corporation it appears that they were recognizing revenue prior to the receipt of a valid promise of payment. A review of revenue recognition policies by company officials indicated the extent to which revenue had been recognized prematurely. As a result of this review, sales for 1992 were restated downward by 20%. Sales in 1993 were said to be inflated by half. Reported net income for 1992 was revised downward by 35%. How did the stock market react to this news? The company's stock price dropped from $24.25 in October of 1993 to $6.875 in December of the same year.

In this chapter, we focus on the complexities associated with revenue recognition. We will discuss the various points at which revenue may be recognized and what factors drive the revenue recognition decision.

As discussed and illustrated in Chapter 4, both internal and external users of financial information focus considerable attention on how business activities affect the income statement. Because the financial statements are interrelated, a study of the measurement and recognition of the elements contained in the income statement is also a study of the measurement and recognition of changes in the elements contained in the balance sheet. Thus, while the focus in this chapter is on the recognition of revenue, it also relates to the recognition of assets and liabilities on the balance sheet.

Recognition refers to the time when transactions are recorded on the books. The FASB's two criteria for recognizing revenues and gains were identified in Chapter 4 and are repeated here for emphasis. Revenues and gains are generally recognized when:

1. They are realized or realizable, and
2. They have been earned through substantial completion of the activities involved in the earnings process.

Both of these criteria generally are met at the point of sale, which most often occurs when goods are delivered or when services are rendered to customers. Usually, assets and revenues are recognized concurrently. Thus, a sale of inventory results in an increase in Cash or Accounts Receivable and an increase in Sales Revenue. However, assets are sometimes received before these revenue recognition criteria are met. For example, if a client pays for consulting services in advance, an asset, cash, is recorded on the books even though revenue has not been earned. In these cases, a liability, Unearned Revenue, is recorded. When the revenue recognition criteria are fully met, revenue is recognized and the liability account is reduced.

While the point-of-sale rule has dominated the interpretation of revenue recognition, there have been notable variations to this rule, especially in specific industries such as construction, real estate, and franchising. Special committees of the AICPA, and later the FASB, have studied these and other areas. For several years, these special studies were conducted under the direction of the AICPA, and publications of the committees' results appeared in the form of **Industry Accounting Guides, Industry Audit Guides,** or **Statements of Position (SOPs).** These publications have been studied by the FASB and, where deemed desirable, have been incorporated in the literature as Statements of Financial Accounting Standards.[1]

1. In the early 1980s, the FASB issued three research reports dealing with revenue recognition. These reports were used by the FASB in its deliberations leading to Concepts Statement No. 5 and several of the special industry standards. The reports were: (1) Yuji Ijiri, *Recognition of Contractual Rights and Obligations* (Stamford: Financial Accounting Standards Board, 1980); (2) Henry R. Jaenicke, *Survey of Present Practice in Recognizing Revenues, Expenses, Gains and Losses* (Stamford: Financial Accounting Standards Board, 1981); (3) L. Todd Johnson and Reed K. Storey, *Recognition in Financial Statements: Underlying Concepts and Practical Conventions* (Stamford: Financial Accounting Standards Board, 1982).

This chapter will explore some of the more common variations in revenue recognition that have arisen through these special industry studies. The focus of the presentation will be on the revenue recognition variations and not on the detailed accounting procedures for a specific industry. The discussion focuses first on revenue recognition **prior to delivery** of goods or performance of services; second on revenue recognition **after delivery** of goods or performance of services; and finally on methods of accounting for sales before revenue recognition occurs. The special industries referred to are construction, real estate, service, and franchising.

REVENUE RECOGNITION PRIOR TO DELIVERY OF GOODS OR PERFORMANCE OF SERVICES

Under some circumstances, revenue can be meaningfully reported prior to the delivery of the finished product or completion of a service contract. Usually this occurs when the construction period of the asset being sold or the period of service performance is relatively long, i.e., more than one year. If a company waits until the production or service period is complete to recognize revenue, the income statement may not report meaningfully the periodic achievement of the company. Under this approach, referred to as the **completed-contract method,** all income from the contract is related to the year of completion, even though only a small part of the earnings may be attributable to effort in that period. Previous periods receive no credit for their efforts; in fact, they may be penalized through the absorption of selling, general and administrative, and other overhead costs relating to the contract but not considered part of the inventory cost.

Percentage-of-completion accounting, an alternative to the completed-contract method, was developed to relate recognition of revenue on long-term construction-type contracts to the activities of a firm in fulfilling these contracts. Similarly, the **proportional performance method** has been developed to reflect revenue earned on service contracts under which many acts of service are to be performed before the contract is completed. Examples of such service contracts include contracts covering maintenance on electronic office equipment, correspondence schools, trustee services, health clubs, professional services such as those offered by attorneys and accountants, and servicing of mortgage loans by mortgage bankers. Percentage-of-completion accounting and proportional performance accounting are similar in their application. However, some special problems arise in accounting for service contracts. The discussion and examples in the following sections relate first to long-term construction-type contracts, then to the special problems encountered with service contracts.

General Concepts of Percentage-of-Completion Accounting

Under the percentage-of-completion method, a company recognizes revenues and costs on a contract as it progresses toward completion, rather than deferring recognition of these items until the contract is completed. The amount of revenue to be recognized each period is based on some measure of progress toward completion. This requires an estimate of costs yet to be incurred. Changes in estimates of future costs arise normally, and the necessary adjustments are made in the year the estimates are revised. Thus, the revenues and costs to be recognized in a given year are affected by the revenues and costs already recognized. As work progresses on the contract, the actual costs incurred are charged to inventory. The amount of profit earned each period also is charged to this asset account. Thus, the inventory account is valued at its net realizable value—the sales (or contract) price less the cost to complete the contract and less the unearned profit on the unfinished contract. (See Chapter 10 for a review of the concepts and computations associated with net realizable value). If a company projects a loss on the contract prior to completion, the full amount of the loss should be recognized immediately. This loss recognition results in a write-down of the asset to its estimated net realizable value. If only a percentage of the loss were recognized, the asset value would exceed the net realizable value. This would violate the lower-of-cost-or-market rule discussed in Chapter 10.

Necessary Conditions to Use Percentage-of-Completion Accounting

Most long-term construction-type contracts should be reported using the percentage-of-completion method. The guidelines presently in force, however, are not specific as to when a company must use percentage-of-completion and when it must use the alternative completed-contract method. The accounting standards that still govern this area were issued by the Committee on Accounting Procedure in 1955.[2] In January 1981, the Construction Contractor Guide Committee of the Accounting Standards Division of the AICPA issued Statement of Position 81-1, "Accounting for Performance of Construction-Type and Certain Production-Type Contracts." In this SOP, the committee strongly recommended which of the two common methods of accounting for these types of contracts should be required, depending on the specific circumstances involved. The committee further stated that the two methods should not be viewed as acceptable alternatives for the same circumstances. The committee identified several elements that should be present if percentage-of-completion accounting is to be used.[3]

1. Dependable estimates can be made of contract revenues, contract costs, and the extent of progress toward completion.
2. The contract clearly specifies the enforceable rights regarding goods or services to be provided and received by the parties, the consideration to be exchanged, and the manner and terms of settlement.
3. The buyer can be expected to satisfy obligations under the contract.
4. The contractor can be expected to perform the contractual obligation.

The completed-contract method should be used only when an entity has primarily short-term contracts, when the conditions for using percentage-of-completion accounting are not met, or when there are inherent uncertainties in the contract beyond the normal business risks.

In February 1982, the FASB issued Statement No. 56 designating the accounting and reporting principles and practices contained in SOP 81-1 and in the AICPA *Audit and Accounting Guide for Construction Contractors* as preferable accounting principles.[4] The Board indicated that it would consider adopting these principles as FASB standards after allowing sufficient time for the principles to be used in practice so that a basis can be provided for determining their usefulness. A critical issue involved in this area is the clear preference in the SOP for using the percentage-of-completion method of accounting.

For many years, the income tax regulations permitted contractors wide latitude in selecting either the percentage-of-completion or completed-contract method. Beginning with the Tax Reform Act of 1986, the tax laws have limited the use of the completed-contract method and have required increased use of the percentage-of-completion method.

2. Committee on Accounting Procedure, *Accounting Research Bulletin No. 45,* "Long-Term Construction-Type Contracts" (New York: American Institute of Certified Public Accountants, 1955).

3. Construction Contractor Guide Committee of the Accounting Standards Division, AICPA, *Statement of Position 81-1,* "Accounting for Performance of Construction-Type and Certain Production-Type Contracts" (New York: American Institute of Certified Public Accountants, 1981), par. 23.

4. *Statement of Financial Accounting Standards No. 56,* "Designation of AICPA Guide and Statement of Position (SOP) 81-1 on Contractor Accounting and SOP 81-2 Concerning Hospital-Related Organizations as Preferable for Purposes of Applying APB Opinion No. 20" (Stamford: Financial Accounting Standards Board, 1982).

This results in greater revenues from taxes without increasing the tax rates, and also results in similar revenue recognition treatment for both taxes and financial reporting.

Measuring the Percentage of Completion

Various methods are currently used in practice to measure the earnings process. They can be conveniently grouped into two categories: input and output measures.

Input Measures. **Input measures** are made in relation to the costs or efforts devoted to a contract. They are based on an established or assumed relationship between a unit of input and productivity. They include the widely used cost-to-cost method and several variations of efforts-expended methods.

Cost-to-Cost Method. Perhaps the most popular of the input measures is the **cost-to-cost method.** Under this method, the degree of completion is determined by comparing costs already incurred with the most recent estimates of total expected costs to complete the project. The percentage that costs incurred bear to total expected costs is applied to the contract price to determine the revenue to be recognized to date as well as to the expected net income on the project in arriving at earnings to date. Some of the costs incurred, particularly in the early stages of the contract, should be disregarded in applying this method, because they do not relate directly to effort expended on the contract. These include such items as subcontract costs for work that has yet to be performed and standard fabricated materials that have not yet been installed. One of the most difficult problems in using this method is estimating the costs yet to be incurred. However, this estimation is required in reporting income, regardless of how the percentage of completion is computed.

To illustrate, assume that in January 1995, Strong Construction Company was awarded a contract with a total price of $3,000,000. Strong expected to earn $400,000 profit on the contract, or in other words, total costs on the contract were estimated to be $2,600,000. The construction was completed over a 3-year period, and the following cost data and cost percentages were compiled during that time:

Year	(1) Actual Cost Incurred	(2) Estimated Cost to Complete	(3) Total Cost (1) + (2)	(4) Cost Percentage (1) ÷ (3)
1995	$1,092,000	$1,508,000	$2,600,000*	42%
1996	832,000			
Total	$1,924,000	676,000	2,600,000*	74
1997	676,000			
Total	$2,600,000	–0–	2,600,000**	100

*Estimated total contract cost
**Actual total contract cost

Note that the cost percentage is computed by dividing cumulative actual costs incurred by total cost, an amount that is estimated for the first two years.

Efforts-Expended Methods. The **efforts-expended methods** are based on some measure of work performed. They include labor hours, labor dollars, machine hours, or material quantities. In each case, the degree of completion is measured in a way similar to that used in the cost-to-cost approach: the ratio of the efforts expended to date to the estimated total efforts to be expended on the entire contract. For example, if the measure of work performed is labor hours, the ratio of hours worked to date to the total estimated hours would produce the percentage for use in measuring income earned.

Output Measures. **Output measures** are made in terms of results achieved. Included in this category are methods based on units produced, contract milestones reached, and values added. For example, if the contract calls for units of output, such as miles of roadway, a measure of completion would be a ratio of the miles completed to the total miles in the contract. Architects and engineers are sometimes asked to evaluate jobs and estimate what percentage of a job is complete. These estimates are, in reality, output measures and usually are based on the physical progress made on a contract.

Accounting for Long-Term Construction-Type Contracts

For both the percentage-of-completion and the completed-contract methods, all direct and allocable indirect costs of the contracts are charged to an inventory account. The difference in recording between the two methods relates to the timing of revenue and expense recognition, that is, when the estimated earned income is recognized with its related effect on the income statement and the balance sheet. During the construction period, the annual reported income under these two accounting methods will differ. However, after the contract is completed, the combined income for the total construction period will be the same under each method of accounting. The balance sheet at the end of the construction and collection period also will be identical.

Usually contracts require progress billings by the contractor and payments by the customer on these billings. The billings and payments are accounted for and reported in the same manner under both methods. The amount of these billings usually is specified by the contract terms and may be related to the costs actually incurred. Generally, these contracts require inspection before final settlement is made. The billings are debited to Accounts Receivable and credited to a deferred account, Progress Billings on Construction Contracts, that serves as an offset to the inventory account, Construction in Progress. The billing of the contract thus transfers the asset value from inventory to receivables, but because of the long-term nature of the contract, the construction costs continue to be reflected in the accounts.

To illustrate accounting for a long-term construction contract, we will continue the Strong Construction Company example from page 765. Recall that construction was completed over a 3-year period and the contract price is $3,000,000. The direct and allocable indirect costs, billings, and collections for 1995, 1996, and 1997 are as follows:

Year	Direct and Allocable Indirect Costs	Billings	Collections[5]
1995	$1,092,000	$1,000,000	$ 800,000
1996	832,000	900,000	850,000
1997	676,000	1,100,000	1,350,000

The following entries for the three years would be made on the contractor's books under either the percentage-of-completion or the completed-contract method.

5. As a protection for the customer, long-term contracts frequently provide for an amount to be retained from the progress payments. This retention is usually a percentage of the progress billings, e.g., 10% to 20%, and is paid upon final acceptance of the construction. Thus, the amount collected is often less than the amount billed in the initial years of the contract.

	1995		1996		1997	
Construction in Progress	1,092,000		832,000		676,000	
Materials, Cash, etc.		1,092,000		832,000		676,000
To record costs incurred.						
Accounts Receivable	1,000,000		900,000		1,100,000	
Progress Billings on Construction Contracts		1,000,000		900,000		1,100,000
To record billings.						
Cash	800,000		850,000		1,350,000	
Accounts Receivable		800,000		850,000		1,350,000
To record cash collections.						

No other entries would be required in 1995 and 1996 under the completed-contract method. In both years, the balance of Construction in Progress exceeds the amount in Progress Billings on Construction Contracts; thus the latter account would be offset against the inventory account in the balance sheet.

Before proceeding further, let's examine the relationship between the accounts Construction in Progress and Progress Billings on Construction Contracts. Amounts recorded in Construction in Progress represent the costs that have been incurred to date relating to a specific contract. If the customer has not been billed, then the entire cost represents a probable future benefit to the company and should be disclosed on the balance sheet as an asset. If, however, the customer has been billed for a portion of these costs, then the company has in effect traded one asset for another. In place of inventory, the company now has a receivable (or cash if the receivable has been paid.)

Thus, if the balance in Construction in Progress exceeds the balance in Progress Billings on Construction Contracts, the excess represents the amount of the construction costs[6] for which the customer has not been billed. The amount for which the customer has been billed is included in either Accounts Receivable or Cash. If Progress Billings on Construction Contracts is greater than Construction in Progress, the difference represents a liability because the customer has been billed (and a receivable has been recorded) for more than the costs actually incurred.

Because the operating cycle of a company that emphasizes long-term contracts is usually more than one year, all of the preceding balance sheet accounts would be classified as current. The balance sheet at the end of 1996 under the completed-contract method would disclose the following balances related to the construction contract:

Current assets:		
Accounts receivable		$250,000
Construction in progress	$1,924,000	
Less progress billings on construction contracts	1,900,000	24,000

If the billings exceeded the construction costs, the excess would be reported in the current liability section of the balance sheet.

Under the completed-contract method, the following entries would be made to recognize revenue and costs and to close out the inventory and billings accounts at the completion of the contract, i.e., in 1997.

Progress Billings on Construction Contracts	3,000,000	
Revenue From Long-Term Construction Contracts		3,000,000
Cost of Long-Term Construction Contracts	2,600,000	
Construction in Progress		2,600,000

6. As we will soon learn, under the percentage-of-completion method, Construction in Progress includes both costs and the portion of expected gross profit earned to date.

The first entry represents the billings on the contract that, at the end of the contract, equal the total revenue from the contract. The second journal entry transfers the inventoried cost from the contract to the appropriate expense account on the income statement. The income statement for 1997 would report the gross revenues and the matched costs, thus recognizing the entire $400,000 profit in one year.

Using Percentage-of-Completion—Cost-to-Cost Method. If the company used the percentage-of-completion method of accounting, the $400,000 profit would be spread over all three years of construction according to the estimated percentage of completion for each year. The information on page 765 details Strong's estimated cost to complete the contract at the end of 1995 and 1996 as well as the total actual costs at the end of 1997. Recall that the percentage of completion for each year, determined on a cost-to-cost basis, is as follows:

	1995	1996	1997
Percentage of completion to date	42%	74%	100%

These percentages may be used to determine directly the gross profit that should be recognized on the income statement; that is, the income statement for 1995 would report only the gross profit from construction contracts in the amount of $168,000 (estimated gross profit—1995, $400,000 × 42% = $168,000). Preferably, the percentages should be used to determine both revenues and costs. The income statement will then disclose revenues, costs, and the resulting gross profit, a method more consistent with normal income statement reporting. The AICPA Audit and Accounting Guide for Construction Contractors recommended this proportional procedure, and the presentations in this chapter will reflect that recommendation.[7] The procedures are as follows:

1. Cumulative revenue to date should be computed by multiplying total estimated contract revenue by the percentage of completion. Revenue for the current period is the difference between the cumulative revenue at the end of the current period and the cumulative revenue recognized in prior periods.
2. Cumulative costs to date should be computed in a manner similar to revenue and should be equal to the total estimated contract cost multiplied by the percentage of completion on the contract. Cost for the current period is the difference between the cumulative costs at the end of the current period and the cumulative costs reported in prior periods.
3. Cumulative gross profit is the excess of cumulative revenue over cumulative costs, and the current period gross profit is the difference between current revenue and current costs.

If the cost-to-cost method is used to estimate earned revenue, the proportional cost for each period will equal the actual cost incurred.

To illustrate, for 1995, 42% of the fixed contract price of $3,000,000 would be recognized as revenue and 42% of the expected total cost of $2,600,000 would be reported as cost. The following revenue recognition entries would be made for each of the three years of the contract. These entries are in addition to the transaction entries illustrated at the top of page 767.

7. Construction Contractor Guide Committee of the Accounting Standards Division, AICPA, *Audit and Accounting Guide for Construction Contractors* (New York: American Institute of Certified Public Accountants, 1980), p. 44.

	1995		1996		1997	
Cost of Long-Term Construction Contracts	1,092,000		832,000		676,000	
Construction in Progress	168,000		128,000		104,000	
Revenue From Long-Term Construction Contracts		1,260,000		960,000		780,000

The gross profit recognized each year is added to the construction in progress account thereby valuing the inventory on the books at its net realizable value. Note that the procedures used in recognizing revenue under the percentage-of-completion method do not affect the progress billings made or the amount of cash collected. These amounts are determined by contract and not by the accounting method used.

Because the construction in progress account contains costs incurred plus recognized profit (the two together equalling total revenues recognized to date), at the completion of the contract, the balance in this account will exactly equal the amount in Progress Billings on Construction Contracts, since the progress billings account reflects the contract price (or total revenues). The following closing entry would complete the accounting process:

Progress Billings on Construction Contracts	3,000,000	
Construction in Progress		3,000,000

Using Percentage-of-Completion—Other Methods. If the cost-to-cost method is not used to measure progress on the contract, the proportional costs recognized under this method may not be equal to the actual costs incurred. For example, assume in 1995 that an engineering estimate measure was used, and 40% of the contract was assumed to be completed. The gross profit recognized would therefore be computed and reported as follows:

Recognized revenue (40% of $3,000,000)	$1,200,000
Cost (40% of $2,600,000)	1,040,000
Gross profit (40% of $400,000)	$ 160,000

Because some accountants believe that the amount of cost recognized should be equal to the costs actually incurred, an alternative to the preceding approach was included in SOP 81-1.[8] Under this **actual cost approach,** revenue is defined as the actual costs incurred on the contract plus the gross profit earned for the period on the contract. Using the data from the previous example, the revenue and costs to be reported on the 1995 income statement would be as follows:

Actual cost incurred to date	$1,092,000
Recognized gross profit (40% of $400,000)	160,000
Recognized revenue	$1,252,000

This contrasts with the $1,200,000 revenue using the **proportional cost approach.** Both approaches report gross profit as $160,000.

In a footnote to this discussion in the SOP, the Committee made it clear that the actual cost approach and the proportional cost approach are equally acceptable. However, because the actual cost approach results in a varying gross profit percentage from period to period whenever the measurement of completion differs from that which would occur if the cost-to-cost method were used, the authors feel that the proportional cost approach

8. *SOP 81-1,* pars. 80 and 81.

is preferable. Unless a different method is explicitly stated, examples and end-of-chapter material will assume the use of the proportional cost approach.

Revision of Estimates. In the previous example, it was assumed that the estimated cost did not vary from the beginning of the contract. This rarely would be the case. As estimates change, catch-up adjustments are made in the year of the change. To illustrate the impact of changing estimates, assume that at the end of 1996, it was estimated that the remaining cost to complete the construction was $726,000 rather than $676,000. This would increase the total estimated cost to $2,650,000, reduce the expected profit to $350,000, and change the percentage of completion at the end of 1996 to 72.60% ($1,924,000 ÷ $2,650,000).

The following analysis shows how this change would affect the revenue and costs to be reported each year assuming that the actual costs in 1997 were $700,000.

	1995	1996	1997
Contract price	$3,000,000	$3,000,000	$3,000,000
Actual cost incurred to date	$1,092,000	$1,924,000	$2,624,000
Estimated cost to complete	1,508,000	726,000	-0-
Total estimated cost	$2,600,000	$2,650,000	$2,624,000
Total expected gross profit	$ 400,000	$ 350,000	$ 376,000
Percentage of completion to date	42%	72.6%	100%

	To Date	Recognized—Prior Years	Recognized—Current Year
1995 Recognized revenue ($3,000,000 × .42)	$1,260,000	-0-	$1,260,000
Cost (actual cost)	1,092,000	-0-	1,092,000
Gross profit	$ 168,000		$ 168,000
1996 Recognized revenue ($3,000,000 × .726)	$2,178,000	$1,260,000	$ 918,000
Cost (actual cost)	1,924,000	1,092,000	832,000
Gross profit	$ 254,000	$ 168,000	$ 86,000
1997 Recognized revenue	$3,000,000	$2,178,000	$ 822,000
Cost (actual cost)	2,624,000	1,924,000	700,000
Gross profit	$ 376,000	$ 254,000	$ 122,000

The entries to record revenue and cost for the three years given the assumed estimate revision would be as follows:

	1995		1996		1997	
Cost of Long-Term Construction Contracts	1,092,000		832,000		700,000	
Construction in Progress	168,000		86,000		122,000	
Revenue From Long-Term Construction Contracts		1,260,000		918,000		822,000

In some cases, an increase in total estimated cost can result in recognition of a loss in the year of the increase. Revising the preceding example, assume that at the end of 1996, the estimated cost to complete construction was $864,000 and this was the actual cost incurred in 1997. The following analysis shows how this change in estimated cost would reduce the percentage of completion at the end of 1996 to 69%, and the cumulative profit at the end of 1996 to $146,000. Since $168,000 was already recognized as gross profit in 1995, a loss of $22,000 would be recognized in 1996.

	1995	1996	1997
Contract price	$3,000,000	$3,000,000	$3,000,000
Actual cost incurred to date	$1,092,000	$1,924,000	$2,788,000
Estimated cost to complete	1,508,000	864,000	-0-
Total estimated cost	$2,600,000	$2,788,000	$2,788,000
Total expected gross profit	$ 400,000	$ 212,000	$ 212,000
Percentage of completion to date	42%	69%	100%

	To Date	Recognized—Prior Years	Recognized—Current Year
1995 Recognized revenue			
($3,000,000 × .42)	$1,260,000	-0-	$1,260,000
Cost (actual cost)	1,092,000	-0-	1,092,000
Gross profit	$ 168,000		$ 168,000
1996 Recognized revenue			
($3,000,000 × .69)	$2,070,000	$1,260,000	$ 810,000
Cost (actual cost)	1,924,000	1,092,000	832,000
Gross profit (loss)	$ 146,000	$ 168,000	$ (22,000)
1997 Recognized revenue	$3,000,000	$2,070,000	$ 930,000
Cost (actual cost)	2,788,000	1,924,000	864,000
Gross profit	$ 212,000	$ 146,000	$ 66,000

The entries to record revenue and cost for the three years given the assumed loss estimate in 1996 would be as follows:

	1995		1996		1997	
Cost of Long-Term Construction Contracts	1,092,000		832,000		864,000	
Construction in Progress	168,000			22,000	66,000	
Revenue From Long-Term Construction Contracts		1,260,000		810,000		930,000

Reporting Anticipated Contract Losses. In the example above, an increase in estimated total cost resulted in recognition of a loss in the year the estimate was revised, but overall, the contract resulted in a profit. In some cases, an increase in estimated total cost is so great that a loss on the entire contract is anticipated; that is, total estimated costs are expected to exceed the total revenue from the contract. When a loss on the total contract is anticipated, generally accepted accounting principles require reporting the loss *in its entirety* in the period when the loss is first anticipated. This is true under either the completed-contract or the percentage-of-completion method.

For example, assume that in the earlier construction example on page 770, the estimated cost to complete the contract at the end of 1996 was $1,176,000. Because $1,924,000 of costs had already been incurred, the total estimated cost of the contract would be $3,100,000 ($1,924,000 + $1,176,000) or $100,000 more than the contract price. Assume also that actual costs equaled expected costs in 1997.

	1995	1996	1997
Contract price	$3,000,000	$3,000,000	$3,000,000
Actual cost incurred to date	$1,092,000	$1,924,000	$3,100,000
Estimated cost to complete	1,508,000	1,176,000	-0-
Total estimated cost	$2,600,000	$3,100,000	$3,100,000
Total expected gross profit (loss)	$ 400,000	$ (100,000)	$ (100,000)
Percentage of completion to date	42%	62%	100%

Using this example, accounting for a contract loss is illustrated first for the completed-contract method, then for the percentage-of-completion method.

Anticipated Contract Loss—Completed-Contract Method. If the completed-contract method is used, the recognition of an anticipated contract loss is simple. The amount of the loss is debited to a loss account, and the inventory account, Construction in Progress, is credited by that amount to reduce the inventory to its expected net realizable value. To record the anticipated loss of $100,000 on the construction contract, the following entry would be made at the end of 1996:

Anticipated Loss on Long-Term Construction Contracts	100,000	
Construction in Progress		100,000

Anticipated Contract Loss—Percentage-of-Completion Method. Recognition of an anticipated contract loss under the percentage-of-completion method is more complex. To properly reflect the entire loss in the year it is first anticipated, the cumulative cost to deduct from cumulative recognized revenue cannot be the actual cost incurred, but must be the cumulative recognized revenue plus the entire anticipated loss. Thus, continuing the construction contract example, the cumulative recognized revenue at the end of 1996 would be $1,860,000 (62% × $3,000,000), and the cumulative cost at the same date would be $1,960,000 ($1,860,000 + $100,000). Because the example assumes that $168,000 profit was recognized on this contract in 1995, the total loss to be recognized in 1996 is $268,000 ($168,000 + $100,000). The following analysis reflects the amounts to be reported for each of the three years of the contract life under the anticipated loss assumption.

	To Date	Recognized—Prior Years	Recognized—Current Year
1995 Recognized revenue ($3,000,000 × .42)	$1,260,000	-0-	$1,260,000
Cost (actual cost)	1,092,000	-0-	1,092,000
Gross profit (loss)	$ 168,000		$ 168,000
1996 Recognized revenue ($3,000,000 × .62)	$1,860,000	$1,260,000	$ 600,000
Cost (recognized revenue plus entire anticipated loss)	1,960,000	1,092,000	868,000
Gross profit (loss)	$ (100,000)	$ 168,000	$ (268,000)
1997 Recognized revenue	$3,000,000	$1,860,000	$1,140,000
Cost (actual cost)	3,100,000	1,960,000	1,140,000
Gross profit (loss)	$ (100,000)	$ (100,000)	$ -0-

The entry to record the revenue, costs, and adjustments to Construction in Progress for the loss in 1996 would be as follows:

Cost of Long-Term Construction Contracts	868,000	
Revenue From Long-Term Construction Contracts		600,000
Construction in Progress		268,000

Note that the construction in progress account under both methods would have a balance of $1,824,000 at the end of 1996 computed as shown below.

Completed Contract Method:

Construction in Progress

1995 cost	1,092,000	1996 loss	100,000
1996 cost	832,000		
Balance	1,824,000		

Percentage of Completion Method:

Construction in Progress

1995 cost	1,092,000	1996 Loss	268,000
1995 gross profit	168,000		
1996 cost	832,000		
Balance	1,824,000		

Accounting for Contract Change Orders. Long-term construction contracts are seldom completed without change orders that affect both the contract price and the cost of performance. **Change orders** are modifications of an original contract that effectively change the provisions of the contract. They may be initiated by the contractor or the customer, and they include changes in specifications or design, method or manner of performance, facilities, equipment, materials, location site, etc. If the contract price is changed as a result of a change order, future computations are made with the revised expected revenue and any anticipated cost changes that will arise because of the change order. Change orders are often unpriced, that is, the work to be performed is defined, but the adjustment to the contract price is to be negotiated later. If it is probable that a contract price change will be negotiated to at least recover the increased costs, the increased costs may be included with the incurred costs of the period and the revenue may be increased by the same amount. Exhibit 18—1 provides an example of the typical note disclosure provided for long-term contracts.

Exhibit 18—1
Martin Marietta Corporation—Disclosure for Long-Term Contracts

NOTES TO CONSOLIDATED FINANCIAL STATEMENTS

Note A (In Part): Accounting Policies

Revenue Recognition—Long-term fixed-price contracts generally are accounted for under percentage-of-completion methods, and sales include a proportion of the earnings expected to be realized in the ratio that costs incurred bear to estimated total costs. Sales are recorded on cost-type contracts as costs are incurred. Under all other contracts, sales are recorded when deliveries are made or as work is performed.

Contracts and programs in progress are reviewed quarterly, and sales and earnings are adjusted in current accounting periods based on revisions in contract value and estimated costs at completion. Performance incentives are incorporated in certain contracts that provide increased or decreased earnings based on performance to established targets. Incentives based upon cost performance are recorded currently, and other incentives and awards are recorded when the amounts reasonably can be estimated or are awarded. Provisions for estimated losses on contracts and programs are recorded when identified.

Accounting for Long-Term Service Contracts—The Proportional Performance Method

Thus far, the discussion in this chapter has focused on long-term construction-type contracts. As indicated earlier, another type of contract that frequently extends over a long period of time is a **service contract.** An increasing percentage of sales in our economy are classified as sales of services as opposed to sales of goods. When the service to be performed is completed as a single act or over a relatively short period of time, no revenue recognition problems arise. The revenue recognition criteria previously defined apply, and all direct and indirect costs related to the service are charged to expense in the period the revenue is recognized. However, when several acts over a period of time are involved, the same revenue recognition problems illustrated for long-term construction-type contracts arise. Although the FASB has not issued a standard dealing with these contracts, the Board did issue an Invitation to Comment on a proposed Statement of Position that had been issued by the AICPA's Accounting Standards Division.[9] The discussion on the following pages reflects the recommendations made by the Accounting Standards Division.

The Division recommends that unless the final act of service to be performed is so vital to the contract that earlier acts are relatively insignificant, e.g., the packaging, loading, and final delivery of goods in a delivery contract, revenue should be recognized under the **proportional performance method.**[10] Both input and output measures are identified as possible ways of measuring progress on a service contract. If a contract involves a specified number of identical or similar acts, e.g., the processing of monthly mortgage payments by a mortgage banker, an output measure derived by relating the number of acts performed to the total number of acts to be performed over the contract life is recommended. If a contract involves a specified number of defined but not identical acts, e.g., a correspondence school that provides evaluation, lessons, examinations, and grading, a cost-to-cost input measurement percentage would be applicable. If future costs are not objectively determinable, output measures such as relating sales value of the individual acts to the total sales value of the service contract may be used. If no pattern of performance can be determined, or if a service contract involves an unspecified number of similar or identical acts with a fixed period for performance, e.g., a maintenance contract for electronic office equipment, the Division recommends the use of the straight-line method, i.e., recognizing revenue equally over the periods of performance.

These measures are used to determine what portion of the service contract fee should be recognized as revenue. Generally, the measures are only indirectly related to the pattern of cash collection; however, they are applicable only if cash collection is reasonably assured and if losses from nonpayment can be objectively determined.

The cost recognition problems of service contracts are somewhat different from those of long-term construction-type contracts. Most service contracts involve three different types of costs: (1) initial direct costs related to obtaining and performing initial services on the contract, such as commissions, legal fees, credit investigations, and paper processing; (2) direct costs related to performing the various acts of service; and (3) indirect costs related to maintaining the organization to service the contract, e.g., general and administrative expenses. Initial direct costs generally are charged i.e., matched, against revenue using the same input or output measure used for revenue recognition. If the cost-to-cost method of input measurement is used, initial direct costs should be excluded from the cost incurred to date in computing the measure. Only direct costs related to the acts of service are relevant for this computation. Direct costs usually are charged to expense as incurred, because they relate directly to the acts for which revenue is recognized. Similarly, all indirect costs should be charged to expense as incurred. As is true for long-term construction-type contracts, any indicated loss on completion of the service contract

9. *FASB Invitation to Comment,* "Accounting for Certain Service Transactions" (Stamford: Financial Accounting Standards Board, 1978).

10. *Ibid.,* pp. 12-13.

is to be charged to the period in which the loss is first indicated. If collection of a service contract is highly uncertain, revenue recognition should not be related to performance but to the collection of the receivable using one of the methods described in the latter part of this chapter.

To illustrate accounting for a service contract using the proportional performance method, assume a correspondence school enters into 100 contracts with students for an extended writing course. The fee for each contract is $500, payable in advance. This fee includes many different services such as providing the text material, evaluating written assignments and examinations, and awarding of a certificate. The total initial direct costs related to the contracts are $5,000. Direct costs for the lessons actually completed during the first period are $12,000. It is estimated that the total direct costs of these contracts over all periods will be $30,000. The facts of this case suggest that the cost-to-cost method is applicable, and the following entries would be made to record these transactions:

Cash	50,000	
Deferred Course Revenue (liability account)		50,000
Deferred Initial Costs (asset account)	5,000	
Cash		5,000
Contract Costs (expense account)	12,000	
Cash		12,000
Deferred Course Revenue	20,000*	
Recognized Course Revenue		20,000
Contract Costs	2,000**	
Deferred Initial Costs		2,000

Computations:
*Cost-to-cost percentage: $12,000/$30,000 = 40%; $50,000 × .40 = $20,000
**$5,000 × .40 = $2,000

The gross profit reported on these contracts for the period would be $6,000 ($20,000 – $12,000 – $2,000). The deferred initial cost and deferred course revenues would normally be reported as current balance sheet deferrals, because the operating cycle of a correspondence school would be equal to the average time to complete a contract or one year, whichever is longer.

Evaluation of the Proportional Performance Method

As noted, the FASB has not issued a standard on service industries. While the proportional performance method has theoretical support for its adoption, it tends to be extremely conservative, especially during a period of rapid growth in a company's revenues. Since no revenue is recognized until performance of the service has begun, the proportional performance method recognizes no revenue at the critical point of signing a service contract. Thus, in the growing years of a company, use of the proportional performance method will result in large losses being reported even though the operation might be very profitable over time. This can lead to the questionable conclusion that a company is no better off after service contracts are sold than it was before.

An alternative method of recognizing revenue for service contracts would be to recognize part of the revenue upon the signing of the contract, and then spread the balance of the revenue over the contract life using the proportional performance concept. The decision as to how much revenue should be recognized at the beginning of the contract would depend on the nature and terms of the contract, including any forfeiture or cancellation provisions.

College Bound Was Bankruptcy Bound

High school students know how important it is to perform well on the educational tests required by many colleges and universities as part of the admissions process. In fact, an entire industry has developed to prepare students to take these tests. One company in this industry was College Bound Inc. It was a fast-growing company that claimed to be the largest educational counseling firm in the United States with 150 test centers nationally. College Bound was founded by George and Janet Ronkin because they could not find a facility that, in their opinion, could adequately prepare their own son to take the college entrance exams.

The company went public in 1988 as a penny stock, and the price of the stock soared to a high of $24 per share in August of 1991. In the early months of 1992, however, the SEC began to question many of College Bound's accounting practices. As a result of its investigations, the SEC determined that much of the rapid growth in revenues reported by College Bound came as a result of "churning bank accounts." This practice involved transferring funds from the home office's bank account to various test centers then back to the home office. College Bound was recognizing as revenue the funds being transferred back from the test centers. The money used for the "churning" was obtained via a convertible note offering in Europe.

The result of these practices was to overstate pretax profits for the fiscal year ended August 1991 by 2.5 times, or $5.2 million. The SEC alleged that the Ronkins were transferring large amounts of company money to their personal accounts. In addition to their compensation of $153,846 each, the Ronkins were said to have transferred over $500,000 to Swiss bank accounts during 1991. The court-appointed receiver, Joseph Del Raso, who was asked by the courts to monitor College Bound during bankruptcy proceedings, determined that most of the company's 150 test centers were not profitable by industry standards and closed over 100 centers in May of 1992.

Questions

1. How would College Bound recognize revenue by simply transferring money from a test center to the home office? What would the journal entry be when the money was transferred from the home office to the test centers?

2. How would the accountant at the home office determine if money being received from a test center was to be recorded as revenue or as repayment of a loan?

Sources:

Michael J. McCarthy, "College Bound Inc., Target of SEC Suit, Files for Bankruptcy Law Protection," *The Wall Street Journal,* April 30, 1992, p. A-4.

Daniel Pearl, "U.S. Judge Freezes Assets of Founders of College Bound," *The Wall Street Journal,* April 24, 1992, p. C-19.

REVENUE RECOGNITION AFTER DELIVERY OF GOODS OR PERFORMANCE OF SERVICES

One of the FASB's two revenue recognition criteria, listed at the beginning of this chapter, states that revenue should not be recognized until the earnings process is substantially completed. Normally, the earnings process is substantially completed by the delivery of goods or performance of services. Collection of receivables is usually routine, and any future warranty costs can be reasonably estimated. In some cases, however, the circumstances surrounding a revenue transaction are such that considerable uncertainty exists as to whether payments will indeed be received. This can occur if the sales transaction is unusual in nature or involves a customer in such a way that default carries little cost or penalty. Under these circumstances, the uncertainty of cash collection suggests that revenue recognition should await the actual receipt of cash. There are at least three different approaches to revenue recognition that depend on the receipt of cash: **installment sales, cost recovery,** and **cash.** These methods differ as to the treatment of costs incurred and the timing of revenue recognition. They are summarized and contrasted with the full accrual method in the table on the next page.

Method	Timing of Revenue and/or Income Recognition	Treatment of Product Costs or Direct Costs Under Service Contracts
Full accrual	At point of sale.	Charge against revenue at time of sale or rendering of service.
Installment sales	At collection of cash. Usually a portion of the cash payment is recognized as income.	Defer to be matched against part of each cash collection. Usually done by deferring the estimated profit.
Cost recovery	At collection of cash, but only after all costs are recovered.	Defer to be matched against total cash collected.
Cash	At collection of cash.	Charge to expense as incurred.

These methods are really not alternatives to each other; however, the guidelines for applying them are not well defined. As the uncertainty of the environment increases, generally accepted accounting principles would require moving from the full accrual method to installment sales, cost recovery, and finally, a strict cash approach. The cash method is the most conservative approach, because it would not permit the deferral of any costs, but would charge them to expense as incurred. In the following pages, each of these revenue recognition methods will be discussed and illustrated.

Installment Sales Method

Traditionally, the most commonly applied method for dealing with the uncertainty of cash collections has been the **installment sales method.** Under this method, income is recognized as cash is collected rather than at the time of sale. This method of accounting was developed after World War II in response to an increasing number of sales contracts that extended the time payment over several years, with full title to the "sold" property being transferred only at the time of final collection. Consumer goods such as electrical appliances, jewelry, automobiles, and recreational equipment were commonly purchased and accounted for in this way. As this method of sales became more popular, and as credit rating evaluations became more sophisticated, the probability of collection on these contracts became more certain. The collection of cash was no longer the critical event, but the point of sale essentially completed the earnings process. Collection costs and the cost of uncollectible accounts could be estimated at the time of sale. Additional protection was afforded the seller because most contracts included a right of repossession. For these reasons, the Accounting Principles Board concluded in 1966 that except for special circumstances, the installment method of recognizing revenue is not acceptable for reporting purposes.[11]

In more recent years, sales of other types of property, such as developed real estate and undeveloped land, also have been made with greatly extended terms. Commonly, these contracts involve little or no down payment, the payments are spread over ten to thirty or forty years, and the probability of default in the early years is high because of a small investment by the buyer in the contract and because the market prices of the property often are unstable. Application of the accrual method to these contracts frequently overstates income in the early years due to the failure to realistically provide for future costs related to the contract, including losses from contract defaults. The FASB considered these types of sales and concluded that accrual accounting applied in these circumstances often results in "front-end loading,"

11. *Opinions of the Accounting Principles Board No. 10,* "Omnibus Opinion—1966" (New York: American Institute of Certified Public Accountants, 1967), par. 12.

i.e., a recognition of all revenue at the time of the sales contract with improper matching of related costs. Thus, the Board has established criteria that must be met before real estate and retail land sales can be recorded using the full accrual method of revenue recognition. If the criteria are not fully met, then the use of the installment sales method, or in some cases the cost recovery or deposit methods, is recommended to reflect the conditions of the sale more accurately.[12] Because the installment sales method often is recommended in new sales environments, it is important for accountants to understand its application.

Accounting for installment sales using the deferred gross profit approach requires determining a gross profit rate for the sales of each year, and establishing an accounts receivable and a deferred revenue account identified by the year of the sale. As collections are made of a given year's receivables, a portion of the deferred revenue equal to the gross profit rate times the collections made is recognized as income. The most common application of this method has been for the sale of merchandise. However, any sale of property or services may be recorded using the concept. The following examples of transactions and journal entries will illustrate this method of recognizing revenue.

Installment Sales of Merchandise. Assume that the Riding Corporation sells merchandise on the installment basis and that the uncertainties of cash collection make the use of the installment sales method necessary. The following data relate to three years of operations. To simplify the presentation, interest charges are excluded from the example.

	1995	1996	1997
Installment sales	$150,000	$200,000	$300,000
Cost of installment sales	100,000	140,000	204,000
Gross profit	$ 50,000	$ 60,000	$ 96,000
Gross profit percentage	33.33%	30%	32%
Cash collections:			
1995 sales	$ 30,000	$ 75,000	$ 30,000
1996 sales		70,000	80,000
1997 sales			100,000

The entries to record the transactions for 1995 would be as follows:

Account	Debit	Credit
Installment Accounts Receivable—1995	150,000	
Installment Sales		150,000
Cost of Installment Sales	100,000	
Inventory		100,000
Cash	30,000	
Installment Accounts Receivable—1995		30,000
Installment Sales	150,000	
Cost of Installment Sales		100,000
Deferred Gross Profit—1995		50,000
Deferred Gross Profit—1995	10,000*	
Realized Gross Profit on Installment Sales		10,000

*$30,000 × 33.33%

The sales and costs related to sales are recorded in a manner identical with the accounting for sales discussed in Chapter 9. At the end of the year, however, the sales and cost of sales accounts are closed to a deferred gross profit account rather than to Income Summary. The realized gross profit is then recognized by applying the gross profit percentage to cash collections. All other general and administrative expenses are normally written off in the period incurred.

12. *Statement of Financial Accounting Standards No. 66,* "Accounting for Sales of Real Estate" (Stamford: Financial Accounting Standards Board, October 1982).

Entries for the next two years are summarized in the schedule below.

	1996		1997	
Installment Accounts Receivable—1996	200,000			
Installment Accounts Receivable—1997			300,000	
Installment Sales		200,000		300,000
Cost of Installment Sales	140,000		204,000	
Inventory		140,000		204,000
Cash	145,000		210,000	
Installment Accounts Receivable—1995		75,000		30,000
Installment Accounts Receivable—1996		70,000		80,000
Installment Accounts Receivable—1997				100,000
Installment Sales	200,000		300,000	
Cost of Installment Sales		140,000		204,000
Deferred Gross Profit—1996		60,000		
Deferred Gross Profit—1997				96,000
Deferred Gross Profit—1995	25,000[1]		10,000[3]	
Deferred Gross Profit—1996	21,000[2]		24,000[4]	
Deferred Gross Profit—1997			32,000[5]	
Realized Gross Profit on Installment Sales		46,000		66,000

Computations:
[1]$75,000 × 33.33% = $25,000
[2]$70,000 × 30% = $21,000
[3]$30,000 × 33.33% = $10,000
[4]$80,000 × 30% = $24,000
[5]$100,000 × 32% = $32,000

Although this method of recording installment sales is the one most commonly followed, it would also be possible to defer both the gross revenue and the gross costs rather than just the net difference. If the latter approach is followed, the resulting entries would be more similar to those illustrated for percentage-of-completion accounting. Each year a portion of the gross revenue and gross costs would be recognized with the difference being the realized gross profit. Both methods produce the same net income.

If a company is heavily involved in installment sales, the operating cycle of the business is normally the period of the average installment contract. Thus, the currently accepted definition of current assets and current liabilities requires the receivables and their related deferred gross profit accounts to be reported in the current asset section of classified balance sheets. The deferred gross profit accounts should be reported as an offset to the related accounts receivable. Thus, at the end of 1995, the current asset section would include the following account balances:

Installment accounts receivable	$120,000	
Less deferred gross profit	40,000	$80,000

Complexities of Installment Sales of Merchandise. In the previous example, no provision was made for interest. In reality, installment sales contracts always include interest, either expressed or implied. The interest portion of the contract payments is recognized as income in the period in which cash is received, and the balance of the payment is treated as a collection on the installment sale. Thus, if in the example on pages 778–779, the $75,000 collection of 1995 sales in 1996 included interest of $40,000, only $35,000 would be used to compute the realized gross profit from 1995 sales. The resulting journal entries made in 1996 relating to the $75,000 collection of 1995 sales would be as follows:

Cash	75,000	
Interest Revenue		40,000
Installment Accounts Receivable — 1995		35,000
Deferred Gross Profit—1995	11,667*	
Realized Gross Profit on Installment Sales		11,667

Computation:
*$35,000 × 33.33% = $11,667

A complete example involving interest is illustrated in the appendix to this chapter covering real estate installment sales.

Additional complexities can arise in installment sales accounting in providing for uncollectible accounts. Because of the right to repossess merchandise in the event of nonpayment, the provision for uncollectible accounts can be less than might be expected. Only the amount of the receivable in excess of the current value of the repossessed merchandise is a potential loss. Accounting for repossessions was discussed in Chapter 10. Theoretically, a proper matching of estimated losses against revenues would require allocating the expected losses over the years of collection. Practically, however, the provision is made and charged against income in the period of the sale. Thus, the accounting entries for handling estimated uncollectible accounts are the same as illustrated in Chapter 8.

Cost Recovery Method

Under the **cost recovery method,** no income is recognized on a sale until the cost of the item sold is recovered through cash receipts. All cash receipts, both interest and principal portions, are applied first to the cost of those items sold. Then, all subsequent receipts are reported as revenue. Because all costs have been recovered, the recognized revenue after cost recovery represents income. This method is used only when the circumstances surrounding a sale are so uncertain that earlier recognition is impossible.

Using the information from the Riding Corporation example, assume that collections are so uncertain that the use of the cost recovery method is deemed appropriate. While the entries to record the installment sale, the receipt of cash, and the deferral of the gross profit are identical for both the installment sales and cost recovery methods, the entry for recognizing gross profit differs.

In 1995 no gross profit would be recognized, because the amount of cash collected ($30,000) is less than the cost of the inventory sold ($100,000). The cash collections in 1996 relating to 1995 sales result in total cash receipts exceeding the cost of sales ($30,000 + $75,000 > $100,000). Thus, in 1996 gross profit of $5,000 would be recognized on 1995 sales. The journal entry to recognize this gross profit in 1996 would be:

Deferred Gross Profit—1995	5,000	
Realized Gross Profit on Installment Sales		5,000

Since the cash collected in 1996 for 1996 sales ($70,000) is less than the cost of inventory sold ($140,000), no gross profit would be recognized in 1996 on 1996 sales. In 1997 the $30,000 collected in cash from the 1995 sales would all be recognized as gross profit. The cash collected relating to 1996 sales, $80,000, when added to the cash received in 1996, $70,000, exceeds the cost of the 1996 sales of $140,000. Thus, $10,000 of gross profit that was deferred in 1996 will be recognized in 1997. The journal entry to recognize gross profit in 1997 would be as follows:

Deferred Gross Profit—1995	30,000	
Deferred Gross Profit—1996	10,000	
Realized Gross Profit on Installment Sales		40,000

Comparing the amount of gross profit that is recognized using the various revenue recognition methods for the period 1995-1997 indicates how the income statement can be materially impacted by the method used.

	Gross Profit Recognized		
Revenue Recognition Method	*1995*	*1996*	*1997*
Full accrual	$50,000	$60,000	$96,000
Installment sales	10,000	46,000	66,000
Cost recovery	-0-	5,000	40,000

Cash Method

If the probability of recovering product or service costs is remote, the cash method of accounting could be used. Seldom would this method be applicable for sales of merchandise or real estate, because the right of repossession would leave considerable value to the seller. However, the cash method might be appropriate for service contracts with high initial costs and considerable uncertainty as to the ultimate collection of the contract price. Under this method, all costs are charged to expense as incurred, and revenue is recognized as collections are made. This extreme method of revenue and expense recognition would be appropriate only when the potential losses on a contract cannot be estimated with any degree of certainty.

ACCOUNTING FOR THE TRANSFER OF ASSETS PRIOR TO THE RECOGNITION OF REVENUE

In addition to the revenue recognition methods discussed in this chapter, some sales arrangements involve an exchange of either goods or monetary assets, such as cash and notes receivable, prior to the point where the earnings process has been completed sufficiently to recognize revenue. Under these circumstances, special accounting procedures must be applied pending the finalization of the sale and subsequent application of one of the methods of revenue recognition. If monetary assets are received prior to finalization of a sale, the deposit method of accounting should be used. If inventory is exchanged in advance of a sale, consignment accounting procedures should be applied. Each of these methods will be discussed briefly.

Deposit Method—General

In some cases, cash is collected before a sales contract is sufficiently defined to recognize revenue. This situation frequently arises in real estate sales contracts. For these cases, a method of accounting referred to as the **deposit method** has been developed.[13] Pending recognition of a sale, the cash received from a buyer is reported as a deposit on the contract and classified among the liabilities on the balance sheet. The property continues to be shown as an asset of the seller, and any related debt on the property continues to be reported as debt of the seller. No revenue or income should be recognized until the sales contract is finalized. At that time, one of the revenue recognition methods illustrated in this chapter may be used, and the deposit account would be closed. If the deposit is forfeited, it should be credited to Miscellaneous Income. An interesting example of the application of the deposit method of accounting is provided in the notes to the financial statements of Service Corporation International (SCI), as presented in Exhibit 18—2. SCI owns and operates funeral homes, cemeteries, and crematories. The company sells (and collects the cash for) funeral packages to individuals while the individuals are still alive. The revenue associated with these packages is "deferred until performance of the specific service,"—whatever that service might be.

13. *Statement of Financial Accounting Standards No. 66*, pars. 65-67.

■ Exhibit 18—2
Service Corporation International—Deposit Method of Accounting

NOTES TO FINANCIAL STATEMENTS (IN PART)

Cemetery operations: Related revenues from pre-need cemetery sales are deferred until performance of the specific service. Deferred revenues on cemetery sales at December 31, 1992 and December 31, 1991 were $157,089,000 and $113,157,000, respectively. Such amounts will be reflected in future revenues when the above described conditions for each sale have been met.

Deposit Method—Franchising Industry

A special application of the deposit method is found in the franchising industry, one of the fastest growing retail industries of recent years. Franchisers create faster growth by selling various rights to use a name and/or a product to operators (franchisees) who manage independent units as separate entrepreneurs from the franchisor.

Sales of franchises usually include several different services, products, and/or plant assets including: (1) intangible rights to use a trademark or name, (2) property owned by the franchisor, (3) pre-opening services such as helping locate suitable business sites, constructing a building, and training employees, and (4) ongoing services, products, and processes as the operations are carried out. Many revenue recognition problems are present in typical franchises; however, most of them may be solved if the elements are identified separately and accounted for in the same manner as they would be if the sale were a separate transaction. The most troublesome revenue recognition problem has been the initial fee. Typically, the franchisor charges a substantial amount for the right to use the franchise name and to provide for pre-opening services. Sometimes these fees are payable immediately in cash, but typically they include a long-term note receivable. Frequently, liberal refund provisions are included in the agreement, especially in the period prior to opening.

In the early days of franchising agreements, franchisers often reported the initial fee as revenue when the monetary assets were received. Future estimated costs were provided as offsets to the revenue. However, this treatment often resulted in questionable front-end loading of revenue similar to that occurring in the real estate and retail land sale industries. As a result, the AICPA issued an Industry Accounting Guide in 1973 that established revenue recognition guidelines for the franchising industry.[14] The essentials of this guide were later incorporated into FASB Statement No. 45.[15] This standard specifies that no revenue is to be recognized prior to **substantial performance** of the services covered by the initial fee. Until that time, any monetary assets received should be offset by a deposit or deferred credit account, and any costs related to the services rendered should be deferred until revenue is recognized, except that such deferred costs shall not exceed anticipated revenue less estimated additional related costs. Once substantial performance is achieved, revenue should be recognized using the method that best reflects the probability of cash collection, e.g., accrual, installment sales, or cost recovery method. The latter two methods "shall be used to account for franchise fee revenue only in those exceptional cases when revenue is collectible over an extended period and no reasonable basis exists for estimating collectibility."[16]

To illustrate, assume that a franchisor charges new franchisees a fee consisting of $10,000 payable in cash when the agreement is signed followed by four annual payments of $3,750 each. Assuming the franchisee could borrow money at 10%, the present value

14. Committee on Franchise Accounting and Auditing, AICPA, *Industry Accounting Guide*, "Accounting for Franchise Fee Revenue" (New York: American Institute of Certified Public Accountants, 1973).

15. *Statement of Financial Accounting Standards No. 45*, "Accounting for Franchise Fee Revenue" (Stamford: Financial Accounting Standards Board, March 1981).

16. *Ibid.*, par. 6.

The Savings & Loan Crisis

The estimated cost to taxpayers to bail out failed savings and loan companies has been estimated as high as $500 billion. Reasons for the crisis include mismanagement of resources, management fraud, and unfavorable economic conditions. Another factor contributing to the S&L problems was their revenue recognition techniques.

When a loan was made, the associated loan origination fee, often as high as 6% of the loan principal, was recognized immediately as revenue. If a financial institution's objective was to increase income for the short term, one strategy would be to loan as much money as possible and collect large loan fees.

The president of one S&L, Texas' Western Savings, elected to follow this strategy. He enticed investors by promising high yields on certificates of deposit that were federally insured. His telephone operations often netted over $20 million in investments per day. Once the money was received from investors, the president would then loan the money to borrowers and collect loan fees as revenue. These fees and other income were the source of a $3 million dividend to the president over a two-year period.

The problem for taxpayers was that the president was making poor-quality loans. Since investors' deposits were federally insured, the collectibility of loans was not a major issue for Western. Million-dollar loans were made with no required down payment. Loans were made for more than the full purchase price of properties. As an example, $64 million was loaned to purchase land that two years earlier had sold for $17.2 million. On this particular deal, Western, holding a sixth lien on the property, received $2 million in loan fees.

Questions:

1. How can a savings & loan company justify recognizing immediately the loan origination fee as revenue rather than recognizing it over the life of the loan?
2. From an accounting point of view, what revenue recognition method should be used when dealing with high-risk loans?
3. Why would investors deposit their money in financial institutions that had lending practices like those illustrated in this case?
4. Do external auditors have a responsibility to evaluate the loan practices of the financial institutions that they audit?

Source: "Easy Money, *The Wall Street Journal*, April 27, 1989.

of the four annual payments is $11,887 ($3,750 × 3.1699).[17] The agreement provides that the franchisor will assist in locating the site for a building, conduct a market survey to estimate potential income, supervise the construction of a building, and provide initial training to employees.

If the down payment is refundable and no services have been rendered at the time the arrangement is made, the deposit method would be used as long as collection on the note is reasonably certain. The following entry would be made to record the transaction:

Cash	10,000	
Notes Receivable	11,887	
Deposit on Franchise (or Unearned Franchise Fee)		21,887

When the initial services are determined to be substantially performed, the revenue recognition method to be used and the resulting journal entries depend on the probability of future cash collection. If the collection of the note is reasonably assured, the full accrual method would be used. Assume that substantial performance of the initial services by the franchisor costs $14,000. The entries to record this event using the full accrual method would be as follows:

Cost of Franchise Fee Revenue	14,000	
Cash		14,000
Deposit on Franchise (or Unearned Franchise Fee)	21,887	
Franchise Fee Revenue		21,887

17. See Chapter 7 for a review of present value calculations.

If the collection of the note is doubtful, the installment sales method could be used. In addition to the entries used under the full accrual method, the installment sales method requires the following entries:

Franchise Fee Revenue	21,887	
Cost of Franchise Fee Revenue		14,000
Deferred Gross Profit on Franchise		7,887
Deferred Gross Profit on Franchise	3,604*	
Realized Gross Profit on Franchise		3,604

Computation:
*$7,887 ÷ $21,887 = 36.04% gross profit percentage .3604 × $10,000 = $3,604

An example of financial statement disclosure provided by a franchise business is presented in Exhibit 18—3 for TCBY Enterprises, a chain of yogurt shops.

Exhibit 18—3
TCBY Enterprises Inc. Disclosure of Franchise Information

NOTES TO FINANCIAL STATEMENTS (IN PART)

The following table summarizes franchise information

	1992	1991	1990
Sales of franchises	15	26	195
Purchases of franchised stores by the Company from franchisees	22	5	20
TCBY locations open as of November 30:			
Franchised	1,401	1,574	1,677
Company-owned	147	136	170
Non-traditional	292	140	97

Franchising Revenues: Franchising revenues consist of initial franchise and license fees and royalty income. Initial franchise and license fees are recognized as revenue when the Company has substantially completed its obligations under the franchise or license agreement. Royalty income is earned on sales by franchisees and is recognized as revenue when the related sales are made.

Consignment Sales

Another method of accounting has developed for use when property is exchanged without a transfer of title and without a sales contract being completed. This type of arrangement is referred to as a **consignment.** Under a consignment, the potential seller, the **consignor,** delivers merchandise to another party, the **consignee,** who then acts as an *agent* for the consignor to sell the goods. Title to the merchandise continues to be held by the consignor until a sale is made, at which time title passes to the ultimate purchaser. The consignee usually is entitled to reimbursement for expenses incurred in relation to this arrangement and also is entitled to a commission if a sale is successfully made.

Because title to the merchandise is held by the consignor, but physical possession is held by the consignee, special accounting records must be maintained by the consignor for control purposes. No revenue is recognized until a sale is made by the consignee. Upon shipment of the merchandise by the consignor, a special inventory account is established on the consignor's books to identify the consigned merchandise. Any consignment expenses paid by the consignor are added to the inventory balance as added costs. The consignee does not make an entry for receipt of the inventory in the general ledger; however, memorandum control records usually are kept. Any reimbursable expense paid by the consignee is charged to a receivable account by the consignee and added to the inventory balance by the consignor. When a sale is made, the consignor recognizes the sale as revenue according to one of the revenue recognition methods, and the consignee recognizes the commission as revenue on the transaction.

To illustrate consignment accounting entries, assume that Harrison Products Inc. sends $500,000 worth of goods on consignment to Benson Industries. Shipping costs of $5,000 are paid by Harrison, and reimbursable advertising costs of $20,000 are paid by Benson Industries. By the end of the year, one-half of the goods on consignment are sold for $400,000 cash. A 10% commission is earned by Benson Industries according to the terms of the consignment. The journal entries shown below would be made on the consignor's and consignee's books.

Transaction	Entries on Consignor's Books (Harrison Products Inc.)			Entries on Consignee's Books (Benson Industries)		
(1) Shipment of goods on consignment.	Inventory on Consignment	500,000		No entry (memorandum control record)		
	Finished Goods Inventory		500,000			
(2) Payment of expenses by consignor	Inventory on Consignment	5,000		No entry		
	Cash		5,000			
(3) Payment of expenses by consignee.	Inventory on Consignment	20,000		Consignor Receivable	20,000	
	Consignee Payable		20,000	Cash		20,000
(4) Sale of merchandise	No entry			Cash	400,000	
				Consignor Payable		400,000
(5) Notification of sale to consignor and payment of cash due.	Commission Expense	40,000		Consignor Payable	400,000	
	Cash	340,000		Cash		340,000
	Consignee Payable	20,000		Commission Revenue		40,000
	Consignment Sales Revenue		400,000	Consignor Receivable		20,000
	Cost of Goods Sold	262,500*				
	Inventory on Consignment		262,500			

**Computation:*
1/2($500,000 + $25,000) = $262,500

If the eventual sale had been on the installment basis, the installment sales entries illustrated earlier in this chapter could have been used by the consignor in place of the accrual entries illustrated.

CONCLUDING COMMENTS

This chapter has explored some special problems that arise in recognizing revenue. Some industries such as franchising, construction, and real estate have been used as illustrative of the types of problems that exist in applying the revenue recognition criteria included in currently accepted accounting standards. While recognizing revenue at the point of sale is still the most traditional method, accounting standards provide for flexibility when a different method of revenue recognition provides more meaningful information to users. Percentage-of-completion, proportional performance, installment sales, cost recovery, and deferral through the deposit method are all part of generally accepted accounting principles under specified conditions.

APPENDIX

Recognition Issues Involving the Sale of Real Estate

The installment sales method of accounting often is used for sales of real estate on a long-term contract basis. These sales frequently are characterized by small down payments with long payoff periods on the balance. Usually the seller retains title to the real estate until the final payment is made, thus giving the seller the right of repossession. In an inflationary economy, this right is valuable and, in most cases, means that ultimate collection of the debt, either through payment or repossession, virtually is assured. However, if circumstances reduce the probability of collection or if the market value of the property is unstable, then the installment sales method may be applied, or in extreme cases, the cost recovery method may be required.

INSTALLMENT SALES METHOD

To illustrate the accounting for real estate sales using the installment method, assume that Emery Industries Inc. sells land and buildings on January 1, 1995, for $4,000,000. Emery receives a down payment of $300,000 and a promissory note for the remaining $3,700,000 plus interest at 12% to be paid in equal installments of $471,752 at the end of each of the next 25 years. The land has a carrying value on Emery's books at the time of the sale of $200,000, and the buildings have a carrying value of $2,000,000. The sale does not meet the FASB's criteria for the full accrual method of revenue recognition, and the installment method of accounting is assumed to be appropriate. The following entries would be made to record the initial transaction:

1995			
Jan. 1	Cash	300,000	
	Notes Receivable	11,793,800[1]	
	Unearned Interest Revenue		8,093,800[2]
	Real Estate Sales		4,000,000
1	Cost of Real Estate Sales	2,200,000	
	Land		200,000
	Building (net of accumulated depreciation)		2,000,000
1	Real Estate Sales	4,000,000	
	Cost of Real Estate Sales		2,200,000
	Deferred Gross Profit on Real Estate Sales		1,800,000

Computations:
[1]$471,752 × 25 = $11,793,800
[2]$11,793,800 – $3,700,000 = $8,093,800

The gross profit percentage for this sale is 45% ($1,800,000 ÷ $4,000,000). This percentage is applied to each cash collection reduced by the amount of interest included in the cash receipt. Thus, $135,000 would be recognized immediately upon receipt of the $300,000 down payment (.45 x $300,000) and the following entry would be made to recognize this profit:

1995			
Jan. 1	Deferred Gross Profit on Real Estate Sales	135,000	
	Realized Gross Profit on Real Estate Sales		135,000

At the end of the first year, cash of $471,752 will be collected in accordance with the contract terms. Included in this amount is interest earned of $444,000 (.12 x $3,700,000). The remainder of the cash collected, $27,752, is payment on the principal amount of the debt; 45% of this portion of the payment, or $12,488 (.45 x $27,752), also would be recognized as realized gross profit in the first year.

1995			
Dec. 31	Cash	471,752	
	Notes Receivable		471,752
31	Unearned Interest Revenue	444,000	
	Interest Revenue		444,000
31	Deferred Gross Profit on Real Estate Sales	12,488	
	Realized Gross Profit on Real Estate Sales		12,488

The following T-accounts summarize these transactions for the first year before closing entries:

Notes Receiviable

Debit	Credit
11,793,800	471,752
Bal. 11,322,048	

Land

Debit	Credit
Beg. Bal. 200,000	200,000

Unearned Interest Revenue

Debit	Credit
444,000	8,093,800
	Bal. 7,649,800

Building (net of accumulated deprecation)

Debit	Credit
Beg. Bal. 2,000,000	2,000,000

Real Estate Sales

Debit	Credit
4,000,000	4,000,000

Deferred Gross Profit on Real Estate Sales

Debit	Credit
135,000	1,800,000
12,488	
	Bal. 1,652,512

Cost of Real Estate Sales

Debit	Credit
2,200,000	2,200,000

Realized Gross Profit on Real Estate Sales

Debit	Credit
	135,000
	12,488
	Bal. 147,488

Interest Revenue

Debit	Credit
	444,000

Cash collections in subsequent years would be divided between interest and principal in the same manner, and a portion of the deferred profit would be recognized each year. Because the collections are constant and the interest revenue is declining as the carrying value of the receivable declines, the gross profit recognized would increase each year.

Care must be taken in evaluating a sale of real estate. In some cases, the contract may be, in reality, a financial arrangement or an operating lease, or it may be a deposit on a possible future sale. Revenue should be recognized only after careful evaluation of the contractual arrangements and application of the criteria in FASB Statement No. 66.

COST RECOVERY METHOD

Assume that collection on the real estate sales contract for Emery Industries Inc. is felt to be so uncertain that the cost recovery method should be used. Under this method, the $2,200,000 carrying value of the real estate must be collected before any revenue or income is recognized, including any recognition of interest revenue on the contract. The same entries would be made to record the sale, the cost of the sale, and the deferred gross profit on the sale as was done under the installment sales method (page 786). The difference between the carrying value of the property and the down payment received equals the unrecovered cost of $1,900,000 ($2,200,000 – $300,000). Unrecovered cost may also be computed as the net balance that would be reported on the balance sheet as follows:

Notes receivable		$11,793,800
Less: Unearned interest revenue	$8,093,800	
Deferred gross profit	1,800,000	9,893,800
		$ 1,900,000

When the first annual payment of $471,752 is collected, the following entries would be made:

1995			
Dec. 31	Cash	471,752	
	Notes Receivable		471,752
31	Unearned Interest Revenue	444,000	
	Unrecognized Interest Revenue		444,000

Note that the interest revenue for 1995 has been earned through the passage of time, but it is not recognized as revenue because the cost has not yet been recovered. The two separate interest offset accounts clarify this earnings process.

The unrecovered cost would now be $1,428,248 ($1,900,000 – $471,752). This agrees with the balance to be reported on the balance sheet as follows:

Notes receivable		$11,322,048
Less: Unearned interest revenue	$7,649,800	
Deferred gross profit	1,800,000	
Unrecognized interest revenue	444,000	9,893,800
Net notes receivable		$ 1,428,248

By the end of 1998, all but $12,992 of the cost will have been recovered by the cash payments computed as follows:

Total cost of sold property		$2,200,000
Less payments received:		
Down payment	$300,000	
1995 payment	471,752	
1996 payment	471,752	
1997 payment	471,752	
1998 payment	471,752	2,187,008
Unrecovered cost		$ 12,992

The 1999 payment would result in a cost recovery of the $12,992 and an interest revenue recognition of $458,760. In each of the remaining collection years, the total cash receipt will be recognized as revenue; first allocated to interest revenue until the unrecognized interest revenue is recognized, and then the balance of the collections will be allocated between interest revenue and the gross profit on the real estate sale.

The selection of a revenue recognition method has a great impact on revenue and income, especially in the first year of a sales contract. The following summary shows how income would vary on the real estate sale of Emery Industries Inc. in 1995 depending on which revenue recognition method is used.

Revenue Recognition Method	Income for 1995
Full accrual	$2,244,000[1]
Installment sales	591,488[2]
Cost recovery	-0-

Computations:
[1]$1,800,000 gross profit + $444,000 interest revenue = $2,244,000
[2]$147,488 gross profit + $444,000 interest revenue = $591,488

In subsequent years, only interest revenue is recognized as revenue under the full accrual method, but interest revenue plus a portion of the payment on the principal is recognized under the installment sales method. After four years, all the cash collected is recognized as revenue under the cost recovery method. The graph below illustrates how revenue for the real estate sale would be recognized over the 25 years assuming all payments were made as scheduled.

Exhibit 18—4 Comparison of Revenue Recognition Methods

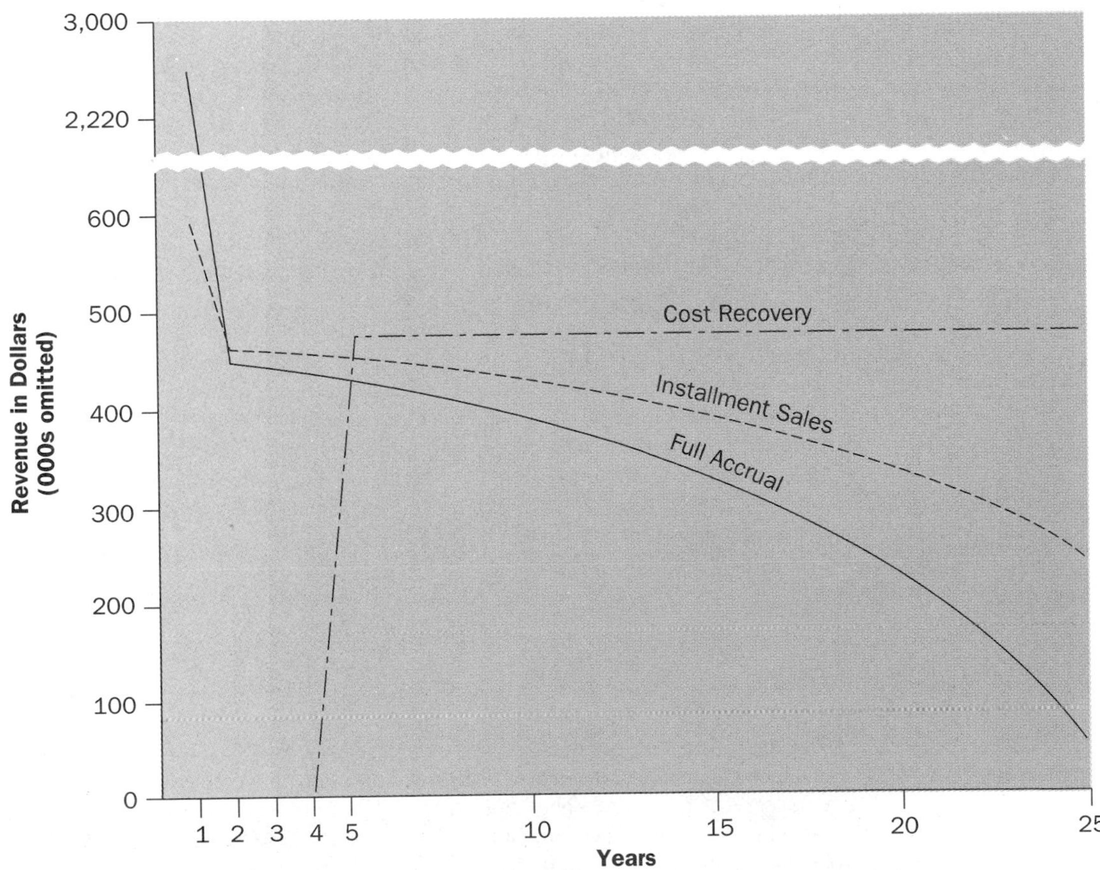

KEY TERMS

Change orders 773
Completed-contract method 763
Consignment 784
Consignee 784
Consignor 784
Cost recovery method 780
Cost-to-cost method 765
Deposit method 781
Efforts-expended methods 765
Input measures 765
Installment sales method 777
Output measures 766
Percentage-of-completion accounting 763
Proportional performance method 763
Substantial performance 782

QUESTIONS

1. Under what conditions is percentage-of-completion accounting recommended for construction contractors?
2. Distinguish between the cost-to-cost method and efforts-expended methods of measuring the percentage of completion.
3. Output measures of percentage of completion are sometimes used in preference to input measures. What are some examples of commonly used output measures?
4. What is the relationship between the construction in progress account and the progress billings on construction contracts account? How should these accounts be reported on the balance sheet?
5. When a measure of percentage of completion other than cost-to-cost is used, the amount of cost charged against revenue using the percentage of completion usually will be different from the costs incurred. How do some AICPA committee members recommend handling this situation so that the costs charged against revenue are equal to the costs incurred?
6. The construction in progress account is used to accumulate all costs of construction. What additional item is included in this account when percentage-of-completion accounting is followed?
7. The gross profit percentage reported on long-term construction contracts often varies from year to year. What is the major reason for this variation?
8. How are anticipated contract losses treated under the completed-contract and percentage-of-completion methods?
9. What input and output measures usually are applicable to the proportional performance method for long-term service contracts?
10. The proportional performance method spreads the profit over the periods in which services are being performed. What arguments could be made against this method of revenue recognition for newly formed, service-oriented companies?
11. Distinguish among the three different approaches to revenue recognition that await the receipt of cash. How does the treatment of costs incurred vary depending on the approach used?
12. Under what general conditions is the installment sales method of accounting preferred to the full accrual method?
13. The normal accounting entries for installment sales require keeping a separate record by year of receivables, collections on receivables, and the deferred gross profit percentages. Why are these separate records necessary?
14. Installment sales contracts generally include interest. Contrast the method of recognizing interest revenue from the method used to recognize the gross profit on the sale.
15. Under what conditions would the cash method of recognizing revenue be acceptable for reporting purposes?
16. What special recognition problems arise in accounting for franchise fees?
17. Consignment accounting is primarily a method of accounting for transfers of inventory prior to the point of revenue recognition. Describe the essential elements of this method from the standpoint of (a) the consignor and (b) the consignee.

DISCUSSION CASES

Case 18—1 (Recognizing revenue on a percentage-of-completion basis)

As the new controller for Enclave Construction Company, you have been advised that your predecessor classified all revenues and expenses by project, each project being considered a separate venture. All revenues from uncompleted projects were treated as unearned revenue, and all expenses applicable to each uncompleted project were treated as "work in process" inventory.

Thus, the income statement for the current year includes only the revenues and expenses related to projects completed during the year.

What do you think about the use of the completed-contract method by the previous controller? What alternative approach might you suggest to company management?

Case 18—2 (Let's spread our losses too!)

The Abbott Construction Company has several contracts to build sections of freeways, bridges, and dams. Because most of these contracts require more than one year to complete, the accountant, Dave Allred, has recommended use of the percentage-of-completion method to recognize revenue and income on these contracts. The president, Kathy Bahr, isn't quite sure how the accounting method works, and she indicates concern about the impact of this decision on income taxes. Bahr also inquires as to what happens when a contract results in a loss. When told by Allred that any estimated loss must be recognized when it is first identified, Bahr becomes upset. "If it is a percentage-of-completion method and we are recognizing profits in part as we go along, why shouldn't we be able to do the same for losses?"

How would you, as the accountant, answer Bahr's concerns?

Case 18—3 (What is the difference between completed-contract and percentage-of-completion accounting?)

In accounting for long-term contracts (those taking longer than one year to complete), the two methods commonly followed are the percentage-of-completion method and the completed-contract method.

1. Discuss how earnings on long-term contracts are recognized and computed under these two methods.
2. Under what circumstances is it preferable to use one method over the other?
3. Why is earnings recognition as measured by interim billings not generally accepted for long-term contracts?

Case 18—4 (When is the membership fee earned?)

The Superb Health Studio has been operating for 5 years but is presently for sale. It has opened 50 salons in various cities in the United States. The normal pattern for a new opening is to advertise heavily and sell different types of memberships: 1-year, 3-year, and 5-year. For the initial membership fee, members may use the pool, exercise rooms, sauna, and other recreational facilities without charge. If special courses or programs are taken, additional fees are charged; however, members are granted certain privileges, and the fees are less than those charged to outsiders. In addition, a minimal $10-a-month dues charge is made to all members. Nonmembers may use the facilities; however, they must pay a substantial daily charge for services they receive.

Your client, Dickson Inc., is considering purchasing the chain of health studios, and asks you to give your opinion on its operations. You are provided with financial statements that show a growing revenue and income pattern over the 5-year period. The balance sheet shows that the physical facilities are apparently owned rather than leased. But you are aware that health studios, like all service institutions, have some challenging revenue recognition problems.

What questions would you want answered in preparing your report for Dickson?

Case 18—5 (When is it revenue?)

Hertzel Advertising Agency handles advertising for clients under contracts that require the agency to develop advertising copy and layouts and place ads in various media, charging clients a commission of 15% of the media cost as its fee. The agency makes advance billings to its clients of estimated media cost plus its 15% commission. Adjustments to these advances usually are small. Frequently both the billings and receipt of cash from these billings occur before the period in which the advertising actually appears in the media.

A conference meeting is held between officers of the agency and the new firm of CPAs recently engaged to perform annual audits. In this meeting, consideration is given to 4 possible points for measuring revenue: (1) at the time the advanced billing is made, (2) when payment is received from the client, (3) in the month when the advertising appears in the media, and (4) when the bill for advertising is received from the media, generally in the month following its appearance. The agency has been following the first method for the past several years on the basis that a definite contract exists and the revenue is earned when billed. When the billing is made, an entry is prepared to record the estimated receivable and liability to the media. Estimated expenses related to the contract are also recorded. Adjusting entries are made later for any differences between the estimated and actual amounts.

As a member of the CPA firm attending this meeting, how would you react to the agency's method of recognizing revenue? Discuss the strengths and weaknesses of each of the 4 methods of revenue recognition and indicate which one you would recommend the agency follow.

Case 18—6 **(Keep shipping, we need the revenue.)**

Datarite, a maker of computer hardware systems, sells its products to dealers who, in turn, sell to the final customer. Datarite offers very liberal credit terms and allows its dealers to take up to 90 days to pay. These terms allow dealers to hold larger inventories. As the end of the fiscal year nears, Datarite needs to increase its current ratio and decrease its debt-to-equity ratio in order to avoid violating its debt covenants. The president of the company has asked that all dealers be shipped extra inventory. This will increase both sales and accounts receivable, thereby allowing Datarite to remain in compliance with its debt covenants. The chief financial officer remarks that shipping inventory that has not been ordered should be accounted for as consigned inventory rather than revenue.

Should the inventory shipments be accounted for as sales or as consigned inventory? Debt covenants exist to protect the interests of creditors. In this instance, are debt covenants effective in monitoring the company's activities?

Case 18—7 **(Which method is appropriate?)**

Green Brothers Furniture sells discount furniture and offers easy credit terms. Its margins are not large but it deals in heavy volume. Its customers are often low-income individuals who cannot obtain credit elsewhere. Green Brothers retains the title to the furniture until full payment is received, and it is not uncommon to have 20% of sales be uncollectible.

Green Brothers is considering expansion and has hired an independent auditor to review its financial statements prior to obtaining outside funding. The auditor questions the use of accrual accounting as a method for recognizing revenue and suggests that Green Brothers use the installment sales method. The auditor justifies this by stating that because of the high rate of uncollectibles, the earnings process is not substantially complete at the point of sale. Financial statements adjusted to the installment sales method result in a 17% decrease in net income for the fiscal year just ended.

The chief financial officer for Green Brothers counters that if uncollectibles can be estimated, even if that estimate is high, the use of the accrual method is appropriate. The accountant also notes that restated financial statements showing the lower net income figure will make obtaining external funding much more difficult.

Which method of revenue recognition would you argue that Green Brothers should use? Why? Remember that your decision could affect this company's ability to obtain favorable external financing.

Case 18—8 **(When is the initial franchise fee really earned?)**

Magleby Inn sells franchises to independent operators throughout the western part of the United States. The contract with the franchisee includes the following provisions:

(a) The franchisee is charged an initial fee of $25,000. Of this amount, $5,000 is payable when the agreement is signed and a $4,000 non-interest-bearing note is payable at the end of each of the 5 subsequent years.
(b) All the initial franchise fee collected by Magleby Inn is to be refunded and the remaining obligation canceled if, for any reason, the franchisee fails to open the franchise.
(c) In return for the initial franchise fee, Magleby agrees to: assist the franchisee in selecting the location for the business; negotiate the lease for the land; obtain financing and assist with building design; supervise construction; establish accounting and tax records; and

provide expert advice over a 5-year period relating to such matters as employee and management training, quality control, and promotion.

(d) In addition to the initial franchise fee, the franchisee is required to pay to Magleby Inn a monthly fee of 2% of sales for recipe innovations and the privilege of purchasing ingredients from Magleby Inn at or below prevailing market prices.

Management of Magleby Inn estimates that the value of the services rendered to the franchisee at the time the contract is signed amounts to at least $5,000. All franchisees to date have opened their locations at the scheduled time and none has defaulted on any of the notes receivable.

The credit ratings of all franchisees would entitle them to borrow at the current interest rate of 10%.

Given the nature of Magleby's agreement with its franchisees, when should revenue be recognized? Discuss the question of revenue recognition for both the initial franchise fee and the additional monthly fee of 2% of sales.

Case 18—9 (I think they're sales!)

The Rain-Soft Water Company distributes its water softeners to dealers upon their request. The contract agreement with the dealers is that they may have 90 days to sell and pay for the softeners. Until the 90-day period is over, any softeners may be returned at the dealer's expense and with no further obligation on the dealer's part. Past experience indicates that 75% of all softeners distributed on this basis are sold by the dealer. In June, 100 units are delivered to dealers at an average billed price of $800 each. The average cost of the softeners to Rain-Soft is $600. Based on the expected sales, Rain-Soft reports profit of $15,000 .

You are asked to evaluate the income statement for its compliance with GAAP. What recommendations would you make?

Case 18—10 (A problem with accruing revenues)

Midwestern Companies, a firm specializing in the production and sale of ethanol plants, used accrual accounting to report revenues from the sale of the plants. However, details of the sale of an ethanol plant have left many questioning Midwestern's accounting practices.

An investor in a partnership would pay $15,000 and sign a note for $45,000. After the initial investment, investors were not required to pay any more money as the cash from the operations of the plant would be applied against the note. The company promised that the plant would operate properly and that those purchasing the plant would be provided with customers.

While the firm reported $36.3 million in revenues from the sale of ethanol plants with costs of $12.2 million, they received only $10.8 million in cash. Thus, on a cash basis, the firm was actually operating at a loss for the period.

1. In selling an ethanol plant, identify the various points at which one could argue that the earnings process is substantially complete. At what point do you think Midwestern was recognizing revenue?
2. Did the use of accrual accounting accurately portray the financial performance of Midwestern?
3. In your opinion, what revenue recognition method should have been used by Midwestern?

Source: "Up & Down Wall Street," *Barron's*, March 5, 1984.

EXERCISES

Exercise 18—11 (Completed-contract method)

On December 1, 1996, bids were submitted for a construction project to build a new municipal building and fire station. The lowest bid was $3,980,000, submitted by the Jessop Construction Company. Jessop was awarded the contract. Jessop uses the completed-contract method to report gross profit. The data on the following page is given to summarize the activities on this contract for 1996 and 1997. Give the entries to record these transactions using the completed-contract method.

Year	Cost Incurred	Estimated Cost to Complete	Billings on Contract	Collections of Billings
1996	$1,720,000	$2,060,000	$1,350,000	$1,150,000
1997	2,020,000	-0-	2,630,000	2,830,000

Exercise 18—12 (Percentage-of-completion analysis)

Espiritu Construction Co. has used the cost-to-cost percentage-of-completion method of recognizing revenue. Tony Espiritu assumed leadership of the business after the recent death of his father, Howard. In reviewing the records, Espiritu finds the following information regarding a recently completed building project for which the total contract was $2,000,000.

	1995	1996	1997
Gross profit (loss)	$ 40,000	$140,000	$ (20,000)
Cost incurred	360,000	?	820,000

Espiritu wants to know how effectively the company operated during the last 3 years on this project and, since the information is not complete, has asked for answers to the following questions:

1. How much cost was incurred in 1996?
2. What percentage of the project was completed by the end of 1996?
3. What was the total estimated gross profit on the project by the end of 1996?
4. What was the estimated cost to complete the project at the end of 1996?

Exercise 18—13 (Percentage-of-completion accounting)

The Quality Construction Company was the low bidder on an office building construction contract. The contract bid was $7,000,000, with an estimated cost to complete the project of $6,000,000. The contract period was 34 months starting January 1, 1995. The company uses the cost-to-cost method of estimating earnings. Because of changes requested by the customer, the contract price was adjusted downward to $6,500,000 on January 1, 1996.

A record of construction activities for the years 1995-1998 follows:

Year	Actual Cost—Current Year	Progress Billings	Cash Receipts
1995	$2,500,000	$2,100,000	$1,800,000
1996	3,300,000	3,100,000	3,000,000
1997	410,000	1,300,000	1,000,000
1998			700,000

The estimated cost to complete the contract as of the end of each accounting period is:

1995	$3,500,000
1996	400,000
1997	-0-

Calculate the gross profit for the years 1995-1997 under the percentage-of-completion method of revenue recognition.

Exercise 18—14 (Percentage-of-completion analysis)

Smokey International Inc. recently acquired the Kurtz Builders Company. Kurtz has incomplete accounting records. On one particular project, only the information below is available.

	1995	1996	1997
Costs incurred during year	$200,000	$250,000	?
Estimated cost to complete	450,000	190,000	-0-
Recognized revenue	220,000	?	?
Gross profit on contract	?	10,000	$(10,000)
Contract price	700,000		

Because the information is incomplete, you are asked the following questions assuming the percentage-of-completion method is used, an output measure is used to estimate the percentage completed, and revenue is recorded using the actual cost approach.

1. How much gross profit should be reported in 1995?
2. How much revenue should be reported in 1996?
3. How much revenue should be reported in 1997?
4. How much cost was incurred in 1997?
5. What are the total costs on the contract?
6. What would be the gross profit for 1996 if the cost-to-cost percentage-of-completion method were used rather than the output measure? (Ignore the revenue amount shown for 1995 and gross profit amount reported for 1996.)

Exercise 18—15 (Reporting construction contracts)

Tara Builders Inc. is building a new home for Margaret Mitchell at a contracted price of $120,000. The estimated cost at the time the contract is signed (January 2, 1996) is $97,000. At December 31, 1996, the total cost incurred is $59,000 with estimated costs to complete of $41,000. Tara has billed $70,000 on the job and has received a $60,000 payment. This is the only contract in process at year-end. Prepare the sections of the balance sheet and the income statement of Tara Builders Inc. affected by these events assuming use of (a) the percentage-of-completion method and (b) the completed-contract method.

Exercise 18—16 (Percentage of completion using architect's estimates)

Central Iowa Builders Inc. entered into a contract to construct an office building and plaza at a contract price of $10,000,000. Income is to be reported using the percentage-of-completion method as determined by estimates made by the architect. The data below summarizes the activities on the construction for the years 1995-1997. For the years 1995-1997, what entries are required to record this information, assuming the architect's estimate of the percentage completed is used to determine revenue (proportional cost approach)?

Year	Actual Cost Incurred	Estimated Cost to Complete	Percentage Complete—Architect's Estimate	Project Billings	Collections on Billings
1995	$3,200,000	$6,000,000	25%	$3,300,000	$3,100,000
1996	4,300,000	1,600,000	75	4,500,000	4,000,000
1997	1,550,000	-0-	100	2,200,000	2,900,000

Exercise 18—17 (Completed-contract method)

On January 1, 1995, the Ishikawa Construction Company entered into a 3-year contract to build a dam. The original contract price for the construction was $18,000,000 and the estimated cost was $16,100,000. The following cost data relates to the construction period.

Year	Cost Incurred	Estimated Cost to Complete	Billings	Cash Collected
1995	$6,000,000	$10,000,000	$6,300,000	$6,000,000
1996	5,300,000	7,400,000	5,700,000	5,400,000
1997	7,650,000	-0-	6,000,000	6,600,000

Prepare the required journal entries for the 3 years of the contract, assuming Ishikawa uses the completed-contract method.

Exercise 18—18 (Percentage-of-completion method with change orders)

The Build-It Construction Company enters into a contract on January 1, 1996, to construct a 20-story office building for $40,000,000. During the construction period, many change orders are made to the original contract. The following schedule summarizes these changes made in 1996:

	Cost Incurred—1996	Estimated Cost to Complete	Contract Price
Basic contract	$8,000,000	$28,000,000	$40,000,000
Change Order #1	50,000	50,000	125,000
Change Order #2	-0-	50,000	-0-
Change Order #3	300,000	300,000	Still to be negotiated; at least cost.
Change Order #4	125,000	-0-	100,000

Compute the revenue, costs, and gross profit to be recognized in 1996, assuming use of the cost-to-cost method to determine the percentage completed. (Round percentage to two decimal places.)

Exercise 18—19 (Service industry accounting)

The Fitness Health Spa charges an annual membership fee of $600 for its services. For this fee, each member receives a fitness evaluation (value $100), a monthly magazine (value $32), and 2-hour's use of the equipment each week. The initial direct costs to obtain the membership are estimated to be $120. The direct cost of the fitness evaluation is $50, and the monthly direct costs to provide the other services are estimated to be $15 per person. In addition, the monthly indirect costs are estimated to average $8 per person. Give the journal entries to record the transactions in 1996 relative to a membership sold on July 1, 1996. The fitness evaluation is given in the first month of membership, and the initial direct cost is to be spread over all direct costs, including the fitness evaluation, using the proportional performance method. (Round percentage of performance to two decimal places and journal entries to the nearest dollar.)

Exercise 18—20 (Installment sales accounting)

Denna Corporation had sales in 1995 of $210,000, in 1996 of $270,000, and in 1997 of $350,000. The gross profit percentage of each year, in order, was 25%, 29%, and 27%. Past history has shown that 10% of total sales are collected in the first year, 40% in the second year, and 30% in the third year. Assuming these collections are made as projected, give the journal entries for 1995, 1996, and 1997, assuming use of the installment sales method. Ignore provisions for doubtful accounts and interest.

Exercise 18—21 (Installment sales analysis)

Complete the following table:

	1995	1996	1997
Installment sales	$50,000	$80,000	$ (7)
Cost of installment sales	(1)	(5)	91,800
Gross profit	(2)	(6)	28,200
Gross profit percentage	(3)	25%	(8)
Cash collections: 1995	(4)	25,000	10,000
1996		20,000	50,000
1997			45,000
Realized gross profit on installment sales	1,100	10,500	(9)

Exercise 18—22 (Cost recovery method)

Bailey Bats Inc. had the following sales and gross profit percentages for the years 1995-1998:

	Sales	Gross Profit Percentage
1995	$47,000	45%
1996	45,000	42
1997	58,000	47
1998	61,000	49

Historically, 55% of sales are collected in the year of the sale, 30% in the following year, 10% in the third year. Assuming collections are as projected, give the journal entries for the years 1995-1998 assuming the use of the cost recovery method. (Ignore provision for doubtful accounts.) Prepare a table comparing the gross profit recognized for 1995-1998 using the full accrual method and the cost recovery method.

Exercise 18—23 (Cost recovery analysis)

Johnson Enterprises uses the cost recovery method for all installment sales. Complete the following table:

	1995	1996	1997
Installment sales	$80,000	$95,000	(1)
Cost of installment sales	(2)	56,050	$68,250
Gross profit percentage	38%	(3)	35%
Cash collections: 1995 sales	25,600	46,400	5,600
1996 sales		22,800	(4)
1997 sales			32,550
Realized gross profit on installment sales	(5)	(6)	16,050

Exercise 18—24 (Franchise accounting)

On September 1, 1996, Jensen Company entered into franchise agreements with three franchisees. The agreements required an initial fee payment of $7,000 plus four $3,000 payments due every 4 months, the first payment due December 31, 1996. The interest rate is 12%. The initial deposit is refundable until substantial performance has been completed. The following table describes each agreement:

Franchisee	Probability of Full Collection	Services Performed by Franchisor at Dec. 31, 1996	Total Cost Incurred to Dec. 31, 1996
A	Likely	Substantially	$ 7,000
B	Doubtful	25%	2,000
C	Doubtful	Substantially	10,000

For each franchisee, identify the revenue recognition method that you would recommend considering the circumstances. What amount of revenue and income would be reported in 1996 for the method selected? Assume $10,000 was received from each franchisee during the year.

Exercise 18—25 (Franchise accounting)

Starbrite Pizzas franchises its name to different people across the country. The franchise agreement requires the franchisee to make an initial payment of $12,000 and sign a $32,000 non-interest-bearing note on the agreement date. The note is to be paid in 4 annual payments of $8,000 each beginning one year from the agreement date. The initial payment is refundable until the date of opening. Interest rates are assumed to be 10%. The franchisor agrees to make market studies, find a location, train the employees, and perform a few other relatively minor services. The following transactions describe the relationship with Libby Loebig, a franchisee:

1996			
July	1	Entered into a franchise agreement.
Sep.	1	Completed a market study at a cost of $5,000.
Nov.	15	Found suitable location. Service cost $3,000.
1997			
Jan.	10	Completed training program for employees, cost $5,000.
	15	Franchise outlet opened.
July	1	Received first annual payment.

Give Starbrite Pizzas' journal entries in 1996-1997 to record these transactions, including any adjusting entries at December 31, 1996.

Exercise 18—26 (Consignment accounting)

In 1996, Rawlings Wholesalers transferred goods to a retailer on consignment. The transaction was recorded as a sale by Rawlings. The goods cost $45,000 and normally are sold at a 30% markup. In 1997, $12,000 (cost) of the merchandise was sold by the retailer at the normal markup, and the balance of the merchandise was returned to Rawlings. The retailer withheld a 10% commission from payment. Prepare the journal entry in 1997 to correct the books for 1996, and prepare the correct entries relative to the consignment sale in 1997.

*Exercise 18—27 (Installment sales accounting—real estate)

On January 1, 1996, the Krystyu Realty Company sold property carried in inventory at a cost of $85,000 for $140,000 with terms of 10% down and the balance in annual installments over a 10-year period at 12% interest. Installment payments are to be made at the end of each year.

1. What is the equal annual payment necessary to pay for this property under the stated terms? (Round to nearest dollar.)
2. Give the entries for the first year assuming the installment sales method is used.

*Relates to Appendix.

*Exercise 18—28 (Cost recovery method—real estate)

Pomona Inc. is a land development company. It has acquired 1,000 acres of choice recreational property for $1,200 per acre, and it is selling developed recreational building lots for $5,000 per acre. The improvement costs amount to $1,200 per acre. The land cost, including improvements, is carried on Pomona's books as inventory. In the first year, Pomona sold 30 one-acre lots, 10% down, the balance to be paid over 10 years in annual installments at an interest rate of 10%. Assume the lots were sold on January 1, 1996.

1. Give the entries required for 1996 and 1997 if the cost recovery method is used to recognize revenue.
2. Prove that the balance reported on the December 31, 1997, balance sheet is equal to the unrecovered cost of the land.

*Relates to Appendix

PROBLEMS

Problem 18—29 (Construction accounting)

Zamponi's Construction Company reports its income for tax purposes on a completed-contract basis and income for financial statement purposes on a percentage-of-completion basis. A record of construction activities for 1996 and 1997 follows:

		1996		1997	
Project	**Contract Price**	**Cost Incurred—1996**	**Estimated Cost to Complete**	**Cost Incurred—1997**	**Estimated Cost to Complete**
A	$1,450,000	$840,000	$560,000	$480,000	-0-
B	1,700,000	720,000	880,000	340,000	$650,000
C	850,000	160,000	480,000	431,500	58,500
D	1,000,000			280,000	520,000

General and administrative expenses for 1996 and 1997 were $60,000 for each year and are to be recorded as a period cost.

Instructions:

1. Calculate the income for 1996 and 1997 that should be reported for financial statement purposes.
2. Calculate the income for 1997 to be reported on a completed-contract basis.

Problem 18—30 (Construction accounting)

The Rushing Construction Company obtained a construction contract to build a highway and bridge over the Snake River. It was estimated at the beginning of the contract that it would take 3 years to complete the project at an expected cost of $50,000,000. The contract price was $60,000,000. The project actually took 4 years, being accepted as completed late in 1997. The following information describes the status of the job at the close of production each year:

	1994	1995	1996	1997	1998
Actual cost incurred	$12,000,000	$18,160,000	$14,840,000	$10,000,000	-0-
Estimated cost to complete	38,000,000	27,840,000	10,555,555	-0-	-0-
Collections on contract	12,000,000	13,500,000	15,000,000	15,000,000	$4,500,000
Billings on contract	13,000,000	15,500,000	17,000,000	14,500,000	-0-

Instructions:

1. What is the revenue, cost, and gross profit recognized for each of the years 1994-1998 under (a) the percentage-of-completion method and (b) the completed-contract method?
2. Give the journal entries for each year assuming that the percentage-of-completion method is used.

Problem 18—31 (Construction accounting)

The Urban Construction Company commenced doing business in January 1996. Construction activities for the year 1996 are summarized in the following table.

Project	Total Contract Price	Contract Expenditures to Dec. 31, 1996	Estimated Additional Costs to Complete Contracts	Cash Collections to Dec. 31, 1996	Billings to Dec. 31, 1996
A	$ 310,000	$187,500	$ 12,500	$155,000	$155,000
B	415,000	195,000	255,000	210,000	249,000
C	350,000	310,000	-0-	300,000	350,000
D	300,000	16,500	183,500	-0-	4,000
	$1,375,000	$709,000	$451,000	$665,000	$758,000

The company is your client. The president has asked you to compute the amounts of revenue for the year ended December 31, 1996, that would be reported under the completed-contract method and the percentage-of-completion method of accounting for long-term contracts.

The following information is available:

(a) Each contract is with a different customer.
(b) Any work remaining to be done on the contracts is expected to be completed in 1997.
(c) The company's accounts have been maintained on the completed-contract method.

Instructions:

1. Prepare a schedule computing the amount of revenue, cost, and gross profit (loss) by project for the year ended December 31, 1996, to be reported under (a) the percentage-of-completion method and (b) the completed-contract method. (Round to two decimal places on percentages.)
2. Prepare a schedule under the completed-contract method, computing the amount that would appear in the company's balance sheet at December 31, 1996, for (a) costs in excess of billings and (b) billings in excess of costs.
3. Prepare a schedule under the percentage-of-completion method that would appear in the company's balance sheet at December 31, 1996, for (a) costs and estimated earnings in excess of billings and (b) billings in excess of costs and estimated earnings.

Problem 18—32 (Construction accounting)

The Kurtz Construction Corporation contracted with the City of Port Huron to construct a dam on the Erie River at a price of $16,000,000. Kurtz expects to earn $1,520,000 on the contract. The percentage-of-completion method is to be used and the completion stage is to be determined by estimates made by the engineer. The following schedule summarizes the activities of the contract for the years 1995-1997:

Year	Cost Incurred	Estimated Cost to Complete	Engineer's Estimate of Completion	Billings on Contract	Collection on Billings
1995	$4,600,000	$9,640,000	31%	$5,000,000	$4,500,000
1996	4,500,000	5,100,000	58	6,000,000	5,400,000
1997	5,250,000	-0-	100	5,000,000	6,100,000

Instructions:

1. Prepare a schedule showing the revenue, cost, and the gross profit earned each year under the percentage-of-completion method, using the engineer's estimate as the measure of completion to be applied to revenues and costs.
2. Prepare all journal entries required to reflect the contract.
3. Prepare journal entries for 1997, assuming the completed-contract method is used.
4. How would the journal entries in (2) differ if the actual costs incurred were used to calculate cost for the period instead of the engineer's estimate?

Problem 18—33 (Construction accounting)

Jana Crebs is a contractor for the construction of large office buildings. At the beginning of 1996, three buildings were in progress. The following data describes the status of these buildings at the beginning of the year:

	Contract Price	Costs Incurred to 1/1/96	Estimated Cost to Complete as of 1/1/96
Building 1	$ 4,000,000	$2,070,000	$1,380,000
Building 2	9,000,000	6,318,000	1,782,000
Building 3	13,150,000	3,000,000	9,000,000

During 1996, the following costs were incurred:

Building 1	$930,000 (estimated cost to complete as of 12/31/96, $750,000)
Building 2	$1,800,000 (job completed)
Building 3	$7,400,000 (estimated cost to complete as of 12/31/96, $2,800,000)
Building 4	$800,000 (contract price, $2,500,000; estimated cost to complete as of 12/31/96, $1,200,000)

Instructions:

1. Compute the total revenue, costs, and gross profit in 1996. Assume that Crebs uses the cost-to-cost percentage-of-completion method. (Round to two decimal places for percentage completed.)
2. Compute the gross profit for 1996 if Crebs uses the completed-contract method.

Problem 18—34 (Construction accounting)

The Power Construction Company was the low bidder on a specialized equipment contract. The contract bid was $6,000,000 with an estimated cost to complete the project of $5,300,000. The contract period was 33 months, beginning January 1, 1995. The company uses the cost-to-cost method to estimate profits.

A record of construction activities for the years 1995-1998 follows:

Year	Actual Cost—Current Year	Progress Billings	Cash Receipts
1995	$3,400,000	$3,200,000	$3,000,000
1996	2,550,000	2,000,000	2,000,000
1997	200,000	800,000	600,000
1998	-0-	-0-	400,000

The estimated cost to complete the contract at the end of each accounting period is:

1995	$2,100,000
1996	150,000
1997	-0-

Instructions:

1. What is the revenue, cost, and gross profit recognized for each of the years 1995-1997 under the percentage-of-completion method?
2. Give the journal entries for each of the years 1995-1997 to record the information from (1).
3. Give the journal entries in 1998 to record any collections and to close out all construction accounts.

Problem 18—35 (Construction accounting)

Seattle Boatbuilders was recently awarded a $14,000,000 contract to construct a luxury liner for Cruiseliners Inc. Seattle estimates it will take 42 months to complete the contract. The company uses the cost-to-cost method to estimate profits.

The following information details the actual and estimated costs for the years 1995-1998:

Year	Actual Cost—Current Year	Estimated Cost to Complete
1995	$6,500,000	$6,800,000
1996	3,300,000	3,900,000
1997	2,400,000	1,900,000
1998	1,700,000	-0-

Instructions:

1. Compute the revenue, cost, and gross profit to be recognized for each of the years 1995-1998 under the percentage-of-completion method.
2. Give the journal entries for each of the years 1995-1998 to record the information from (1).

Problem 18—36 (Installment sales accounting)

London Corporation has been using the cash method to account for income since its first year of operation in 1996. All sales are made on credit with notes receivable given by the customers. The income statements for 1996 and 1997 included the following amounts:

	1996	1997
Revenues—collection on principal	$32,000	$50,000
Revenues—interest	3,600	5,500
Cost of goods purchased*	45,200	52,020

*Includes increase in inventory of goods on hand of $2,000 in 1996 and $8,000 in 1997.

The balances due on the notes at the end of each year were as follows:

	1996	1997
Notes receivable—1996	$62,000	$36,000
Notes receivable—1997	-0-	60,000
Unearned interest revenue—1996	7,167	5,579
Unearned interest revenue—1997	-0-	8,043

Instructions: Give the journal entries for 1996 and 1997 assuming the installment sales method was used rather than the cash method.

Problem 18—37 (Installment sales)

Bain's Furniture sells furniture and electronic items. The majority of its business is on credit, and the following information is available relating to sales transactions for 1995, 1996, and 1997.

	1995	1996	1997
Installment sales (net of interest)	$104,000	$116,000	$121,000
Gross profit percentage	38%	41%	39%
Cash collections on installment sales:			
Principal—1995	$ 57,200	$ 29,120	$ 15,000
Principal—1996		71,920	26,680
Principal—1997			76,230
Interest—1995	9,780	17,870	3,030
Interest—1996		6,610	18,142
Interest—1997			6,378

Instructions: Prepare the journal entries for the years 1995-1997 assuming Bain's uses the installment sales method for revenue recognition and records receivables net of interest.

Problem 18—38 (Consignment accounting)

Tingey Industries sells merchandise on a consignment basis to dealers. Shipping costs are chargeable to Tingey, although in some cases, the dealer pays them. The selling price of the merchandise averages 25% above cost of merchandise exclusive of freight. The dealer is paid a 10% commission on the sales price for all sales made. All dealer sales are made on a cash basis. The following consignment sales activities occurred during 1996:

Manufacturing cost of goods shipped on consignment		$250,000
Freight costs incurred:		
Paid by Tingey Industries	$15,000	
Paid by dealer	5,000	20,000
Sales price of merchandise sold by dealers		210,000
Payments made by dealers after deducting commission and freight costs		139,000

Instructions:

1. Prepare summary entries on the books of the consignor for these consignment sales transactions.
2. Prepare summary entries on the books of the dealer consignee assuming there is only one dealer involved.
3. Prepare the parts of Tingey Industries' financial statements at December 31, 1996, that relate to these consignment sales.

Problem 18—39 (Revenue recognition analysis)

The Wasatch Construction Company entered into a $4,500,000 contract in early 1996 to construct a multipurpose recreational facility for the City of Helper. Construction time extended over a 2-year period. The table on the next page describes the pattern of progress payments made by the City of Helper and costs incurred by Wasatch Construction by semiannual periods. Estimated costs of $3,600,000 were incurred as expected.

Period	Progress Payments for Period	Progress Cost for Period
(1) Jan. 1 - June 30, 1996	$ 750,000	$ 900,000
(2) July 1 - Dec. 31, 1996	1,050,000	1,200,000
(3) Jan. 1 - June 30, 1997	1,950,000	1,080,000
(4) July 1 - Dec. 31, 1997	750,000	420,000
Total	$4,500,000	$3,600,000

The Wasatch Construction Company prepares financial statements twice each year, June 30 and December 31.

Instructions:

1. Based on the foregoing data, compute the amount of revenue, costs, and gross profit for the 4 semiannual periods under each of the following methods of revenue recognition:
   (a) Percentage of completion.
   (b) Completed contract.
   (c) Installment sales (gross profit only).
   (d) Cost recovery (gross profit only).
2. Which method do you feel best measures the performance of Wasatch on this contract?

*Problem 18—40 (Cost recovery accounting—real estate)

After a 2-year search for a buyer, Choapas Inc. sold its idle plant facility to Reeve Company for $700,000 on January 1, 1993. On this date, the plant had a depreciated cost on Choapas' books of $500,000. Under the agreement, Reeve paid $200,000 cash on January 1, 1993, and signed a $500,000 interest-bearing note. The note was payable in installments of $100,000, $150,000, and $250,000 on January 1, 1994, 1995, and 1996, respectively. The note was secured by a mortgage on the property sold. Choapas appropriately accounted for the sale under the cost recovery method, since there was no reasonable basis for estimating the degree of collectibility of the note receivable. Reeve repaid the note with 3 late installment payments, which were accepted by Choapas, as follows:

Date of Payment	Principal	Interest	Total Payment
July 1, 1994	$100,000	$90,000	$190,000
Dec. 31, 1995	150,000	75,000	225,000
Feb. 1, 1997	250,000	32,500	282,500

Instructions: Prepare the journal entries required for the years 1993-1997 for the sale and subsequent collections.

*Relates to Appendix.

CHAPTER 19

Accounting for Leases

CHAPTER TOPICS

- Economic Advantages of Leasing
- Lease Classification Criteria
- Accounting for Leases—Lessee
- Accounting for Leases—Lessor
- Disclosure Requirements for Leases
- Accounting for Sale-Leaseback Transactions
- Criteria for Classifying Real Estate Leases (Appendix 19-1)
- Leveraged Leases (Appendix 19-2)

In 1993, the average American worker toiled for 26 weeks to earn the $18,100 required to purchase the average new car. Car prices have risen 69% over the last ten years, while household incomes have not kept pace. The result is fewer and fewer Americans who can afford to purchase new cars. The automakers' answer to this problem is leasing. As car prices continue to increase, more and more car buyers are turning to leasing to finance their new cars. Ford leases about 20% of its cars and light trucks. About 49% of Cadillac Seville's, with a sticker price of $43,143, are leased. Jaguar, a European-based car maker, leases approximately 70% of the cars it delivers in the United States.

Why the attraction to leasing? For consumers, leasing requires a low or no downpayment. Also, monthly payments are lower than if the vehicle had been purchased and financed. What are the advantages to the auto dealer? Leases eventually come to an end and the customer will be back, hopefully to lease again. In addition, individuals tend to lease cars that they typically could not afford to purchase, the results being the dealers move the high-margin cars off the lot with leasing. Another major advantage to the dealer is a supply of two- to three-year old used cars that can then be sold, or leased again. In January of 1994, Ford unveiled a plan to enter the used car leasing market. Other auto companies are expected to follow Ford's lead into the used car leasing market.

In this chapter, we will focus on how leases are accounted for from both the lessor's and the lessee's perspectives. We will discuss the issues associated with classifying a lease as a capital or an operating lease and the disclosure issues associated with that classification. In addition, we will discuss how businesses can have definite obligations to pay significant amounts of money in the future relating to lease obligations and yet not disclose those obligations as liabilities on the balance sheet.

A **lease** is a contract specifying the terms under which the owner of property, the **lessor,** transfers the right to use the property to a **lessee.** Leasing is widely used in our economy as a method of obtaining various kinds of assets. Individuals may lease houses, apartments, automobiles, televisions, appliances, furniture, and almost any other consumer good on the market. Business enterprises lease land, buildings, and almost any type of equipment. For example, Hartmarx Corporation in its 1992 financial statements reported leased assets including "office, manufacturing, warehouse/distribution, showroom and retail space, automobiles, computers and other equipment." Indeed, almost any asset that can be acquired through purchase can be obtained through leasing. Of the 600 companies surveyed in the annual AICPA publication, *Accounting Trends & Techniques,* 534 companies, or approximately 90%, reported some form of lease arrangement.[1]

Some leases are simple rental agreements, while others closely resemble a debt-financed purchase of property. A major issue for the accounting profession has been whether this latter type of lease should be accounted for as a rental agreement in accordance with its legal form, or as a purchase of property that reflects the economic substance of the transaction. To illustrate the issue, assume that Monroe Co. decides to acquire equipment costing $10,000. The equipment has a useful life of 5 years with no expected residual value. Monroe Co. can purchase the equipment by issuing a 5-year, 10%, $10,000 note with principal and interest to be paid in 5 equal installments of $2,368. Alternatively, Monroe Co. can lease the asset for 5 years, making 5 annual "rental" payments of $2,368. In substance, the lease is equivalent to purchasing the asset, the only difference being the legal form of the transaction. However, if the lease is accounted for as a simple rental agreement, Monroe Co. will not report the equipment as an asset nor the obligation to the lessor as a liability. Under conditions such as these, recording the transaction as a rental agreement does not reflect the underlying economic substance of acquiring and using the equipment.

As illustrated by this simple example, leasing can be used to avoid reporting a liability on the balance sheet. As discussed in Chapter 14, "off-balance-sheet financing" continues to be a perplexing problem for the accounting profession, and leasing is probably the oldest and most widely used means of keeping debt off the balance sheet. The FASB has attempted to eliminate this practice by requiring leases that meet certain criteria to be treated as **capital leases**—in effect, debt-financed purchases of property.

ECONOMIC ADVANTAGES OF LEASING

It would be unfair and incorrect to imply that the only reason companies lease property is to avoid reporting the lease obligation in the financial statements. While the accounting issue is one factor, other financial and tax considerations also play an important role in the leasing decision. While every situation is different, there are two primary advantages to the lessee of leasing over purchasing:

1. *Accounting Trends & Techniques,* 1993 (New York: American Institute of Certified Public Accountants, 1993), p. 227.

1. **No down payment.** Most debt-financed purchases of property require a portion of the purchase price to be paid immediately by the borrower. This provides added protection to the lender in the event of default and repossession. Lease agreements, in contrast, frequently are structured so that 100% of the value of the property is financed through the lease. This aspect of leasing makes it an attractive alternative to a company that does not have sufficient cash for a down payment or wishes to use available capital for other operating or investing purposes.
2. **Avoids risks of ownership.** There are many risks accompanying the ownership of property. They include casualty loss, obsolescence, changing economic conditions, and physical deterioration. The lessee may terminate a lease, although usually with a certain penalty, and thus avoid assuming the risk of these events. This flexibility is especially important in businesses where innovation and technological change make the future usefulness of particular equipment or facilities highly uncertain. A prime example of this condition in recent years has been in high-tech industries with rapid change in areas such as computer technology, robotics, and telecommunications.

The lessor also may find benefits to leasing its property rather than selling it. Advantages of the lease to the lessor include the following:

1. **Increased sales.** For the reasons suggested in the preceding paragraphs, customers may be unwilling or unable to purchase property. By offering potential customers the option of leasing its products, a manufacturer or dealer may significantly increase its sales volume.
2. **Ongoing business relationship with lessee.** When property is sold, the purchaser frequently has no more dealings with the seller of the property. In leasing situations, however, the lessor and lessee maintain contact over a period of time, and long-term business relationships often can be established through leasing.
3. **Residual value retained.** In many lease arrangements, title to the leased property never passes to the lessee. The lessor benefits from economic conditions that may result in a significant residual value at the end of the lease term. The lessor may lease the asset to another lessee or sell the property and realize an immediate gain. Many lessors have realized significant profits from unexpected increases in residual values.

NATURE OF LEASES

Leases vary widely in their contractual provisions. Reasons for this variability include cancellation provisions and penalties, lease term, bargain renewal and purchase options, economic life of assets, residual asset values, minimum lease payments, interest rates implicit in the lease agreement, and the degree of risk assumed by the lessee, including payments of certain costs such as maintenance, insurance, and taxes. These and other relevant facts must be considered in determining the appropriate accounting treatment of a lease.

The many variables affecting lease capitalization have been given precise definitions that must be understood in order to account for the various types of leases found in practice. Each of these variables is defined and briefly discussed below.

Cancellation Provisions

Some leases are **noncancellable,** meaning that these lease contracts are cancellable only upon the outcome of some remote contingency or that the cancellation provisions and penalties of these leases are so costly to the lessee that, in all likelihood, cancellation will not occur. Only noncancellable leases are subject to capitalization.

Lease Term

An important variable in lease agreements is the **lease term;** that is, the time period from the beginning to the end of the lease. The **beginning of the lease term** occurs when the leased property is transferred to the lessee. The **end of the lease term** is the end of the fixed noncancellable period of the lease plus all periods, if any, covered by **bargain renewal options,** or other provisions that, at the inception of the lease strongly indicate that the lease will be renewed.[2] If a bargain purchase option, as defined in the next section, is included in the lease contract, the lease term includes any renewal periods preceding the date of the bargain purchase option. In no case does the lease term extend beyond the date of a bargain purchase option.

Bargain Purchase Option

Leases often include a provision giving the lessee the right to purchase leased property at some future date. A definite purchase or option price may be specified, although in some cases the price is expressed as the fair market value at the date the option is exercised. If the specified option price is expected to be considerably less than the fair market value at the date the purchase option may be exercised, a **bargain purchase option** is indicated.

Residual Value

The market value of the leased property at the end of the lease term is referred to as its **residual value.** In some leases, the lease term extends over the entire **economic life of the asset,** or the period in which the asset continues to be productive, and there is little, if any, residual value. In other leases, the lease term is shorter, and a residual value does exist. If the lessee can purchase the asset at the end of the lease term at a materially reduced price from its residual value, a bargain purchase option is present, and it can be assumed that the lessee would exercise the option and purchase the asset.

Some lease contracts require the lessee, or a designated third party, to guarantee a minimum residual value. If the market value at the end of the lease term falls below the **guaranteed residual value,** the lessee or third party must pay the difference. This provision protects the lessor from loss due to unexpected declines in the market value of the asset. For example, assume a piece of equipment is expected to have a $25,000 residual value at the end of the lease term, and the lessee guarantees that amount. However, at the end of the lease term, the residual value is only $15,000. The lessee is obligated to pay the $10,000 difference to the lessor, because the lessor is, in effect, guaranteed the full amount of the residual value that was estimated at the beginning of the lease. The lessee or the third party may buy the property for the $25,000 guaranteed amount, but the terms do not require the purchase. As will be demonstrated later in the chapter, a guarantee of residual value by a third party requires lessees to account for leases differently than would be true if the lessee were making the guarantee.

If there is no bargain purchase option or guarantee of the residual value, the lessor reacquires the property and may offer to renew the lease, lease the asset to another lessee, or sell the property. The actual amount of the residual value is unknown until the end of the lease term; however, it must be estimated at the inception of the lease. The residual value under these circumstances is referred to as the **unguaranteed residual value.**

Minimum Lease Payments

The rental payments required over the lease term plus any amount to be paid for the residual value either through a bargain purchase option or a guarantee of the residual value are referred to as the **minimum lease payments.** If all of these payments are made by the

2. In some lease situations, such as sale-lease backs, the lessee lends the lessor money to finance the lease or acts as a guarantor for third-party financing. As long as these financial arrangements are in place, the lease-term extends through ordinary renewal option periods. Thus, the lease term for a 10-year lease, with a 10-year ordinary renewal and a 20-year loan on the leased property from the lessee to the lessor, would be 20 years. *Statement of Financial Accounting Standards No. 98,* "Accounting for Leases: . . . Definition of Lease Term" (Norwalk: Financial Accounting Standards Board, 1988), par. 22a.

lessee, the minimum lease payments are the same for the lessee and the lessor. However, if a third party guarantees the residual value, the lessee would not include the guarantee as part of the minimum lease payments, but the lessor would.

Rental payments sometimes include charges for such items as insurance, maintenance, and taxes incurred for the leased property. These are referred to as **executory costs,** and they are not included as part of the minimum lease payments. If the lessor includes a charge for profit on these costs, the profit also is considered an executory cost.

To illustrate the computation of minimum lease payments, assume that Dorney Leasing Co. leases road equipment for 3 years at $3,000 per month. Included in the rental payment is $500 per month for executory costs to insure and maintain the equipment. At the end of the 3-year period, Dorney is guaranteed a residual value of $10,000 by the lessee.

Minimum lease payments:	
Rental payments exclusive of executory costs ($2,500 × 36)	$ 90,000
Guaranteed residual value	10,000
Total minimum lease payments	$100,000

Because the minimum lease payments are to be made in future periods, the present value of these payments is needed to account for capitalized leases. Two different discount rates must be considered in computing the present value of minimum lease payments: the lessee's incremental borrowing rate and the implicit interest rate. The **incremental borrowing rate** is the rate at which the lessee could borrow the amount of money necessary to purchase the leased asset, taking into consideration the lessee's financial situation and the current conditions in the marketplace. The **implicit interest rate** is the rate that would discount the rental payments and the residual value (either guaranteed or unguaranteed) to the fair market value of the asset at the inception of the lease. The lessor uses the implicit interest rate in determining the present value of the minimum lease payments. The lessee, however, uses either the implicit rate or the incremental borrowing rate, whichever is lower. If the lessee cannot compute the implicit rate, the incremental borrowing rate is used.

To illustrate using the Dorney Leasing Co. example, assume that the $3,000 rental payments to Dorney are made at the beginning of each month, the implicit interest rate in the lease contract is 12% per year, and the lessee's incremental borrowing rate is 14%. Assuming the lessee knows the implicit rate, both the lessor and lessee would discount the minimum lease payments using the 12% rate. The present value of the $100,000 minimum lease payments would be:

Present value of 36 payments of $2,500 ($3,000 less executory costs of $500) at 1% interest (12% annual interest divided by 12 months per year) paid at the beginning of each month:	
$PVn = R(PVAF_{\overline{n}\rceil i})$	
PVn = $2,500 (29.4086* + 1) =	$76,022
Present value of $10,000 guaranteed residual value at the end of 3 years at 12% annual interest:	
$PV = A(PVF_{\overline{n}\rceil i})$	
PV = $10,000 (0.7118**) =	7,118
Present value of minimum least payments	$83,140

*From Table IV, page 270
**From Table II, page 268

The present value of $83,140 would be the selling price or fair market value of the asset at the inception of the lease. The use of present value formulas and tables in discounting minimum lease payments is illustrated later in the chapter.

LEASE CLASSIFICATION CRITERIA

Leasing was one of the topics on the original agenda of the FASB, and in 1976 the Board issued Statement No. 13, "Accounting for Leases." The objective of the FASB in issuing Statement No. 13 was to reflect the economic reality of leasing by requiring that the majority of long-term leases be accounted for as capital acquisitions by the lessee and sales by the lessor. To accomplish this objective, the FASB identified criteria to determine whether a lease is merely a rental contract (an operating lease) or is, in substance, a purchase of property (a capital lease). In considering this issue, the FASB was concerned with the fact that under the APB pronouncements, leases were often reported differently by the lessee and the lessor. The Board felt that in most cases, there should be symmetrical treatment between the two parties; i.e., if the lessee treated the agreement as a purchase of property, the lessor should treat it as a sale of property. For this reason, the Board specified four criteria that apply to both the lessee and the lessor, any one of which would identify the lease agreement as a purchase and sale of property or, in other words, a capital lease. Two additional criteria were specified for lessors, both of which must be met before the lease can be treated as a sale by the lessor. The lease classification criteria and their applicability to lessees and lessors are summarized in Exhibit 19—1.

Exhibit 19—1
Lease Classification Criteria

General criteria applicable to both the lessee and the lessor:

1. The lease transfers ownership of the property to the lessee by the end of the lease term.
2. The lease contains a bargain purchase option.
3. The lease term is equal to 75% or more of the estimated economic life of the leased property.
4. The present value of the minimum lease payments, excluding that portion representing executory costs, equals or exceeds 90% of the fair market value of the property.

Additional criteria applicable to lessors:

5. Collectibility of the minimum lease payments is reasonably predictable.
6. No important uncertainties surround the amount of unreimbursable costs yet to be incurred by the lessor.

Lessee: Capital lease if any one of criteria 1, 2, 3, or 4 is met.
Lessor: Capital lease if any one of criteria 1, 2, 3, or 4 is met *and* both 5 and 6 are met.

Classification Criteria—Lessee and Lessor

The four general criteria that apply to all leases for both the lessee and lessor relate to transfer of ownership, bargain purchase options, economic life, and fair market value. The **transfer of ownership** criterion is met if the lease agreement includes a clause that transfers full ownership of the property to the lessee by the end of the lease term. Of all the classification criteria, transfer of ownership is the most objective and, therefore, the easiest to apply.

The second general criterion is met if the lease contains a **bargain purchase option** that makes it reasonably assured that the property will be purchased by the lessee at some future date. This criterion is more difficult to apply than the first criterion, because the future fair market value of the leased property must be estimated at the inception of the lease and compared with the purchase option price to determine if a bargain purchase is indeed indicated.

The third criterion relates to the **economic life** of the asset. This criterion is met if the lease term is equal to 75% or more of the estimated economic life of the leased property. As defined earlier, the lease term includes renewal periods if renewal seems assured. This criterion is difficult to apply objectively because of the uncertainty of an asset's economic life. Also, it can be easily manipulated to achieve whatever result is desired. An exception to the economic life criterion was made for certain used property. The FASB recognized that used property may be leased near the end of the property's economic life, and this criterion would result in classifying all such leases as capital leases. The Board provided that this criterion would not be applicable to leases occurring in the last 25% of the leased property's economic life. In addition, this criterion cannot apply to land leases, since land has an unlimited life.

The fourth general criterion focuses on the **fair market value** of the property in relation to the provisions of the lease. This criterion is met if, at the beginning of the lease term, the present value of the minimum lease payments equals or exceeds 90% of the fair market value of the leased asset. This criterion was intended to be a key factor in determining the existence of a capital lease. If the lessee is obligated to pay, in present-value terms, almost all of the fair market value of the leased property, the lease is in substance a purchase of the property. But the application of this criterion also has been difficult and subject to manipulation by lessees and lessors. The key variable in this criterion is the discounted minimum lease payments.

Since larger minimum lease payments cause the fair market value criterion to be met, the use of third parties to guarantee residual values has led to a lack of consistency between lessees and lessors in many lease arrangements. Many lessors want to report the lease as a sale and thus recognize income at the inception of the lease. However, lessees generally want to report the lease as a rental contract and gain the advantage of off-balance-sheet financing. Since third-party guarantees are considered minimum lease payments to the lessor but not to the lessee, a careful structuring of the lease terms can allow both parties to achieve their goals.

This variable, more than any other, has been used in lease arrangements to avoid the intent of the FASB to achieve increased consistency in reporting. In fact, a new industry of third-party financing has arisen to take advantage of this difference in defining minimum lease payments between the lessee and the lessor.

The rate used to discount the future minimum lease payments is critical in determining whether the fair market value criterion is met. The lower the discount rate used, the higher the present value of the minimum lease payments and the greater the likelihood that the fair market value criterion of 90% will be met. As explained earlier in the chapter, the FASB specified that the lessor should use the implicit interest rate of the lease agreement. The lessee also uses the lessor's implicit interest rate if it is known and if it is lower than the lessee's incremental borrowing rate. If the lessee cannot determine the lessor's implicit interest rate, the lessee must use its incremental borrowing rate. The use of different discount rates between lessees and lessors is another cause of inconsistent accounting treatment between lessees and lessors.

Because incremental borrowing rates are often higher than the implicit interest rates, and because lessees generally do not want to capitalize leases, many lessees use the borrowing rate and do not attempt to estimate the implicit rate. If there is no residual value, the lessee can determine the implicit rate in most cases, because the market value of the leased asset usually is known. If a residual value exists, however, the lessee must obtain that value from the lessor.

Additional Classification Criteria—Lessor

In addition to meeting one of the four general criteria, a lease must meet two additional criteria in order to be classified by the lessor as a capital lease.[3] As indicated in Exhibit 19—1, the first of the two lessor-specific criteria relates to **collectibility.** Collection of the minimum lease payments, either from the lessee or a third-party guarantor, must be reasonably predictable.

The second additional criterion requires **substantial completion** of performance by the lessor. This means that any unreimbursable costs yet to be incurred by the lessor under the terms of the lease are known or can be reasonably estimated. This criterion is to be applied at the inception of the lease or at the date the leased asset is acquired by the lessor if acquisition occurs after the inception date. If the leased asset is constructed by the lessor, the criterion is applied at the later of the inception date or the date construction is completed.

Application of General Lease Classification Criteria

To illustrate the application of the classification criteria specified in FASB Statement No. 13, four different leasing situations are presented in Exhibit 19—2. A summary analysis of each lease also is presented in the exhibit. Following is a brief explanation of the analysis for each of the four leases.

Exhibit 19—2 Application of FASB Statement No. 13 Criteria to Lease Situations

Lease Provisions	Lease #1	Lease #2	Lease #3	Lease #4
Cancellable	No	No	No	Yes
Title passes to lessee	No	Yes	No	Yes
Bargain purchase option	No	No	Yes	No
Lease term	10 years	10 years	8 years	10 years
Economic life of asset	14 years	15 years	13 years	12 years
Present value of minimum lease payments as a percentage of fair market value—incremental borrowing rate	80%	79%	95%	76%
Present value of minimum lease payments as a percentage of fair market value—implicit interest rate	92%	91%	92%	82%
Lessee knows implicit interest rate	No	No	Yes	Yes
Unguaranteed residual value	Yes	No	No	No
Residual value guaranteed by third party	No	Yes	No	No
Present value of minimum lease payments exclusive of third-party guaranteed residual value as a percentage of fair market value—implicit interest rate	92%	80%	92%	82%
Rental payments collectible and lessor costs certain	Yes	Yes	No	Yes
Analysis of Leases:				
Lessee				
Treat as capital lease	No	Yes	Yes	No
Criteria met	None	1	2 and 4	must be non-cancellable
Use incremental borrowing rate	NA	Yes	No	
Amortization period	NA	15 years	13 years	
Lessor				
Treat as capital lease	Yes	Yes	No	No
First four criteria met	4	1 and 4	2 and 4	must be non-cancellable
Lessor criteria met	Yes	Yes	No	

Lease #1 will be treated as an operating lease by the lessee but as a capital lease by the lessor. The lease does not meet any of the first three general criteria. Since the lessee

3. *Statement of Financial Accounting Standards No. 13,* par. 8. If the lease involves real estate, these criteria are replaced by a criterion that requires a transfer of title at the end of the lease term. *Statement of Financial Accounting Standards No. 98,* par. 22c.

does not know the implicit interest rate of the lessor, the incremental borrowing rate is used to test for criterion 4. The present value of the minimum lease payments using the incremental borrowing rate is less than 90% of the fair market value of the property; thus criterion 4 is not met for the lessee. Because the lessor uses the implicit interest rate, criterion 4 is met. The two additional criteria applicable to the lessor are also met.

Lease #2 will be treated as a capital lease by both the lessee and the lessor, because title passes to the lessee at the end of the lease term (criterion 1) and the additional lessor criteria are both met. Because there is a third-party guaranteed residual value, the minimum lease payments are higher for the lessor than the lessee, and criterion 4 is met by the lessor but not by the lessee. Thus, if title had not passed, Lease #2 would be treated as an operating lease by the lessee but a capital lease by the lessor.

Lease #3 will be treated as a capital lease by the lessee, but as an operating lease by the lessor. The bargain purchase option meets criterion 2, and since the lessee knows the implicit interest rate, both the lessee and lessor computations meet criterion 4. However, since there is some uncertainty as to the collectibility of the rental payments and the amount of lessor costs to be incurred, the lease fails to meet the additional criteria applicable to the lessor.

Lease #4 will be treated as an operating lease by both the lessee and the lessor. The lease is a cancellable lease, and even though title passes to the lessee at the end of the lease, it would be classified as a rental agreement.

ACCOUNTING FOR LEASES—LESSEE

All leases as viewed by the lessee may be divided into two types: **operating leases** and **capital leases.** If a lease meets any one of the four classification criteria discussed previously, it is treated as a capital lease. Otherwise, it is accounted for as an operating lease.

Accounting for operating leases involves the recognition of rent expense over the term of the lease. The leased property is not reported as an asset on the lessee's balance sheet nor is a liability recognized for the obligation to make future payments for use of the property. Information concerning the lease is limited to disclosure in notes to the financial statements. Accounting for a capital lease essentially requires the lessee to report on the balance sheet the present value of the future lease payments, both as an asset and a liability. The asset is amortized as though it had been purchased by the lessee. The liability is accounted for in the same manner as would be a mortgage on the property. The difference in the impact of these two treatments on the financial statements often can be significant, as noted in the boxed item on page 819.

Accounting for Operating Leases—Lessee

Operating leases are considered to be simple rental agreements with debits being made to an expense account as the payments are made. For example, assume the lease terms for manufacturing equipment were $40,000 a year on a year-to-year basis. The entry to record the payment for a year's rent would be:

Rent Expense	40,000	
Cash		40,000

Rent payments frequently are made in advance. If the lease period does not coincide with the lessee's fiscal year, or if the lessee prepares interim reports, a prepaid rent account would be required to record the unexpired portion of rent at the end of the accounting period involved. The prepaid rent account should be adjusted at the end of each period.

Operating Leases With Varying Rental Payments. Some operating leases specify rental terms that provide for varying rental payments over the lease term. Most commonly, these types of agreements call for lower initial payments and scheduled rent increases later in the life of the lease. They may even provide an inducement to prospective lessees in the form of a "rent holiday" (free rent). In some cases, however, the lease may provide for higher initial rentals. FASB Statement No. 13 requires that when rental payments vary over the lease term, rental expense be recognized on a straight-line basis "unless another systematic and rational basis is more representative of the time pattern in which use benefit is derived from the leased property, in which case that basis shall be used."[4]

When recording rent expense under these agreements, differences between the actual payments and the debit to expense would be reported as Rent Payable or Prepaid Rent, depending on whether the payments were accelerating or declining. For example, assume the terms of the lease for an aircraft by International Airlines provide for payments of $150,000 a year for the first 2 years of the lease and $250,000 for the next 3 years. The total lease payments for the 5 years would be $1,050,000, or $210,000 a year on a straight-line basis. The required entries in the first 2 years would be:

Rent Expense	210,000	
Cash		150,000
Rent Payable		60,000

The entries for each of the last 3 years would be:

Rent Expense	210,000	
Rent Payable	40,000	
Cash		250,000

The portion of Rent Payable due in the subsequent year would be classified as a current liability.

Accounting for Capital Leases—Lessee

are considered to be more like a purchase of property than a rental. Consequently, accounting for capital leases by lessees requires entries similar to those required for the purchase of an asset with long-term credit terms. The amount to be recorded as an asset and as a liability is the present value of the future minimum lease payments as previously defined. The discount rates used by lessees to record capital leases are the same as those used to apply the classification criteria previously discussed, i.e., the lower of the implicit interest rate (if known) and the incremental borrowing rate. The minimum lease payments consist of the total rental payments, bargain purchase options, and lessee-guaranteed residual values.

An important exception to the use of the present value of future minimum lease payments as a basis for recording a capital lease was included by the FASB in Statement No. 13 as follows:

However, if the amount so determined exceeds the fair value of the leased property at the inception of the lease, the amount recorded as the asset and obligation shall be the fair value.[5]

This means that if the leased asset has a determinable sales price, the present value of the future minimum lease payments should be compared with that price. If the sales price is lower, it should be used as the capitalized value of the lease, and an implicit interest rate would have to be computed using the sales price as the capitalized value of the asset.

4. *Ibid.*, par. 15.
5. *Ibid.*, par. 10.

Illustrative Entries for Capital Leases. Assume that Marshall Corporation leases equipment from Universal Leasing Company with the following terms:

Lease period: 5 years, beginning January 1, 1996. Noncancellable.
Rental amount: $65,000 per year payable annually in advance; includes $5,000 to cover executory costs.
Estimated economic life of equipment: 5 years.
Expected residual value of equipment at end of lease period: None.

Because the rental payments are payable in advance, the formula to find the present value of the lease is the annuity-due formula described in Chapter 7. Assuming the Marshall Corporation's incremental borrowing rate and the implicit interest rate on the lease are both 10%, the present value for the lease would be $250,194 computed as follows:[6]

$$PVn = R(PVAF_{\overline{n}|i})$$
$$PVn = \$60{,}000(\text{Table VI}_{\overline{5}|10\%})$$
$$PVn = \$60{,}000(4.1699)$$
$$PVn = \$250{,}194$$

The journal entries to record the lease at the beginning of the lease term would be:

1996				
Jan.	1	Leased Equipment	250,194	
		Obligations Under Capital Leases		250,194[7]
		To record the lease.		
	1	Lease Expense	5,000	
		Obligations Under Capital Leases	60,000	
		Cash		65,000
		To record the first lease payment.		

The asset value is amortized in accordance with the lessee's normal method of depreciation for owned assets. The amortization period to be used depends on which of the criteria is used to qualify the lease as a capital lease. If the lease qualifies under either of the first two criteria, ownership transfer or bargain purchase option, the economic life of the asset should be used. If the lease qualifies under either of the last two criteria, economic life or investment recovery, the lease term should be used for amortization purposes. If the lease qualifies under a combination of one of the first two criteria and one of the last two criteria, the economic life of the asset should be used for amortization purposes.

In the preceding example, the lease qualifies under the third criterion and presumably the fourth, since the lessor would not lease the asset over its entire economic life if the present value of the lease payments were less than the fair market value of the asset at the inception of the lease. The liability should be reduced each period to produce a constant rate of interest expense on the remaining balance of the obligation. The lessee's incremental borrowing rate, or the lessor's implicit interest rate if lower, is the constant interest rate for the lessee under the provisions of FASB Statement No. 13. Exhibit 19—3 shows how the $60,000 payments (excluding executory costs) would be allocated between payment on the obligation and interest expense. To simplify the schedule, it is assumed that all lease payments after the first payment are made on December 31 of each year. If the payments were made in January, an accrual of interest at December 31 would be required.

6. All computations of present value in this chapter will be rounded to the nearest dollar. This will require some adjustment at times to the final figures in the tables to balance the amounts.

7. It also is possible to record the liability at the gross amount of the payments ($300,000) and offset it with a discount account—Discount on Lease Contract. The net method is more common in accounting for leases by the lessee and will be used in this chapter.

Exhibit 19—3
Schedule of Lease Payments [Five-Year Lease, $60,000 Annual Payments (Net of Executory Costs), 10% Interest]

		Lease Payment			
Date	**Description**	**Amount**	**Interest Expense***	**Principal**	**Lease Obligation**
1-1-96	Initial balance				$250,194
1-1-96	Payment	$ 60,000		$60,000	190,194
12-31-96	Payment	60,000	$19,019	40,981	149,213
12-31-97	Payment	60,000	14,921	45,079	104,134
12-31-98	Payment	60,000	10,413	49,587	54,547
12-31-99	Payment	60,000	5,453	54,547	-0-
		$300,000	$49,806	$250,194	

*Preceding lease obligation × 10%.

If the normal company depreciation policy for this type of equipment is straight-line, the required entry at December 31, 1996, for amortization of the leased asset would be:

1996			
Dec. 31	Amortization Expense on Leased Equipment	50,039	
	Accumulated Amortization on Leased Equipment		50,039

Computation:
$250,194 ÷ 5 = $50,039

Similar entries would be made for each of the remaining 4 years. Although the credit could be made directly to the asset account, the use of a contra asset account provides the necessary disclosure information about the original lease value and accumulated amortization to date.

In addition to the entry recording amortization, another entry is required at December 31, 1996, to record the second lease payment, including a prepayment of 1997's executory costs. As indicated in Exhibit 19—3, the interest expense for 1996 would be computed by multiplying the incremental borrowing rate of 10% by the initial present value of the obligation less the immediate $60,000 first payment, or ($250,194 – $60,000) × .10 = $19,019.

1996			
Dec. 31	Prepaid Executory Costs	5,000	
	Obligations Under Capital Leases	40,981	
	Interest Expense	19,019	
	Cash		65,000

Because of the assumption that all lease payments after the first payment are made on December 31, the portion of each payment that represents executory costs must be recorded as a prepayment and charged to lease expense in the following year.

Based on the preceding journal entries and using information contained in Exhibit 19—3, the December 31, 1996, balance sheet of Marshall Corporation would include information concerning the leased equipment and related obligation as illustrated below.

Marshall Corporation
Balance Sheet (Partial)
December 31, 1996

Assets		**Liabilities**	
Current assets:		Current liabilities:	
Prepaid executory costs—leased equipment	$ 5,000	Obligations under capital leases, current portion	$ 45,079
Land, buildings, and equipment:		Noncurrent liabilities:	
Leased equipment	$250,194	Obligations under capital leases, exclusive of $45,079 included in current liabilities	$104,134
Less accumulated amortization	50,039		
Net value	$200,155		

Note that the principal portion of the payment due December 31, 1997, is reported as a current liability on the December 31, 1996, balance sheet.[8]

The income statement would include the amortization on leased property of $50,039, interest expense of $19,019, and executory costs of $5,000 as expenses for the period. The total expense of $74,058 exceeds the $65,000 rental payment made in the first year. As the amount of interest expense declines each period, the total expense will be reduced and, for the last 2 years, will be less than the $65,000 payments (Exhibit 19—4). The total amount debited to expense over the life of the lease will, of course, be the same regardless of whether the lease is accounted for as an operating lease or as a capital lease. If a declining-balance method of amortization is used, the difference in the early years between the expense and the payment would be even larger. In addition to the financial statement disclosure, a note to the financial statements would be necessary to explain the terms of the lease and future rental payments in more detail.

Exhibit 19—4
Schedule of Expenses Recognized—Capital and Operating Leases Compared

	Expenses Recognized—Capital Lease				Expenses Recognized—Operating Lease	
Year	**Interest**	**Executory Costs**	**Amortization**	**Total**		**Difference**
1996	$19,019	$ 5,000	$ 50,039	$ 74,058	$ 65,000	$ 9,058
1997	14,921	5,000	50,039	69,960	65,000	4,960
1998	10,413	5,000	50,039	65,452	65,000	452
1999	5,453	5,000	50,039	60,492	65,000	(4,508)
2000	-0-	5,000	50,038	55,038	65,000	(9,962)
	$49,806	$25,000	$250,194	$325,000	$325,000	$ -0-

If in this example, the fair market value of the leased asset had been less than $250,194, the exception discussed previously would be applied, and the lower fair market value would be used for the capitalized value of the lease. For example, assume the fair market value, or sales price, of the leased asset is $242,250. By using the present-value tables and the method illustrated in Chapter 7, the implicit interest rate of the lease can be computed as being approximately 12%. A table similar to Exhibit 19—3 could then be constructed using $242,250 as the initial balance and 12% as the interest rate. For complex lease situations involving something other than equal annual lease payments, computation of the implicit rate of interest must be done from the present-value formulas themselves. This computation is facilitated by use of a computer.

Accounting for Lease With Bargain Purchase Option. Frequently, the lessee is given the option of purchasing the property at some future date at a bargain price. As discussed previously, the present value of the bargain purchase option is part of the minimum lease payments and should be included in the capitalized value of the lease. Assume in the preceding example that there was a bargain purchase option of $75,000 exercisable after 5 years, and the economic life of the equipment was expected to be 10 years. The other lease terms remain the same. The present value of the minimum lease payments would be increased by the present value of the bargain purchase amount of $75,000 or $46,568 computed as follows:

8. There have been some theoretical arguments advanced against this method of allocating lease obligations between current and noncurrent liabilities. See Robert J. Swierenga, "When Current Is Noncurrent and Vice Versa," *Accounting Review* (January 1984), pp. 123-130. Professor Swierenga identifies two methods of making the allocation: the "change in present value" (CPV) approach that is used in the example, and the "present value of the next year's payment" (PVNYP) approach that allocates a larger portion of the liability to the current category. A later study shows that the CPV method is followed almost universally in practice. A. W. Richardson, "The Measurement of the Current Portion of Long-Term Lease Obligations—Some Evidence From Practice," *Accounting Review* (October 1985), pp. 744-752. While there is theoretical support for both positions, this text uses the CPV method in chapter examples and problem materials.

$PV = A (PVF_{\overline{n}|i})$
$PV = \$75,000 (\text{Table II}_{\overline{5}|10\%})$
$PV = \$75,000 (0.6209)$
$PV = \$46,568$

The total present value of the lease is $296,762 ($250,194 + $46,568). This amount will be used to record the initial asset and liability. The asset balance of $296,762 will be amortized over the asset life of 10 years because of the existence of the bargain purchase option; this makes the transaction, in reality, a sale. The liability balance will be reduced as shown in Exhibit 19—5.

Exhibit 19—5
Schedule of Lease Payments [Five-Year Lease With Bargain Purchase Option of $75,000 After Five Years, $60,000 Annual Payments (Net of Executory Costs), 10% Interest]

		Lease Payment			
Date	**Description**	**Amount**	**Interest Expense**	**Principal**	**Lease Obligation**
1-1-96	Initial balance				$296,762
1-1-96	Payment	$ 60,000		$ 60,000	236,762
12-31-96	Payment	60,000	$23,676	36,324	200,438
12-31-97	Payment	60,000	20,044	39,956	160,482
12-31-98	Payment	60,000	16,048	43,952	116,530
12-31-99	Payment	60,000	11,653	48,347	68,183
12-31-00	Payment	75,000	6,817	68,183	-0-
		$375,000	$78,238	$296,762	

At the date of exercising the option, the net balance in the asset account Leased Equipment and its related accumulated amortization account would be transferred to the regular equipment account. The entries at the exercise of the option would be:

2000				
Dec.	31	Obligations Under Capital Leases	68,183	
		Interest Expense	6,817	
		Cash		75,000
		To record exercise of bargain purchase option.		
		Equipment	148,381	
		Accumulated Amortization on Leased Equipment	148,381	
		Leased Equipment		296,762
		To transfer remaining balance in leased asset account to equipment account.		

Computation:
Accumulated amortization: One-half amortized after 5 years of a 10-year life: $296,762 ÷ 2 = $148,381

If the equipment is not purchased and the lease is permitted to lapse, a loss equal to the difference between the equipment's book value and the amount of the bargain purchase option ($148,381 – $75,000 = $73,381) would have to be recognized by the following entry:

2000				
Dec.	31	Loss From Failure to Exercise Bargain Purchase Option	73,381	
		Obligations Under Capital Leases	68,183	
		Interest Expense	6,817	
		Accumulated Amortization on Leased Equipment	148,381	
		Leased Equipment		296,762

Accounting for Lease With Lessee-Guaranteed Residual Value. If the lease terms require the lessee to guarantee a residual value, the lessee treats the guarantee similar to a bargain purchase option and includes the present value of the guarantee as part of the capitalized value of the lease. At the expiration of the lease term, the amount of the guarantee will be reported as a liability under the lease. If the lessee is required to pay the guaranteed amount, the liability will be reduced accordingly. If only part of the guaranteed amount is paid, the difference can be reflected as an adjustment to the current lease expense.

Accounting for Purchase of Asset During Lease Term. When a lease does not provide for a transfer of ownership or a purchase option, it is still possible that a lessee may purchase leased property during the term of the lease. Usually the purchase price will differ from the recorded lease obligation at the purchase date. The FASB issued Interpretation No. 26 to cover this situation. The Board decided that no gain or loss should be recorded on the purchase, but the difference between the purchase price and the obligation still on the books should be charged or credited to the acquired asset's carrying value.[9]

To illustrate, assume that on December 31, 1998, rather than making the lease payment due on that date, the lessee purchased the leased property described on page 814 for $120,000. At that date, the remaining liability recorded on the lessee's books is $114,547 (lease obligation of $104,134 + interest payable of $10,413), and the net book value of the recorded leased asset is $100,077, the original capitalized value of $250,194 less $150,117 amortization ($50,039 × 3). The entry to record the purchase on the lessee's books would be:

1998				
Dec.	31	Interest Expense	10,413	
		Obligations Under Capital Leases	104,134	
		Equipment	105,530	
		Accumulated Amortization on Leased Equipment	150,117	
		Leased Equipment		250,194
		Cash		120,000

The purchased equipment is capitalized at $105,530, which is the book value of the leased asset, $100,077, plus $5,453, the excess of the purchase price over the carrying value of the lease obligation ($120,000 – $114,547).

Treatment of Leases on Lessee's Statement of Cash Flows

Operating leases present no special problems to the lessee in preparing a statement of cash flows. The lease payments reduce net income and thus require no adjustment to net income under the indirect method except for any accrued or prepaid rent expense. The cash payments would be reported as operating expense outlays under the direct method.

Adjustments for capital leases by the lessee, however, are more complex. The amortization of leased assets would be treated the same as depreciation, i.e., added to net income under the indirect method and ignored under the direct method. The portion of the cash payment allocated to interest expense would require no adjustment under the indirect method and would be reported as part of the cash payment for interest expense under the direct method. The portion of the cash payment allocated to the lease liability would be reported as a financing outflow under either method. Leases would not be reported as an investment on the statement of cash flows, because the entire arrangement is considered a financing event. If the asset is purchased rather than leased, any down payment made at the purchase date would be reported as an investment in assets with the balance being financed disclosed in the notes to the financial statements. Later payments would be reported as financing cash outflows in the same way lease payments are reported.

9. *FASB Interpretation No. 26,* "Accounting for Purchase of a Leased Asset by the Lessee During the Term of the Lease" (Stamford: Financial Accounting Standards Board, 1978), par. 5.

Avoiding a Liability

The effect on the financial statements of operating versus capital leases can be significant. One study estimated that if McDonalds were required to capitalize all noncancellable leases that it currently classifies as operating, the company's debt-to-equity ratio would increase 30%. Examining firms in seven different industries, the study concluded that for those firms who use leases extensively, the effect on their return on assets and debt-to-equity ratios would be even more significant. For those firms, the average decrease in the return on total assets was 34% while the debt-to-equity ratio increased by 191%.

With the issuance of FASB Statement No. 13, it was thought that firms would reflect the economic reality of their lease agreements. However, this standard has been relatively ineffective in meeting its objective. Instead of complying with the spirit of the standard, firms seem to have gone to great lengths to structure leases that do not meet the criteria for balance sheet disclosure.

Questions:

1. If a major objective of financial statement information is to provide useful information to investors and creditors, are those groups currently receiving financial statements that contain relevant and reliable information regarding leased assets?
2. Do you think the FASB has achieved its objective of requiring leases that are, in effect, purchases to be disclosed on the balance sheet?
3. It often seems that whenever the FASB provides detailed rules for applying a specific standard, companies spend a great deal of time looking for loopholes in those rules. What can the FASB do to get companies to comply with the intent of a standard?
4. If the FASB were to ask you for advice in revising its standard on leasing, what would your advice be?

Source: Imhoff, Lipe, and Wright, "Operating Leases: Impact of Constructive Capitalization," *Accounting Horizons,* March 1991, pp. 51-63.

ACCOUNTING FOR LEASES—LESSOR

The lessor in a lease transaction gives up the physical possession of the property to the lessee. If the transfer of the property is considered temporary in nature, the lessor will continue to carry the leased asset as an owned asset on the balance sheet, and the revenue from the lease will be reported as it is earned. Depreciation of the leased asset will be matched against the revenue. This type of lease is described as an **operating lease** and cash receipts from the lessee are treated similar to the operating lease procedures described for the lessee. However, if a lease has terms that make the transaction similar in substance to a sale or a permanent transfer of the asset to the lessee, the lessor should no longer report the asset as though it were owned, but should reflect the transfer to the lessee.

As indicated on page 809, if a lease meets one of the four criteria that apply to both lessees and lessors, plus both of the lessor-only conditions, i.e., collectibility and substantial completion, it is classified by the lessor as a capital lease and recorded as either a direct financing lease or a sales-type lease.

Direct financing leases involve a lessor who is primarily engaged in financing activities, such as a bank or finance company. The lessor views the lease as an investment. The revenue generated by this type of lease is interest revenue. **Sales-type leases,** on the other hand, involve manufacturers or dealers who use leases as a means of facilitating the marketing of their products. Thus, there are two different types of revenue generated by this type of lease: (1) an immediate profit or loss, which is the difference between the cost of the property being leased and its sales price, or fair value, at the inception of the lease, and (2) interest revenue to compensate for the deferred payment provisions.

For either an operating, direct financing, or sales-type lease, a lessor may incur certain costs, referred to as **initial direct costs,** in connection with obtaining the lease. These costs include:[10]

10. *Statement of Financial Accounting Standards No. 91,* "Accounting for Nonrefundable Fees and Costs Associated With Originating or Acquiring Loans and Initial Direct Costs of Leases" (Stamford: Financial Accounting Standards Board, 1986), par. 24.

1. Costs to originate a lease that result directly from and are essential to acquire that lease and would not have been incurred if that leasing transaction had not occurred.
2. Certain costs directly related to the following specified activities performed by the lessor for that lease: evaluating the prospective lessee's financial condition; evaluating and recording guarantees, collateral, and other security arrangements; negotiating lease terms; preparing and processing lease documents; and closing the transaction.

Initial direct costs are accounted for differently depending on which of the three types of leases is involved. Exhibit 19—6 summarizes the accounting treatment for initial direct costs. These costs will be discussed further as each type of lease is presented.

Exhibit 19—6
Accounting for Initial Direct Costs

Type of Lease	Accounting Treatment of Costs.
Operating	Recorded as an asset and amortized over lease term.
Direct financing	Recorded as an asset and amortized over lease term with unearned interest so as to produce a constant rate of return on the net investment in the lease.
Sales-type	Immediately recognized as reduction in manufacturer's or dealer's profit.

Accounting for Operating Leases—Lessor

Accounting for operating leases for the lessor is very similar to that described for the lessee. The lessor recognizes revenue as the payments are received. If there are significant variations in the payment terms, entries will be necessary to reflect a straight-line pattern of revenue recognition. Initial direct costs incurred in connection with an operating lease are deferred and amortized on a straight-line basis over the term of the lease, thus matching them against rent revenue.

To illustrate accounting for an operating lease on the lessor's books, assume that the equipment leased for 5 years by Marshall Corporation (page 814) on January 1, 1996, for $65,000 a year, including executory costs of $5,000 per year, had a cost of $400,000 to the lessor. Initial direct costs of $15,000 were incurred to obtain the lease. The equipment has an estimated life of 10 years, with no residual value. Assuming no purchase or renewal options or guarantees by the lessee, the lease does not meet any of the four general classification criteria and would be treated as an operating lease. The entries to record the payment of the initial direct costs and the receipt of rent would be:

1996				
Jan.	1	Deferred Initial Direct Costs	15,000	
		Cash		15,000
	1	Cash	65,000	
		Rent Revenue		60,000
		Executory Costs		5,000

Assuming the lessor depreciates the equipment on a straight-line basis over its expected life of 10 years and amortizes the initial direct costs on a straight-line basis over the 5-year lease term, the depreciation and amortization entries at the end of the first year would be:

1996				
Dec.	31	Amortization of Initial Direct Costs	3,000	
		Deferred Initial Direct Costs		3,000
	31	Depreciation Expense on Leased Equipment	40,000	
		Accumulated Depreciation on Leased Equipment		40,000

Executory costs would be recognized as expense when paid or accrued. If the rental period and the lessor's fiscal year do not coincide, or if the lessor prepares interim reports, an adjustment would be required to record the unearned rent revenue at the end of the accounting period. Amortization of the initial direct costs would be adjusted to reflect a partial year.

Accounting for Direct Financing Leases

Accounting for direct financing leases for lessors is very similar to that used for capital leases by lessees, but with the entries reversed to provide for interest revenue rather than interest expense and reduction of an asset rather than a liability. In practice, the receivable usually is recorded by the lessor at the gross amount of the lease payments with an offsetting valuation account for the unearned interest revenue, rather than at a net figure as is true for lessee accounting. **Unearned interest revenue** is computed as the difference between the **gross investment** (total lease payments) and the fair market value, or cost, of the leased asset. The difference between the gross investment and the unearned interest revenue is the **net lease investment.**

Illustrative Entries for Direct Financing Leases. Referring to the lessee example on page 814, assume that the cost of the equipment to the Universal Leasing Company was the same as its fair market value, $250,194, and the purchase by the lessor had been entered into the account Equipment Purchased for Lease. The entry to record the initial lease would be:

1996				
Jan.	1	Lease Payments Receivable	300,000	
		Equipment Purchased for Lease		250,194
		Unearned Interest Revenue		49,806

The first payment would be recorded as follows:

Jan.	1	Cash	65,000	
		Lease Payments Receivable		60,000
		Executory Costs		5,000

The lessor is paying the executory costs, but charging them to the lessee. The lessor can record the receipt of the executory costs by debiting Cash and crediting the expense account Executory Costs. As the lessor pays the costs, the expense account is debited. The lessor is serving as a conduit for these costs to the lessee, and will have an expense only if the lessee fails to make the payments.

Interest revenue will be recognized over the lease term as shown in Exhibit 19—7.

Exhibit 19—7
Schedule of Lease Receipts and Interest Revenue [Five-Year Lease, $60,000 Annual Payments (Exclusive of Executory Costs), 10% Interest]

Date	Description	Interest Revenue*	Lease Receipt	Lease Payments Receivable	Unearned Interest Revenue
1-1-96	Initial balance			$300,000	$49,806
1-1-96	Receipt		$ 60,000	240,000	49,806
12-31-96	Receipt	$19,019	60,000	180,000	30,787
12-31-97	Receipt	14,921	60,000	120,000	15,866
12-31-98	Receipt	10,413	60,000	60,000	5,453
12-31-99	Receipt	5,453	60,000	-0-	-0-
		$49,806	$300,000		

*(Preceding lease payment receivable less unearned interest revenue) × 10%.

At the end of the first year, the following entries would be made to record receipt of the second lease payment, to recognize interest revenue for 1996, and to recognize the advance payment for next year's executory costs as a deferred credit.

1996				
Dec.	31	Cash	65,000	
		Lease Payments Receivable		60,000
		Deferred Executory Costs (a liability)		5,000
	31	Unearned Interest Revenue	19,019	
		Interest Revenue		19,019

Based on the journal entries, the asset portion of the balance sheet of the lessor at December 31, 1996, will report the lease receivable less the unearned interest revenue as follows:

Universal Leasing Company
Balance Sheet (Partial)
December 31, 1996

Assets		
Current assets:		
Lease payments receivable	$ 60,000	
Less unearned interest revenue	14,921	$ 45,079
Noncurrent assets:		
Lease payments receivable (exclusive of $60,000 included in current assets)	$120,000	
Less unearned interest revenue	15,866	$104,134

If a direct financing lease contains a bargain purchase option, the amount of the option is added to the receivable, and the interest included in the option amount is added to the unearned interest revenue account. The periodic entries and computations are made as though the bargain purchase amount was an additional rental payment.

Lessor Accounting for Direct Financing Lease With Residual Value. If leased property is expected to have residual value, the gross amount of the expected residual value is added to the receivable account. It does not matter whether the residual value is guaranteed or unguaranteed. If guaranteed, it is treated in the accounts exactly like a bargain purchase option. If unguaranteed, the lessor is expected to have an asset equal in value to the residual amount at the end of the lease term. The estimated residual value is added to the asset account and the interest attributable to the unguaranteed residual value is added to the unearned interest revenue account.

To illustrate the recording of residual values, assume the same facts for the Universal Leasing Company as the example on pages 816–817 except that the asset has a residual value at the end of the 5-year lease term of $75,000 (either guaranteed or unguaranteed) rather than a bargain purchase option. Assume the cost of the equipment to the Universal Leasing Company was again the same as its fair market value, $296,762.

The entries to record this lease and the first payment would be:

1996				
Jan.	1	Lease Payments Receivable	375,000	
		Equipment Purchased for Lease		296,762
		Unearned Interest Revenue		78,238
	1	Cash	65,000	
		Lease Payments Receivable		60,000
		Executory Costs		5,000

The difference between the Lease Payments Receivable of $375,000 and the cost of the equipment leased of $296,762 is the Unearned Interest Revenue of $78,238. The amortization of the unearned interest revenue would be identical to the interest expense computation illustrated in Exhibit 19—5 for the lessee.

At the end of the first year, the lessor would make the following entries:

1996				
Dec.	31	Cash	65,000	
		Lease Payments Receivable		60,000
		Deferred Executory Costs		5,000
	31	Unearned Interest Revenue	23,676	
		Interest Revenue		23,676

At the end of the lease term, the lessor would make the following entry to record the recovery of the leased asset assuming the residual value was the same as originally estimated:

2000				
Dec.	31	Equipment	75,000	
		Unearned Interest Revenue	6,817	
		Lease Payments Receivable		75,000
		Interest Revenue		6,817

The unguaranteed residual value should be reviewed at least annually by the lessor and adjusted for any decline that is considered other than temporary. Any adjustment is accounted for as a change in estimate.

Initial Direct Costs Related to Direct Financing Lease. If the lessor incurs any initial direct costs in conjunction with a direct financing lease, those costs are recorded as a separate asset and amortized, along with unearned interest revenue, to produce a constant rate of return on the net lease investment.[11] Because the net lease investment is increased by the initial direct costs, a lower implicit interest rate will be used to compute the amortization. In effect, this treatment spreads the initial costs over the lease term and reduces the amount of interest revenue that would otherwise be recognized.

Accounting for Sales-Type Leases

Accounting for sales-type leases adds one more dimension to the lessor's revenue, an immediate profit or loss arising from the difference between the sales price of the leased property and the lessor's cost to manufacture or purchase the asset. If there is no difference between the sales price and the lessor's cost, the lease is not a sales-type lease. The lessor also will recognize interest revenue over the lease term for the difference between the sales price and the gross amount of the minimum lease payments. The three values that must be identified to determine these income elements, therefore, can be summarized as follows:

1. The minimum lease payments as defined previously for the lessee, i.e., rental payments over the lease term net of any executory costs included therein plus the amount to be paid under a bargain purchase option or guarantee of the residual value.
2. The fair market value of the asset.
3. The cost or carrying value of the asset to the lessor increased by any initial direct costs to lease the asset.

The manufacturer's or dealer's profit is the difference between the fair market value of the asset and the cost or carrying value of the asset to the lessor. If cost exceeds the fair market value, a loss will be reported. The difference between the gross rentals and the fair market value of the asset is interest revenue and arises because of the time delay in pay-

11. *Statement of Financial Accounting Standards No. 98,* "Accounting for Leases—Initial Direct Costs of Direct Financing Leases" (Norwalk: Financial Accounting Standards Board, 1988) par. 22i.

ing for the asset as described by the lease terms. The relationship between these three values can be demonstrated as follows:

(1) Minimum lease payments	
	Financial Revenue (Interest)
(2) Fair market value of leased asset	
	Manufacturer's or Dealer's Profit (Loss)
(3) Cost or carrying value of leased asset to lessor	

To illustrate this type of lease, assume the lessor for the equipment described on page 814 is American Manufacturing Company rather than Universal Leasing. The fair market value of the equipment is equal to its present value (the future lease payments discounted at 10%), or $250,194. Assume the equipment cost American $160,000 and initial direct costs of $15,000 were incurred. The three values and the related revenue amounts would be as follows:

(1) Minimum lease payments: ($65,000 – $5,000) × 5	$300,000	
		$49,806 (Interest Revenue)
(2) Fair market value of equipment	$250,194	
		$75,194 (Manufacturer's Profit)
(3) Cost of leased equipment to lessor, plus initial direct costs	$175,000	

Illustrative Entries for Sales-Type Leases. The interest revenue ($49,806) is the same as that illustrated for a direct financing lease on page 821, and it is recognized over the lease term by the same entries and according to Exhibit 19—7. The manufacturer's profit is recognized as revenue immediately in the current period by including the fair market value of the asset as a sale and debiting the cost of the equipment carried in the finished goods inventory to Cost of Goods Sold. The initial direct costs previously deferred are recognized as an expense immediately by increasing Cost of Goods Sold by the amount expended for these costs. This reduces the amount of immediate profit to be recognized. The reimbursement of executory costs is treated in the same way as illustrated for direct financing leases.

The entries to record this information on American Manufacturing Company's books at the beginning of the lease term would be:

1996				
Jan.	1	Lease Payments Receivable	300,000	
		Cost of Goods Sold	175,000	
		Finished Goods Inventory		160,000
		Deferred Initial Direct Costs		15,000
		Unearned Interest Revenue		49,806
		Sales		250,194
	1	Cash	65,000	
		Lease Payments Receivable		60,000
		Executory Costs		5,000

The 1996 income statement would include the sales and cost of sales amounts yielding the manufacturer's profit of $75,194 and interest revenue of $19,019. A note to the statements would describe in more detail the nature of the lease and its terms.

In the preceding example, it was implied that the fair market value of the leased equipment was determined by discounting the minimum lease payments at a rate of 10%. Normally, the fair market value is known, and the minimum lease payments are set at an amount that will yield the desired rate of return to the lessor.

Accounting for Sales-Type Leases With Bargain Purchase Option or Guarantee of Residual Value. If the lease terms provide for the lessor to receive a lump-sum payment at the end of the lease term in the form of a bargain purchase option or a guarantee of residual value, the minimum lease payments include these amounts. The receivable is thus increased by the gross amount of the future payment, the unearned interest revenue account is increased by the interest on the end-of-lease payment, and sales are increased by the present value of the additional amount.

To illustrate a sales-type lease with a bargain purchase option, assume American Manufacturing was the lessor on the lease described on page 816 and Exhibit 19—5. The initial entries when either a bargain purchase option or a guarantee of residual value of $75,000 is payable at the end of the 5-year lease term would be:

1996				
Jan.	1	Lease Payments Receivable	375,000	
		Cost of Goods Sold	175,000	
		Finished Goods Inventory		160,000
		Deferred Initial Direct Costs		15,000
		Unearned Interest Revenue		78,238
		Sales		296,762
	1	Cash	65,000	
		Lease Payments Receivable		60,000
		Executory Costs		5,000

Because the lease now includes a bargain purchase option, Sales increases by $46,568 (present value of the bargain purchase amount) over the amount recorded on page 824. The manufacturer's profit is also increased by this amount, and the difference between the $75,000 gross payment and the $46,568 increase in Sales is recorded as a $28,432 increase in Unearned Interest Revenue.

Accounting for Sales-Type Leases With Unguaranteed Residual Value. When a sales-type lease does not contain a bargain purchase option or a guaranteed residual value, but the economic life of the leased asset exceeds the lease term, the residual value of the property will remain with the lessor. As indicated earlier, this is called an unguaranteed residual value. Because the sales account reflects the present value of the minimum lease payments, an unguaranteed residual value would not be included in the sales account. However, cost of goods sold would be reduced by the present value of the unguaranteed residual value to recognize the fact that the lessor will be receiving back the leased asset (worth a present value of $46,568) at the end of the lease term. The entry to record the initial lease described above with an unguaranteed residual value, therefore, would be:

1996				
Jan.	1	Lease Payments Receivable	375,000	
		Cost of Goods Sold	128,432	
		Finished Goods Inventory		160,000
		Deferred Initial Direct Costs		15,000
		Unearned Interest Revenue		78,238
		Sales		250,194

Note that the gross profit on the transaction is the same regardless of whether the residual value is guaranteed or unguaranteed as demonstrated on the next page.

	Guaranteed Residual Value	Unguaranteed Residual Value
Sales	$296,762	$250,194
Cost of goods sold	175,000	128,432
Gross profit	$121,762	$121,762

Sale of Asset During Lease Term

If the lessor sells an asset to the lessee during the lease term, a gain or loss is recognized on the difference between the receivable balance, after deducting any unearned finance charges, and the selling price of the asset. Thus, if the leased asset described in Exhibit 19—7, page 821, is sold on December 31, 1998, for $140,000 before the $60,000 rental payment is made, a gain of $25,453 would be reported. The following journal entry would be made to record the sale:

1998			
Dec. 31	Unearned Interest Revenue	15,866	
	Cash	140,000	
	Interest Revenue		10,413
	Lease Payments Receivable		120,000
	Gain on Sale of Leased Asset		25,453

It should be remembered that although the lessor does recognize a gain or loss on the sale, the lessee defers any gain or loss in the value placed on the purchased asset.

Treatment of Leases on Lessor's Statement of Cash Flows

Operating leases present no special problems to the lessor in preparing a statement of cash flows except for initial direct costs. The payment of these costs would be reported as an investing cash outflow under all methods. Under the indirect method, the amortization of initial direct costs would be added to net income in the same way income is adjusted for depreciation. Under the direct method, the amortization would be ignored. The lease receipts would be reported as part of net income and would require no adjustment under the indirect method and would be reported as part of the revenue receipts under the direct method.

Capital leases must be analyzed carefully to determine their impact on the statement of cash flows. Financing leases would require adjustments similar to those made by the lessee for capital leases except that for the lendor (lessor), the transaction is viewed as an investing activity rather than a financing activity as was the case for the borrower (lessee). The portion of the receipt that represents interest will be included in net income and requires no adjustment under the indirect method. It would be part of cash inflows from interest under the direct method. The portion of the payment representing the principal would be reported as an investing inflow under either method.

Under sales-type leases, the manufacturer's profit, net of initial direct costs, is reported in net income, but the cash inflow comes as the lease payments are received. Under the indirect method, this requires a deduction from net income for the manufacturer's profit at the inception of the lease. This would automatically occur as the changes in inventory, deferred initial costs, and net lease payments receivable are reflected in the operating section of the statement of cash flows. Since the transaction is being accounted for as a sale, all further receipts under the indirect method are reported as operating inflows, either as interest revenue or as reductions in the net lease payments receivable. Under the direct method, the entire lease receipt would be included in cash flows from operating activities. A summary of the treatment of lease impact on the statement of cash flows is included in Exhibit 19—8.

Exhibit 19—8
Summary of Lease Impact on Statement of Cash Flows

	Operating Activities			
Lessee	**Indirect Method**	**Direct Method**	**Investing Activities**	**Financing Activities**
Operating lease payments	NI	– Cash		
Capital lease:				
Lease payments—interest	NI	– Cash		
Lease payments—principal				– Cash
Amortization of asset	+ NI	No impact		
Lessor				
Operating leases:				
Initial direct costs (IDC)			– Cash	
Amortization of IDC	+ NI	No impact		
Lease receipts	NI	+ Cash		
Direct financing lease:				
Initial direct costs			– Cash	
Amortization of IDC	+ NI	No impact		
Lease receipts—interest	NI	+ Cash		
Lease receipts—principal			+ Cash	
Sales-type lease:				
Initial direct costs			– Cash	
Manufacturer's or dealer's profit (net of IDC)	– NI	No impact		
Lease receipts—interest	NI	+ Cash		
Lease receipts—principal	+ NI	+ Cash		

Key:
NI = Included in net income
+ NI = Added as an adjustment to net income
– NI = Deducted as an adjustment to net income
+ Cash = Reported as a receipt of cash
– Cash = Reported as a payment of cash

DISCLOSURE REQUIREMENTS FOR LEASES

The Financial Accounting Standards Board has established specific disclosure requirements for all leases, regardless of whether they are classified as operating or capital leases. The required information supplements the disclosures required in the financial statements and usually is included in a single note to the financial statements. For example, Microsoft Corporation reports information concerning its operating leases in the note entitled "Leases." (See Appendix A at the end of the text.)

The following information is required for all leases that have initial or remaining noncancellable lease terms in excess of one year:

Lessee

1. Gross amount of assets recorded as capital leases and related accumulated depreciation as of the date of each balance sheet presented by major classes according to the nature of the function.
2. Future minimum rental payments required as of the date of the latest balance sheet presented in the aggregate and for each of the five succeeding fiscal years. These payments should be separated between operating and capital leases. For capital leases, executory costs should be excluded.
3. Rental expense for each period for which an income statement is presented. Additional information concerning minimum rentals, contingent rentals, and sublease rentals is required for the same periods.

4. A general description of the lease contract including information about restrictions on such items as dividends, additional debt, and further leasing.
5. For capital leases, the amount of imputed interest necessary to reduce the lease payments to present value.

A note accompanying the 1992 financial statements of The Kroger Co., presented in Exhibit 19—9, illustrates the required lessee disclosures for both operating and capital leases.

Exhibit 19—9
The Kroger Co.—Lessee Disclosures

LEASES

The Company operates primarily in leased facilities. Lease terms generally range from 10 to 25 years with options to renew at varying terms. Certain of the leases provide for contingent payments based upon a percent of sales.

Rent expense (under operating leases) consists of:

	1992	1991	1990
Minimum rentals	$270,763	$253,345	$238,006
Contingent payments	17,350	12,983	14,494
	$288,113	$266,328	$252,500

Assets recorded under capital leases consists of:

	1992	1991
Distribution and manufacturing facilities	$ 38,742	$ 46,680
Store facilities	178,502	179,390
Less accumulated amortization	(98,684)	(96,827)
	$118,560	$129,243

Minimum annual rentals for the five years subsequent to 1992 and in the aggregate are:

	Capital Leases	Operating Leases
1993	$ 26,679	$ 261,965
1994	26,236	250,205
1995	25,678	237,134
1996	24,881	220,160
1997	24,075	202,487
Thereafter	220,046	1,727,409
	347,595	$2,899,360
Less estimated executory costs included in capital leases	(29,533)	
Net minimum lease payments under capital leases	318,062	
Less amount representing interest	(161,725)	
Present value of net minimum lease payments under capital leases	$ 156,337	

Lessor

1. The following components of the net investment in sales-type and direct financing leases as of the date of each balance sheet presented:
   (a) Future minimum lease payments receivable with separate deductions for amounts representing executory costs and the accumulated allowance for uncollectible minimum lease payments receivable.

   (b) Unguaranteed residual values accruing to the benefit of the lessor.
   (c) Unearned revenue.
   (d) For direct financing leases only, initial direct costs.
2. Future minimum lease payments to be received for each of the five succeeding fiscal years as of the date of the latest balance sheet presented, including information on contingent rentals.
3. The amount of unearned revenue included in income to offset initial direct costs for each year for which an income statement is prepared.
4. For operating leases, the cost of assets leased to others and the accumulated depreciation related to these assets.
5. A general description of the lessor's leasing arrangements.

An example of lessor disclosure of sales-type, direct financing and leveraged leases for Sun Company, Inc. is shown in Exhibit 19—10.

■ Exhibit 19—10
Sun Company, Inc.—
Lessor Disclosures

NOTES TO CONSOLIDATED FINANCIAL STATEMENTS

9. Long-Term Receivables and Investments

	December 31 1992	December 31 1991
	(Millions of Dollars)	
Investment in:		
Leveraged leases	$ 43	$ 58
Direct financing and sales-type leases	87	123
	$130	$181
Accounts and notes receivable	64	72
Investments in affiliated companies	56	52
Other investments, at cost	29	29
	$279	$334

Sun, as lessor, has entered into leveraged, direct financing and sales-type leases of a wide variety of equipment including aircraft, railroad rolling stock and various other transportation and manufacturing equipment. The components of Sun's investment in these leases at December 31, 1992 and 1991 are set forth below (in millions of dollars):

	Leveraged Leases		Direct Financing and Sales-Type Leases	
December 31	**1992**	**1991**	**1992**	**1991**
Minimum rentals receivable	$ 28*	$ 42*	$114	$159
Estimated unguaranteed residual value of leased assets	30	38	15	34
Unearned and deferred income	(15)	(22)	(42)	(70)
Investment in leases	$ 43	$ 58	$ 87	$123
Deferred taxes arising from leveraged leases	(29)	(43)		
Net investment in leveraged leases	$ 14	$ 15		

*Net of principal of and interest on related nonrecourse debt aggregating $65 and $98 million in 1992 and 1991, respectively.

Continued

The following is a schedule of minimum rentals receivable by years at December 31, 1992 (in millions of dollars):

	Leveraged Leases	Direct Financing and Sales-Type Leases
Year ending December 31:		
1993	$ 3	$ 18
1994	2	17
1995	3	15
1996	5	14
1997	5	9
Later years	10	41
	$28	$114

ACCOUNTING FOR SALE-LEASEBACK TRANSACTIONS

A common type of lease arrangement is referred to as a **sale-leaseback** transaction. Typical of this type of lease is an arrangement whereby one party sells the property to a second party, and then the first party leases the property back. Thus, the seller becomes a seller-lessee and the purchaser a purchaser-lessor. The accounting problem raised by this transaction is whether the seller-lessee should recognize the profit from the original sale immediately or defer it over the lease term. The Financial Accounting Standards Board has recommended that if the initial sale produces a profit, it should be deferred and amortized in proportion to the amortization of the leased asset if it is a capital lease or in proportion to the rental payments if it is an operating lease. If the transaction produces a loss because the fair market value of the asset is less than the undepreciated cost, an immediate loss should be recognized.[12]

To illustrate the accounting treatment for a sale at a gain, assume that on January 1, 1996, Hopkins Inc. sells equipment having a carrying value of $750,000 on its books to Ashcroft Co. for $950,000 and immediately leases back the equipment. The following conditions are established to govern the transaction:

1. The term of the lease is 10 years, noncancellable. A down payment of $200,000 is required plus equal rental payments of $107,108 at the beginning of each year.
2. The equipment has a fair value of $950,000 on January 1, 1996, and an estimated economic life of 20 years. Straight-line depreciation is used on all owned assets.
3. The lessee has an option to renew the lease for $10,000 per year for 10 years, the rest of its economic life. Title passes at the end of the lease term.

Analysis of this lease shows that it qualifies as a capital lease under both the third and fourth criteria. It meets the third "75% of economic life" criterion because of the bargain renewal option, which makes both the lease term and the economic life of the equipment 20 years. It meets the fourth "90% of fair market value" criterion, because the present value of the rental payments is equal to the fair market value of the equipment ($950,000).[13] The purchaser-lessor's books for the first year of the lease are shown on page 831.

12. *Ibid.*, pars. 32-33.
13. *Computation of present value of lease:*
(a) Present value of 10 years' rentals:
$R(PVAF_{\overline{10}|10\%}) = \$107,108 \times 6.7590 = \$723,943$.
(b) Present value of second 10 years' rentals:
$R(PVAF_{\overline{10}|10\%}) = \$10,000 \times 6.7590 = \$67,590$, present value at beginning of second 10 years' lease period.
Present value at beginning of lease, 10 years earlier:
$A(PVF_{\overline{10}|10\%}) = \$67,590 \times 0.3855 = \$26,056$.
(c) Total present value, $723,943 + $26,056 + $200,000 down payment = $950,000 (rounded).

Hopkins Inc. (Seller-Lessee)

			Debit	Credit
1996				
Jan.	1	Cash	950,000	
		Equipment		750,000
		Unearned Profit on Sale-Leaseback		200,000
		Original sale of equipment.		
	1	Leased Equipment	950,000	
		Obligations Under Capital Lease		642,892
		Cash		307,108
		Lease of equipment, including first payment.		
Dec.	31	Amortization Expense on Leased Equipment	47,500	
		Accumulated Amortization on Leased Equipment		47,500
		Amortization of equipment over 20-year period ($950,000 ÷ 20).		
	31	Interest Expense	64,289	
		Obligations Under Capital Lease	42,819	
		Cash		107,108
		Second lease payment (interest expense: $642,892 × 10% = $64,289).		
	31	Unearned Profit on Sale-Leaseback	10,000	
		Revenue Earned on Sale-Leaseback		10,000
		Recognition of revenue over 20-year life in proportion to the amortization of the leased asset.		

Ashcroft Co. (Purchaser-Lessor)

			Debit	Credit
Jan.	1	Equipment	950,000	
		Cash		950,000
		Purchase of equipment.		
	1	Cash	307,108	
		Lease Payments Receivable	1,063,972	
		Equipment		950,000
		Unearned Interest Revenue		421,080
		Direct financing leaseback to Hopkins Inc. [total receivable = (10 × $107, 108) + (10 × $10,000) = $1,171,080; $1,171,080 – $107,108 = $1,063,972].		
Dec.	31	Cash	107,108	
		Unearned Interest Revenue	64,289	
		Lease Payments Receivable		107,108
		Interest Revenue		64,289
		Receipt of second lease payment (see computations for Hopkins Inc.).		

The amortization entries and recognition of the deferred gain on the sale for Hopkins Inc. would be the same each year for the 20-year lease term. The interest expense and interest revenue amounts would decline each year using the effective interest method of computation.

If the lease had not met the criteria, it would have been recorded as an operating lease. The gain on the sale would have been deferred and recognized in proportion to the lease payments. If the initial sale had been at a loss, an immediate recognition of the loss would have been recorded.

LEASING STUD SERVICES

Today a business can lease cars, buildings, equipment, and machinery. You name it, you can probably lease it. Bill Roloson, a farmer from Canada, can verify that almost anything can be leased. Bill is in the horse racing and horse breeding business. When his stallion, Rebel Blue Chip, died in 1993, he began searching for a replacement to sire future winners. His search led him to the stallion, Hunterstown, a horse that had been put out to pasture in 1990 because of lameness. Roloson contacted Hunterstown's owner, Getrude Seiling, and arranged to lease the horse for stud for five years.

Upon arrival at Prince Edward Island in Canada, the horse was given a workout. Much to Roloson's surprise, Hunterstown's lameness seemed to have healed. Instead of using Hunterstown for breeding, Roloson wanted to begin racing the stallion again. The lease agreement with Seiling was renegotiated to cover race earnings and Hunterstown began winning races. Roloson then faced the decision of continuing to race the horse or take the horse back to Prince Edward Island for stud duty. Roloson stated, "We'd planned to bring him back for at least a month on April 1, but that's up in the air, depending on how he's racing."

Questions:

1. Can you capitalize the lease of an animal?
2. In this instance, what would be Hunterstown's expected useful life? Would your answer vary depending upon whether Hunterstown was used for breeding or for racing?
3. When circumstances changed and the lease for the horse was renegotiated, could that affect whether or not the horse was capitalized? How?

Source: Paul Delean, "Hunterstown's Remarkable Return: Horse Returned to Racetrack After Three Years at Stud," *The Gazzette (Montreal)*, p. F7.

CONCLUDING COMMENT

This chapter has discussed the basics of accounting for leases. Special considerations applicable to real estate leases and leveraged leases are discussed in Appendixes 19—1 and 19—2, respectively, at the end of the chapter. **Leveraged leases** often are very complex arrangements involving third parties who assist in financing lease transactions.

Comparatively few leases have been capitalized as a result of FASB Statement No. 13 because of the liberal interpretations applied by many companies to the criteria used to define a capital lease. Many modifications and interpretations of the lease standard have been made by the FASB since the standard was first issued in an attempt to reduce the manipulation of the criteria. However, this method of off-balance-sheet financing is still used frequently. The FASB project on financial instruments may address the lease question as part of the larger financing issue. In the meantime, full disclosure of lease arrangements seems to be a minimum requirement to meet the spirit of FASB Statement No. 13.

APPENDIX 19-1
Criteria for Classifying Real Estate Leases

A significant percentage of leases involve real estate. If the real estate includes both nondepreciable land and depreciable buildings and equipment, special problems arise in determining how the lease should be treated. Some of the criteria used to evaluate a lease do not apply to leases of land. The FASB treated leases of real estate separately in Statement No. 13. This treatment is summarized in Exhibit 19—11 and in subsequent sections.

LEASES INVOLVING LAND ONLY OR BUILDINGS ONLY

Leases of land should be classified as capital leases only if title to the land is certain to be transferred in the future or if transfer is reasonably assured based on the existence of a bargain purchase option. Thus, only the first two general criteria listed on page 809 apply to the leasing of land. The third criterion cannot apply because land has an unlimited life. The fourth criterion was not felt to be applicable because under this criterion, no actual ownership transfer is contemplated. Ownership transfer is an important consideration because the residual value of the land to the lessor would be material, since there is no depreciation on land. Leases of land that meet either of the first two general criteria are capitalized on the lessee's books and treated as sales-type or direct financing leases on the lessor's books if both of the lessor's supplementary criteria also are met. Other leases of land are treated as operating leases.

No special problems arise when a lease involves only the building. The four general criteria for lessees and lessors and the two additional criteria for the lessor can be applied as discussed previously.

LEASES INVOLVING LAND AND BUILDINGS

If a lease involves both land and buildings, the accounting treatment depends on which criteria the lease meets. If it meets either of the first two criteria, both the land and the buildings should be classified as capital leases using the fair market values of the properties to allocate the capital value between them. The building lease portion will be amortized by the lessee and the land will be left at originally allocated cost. The lessor treats the lease as a sale of a single unit and accounts for it as a sales-type or direct financing lease depending on the circumstances.

If the lease does not meet either of the first two criteria, then additional tests are prescribed by the FASB to determine if any portion should be capitalized. If the land fair market value is less than 25% of the total fair value, the lease is treated as a single unit and the third and fourth criteria are applied to the single unit to determine if it should be treated as an operating or a capital lease. The estimated economic life of the building is used in applying the third classification criterion. If the fair market value of the land exceeds 25% of the total fair value, the land portion is treated as an operating lease and the third and fourth criteria are applied to the building as a separate unit. If the test is met for the building, the building portion is classified as a capital lease; otherwise, it is treated as an operating lease.

LEASES INVOLVING REAL ESTATE AND EQUIPMENT

If a lease includes both real estate and equipment, the equipment is considered separately in determining the appropriate classification by the lessee and lessor and is accounted for separately over the term of the lease. The real estate portion of the lease is then classified and accounted for in accordance with the criteria applicable to leases of real estate.

PROFIT RECOGNITION ON SALES-TYPE REAL ESTATE LEASES

The provisions of profit recognition on sales of real estate have an impact on the lessor's classification of real estate leases. Under the guidelines for sales of real estate, a substantial down payment (approximately 25%) must be made before the profit on the sale can be recognized in full. The FASB amended Statement No. 13 to specify that leases that fail to meet the criteria for full and immediate profit recognition if the real estate had been sold should be classified as operating leases and no immediate profit should be recognized. This amendment does not apply to direct financing leases or sales-type leases where a loss is indicated.

Exhibit 19—11 Flowchart for Treatment of Real Estate Leases

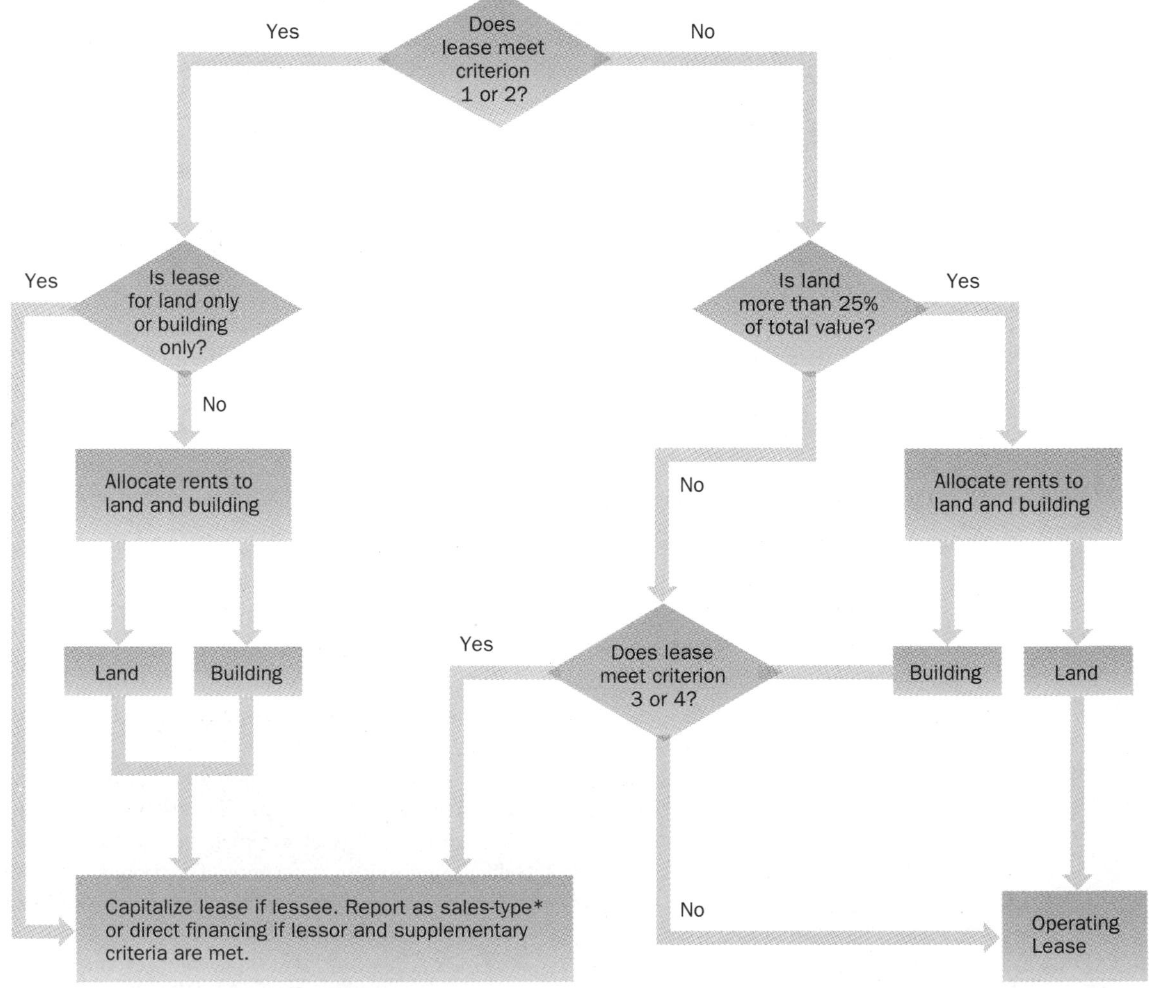

APPENDIX 19-2

Leveraged Leases

As indicated in the chapter, there are several potential economic advantages to a lessor in leasing property to others. A lessor who wishes to maximize its ability to lease often has to obtain outside financing for the investment in leased assets. A popular type of lease that has developed over the past twenty-five years to accommodate this type of situation is the **leveraged lease.** There generally are three parties in a leveraged lease: the **lessee;** the **owner-lessor,** or equity participant; and the **third-party, long-term creditor,** or debt participant. Only direct financing leases are treated as leveraged leases.

A leveraged lease generally requires a down payment by the owner-lessor equivalent to 20%-30% of the purchase price. The rest of the financing is provided by the debt participant as a nonrecourse loan on the general credit of the lessor. The interest rate charged on the loan is dependent on the credit rating of the owner-lessor. The owner-lessor enters into the lease arrangement with the lessee, receives rental payments, makes required principal and interest payments on the debt, and recognizes the difference as income. No special accounting is required by the lessee. The lessor records the investment in the leveraged lease net of the nonrecourse debt. The interaction of deferred income taxes, rental payments, and debt-related costs can result in complex accounting entries for the lessor. These complexities are not treated in this text.[14]

14. For additional discussion and illustrations concerning leveraged leases, see *Statement of Financial Accounting Standards No. 13,* Appendix E, par. 123.

KEY TERMS

QUESTIONS

1. What are the principal advantages to a lessee in leasing rather than purchasing property?
2. What are the principal advantages to a lessor in leasing rather than selling property?
3. Why is the concept of residual value an important one in capital leases?
4. How is the lease term measured?
5. What criteria must be met before a lease can be properly accounted for as a capital lease on the books of the lessee?
6. The third and fourth criteria for classifying a lease as a capital transaction are not as restrictive as originally intended. Explain how each of these criteria can be circumvented.
7. In determining the classification of a lease, a lessor uses the criteria of the lessee plus two additional criteria. What are these additional criteria and why are they included in the classification of leases by lessors?
8. Under what circumstances are the minimum lease payments for the lessee different from those of the lessor?
9. (a) What discount rate is used to determine the present value of a lease by the lessee? (b) by the lessor?
10. What is the basic difference between an operating lease and a capital lease from the viewpoint of the lessee?
11. If an operating lease requires the payment of uneven rental amounts over its life, how should the lessee recognize rental expense?
12. What amount should be recorded as an asset and a liability for capital leases on the books of the lessee?
13. The FASB has identified a situation in which the present value of future minimum lease payments would not be used as the amount for the initial recording of an asset and liability for lessees under capital leases. Describe this situation and how an interest rate would be calculated for determining interest expense.
14. Why do asset and liability balances for capital leases usually differ after the first year?
15. A capitalized lease should be amortized in accordance with the lessee's normal depreciation policy. What life should be used for lease amortization?
16. The use of the capital lease method for a given lease will always result in a lower net income than the operating lease method. Do you agree? Explain fully.
17. If a lease contains a bargain purchase option, what entries are required on the books of the lessee under each of the following conditions?
    (a) The bargain purchase option is exercised.
    (b) The bargain purchase option is not exercised, and no renewal of the lease is made.
    (c) The bargain purchase option is not exercised, but a renewal of the lease is obtained.
18. (a) How does a capital lease for equipment affect the lessee's statement of cash flows? (b) How would the treatment on the statement of cash flows differ if the contract was identified as a purchase of equipment with a down payment and a long-term note payable for the balance?
19. Distinguish a sales-type lease from a direct financing lease.
20. Under what circumstances would a lessor recognize as interest revenue over the lease term an amount greater than the difference between the gross amount of lease receivables and the cost of the asset to the lessor?
21. Terms of leases may provide for guaranteed residual values by third parties. Why have such agreements been popular in many leasing situations?
22. Unguaranteed residual values accrue to the lessor at the expiration of the lease. How are these values treated in a sales-type lease?
23. Why is the principal portion of a lease receipt of a financing lease treated as an investment inflow on the lessor's books, while the principal portion of a lease payment is treated as a financial cash outflow on the lessee's books?
24. Describe how the manufacturer's profit on a sales-type lease is accounted for by the lessor in a statement of cash flows under both the direct and the indirect methods.
25. Describe the specific lease disclosure requirements for lessees.
26. What disclosure is required by the FASB for lessors under sales-type and direct financing leases?

27. When should the profit or loss be recognized by the seller-lessee in a sale-leaseback arrangement?

*28. Real estate leases can include land and/or buildings. Explain how the four criteria for determining lease capitalization are applied to the following:
   (a) Leases involving land only.
   (b) Leases involving land and buildings.
   (c) Leases involving buildings only.

**29. What characteristics are unique to a leveraged lease?

*Relates to Appendix 19—1
**Relates to Appendix 19—2

DISCUSSION CASES

Case 19—1 (How should the lease be recorded?)

Louise Corporation entered into a leasing arrangement with Wilder Leasing Corporation for a certain machine. Wilder's primary business is leasing, and it is not a manufacturer or dealer. Louise will lease the machine for a period of 3 years, which is 50% of the machine's economic life. Wilder will take possession of the machine at the end of the initial 3-year lease. Louise does not guarantee any residual value for the machine.

Louise's incremental borrowing rate is 10%, and the implicit rate in the lease is 8 1/2%. Louise has no way of knowing the implicit rate used by Wilder. Using either rate, the present value of the minimum lease payments is between 90% and 100% of the fair value of the machine at the date of the lease agreement.

Louise has agreed to pay all executory costs directly, and no allowance for these costs is included in the lease payments.

Wilder is reasonably certain that Louise will pay all lease payments, and because Louise has agreed to pay all executory costs, there are no important uncertainties regarding costs to be incurred by Wilder.

1. With respect to Louise (the lessee), answer the following:
   (a) What type of lease has been entered into? Explain the reason for your answer.
   (b) How should Louise compute the appropriate amount to be recorded for the lease or asset acquired?
   (c) What accounts will be created or affected by this transaction, and how will the lease or asset and other costs related to the transaction be matched with earnings?
   (d) What disclosures must Louise make regarding this lease or asset?
2. With respect to Wilder (the lessor), answer the following:
   (a) What type of leasing arrangement has been entered into? Explain the reason for your answer.
   (b) How should this lease be recorded by Wilder, and how are the appropriate amounts determined?
   (c) How should Wilder determine the appropriate amount of earnings to be recognized from each lease payment?
   (d) What disclosures must Wilder make regarding this lease?

(AICPA adapted)

Case 19—2 (Should we buy or lease?)

The Meeker Machine and Die Company has learned that a sophisticated piece of computer-operated machinery is available to either buy or rent. The machinery will result in 3 employees being replaced, and quality of the output has been tested to be superior in every demonstration. There is no doubt that this machinery represents the latest in technology; however, new inventions and research make it difficult to estimate when the machinery will be made obsolete by new technology. The physical life expectancy of the machine is 10 years; however, the estimated economic life is between 2 and 5 years.

Meeker has a debt-to-equity ratio of .75. If the machine is purchased and the minimum down payment is made, the debt-to-equity ratio will increase to 1.1. The monthly payments if the machine is purchased are 20% lower than the rental payments if it is leased. The incremental borrowing rate for Meeker is 11%. The rate implicit in the lease is 12%. What factors should Meeker consider in deciding how to finance the acquisition of the machine?

Case 19—3 **(How should the leases be classified and accounted for?)**

On January 1, Toronto Company, a lessee, entered into three noncancellable leases for new equipment, Lease J, Lease K, and Lease L. None of the three leases transfers ownership of the equipment to Toronto at the end of the lease term. For each of the three leases, the present value at the beginning of the lease term of the minimum lease payments is 75% of the fair value of the equipment to the lessor at the inception of the lease. This excludes that portion of the payments representing executory costs, such as insurance, maintenance, and taxes to be paid by the lessor, including any profit thereon.

The following information is peculiar to each lease:

(a) Lease J does not contain a bargain purchase option; the lease term is equal to 80% of the estimated economic life of the equipment.
(b) Lease K contains a bargain purchase option; the lease term is equal to 50% of the estimated economic life of the equipment.
(c) Lease L does not contain a bargain purchase option; the lease term is equal to 50% of the estimated economic life of the equipment.

1. How should Toronto Company classify each of the 3 leases and why? Discuss the rationale for your answer.
2. What amount, if any, should Toronto record as a liability at the inception of the lease for each of the 3 leases?
3. Assuming that the minimum lease payments are made on a straight-line basis, how should Toronto record each minimum lease payment for each of the 3 leases?

(AICPA adapted)

Case 19—4 **(More leases mean lower profits)**

Ultrasound, Inc., has introduced a new line of equipment that may revolutionize the medical profession. Because of the new technology involved, potential users of the equipment are reluctant to purchase the equipment, but they are willing to enter into a lease arrangement as long as they can classify the lease as an operating lease. The new equipment will replace equipment that Ultrasound has been selling in the past. It is estimated that a 25% loss of actual equipment sales will occur as a result of the leasing policy for the new equipment.

Management must decide how to structure the leases so that the lessees can treat them as operating leases. Some members of management want to structure the leases so that Ultrasound, as lessor, can classify the lease as a sales-type lease and thus avoid a further reduction of income. Others feel they should treat the leases as operating leases and minimize the income tax liability in the short term. They are uncertain, however, as to how the financial statements would be affected under these two different approaches. They also are uncertain as to how leases could be structured to permit the lessee to treat the lease as an operating lease and the lessor to treat it as a sales-type lease. You are asked to respond to their questions.

Case 19—5 **(Structuring a lease to avoid liability disclosure)**

Johnson Pharmaceuticals is in need of cash. One option being considered by the board of directors is to sell the plant facilities to a group of venture capitalists and then lease the facilities back for a long-term period with the option of repurchasing the plant facilities at the end of the lease.

The chairman has commented that this option will provide Johnson Pharmaceuticals with the needed cash but will result in a large lease liability on the balance sheet. As the chief financial officer, you comment that if the company carefully structures the terms of the lease agreement, it may be able to avoid disclosing the lease liability.

The chairman has asked you to prepare a memo discussing the specific ways in which a lease agreement can be structured so as to avoid disclosing the liability on the balance sheet.

Case 19—6 **(Recognizing profits on a sale-leaseback transaction)**

John Carson, president of Carson Enterprises, recently arranged a financing deal with a group of foreign investors whereby he sold his movie company for $13,000,000 and immediately leased the company back, recognizing a $4,000,000 profit on the sale. Mr. Carson has just entered your office to tell you, as his accountant, the good news.

After hearing the details of the transaction, you tell Mr. Carson that he must defer recognizing the gain immediately and instead recognize it piecemeal over the term of the lease agreement. Mr. Carson counters that if he had simply sold the company to the investors, he would be able to book the profits. He asks you: "What difference does it make if I lease the company back or not? Shouldn't the sale and the lease be treated as two separate transactions?" How do you respond?

Case 19—7 **(Recognizing a profit from leasing)**

In June of 1988, British & Commonwealth PLC (B&C) acquired Atlantic Computers, the world's third largest computer-leasing company. In April of 1990, B&C placed Atlantic Computers into administrative receivership and wrote off its $900 million investment in the company. The reason for the write-off? Atlantic's method of accounting for leases.

Atlantic had developed what was called a "flexlease," which allowed customers to upgrade their computers at specified points during the lease period. The flexlease involved two separate contracts—one with a financing institution and the second with Atlantic. When customers elected to exercise their flex options, Atlantic would take back the equipment, pay off the remainder of the contract to the lender, and sell the equipment in the used computer market.

Even though the original lease arrangement did not meet the criteria for a sales-type lease, Atlantic was estimating the profits to be made from the sale of those computers that would be returned assuming customers exercised their flex options, and recognizing these sales profits when the original lease contract was signed.

1. Is there anything wrong with Atlantic's method of accounting for the profits to be made on the flexleases?
2. When would be the most appropriate time for Atlantic to recognize profits from the sale of a computer that was returned under a flex option?
3. Why would British & Commonwealth PLC get rid of Atlantic rather than simply change the accounting practice?

Source: *Computerworld,* April 30, 1990, p. 99.

EXERCISES

Exercise 19—8 **(Criteria for capitalizing leases)**

Atwater Manufacturing Co. leases its equipment from Westside Leasing Company. In each of the following cases, assuming none of the other criteria for capitalizing leases are met, determine whether the lease would be a capital lease or an operating lease under FASB Statement No. 13. Your decision is to be based only on the terms presented, considering each case independently of the others.

(a) At the end of the lease term, the market value of the equipment is expected to be $20,000. Atwater has the option of purchasing it for $5,000.
(b) The fair market value of the equipment is $75,000. The present value of the lease payments is $71,000 (excluding any executory costs).
(c) Ownership of the property automatically passes to Atwater at the end of the lease term.
(d) The economic life of the equipment is 12 years. The lease term is 9 years.
(e) The lease requires payments of $9,000 per year in advance plus executory costs of $500 per year. The lease period is 3 years, and Atwater's incremental borrowing rate is 12%. The fair market value of the equipment is $28,000.
(f) The lease requires payments of $6,000 per year in advance, which includes executory costs of $500 per year. The lease period is 3 years, and Atwater's incremental borrowing rate is 10%. The fair market value of the equipment is $16,650.

Exercise 19—9 (Entries for lease—lessor and lessee)

The Doxey Company purchased a machine on January 1, 1996, for $1,250,000 for the express purpose of leasing it. The machine was expected to have a 7-year life from January 1, 1996, no salvage value, and to be depreciated on a straight-line basis. On March 1, 1996, Doxey leased the machine to Mondale Company for $300,000 a year for a 4-year period ending February 28, 2000. Doxey paid a total of $15,000 for maintenance, insurance, and property taxes on the machine for the year ended December 31, 1996. Mondale paid $300,000 to Doxey on March 1, 1996. Doxey retains title to the property and plans to lease it to someone else after the 4-year lease period. Give all the 1996 entries relating to the lease on (a) Doxey Company's books and (b) Mondale Company's books. Assume both sets of books are maintained on the calendar-year basis.

Exercise 19—10 (Entries for operating lease—lessee)

Jonas Inc. leases equipment on a 5-year lease. The lease payments are to be made in advance as shown in the following schedule.

January 1, 1996	$100,000
January 1, 1997	100,000
January 1, 1998	140,000
January 1, 1999	170,000
January 1, 2000	210,000
Total	$720,000

The equipment is to be used evenly over the 5-year period. For each of the 5 years, give the entry that should be made at the time the lease payment is made to allocate the proper share of rent expense to each period. The lease is classified as an operating lease by Jonas Inc.

Exercise 19—11 (Entries for lessee)

Bingham Smelting Company entered into a 15-year noncancellable lease beginning January 1, 1996, for equipment to use in its smelting operations. The term of the lease is the same as the expected economic life of the equipment. Bingham uses straight-line depreciation for all plant assets. The provisions of the lease call for annual payments of $290,000 in advance plus $20,000 per year to cover executory costs, such as taxes and insurance, for the 15-year period of the lease. At the end of the 15 years, the equipment is expected to be scrapped. The incremental borrowing rate of Bingham is 10%. The lessor's computed implicit interest rate is unknown to Bingham.

Record the lease on the books of Bingham and give all the entries necessary to record the lease for its first year plus the entry to record the second lease payment on December 31, 1996. (Round to the nearest dollar.)

Exercise 19—12 (Entries for lease—lessee)

On January 2, 1996, the Jacques Company entered into a noncancellable lease for a new equipment. The equipment was built to the Jacques Company's specifications and is in an area where rental to another lessee would be difficult. Rental payments are $300,000 a year for 10 years, payable in advance. The equipment has an estimated economic life of 20 years. The taxes, maintenance, and insurance are to be paid directly by the Jacques Company, and the title to the equipment is to be transferred to Jacques at the end of the lease term. Assume the cost of borrowing funds for this type of an asset by Jacques Company is 12%.

1. Give the entry on Jacques' books that should be made at the inception of the lease.
2. Give the entries for 1996 and 1997 assuming the second payment and subsequent payments are made on December 31 and assuming double-declining-balance amortization.

Exercise 19—13 (Schedule of lease payments)

Carter Construction Co. is leasing equipment from Vasquez Inc. The lease calls for payments of $50,000 a year plus $4,000 a year executory costs for 5 years. The first payment is due on January 1, 1996, when the lease is signed, with the other 4 payments coming due on December

31 of each year. Carter has also been given the option of purchasing the equipment at the end of the lease at a bargain price of $100,000. Carter has an incremental borrowing rate of 10%, the same as the implicit interest rate of Vasquez. Carter has hired you as an accountant and asks for a schedule of its obligations under the lease contract. Prepare a schedule that shows all the lessee's obligations.

Exercise 19—14 (Entry for purchase by lessee)

The Cordon Enterprise Company leases many of its assets and capitalizes most of the leased assets. At December 31, the company had the following balances on its books in relation to a piece of specialized equipment:

Leased Equipment	$70,000
Accumulated Amortization—Leased Equipment	49,300
Obligations Under Capital Leases	26,000

Amortization has been recorded up to the end of the year, and no accrued interest is involved. At December 31, Cordon decided to purchase the equipment for $32,000 and paid cash to complete the purchase. Give the entry required on Cordon's books to record the purchase.

Exercise 19—15 (Entry for purchase by lessee)

Smithston Corporation leased equipment to Dayplanner Co. on January 1, 1996. The terms of the lease called for annual lease payments to be made at the first of each year. Smithston's implicit interest rate for the transaction is 12%. On July 1, 1998, Dayplanner purchased the equipment and paid $58,000 to complete the transaction. After the 1998 payment was made, the following balances relating to the leased equipment were on the books of Smithston as of January 1, 1998:

Lease Payments Receivable	$ 84,500
Unearned Interest Revenue	18,750

Prepare the journal entry that should be made by Smithston to record the sale including the accrual of interest through July 1.

Exercise 19—16 (Computation of implicit interest rate)

Tueller Leasing leases equipment to Tsoi Manufacturing. The fair market value of the equipment is $473,130. Lease payments, excluding executory costs, are $70,000 per year, payable in advance, for 10 years. What is the implicit rate of interest Tueller Leasing should use to record this capital lease on its books?

Exercise 19—17 (Direct financing lease—lessor)

The Deseret Finance Company purchased a printing press to lease to the Quality Printing Company. The lease was structured so that at the end of the lease period of 15 years, Quality would own the printing press. Lease payments required in this lease were $190,000 (excluding executory costs) per year, payable in advance. The cost of the press to Deseret was $1,589,673, which is also its fair market value at the time of the lease.

1. Why is this a direct financing lease?
2. Give the entry to record the lease transaction on the books of Deseret Finance Company.
3. Give the entry at the end of the first year on Deseret Finance Company's books to recognize interest revenue.

Exercise 19—18 (Direct financing lease with residual value)

The Massachusetts Casualty Insurance Company decides to enter the leasing business. It acquires a specialized packaging machine for $300,000 cash and leases it for a period of 6 years, after which the machine is returned to the insurance company for disposition. The expected unguaranteed residual value of the machine is $20,000. The lease terms are arranged so that a return of 12% is earned by the insurance company.

1. Calculate the annual rent, payable in advance, required to yield the desired return.
2. Prepare entries for the lessor for the first year of the lease assuming the machine is acquired and the lease is recorded on January 1, 1996. The first lease payment is made on January 1, 1996, and subsequent payments are made each December 31.
3. Assuming the packaging machine is sold by Massachusetts to the lessee at the end of the 6 years for $32,000, give the required entry to record the sale.

Exercise 19—19 (Table for direct financing lease—lessor)

The Pioche Savings and Loan Company acquires a piece of specialized hospital equipment for $1,500,000 that it leases on January 1, 1996, to a local hospital for $391,006 per year, payable in advance. Because of rapid technological developments, the equipment is expected to be replaced after 4 years. It is expected that the machine will have a residual value of $200,000 to Pioche Savings at the end of the lease term. The implicit rate of interest in the lease is 10%.

1. Prepare a 4-year table for Pioche Savings and Loan similar to Exhibit 19—7 on page 821.
2. How would the table differ if the local hospital guaranteed the residual value to Pioche?

Exercise 19—20 (Direct financing lease with residual value)

The Mario Automobile Company leases automobiles under the following terms. A 3-year lease agreement is signed in which the lessor receives annual rental of $4,000 (in advance). At the end of the 3 years, the lessee agrees to make up any deficiency in residual value below $3,500. The cash price of the automobile is $13,251. The implicit interest rate is 12%, which is known to the lessee, and the lessee's incremental borrowing rate is 14%. The lessee estimates the residual value at the end of 3 years to be $4,200 and depreciates its automobiles on a straight-line basis.

1. Give the entries on the lessee's books required in the first year of the lease including the second payment on April 30, 1997. Assume the lease begins May 1, 1996, the beginning of the lessee's fiscal year.
2. What balances relative to the lease would appear on the lessee's balance sheet at the end of year 3?
3. Assume the automobile is sold by the lessee for $3,100. Prepare the entries to record the sale and settlement with the lessor.

Exercise 19—21 (Sales-type lease—lessor)

Salcedo Co. leased equipment to Erickson Inc. on April 1, 1996. The lease is appropriately recorded as a sale by Salcedo. The lease is for an 8-year period ending March 31, 2004. The first of 8 equal annual payments of $175,000 (excluding executory costs) was made on April 1, 1996. The cost of the equipment to Salcedo is $940,000. The equipment has an estimated useful life of 8 years with no residual value expected. Salcedo uses straight-line depreciation and takes a full year's depreciation in the year of purchase. The cash selling price of the equipment is $1,026,900.

1. Give the entry required to record the lease on Salcedo's books.
2. How much interest revenue will Salcedo recognize in 1996?

Exercise 19—22 (Sales-type lease—lessor)

The Jacinto Leasing and Manufacturing Company uses leases as a means of financing sales of its equipment. Jacinto leased a machine to Hudson Construction for $22,000 per year, payable in advance, for a 10-year period. The cost of the machine to Jacinto was $108,000. The fair market value at the date of the lease was $120,000. Assume a residual value of $0 at the end of the lease.

1. Give the entry required to record the lease on Jacinto's books.
2. How much profit will Jacinto recognize initially on the lease, excluding any interest revenue?
3. How much interest revenue would be recognized in the first year?

Exercise 19—23 (Effect of lease on reported income—lessee and lessor)

On February 20, 1996, Topham Inc. purchased a machine for $1,200,000 for the purpose of leasing it. The machine is expected to have a 10-year life, no residual value, and is depreciated on the straight-line basis to the nearest month. The machine was leased to Lutts Company on March 1, 1996, for a 4-year period at a monthly rental of $18,000. There is no provision for the renewal of the lease or purchase of the machine by the lessee at the expiration of the lease term. Topham paid $60,000 of commissions associated with negotiating the lease in February 1996.

1. What expense should Lutts record as a result of the lease transaction for the year ended December 31, 1996? Show supporting computations in good form.
2. What income or loss before income taxes should Topham record as a result of the lease transaction for the year ended December 31, 1996? Show supporting computations in good form.

Exercise 19—24 (Cash flow treatment of capital leases—lessee)

The following information relates to a capital lease between Simpson Electric Co. (lessee) and Harris Manufacturing Inc. (lessor). The lease term began on January 1, 1996. Simpson capitalized the 10-year lease and recorded $90,000 as an asset. The annual lease payment, made at the beginning of each year, is $13,316 at 10% interest. Simpson uses the straight-line method to depreciate its owned assets. How will this lease be reported on Simpson's statement of cash flows for 1996 if the 2nd lease payment is made on December 31, 1996, and Simpson uses the indirect method?

Exercise 19—25 (Lease disclosures—lessee)

The following lease information was obtained by a staff auditor for a client, Kroller Inc., at December 31, 1997. Indicate how this information should be presented in Kroller's 2-year comparative financial statements. Include any notes to the statements required to meet generally accepted accounting principles. Lease payments are made on December 31 of each year.

Leased building; minimum lease payments per year; 10 years remaining life	$ 45,000
Executory costs per year	2,000
Capitalized lease value, 12% interest	343,269
Accumulated amortization of leased building at December 31, 1997	114,423
Amortization expense for 1997	22,885
Obligations under capital leases; balance at December 31, 1997	239,770
Obligations under capital leases; balance at December 31, 1996	254,259

Exercise 19—26 (Lease disclosure on the financial statements)

Acme Enterprises leased equipment from Monument Equipment Co. on January 1, 1996. The terms of the lease agreement require 5 annual payments of $20,000 with the first payment being made on January 1, 1996, and each subsequent payment being made on December 31 of each year. Because the equipment has an expected useful life of 5 years, the lease qualifies as a capital lease for Acme. Acme does not know Monument's implicit interest rate and therefore uses its own incremental borrowing rate of 12% to calculate the present value of the lease payments. Acme uses the sum-of-the-years-digits method for amortizing leased assets. The expected salvage value of the leased asset is $0.

1. Prepare a schedule that shows all of the lessee's obligations.
2. Prepare an asset amortization schedule for the leased asset.
3. Compare the amount shown on the year-end balance sheet for the leased asset with that of the lease obligation for the years 1996 through 2000 and explain why the amounts differ.

Exercise 19—27 (Sale-leaseback accounting)

On July 1, 1996, Baker Corporation sold equipment it had recently purchased to an unaffiliated company for $570,000. The equipment had a book value on Baker's books of $450,000 and a remaining life of 5 years. On that same day, Baker leased back the equipment at $135,000 per year, payable in advance, for a 5-year period. Baker's incremental borrowing rate is 10%, and it does not know the lessor's implicit interest rate. What entries are required for Baker to record the transactions involving the equipment during the first full year assuming the second lease payment is made on June 30, 1997? Ignore consideration of the lessee's fiscal year. The lessee uses the double-declining-balance method of depreciation for similar assets it owns outright.

Exercise 19—28 (Sale-leaseback transaction)

Smalltown Grocers sold its plant facilities to United Grocers, Inc., for $813,487. United immediately leased the building back to Smalltown for 20 annual payments of $96,000 with the first payment due immediately. The terms of the lease agreement provide a bargain purchase option wherein Smalltown has the option of purchasing the building at the end of the lease term for $100,000. If United's implicit interest rate is 12% (lower than Smalltown's incremental borrowing rate), prepare the entries that should be made by United to record the purchase of the building and the receipt of the first two payments from Smalltown Grocers assuming this leasing arrangement qualifies as a capital lease for United.

***Exercise 19—29 (Entries for real estate lease with residual value—lessee)**

Atlantus Corporation leases its land and buildings from an investment company. The terms of the lease are as follows:

(a) Lease term is 20 years, after which title to the property can be acquired for 25% of the market value at that date. The estimated remaining life of the building is 30 years.
(b) Annual lease payments payable in advance are $250,000 (excluding executory costs). Expected residual value of the property in 20 years is $800,000.
(c) Assume the current market value of the combined land and buildings is $2,370,945, of which the market value of the land is $350,000. The implicit interest rate of the lease is 10%.

What entries would be required on Atlantus Corporation's books for the first year of the lease? Assume the second lease payment is made on the last day of the first year.

*Relates to Appendix 19—1

***Exercise 19—30 (Lease of real estate—lessee)**

Maycomb Industries leases its land and buildings on a 10-year lease from E. L. Kimball. The property includes 10 acres of land that is used for parking and an amusement area. The market value of the leased land is $500,000, and the market value of the leased buildings is $1,200,000. The annual rent for the property, payable in advance, is $251,516. There is no provision in the lease for Maycomb to purchase the property at the conclusion of the lease. The buildings are estimated to have a 12-year remaining life and are depreciated on a straight-line basis.

1. Does the lease of Maycomb Industries qualify as a capital lease? If yes, what criteria apply?
2. Record the lease on Maycomb's books and give the entries for the first full year of the lease assuming the first payment is made on January 1, 1996, and the second payment is made on December 31, 1996.

*Relates to Appendix 19—1

PROBLEMS

Problem 19—31 (Entries for capital lease—lessee; lease criteria)

The Miner Company leased a machine on July 1, 1996, under a 10-year lease. The economic life of the machine is estimated to be 15 years. Title to the machine passes to Miner Company at the expiration of the lease, and thus the lease is a capital lease. The lease payments are $83,000 per year, including executory costs of $3,000 per year, all payable in advance annually. The incremental borrowing rate of the company is 10%, and the lessor's implicit interest rate is unknown. The Miner Company uses the straight-line method of amortization and uses the calendar year for reporting purposes.

Instructions:

1. Give all entries on the books of the lessee relating to the lease for 1996.
2. Assume that the lessor retains title to the machine at the expiration of the lease, that there is no bargain renewal or purchase option, and that the fair market value of the equipment is $575,000 as of the lease date. Using the criteria for distinguishing between operating and capital leases according to FASB Statement No. 13, what would be the amortization expense for 1996?

Problem 19—32 (Operating lease—lessee and lessor)

Calderwood Industries leases a large specialized machine to the Youngstown Company at a total rental of $1,800,000, payable in 5 annual installments in the following declining pattern: 25% for each of the first 2 years, 22% in the third year, and 14% in each of the last 2 years. The lease begins January 1, 1996. In addition to the rent, Youngstown is required to pay annual executory costs of $15,000 to cover unusual repairs and insurance. The lease does not qualify as a capital lease for reporting purposes. Calderwood incurred initial direct costs of $15,000 in obtaining the lease. The machine cost Calderwood $2,100,000 to construct and has an estimated life of 10 years with an estimated residual value of $100,000. Calderwood uses the straight-line depreciation method on its equipment. Both companies report on a calendar-year basis.

Instructions:

1. Prepare the journal entries on Calderwood's books for 1996 and 2000 related to the lease.
2. Prepare the journal entries on Youngstown's books for 1996 and 2000 related to the lease.

Problem 19—33 (Entries for capital lease—lessee)

Aldridge Enterprises has a long-standing policy of acquiring company equipment by leasing. Early in 1996, the company entered into a lease for a new milling machine. The lease stipulates that annual payments will be made for 5 years. The payments are to be made in advance on December 31 of each year. At the end of the 5-year period, Aldridge may purchase the machine. Company financial records show the incremental borrowing rate to be less than the implicit interest rate. The estimated economic life of the equipment is 12 years. Aldridge uses the calendar year for reporting purposes and uses straight-line depreciation for other equipment. In addition, the following information about the lease is also available:

Annual lease payments	$55,000
Purchase option price	$25,000
Estimated fair market value of machine after 5 years	$75,000
Incremental borrowing rate	10%
Date of first lease payment	Jan. 1, 1996

Instructions:

1. Compute the amount to be capitalized as an asset for the lease of the milling machine.
2. Prepare a schedule that shows the computation of the interest expense for each period.
3. Give the journal entries that would be made on Aldridge's books for the first 2 years of the lease.
4. Assume that the purchase option is exercised at the end of the lease. Give the Aldridge journal entry necessary to record the exercise of the option.

Problem 19—34 (Entries for capital lease—lessee; guaranteed residual value)

For some time, Balster Inc. has maintained a policy of acquiring company equipment by leasing. On January 1, 1996, Balster entered into a lease with Edgemont Fabricators for a new concrete truck that had a selling price of $265,000. The lease stipulates that annual payments of $52,500 will be made for 6 years. The first lease payment is made on January 1, 1996, and subsequent payments are made on December 31 of each year. Balster guarantees a residual value of $45,890 at the end of the 6-year period. Balster has an incremental borrowing rate of 13%, and the implicit interest rate to Edgemont is 12% after considering the guaranteed residual value. The economic life of the truck is 9 years. Balster uses the calendar year for reporting purposes and uses straight-line depreciation to depreciate other equipment.

Instructions:

1. Compute the amount to be capitalized as an asset on the lessee's books for the concrete truck.
2. Prepare a schedule showing the reduction of the liability by the annual payments after considering the interest charges.
3. Give the journal entries that would be made on Balster's books for the first 2 years of the lease.
4. Assume that the lessor sells the truck for $35,000 at the end of the 6-year period to a third party. Give the Balster journal entries necessary to record the payment to satisfy the residual guarantee and to write off the leased equipment accounts. Write off any remaining liability to lease expense—adjustment.

Problem 19—35 (Accounting for direct financing lease—lessee and lessor)

The Trost Leasing Company buys equipment for leasing to various manufacturing companies. On October 1, 1995, Trost leases a press to the Shumway Shoe Company. The cost of the machine to Trost was $196,110, which approximated its fair market value on the lease date. The lease payments stipulated in the lease are $33,000 per year in advance for the 10-year period of the lease. The payments include executory costs of $3,000 per year. The expected economic life of the equipment is also 10 years. The title to the equipment remains in the hands of Trost Leasing Company at the end of the lease term, although only nominal residual value is expected at that time. Shumway's incremental borrowing rate is 10%, and it uses the straight-line method of depreciation on all owned equipment. Both Shumway and Trost have fiscal years ending September 30, and lease payments are made on this date.

Instructions:

1. Prepare the entries to record the lease and the first lease payment on the books of the lessor and lessee assuming the lease meets the criteria of a direct financing lease for the lessor and a capital lease for the lessee.
2. Compute the implicit rate of interest of the lessor.
3. Give all entries required to account for the lease on both the lessee's and lessor's books for the fiscal years 1996, 1997, and 1998.

Problem 19—36 (Lease computations—lessee and lessor)

Computer Controls Corporation is in the business of leasing new sophisticated computer systems. As a lessor of computers, Computer Controls purchased a new system on December 31, 1996. The system was delivered the same day (by prior arrangement) to Edwards Investment Company, a lessee. The corporation accountant revealed the following information relating to the lease transaction:

Cost of system to Computer Controls	$550,000
Estimated useful life and lease term	8 years
Expected residual value (unguaranteed)	$40,000
Computer Controls' implicit rate of interest	12%
Edwards' incremental borrowing rate	14%
Date of first lease payment	Dec. 31, 1996

Additional information is as follows:

(a) At the end of the lease, the system will revert to Computer Controls.
(b) Edwards is aware of Computer Controls' rate of implicit interest.
(c) The lease rental consists of equal annual payments.
(d) Computer Controls accounts for leases using the direct financing method. Edwards intends to record the lease as a capital lease. Both the lessee and the lessor report on a calendar-year basis and elect to depreciate all assets on the straight-line basis.

Instructions:

1. Compute the annual rental under the lease. (Round to the nearest dollar.)

2. Compute the amounts of the lease payments receivable and the unearned interest revenue that Computer Controls should disclose at the inception of the lease.
3. What are the total expenses related to the lease that Edwards should record for the year ended December 31, 1996?

Problem 19—37 (Sales-type lease—lessor)

Aquatran Incorporated uses leases as a method of selling its products. In early 1996, Aquatran completed construction of a passenger ferry for use on the Upper New York Bay between Manhattan and Staten Island. On April 1, 1996, the ferry was leased to the Manhattan Ferry Line on a contract specifying that ownership of the ferry will transfer to the lessee at the end of the lease period. Annual lease payments do not include executory costs. Other terms of the agreement are as follows:

Original cost of the ferry	$1,500,000
Fair market value of ferry at lease date	2,107,102
Lease payments (paid in advance)	225,000
Estimated residual value	78,000
Incremental borrowing rate—lessee	10%
Date of first lease payment	April 1, 1996
Lease period	20 years

Instructions:

1. Compute the amount of financial revenue that will be earned over the lease term and the manufacturer's profit that will be earned immediately by Aquatran.
2. Give the entry to record the lease on Aquatran's books. Compute the implicit rate of interest on the lease.
3. Give the journal entries necessary on Aquatran's books to record the operating of the lease for the first 3 years exclusive of the initial entry. Aquatran's accounting period is the calendar year.
4. Indicate the balance of each of the following accounts at December 31, 1998: Unearned Interest Revenue and Lease Payments Receivable.

Problem 19—38 (Sales-type lease—lessor)

Universal Enterprises adopted the policy of leasing as the primary method of selling its products. The company's main product is a small jet airplane that is very popular among corporate executives. Universal constructed such a jet for Executive Transport Services (ETS) at a cost of $8,329,784. Financing of the construction was accomplished through borrowings at a 13% rate. The terms of the lease provided for annual advance payments of $1,331,225 to be paid over 20 years with the ownership of the airplane transferring to ETS at the end of the lease period. It is estimated that the plane will have a residual value of $800,000 at that date. The lease payments began on October 1, 1996. Universal incurred initial direct costs of $150,000 in finalizing the lease agreement with ETS. The sales price of similar airplanes is $11,136,734.

Instructions:

1. Compute the amount of manufacturer's profit that will be earned immediately by Universal.
2. Prepare the journal entry to record the lease on Universal's books at October 1, 1996.
3. Prepare the journal entries to record the lease for the years 1996-1998 exclusive of the initial entry. Universal's accounting period is the calendar year.
4. How much revenue did Universal earn from this lease for each of the first 3 years of the lease?

Problem 19—39 (Entries for capital lease—lessee and lessor)

The Alta Corporation entered into an agreement with Snowfire Company to lease equipment for use in its ski manufacturing facility. The lease is appropriately recorded as a purchase by Alta and as a sale by Snowfire. The agreement specifies that lease payments will be made on an annual basis. The cost of the machine is reported as inventory on Snowfire's accounting records. Because of extensive changes in ski manufacturing technology, the machine is not expected to have any residual value. Alta uses straight-line depreciation and computes depreciation to the nearest month. After 3 years, Alta purchases the machine from Snowfire.

Annual lease payments do not include executory costs. Other terms of the agreement are as follows:

Machine cost recorded in inventory	$3,700,000
Price at purchase option date	3,250,000
Lease payments (paid in advance)	710,000
Contract interest rate	10%
Contract date/first lease payment	Oct. 1, 1996
Date of Alta purchase	Oct. 1, 1999
Lease period	8 years

Instructions: Prepare journal entries on the books of both the lessee and the lessor as follows:

1. Make entries in 1996 to record the first lease payment, and make adjustments necessary at December 31, the end of each company's fiscal year.
2. Record all entries required in 1997. The companies do not make reversing entries.
3. Prepare the entry in 1999 to record the sale and purchase assuming no previous entries have been made during the year in connection with the lease.

Problem 19—40 (Accounting for capital lease—lessee and lessor)

The Crosby Equipment Company both leases and sells its equipment to its customers. The most popular line of equipment includes a machine that costs $340,000 to manufacture. The standard lease terms provide for 5 annual payments of $130,000 each (excluding executory costs), with the first payment due when the lease is signed and subsequent payments due on December 31 of each year. The implicit rate of interest in the contract is 10% per year. Dannell Tool Co. leases one of these machines on January 2, 1996. Initial direct costs of $17,000 are incurred by Crosby on January 2, 1996, to obtain the lease. Dannell's incremental borrowing rate is determined to be 12%. The equipment is very specialized, and it is assumed it will have no salvage value after 5 years. Assume the lease qualifies as a capital lease and a sales-type lease for lessee and lessor, respectively. Also assume that both the lessee and the lessor are on a calendar-year basis and that the lessee is aware of the lessor's implicit interest rate.

Instructions:

1. Give all entries required on the books of Dannell to record the lease of equipment from Crosby for the year 1996. The depreciation on owned equipment is computed once a year on the straight-line basis.
2. Give entries required on the books of Crosby to record the lease of equipment to Dannell for the year 1996.
3. Prepare the balance sheet section involving lease balances for both the lessee's and lessor's financial statements at December 31, 1996.
4. Determine the amount of expense Dannell will report relative to the lease for 1996 and the amount of revenue Crosby will report for the same period.

Problem 19—41 (Accounting for leases—lessee and lessor with third-party guarantee)

Atwater Equipment Co. manufactures, sells, and leases heavy construction equipment. England Construction Company, a regular customer, leased equipment on July 1, 1996, that had cost Atwater $252,000 to manufacture. The lease payments are $63,161 beginning on July 1, 1996, and continuing annually, with the last payment being made on July 1, 2000. If England were to purchase the equipment outright, the fair market value would be $291,881. Because of the heavy wear expected on construction equipment, the lease contains a guaranteed residual value clause wherein the lessee guarantees a residual value on June 30, 2001, of $65,000. England contracted with Weathertop Financial Services to serve as a third-party guarantor of the residual value. Atwater's implicit interest rate is 12%, which is lower than England's incremental borrowing rate of 14%.

Instructions:

1. Assuming that the equipment reverts to Atwater upon completion of the lease term and that the equipment has an expected useful life of 10 years, prepare the entries that should be made on the books of both Atwater and England in recording the lease on July 1, 1996.
2. Prepare the journal entries that should be made by Atwater and England on July 1, 1997.
3. What financial statement disclosure would be made by Weathertop in its role as a third-party guarantor?

Problem 19—42 (Accounting for lease—lessee and lessor)

Astle Manufacturing Company manufactures and leases a variety of items. On January 2, 1996, Astle leased a piece of equipment to Haws Industries Co. The lease is for 6 years with an annual amount of $33,500, payable in advance. The lease payment includes executory costs of $1,500 per year. The equipment has an estimated useful life of 9 years, and it was manufactured by Astle at a cost of $120,000. It is estimated that the equipment will have a residual value of $60,000 at the end of the 6-year lease term. There is no provision for purchase or renewal by Haws at the end of the lease term, however, a third party has guaranteed the residual value of $60,000. The equipment has a fair market value at the lease inception of $187,176. The implicit rate of interest in the contract is 10%, the same rate at which Haws can borrow money at its bank. All lease payments after the first one are made on December 31 of each year. Both companies use the straight-line method of depreciation.

Instructions:

1. Give all the entries relating to the lease on the books of the lessor and lessee for 1996.
2. Show how the lease would appear on the balance sheet of Astle Manufacturing Company and Haws Industries Co. (if applicable) as of December 31, 1996.
3. Assume Astle sold the equipment at the end of the 6-year lease for $70,000. Give the entry to record the sale assuming all lease entries have been properly made.

Problem 19—43 (Cash flow treatment of capital leases—lessor)

The following information relates to a capital lease between Bradshaw Electric Co. (lessee) and Smoot Manufacturing Inc. (lessor). The lease term began on January 1, 1996. Smoot recorded the lease as a sale and made the following entries related to the lease during 1996. Assume this was the only lease Smoot had during the year.

Jan.	1	Deferred Initial Direct Costs	4,000	
		Cash		4,000
	1	Lease Payments Receivable	133,156	
		Cost of Goods Sold	65,000	
		Finished Goods Inventory		61,000
		Deferred Initial Costs		4,000
		Sales		90,000
		Unearned Interest Revenue		43,156
	1	Cash	13,316	
		Lease Payments Receivable		13,316
Dec.	31	Cash	13,316	
		Lease Payments Receivable		13,316
	31	Unearned Interest Revenue	7,666	
		Interest Revenue		7,666

Instructions:

1. Prepare a partial statement of cash flows for 1996 for Smoot Manufacturing Inc. under the indirect method. Assume Smoot reported net income of $132,666 inclusive of the lease revenue in the above entries.
2. Prepare the partial operating activities section of the statement of cash flows for 1996 for Smoot Manufacturing Inc. under the direct method. Assume that cash provided by operating activities exclusive of the lease transactions is $100,000.

Problem 19—44 (Disclosure requirements—operating leases)

Jaquar Mining and Manufacturing Company leases from Emory Leasing Company three machines under the following terms:

Machine #1	Lease period—10 years, beginning April 1, 1991.
	Lease payment—$18,000 per year, payable in advance.
Machine #2	Lease period—10 years, beginning July 1, 1995.
	Lease payment—$30,000 per year, payable in advance.
Machine #3	Lease period—15 years, beginning January 1, 1996.
	Lease payment—$12,500 per year, payable in advance.

All of the leases are classified as operating leases.

Instructions: Prepare the note to the 1997 financial statements that would be required to disclose the lease commitments of Jaquar Mining and Manufacturing Company. Jaquar uses the calendar year as its accounting period.

Problem 19—45 (Sale-leaseback of a building)

On January 3, 1996, Juniper Inc. sold a building with a book value of $1,800,000 to Cedarcrest Industries for $1,757,340. Juniper immediately entered into a leasing agreement whereby Juniper would lease the building back for an annual payment of $260,000. The term of the lease is 10 years, the expected remaining useful life of the building. The first annual lease payment is to be made immediately, and future payments will be made on January 1 of each succeeding year. Cedarcrest's implicit interest rate is 10%.

Instructions:

1. Prepare the journal entries that should be made by both Juniper and Cedarcrest on January 3, 1996, relating to this sale-leaseback transaction.
2. Prepare the journal entries that should be made by both parties at the end of 1996 to accrue interest and to amortize the leased building. (Assume a salvage value of $0 and use of the straight-line method.)

CHAPTER 20

Accounting for Income Taxes

CHAPTER TOPICS

- Overview of Deferred Income Taxes
- Annual Computation of Deferred Tax Liabilities and Assets
- Carryback and Carryforward of Operating Losses
- Scheduling for Enacted Future Tax Rates
- Financial Statement Presentation ond Disclosure
- Deferred Income Taxes and the Statement of Cash Flows
- Evaluation of the Asset and Liability Method
- Intraperiod Income Tax Allocation (Appendix 20-1)
- The Investment Tax Credit (Appendix 20-2)

Accounting for deferred taxes has been a bit like a roller coaster ride in the past few years. In February 1992, the FASB issued Statement No. 109, "Accounting for Income Taxes," in response to five years of complaints and controversy surrounding the standard it superseded, FASB Statement No. 96. Statement No. 96 was so unpopular that some observers predicted it would result in an unraveling of public confidence in the FASB, with the possibility that the FASB would be replaced just as its two predecessor bodies, the CAP and the APB, had been. The two primary complaints against Statement No. 96 were that it was overly complicated and that it severely restricted the recognition of deferred tax assets.

Statement No. 96 was issued in 1987 and mandated that the deferred tax amounts reported in the balance sheet should be valued using enacted future tax rates. Previously, deferred tax items had been valued using tax rates in effect when the deferred taxes arose. This accounting change, coupled with the fact that the Tax Reform Act of 1986 had lowered the maximum corporate tax rate from 46% to 34%, caused significant downward revisions in the reported amounts of deferred taxes. For a firm with a deferred tax liability, the combined result was a decrease in the reported liability (a debit), and the recognition of a corresponding one-time gain (a credit). The business press of the period was full of articles warning investors of the large cosmetic accounting gains that companies were expected to report.[1] General Electric adopted Statement No. 96 in 1987; as a result, General Electric's finance subsidiary showed a gain of $518 million, increasing the subsidiary's net income by 106%. IBM adopted Statement No. 96 in 1988 and showed a gain of $315 million. Exxon made the adoption in 1989 and increased net income by 18% with a $535 million gain.

In response to one of the major criticisms of Statement No. 96, Statement No. 109, as explained more fully in the chapter, allows the recognition of most deferred tax assets. Once again, the business press warned investors to beware of firms reporting one-time accounting gains because of the change in accounting for deferred taxes.[2] These gains come about because previously unrecorded deferred tax assets are recognized (a debit), along with a corresponding gain (a credit). For example, on September 30, 1992, IBM announced that it would report a $1.9 billion gain as a result of adopting Statement No. 109. Interestingly, this gain was used to partially offset a $2.1 billion write-off of buildings and equipment.[3]

This chapter begins with a discussion of the concepts and issues associated with deferred taxes. The rest of the chapter focuses on the important provisions of FASB Statement No. 109 and relevant income tax laws.

DEFERRED INCOME TAXES: AN OVERVIEW

When taking introductory financial accounting, many students are surprised to learn that corporations in the United States compute two different income numbers — **financial income** for reporting to stockholders and **taxable income** for reporting to the Internal Revenue Service. The existence of these two "sets of books" seems unethical to some, illegal to others. However, the difference between the information needs of the stockholders and the efficient revenue collection needs of the government makes the computation of the two different income numbers essential. The different purposes of these reporting systems was summarized by the United States Supreme Court in the Thor Power Tool case (1979):

The primary goal of financial accounting is to provide useful information to management, shareholders, creditors, and others properly interested; the major responsibility of the accountant is to protect these parties from being misled. The primary goal of the income tax system, in contrast, is the equitable collection of revenue.

In summary, U.S. corporations compute income in two different ways, and rightly so. But, the existence of these two different numbers that can each be called "income before taxes" makes it surprisingly difficult to define what is meant by "income tax expense" and to compute an appropriate balance sheet value for income tax liabilities and prepaid income tax assets. This accounting difficulty stems from two basic considerations:

1. How to account for revenues and expenses that have already been recognized and reported to shareholders in a company's financial statements but that will not affect taxable income until subsequent years.

1. For an example, see Lee Berton, "FASB Is Expected to Issue Rule Allowing Many Firms to Post Big, One-Time Gains," *The Wall Street Journal,* November 4, 1987, p. 4.

2. See Mary Beth Grover, "Cosmetics," *Forbes,* March 30, 1992, p. 78.

3. See Michael W. Miller and Laurence Hooper, "IBM Announces Write-Off for Total of $2.1 Billion," *The Wall Street Journal,* September 30, 1992, p. A3.

2. How to account for revenues and expenses that have already been reported to the Internal Revenue Service but that will not be recognized in the financial statements until subsequent years.

Two simple examples will be used to illustrate the accounting issues resulting from this difference between financial accounting income and taxable income.

Example 1. Simple Deferred Income Tax Liability

In 1996, Ibanez Company earned revenues of $30,000. Ibanez has no expenses other than income taxes. Assume that, in this case, the income tax law specifies that income is taxed when received in cash and that Ibanez received $10,000 cash in 1996 and expects to receive $20,000 in 1997. The income tax rate is 40%.

The two amounts to be determined are total income tax liability at the end of the year and total income tax expense for the year. Obviously, the income tax liability is at least $4,000 since that is how much the IRS is expecting based on Ibanez's reported taxable income of $10,000. In addition, it would be misleading to the shareholders not to tell them of the expected tax to be paid on the additional $20,000 to be received in cash in 1997. Remember, this $20,000 in income has been reported to the shareholders because it was earned in 1996, but it has not yet been reported to the IRS. The expected tax on the $20,000 is $8,000 ($20,000 × .40) and is called a **deferred tax liability**. This liability can be thought of as the expected income tax on income earned but not yet taxed. The journal entries to record all of the tax-related information for Ibanez for 1996 are as follows:

Income Tax Expense—Current	4,000	
Income Taxes Payable		4,000
Income Tax Expense—Deferred	8,000	
Deferred Tax Liability		8,000

It is important to recognize the difference between the two recorded liabilities. Income Taxes Payable is an existing legal liability which the IRS fully expects to collect by April 15, 1997. Deferred Tax Liability is not an existing legal liability — as far as the IRS is concerned, it doesn't exist. However, since Ibanez knows that $20,000 of the revenues earned in 1996 will be taxed in 1997, recognition of the deferred tax liability is necessary to ensure that all expenses associated with 1996 revenues are reported in the 1996 income statement and that all obligations are reported in the December 31, 1996 balance sheet.

As can be seen from the income tax journal entries for 1996, total income tax expense of $12,000 is the sum of the current and deferred tax expenses. The 1996 income statement for Ibanez Company is as follows:

Revenues		$30,000
Income tax expense:		
Current	$4,000	
Deferred	8,000	12,000
Net income		$18,000

Some have argued that reported income tax expense should just be the amount currently payable according to IRS rules. This type of disclosure would lead to a rude surprise in 1997 for the Ibanez shareholders—Ibanez will owe $8,000 in income tax in 1997 even if no new revenues are generated in 1997.

Example 2. Simple Deferred Tax Asset

In 1996, its first year of operations, Gupta Company generated service revenues totaling $60,000, all taxable in 1996. Gupta Company offers a warranty on its service. No warranty claims were made in 1996, but Gupta estimates that in 1997 warranty costs of $10,000 will be incurred for warranty claims relating to 1996 service revenues. The $10,000 estimated warranty expense is reported in the 1996 financial statements as required by GAAP. For tax purposes, however, assume that the IRS does not allow any tax deduction until the actual warranty services are performed. Also assume that the income tax rate is 40% and that Gupta Company had no expenses in 1996 other than warranty costs and income taxes.

Income taxes payable as of the end of 1996 is $24,000 ($60,000 × .40) since Gupta is required to report $60,000 in revenues to the IRS but is not allowed to take any warranty deduction until 1997. What about the $10,000 warranty deduction Gupta expects to take in 1997? Gupta can expect this deduction to lower the 1997 tax bill by $4,000 ($10,000 × .40). This $4,000 is a **deferred tax asset** and represents the expected benefit of a tax deduction for an expense item which has already been incurred and reported to the shareholders but is not yet deductible according to IRS rules. The journal entries to record all of the tax-related information for Gupta for 1996 is as follows:

Income Tax Expense—Current	24,000	
Income Taxes Payable		24,000
Deferred Tax Asset	4,000	
Income Tax Benefit—Deferred		4,000

Total income tax expense of $20,000 is the difference between the current tax expense and the deferred tax benefit. The 1996 income statement for Gupta Company is as follows:

Revenues		$60,000
Warranty expense		10,000
Income before taxes		$50,000
Income tax expense:		
Current	$24,000	
Deferred benefit	(4,000)	20,000
Net income		$30,000

As explained in detail later in the chapter, deferred tax assets can be much more complicated than this simple example indicates. The complications revolve around whether Gupta will ever be able to realize the benefit from the $10,000 future warranty tax deduction. Dissatisfaction over the FASB's handling of this issue contributed to the demise of Statement No. 96 and the adoption of Statement No. 109.

Permanent and Temporary Differences

Before more detailed deferred tax examples are presented, some of the specific differences between financial accounting standards and tax rules will be described.

Some differences between financial and taxable income are **permanent differences.** These differences are caused by specific provisions of the tax law that exempt certain types of revenues from taxation and prohibit the deduction of certain types of expenses. Nontaxable revenues and nondeductible expenses are never included in determining taxable income, but they are included in determining financial income under generally accepted accounting principles. Permanent differences are created by political and social pressures to favor certain segments of society or to promote certain industries or economic activities. Examples of nontaxable revenues include proceeds from life insurance policies and interest received on municipal bonds. Examples of nondeductible expenses include fines for violation of laws, and payment of life insurance premiums. Permanent differences do not create accounting problems. Because they are never included in the computation of taxable income, they have no impact on either current or future (deferred) tax obligations.

More commonly, differences between pretax financial income and taxable income arise from business events that are recognized for both financial reporting and tax purposes, but in different time periods. In some cases, income tax payments are deferred to a period later than when the effect of the event on financial income is recognized. In other cases, income tax payments are required before the effect of the event on financial income is recognized. These differences are referred to as **temporary differences** because, over time, their impact on financial income and taxable income will be the same.

A common example of a temporary difference, and one that historically has been the most significant for U.S. companies, is the computation of depreciation. As indicated in Chapter 12, depreciation for federal income tax purposes is referred to as *cost recovery* and has varied over time as to the degree of acceleration in the recovery of asset costs. On the other hand, the most common depreciation method used to determine financial income is the straight-line method, which recognizes an even amount of depreciation expense each year the asset is in service. In the early years of asset life, straight-line depreciation reported on the income statement usually is less than the cost recovery deduction on the income tax return. In the latter portion of an asset's life, however, this pattern reverses; that is, the depreciation expense on the income statement exceeds the cost recovery deduction on the tax return.

There are many other temporary differences besides depreciation, and new income tax laws continue to create additional ones as income taxes are used to meet changing economic and policy objectives. Some examples of temporary differences are given in Exhibit 20—1. This list is just a sample of the differences between financial accounting standards and income tax laws that can create temporary differences between financial and taxable income.

Exhibit 20—1
Examples of Temporary Differences

1. Differences That Create Deferred Tax Liabilities for Future Taxable Amounts

(a) Revenues or gains are taxable after they are recognized for financial reporting purposes.

- Installment sales method used for tax purposes, but accrual method of recognizing sales revenue used for financial reporting purposes.
- Completed-contract method of recognizing construction revenue used for tax purposes, but percentage-of-completion method used for financial reporting purposes.

(b) Expenses or losses are deductible for tax purposes before they are recognized for financial reporting purposes.

- MACRS used for tax purposes, but straight-line method of depreciation used for financial reporting purposes.
- Intangible drilling costs for extractive industry written off as incurred for tax purposes, but capitalized for financial reporting purposes.

2. Differences That Create Deferred Tax Assets for Future Deductible Amounts

(a) Revenues or gains are taxable before they are recognized for financial reporting purposes.

- Rent revenue received in advance of period earned recognized as revenue for tax purposes, but deferred to be recognized in future periods for financial reporting purposes.
- Subscription revenue received in advance of period earned recognized as revenue for tax purposes, but deferred to be recognized in future periods for financial reporting purposes.

(b) Expenses or losses are deductible for tax purposes after they are recognized for financial reporting purposes.

- Warranty expense deductible for tax purposes only when actually incurred, but accrued in the year of product sale for financial reporting purposes.
- Marketable securities valued at cost for tax purposes, but valued at market for financial reporting purposes.

History of the Accounting for Deferred Taxes

In the history of accounting standard setting, few issues have caused as much commotion as that of accounting for deferred income taxes. The debate began with a basic conceptual issue: are income taxes paid by a business to be considered as expenses of doing business or as a distribution of income to government entities? If viewed as a distribution of income, the amount of income taxes paid each period could be shown as the portion of financial income that is not available to the owners of the business. This amount would be determined by the tax laws in effect each period, and the existence of temporary differences would be of no consequence in the financial statements. If income taxes are considered to be business expenses, however, then the underlying concept of accrual accounting requires that the impact of temporary differences be reflected in the financial statements.

As the number of differences between pretax financial income and taxable income began to increase in the late 1940s and early 1950s, there were many articles in the accounting literature arguing the merits of these two positions. When the AICPA Committee on Accounting Procedures issued a consolidated set of accounting procedures in 1953, *Accounting Research Bulletin (ARB) No. 43*, it chose to consider income taxes as expenses, concluding that

> Income taxes are an expense that should be allocated, as other expenses are allocated. What the income statement should reflect under this head, as under any other head, is the expense properly allocable to the income included in the income statement for the year.[4]

Once the decision was made to classify income taxes as expenses, the next critical conceptual issue was how to measure income tax expense each period, and then how to report the difference between the amount shown as income tax expense on the income statement and the amount of income taxes actually paid based on taxable income. No guidance on this issue was included in ARB No. 43, but in 1967, the Accounting Principles Board issued Opinion No. 11, "Accounting for Income Taxes," the standard that governed this area for over 20 years. Under APB Opinion No. 11, the deferred method was used in accounting for income taxes. Under this method, income tax expense is the amount of tax that *would have been paid* based on financial income and using current year tax rates. The deferred method of allocation emphasizes the income statement—income tax expense is computed directly on the current year's financial income and the deferred tax on the balance sheet (debit or credit) is a residual amount, the difference between the expense and the taxes payable for the period. Changes in future tax rates are not considered even though the actual tax effect will depend on the rates in effect when differences reverse. Thus, under the deferred method, over time deferred tax balances become meaningless as a measure of assets (future tax benefits) or liabilities (future tax payments).

The FASB expressed concern over the deferred method of reporting income taxes in Statement of Financial Accounting Concepts No. 3, "Elements of Financial Statements of Business Enterprises," issued in 1980. The Board concluded that deferred income tax amounts reported on the balance sheet did not meet the newly established conceptual framework definitions of assets and liabilities.[5] Other criticisms leveled against the deferred method included inconsistencies in the various accounting requirements, emphasis on procedures with little theoretical justification, and the excessive time and cost involved in applying APB Opinion No. 11 relative to the benefits.[6]

These concerns led the FASB to add income taxes to its agenda in 1982. For five years the Board issued Discussion Memorandums, held public hearings, and considered the many arguments. The Board was determined to make income tax accounting meet the asset and liability definitions of the conceptual framework. The result was the issuance in December 1987 of FASB Statement No. 96, which abandoned the deferred method of interperiod tax allocation in favor of the asset and liability method. The stated objectives of the asset and liability method are as follows:

> One objective of accounting for income taxes is to recognize the amount of taxes payable or refundable for the current year. A second objective is to recognize deferred tax liabilities and assets for the future tax consequences of events that have been recognized in an enterprise's financial statements or tax returns.[7]

The second objective points out a fundamental difference between the asset and liability method and the deferred method. The asset and liability method emphasizes the

4. *Statement and Revision of Accounting Research Bulletin No. 43,* "Income Taxes" (New York: AICPA, 1953), Ch. 10, Section B., par. 4.

5. *Statement of Financial Accounting Concepts No. 3,* "Elements of Financial Statements of Business Enterprises" (Stamford: Financial Accounting Standards Board, 1980), par. 164.

6. *Statement of Financial Accounting Standards No. 96,* "Accounting for Income Taxes" (Stamford: Financial Accounting Standards Board, 1987), pars. 197-198.

7. *Statement of Financial Accounting Standards No. 109,* "Accounting for Income Taxes" (Norwalk: Financial Accounting Standards Board, 1992), par. 6.

reporting of balance sheet amounts that measure the future tax consequences of temporary differences. Deferred tax assets and liabilities are measured and recorded by applying currently enacted tax rates and laws that will be in effect when the differences reverse,[8] and the income tax expense reported on the income statement is a residual amount. Further, when tax rate changes are enacted in subsequent periods, deferred tax asset and liability balances are adjusted to reflect the impact of the changes.

After FASB Statement No. 96 was issued and before its mandatory implementation date, many companies became concerned when they began to see the effect the standard would have on their financial statements and the cost they would incur in implementing it. From a theoretical perspective, some opposed the inconsistent treatment of deferred tax liabilities and deferred tax assets. Others complained that since the deferred tax liability amount is not discounted to its present value and may never be paid anyway, it doesn't represent a true liability. Others argued that the FASB is fundamentally misguided in emphasizing deferred tax reporting on the balance sheet, when historically the topic of deferred taxes arose in the context of proper reporting of tax expense on the income statement. Practitioners objected to the complex scheduling requirements and to the requirement to devise hypothetical tax strategies. One firm, Citicorp, estimated that it would cost $3,000,000 to implement the standard. The objections became so strong that the FASB postponed the implementation date from 1988 to 1989,[9] from 1989 to 1991,[10] and then from 1991 to 1992.[11]

In response to the issuance of Statement No. 96, the FASB "received (a) requests for about 20 different limited-scope amendments to Statement No. 96, (b) requests to change the criteria for recognition and measurement of deferred tax assets to anticipate, in certain circumstances, the tax consequences of future income, and (c) requests to reduce the complexity of scheduling the future reversals of temporary differences and considering hypothetical tax-planning strategies."[12] These requests to amend FASB Statement No. 96 were considered at 41 public Board meetings and three Implementation Group meetings. On June 5, 1991, the FASB issued an Exposure Draft that proposed superseding FASB Statement No. 96 and several other accounting pronouncements. Finally, in February 1992, FASB Statement No. 109 was issued. Many are hoping that this whole area of accounting for deferred taxes will settle down for a while so that users and preparers of financial statements can catch their collective breaths.

Questions:

1. Many are concerned that the extended flap over deferred tax accounting has hurt the credibility of the FASB. What dangers are there in a loss of prestige by the FASB?
2. Should pressures from practitioners be allowed to influence the FASB's deliberations?
3. In your opinion, have all the time and resources spent in the area of deferred taxes by the FASB, practitioners, and other interest groups been worth the benefits?

The examples in the exhibit are presented in two major categories. The first category includes differences, called **taxable temporary differences,** that will result in *taxable amounts* in future years. Income taxes expected to be paid on future taxable amounts are reported in the balance sheet as a **deferred tax liability.** The second category includes differences, called **deductible temporary differences,** that will result in *deductible amounts* in future years. Income tax benefits (savings) expected to be realized from future deductible amounts are reported in the balance sheet as a **deferred tax asset.**

Illustration of Permanent and Temporary Differences

To illustrate the effect of permanent and temporary differences on the computation of income taxes, assume that for the year ending December 31, 1996, Monroe Corporation reported income before taxes of $420,000. Assume this amount includes $20,000 of non-

8. Changes in tax rates and other provisions of the tax law often are legislated prior to the years in which they become effective. For example, the 1986 Tax Reform Act legislated a phased tax rate reduction over three years.

9. *Statement of Financial Accounting Standards No. 100,* "Accounting for Income Taxes—Deferral of the Effective Date of FASB Statement No. 96" (Norwalk: Financial Accounting Standards Board, December 1988).

10. *Statement of Financial Accounting Standards No. 103,* "Accounting for Income Taxes—Deferral of the Effective Date of FASB Statement No. 96" (Norwalk: Financial Accounting Standards Board, December 1989).

11. *Statement of Financial Accounting Standards No. 108,* "Accounting for Income Taxes—Deferral of the Effective Date of FASB Statement No. 96" (Norwalk: Financial Accounting Standards Board, February 1992).

12. *Exposure Draft of Proposed Statement of Financial Accounting Standards,* "Accounting for Income Taxes" (Norwalk: Financial Accounting Standards Board, June 5, 1991), Appendix C, par. 266.

taxable revenues and $5,000 of nondeductible expenses, both permanent differences. In addition, assume that Monroe has two temporary differences: (1) the depreciation (cost recovery) deduction on the 1996 income tax return exceeds depreciation expense on the income statement by $30,000, and (2) rent revenue included on the 1996 tax return is $14,000 more than the amount recognized on the income statement. The latter difference arises because current federal income tax laws require recognition of rent revenue when the payment is received, not when the rent is earned. Assuming a corporate income tax rate of 35% for 1996, income taxes payable for the year would be computed as follows:

Pretax financial income (from income statement)		$420,000
Add (deduct) permanent differences:		
Nontaxable revenues	$(20,000)	
Nondeductible expenses	5,000	(15,000)
Pretax financial income subject to tax		$405,000
Add (deduct) temporary differences:		
Excess of tax depreciation over book depreciation		(30,000)
Excess of tax rent revenue over book rent revenue		14,000
Taxable income		$389,000
Tax on taxable income (income taxes payable):		
$389,000 × .35		$136,150

As illustrated, the permanent differences are not included in either the financial income subject to tax or the taxable income. In addition, since these permanent differences never reverse, they have no impact on income taxes payable in subsequent periods and are thus not associated with any deferred tax consequences. Temporary differences are the cause of the complexity and controversy in accounting for income taxes, because they impact financial income and taxable income in different periods. In general, the accounting for temporary differences is referred to as **interperiod tax allocation.**

ANNUAL COMPUTATION OF DEFERRED TAX LIABILITIES AND ASSETS

As illustrated with the earlier examples, the basic concepts underlying deferred tax accounting are fairly simple. The examples that follow introduce some of the complexities associated with the specific provisions of Statement No. 109. Before launching into these examples, take a moment to reflect on how lucky you are not to have taken this class a few years ago. At the time, this chapter was based on Statement No. 96 which was much more difficult to understand and to implement and was hated by practitioners, financial statement users, students, and professors.

As discussed in the boxed item on pages 856–857, FASB Statement No. 109 reflects the Board's preference for the **asset and liability method of interperiod tax allocation,** which emphasizes the measurement and reporting of balance sheet amounts. The following steps summarize the procedure to be followed each year to compute the amount of deferred tax liabilities and assets to be included in the financial statements under the provisions of FASB Statement No. 109.[13]

1. Identify the types and amounts of existing temporary differences.
2. Measure the deferred tax liability for taxable temporary differences using the applicable tax rate.
3. Measure the deferred tax asset for deductible temporary differences using the applicable tax rate.

13. FASB Statement No. 109, par. 17.

4. Reduce deferred tax assets by a valuation allowance if it is more likely than not (a likelihood of more than 50 percent) that some portion or all of the deferred tax assets will not be realized. The valuation allowance should reduce the deferred tax asset to the amount that is more likely than not to be realized.

Several examples will illustrate the computation of deferred tax assets and liabilities under the provisions of Statement No. 109.

Example 3. Deferred Tax Liability

If a company has only deferred tax liabilities to consider, the accounting for deferred taxes is relatively straightforward. To illustrate assume that Roland, Inc. begins operations in 1996. For 1996, Roland computes pretax financial income of $75,000. The only difference between financial accounting income and taxable income is depreciation. Roland uses the straight-line method of depreciation for financial reporting purposes and an accelerated cost recovery method on its tax return. The depreciation amounts for existing plant assets for the years 1996 through 1999 are as follows:

Year	Financial Reporting	Income Tax Reporting
1996	$ 25,000	$ 40,000
1997	25,000	30,000
1998	25,000	25,000
1999	25,000	5,000
	$100,000	$100,000

The enacted tax rate for 1996 and future years is 40%. At the end of 1996, aggregate tax depreciation exceeds aggregate book depreciation by $15,000 ($40,000 – $25,000). This is a *taxable temporary difference* that will result in a taxable amount of $15,000 in future years as the difference reverses. With the currently enacted 40% tax rate, income tax on this future taxable amount will total $6,000 ($15,000 × .40). Accordingly, a deferred tax liability of $6,000 will be reported on the December 31, 1996 balance sheet. Because the depreciable asset is a noncurrent operating asset, the associated deferred tax liability is also classified as noncurrent.

The journal entries to record Roland's income taxes for 1996 would be as follows:

Income Tax Expense—Current	24,000	
Income Taxes Payable [($75,000 – $15,000) × .40]		24,000
Income Tax Expense—Deferred	6,000	
Deferred Tax Liability—Noncurrent		6,000

Income taxes would be shown on Roland's 1996 income statement as follows:

Roland, Inc.
1996 Partial Income Statement

Income before income taxes		$75,000
Income tax expense:		
Current	$24,000	
Deferred	6,000	30,000
Net income		$45,000

The December 31, 1996 balance sheet would report a current liability of $24,000 for income taxes payable and, as noted above, a noncurrent deferred tax liability of $6,000.

In each subsequent year, the ending deferred tax liability is determined and compared with the beginning balance. The difference between the beginning and ending balance is recorded as an adjustment to the deferred tax liability account. For example, at the end of 1997, aggregate tax depreciation exceeds aggregate book depreciation by $20,000 ($70,000 – $50,000). The deferred tax liability account, therefore, must be adjusted to a balance of $8,000 ($20,000 × .40). The amount of the adjustment is $2,000 ($8,000 less the beginning balance of $6,000), recorded as follows:

Income Tax Expense—Deferred	2,000	
Deferred Tax Liability—Noncurrent		2,000

Because the depreciation expense for tax and financial reporting purposes are the same for 1998, no adjustment to the deferred tax liability account would be necessary for that year. At the end of 1999, the accumulated difference of $20,000 reverses, and aggregate tax depreciation and aggregate book depreciation are the same ($100,000). Thus the deferred tax liability must be reduced to zero with the following adjustment:

Deferred Tax Liability—Noncurrent	8,000	
Income Tax Benefit		8,000

The income tax benefit reduces the current income tax expense for 1999.

Effect of Currently Enacted Changes in Future Tax Rates. The example assumed a constant future tax rate of 40%. If changes in future tax rates have been enacted, the deferred tax liability (or asset) is measured using the enacted tax rate for the future years when the temporary difference is expected to reverse. To illustrate, assume that in 1996, Congress enacts legislation that reduces corporate tax rates for 1997 and subsequent years. In the Roland, Inc. example, all of the temporary difference reverses in 1999, and the deferred tax liability should be measured using the tax rate enacted for that year. If the enacted tax rate for 1999 is 35%, the deferred tax liability at the end of 1996 would be $5,250 ($15,000 × .35) rather than $6,000 as computed above. At the end of 1997 the deferred tax liability would be $7,000 ($20,000 × .35) and the required adjustment would be $1,750 ($7,000 – $5,250).

Subsequent Changes in Enacted Tax Rates. When rate changes are enacted after a deferred tax liability or asset has been recorded, FASB Statement No. 109 requires that the beginning deferred account balance be adjusted to reflect the new tax rate. Again using the Roland, Inc. example, assume that the enacted tax rate for 1999 changed from 40% to 35% during 1997. The balance in the deferred tax liability at the beginning of 1997 is $6,000 ($15,000 × .40). The following entry would be made to reflect the newly enacted 35% tax rate for 1999.

Deferred Tax Liability—Noncurrent	750	
Income Tax Benefit—Rate Change ($15,000 × .05)		750

The income effect of the change is reflected in income tax expense. In this case, the effect is a tax benefit resulting from a lower tax rate and would be shown as a reduction in income tax expense in the 1997 income statement.

Example 4. Deferred Tax Asset

Assume that Sandusky, Inc. begins operations in 1996. For 1996, Sandusky computes pre-tax financial income of $22,000. The only difference between financial and taxable income is the recognition of warranty expense. Sandusky accrues estimated warranty expense in the year of sale for financial reporting purposes but deducts only actual warranty expenditures for tax purposes. Accrued warranty expense for 1996 was $18,000; no actual warranty expenditures were made in 1996. Therefore, taxable income in 1996 is $40,000 ($22,000 + $18,000). The difference in 1996 between warranty expense for financial reporting and tax purposes is a *deductible temporary difference*, because it will result in future tax deductions of $18,000. The deferred tax asset implied by this difference is $7,200 ($18,000 × .40). Warranty expenditures for 1996 sales are expected to be $6,000 in each of the years 1997-1999. Since the underlying warranty obligation is assumed to be one-third current and two-thirds noncurrent, the associated deferred tax asset would be classified in the same ratio.

The future tax deduction of $18,000 will provide a tax benefit only if Sandusky has taxable income in future periods against which the deduction can be offset. Accordingly, in order to record a deferred tax asset, one must assume that sufficient taxable income will exist in future years. Conditions under which this assumption may or may not be reasonable are described later in the chapter in the section titled "Valuation Allowance for Deferred Tax Assets."

Assuming that future taxable income will be sufficient to allow for full realization of the tax benefits of the $18,000 future tax deduction, the journal entries to record Sandusky's income taxes for 1996 would be as follows:

Income Tax Expense—Current	16,000	
Income Taxes Payable [($22,000 + $18,000) × .40]		16,000
Deferred Tax Asset—Current	2,400*	
Deferred Tax Asset—Noncurrent	4,800**	
Income Tax Benefit		7,200

*1/3 of underlying warranty obligation is current (1/3 × $7,200)
**2/3 of underlying warranty obligation is noncurrent (2/3 × $7,200)

Sandusky's 1996 income statement would present income tax expense as follows:

Sandusky, Inc.
Partial 1996 Income Statement

Income before income taxes		$22,000
Income tax expense:		
Current expense	$16,000	
Deferred benefit	(7,200)	8,800
Net income		$13,200

Sandusky's December 31, 1996 balance sheet would report deferred tax assets of $2,400 under current assets and $4,800 under noncurrent assets. Income taxes payable for 1996 would be shown with current liabilities.

Example 5. Deferred Tax Liabilities and Assets

Hsieh Company began operation on January 1, 1996. As of December 31, 1996, the actual differences between Hsieh Company's financial accounting and income tax records for 1996, and the estimated differences for 1997-1999, are summarized as follows:

	Financial Reporting		Income Tax Reporting	
	Depreciation Expense	Warranty Expense	Depreciation Deduction	Warranty Deduction
1996 (actual)	$25,000	$18,000	$40,000	$ 0
1997 (est.)	25,000	0	25,000	6,000
1998 (est.)	25,000	0	25,000	6,000
1999 (est.)	25,000	0	10,000	6,000

The enacted income tax rate for all years is 40%.

As of December 31, 1996, aggregate tax depreciation exceeds aggregate book depreciation by $15,000 ($40,000 – $25,000). As explained previously, this represents a future taxable amount. The income tax expected to be paid on this amount is $6,000 ($15,000 × .40). This $6,000 is a deferred tax liability as of December 31, 1996. Because the difference relates to a noncurrent item, the deferred tax liability is a noncurrent liability.

As of December 31, 1996, Hsieh has recognized an $18,000 warranty expense for financial accounting purposes which it plans to deduct for tax purposes over the next three years. Assuming that future taxable income will be sufficient to allow the tax benefit of this deduction to be fully realized, this future deductible amount creates a deferred tax asset of $7,200 ($18,000 × .40). Since the underlying warranty liability is part current ($6,000) and part noncurrent ($12,000), the deferred tax asset would also be classified as part current ($2,400 = $6,000 × .40) and part noncurrent ($4,800 = $12,000 × .40). The journal entry to record the deferred portion of Hsieh's 1996 income tax expense is as follows:

Deferred Tax Asset—Current	2,400	
Deferred Tax Asset—Noncurrent	4,800	
Income Tax Benefit		1,200
Deferred Tax Liability—Noncurrent		6,000

For reporting purposes, current deferred tax assets and current deferred tax liabilities are netted against one another and reported as a single amount. Similarly, noncurrent deferred tax assets and liabilities are netted and reported as a single amount.[14] In this example, the amounts to be reported in Hsieh's December 31, 1996 balance sheet are a $2,400 current deferred tax asset and a $1,200 noncurrent deferred tax liability ($6,000 liability – $4,800 asset). The income tax benefit would be shown as a $1,200 reduction of current income tax expense in the 1996 income statement.

Valuation Allowance for Deferred Tax Assets

A deferred tax asset represents future income tax benefits. But the tax benefits will be realized only if there is sufficient taxable income from which the deductible amount can be deducted. FASB Statement No. 109 requires that the deferred tax asset be reduced by a valuation allowance if, based on all available evidence, it is *more likely than not* that some portion or all of the deferred tax asset will not be realized. As applied to deferred tax assets, *more likely than not* means a likelihood of more than 50 percent.[15] The **valuation allowance** is a contra-asset account that reduces the asset to its expected realizable value.

In the Hsieh Company example, it was assumed that there would be sufficient taxable income to allow for the full realization of the benefits from the $18,000 warranty deduction and thus no valuation allowance was established. Some possible sources of taxable income to be considered in evaluating the realizable value of a deferred tax asset are:[16]

14. FASB Statement No. 109, par. 42.
15. *Ibid.*, par. 17e.
16. *Ibid.*, par. 21.

1. Future reversals of existing taxable temporary differences.
2. Future taxable income exclusive of reversing temporary differences.
3. Taxable income in prior (carryback) years.

The first source of future taxable income, reversals of taxable temporary differences, can be identified without making assumptions about the profitability of future operations. In 1996, Hsieh Company has a $15,000 excess of aggregate tax depreciation over aggregate book depreciation, which will result in a future taxable amount. The reversal of this temporary difference will provide taxable income in the future against which the $18,000 warranty deduction can be offset. If it appears more likely than not that no other income will be available, then only $15,000 of the $18,000 warranty deduction is expected to be realized. Accordingly, the total deferred tax asset is $7,200 ($18,000 × .40), but the realizable amount is only $6,000 ($15,000 × .40). The $1,200 difference would be recorded as a valuation allowance, an offset to the reported deferred tax asset. For classification purposes, the valuation allowance is to be allocated proportionately between the current and noncurrent portions of the deferred tax asset.[17] In this example, since one-third of the deferred tax asset is current ($6,000/$18,000), one-third, or $400 ($1,200 × 1/3) of the valuation would be classified as current. The remaining $800 ($1,200 – $400) of the valuation allowance is noncurrent. The journal entry recording the deferred portion of income tax expense for 1996 is as follows:

Deferred Tax Asset—Current	2,400	
Deferred Tax Asset—Noncurrent	4,800	
Allowance to Reduce Deferred Tax Asset to Realizable Value—Current		400
Allowance to Reduce Deferred Tax Asset to Realizable Value—Noncurrent		800
Deferred Tax Liability—Noncurrent		6,000

In 1997 and subsequent years, the company should reconsider available evidence to determine whether the valuation account should be adjusted.

Future reversal of existing taxable differences is only one source of taxable income through which the benefit of a deferred tax asset can be realized. Other sources include taxable income expected from profitable operations in future years and taxable income in prior carryback years. This latter source relates to specific carryback provisions of the tax law, which are explained later in the chapter.

Statement No. 109 stipulates that both positive and negative evidence be considered when determining whether deferred tax assets will be fully realized.[18] Examples of negative evidence include cumulative losses in recent years, a history of the expiration of unused tax loss carryforwards, and unsettled circumstances that might cause a currently profitable company to report losses in future years. Positive evidence includes the existence of an order backlog sufficient to yield enough taxable income for the deferred tax asset to be realized, the existence of appreciated assets, and a strong earnings history.

The FASB was very reluctant to allow firms to consider possible future taxable income when evaluating the realizability of deferred tax assets because, as stated in FASB Statement No. 96:

Incurring losses or generating profits in future years are future events that are not recognized in financial statements for the current year. Those future events shall not be anticipated, regardless of probability, for purposes of recognizing and measuring a deferred tax liability or asset in the cur-

17. *Ibid.*, par. 41.
18. *Ibid.*, par. 20.

rent year. The tax consequences of those future events shall be recognized and reported in the financial statements in future years when the events occur.[19]

However, because many firms complained that it was unfair to require them to report deferred tax liabilities but not allow them to report deferred tax assets, the FASB reconsidered and revised its position. Statement No. 109 explicitly allows a firm to consider potential future income in evaluating the realizability of deferred tax assets.

CARRYBACK AND CARRYFORWARD OF OPERATING LOSSES

Because income tax is based on the amount of income earned, no tax is payable if a company experiences an operating loss. As an incentive to those businesses that experience alternate periods of income and losses, United States tax laws provide a way to ease the risk of loss years. This is done through a carryback and carryforward provision that permits a company to apply a net operating loss occurring in one year against income of other years. Specifically, the Internal Revenue Code provides for a three-year carryback and a fifteen-year carryforward.[20]

Net Operating Loss (NOL) Carryback

A **net operating loss (NOL) carryback** is applied to the income of the three preceding years in reverse order, beginning with the third year and moving to the first year. If unused net operating losses are still available, they may be carried forward up to fifteen years to offset any future income. Amended income tax returns must be filed for each year to which the carryback is applied to receive refunds of previously paid income taxes. Net operating loss carrybacks result in a journal entry establishing a current receivable for the tax refund claim. The benefit that arises from such refunds is used to reduce the loss in the current period. This treatment is supported in theory because it is the current year's operating loss that results in the tax refund.

To illustrate, assume the Prairie Company had the following pattern of income and losses for the years 1994-1997.

Year	Income (Loss)	Income Tax Rate	Income Tax
1994	$ 15,000	40%	$6,000
1995	10,000	35	3,500
1996	14,000	30	4,200
1997	(29,000)	30	0

The $29,000 net operating loss in 1997 would be carried back to 1994 first, then to 1995, and finally, $4,000 to 1996. An income tax refund claim of $10,700 would be filed for the 3 years [$6,000 + $3,500 + .30($4,000)]. The entry to record the income tax receivable in 1997 would be:

Income Tax Refund Receivable	10,700	
Income Tax Benefit From NOL Carryback		10,700

The refund will be reflected on the income statement as a reduction of the operating loss as follows:

19. FASB Statement No. 96, par. 15.

20. As an alternative, a taxpayer can elect to forego the carryback and carry the entire loss forward for up to fifteen years. This election is seldom made, because carrybacks result in current refunds of taxes.

Prairie Company
1997 Partial Income Statement

Net operating loss before income tax benefit	$(29,000)
Income tax benefit from NOL carryback	10,700
Net loss	$(18,300)

The 1997 net operating loss reduces the 1994 and 1995 taxable income to zero and the 1996 taxable income to $10,000 ($14,000 – $4,000). If another net operating loss occurs within the next two years, it may be carried back to the remaining $10,000 from 1996.

Net Operating Loss (NOL) Carryforward

If an operating loss exceeds income for the three preceding years, the remaining unused loss may be applied against income earned over the next fifteen years as a **net operating loss (NOL) carryforward**. Under FASB Statement No. 109, a deferred tax asset is recognized for the potential future tax benefit from a loss carryforward. Full realization of the benefit, however, depends on the company having income equal to the carryforward in the next fifteen years. As is true for other deferred tax assets, a valuation allowance is used to reduce the asset if it is more likely than not that some or all of the future benefit will not be realized.

To illustrate the carryforward provisions, assume that in 1998 Prairie Company incurred another operating loss of $40,000. This loss would be carried back to the years 1995, 1996, and 1997 in that order. However, the only income remaining against which operating losses can be applied is $10,000 from 1996. After applying $10,000 to the 1996 income, $30,000 is left to carry forward against future income. The tax benefit from the carryback is $3,000 ($10,000 × .30). Assuming the enacted tax rate for future years is 30 percent, the potential tax benefit from the carryforward is $9,000 ($30,000 × .30). The entry in 1998 to record the tax benefits would be:

Income Tax Refund Receivable	3,000	
Deferred Tax Asset—NOL Carryforward	9,000	
Income Tax Benefit From NOL Carryback		3,000
Income Tax Benefit From NOL Carryforward		9,000

The deferred tax asset of $9,000 would be reported on the balance sheet as a current asset if it is expected to be realized in 1999. Any portion that is expected to be realized after 1999 would be classified as noncurrent. The $12,000 in tax benefits would be shown on the 1998 income statement as a reduction of the operating loss.

The journal entry above indicates that it is more likely than not that the carryforward benefit will be realized in full. If, however, it is more likely than not that some portion or all of the deferred tax asset will not be realized, a valuation account is needed to reduce the asset to its estimated realizable value. For example, assume that Prairie Company's recent losses resulted from a declining market for its products, and the weight of available evidence indicates continuing losses in subsequent years. As a result, management believes it is more likely than not that none of the asset will be realized. In this case, the journal entry to record the carryback and carryforward would be:

Income Tax Refund Receivable	3,000	
Deferred Tax Asset—NOL Carryforward	9,000	
Income Tax Benefit from NOL Carryback		3,000
Allowance to Reduce Deferred Tax Asset to Realizable Value—NOL Carryforward		9,000

As a result of this entry, the net deferred tax asset is zero—the expected realizable value. If market conditions improve, and the company does have taxable income in subsequent years, the valuation account would be adjusted. The allowance account would be decreased (debited) and an income tax benefit account would be credited.

Under APB Opinion No. 11, future tax benefits from an NOL carryforward could be reported as an asset only if future income were "assured beyond reasonable doubt." Although such a criterion is not easily met, there have been cases in which NOL carryforward benefits were reported as an asset. In Statement No. 96, the FASB was even more restrictive and prohibited reporting income tax benefits from carryforwards as an asset under any circumstances. The adoption of the *more likely than not* approach for deferred tax assets in FASB Statement No. 109 led the Board to conclude that a similar approach should be used for net operating loss carryforwards. That is, NOL carryforwards are reported as assets if it is more likely than not that future income will be sufficient to allow for the realization of the tax benefit. This is a significant change in accounting for NOL carryforwards. Under Statement No. 109, millions of dollars of previously unreported income tax carryforwards are now included in the assets of companies. For example, IBM indicated in the notes to its 1990 financial statements that in addition to $110 million of unrecognized deferred tax assets under FASB Statement No. 96, it had $700 million of unrecognized tax credit carryforwards. As reported at the beginning of the chapter, IBM announced in September 1992 that it would recognize a gain of $1.9 billion as a result of the deferred tax assets it would be able to recognize because of its adoption of Statement No. 109.

SCHEDULING FOR ENACTED FUTURE TAX RATES

Recall that the two major complaints about FASB Statement No. 96 were that it did not allow for the recognition of most deferred tax assets and that it was too complicated. The complaints about nonrecognition of deferred tax assets came primarily from companies and users of financial statements who thought the inconsistent treatment of deferred tax assets and liabilities was misleading and unfair. Complaints about the complexities of Statement No. 96 came primarily from preparers of financial statements. Those complaints focused on one topic—scheduling of the periods in which temporary differences are expected to reverse. Under the provisions of Statement No. 96, scheduling was required each year to determine which deferred tax assets could be realized since no future income could be assumed and these assets were realizable only through the carryback and carryforward provisions of the tax law. In addition, under the provisions of Statement No. 96, scheduling was necessary to determine how deferred tax assets and liabilities should be classified based on the expected period of their reversal.

Statement No. 109 eliminates much of the need for scheduling through the "more likely than not" criterion for future income and because deferred tax assets and liabilities are classified according to the classification of the underlying items instead of according to the expected reversal period. However, scheduling is still required in a limited number of cases. One such case arises when differences in enacted future tax rates make it necessary to schedule the timing of a reversal in order to match that reversal with the tax rate expected to be in effect when it occurs.

Consider again the Hsieh Company example introduced on page 861. When that example was covered before, it was assumed that the enacted income tax rate was 40% for all periods. Assume now that the enacted tax rates are as follows: 1996, 40%; 1997, 35%; 1998, 30%; and 1999, 25%. As of December 31, 1996, using the 40% rate to value the deferred tax asset stemming from the future deductible amount of $18,000 and the deferred tax liability resulting from the future taxable amount of $15,000 would be misleading since it is known that the tax rate will not be 40% when those temporary differences reverse. A more accurate valuation can be obtained by applying tax rates expected to be in effect when the differences reverse, as follows:

	Enacted Tax Rate	Deductible Amount	Asset Valuation	Taxable Amount	Liability Valuation
1997	35%	$ 6,000	$2,100	$ 0	$ 0
1998	30%	6,000	1,800	0	0
1999	25%	6,000	1,500	15,000	3,750
Total		$18,000	$5,400	$15,000	$3,750

The noncurrent deferred tax liability is $3,750 ($15,000 × .25), the expected tax to be paid on the taxable amount when it is taxed in 1999. The current deferred tax asset is $2,100 ($6,000 × .35) and the noncurrent deferred tax asset is $3,300 [($6,000 × .30) + ($6,000 × .25)]. The journal entry to record the deferred portion of income tax expense for 1996 would be as follows:

Deferred Tax Asset—Current	2,100	
Deferred Tax Asset—Noncurrent	3,300	
Income Tax Benefit		1,650
Deferred Tax Liability—Noncurrent		3,750

In this example it was assumed that future income is more likely than not to be sufficient to allow for full deductibility of the $6,000 deductible amount each year. Accordingly, the tax benefit is computed as the deductible amount times the tax rate for that year. However, if the future income were not deemed sufficient to allow for offset of the deductible amounts, and if the deferred tax asset could only be realized through the carryback provision of the tax law, the deferred tax asset would be valued using the tax rate in the carryback year. For example, if future income is unlikely but 1996 taxable income exceeds $18,000, then the deductible amounts will be realized only through carryback and offset against 1996 taxable income. If this is the case, the deferred tax asset would be valued using the tax rate in effect for 1996, the carryback year.

FINANCIAL STATEMENT PRESENTATION AND DISCLOSURE

In classified balance sheets, deferred tax assets and liabilities must be reported as either current or noncurrent. As discussed previously, FASB Statement No. 109 provides for some offsetting of deferred assets and liabilities. In order for offsetting to be acceptable, the asset and liability must both be current or both be noncurrent. A current asset cannot be offset against a noncurrent liability.Most companies are subject to state and municipal income taxes as well as federal income taxes. If a business enterprise pays income taxes in more than one tax jurisdiction, no offsetting is permitted across jurisdictions.

The income statement must show, either in the body of the statement or in a note, the following selected components of income taxes related to continuing operations:[21]

1. Current tax expense or benefit.
2. Deferred tax expense or benefit.
3. Investment tax credits.
4. Government grants recognized as tax reductions.
5. Benefits of operating loss carryforwards.
6. Adjustments of a deferred tax liability or asset for enacted changes in tax laws or rates or a change in the tax status of an enterprise.
7. Adjustments in the beginning-of-the-year valuation allowance because of a change in circumstances.

21. FASB Statement No. 109, par. 45.

International Accounting for Deferred Taxes

Tired of the complexities and controversies surrounding the accounting for deferred taxes? The solution used to be to move to Sweden. For many years, the Swedish approach was quite simple and is summarized in the following quotation from the 1989 annual report of Volvo: "Following Swedish accounting practice, no provision is generally made for deferred income taxes." This no-deferral approach and the asset and liability approach adopted by the FASB represent the extremes in deferred tax accounting. Practices in other countries fall somewhere in between. In the United Kingdom, for example, a deferred tax liability is recorded only to the extent that the deferred taxes are actually expected to be paid in the future.

In many countries, the importance of deferred tax accounting is greatly reduced because of a close correspondence between financial accounting standards and tax rules. In Japan, companies normally use the same depreciation methods for both financial reporting and taxes. The same is true in France and Germany.

The International Accounting Standards Committee has established a broad international standard for deferred tax accounting in International Accounting Standard No. 12. The standard requires that deferred taxes be included in the computation of income tax expense and that deferred taxes be reported on the balance sheet, but leaves open the method used to compute the deferred taxes.

Now, back to Sweden. Volvo's approach to deferred tax accounting illustrates a common trend throughout the world in many areas in which there is divergent international practice. In its 1990 annual report, Volvo disclosed that it had decided to abandon the no-deferral approach and begin recording deferred taxes "as part of [its] program of adapting Volvo's financial reporting to international accounting practice." As companies increasingly do business and raise capital across international boundaries, information needs of international financial statement users will result in a natural harmonization of accounting practices. In recent years, international practice has slowly become more consistent with U.S. GAAP — only time will tell whether this trend will continue.

Questions:

1. From a purely theoretical standpoint, which deferred tax accounting approach seems most reasonable to you: the no-deferral approach, the British partial allocation approach, or the full liability approach adopted by the FASB?
2. From a practical standpoint, which of the approaches mentioned above would be the most difficult to implement?

Source:
International Accounting Standard No. 12, "Accounting for Taxes on Income" (London: International Accounting Standards Committee, 1979).

The kind of disclosure typically made for income taxes is illustrated by an excerpt from the notes to the 1992 financial statements of General Electric, presented in Exhibit 20—2.

The current portion of income tax expense (called "estimated amounts payable" in the General Electric example) can be viewed as the one place in the financial statements where the financial accounting records and the tax records coincide. Roughly speaking, the \$1.071 billion that General Electric reports as the current portion of income tax expense for 1992 is the same number that appears on General Electric's 1992 consolidated tax return under the heading of "Total Tax" for the year. Note that, because of the existence of deferred taxes, the amount of reported income tax expense is significantly greater than the amount of income tax actually owed for the year.

As another example of disclosure, IBM reported in the notes to its 1992 financial statements that it had increased the valuation allowance for its deferred tax assets by \$1.647 billion in 1992. This increase had the effect of increasing income tax expense for the year by the same amount. The reason given for the increase was that "the valuation allowance applies to state and local net operating loss carryforwards and net deferred tax assets, U.S. federal tax credit carryforwards, and net operating losses in certain foreign jurisdictions that may expire before the company can utilize them."

In addition to the above disclosures, the reported amount of income tax expense related to continuing operations must be reconciled with the amount of income tax expense

Exhibit 20—2
General Electric Company—Disclosure of Income Taxes

NOTE 9 — PROVISION FOR INCOME TAXES

(in millions)	1992	1991	1990
Estimated amounts payable	$1,071	$896	$1,364
Deferred tax expense from temporary differences	929	866	272
Investment credit deferred (amortized) — net[22]	(32)	(20)	(40)
	$1,968	$1,742	$1,596

that would result from applying federal tax rates to pretax financial income from continuing operations. This reconciliation provides information to readers of the financial statements regarding how the entity has been affected by special provisions of the tax code such as permanent differences, tax credits, and operating loss carrybacks and carryforwards. For example, IBM reported in the notes to its 1992 financial statements that, excluding the effects of restructuring charges, its effective tax rate for 1992 was 46%, significantly higher than the 34% U.S. federal statutory rate. IBM disclosed that the primary cause of this difference was a higher effective tax rate on income generated in foreign countries.

Firms also disclose the specific accounting differences between the financial statements and the tax return that give rise to deferred tax assets and deferred tax liabilities. The most common source of deferred tax items is depreciation — 456 of 600 firms surveyed in 1992 reported deferred taxes related to tax/book differences in depreciation.[23] As an additional illustration, IBM disclosed that, as of December 3, 1992, it had a $3.882 billion deferred tax asset related to restructuring charges. These non-cash charges involved large asset write-downs and provisions for employee severance costs. Since no tax deduction is allowed for these non-cash charges, IBM has recorded a deferred tax asset in anticipation of taking the tax deductions when the employee severance costs are paid and the losses on asset devaluations are realized. IBM also disclosed that it had a $3.785 billion deferred tax liability related to sales-type leases and installment sales. Essentially, these sales are recognized for financial accounting purposes before it is required that they be reported to the tax authorities. Overall, as of December 31, 1992, IBM had $12.039 billion in deferred tax assets (net of a $1.976 billion valuation allowance) and $9.029 billion in deferred tax liabilities.

As noted at the beginning of this chapter, the adoption of Statement No. 109 has had a significant impact on the financial statements of many firms. The provisions of the statement have been applied for periods beginning after December 15, 1992, although many firms adopted the statement earlier. FASB Statement No. 109 allows some flexibility in making the transition from previous income tax accounting to the new standard. Most companies that adopted FASB Statement No. 96 early showed the adjustment as a cumulative change in accounting principles on the income statement. Statement No. 109 provides for the same type of cumulative adjustment for companies going from APB Opinion No. 11 to Statement No. 109 or for those going from FASB Statement No. 96 to Statement No. 109. Statement No. 109 also permits restatement of prior years' financial statements, but restatement is optional.

22. The accounting for investment tax credits is discussed in Appendix 20-2.
23. *Accounting Trends & Techniques—1993 edition,* (New York: American Institute of Certified Public Accountants, 1993), p. 347.

DEFERRED TAXES AND THE STATEMENT OF CASH FLOWS

FASB Statement No. 95, "Statement of Cash Flows," requires separate disclosure of the amount of cash paid for income taxes during a period. The Statement requires this separate disclosure for just two items — cash paid for income taxes and cash paid for interest. Financial statements are used to assess the amount and timing of future cash flows and, in the case of interest and income taxes, the FASB argued that this specific cash flow information should be readily available and easily disclosed by most firms.[24] As an example of this disclosure see the "Income Taxes" note to the 1993 financial statements of Microsoft included in Appendix A. For the year ended June 30, 1993, Microsoft reported income tax expense of $448 million, income taxes payable for the year of $475 million, and cash paid during the year for income taxes of $187 million.

Income taxes affect the operating activities section of the statement of cash flows.[25] When the direct method is used, cash paid for income taxes is shown as a separate line item. For example, Compaq Computer reports "Income taxes paid" of $2.8 million in the operating activities section (prepared using the direct method) of its 1992 statement of cash flows. When the indirect method is used, the treatment of income taxes is a bit more complicated. Adjustments to convert net income into cash from operations are needed for changes in income taxes payable and receivable accounts and for changes in deferred tax asset and liability accounts. In addition, supplemental disclosure of the amount of cash paid for income taxes is required.

As an illustration of how income taxes are handled in the statement of cash flows, consider the following information for Collazo Company for 1996:

Revenue (all cash)		$30,000
Income tax expense:		
Current	$10,300	
Deferred	1,700	12,000
Net income		$18,000

Cash paid for income taxes during 1996 totaled $13,300. In addition, Collazo had the following balance sheet amounts at the beginning and end of the year:

	December 31 1996	December 31 1995
Income Tax Refund Receivable	$2,000	$ 0
Income Taxes Payable	0	1,000
Deferred Tax Liability	9,700	8,000

The operating activities section of Collazo's statement of cash flows is as follows if the direct method is used:

Cash collected from customers	$30,000
Income taxes paid	(13,300)
Cash provided by operating activities	$16,700

If the indirect method is used, the operating activities section is as follows:

24. *Statement of Financial Accounting Standards No. 95,* "Statement of Cash Flows" (Stamford: Financial Accounting Standards Board, November 1987), par. 121.

25. The FASB considered allocating income taxes paid among the operating, investing, and financing activities sections of the statement of cash flows. For example, any income tax effects from the disposal of equipment could be disclosed in the investing activities section. However, it was concluded that this allocation would be unnecessarily complex and the cost of doing it would outweigh the benefit. See FASB Statement No. 95, par. 92.

Net income	$18,000
(Increase) decrease in income tax refund receivable	(2,000)
Increase (decrease) in income taxes payable	(1,000)
Increase (decrease) in deferred tax liability	1,700
Cash provided by operating activities	$16,700

In addition, if the indirect method is used, the amount of cash paid for income taxes, $13,300, must be separately disclosed, either in the statement of cash flows or in the notes to the financial statements.

EVALUATION OF THE ASSET AND LIABILITY METHOD

Accounting for income taxes has been, and will continue to be, a complex financial accounting issue. This chapter has introduced the major concepts and applications of this topic.

The major advantages of the asset and liability method of accounting for deferred taxes are as follows:

1. Because the assets and liabilities recorded under this method are in agreement with the FASB definitions of financial statement elements, the method is conceptually consistent with other standards.
2. The asset and liability method is a flexible method that recognizes changes in circumstances and adjusts the reported amounts accordingly. This flexibility may improve the predictive value of the financial statements.

One drawback of the asset and liability method is that, in some ways, it is still too complicated, even after the significant simplification brought about by Statement No. 109. Many financial statement users claim that they ignore deferred tax assets and liabilities anyway and thus efforts devoted to deferred tax accounting are just a waste of time. For example, one financial statement analysis textbook reports that "because of the uncertainty over whether (and when) a deferred tax liability will be paid, some individuals elect to exclude deferred tax liabilities from liabilities when performing analysis."[26] On the other hand, research using stock market data suggests that investors compute values of companies as if the reported deferred tax liabilities are bona fide liabilities.[27]

Some users of financial statements have criticized Statement No. 109, as well as earlier standards, for failing to recognize the effect of discounting on the recognition of deferred assets and liabilities. Since the time value of money is ignored under the provisions of Statement No. 109, the financial statements do not reflect the real economic benefit firms experience by taking advantage of the income tax code to delay the payment of taxes. Requiring firms to report the discounted present value of deferred tax assets and liabilities might improve the usefulness of deferred tax accounting, but would involve a significant increase in complexity. Rather than wrestle with the issue of discounting in conjunction with the already complex issue of deferred taxes, the FASB decided to prohibit discounting for now, but is currently examining the discounting issue in a broader context. A discussion memorandum on the use of present value-based measurements in accounting was issued in December 1990.

Like many other areas of accounting, deferred tax accounting is not perfect. However, the asset and liability approach embodied in Statement No. 109 represents a substantial improvement over the deferred approach. As accounting standards evolve in the future, it is likely that the area of deferred tax accounting will be revisited and improved further. Don't worry, though; most informed observers don't think this will happen in the near future. After the Statement No. 96 fiasco, the accounting profession seems eager to move on to other issues for a while.

26. Charles H. Gibson, *Financial Statement Analysis: Using Financial Accounting Information,* 5th edition (Cincinnati: South-Western Publishing Co., 1992), p. 278.

27. Dan Givoly and Carla Hayn, "The Valuation of the Deferred Tax Liability: Evidence from the Stock Market," *The Accounting Review,* April 1992, pp. 394-410.

APPENDIX 20-1

Intraperiod Income Tax Allocation

As discussed in Chapter 4, when a company reports irregular or extraordinary items on its income statement, or when a prior-period adjustment affects retained earnings, **intraperiod tax allocation** is appropriate. Under this approach, the income tax effect of each of these special items is reported with the individual item rather than being included with the income tax expense related to current operations. It was assumed in Chapter 4 that a single rate applied to each category of income and that no special tax limitations were present for any of the income categories. With this assumption, intraperiod income tax allocation is not difficult.

When this simplifying assumption is not realistic and different levels of income are taxed at varying rates, decision rules must be developed to make the allocation among the various categories of income. Paragraph 38 of FASB Statement No. 109 establishes the priority for intraperiod tax allocation.

In summary, a "with and without" approach is applied as follows:[28]

1. Income taxes are computed for current operations *without* any of the irregular or extraordinary items.
2. Income taxes are computed *with* all income items considered. The difference between (1) and (2) is the total tax allocation to irregular and extraordinary items.
3. Income taxes are computed on total income *without* irregular and extraordinary *losses* considered to determine the tax effect of all losses. If there are several losses, the incremental tax effect of each loss category is considered, and the total tax impact of all loss categories is allocated among the separate losses in the ratio of their separate incremental impacts.
4. The difference between the income tax benefit allocated to all losses and the total irregular and extraordinary allocation (2) is attributed to irregular and extraordinary gains. If there are several gains, the incremental tax effect of all gain categories is considered, and further allocation to gain items is made in the same manner as losses.

An example will illustrate the application of these decision rules. Assume Marble Corp. reports the following pretax income components on its income statement:

Income from continuing operations	$ 75,600
Loss on disposal of business segment	(19,000)
Extraordinary gain on early extinguishment of debt	30,000
Extraordinary loss on litigation claim	(16,000)
Cumulative effect of change in depreciation method	15,000
Total income before considering income taxes	$ 85,600

28. To simplify the discussion of intraperiod income tax allocation, it is assumed that financial and taxable income are equal, thus there are no deferred taxes. In many actual situations, deferred taxes may apply both to current operations and to irregular categories of income such as discontinued operations. The interplay of deferred taxes with intraperiod tax allocation adds another dimension of complexity not considered in this introductory presentation of accounting for income taxes.

Assume the tax department has applied the current tax regulations and rates to Marble's various income categories, and computed the following tax information using the with-and-without concepts required for intraperiod tax allocation:

Tax on total income ($85,600)	$30,200
Tax on income from continuing operations ($75,600)	26,750
Tax on total income before considering all irregular and extraordinary losses ($85,600 + $19,000 + $16,000 = $120,600)	42,500

Based on this assumed tax information, the net income for the year is $55,400 ($85,600 – $30,200). The total intraperiod tax allocation is $3,450 tax expense ($30,200 – $26,750). The total tax benefit allocated to the two loss categories is $12,300 ($42,500 – $30,200), and the total tax expense allocated to the two gain categories is $15,750 ($12,300 + $3,450). This allocation can be shown graphically as follows:

Tax on income from continuing operations	$26,750	
		$ 15,750 (Tax on all gains)
Tax on total income before considering all irregular and extraordinary losses	$42,500	
		$(12,300) (Tax benefit from all losses)
Tax on total income	$30,200	
		$ 3,450 (Net tax allocated to irregular and extraordinary items)

The loss and gain tax effects are further allocated to the specific gain and loss categories using the following assumed information also provided by the tax department. The incremental tax benefit or expense is determined by considering each component separately.

Incremental tax benefit—disposal loss	$ 9,000
Incremental tax benefit—extraordinary loss	6,000
Total tax benefits from losses	$15,000
Incremental tax expense—extraordinary gain	$10,200
Incremental tax expense—cumulative change	3,800
Total tax expense on gains	$14,000

Allocation of the $12,300 tax benefit to loss categories would be as follows:

Disposal loss ($9,000 ÷ $15,000) × $12,300	$ 7,380
Extraordinary loss ($6,000 ÷ $15,000) × $12,300	4,920
Total tax benefit	$12,300

Allocation of the $15,750 tax expense to gain categories would be as follows:

Extraordinary gain ($10,200 ÷ $14,000) × $15,750	$11,475
Cumulative change ($3,800 ÷ $14,000) × $15,750	4,275
Total tax expense	$15,750

The bottom portion of Marble Corp.'s income statement would be reported as follows:

Income from continuing operations before income taxes	$75,600
Income taxes	26,750
Income from continuing operations	$48,850
Loss on disposal of business segment (net of income tax benefit of $7,380)	(11,620)
Extraordinary gain from early extinguishment of debt (net of income taxes of $11,475)	18,525
Extraordinary loss on litigation claim (net of income tax benefit of $4,920)	(11,080)
Cumulative effect of change in depreciation method (net of income taxes of $4,275)	10,725
Net income	$55,400

If there are taxable direct entries to owners' equity accounts, the incremental approach is used to allocate tax benefits or tax expense to the equity accounts. For example, prior-period adjustments usually are affected by income taxes and must be shown in the statement of retained earnings net of the tax effect.

APPENDIX 20-2

The Investment Tax Credit

Tax credits are direct reductions in the amount of taxes due. They represent another way legislative bodies can stimulate economic growth. Unlike temporary differences that affect the amount of taxable income used to compute the taxes payable, tax credits are applied directly to the computed income tax liability. They represent the last adjustment made in computing income taxes payable.

One of the more common tax credits of the past thirty years has been the **investment tax credit (ITC).** In order to encourage investment in productive assets, the Revenue Act of 1962 permitted taxpayers to reduce their federal income tax by a credit equal to a specified percentage of the cost of certain depreciable assets acquired after December 31, 1961. Since this provision was first included in the tax code, there have been many modifications of the investment tax credit, including its temporary suspension. Whenever the economy has needed a stimulus, however, Congress has returned to the ITC as a way of encouraging business to invest in new productive assets and thus increase the gross national product. As part of the Tax Reform Act of 1986, Congress repealed the investment tax credit for property placed in service after December 31, 1985.

Although the investment tax credit was suspended by the 1986 Act, history suggests that it could be reinstated at any future time. In addition, because many companies deferred the benefits from the investment tax credit, current financial statements still reflect amortization of these balances. With these circumstances in mind, a brief discussion of the accounting implications of the credit is warranted.

ACCOUNTING FOR THE INVESTMENT TAX CREDIT

There are two methods that can be used to record the tax reduction resulting from the ITC: (1) the credit can be used to reduce the income tax expense for the year in which it is received, commonly referred to as the **flow-through method of investment tax credit,** or (2) the credit can be deferred and reflected as a reduction of tax expense over the period during which the asset is depreciated, commonly referred to as the **deferred method of investment tax credit.**

Flow-Through Method

Using the flow-through method, the investment tax credit is treated as a reduction of income tax expense in the year the credit is allowed. To illustrate, assume that a business acquired machinery in 1996 for $100,000, and the applicable investment tax credit rate is 10%. The federal income tax for 1996 is $75,000 reduced by an investment tax credit of $10,000 (10% of $100,000). The entry to record the federal income tax for 1996 would be:

Income Tax Expense	65,000	
Income Taxes Payable		65,000
Recognition of income tax of $75,000 less investment tax credit of $10,000.		

Deferred Method

Under the deferred method of accounting for the investment tax credit, the credit is viewed as a reduction of income tax expense over the life of the asset rather than in the year the credit is applied to the tax liability. Using the information in the previous example, the entry to record income tax in 1996 under the deferred method would be:

Income Tax Expense	75,000	
Deferred Investment Tax Credit		10,000
Income Taxes Payable		65,000

The following entry would be made each year to amortize the investment tax credit over the 5-year life of the asset:

Deferred Investment Tax Credit	2,000	
Income Tax Expense		2,000

EVALUATION OF ACCOUNTING TREATMENT OF INVESTMENT TAX CREDIT

The Accounting Principles Board favored the deferred method and approved it in Opinion No. 2. Lack of support for this view from many prominent accountants led to the issuance in 1964 of Opinion No. 4 in which the Board accepted both methods, although still stating a preference for the deferred method. In 1968, a further attempt was made by the Accounting Principles Board to restore the deferred method as a single uniform method. Again, differences of opinion resulted in failure to adopt the original conclusions. In 1971, the Board once again made a serious effort to restore the deferred method. However, it had to postpone its work as a result of congressional action permitting the taxpayer to choose the method to be used in recognizing the benefit arising from the credit.

Good theoretical arguments can be presented for either method. Those who advocate using the deferred method argue that the cost of the asset is effectively reduced by the investment credit, and the tax benefit should be spread over the acquired asset's useful life. Those who advocate using the flow-through method argue that the tax credit is in reality a tax reduction in the current period. They argue that tax regulations establish the tax liability each year, and that amount is the proper expense to match against current revenues. This latter treatment affects current income more and is favored by political leaders when the investment tax credit is being used to stimulate a sluggish economy.

It is unfortunate that this issue has become such a political item. It is an example of an area where there seems to be no justification for having two methods. It is difficult to see how different economic circumstances among companies would justify dual treatment. If the investment tax credit is reinstated by Congress, the authors recommend that a uniform accounting method for its treatment should be adopted by the accounting profession.

KEY TERMS

Asset and liability method of interperiod tax allocation 858
Deductible temporary differences 857
Deferred method of investment tax credit 875
Deferred tax asset 854
Deferred tax liability 853
Financial income 852
Flow-through method of investment tax credit 875
Interperiod tax allocation 858
Intraperiod tax allocation 872
Investment tax credit (ITC) 875
Net operating loss (NOL) carryback 864
Net operating loss (NOL) carryforward 865
Permanent differences 854
Taxable income 852
Taxable temporary differences 857
Temporary differences 855
Valuation allowance 862

QUESTIONS

1. Accounting methods used by a company to determine income for financial reporting purposes frequently differ from those used to determine taxable income. What is the justification for these differences?
2. Distinguish between a nondeductible expense and a temporary difference that results in a taxable income greater than pretax financial income reported in the income statement.
3. Distinguish between taxable temporary differences and deductible temporary differences and give at least two examples of each type.
4. One possibility for reporting income tax expense in the income statement for a given year is to merely report the amount of income tax payable in that year. What is wrong with this approach?
5. How is income tax expense computed under the deferred method?
6. How is income tax expense computed under the asset and liability method?
7. What were the principal points of dissatisfaction with the deferred method of interperiod tax allocation as applied under APB Opinion No. 11?
8. What were the principal points of dissatisfaction with the asset and liability method as applied under FASB Statement No. 96?
9. Describe how a change in enacted future tax rates is accounted for under the asset and liability method.
10. When is a valuation allowance necessary?
11. How does the FASB define the probability term "more likely than not" in Statement No. 109?
12. What are the sources of income through which the tax benefit of a deferred tax asset can be realized?
13. In applying the net operating loss carryback and carryforward provisions, what order of application is followed for federal tax purposes?
14. How is the classification of assets arising from NOL carryforwards determined under Statement No. 109?
15. Under what conditions would scheduling the temporary difference reversals be required under Statement No. 109?
16. What was the most significant change in accounting for income tax carryforwards made by FASB Statement No. 109?
17. Why is accounting for income taxes not as significant an issue in some foreign countries as it is in the United States? Does this difference make it more difficult to legislate common international accounting standards for income taxes?
18. How do changes in the balances of deferred income taxes affect the amount of cash paid for income taxes?
19. If a company experiences a current operating loss, it may carry the loss backward and forward. What impact do these carrybacks and carryforwards have on the reported operating loss? On the statement of cash flows?
20. What are the major advantages of the asset and liability method?
21. Why doesn't Statement No. 109 incorporate time value of money considerations?
22. What rules govern the netting of deferred tax assets and deferred tax liabilities?

*23. Describe the with-and-without method of intraperiod tax allocation.

*24. What is the proper sequence for computing intraperiod tax allocation?

**25. Two methods of accounting for investment tax credits are acceptable. Identify and briefly describe both methods.

*Relates to Appendix 20—1
**Relates to Appendix 20—2

DISCUSSION CASES

Case 20—1 (What are deferred income taxes?)

Hurst Inc. is a new corporation that has just completed a highly successful first year of operation. Hurst is a privately held corporation, but its president, Byron Hurst, has indicated that if the company continues to do as well for the next 4 or 5 years, it will go public. By all indications, the company should continue to be highly profitable on both a short-term and a long-term basis.

The controller of the new company, Lori James, plans on using the MACRS method of depreciating Hurst's assets and using the installment sales method of recognizing income for tax purposes. For financial statement presentation, straight-line depreciation will be used and all sales will be fully recognized in the year of sale. There are no other differences between book and taxable income.

Hurst has hired your firm to prepare its financial statements. You are now preparing the income statement. The controller wants to show, as "income tax expense," the amount of the tax liability actually due. "After all," James reasons, "that's the amount we'll actually pay, and in light of our plans for continued expansion, it's highly unlikely that the temporary differences will ever reverse."

Draft a memo to the controller outlining your reaction to the plan. Give reasons in support of your decision.

Case 20—2 (How do deferred taxes work?)

The Primrose Company appropriately uses the asset and liability method for interperiod income tax allocation.

Primrose reports depreciation expense for certain machinery purchased this year using the modified accelerated cost recovery system (MACRS) for income tax purposes and the straight-line basis for accounting purposes. The tax deduction is the larger amount this year.

Primrose received rent revenues in advance this year. These revenues are included in this year's taxable income. However, for accounting purposes, these revenues are reported as unearned revenues, a current liability.

1. What is the theoretical basis for deferred income taxes under the asset and liability concept as specified by FASB Statement No. 109?
2. How would Primrose determine and account for the income tax effect for depreciation and rent? Why?

Case 20—3 (Why aren't deferred taxes discounted?)

Tyler Dee is the controller for Martinez Company. Martinez is a major employer in the area, and Tyler has just come from a meeting of a local civic group. The meeting was an opportunity for Tyler to present and explain Martinez's financial statements for the fiscal year recently ended. A significant amount of time was spent discussing the large deferred tax liability reported by Martinez. Several members of the civic group questioned Tyler about the nature of this liability. In particular, Tyler was asked why the liability wasn't discounted to reflect the time value of money. Tyler had no real answer, except to mumble something like, "That's just the way the standard is written."

How might Tyler have better explained the lack of discounting of deferred taxes?

Case 20—4 (Raising tax rates: does it help me or hurt me?)

When the corporate tax rate was lowered from 46% to 34% in 1986, most firms which had adopted the asset and liability method of deferred tax accounting reported one-time gains as a result of the revaluation of their deferred tax items. In fact, one writer claimed that this lowering of income tax rates "freed a large chunk of money that had been accumulated to pay deferred taxes at the former, higher rate."

In early 1993, the United States Congress was considering raising the corporate income tax rate. One proposal was to raise the top corporate rate from 34% to 36%. Accounting experts pointed out that the increase in the tax rate would cause some firms to report one-time losses and other firms to report one-time gains.

1. Why did the lowering of tax rates in 1986 result in most firms reporting gains, whereas an increase in tax rates in 1993 would cause some firms to report gains and some firms to report losses?
2. Comment on the writer's statement that the lowering of income tax rates "freed a large chunk of money."

Sources:
Rick Wartzman, "Rise in Corporate Taxes Would Force Many Big Companies to Take Charges," *The Wall Street Journal,* February 11, 1993, p.A2.
Lee Berton, "FASB Is Expected to Issue Rule Allowing Firms to Post Big, One-Time Gains," *The Wall Street Journal,* November 4, 1987, p.4.

Case 20—5 (No carrybacks or carryforwards in Cardassia)

The president of Cardassia has recently been doing some recreational reading and came across an article on the adoption of FASB Statement No. 109 in the United States. The president liked the article so much that she has decided to adopt Statement No. 109 as the standard for deferred tax accounting in Cardassia.

You have been hired as the government minister in charge of accounting, taxation, and nuclear waste disposal for the country of Cardassia. It is your duty to figure out how to implement Statement No. 109. You note that the accounting rules and tax code in Cardassia are very similar to those in the United States, except that Cardassian income tax law does not allow the carryback or carryforward of net operating losses.

How will this difference in Cardassian tax law affect the accounting for deferred tax liabilities? Deferred tax assets?

***Case 20—6 (Should health of the economy govern GAAP?)**

The investment tax credit has created much controversy and discussion in the accounting profession, business, and government. The government's involvement has been an intriguing one. The purpose of the investment tax credit has been to stimulate investment in new business property and thus promote a steady growth in the Gross National Product and avoid severe recession or depression. In order to have the most significant impact possible on a company's income, legislative officials who enacted the investment tax credit legislation indicated a preference for the flow-through method of accounting. Many people in the business community agree with this approach because of its favorable impact on reported income. Accounting theorists, on the other hand, argue that the deferred method of accounting for the credit is preferable because it reflects more clearly the economic reality of the credit. Evaluate these two positions. What role, if any, should public policy and the impact of accounting principles on the economy have upon the establishment of GAAP?

*Relates to Appendix 20—2

Case 20—7 (Why different probability terms for contingent assets and liabilities?)

Because you are an accounting student, one of your business major friends asks you to explain to him why the accounting profession records contingent liabilities only when their occurrence is probable, but records deferred income tax assets as long as it is more likely than not that a future benefit will be realized from the deferral. He's confused by the probability terms used to record these items and wonders why the recognition of assets seems less conservative than the recognition of liabilities. How would you answer your friend?

Case 20—8 (Is a valuation allowance needed?)

Assume you go to work for one of the Big 6 accounting firms upon your graduation from college, and on your first assignment, you are asked to review the deferred income tax asset account to determine whether a valuation allowance seems to be warranted. You remember talking about deferred income taxes in your intermediate accounting class, but the problems always told you whether an allowance was required or not. Now you must examine the facts to help determine the need for an allowance. What factors would you consider in making your recommendation?

EXERCISES

Exercise 20—9 (Identification of temporary differences)

Indicate which of the following items are temporary differences and which are nontaxable or nondeductible. For each temporary difference, indicate whether the item considered alone would create a deferred tax asset or a deferred tax liability.

(a) Tax depreciation in excess of book depreciation, $150,000.
(b) Excess of income on installment sales over income reportable for tax purposes, $130,000.
(c) Premium payment for life insurance policy on president, $95,000.
(d) Rent collected in advance of period earned, $75,000.
(e) Warranty provision accrued in advance of period paid, $40,000.
(f) Interest revenue received on municipal bonds, $30,000.

Exercise 20—10 (Calculation of taxable income)

Using the information given in Exercise 20—9, and assuming pretax financial income of $2,060,000, calculate taxable income.

Exercise 20—11 (Deferred tax liability)

Gideon, Inc. began operating on January 1, 1996. At the end of the first year of operations, Gideon reported $750,000 income before income taxes on its income statement, but only $660,000 taxable income on its tax return. Analysis of the $90,000 difference revealed that $30,000 was a permanent difference and $60,000 was a temporary tax liability difference related to a current asset. The enacted tax rate for 1996 and future years is 35%.

1. Prepare the journal entries to record income taxes for 1996.
2. Assume that at the end of 1997, the accumulated temporary tax liability difference related to future years is $80,000. Prepare the journal entry to record any adjustment to deferred tax liabilities at the end of 1997.

Exercise 20—12 (Deferred tax asset)

Lofthouse Machinery Co. includes a two-year warranty on its machinery sales. At the end of 1996, an analysis of the warranty records reveals an accumulated temporary difference of $120,000 for warranty expenses—book expenses related to warranties have exceeded tax deductions allowed. The enacted income tax rate for 1996 and future years is 40%. Management concludes that it is more likely than not that Lofthouse will have future income to realize the future tax benefit from this temporary difference. They also conclude that 20% of the warranty liability is current and 80% noncurrent.

1. How would the deferred tax information be reported on the Lofthouse balance sheet at December 31, 1996?
2. If management assumed that only 60% of the tax benefit from the temporary difference could be realized, how would the deferred tax information be reported on the balance sheet at December 31, 1996? (Recall that the valuation allowance is allocated proportionately between the current and noncurrent portions of the deferred tax asset.)

Exercise 20—13 (Determinants of "more likely than not")

Cobb Company computed a pretax financial loss of $10,000 for the first year of its operations ended December 31, 1996. This loss did not include $25,000 in unearned rent revenue that was recognized as taxable income in 1996 when the cash was received.

1. Prepare the journal entries necessary to record income tax for the year. The income tax rate is 40%. Assume it is more likely than not that future taxable income will be sufficient to allow for the full realization of any deferred tax assets and that unearned rent revenue is a current liability.
2. If future taxable income from operations was not expected to be sufficient to allow for the full realization of any deferred tax assets, what other sources of income may be considered to determine the need for a valuation allowance?

Exercise 20—14 (Deferred tax asset valuation allowance)

Rowberry Company computed a pretax financial loss of $5,000 for the first year of its operations ended December 31, 1996. Included in the loss was $18,000 in uncollectible accounts expense that was accrued on the books in 1996 using an allowance system based on a percentage of sales. For income tax purposes, deductions for uncollectible accounts are allowed when specific accounts receivable are determined to be uncollectible and written off. No accounts receivable have been written off as uncollectible in 1996.

1. Prepare the journal entries necessary to record income taxes for the year. The enacted income tax rate is 40% for 1996 and all future years. Assume that it is more likely than not that future taxable income will be sufficient to allow for the full realization of any deferred tax assets. Accounts Receivable and the related allowance account are reported under current assets in the balance sheet.
2. Repeat part (1), assuming that it is more likely than not that future taxable income will be zero before considering the actual bad debt losses in future years.

Exercise 20—15 (Changing tax rates)

Goshute Company computed pretax financial income of $50,000 for the year ended December 31, 1996. Taxable income for the year was $15,000. Accumulated temporary differences as of December 31, 1995, were $120,000. A deferred tax liability of $48,000 was included in the December 31, 1995, balance sheet. Accumulated temporary differences as of December 31, 1996, are $155,000. The differences are related to noncurrent items.

1. Prepare the journal entries necessary to record income tax for 1996. The enacted income tax rate is assumed to be 40% for 1996 and future years.
2. On January 1, 1997, the income tax rate is changed to 35% for 1997 and all future years. Prepare the necessary journal entry, if any.

Exercise 20—16 (Deferred tax liability)

The McCall Exploration Company reported pretax financial income of $596,500 for the calendar year 1996. Included in the "Other income" section of the income statement was $86,000 of interest revenue from municipal bonds held by the company. The income statement also included depreciation expense of $610,000 for a machine that cost $4,000,000. The income tax return reported $800,000 as MACRS depreciation on the machine.

The enacted tax rate is 40% for 1996 and future years. Prepare the journal entries necessary to record income taxes for 1996.

Exercise 20—17 (Deferred tax asset)

Pro-Tech-Tronics Company computed pretax financial income of $35,000 for the first year of its operations ended December 31, 1996. Unearned rent revenue of $55,000 had been recognized as taxable income in 1996 when the cash was received but had not yet been recognized in the financial accounting records.

The unearned rent is expected to be recognized on the books in the following pattern:

1997	$15,000
1998	20,000
1999	12,000
2000	8,000
	$55,000

The enacted tax rates for this year and the next four years are as follows:

1996	34%	1999	30%
1997	34%	2000	32%
1998	30%		

Prepare the journal entries necessary to record income taxes for 1996. Assume that there will be sufficient income in each future year to realize any deductible amounts.

Exercise 20—18 (Deferred tax assets and liabilities)
Fibertek, Inc., computed a pretax financial income of $40,000 for the first year of its operations ended December 31, 1996. Included in financial income was $25,000 of nondeductible expenses, $22,000 gross profit on installment sales that was deferred for tax purposes until the installments were collected, and $18,000 in doubtful accounts expense that had been accrued on the books in 1996.

The temporary differences are expected to reverse in the following patterns:

Year	Gross Profit on Collections	Bad Debt Write-Offs
1997	$ 5,000	$ 6,000
1998	7,000	12,000
1999	4,000	
2000	6,000	
	$22,000	$18,000

The enacted tax rates for this year and the next four years are as follows:

1996	40%	1999	30%
1997	35%	2000	32%
1998	32%		

Prepare the journal entries necessary to record income taxes for 1996. Assume that there will be sufficient income in each future year to realize any deductible amounts. For classification purposes, the bad debt write-offs are considered to be associated with a current asset and the receivable for installment sales is classified as both current and noncurrent, depending on the expected timing of the receipt.

Exercise 20—19 (Deferred tax assets and liabilities)
Energizer Manufacturing Corporation reports taxable income of $829,000 on its income tax return for the year ended December 31, 1996, its first year of operations. Temporary differences between financial income and taxable income for the year are:

Tax depreciation in excess of book depreciation	$ 80,000
Accrual for product liability claims in excess of actual claims (estimated product claims payable is a current liability)	125,000
Reported installment sales income in excess of taxable installment sales income (installments receivable is a current asset)	265,000

The enacted income tax rate is 40% for 1996 and all future years. Prepare the journal entries necessary to record income taxes for 1996.

Exercise 20—20 (Computation of deferred asset and liability balances)
Nashua Engineering reported taxable income of $20,000 for 1996, its first fiscal year. The enacted tax rate for 1996 is 40%. Enacted tax rates and deductible amounts for 1997-1999 are as follows:

	Enacted Tax Rate	Deductible Amount
1997	35%	$ 7,000
1998	32%	12,000
1999	30%	8,000

1. Prepare the journal entries necessary to record income taxes for 1996. Assume that there will be sufficient income in each future year to realize any deductible amounts. For classification purposes, assume that all deductible amounts relate to noncurrent items.
2. Repeat (1) assuming that it is more likely than not that taxable income for all future periods will be zero or less.

Exercise 20—21 (Computation of deferred asset and liability balances)
Dixon Type and Supply Company reported taxable income of $60,000 for 1996, its first fiscal year. The enacted tax rate for 1996 is 40%. Enacted tax rates and deductible amounts for 1997-2000 are as follows:

	Enacted Tax Rate	Deductible Amount
1997	35%	$14,000
1998	32%	24,000
1999	30%	16,000
2000	32%	40,000

1. Prepare the journal entries necessary to record income taxes for 1996. Assume that there will be sufficient income in each future year to realize any deductible amounts. For classification purposes, assume that all deductible amounts relate to noncurrent items.
2. Repeat (1) assuming it is more likely than not that taxable income for all future periods will be zero or less.

Exercise 20—22 (Net operating loss carryback)
The following historical financial data are available for the Bradshaw Manufacturing Company:

Year	Income	Tax Rate	Tax Paid
1993	$175,000	40%	$ 70,000
1994	230,000	42%	96,600
1995	310,000	35%	108,500

In 1996, the Bradshaw Company suffered a $750,000 net operating loss due to an economic recession. The company elects to use the carryback provision in the tax law.

1. Using the information given, calculate the refund due arising from the loss carryback and the amount of the loss available to carry forward to future periods. Assume the enacted tax rate is 34% for 1996 and all future years.
2. Prepare the entry necessary to record the loss carryback and carryforward. Assume there will be sufficient taxable income in the carryforward period to realize all benefits from NOL carryforwards.
3. Using the answers from (1) and (2), prepare the bottom portion of the 1996 income statement reflecting the effect of the loss carryback and carryforward.

Exercise 20—23 (NOL carryforward)
The following historical financial data are available for the Terry Company:

Year	Income	Tax Rate	Tax Paid
1993	$300,000	30%	$90,000
1994	100,000	35%	35,000
1995	10,000	35%	3,500

In 1996 the Terry Company suffered a $2 million net operating loss. The company will use the carryback provision of the tax law.

1. Using the information given, calculate the refund due for the loss carryback and the amount of the loss available to carry forward to future periods. Assume the enacted tax rate for 1996 and all future years is 40%.
2. Prepare journal entries to record the loss carryback and carryforward. Assume it is more likely than not that future taxable income will be sufficient to allow for the full realization of any deferred tax assets.
3. Evaluate the reasonableness of the assumption in (2).

Exercise 20—24 (Cash flow and income taxes)
Joyce Smithers, Inc. reported the following amounts related to income taxes on its 1996 income statement:

Income tax expense—current	$32,000
Income tax expense—deferred provision	(8,000)

Smithers also reported the following amounts on its December 31, 1995 and 1996 balance sheets.

	1996	1995
Deferred tax liability	$26,000	$34,000
Income tax payable	8,000	4,000

If Smithers uses the indirect method of reporting cash flows, what information concerning income taxes would Smithers include in its statement of cash flows and related disclosure?

Exercise 20—25 (Cash flow and income taxes)
Owyhee Motors reported the following amounts related to income taxes on its 1996 income statement:

Income tax benefit from NOL carryback	$12,000
Income tax benefit from NOL carryforward	28,000

Owyhee also reported the following on its December 31, 1995 and 1996 balance sheets.

	1996	1995
Deferred tax asset-NOL carryforward	$28,000	$ 0
Income tax refund receivable	12,000	4,000

1. If Owyhee uses the indirect method of reporting cash flows, what information concerning income taxes would Owyhee include in the statement of cash flows and related disclosure?
2. If Owyhee uses the direct method of reporting cash flows, what information concerning income taxes would Owyhee include in the statement of cash flows and related disclosure?

***Exercise 20—26 (Intraperiod income tax allocation)**
The Hughes Enterprise Company paid $360,000 in income taxes for the year ended December 31, 1996. $20,000 of these taxes related to an extraordinary gain that was taxed at 25%. Hughes discontinued one of its business segments during 1996, and realized a tax savings of $50,000 from the loss on disposition of the segment. The loss was treated for tax purposes as an ordinary loss, and was deducted from ordinary income that was taxed at 40%. Included in the $360,000 tax payment was $10,000 resulting from a gain on the sale of equipment. The tax rate on the gain was 25%. All other income items were from normal operations and were taxed at 40%. Hughes had 40,000 shares of common stock outstanding.

Prepare the income statement for Hughes Enterprise beginning with "Income from continuing operations before income taxes." Include the appropriate intraperiod tax allocation procedures.

*Relates to Appendix 20—1

***Exercise 20—27 (Investment tax credit)**

Brossard Electric Company purchased a new machine on January 1, 1996, for $350,000. The machine had a 10-year life and was depreciated by the straight-line method. Assuming a 10% investment tax credit, give the entries to record the recognition of income taxes for the first 2 years under (1) the flow-through method and (2) the deferred method. (Income tax before the credit in 1996 and 1997 was $217,500 and $312,000 respectively.)

*Relates to Appendix 20—2

***Exercise 20—28 (Investment tax credit)**

The Ferre Corporation purchased a stamping press for $1,360,000 on January 1, 1996. The press had an estimated useful life of 12 years and no salvage value. The corporation uses the straight-line method of depreciation. Assuming an income tax liability for the current year of $476,000 before an eligible investment tax credit of 6%, give the entries to record income tax for 1996 using (1) the flow-through method and (2) the deferred method.

*Relates to Appendix 20—2

PROBLEMS

Problem 20—29 (Life cycle of a temporary difference)

A. J. Johnson & Co. recorded certain revenues on its books in 1996 and 1997 of $15,400 and $16,600 respectively. However, such revenues were not subject to income taxation until 1998. Company records reveal pretax financial income and taxable income for the 3-year period as follows:

	Financial Income	Taxable Income
1996	$44,200	$28,800
1997	38,200	21,600
1998	21,100	53,100

Assume Johnson's tax rate is 40% for all periods.

Instructions: Prepare the journal entries necessary at the end of each year to record income taxes.

Problem 20—30 (Deferred tax liability)

Tristar Corporation reported taxable income of $1,996,000 for the year ended December 31, 1996. The controller is unfamiliar with the required treatment of temporary and permanent differences in reconciling taxable income to pretax financial income and has contacted your firm for advice. You are given company records that list the following differences:

Tax depreciation in excess of book depreciation	$275,000
Proceeds from life insurance policy upon death of officer	125,000
Interest revenue on municipal bonds	98,000

Instructions:

1. Compute pretax financial income.
2. Given an income tax rate of 40%, prepare the journal entry to record income taxes for the year.
3. Prepare a partial income statement beginning with "income from continuing operations before income taxes."

Problem 20—31 (Deferred tax liability)

Timpany Motors, Inc., computed a pretax financial income of $75,000 for its first year of operations ended December 31, 1996. In preparing the income tax return for the year, the tax accountant determined the following differences between 1996 financial income and taxable income:

Nondeductible expenses	$30,000
Nontaxable revenues	12,500
Temporary difference—installment sales reported in financial income but not in taxable income	28,000

The temporary difference is expected to reverse in the following pattern as the cash is collected:

1997	$ 6,000
1998	13,500
1999	8,500
	$28,000

The enacted tax rates for this year and the next three years are as follows:

1996 — 40%	1998 — 34%
1997 — 36%	1999 — 30%

Instructions:

1. Prepare journal entries to record income taxes payable and deferred income taxes.
2. Prepare the income statement for Timpany Motors beginning with "Income from continuing operations before income taxes" for the year ended December 31, 1996.

Problem 20—32 (Deferred tax asset)

Davidson Gasket Inc. computed a pretax financial loss of $15,000 for the first year of its operations, ended December 31, 1996. Analysis of the tax and book bases of its liabilities disclosed $55,000 in unearned rent revenue on the books that had been recognized as taxable income in 1996 when the cash was received. Also disclosed was $20,000 in warranties payable that had been recognized as expense on the books in 1996 when product sales were made, but that are not deductible on the tax return until paid.

These temporary differences are expected to reverse in the following pattern:

Year	Rent Earned on Books	Warranty Payments
1997	$13,000	$ 5,000
1998	25,000	8,000
1999	12,000	7,000
2000	5,000	
	$55,000	$20,000

The enacted tax rates for this year and the next four years are as follows:

1996 — 38%	1999 — 30%
1997 — 36%	2000 — 30%
1998 — 32%	

Instructions:

1. Prepare journal entries to record income taxes payable and deferred income taxes. Assume there will be sufficient income in each future year to realize any deductible amount.
2. Prepare the income statement for Davidson Gasket Inc. beginning with "Income from continuing operations before income taxes" for the year ended December 31, 1996.
3. If future taxable income from operations was not expected to be sufficient to allow for the full realization of any deferred tax assets, what other sources of income may be used to avoid establishing a valuation allowance?

Problem 20—33 (Deferred tax assets and liabilities)

As of December 31, 1996, its first year in business, Khaleeq Company had taxable temporary differences totaling $60,000. Of this total, $20,000 relates to current items. Khaleeq also had deductible temporary differences totaling $17,000, $5,000 of which relates to current items. Pretax financial income for the year was $100,000. The enacted tax rate for 1996 and all future years is 40%.

Instructions:

1. Prepare the journal entries to record income taxes for 1996.
2. Repeat (1), but assume that all the taxable temporary differences are noncurrent, and that all the deductible temporary differences are current.

Problem 20—34 (Netting of deferred tax assets and liabilities)

Stratco Corporation computed a pretax financial income of $40,000 for the first year of its operations ended December 31, 1996. Included in financial income was $50,000 of nontaxable revenue, $20,000 gross profit on installment sales that was deferred for tax purposes until the installments were collected, and $50,000 in warranties payable that had been recognized as expense on the books in 1996 when product sales were made.

The temporary differences are expected to reverse in the following pattern:

Year	Gross Profit on Collections	Warranty Payments
1997	$ 5,000	$ 9,000
1998	7,000	16,500
1999	2,000	20,500
2000	6,000	4,000
	$20,000	$50,000

The enacted tax rates for this year and the next four years are as follows:

1996 — 40%
1997 — 35%
1998 — 32%
1999 — 30%
2000 — 30%

Instructions:

1. Prepare journal entries to record income taxes payable and deferred income taxes. Assume there will be sufficient income in each future year to realize any deductible amount.
2. Prepare the income statement for Stratco beginning with "Income from continuing operations before income taxes" for the year ended December 31, 1996.

Problem 20—35 (Valuation allowance)

Cheng Company computed taxable income of $7,000 for the first year of its operations ended December 31, 1996. Tax depreciation exceeded depreciation for financial reporting purposes by $20,000. Receipt of $15,000 cash was reported as revenue for tax purposes but is reported as a current liability, Unearned Revenue, for financial reporting. The enacted tax rate for 1996 and all future years is 40%.

Instructions:

1. Prepare the journal entries to record income taxes for 1996. Assume that it is more likely than not that future taxable income will be sufficient to allow for the full realization of any deferred tax assets.
2. Repeat (1), assuming that it is more likely than not that future taxable income will be zero, exclusive of the expected reversal of the depreciation temporary difference.

Problem 20—36 (Adjustment for changing tax rates)

Moritz Company analyzed its temporary differences as of December 31, 1996. The enacted tax rate was 40% for 1996 and all future tax years.

The total amount of taxable temporary differences as of the end of 1996 was $110,000. All of the temporary differences relate to noncurrent items.

Instructions:

1. Assume that in early 1997 the taxing authority changed the rates for 1997 and beyond to 34%. Prepare the 1997 journal entry to record the tax rate decrease.
2. Assume that, instead of being decreased, the tax rate was increased to 46% in early 1997. Prepare the 1997 journal entry to record the tax rate increase.

Problem 20—37 (Operating loss carryback and carryforward)

The following information is taken from the financial statements of Columbia Enterprises:

Year	Taxable and Pretax Financial Income	Income Tax Rate	Income Tax Paid
1992	$24,000	40%	$ 9,600
1993	27,400	40%	10,960
1994	31,500	34%	10,710
1995	21,240	34%	7,222
1996	(86,000)	36%	0

The company elects to use the carryback provisions of the tax law.

Instructions:

1. Given the information from the financial statements, compute the amount of income tax refund due as a result of the operating loss.
2. What is the amount, if any, of the operating loss carryforward? How would the operating loss carryforward be reflected in the financial statements?
3. (a) Assume the foregoing information except that the loss in 1996 was $61,000. Calculate the refund due and prepare the journal entry to record the claim for income tax refund.
   (b) Assume that in addition to (a), there was a loss in 1997 of $24,000. How much could be carried back and how much could be carried forward?

Problem 20—38 (Net operating loss carryback and carryforward)

The following financial history shows the income and losses for Steele and Associates for the 10-year period 1987-1996:

Year	Taxable and Pretax Financial Income (Before NOL)	Income Tax Rate	Income Tax Paid
1987	$ 8,800	50%	$ 4,400
1988	12,300	50%	6,150
1989	14,800	44%	6,512
1990	(29,250)	44%	0
1991	7,200	44%	3,168
1992	(21,750)	46%	0
1993	16,600	46%	?
1994	32,000	40%	12,800
1995	(58,700)	40%	0
1996	65,000	40%	?

Assume that no adjustments to taxable income are necessary for purposes of the net operating loss carryback and the company elects to use the carryback provisions of the tax code.

Instructions:

1. Given the foregoing information, compute the amount of income tax refund for each year as a result of each loss carryback and the amount of the carryforward (if any).
2. How would the loss carryforward as of December 31, 1995, be reflected in the 1995 financial statements?
3. Calculate the amount of income tax paid, showing the benefit of the loss carryforward, for the years 1993 and 1996.
4. For 1996, give the entry (or entries) to record income taxes assuming that the deferred tax asset stemming from the 1995 NOL carryforward was fully recognized in 1995.

***Problem 20—39 (Intraperiod tax allocation)**

Assume Energy Corp. has the following income components on its income statement. Amounts are before tax.

Income from continuing operations	$37,500
Gain on disposal of business segment	19,000
Extraordinary gain on early extinguishment of debt	23,000
Extraordinary loss on property loss	(32,000)
Cumulative effect of change in depreciation method	(13,000)
Total income before considering income taxes	$34,500

Assume that the tax department has applied the current tax regulations and rates to Energy's various income categories, and computed the following tax information using the with-and-without concept required for intraperiod tax allocation:

Tax on total income ($34,500)	$13,100
Tax on income from continuing operations ($37,500)	15,200
Tax on total income before considering all irregular and extraordinary losses	27,030

Instructions:

1. Compute the total tax to be allocated to all income components after income from continuing operations, the total tax benefit allocated to the two loss categories, and the total tax expense allocated to the two gain categories.
2. Assume the tax department has computed the following incremental tax benefits and expenses on each individual gain or loss component:

Incremental tax expense—gain components	
Gain on disposal	$5,700
Extraordinary gain	6,500
Incremental tax benefit—loss components	
Extraordinary loss	9,600
Cumulative effect	5,000

Allocate the total tax benefit and tax expense from (1) to the separate gain and loss components.

*Relates to Appendix 20—1

***Problem 20—40 (Intraperiod tax allocation cases)**

Assume the following intraperiod tax allocation information for Cases A, B, and C:

	Case A	Case B	Case C
Tax on income from continuing operations	$23,000	$57,000	$7,000
Tax on total income before considering all irregular and extraordinary losses	36,900	61,000	9,500
Tax on total income	32,000	46,000	7,000
Incremental tax expense—gains:			
Gain on disposal	4,300	1,700	800
Extraordinary gain—A	6,500	3,200	3,000
Extraordinary gain—B	3,900		
Incremental tax benefit—losses:			
Extraordinary loss	(2,500)	(12,500)	(1,600)
Cumulative effect of accounting changes	(3,000)	(6,000)	(900)

Instructions: Compute the tax expense and benefits in Cases A through C for all irregular and extraordinary items.

*Relates to Appendix 20—1

***Problem 20—41 (Investment tax credit)**

Granite Sand and Gravel purchased a gravel-sifting machine from Steelco Fabrications in 1996. Granite also purchased from Steelco the patent on the machine. In conjunction with the acquisition, Granite hired an independent appraiser to assess the fair market values of the machine and the patent at the purchase date. Company records revealed the following information:

Machine and patent purchase price		$530,000
Fair market value of the machine		$425,000
Fair market value of the patent		$125,000
Useful life of the machine		10 years
Useful life of the patent		15 years
Precredit tax liability:	1996	$650,800
	1997	$1,180,200

Assume that an investment tax credit of 10% is allowable in 1996 for all purchases of tangible long-lived assets.

Instructions: Give the journal entries to record the acquisition of the machine and the patent, the recognition of income taxes in 1996 and 1997, and any amortization of deferred investment tax credits under both (1) the flow-through method and (2) the deferred method. (Assume that the company records depreciation for a full year in the year of acquisition.)

*Relates to Appendix 20—2

CHAPTER 21

Accounting for Pensions and Other Postretirement Benefits

CHAPTER TOPICS

- Nature and Characteristics of Employer Pension Plans
- Determining Net Periodic Pension Cost
- Disclosure of Pension Plans
- Postretirement Benefits Other Than Pensions

Press reports in the United States often talk about the rising "national debt." As of September 30, 1991, borrowing from the public by the U.S. Treasury totaled $2.687 trillion. This obligation is the most publicized liability of the U.S. government, but it is not the only large one. As of the same date, the present value of the government liability under military and civilian pension plans and for veterans' benefits was $1.483 trillion. These liabilities are certainly large (a trillion dollar bills laid end to end would stretch from the earth to the moon and back 197 times), but all other government liabilities are dwarfed by the social security pension obligation. Of course, in one sense it is not correct to view social security as a pension plan; it is a social insurance arrangement in which current workers pay for the benefits of past workers in the hopes that they (the current workers) will be supported by the contributions of future workers. With that qualification, it is still interesting to evaluate the status of social security as if it were a pension plan. As of September 30, 1991, the U.S. Treasury estimated that the present value of future benefits to existing workers exceeded the present value of expected future contributions from those workers and their employers by $6.595 trillion.[1]

A widely recognized phenomenon of the 20th century has been the increasing life expectancy of people in almost all countries of the world. For example, in 1900 the average life expectancy of people in the United States was 49 years; by 1991 it had increased to 75.7 years.[2] As people live longer, they must deal with the problem of financing their extended retirement years. The magnitude of the problem in the United States will increase in the next 15 to 20 years as the "baby-boomer" population of the 1940s and 50s moves into retirement. It is estimated that the proportion of the U.S. population that is over 65 will increase from the current 13% to 20% by the year 2030.

Financing retirement years is accomplished by establishing some type of **pension plan** that sets aside funds during an employee's working years so that at retirement the funds and earnings from investment of the funds may be returned to the employee in lieu of earned wages. In the United States, three major categories of pension plans have emerged:

1. Government plans, primarily social security
2. Individual plans, such as individual retirement accounts (IRAs)
3. Employer plans

The third category, employer pension plans, involves several difficult and controversial accounting and reporting issues. In 1985, the FASB issued two new pension accounting standards, Statement No. 87, "Employers' Accounting for Pensions," and Statement No. 88, "Employers' Accounting for Settlements and Curtailments of Defined Benefit Pension Plans and for Termination Benefits." These standards, particularly Statement No. 87, significantly changed the way in which pension costs are determined and reported by employers.

A related issue to employer pension plans is the employer's accounting for **postretirement benefits other than pensions**. These benefits extend beyond the active years of employment and include such items as health care, life insurance, legal services, special discounts on items produced or sold by the employer, and tuition assistance. Historically, most companies recognized the costs of these benefits on a pay-as-you-go, or cash, basis. The Financial Accounting Standards Board considered postretirement benefits as a separate project and, in December 1990, issued FASB Statement No. 106, "Employers' Accounting for Postretirement Benefits Other Than Pensions." Generally, this standard requires companies to accrue the cost of postretirement benefits as deferred compensation and to disclose the nature of the company's future obligation for postretirement benefits.

This chapter focuses first on employers' accounting for pension plans. Many of the provisions of the postretirement benefits standard are similar to those of the pension standard. The differences between them will be presented in the latter part of the chapter.

NATURE AND CHARACTERISTICS OF EMPLOYER PENSION PLANS

The subject of employers' accounting for pensions is very complex, partly because of the many variations in plans that have been developed. Most pension plans are specifically designed for one employer and are known as **single-employer pension plans**. If several companies contribute to the same plan, it is called a multiemployer pension plan. This chapter, like the accounting standards, focuses on accounting for single-employer plans.

1. Consolidated Financial Statements of the United States Government (Prototype) for the fiscal year ended September 30, 1991 (Department of the Treasury).
2. *Statistical Abstract of the United States—1993, 113th Edition* (U.S. Department of Commerce).

Funding of Employer Pension Plans

The basic purpose of all employer pension plans is the same—to provide retirement benefits to employees. A principal issue concerning pension plans is how to provide sufficient funds to meet the needs of retirees. The social security system of the federal government has frequently been criticized because it is not a "funded" plan. FICA taxes (contributions) paid by employers and employees in the current year are used to pay benefits to individuals who are currently retired. This means that the current employees must have faith that a future generation will do the same for them. Such a system creates much doubt and uncertainty.

Private plans are not permitted to operate in this way. Federal law, such as the Employee Retirement Income Security Act (ERISA) of 1974, requires companies to fund their pension plans in an orderly manner so that the employee is protected at retirement. Some pension plans are funded entirely by the employer and are referred to as **noncontributory pension plans**. In other cases, the employee also contributes to the cost of the pension plan, referred to as a **contributory pension plan**.[3] The amounts and timing of contributions depend on the particular circumstances and plan provisions. While the provisions of pension plans vary widely and in many cases are very complex, there are two basic classifications of pension plans: (1) defined contribution plans and (2) defined benefit plans.

Defined Contribution Pension Plans

Defined contribution pension plans are relatively simple in their construction and raise very few accounting issues for employers. Under these plans, a periodic contribution amount is paid by the employer into a separate trust fund, which is administered by an independent third-party trustee. The contribution may be defined as a fixed amount each period, a percentage of the employer's income, a percentage of employee earnings, or a combination of these or other factors. As contributions to the fund are made, they are invested by the fund administrator. When an employee retires, the accumulated value in the fund is used to determine the pension payout to the employee. The employee's retirement income therefore depends on how the fund has been managed. If investments have been made wisely, the employee will fare better than if the investments were managed poorly. In effect, the investment risk is borne by the employee. The employer's obligation extends only to making the specified periodic contribution. This amount is charged to pension expense and no further accounting is required for the plan. As an example of this type of plan, many college professors belong to a defined contribution plan called TIAA/CREF. The college or university makes contributions on behalf of the professor who then must rely on the good judgment of the TIAA/CREF fund managers to ensure his or her retirement security. As of October 1993, TIAA/CREF was the largest private pension plan in the world with assets in excess of $125 billion.

Defined Benefit Pension Plans

Defined benefit pension plans are much more complex than defined contribution plans. Under defined benefit plans, the employee is guaranteed a specified retirement income often related to his or her number of years of employment and average salary over a certain number of years. The periodic amount of the employer's contribution is based on the expected future benefits to be paid to employees and is affected by a number of variables. Because the benefits are defined, the contributions (funding) must vary as conditions change. Exhibit 21—1 illustrates the basic nature of a defined benefit plan. A defined contribution plan could be illustrated in the same manner except that the contributions (rather than the benefits) would be defined. This difference, however, is significant and accounts for the complexity of defined benefit plans.

3. Employee contributions are not considered in subsequent discussions and examples, since the chapter is concerned with employers' accounting for pensions.

Exhibit 21—1 Defined Benefit Pension Plans

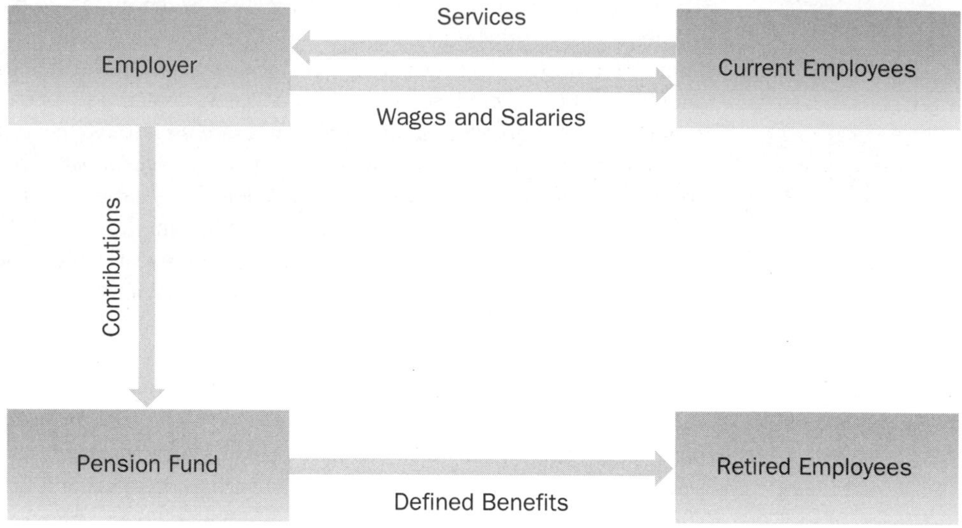

Under defined benefit plans, the investment risk is, in substance, borne by the employer. While a separate trust fund usually is maintained for contributions and investment earnings, the employer ultimately is responsible to ensure that employees receive the defined benefits provided by the plan. **Pension plan assets** may be viewed essentially as funds set aside to meet the employer's future pension obligation just as funds may be set aside for other purposes, e.g., to retire bonds at maturity. One major difference, however, is that a future obligation to retire bonds is a definite amount, while the employer's future obligation for retirement benefits is based on many estimates and assumptions. In addition, U.S. federal law requires minimum pension plan funding, whereas sinking fund requirements are privately negotiated between the borrower and the bondholders.

Defined Benefits. Defined benefit pension plans provide for an increase in future retirement benefits as additional services are rendered by an employee. In effect, the employee's total compensation for a period consists of current wages or salaries plus deferred compensation represented by the right to receive a defined amount of future benefits. The amount of future benefits earned by employees for a particular period is determined by actuaries, not accountants. However, an understanding of the basic concepts used in measuring future retirement benefits is necessary for understanding the accounting issues relating to pensions.

The amount of future benefits earned for a period is based on the plan's **benefit formula**, which specifies how benefits are **attributed** (assigned) to years of employee service. Some plans attribute equal benefits to each year of service rendered, e.g., a pension benefit of $20 per month for each year of employee service rendered. Thus an employee who retires after 30 years of service would be entitled to a monthly benefit of $600 ($20 per month × 30 years of service). The benefit attributed to each year of service would be $20 multiplied by the number of months of life expectancy after retirement. Some plans attribute different benefits to different years of service, e.g., a pension benefit of $20 per month for each year of service up to 20 years and $25 per month for each additional year of service. Many plans include a benefit formula based on current or future employee earnings. For example, a plan might provide monthly benefits of 2% of an employee's average annual earnings for the 5 years preceding retirement.

The measurement of future benefits is highly subjective. The amount of benefits earned by employees for a period is based on many variables, including the average age of employees, length of service, expected turnover, vesting provisions, and life expectancy. Thus, the actuaries must estimate how many of the current employees will retire and when they will retire, the number of employees who will leave the company prior to retirement, the life expectancy of employees after retirement, and other relevant factors.

Vesting of Pension Benefits. A key element in all pension plans is the **vested benefits** provision. Vesting occurs when an employee has met certain specified requirements and is eligible to receive pension benefits at retirement regardless of whether the employee continues working for the employer. In early pension plans, vesting did not occur for many years. In extreme cases, vesting occurred only when an employee reached retirement. A major outcome of federal regulation is the much earlier vesting privileges for employees. Most pension plans provide for full vesting after 10 years of employment. Colleges and universities typically require professors to remain at the school for three to five years in order for pension contributions to vest. It is not uncommon for a professor to forfeit non-vested pension contributions when moving from one school to another.

Funding of Defined Benefit Plans. The periodic amounts to be contributed to a defined benefit plan by the employer are directly related to the future benefits expected to be paid to current employees. The methods of funding pension plans vary widely. Most defined benefit plans require periodic contributions that accumulate to the balance needed to pay the promised retirement benefits to employees. Some plans specify an even amount for each year of employee service. Others require a lower amount in the early years of employee service, with an accelerating schedule over the years. Still other plans provide for a higher amount at first, then a declining pattern of funding. The contribution amounts are determined by actuarial formulas and must be adjusted as estimates and assumptions are revised to reflect changing conditions.

All funding methods are based on present values. The additional future benefits earned by employees each year must be discounted to their present value, referred to as the **actuarial present value**, using an assumed rate of return on pension fund investments. In many cases, employers contribute an amount equal to the present value of future benefits attributed to current services. As noted above, however, funding patterns vary and the amount contributed for a particular period may be less than or greater than the present value of the additional benefits earned for the period. Assume, for example, that the present value of future benefits earned in the current period is determined to be $30,000 using a discount rate of 10%. If the funding method requires a contribution of only $25,000 for the period, the employer has an **unfunded** obligation of $5,000. At the end of the following year, this obligation will have increased to $5,500 to reflect the interest cost of 10%. When contributions exceed the present value of the future benefits, lower contributions will be required in subsequent periods as a result of earnings on the "overfunded" amount.

The Pension Benefit Guaranty Corporation (PBGC) is charged with monitoring the funding status of pension plans in the United States. The PBGC provides federal insurance for participants in U.S. pension plans much as the FDIC provides insurance for bank depositors. Each year the PBGC publishes a top-50 list of underfunded pension plans. In 1993, as in prior years, the firm heading the list was General Motors with an unfunded pension liability of $20.2 billion.[4] The number two firm on the list was Bethlehem Steel with a $2.4 billion unfunded liability.

4. Albert R. Karr. "Pension Plans' Underfunding Worsened in '92." *The Wall Street Journal,* November 23, 1993, p. A3.

ISSUES IN ACCOUNTING FOR DEFINED BENEFIT PLANS

Although the provisions of defined benefit pension plans can be extremely complex, and the application of accounting standards to a specific plan can be highly technical, the accounting issues themselves are identified easily. Following is a list of these issues, all of which relate to accounting and reporting by employers.

1. The amount of net periodic pension cost to be recognized as expense.
2. The amount of pension liability to be reported on the balance sheet.
3. The amount of pension fund assets to be reported on the balance sheet.
4. Accounting for pension settlements, curtailments, and terminations.
5. Disclosures needed to supplement the amounts reported in the financial statements.

The issue of funding pension plans is purposely omitted from the list. Funding decisions are affected by tax laws, governmental regulations, actuarial computations, and contractual terms, not by accounting standards. They should not directly affect the amount that is reported as net periodic pension cost (expense) under the accrual concept.

The next section of the chapter illustrates the basic computational and accounting issues related to pensions in the context of a simple illustration. The simple example is then followed by a more complex illustration that introduces the intricacies for which pension accounting is famous.

SIMPLE ILLUSTRATION OF PENSION ACCOUNTING

Thakkar Company has established a defined benefit pension plan. As of January 1, 1996, only one employee, Lorien Bach, is enrolled in the plan. Some characteristics of the plan and of Bach as of January 1, 1996, are outlined below:

- Bach is 35 years old and has worked for Thakkar for 10 years.
- Bach's salary for 1995 was $40,000.
- Thakkar's pension plan pays a benefit based on an employee's highest salary. Pension payments begin after an employee turns 65 and payments are made at the end of the year. The annual payment is equal to:

  2% of the highest salary times number of years with the company
- Bach is an unusually predictable person; it is known with certainty that she will not quit, be fired, or die before age 65. Also, it is known with certainty that she will live exactly 75 years and will therefore collect 10 annual pension payments after she retires. Bach's benefits have already fully vested.
- In valuing pension fund liabilities, Thakkar uses a discount rate of 10%.
- As of January 1, 1996, Thakkar Company has a pension fund containing $10,000. During 1996, Thakkar made additional contributions to the fund totaling $1,500. Also, the fund earned a return of $350 during the year. Over the long run, Thakkar expects to earn an average return of 12% on pension fund assets.

Estimation of Pension Liability

The first step in estimating Thakkar Company's pension liability is to compute the amount of the annual pension payment to be made to Bach when she retires. The amount of the payment depends on Bach's years of service and highest salary. As of January 1, 1996, Bach has put in 10 years of service and, assuming that her most recent salary of $40,000 is her highest salary to date, the forecasted amount of her annual pension payment can be computed as follows:

(2% × 10 years) × $40,000 = $8,000

It is known that Bach will live long enough after retirement at age 65 to collect 10 annual pension payments and thus the total amount of pension benefits that Thakkar expects to pay to Bach is \$80,000 (10 years × \$8,000). However, \$80,000 is an overstatement of the value of Thakkar's pension liability since the payments won't begin for another 30 years. To properly compute the present value of the payments to Bach, allowance must be made for the fact that the first payment won't be made until Bach is 66 years old (pension payments are made at the end of the year), the payments are spread over 10 years, and Thakkar Company's discount rate is 10%. This discount rate can be thought of as the implicit rate of interest Thakkar would have to pay to a financial institution (such as an insurance company) to purchase annuity contracts settling the pension obligation to Bach.[5] In the appendix to this chapter, it is shown that, using the 10% discount rate, the present value of the expected pension payments to Bach is equal to \$2,817.

The \$2,817 amount can be thought of as follows: If Thakkar Company were to deposit \$2,817 on January 1, 1996, in a bank account yielding 10%, by the end of 30 years when Bach retires, that \$2,817 will have accumulated to an amount large enough to support payments to Bach of \$8,000 per year for the succeeding 10 years. The \$2,817 is the **actuarial present value** of Thakkar's pension liability. An actuarial present value takes into account both time value of money considerations and actuarial assumptions (i.e., how long until Bach retires, how long will Bach live after retirement). In practice, such calculations are performed by professionals called *actuaries*. Financial accountants do not need to know how to perform the detailed actuarial present value calculations, but should understand the general concepts underlying the calculations.

The \$2,817 pension liability computed above is called the **accumulated benefit obligation (ABO).** The ABO is the actuarial present value of the expected future pension payments, using the *current* salary as the basis for forecasting the amount of the pension benefit payments. The ABO approach ignores the impact of expected future salary increases on the amount of the benefit payments. An alternative measure of the pension liability that does consider the impact of future salary increases is called the **projected benefit obligation (PBO).**

To illustrate the difference between the PBO and the ABO, assume that Thakkar Company expects Bach's 1995 salary of \$40,000 to increase 5% every year until retirement. As a result, Bach's salary is expected to increase to \$172,876 by the year 2025, Bach's last year of employment.[6] The pension benefit payment based on this salary would be:

(2% × 10 years) × \$172,876 = \$34,575 (rounded)

The PBO at January 1, 1996, is \$12,175 (see the appendix to this chapter for details of the computation). This is the present value of the 10 future annual payments of \$34,575 that Bach is expected to receive. The diagram in Exhibit 21—2 illustrates the relationship between the future payments and the PBO.

Both the PBO and the ABO computations are based on the amount of pension benefits that have already been earned—in this case, on the 10 years of service Bach has provided to Thakkar. The difference between the PBO and the ABO comes in the estimate of Bach's highest salary. The ABO computations ignore likely future salary increases; the PBO computations include estimates of those increases. The quantitative difference between these two approaches can be substantial. For Thakkar, the \$2,817 ABO is substantially lower than the \$12,175 value computed for the PBO.

5. *Statement of Financial Accounting Standards No. 87,* "Employers' Accounting for Pensions" (Stamford: Financial Accounting Standards Board, 1985), par. 44. The SEC has suggested that the appropriate discount rate is the return on highly rated fixed income debt securities. See EITF Topic D-36, Sept. 23, 1993.

6. $FV = P(FVF_{\overline{n}|i})$
$= \$40,000(\text{Table I}_{\overline{30}|5\%})$
$= \$40,000(4.3219)$
$= \$172,876$

■ **Exhibit 21—2** Thakkar Company—Projected Benefit Obligation, January 1, 1996

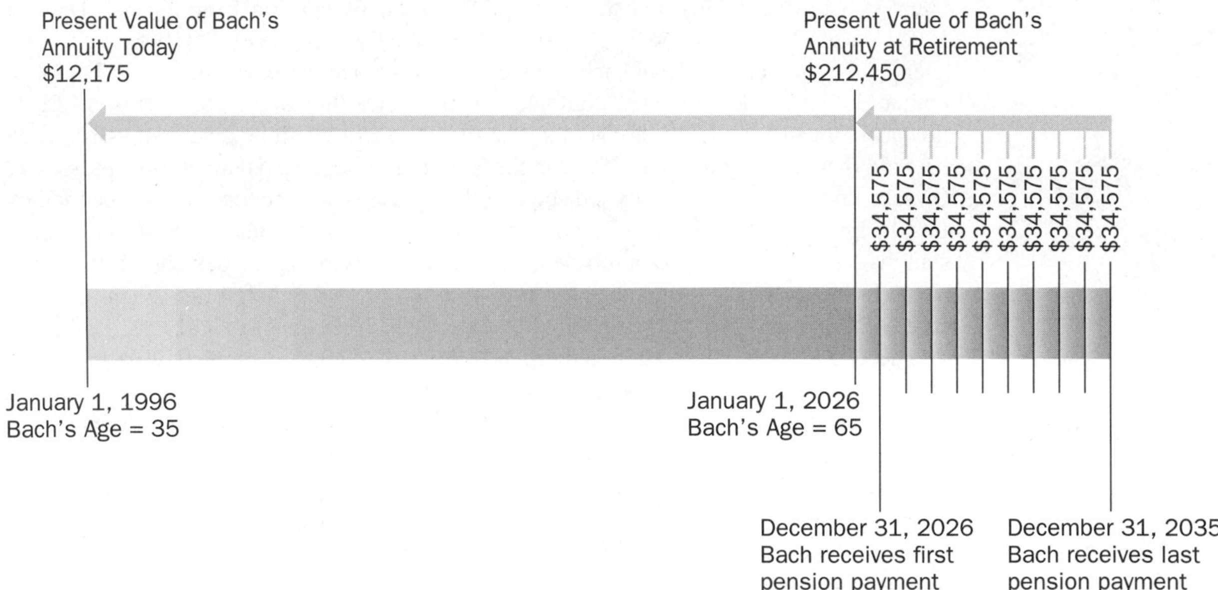

The numerical relationship between the ABO and the PBO is often presented as follows:

Accumulated Benefit Obligation, 1/1/96	$ 2,817
Additional amounts related to projected pay increases	9,358
Projected Benefit Obligation, 1/1/96	$12,175

So, which is a better measure of a firm's pension obligation, the PBO or the ABO? FASB Statement No. 87 identifies the PBO as the measure appropriate for use in most calculations. The ABO is also disclosed and sometimes enters into the calculation of the reported pension liability (in a way that is explained later in the chapter). This choice of the PBO as the primary measure of a firm's pension obligation was not without some controversy.[7] It was argued that use of the PBO is not appropriate because it embodies future salary increases and the historical cost accounting model does not include recognition of future events. This argument was countered with the observation that use of a discount rate also results in recognition of future events since the discount rate includes a premium for expected future inflation. It was argued that to allow recognition of the impact of expected future inflation but not allow consideration of expected salary increases would result in a gross understatement of the pension obligation in some cases. Hence, the projected benefit obligation is the primary measure of a firm's pension obligation.

As of January 1, 1996, the pension obligation for Thakkar, as measured by the PBO, is $12,175 and, from the information given at the beginning of the illustration, the total fair value of the pension plan assets is $10,000. One possible way to present this information in a balance sheet is to list the pension plan assets among the noncurrent assets and the pension liability as a noncurrent liability. However, FASB Statement No. 87 stipulates that these two items be offset against one another and a single net amount be shown as

7. Adoption of FASB Statement No. 87 was opposed by three of the seven members of the Board. A description of the dissenting views is included at the end of the primary text of the Statement (following paragraph 77).

either a net pension asset or a net pension liability.[8] Thakkar would calculate the appropriate balance sheet amount in the following way:

Accumulated Benefit Obligation, 1/1/96	$ 2,817
Additional amounts related to projected pay increases	9,358
Projected Benefit Obligation, 1/1/96	$12,175
Plan assets at fair value, 1/1/96	10,000
Accrued Pension Liability, 1/1/96	$ 2,175

If the fair value of plan assets had exceeded the projected benefit obligation, the resulting net asset would have been labeled "Prepaid pension cost."

Why does Statement No. 87 require offsetting of pension liabilities and assets instead of separate recognition of each? The answer, in one word, is tradition. Accepted practice before Statement No. 87 was to offset pension liabilities and assets and, to avoid too great a change, the FASB decided to maintain that feature. Statement No. 87 is viewed as an improvement over prior standards, but not too different from those prior standards, in order to preserve the "gradual, evolutionary" nature of accounting standard setting.[9] The separate components of accrued pension liability and prepaid pension cost are disclosed in the notes to the financial statements in a manner similar to the table shown above.

Computation of Pension Cost for 1996

In the simple Thakkar Company example, measurement of pension cost[10] for the year involves consideration of three factors:

1. Implied interest on the beginning-of-the-period pension obligation,
2. New pension benefits earned by employees through service during the year, and
3. Investment return on the pension plan assets.

These three factors will be considered in turn.

Interest Cost. The projected benefit obligation on January 1, 1996 is $12,175. This represents an amount owed by Thakkar to its employee Bach. The 10% discount rate used in the computation of the PBO is called the **settlement interest rate** and can be viewed as the implied interest rate on this debt. Accordingly, one aspect of annual pension cost is the increase in the PBO resulting from interest on this pension obligation, computed as follows:

PBO, Beginning of Period		Discount Rate		Interest Cost
$12,175	×	.10	=	$1,218

Service Cost. Bach's work for Thakkar Company during the year results in an increase in the forecasted annual pension benefit payments from Thakkar to Bach since those payments are now computed based on 11 years of service instead of 10 years. The impact of this extra year of service is to increase the December 31, 1996 projected benefit obligation by $1,339 over what it would have been if Bach had just vacationed for the entire year. (See the end-of-chapter appendix for the computations.) Therefore, the service cost element of pension cost for the year is $1,339. In practice, of course, service cost computations are very complex and are done by actuaries.

8. *Statement of Financial Accounting Standards No. 87,* par. 35. In a more complicated example, other items would also be included in the computation of the net pension asset or liability. These items are discussed later in the chapter.

9. *Ibid.,* par. 107.

10. The text discussion refers to pension *cost* instead of pension *expense*. This follows the usage in Statement No. 87. Periodic pension cost may be expensed immediately or it may be capitalized as part of an asset such as inventory.

Return on Pension Plan Assets. Pension cost is reduced by the return on pension plan assets for the year. Just as liabilities and assets are offset to arrive at a net measure of accrued pension liability or prepaid pension cost, the return on pension plan assets is offset against interest and service costs to compute a single net pension cost number. Instead of using the actual return, $350 in this case, Statement No. 87 indicates that the expected long-term return should be used. This return is typically computed by multiplying the fair value of pension plan assets as of the beginning of the year by some estimate of the average rate of return the pension fund is expected to earn over the long run. For Thakkar Company, this long-term expected rate of return has been estimated to be 12%. Accordingly, for 1996, Thakkar's net pension cost is reduced by $1,200 ($10,000 × .12). The $850 ($1,200 – $350) difference between the actual return and the expected return is a deferred loss — an indication that the actual performance of the pension fund has not met the long-term expectation. The accounting treatment of this deferred loss is explained later in the chapter.

Net pension cost for 1996 for Thakkar is computed as follows:

Interest cost	$1,218
Service cost	1,339
Less: Expected return on plan assets	(1,200)
Net pension cost	$1,357

The Thakkar Company illustration contains only the most basic elements of accounting for pensions. In more complex cases, pension cost is affected by amortization of deferred gains and losses from prior periods, amortization of the impact of a change in the terms of the pension plan, and amortization of the impact of changes in the actuarial assumptions. The accounting for these components of pension cost is illustrated in a subsequent example.

Basic Pension Journal Entries

The basic accounting entries for pensions are very straightforward. An entry is made to accrue the pension cost, and another entry is made to record the contribution to the pension fund. For convenience, a single account, **Prepaid/Accrued Pension Cost,** is used to reflect changes in the net pension asset or liability. Since Thakkar started the year with a credit balance of $2,175 in this account, it can be viewed as a liability account in this example. Thakkar Company would make the following journal entries for 1996:

Pension Cost	1,357	
Prepaid/Accrued Pension Cost		1,357
To record 1996 pension cost.		
Prepaid/Accrued Pension Cost	1,500	
Cash		1,500
To record 1996 contribution to pension plan.		

As a result of these entries, pension cost of $1,357 would be reported as an expense on the income statement. The combined effect of the two entries is to decrease Accrued Pension Cost liability by $143 ($1,500 – $1,357); the balance in Accrued Pension Cost is $2,032 ($2,175 beginning balance – $143 decrease).

Computation of Accrued Pension Liability

As of December 31, 1996, the projected benefit obligation for Thakkar is $14,732 (see the appendix) and the total fair value of the pension plan assets is $11,850 ($10,000 + $350 return + $1,500 new contributions). As illustrated previously, the PBO and the fair value of plan assets are offset to arrive at a single balance sheet amount. This single amount also should include deferred gains and losses arising from differences between actual and expected returns on pension plan assets. As of December 31, 1996, Thakkar Company would perform the following calculation:

Accumulated Benefit Obligation, 12/31/96	$ 3,577*
Additional amounts related to projected pay increases	11,155
Projected Benefit Obligation, 12/31/96	$14,732
Plan assets at fair value, 12/31/96	11,850
Excess of PBO over assets	$ 2,882
Less: Deferred loss on plan assets	(850)
Accrued pension liability, 12/31/96	$ 2,032

*Based on 1996 salary which is assumed to be $42,000, representing a 5% increase over 1995.

The net accrued pension liability of $2,032 would be shown in the noncurrent liability section of Thakkar's balance sheet. The table above would be included in the notes to the financial statements.

Key Points from the Thakkar Company Example

Before considering a more complicated example, take a moment now to review some important points illustrated with the Thakkar Company example:

- The actuarial computations are complicated, even in the simplest possible example. For proof, see the appendix at the end of the chapter. The good news is that in practice these computations are done by actuaries.
- The balance sheet and income statement amounts related to pensions are sensitive to the actuarial assumptions made. This is illustrated in the appendix.
- The balance sheet amount is a conglomeration of several items: the projected benefit obligation, the fair value of pension plan assets, and deferred items. The details of the computation are disclosed in the notes to the financial statements.
- Net pension cost is also a conglomeration of several items. The three main items are interest cost, service cost, and the expected return on plan assets.

In the next section, the discussion of pension accounting continues with a more complex example. That example provides more detailed coverage of the treatment of deferred items, and also introduces the minimum liability provisions that result in the messiest aspects of pension accounting. A work sheet approach is introduced that greatly simplifies the handling of complex pension situations.

COMPREHENSIVE PENSION ILLUSTRATION

The Thakkar Company example included only three factors in the computation of pension cost. In a more general case, a company could recognize as many as six different components of **net periodic pension cost.** The six components are:

1. Service cost.
2. Interest cost.
3. Actual return on pension plan assets (if any).
4. Amortization of unrecognized prior service cost (if any).
5. Deferral of current period gain or loss and amortization of unrecognized net gain or loss.
6. Effects (if any) of transition to Statement No. 87.

Before discussing these components of pension cost in depth, it is useful to review two key measurements in pension accounting, the **projected benefit obligation (PBO)** and the **fair value of pension plan assets.** The **projected benefit obligation** is a present-value measure of the future benefits expected to be paid to employees based on their employment to date but taking into consideration, if applicable, expected increases in wages that would affect their retirement benefits. The measurement is based on actuarial estimation of such factors as life expectancy, employee turnover, and interest rates. The projected benefit obligation increases each year as additional benefits are earned by employees through another year of service (service cost) and by the passage of time that brings employees one year closer to receiving their benefits (interest cost). The projected benefit obligation decreases each year by the pension payments to retired employees. In addition, the obligation may increase or decrease by changes in any of the actuarial assumptions enumerated previously. These changes may be summarized as follows:

Projected benefit obligation, beginning of year	+	Service cost and interest cost	−	Retirement benefits paid	±	Change in actuarial assumptions	=	Projected benefit obligation, end of year

The **fair value of pension plan assets** is based on the market value of pension plan assets at a given measurement date. The fair value of pension plan assets increases each year by employer contributions to the fund and decreases by the retirement benefits paid. The fair value also changes by the amount of earnings on the pension plan assets, including changes in the market value of the assets. These changes may be summarized as follows:

Fair value of pension plan assets, beginning of year	+	Employer contributions	−	Retirement benefits paid	±	Actual return on pension plan assets	=	Fair value of pension plan assets, end of year

These two valuations are used extensively in computing pension cost. Because FASB Statement No. 87 permits the asset (fair value of pension plan assets) and the liability (projected benefit obligation) to be offset against each other, they are not recorded in the employer's formal accounting system nor reported in the employer's balance sheet. However, informal memorandum records of these and other deferred pension balances must be maintained in order to compute pension cost. These memorandum records include accounts for the following five items:

1. Projected benefit obligation
2. Fair value of pension plan assets
3. Deferred pension gains and losses
4. Unrecognized prior service cost
5. Unamortized transition gains or losses

Any reasonable recordkeeping method can be used to maintain these accounts. This chapter illustrates a pension work sheet that displays all accounts related to pensions, both formal and informal, in a side-by-side format.[11]

Throughout the discussion of the components of pension cost, an illustration for a hypothetical company, Thornton Electronics, Inc., will be used.

11. This work sheet approach is based on an article by Paul B. W. Miller. See "The New Pension Accounting (part 2)," *Journal of Accountancy*, February 1987, pp. 84-94.

Thornton Electronics — 1996

Thornton's pension-related balances as of January 1, 1996, are as follows:

Balances at January 1, 1996:	
Projected benefit obligation	$1,500,000
Fair value of pension plan assets	1,385,000
Unrecognized prior service costs	495,000
Unamortized transition gain	420,000
Accrued pension liability	40,000

The projected benefit obligation, the fair value of pension plan assets, and the net accrued pension liability have been explained previously. The two new items, unrecognized prior service cost and unamortized transition gain, are described below.

Unrecognized Prior Service Cost. When a pension plan is initially adopted or amended to provide increased benefits, employees are granted additional benefits for services performed in years prior to the plan adoption or amendment. The cost of these additional benefits to the employer is called **prior service cost.** The amount of prior service cost is determined by actuaries and represents the increase in the projected benefit obligation arising from the adoption or amendment of the plan. Although prior service costs arise from services rendered in prior periods, there has been general agreement in the accounting profession that the cost should not be recognized at the plan adoption or amendment date, but rather should be **amortized over future periods.** This is based on the assumption that the employer will receive future economic benefits accruing from the plan adoption or amendment in the form of improved employee morale, loyalty, and productivity.

Unamortized Transition Gain or Loss. The **transition gain or loss** is defined as the difference between the projected benefit obligation and the fair value of the pension plan assets at the time FASB Statement No. 87 was adopted by a company. For most companies, this occurred in their 1987 fiscal year. If the projected benefit obligation was the larger of these two values at the transition date, the difference was a loss. If the fair value of the pension plan assets was the larger value, the difference was a gain. The resulting transition gain or loss is not recorded on the books, but is entered as a memorandum entry and is recognized by amortization over future periods. Transition gains and losses arise strictly from companies switching from an old accounting standard to FASB Statement No. 87. Since all companies have now made this switch, no new transition gains or losses are being created. However, amortization of existing transition items will still be part of many companies' pension cost until the year 2003.

The January 1, 1996, pension information for Thornton Electronics would appear in the pension work sheet as shown in Exhibit 21—3.

The work sheet is divided into two sections: the formal account section where the net effect of pension-related items on the balance sheet and income statement is shown, and

Exhibit 21—3 Thornton Electronics, Inc.—Pension Work Sheet, January 1, 1996

	FORMAL ACCOUNTS			MEMORANDUM ACCOUNTS				
	Net Pension Cost	Cash	Prepaid/ Accrued Pension Cost	Periodic Pension Cost Items	Projected Benefit Obligation	Fair Value of Pension Assets	Unamortized Transition Gain/Loss	Unrecognized Prior Service Cost
Balance, January 1, 1996			($40,000)		($1,500,000)	$1,385,000	($420,000)	$495,000

Note: Positive amounts are debits; negative amounts are credits.

the memorandum account section where detailed pension information, to be disclosed in the notes to the financial statements, is listed. The formal balance sheet account, Prepaid/Accrued Pension Cost, summarizes in one number all the asset and liability information contained in the memo records. When preparing a pension work sheet, make sure to confirm that the net balance in the formal prepaid/accrued pension cost account ($40,000 credit) is equal to the sum of the balances in the memo records ($1,500,000 credit + $1,385,000 debit + $420,000 credit + $495,000 debit). Note that if the transition item had been a deferred loss instead of a deferred gain, its balance would have been a debit instead of a credit. In the work sheet, a credit balance is indicated by parentheses.

Information summarizing the 1996 pension activity of Thornton Electronics is listed below:

1996 Pension Activity for Thornton Electronics	
Service cost as reported by actuaries	$ 75,000
Contributions to pension plan	115,000
Benefits paid to retirees	125,000
Fair value of pension plan assets at December 31, 1996	1,513,500
Settlement interest rate	11.0%
Long-term expected rate of return on pension plan assets	10.0%

The 1996 pension information has been entered in the pension work sheet shown in Exhibit 21—4. Each entry is explained below.

Service Cost. Recall that service cost is the present value of additional benefits earned by employees during the period. As explained earlier, service cost for the period is determined by actuaries based on the pension plan's benefit formula. Thornton Electronics' actuaries reported 1996 service cost of $75,000. This $75,000 is recorded in work sheet entry (a) as an increase in net periodic pension cost (a debit) and an increase to the projected benefit obligation (a credit). This entry does not directly impact the formal accounting records. The indirect impact will be reflected in a year-end summary journal entry in the formal accounting records.

Exhibit 21—4 Thornton Electronics, Inc.—Pension Work Sheet for 1996

	FORMAL ACCOUNTS			MEMORANDUM ACCOUNTS				
	Net Pension Cost	Cash	Prepaid/ Accrued Pension Cost	Periodic Pension Cost Items	Projected Benefit Obligation	Fair Value of Pension Assets	Unamortized Transition Gain/Loss	Unrecognized Prior Service Cost
Balance, January 1, 1996			($40,000)		($1,500,000)	$1,385,000	($420,000)	$495,000
(a) Service Cost				75,000	(75,000)			
(b) Interest Cost				165,000	(165,000)			
(c) Actual Return on Assets				(138,500)		138,500		
(d) Benefits Paid					125,000	(125,000)		
(e) PSC Amortization				90,000				(90,000)
(f) Transition Amortization				(70,000)			70,000	
Summary Journal Entries								
(1) Annual Pension Cost Accrual	121,500		(121,500)					
(2) Annual Pension Contribution		(115,000)	115,000			115,000		
Balance, December 31, 1996			($46,500)		($1,615,000)	$1,513,500	($350,000)	$405,000

Note: Positive amounts are debits; negative amounts are credits.

Components of Prepaid/Accrued Pension Cost

Interest Cost. The interest cost represents the fact that the present value of Thornton's pension obligation is increased by the interest on the beginning projected benefit obligation. The settlement interest rate is used to discount the projected benefit obligation and is also used to compute the interest cost. The interest cost for 1996 is $1,500,000 × 11.0%, or $165,000. The interest cost is shown in entry (b) as a debit to net periodic pension cost and a credit to the projected benefit obligation.

Actual Return on Pension Plan Assets. The assets created by employer contributions to a pension plan usually earn a return that reduces the reported amount of annual pension cost. The return is composed of such elements as interest revenue, dividends, rentals, and changes in the market value of the assets. If a decline in the market value of the pension plan assets exceeds the earnings on the assets, the actual return will be a negative figure that would increase the pension cost rather than decrease it. The actual return can be computed by comparing the fair value of the pension plan assets at the beginning and end of the year. After adjusting for current-year contributions and benefits paid to retirees, any change is the actual return on pension plan assets. The actual return on pension plan assets for Thornton Electronics in 1996 is $138,500, computed as follows:

Fair value of pension plan assets December 31, 1996	$1,513,500
Fair value of pension plan assets January 1, 1996	1,385,000
Increase in fair value	$ 128,500
Add benefits paid	125,000
Deduct contributions made	(115,000)
Actual return on pension plan assets	$ 138,500

The actual return on pension plan assets is always computed in determining net periodic pension cost. However, as illustrated later, the actual return may be adjusted to the expected return when there is a difference between the two amounts. In this case, the actual return of $138,500 is equal to the expected return ($1,385,000 × .10).

The actual return of $138,500 is shown in entry (c) as a credit to net periodic pension cost (representing a decrease) and a debit to the fair value of pension assets (representing an increase). Note that benefits paid from fund assets do not reduce the formal account Cash—benefit payments are shown in entry (d) as a decrease in both plan assets and the remaining projected benefit obligation. The entry to reduce cash because of contributions to the pension fund is shown later.

Amortization of Unrecognized Prior Service Cost. Prior service cost is the cost of benefits granted to employees for past service when a pension plan is adopted or amended. In some sense, prior service cost represents "pension goodwill" acquired by making the new or amended pension plan more attractive to existing employees. The accounting question is whether to expense prior service cost in the period of the plan adoption or to amortize the cost over future periods.

FASB Statement No. 87 states that **unrecognized prior service cost** should be amortized by "assigning an equal amount to each future period of service of each employee active at the date of the amendment who is expected to receive benefits under the plan."[12] The future period of service is referred to as the **expected service period.** Because employees will have varying years of remaining service, this amortization method will result in a declining amortization charge. For example, assume a company has 4 employ-

12. *Statement of Financial Accounting Standards No. 87*, par. 25.

ees at the time of a plan amendment. The prior service cost is $30,000. Assume further that the employees had the following expected remaining years of service life:

Employee 1	1 year
Employee 2	2 years
Employee 3	4 years
Employee 4	5 years

The amortization fractions would be computed as follows:

Employee	Future Service Years	Year 1	Year 2	Year 3	Year 4	Year 5
1	1	1				
2	2	1	1			
3	4	1	1	1	1	
4	5	1	1	1	1	1
	12	4	3	2	2	1
Amortization fraction		4/12	3/12	2/12	2/12	1/12
Amortization amount (fraction × $30,000)		$10,000	$7,500	$5,000	$5,000	$2,500

When a company has many employees retiring or terminating in a systematic pattern, a method similar to the sum-of-the-years-digits depreciation method can be used. The FASB included an illustration of how this computation would be made in Statement No. 87, Appendix B.[13] A simplified version of the Board's illustration is included in Exhibit 21—5. Assume that Thornton Electronics, Inc., has 150 employees who are expected to receive benefits for prior services under a plan amendment adopted at the end of 1995. Ten percent of the employees (15 employees) are expected to leave (either retire or quit with vesting privileges) in each of the next 10 years. Employees hired after the plan amendment date do not affect the amortization. Note that under these assumptions, 825 service years will be rendered by the affected employees. The fraction used to determine the amortiza-

Exhibit 21—5
Determination of Amortization Fraction Based on Service Years Rendered in Each Year

Employees	Future Service Years	Year 1	2	3	4	5	6	7	8	9	10
A1-A15	15	15									
B1-B15	30	15	15								
C1-C15	45	15	15	15							
D1-D15	60	15	15	15	15						
E1-E15	75	15	15	15	15	15					
F1-F15	90	15	15	15	15	15	15				
G1-G15	105	15	15	15	15	15	15	15			
H1-H15	120	15	15	15	15	15	15	15	15		
I1-I15	135	15	15	15	15	15	15	15	15	15	
J1-J15	150	15	15	15	15	15	15	15	15	15	15
	825	150	135	120	105	90	75	60	45	30	15
Amortization fraction		150/825	135/825	120/825	105/825	90/825	75/825	60/825	45/825	30/825	15/825

13. *Ibid.*, Appendix B, illustration 3.

tion has a numerator that declines by 15 employees each year and a denominator that is the sum of the service years, or 825. If the increase in the projected benefit obligation, or prior service cost, arising from the plan amendment at the end of 1995 was $495,000, the amortization for 1996 would be 150/825 × $495,000, or $90,000. The annual amortization for the 10 years is shown in Exhibit 21—6.

Exhibit 21—6
Declining Amortization of Unrecognized Prior Service Cost

Year	Beginning-of-Year Balance	Amortization Rate	Amortization	End-of-Year Balance
1996	$495,000	150/825	$90,000	$405,000
1997	405,000	135/825	81,000	324,000
1998	324,000	120/825	72,000	252,000
1999	252,000	105/825	63,000	189,000
2000	189,000	90/825	54,000	135,000
2001	135,000	75/825	45,000	90,000
2002	90,000	60/825	36,000	54,000
2003	54,000	45/825	27,000	27,000
2004	27,000	30/825	18,000	9,000
2005	9,000	15/825	9,000	0

It is not necessary to construct a future-years-of-service table (Exhibit 21—5) each time an amortization schedule is desired. The formula for the sum-of-the-years-digits method illustrated in Chapter 12 can be used with a slight modification to reflect the decreased number of employees each period. Thus, the total service years for Thornton Electronics, Inc., could be computed with the following formula:

$$\frac{N(N+1)}{2} \times D = \text{Total future years of service}$$

where

N = number of remaining years of service
D = decrease in number of employees working each year

or

$$\frac{10(11)}{2} \times 15 = 825$$

The numerator would begin with the total employees at the time of the plan amendment and decline by D each period.

Although the FASB indicated a preference for this method, it also indicated that consistent use of an alternative amortization approach that more rapidly reduces the unrecognized prior service cost is acceptable.[14] As an example of such an alternative, a straight-line amortization of prior service cost over the average remaining service period of employees was presented in Statement No. 87, Appendix B.[15] To illustrate the straight-line approach using the Thornton Electronics example, the average remaining service life would be 5.5 years (825/150 employees), and the amortization schedule would be as shown in Exhibit 21—7.[16]

14. *Ibid.*, par. 26.
15. *Ibid.*, Appendix B, illustration 3, Case 2.
16. The straight-line amortization rate can be obtained more directly by using the simplified version of the formula above. Since the number of employees is equal to DN in the formula, simplification results in

$$\text{Average life} = (N + 1) \div 2$$

Thus, for Thornton it would be 11 ÷ 2 = 5.5 years. If N were 15, the average life would be 16 ÷ 2, or 8 years.

Exhibit 21—7
Straight-Line Amortization of Unrecognized Prior Service Cost

Year	Beginning-of-Year Balance	Amortization	End-of-Year Balance
1996	$495,000	$90,000	$405,000
1997	405,000	90,000	315,000
1998	315,000	90,000	225,000
1999	225,000	90,000	135,000
2000	135,000	90,000	45,000
2001	45,000	45,000	0

A separate amortization schedule is necessary for each plan amendment. There is no need to alter the schedule for new employees, as they would not receive benefits from prior services. If the planned termination or retirement pattern does not occur, adjustments may be necessary later to completely amortize the prior service cost.

For the Thornton Electronics example, the amortization amount based on the number of service years remaining is used. For 1996, this amount is $90,000. In entry (e), the $90,000 is shown as an increase in net periodic pension cost and a decrease in unrecognized prior service cost. This entry is analogous to the amortization of an intangible asset.

Amortization of Transition Gain or Loss. The transition gain or loss created upon adoption of FASB Statement No. 87 is amortized on a straight-line basis over the average remaining service life of the participating employees as of the adoption date. Alternatively, if the average service life is less than 15 years, the employer is permitted to use a 15-year amortization period. Amortization of transition losses increases net periodic pension cost, while amortization of transition gains decreases net periodic pension cost.

Thornton Electronics made its transition to FASB Statement No. 87 on January 1, 1987 and its transition gain on that date was $1,050,000. Thornton elected to amortize this gain over 15 years, or $70,000 per year. Thus, the unamortized transition gain at January 1, 1996 is $420,000 [$1,050,000 – (9 × $70,000)]. Amortization for the year is recorded in work sheet entry (f).

Summary Journal Entries. All of the Thornton work sheet entries discussed to this point have impacted only the memorandum accounts. The net effect on the formal accounts is summarized in the two journal entries, (1) and (2), included at the bottom of the pension work sheet in Exhibit 21—4.

Using data from the memorandum records, pension cost for the year is computed to be $121,500. The journal entry to record net pension cost for the year is as follows:

Pension Cost	121,500	
Prepaid/Accrued Pension Cost		121,500
To record accrual of net pension cost for 1996.		

The $121,500 increase in the reported accrued pension liability reflects the net effect of all the changes in the memorandum accounts—the projected benefit obligation, the pension fund, the unamortized transition gain, and the unrecognized prior service cost. Clearly, it is impossible to understand the events underlying this one number without seeing the notes to the financial statements. Because of the impact of the amortization of deferred items, this $121,500 amount should NOT be viewed as the increase in the pension obligation or unfunded pension obligation for the year.

The second formal journal entry records the cash contribution to the pension fund:

Prepaid/Accrued Pension Cost	115,000	
Cash		115,000
To record 1996 contribution to the pension plan.		

Note that on the work sheet this entry includes two debit amounts and doesn't seem to follow the fundamental rule of double-entry accounting: debits equal credits. However, both debits are reflecting the same event, once in the memorandum accounts and once in the formal accounts. One debit, the debit to the fair value of pension assets, reflects an increase in pension fund assets. The second debit, the debit to prepaid/accrued pension cost shown in the preceding formal journal entry, reflects the impact of this increase in the pension fund, a memorandum account, on the net pension liability, a formal account.

The closing balance in the prepaid/accrued pension cost account is a credit of $46,500. Accordingly, this amount is shown as a liability in Thornton's December 31, 1996 balance sheet. The pension work sheet illustrates that this $46,500 liability is much more complex than most liabilities. The Prepaid/Accrued Pension Cost liability contains elements of current market values (in both the projected benefit obligation and the fair value of pension assets), a deferred gain (transition gain), and an intangible asset (unrecognized prior service cost).

THORNTON ELECTRONICS — 1997

The Thornton Electronics example continues with the information for 1997 shown below:

1997 Pension Plan Information for Thornton Electronics, Inc.

Service cost as reported by actuaries	$ 87,000
Contributions to pension plan	120,000
Benefits paid to retirees	132,000
Actual return on pension plan assets	26,350
Actuarial change increasing projected benefit obligation	80,000
Settlement interest rate	11.0%
Long-term expected rate of return on pension plan assets	10.0%

The pension work sheet to record the 1997 pension information is shown in Exhibit 21-8. Entries (a) through (f) are similar to those shown previously for 1996. Note that the amount of prior service cost amortization has decreased because the remaining service years of the employees in place at the time of the plan amendment has declined (see Exhibit 21—6). Entries (g) and (h) relate to unrecognized gains and losses and are explained below.

Deferral of Gains and Losses. Because pension costs include many assumptions and estimates, frequent adjustments must be made for variations between the actual results and the estimates or projections that were used in determining net periodic pension cost for previous periods. For example, the market value of pension plan assets may increase at a much higher or lower rate than anticipated, the employee turnover rate may differ from that projected in earlier periods, or changes in the interest rate may differ significantly from expectations. Such differences between expected results and actual experience give rise to a **pension gain or loss.**

Recognition of these pension gains and losses was a subject of controversy during the FASB's study of pensions. Immediate recognition was opposed by many accountants who were concerned about the volatility of pension cost. The FASB decided to minimize the volatility of net periodic pension cost by allowing deferral of some gains and losses and amortization over future periods rather than requiring recognition of gains and losses in the period they arise.[17] The FASB's position, as reflected in FASB Statement No. 87, represents a compromise and has created some unusual and complex accounting practices.

17. Alternately, a company may elect to recognize all gains or losses immediately. If this election is made, the company must (1) apply the immediate recognition method consistently, (2) recognize all gains or losses immediately, and (3) disclose the fact that immediate recognition is being followed. *Special Report,* "A Guide to Implementation of Statement No. 87 on Employers' Accounting for Pensions—Questions and Answers," (Stamford: Financial Accounting Standards Board, 1986), p. 23. For purposes of this chapter, all illustrations and end-of-chapter material will assume that the deferred recognition method is used.

■ **Exhibit 21—8**
Thornton Electronics, Inc.—Pension Work Sheet for 1997

	FORMAL ACCOUNTS		
	Net Pension Cost	**Cash**	**Prepaid/ Accrued Pension Cost**
Balance, January 1, 1997			($46,500)
(a) Service Cost			
(b) Interest Cost			
(c) Actual Return on Assets			
(d) Benefits Paid			
(e) PSC Amortization			
(f) Transition Amortization			
(g) Deferred Loss			
(h) PBO change			
Summary Journal Entries			
(1) Annual Pension Cost Accrual	124,300		(124,300)
(2) Annual Pension Contribution		(120,000)	120,000
Balance, December 31, 1997			($50,800)

Note: Positive amounts are debits; negative amounts are credits.

Although actuarial estimates may change for several reasons, only two will be considered in this illustration: (1) the current-year difference between the actual and expected return on pension plan assets and (2) actuarial changes in determining the projected benefit obligation.

Deferral of Current-Year Difference Between Actual and Expected Return on Pension Plan Assets. In estimating the return on pension plan assets, FASB Statement No. 87 indicates that the expected *long-term* rate of return on assets should be used rather than a more volatile short-term rate. Thus, in the short run, the **actual return on pension plan assets** usually will differ from the expected return. By deferring the difference between the expected return and the actual return, pension cost will tend to be reduced by the expected long-term rate of return rather than by the more volatile short-term return rates. If the actual return on pension plan assets exceeds the expected return, the difference is a deferred gain; if the expected return exceeds the actual return, the difference is a deferred loss.

The **expected return on pension plan assets** is computed by multiplying the market-related value of pension plan assets by the expected long-term rate of return. The FASB defines **market-related value of pension plan assets** as either (1) the fair market value of pension plan assets at the beginning of the current year or (2) a weighted average value based on market values of pension plan assets over a period not to exceed five years.[18] If asset values have been increasing, the weighted average value will be lower than the beginning fair market value, resulting in a lower expected return.

When the actual return on pension plan assets exceeds the expected return, the difference, a deferred gain, is added to the pension cost as part of the gain or loss component. When the actual return is less than the expected return, the difference, a deferred loss, is deducted from pension cost. Because the actual return on pension plan assets is deducted in computing pension cost, the net effect of the deferred pension gain or loss adjustment is that the expected return, rather than the actual return, is used to reduce pension cost, thus achieving a smoothing of pension costs over time.

18. Different methods of calculating market-related value may be used for different classes of assets. However, a company must apply the methods consistently from year to year.

MEMORANDUM ACCOUNTS

Periodic Pension Cost Items	Projected Benefit Obligation	Fair Value of Pension Assets	Unamortized Transition Gain/Loss	Unrecognized Prior Service Cost	Unrecognized Net Pension Gain/Loss
	($1,615,000)	$1,513,500	($350,000)	$405,000	$ 0
87,000	(87,000)				
177,650	(177,650)				
(26,350)		26,350			
	132,000	(132,000)			
81,000				(81,000)	
(70,000)			70,000		
(125,000)					125,000
	(80,000)				80,000
		120,000			
	($1,827,650)	$1,527,850	($280,000)	$324,000	$205,000

Components of Prepaid/Accrued Pension Cost

To illustrate the computation of the pension gain or loss arising from differences between actual and expected return, assume Thornton Electronics computes the expected return on pension plan assets using the fair market value of pension plan assets at the beginning of the year. The expected return on pension plan assets for 1997 is $151,350 ($1,513,500 × .10). Since the actual return for the year is $26,350, the $125,000 difference is treated as a deferred pension loss and is subtracted from pension cost.

As mentioned above, combining the effects of the actual return and the unrecognized loss results in a net reduction in pension cost equal to the expected return of $151,350 (Actual return of $26,350 + Unrecognized loss of $125,000). The unrecognized loss is recorded in entry (g) in the 1997 pension work sheet as a credit (decrease) to annual pension cost and a debit to the memorandum account Unrecognized Net Pension Gain/Loss.

Differences in Actuarial Estimates of Projected Benefit Obligation. As indicated earlier, the actuarial computation of the projected benefit obligation involves many estimates, including future interest rates, life expectancy rates, and future salary rates. The effects of changing these estimates are deferred and accumulated for possible amortization to pension cost over future periods. During 1997, Thornton's actuaries reevaluated their actuarial assumptions in light of experience with Thornton's employees and calculated that the projected benefit obligation should be increased by $80,000. This increase is identified as a loss and is deferred to future periods. No adjustment is made to pension cost in the current period for this deferral as was necessary for the deferral of the difference in the return on pension plan assets. The deferred loss arising from the adjustment to the projected benefit obligation becomes part of the **unrecognized net pension gain or loss** for future amortization.

This change in actuarial estimate is recorded in work sheet entry (h) as a credit (increase) to the projected benefit obligation and a debit to Unrecognized Net Pension Gain/Loss. Note that the change has no impact on pension cost or on the reported accrued pension liability for 1997; only memorandum accounts are affected. However, the change will impact future years in two ways. First, since the PBO is higher, interest cost in future years will be higher. Second, depending on future developments, the deferred loss may be amortized to pension cost in future years. Circumstances under which deferred losses and gains are amortized are described later in the chapter.

From the work sheet in Exhibit 21—8, it can be seen that the summary journal entries for 1997 are as follows:

Pension Cost	124,300	
Prepaid/Accrued Pension Cost		124,300
To record accrual of net pension cost for 1997.		
Prepaid/Accrued Pension Cost	120,000	
Cash		120,000
To record 1997 contribution to the pension plan.		

THORNTON ELECTRONICS — 1998

The Thornton Electronics pension information for 1998 is shown below:

1998 Pension Plan Information for Thornton Electronics, Inc.

Service cost as reported by actuaries	$ 115,000
Contributions to pension plan	125,000
Benefits paid to retirees	140,000
Actual return on pension plan assets	180,000
Settlement interest rate	11.0%
Long-term expected rate of return on pension plan assets	10.0%
Accumulated benefit obligation, December 31, 1998	1,850,000
Vested benefit obligation, December 31, 1998	1,500,000

This information is recorded in the 1998 pension work sheet shown in Exhibit 21—9. Entries (a) through (g) are similar to those made in previous years. Again, note that the prior service cost amortization amount is lower than in prior years reflecting the continuing decline in the expected remaining service lives of those employees who were in place when the plan amendment was initiated (see Exhibit 21—6). Entry (g) reflects the fact that the actual return on plan assets of $180,000 for the year exceeded the expected return of

Exhibit 21—9
Thornton Electronics, Inc.—Pension Work Sheet for 1998

	FORMAL ACCOUNTS			
	Net Pension Cost	**Cash**	**Prepaid/ Accrued Pension Cost**	**Deferred Pension Cost**
Balance, January 1, 1998			($50,800)	
(a) Service Cost				
(b) Interest Cost				
(c) Actual Return on Assets				
(d) Benefits Paid				
(e) PSC Amortization				
(f) Transition Amortization				
(g) Deferred Gain				
(h) Amort. of Deferred Loss				
Summary Journal Entries				
(1) Annual Pension Cost Accrual	169,704		(169,704)	
(2) Annual Pension Contribution		(125,000)	125,000	
(3) Minimum Liability Adjustment			(61,646)	61,646
Balance, December 31, 1996			($157,150)	$61,646

Note: Positive amounts are debits; negative amounts are credits.

$152,785 ($1,527,850 × .10). The excess of $27,215 is considered an unexpected gain and is credited to the Unrecognized Net Pension Gain/Loss account in the memorandum records. The same amount is debited to net periodic pension cost.

Memorandum entry (h) and formal journal entry (3) relate to amortization of unrecognized pension gains and losses and to the minimum liability adjustment, respectively, and are explained below.

Amortization of Unrecognized Net Pension Gain or Loss from Prior Years. Under certain conditions, an employer's net periodic pension cost will include the amortization of unrecognized net pension gain or loss. The unrecognized pension gain or loss from prior years is amortized over future years if it accumulates to more than an amount defined by the FASB as a **corridor amount.** Amortization is required only for an unrecognized net gain or loss that exceeds 10% of the greater of the projected benefit obligation or the market-related value of the plan assets as of the beginning of the year. The Board indicated that any systematic method of amortization that equaled or exceeded the straight-line amortization over the remaining expected service years of the employees would be acceptable as long as the procedure is applied consistently to both gains and losses. The amortization of a deferred gain reduces the net periodic pension cost while the amortization of a deferred loss increases the net periodic pension cost. It is important to remember that only unrecognized gains and losses from *prior* years are subject to amortization. Accordingly, the corridor comparison applies only to the beginning balances in the projected benefit obligation, the fair value of pension assets, and the unrecognized net pension gain/loss.

This corridor amortization is a compromise between immediate recognition of gains and losses (which is viewed as causing too much volatility in earnings) and permanent deferral. Permanent deferral makes sense as long as the gains and losses tend to cancel out, but it becomes less reasonable when a "large" deferred gain or loss accumulates. The corridor amount is simply an arbitrary definition of what amount of deferred gain or loss is considered "large."

MEMORANDUM ACCOUNTS

Periodic Pension Cost Items	Projected Benefit Obligation	Fair Value of Pension Assets	Unamortized Transition Gain/Loss	Unrecognized Prior Service Cost	Unrecognized Net Pension Gain/Loss
	($1,827,650)	$1,527,850	($280,000)	$324,000	$205,000
115,000	(115,000)				
201,042	(201,042)				
(180,000)		180,000			
	140,000	(140,000)			
72,000				(72,000)	
(70,000)			70,000		
27,215					(27,215)
4,447					(4,447)
		125,000			
	($2,003,692)	$1,692,850	($210,000)	$252,000	$173,338

Components of Prepaid/Accrued Pension Cost

To illustrate the computation of the corridor amount, Thornton would apply the 10% corridor threshold to the projected benefit obligation at the beginning of the year since the PBO exceeds the market value of pension plan assets at the beginning of the year.[19] Thus, the corridor amount is $182,765 ($1,827,650 × .10). Because the unrecognized deferred loss at January 1, 1998 is $205,000, only the excess of $22,235 ($205,000 – $182,765) is subject to amortization. The average remaining employee service life on January 1, 1998 is assumed to be five years, so the 1998 amortization is $4,447 ($22,235 / 5). This amount represents amortization of a loss and is an addition to the other components in computing pension cost. The loss amortization is recorded in entry (h) in the 1998 pension work sheet as a debit to net periodic pension cost and a credit to unrecognized loss. Note the size of the loss amortization amount ($4,447) in relation to the size of the unrecognized loss itself ($205,000). Clearly, this deferral of gains and losses and subsequent corridor amortization accomplishes the goal of reducing volatility in annual pension cost.

Minimum Pension Liability. The computation of the annual pension cost is based on the concept of accrual accounting. However, FASB Statement No. 87 allows companies to defer many gains and losses over an extended service period thus minimizing the impact of these items on the financial statements. In formulating the pension standard, the FASB was concerned that the balance sheet would not disclose unfunded pension liabilities directly in the statement. To compensate for this omission, FASB Statement No. 87 identifies the concept of a **minimum pension liability** to reflect existing unfunded pension costs and establishes rules for an employer to apply in determining if an entry to record a minimum pension liability is required.

FASB Statement No. 87 requires the employer to report a minimum pension liability that is at least equal to the **unfunded accumulated benefit obligation,** which is determined as follows:

Unfunded ABO (minimum pension liability) = ABO − Fair value of pension plan assets

If the employer already has an accrued pension liability resulting from accrued pension costs in excess of the amount funded, no **additional pension liability** is recognized if the accrued pension cost is equal to or greater than the minimum pension liability (unfunded ABO). If accrued pension costs are less than the minimum liability, then an additional liability is recognized for the difference. In this situation, the additional pension liability equals the minimum pension liability minus the accrued pension cost.

If a prepaid pension cost balance exists because funding has exceeded the accrual, the *total* amount of the liability to be reported is the minimum pension liability (unfunded ABO) plus the prepaid balance reported as an asset. Thus, the *net* pension liability reported is the minimum pension liability. To illustrate, assume that the unfunded ABO at December 31 is determined to be $250,000 and the accounts reflect prepaid pension cost of $36,000. The prepaid cost of $36,000 would be reported with the assets on the balance sheet, and a separate liability of $286,000 would be reported. The result is a net pension liability equal to the minimum pension liability of $250,000 required by Statement No. 87.

Exhibit 21—10 illustrates the computation of the pension liability under four different conditions. The entries to record the liability are discussed and illustrated in the next section.

When the value of the pension plan assets is greater than the present value of the accumulated benefit obligation, the pension plan is said to be **overfunded.** In this situation, however, **no recognition of the net asset position on the balance sheet is permitted.** The FASB's decision to exclude the reporting of net pension plan assets under these circumstances

19. For simplicity, the fair market value of pension assets is used as the market-related value. Recall that an alternate measure is the weighted average of the fair market values of pension assets from prior years.

Exhibit 21—10 Pension Liability Computation

Case	(1) Accumulated Benefit Obligation	(2) Fair Value of Pension Plan Assets	(3) Minimum Pension Liability	(4) Prepaid Pension Costs	(5) Accrued Pension Costs	(6) Additional Pension Liability	(7) Total Pension Liability
1	$2,564,500	$1,685,600	$878,900		$125,000	$753,900	$878,900
2	2,564,500	2,480,000	84,500		125,000	0	125,000
3	2,150,000	2,480,000	0		125,000	0	125,000
4	2,564,500	2,480,000	84,500	$32,000		116,500	84,500

(1) Present value of future benefits attributable to service already rendered by employees. The measurement of future benefits is based on current, rather than future, salary levels.
(2) Fair market value of pension plan assets.
(3) The minimum amount of net pension liability to be reported on the balance sheet (ABO - Fair value of pension plan assets).
(4) Excess of pension contributions over accrued pension costs reported as an asset.
(5) Excess of accrued pension costs over pension contributions reported as a liability.
(6) Additional pension liability, if any, necessary to reflect the minimum liability required by FASB Statement No. 87.
(7) Total amount of pension liability to be reported on the balance sheet.

is another reflection of inconsistency in the interest of conservatism, and reflects the intense pressure that was exerted on the Board by various groups. In Appendix A of Statement No. 87, the Board stated that it "believes that . . . an employer with . . . an overfunded pension obligation has an asset."[20] The Board concluded, however, that recognition of all changes in plan asset values and in the present value of the obligation would not be practical at the present time and would be too drastic a change from previous reporting practices.

Deferred Pension Cost

If an employer is required to record an additional pension liability as a result of applying the minimum liability provisions, FASB Statement No. 87 indicates that the offsetting charge should be to a **deferred pension cost** account (intangible asset) to the extent of any unrecognized prior service cost or any unamortized transition loss. If the additional liability exceeds these unrecognized amounts, the excess should be recorded as a separate **contra equity adjustment.** The deferred account represents that portion of the additional liability that can be related to prior periods because of either the adoption of a plan or a plan amendment, or because of the transition to the new standards. These unrecognized costs will be recognized in future periods through the amortization procedures discussed earlier, and thus the deferred account is not directly amortized. It is adjusted each period to reflect the increases or decreases in the recorded minimum liability.

The contra equity adjustment account represents that portion of the additional liability that reflects either changes in the value of pension plan assets or changes in the benefit obligation that are not related to unrecognized prior service costs or to the transition adjustment. These unrecognized losses are recognized through the gains and losses component of pension cost. The contra equity account is also adjusted each period when the minimum liability is recorded.

To illustrate accounting for the minimum liability and its offsetting asset or equity adjustment, assume the Clapton Corporation computes the following balances as of December 31, 1996:

Accumulated benefit obligation	$1,250,000
Fair value of pension plan assets	1,140,000
Accrued pension cost	16,000
Unrecognized prior service cost	80,000

20. *Statement of Financial Accounting Standards No. 87*, par. 98.

The minimum pension liability is $110,000 ($1,250,000 – $1,140,000), and the recorded liability for accrued pension cost is only $16,000. An additional pension liability of $94,000 ($110,000 – $16,000) would be recorded as follows:

Deferred Pension Cost	80,000	
Excess of Additional Pension Liability Over Unrecognized Prior Service Cost	14,000	
Additional Pension Liability		94,000
To recognize additional pension liability.		

For reporting purposes, the $16,000 accrued pension cost and the $94,000 additional pension liability may be combined into one pension liability of $110,000 on the balance sheet.

The minimum liability is accounted for in subsequent periods in a similar manner. For example, assume that the computed minimum liability for Clapton Corporation at December 31, 1997, is $104,000 and accrued pension cost at that date is $18,000. The balance in the additional pension liability account would be adjusted to $86,000 ($104,000 – $18,000). If the unrecognized prior service cost at December 31, 1997, has declined to $70,000, the deferred pension cost would be adjusted to $70,000. The excess of additional pension liability over unrecognized prior service cost would be adjusted to $16,000 ($86,000 – $70,000). The following journal entry would be made to adjust the accounts at the end of 1997:

Additional Pension Liability	8,000[1]	
Excess of Additional Pension Liability Over Unrecognized Prior Service Cost	2,000[2]	
Deferred Pension Cost		10,000[3]
To adjust additional pension liability and related asset and contra equity accounts.		

Computations:

	Beginning Balance	Ending Balance	Adjustment
1	$94,000 cr	$86,000 cr	$ 8,000 dr
2	14,000 dr	16,000 dr	2,000 dr
3	80,000 dr	70,000 dr	10,000 cr

The deferred pension cost balance of $70,000 (the amount of unrecognized prior service cost) would be reported on the balance sheet as an intangible asset. The contra equity account balance of $16,000 would be deducted in the stockholders' equity section. The combined pension liability of $104,000 ($18,000 accrued pension cost + $86,000 additional pension liability) would be reported as a liability, usually under the noncurrent liabilities section.

If Clapton Corporation had an unamortized transition loss, that amount would be treated the same as unrecognized prior service cost in recording the minimum pension liability. The combined amount of any unrecognized prior service cost and unamortized transition loss determines the maximum amount of deferred pension cost. Unamortized transition gains are ignored in the computation of the maximum amount of deferred pension cost.

One of the more difficult aspects of the pension standards is identifying which obligation and asset values are used for the different pension amounts. It is important to note that the *accumulated benefit obligation* is used only in determining the minimum pension liability. In all other determinations involving future benefits discussed in this chapter, the *projected benefit obligation* is used.

Applying the minimum liability computation to the December 31, 1998 data of Thornton Electronics yields work sheet entry (3) in Exhibit 21–9. The accumulated benefit obligation of $1,850,000 exceeds the fair market value of the plan assets by $157,150

($1,850,000 – $1,692,850). Since the preliminary balance in the accrued liability is only $95,504, an additional liability of $61,646 ($157,150 – $95,504) must be recorded. An intangible asset, Deferred Pension Cost, is recognized for the entire amount since unrecognized prior service cost of $252,000 exceeds the amount of the additional liability.

The formal journal entries to record pension-related data for 1998 are as follows:

Annual Pension Cost	169,704	
Prepaid/Accrued Pension Cost		169,704
To record accrual of net pension cost for 1998.		
Prepaid/Accrued Pension Cost	125,000	
Cash		125,000
To record 1998 contribution to the pension plan.		
Deferred Pension Cost (intangible asset)	61,646	
Prepaid/Accrued Pension Cost		61,646
To recognize additional pension liability.		

DISCLOSURE OF PENSION PLANS

All useful information concerning an employer's pension plans cannot be provided in the body of the financial statements. A major objective of the pension accounting standard is:

To provide disclosures that will allow users to understand better the extent and effect of an employer's undertaking to provide employee pensions and related financial arrangements.[21]

Statement No. 87 therefore requires extensive disclosure in the notes accompanying the general-purpose financial statements. Following is a list of the required disclosures for defined benefit plans.[22]

1. A description of the plan including employee groups covered, type of benefit formula, funding policy, types of assets held and significant nonbenefit liabilities, if any, and the nature and effect of significant matters affecting comparability of information for all periods presented.
2. The amount of the net periodic pension cost for the period showing separately the service cost component, the interest cost component, the actual return on assets for the period, and the net total of the other components.
3. A schedule reconciling the funded status of the plan with amounts shown in the employer's statement of financial position, showing separately:
   (a) The fair value of pension plan assets.
   (b) The projected benefit obligation, the accumulated benefit obligation, and the vested benefit obligation.
   (c) The amount of unrecognized prior service cost.
   (d) The amount of unrecognized net pension gain or loss.
   (e) The amount of any remaining unrecognized transition adjustment.
   (f) The amount of any additional liability arising from application of the minimum liability provision.
   (g) The net result of the preceding items recognized in the statement of financial position.
4. The assumed discount rate (settlement interest rate), the rate of compensation increase used to measure the projected benefit obligation, and the expected long-term rate of return on pension plan assets.

21. *Statement of Financial Accounting Standards No. 87*, par. 6c.
22. *Ibid.*, par. 54.

5. The amounts and types of securities included in plan assets and approximate amount of annual benefits to employees covered by annuity contracts.

For Thornton Electronics, most of the information needed for the disclosure of the details of the computation of annual pension cost and reconciliation of the funded status of the pension plan can be obtained from the 1998 pension work sheet in Exhibit 21–9. In addition, the vested benefit obligation of $1,500,000 and the accumulated benefit obligation of $1,850,000 are disclosed.

The note disclosure of the computation of annual pension cost is as follows:

Thornton Electronics
Net Annual Pension Cost
For the Year Ended December 31, 1998

Service cost		$115,000
Interest cost		201,042
Return on pension plan assets:		
Actual	$(180,000)	
Deferred gain	27,215	(152,785)
Amortization of prior service cost		72,000
Amortization of transition gain		(70,000)
Amortization of deferred loss		4,447
Net pension cost		$169,704

Note disclosure reconciling the December 31, 1998 funded status of the Thornton pension plan is as follows:

Thornton Electronics
Reconciliation of Funded Status of Pension Plan
December 31, 1998

Vested benefit obligation, December 31, 1998	$(1,500,000)
Accumulated benefit obligation, December 31, 1998	$(1,850,000)
Additional amounts related to projected pay increases	(153,692)
Projected benefit obligation, December 31, 1998	$(2,003,692)
Fair value of pension plan assets, December 31, 1998	1,692,850
Excess of obligation over assets (underfunding)	(310,842)
Unamortized transition gain, December 31, 1998	(210,000)
Unrecognized net pension loss, December 31, 1998	173,338
Unrecognized prior service cost, December 31, 1998	252,000
Adjustment required to recognize minimum liability	(61,646)
Accrued pension liability, December 31, 1998	$ (157,150)

Companies with more than one pension plan are required to disclose the details of overfunded and underfunded plans separately. For purposes of this distinction, overfunded plans are those for which the accumulated benefit obligation exceeds the fair value of plan assets. In addition, disclosure for plans covering employees outside the United States should be separate from disclosure of U.S. plans.[23] This type of disclosure is illustrated in Exhibit 21—11 using an exerpt from the notes to the 1993 financial statements of Pitney Bowes.

Pension Settlements and Curtailments

If a pension plan is settled or the benefits are curtailed, a question arises as to how a resulting gain or loss should be treated by the employer. **Settlement of a pension plan** occurs

23. *Ibid.*, par. 56.

when an employer takes an irrevocable action that relieves the employer of primary responsibility for all or part of the obligation. Examples of a settlement transaction include the purchase by the employer of an annuity from an insurance company that would cover vested benefits, or a lump-sum cash payment to the employees in exchange for their rights to receive specified pension benefits. A **curtailment of a pension plan** arises from an event that significantly reduces the benefits that will be provided for present employees' future services. Curtailments include: (1) the termination of employees' services earlier than expected, for example, as a result of closing a plant or discontinuing a segment of the business and (2) the termination or suspension of a pension plan so that employees do not earn additional benefits for future services.[24]

Exhibit 21—11 Pitney Bowes—Pension Plan Disclosure

9. Retirement Plans

The company has several defined benefit and defined contribution pension plans covering substantially all employees worldwide. Benefits are primarily based on employees' compensation and years of service. Company contributions are determined based on the funding requirements of U.S. federal and other governmental laws and regulations.

Total pension expense amounted to $50.9 million in 1993, $44.8 million in 1992 and $33.1 million in 1991. Net pension expense for defined benefit plans for 1993, 1992 and 1991 included the following components:

	United States			Foreign		
	1993	1992	1991	1993	1992	1991
Service cost – benefits earned during period	$ 30,797	$ 27,319	$ 25,843	$ 5,971	$ 6,913	$ 7,943
Interest cost on projected benefit obligations	62,241	56,133	46,452	9,163	10,005	9,736
Actual return on assets	(85,971)	(37,861)	(100,173)	(31,494)	(2,684)	(21,211)
Net amortization and (deferral)	30,804	(11,085)	55,368	19,896	(10,978)	8,092
Net periodic defined benefit pension expense	$ 37,871	$ 34,506	$ 27,490	$ 3,536	$ 3,256	$ 4,560

The funded status at December 31, 1993 and 1992 for the company's defined benefit plans was:

	United States		Foreign	
	1993	1992	1993	1992
Actuarial present value of:				
Vested benefits	$561,874	$442,606	$ 97,471	$ 85,619
Accumulated benefit obligations	$632,317	$495,766	$ 97,714	$ 85,663
Projected benefit obligations	$854,589	$707,685	$124,286	$107,970
Plan assets at fair value, primarily stocks and bonds, adjusted by:	689,622	584,078	136,900	112,289
Unrecognized net loss (gain)	90,078	35,597	(10,889)	(1,003)
Unrecognized net asset	(23,236)	(26,566)	(20,281)	(23,160)
Unamortized prior service costs from plan amendments	30,159	35,807	10,952	11,551
	786,623	628,916	116,682	99,677
Net pension liability	$ 67,966	$ 78,769	$ 7,604	$ 8,293
Assumptions for defined benefit plans*:				
Discount rate	7.50%	8.50%	6.7%– 9.5%	8.0%– 9.5%
Rate of increase in future compensation levels	5.00%	6.00%	4.0%– 7.0%	4.0%– 7.0%
Expected long-term rate of return on plan assets	9.50%	9.50%	8.5%–10.0%	8.5%–10.0%

*Pension costs are determined using assumptions as of the beginning of the year while the funded status of the plans is determined using assumptions as of the end of the year.

24. *Statement of Financial Accounting Standards No. 88*, "Employers' Accounting for Settlements and Curtailments of Defined Benefit Pension Plans and for Termination Benefits" (Stamford: Financial Accounting Standards Board, 1985), par. 6.

As discussed throughout this chapter, FASB Statement No. 87 provides for delayed recognition of pension gains and losses arising from the ordinary operations of the pension plan. In addition, the statement provides for delayed recognition of prior service costs and transition adjustments. Thus, at any given time, unrecognized gains, losses, and prior service costs usually exist.

The FASB felt it was clear that if a pension plan is completely terminated and all pension obligations are settled and plan assets are disbursed, then previously unrecognized pension amounts should be recognized. What wasn't clear, however, is what happens when partial settlements or curtailments take place. The FASB considered this issue and presented its recommendations in FASB Statement No. 88. The statement also addresses the issue of termination benefits, i.e., benefits provided to employees in connection with the termination of their employment.

Settlements. Pension plans occasionally become overfunded because a rising stock market causes the value of plan assets to exceed the pension obligation. To take advantage of this situation, companies sometimes **settle** their pension plans by purchasing annuity contracts from insurance companies for less than the amount in the pension fund. Subject to regulations such as ERISA, the excess funds can then be used for other corporate purposes.

The accounting issue surrounding settlements centers on whether the gain should be recognized immediately or deferred and recognized in future periods. Prior to Statement No. 88, settlement gains that were accompanied by asset withdrawals from the pension fund, referred to as "asset reversion transactions," were deferred and offset against future pension costs. The Board, however, decided that if the settlement (1) was an irrevocable action, (2) relieved the employer of primary responsibility for the pension benefit obligation, and (3) eliminated significant risks related to the obligation and the assets used to effect the settlement, the previously unrecognized net gain or loss should be recognized in the current period. If only part of the projected benefit obligation is settled, a pro rata portion of the gain should be recognized currently.[25]

Curtailments. As indicated previously, a pension plan curtailment is an event that significantly reduces the expected years of future service of present employees or eliminates for a significant number of employees the accrual of defined benefits for their future services. Examples include termination of employees' services earlier than expected, such as occurs when a segment of the business is discontinued, or termination or suspension of a plan so that no further benefits are earned for future services.

Any unrecognized prior service cost or transition adjustment associated with years of service no longer expected to be rendered as a result of the curtailment is recognized as a loss. In addition, the projected benefit obligation of the pension plan may be changed as a result of the curtailment, giving rise to an additional gain or loss. The Board provided for offsetting previously unrecognized pension gains and losses against the gain or loss from changes in the projected benefit obligation and called the difference curtailment gains or losses. If the sum of all gains and losses attributed to the curtailment, including the write-off of unrecognized prior service cost, is a loss, it is recognized in the period when it is probable that the curtailment will occur and the effects are estimable. If the sum of all gains and losses attributed to the curtailment is a gain, it is recognized when the related employees are terminated or when the plan suspension or amendment is adopted.[26]

25. *Ibid.*, par. 9.
26. *Ibid.*, pars. 12-14.

Pension Plan Settlements

On June 11, 1985, UAL Corp., parent company of United Airlines, announced its intention to settle some of its pension benefit obligations by purchasing annuity contracts, and to convert the excess $962 million in pension fund assets to corporate use. As a result of this settlement, UAL recognized a gain of $137 million for the year 1985. This gain reduced UAL's 1985 net loss (before taxes) from $232 million to $95 million. The UAL pension plan settlement was only one of over 1,000 settlements initiated from 1980 through 1986. Asset reversion from excess pension fund assets exceeded $6 billion in 1985 alone.

Two questions that can be asked are why these firms settled the pension plans and what effect the settlements had on employee and corporate wealth. In addressing the question of why, Thomas (1989) identifies two major groups of firms settling overfunded pension plans: those that had experienced recent significant declines in cash flow from operations, and those that were in tight financial condition because of financial restructuring in the wake of a hostile takeover. Thus, the evidence suggests that while firms viewed settlement of an overfunded pension plan as one source of funds, in general this source was not used except by firms in extreme circumstances when other funding sources may have already been depleted.

Mittelstaedt and Regier (1990) summarize the research on what effect these excess asset reversions had on firms' stock prices. They confirm that firms' stock prices generally increased on announcement of an asset reversion, but suggest that this result is primarily due to two factors:

1. Many asset reversions were announced in conjunction with other significant news (dividend increases, changes in corporate strategy, etc.) and these other items may have been responsible for the stock price increases.
2. The most significant stock price increases were for settlements prior to 1984. Before 1984, it was uncertain whether the courts would allow firms to keep excess pension fund assets. Accordingly, during that time period, financial analysts and investors were uncertain about who owned excess pension assets—the firm or the employees. By explicitly announcing a pension plan settlement and excess asset reversion, a firm increased the probability that it could claim the excess assets. As a result of this change in perception about whether the firm could claim the excess assets, the value of the firm went up and its stock price increased. After 1984, the legal environment was such that there was a strong presumption in the market that the excess assets did in fact belong to the firm. Thus, announcements in this period contained no new information and did not significantly impact stock prices.

Excess pension asset reversions have decreased dramatically since 1986, largely as a result of government action. These settlements were viewed by many as transfers of pension fund assets from employees to their employers. As a result, the Tax Reform Act of 1986 imposed a 10% excise tax on excess asset reversions. The excise tax was increased to 15% in 1988.

Questions:

1. Why would the announcement of a pension plan settlement and excess asset reversion have no impact on the announcing company's stock price?
2. Are there other, less dramatic means a company can use to remove assets from an overfunded pension plan?

Sources:

H. Fred Mittelstaedt and Philip R. Regier, "Further Evidence on Excess Asset Reversions and Shareholder Wealth," *Journal of Risk and Insurance* (September 1990), p. 471.

Jacob K. Thomas, "Why Do Firms Terminate Overfunded Pension Plans?" *Journal of Accounting and Economics* (November 1989), p. 361.

POSTRETIREMENT BENEFITS OTHER THAN PENSIONS

In December 1990, five years after the pension standards were issued, the FASB issued a third major standard in the area of retirement benefits, FASB Statement No. 106, "Employers' Accounting for Postretirement Benefits Other Than Pensions." Although the standard's primary focus is on health care benefits, it also applies to other postretirement benefits, such as the cost of life insurance contracts, legal assistance benefits, and tuition assistance. The standard relates only to single-employer defined benefit postretirement plans. The benefits are defined either in monetary amounts, such as a designated amount of life insurance, or as benefit coverage, such as specified coverage for hospital or doctor care.

The Board devoted several years to studying these postretirement benefits, and after extensive exposure, hearings, and discussion, agreed unanimously that, in general, the costs of the benefits should be accounted for by employers in the same way as pension costs, i.e., on an accrual basis. Statement No. 106, however, is creating more concern among businesses than the pension standards did because of some important differences between pensions and other postretirement benefits.

Nature of Postretirement Health Care Plans

The Board spent much of its time considering the unique features of postretirement health care benefits as compared with pension benefits. Because the details of Statement No. 106 were affected by these features, they will be considered first before the differences between accounting for pensions and other postretirement benefits are discussed.

Informal Rather Than Formal Plans. Many company postretirement benefit plans are not written into formal contracts. Companies often begin paying for postretirement health care benefits as a continuation of health care coverage for active employees. In some cases, the practice becomes part of union contract bargaining, and informal plans are changed to formal union negotiated contractual plans. Even though a plan may be informal, and thus not legally binding, the courts have sometimes interpreted the informal plan as a contract, and have required companies to honor the plan.

Nonfunded Rather Than Funded Plans. Most company plans for postretirement benefits are not funded. Thus, companies rely on current revenues to meet current costs of the plan. Unlike pension contributions, postretirement benefit plan contributions usually are not deductible for income tax purposes. As discussed earlier, ERISA, a federal law, requires companies to fund their pension liability during an employee's working years. There has been no similar federal legislation to encourage funding of postretirement benefit costs. In some instances, a separate insurance carrier, such as Blue Cross, is used to cover the risk. But in many cases, especially for larger companies, a form of self-insurance has developed.

Pay-As-You-Go Accounting Rather Than Accrual Accounting. Because postretirement benefit plans usually are not funded, almost all companies previously charged these costs against revenue in the period the benefit costs were incurred rather than in the period when the employee service was rendered. This policy results in uneven charges against revenue and does not recognize a liability for unfunded postretirement benefits. The total of unfunded postretirement benefits for all companies has been estimated to amount to over one trillion dollars.[27]

Uncertainty of Future Benefits Rather Than Clearly Defined Benefits. Defined benefit pension plans establish terms that make the amount of their future pension obligation measurable with reasonably high reliability. Salary trends, mortality tables, and discount rates are reasonably objective, and have been used to implement FASB Statements 87 and 88. Health care costs, however, involve many variables that make accrual accounting difficult to implement. Over the years, factors such as longer life expectancy, improved medical treatment facilities, and early retirements have combined to cause health care costs for retired employees to increase dramatically. The amount of these costs absorbed by government Medicare programs has varied over time, and will continue to vary as Congress works to bring government finances under control. As the Medicare plans cover less of these costs, employers and individuals are required to absorb higher costs. The

27. Lee Berton, "FASB Plan Would Make Firms Deduct Billions for Potential Retiree Benefits," *The Wall Street Journal,* August 17, 1988, p. 3.

magnitude of this change can be reflected in comparing employer cost per employee for health care in 1988 and 1990. In the earlier year, $2,160 was spent in health care costs per employee. Two years later this number had jumped to $3,161.[28]

Other variables that must be considered before an accrual entry can be made for postretirement benefits include age of retirees, geographical location of retirement, geographical differences in health costs, dependent coverage, sex of retiree, costs of new medical technology, emergence of new diseases, age of retirement, etc. Estimating future benefit costs based on these variables can be costly and time-consuming for companies. It was the magnitude of these record-keeping costs, plus the impact of the accrual concept on the financial statements, that led many business groups to oppose this standard during its exposure period. Although the Board agreed to some compromises between the exposure draft and the final standard, the underlying theory of pension accounting introduced in FASB Statement No. 87 was retained.

Non-Pay-Related Rather Than Pay-Related. Most postretirement benefits are granted to employees after a certain number of service years or when an employee reaches a specified preretirement age. The amount of benefits to be received is unrelated to the level of compensation. The date when an employee becomes eligible for these benefits is known as the **full eligibility date.** No postretirement benefits are granted unless the employee meets this service or age requirement. After that date is reached, the employee is eligible to receive 100% of the postretirement benefits regardless of any future service or regardless of pay level reached. Thus, the period over which an employee earns postretirement benefits extends from the hire date to the full eligibility date.

In contrast, since most pension plans increase an employee's benefits for each additional year of service rendered and for salary increases, the employee continues to earn pension benefits until retirement. Accordingly, the period over which postretirement benefits are earned differs from that over which pension benefits are earned. There are, of course, many exceptions to this description of pensions and postretirement benefits. Some pension plans are non-pay-related and some health care postretirement benefit plans are pay-related. To avoid complicating the discussion, the more general situation of non-pay-related postretirement benefits will be assumed in the following analysis.

Overview of FASB Statement No. 106

Most companies must adopt accrual accounting for postretirement benefits beginning with their 1993 financial statements. The same six components for net periodic pension cost listed on page 901 are required for net periodic postretirement benefit cost. Service cost and prior service cost are charged (attributed) to the years from the hire date to the full eligibility date rather than from the hire date to the retirement date as is true for pension costs.[29] Any retirement benefit fund assets may be offset against retirement benefit obligations if the assets are clearly restricted for the payment of postretirement benefits. Under- or overfunding at the transition date must be computed and may be recognized immediately as a change in accounting principle, or may be deferred and recognized over the remaining service life of the employees or 20 years, whichever is longer. As indicated on page 908, the transition gain or loss for pensions had to be deferred and written off over the remaining employee service life or 15 years, whichever is longer.

28. Ron Winslow, "Costs of Medical Care Continue to Soar, Defying Corporate Efforts to Find Cures," *The Wall Street Journal*, January 29, 1991, p. B1.

29. If the period of service needed to earn the postretirement benefits does not include previous years, the attribution period will be from a later date referred to as the beginning of the credited service period. FASB Statement No. 106, par. 44.

Accounting for Postretirement Benefits Other Than Pensions: Cost vs. Benefit

Accounting standard setting always involves a trade-off between costs and benefits. A difficult aspect of standard setting is that the nature of the costs and benefits associated with a standard make them very hard to compare. The benefits from a new standard are typically difficult to quantify and those benefits are spread over a large group (i.e., all financial statement users). On the other hand, the costs are usually easier to quantify and are concentrated on a smaller group, the firms preparing financial statements.

This asymmetry between costs and benefits makes disagreement and controversy almost inevitable. Predictably, such disagreement and controversy have surrounded the FASB's project on postretirement benefits other than pensions. In Statement No. 106, the FASB explicitly addresses the issue of costs and benefits to a greater extent than in any previous statement. The benefits of improved accounting disclosure and the increased costs of providing the data are certainly difficult to quantify, but the thorniest issues associated with the standard are actually nonaccounting ones: How will the standard impact the benefit packages offered by firms, and how will the standard influence government regulation?

Critics of the standard are already offering evidence suggesting that firms are reducing retiree health benefits in order to lower the expense that will now have to be reported. Published comments like the following are typical: "Some companies are reducing their health care costs for retirees to ease the effect of the FASB rule." In addition, firms have expressed fears that the explicit recognition of a liability for nonpension retirement benefits will increase the probability that government will mandate or regulate such plans.

Questions:

1. List several reasons for a firm to reduce its retiree health benefits in response to the FASB's requirement that such plans be accounted for on an accrual rather than a pay-as-you-go basis. Critically evaluate each reason.
2. In general, FASB Statement No. 106 will result in firms reporting lower earnings and higher liabilities. Would you expect stock prices to decline for companies with large postretirement benefit plans? Would you expect it to be harder for these firms to obtain loans?

Sources:

Lee Berton, "FASB Issues Rule Change On Benefits," *The Wall Street Journal*, December 20, 1990, p. A3.

Statement of Financial Accounting Standards No. 106, "Employers' Accounting for Postretirement Benefits Other Than Pensions" (Norwalk: Financial Accounting Standards Board, December 1990), pars. 118-132.

No minimum liability provision is required for postretirement health care benefits. Because most plans are nonfunded or only minimally funded, the amortization of the transition adjustment will increase postretirement costs and thus result in recognition of the liability over a reasonably short period of time. The disclosure required for postretirement benefit plans includes all the requirements for pension plans plus information about health cost trend assumptions and sensitivity analysis of how postretirement costs and the postretirement obligation would vary if the health care costs trend rate were increased by 1%.

Components of Net Periodic Postretirement Benefit Cost

Because much of the accounting for postretirement health care costs parallels the accounting for pension costs presented in this chapter, only the major differences in accounting for the six components of net periodic postretirement costs will be explained further. Exhibit 21—12 summarizes the major differences in accounting for these two types of retirement benefits. Undoubtedly, application of this controversial standard will reveal many other areas for clarification and possible exceptions.

Service Cost. Service costs in most defined benefit pension plans are computed by measuring the cost to the employer of additional benefits earned during a period (see page 904). Because most postretirement benefits do not increase with length of service or level of pay, a different definition of service cost is required.

■ Exhibit 21—12 Major Differences in Accounting for Pensions and Other Postretirement Benefits

Item	Pension	Other Postretirement Benefits
Service cost	Present value of increased benefits coming from one additional year of service.	Present value of equal attribution of postretirement benefit costs for period from hiring date to full eligibility date.
Interest cost	Interest on beginning-of-year projected benefit obligation at settlement rate of interest.	Interest on beginning-of-year accumulated postretirement benefit obligation at assumed discount rate.
Total obligation	Projected benefit obligation or accumulated benefit obligation depending on component being measured.	Accumulated postretirement benefit obligation.
Minimum liability	Must be reported if accumulated benefit obligation exceeds the fair value of plan assets adjusted for prepaid and accrued pension costs.	No provisions for minimum liability.
Transition amortization period	Average remaining service life of employees or 15 years, whichever is longer.	Immediate recognition or delayed recognition over the remaining service life or 20 years, whichever is longer.
Effective date	Years beginning after December 15, 1986.	Years beginning after December 15, 1992, for most companies.
Disclosure requirements	Description of plan, detail of pension cost, rate assumptions, and reconciliation of funded status of the plan with amounts reported on the balance sheet.	Same as pensions with additional information about the health cost trend rate used and sensitivity information about effect of rate change.

The FASB defined two new terms to describe the nature of service costs for postretirement benefits: **expected postretirement benefit obligation (EPBO)** and **accumulated postretirement benefit obligation (APBO).** The expected postretirement benefit obligation is the actuarial present value as of a particular date of the postretirement benefits expected to be paid by the employer to or for the employee, the employee's beneficiaries, and any covered dependents pursuant to the terms of the plan. The amount of the EPBO for an employee in non-pay-related plans differs each year only by the discount factor unless the actuarial assumptions are changed.

The accumulated postretirement benefit obligation as of a particular date is the actuarial present value of all future benefits attributed (charged) to an employee's service up to that date, assuming the plan remains in effect and all the assumptions about the future are fulfilled. Prior to an employee's full eligibility date, the accumulated postretirement benefit obligation as of a specific date for an employee is the portion of the expected postretirement benefit obligation attributed to that employee's service rendered to that date; on and after the full eligibility date, the accumulated and expected postretirement benefit obligations for an employee are the same.

To illustrate these definitions, assume that the Haymond Electrical Company has a postretirement benefit plan and that John Jenkins is hired as an employee at age 50. The plan provides for full benefits after age 60 and Jenkins plans to retire at age 65. The assumed discount rate to compute present values is 8%. The expected postretirement benefit obligation measurement for Jenkins at the full eligibility date (age 60) is $87,000. Exhibit 21—13 illustrates how the EPBO and APBO would be calculated for the 15 years of employment; 10 years to full eligibility and another 5 years to retirement. Note that the fraction of the EPBO included in the APBO increases by $^1/_{10}$ each year. After 10 years, the EPBO and APBO are the same.

■ Exhibit 21—13 Computation of Expected and Accumulated Postretirement Benefit Obligations for John Jenkins

Year	Interest Factor—8%	EPBO	Portion	APBO
0	0.4632	40,298	0	0
1	0.5002	43,517	1/10	4,352
2	0.5403	47,006	2/10	9,401
3	0.5835	50,765	3/10	15,229
4	0.6302	54,827	4/10	21,931
5	0.6806	59,212	5/10	29,606
6	0.7350	63,945	6/10	38,367
7	0.7938	69,061	7/10	48,343
8	0.8573	74,585	8/10	59,668
9	0.9259	80,553	9/10	72,498*
10	1.0000	87,000	10/10	87,000
11	1.0800	93,960		93,960
12	1.1664	101,268		101,268
13	1.2597	109,594		109,594
14	1.3605	118,364		118,364
15	1.4693	127,829		127,829

*Computation example: $87,000 × .9259 = $80,553; $80,553 × 9/10 = $72,498

■ Exhibit 21—14 Computation of Service Cost and Interest Cost for John Jenkins

Year	Interest Factor—8%	EPBO	Portion	APBO	Service Cost	Interest Cost
0	0.4632	40,298	0	0	0	0
1	0.5002	43,517	1/10	4,352	4,352	0
2	0.5403	47,006	2/10	9,401	4,701	348
3	0.5835	50,765	3/10	15,229	5,076	752
4	0.6302	54,827	4/10	21,931	5,483	1,218
5	0.6806	59,212	5/10	29,606	5,921	1,754
6	0.7350	63,945	6/10	38,367	6,395	2,368
7	0.7938	69,061	7/10	48,343	6,906	3,069
8	0.8573	74,585	8/10	59,668	7,459	3,867
9	0.9259	80,553	9/10	72,498	8,055*	4,773**
10	1.0000	87,000	10/10	87,000	8,700	5,800
11	1.0800	93,960		93,960	0	6,960
12	1.1664	101,268		101,268	0	7,517
13	1.2597	109,594		109,594	0	8,101
14	1.3605	118,364		118,364	0	8,768
15	1.4693	127,829		127,829	0	9,469
					63,048	64,764

*Computation example: $8,700 × .9259 = $8,055
**Computation example: $59,668 × .08 = $4,773
Note: In the absence of rounding error, the accumulated sum of service cost and interest cost would equal the APBO.

Exhibit 21—14 is an expansion of Exhibit 21—13 to show the computation of the service and interest cost components of the net periodic postretirement benefit cost for the Haymond plan. The service cost for each year between the hire date and the full eligibility date is a portion of the expected postretirement benefit attributed to each year. Since Jenkins had 10 years before the full eligibility date, the present value of 1/10 of the computed EPBO at the full eligibility date for each year is defined as the service cost. No service cost accrues after the tenth year. If Jenkins had been employed by Haymond at age 45 rather than age 50, the portion of EPBO each year allocated to service cost would be 1/15 rather than 1/10.

In the above example, the EPBO at the full eligibility date for Jenkins was $87,000. Because this amount is attributed to the period between the hire date and the full eligibility date, and because the Haymond plan provides for full benefits after a single date is reached, $1/10$ of the $87,000, or $8,700, is attributed to each year of service between these dates. The service cost in any given year is the present value of this equal amount for that year. Thus, for year 1 the service cost is $4,352 ($8,700 × .5002) and for year 5, it is $5,921 ($8,700 × .6806). If the postretirement benefit plan provides for different percentages of benefits for different years of service, the service cost must be computed using the specific provisions of the plan.[30]

Interest Cost. The interest cost component of the net periodic postretirement benefit is computed by applying an assumed discount (interest) rate to the beginning accumulated postretirement benefit obligation. The assumed discount rate should reflect the rates of return on high-quality, fixed income investments currently available whose cash flows match the timing and amount of expected benefit payments.[31] Thus, for year 3 in Exhibit 21—14, the interest cost is $752 ($9,401 × 8%). Note that after the full eligibility date is reached, the interest cost component continues to grow even though there is no more service cost accrued.

Actual Return on Postretirement Plan Assets. Since most plans in the past have not been funded, this offset against net periodic postretirement benefit cost will not be present for many employers until funding begins. As is true for pension accounting, the actual return is adjusted to the expected return through the gain or loss computation. If the fund holding the assets is a taxable entity, the actual return on plan assets shall reflect the tax expense or benefit for the period.

Amortization of Postretirement Prior Service Costs. These costs arise from plan initiations and amendments as they do for pensions. If the amendment includes provisions that count service years prior to the amendment date, the additional expected postretirement benefit obligation related to those years is calculated and amortized over the period from the date of the amendment to the full eligibility date. If the amendment provision only relates to future service periods, the additional costs are added to the service cost for the future years.

Gains and Losses Arising From Changes in the APBO and Plan Assets. These gains and losses arise from experiences different from those assumed in initiating the plan or from changes in actuarial assumptions. They may be recognized immediately or deferred and amortized over future service periods if they exceed a "corridor" amount similar to that used for pensions. The corridor amount is 10% of the larger of the APBO or the market-related value of the postretirement plan assets as of the beginning of the year. Consistent treatment over the years is required.

Amortization of Transition Adjustment. As with pensions, a transition adjustment is computed when the postretirement standard is applied. The adjustment arises from over- or underfunded APBO for all the earned benefits of all plan participants at the transition date. The FASB decided to allow adopting companies to either recognize the transition asset or obligation immediately in the year the standard is applied, or delay the recognition and amortize it over the average remaining service life of active participants or 20 years, whichever is longer.[32] If immediate recognition is selected, the offset to the asset or obligation is to be accounted for as a cumulative change adjustment to income in the transition year.[33]

30. See Appendix C of FASB Statement No. 106 for several illustrations of the computation of service cost under different assumed postretirement benefit plans.

31. *Statement of Financial Accounting Standards No. 106,* par. 31.

32. If most plan participants are inactive, i.e., retired, amortization should be based on the life expectancy of the plan participants.

33. The adjustment to income would be net of any income tax effects. If the transition adjustment remains nondeductible for tax purposes, a timing difference deferred tax could result. See Chapter 20 for discussion of accounting for income taxes.

As was true for pension accounting, the transition adjustment amount is affected by any prepaid or accrued postretirement benefits on the books. The transition date established by the standard for most business entities is the financial statements for years beginning after December 15, 1992 (calendar year 1993) for most companies, and December 15, 1994 (calendar year 1995) for smaller companies.

To illustrate, assume that Haymond Electrical Company had not funded nor recorded postretirement benefits, but elected to make the transition to the accrual method at the end of year 5. The transition obligation for John Jenkins as illustrated in Exhibit 21—13, would be $29,606. Haymond has the choice of immediately recognizing this amount as a postretirement obligation and a charge to the current income, to delay recognition over the 10 years to Jenkin's retirement ($2,960 per year), or to delay recognition over 20 years ($1,480 per year).

The wide range of choices allowed by the FASB for reporting the transition adjustment will make it difficult to compare companies' financial statements during the transition period. Some companies elected to recognize their postretirement benefit obligation before the standard was issued. For example, in 1988, LTV Corp. accrued $2.26 billion as the potential cost of medical and life insurance benefits for its 118,000 current and retired employees. LTV was in bankruptcy proceedings, and decided to eliminate this material future charge against income as part of the reorganization.[34] The exposure draft would have eliminated this option once the standard was issued, but the Board decided to allow this alternative to all companies up to the effective date. No change can be made once a specific alternative is selected.

Disclosure of Postretirement Benefit Plans

The same work sheet reconciliation illustrated for pensions could be used for postretirement benefits. This information is part of the disclosure requirement of the standard. The health cost trend rate must be based on stated assumptions about the many variables discussed earlier. In most instances, the company must estimate the future variables. The one exception is future government regulations. The Board decided that anticipating federal legislation was too subjective, and allowed companies to base its forecast of the government's activity on enacted legislation.

Accounting for Postemployment Benefits

The material in this chapter has focused on the accounting for postretirement benefits—pensions and other benefits provided benefits to employees after they retire. In addition to these types of benefits, firms also often provide benefits to employees who have left the company but have not retired. Examples of such employees are those who have been laid off or put on extended furlough. Benefits provided to these employees are called postemployment benefits and include things like severance pay, job training, and continued health care coverage. FASB Statement No. 112 stipulates that if a company's benefit plan is structured so that the right to receive postemployment benefits is earned through service (i.e., the right vests after a certain number of years or the amount of the benefit increases with more years of service), then the postemployment benefit obligation should be estimated and accrued in the period the employees provide the service. This accounting treatment follows that used for sick-leave and vacation pay under FASB Statement No. 43.[35]

34. Karen Blumental and Lee Berton, "LTV to Reserve $2.26 Billion for Retirees," *The Wall Street Journal,* November 22, 1988, p. A3.

35. *Statement of Financial Accounting Standards No. 112,* "Employers' Accounting for Postemployment Benefits" (Norwalk: Financial Accounting Standards Board, November 1992), par. 6.

If a company's benefit plan is structured so that postemployment benefits are not explicitly earned and thus are granted without regard to years of service, then the postemployment obligation should be accounted for in the same way as a loss contingency as outlined in FASB Statement No. 5. If information available before the issuance of the financial statements indicates that payment of postemployment benefits is probable AND the amount can be reasonably estimated, then a postemployment liability should be recognized.

CONCLUSION

Accounting for pensions has become more standardized as a result of FASB Statements 87 and 88. The Board felt that it compromised its final position in these statements and that pension obligations theoretically should be recognized for any underfunded plan. Similarly, the Board decided not to require an adjustment for a minimum liability for other postretirement benefits. Both of these concessions demonstrate the "evolutionary change" approach recognized in FASB Concepts Statement No. 5, par. 2. As further experience is gained with FASB Statement No. 106, additional changes are likely. Many employers and other preparers of financial statements have been critical of the implementation cost of many of the FASB standards in relation to the benefits realized. In FASB Statement No. 106, the Board devoted four pages to analyzing the costs and benefits related to implementing this standard.[36] They concluded that the recommendations in this standard will result in a significant improvement in financial reporting. They reminded employers that many of the required implementation costs "reflect costs that a prudent employer would incur in monitoring and managing the consequences of its postretirement benefit arrangement."[37]

The Board also has been quick to remind critics that the pension and postretirement health care costs were not created by the new standards. The arrangements were entered into by employers, but reporting these arrangements has been inadequate. Some employers have indicated they will be forced to reduce the postretirement benefits provided to employees because of the new reporting standard. Although this has many interesting social policy considerations, the qualitative characteristic of neutrality specified in the FASB's conceptual framework does not permit these issues to govern the acceptability of a standard.

36. *FASB Statement No. 106,* pars. 118-132.
37. *Ibid.,* par. 126.

APPENDIX 21

Present Value Calculations - Thakkar Company

This appendix contains the detailed present value calculations underlying the pension liability numbers reported in the Thakkar Company example used in the body of the chapter. The tables referred to are at the end of Chapter 7.

Accumulated Benefit Obligation - January 1, 1996

- Length of service: 10 years
- Highest salary: $40,000 (future salary increases ignored)
- Annual pension payment: $8,000 = [(2% × 10 years) × $40,000]
- Number of pension payments to be received after retirement: 10
- Length of time until retirement: 30 years
- Discount rate: 10%

The present value of the annuity stream of ten $8,000 pension payments is computed as follows:

$PVn = R\,(PVAF_{\overline{n|}\,i})$

where:

R = $8,000 annual payment
n = 10 years
i = 10% discount rate
PVn = $8,000 (Table IV $_{\overline{10|}\,10\%}$)
PVn = $8,000 (6.1446)
PVn = $49,157 (rounded to the nearest dollar)

Recall from Chapter 7 that the formula for the present value of an annuity is derived under the assumption that the first annuity payment is made at the end of the first period. Viewed in another way, since the first pension payment to Bach is made on December 31, 2026, $49,157 is the present value of the stream of ten payments as of January 1, 2026. Thakkar Company wishes to calculate the present value of the stream of payments as of January 1, 1996. This can be done by computing the present value of the lump sum of $49,157, as follows:

$PV = A(PVF_{\overline{n|}\,i})$

where:

A = $49,157
n = 30 years (difference between 1/1/2026 and 1/1/1996)
i = 10% discount rate

PV = $49,157 (Table II $_{\overline{30|}\,10\%}$)
PV = $49,157 (0.05731)*
PV = $2,817 (rounded to the nearest dollar)

*This factor has been expanded to five decimal places to avoid rounding error.

Exhibit 21—15 Thakkar Company—Accumulated Benefit Obligation, January 1, 1996

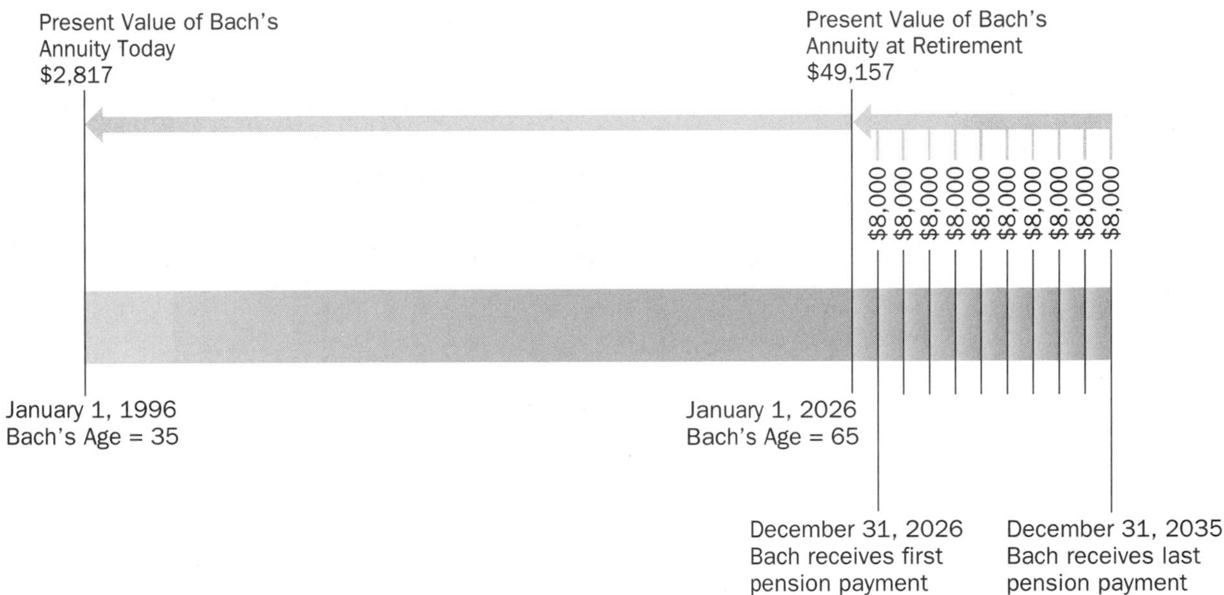

Let's review the information and assumptions needed in arriving at the actuarial present value for Thakkar's pension liability.

1. How long has Bach worked for Thakkar?
2. What salary will Bach's pension benefit be based on? In this example, Bach's most recent salary was used as an indicator of the highest salary.
3. How long until Bach retires?
4. How long will Bach live after retirement?
5. What is the appropriate discount rate?

Under the assumptions made, the actuarial present value was $2,817. To illustrate how sensitive this calculation is to the assumptions made, the table below summarizes how the actuarial present value would change if different values for the discount rate and the length of Bach's life after retirement were used.

Discount	Years of Life after Retirement				
Rate	**5**	**10**	**15**	**20**	**25**
6%	5,867	10,252	13,528	15,976	17,806
8%	3,174	5,335	6,805	7,806	8,487
10%	1,738	**2,817**	3,487	3,903	4,162
12%	963	1,509	1,819	1,995	2,094
14%	539	819	964	1,040	1,079

As an illustration of the impact of the discount rate assumption on the magnitude of the ABO, restrict your attention to the 10-year column. Note that each 2% decrease in the discount rate nearly doubles the amount of the pension liability. The impact of changes in the discount rate assumption is particularly large in this Thakkar example because the expected pension payments are so many years in the future. However, the general point is valid with all computations of the actuarial present value of a pension liability — the final result is sensitive to the assumptions made.

Projected Benefit Obligation - January 1, 1996

- Length of service: 10 years
- Estimated salary growth rate: 5%
- Length of time until retirement: 30 years
- Projected highest salary: $172,876 = $40,000 (Table I $\overline{30|}\,5\%$) = $40,000 (4.3219)
- Annual pension payment: $34,575 = [(2% × 10 years) × $172,876]
- Number of pension payments to be received after retirement: 10
- Discount rate: 10%

The present value of the annuity stream of ten $34,575 pension payments is computed as follows:

PVn = R(PVAF $\overline{n|}\,i$)

where:

R = $34,575 annual payment
n = 10 years
i = 10% discount rate

PVn = $34,575 (Table IV $\overline{10|}\,10\%$)
PVn = $34,575 (6.1446)
PVn = $212,450 (rounded to the nearest dollar)

Compute the present value of the stream of payments as of January 1, 1996 as follows:

PV = A(PVF $\overline{n|}\,i$)

where:

A = $212,450
n = 30 years (difference between 1/1/2026 and 1/1/1996)
i = 10% discount rate

PV = $212,450 (Table II $\overline{30|}\,10\%$)
PV = $212,450 (0.05731)
PV = $12,175 (rounded to the nearest dollar)

As illustrated with the ABO computations, PBO actuarial present values are sensitive to the underlying assumptions. The additional assumption about future salary increases makes the PBO even more sensitive. The table below contains PBO values for different combinations of discount rate and salary growth rate assumptions, holding all other values constant:

Discount	**Salary Growth Rate**					
Rate	**0%**	**1%**	**3%**	**5%**	**7%**	**9%**
6%	10,252	13,818	24,884	44,307	78,039	136,017
8%	5,335	7,190	12,949	23,056	40,609	70,778
10%	**2,817**	3,797	6,838	**12,175**	21,444	37,376
12%	1,509	2,034	3,662	6,521	11,485	20,017
14%	819	1,104	1,988	3,540	6,235	10,866

The 0% column is equivalent to the ABO since it reflects the assumption of no future salary increases—it corresponds to the 10-year column in the earlier table of ABO values.

The range of discount rate and salary growth rate assumptions used in this hypothetical illustration is generally in line with what is observed for actual companies. In 1992, large U.S. corporations reported using discount rates ranging from 4.5% to 11.0% and

■ **Exhibit 21—16** Thakkar Company—Projected Benefit Obligation, January 1, 1996

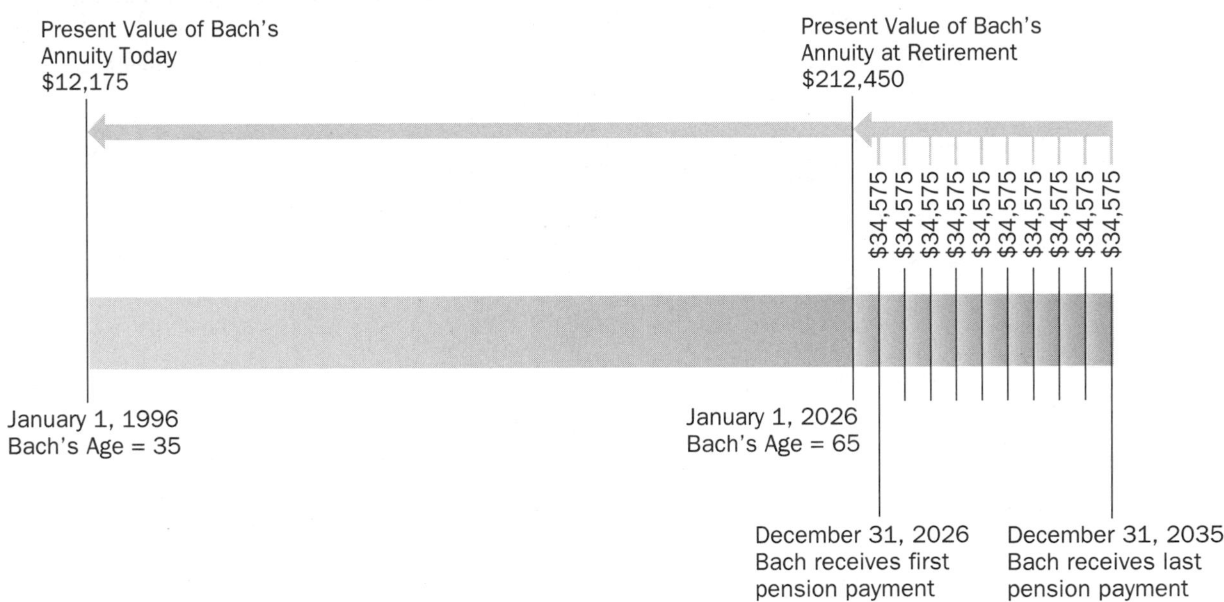

salary growth rate assumptions from 1.0% to 10.0%. Extreme combinations of discount rate and salary growth rate assumptions are unlikely to occur in practice. For example, it is very unusual for the assumed salary growth rate to exceed the discount rate. The most typical case is for the discount rate to exceed the salary growth rate by from 2% to 4%.

Computation of Service Cost for 1996

Service cost for 1996 is the increase in the projected benefit obligation caused by the addition of one more service year in the computation of the expected amount of the pension benefit payments. The details of this computation for the Thakkar Company example are shown below.

Projected Benefit Obligation, 12/31/96, WITH an extra year of service

Annual pension payment: $38,033 = [(2% × 11 years) × $172,876].

Computation of the present value of the annuity stream of ten $38,033 payments:

PVn = $38,033 (Table IV $_{\overline{10|}\,10\%}$)
PVn = $38,033 (6.1446)
PVn = $233,698 (rounded to the nearest dollar)

Computation of the present value of the lump sum of $233,698:

PV = $233,698 (Table II $_{\overline{29|}\,10\%}$)
PV = $233,698 (0.06304)*
PV = $14,732 (rounded to the nearest dollar)

*This factor has been expanded to five decimal places to avoid rounding error.

Projected Benefit Obligation, 12/31/96, WITHOUT an extra year of service:

Annual pension payment: $34,575 = [(2% × 10 years) × $172,876].
Computation of the present value of the annuity stream of ten $34,575 payments:

PVn = $34,575 (Table IV $\overline{10|}$ 10%)
PVn = $34,575 (6.1446)
PVn = $212,450 (rounded to the nearest dollar)

Computation of the present value of the lump sum of $212,450:

PV = $212,450 (Table II $\overline{29|}$ 10%)
PV = $212,450 (0.06304)
PV = $13,393 (rounded to the nearest dollar)

Service Cost for 1996:

PBO, 12/31/96, WITH an extra year of service	$14,732
PBO, 12/31/96, WITHOUT an extra year of service	13,393
Increase in PBO resulting from 1996 service	$ 1,339

The interest cost and service cost for 1996 can be used to reconcile the change in the PBO between January 1 and December 31.

Projected Benefit Obligation, 1/1/96	$12,175
Interest cost ($12,175 × .10)	1,218
Service cost	1,339
Projected Benefit Obligation 12/31/96	$14,732

KEY TERMS

Accumulated benefit obligation (ABO) 897
Accumulated postretirement benefit obligation (APBO) 925
Actual return on pension plan assets 910
Actuarial present value 895
Additional pension liability 914
Contributory pension plan 893
Corridor amount 913
Curtailment of a pension plan 919
Deferred pension cost 915
Defined benefit pension plans 893
Defined contribution pension plans 893
Expected postretirement benefit obligation (EPBO) 925
Expected return on pension plan assets 910
Expected service period 905
Fair value of pension plan assets 902
Full eligibility date 923
Market-related value of pension plan assets 910
Minimum pension liability 914
Net periodic pension cost 901
Noncontributory pension plans 893
Pension gain or loss 909
Pension plan 892
Pension plan assets 894
Postretirement benefits other than pensions 892
Prepaid/Accrued Pension Cost 900
Prior service cost 903
Projected benefit obligation (PBO) 897
Service cost 899
Settlement of a pension plan 919
Settlement interest rate 899
Single-employer pension plans 892
Transition gain or loss 903
Unrecognized net pension gain or loss 911
Unrecognized prior service cost 905
Vested benefits 895

QUESTIONS

1. What is meant by the term *vesting?*
2. Distinguish between: (a) a defined benefit plan and a defined contribution plan, (b) a contributory plan and a noncontributory plan, (c) a single-employer plan and a multiemployer plan.
3. Distinguish between the accumulated benefit approach and the projected benefit approach in determining the amount of future benefits earned by employees under a defined benefit pension plan.
4. What factors must be considered by actuaries in determining the amount of future benefits under a defined benefit plan?
5. Explain how prior-period pension costs arise (a) at the inception of a pension plan, and (b) at the time of a plan amendment.
6. What five accounting issues were addressed by the FASB in relation to defined benefit plans?
7. List and briefly describe the six basic components of net periodic pension cost.
8. How is the service cost portion of net periodic pension cost to be measured according to FASB Statement No. 87?
9. Since prior service costs are related to years of service already rendered, why are they considered to be a future pension cost?
10. How does the FASB recommend that prior service cost be amortized?
11. Does pension cost include the actual return on plan assets or the expected return? Explain.
12. The FASB identified two parts to the gain or loss component of pension cost. Identify the parts and explain how they are computed and used.
13. Why is a corridor amount identified in recognizing gain or loss from pension plans?
14. (a) How is the transition gain or loss arising from adoption of FASB Statements 87 and 88 computed? (b) How is the unrecognized transition gain or loss amortized?
15. The FASB permits the use of an average market value of plan assets for some pension computations. In other cases, the fair market value at a specific measurement date must be used. Under what circumstances is the average market value permissible?
16. (a) Under what conditions does FASB Statement No. 87 provide for recording a contra equity account? (b) How is it adjusted from period to period?
17. Distinguish between a pension settlement and a pension curtailment.
18. How are gains and losses arising from pension settlements recognized according to FASB Statement No. 88?
19. What is the function of the pension disclosure requirement included in the pension standards?
20. What is meant by postretirement benefits, and what is the primary issue in accounting for their costs?
21. Describe the differences between pension plans and other postretirement benefit plans.
22. Describe the major differences in the accounting for pensions and other postretirement benefits.
23. What is the full eligibility date, and why is it an important date in accounting for postretirement benefits?

DISCUSSION CASES

Case 21—1 (What theoretical support is there for the pension standards?)

The topic of pensions and other postretirement benefits was considered at length in an accounting theory class. The discussion centered on the following terms:

(a) Representational faithfulness
(b) Substance over form
(c) Verifiability
(d) Usefulness
(e) Present value
(f) Conservatism
(g) Adequate disclosure

How are these terms helpful in justifying the accounting for pension and other postretirement benefit plans on the employer's books? Based on your understanding of these terms, assess the treatment of pension and other postretirement benefit plans by the FASB in Statements 87, 88, and 106.

Case 21—2 (Why fix something that isn't broken?)

The FASB's study of pension accounting for employers generated considerable interest among business executives. During the extended discussion period, pressure was brought to bear against the FASB by several individuals and the companies they represented to leave pension accounting alone. These business executives felt that the existing standards (APB Opinion No. 8) were adequate and that further tinkering with the pension provisions was unnecessary. What are some of the factors that caused the FASB to "hold on" to the pension issue until a standard was released?

Case 21—3 (Are those postretirement benefits really accruable?)

George Logan, controller of Dyatine, Inc., has just finished reading a *Wall Street Journal* article about accounting for postretirement health costs. Dyatine has informally agreed to pay the medical costs of its retirees and their spouses for as long as they live. Because the company has a young work force, very little has been paid under this program. Last year, an analysis of the potential liability indicated that there would not be significant risk of payment for at least ten years. No liability for future benefits has been accrued on Dyatine's books. But, according to the article, this must change under FASB Statement No. 106. George has always felt that Dyatine was being generous with its employees, and that if economic circumstances changed, the plan easily could be altered or terminated. George calls his CPA, Debra Adams, to ask her how she feels about the FASB standard. He is surprised to learn that Debra is very supportive of the standard. He asks for reasons and Debra, in turn, asks George to support his position. Prepare a summary of the pros and cons surrounding the implementation of FASB Statement No. 106.

Case 21—4 (Does accounting have political consequences?)

C. B. Seabright, a U.S. congresswoman, has just received from her staff an analysis of FASB Statement No. 106, "Employers' Accounting for Postretirement Benefits Other Than Pensions." Seabright is very influential in the formation of tax legislation and also in federal regulation of employer-provided health care plans. How might FASB Statement No. 106 impact Seabright's legislative agenda?

Case 21—5 (Let the user beware!)

Joseph Hudson is a financial analyst. Hudson recently received the annual reports of Company A and Company B. Both A and B are in the same industry, one that Hudson specializes in. Hudson was interested to note that Company A had substantially lower earnings in the prior year than Company B, but Company A's earnings were slightly higher than B's in the current year. Hudson was ready to recommend A as a company on the rebound when he remembered that both Company A and Company B had substantial postretirement benefit plans other than pensions and both had adopted FASB Statement No. 106 in the prior year. What might explain the earnings trends for A and B? Why do accounting standards allow like items to be accounted for differently by different firms? How can users of financial statements avoid confusion over the use of differing accounting methods by similar firms?

EXERCISES

Exercise 21—6 (Computing defined benefit pension payments)

Francisco Company has established a defined benefit pension plan for its lone employee, Derrald Ryan. Annual payments under the pension plan are equal to Derrald's highest lifetime salary multiplied by (3% x Number of years with the company). Derrald's salary in 1995 was $60,000. Derrald is expected to retire in 20 years and his salary increases are expected to average 4% per year during that period. As of the beginning of 1996, Derrald had worked for Francisco Company for 12 years.

1. What is the amount of the annual pension payment that should be used in computing Francisco's accumulated benefit obligation as of January 1, 1996?
2. What is the amount of the annual pension payment that should be used in computing Francisco's projected benefit obligation as of January 1, 1996?

Exercise 21—7 (Computation of pension service cost)

Pension plan information for Springfield Metro Company is as follows:

January 1, 1996	Projected benefit obligation	$3,620,000
	Accumulated benefit obligation	2,850,000
During 1996	Pension benefits paid to retired employees	136,000
December 31, 1996	Projected benefit obligation	4,150,000
	Accumulated benefit obligation	3,125,000
Discount (settlement) rate		12%

Assuming no change in actuarial assumptions, what is the pension service cost for 1996?

Exercise 21—8 (Computing the amount of prepaid/accrued pension cost)

Using the information given for the following three independent cases, compute the amount of prepaid/accrued pension cost that would be reported in the balance sheet. Clearly indicate whether the amount would be shown as an asset or as a liability.

	Case 1	Case 2	Case 3
Unamortized transition loss	$ 40	$ 100	$ 30
Unrecognized prior service cost	250	60	10
Projected benefit obligation	1,000	900	1,000
Unrecognized net pension gain	70	120	200
Accumulated benefit obligation	750	800	850
Fair value of pension assets	700	1,300	900

Exercise 21—9 (Amortization of prior service cost—plan amendment)

Queensland Company has 5 employees belonging to its pension plan. Expected years of future service for these employees are as follows:

Employee	Future Service Years
1	3
2	6
3	7
4	9
5	10

On January 1, 1996, Queensland initiated an amendment to its pension plan that increased the projected benefit obligation for the plan by $390,000. If Queensland amortizes the prior service cost of the pension plan by assigning an equal amount to each future period of service of each employee who is active at the date of the amendment and expected to receive benefits under the plan, determine the amortization for the years 1996, 1998, 2002, and 2005.

Exercise 21—10 (Amount of funding and amortization of prior service cost)

Stratosphere, Inc., has a work force of 200 employees. A new pension plan is negotiated on January 1, 1996, with the labor union. Based on the provisions of the pension agreement, prior service cost related to the new plan amounts to $3,726,000. The cost is to be funded evenly with annual contributions over a 10-year period, with the first payment due at the end of 1996. The cost is to be amortized over the average remaining service life of the covered employees. The interest rate for funding purposes is 10%. It is anticipated that, on the average, 10 employees will retire each year over the next 20 years.

1. Compute the annual amount Stratosphere will pay to fund its prior service cost.
2. Compute the amount of amortization of prior service cost for 1996, 1998, and 2003.

Exercise 21—11 (Amortization of prior service cost—straight-line method)

Osvaldo Awning Co. has unrecognized prior service cost of $1,262,000 arising from a pension plan amendment. The board of directors decided to amortize this cost over the average remaining service period for its 45 employees on a straight-line basis. It is assumed that employees will retire at the rate of 3 employees each year over a 15-year period. (1) Compute the average remaining service life and the annual amortization of prior service cost for Osvaldo. (2) Assuming that pension cost other than amortization of prior service cost was $370,000 for the year, and $450,000 was contributed by the employer to the pension fund, prepare the formal summary journal entries relating to the pension plan for the current year.

Exercise 21—12 (Computation of actual return on plan assets)

The Longlee Electrical Company maintains a fund to cover its pension plan. The following data relates to the fund for 1996:

January 1	Fair value of pension plan assets	$875,000
	Market-related value of plan assets (5-year weighted average)	715,000
During year	Pension benefits paid	62,000
	Contributions made to the fund	50,000
December 31	Fair value of pension plan assets	980,000
	Market-related value of plan assets (5-year weighted average)	730,000

Compute the 1996 actual return on plan assets for Longlee Electrical.

Exercise 21—13 (Return on plan assets—expected and actual)

Tingey Originals has a pension plan covering its 75 employees. Tingey anticipates a 12% return on its pension plan assets. The fund trustee furnishes Tingey with the following information relating to the pension fund for 1996:

January 1	Fair value of pension plan assets	$1,350,000
	Market-related value of pension plan assets (5-year weighted average)	1,220,000
During year	Actual return on pension plan assets	155,000
December 31	Fair value of pension plan assets	1,470,000
	Market-related value of pension plan assets (5-year weighted average)	1,210,000

Compute the difference between the actual and expected return on plan assets. How should the difference be treated in determining pension cost for 1996, assuming Tingey bases expected return on the market-related value of the plan assets?

Exercise 21—14 (Amortization of unrecognized gain on plan assets)

Melba Enterprises has an unrecognized gain of $425,000 relating to its pension plan as of January 1, 1996. Management has chosen to amortize this deferral on a straight-line basis over the 10-year average remaining service life of its employees, subject to the limitation of the corridor amount. Additional facts about the pension plan as of January 1, 1996, are as follows:

Projected benefit obligation	$1,950,000
Accumulated benefit obligation	1,850,000
Fair value of pension plan assets	1,500,000
Market-related value of pension plan assets (5-year weighted average)	1,350,000

Compute the minimum amortization of unrecognized gain to be recognized by Melba in 1996.

Exercise 21—15 (Computation of gain or loss component)

The gain or loss component of pension cost consists of (a) a deferral of the difference between actual and expected return on pension plan assets and (b) amortization of unrecognized pension gains and losses. Determine the proper addition (deduction) to pension cost related to the gain or loss component under each of the following independent conditions.

	A	B	C	D
(1) Actual return on pension plan assets	$200,000	$200,000	$500,000	$500,000
(2) Expected return on pension plan assets	$180,000	$230,000	$400,000	$550,000
(3) Unrecognized (gain) loss at beginning of year	$200,000	$275,000	$(100,000)	$(75,000)
(4) Average service life of employees used for amortization	10 years	5 years	8 years	12 years
(5) Corridor amount	$100,000	$150,000	$50,000	$175,000

Exercise 21—16 (Computation of pension cost and journal entries)

The accountants for Bern Financial Services provide you with the following detailed information at December 31, 1996. Based on this data, prepare the journal entries related to the accrual and funding of pension cost for 1996.

Service cost	$45,000
Actual return on pension plan assets	75,000
Interest cost	52,000
Excess of expected return over actual return on pension plan assets	20,000
Amortization of deferred pension loss from prior years	15,000
Amortization of transition loss	8,000
Amortization of prior service cost	30,000
Contribution to pension fund	72,000

Exercise 21—17 (Pension cost computation)

Fredco's defined benefit pension plan had a projected benefit obligation of $10,000,000 at the beginning of the year. This was based on a 10% discount rate (settlement interest rate). The fair value of pension plan assets at the beginning of the year was $10,400,000. These assets were expected to earn a long-term rate of return on the fair value of 8%. During the year, service cost was $800,000. At the date of transition to FASB Statement No. 87, a net pension asset of $500,000 existed. This was equal to the amount by which the plan was overfunded at that date. At the transition date, the average service life of the employees expected to receive the benefits was 20 years. There was no unrecognized prior service cost or unrecognized net pension gain (loss) at the beginning of the year. The actual return on pension plan assets for the year was $900,000. The accumulated benefit obligation was $9,500,000 at the beginning of the year. Compute Fredco's net periodic pension cost for the year.

Exercise 21—18 (Preparing a pension work sheet)

The following information relates to the defined benefit pension plan of Mascare Company.

January 1, 1996:	
Projected benefit obligation	$ 9,000
Fair value of pension assets	11,000
Expected return on plan assets	8%
Settlement discount rate	10%
For the year ended December 31, 1996:	
Service cost	$1,200
Benefit payments to retirees	500
Contributions to pension fund	100
Actual return on plan assets	1,500

Prepare a pension work sheet for Mascare Company for 1996.

Exercise 21—19 (Computing and recording minimum pension liability)

Tacoma Energy Corp. has had a retirement program for its employees for several years. It adopted FASB Statement No. 87 beginning January 1, 1988. The following information relates to the plan for 1996:

Balances at December 31, 1996:	
Projected benefit obligation	$967,500
Accumulated benefit obligation	825,000
Fair value of pension plan assets	790,000
Market-related value of pension plan assets (5-year weighted average)	750,000
Prepaid pension cost	21,000
Unamortized transition loss	76,000
Unrecognized prior service cost	80,000
Unrecognized net pension loss	42,500

In prior years, no additional liability was required. Compute the minimum pension liability, if any for 1996, and prepare any necessary journal entries to record the liability.

Exercise 21—20 (Computing minimum pension liability)

Chateau Furniture and Cabinet Mfg. Co. computes the following balances for its defined benefit pension plan as of the end of its fiscal year:

	(In Thousands)
Projected benefit obligation	$1,625
Accumulated benefit obligation	1,380
Fair value of pension plan assets	1,460
Market-related value of pension plan assets (5-year weighted average)	1,336
Accrued pension cost	61
Unamortized transition loss	115
Unrecognized prior service cost	180
Unrecognized net pension (gain)	(191)

1. According to FASB Statement No. 87, what is the amount of additional liability, if any, required to reflect the minimum pension liability?
2. Some FASB members felt that the minimum pension liability should consider expected future salary levels rather than the current levels. If this approach had been adopted in the standard, what additional liability adjustment, if any, would have been required?

Exercise 21—21 (Reconciliation of funding status)

From the following information for each of three independent cases, prepare the reconciliation that would be included in the pension note according to FASB Statement No. 87.

	(In Thousands)		
	Case 1	Case 2	Case 3
Projected benefit obligation	$12,500	$6,290	$890
Accumulated benefit obligation	9,700	4,100	750
Fair value of pension plan assets	15,300	4,200	650
Market-related value of pension plan assets	12,800	5,000	560
Unamortized transition (gain) or loss	(400)	1,200	(75)
Unrecognized net (gain) or loss from prior years	(200)	(500)	100
Unrecognized prior service cost	1,200	1,100	200
Recorded additional liability	-0-	-0-	85
Prepaid/(accrued) pension cost	3,400	(290)	(15)

Exercise 21—22 (Postretirement benefit service cost and interest cost)

Knox Company has a postretirement benefit plan. Employees are eligible for full benefits after working for the company for 10 years. On January 1, 1996, Knox hired Employee A. At the time of the hire, Knox estimated the expected postretirement benefit obligation at the full eligibility date for Employee A to be $100,000. On January 1, 1998, Knox hired Employee B; the expected postretirement benefit obligation at the full eligibility date for Employee B was estimated to be $113,000. Knox uses a 10% discount rate in computing present values.

Prepare a schedule showing the service cost and interest cost associated with the postretirement benefits for Employees A and B for each of the years 1996-2008.

Exercise 21—23 (Computation of postretirement benefit cost)

Summary information for Lafe Company as of January 1, 1996, is listed below.

Accumulated postretirement benefit obligation	$800,000
Fair value of plan assets	0
Unamortized transition loss	$680,000
Remaining amortization period for transition loss	17 years

Postretirement benefit plan data for 1996 is listed below.

Service cost	$75,000
Contributions to plan	20,000
Benefits paid on behalf of retirees	14,000
Actual return on plan assets	300
Assumed discount rate	9.0%
Long-term expected rate of return on plan assets	8.5%

Lafe uses the fair market value of plan assets at the beginning of the year as the market-related value of plan assets.

Prepare the journal entries for recording net postretirement benefit cost and benefit plan funding for 1996.

Exercise 21—24 (Computation of prepaid/accrued postretirement benefit cost)

Orrin Company has an informal health benefit plan for its retirees. The following balances relate to the benefits from this plan as of December 31, 1996.

Unamortized transition loss	$650,000
Unrecognized net postretirement benefit gain	76,000
Accumulated postretirement benefit obligation	945,000
Unrecognized prior service postretirement costs	111,000
Fair value of postretirement plan assets	57,000

What amount should be shown on Orrin Company's December 31, 1996, balance sheet as "Prepaid/Accrued Postretirement Benefit Cost"?

Exercise 21—25 (Deferral of transition loss and financial statement effect)

As of January 1, 1993, Jason Company adopted FASB Statement No. 106, "Employers' Accounting for Postretirement Benefits Other Than Pensions." On that date, Jason had $230,000 in its postretirement benefit fund. Jason computed its accumulated postretirement benefit obligation as of January 1, 1993, to be $3,500,000. Jason elected to defer the transition loss and amortize it over 20 years. Jason reported net income of $4,000,000 for the year ended December 31, 1993; this represented an increase of approximately 10% compared to the prior year. What would net income have been if Jason had elected to recognize the transition loss immediately? How would Jason's December 31, 1993, balance sheet have been affected? (Ignore income taxes.)

***Exercise 21—26 (Computing the accumulated and projected benefit obligations)**

Wu Company has established a defined benefit pension plan for its lone employee, Ronald Dalton. Annual payments under the pension plan are equal to Ronald's highest lifetime salary multiplied by (2% × Number of years with the company). As of the beginning of 1996, Ronald had worked for Wu Company for 10 years. Ronald's salary in 1995 was $50,000. Ronald is expected to retire in 25 years and his salary increases are expected to average 3% per year during that period. Ronald is expected to live for 15 years after retiring and will receive the first annual pension payment one year after he retires.

1. Compute Wu Company's accumulated benefit obligation as of January 1, 1996, assuming an 8% discount rate.
2. Compute Wu Company's projected benefit obligation as of January 1, 1996, assuming an 8% discount rate.
3. Compute Wu Company's accumulated benefit obligation as of January 1, 1996, assuming a 12% discount rate.
4. Compute Wu Company's projected benefit obligation as of January 1, 1996, assuming a 12% discount rate.

*Relates to Appendix.

PROBLEMS

Problem 21—27 (Entries to record accrual and funding of pension costs)

The Allied Rental Company reported the following information related to its pension plan for the years 1996-1999. The fund is administered by a separate outside trustee.

Year	Pension Cost Accrual	Contribution	Benefit Payments to Retirees	Actual Return on Pension Plan Assets
1996	$560,700	$625,000	$300,000	$350,000
1997	725,000	670,000	300,000	400,000
1998	685,000	620,000	275,000	450,000
1999	726,500	625,000	400,000	525,000

Instructions:

1. Prepare the required summary journal entries for each year to record applicable pension items.
2. Assuming Allied had an accrued pension liability of $25,000 at January 1, 1996, compute the prepaid/accrued pension account balance at December 31, 1999.
3. Assuming that the fair value of the pension plan assets at January 1, 1996, was $2,600,000, compute the fair value of the pension plan assets at December 31, 1999.

Problem 21—28 (Computation of prior service cost funding and amortization)

The Staybrite Electronics Co. amended its pension plan effective January 1, 1996. The increase in the projected benefit obligation occurring as a result of the plan amendment is $6,290,000. Staybrite arranged to fund the prior service cost by equal annual contributions over the next 15 years at 10% interest. The first payment will be made December 31, 1996. The company decides to amortize the prior service cost on a straight-line basis over the average remaining service life of its employees. The company has 225 employees at January 1, 1996, who are entitled to the benefits of the amendment. It is estimated that, on the average, 15 employees will retire each year.

Instructions:

1. Compute the amount Staybrite will pay each year to fund the prior service cost arising from the plan amendment.
2. Compute Staybrite's annual prior service cost amortization based on average remaining years of employee service.

Problem 21—29 (Computation of gain or loss component)

The Birnberg Equipment Co. has a defined benefit pension plan. As of January 1, 1996, the following balances were computed for the pension plan:

Unrecognized pension gain	$ 500,000
Fair value of pension plan assets	3,100,000
Market-related value of plan assets (5-year weighted average)	2,600,000
Projected benefit obligation	3,600,000
Accumulated benefit obligation	3,300,000

It was anticipated that the pension plan would earn 11% of the market-related value of plan assets in 1996. The actual return on pension plan assets was $275,000. The company has elected to amortize the unrecognized pension gains and losses over 10 years.

Instructions:

1. Compute the amount of gain or loss deferral for 1996.
2. Compute the amount of amortization of unrecognized pension gain or loss for 1996.
3. If net periodic pension cost, exclusive of the gain or loss component, is $626,000, what is the net periodic pension cost after including the gain or loss component?
4. What is the unrecognized pension gain or loss that Birnberg will carry forward to 1997 as a result of changes in the return on pension plan assets?

Problem 21—30 (Computation, recording, and funding of pension cost)

Averon Industrial, Inc., computed the following components of pension cost for the years 1996-1998.

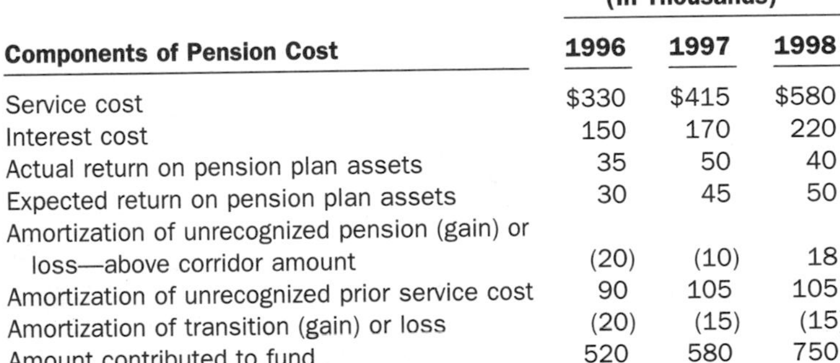

	(In Thousands)		
Components of Pension Cost	**1996**	**1997**	**1998**
Service cost	$330	$415	$580
Interest cost	150	170	220
Actual return on pension plan assets	35	50	40
Expected return on pension plan assets	30	45	50
Amortization of unrecognized pension (gain) or loss—above corridor amount	(20)	(10)	18
Amortization of unrecognized prior service cost	90	105	105
Amortization of transition (gain) or loss	(20)	(15)	(15)
Amount contributed to fund	520	580	750

Instructions:

1. Compute the net periodic pension cost for the years 1996-1998.
2. Prepare the journal entries to record the computed pension cost in (1) and the funding of the pension plan.
3. If the prepaid pension cost balance at January 1, 1996, was $75,000, compute the balance of the prepaid/accrued pension cost account at December 31, 1998.

Problem 21—31 (Computation of transition amortization and minimum liability)

The following information was provided relative to the pension plan for Atlas Wholesale Company for the years 1996-1998:

	January 1, 1996	December 31, 1996	December 31, 1997	December 31, 1998
Accrued pension cost	$ 625			
Projected benefit obligation	27,525	$29,700	$32,600	$39,000
Accumulated benefit obligation	22,900	23,800	29,300	37,000
Fair value of pension plan assets	20,600	24,200	27,900	31,500
Market-related value of pension plan assets (5-year weighted average)	17,900	18,600	21,300	26,950
Net pension cost exclusive of transition amortization		1,920	2,410	2,860
Contributions made to pension fund		1,970	3,510	2,410
Unrecognized net pension loss (gain)	2,520	1,145	1,445	3,795
Unrecognized net transition loss	3,780	3,360	2,940	2,520

Instructions:

1. Compute the amount of net periodic pension cost for each of the 3 years.
2. Prepare the journal entries for recording the net pension cost and the pension funding for the 3 years.
3. Compute any additional liability to be recorded for each of the 3 years under the minimum liability requirements of FASB Statement No. 87.
4. Identify the pension balance sheet accounts and their amounts as of December 31, 1998. There is no unrecognized prior service cost at this date.

Problem 21—32 (Computing and recording additional pension liability)

The following balances relate to the defined benefit pension plan of Cameron Industries:

	12/31/96	12/31/97
Fair value of pension plan assets	$149,000	$160,000
Market-related value of pension plan assets (5-year weighted average)	145,000	152,000
Projected benefit obligation	173,200	191,600
Accumulated benefit obligation	159,100	172,900
Prepaid/(accrued) pension cost	4,200	(1,950)
Unrecognized prior service cost	8,200	6,300
Unrecognized net pension loss	20,200	23,350

Instructions:

1. Determine the additional pension liability, if any, at December 31, 1996, and December 31, 1997.
2. Prepare journal entries for the additional pension liability adjustment, if any, at December 31, 1996, and December 31, 1997. Assume that the company had not previously recognized additional pension liability under FASB Statement No. 87.

Problem 21—33 (Adjusting additional pension liability)

At the end of 1994, Adamson Corporation recorded an additional pension liability of $700,000 for the first time, the offset being charged to Deferred Pension Cost. Minimum pension liability computations for 1995-1998 indicated the following additional pension liability amounts:

December 31, 1995	$ 800,000
December 31, 1996	1,100,000
December 31, 1997	400,000
December 31, 1998	600,000

No plan amendments occurred during these years. The amount of the unamortized transition loss is as follows:

December 31, 1995	$1,000,000
December 31, 1996	750,000
December 31, 1997	500,000
December 31, 1998	250,000

Instructions: For each of the 4 years, prepare the journal entry to adjust the minimum pension liability account to the balance indicated above.

Problem 21—34 (Journal entries and minimum pension liability)

The following balances relate to the pension plan of Rienstem Transportation Co. at December 31, 1996 and 1997:

	(In Thousands)	
	December 31, 1996	December 31, 1997
Projected benefit obligation	$3,075	$3,160
Accumulated benefit obligation	2,804	2,907
Fair value of pension plan assets	2,754	2,532
Market-related value of pension plan assets	2,550	2,750
Unrecognized prior service cost	240	215
Prepaid/(accrued) pension cost	15	(30)
Unrecognized net pension loss	272	537
Unrecognized transition gain	176	154

Instructions:

1. Determine if a minimum pension liability adjustment is required at December 31, 1996 and 1997.
2. Prepare journal entries at December 31, 1996 and 1997, to record any additional liability.

Problem 21—35 (Disclosure of pension plan information)

The following information relates to the pension plan of Circle Manufacturing Company at December 31, 1996.

	(In Thousands)
Balances at December 31, 1996:	
Projected benefit obligation	$11,750
Fair value of pension plan assets	10,800
Accumulated benefit obligation	9,900
Vested benefit obligation	7,400
Unrecognized transition loss	750
Unrecognized net pension loss (arose in 1996)	160
Accrued pension cost	40
1996 activity:	
Service cost	875
Interest cost	1,100
Actual return on pension plan assets	1,250
Expected return on pension plan assets	1,310
Amortization of transition loss	75

Instructions: Prepare the pension note at December 31, 1996, that discloses the component parts of pension cost and the reconciliation of the funded status of the plan.

Problem 21—36 (Preparing a pension work sheet)

The following information relates to the defined benefit pension plan of Haan Company:

January 1, 1996:	
Projected benefit obligation	$3,500
Unamortized transition gain	450
Unrecognized prior service cost	200
Fair value of pension assets	3,000
Accumulated benefit obligation	2,800
Expected return on plan assets	7%
Settlement discount rate	10%
For 1996:	
Service cost	$400
Benefit payments to retirees	170
Contributions to pension fund	230
Actual return on plan assets	130
Prior service cost amortization	40
Transition gain amortization	50

Instructions: Prepare a pension work sheet for Haan Company for 1996.

Problem 21—37 (Comprehensive computation of pension cost components)

The actuaries for Viewmont Cable Company provided Viewmont's accountants with the following information related to the company's pension plan:

	(In Thousands)
December 31, 1996:	
Increase in PBO arising from plan amendment	$ 732
January 1, 1997:	
Projected benefit obligation	$3,800
Accumulated benefit obligation	$3,420
Fair value of pension plan assets	$2,530
Market-related value of pension plan assets (5-year weighted average)	$2,100
Accrued pension cost	$532
Unamortized transition loss	$66
Settlement discount rate	12%
Remaining life for amortization of transition loss	3 years
Average service life for amortization of gain and prior service costs	12 years
Unamortized pension gain—prior year	$60
Expected rate of return	10%
For year 1997:	
Benefit payments to retirees	$185
Contributions to pension plan	$300
December 31, 1997:	
Projected benefit obligation	$4,161
Fair value of pension plan assets	$2,865

Instructions: Based on the data provided, prepare a pension work sheet for Viewmont Cable Company for 1997. The five-year weighted average value of plan assets is used in computing the expected return.

Problem 21—38 (Pension cost components and reconciliation of funded status)

As of January 1, 1996, information related to the defined benefit pension plan of Leffingwell Company was as follows:

Projected benefit obligation	$1,615,000
Fair value of pension assets	1,513,500
Unamortized transition gain	350,000
Unrecognized prior service cost	405,000
Unrecognized net pension gain or loss	0
Remaining amortization period for transition gain	7 years

Pension data for the years 1996 and 1997 are listed below:

1996 Pension plan information:	
Service cost as reported by actuaries	$ 87,000
Contributions to pension plan	120,000
Benefits paid to retirees	132,000
Actual return on pension plan assets	26,350
Amortization of prior service cost	81,000
Actuarial change increasing projected benefit obligation	80,000
Settlement interest rate	11.0%
Long-term expected rate of return on pension plan assets	10.0%
Accumulated benefit obligation, December 31, 1996	$1,580,000
Vested benefit obligation, December 31, 1996	1,200,000
1997 Pension plan information:	
Service cost as reported by actuaries	$ 115,000
Contributions to pension plan	125,000
Benefits paid to retirees	140,000
Actual return on pension plan assets	180,000
Amortization of prior service cost	72,000
Settlement interest rate	11.0%
Long-term expected rate of return on pension plan assets	10.0%
Accumulated benefit obligation, December 31, 1997	$1,850,000
Vested benefit obligation, December 31, 1997	1,500,000

As of January 1, 1997, the remaining expected service life of employees was 5.0 years. Also, Leffingwell uses the fair market value of pension plan assets at the beginning of the year as the market-related value of pension plan assets.

Instructions:

1. For both 1996 and 1997, prepare the pension note that discloses the component parts of pension cost and the reconciliation of the funded status of the plan.
2. Prepare the journal entries for recording net pension cost and pension funding for 1996 and 1997.
3. Compute any additional liability to be recorded for each of the years. Prepare the necessary journal entry.

Problem 21—39 (Postretirement benefit cost components and reconciliation of funded status)

Summary information for Munson Company as of January 1, 1996, is listed below.

Accumulated postretirement benefit obligation	$1,200,000
Fair value of plan assets	$170,000
Unamortized transition loss	$875,500
Remaining amortization period for transition loss	17 years
Accrued postretirement cost	$ 154,500

Postretirement benefit plan data for the years 1996 and 1997 are listed below.

1996 Postretirement benefit plan information:	
Service cost	$113,000
Contributions to plan	35,000
Benefits paid on behalf of retirees	35,000
Actual return (loss) on plan assets	(38,000)
Actuarial change increasing accumulated postretirement benefit obligation	112,000
Assumed discount rate	10.0%
Long-term expected rate of return on plan assets	9.0%

1997 Postretirement benefit plan information:	
Service cost	$121,000
Contributions to plan	100,000
Benefits paid on behalf of retirees	42,000
Actual return on plan assets	47,000
Assumed discount rate	10.0%
Long-term expected rate of return on plan assets	9.0%

As of January 1, 1997, the average remaining time to full benefit eligibility for Munson's employees was 6 years. Also, Munson uses the fair market value of plan assets at the beginning of the year as the market-related value of plan assets.

Instructions:

1. For both 1996 and 1997, prepare the note that discloses the component parts of postretirement benefit cost and the reconciliation of the funded status of the plan.
2. Prepare the journal entries for recording net postretirement benefit cost and benefit plan funding for 1996 and 1997.

*Problem 21—40 (Computing pension service cost)

Kendall Company has established a defined benefit pension plan for its lone employee, Jim Tanaka. Annual payments under the pension plan are equal to Jim's highest lifetime salary multiplied by (2% × Number of years with the company). As of the beginning of 1996, Jim had worked for Kendall Company for 15 years. Jim is expected to retire at the end of the year 2006 and his salary increases are expected to average 5% per year until then. Jim is expected to live for 20 years after retiring and will receive the first annual pension payment one year after he retires. Jim worked for Kendall Company for the entire year of 1996 and his 1996 salary was $84,000. Jim's 1995 salary was $80,000.

Instructions:

1. Assuming an 8% discount rate, compute pension service cost for 1996.
2. Assuming a 12% discount rate, compute pension service cost for 1996.

*Relates to Appendix.

CHAPTER 22

Accounting Changes and Error Corrections

CHAPTER TOPICS

- Change in Accounting Estimate
- Change in Accounting Principle
- Change in Accounting Entity
- Accounting for Error Corrections

In 1992 General Motors took a one-time charge of $33 billion, which caused a $21 billion after-tax decrease in earnings and a $33.38 per share decrease. The charge was a result of the company's adoption of Statement of Financial Accounting Standards No. 106, "Employers' Accounting for Postretirement Benefits Other Than Pensions." Although the standard gave companies the option of spreading the charge over 20 years, many companies chose to take the "big hit" in one year rather than negatively impacting earnings for 19 additional years.

A few other companies that elected the one-time charge method and the size of the resulting charges are as follows:

	One-Time Charge (in millions)
IBM	$2,263
General Electric	1,799
Bell Atlantic	1,550
Pepsico	357
CocaCola	7
Tiffany & Co.	6

The overall impact to corporate profits is a record for a new accounting rule and could decrease profits of major U.S. companies by as much as $1 trillion.[1]

1. Lee Berton and Robert J. Brennan, "New Medical-Benefits Accounting Rule Seen Wounding Profits, Hurting Shares," *The Wall Street Journal,* April 22, 1992, Sec. C, p. 1, cols. 3-5.

As the experience of these companies illustrates, the financial statements of companies sometimes report significantly different results from year to year. This may be due to changes in economic circumstances, but it also may be due to changes in accounting methods or to corrections of errors in recording past transactions.

Changing the accounting methods used can have a dramatic impact on the financial statements of a company. Because of this impact, one can argue that accounting changes detract from the informational characteristics of *comparability* and *consistency* discussed in Chapter 2. So why are these accounting changes made? The main reasons for such changes may be summarized as follows:

1. A company, as a result of experience or new information, may change its estimates of revenues or expenses, for example, the estimate of uncollectible accounts receivable, or the estimated service lives of depreciable assets.
2. Due to changes in economic conditions, companies may need to change methods of accounting to more clearly reflect the current economic situation.
3. Accounting standard-setting bodies may require the use of a new accounting method or principle, such as new reporting requirements for postretirement benefits.
4. The acquisition or divestiture of companies, which was particularly prevalent in the 1980s and early 1990s, may cause a change in the reporting entity.
5. Management may be pressured to report profitable performance. Making accounting changes can often result in higher net income, thereby reflecting favorably on management.

Whatever the reason, accountants must keep the primary qualitative characteristic of *usefulness* in mind. They must determine if the reasons for accounting changes are appropriate, and then how best to report the changes to facilitate understanding of the financial statements.

The detection of errors in accounting for past transactions presents a similar problem. The errors must be corrected and appropriate disclosures made so that the readers of the financial statements will clearly understand what has happened. The purpose of this chapter is to discuss the different types of accounting changes and error corrections and the appropriate accounting procedures that should be used.

ACCOUNTING CHANGES

The accounting profession has identified three main categories of **accounting changes**.[2]

1. Change in accounting estimate
2. Change in accounting principle
3. Change in reporting entity

As pointed out in Chapter 1, a major objective of published financial statements is to provide users with information to help them predict, compare, and evaluate future earning power and cash flows of the reporting entity. When a reporting entity adjusts its past estimates of revenues earned or costs incurred, changes its accounting principles from one method to another, or changes its nature as a reporting entity, it becomes more difficult for a user to predict the future from past historical statements. The basic accounting issue is whether accounting changes should be reported as adjustments of the prior periods' statements, and thus increase their comparability with the current and future statements, or whether the changes should affect only the current and future years.

Several alternatives have been suggested for reporting accounting changes.

2. *Opinions of the Accounting Principles Board, No. 20,* "Accounting Changes" (New York: American Institute of Certified Public Accountants, 1971).

1. Restate the financial statements presented for prior periods to reflect the effect of the change. Adjust the beginning retained earnings balance for the current period for the cumulative effect of the change.
2. Make no adjustment to statements presented for prior periods. Report the cumulative effect of the change in the current year as a direct entry to Retained Earnings.
3. Same as (2), except report the cumulative effect of the change as a special item in the income statement instead of directly to Retained Earnings.
4. Report the cumulative effect in the current year as in (3), but also present limited pro forma information for all prior periods included in the financial statements reporting "what might have been" if the change had been made in the prior years.
5. Make the change effective only for current and future periods with no catch-up adjustment.

Each of these methods for reporting an accounting change has been used by companies in the past, and arguments can be made for each of the various approaches. For example, some accountants argue that accounting principles should be applied consistently for all reported periods. Therefore, if a new accounting principle is used in the current period, the financial statements presented for prior periods should be restated so that the results shown for all reported periods are based on the same accounting principles. Other accountants contend that restating financial statements may dilute public confidence in those statements. Principles applied in earlier periods were presumably appropriate at that time and should be considered final. The only exception would be for changes in a reporting entity. In addition, restating financial statements is costly, requires considerable effort, and is sometimes impossible due to lack of data.

Because of the diversity of practice and the resulting difficulty in user understandability of the financial statements, the Accounting Principles Board issued Opinion No. 20. The Board's objective was to bring increased uniformity to reporting practice. Evidence of compromise exists in the final opinion, as the Board attempted to reflect both its desire to increase comparability of financial statements and to improve user confidence in published financial statements. Depending on the type of accounting change, different accounting treatment is required, as explained in the following sections.

Change in Accounting Estimate

Contrary to what many people believe, accounting information cannot always be measured and reported precisely. Also, to be reported on a timely basis for decision making, accounting data often must be based on estimates of future events. The financial statements incorporate these estimates, which are based on the best professional judgment given the information available at that time. At a later date, however, additional experience or new facts sometimes make it clear that the estimates need to be revised to more accurately reflect the existing business circumstances. When this happens, a **change in accounting estimate** occurs.

Examples of areas where changes in accounting estimates often are needed include:

1. Uncollectible receivables
2. Useful lives of depreciable or intangible assets
3. Residual values for depreciable assets
4. Warranty obligations
5. Quantities of mineral reserves to be depleted
6. Actuarial assumptions for pensions or other postemployment benefits
7. Number of periods benefited by deferred costs

Accounting for a change in estimate has already been discussed in Chapter 4 and throughout the text in areas where changes in estimates are common. By way of review, all changes in estimates should be reflected either in the current period or in current and future periods. No retroactive adjustments or pro forma statements are to be prepared for a change in accounting estimate. Changes in estimates are considered to be part of the normal accounting process and not corrections or changes of past periods.

However, disclosures such as the one in Exhibit 22—1, reported by Southwest Airlines, are useful in helping readers of financial statements understand the impact of changes in estimates.

Exhibit 22—1
Southwest Airlines Company—Disclosure of Change in Estimate

NOTES TO FINANCIAL STATEMENTS (in part)

Two—Change in Accounting Estimate:

Effective January 1, 1992, the Company revised the estimated useful lives of its 737-200 aircraft from 15 years to 15-19 years. This change was the result of the Company's assessment of the remaining useful lives of its 737-200 aircraft following the recent promulgations of rules by the FAA for the phaseout of stage 2 aircraft by December 31, 1999. The effect of this change was to reduce depreciation expense approximately $3,680,000, $.02 per share, for the year ended December 31, 1992.

Change in Accounting Principle

A **change in accounting principle** involves a change from one generally accepted principle or method to another.[3] A change in principle, as defined in APB Opinion No. 20, does not include the initial adoption of an accounting principle as a result of transactions or events that had not occurred (or were immaterial) in previous periods. Also, a change from a principle that is not generally accepted to one that is generally accepted is considered to be an error correction rather than a change in accounting principle.

If an asset is affected by both a change in principle and a change in estimate during the same period, APB Opinion No. 20 requires that the change be treated as a change in estimate rather than a change in principle.[4] For example, if a company changes its depreciation method at the same time it recognizes a change in estimated asset life, this would involve both a change in method and a change in estimate. According to APB Opinion No. 20, such circumstances would be treated as a change in estimate.

As indicated in previous chapters, companies may select among alternative accounting principles to account for business transactions. For example, for financial reporting purposes, a company may depreciate its buildings and equipment using the straight-line depreciation method, the double-declining-balance method, the sum-of-the-years-digits method, or any other consistent and rational allocation procedure. Long-term construction contracts may be accounted for by the percentage-of-completion or the completed-contract method. Inventory may be accounted for using FIFO, LIFO, or other acceptable methods. These alternative methods are often equally available to a given company, but in most instances, criteria for selection among the methods are inadequate. As a result, companies have found it rather easy to justify changing from one accounting principle or method to another.

Current Recognition of Cumulative Effect of Change in Principle. The APB concluded that, in general, companies should not change their accounting principles from one period to the next. "Consistent use of accounting principles from one period to another enhances the utility of financial statements to users by facilitating analysis and understanding of comparative accounting data."[5] A company may change its accounting principles,

3. The classification "change in accounting principle" includes changes in methods used to account for transactions. No attempt was made by the APB in Opinion No. 20 to distinguish between a principle and a method.
4. Opinions of the Accounting Principles Board, No. 20, par. 32.
5. *Ibid.*, par. 15.

however, if it can justify a change because of a new pronouncement by the authoritative accounting standard-setting body or because of a change in its economic circumstances. Just what constitutes an acceptable change in economic circumstances is not clear. It presumably could include a change in the competitive structure of an industry, a significant change in the rate of inflation in the economy, a change resulting from government restrictions due to economic or political crisis, and so forth.

In general, the effect of a change from one accepted accounting principle to another is reflected by **reporting the cumulative effect of the change in the income statement** in the period of the change. This cumulative adjustment is shown as a separate item on the income statement after extraordinary items and before net income. When a change in accounting principle occurs, the financial statements for all prior periods reported for comparative purposes with the current- year financial statements are presented as previously reported. To enhance trend analysis, however, pro forma information also is required to reflect the income before extraordinary items and net income that would have been reported if the new accounting principle had been in effect for the respective prior years. Pro forma earnings per share figures also should be reported.

To illustrate the general treatment of a change in accounting principle, assume Telstar Company, a high-power telescope sales and manufacturing firm, elected in 1996 to change from the double-declining-balance (DDB) method of depreciation to the straight-line method to make its financial reporting more consistent with the majority of its competitors. For tax purposes, assume Telstar had elected to use the straight-line method and will continue to do so. Assume further that Telstar presents comparative income statements for three years, and that the past difference in book and tax depreciation is the only difference in accounting treatment impacting Telstar's financial and taxable income.

These and other assumptions are necessary because, in most instances, a change in accounting principle involves temporary differences between book and tax income, creating the need for interperiod tax allocation. The exact amounts of any deferred income tax liabilities or potential deferred income tax assets are dependent on several factors, such as current tax laws and current and future tax rates. Therefore, in this chapter, including the end-of-chapter material, the impact of income tax either is ignored or the assumed amounts are provided to simplify the illustrations and focus on the effects of accounting changes and error corrections.

For Telstar, the change to straight-line depreciation for reporting purposes means that tax and book depreciation will be the same in future years. It is assumed, however, that the greater depreciation charged on the books in prior years, as compared to the tax depreciation taken, resulted in a previously recorded deferred tax asset. This and other relevant information for Telstar are presented below.

Year	Double Declining-Balance Depreciation	Straight-Line Depreciation	Depreciation Difference	Assumed Tax Effects	Effects on Income (Net of Taxes)
Prior to 1994	$163,000	$ 90,000	$ 73,000	$21,900	$51,100
1994	60,000	32,000	28,000	8,400	19,600
1995	65,000	35,000	30,000	9,000	21,000
	$288,000	$157,000	$131,000	$39,300	$91,700

The data indicate that depreciation expense for the years prior to 1996 would have been $131,000 ($288,000 − $157,000) less if the straight-line method had been used. Thus, income would have been $131,000 higher, less the applicable assumed income taxes of $39,300. Based on these data, the journal entry to record the cumulative effect adjustment and to eliminate the previously recorded deferred tax asset is as follows:

Accumulated Depreciation	131,000	
Deferred Tax Asset		39,300
Cumulative Effect of Change in Accounting Principle		91,700

The $131,000 debit to Accumulated Depreciation represents the excess depreciation charged to the books in prior years. The $39,300 credit would eliminate the previously established deferred tax asset amount. The $91,700 after-tax cumulative effect would be reported as additional income in the income statement for 1996, the year of the change.

Continuing the Telstar example, assume that net income for the two preceding years as originally reported was $450,000 in 1994 and $500,000 in 1995, and that all net income in both years was from continuing operations. Using the new depreciation method, in 1996 Telstar reported $560,000 income from continuing operations and an extraordinary gain of $70,000 net of income taxes of $30,000. Following is a partial income statement for 1996 with comparative information for 1995 and 1994.

Telstar Company
Partial Comparative Income Statement
For Years Ended December 31

	1996	1995	1994
Income from continuing operations	$560,000	$500,000	$450,000
Extraordinary gain (net of income taxes of $30,000)	70,000		
Cumulative effect on prior years of change in accounting principle—change to the straight-line method of depreciation from double-declining-balance method (net of income taxes of $39,300)	91,700		
Net income	$721,700	$500,000	$450,000

Note that in 1996 the cumulative effect is shown net of tax and as a separate item after the extraordinary item. As explained in Chapter 4, all below-the-line items, such as extraordinary gains or losses and the cumulative effect of a change in accounting principle, are to be reported net of related income taxes. This is referred to as **intraperiod tax allocation.** With this disclosure technique, the appropriate amount of income taxes is associated with income from continuing operations and with the individual below-the-line items reported separately. Also note that the amounts of income from continuing operations for the two prior years are presented as originally reported. In addition, the disclosure of pro forma (as if) income for the prior years is required and would be shown on the face of the income statement (using the assumed data) as follows:

Pro Forma Income Data

	1995	1994
Net income from continuing operations as previously reported	$500,000	$450,000
Effect of change in accounting principle (net of tax)	21,000	19,600
Pro forma income (restated)	$521,000	$469,600

Pro forma earnings per share amounts reflecting the revised income figures also would be presented.

The Change From FIFO to LIFO

In 1974, more firms switched their inventory to LIFO than in any other year. As noted in Chapter 9, if LIFO is used for tax purposes, it must also be used for financial reporting purposes. In periods of rising prices, as was the case in 1974, LIFO results in a lower reported net income figure for both financial and tax purposes. Thus, the use of LIFO can result in significant tax savings.

Given these potential savings, one author wondered why more firms didn't switch. Professor Gary Biddle examined 105 firms that did not switch to LIFO during 1974 and estimated that those firms paid, on average, $12 million each in additional taxes simply because they used FIFO rather than LIFO. He concludes by stating, "It is puzzling why so many firms in so many industries have continued to use FIFO."

Questions:

1. If inventory costing $100 is purchased by a firm, how much is paid for that inventory if the FIFO inventory method is used? How much if the LIFO method is used?
2. Why might firms elect not to switch to LIFO given the tax savings they could receive?
3. How is a change to LIFO reported in the financial statements?

Source: Gary Biddle, "Paying FIFO Taxes: Your Favorite Charity," *The Wall Street Journal*, January 19, 1981, p. 18.

In a few cases, past records are inadequate to prepare pro forma statements for individual years. This fact should be disclosed when applicable. For example, a change to the LIFO method of inventory valuation is usually made effective with the beginning inventory in the year of change rather than with some prior year, because of the difficulty in identifying prior-year layers or dollar-value pools. Thus, the beginning inventory in the year of change becomes the same as the previous inventory valued using another costing method, and this becomes the base LIFO layer. No cumulative effect adjustment is required.

Restatement of Prior Periods for Change in Principle. If a change in accounting principle is caused by a new pronouncement by an authoritative accounting body, the cumulative effect may be reported retroactively or currently, depending on the instructions contained in the pronouncement. The APB generally favored the reporting procedures described in the previous section, i.e., current recognition of the cumulative effect. However, the Board identified the following four specific changes as being of such a nature that the "advantages of retroactive treatment in prior-period reports outweigh the disadvantages."[6]

1. A change from LIFO method of inventory pricing to another method.
2. A change in the method of accounting for long-term construction contracts.
3. A change to or from the "full cost" method of accounting used in extractive industries.
4. Changes made at the time of an initial distribution of company stock.[7]

In addition to these exceptions, several FASB statements require retroactive restatement.

In those cases where retroactive restatement is required, the cumulative effect of the change is recorded directly as an adjustment to the beginning retained earnings balance for the earliest year presented. Income statement data reported for comparative purposes also must be adjusted to reflect the new principle.

6. *Opinions of the Accounting Principles, Board No. 20*, par. 27.
7. This exception is available only once for a company, and it may be used for (a) obtaining additional equity capital from investors, (b) effecting business combinations, or (c) registering securities, whenever a company first issues financial statements. *Ibid.*, par. 29.

To illustrate the procedures required for restatement, assume that in 1996 the Forester Company changed from the LIFO inventory costing method to the FIFO method for both financial reporting and income tax purposes. There are no deferred tax consequences because both the old and new methods apply to both financial and tax reporting. However, additional taxes will be payable for prior years as a result of the change in inventory method used for tax purposes. The following data are applicable, and a tax rate of 30% is assumed for all years.

Year	Pretax Income FIFO	Pretax Income LIFO	Pretax Income Difference	Income Tax Effect (30%)	Effect on Income (Net of Tax)
Prior to 1994	$190,000	$160,000	$30,000	$ 9,000	$21,000
1994	110,000	75,000	35,000	10,500	24,500
1995	120,000	100,000	20,000	6,000	14,000
Totals—beginning of 1996	$420,000	$335,000	$85,000	$25,500	$59,500
1996 results	$125,000	$100,000	$25,000	$ 7,500	$17,500

The entry in 1996 to record the prior-period effects of the change in accounting principle would be:

Inventory	85,000	
Income Taxes Payable		25,500
Retained Earnings		59,500

The $85,000 debit to Inventory adjusts the beginning 1996 inventory to its FIFO cost. The $59,500 reflects the after-tax effect on cost of goods sold in years prior to 1996. Cost of goods sold would have been lower using FIFO and pretax income would have been higher, resulting in additional taxes of $25,500. Assumed comparative income statement data, restated for 1995 and 1994, would be presented as follows:

Forester Company
Partial Comparative Income Statement
For Years Ended December 31

	1996	1995	1994
Income before income taxes	$125,000	$120,000	$110,000
Income taxes (30%)	37,500	36,000	33,000
Net income	$ 87,500	$ 84,000	$ 77,000
Earnings per share (10,000 shares outstanding)	$8.75	$8.40	$7.70

The adjustment for the cumulative effect of the change in principle would be reported in Forester Company's statement of retained earnings. Assuming a beginning retained earnings balance in 1994 of $351,000 and no dividends, a comparative retained earnings statement would appear as follows shown on the next page.

Note that no pro forma information is required with the retroactive approach, because the statements for prior years are restated directly. If prior-year income statements cannot

Forester Company
Comparative Statement of Retained Earnings
For Years Ended December 31

	1996	1995	1994
Retained earnings at beginning of year, as previously reported	$473,500	$403,500	$351,000
Add adjustment for cumulative effect on prior years of retroactively applying the FIFO method of inventory costing (see Note A)	59,500	45,500	21,000
Adjusted retained earnings, beginning of year	$533,000	$449,000	$372,000
Net income	87,500	84,000	77,000
Retained earnings, end of year	$620,500	$533,000	$449,000

Note A Change in Accounting Principle Forester Company has changed its inventory costing method from last-in, first-out (LIFO) to first-in, first-out (FIFO), effective January 1, 1996. The new inventory method was adopted to better reflect company earnings and inventory values. The financial statements have been restated to apply the new method retroactively. Because income tax laws permit the use of LIFO for tax purposes only if it is also used for financial reporting, the FIFO method has also been adopted for income tax reporting. As a result, an additional tax liability of $25,500 was incurred for years prior to 1996. The effect of the accounting change on income in 1996 (net of taxes of $7,500) was an increase of $17,500, or $1.75 per share. The net-of-tax effect in 1995 was an increase of $14,000, and in 1994, an increase of $24,500. The retained earnings balances for 1996, 1995, and 1994 have been adjusted to reflect the cumulative effect of retroactively applying the new method of inventory costing, net of applicable taxes.

be presented because of inadequate data, that fact should be disclosed. Under those circumstances, the cumulative effect would be reported only in the retained earnings statement.

Change in Reporting Entity

Companies sometimes change their structures or report their operations in such a way that the financial statements are, in effect, those of a different reporting entity. Specifically, a **change in reporting entity** includes: (a) presenting consolidated or combined statements in place of statements of individual companies; (b) changing specific subsidiaries comprising the group of companies for which consolidated statements are presented; (c) changing the companies included in combined financial statements; and (d) a business combination accounted for as a pooling of interests.[8]

Because of the basic objective of comparability, the APB required that financial statements be adjusted retroactively to disclose what the statements would have looked like if the current entity had been in existence in the prior years. Thus, previous years' financial statements presented for comparison with the current year (the year of change) must be restated to reflect results of operations, financial condition, and cash flows as if the current reporting entity had been in existence in those years. Also, in the period of the change, the financial statements should disclose the nature of, and reasons for, the change, as illustrated in the note included in Synbiotics Corporation's 1993 annual report, as shown in Exhibit 22—2.

The statements also should disclose the effect of the change on income from continuing operations, net income, and the related earnings per share amounts for all periods presented. Subsequent years' statements do not need to repeat the disclosure.[9] Changes in reporting entities are covered in more depth in advanced accounting texts.

8. *Ibid.*, par.12.
9. *Ibid.*, par. 35.

■ Exhibit 22—2
Synbiotics Corporation—Disclosure of Change in Reporting Entity

NOTES TO FINANCIAL STATEMENTS

One (In Part)—Significant Accounting Policies:

The financial statements of Synbiotics Corporation (the Company) as of March 31, 1991, were consolidated to include the accounts of its then 53 percent owned subsidiary UniSyn Technologies, Inc. (UniSyn), formerly UniSyn Fibertec Corporation, and the accounts of its then 79 percent owned subsidiary ImmunoPharmaceutics, Inc. (IPI).

During fiscal 1993 and 1992, UniSyn issued approximately 1,680,000 shares of voting convertible preferred stock to outside investors, and issued 1,200,000 shares of voting convertible preferred stock in conjunction with the acquisition of a subsidiary, reducing the Company's effective ownership to approximately 29 percent. As of March 31, 1993, UniSyn had approximately 6,339,000 shares of voting stock issued and outstanding, of which approximately 1,833,000 were owned by the Company.

During fiscal 1993 and 1992, IPI issued approximately 3,719,000 shares of voting convertible preferred stock to outside investors, reducing the Company's effective ownership to approximately 43 percent. In conjunction with the 1992 issuances, the Company converted all of its common shares of IPI into voting convertible preferred shares. As of March 31, 1993, IPI had approximately 8,322,000 shares of voting stock issued and outstanding, of which approximately 3,573,000 were owned by the Company.

As a result of the above transactions, the Company utilizes the equity method to account for its investments in UniSyn and IPI. The accompanying financial statements have been restated to reflect the change in accounting for the Company's investments in affiliated companies, due to the change in reporting entity, as if the transactions had occurred on April 1, 1990.

ERROR CORRECTIONS

Error corrections are not considered accounting changes, but their treatment is specified in APB Opinion No. 20 and reaffirmed in FASB Statement No. 16.[10] In effect, **accounting errors** made in prior years that have not already been "counterbalanced" or reversed are reported as prior-period adjustments and recorded directly to Retained Earnings. Examples of errors include mathematical mistakes, improper application of accounting principles, or omissions of material facts.

Kinds of Errors

There are a number of different kinds of errors. Some errors are discovered in the period in which they are made, and these are easily corrected. Others may not be discovered currently and are reflected on the financial statements until discovered. Some errors are never discovered; however, the effects of these errors may be counterbalanced in subsequent periods, and after this takes place, account balances are again accurately stated. Errors may be classified as follows:

1. **Errors discovered currently in the course of normal accounting procedures.** Examples of this type of error are clerical errors, such as an addition error, posting to the wrong account, misstating an account, or omitting an account from the trial balance. These types of errors usually are detected during the regular summarizing process of the accounting cycle and are readily corrected.
2. **Errors limited to balance sheet accounts.** Examples include debiting Accounts Receivable instead of Notes Receivable, crediting Interest Payable instead of Notes Payable, or crediting Interest Payable instead of Salaries Payable. Another example is not recording the exchange of convertible bonds for stock. Such errors are frequently discovered and corrected in the period in which they are made. When such errors are not found until a subsequent period, corrections must be made at that time and balance sheet data subsequently restated for comparative reporting purposes.

10. *Statement of Financial Accounting Standards No. 16,* "Prior-Period Adjustments" (Stamford: Financial Accounting Standards Board, 1977), p. 5.

3. **Errors limited to income statement accounts.** The examples and correcting procedures for this type of error are similar to those in (2). For example, Office Salaries may be debited instead of Sales Salaries. This type of error should be corrected as soon as it is discovered. Even though the error would not affect net income, the misstated accounts should be restated for analysis purposes and comparative reporting.
4. **Errors affecting both income statement accounts and balance sheet accounts.** Certain errors, when not discovered currently, result in the misstatement of net income and thus affect both the income statement accounts and the balance sheet accounts. The balance sheet accounts are carried into the succeeding period; hence, an error made currently and not detected will affect earnings of the future. Such errors may be classified into two groups:
   (a) **Errors in net income that, when not detected, are automatically counterbalanced in the following fiscal period.** Net income amounts on the income statements for two successive periods are inaccurately stated; certain account balances on the balance sheet at the end of the first period are inaccurately stated, but the account balances in the balance sheet at the end of the succeeding period are accurately stated. In this class are errors such as the misstatement of inventories and the omission of adjustments for prepaid and accrued items at the end of the period.
   (b) **Errors in net income that, when not detected, are not automatically counterbalanced in the following fiscal period.** Account balances on successive balance sheets are inaccurately stated until such time as entries are made compensating for or correcting the errors. In this class are errors such as the recognition of capital expenditures as revenue expenditures and the omission of charges for depreciation and amortization.

When errors affecting income are discovered, careful analysis is necessary to determine the required action to correct the account balances. As indicated, most errors will be caught and corrected prior to closing the books. The few material errors not detected until subsequent periods and those that have not already been counterbalanced must be treated as prior-period adjustments.

The following sections describe and illustrate the procedures to be applied when error corrections require prior-period adjustments. It is assumed that each of the errors is material. Errors that are discovered usually affect the income tax liability for a prior period. Amended tax returns are usually prepared either to claim a refund or to pay any additional tax assessment. For simplicity, the examples on the following pages and the exercises and problems ignore the income tax effects of errors.

Illustrative Example of Error Correction

Assume Supply Master, Inc. began operations at the beginning of 1994. An auditing firm is engaged for the first time in 1996. Before the accounts are adjusted and closed for 1996, the auditor reviews the books and accounts and discovers the errors summarized on pages 962 and 963. Effects of these errors on the financial statements, before any correcting entries, are indicated as follows: a plus sign (+) indicates an overstatement; a minus sign (−) indicates an understatement. Each error correction is discussed in the following paragraphs.

(1) Understatement of Merchandise Inventory. It is discovered that the merchandise inventory as of December 31, 1994, was understated by $1,000. The effects of the misstatement were as follows:

Income Statement	Balance Sheet
1994: Cost of goods sold overstated (ending inventory too low) Net income understated	Assets understated (inventory too low) Retained earnings understated
1995: Cost of goods sold understated (beginning inventory too low) Net income overstated	Balance sheet items not affected, retained earnings understatement for 1994 being corrected by net income overstatement for 1995

Since this type of error counterbalances after two years, no correcting entry is required in 1996.

If the error had been discovered in 1995 instead of 1996, an entry would have been made to correct the account balances so that operations for 1995 would be reported accurately. The beginning inventory for 1995 would have been increased by $1,000, the amount of the asset understatement and Retained Earnings would have been credited for this amount, representing the income understatement in 1994. The correcting entry in 1995 would have been:

Merchandise Inventory	1,000	
Retained Earnings		1,000

(2) Failure to Record Merchandise Purchases. It is discovered that purchase invoices as of December 28, 1994 for $850 were not recorded until 1995. The goods were included in the inventory at the end of 1994. The effects of failure to record the purchases were as follows:

Income Statement	Balance Sheet
1994: Cost of goods sold understated (purchases too low) Net income overstated	Liabilities understated (accounts payable too low) Retained earnings overstated
1995: Cost of goods sold overstated (purchases too high) Net income understated	Balance sheet items not affected, retained earnings overstatement for 1994 being corrected by net income understatement for 1995

Since this is a counterbalancing error, no correcting entry is required in 1996.

If the error had been discovered in 1995 instead of 1996, a correcting entry would have been necessary. In 1995, Purchases was debited and Accounts Payable credited for $850 for merchandise acquired in 1994 and included in the ending inventory of 1994. Retained Earnings would have to be debited for $850, representing the net income overstatement for 1994, and Purchases would have to be credited for the same amount to reduce the purchases balance in 1995. The correcting entry in 1995 would have been:

Retained Earnings	850	
Purchases		850

(3) Failure to Record Merchandise Sales. It is discovered that sales on account for the last week of December 1995 for $1,800 were not recorded until 1996. The goods sold were not included in the inventory at the end of 1995. The effects of the failure to report the revenue in 1995 were:

Income Statement	Balance Sheet
1995: Revenue understated (sales too low) Net income understated	Assets understated (accounts receivable too low) Retained earnings understated

When the error is discovered in 1996, Sales is debited for $1,800 and Retained Earnings is credited for this amount, representing the net income understatement for 1995. The following entry is made:

Sales	1,800	
Retained Earnings		1,800

(4) Failure to Record Accrued Expense. Accrued sales salaries of $450 as of December 31, 1994, were overlooked in adjusting the accounts. Sales Salaries is debited for salary payments. The effects of the failure to record the accrued expense of $450 as of December 31, 1994, were as follows:

Income Statement	Balance Sheet
1994: Expenses understated (sales salaries too low) Net income overstated	Liabilities understated (accrued salaries not reported) Retained earnings overstated
1995: Expenses overstated (sales salaries too high) Net income understated	Balance sheet items not affected, retained earnings overstatement for 1994 being corrected by net income understatement for 1995

No entry is required in 1996 to correct the accounts for the failure to record the accrued expense at the end of 1994, the misstatement in 1994 having been counterbalanced by the misstatement in 1995. If the error had been discovered in 1995, an entry would have been required to correct the accounts for the failure to record the accrued expense at the end of 1994 if the net income for 1995 is not to be misstated. If accrued expenses are to be properly recorded at the end of 1995, Retained Earnings would be debited for $450, representing the net income overstatement for 1994, and Sales Salaries would be credited for the same amount, representing the amount to be subtracted from salary payments in 1995. The correcting entry made in 1995 would be:

Retained Earnings	450	
Sales Salaries		450

(5) Failure to Record Prepaid Expense. It is discovered that Miscellaneous General Expense for 1994 included taxes of $275 that should have been deferred in adjusting the accounts on December 31, 1994. The effects of the failure to record the prepaid expense were as follows:

Income Statement	Balance Sheet
1994: Expenses overstated (miscellaneous general expense too high) Net income understated	Assets understated (prepaid taxes not reported) Retained earnings understated
1995: Expenses understated (miscellaneous general expense too low) Net income overstated	Balance sheet items not affected, retained earnings understatement for 1994 being corrected by net income overstatement for 1995

Analysis Sheet to Show Effects

	At End of 1994			
	Income Statement		Balance Sheet	
	Section	Net Income	Section	Retained Earnings
(1) Understatement of merchandise inventory of $1,000 on December 31, 1994.	Cost of Goods Sold +	−	Current Assets −	−
(2) Failure to record merchandise purchases on account of $850 in 1994; purchases were recorded in 1995.	Cost of Goods Sold −	+	Current Liabilities −	+
(3) Failure to record merchandise sales on account of $1,800 in 1995. (It is assumed that the sales for 1995 were recognized as revenue in 1996.)				
(4) Failure to record accrued sales salaries of $450 on December 31, 1994; expense was recognized when payment was made.	Selling Expense −	+	Current Liabilities −	+
(5) Failure to record prepaid taxes of $275 on December 31, 1994; amount was included In Miscellaneous General Expense.	General Expense +	−	Current Assets −	−
(6) Failure to record accrued interest on notes receivable of $150 on December 31, 1994; revenue was recognized when collected in 1995.	Other Revenue −	−	Current Assets −	−
(7) Failure to record unearned service fees of $225 on December 31, 1995; amount received were included in Miscellaneous Revenue.				
(8) Failure to record depreciation of delivery equipment. On December 31, 1994, $1,200.	Selling Expense −	+	Noncurrent Assets +	+
On December 31, 1995, $1,200.				

Since this is a counterbalancing error, no entry to correct the accounts is required in 1996.

If the error had been discovered in 1995 instead of 1996, a correcting entry would have been necessary. If prepaid taxes were properly recorded at the end of 1995, Miscellaneous General Expense would have to be debited for $275, the expense relating to operations of 1995, and Retained Earnings would have to be credited for the same amount, representing the net income understatement for 1996. The correcting entry in 1995 would have been:

Miscellaneous General Expense	275	
Retained Earnings		275

(6) Failure to Record Accrued Revenue. Accrued interest on notes receivable of $150 was overlooked in adjusting the accounts on December 31, 1994. The revenue was recognized when the interest was collected in 1995. The effects of the failure to record the accrued revenue were:

of Errors on Financial Statements

At End of 1995				At End of 1996			
Income Statement		**Balance Sheet**		**Income Statement**		**Balance Sheet**	
Section	**Net Income**	**Section**	**Retained Earnings**	**Section**	**Net Income**	**Section**	**Retained Earnings**
Cost of Goods Sold −	+						
Cost of Goods Sold +	−						
Sales −	−	Accounts Receivable −	−	Sales +	+		
Selling Expense +	−						
General Expense −	+						
Other Revenue +	+						
Other Revenue +	+	Current Liabilities −	+	Other Revenue −	−		
		Noncurrent Assets +	+			Noncurrent Assets +	+
Selling Expense −	+	Noncurrent Assets +	+			Noncurrent Assets +	+

	Income Statement	**Balance Sheet**
1994:	Revenue understated (interest revenue too low) Net income understated	Assets understated (interest receivable not reported) Retained earnings understated
1995:	Revenue overstated (interest revenue too high) Net income overstated	Balance sheet items not affected, retained earnings understatement for 1994 being corrected by net income overstatement for 1995

Since the balance sheet items at the end of 1995 were correctly stated, no entry to correct the accounts is required in 1996.

If the error had been discovered in 1995 instead of 1996, an entry would have been necessary to correct the account balances. If accrued interest on notes receivable had been properly recorded at the end of 1995, Interest Revenue would have to be debited for $150, the amount to be subtracted from receipts of 1995, and Retained Earnings would have to be credited for the same amount, representing the net income understatement for 1994. The correcting entry in 1995 would have been:

Interest Revenue	150	
Retained Earnings		150

(7) Failure to Record Unearned Revenue. Fees of $225 received in advance for miscellaneous services as of December 31, 1995, were overlooked in adjusting the accounts. Miscellaneous Revenue had been credited when fees were received. The effects of the failure to recognize the unearned revenue of $225 at the end of 1995 were as follows:

Income Statement	Balance Sheet
1995: Revenue overstated (miscellaneous revenue too high)	Liabilities understated (unearned service fees not reported)
Net income overstated	Retained earnings overstated

An entry is required to correct the accounts for the failure to record the unearned revenue at the end of 1995 if the net income for 1996 is not to be misstated. If the unearned revenue were properly recorded at the end of 1996, Retained Earnings would be debited for $225, representing the net income overstatement for 1995, and Miscellaneous Revenue would be credited for the same amount, representing the revenue that is to be identified with 1996. The correcting entry is:

Retained Earnings	225	
Miscellaneous Revenue		225

(8) Failure to Record Depreciation. Delivery equipment was acquired at the beginning of 1994 at a cost of $6,000. The equipment has an estimated 5-year life, and depreciation of $1,200 was overlooked at the end of 1994 and 1995. The effects of the failure to record depreciation for 1994 were as follows:

Income Statement	Balance Sheet
1994: Expenses understated (depreciation of delivery equipment too low)	Assets overstated (accumulated depreciation of delivery equipment too low)
Net income overstated	Retained earnings overstated
1995: Expenses not affected	Assets overstated (accumulated depreciation of delivery equipment too low)
Net income not affected	Retained earnings overstated

It should be observed that the misstatements arising from the failure to record depreciation are not counterbalanced in the succeeding year.

Failure to record depreciation for 1995 affected the statements as shown below.

Income Statement	Balance Sheet
1995: Expenses understated (depreciation of delivery equipment too low)	Assets overstated (accumulated depreciation of delivery equipment too low)
Net income overstated	Retained earnings overstated

When the omission is recognized, Retained Earnings must be decreased by the net income overstatements of prior years and accumulated depreciation must be increased by the depreciation that should have been recorded. The correcting entry in 1996 for depreciation that should have been recognized for 1994 and 1995 is as follows:

Retained Earnings	2,400	
Accumulated Depreciation—Delivery Equipment		2,400

SUMMARY OF ACCOUNTING CHANGES AND CORRECTION OF ERRORS

The following summary presents the appropriate accounting procedures applicable to each of the four main categories covered in APB Opinion No. 20. Naturally, accountants must apply these guidelines with judgment and should seek to provide the most relevant and reliable information possible.

Summary of Procedures for Reporting Accounting Changes and Correction of Errors

Category	**Accounting Procedures**
I. Change in estimate	1. Adjust only current-period results or current and future periods. 2. No separate, cumulative adjustment or restated financial statements. 3. No pro forma disclosure needed.
II. Change in accounting principle	
a. Current recognition of cumulative effect	1. Adjust for cumulative effect, i.e., a "catch-up" adjustment in current period as special item in income statement. 2. No restated financial statements. 3. Pro forma data required showing income and EPS information for all periods presented.
b. Restatement of prior periods	1. Direct cumulative adjustment to beginning retained earnings balance. 2. Restate financial statements to reflect new principle for comparative purposes. 3. No pro forma information required, because prior-period statements are changed directly.
III. Change in reported entity	1. Restate financial statements as though new entity had been in existence for all periods presented.
IV. Error correction	1. If detected in period error occurred, correct accounts through normal accounting cycle adjustments. 2. If detected in a subsequent period, adjust for effect of material errors by making prior-period adjustments directly to Retained Earnings.

KEY TERMS

Accounting changes 950
Accounting errors 958
Change in accounting estimate 951
Change in accounting principle 952
Change in reporting entity 957

QUESTIONS

1. How do accounting changes detract from the informational characteristics of comparability and consistency as described in FASB Concepts Statement No. 2?
2. List the three categories of accounting changes and explain briefly why such changes are made.
3. What alternative procedures have been suggested as solutions for reporting accounting changes?
4. (a) List several examples of areas where changes in accounting estimates are often made. (b) Explain briefly the proper accounting treatment for a change in estimate. (c) Why is this procedure considered proper for recording changes in accounting estimates?
5. (a) List several examples of changes in accounting principle that a company may make. (b) Explain briefly the proper accounting treatment for recognizing currently a change in accounting principle.
6. What information should pro forma statements include?
7. Why does a change in accounting principle require justification?
8. (a) When should the effects of a change in accounting principle be reported as a restatement of prior periods? (b) Although no justification was given by the APB for selecting certain items for special treatment, what might be a possible reason?
9. The Dallas Company purchased a delivery van in 1993. At the time of purchase, the van's service life was estimated to be 7 years with a salvage value of $500. The company has been using the straight-line method of depreciation. In 1996, the company determined that because of extensive use, the van's service life would be only 5 years with no salvage value. Also, the company has decided to change the depreciation method used from straight-line to the sum-of-the-years-digits method. How would these changes be treated?
10. (a) List the 4 types of changes in reporting entities that might occur. (b) How are these changes treated? (c) What assumption does the treatment of a change in reporting entity make?
11. Describe the effect on current net income, beginning retained earnings, individual asset accounts, and contra asset accounts when:
    (a) Depreciation is changed from the straight-line method to an accelerated method.
    (b) Depreciation is changed from an accelerated method to the straight-line method.
    (c) Income on construction contracts that had been reported on a completed-contract basis is now reported on the percentage-of-completion basis.
    (d) The valuation of inventories is changed from a FIFO to a LIFO basis.
    (e) It is determined that warranty expenses in prior years should have been 5% of sales instead of 4%.
    (f) The valuation of inventories is changed from a LIFO to a FIFO basis.
    (g) Your accounts receivable clerk has learned that a major customer has declared bankruptcy.
    (h) Your patent lawyer informs you that your rival has perfected and patented a new invention making your product obsolete.
12. (a) How are accounting errors to be treated? (b) What are counterbalancing errors?
13. The Mendez Manufacturing Co. failed to record accrued interest for 1993, $800; 1994, $700; and 1995, $950. What is the amount of overstatement or understatement of retained earnings at December 31, 1996?
14. Goods purchased FOB shipping point were shipped to Merkley & Co. on December 31, 1996. The purchase was recorded in 1996, but the goods were not included in ending inventory. (a) What effect would this error have had on reporting income for 1996 had it not been discovered? (b) What entry should be made on the books to correct this error assuming the books have not yet been closed for 1996?

DISCUSSION CASES

Case 22—1 (Accounting changes)

Situation A Tucker Corporation has determined that the depreciable lives of several operating machines are too long and therefore do not fairly match the cost of the assets with the revenues produced. Tucker therefore decides to reduce the depreciable lives of these machines by 3 years.

Situation B Trent Company decides that at the beginning of the year, it will adopt the straight-line method of depreciation for plant equipment. The straight-line method will be used for new acquisitions as well as for the previously acquired plant equipment, which had been accounted for using an accelerated depreciation method.

What types of accounting changes were involved in the two situations? Describe the method of reporting the changes under current GAAP. Where applicable, explain how the reported amounts are computed.

Case 22—2 (Change in principle or change in estimate?)

Jill Stanton, President of Central Company, is confused about why your accounting firm has recommended that she report certain events as changes in principle instead of changes in estimate, which is what Jill thought they should be. She has asked you for an explanation. Describe a change in an accounting principle and a change in accounting estimate. Explain how each would be reported in the income statement of the period of change.

Case 22—3 (Why do they make the change?)

An interesting phenomenon can sometimes occur when companies are in danger of not meeting their projected earnings goals. Management suddenly realizes that they have been far too conservative in their previous estimates associated with bad debts, estimated useful lives of equipment, and residual values, to name a few. With this newfound realization, management proceeds to revise these estimates to, as is often stated, "more closely reflect economic reality."

What is the primary difference in financial statement disclosure between a change in estimate and a change in principle? Why do you think managers who are in danger of not meeting their goals would prefer to revise an accounting estimate rather than change an accounting principle?

Case 22—4 (Continuing that upward trend)

Hornberger Co. has demonstrated a consistently increasing earnings trend over the past ten years. Stockholders have come to expect this steady increase, and management has gone to great lengths to emphasize the smooth growth pattern associated with Hornberger's earnings.

At the year-end board of directors meeting, you, as the chief financial officer, present to the board the preliminary results for the year just ended. These results indicate a slight decline in both income from operations and net income when compared to the previous year. The chairman of the board quickly reviews the firm's earnings history and then suggests the following items for consideration:

(a) Increase the estimated useful life of the company's plant facilities from 15 to 25 years.
(b) Change the firm's estimate of bad debts from 4% of credit sales to 2.5% of credit sales.
(c) Change the firm's amortization period for goodwill from the industry average of 10 years to the maximum allowed by GAAP of 40 years.

These changes will result in income for the period that is slightly higher than that reported for the past year and will continue the upward trend. The board votes on the proposed changes and instructs you to revise the income statement to reflect the changed estimates.

How would each of the above changes be reported in the current year's annual report to shareholders? Why would the chairman of the board suggest changing accounting estimates rather than accounting principles? As the accountant, do you have a responsibility to review management's estimates for reasonableness and to evaluate the motives behind management's decision to change an accounting estimate?

Case 22—5 (How long can airplanes fly?)

Delta Air Lines depreciates its airplanes over a 15-year period and estimates a salvage value of 10% of the cost of the plane. On the other hand, Pan Am depreciates identical airplanes over a 25-year period and provides for a 15% salvage value. These different assumptions can result in markedly different operating results. For example, if one Boeing 727 costs $10 million, Delta will depreciate $260,000 more per year for 15 years than will Pan Am.

Which company's estimate of useful life more closely reflects reality? Would you feel comfortable as a passenger in an airplane that is 25 years old? Does the fact that Pan Am recently filed for bankruptcy protection provide any information as to why its estimates might be so substantially different from those of financially sound Delta?

Case 22—6 (Can you fool the market?)

During the 1980s, Blockbuster Entertainment became one of the largest national video rental chains in the U.S. With its rapid growth came significantly increased stock prices. Then, in 1988, Blockbuster changed the amortization period for its video tapes from 9 months to 36 months. Why do you think Blockbuster changed its estimate of the useful life of its video tapes? What do you think happened to Blockbuster's market value?

EXERCISES

Exercise 22—7 (Change in estimate and in accounting principle)

Manchester Manufacturing purchased a machine on January 1, 1992, for $50,000. At the time, it was determined that the machine had an estimated useful life of 10 years and an estimated residual value of $2,000. The company used the double-declining-balance method of depreciation. On January 1, 1996, the company decided to change its depreciation method from double-declining-balance to straight-line. The machine's remaining useful life was estimated to be 5 years with a residual value of $1,000.

1. Give the entry required to record the company's depreciation expense for 1996.
2. Give the entry, if any, to record the effect of the change in depreciation methods.

Exercise 22—8 (Change in estimate)

The Curtis Company purchased a machine on January 1, 1993, for $1,500,000. At the date of acquisition, the machine had an estimated useful life of 6 years with no residual value. The machine is being depreciated on a straight-line basis. On January 1, 1996, Curtis determined, as a result of additional information, that the machine had an estimated useful life of 8 years from the date of acquisition with no residual value.

1. Give the journal entry, if any, to record the cumulative effect on prior years of changing the estimated useful life of the machine.
2. What is the amount of depreciation expense on the machine that should be charged to Curtis Company's income statement for the year ended December 31, 1996?

Exercise 22—9 (Change in accounting estimate)

Albrecht Inc. began business in 1993. An examination of the company's allowance for doubtful accounts reveals the following:

	Estimated Bad Debts	Actual Bad Debts
1993	$11,000	$4,500
1994	13,000	6,800
1995	16,500	8,950
1996	No adjustment yet	9,500

In the past, the company has estimated that 3% of credit sales will be uncollectible. The accountant for Albrecht Inc. has determined that the percentage used in estimating bad debts has been inappropriate. She would like to revise the estimate downward to 1.5%. The president of the company has stated that if the previous estimates of bad debt expense were incorrect, the financial statements should be restated using the more accurate estimate.

1. Assuming credit sales for 1996 are $600,000, provide the adjusting entry to record bad debt expense for the year.
2. What catch-up entry, if any, would be made to correct the inaccurate estimates for previous years?
3. How would you respond to the president's request to restate the prior years' financial statements?

Exercise 22—10 (Change in accounting estimate)

On January 1, 1996, management of Micro Storage Inc. determined that a revision in the estimates associated with the depreciation of storage facilities was appropriate. These facilities, purchased on January 5, 1994, for $600,000, had been depreciated using the straight-line method with an estimated salvage value of $60,000 and an estimated useful life of 20 years. Management has determined that the storage facilities' expected *remaining* useful life is 10 years and they have an estimated salvage value of $100,000.

1. How much depreciation was recognized by Micro Storage in 1994 and 1995?
2. How much depreciation will be recognized by Micro Storage in 1996 as a result of the changes in estimates?
3. What journal entry is required to account for the change in estimate at the beginning of 1996?

Exercise 22—11 (Change in estimate of natural resources)

Western Mining Company purchased a tract of land with estimated silver ore deposits totaling 400,000 tons. The purchase price for the land was $1.5 million. During the first year of operation, Western mined 50,000 tons of ore. During the second year, Western mined 110,000 tons of ore. At the beginning of the third year, new geological engineering estimates determined that a total of 300,000 tons of silver ore remained. During year three, 125,000 tons of ore were mined.

1. What was the original depletion rate used by Western in years one and two?
2. Make the accounting entries for depletion expense for Western Mining Company at the end of years one and two?
3. What is the depletion rate for year three and what accounting entry should be made to reflect the change in accounting estimate in year three?

Exercise 22—12 (Change in accounting principle)

Modern Lighting Inc. has, in the past, depreciated its computer hardware using the straight-line method assuming a 10% salvage value and an expected useful life of 5 years. As a result of the rapid obsolescence associated with the computer industry, Modern Lighting has determined that it receives most of the benefit from its computer systems in the first few years of ownership. Therefore, Modern Lighting proposes changing to the sum-of-the-years-digits method for depreciating its computer hardware. The following information is available regarding all of Modern Lighting's computer purchases:

	Cost
1993	$40,000
1994	25,000
1995	30,000

1. Compute the depreciation taken by Modern Lighting during 1993, 1994, and 1995. Assume all purchases were made at the beginning of the year.
2. Compute the amount of depreciation expense assuming sum-of-the-years-digits had been used.
3. Prepare the journal entry required to adjust the accounts on January 1, 1996. (Ignore income tax effects.)

Exercise 22—13 (Change in accounting principle)

High Quality Construction Company has used the completed-contract method of accounting since it began operations in 1989. In 1996, for justifiable reasons, management decided to adopt the percentage-of-completion method.

The following schedule, reporting income for the past 3 years, has been prepared by the company.

	1993	1994	1995
Total revenues from completed contracts	$500,000	$1,200,000	$1,000,000
Less cost of completed contracts	350,000	925,000	760,000
Income from operations	$150,000	$ 275,000	$ 240,000
Extraordinary loss	-0-	-0-	45,000
Income	$150,000	$ 275,000	$ 195,000

Analysis of the accounting records disclosed the following income by projects, earned in the years 1993-1995 using the percentage-of-completion method.

	1993	1994	1995
Project A	$150,000		
Project B	100,000	$175,000	
Project C	70,000	200,000	$ 10,000
Project D		10,000	60,000
Project E			(40,000)

Give the journal entry required in 1996 to reflect the change in accounting principle. (Ignore income tax effects.)

Exercise 22—14 (Change in accounting principle)

Diversified Manufacturing Company decides to change from an accelerated depreciation method it has used for both reporting and tax purposes to the straight-line method for reporting purposes. From the following information, prepare the income statement for the year ended December 31, 1996:

Year	Net Income as Reported	Excess of Accelerated Depreciation Over Straight-Line Depreciation	Income Effect (Net of Tax)
Prior to 1993		$12,500	$ 7,500
1993	$62,500	6,250	3,750
1994	54,500	7,500	4,500
1995	78,000	11,250	6,750
		$37,500	$22,500

In 1996, net sales were $190,000; cost of goods sold, $92,500; selling expenses, $47,500; and general and administrative expenses, $14,000. The income tax on operating income was $14,400. In addition, Diversified had a tax deductible extraordinary loss of $12,000 net of $8,000 income tax savings.

Exercise 22—15 (Change in accounting principle involving LIFO)

Assume the change in net income as shown in Exercise 22—14 is the result of a change from the LIFO method of inventory pricing to another method. During 1996, dividends of $17,500 were paid. Based on this information, prepare the retained earnings statement for 1996. The December 31, 1995, retained earnings balance as reported was $260,000.

Exercise 22—16 (Changes in estimates and accounting principles)

Due to changing economic conditions and to make its financial statements more comparable to those of other companies in its industry, the management of Kelsea Inc. decided in 1996 to review its accounting practices.

On January 1, management decided to change its allowance for uncollectible accounts from 2% to 3 1/2% of its outstanding receivables balance.

On July 1, Kelsea decided to begin using the straight-line method of depreciation on its mainframe computer instead of the sum-of-the-years-digits method. Based on further information, it also was decided that the computer has 10 more years of useful life. Kelsea bought the computer on January 1, 1986, at a cost of $550,000. At that time, Kelsea estimated it would have a 15-year useful life. The computer has no expected salvage value. Prior years' depreciation is as follows:

1986	$68,750	1991	$45,833
1987	64,167	1992	41,250
1988	59,583	1993	36,667
1989	55,000	1994	32,083
1990	50,417	1995	27,500

On October 1, Kelsea determined that starting with the current year, it would depreciate the company's printing press using hours of use as the depreciation base. The press, which had been purchased on January 1, 1983, at a cost of $930,000, was being depreciated for 25 years using the straight-line method. No salvage value was anticipated. It is estimated that this type of press provides 200,000 total hours of use and, as of January 1, 1996, it had been used 76,000 hours. At the end of 1996, the plant manager determined that the press had been run 6,250 hours during the year. Ignore income taxes relating to this change.

1. Evaluate each of the foregoing changes and determine whether it is a change in estimate or a change in accounting principle.
2. Give the journal entries required at December 31, 1996, to account for the above changes. Kelsea's receivable balance at December 31, 1996, was $345,000. Allowance for Doubtful Accounts carried a $1,000 debit balance before adjustment.

Exercise 22—17 (Accounting errors)

The following errors in the accounting records of the Reed & Kinsey Partnership were discovered on January 10, 1996:

Year of Error	Ending Inventories Overstated	Depreciation Understated	Accrued Rent Revenue Not Recorded	Accrued Interest Expense Not Recorded
1993	$20,000		$ 6,000	
1994		$5,000	22,000	
1995	24,000			$2,000

The partners share net income and losses as follows: 40%, Reed; 60%, Kinsey.

1. Prepare a correcting journal entry on January 10, 1996, assuming that the books were closed for 1995.
2. Prepare a correcting journal entry on January 10, 1996, assuming that the books are still open for 1995 and that the partnership uses the perpetual inventory system.

Exercise 22—18 (Analysis of errors)

State the effect of each of the following errors made in 1995 on the balance sheets and the income statements prepared in 1995 and 1996:

(a) The ending inventory is understated as a result of an error in the count of goods on hand.
(b) The ending inventory is overstated as a result of the inclusion of goods acquired and held on a consignment basis. No purchase was recorded on the books.
(c) A purchase of merchandise at the end of 1995 is not recorded until payment is made for the goods in 1996; the goods purchased were included in the inventory at the end of 1995.

(d) A sale of merchandise at the end of 1995 is not recorded until cash is received for the goods in 1996; the goods sold were excluded from the inventory at the end of 1995.
(e) Goods shipped to consignees in 1995 were reported as sales; goods in the hands of consignees at the end of 1995 were not recognized for inventory purposes; sale of such goods in 1996 and collections on such sales were recorded as credits to the receivables established with consignees in 1995.
(f) The total of one week's sales during 1995 was credited to Gain on Sales—Machinery.
(g) No depreciation is taken in 1995 for equipment sold in April 1995. The company reports on a calender-year basis and computes depreciation to the nearest month.
(h) No depreciation is taken in 1995 for equipment purchased in October 1995. The company reports on a calender-year basis and computes depreciation to the nearest month.
(i) Customer notes receivable are debited to Accounts Receivable.

Exercise 22—19 (Error and change in accounting principle)
Comparative statements for Bodie Corporation are as follows:

Bodie Corporation
Income Statement and Statement of Retained Earnings
For the Years Ended December 31

	1995	1994
Sales	$4,600,000	$4,350,000
Cost of goods sold	2,346,000	2,305,500
Gross profit	$2,254,000	$2,044,500
Expenses	1,598,000	1,533,000
Net income	$ 656,000	$ 511,500
Beginning retained earnings	$1,441,000	$1,077,500
Net income	656,000	511,500
Dividends	(157,000)	(148,000)
Ending retained earnings	$1,940,000	$1,441,000

In 1995, Bodie Corporation discovers that ending inventory for 1994 was understated by $11,000. In addition, Bodie decides to change its depreciation method from double-declining-balance to straight-line. The differences in the two depreciation methods for the assets involved are as follows:

	1995	1994
Double-declining-balance	$358,400	$448,000
Straight-line	350,000	350,000

Expenses in the income statements presented above include depreciation based on the double-declining-balance method.

Prepare comparative income and retained earnings statements for 1994 and 1995. Ignore income tax effects, and assume the 1995 books have not been closed.

Exercise 22—20 (Journal entries to correct accounts)
The first audit of the books for the Calienti Corporation was made for the year ended December 31, 1996. In reviewing the books, the auditor discovered that certain adjustments had been overlooked at the end of 1995 and 1996 and also that other items had been improperly recorded. Omissions and other failures for each year are summarized as follows.

	December 31,	
	1995	1996
Sales salaries payable	$1,300	$1,100
Interest receivable	325	215
Prepaid insurance	450	300
Advances from customers (Collections from customers had been included in sales but should have been recognized as advances from customers, since goods were not shipped until the following year.)	1,750	2,500
Equipment (Expenditures had been recognized as repairs but should have been recognized as cost of equipment; the depreciation rate on such equipment is 10% per year, but depreciation in the year of the expenditure is to be recognized at 5%.)	1,400	1,200

Prepare journal entries to correct revenue and expense accounts for 1996 and record assets and liabilities that require recognition on the balance sheet as of December 31, 1996. Assume the nominal accounts for 1996 have not yet been closed into the income summary account.

Exercise 22—21 (Error analysis)

In early 1995, while reviewing Huffman, Inc.'s 1994 financial records, Huffman's accountant discovered several errors. For each of the errors listed below, indicate the effect on net income (i.e., understatement, overstatement, or no effect) for both 1994 and 1995, assuming no correction is made and the company uses a periodic system for inventory.

1. Certain items of ending inventory were accidentally not counted at the end of 1994.
2. Machinery was sold in May of 1994, but the company continued to deduct depreciation for the remainder of 1994 although the asset was removed from the books in May.
3. 1994 year-end purchases of inventory were not recorded until the beginning of 1995 although the inventory was correctly counted at the end of 1994.
4. Goods sold on account in 1994 were not recorded as sales until 1995.
5. Insurance costs incurred but unpaid in 1994 were not recorded until paid in 1995.
6. Interest receivable in 1994 was not recorded until 1995.
7. 1994 year-end purchases were not recorded until the beginning of 1995. The inventory associated with these purchases was omitted from the ending inventory count in 1994.
8. A check for January 1995 rent was received and recorded as revenue at the end of 1994.
9. Interest accrued in 1994 on a note payable was not recorded until it was paid in 1995.

PROBLEMS

Problem 22—22 (Change in accounting principle)

Yuki, Inc., acquired the following assets on January 3, 1993:

Equipment, estimated useful life 5 years; residual value $13,000	$513,000
Building, estimated useful life 40 years; no residual value	900,000

The equipment has been depreciated using the sum-of-the-years-digits method for the first 3 years. In 1996, the company decided to change the method of depreciation to straight-line. No change was made in the estimated service life or residual value. The company also decided to change the total estimated useful life of the building from 40 to 45 years with no change in the estimated residual value. The building is depreciated on the straight-line method. The company has 200,000 shares of capital stock outstanding. Partial results of operations for 1996 and 1995 are as follows:

	1996	1995
Income before cumulative effect of change in computing depreciation for 1996; depreciation for 1996 was computed on a straight-line basis for equipment and building*	$890,000	$856,000
Earnings per share before cumulative effect of change in computing depreciation for 1996	$4.45	$4.28

*The computations for depreciation expense for 1996 and 1995 for the building were based on the original estimate of useful life of 40 years.

Instructions:

1. Compute the cumulative effect of the change in accounting principle to be reported in the income statement for 1996, and prepare the journal entry to record the change. (Ignore income tax effects.)
2. Present comparative data for the years 1995 and 1996, starting with income before cumulative effect of accounting change. Prepare pro forma data. (Ignore income tax effects.)

Problem 22—23 (Accounting changes)

Barney Corporation has released the following condensed financial statements for 1994 and 1995 and has prepared the following proposed statements for 1996:

Barney Corporation
Comparative Balance Sheet
December 31

	1996	1995	1994
Assets			
Current assets	$249,000	$219,000	$165,000
Land	60,000	45,000	30,000
Equipment	150,000	150,000	150,000
Accumulated depreciation—equipment	(45,000)	(30,000)	(15,000)
Total assets	$414,000	$384,000	$330,000
Liabilities and Stockholders' Equity			
Current liabilities	$177,000	$177,000	$147,000
Common stock	60,000	60,000	60,000
Retained earnings	177,000	147,000	123,000
Total liabilities and stockholders' equity	$414,000	$384,000	$330,000

Barney Corporation
Comparative Income Statement
For Years Ended December 31

	1996	1995	1994
Sales	$315,000	$300,000	$255,000
Cost of goods sold	$240,000	$225,000	$189,000
Other expenses except depreciation	30,000	36,000	33,000
Depreciation expense—equipment	15,000	15,000	15,000
Total costs	$285,000	$276,000	$237,000
Net income	$ 30,000	$ 24,000	$ 18,000

Barney Corporation acquired the equipment for $150,000 on January 1, 1994, and began depreciating the equipment over a 10-year estimated useful life with no salvage value, using the straight-line method of depreciation. The double-declining-balance method of depreciation, under the same assumptions, would have required the following depreciation expense:

1994	20% × $150,000 = $30,000
1995	20% × $120,000 = $24,000
1996	20% × $ 96,000 = $19,200

Instructions: In comparative format, prepare a balance sheet and a combined statement of income and retained earnings for 1996, giving effect to the following changes. Ignore any income tax effect. Barney Corporation has 10,000 shares of common stock outstanding. The following situations are independent of each other.

(a) For justifiable reasons, Barney Corporation changed to the double-declining-balance method of depreciation in 1996. The effect of the change should be included in the net income of the period in which the change was made.
(b) During 1996, Barney Corporation determined that the equipment was fast becoming obsolete and decided to change the estimated useful life from 10 years to 5 years. The books for 1996 had not yet been closed.
(c) During 1996, Barney Corporation found that additional equipment, also acquired on January 1, 1994, costing $24,000, had been recorded in the land account and had not been depreciated. This error should be corrected using straight-line depreciation over a 10-year period.

Problem 22—24 (Change in accounting estimate and principle)
The following information relates to depreciable assets of Brillantez Electronics:

(a) Machine A was purchased for $30,000 on January 1, 1991. The entire cost was expensed in the year of purchase. The machine had a 15-year useful life and no residual value.
(b) Machine B cost $105,000 and was purchased January 1, 1992. The straight-line method of depreciation was used. At the time of purchase, the expected useful life was 12 years with no residual value. In 1996, it was estimated that the total useful life of the asset would be only 8 years and that there would be a $5,000 residual value.
(c) Building A was purchased January 1, 1993, for $600,000. The straight-line method of depreciation was originally chosen. The building was expected to be useful for 20 years and to have zero residual value. In 1996, a change was made from the straight-line depreciation method to the sum-of-the-years-digits method. Estimates relating to the useful life and residual value remained the same.

Income before depreciation expense was $520,000 for 1996. Depreciation on assets other than those described totaled $50,000. Net income for 1995 was $415,000.

Instructions: (Ignore all income tax effects.)
1. Prepare all entries for 1996 relating to depreciable assets.
2. Prepare partial income statements for 1995 and 1996. Begin with income before the cumulative effects of any accounting changes. Show all computations.

Problem 22—25 (Change in estimate and accounting principle)
Johnston Doors began operations on January 4, 1993. During the first month, Johnston purchased the following assets, all of which were depreciated using the straight-line method.

Equipment:	Cost, $48,000; estimated salvage value, $5,000; estimated useful life, 10 years.
Building:	Cost, $85,000; estimated salvage value, $15,000; estimated useful life, 15 years.

At the end of 1996, Johnston reviewed its accounting records and determined that the building should have a total useful life of 20 years. In addition, because of significant wear on the equipment, Johnston proposes changing to the sum-of-the-years-digits method for depreciating equipment.

Johnston also has found that its estimated bad debt expense has been consistently higher than actual bad debts. Management proposes lowering the percentage from 3% of credit sales to 2%. If 2% had been used since 1993, the balance in Allowance for Doubtful Accounts at the beginning of 1996 would have been $3,200 rather than $6,900. Credit sales for 1996 totaled $250,000, and accounts written off as uncollectible during 1996 totaled $5,500.

Instructions: (Ignore income tax effects.)

1. What is the proper accounting treatment for each of the proposed changes?
2. Prepare the journal entry necessary to record the cumulative adjustment associated with changing depreciation methods.
3. Prepare the journal entries necessary to record the depreciation expense for the year for both equipment and buildings.
4. Prepare the journal entry to record the write-off of accounts deemed uncollectible during 1996 and the adjusting entry at year-end to record the bad debt expense for the period.
5. What adjustment is made to the allowance account at the beginning of 1996 as a result of changing the bad debt percentage?

Problem 22—26 (Reporting accounting changes)

Listed below are three independent, unrelated sets of facts concerning accounting changes.

Case 1 The Runyon Development Company determined that the amortization rate on its patents is unacceptably low due to current advances in technology. The company decided at the beginning of 1996 to increase the amortization rate on all existing patents from 10% to 20%. Patents purchased on January 1, 1991, for $3,000,000 had a book value of $1,500,000 on January 1, 1996.

Case 2 Cartwright Corporation decided on January 1, 1996, to change its depreciation method for manufacturing equipment from an accelerated method to the straight-line method. The straight-line method is to be used for new acquisitions as well as for previously acquired equipment. It has been determined that the excess of accelerated depreciation over straight-line depreciation for the years 1993 through 1995 totals $343,000.

Case 3 On December 31, 1995, Enterprise Inc. owned 35% of the Packard Company, at which time Enterprise reported its investment using the equity method. During 1996, Enterprise increased its ownership in Packard by 25%. Accordingly, Enterprise is planning to prepare consolidated financial statements for Enterprise and Packard for the year ended December 31, 1996.

Instructions: For each of the situations described:

1. Identify the type of accounting change.
2. Explain how the accounting change should be reported in 1996. Where applicable, prepare the journal entries to record the accounting change. (Ignore income tax effects.)
3. Explain the effect of the change on the December 31, 1996, balance sheet and the 1996 income statement.

Problem 22—27 (Change in accounting principle)

During 1996, All Seasons Company changed its method of depreciating equipment from an accelerated depreciation method to the straight-line method. The following information shows the effect of this change:

Year	Net Income as Reported	Excess of Accelerated Depreciation Over Straight-Line Depreciation	Assumed Tax Effects
Prior to 1994		$ 68,000	$27,200
1994	$190,000	14,000	5,600
1995	210,000	17,000	6,800

Instructions:

1. Compute the effect of the change in accounting principle on income (net of tax).
2. Prepare a partial income statement for 1996 assuming income before extraordinary items was $225,000 and an extraordinary loss of $21,600 (net of $14,400 income tax reduction) was incurred. Assume 100,000 shares of common stock are outstanding.
3. Present pro forma income data for the years 1994-1996. Assume 100,000 shares of common stock were outstanding in all years.

Problem 22—28 (Change in estimate)

On January 3, 1995, Sandy's Fashions, a chain of moderately priced women's clothing, purchased a large quantity of personal computers. The cost of these computers was $120,000. On the date of purchase, Sandy's management estimated that the computers would last approximately 5 years and would have a salvage value at that time of $12,000. The company used the double-declining-balance method to depreciate the computers.

During January of 1996, Sandy's management realized that technological advancements had made the computers virtually obsolete and that they would have to be replaced. Management proposed changing the estimated useful life of the computers to 2 years.

Instructions: Prepare the journal entry necessary at the end of 1996 to record depreciation on the computers.

Problem 22—29 (Change in accounting principle—LIFO to FIFO)

On January 1, 1996, Overland Inc. decided to change from the LIFO method of inventory costing to the FIFO method. The reported income for the 4 years Overland had been in business was as follows:

1992	$250,000	1994	$310,000
1993	$260,000	1995	$330,000

Analysis of the inventory records disclosed that the following inventories were on hand at the end of each year as valued under both the LIFO and FIFO methods.

	LIFO Method	FIFO Method
January 1, 1992	-0-	-0-
December 31, 1992	$228,000	$256,000
December 31, 1993	240,000	238,000
December 31, 1994	270,000	302,000
December 31, 1995	288,000	352,000

The income tax effect of the change in inventory method is assumed to be as follows:

1992	$ 11,200	1994	$13,600
1993	$(12,000)	1995	$12,800

Instructions:

1. Compute the restated net income for the years 1992-1995.
2. Prepare the retained earnings statement for Overland Inc. for 1996 if the 1995 ending balance had been previously reported at $600,000, 1996 net income using the FIFO method is $360,000, and dividends of $200,000 were paid during 1996.

Problem 22—30 (Change in principle—inventory methods)

Shoestring, Inc. had the following pre-tax net income under three different inventory methods:

Year	FIFO	LIFO	Weighted Average
Prior to 1993	$331,000	$264,000	$282,000
1993	117,000	108,000	114,000
1994	129,000	114,000	123,000
1995	133,000	126,000	129,000

Assume that the following independent changes are made during 1995:

1. Shoestring, Inc. changes its inventory method from FIFO to LIFO.
2. Shoestring, Inc. changes its inventory method from LIFO to FIFO.
3. Shoestring, Inc. changes its inventory method from FIFO to weighted average.

Instructions:

For each of the changes described above, prepare the journal entries necessary to account for the change. Also show the appropriate pro forma or restated comparative income statement and/or statement of retained earnings for the years 1993 through 1995. Assume a tax rate of 40% for all years, a beginning retained earnings balance of $483,200 in 1993, and no payments for dividends.

Problem 22—31 (Correction of errors)

Hiatt Textile Corporation is planning an expansion of its current plant facilities. Hiatt is in the process of obtaining a loan at City Bank. The bank has requested audited financial statements. Hiatt has never been audited before. It has prepared the following comparative financial statements for the years ended December 31, 1996 and 1995.

Hiatt Textile Corporation
Comparative Balance Sheet
December 31, 1996 and 1995

	1996	1995
Assets		
Current assets:		
Cash	$ 602,500	$ 400,000
Accounts receivable	980,000	740,000
Allowance for doubtful accounts	(92,500)	(45,000)
Inventory	517,500	505,000
Total current assets	$2,007,500	$1,600,000
Plant assets:		
Property, plant, and equipment	$ 417,500	$ 423,750
Accumulated depreciation	(304,000)	(266,000)
Total plant assets	$ 113,500	$ 157,750
Total assets	$2,121,000	$1,757,750
Liabilities and Stockholders' Equity		
Liabilities:		
Accounts payable	$ 303,500	$ 490,250
Stockholders' equity:		
Common stock, par value $25; authorized, 30,000 shares; issued and outstanding, 26,000 shares	$ 650,000	$ 650,000
Retained earnings	1,167,500	617,500
Total stockholders' equity	$1,817,500	$1,267,500
Total liabilities and stockholders' equity	$2,121,000	$1,757,750

Hiatt Textile Corporation
Comparative Income Statement
For the Years Ended December 31, 1996 and 1995

	1996	1995
Sales	$2,500,000	$2,250,000
Cost of goods sold	1,075,000	987,500
Gross margin	$1,425,000	$1,262,500
Operating expenses	$ 575,000	$ 512,500
General and administrative expenses	300,000	262,500
	$ 875,000	$ 775,000
Net income	$ 550,000	$ 487,500

The following facts were disclosed during the audit:

(a) On January 20, 1995, Hiatt had charged a 5-year fire insurance premium to expense. The total premium amounted to $15,500.

(b) Over the last two years, the amount of loss due to bad debts has steadily decreased. Hiatt has decided to reduce the amount of bad debt expense from 2% to 1 ½% of sales, beginning with 1996. (A charge of 2% has already been made for 1996.)

(c) The inventory account (maintained on a periodic basis) has been in error the last 2 years. The errors were as follows:

1995: Ending inventory overstated by $37,750
1996: Ending inventory overstated by $49,500

(d) A machine costing $75,000, purchased on January 4, 1995, was incorrectly charged to operating expense. The machine had a useful life of 10 years and a residual value of $12,500. The straight-line depreciation method is used by Hiatt.

Instructions:

1. Prepare the journal entries to correct the books at December 31, 1996. The books for 1996 have not been closed. (Ignore income taxes.)
2. Prepare a schedule showing the computation of corrected net income for the years ended December 31, 1995 and 1996, assuming that any adjustments are to be reported on the comparative statements for the two years. Begin your schedule with the net income for each year. (Ignore income taxes.)

Problem 22—32 (Analysis and correction of errors)

A CPA is engaged by the Alpine Corp. in 1996 to examine the books and records and to make whatever corrections are necessary. An examination of the accounts discloses the following:

(a) Dividends had been declared on December 15 in 1993 and 1994 but had not been entered in the books until paid.

(b) Improvements in buildings and equipment of $4,800 had been debited to expense at the end of April 1992. Improvements are estimated to have an 8-year life. The company uses the straight-line method in recording depreciation and computes depreciation to the nearest month.

(c) The physical inventory of merchandise had been understated by $1,500 at the end of 1993 and by $2,150 at the end of 1994.

(d) The merchandise inventories at the end of 1994 and 1995 did not include merchandise that was then in transit and to which the company had title. These shipments of $1,900 and $2,750 were recorded as purchases in January of 1995 and 1996 respectively.

(e) The company had failed to record sales commissions payable of $1,050 and $850 at the end of 1994 and 1995 respectively.

(f) The company had failed to recognize supplies on hand of $600 and $1,250 at the end of 1994 and 1995 respectively.

The retained earnings account appeared as follows on the date the CPA began the examination:

Account: RETAINED EARNINGS

Date		Item	Debit	Credit	Balance Debit	Balance Credit
1993						
Jan.	1	Balance				40,500
Dec.	31	Net income for year		9,000		49,500
1994						
Jan.	10	Dividends paid	7,500			42,000
Mar.	6	Stock sold—excess over par		16,000		58,000
Dec.	31	Net loss for year	5,600			52,400
1995						
Jan.	10	Dividends paid	7,500			44,900
Dec.	31	Net loss for year	6,200			38,700

Instructions:

1. Journalize the necessary corrections.
2. Prepare a statement of retained earnings covering the 3-year period beginning January 1, 1993. The statement should report the corrected retained earnings balance on January 1, 1993, the annual changes in the account, and the corrected retained earnings balances as of December 31, 1993, 1994, and 1995.
3. Set up an account for retained earnings before correction, and post correcting data to this account for part (1). Balance the account, showing the corrected retained earnings as of January 1, 1996.

Problem 22—33 (Accounting changes and correction of errors)

Stevens Company is in the process of adjusting its books at the end of 1996. Stevens' records reveal the following information:

(a) Stevens failed to accrue sales commissions at the end of 1994 and 1995 as follows:

1994	$27,000
1995	15,333

The sales commissions were paid in January of the following year.

(b) On December 31, 1996, Stevens changed its depreciation method for machinery from double-declining-balance to the straight-line method. Stevens has already recorded the 1996 depreciation using the double-declining-balance method. The following information also was provided:

	Double-Declining-Balance Depreciation	Straight-Line Depreciation	Depreciation Difference
Prior to 1996	$233,333	$133,333	$100,000
1996	40,000	33,333	6,667

(c) Errors in ending inventories for the last 3 years were discovered to be as follows:

1994	$43,333 understated
1995	56,667 understated
1996	10,000 overstated

The incorrect amount has already been recorded for 1996.

(d) Early in 1996, Stevens changed from the percentage-of-completion method of accounting for long-term construction contracts to the completed-contract method. The income for 1996 was recorded using the completed-contract method. The following information also was available:

	Pretax Income	
	Percentage of Completion	**Completed Contract**
Prior to 1996	$583,333	$166,667
1996	200,000	66,667

Instructions:

1. Prepare the necessary journal entries at December 31, 1996, to record the above information. Assume the books are still open for 1996. (Ignore all income tax effects.)
2. Assuming income from continuing operations before taxes of $500,000, taxes of $150,000 on operating income, and no applicable taxes on the cumulative effect of changing depreciation methods, prepare a partial income statement (beginning with income from continuing operations before taxes) for Stevens Company for 1996. (Ignore earnings per share.)
3. Assuming Retained Earnings at the beginning of 1996 was $1,985,000 and that dividends of $125,000 were declared during 1996, prepare a statement of retained earnings for Stevens Company, reflecting appropriate adjustments from (1). Assume no applicable taxes on the cumulative effect of changing to the completed-contract method.

Other Dimensions of Financial Reporting

CHAPTER 23

Earnings Per Share

CHAPTER TOPICS

- History of Earnings Per Share (EPS) Disclosure Requirements
- Simple and Complex Capital Structures
- Basic Earnings Per Share
- Fully Diluted Earnings Per Share
- Effect of Actual Exercise or Conversion
- Effect of Net Losses on EPS
- Computations for Multiple Potentially Dilutive Securities
- Primary Earnings Per Share
- Financial Statement Presentation
- Comprehensive Illustration Using Multiple Potentially Dilutive Securities (Appendix)

In Japan, stocks trade at an average of forty times their reported earnings per share. In the United States, that average is approximately fourteen (the market value of a firm's stock divided by the firm's earnings per share is called the price-earnings ratio). *The Wall Street Journal* reports price-earnings ratios on a daily basis because analysts consider the price-earnings ratio when evaluating stocks. While the market determines the ultimate trading price of stocks, the earnings per share figure provided by accountants can significantly influence a firm's perceived value.

As indicated in Chapter 2, a primary objective of financial reporting is to provide information that is useful in making credit and investment decisions. Investors are interested in gauging how well a company is performing in comparison with other companies and with itself over time. When evaluating a company, it is not enough to know that net income is increasing or decreasing. Investors are concerned with how income is changing relative to their investment and to the current stock market valuation.

In an attempt to include both income and investment information in the same measurement, a computation known as **earnings per share** has been developed. While this measurement has some limitations, which will be discussed later in this chapter, its presentation on the income statement has been required by generally accepted accounting principles since 1969.

Potential investors might use the earnings per share figure when choosing among different investment options. For example, if Company A earns $3 per share on common stock with a $21-per-share market price, and Company B earns $6 per share on common stock with a $54-per-share market value, an investor can state that Company A stock is selling at seven times earnings and Company B stock is selling at nine times earnings. Thus, investors as a group perceive Company B stock to have more growth potential than Company A. If an individual investor disagrees with this market evaluation, Company A stock may seem to be a better buy because of its lower market price relative to earnings.

Investors are also interested in dividends and can use earnings per share data to compute a **dividend payout percentage (or payout rate).** This percentage is computed by dividing earnings per share into dividends per share. Thus, if Company A in the previous example pays a dividend of $2 per share, and Company B pays $3 per share, the payout percentage would be 66 $^{2}/_{3}$% for Company A and 50% for Company B.

Earnings per share data receive wide recognition in the annual reports issued by companies, in the press, and in financial reporting publications. This measurement is frequently regarded as an important determinant of the market price of common stock.

EVOLUTION OF REQUIREMENTS FOR EARNINGS PER SHARE DISCLOSURE

Earnings per share figures were historically computed and used primarily by financial analysts. Sometimes the computation was disclosed in the unaudited section of the annual report along with a message from the company's president. However, because this measurement was not reviewed by an independent third party, figures used to develop earnings per share were often different from those attested to by the auditor. The situation became more complex when some companies and analysts began computing earnings per share not only on the basis of common shares actually outstanding, but also on the basis of what shares would be outstanding if certain convertible securities were converted and if certain stock options were exercised. Usually the conversion or exercise terms were very favorable to the holders of these securities, and earnings per share would decline if common stock were issued upon conversion or exercise. This result, a reduced earnings per share, is referred to as a **dilution of earnings.** In some cases, however, the exercise of options or conversion of securities might result in an increased earnings per share. This result is referred to as an **antidilution of earnings.** Securities that would lead to dilution are referred to as **dilutive securities,** and those that would lead to antidilution are referred to as **antidilutive securities.** Rational investors would not convert or exercise antidilutive securities because they could do better by purchasing common stock in the marketplace.

These forward-looking computations of earnings per share attempted to provide information as to what future earnings per share *might* be assuming conversions and exercises took place. Because these "as if" conditions were based on assumptions, they could be computed in several ways. Recognizing the diversity of reporting practices, the Accounting Principles Board became involved in establishing guidelines for the computation and disclosure of earnings per share figures. The result was the issuance in 1969 of APB Opinion No. 15, "Earnings Per Share," which concluded:

The Board believes that the significance attached by investors and others to earnings per share data, together with the importance of evaluating the data in conjunction with the financial statements, requires that such data be presented prominently in the financial statements. The Board has therefore concluded that earnings per share or net loss per share data should be shown on the face of the income statement. The extent of the data to be presented and the captions used will vary with the complexity of the company's capital structure. . . .[1]

For the first few years after Opinion No. 15 was issued, all business entities were required to include earnings per share data in their income statements. However, in 1978, the FASB issued Statement No. 21, which eliminated this requirement for nonpublic entities. A nonpublic company is defined as any enterprise other than "one (a) whose debt or equity securities trade in a public market on a foreign or domestic stock exchange or in the over-the-counter market . . . or (b) that is required to file financial statements with the Securities and Exchange Commission."[2]

In the process of establishing rules for computing earnings per share, the Accounting Principles Board felt it necessary to be very specific about how future-oriented "as if" figures were to be computed. Many interpretations and amendments were issued with the intent of clarifying the computations for a variety of securities and under varied circumstances. In some areas, the rules became arbitrary and complex, and the resulting earnings per share computations have received much criticism as to their usefulness. Indeed, for companies with complex capital structures, the historical or **basic earnings per share** figure based on actual shares of common stock outstanding was not even reported. In its place, the APB substituted two earnings per share amounts: (1) **primary earnings per share,** based on the assumed conversion or exercise of certain securities identified as common stock equivalents and (2) **fully diluted earnings per share,** based on the assumed conversions of all convertible securities or exercise of all stock options that would reduce or dilute primary earnings per share.

Although more than 25 years have passed since APB Opinion No. 15 was issued, little evidence to support the usefulness of these forward-type earnings per share figures has emerged. Indeed, many critical articles have appeared in print suggesting this measurement be modified or eliminated from reporting.[3] Shortly after APB Opinion No. 15 was issued, the Canadian Institute of Chartered Accountants reviewed what the APB had done and concluded that only a historical or basic earnings per share and a fully diluted earnings per share had potential value. Many countries followed the Canadian lead, and thus internationally, two different approaches to measuring and reporting earnings per share have emerged. In an attempt to reduce the number of different reporting requirements of its constituent countries, the International Accounting Standards Committee (IASC) in 1993 appointed a steering committee to consider earnings per share. The committee concluded that the Canadian approach of a basic and fully diluted earnings per share was preferred to the American primary and fully diluted earnings per share.

In June 1993, the Financial Accounting Standards Board issued a prospectus suggesting that a project be added to the FASB's agenda to consider the IASC position on earnings per share and to determine the wisdom of modifying APB Opinion No. 15. The prospectus suggests a wide range of options—from adopting the IASC position to reopening the entire subject of earnings per share with the objective of issuing a new standard to replace the old opinion. In March 1994, the FASB added the topic of earnings per share to its agenda,

1. *Opinions of the Accounting Principles Board No. 15,* "Earnings Per Share" (New York: American Institute of Certified Public Accountants, 1969), par. 12.

2. *Statement of Financial Accounting Standards No. 21,* "Suspension of the Reporting of Earnings Per Share and Segment Information by Nonpublic Enterprises" (Stamford: Financial Accounting Standards Board, 1978), par. 13.

3. For example, see R. David Mautz, Jr. and Thomas Jeffrey Hogan, "Earnings Per Share Reporting: Time for an Overhaul?" *Accounting Horizons,* September 1989, pp. 21-27.

anticipating issuance of a new standard in 1995. Although a new standard will not be issued before this edition of the text is published, strong sentiment exists to eliminate primary earnings per share and replace it with an historical-based basic earnings per share. Fully diluted earnings per share would also be required for companies with a complex capital structure.

In anticipation of a change in standards, basic earnings per share for either a simple or a complex capital structure is discussed first, followed by fully diluted earnings per share. Primary earnings per share, with the concept of common stock equivalency, is presented last as a further refinement of the dilution concept.

SIMPLE AND COMPLEX CAPITAL STRUCTURES

The capital structure of a company may be classified as simple or complex. If a company has only common stock, or common and nonconvertible preferred stock outstanding, and there are no convertible securities, stock options, warrants, or other rights outstanding, it is classified as a company with a **simple capital structure.** Earnings per share is computed by dividing the net income for the period by the weighted average number of common shares outstanding for the period. No future-oriented "as if" conditions need to be considered. If net income includes extraordinary gains or losses or other below-the-line items, as discussed in Chapter 4, a separate earnings per share figure is required for each major component of income, as well as for net income. These historical earnings per share amounts are referred to as **basic earnings per share.**

Even if convertible securities, stock options, warrants or other rights do exist, the capital structure may be classified as simple if there is no potential dilution to earnings per share from the conversion or exercise of these items. Potential earnings per share dilution exists if the earnings per share would decrease or the loss per share would increase as a result of the conversion of securities or exercise of stock options, warrants, or other rights based on the conditions existing at the financial statement date. A company with potential earnings per share dilution is considered to have a **complex capital structure.**

BASIC EARNINGS PER SHARE

The basic earnings per share computation presents no problem when only common stock has been issued and the number of shares outstanding has remained the same for the entire period. The numerator is the net income (loss), and the denominator is the number of shares outstanding for the entire period. Frequently, however, either the numerator, the denominator, or both must be adjusted because of the circumstances described in the following sections.

Issuance or Reacquisition of Common Stock

When common shares have been issued or have been reacquired by a company during a period, the resources available to the company have changed, and this change should affect earnings. Under these circumstances, a weighted average for shares outstanding should be computed.

The weighted average number of shares may be computed by determining month-shares of outstanding stock and dividing by 12 to obtain the weighted average for the year. For example, if a company has 10,000 shares outstanding at the beginning of the year, issues 5,000 more shares on May 1, and reacquires 2,000 shares on November 1, the weighted average number of shares would be computed as follows. Note that a separate period computation is required each time stock is sold or reacquired.

			Month-Shares
Jan. 1 to May 1		10,000 × 4 months	40,000
May 1 to Nov. 1	(10,000 + 5,000)	15,000 × 6 months	90,000
Nov. 1 to Dec. 31	(15,000 − 2,000)	13,000 × 2 months	26,000
Total month-shares			156,000
Weighted average number of shares: 156,000 ÷ 12			13,000

The same answer can be obtained by applying a weight to each period equivalent to the portion of the year since the last change in shares outstanding, as follows:

Jan. 1 to May 1	10,000 × 4/12 year	3,333
May 1 to Nov. 1	15,000 × 6/12 year	7,500
Nov. 1 to Dec. 31	13,000 × 2/12 year	2,167
Weighted average number of shares		13,000

If stock transactions occurred during a month, the weighted average computation could be made either on a daily basis or to the nearest month. In examples and end-of-chapter material, assume computations to the nearest month unless otherwise specified.

Stock Dividends and Stock Splits

When the number of common shares outstanding has changed during a period as a result of a stock dividend, a stock split, or a reverse split, a retroactive recognition of this change must be made in determining the weighted average number of shares outstanding. To illustrate, assume that a company had 2,600 shares outstanding as of January 1 and that the following events affecting common stock occurred during the year:

Date	Economic Event	Change in Shares Outstanding
Feb. 1	Exercise of stock option	+ 400
May 1	10% stock dividend (3,000 × 10%)	+ 300
Sep. 1	Sale of stock for cash	+1,200
Nov. 1	Purchase of treasury stock	− 400
Dec. 15	3-for-1 stock split	+8,200

The computation of the weighted average number of shares for the year would be as follows:

Dates	Shares Outstanding		Stock Dividend		Stock Split		Portion of Year		Weighted Average
Jan. 1 to Feb. 1	2,600	×	1.10	×	3.0	×	1/12	=	715
Feb. 1—option	400								
Feb. 1 to May 1	3,000	×	1.10	×	3.0	×	3/12	=	2,475
May 1—stock dividend	300								
May 1 to Sep. 1	3,300			×	3.0	×	4/12	=	3,300
Sep. 1—sale	1,200								
Sep. 1 to Nov. 1	4,500			×	3.0	×	2/12	=	2,250
Nov. 1—treasury stock	(400)								
Nov. 1 to Dec. 1	4,100			×	3.0	×	1/12	=	1,025
Dec. 1—split	8,200								
Dec. 1 to Dec. 31	12,300					×	1/12	=	1,025
Weighted average number of shares									10,790

In the preceding illustration, the shares outstanding for January 1 to May 1 were multiplied by 1.10 to reflect the 10% stock dividend, and the shares outstanding for January 1 to December 1 were multiplied by 3 to reflect the 3-for-1 stock split. When comparative financial statements are presented, the common shares outstanding for all periods shown must be adjusted to reflect any stock dividend or stock split in the current period.

Only with the retroactive recognition of changes in the number of shares can earnings per share presentations for prior periods be stated on a basis comparable with the earnings per share presentation for the current period. Similar retroactive adjustments must be made even if a stock dividend or stock split occurs after the end of the period but before the financial statements are prepared; disclosure of this situation should be made in a note to the financial statements.

Preferred Stock Included in Capital Structure

Basic earnings per share reflects only income available to common stockholders and does not include preferred stock. It would be inappropriate to report earnings per share on preferred stock in view of the limited dividend rights of such stock. When a capital structure includes preferred stock, dividends on preferred stock should be deducted from income before extraordinary or other special items and from net income in arriving at the earnings related to common shares. If preferred dividends are not cumulative, only the dividends declared on preferred stock during the period are deducted. If preferred dividends are cumulative, the full amount of dividends on preferred stock for the period, whether declared or not, should be deducted from income in arriving at the earnings or loss balance related to the common stock. If there is a loss for the period, preferred dividends for the period, including any undeclared dividends on cumulative preferred stock, are added to the loss in arriving at the full loss related to the common stock.

To illustrate the computation of earnings per share at December 31, 1997, for a company with a simple capital structure for a comparative two-year period, assume the following data:

Summary of Changes in Capital Balances

	8% Cumulative Preferred Stock $100 Par		Common Stock No Par		Retained Earnings
	Shares	**Amount**	**Shares**	**Amount**	
Dec. 31, 1995, balances	10,000	$1,000,000	200,000	$1,000,000	$4,000,000
June 30, 1996, issuance of 100,000 shares of common stock			100,000	600,000	
June 30, 1996, dividend on preferred stock, 8%					(80,000)
June 30, 1996, dividend on common stock, $.30					(90,000)
Dec. 31, 1996, net income for year, including extraordinary gain of $75,000					380,000
Dec. 31, 1996, balances	10,000	$1,000,000	300,000	$1,600,000	$4,210,000
May 1, 1997, 50% stock dividend on common stock			150,000	800,000	(800,000)
Dec, 31, 1997, net loss for year					(55,000)
Dec. 31, 1997, balances	10,000	$1,000,000	450,000	$2,400,000	$3,355,000

Because comparative statements are presented, the denominator of weighted shares outstanding for 1996 must be adjusted for the 50% stock dividend issued in 1997 as follows:

1996

Jan. 1-June 30	200,000 × 1.5 (50% stock dividend in 1997) × 6/12 year	150,000
July 1-Dec. 31	200,000 + 100,000 (issuance of stock on June 30, 1996) × 1.5 (50% stock dividend in 1997) × 6/12 year	225,000
		375,000

1997

Jan. 1-May 1	300,000 × 1.5 (50% stock dividend in 1997) × 4/12 year	150,000
May 1-Dec. 31	450,000 (300,000 + 150,000) × 8/12 year	300,000
		450,000

Continuing the example, earnings per share for 1996 is shown separately for income from continuing operations, the extraordinary gain, and net income. The preferred dividends must be deducted from both income from continuing operations and net income in computing earnings per share for these income components. For 1997, the reported net loss must be increased by the full amount of the preferred dividend even though the dividend was not declared. If the preferred stock were noncumulative, no adjustment for the undeclared preferred dividend would be necessary in 1997. The adjusted income (loss) figures for computing basic earnings per share are determined as follows:

1996

Income from continuing operations ($380,000 net income − $75,000 extraordinary gain)	$305,000
Less preferred dividend	80,000
Income from continuing operations identified with common stock	$225,000
Net income	$380,000
Less preferred dividend	80,000
Net income identified with common stock	$300,000

1997

Net loss	$ 55,000
Add preferred dividend	80,000
Net loss identified with common stock	$135,000

The basic earnings per share amounts can now be computed as follows:

1996

Basic earnings per common share:	
Continuing operations ($225,000 ÷ 375,000)	$.60
Extraordinary gain ($75,000 ÷ 375,000)	.20
Net income per share ($300,000 ÷ 375,000)	$.80

1997

Basic loss per share ($135,000 ÷ 450,000)	$.30

Forget Earnings Per Share?

If earnings per share influences the value at which stocks are traded, then corporate executives should seek to maximize reported EPS. Joel Stern, managing partner of a Manhattan-based consulting firm, writes that most executives strive to do exactly that. He points out, however, that "investors care about both the quality and quantity of earnings in setting stock price; EPS represents only half the story."

An example of the choice of inventory costing methods illustrates the dangers associated with focusing solely on the quantity of earnings. If prices are rising and a firm chooses FIFO as its inventory method, net income will be higher than under the LIFO method. However, the adoption of LIFO results in actual cash savings to the firm in the form of lower taxes. Research demonstrates that the market responds more favorably to the adoption of LIFO because of the quality of the reported earnings.

Stern concludes that investors should focus on economic value—the cash-generating ability of a firm—rather than "those bookkeeping entries that have no bearing on economic values."

Questions:

1. FASB Concept Statement No. 1 states that financial reporting should provide information to help users in assessing the future cash flows of a business. It also states that accrual accounting provides a better indication of future cash flows than does cash-basis accounting. How would Mr. Stern respond to the FASB's position?
2. Cite several ways in which earnings per share can be manipulated by management to portray a more favorable performance by a firm than is actually the case.
3. How should the market react to these "accounting tricks"?
4. Why don't accountants provide solely cash-basis information?

Source: Joel Stern, "Think Cash and Risk—Forget Earnings Per Share," *Planning Review,* January-February 1988.

FULLY DILUTED EARNINGS PER SHARE

When a company has a complex capital structure, additional information may be provided to users of the financial statements to reflect all potential dilution arising from the assumption that additional common stock is issued from exercise of options or conversion of convertible securities. APB Opinion No. 15 identifies this earnings per share figure as **fully diluted,** implying a maximum dilution that could occur. Dilution occurs if inclusion of a potentially dilutive security reduces the basic earnings per share or increases the basic loss per share. If the opposite results occur, the security is classified as an **antidilutive security.** In general, securities classified as antidilutive are not included in computing fully diluted earnings per share.

The adjustment of the numerator and/or denominator of basic earnings per share to compute fully diluted earnings per share depends on the nature of the security and its terms. The adjustment process consists of a "what if" scenario. What would happen to the numerator and denominator if options had been exercised and convertible securities had been converted at the beginning of the year being evaluated. The two major types of potentially dilutive securities are (1) common stock options, warrants, and rights and (2) convertible bonds and convertible preferred stock. Because the purpose of a fully diluted earnings per share figure is to disclose how exercise or conversion would affect future earnings per share, all computations of fully diluted earnings per share are made as if the exercise or conversion took place at the beginning of the company's fiscal year or at the issue date of the stock option or convertible security, whichever comes later. Thus, if a convertible bond has been outstanding the entire year, the fully diluted earnings per share computation will be made as if the conversion of the bonds took place at the beginning of the year. However, if the convertible bond is issued on May 1, and the fiscal year is the calendar year, all conversion computations will be made for 8 months, or $2/3$ of a year.

APB Opinion No. 15 specified that fully diluted earnings per share needs to be disclosed only if it is materially different from basic earnings per share. The opinion defined this materiality as 3%. Because the FASB is tentatively planning to discontinue this materiality test, the text and end-of-chapter materials will include fully diluted earnings per share as long as it is dilutive regardless of its degree of materiality. The computation of fully diluted earnings per share for each of the two basic types of potentially dilutive securities will be illustrated separately.

Stock Options, Warrants, and Rights

As explained in Chapter 15, stock options, warrants, and rights provide no cash yield to investors, but have value because they permit the acquisition of common stock at specified prices for a certain period of time. As noted previously, options, warrants, and rights are included in the computation of fully diluted earnings per share for a particular period only if they are dilutive. If the price for which stock can be acquired (exercise price) is lower than the current market price, the options, warrants, or rights probably would be exercised and their effect would be dilutive. If the exercise price is higher than the current market price, no exercise would take place; thus, there is no potential dilution from these securities.[4]

It is assumed that exercise of options, warrants, or rights takes place as of the beginning of the year or at the date they are issued, whichever comes later. Additional cash resources would thus have been available for the company's use. In order to compute fully diluted earnings per share when these types of securities exist, either net income must be increased to take into consideration the increase in revenue such additional resources would produce, or the cash must be assumed to be used for some nonrevenue-producing purpose. The APB selected the latter approach and recommended it be assumed that the cash proceeds from the exercise of options, warrants, or rights be used to purchase common stock on the market (treasury stock) at the end-of-year market price.[5] It is further assumed that the shares of treasury stock are issued to those exercising their options, warrants, or rights, and the remaining shares required to be issued will be added as incremental shares to the actual number of shares outstanding to compute fully diluted earnings per share. This method of including warrants, options, and rights in the EPS computation is known as the **treasury stock method.**

To illustrate, assume that at the beginning of the current year, employees were granted options to acquire 5,000 shares of common stock at $40 per share. The market price of the stock at year-end is $50, so exercise is assumed and the effect will be dilutive. The proceeds received by the corporation from the issuance of stock to the employees would be $200,000 (5,000 shares × $40 exercise price). Since the year-end market price of the stock was $50, these proceeds would purchase 4,000 shares of treasury stock ($200,000 ÷ $50). If it is assumed that these 4,000 shares are issued to the employees, an additional 1,000 shares would have to be issued, and the number of shares of stock for computing fully diluted earnings per share would be increased by 1,000 shares.

Illustration of Fully Diluted EPS With Stock Options The use of the treasury stock method in computing fully diluted earnings per share is illustrated with the following data for the Rasband Corporation:

4. The Board stated that, as a practical matter, no assumption of exercise is necessary until the market price has exceeded the exercise price for substantially all of three consecutive months ending with the last month to which earnings per share relates. "Substantially all" has been defined as 11 of the 13 weeks. This is a one-time test. Once the requirement is met, future computations of EPS will include the options, warrants, or rights unless they are antidilutive. See APB Opinion No. 15, par. 36.

5. The APB specified that if the end-of-year market price was lower than the average for the year, the higher average price should be used. This exception to using the ending market price becomes less important if a primary earnings per share is not required and will likely be dropped in the new standard.

Summary of relevant information:

Net income for the year	$92,800
Common shares outstanding (no change during year)	100,000
Options outstanding to purchase equivalent shares	20,000
Exercise price per share on options	$6
Year-end market price for common shares	$10

Basic earnings per share:

Net income for the year	$92,800
Actual number of shares outstanding	100,000
Basic earnings per share ($92,800 ÷ 100,000)	$.93

Application of proceeds from assumed exercise of options outstanding to purchase treasury stock:

Proceeds from assumed exercise of options outstanding (20,000 × $6)	$120,000
Number of outstanding shares assumed to be repurchased with proceeds from options ($120,000 ÷ $10)	12,000

Number of shares to be used in computing fully diluted earnings per share:

Actual number of shares outstanding		100,000
Incremental shares:		
Issued on assumed exercise of options	20,000	
Less assumed repurchase of shares from proceeds of options	12,000	8,000
Total		108,000
Fully diluted earnings per share ($92,800 ÷ 108,000)		$.86

If the stock options had been issued to the company's employees on April 1 of the current year, the incremental shares would be 3/4 of 8,000, or 6,000 shares, and the fully diluted earnings per share would be $.88 ($92,800/106,000).

If the market price of the company's stock is less than the option exercise price, the treasury stock computation would cause the earnings per share to increase when compared to basic earnings per share because the incremental shares would be negative rather than positive. To illustrate, assume the ending market price for Rasband Corporation is $5 rather than $10. In this case, 24,000 shares could be purchased with the $120,000 proceeds from the stock options. Since only 20,000 shares would be issued on exercise of the options, the number of shares for computing fully diluted earnings per share would be 96,000 and the fully diluted earnings per share would be $.97. When compared with basic earnings per share of $.93, the result is antidilution.

Thus, the test for antidilution of stock options, warrants, and rights is simply to compare the ending market price with the exercise price. If the market price exceeds the exercise price, the options are dilutive and would be included "as if" exercised in computing fully diluted earnings per share. If the market price is less than the exercise price, the options are antidilutive and would not be used in computing fully diluted earnings per share.

Limitation on Use of Treasury Stock Method If the number of common shares of stock involved in exercising options, warrants, or rights is large, the market price of the shares may not be a reliable figure, because any attempt to purchase a large block of stock would drive the stock price upward. The Accounting Principles Board recognized this possibility and declared the treasury stock method inappropriate for proceeds in excess of those required to purchase 20% of the shares outstanding at the end of the year. Proceeds beyond those required to purchase 20% of the common stock are assumed to be applied first to reduce any short-term or long-term borrowings, which would increase net income by decreasing interest expense. Any remaining proceeds are assumed to be invested in U.S. Government securities or commercial paper, which would increase net income through interest revenue. Currently, the FASB is considering deletion of this limitation.

To illustrate the computation of fully diluted earnings per share under these circumstances, assume the following data for the Mirage Corporation:

Summary of relevant information:		
Net income for the year		$4,000,000
Common shares outstanding (no change during year)		3,000,000
10% bonds payable		$5,000,000
Options outstanding to purchase equivalent shares		1,000,000
Limitation on assumed repurchase of shares (3,000,000 × 20%)		600,000
Exercise price per share on options		$15
Year-end market price for common shares		$20
Income tax rate		40%
Basic earnings per share:		
Net income for the year		$4,000,000
Actual number of shares outstanding		3,000,000
Basic earnings per share ($4,000,000 ÷ 3,000,000)		$1.33
Application of proceeds from assumed exercise of options outstanding:		
Proceeds from assumed exercise of options outstanding (1,000,000 × $15)		$15,000,000
Maximum applied toward repurchase of outstanding shares (600,000 × $20)		12,000,000
Balance of proceeds applied to retirement of 10% bonds		$ 3,000,000
Net income to be used in computing fully diluted earnings per share:		
Net income		$4,000,000
Add interest on 10% bonds assumed retired, net of income tax:		
Interest ($3,000,000 × 10%)	$300,000	
Less income tax savings ($300,000 × 40%)	120,000	180,000
Adjusted net income		$4,180,000
Number of shares to be used in computing fully diluted earnings per share:		
Actual number of shares outstanding		3,000,000
Incremental shares:		
Issued on assumed exercise of options	1,000,000	
Less assumed repurchase of shares from proceeds of options	600,000	400,000
Total		3,400,000
Fully diluted earnings per share ($4,180,000 ÷ 3,400,000)		$1.23

Partially paid stock subscriptions are to be considered the equivalent of warrants for purposes of computing earnings per share amounts. The unpaid balance is assumed to be the proceeds used to purchase stock under the treasury stock method. The number of incremental shares for partially paid stock subscriptions is the difference between the number of shares subscribed and the number of shares assumed to be purchased under the treasury stock method.[6]

Convertible Securities

In order to compute fully diluted earnings per share when convertible securities exist, adjustments must be made **both** to net income and to the number of shares of common stock outstanding. These adjustments must reflect what these amounts would have been if the conversion had taken place at the beginning of the current year or at the date of issuance of the convertible securities, whichever comes later. This method of including convertible securities in the EPS computation is referred to as the **if-converted method.** If the securities are bonds, net income is adjusted by adding back the interest expense, net of tax, to net income; the number of shares of common stock outstanding is increased by the number of shares that would have been issued on conversion.[7] Any amortization of initial premium or discount is included in the interest expense added back. If the convertible securities are shares of preferred stock, no reduction is made from net income for preferred dividends, as is done with the computation of basic earnings per share; the number of shares of common stock outstanding is increased by the number of shares that would have been issued upon conversion. Because preferred stock dividends are not deductible as an expense for tax purposes, no adjustment for tax effects is required. If the convertible securities were issued during the year, adjustments would be made for only the portion of the year since the issuance date.

In order to test for dilution, each potentially dilutive convertible security must be evaluated individually. If there is only one such security, comparison is made between earnings per share before considering the convertible security with the earnings per share after including it. As indicated earlier, if the earnings per share decreases or loss per share increases, the convertible security is defined as dilutive. Antidilutive securities are excluded from the computation of fully diluted earnings per share. An example using multiple dilutive securities is included in the appendix to this chapter.

Illustration of Fully Diluted EPS With Convertible Securities The following examples for the Reid Corporation illustrate the computation of fully diluted earnings per share when convertible securities exist.

Summary of relevant information:	
8% convertible bonds issued at par	$500,000
Net income for the year	$83,000
Common shares outstanding (no change during year)	100,000
Conversion terms of convertible bonds—80 shares for each $1,000 bond	
Assumed tax rate	40%

Basic earnings per share:	
Net income	$83,000
Actual number of shares outstanding	100,000
Basic earnings per share ($83,000 ÷ 100,000)	$.83

6. *Accounting Interpretations of APB Opinion No. 15, Interpretation No. 83,* "Stock Subscriptions Are Warrants" (New York: American Institute of Certified Public Accountants, 1970).

7. In addition to adjustments for interest, adjustments to net income for nondiscretionary or indirect items would have to be made in many situations. These items would include profit-sharing bonuses and other payments whose amount is determined by the net income reported. For simplicity, no indirect effects are illustrated in this chapter.

Fully diluted earnings per share:

Net income		$ 83,000
Add interest on convertible bonds, net of income tax:		
Interest ($500,000 × 8%)	$40,000	
Less income tax savings ($40,000 × 40%)	16,000	24,000
Adjusted net income		$107,000
Actual number of shares outstanding		100,000
Additional shares issued on assumed conversion of bonds (500 × 80)		40,000
Adjusted number of shares		140,000
Fully diluted earnings per share ($107,000 ÷ 140,000)		$.76

Computation of Fully Diluted EPS for Securities Issued During Year If the convertible bonds had been issued by Reid Corporation on June 30 of the current year, the adjustment would be made to reflect only the period subsequent to the issuance date, or ½ of a year.

Fully diluted earnings per share (1/2 year):

Net income		$ 83,000
Add interest on convertible bonds, net of income tax:		
Interest ($500,000 x 8% × ½ year)	$20,000	
Less income tax ($20,000 × 40%)	8,000	12,000
Adjusted net income		$ 95,000
Actual number of shares outstanding		100,000
Additional shares issued on assumed conversion of bonds (500 × 80 × ½)		20,000
Adjusted number of shares		120,000
Fully diluted earnings per share ($95,000 ÷ 120,000)		$.79

Convertible preferred stock is treated in a similar manner to convertible debt securities (bonds). To illustrate application of the "if-converted" method to preferred stock, assume the same facts as given previously for Reid Corporation except that instead of 8% convertible bonds, the company has 8% preferred stock outstanding, par value $500,000, convertible into 40,000 shares of common stock. Note that since Reid would have no bond interest under the change in assumptions, the reported net income would be $107,000 ($83,000 + $24,000 bond interest net of tax savings.) Assume the preferred stock was outstanding for the entire year.

Basic earnings per share:

Net income, without the deduction for interest on bonds	$107,000
Less preferred dividends	40,000
Net income identified with common stock	$ 67,000
Actual number of shares outstanding	100,000
Basic earnings per share ($67,000 ÷ 100,000)	$.67

Fully diluted earnings per share:

Net income assuming no payment of preferred dividends due to conversion	$107,000
Actual number of shares outstanding	100,000
Additional shares issued on assumed conversion of preferred stock	40,000
Adjusted number of shares	140,000
Fully diluted earnings per share ($107,000 ÷ 140,000)	$.76

In this example, fully diluted earnings per share ($.76) is greater than basic earnings per share ($.67). Thus the convertible preferred stock is antidilutive and would not be considered in the computation of earnings per share. Assuming the corporation had no other potentially dilutive securities outstanding, only basic earnings per share would be presented on the income statement.

Shortcut Test for Antidilution It is possible to determine if a convertible security is antidilutive without actually computing primary or fully diluted earnings per share assuming conversion. If a company has net income rather than loss, the antidilutive test is performed by computing what the conversion contributes to per share earnings. For example, if the 8% bonds are converted, net income to the common shareholders increases by $24,000 (see page 995), and the number of common shares outstanding increases by 40,000 shares. The contribution of this conversion to earnings is $.60 per share, ($24,000 ÷ 40,000). Since this amount is less than the preconversion basic earnings per share of $.83, the bonds are dilutive. On the other hand, if the preferred stock is converted, the preferred dividends of $40,000 would no longer be deducted from net income in computing earnings per share, and the number of common shares outstanding will increase by 40,000 shares. The contribution of this conversion to earnings is $1.00 per share ($40,000 ÷ 40,000). Since the preferred stock conversion contributes more per share than preconversion basic earnings of $.67, the preferred stock is antidilutive.

EFFECT OF ACTUAL EXERCISE OR CONVERSION

If exercise or conversion actually takes place during the year, the weighted average number of shares issued will be included in all earnings per share computations. In addition, however, an adjustment is made to reflect what the earnings per share would have been if conversion or exercise had taken place at the beginning of the period or issuance date, whichever comes later. This adjustment is required for all securities actually converted or exercised during the period for computing fully diluted earnings per share whether dilutive or not.

When options or warrants are exercised, the adjustment for the period before exercise for fully diluted earnings per share uses the market price at exercise date. To illustrate the computation of fully diluted earnings per share when stock options are exercised during the year, assume the following data for Weatherby, Inc.

Summary of relevant information:	
Net income for the year	$2,300,000
Common shares outstanding at beginning of year	400,000
Options outstanding at beginning of year to purchase equivalent shares	100,000
Exercise price per share on options	$9.00
Proceeds from actual exercise of options on October 1 of current year	$900,000
Market price of common stock at exercise date, October 1	$15.00

Number of shares to be used in computing basic earnings per share:	
Actual number of shares outstanding for full year	400,000
Weighted shares issued on October 1 (100,000 × 1/4 year)	25,000
Weighted average number of shares for basic earnings per share	425,000
Basic earnings per share ($2,300,000 ÷ 425,000)	$5.41

Number of shares to be used in computing fully diluted earnings per share:		
Weighted average number of shares for basic earnings per share		425,000
Incremental shares if options had been exercised on January 1 (included whether dilutive or not):		
Issued on assumed exercise of options	100,000	
Less assumed repurchase of shares with proceeds ($900,000 ÷ $15)	60,000	
Incremental shares assumed to be issued	40,000	
Weighted average of incremental shares assumed to be issued (40,000 × 3/4 year)		30,000
Weighted average number of shares for fully diluted earnings per share		455,000
Fully diluted earnings per share ($2,300,000 ÷ 455,000)		$5.05

EFFECT OF NET LOSSES ON EPS

If a company has a net loss, no dual computation of earnings per share is necessary, since inclusion of stock options or convertible securities would decrease the loss per share and thus always would be antidilutive. To illustrate this situation, assume the following data for the Boggs Co.

Summary of relevant information:	
Net loss for the year	($50,000)
Number of shares of stock outstanding—full year	100,000
Number of shares of convertible preferred stock	10,000
Conversion terms—2 shares of common for 1 share of preferred	
Dividends on preferred stock	$8,000

The computation of basic and fully diluted earnings per share would be as follows:

Basic loss per share:	
Net loss	($50,000)
Dividends on preferred stock	(8,000)
Total loss to common shareholders	($58,000)
Actual number of shares outstanding	100,000
Basic loss per share ($58,000 ÷ 100,000)	($.58)

Fully diluted loss per share:	
Net loss	($50,000)
Actual number of shares outstanding	100,000
Incremental shares on assumed conversion of preferred stock	20,000
Adjusted number of shares	120,000
Fully diluted loss per share ($50,000 ÷ 120,000)	($.42)

Because the fully diluted loss per share is less than the basic loss per share, only the basic loss per share would be reported on the income statement.

MULTIPLE POTENTIALLY DILUTIVE SECURITIES

The illustrations in the chapter thus far have dealt primarily with one type of potentially dilutive security at a time. For a company having several different issues of convertible securities and/or stock options and warrants, the APB requires selection of the combination of securities producing the lowest possible earnings per share figure. To avoid having to test a large number of different combinations to find the lowest one, companies can compute the incremental earnings per share for each potentially dilutive security. Because the smaller the incremental computation, the greater the impact on basic earnings per share, the securities are then ranked in order from the smallest incremental EPS to the largest. Then each security—beginning with the one having the smallest incremental EPS—is introduced into the computation until the earnings per share is lower than the next security's incremental computation. At that point, all remaining securities in the list would be antidilutive. Any dilutive stock options and warrants are considered first before introducing convertible securities into the computations.

To illustrate, assume a company had no stock options but did have four convertible securities that would have the following effects on fully diluted earnings per share if each were considered separately.

	Effects of Assumed Conversion		
	Increase in Net Income	Increase in No. of Shares	Incremental EPS
Convertible Security A	$ 75,000	50,000	$1.50
Convertible Security B	150,000	60,000	2.50
Convertible Security C	110,000	20,000	5.50
Convertible Security D	600,000	100,000	6.00

Assume further that basic earnings per share was $6.50 ($2,275,000 income divided by 350,000 outstanding shares). Each of the four securities considered separately result in an incremental earnings per share figure lower than basic earnings per share and thus would be dilutive. However, when considering all four securities together, only the first two (A and B) would be dilutive and therefore included in fully diluted earnings per share. This is determined by adding one security at a time to the basic earnings per share figure as follows:

	Net Income (Adjusted)	No. of Shares (Adjusted)	Fully Diluted EPS
Simple capital structure	$2,275,000	350,000	$6.50
Convertible Security A	75,000	50,000	
	$2,350,000	400,000	$5.87
Convertible Security B	150,000	60,000	
	$2,500,000	460,000	$5.43
Convertible Security C	110,000	20,000	
	$2,610,000	480,000	$5.44
Convertible Security D	600,000	100,000	
	$3,210,000	580,000	$5.53

It would not be necessary to continue the computation beyond Security B, since the EPS at that point ($5.43) is lower than the incremental EPS impact of Security C ($5.50). Inclusion of Securities C and D would be antidilutive as the computations show.

When a company has multiple potentially dilutive convertible securities, an orderly approach to computing earnings per share is necessary. Exhibit 23—1 should prove helpful in understanding this illustration and in solving complex earnings per share problems. The exhibit summarizes the steps in computing basic and fully diluted earnings per share.

■ Exhibit 23—1
Steps in Computing Earnings Per Share

1. Compute basic earnings per share using a weighted average number of shares for common stock outstanding during the year.
2. For companies with complex capital structures, determine whether stock options, warrants, rights, and convertible securities are dilutive.
   (a) Stock options, warrants, and rights: Dilutive if the exercise price is less than the ending market price of the common stock.
   (b) Convertible securities: Compute incremental earnings per share for each security individually. Those with an incremental value greater than basic earnings per share after considering any stock options, warrants, or rights, are antidilutive and are excluded.
3. Compute fully diluted earnings per share:
   (a) Include all dilutive stock options, warrants, and rights first. Apply proceeds using the treasury stock method at the end-of-year common stock market price to compute incremental shares.
   (b) Include dilutive convertible securities one at a time, beginning with the security that has the smallest incremental EPS. Compute a new earnings per share figure. Continue selecting and applying convertible securities until the next security in the list has an incremental EPS value greater than the last computed earnings per share. Discontinue the process at that point. All other securities in the list are antidilutive for purposes of computing the lowest possible fully diluted earnings per share figure.

   Report basic and fully diluted earnings per share on the face of the income statement.

To illustrate the steps in Exhibit 23—1 for computing basic and fully diluted earnings per share, assume the following facts related to Wildwood, Inc.

Summary of relevant information:	
Net income for the year	$136,000
Common shares outstanding (no change during the year)	125,000
Options outstanding to purchase equivalent shares	30,000
Exercise price per share on options	$10
End-of-year market price for common shares	$15
9% convertible bonds, issued at par	$600,000
Conversion terms for bonds, 100 shares for each $1,000 bond	
Tax rate	30%

Step 1 Compute basic earnings per share	
Net income for the year	$136,000
Actual number of shares outstanding	125,000
Basic earnings per share ($136,000 ÷ $125,000)	$1.09

Step 2 Determine whether stock options and convertible bonds are dilutive

(a) Stock options: The options are dilutive since the exercise price is less than the market price at year-end.
(b) Convertible bonds: The bonds are potentially dilutive since the EPS impact of $.63, as computed below, is less than basic earnings per share of $1.09.

Net Income Impact	Number of Shares	EPS Impact
$600,000 × .09 × .70 = $37,800	60,000	$.63

Step 3 Compute fully diluted earnings per share

Description		Net Income	Number of Shares	EPS
Basic earnings per share		$136,000	125,000	$1.09
Options as if exercised at beginning of year:				
Number of shares assumed issued	30,000			
Number of treasury shares assumed repurchased [(30,000 × $10) ÷ $15]	(20,000)			
Incremental shares	10,000		10,000	
		$136,000	135,000	$1.01
9% Convertible bonds		37,800	60,000	
Fully diluted earnings per share		$173,800	195,000	$ .89

PRIMARY EARNINGS PER SHARE

In the earlier sections of this chapter, mention was made of primary earnings per share. When the Accounting Principles Board studied earnings per share in the mid-1960s, they decided to identify an earnings per share number somewhere between basic and fully diluted EPS. The objective of the APB was to produce an earnings per share figure based on those securities most likely to be exercised and converted rather than all that could be exercised and converted. Because it cannot be determined with certainty which securities are going to be converted or exercised until the actual conversion or exercise takes place, an attempt was made to examine the terms and economic conditions existing at the date the security was issued and identify those securities that should be considered in this intermediate figure. Definitions were established to identify these securities, and they were given a name, **common stock equivalents.** The APB identified the intermediate earnings per share number that considered only potentially dilutive securities that met the definition of common stock equivalents as **primary earnings per share.**

Definition of Common Stock Equivalents

By definition, the APB classified all stock options, warrants, and rights as common stock equivalents. If they were dilutive, they were considered in the primary earnings per share figure in the same manner as they were considered in computing fully diluted earnings per share. As described for fully diluted earnings per share, a stock option is considered dilutive if the ending market price of a stock exceeds the option exercise price. The APB modified the rule slightly for primary earnings per share by replacing ending market price with **annual average market price**. Thus, stock options, warrants, and rights are included in both fully diluted and primary earnings per share, but an adjustment to the number of incremental shares used in computing fully diluted earnings per share may be required when the ending stock market price exceeds the average price.

A convertible security, whether bonds or preferred stock, that at the time of its issuance has terms indicating the purchaser is placing a premium on the conversion feature is also recognized as a common stock equivalent. Specifically, a convertible security is considered a common stock equivalent if, at the time of issuance, it has an effective yield of less than 66 2/3% of the then current average Aa corporate bond yield.[8] The effective

8. *Statement of Financial Accounting Standards No. 85,* "Yield Test for Determining Whether a Convertible Security Is a Common Stock Equivalent" (Stamford: Financial Accounting Standards Board, 1985).

yield is the rate that would discount all future cash flows from the security to the issue price. For example, assume that Brown Inc. purchased a $10,000, 14%, 10-year convertible bond when the effective market interest yield was 12%. The purchase price of the bond would be $11,130 computed as follows:

Present value of the interest:	
$1,400 × 5.6502 (Table IV; 12%, 10 years)	$ 7,910
Present value of the principal:	
$10,000 × .3220 (Table II; 12%, 10 years)	3,220
Market price discounted at the effective interest rate	$11,130

Usually the purchase price is known and the effective yield must be computed. Because the computation involves an annuity and a single payment, a computer or a bond yield table is required to determine the effective yield. If a security has no maturity date, the effective yield is the same as the cash yield, or the annual return divided by the issue price of the security. Most preferred stock fits this situation. Thus if 8%, $100 par preferred stock is sold for $105, the cash and effective yield would be 7.6% ($8 ÷ $105).

The identification of a convertible security as a common stock equivalent is made at the time of its issuance, and it retains this identity as long as it remains outstanding, regardless of changes in the interest rate. Convertible securities are included in primary earnings per share only if they are dilutive.

For example, assume at December 31, 1996, the Aa corporate bond yield is 11%. A $1,000, 20-year, convertible bond with a stated interest rate of 7% is sold at a price providing an effective yield of 6.42%. Since the yield is less than 66 2/3% of the Aa corporate bond yield of 11%, or 7 1/3%, the bond is recognized as a common stock equivalent. The bond will retain this classification even though future bond interest rates fall and the effective yield exceeds 66 2/3% of the Aa corporate bond yield.

Those convertible securities that do not meet the definition of dilutive common stock equivalents, while used to compute fully diluted earnings per share, are not used to compute primary earnings per share. Under APB Opinion No. 15, if a company with a complex capital structure computes a primary earnings per share number that is materially lower than the basic earnings per share, the primary earnings per share is reported rather than the basic earnings per share. A fully diluted earnings per share figure is also required to be reported. Thus, APB Opinion No. 15 requires a dual presentation of earnings per share, both assuming some conversion or exercise of potentially dilutive securities. Under APB Opinion No. 15, basic earnings per share is disclosed only for simple capital structures and for complex capital structures where the potentially dilutive securities are antidilutive.

Although the FASB is likely to eliminate primary earnings per share in the future because of the criticism it has received as a meaningful measure of earnings, it will still be a required computation until a new standard takes effect. The following steps must be added to Exhibit 23—1 if a primary earnings per share is to be computed and reported as required by APB Opinion No. 15.

Additional Steps to Compute Primary EPS:

4. Compute new incremental shares using average market price for the presumed exercise of any options, warrants, and rights. Replace incremental shares in the fully diluted earnings per share with this new number.
5. Identify dilutive convertible securities used in computing fully diluted earnings per share that do not meet the definition of common stock equivalents. Exclude these securities from both the fully diluted numerator and denominator to determine primary earnings per share.

To illustrate, these steps will be applied using the Wildwood, Inc. example (see page 999) and the following additional information:

Annual average market price for common shares	$12
Aa corporate bond yield when 9% bonds were issued	11%

Step 4 (compute new incremental shares using average market price) and Step 5 (exclude convertible securities that do not meet common stock equivalency test) are applied as follows:

Description		Net Income	Number of Shares	EPS
Fully diluted earnings per share		$173,800	195,000	$ .89
Step 4 Options adjustment:				
Fully diluted incremental shares			(10,000)	
Primary incremental shares:				
Number of shares assumed issued	30,000			
Number of treasury shares assumed repurchased [(30,000 × $10) ÷ $12]	(25,000)			
Incremental shares	5,000		5,000	
Step 5 Exclude 9% convertible bonds*		(37,800)	(60,000)	
		$136,000	130,000	$1.05

*$\frac{2}{3}$ × 11% = 7.33%, which is less than 9%; bonds are not common stock equivalent.

Under APB Opinion No. 15, Wildwood would report primary EPS of $1.05.

FINANCIAL STATEMENT PRESENTATION

When earnings of a period include extraordinary items, income or loss from discontinued operations, or a cumulative effect of a change in accounting principle, earnings per share amounts should be presented for amounts before these special items, for each of these significant items, and for net income. For a complex capital structure, each of these items should be presented on both a primary and a fully diluted basis.

A schedule or note should be provided explaining how the earnings per share figures are calculated. Those securities included as common stock equivalents in arriving at primary earnings per share, as well as those included in the computation of fully diluted earnings per share, should be identified. All assumptions made and the resulting adjustments required in developing the earnings per share data should be disclosed. Additional disclosures should be made of the number of shares of common stock issued upon conversion, exercise, or satisfaction of required conditions for at least the most recent annual fiscal period. To illustrate, pertinent sections of the financial statements of Unisys Corporation are reproduced on page 1004.

A common stock equivalent or other dilutive security may dilute one of the several per-share amounts required to be disclosed on the face of the income statement, while increasing another amount. In such a case, the common stock equivalent or other dilutive securities should be recognized for all computations, even though they have an antidilutive effect on one or more of the per-share amounts.[9]

9. *Opinions of the Accounting Principles Board No. 15*, par. 30.

Utility of Earnings Per Share Numbers

On June 25, 1993, a memorandum was issued by the FASB to convey a project on earnings per share (EPS) that could result in enhanced international comparability and simplification of EPS calculations. With the complex calculations associated with EPS, some wonder if the benefits of the information exceed the costs. Ralph Walters, as an FASB member, dissented from FASB Statement No. 55, stating that primary EPS "is not relevant because it furnishes little or no incremental information about the probability, timing or amount of dilution. It is not reliable, that is, representationally faithful, because it implies imminent or predictable dilution, whereas research suggests that it has been a poor predictor of dilution." In addition, the FASB understands that cross-border financing and investing has become more prevalent. Greater consistency between U.S. accounting standards and those issued by other national standard setters, such as the IASC, is crucial if international comparability is to be achieved.

An IASC Steering Committee is considering an approach to EPS that would require financial statements of public companies to present basic and fully diluted EPS. *Basic EPS* is defined as earnings divided by weighted average common stock outstanding, without potential dilution from securities other than common stock. *Fully diluted EPS* would include securities with the right to a future issuance of common shares that would cause a reduction of basic EPS. Under this approach, primary EPS would not be presented—this is in accordance with current international practice.

The FASB realizes that some of the most complex aspects of the standards relate to the determination of (a) whether a security is a common stock equivalent, and (b) differences in the computational method between primary and fully diluted EPS. If an approach such as the basic/fully diluted approach being considered by the IASC Steering Committee were adopted, the need to determine whether a security is a common stock equivalent should be eliminated.

Current practice varies internationally for computing EPS. However, the basic/fully diluted approach is taken by many countries that do prescribe an EPS calculation; e.g., Australia, Canada, and the United Kingdom. There is an increasing trend toward adoption of an EPS requirement by countries that do not presently have one, with the basic/fully diluted approach as the preferred method. The United States is the notable exception to this trend.

Questions:

1. What would be the advantages if the FASB required all firms to provide only basic and fully diluted EPS in the audited financial statements?
2. What problems might the FASB face in implementing a project based on the basic/fully diluted approach?
3. How important is international comparability in today's capital markets?
4. Research indicates that EPS is not news when it is released to financial markets. Yet analysts consistently cite EPS figures when evaluating investment options. If you were allowed to establish disclosure requirements for EPS, what would you require?

Earnings per share data should be presented for all periods covered by the income statement. If potential dilution exists in any of the periods presented, the dual presentation of primary and fully diluted earnings per share should be made for all periods presented.[10] Whenever net income of prior periods has been restated as a result of a prior-period adjustment, the earnings per share for these prior periods should be restated and the effect of the restatements disclosed in the current year.[11]

It is important that great care be exercised in interpreting earnings per share data regardless of the degree of refinement applied in the development of the data. These values are the products of the principles and practices employed in the accounting process and are subject to the same limitations found in the net income measurement reported on the income statement.

10. *Ibid.*, par. 17.
11. *Ibid.*, par. 18.

■ Exhibit 23—2
Unisys Corporation—Additional Disclosure to Earnings Per Share Data

UNISYS CORPORATION

	1992	1991	1990
(Millions, except per share date)			
Earnings (loss) on common shares	$239.1	$(1,514.5)	$(551.0)
Earnings (loss) per common share			
Primary			
Before extraordinary item	$ 1.06	$ (9.37)	$ (3.45)
Extraordinary item	.40		
Total	$ 1.46	$ (9.37)	$ (3.45)
Fully diluted			
Before extraordinary item	$ 1.04	$ (9.37)	$ (3.45)
Extrordinary item	.36		
Total	$ 1.40	$ (9.37)	$ (3.45)

NOTES TO CONSOLIDATED FINANCIAL STATEMENTS

1. (In Part): Summary of Significant Accounting Policies
Earnings per common share

In 1992, the computation of primary earnings per share is based on the weighted average number of outstanding common shares and additional shares assuming the exercise of stock options. The computation of fully diluted earnings per share further assumes the conversion of the 8 1/4% convertible subordinated notes due August 1, 2000. In 1991 and 1990, both primary and fully diluted earnings per common share were based on the weighted average number of outstanding common shares. The inclusion of additional shares assuming the converssion of Series A Cumulative Convertible Preferred Stock would have been antidilutive in all three years. Accounting rules governing the computation of earnings per share require that dividends on cumulative preferred stock, whether declared or not, be deducted in the earnings per share computation. The shares used in the computations for the three years ended December 31, 1992 were as follows (in thousands):

	1992	1991	1990
Primary	163,725	161,552	159,683
Fully diluted	181, 813	161,552	159,683

APPENDIX

Comprehensive Illustration Using Multiple Potentially Dilutive Securities

The steps outlined in Exhibit 23—1 for computing earnings per share for multiple securities will be used in the comprehensive problem that follows. The Circle West Transportation Co. has the following outstanding stocks and bonds at January 1, 1997. All securities had been sold at par or face value. Thus, the effective yield is equal to the stated interest or dividend rate for each security.

Date of Issue	Type of Security	Par or Face Value	No. of Shares or Total Face Value	Conversion Terms	Aa Bond Rate at Date of Issue
1985-1996	Common stock	$.25	200,000	none	
May 1, 1991	12% debentures	1,000	$750,000	none	9%
Jan. 1, 1995	6% cumulative preferred stock	100	40,000	4 shares of common for each preferred share	14%
Jan. 1, 1996	8% debentures	1,000	$1,000,000	15 shares of common for each $1,000 debenture	13%
June 30, 1996	10% debentures	1,000	$600,000	30 shares of common debenture	12%
Dec. 31, 1996	8% cumulative preferred stock	50	12,500	none	11%

Circle West also had stock options outstanding at January 1, 1997, for the purchase of 20,000 shares of common. During 1997, options were granted for an additional 40,000 shares. The terms of these stock options are as follows:

Date of Issue	Exercisable Date	Exercise Price	Number of Options
Jan. 1, 1994	June 30, 1997	$30	20,000
June 30, 1997	June 30, 1999	60	40,000

Common stock market prices for 1997 were as follows:

Average for year	$60	
Average for first 3/4 of year	55	
Average for last half of year	61	
October 1 price	62	
December 31 price	65	(Market price exceeded October 1 price for entire fourth quarter)

During 1997, Circle West issued the following common stock:

Apr. 1 30,000 shares sold at $56.
Oct. 1 20,000 shares issued from exercise of Jan. 1, 1994, options.

On December 1, 1997, Circle West paid a full year's dividend on the 6% preferred stock and on the 8% preferred stock. Assume that the company had net income of

$1,026,000 in 1997, all of which was income from continuing operations. The income tax rate is 40%.

The steps for computing earnings per share will be applied to the data for Circle West Transportation Company to compute the various earnings per share amounts.

Step 1 Compute basic earnings per share

Net income		$1,026,000
Less preferred dividends:		
6% stock (40,000 × $100 × .06)	$240,000	
8% stock (12,500 × $50 × .08)	50,000	290,000
Net income identified with common stock		$ 736,000

Weighted average number of shares:

Jan. 1 to Apr. 1		200,000 × 1/4	50,000	
Apr. 1 to Oct. 1	(200,000 + 30,000)	230,000 × 1/2	115,000	
Oct. 1 to Dec. 31	(230,000 + 20,000)	250,000 × 1/4	62,500	
Total weighted average number of shares			227,500	
Basic earnings per share ($736,000 ÷ 227,500)				$3.24

Step 2 Determine whether options and convertible securities are dilutive for computing fully diluted earnings per share

(a) Stock options: Both stock options are dilutive, since the exercise prices ($30 and $60) are less than the applicable ending market prices ($62 on October 1 for the exercised options and $65 at year-end for the unexercised options).

(b) Convertible securities:

	Net Income Impact	Number of Shares	Incremental EPS
6% preferred stock	$240,000	160,000	$1.50
10% debentures	36,000*	18,000	2.00
8% debentures	48,000	15,000	3.20

*$600,000 × .10 × .60 (income tax rate)

All three convertible securities are potentially dilutive, since their impact on earnings per share is less than the $3.24 basic earnings per share.

Step 3 Compute fully diluted earnings per share

Description	Net Income	Number of Shares	Part of Year	Weighted Average	EPS
Basic earnings per share	$ 736,000			227,500	$3.24
Jan. 1, 1994, options—exercised Oct. 1, as if exercised Jan. 1, 1997:					
Number of shares assumed issued		20,000			
Number of treasury shares assumed repurchased [(20,000 × $30) ÷ $60]		(10,000)			
Incremental shares		10,000	3/4	7,500	

Step 3 Continued

June 30, 1997 options:					
Number of shares assumed issued		40,000			
Number of treasury shares assumed repurchased [(40,000 x $60) ÷ $65]		(36,923)			
Incremental shares		3,077	1/2	1,538	
	$ 736,000			236,538	$3.11
6% preferred stock	240,000	160,000	1	160,000	
	$ 976,000			396,538	$2.46
10% debentures	36,000			18,000	
Fully diluted earnings per share	$1,012,000			414,538	$2.44

8% debentures: Because impact value of $3.20 exceeds latest EPS of $2.44, the debentures are antidilutive and not included in fully diluted EPS.

Step 4 Compute new incremental shares using average market price

Step 5 Exclude convertible securities that do not meet common stock equivalency test

Description	Net Income	Number of Shares	Part of Year	Weighted Average	EPS
Fully diluted earnings per share	$1,012,000			414,538	$2.44
Step 4 Options adjustment:					
Fully diluted incremental shares:					
Jan. 1, 1994 options				(7,500)	
June 30, 1997 options				(1,538)	
Primary incremental shares:					
Jan. 1, 1994 options:					
Number of shares assumed issued		20,000			
Number of treasury shares assumed repurchased [40,000 × $60)/$61]		(10,909)			
Incremental shares		9,091	3/4	6,818	
June 30, 1997 options:					
Number of shares assumed issued		40,000			
Number of treasury shares assumed repurchased [(40,000 × $60)/$61]		(39,344)			
Incremental shares		656	1/2	328	
Step 5:					
10% convertible debentures	(36,000)			(18,000)	
Primary EPS	$ 976,000			394,646	$2.47

*2/3 × 12% = 8%; 8% < 10%. Debentures not common stock equivalent.
2/3 × 12% = 8%; 8% > 6%. Preferred stock is common stock equivalent and therefore requires no adjustment to fully diluted earnings per share.

Under APB Opinion No. 15, Circle West would report primary EPS of $2.47 and fully diluted EPS of $2.44.

KEY TERMS

QUESTIONS

1. Earnings per share computations have received increased prominence on the income statement. How would an investor use such information in making investment decisions?
2. Why are earnings per share figures computed on the basis of common stock transactions that have not yet happened rather than on the basis of strictly historical common stock data?
3. An enterprise split its common stock 3-for-1 on July 1. Its accounting year ends December 31. Prior to the split, there were 10,000 shares of common stock outstanding. What is the weighted average number of shares that should be used to compute earnings per share in the current and preceding year?
4. Why are earnings per share figures adjusted retroactively for stock dividends, stock splits, and reverse stock splits?
5. What is meant by "dilution of earnings per share"?
6. What is an antidilutive security? Why are such securities generally excluded from the computation of earnings per share?
7. What distinguishes a simple from a complex capital structure?
8. What is the treasury stock method of accounting for outstanding stock options and warrants in computing fully diluted earnings per share?
9. What modification to the treasury stock method is required under APB Opinion No. 15 if the number of shares obtainable from the exercise of outstanding options and warrants exceeds 20% of the number of shares outstanding?
10. Convertible debt that is dilutive requires an adjustment to income. What is the nature of the adjustment?
11. What is the meaning of the "if-converted method" of computing earnings per share?
12. If stock options are actually exercised during the year, how is fully diluted earnings per share affected?
13. Why are all convertible securities and options antidilutive when a company is operating at a loss?
14. If a company has multiple potentially dilutive securities, how are the computations made to ensure obtaining the lowest earnings per share figure?
15. What limitations should be recognized in using earnings per share data?
16. Compare the concept of primary earnings per share with the concept of fully diluted earnings per share.
17. What constitutes a common stock equivalent for calculating primary earnings per share?
18. (a) Under what conditions are stock options and warrants recognized as common stock equivalents? (b) Under what conditions is a convertible security recognized as a common stock equivalent?
19. How is the treasury stock method for stock options and warrants modified in computing primary earnings per share as compared with computing fully diluted earnings per share?

DISCUSSION CASES

Case 23—1 (But why is EPS different if income is the same?)

Fredrica Brown has $200,000 which she plans to invest in growth common stock. She has narrowed her choice to two companies in the same industry, White Inc. and Adam Inc. Each company has a documented history of growth and an established, strong position within the industry. Last year each company reported net income of $10 million and a return on owners' investment of 17%; however, White reported earnings per share of $10 and Adam reported earnings per share of $20.

Fredrica requests that you explain why the EPS differs when other measures of activity and profitability are similar. What factors contribute to and limit the comparability of these data?

Case 23—2 **(But let's maintain earnings per share.)**

On January 1, 1994, Farnsworth Company had 1,000,000 shares of common stock and 100,000 shares of $8 cumulative preferred stock issued and outstanding. A principal goal of Farnsworth's management is to maintain or increase earnings per share.

On January 1, 1995, Farnsworth Company retired 50,000 shares of the preferred stock with excess cash and additional funds provided from the sale of a subsidiary.

At the beginning of 1996, the company borrowed $5,000,000 at 10% and used the proceeds to retire 200,000 shares of common stock. Operating income, before interest and income taxes (income tax rate is 40%), is as follows:

	1996	1995	1994
Operating income	$6,500,000	$7,000,000	$7,500,000

Did Farnsworth Company maintain its earnings per share even though income declined? What was the impact of the preferred and common stock transactions on earnings per share?

Case 23—3 **(Are we in trouble or not?)**

Tolman Yacht Company has just completed its determination of earnings per share for the year. As a result of issuing convertible securities during the year, the capital structure of Tolman is now defined as being complex. The primary earnings per share for this year is $2.90, but the fully diluted earnings per share is only $2.50, both figures down from the prior year's $3.25 basic earnings per share figure.

Sung Wong and Martha Chou, two stockholders, have received their financial statements from Tolman and are discussing the earnings per share figures over lunch. The following dialogue ensues:

Wong I guess Tolman must be having trouble. I see its earnings per share is down significantly.

Chou Maybe so, but this year there are two figures where before there was only one.

Wong Something to do with the convertible bonds and preferred stock issued during the year making it a complex capital structure. But both of the earnings per share figures are lower than the single figure the year before.

Chou That's true. But income for the current year is higher than last year. I'm confused.

Enlighten the stockholders.

Case 23—4 **(Don't change the 20% treasury stock rule!)**

When the FASB announced some tentative changes to be made to the manner in which earnings per share figures were to be computed, some companies became quite concerned about its impact on their reported amounts. A trade group of software developers was reported by the *Wall Street Journal* as being convinced that the earnings per share proposal "shows that the rulemaker is determined to hurt high-tech and growth companies that need good results to go to the public." The change that concerned this group was the removal of the restriction on using the treasury stock method when over 20% of the outstanding common stock would be reacquired due to stock options. Under what circumstances would removal of this restriction adversely affect companies' EPS calculations? (*The Wall Street Journal,* June 3, 1994)

Case 23—5 **(How does a complex capital structure affect EPS?)**

Big Horn Construction Company has gradually grown in size since its inception in 1919. The third generation of Jensens who now manage the enterprise are considering selling a large block of stock to raise capital for new equipment purchases and to help finance several big projects. The Jensens are concerned about how the earnings per share information should be presented on the income statement and have many questions concerning the nature of earnings per share.

(1) Discuss the earnings per share presentation that would be required if Big Horn Construction has (a) a simple capital structure or (b) a complex capital structure. What factors determine whether a capital structure is simple or complex?

(2) Assume Big Horn Construction Company has a complex capital structure. Discuss the effect, if any, of each of the following transactions on the computation of earnings per share:
   (a) The firm acquires some of its outstanding common stock to hold as treasury stock.
   (b) The firm pays a dividend of $.50 per common stock share.
   (c) The firm declares a dividend of $.75 per share on cumulative preferred stock.
   (d) A 3-for-1 common stock split occurs during the year.
   (e) Retained earnings are appropriated for a disputed construction contract that may be litigated.

(3) Are primary earnings per share for a complex structure with common stock equivalents the same as earnings per share for a simple structure? Discuss why APB Opinion No. 15 does not provide for a basic earnings per share for a complex capital structure and why the FASB is considering replacing primary earnings per share with basic earnings per share.

EXERCISES

Exercise 23—6 (Weighted average number of shares)

Compute the weighted average number of shares outstanding for Troy Company, which has a simple capital structure, assuming the following transactions in common stock occurred during the year:

Date	Transactions in Common Stock	Number of Shares $10 Par Value
Jan. 1	Shares outstanding	44,000
Feb. 1	Issued for cash	56,000
May 1	Acquisition of treasury stock	(25,000)
Aug. 1	25% stock dividend	25% of shares outstanding
Sep. 1	Resold part of treasury stock shares	10,000
Nov. 1	Issued 2-for-1 stock split	

Exercise 23—7 (Weighted average number of shares)

Transactions involving the common stock account of the Higrade Gas Company during the 2-year period 1996 and 1997 were as follows:

1996

Jan. 1	Balance 200,000 shares of $10 par common stock.
Apr. 1	$2,500,000 of convertible bonds were converted with 50 shares issued for each $1,000 bond.
July 1	A 10% stock dividend was declared.
Oct. 1	Option to purchase 7,000 shares for $20 a share was exercised.

1997

Apr. 1	A 2-for-1 stock split was declared.
Oct. 1	80,000 shares were sold for $30 a share.

From the information given, compute the comparative number of weighted average shares outstanding for 1996 and 1997 to be used for earnings per share computations at the end of 1997. Assume that conversion of bonds and exercise of options at January 1, 1996, would not have resulted in material dilution, and there are no other convertible securities or options outstanding. Thus, only a basic earnings per share is required.

Exercise 23—8 (Weighted average number of shares)

Assume the following transactions affected owners' equity for Cervantes Inc. during 1996.

Feb. 1	20,000 shares of common stock were sold in the market.
Apr. 1	Purchased 5,000 shares of common stock to be held as treasury stock. Paid cash dividends of $.50 per share.
May 1	Split common stock 3-for-1.
July 1	35,000 shares of common stock were sold.
Oct. 1	A 5% stock dividend was issued.
Dec. 31	Paid a cash dividend of $.75 per share. The total amount paid for dividends on December 31 was $511,875.

Compute the weighted average number of shares to be used in computing basic earnings per share for 1996. Because no beginning share figures are available, you must work backwards from December 31, 1996, to compute shares outstanding.

Exercise 23—9 (Basic earnings per share—simple capital structure)

At December 31, 1996, the Munter Corporation had 50,000 shares of common stock issued and outstanding, 30,000 of which had been issued and outstanding throughout the year and 20,000 of which had been issued on October 1, 1996. Operating income before income taxes for the year ended December 31, 1996, was $703,200. In 1996 and 1997, a dividend of $80,000 was paid on 80,000 shares of 10% cumulative preferred stock, $10 par.

On April 1, 1997, 30,000 additional shares were issued. Total income before income taxes for 1997 was $477,000, which included an extraordinary gain before income taxes of $37,000. Assuming a 30% tax rate, what is Munter's basic earnings per common share for 1996 and for 1997, rounded to the nearest cent? Show computations in good form.

Exercise 23—10 (Basic earnings per share—simple capital structure)

The income statement for the Fignon Co. for the year ended December 31, 1996, reported the following:

Income from continuing operations before income taxes	$35,000
Income taxes	14,000
Income from continuing operations	$21,000
Loss from disposal of segment (net of income taxes)	(6,400)
Net income	$14,600

Compute basic earnings per share amounts for 1996 under each of the following assumptions (consider each assumption separately):

(a) The company has only one class of common stock with 20,000 shares outstanding.

(b) The company has shares outstanding as follows: preferred 8% stock, $15 par, cumulative, 5,000 shares; common, $12 par, 20,000 shares. Only the current year's preferred dividends are unpaid.

(c) Same as (b) except Crosby Co. *also* has preferred 7% stock, $10 par, noncumulative, 2,000 shares. Only $3,000 in dividends on the noncumulative preferred has been declared.

Exercise 23—11 (Dilutive securities)

The Claney Corporation has basic earnings per common share of $2.09 for the period ended December 31, 1996. For each of the following examples, decide whether the convertible security would be dilutive or antidilutive in computing fully diluted earnings per share. Consider each example individually. The tax rate is 30%.

(a) 8 1/2% debentures, $1,000,000 face value, are convertible into common stock at the rate of 40 shares for each $1,000 bond.

(b) $5 preferred stock (no par) is convertible into common stock at the rate of 2 shares of common stock for 1 share of preferred stock. There are 50,000 shares of preferred stock outstanding.

(c) Options to purchase 200,000 shares of common stock are outstanding. The exercise price is $25 per share. Current market price is $20 per share.

(d) $400,000 of 10% debentures are convertible at the rate of 25 shares of common stock for each $1,000 bond.

(e) Preferred 6% stock, $100 par, 5,000 shares outstanding, convertible into 3 shares of common stock for each 1 share of preferred stock.

Exercise 23—12 (Number of shares—stock options)

On January 1, 1996, Wander Corporation had 56,000 shares of common stock outstanding that did not change during 1996. In 1995 Wander Corporation granted options to certain executives to purchase 9,000 shares of its common stock at $7 each. The market price of common was $10.50 per share on December 31, 1996. Compute the number of shares to be used in computing fully diluted earnings per share for 1996.

Exercise 23—13 (Number of shares—stock options)

Barone Company has employee stock options outstanding to purchase 40,000 common shares at $12 per share. All options were outstanding during the entire year. The price of the company's common stock at the end of the year was $20. Compute the incremental shares that would be used in arriving at fully diluted earnings per share. Barone has 80,000 shares outstanding at the date the option is granted.

Exercise 23—14 (Fully diluted earnings per share—convertible bonds)

On January 2, 1996, Saftner Co. issued at par $30,000 of 10% bonds convertible in total into 2,000 shares of Saftner's common stock. No bonds were converted during 1996. Throughout 1996, Saftner had 5,000 shares of common stock outstanding. Saftner's 1996 net income was $45,000. Saftner's tax rate is 40%.

No other potentially dilutive securities other than the convertible bonds were outstanding during 1996. For 1996, compute Saftner's basic and fully diluted earnings per share.

Exercise 23—15 (Fully diluted earnings per share—convertible bonds)

The Delgado Manufacturing Company reports long-term liabilities and stockholders' equity balances at December 31, 1996, as follows:

Convertible 5% bonds (par)	$ 600,000
Common stock, $25 par, 100,000 shares issued and outstanding	2,500,000

Additional information is determined as follows:

Conversion terms of bonds—50 shares for each $1,000 bond	
Operating income—1996	$199,800
Extraordinary gain (net of tax)	43,520
Net income—1996	$243,320

Compute the basic and fully diluted earnings per share for the company for 1996, assuming that the income tax rate is 40%. No changes occurred in the debt and equity balances during 1996.

Exercise 23—16 (Earnings and loss per share—convertible preferred stock, operating loss)

During all of 1996, Malone Inc. had outstanding 100,000 shares of common stock and 5,000 shares of $7 preferred stock. Each share of the preferred stock is convertible into 4 shares of common stock. For 1996, Malone had a $230,000 loss from operations; no dividends were paid or declared.

Compute the basic and fully diluted earnings (loss) per share for Malone assuming:

1. The preferred stock is noncumulative.
2. The preferred stock is cumulative.

Exercise 23—17 (Earnings per share with actual conversion)

Atlas, Inc., has the following capital structure at January 1, 1996:

	Outstanding
Common stock, $10 par	800,000 shares
11% stated interest rate convertible bonds issued at par; each $1,000 bond is convertible into 80 shares of common stock	$5,000,000

During 1996, Atlas had the following stock transactions:

May 1	Issued 50,000 shares of common stock for $30 per share.
Aug. 1	Purchased 100,000 shares of treasury stock at $35 per share.
Oct. 1	Converted $2,000,000 of bonds.

Net income for 1996 was $950,000. The income tax rate was 30%. Compute basic and fully diluted earnings per share for Atlas for 1996.

Exercise 23—18 (Common stock equivalents)

Which of the following securities would qualify as common stock equivalents? If a common stock equivalent, would it be used in computing primary earnings per share? Give reasons supporting each answer.

(a) Employee stock options to purchase 1,000 shares of common stock at $40 are outstanding. The market price of the common stock has been in excess of $45 throughout the year.
(b) Warrants to purchase 2,000 shares at $30 are issued. The current market price is $27.
(c) 8%, $1,000 convertible bonds are sold; sales price, to yield 6.67%. The Aa corporate bond yield is 10 1/4%.
(d) Preferred stock, 7%, convertible, is sold at par. The Aa corporate bond yield is 10 1/4%.

Exercise 23—19 (Earnings per share—APB Opinion No. 15)

At December 31, 1996, the books of Yorke Corporation include the following balances:

Long-term liabilities:	
Bonds payable, 8%, each $1,000 bond is convertible into 50 shares of common stock; bonds sold at par and were issued November 3, 1995	$ 500,000
Stockholders' equity:	
Preferred stock, 7%, par $50, cumulative, nonconvertible, 10,000 shares outstanding	500,000
Paid-in capital in excess of par, preferred stock	300,000
Common stock, par $10, authorized 300,000 shares; 199,500 shares outstanding	1,995,000
Paid-in capital in excess of par, common stock	450,000
Retained earnings	519,000

The records of Yorke reveal the following additional information:

(a) 150,000 shares of common stock were outstanding January 1, 1996.
(b) 40,000 shares of common stock were sold for cash on April 30, 1996.
(c) Issued 5% stock dividend on July 1, 1996.
(d) Aa corporate bond yield was 12% when bonds were issued.
(e) Operating income before extraordinary items (after tax) was $715,000.
(f) Extraordinary loss (net of tax), $16,000.
(g) Income tax rate, 40%.
(h) Bond indenture does not provide for increase in shares at conversion due to stock dividends declared subsequent to the bond issue date.

1. Is this a simple or complex capital structure?
2. Compute earnings per share amounts as required by APB Opinion No. 15. How should earnings per share data be presented under this opinion?

Exercise 23—20 (Earnings per share—convertible securities)

Information relating to the capital structure of the Roninger Corporation at December 31, 1995 and 1996, is as follows:

	Outstanding
Common stock	120,000 shares
Convertible preferred stock noncumulative (issued in 1994)	18,000 shares
7.5% convertible bonds (issued in 1995)	$1,200,000
Stock options to purchase 20,000 shares at $15. Market price of Roninger stock was $20 at December 31, 1996 and averaged $18 during the year	

Roninger Corporation paid dividends of $5 per share on its preferred stock. The preferred stock is convertible into 40,000 shares of common stock and is considered a common stock equivalent. The 7.5% convertible bonds are convertible into 35,000 shares of common stock, but are *not* considered to be common stock equivalents. The net income for the year ended December 31, 1996, is $640,000. Assume that the income tax rate is 40%. Compute basic, fully diluted, and primary earnings per share for the year ended December 31, 1996.

PROBLEMS

Problem 23—21 (Weighted average number of shares)

Inman's Wholesale Products Inc. had 75,000 shares of common stock outstanding at the end of 1995. During 1996 and 1997, the following transactions took place:

1996	
Mar. 31	Sold 5,000 shares at $27.
Apr. 26	Paid cash dividend of $.50 per share.
July 31	Paid cash dividend of $.25 per share, and issued a 10% stock dividend.
Nov. 1	Sold 7,000 shares at $30.

1997	
Feb. 28	Purchased 5,000 shares of common stock to be held in treasury.
Mar. 1	Paid cash dividend of $.50 per share.
Apr. 30	Issued 3-for-1 stock split.
Nov. 1	Sold 6,000 shares of treasury stock.
Dec. 20	Declared cash dividend of $.25 per share.

Inman's Wholesale Products Inc. has a simple capital structure.

Instructions: Compute the weighted average number of shares for 1996 and 1997 to be used in the earnings per share computation at the end of 1997.

Problem 23—22 (Basic earnings per share—simple capital structure)

The following condensed financial statements for the Tomac Corporation were prepared by the accounting department:

Tomac Corporation
Income Statement
For the Year Ended December 31, 1996

Sales		$12,000,000
Cost of goods sold		10,000,000
Gross profit on sales		$ 2,000,000
Expenses:		
Selling expense	$500,000	
Administrative expense	340,000	
Interest expense	24,000	864,000
Income from continuing operations before income taxes		$ 1,136,000
Income taxes		446,000
Income from continuing operations		$ 690,000
Extraordinary loss, net of tax savings		(60,000)
Net income		$ 630,000

Tomac Corporation
Balance Sheet
December 31, 1996

Assets	$5,300,000
Liabilities:	
Current liabilities	$1,450,000
6% bonds, due December 31, 2003	900,000
Stockholders' equity:	
Common stock, $10 par, 200,000 shares authorized, issued and outstanding	2,000,000
Additional paid-in capital	600,000
Retained earnings	350,000
Total liabilities and stockholders' equity	$5,300,000

Instructions: Compute the basic earnings per share under each of the following separate assumptions (the company has a simple capital structure):

1. No change in the capital structure occurred in 1996.
2. On December 31, 1995, there were 120,000 shares outstanding. On May 1, 1996, 60,000 shares were sold at par and on October 1, 1996, 20,000 shares were sold at par.
3. On December 31, 1995, there were 160,000 shares outstanding. On July 1, 1996, the company issued a 25% stock dividend.

Problem 23—23 (Basic earnings per share—simple capital structure)

Great Northern Inc. reported the following comparative information in the stockholders' equity section of its 1997 balance sheet.

	Dec. 31 1997	Dec. 31 1996	Dec. 31 1995
12% preferred stock, $50 par	$ 82,500	$ 67,500	$ 50,000
Paid-in capital in excess of par—preferred	13,400	9,200	5,000
Common stock, $5 par*	410,600	399,600	325,000
Paid-in capital in excess of par—common	64,300	58,800	35,000
Paid-in capital from treasury stock	1,800	800	800
Retained earnings	471,200	396,460	290,200
Total stockholders' equity	$1,043,800	$932,360	$706,000

*Par value after June 1, 1997, stock split.

In addition, company records show that the following transactions involving stockholders' equity were recorded in 1996 and 1997:

1996	
May 1	Sold 4,500 shares of common stock for $12, par value $10.
June 30	Sold 350 shares of preferred stock for $62, par value $50.
Aug. 1	Issued an 8% stock dividend on common stock. The market price of the stock was $15.
Sep. 1	Declared cash dividends of 12% on preferred stock and $1.50 on common stock.
Dec. 1	Income from operations for the year totaled $316,200. In addition, Great Northern had an extraordinary gain of $12,500, net of tax.

1997	
Jan. 31	Sold 1,100 shares of common stock for $15.
May 1	Sold 300 shares of preferred stock for $64.
June 1	Issued a 2-for-1 split of common stock, reduced par value to $5.
Sep. 1	Purchased 500 shares of common stock for $9 to be held as treasury stock.
Oct. 1	Declared cash dividends of 12% on preferred stock and $2 per share on outstanding common stock.
Nov. 1	Sold 500 shares of treasury stock for $11.
Dec. 31	Net income for the year included an extraordinary loss net of income tax of $19,000.

Instructions: Compute the basic earnings per share amounts for 1996 and 1997 to be presented in the income statement for 1997.

Problem 23—24 (Fully diluted earnings per share—stock options)

The records of Mountain Crest Company reveal the following capital structure as of December 31, 1995:

$10 preferred stock, $80 par, 7,500 shares issued and outstanding	$ 600,000
Additional paid-in capital on preferred stock	90,000
Common stock, $10 par, 200,000 shares issued and outstanding	2,000,000
Additional paid-in capital on common stock	350,000
Retained earnings	886,000

To stimulate work incentive and to bolster trade relations, Mountain Crest on May 1, 1996, issued stock options to select executives, creditors, and others allowing the purchase of 26,000 shares of common stock for $28 a share. Market prices for the stock at various times during 1996 were:

Option issuance date	$25
Year-end	75
Average, May 1 to Dec. 31	50

A dividend on preferred stock was paid during the year, and there are no dividends in arrears at year-end. There are no other capital transactions during the year. Net income for 1996 was $631,000.

Instructions: Compute basic and fully diluted earnings per share for 1996.

Problem 23—25 (Fully diluted earnings per share—stock options)

The Ugrumov Technology Co. provides the following data at December 31, 1996:

Operating revenue	$1,120,000
Operating expenses	$ 600,000
Income tax rate	30%
Common stock outstanding during the entire year	26,000 shares

On January 1, 1996, there were options outstanding to purchase 15,000 shares of common stock at $25 per share. At December 31, 1996, the market price was $35 per share. The balance sheet reports $240,000 of 7% nonconvertible bonds at December 31, 1996. (Interest expense is included in operating expenses.)

Instructions: Compute for 1996:

1. Basic earnings per share.
2. Fully diluted earnings per share.

Problem 23—26 (Fully diluted earnings per share with exercise of stock options)
As of January 1, 1996, the Bayer Corporation had 30,000 shares of $5 par common stock outstanding. The company had issued stock options in 1994 to its management personnel permitting them to acquire 6,000 shares of common stock at $9 per share. At the time of the issuance, common stock was selling for $9 per share. The market price of common stock was $23 on September 1, 1996, and $25 on December 31, 1996. Income from operations for 1996 was $131,700. The company also had an extraordinary gain of $25,000, net of taxes. Terms of the options make them currently exercisable. On September 1, 1996, options to acquire 2,000 shares were exercised. The other 4,000 options are still outstanding at December 31, 1996.

Instructions: Compute basic and fully diluted earnings per share for the year ended December 31, 1996.

Problem 23—27 (Fully diluted earnings per share—conversion of debentures)
The following information relates to the December 31, 1995, balance sheet for Chiapucci Incorporated:

6% convertible 10-year debentures issued at par	$1,000,000
Common stock, $12 par, 110,000 shares issued and outstanding	$1,320,000
Retained earnings	842,000
Total stockholders' equity	$2,162,000

The convertible debentures include terms stating that each $1,000 bond can be converted into 30 shares of common stock.

The following events occurred during 1996:

(a) On August 31, 1996, the complete issue of convertible debentures was converted into common stock.
(b) Chiapucci reported net income of $540,000 in 1996. The company's income tax rate was 30%.
(c) No other common stock transactions took place during the year other than the debenture conversion.

Instructions:

1. Compute earnings per share for Chiapucci for the year ended December 31, 1996.
2. Assume Chiapucci had a net loss of $220,000. Show why the convertible debentures are antidilutive under loss conditions.

Problem 23—28 (Fully diluted earnings per share—complex capital structure)
Carrizo Corporation's capital structure is as follows:

	December 31	
	1997	**1996**
Outstanding shares of:		
Common stock	336,000	280,000
Nonconvertible, noncumulative preferred stock	10,000	10,000
10% convertible bonds	$1,000,000	$1,000,000

The following additional information is available:

(a) On September 1, 1997, Carrizo sold 56,000 additional shares of common stock.
(b) Net income for the year ended December 31, 1997, was $860,000.
(c) During 1997, Carrizo declared and paid dividends of $5 per share on its preferred stock.
(d) The 10% bonds are convertible into 40 shares of common stock for each $1,000 bond.

(e) Unexercised options to purchase 30,000 shares of common stock at $22.50 per share were outstanding at the beginning and end of 1997. The market price of Carrizo's common stock was $36 per share at December 31, 1997.
(f) Warrants to purchase 20,000 shares of common stock at $38 per share were attached to the preferred stock at the time of issuance. The warrants, which expire on December 31, 2002, were outstanding at December 31, 1997.
(g) Carrizo's effective income tax rate was 40% for 1996 and 1997.

Instructions: For the year ended December 31, 1997, compute the following:
1. Basic earnings per share.
2. Fully diluted earnings per share.

(AICPA adapted)

Problem 23—29 (Earnings per share—complex capital structure)

The "Stockholders' equity" section of Alta Company's balance sheet as of December 31, 1996, contains the following:

$2 cumulative preferred stock, $25 par, convertible, 1,600,000 shares authorized, 1,400,000 shares issued, 750,000 converted to common, 650,000 shares outstanding	$16,250,000
Common stock, $.25 par, 15,000,000 shares authorized, 8,800,000 shares issued and outstanding	2,200,000
Additional paid-in capital	32,750,000
Retained earnings	40,595,000
Total stockholders' equity	$91,795,000

Included in the liabilities of Alta Company are 9% convertible subordinated debentures, face value $20,000,000, issued at par in 1995. The debentures are due in 2004 and until then are convertible into the common stock of Alta Company at the rate of 60 shares of common stock for each $1,000 debenture. To date none of these have been converted.

On April 2, 1996, Alta Company issued 1,400,000 shares of convertible preferred stock at $40 per share. Quarterly dividends to December 31, 1996, have been paid on these shares. The preferred stock is convertible into common stock at the rate of 2 shares of common for each share of preferred. On October 1, 1996, 150,000 shares and on November 1, 1996, 600,000 shares of the preferred stock were converted into common stock.

During July 1995, Alta Company granted options to its officers and key employees to purchase 500,000 shares of the company's common stock at a price of $20 a share. No options were exercised in 1996.

During 1996 dividend payments and average market prices of the Alta common stock were as follows:

	Dividend Per Share	Average Market Price Per Share
First quarter	$.10	$20
Second quarter	.15	25
Third quarter	.10	30
Fourth quarter	.15	35
Average for the year		30

The December 31, 1996, closing price of the common stock was $25 per share.

Assume that the Aa corporate bond yield was 12% throughout 1995 and 1996. Alta Company's net income for the year ended December 31, 1996, was $12,750,000. The provision for income tax was computed at a rate of 40%.

Instructions: Compute basic, fully diluted, and primary earnings per share for the year ended December 31, 1996.

*Problem 23—30 (Earnings per share—complex capital structure)

At December 31, 1996, the Norbalco Company had 400,000 shares of common stock outstanding. Norbalco sold 100,000 shares on October 1, 1997. Net income for 1997 was $2,565,000; the income tax rate was 30%. In addition, Norbalco had the following debt and equity securities on its books at December 31, 1996:

(a) 20,000 shares of $100 par, 10% cumulative preferred stock. Aa corporate bond yield was 11% at time of sale. Stock was sold at 102.
(b) 30,000 shares of 8% convertible cumulative preferred stock, par $100, sold at 110 when Aa corporate bond yield was 11%. Each share of preferred stock is convertible into two shares of common.
(c) $2,000,000 face value of 8% bonds sold at par when Aa corporate bond yield was 10%.
(d) $3,000,000 face value of 6% convertible bonds sold to yield 7% when Aa corporate bond yield was 8%. Unamortized bond discount is $100,000 at December 31, 1996. Each $1,000 bond is convertible into 20 shares of common.

Also, options to purchase 10,000 shares were issued May 1, 1997. Exercise price is $30 per share; market value at date of option was $29; market value at end of year, $40; average market value May 1 to December 31, 1997, $35.

Instructions: For the year ended December 31, 1997, compute the following:

1. Basic earnings per share.
2. Fully diluted earnings per share.
3. Primary earnings per share.

*Relates to Appendix

*Problem 23—31 (Earnings per share—multiple convertible securities)

Data for the Dwight Powder Company at the end of 1997 are listed below. All bonds are convertible as indicated and were issued at their face amounts.

Description of Bonds	Amount	Date Issued	Aa Corporate Bond Yield on Date Issued	Conversion Terms
10-year, 6 1/2% convertible bonds	$ 700,000	1/1/91	9 1/2%	100 shares of common for each $1,000 bond
20-year, 7% convertible bonds	1,000,000	1/1/92	11%	50 shares of common for each $1,000 bond
25-year, 10 1/2% convertible bonds	1,600,000	6/30/96	14 1/4%	32 shares of common for each $1,000 bond

Additional information:

Common shares outstanding at December 31, 1996	700,000
Net income for 1997	$1,406,000
Income tax rate	40%

Instructions:

1. Compute basic and fully diluted earnings per share for 1997, assuming that no additional shares of common stock were issued during the year.
3. Compute basic, fully diluted, and primary earnings per share assuming that the 10-year bonds were converted on July 1, 1997, and that net income for the year was $1,419,650 (reflects reduction in interest due to bond conversion).

*Relates to Appendix

*Problem 23—32 (Earnings per share—multiple convertible securities)

Sawyer Company had the following capital structure at December 31, 1996 and 1997:

	1997	1996
Shares of stock outstanding:		
Common stock	756,000	600,000
$6 convertible preferred stock	10,000	20,000
Bonds outstanding:		
8 1/2%, 10-year convertible bonds	$1,500,000	$2,000,000

The following additional information is available:

(a) The conversion terms of the preferred stock and bonds at January 1, 1997, were as follows: Preferred stock, 5 shares of common for each share of preferred. Convertible bonds, 40 shares of common for each $1,000 bond. These terms are to be adjusted for any issued stock dividends or stock splits.

(b) On May 1, 1997, Sawyer sold an additional 50,000 shares of common stock, and on August 1, 1997, a 5% stock dividend on common shares was declared.

(c) On October 1, 1997, 10,000 shares of preferred stock were converted to 52,500 shares of common stock (5.25 shares common for each 1 share of preferred). The preferred stock was issued at $100 par in 1990 when the Aa corporate interest rate was 9.5%.

(d) On December 1, 1997, 25% of the convertible bonds were converted. The bonds were issued at par in 1996 when the Aa corporate interest rate was 13%.

(e) On December 31, 1997, Sawyer declared and paid a $6 per share dividend on outstanding preferred stock. Income for the year was $1,400,000.

(f) Stock options (issued and unexercised) to purchase 60,000 shares of common stock at $25 per share were outstanding at the beginning of 1997. Average market price was $40, and the market price at December 31, 1997, was $48.

(g) Stock warrants to purchase 40,000 shares of common stock at $46 per share were attached to the preferred stock. The warrants expire on December 31, 2001, and were outstanding at December 31, 1997.

(h) The effective tax rate was 35% for both years.

(i) On February 1, 1998, before the 1997 financial statements were issued, Sawyer split its common stock 2 for 1.

Instructions: For the year ended December 31, 1997, compute the following. (Carry EPS figures to 3 decimal places.)

1. Basic earnings per share.
2. Fully diluted earnings per share.
3. Primary earnings per share.

*Relates to Appendix

CHAPTER 24

Reporting the Impact of Changing Prices – Domestic and Foreign

CHAPTER TOPICS

- Reporting the Effects of Changing Prices
- Constant Dollar Accounting
- Current Cost Accounting
- The FASB Experiment (Statement No. 33)
- Future Prospects for Reporting Price-Level Adjusted Data
- Translating Foreign Financial Statements

A troublesome problem for both individuals and businesses is how to deal with changing prices. Most consumers are well aware that the prices of goods and services have risen significantly over the past fifty years. This increase in the general price level is called **inflation.** While America gets nervous when inflation climbs above 6%, other countries around the world would be pleased with single-digit inflation. Russia, for example, experienced 12% inflation in the month of January 1994. Victor Chernomydrin, Russia's prime minister, pledged in January to keep inflation below 18% per month. However, with all the political and economic uncertainty associated with Russia's future, experts fear that inflation of 50% per month is not unexpected.

The following schedule shows the general price level in the United States since 1975, as measured by the Consumer Price Index (CPI). The schedule illustrates how inflation has subsided in the United States over the past decade. As the Russian example illustrates, however, the rate of inflation has been much higher in other parts of the world, at times over 100% a year.

Year	Consumer Price Index 1982-84 = 100	Rate of Inflation*
1975	53.8	9.1%
1976	56.9	5.8
1977	60.6	6.5
1978	65.2	7.7
1979	72.6	11.3
1980	82.4	13.5
1981	90.9	10.4
1982	96.5	6.1
1983	99.6	3.2
1984	103.9	4.3
1985	107.6	3.6
1986	109.6	1.9
1987	113.6	3.7
1988	115.3	4.1
1989	124.0	4.8
1990	130.7	5.4
1991	136.2	4.2
1992	140.3	3.0

*$\frac{CPI_t - CPI_{t-1}}{CPI_{t-1}}$

Financial statements of business enterprises have traditionally reflected transactions in terms of the number of dollars exchanged. These statements are often referred to as **historical cost/nominal dollar,** or simply **historical cost,** statements, meaning statements reporting unadjusted original dollar amounts. The justification for reporting original dollar amounts is objectivity. Historical costs generally are based on arm's-length transactions that are considered to measure appropriate exchange values at a transaction date.

The problem is that historical cost statements do not reflect the impact of price changes subsequent to the transaction date. To some, this is a serious limitation of traditional accounting, especially in periods of high inflation or rapidly increasing replacement costs for certain assets. When the inflation rate is low, the concern over accounting for changing prices tends to diminish.

Regardless of existing economic conditions and the related level of interest in accounting for changing prices, there are some basic concepts that should be understood. This chapter explains these concepts and provides simple examples to illustrate the procedures involved in accounting for changing prices. In addition, companies that own foreign subsidiaries must convert the subsidiaries' financial statements from their local currency to U.S. dollars before the financial statements can be consolidated. The procedures for accomplishing this conversion are similar to those used in accounting for changing prices, and they are also presented in this chapter.

REPORTING THE EFFECTS OF CHANGING PRICES

Two kinds of price changes have been identified. The first deals with changes in the general price level for all commodities and services. The second kind of price change relates to changes in prices of specific items. Prices for individual items may fluctuate up or down and by differing magnitudes; the average of all specific price changes determines the change in the general price level. With respect to terminology, accounting for the first kind of price change is referred to as **constant dollar accounting,** or general price-level adjusted accounting. Accounting for the second kind of price change is referred to as **current cost accounting,** or current value accounting. This distinction is important in order to understand the reporting alternatives identified in the next section.

Reporting Alternatives

The major financial reporting alternatives, including the currently used historical cost/nominal dollar basis, may be classified as follows:

	Historical Cost Valuation	**Current Cost Valuation**
Nominal Dollar Measurement	HC/ND Historical Cost/ Nominal Dollar	CC/ND Current Cost/ Nominal Dollar
Constant Dollar Measurement	HC/CD Historical Cost/ Constant Dollar	CC/CD Current Cost/ Constant Dollar

The two distinct aspects of changing prices are highlighted by the matrix: the change in the unit of measurement (nominal and constant dollars) and the change in basis of valuation (historical and current costs). These distinctions are important, since the accounting for and the effects on the financial statements are significantly different.

The first cell reflects financial statements that are currently reported in terms of nominal dollars using historical cost valuation. The dollar measurement is not adjusted for changes in the general price level, and the valuation basis represents the historical exchange prices of transactions, not the current costs of the items reported. This is contrasted to the cell labeled HC/CD. Reporting on this basis maintains historical cost valuation but measures the items in terms of constant dollars. This means that the original or nominal dollars are adjusted to constant dollars—dollars of equivalent purchasing power. Sometimes constant dollars are referred to as general purchasing **power dollars** because they represent quantities of goods or services that can be purchased given a general price level. This concept is explained in greater detail later in this chapter.

The cell identified as CC/ND does not adjust the dollar measurement; it reports nominal dollars. However, it changes the valuation basis from historical costs to current costs. This basis of reporting reflects changes in specific prices but does not account for changes in the general price level. The term **current cost** is used throughout this chapter in a general sense to mean the current value of an asset. Measures of current cost include: replacement cost, reproduction cost, sales value, net realizable value, and net present value of expected cash flows. Note that a number of these current cost measurements are currently being used in financial statements. For example, accounts receivable are reported at their net realizable value, and long-term bonds are reported at their net present value. The terms "current cost" and "current value" are used interchangeably.

The cell identified as CC/CD combines current cost valuation with constant dollar measurement. Reporting on this basis reflects both specific price changes and general purchasing power changes.

In summary, reporting on the traditional basis (represented by HC/ND) does not reflect the impact of general price changes or specific price changes until assets are sold or otherwise disposed of. Reporting on the HC/CD basis considers general purchasing power changes but not specific price changes. The CC/ND basis is just the opposite. It reports the impact of specific price changes because of its current cost valuation but does not reflect changes in the general purchasing power of the dollar. Only by reporting on a CC/CD basis are both types of price changes accounted for.

The extent and manner of reporting the impact of changing prices is also an issue. One possibility is to choose one of the three nontraditional cells and require preparation of primary financial statements on the basis selected. Another alternative is to continue reporting the primary financial statements on the historical cost/nominal dollar basis, but also provide supplemental information adjusted to constant dollars and/or to reflect current costs. If the latter alternative were chosen, a remaining question would be whether to restate all items or only selected items.

Historical Perspective

The issues involved and the proposed alternatives for reporting the effects of changing prices are not new. In the 1920s and 1930s, Henry Sweeney and others advocated constant dollar accounting under the names of "stabilized" or price-level accounting.[1]

In 1963, the AICPA published Accounting Research Study No. 6, "Reporting the Financial Effects of Price-Level Changes." This study recommended that supplementary data be presented showing comprehensive restatement of all elements of financial statements using a general price index.[2] Later, in 1969, the APB issued Statement No. 3, which again recognized the potential benefits of general price-level adjusted information and suggested supplemental disclosure of such data.[3]

At the end of 1974, the FASB issued an exposure draft entitled "Financial Reporting in Units of General Purchasing Power." This proposed statement would have required constant dollar accounting, although still as supplemental information.[4] However, before the FASB adopted a final statement, the SEC issued ASR No. 190, which required many companies to disclose current replacement costs of selected assets.[5] Because this conflicted with the FASB's constant dollar exposure draft, the Board withdrew its proposal.

In 1979, after careful evaluation, the FASB decided to experiment with alternative ways of reporting the impact of changing prices by issuing Statement No. 33, "Financial Reporting and Changing Prices.[6] This statement required certain companies to disclose supplemental information for selected items on *both* a constant dollar and a current cost basis. Subsequently, the SEC modified its requirements, as established in ASR No. 190, to comply with the more comprehensive FASB Statement No. 33.

By 1986, the double-digit inflation of the 1970s had subsided, thereby reducing the value of information related to changing prices. Many companies, citing the enormous

1. Henry W. Sweeney, *Stabilized Accounting,* (New York: Harper & Brothers, 1936).
2. *Accounting Research Study No. 6,* "Reporting the Financial Effects of Price-Level Changes" (New York: American Institute of Certified Public Accountants, 1963).
3. *Statement of the Accounting Principles Board No. 3,* "Financial Statements Restated for General Price-Level Changes" (New York: American Institute of Certified Public Accountants, 1969).
4. *FASB Exposure Draft,* "Financial Reporting in Units of General Purchasing Power" (Stamford: Financial Accounting Standards Board, 1974).
5. Securities and Exchange Commission, *Accounting Series Release No. 190,* "Disclosure of Certain Replacement Cost Data" (Washington: U.S. Government Printing Office, 1976).
6. *Statement of Financial Accounting Standards No. 33,* "Financial Reporting and Changing Prices" (Stamford: Financial Accounting Standards Board, 1979). Also see Robert W. Berliner and Dale L. Gerboth, "FASB Statement No. 33 'The Great Experiment,'" *Journal of Accountancy* (May 1980), pp. 48-54.

costs of providing the required supplemental information versus its declining benefit, lobbied the FASB. As a result, the FASB issued Statement No. 89, which superseded Statement No. 33 and which made voluntary the supplementary disclosure of current cost/constant dollar information. The FASB concluded that such disclosures should be encouraged, but not required.[7]

Since some companies will continue to report changing price data, and since this topic will no doubt continue to be debated, accounting students should be familiar with the underlying concepts of constant dollar accounting and current cost accounting.

CONSTANT DOLLAR ACCOUNTING

Recording transactions in terms of the number of nominal dollars exchanged ignores the fact that the dollar is *not* a stable monetary unit. As a unit of measurement, the dollar has significance only in reference to a particular price level. Thus, nominal dollar measurements represent diverse amounts of purchasing power. Unless statements are adjusted, readers are likely to regard dollars in terms of current general purchasing power rather than the general purchasing power at the time the dollars were exchanged. The objective of constant dollar accounting is to convert all dollar measurements into **equivalent purchasing power units** so that a company's position and progress may be viewed in proper perspective.

To illustrate, it would not seem proper to add 100 U.S. dollars to 100 British pounds. It would seem necessary to first convert one of the figures to its exchange equivalent before adding, subtracting, or comparing amounts. Similarly, the number of dollars spent years ago for land or buildings should be converted into current equivalent purchasing power units to arrive at meaningful asset totals. This conversion of nominal dollar amounts to equivalent purchasing power units is the essence of constant dollar accounting. Historical costs, the original exchange values, are maintained as the valuation basis, but are adjusted for changes in the general price level. The basis of measurement changes from nominal dollar amounts to constant dollar amounts or equivalent purchasing power units. The conversion is accomplished using a general price index.

Price Indexes

The value or purchasing power of a monetary unit is inversely related to the price of goods or services for which it can be exchanged. Over a period of time, the prices of specific goods or services will move up or down depending on the relative scarcity and desirability of the goods or services. It would be possible to adjust for specific items, but those price changes may be different than changes in the general price level.

The general price level cannot be measured in absolute terms, but relative changes from period to period and the direction of change can be determined. To measure changes in the general price level, a sample of commodities and services is selected and the current prices of these items are compared with their prices during a base period. The prices during the base period are assigned a value of 100, and the prices of all other periods are expressed as percentages of this amount. The resulting series of numbers is called a **price index.**

Price indexes are valuable aids in measuring inflation or deflation. However, these measurements do have limitations. In the first place, all price indexes are based on sam-

7. *Statement of Financial Accounting Standards No. 89*, "Financial Reporting and Changing Prices" (Stamford: Financial Accounting Standards Board, 1986).

ples. Since all prices do not fluctuate in the same degree or direction, the selection of commodities to be included in the sample affects the computed amounts. In addition, improvements in products affect the general level of prices, but such qualitative changes are difficult to measure.

Although there is no perfect way to measure the changing value of the dollar, indexes have been developed that provide reasonable estimates of changes in the dollar's general purchasing power. Among these are the Consumer Price Index and the Wholesale Price Index, both provided by the Bureau of Labor Statistics, and the GNP (Gross National Product) Implicit Price Deflator provided by the Department of Commerce.

Each of these indexes exhibits a similar pattern of price-level change, but reports different values. This is because each index is based on a different sample. The index recommended by the FASB is the Consumer Price Index for all Urban Consumers (CPI-U), which is published monthly.

Mechanics of Constant Dollar Restatement

Constant dollar accounting requires that nominal dollar amounts be restated to equivalent purchasing power units, i.e., constant dollars, usually for the current period. The general formula for restatement is:

$$\text{Nominal dollar amount} \times \frac{\text{Price index converting } \textbf{to}}{\text{Price index converting } \textbf{from}} = \text{Constant dollar amount}$$

To illustrate the conversion process, assume that a company issued capital stock worth \$50,000 in exchange for inventory valued at \$50,000. Further assume that the current end-of-year price index is 105 and that the exchange took place when the general price index was 100. The company holds inventory during the year without engaging in any other activities. A conventional balance sheet prepared at the end of the year will show both inventory and invested capital at their nominal amounts, \$50,000. In preparing a constant dollar balance sheet at the end of the year, however, inventory and capital stock will be reported as follows:

1. Inventory needs to be restated for the change in the general price level since its acquisition. Inventory, with a nominal acquisition cost of \$50,000, is expressed in constant dollars as \$52,500:

$$\$50{,}000 \times \frac{\text{Index converting to (105)}}{\text{Index converting from (100)}} = \$52{,}500$$

2. Capital stock also requires restatement so that it expresses the stockholders' investment in terms of the current general price level. The capital stock balance is expressed in constant dollars as \$52,500:

$$\$50{,}000 \times \frac{\text{Index converting to (105)}}{\text{Index converting from (100)}} = \$52{,}500$$

Conversion ratios may be used that express the relationship of one index to another. Thus, in the example cited, 105/100 may be stated as a conversion ratio of 1.05. The procedures used in converting nominal dollars to constant dollars are similar to the procedures illustrated in Chapter 10 when dealing with foreign currency transactions. Recall that these transactions required the company to convert an invoice denominated in a foreign currency, French francs for example, into U.S. dollars using a specified exchange rate.

In the example presented, the price index converted "to" was the end-of-year index. Alternatively, an average index for the current year could have been used. If such an approach were taken, the conversion factor would have been 102.5/100 rather than 105/100. Another approach would be to restate all amounts in terms of the price level of an earlier period, e.g., the year of purchase of an item or a base year. Then, events occurring during the current year would be restated in terms of constant dollars of the earlier period selected. Nominal dollars can be restated to constant dollars of any period by modifying the indexes used for the conversion factor.

If current-year constant dollars are used to prepare comparative summaries, all past-year data, including monetary assets and liabilities (defined in the next section), must be "rolled forward" to the current year. In this manner, data presented for several years will all be stated in terms of the same purchasing power units. To illustrate, assume that land was purchased in 1990 for $100,000. Assume further that the general price level was 150 when the land was purchased, 200 at the end of 1995, and 215 at the end of 1996. In reporting the land on the balance sheet at the end of 1995, the land would be reported in current end-of-year constant dollars as follows:

$$\text{Land}\left(\$100{,}000 \times \frac{200}{150}\right) = \$133{,}333$$

However, in reporting comparative amounts at the end of 1996 in current end-of-year constant dollars, the 1995 amount would have to be rolled forward as follows:

$$\text{Land}\left(\$133{,}333 \times \frac{215}{200}\right) = \$143{,}333$$

Alternatively, the 1996 amount could be computed directly as follows:

$$\$100{,}000 \times \frac{215}{150} = \$143{,}333$$

Thus, the comparative balance sheet at December 31, 1996, would show the following:

	1996	**1995**
Land	$143,333	$143,333

This correctly shows no increase in the land account during 1995 and 1996 when amounts are all stated in terms of the same constant dollars. For comparative balance sheet purposes at the end of 1997, the $143,333 would again have to be rolled forward to reflect 1997 dollars.

As indicated earlier, all terms may be reported in terms of constant dollars of an earlier base year. This would eliminate the need for a roll-forward adjustment because all items would be stated in terms of a base year's constant dollars. Even though restating amounts to current-year constant dollars requires a roll-forward procedure, it provides information that relates to the current general price level as opposed to some earlier price level. Current price levels are usually more understandable and relevant for decision-making purposes.

To illustrate the application of constant dollar accounting to the balance sheet, consider a simple example—Campus Supply, at the top of page 1028. All amounts are restated to current end-of-year constant dollars. Assume that the beginning-of-year index was 220 and that the end-of-year index was 260. The entire ending inventory was purchased when the index was 225; the land was bought when the index was 125; all capital stock was issued when the index was 110.

Campus Supply
Balance Sheet
December 31, 1996
(Constant Dollar Basis)

	HC/ND Amounts	Conversion Factor	HC/CD Amounts
Assets			
Cash	$22,000		$22,000
Accounts receivable	14,000		14,000
Inventory	9,000	260/225	10,400
Land	20,000	260/125	41,600
Total assets	$65,000		$88,000
Liabilities and Stockholders' Equity			
Accounts payable	$ 4,000		$ 4,000
Mortgage payable	15,000		15,000
Capital stock	22,000	260/110	52,000
Retained earnings	24,000		17,000*
Total liabilities and stockholders' equity	$65,000		$88,000

*$88,000 − ($4,000 + $15,000 + $52,000)

Note that conversion is not made for cash, receivables, and payables. As explained in the next section, these "monetary items" are fixed in amount regardless of changes in the price level, except when rolling forward past-year data for comparative statements. It also should be observed that Retained Earnings cannot be converted directly, since it represents a composite of many different price levels.

Purchasing Power Gains and Losses

In preparing an income statement on the historical cost/constant dollar basis, revenues and expenses are restated by applying the appropriate indexes in the same manner as illustrated in the preceding section. In addition, reported income is adjusted for any **purchasing power gain or loss** that results from holding monetary items. **Monetary items** are assets, liabilities, and equities whose balances are fixed in terms of numbers of dollars regardless of changes in the general price level. All items not representing a right to receive or an obligation to pay a fixed sum are **nonmonetary items.**

Monetary assets include cash and items such as accounts and notes receivable, loans to employees, cash surrender value of life insurance, and certain marketable securities, such as bonds, that are expected to be held to maturity and redeemed at a fixed number of dollars. Regardless of changes in the general price level, these balances are fixed and provide for the recovery of neither more nor less than the stated amounts. Monetary liabilities include such items as accounts and notes payable, cash dividends payable, and fixed payments for accruals under pension plans. Regardless of changes in the price level, these balances are fixed and call for the payment of neither more nor less than the stated amounts. Nonconvertible preferred stock is a monetary equity item, while common stock is a nonmonetary item. (For a more extensive classification of monetary and nonmonetary items, see Appendix D of FASB Statement No. 33.)

To illustrate the concept of purchasing power gain or loss, assume that a person placed $1,000 cash under the mattress for "safekeeping" when the price index was 100. If the price index were to rise to 110 a year later, the individual would have suffered a purchasing power loss, because it would require $1,100 to purchase the same amount of goods that $1,000 would have bought a year ago. On the other hand, a debt of $1,000 payable a year later, again assuming an increase in the price index from 100 to 110, would result in a purchasing power gain. The equivalent purchasing power would be $1,100, yet the debt can be settled for the fixed amount of $1,000.

Nonmonetary assets include such items as inventories and supplies; land, buildings, and equipment; and intangible assets. These items are nonmonetary because, with changes in the general price level, the nominal dollar amounts at which they are reported on the conventional financial statements will differ from the resources they actually represent. On the other hand, nonmonetary liabilities generally include such items as obligations to furnish goods or services, advances on sales contracts, and warranties on goods sold. These items are nonmonetary because, with changes in the general price level, the dollar demands they actually make will differ from the dollar amounts reported on conventional financial statements.

The difference between a company's monetary assets and its monetary liabilities and equities is referred to as its **net monetary position.** With the number of dollars relating to monetary items remaining fixed and reflecting current dollars regardless of the change in the price level, purchasing power gains and losses arise as prices change. In any given period, the gain or loss from holding monetary assets is offset by the loss or gain from maintaining monetary liabilities and equities. The net gain or loss for a period, then, depends on whether a company's position in net monetary items is positive—monetary assets exceed monetary liabilities and equities—or negative—monetary liabilities and equities exceed monetary assets. Gains and losses are associated with a company's net monetary position as follows:

	Rising Prices	**Declining Prices**
Positive Net Monetary Position	Loss	Gain
Negative Net Monetary Position	Gain	Loss

Constant dollar accounting requires that purchasing power gains and losses be determined. The steps to be followed in determining these gains and losses are explained and illustrated using the financial information for Campus Supply on page 1028 and the following additional information.

Sales for the year were $90,000, purchases were $60,000, and other expenses were $24,000. These revenues and expenses were incurred evenly throughout the year.

The net monetary positions as of January 1, 1996, and December 31, 1996, are as follows:

	Jan. 1, 1996	**Dec. 31, 1996**
Cash	$ 19,000	$ 22,000
Accounts receivable	11,000	14,000
Accounts payable	(3,000)	(4,000)
Mortgage payable	(16,000)	(15,000)
Net monetary position	$ 11,000	$ 17,000

The purchasing power gain or loss is calculated as follows assuming conversion to end-of-year constant dollars:

1. The company's net monetary position at the beginning of the period is restated to end-of-year constant dollars. Campus Supply's net monetary position as of January 1, 1996, is $11,000. This amount can be restated to end-of-year dollars by multiplying it by the ratio of the year-end price index to the index at the beginning of the year: $11,000 × 260/220 = $13,000.
2. Transactions involving monetary items during the year are expressed in terms of year-end constant dollars and are added to, or subtracted from, the beginning net monetary position. For Campus Supply, monetary items were increased by sales and decreased by purchases and other expenses. Because these items were incurred evenly during the year, the ratio of the year-end price index to the average index for 1996 can be used to restate them to end-of-year dollars.

	HC/ND	Conversion Factor	HC/CD
Sales	$ 90,000	260/240	$ 97,500
Purchases	(60,000)	260/240	(65,000)
Other expenses	(24,000)	260/240	(26,000)
Increase in net monetary position	$ 6,000	260/240	$ 6,500

If no gain or loss in purchasing power had occurred during the year, the ending net monetary position would be $19,500 computed as follows:

	HC/CD
Net monetary position, January 1, 1996	$13,000
Increase in net monetary position	6,500
Net monetary position, December 31, 1996	$19,500

3. The actual net monetary position at the end of the year is compared with the results from Step 2. If the actual net monetary position is less than the amount computed in Step 2, the company has sustained a loss in purchasing power. If it is greater, the company has experienced a gain. Campus Supply's actual net monetary position at the end of 1996 is $17,000. Since this amount is less than the $19,500 computed above, the company has sustained a $2,500 purchasing power loss. The foregoing calculations can be summarized in the following schedule:

Campus Supply
Schedule of Purchasing Power Loss
For the Year Ended December 31, 1996

	HC/ND	Conversion Factor	HC/CD*
Net monetary position, January 1, 1996	$11,000	260/220	$13,000
Increase in net monetary position	6,000	260/240	6,500
			$19,500
Net monetary position, December 31, 1996	$17,000		17,000
Purchasing power loss			$ 2,500

*End-of-year dollars

This schedule shows several things. First, the beginning net monetary position plus the net increase (or less the net decrease) will always equal the ending net monetary position, all stated in nominal dollars. This amount can be computed directly from the balance sheet data. Second, the $19,500 represents the amount that the ending monetary position should be in terms of current end-of-year purchasing power units (constant dollars) if no gain or loss had occurred. However, the actual net monetary position is $17,000, because monetary items are fixed in amount. The result is a purchasing power loss of $2,500, the difference between what the monetary position would be if purchasing power had been maintained and the actual amount. On a constant dollar income statement, the purchasing power gain or loss is added to or subtracted from the constant dollar operating income and becomes a part of the ending retained earnings balance.

As indicated earlier, the objective of constant dollar accounting is to convert all nominal dollar amounts to dollars of equivalent purchasing power. Thus, nominal dollars may be converted to constant dollars of a prior period or to average dollars for the current year. The latter approach is frequently encountered in practice and is illustrated in the following schedule for Campus Supply:

Campus Supply
Schedule of Purchasing Power Loss
For the Year Ended December 31, 1996

	HC/ND	Conversion Factor	HC/CD*
Net monetary position, January 1, 1996	$11,000	240/220	$12,000
Increase in net monetary position	6,000		6,000
			$18,000
Net monetary position, December 31, 1996	$17,000	240/260	15,692
Purchasing power loss			$ 2,308

*Average dollars

When average-for-the-year constant dollars are used to determine purchasing power gain or loss, both beginning and ending amounts must be restated in terms of the average price index. No restatement was required for the ending balance in the previous example, since this amount reflected end-of-year dollars. When using an average current-year index, the net increase or decrease in monetary position is not converted, since revenues and expenses are assumed to occur evenly throughout the period; therefore, these amounts already reflect average price levels for the year. The purchasing power loss of $2,308 differs from the $2,500 loss in the previous example because it reflects a different price level. The $2,308 can be restated to end-of-year dollars as follows: $2,308 × 260/240 = $2,500.

Arguments For and Against Constant Dollar Accounting

Proponents of constant dollar accounting maintain that meaningful comparisons of accounting data are not possible unless the measuring units are comparable. They argue that the purchasing power of the dollar is not stable, fluctuating with changes in the general price level. Constant dollar accounting corrects this deficiency by measuring transactions in terms of equivalent purchasing power units, thus giving proper recognition to changes in the general price level. Those in favor of constant dollar accounting also point out that recognition of purchasing power gains and losses highlights the impact of inflation with respect to monetary assets, liabilities, and equities. They conclude that constant dollar information is relevant to decision makers and can be provided on a reliable basis without undue cost.

Those opposed to constant dollar accounting note that changes in specific prices of goods are not considered. Constant dollar accounting reflects only changes in the general price level. It ignores many underlying reasons for specific price changes—for example, those due to improvements in quality and specialized industry circumstances. In addition, the general price index used may not be relevant to particular industries. Constant dollar opponents also point out that price indexes are based on statistical averages and have many weaknesses. They question the reliability of the data, especially if used indiscriminately. Many accountants also question whether the benefits exceed the costs of providing constant dollar data. They fear companies will incur substantial costs, only to have users of the data be confused by or uninterested in the information.

CURRENT COST ACCOUNTING

The objective of current cost accounting is different from constant dollar accounting. Constant dollar accounting seeks to use comparable measuring units to reflect equivalent purchasing power for a specified general price level. Current cost accounting attempts to measure the current values of assets, liabilities, and equities. The current values may be measured in nominal dollars or in constant dollars, but they are intended to represent the current exchange prices of goods or services, not historical costs.

Current cost accounting measures changes in specific prices rather than changes in the general price level. While the general price level may have increased an average 12% during the past year, the current values of land may be up 22%, inventories may be up only 8%, and certain types of equipment, perhaps due to technological advancements, may have even decreased in value.

Concept of Well-Offness

From an income measurement perspective, current cost accounting is based on a concept of *well-offness*. This concept is attributed to an economist, J. R. Hicks, and maintains that operating gross profit, often called economic income, is the amount a firm can spend during a period and be as well-off at the end of the period as at the beginning. Operationalized, economic income (loss) is the difference between the sales price of an item and the cost to replace that item. Alternatively, it may be viewed as the change in net assets during a period measured on a current value basis. For example, if an entity's net assets, in terms of current costs, equaled $250,000 at the beginning of a period and $300,000 at the end of the period, given no additional investments or withdrawals and holding the general price level constant, economic income would be $50,000.

Current cost may be defined in several ways. Among the most common are: (1) input prices, i.e., replacement or reproduction costs; (2) exit prices, i.e., sales values; (3) net realizable values, i.e., expected sales prices less costs to complete and sell; and (4) economic values, i.e., present values of future cash flows. These distinctions are technical refinements in implementing the general approach of reflecting current values in financial statements.

Different circumstances may require different approaches to presenting current cost information. For example, the current cost of inventory or plant assets is generally thought of as the cost to replace or reproduce those assets at the balance sheet date. However, assets such as timber can be replaced only over a long period of time; minerals and oil and gas reserves may not be renewable at all. In these circumstances, economic values probably offer better representations of current costs than do replacement costs. This again points out the need for accountants to use judgment, within the guidelines established by the profession, in applying accounting principles.

Holding Gains or Losses

Current cost accounting not only emphasizes economic income but also makes it possible to isolate any gains or losses resulting from holding nonmonetary assets. Traditionally, accountants have recognized income at the point of sale, measuring the difference between the sales price and the historical cost of the item sold. Under current cost accounting, changes in asset values during a period would be recognized whether the assets were sold or not. The recognition of **holding gains or losses** is therefore an essential ingredient of current cost accounting.

Two types of gains and losses from holding assets need to be accounted for. **Realized holding gains and losses** indicate the differences between the current costs and the historical costs of assets sold or used during a period. **Unrealized holding gains and losses** are increases (or decreases) in the current values of assets held during a period but not sold or used. For example, in the earlier illustration, assume that the land of Campus Supply had a current value of $60,000 at the end of 1996. On a December 31, 1996, current cost balance sheet, the land would be reported at its current value of $60,000 rather than its historical cost of $20,000, or its end-of-year constant dollar value of $41,600, thus disclosing a $40,000 unrealized holding gain.

To further illustrate the concept of holding gains or losses, assume that Current Value Company made a sale of $100,000. The cost of goods sold was $65,000, and the cost to replace the inventory sold was $80,000. The total gross profit recognized under historical cost accounting is $35,000 (sales price minus historical cost of inventory sold). However, the $35,000 includes an operating gross profit of $20,000 (sales price minus current cost of inventory sold) and an inventory holding gain of $15,000. The realized holding gain of $15,000 represents the difference between the historical cost and the replacement cost of the inventory sold. This may be illustrated as follows:

Sales	$100,000	
		$20,000 Operating gross profit
Current cost of inventory	$80,000	
		15,000 Realized holding gain
Cost of goods sold	65,000	
Total gross profit		$35,000

If, in the example, Current Value Company had additional inventory that was not sold but that had a change in value, it would have an unrealized holding gain or loss. Assume inventory that was not sold cost $50,000 and had a replacement cost of $75,000. There would be a $25,000 unrealized holding gain on the inventory.

To show how these concepts would be applied over time, assume $10,000 of inventory was purchased by a company at the beginning of Year 1. At the end of Year 1, no inventory had been sold but its current cost was $12,000. At the end of Year 2, the inventory was sold for $18,000 and was replaced at a cost of $15,000. A comparison of the historical cost and current cost approaches over time is shown in the following illustration. For simplicity, assume that the only expense is cost of goods sold.

	Historical Cost			Current Cost		
	Year 1	Year 2	Total	Year 1	Year 2	Total
Sales revenue	-0-	$18,000	$18,000	-0-	$18,000	$18,000
Cost of goods sold	-0-	10,000	10,000	-0-	15,000	15,000
Operating income	-0-	$ 8,000	$ 8,000	-0-	$ 3,000	$ 3,000
Holding gain (loss)	-0-	-0-	-0-	$2,000	3,000	5,000
Net income	-0-	$ 8,000	$ 8,000	$2,000	$ 6,000	$ 8,000

Note that total income recognized is the same under either method. Under current cost accounting, however, changes in the prices of inventory are recognized as they occur. The $2,000 increase in the value of the inventory during Year 1 was an unrealized holding gain, since the inventory had not been sold.

In Year 2, the difference between the current cost of the inventory and its historical cost, $5,000, is a realized holding gain. Note that this realized holding gain includes the $2,000 unrealized holding gain recognized in Year 1 as well as $3,000 realized in Year 2. There is no unrealized holding gain on the inventory in Year 2, since the ending inventory was acquired at the end of Year 2 resulting in the historical cost and the current value being the same.

Current cost net income in this example consists of operating income and holding gains, both realized and unrealized. The total net income would be reflected in retained earnings and would offset changes in net asset values shown on the balance sheet. Some accountants argue, however, that holding gains and losses should be reported as a special account in the owners' equity section of the balance sheet and should not be included in the determination of net income. Another position is that only realized holding gains and losses should be reported as income, and unrealized gains or losses should be reported in an owners' equity account.

Mechanics of Current Cost Accounting

The major problem in current cost accounting is determining appropriate current values. There are two recommended approaches: (1) **indexing** through internally or externally developed specific price indexes for the class of goods or services being measured, and (2) **direct pricing** from current invoice prices, vendors' price lists, or standard manufacturing costs that reflect current costs. If indexing is used, restatement is mechanically the same as for constant dollar accounting. The difference is that specific price indexes are used rather than a general price index. The direct pricing approach assigns current values, determined by analysis and estimate, to particular assets.

Arguments For and Against Current Cost Accounting

Many accountants were not in favor of the replacement cost reporting requirements of ASR No. 190. Some were opposed to FASB Statement No. 33, being especially critical of its complexity and the confusion it might cause. However, proponents of current cost accounting argue that historical cost financial statements, even if adjusted for general price-level changes, do not adequately reflect the economic circumstances of a business. The balance sheet is deficient because only historical costs are presented, and these measurements do not reflect the current financial picture of an enterprise. The income statement is deficient because charges against revenues are based on historical costs that may differ from current costs. Also, increases in net asset values are not recognized at the time of a change in asset value but must await realization at time of sale. Under current cost accounting, assets are reported at their current values, thus more closely reflecting the actual financial position of a business. Expenses are based on the expiration of current costs of assets utilized, thus providing a more meaningful income measure, and changes in values of assets held are recognized as they occur.

Opponents of current cost accounting argue that determining current values is too subjective. For example, the current cost of a particular item may not be readily available and may have to be determined by appraisal or estimation. It may be difficult or impossible to even find an identical replacement item to consider its replacement cost. If an identical asset is not used, a subjective adjustment for differences in the quality of a similar but not identical item would have to be made.

Financing an International Media Giant

In the mid-1980s, Rupert Murdock set out to assemble a global media company with subsidiaries located in countries such as the United States, England, and Australia, to name a few. His objective was to have a far-reaching media empire with ownership in newspapers, television and radio stations, and film studios.

To finance his ambitious goals, Mr. Murdock incurred $2.6 billion in debt to finance the purchase of 14 magazines, Twentieth Century-Fox, and Metromedia Broadcasting. The addition of this debt would have had disastrous effects on the balance sheet of Murdock's company, News Corp.

However, being based in Australia, with its own set of accounting standards, News Corp. was able to write up to fair market value the worth of its newspapers and other assets to mitigate the effect on the debt-to-equity ratio. The effect of this write-up on net worth was an increase of $455 million. The debt-to-equity ratio in Australia after this move was .8 to 1. In the United States, where this practice is not allowed, the debt-to-equity ratio was 3.4 to 1.

Questions:

1. What are the advantages and disadvantages to investors and creditors of having the balance sheet reflect current values?
2. What are the risks to an investor of trying to interpret financial statements prepared in another country?
3. If you were the external auditor for News Corp., would you feel comfortable in expressing an opinion on the financial statements of this company?

Source: *Forbes*, March 10, 1986 by Allan Sloan.

Another disadvantage is the increased subjectivity of the income measurement if changes in current values are recognized as income prior to transactions that confirm arm's-length exchange values.

Additional arguments against current cost accounting include the lack of understanding of current cost financial statements; the question of whether the benefits are worth the extra costs involved; and the uncertainty of whether financial statement users will be better served by current cost accounting.

CURRENT COST/CONSTANT DOLLAR ACCOUNTING

A number of accountants argue against both constant dollar and current cost accounting, pointing out that each approach solves only one of the problems of accounting for changing prices. Constant dollar accounting adjusts for general price changes; current cost accounting recognizes the impact of specific price changes. Current cost/constant dollar accounting combines both approaches and reflects current cost valuation on a constant dollar basis. Such an approach recognizes that adjustments for specific and general price changes are neither mutually exclusive nor competing alternatives. Conceptually, this is the best reporting alternative if the objective is to give full effect to the impact of changing prices on business enterprises. Its primary disadvantage, in addition to the shortcomings ascribed to the other approaches considered separately, is its complexity.

Again referring to the Campus Supply example, on a December 31, 1996, current cost/constant dollar balance sheet, the land would be reported at its current cost stated in end-of-year constant dollars of $60,000. Note that this is the same amount as reported under the current cost/nominal dollar approach. For the $60,000 to be a current cost, it would have to be a year-end amount. Conversion would be required, however, if average-year or base-year dollars were used.

In the example, the $60,000 current cost/constant dollar land amount is $40,000 higher than the $20,000 reported under the historical cost/nominal dollar approach. As explained earlier, this is an unrealized holding gain. However, only part of the $40,000 total unrealized holding gain is real; a portion of it is an inflationary component or fictitious holding gain due to changes in the general purchasing power of the dollar. This concept can be illustrated by the following diagram:

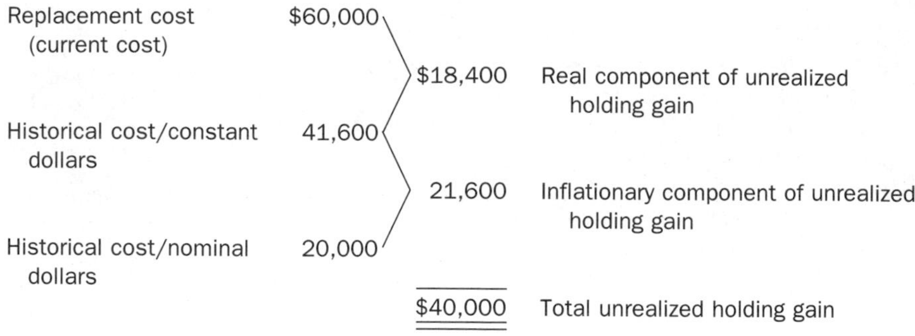

However, it should be noted that in presenting financial statements on a current cost/constant dollar basis, the inflationary component is not reported separately. The constant dollar adjustment is made for all nonmonetary items, and only the real component of unrealized holding gains is shown as a separate item. In the Campus Supply example, only the $18,400 holding gain on the land would be disclosed.

This example shows the impact of both general and specific price changes on only one item. It is indeed a complex problem to determine and report such information for all items on a balance sheet as well as to trace the impact of real and inflationary and realized and unrealized holding gains and losses through the income and retained earnings statements.

THE FASB EXPERIMENT

FASB Statement No. 33 was issued in September 1979 as an experiment in requiring supplementary information concerning the effects of changing prices on business enterprises. The statement initially required large, public companies to disclose both constant dollar and current cost information for the current year as well as summary data for the most recent five-year period. Subsequently, requirements for the disclosure of certain constant dollar data were eliminated, and other disclosure requirements were modified.

When Statement No. 33 was issued, the FASB indicated that it would review the results of the reporting requirements after five years. The Board completed that review and concluded in 1986 that further supplementary disclosures should be encouraged, but not required. The primary basis for that decision seemed to be a lack of public interest in and use of the supplemental data and a feeling that whatever benefits may be derived from the disclosures are not equal to the costs of providing the information.

The decision of the FASB to, in effect, rescind Statement No. 33 was not unanimous. Some members of the Board, and no doubt others, believe that inflation and specific price changes cause historical cost statements to show illusory profits and to hide the erosion of capital. These accountants view supplemental disclosures of changing prices as being relevant information necessary to prevent users from making incorrect economic decisions.

PROSPECTS FOR THE FUTURE

Some companies may continue to disclose supplemental information concerning changing prices. For example, changing price disclosures for Glenfed Inc. were shown in Chapter 4. Most companies, however, have discontinued the supplementary disclosures, since there is no reporting requirement. If inflation rates increase to higher levels, however, this topic may again become controversial, with increased pressure to consider additional reporting on a basis other than historical cost/nominal dollar.

While public concern about the impact of inflation has subsided, concern regarding the changing market value of a firm's assets and liabilities has increased. The savings and loan crisis has heightened the need for information relating to the current value of a firm's resources and obligations. To this end, the FASB, with gentle pressure from the SEC, issued SFAS No. 115, "Accounting for Certain Investments in Debt and Equity Securities," in May 1993. This standard requires firms to report most of their investments at current value. Firms are also required to recognize both realized and unrealized losses on these investments. This emphasis from both public and private standard setter on disclosing market value information highlights how the public's demand for quality information influences the standard-setting process.

FOREIGN CURRENCY FINANCIAL STATEMENTS

In Chapter 10, the issues associated with foreign exchange rates and their impact on accounting for transactions were introduced. In this section, the concepts associated with foreign currency are extended to include all financial statements. Foreign currency financial statements are financial statements prepared in a currency other than the local currency. For example, IBM has many European subsidiaries whose internal financial statements are prepared in French francs, German marks, etc. Those financial statements, when submitted to IBM headquarters in the United States, must be converted into U.S. dollars. The FASB has developed two methods for converting foreign currency financial statements—translation and remeasurement. **Translation** is used when the foreign subsidiary is a relatively self-contained unit that is independent from the parent company's operations. **Remeasurement** is appropriate when the subsidiary does not operate independently of the parent company. The translation process simply converts the foreign currency financial statements into the currency of the parent company (much like constant dollar accounting converts nominal dollars to constant dollars), while remeasurement involves remeasuring the financial statements as though the transactions had been originally recorded in dollars.

To determine the method of conversion, the **functional currency** of the foreign subsidiary must first be determined. The functional currency concept is developed in FASB Statement No. 52, which states that the functional currency of the foreign entity is the currency of the primary economic environment in which the entity operates. In most instances, the functional currency is the currency with which the entity generates and expends cash. Other factors may be examined when determining a firm's functional currency in addition to cash flows. FASB Statement No. 52 provides the following guidelines:[8]

1. If the sales price of the foreign entity's products is determined by worldwide competition rather than the local market, then the functional currency may be the parent's currency.
2. If costs for the foreign entity's product are primarily local costs, then the functional currency may be the foreign entity's local currency.
3. If the sales market is mostly in the parent's country or sales are denominated in the parent's currency, then the functional currency may be the parent's currency.
4. If financing is denominated in the foreign entity's local currency, then the functional currency may be the foreign entity's local currency.

8. *Statement of Financial Accounting Standards No. 52,* "Foreign Currency Translation" (Stamford: Financial Accounting Standards Board, 1981), Appendix A.

Management has the responsibility of weighing all relevant factors and determining the appropriate functional currency for the foreign entity. If management determines that the foreign entity's functional currency is its local currency, then the financial statements must be translated into U.S. dollars. The translation process, which uses the current exchange rate for conversion, maintains the relationship of the individual balance sheet and income statement components and allows foreign entities to be evaluated using the same measurement scales as the parent company.

If the functional currency is determined to be the parent's currency, then the financial statements must be remeasured into U.S. dollars. Remeasurement, which uses both historical and current exchange rates, produces financial statements that appear as if the foreign entity's transactions had been initially recorded in U.S. dollars. Most foreign entities generate and expend cash using their local currency, which differs from the parent's currency. The result is that most foreign financial statements that are converted into U.S. dollars involve the translation process. As a result, this chapter discusses the translation process. Remeasurement is typically discussed in advanced accounting courses.

Translation

Translation involves converting financial statement information from a subsidiary's functional currency to the parent company's reporting currency. For example, if IBM's French subsidiary has a functional currency of the French franc, then those francs must be translated into U.S. dollars. FASB Statement No. 52 specifies that translation must occur using the current exchange rate for assets and liabilities, while the weighted average rate is used in translating income statement items. Capital stock is translated at the historical rate, i.e., the spot rate on the date the subsidiary was acquired, and dividends are translated at the spot rate on the date of their declaration. Retained earnings is translated in the first year using historical rates, but in subsequent years, it is computed by taking the balance in retained earnings from the prior period's translated financial statements, adding translated net income, and subtracting translated dividends. As a result of the translation process, debits on a trial balance typically will not equal credits. The balancing figure is termed a translation adjustment and is disclosed in the stockholders' equity section of the balance sheet.

To illustrate the translation process, consider the following example. USA Co. purchased French Inc. on January 1, 1995. On that date, the exchange rate for one French franc was \$.25. On December 31, 1995, the following trial balance for French Inc. is available. The current exchange rate is \$.28, and the average exchange rate for the year was \$.27. Dividends were declared and paid when the exchange rate was \$.275.

Cash	10,000	francs	Accounts Payable	50,000	francs
Accounts Receivable	35,000		Long-Term Debt	80,000	
Inventory	65,000		Capital Stock	30,000	
Equipment	90,000		Retained Earnings	20,000	
Cost of Goods Sold	60,000		Sales	120,000	
Expenses	30,000				
Dividends	10,000				
Total debits	300,000	francs	Total credits	300,000	francs

If French Inc. determines its functional currency to be the French franc, translation is required to convert the financial statements into U.S. dollars. As stated previously, the current rate is used to translate assets and liabilities, and the average rate is used to translate income statement items. The translation process is as follows:

December 31, 1995	Trial Balance (In French Francs)	Exchange Rate	Trial Balance (In U.S. Dollars)
Cash	10,000	$.28	$ 2,800
Accounts Receivable	35,000	.28	9,800
Inventory	65,000	.28	18,200
Equipment	90,000	.28	25,200
Cost of Goods Sold	60,000	.27	16,200
Expenses	30,000	.27	8,100
Dividends	10,000	.275	2,750
	300,000		$83,050
Accounts Payable	50,000	$.28	$14,000
Long-Term Debt	80,000	.28	22,400
Capital Stock	30,000	.25	7,500
Retained Earnings	20,000	.25	5,000
Sales	120,000	.27	32,400
Translation Adjustment			1,750
	300,000		$83,050

In this example, French Inc. requires a credit translation adjustment. This adjustment reflects the effect of exchange rate changes on the financial statement elements of French Inc. The financial statements of French Inc. can be prepared directly from the translated trial balance, with the translation adjustment being reported in the stockholders' equity section of the balance sheet.

In 1996, similar procedures are followed. Care must be taken when dealing with the retained earnings account, however. Recall that in subsequent years this account balance is computed rather than calculated using exchange rates. The balance in the retained earnings account on December 31, 1996, prior to the closing entries being made, is 40,000 francs, or $10,350 (a beginning balance of $5,000 plus net income for 1995 of $8,100 less dividends for 1995 of $2,750). This $10,350 is the amount of retained earnings that appears on the December 31, 1996, translated trial balance. The translation process for 1996 is illustrated below. The exchange rate on December 31, 1996, is $.24, and the average rate for the year was $.26. Dividends were declared and paid when the exchange rate was $.25.

December 31, 1996	Trial Balance (In French Francs)	Exchange Rate	Trial Balance (In U.S. Dollars)
Cash	15,000	$.24	$ 3,600
Accounts Receivable	50,000	.24	12,000
Inventory	85,000	.24	20,400
Equipment	100,000	.24	24,000
Cost of Goods Sold	90,000	.26	23,400
Expenses	55,000	.26	14,300
Dividends	5,000	.25	1,250
Translation Adjustment			900
	400,000		$99,850
Accounts Payable	90,000	$.24	$21,600
Long-Term Debt	100,000	.24	24,000
Capital Stock	30,000	.25	7,500
Retained Earnings	40,000	computed	10,350
Sales	140,000	.26	36,400
	400,000		$99,850

Inflation in Foreign Countries

Petroleo Brasileiro is Brazil's largest oil and energy company. In 1987, Petroleo Brasileiro reported operating income before any adjustments for changing prices of 122,266 million cruzados. (On December 31, 1987, one cruzado equaled $.0139.) However, price-level restatements and monetary and exchange adjustments resulted in a reduction to operating income of 112,123 million cruzados, leaving adjusted operating income at 10,143 million cruzados.

Questions:

1. Brazil was experiencing high inflation during 1987. What would be the effect of inflation on Petroleo Brasileiro's positive net monetary position?
2. Did the adjustment to income from inflation materially impact the energy company's operating income?
3. If inflation is running at a low rate, is there a need for price-level adjusted accounting information?

Source: Petroleo Brasileiro 1987 income statement.

The financial statements for French Inc. for 1996 are produced from the translated trial balance and are reproduced below.

Income Statement
For the Year Ended December 31, 1996

Sales	$36,400
Cost of goods sold	23,400
Gross margin	$13,000
Expenses	14,300
Net loss	$ (1,300)
Retained earnings, January 1, 1996	10,350
	$ 9,050
Less dividends	1,250
Retained earnings, December 31, 1996	$ 7,800

Balance Sheet
December 31, 1996

Assets	
Cash	$ 3,600
Accounts receivable	12,000
Inventory	20,400
Equipment	24,000
Total assets	$60,000
Liabilities and Equity	
Accounts payable	$21,600
Long-term debt	24,000
Capital stock	7,500
Retained earnings	7,800
Translation adjustment	(900)
Total liabilities and equity	$60,000

The impact of translation on financial statement ratios depends on whether the same rates were used to convert the numerator and denominator in the ratios. Because the same rate is used to translate assets and liabilities, the current ratio, for example, will be the same before and after translation. Because a weighted average exchange rate is used to convert all income statement items, the profit margin, for example, will also be the same both before and after translation. Using the above example, the 1996 current ratio in francs and dollars for French Inc. is as follows:

	French Francs	U.S. Dollars
$\frac{\text{Current assets}}{\text{Current liabilities}}$	$\frac{150{,}000}{90{,}000} = 1.67$	$\frac{\$36{,}000}{\$21{,}600} = 1.67$

SUMMARY

If a company has foreign subsidiaries, exchange rates also effect the conversion of the foreign entity's financial statements into U.S. dollars. The method of conversion depends on the foreign entity's functional currency. The functional currency is typically the currency in which the foreign entity generates and expends cash. If the functional currency is determined to be the foreign entity's local currency, the financial statements are translated. If the functional currency is determined to be the parent's currency, the financial statements are remeasured. The difference between the two methods is in the use of different exchange rates. When foreign financial statements are translated, the resulting translation adjustment is reported in the stockholders' equity section of the balance sheet.

KEY TERMS

QUESTIONS

1. (a) Why have accountants traditionally preferred to report historical costs rather than current costs in conventional statements? (b) What are some of the limitations of historical cost statements?
2. What are the 3 alternatives to reporting historical cost/nominal dollar financial statements and how do they differ from conventional reporting practice?
3. (a) What are general purchasing power dollars? (b) How are they different from equivalent purchasing power units?
4. Historically, what has caused an increased interest in reporting financial statements adjusted for price changes?
5. (a) How does constant dollar reporting differ from current cost reporting? (b) What is the objective of constant dollar reporting and how is this objective accomplished?
6. (a) How are general price indexes computed? (b) What are some of their limitations? (c) Which index is recommended by the FASB?
7. If equipment was purchased for $85,000 at the beginning of the year when the CPI-U was 160, how would the equipment be recorded on a constant dollar, end-of-year balance sheet if the year-end CPI-U was 180?
8. Distinguish between monetary assets and nonmonetary assets and indicate which of the following are monetary assets.
   (a) Cash
   (b) Investment in common stock
   (c) Investment in bonds
   (d) Merchandise on hand
   (e) Prepaid expenses
   (f) Buildings
   (g) Patents
   (h) Sinking fund—uninvested cash
   (i) Sinking fund—investments in real estate
   (j) Deferred development costs
9. Assume a company holds property or maintains the obligations listed below during a year in which there is an increase in the general price level. State in each case whether the real position of the company at the end of the year is better, worse, or unchanged.
   (a) Cash
   (b) Cash surrender value of life insurance
   (c) Land
   (d) Unearned subscription revenue
   (e) Accounts receivable
   (f) Notes payable
   (g) Inventory
   (h) Long-term warranties on sales
10. Indicate whether a company sustains a gain or loss in purchasing power under each of the following conditions.
    (a) A company maintains an excess of monetary assets over monetary liabilities during a period of general price-level increase.
    (b) A company maintains an excess of monetary liabilities over monetary assets during a period of general price-level increase.
    (c) A company maintains an excess of monetary assets over monetary liabilities during a period of general price-level decrease.
    (d) A company maintains an excess of monetary liabilities over monetary assets during a period of general price-level decrease.
11. (a) What is the objective of current cost accounting? (b) Give examples of definitions of current costs.
12. Define the concept of "well-offness."
13. (a) Distinguish between realized and unrealized holding gains and losses. (b) Distinguish between the real and inflationary components of total holding gains and losses.
14. What are the two recommended approaches used to determine appropriate current values?
15. Briefly explain the advantages and disadvantages of current cost accounting as compared to constant dollar and historical cost accounting.
16. Distinguish between the current cost/constant dollar approach and the current cost/nominal dollar approach to financial reporting.
17. A foreign subsidiary's functional currency determines whether its financial statements should be translated or remeasured. Identify the primary factor in determining a firm's functional currency. What other factors can influence management's determination as to the firm's functional currency?

18. When financial statements are translated, which exchange rate is used for translating assets and liabilities? Which exchange rate is used for translating common stock? Which exchange rate is used for translating income statement items?

19. When financial statements are translated, what is the difference between the resulting debits and credits called? Where is this difference disclosed on the balance sheet?

DISCUSSION CASES

Case 24—1 (Which reporting alternative is best?)

At a recent executive committee meeting, the officers of Celebrar Corporation entered into a lively discussion concerning changing prices in the economy and financial reporting. Kyle Jones, the controller, argued that the FASB was smart to experiment with reporting alternatives in Statement No. 33, since something must be done to reflect price changes. The economic analyst, Marie Colton, argued strongly for a current cost approach. Colton had little good to say about "irrelevant" historical costs, even if adjusted to constant dollars. On the other hand, Ted Starley, the marketing V.P., felt comfortable with historical cost data. Starley understands that approach and has confidence in the objectivity of the numbers reported. As president of the company, what position do you take?

Case 24—2 (Constant dollar theory)

Published financial statements of U.S. companies are currently prepared on a "stable-dollar" assumption, even though the general purchasing power of the dollar has declined considerably because of inflation over the past several years. To account for this changing value of the dollar, many accountants suggest that financial statements should be adjusted for general price-level changes. Two independent statements regarding constant dollar financial statements follow. Each statement contains some fallacious reasoning.

Statement 1

The accounting profession has not seriously considered constant dollar financial statements before, because the rate of inflation usually has been so small from year to year that the adjustments would have been immaterial in amount. Constant dollar financial statements represent a departure from the historical cost basis of accounting. Financial statements should be prepared from facts, not estimates.

Statement 2

If financial statements were adjusted for general price-level changes, depreciation charges in the earnings statement would permit the recovery of dollars of current purchasing power and thereby equal the cost of new assets to replace the old ones. Constant dollar adjusted data would yield balance sheet amounts closely approximating current values. Furthermore, management can make better decisions if constant dollar financial statements are published.

Evaluate each of the independent statements, identify the areas of fallacious reasoning in each, and explain why the reasoning is incorrect.

Case 24—3 (Current valuation of assets)

The financial statements of a business entity could be prepared by using historical cost or current value as a measurement basis. In addition, the basis could be stated in terms of unadjusted dollars or dollars restated for changes in purchasing power. The various combinations of these two separate and distinct areas are shown in the following matrix:

	Unadjusted dollars	Dollars restated for changes in purchasing power
Historical cost	1	2
Current value	3	4

Block 1 of the matrix represents the traditional method of accounting for transactions, wherein the absolute (unadjusted) amount of dollars given up or received is recorded for the asset or liability obtained (relationship between resources). Amounts recorded in the method described in block 1 reflect the original cost of the asset or liability and do not take into account any change in value of the unit of measure (standard of comparison). This method assumes the validity of the accounting concepts of going concern and stable monetary unit. Any gain or loss (including holding and purchasing power gains or losses) resulting from the sale or satisfaction of amounts recorded under this method is deferred in its entirety until sale or satisfaction.

For each of the remaining matrix blocks, respond to the following questions. Limit your discussion to nonmonetary assets only.

1. How will this method of recording assets affect the relationship between resources and the standard of comparison?
2. What is the theoretic justification for using each method?

Case 24—4 (Translation or remeasurement?)

As the chief financial officer for Harvestors Inc., you are responsible for preparing the consolidated financial statements for your firm. Your first problem is how to consolidate the French subsidiary your company purchased during the past year. You have recently received the subsidiary's year-end financial statements and find that they are stated in French francs. Before you can consolidate the financial statements, you must first convert them from French francs to U.S. dollars. You know that foreign financial statements can be either translated or remeasured and must now determine which method is appropriate.

What factors should you consider in determining whether the financial statements should be translated or remeasured? Who has the final say in determining which method is used? What are the major differences between translation and remeasurement?

EXERCISES

Exercise 24—5 (Classification of monetary and nonmonetary items)

Classify the following accounts as either monetary or nonmonetary.

Assets

Current assets:
- Cash
- Marketable securities (stocks)
- Receivables (net of allowance)
- Inventories
- Prepaid rent
- Discount on notes payable
- Deferred tax asset

Long-term investments:
- Affiliated companies, at cost
- Cash surrender value of life insurance
- Bond retirement fund
- Investment in bonds

Land, buildings, and equipment:
- Land
- Buildings
- Equipment

Intangible assets:
- Patents
- Goodwill
- Advances paid on purchase contracts

Liabilities and Stockholders' Equity

Current liabilities:
- Accounts and notes payable
- Dividends payable
- Refundable deposits on returnable containers
- Advances on sales contracts

Long-term liabilities:
- Bonds payable
- Premium on bonds payable

Stockholders' equity:
- Preferred stock (at fixed liquidation price)
- Common stock
- Retained earnings

Exercise 24—6 (Computing purchasing power gains or losses)

On January 1, 1996, Camden Corporation had monetary assets of $5,000,000 and monetary liabilities of $2,000,000. During 1996, Camden's monetary inflows and outflows were relatively constant and equal so that it ended the year with net monetary assets of $3,000,000.

1. Assume that the CPI-U was 200 on January 1, 1996, and 220 on December 31, 1996. In end-of-year constant dollars, what is Camden's purchasing power gain or loss for 1996?
2. Assume that the CPI-U was 200 on January 1, 1996, and 180 on December 31, 1996. In average-year constant dollars, what is Camden's purchasing power gain or loss for 1996?

Exercise 24—7 (Adjusting expenses to constant dollars)

Assuming prices rise evenly by 6% during the year, compute the amount of expenses stated in terms of year-end constant dollars in each of the following independent cases:

1. Expenses of $1,000,000 were paid at the beginning of the year for services received during the first half of the year.
2. Expenses of $250,000 were paid at the end of each quarter for services received during the quarter.
3. Expenses of $250,000 were paid at the beginning of each quarter for services received during the quarter.
4. Expenses of $1,000,000 were paid evenly throughout the year for services received during the year.

Exercise 24—8 (Constant dollar depreciation)

The financial statements for Superior Corp. showed the original cost of depreciable assets purchased over the years as $3,500,000 at December 31, 1995, and $4,200,000 at December 31, 1996. These assets are being depreciated on a straight-line basis over a 10-year period with no residual value. Acquisitions of $700,000 were made on January 1, 1996. A full year's depreciation was taken in the year of acquisition.

Superior presents constant dollar financial statements as supplemental information to its historical cost financial statements. The December 31, 1995, depreciable asset balance (before accumulated depreciation) restated to reflect 1996 average purchasing power was $4,060,000.

Compute the amount of depreciation expense that should be shown in the constant dollar income statement for 1996 if the general price-level index was 110 at December 31, 1995, and 130 at December 31, 1996. Assume that the constant dollar financial statements are to be expressed in average 1996 dollars.

Exercise 24—9 (Constant dollar restatement of income and retained earnings statement)

A comparative income statement for the Linquist Company for the first 2 years of operations appears below.

	Results of Operations			
	First Year		Second Year	
Sales		$750,000		$900,000
Cost of goods sold:				
Beginning inventory	—		$300,000	
Purchases	$750,000		500,000	
Goods available for sale	$750,000		$800,000	
Ending inventory	300,000	450,000	400,000	400,000
Gross profit on sales		$300,000		$500,000
Operating expenses:				
Depreciation	$ 30,000		$ 30,000	
Other	240,000	270,000	350,000	380,000
Net income		$ 30,000		$120,000
Dividends		15,000		30,000
Increase in retained earnings		$ 15,000		$ 90,000

Prepare a comparative income and retained earnings statement expressing items in constant dollars at the end of the second year, considering the following data:

(a) Prices rose evenly, and index numbers expressing the general price-level changes were:

Beginning of first year	100
End of first year	110
End of second year	140

(b) Sales and purchases were made and expenses were incurred evenly each year.
(c) Inventories were reported at cost using first-in, first-out pricing; average indexes for the year are applicable in restating inventories.
(d) Depreciation relates to equipment acquired at the beginning of the first year.
(e) Dividends were paid at the middle of each year.
(f) Assume no purchasing power gain or loss in either year.

Exercise 24—10 (Constant dollar restatement of balance sheet)

Comparative balance sheet data for Fletch Inc. since its formation are presented below. The general price level during the 2-year period went up steadily; index numbers expressing the general price-level changes are listed following the balance sheet. Restate the comparative balance sheet data in terms of constant dollars at the end of the second year.

	End of First Year	End of Second Year
Cash	$ 90,000	$ 75,000
Receivables	60,000	84,000
*Land, buildings, and equipment (net)	156,000	138,000
	$306,000	$297,000
Payables	$ 81,000	$ 54,000
Capital stock	192,000	192,000
Retained earnings	33,000	51,000
	$306,000	$297,000

*Acquired at the beginning of the first year

General Price Index	
Beginning of first year	106
End of first year	120
End of second year	130

Exercise 24—11 (Adjustment to average-year constant dollars)

The historical cost/constant dollar income statement of the Dunn Corporation shows a purchasing power loss of $3,000 based on end-of-year constant dollars. Price indexes were as follows:

Beginning of year	120
Average	145
End of year	170

Calculate the purchasing power loss in average-year dollars.

Exercise 24—12 (Current cost income)

On January 1, 1996, Outerspace Corp. purchased 1,000 robots at $25 per robot. As of December 31, 1996, Outerspace had sold three-fourths of the robots at $32 per robot, and the robot manufacturer (supplier) was selling to retailers (Outerspace) at $28 per robot.

Compute the operating gross profit for 1996 on a current cost basis. Also identify the amount of realized holding gain and unrealized holding gain. Ignore income taxes.

Exercise 24—13 (Current cost depreciation)

Detmer Company began operating on December 31, 1993, at which time it purchased operating machinery for $3,000,000. These assets were expected to have a 15-year life with no residual value and are to be depreciated using the straight-line method.

The following information is available:

(a) Current value of assets (as if new)	
December 31, 1995	$5,000,000
December 31, 1996	5,500,000
(b) General price-level index values:	
December 31, 1993	120
December 31, 1995	140
December 31, 1996	155
1996 average (rounded)	148

Compute the following:

1. Current-value depreciation expense for 1996 in terms of average dollars from 1996.
2. Realized holding gains from the use (and depreciation) of the asset during 1996 measured in terms of average dollars from 1996.

Exercise 24—14 (Current cost/constant dollar balance sheet)

The current cost/nominal dollar balance sheet for the Josh Corporation at December 31, 1996, is shown below. The equipment and land were purchased at year-end. The inventory is valued at year-end current prices. The capital stock was issued when the consumer price index was 240. The consumer price index at December 31, 1996, was 270. Prepare a current cost/constant dollar balance sheet for the Josh Corporation at December 31, 1996, stated in end-of-year constant dollars.

Josh Corporation
Balance Sheet
December 31, 1996
(Current Cost/Nominal Dollar Basis)

Assets		Liabilities and Stockholders' Equity	
Cash	$ 10,000	Accounts payable	$ 20,000
Accounts receivable	15,000	Interest payable	10,000
Inventory	30,000	Total liabilities	$ 30,000
Equipment (net)	50,000	Capital stock	$ 80,000
Land	45,000	Retained earnings	40,000
		Total stockholders' equity	$120,000
Total assets	$150,000	Total liabilities and stockholders' equity	$150,000

Exercise 24—15 (Reporting alternatives)

Gifford Company purchased land for $150,000 in 1995 when the price index was 150. At the end of 1996 when the price index was 175, the land had a fair market value of $180,000. How would the land be reported on the balance sheet under each of the following approaches?

1. Historical cost/nominal dollar
2. Historical cost/constant dollar
3. Current cost/nominal dollar
4. Current cost/constant dollar (year-end dollars)

Exercise 24—16 (Translating foreign currency financial statements–date of acquisition)
On January 3, 1996, American Can Co. purchased International Metals, a Canadian company. On the day of the purchase, the exchange rate for one Canadian dollar was $.79 (U.S.). International Metals' balance sheet on the date of the purchase is presented below.

	(In Canadian Dollars)
Assets	
Cash	$ 58,000
Accounts receivable	112,500
Inventory	91,800
Plant assets	135,400
Total assets	$397,700
Liabilities and Equity	
Accounts payable	$165,600
Long-term debt	88,000
Capital stock	65,100
Retained earnings	79,000
Total liabilities and equity	$397,700

Prepare a translated balance sheet as of January 3, 1996.

Exercise 24—17 (Translating foreign currency financial statements)
The following financial statement for International Data Products, a Japanese subsidiary of National Data Products, is available.

Trial Balance

	(In Japanese Yen)
Cash	6,000,000
Accounts Receivable	18,500,000
Inventory	21,250,000
Equipment	27,700,000
Cost of Goods Sold	36,000,000
Expenses	15,500,000
Dividends	5,000,000
Total assets	129,950,000
Accounts Payable	24,000,000
Long-Term Debt	12,000,000
Capital Stock	20,000,000
Retained Earnings	15,950,000
Sales	58,000,000
Total liabilities and equity	129,950,000

The exchange rate when the subsidiary was purchased was $.0055. The current exchange rate is $.007, the average exchange rate for the year was $.0065, and the exchange rate on the date dividends were declared and paid was $.0067. The computed retained earnings balance from the previous year's translated financial statements was $105,000.

1. Prepare a translated trial balance for International Data Products using the information provided.
2. Prepare an income statement and a balance sheet for International Data Products using the information contained in the translated trial balance.

PROBLEMS

Problem 24—18 (Constant dollar adjustments and replacement costs)

Valuation to reflect constant dollar adjustments would yield differing amounts on a firm's financial statements as opposed to replacement costs.

Transactions regarding one asset of a company who operates on a calendar-year basis are as follows:

1994 Purchased land for $48,000 cash on December 31. Replacement cost at year-end was $48,000.
1995 Held land all year. Replacement cost at year-end was $62,400.
1996 December 31—sold land for $81,600.

General price-level index at:

December 31, 1994	120
December 31, 1995	132
December 31, 1996	144

Instructions: Duplicate the following schedule and complete the information required based on the foregoing transactions. Express all constant dollar amounts in year-end dollars. Do not distinguish between realized and unrealized holding gains.

	Historical Cost		Replacement Cost	
	Nominal Dollar	Constant Dollar	Unadjusted for Inflation	Adjusted for Inflation
Valuation of land:				
December 31, 1994	______	______	______	______
December 31, 1995	______	______	______	______
Gain on income statement:				
1994	______	______	______	______
1995	______	______	______	______
1996	______	______	______	______
Total	______	______	______	______

Problem 24—19 (Constant dollar adjustment for cost of goods sold and depreciation)

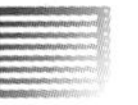

The following information was taken from the books of the Top Value Company during its first 2 years of operations:

	Useful Life	1995	1996
Beginning inventory		$150,000	$200,000
Purchases		550,000	500,000
Ending inventory		200,000	160,000
Building (acquired 1/1/95)	25 years	400,000	—
Office equipment (acquired 7/1/95)	12 years	30,000	—
Machinery (acquired 10/1/95)	8 years	16,000	—
Price index (1/1)		190	202
Price index (12/31)*		202	214

*Assume prices rose evenly throughout the year.

Instructions:

1. Calculate the cost of goods sold for 1995 and 1996 in terms of respective year-end dollars assuming a LIFO inventory cost flow with average costs used for any increments. Assume the 1995 beginning inventory was purchased on January 1, 1995. Round to the nearest dollar amount.
2. Restate depreciable assets and accumulated depreciation (straight-line, ignore salvage values) reporting the depreciation for 1995 and 1996 in terms of 1995 and 1996 year-end dollars, respectively.

Problem 24—20 (Converting nominal dollar financial data to constant dollars)

Midwest Inc., a retailer, was organized during 1993. Midwest's management has decided to supplement its December 31, 1996, historical dollar financial statements with constant dollar financial statements. The following general ledger trial balance (historical dollar) and additional information have been furnished:

Midwest Inc.
Trial Balance
December 31, 1996

	Debits	Credits
Cash and Receivables (net)	$ 432,000	
Trading Securities (U.S. Treasury bonds)	320,000	
Inventory	352,000	
Equipment	520,000	
Accumulated Depreciation—Equipment		$ 131,200
Accounts Payable		240,000
6% First-Mortgage Bonds, due 2001		400,000
Common Stock, $8 par		800,000
Retained Earnings, December 31, 1995 (deficit)	36,800	
Sales		1,520,000
Cost of Sales	1,206,400	
Depreciation	52,000	
Other Operating Expenses and Interest	$ 172,000	
Total	$3,091,200	$3,091,200

(a) Monetary assets (cash and receivables) exceeded monetary liabilities (accounts payable and bonds payable) by $356,000 at December 31, 1995.

(b) Purchases ($1,152,000 in 1996) and sales are made evenly throughout the year.

(c) Depreciation is computed on a straight-line basis, with a full year's depreciation being taken in the year of acquisition and none in the year of retirement. The depreciation rate is 10%, and no residual value is anticipated. Acquisitions and retirements have been made evenly over each year, and the retirements in 1996 consisted of assets purchased during 1994 that were scrapped. No cash was received.

An analysis of the equipment account reveals the following:

Year	Beginning Balance	Additions	Retirements	Ending Balance
1994		440,000		440,000
1995	440,000	8,000		448,000
1996	448,000	120,000	48,000	520,000

(d) The bonds were issued in 1994, and the trading securities were purchased evenly throughout 1996. Other operating expenses and interest were incurred evenly throughout the year and paid in cash.

(e) Assume that the relevant price-index values were as follows:

Annual Average		Quarterly Average	
1994	110	1995	
1995	122	Fourth	123
1996	128	1996	
		First	124
		Second	128
		Third	127
		Fourth	130

Instructions: In completing the following requirements, use constant dollars from the fourth quarter of 1996.

1. Prepare a schedule to convert the equipment account balance at December 31, 1996, from nominal to constant dollars.
2. Prepare (in nominal dollars) an analysis of the accumulated depreciation—equipment account for the years 1994 through 1996.
3. Prepare a schedule to express the accumulated depreciation—equipment account balance as of December 31, 1996, in terms of constant dollars.
4. Prepare a schedule to compute Midwest's purchasing power gain or loss on its net holdings or monetary assets for 1996.

Problem 24—21 (Analysis of EPS & ROI in terms of constant dollars)

To obtain a more realistic appraisal of her investment, Sheri West, your client, has asked you to adjust certain financial data of the International Company for general price-level changes. On January 1, 1994, West invested $50,000 in the International Company in return for 10,000 shares of common stock. Immediately after her investment, the trial balance data appeared as follows:

	Debit	Credit
Cash and Receivables	$ 75,000	
Merchandise Inventory	4,000	
Building	50,000	
Accumulated Depreciation—Building		$ 8,000
Equipment	36,000	
Accumulated Depreciation—Equipment		7,200
Land	10,000	
Current Liabilities		50,000
Capital Stock, $5 par		100,000
Retained Earnings		9,800
	$175,000	$175,000

Balances in certain selected accounts as of December 31, 1994-1996, were as follows:

	1994	1995	1996
Sales	$39,650	$39,000	$42,350
Inventory	4,500	5,600	5,347
Purchases	14,475	16,350	18,150
Operating expenses (excluding depreciation)	10,050	9,050	9,075

Assume the 1994 price level as the base year and all changes in the price level take place at the beginning of each year. Further assume the 1995 price level is 10% above the 1994 price level and the 1996 price level is 10% above the 1995 level.

The building was constructed in 1990 at a cost of $50,000 with an estimated life of 25 years. The price level at that time was 80% of the 1994 price level.

The equipment was purchased in 1992 at a cost of $36,000 with an estimated life of 10 years. The price level at that time was 90% of the 1994 price level.

The LIFO method of inventory valuation is used. The original inventory was acquired in the same year the building was constructed and was maintained at a constant $4,000 until 1994. In 1994 a gradual buildup of the inventory was begun in anticipation of an increase in the volume of business.

West considers the return on her investment as the dividend she actually receives. In 1994 and also in 1996 the International Company paid cash dividends to stockholders in the amount of $8,000.

Instructions:

1. Compute the 1996 earnings per share of common stock in terms of 1994 dollars.
2. Compute the percentage return on West's investment for 1994 and 1996 in terms of 1994 dollars.

Problem 24—22 (Restatement of balance sheet to constant dollars)

The Layton Co. began operations in 1965. At the end of 1996 it was decided to furnish stockholders with a balance sheet restated in terms of constant 1996 dollars as a supplement to the conventional financial statements. This is the first time such a statement was prepared. The balance sheet prepared in conventional form at the end of 1996 follows:

Layton Co.
Balance Sheet
December 31, 1996

Assets		Liabilities and Stockholders' Equity	
Cash	$ 187,600	Accounts payable	$ 379,900
Accounts receivable	342,400	Mortgage note payable	450,000
Inventory	742,300	Bonds payable	1,250,000
Land	1,720,000	Capital stock	1,000,000
Building	2,115,000	Additional paid-in capital	200,000
Less accumulated depreciation	(705,000)	Retained earnings	1,122,400
Total assets	$4,402,300	Total liabilities and stockholders' equity	$4,402,300

All the stock was issued in 1965. Land was purchased subject to a mortgage note of $1,000,000 at the time the company was formed. The present building is being depreciated on a straight-line basis with a 30-year life and no salvage value. The bonds were issued in 1975. The company uses the first-in, first-out method in pricing inventories.

Instructions: Prepare a balance sheet for the Layton Co. restated in terms of 1996 constant dollars. Use the following indexes in making adjustments; assume the index for each year is regarded as representative of the price level for the entire year.

Year	Price Index	Price Year	Index
1965	54.9	1993	160.1
1975	70.7	1994	168.0
1985	93.0	1995	178.6
1987	100.0	1996	185.2
1992	146.5		

Problem 24—23 (Restatement of income statement to constant dollars)

The income statement prepared at the end of the year for Novasano Corporation follows:

Novasano Corporation
Income Statement
For the Year Ended December 31, 1996

Sales		$350,000
Less sales discount		15,000
Net sales		$335,000
Cost of goods sold:		
Inventory, January 1	$125,000	
Purchases	180,000	
Goods available for sale	$305,000	
Inventory, December 31	120,000	
Total cost of goods sold		185,000

Novasano Corporation
Income Statement continued

Gross profit on sales		$150,000
Operating expenses:		
Depreciation	$ 21,250	
Other operating expenses	50,000	
Total operating expenses		71,250
Income before income tax		$ 78,750
Income tax		31,300
Net income		$ 47,450

The following additional information is available:

(a) The price index rose evenly throughout the year from 120 on January 1 to 130 on December 31.

(b) Sales were made evenly throughout the year; expenses were incurred evenly throughout the year.

(c) The inventory was valued at cost using first-in, first-out pricing; average indexes for the year are used in restating inventories. The beginning inventory was acquired in the preceding period when the average index was 122.

(d) The depreciation charge relates to the following items:

	Asset Cost	Index at Date of Acquisition	Depreciation Rate
Building	$75,000	95	3%
Equipment	80,000	95	12 1/2%
Equipment	20,000	98	12 1/2%
Equipment*	39,000	120	16 2/3%

*Acquired at the beginning of the current year.

(e) Semiannual dividends of $7,500 were declared and paid at the end of June and at the end of December.

(f) The balance sheet position for the company changed during the year as follows:

	January 1	December 31
Current assets	$180,000	$174,700
Building and equipment (net)	120,000	137,750
	$300,000	$312,450
Current liabilities	$ 55,000	$ 35,000
Capital stock	200,000	200,000
Retained earnings	45,000	77,450
	$300,000	$312,450

Instructions: Prepare an income statement in which items are stated in end-of-year dollars accompanied by a schedule summarizing the purchasing power gain or loss for 1996.

Problem 24—24 (Restatement of financial statements to constant dollars)

Financial statements are prepared for the Missouri Company at the end of each year in nominal dollars and are also measured in constant dollars. Balance sheet data summarized in nominal dollars and in constant dollars at the end of 1995 are given below.

	Nominal Dollars		Constant Dollars (Reporting Purchasing Power at End of Year)	
Assets				
Cash		$ 23,000		$ 23,000
Accounts receivable		70,000		70,000
Inventory		105,000		106,500
Buildings and equipment	$120,000		$153,600	
Less accumulated depreciation	48,000	72,000	61,440	92,160
Land		50,000		64,000
Total assets		$320,000		$355,660
Liabilities				
Accounts payable		$ 48,000		$ 48,000
Long-term liabilities		40,000		40,000
Total liabilities		$ 88,000		$ 88,000
Stockholders' Equity				
Capital stock		$150,000		$192,000
Retained earnings		82,000		75,660
Total stockholders' equity		$232,000		$267,660
Total liabilities and stockholders' equity		$320,000		$355,660

Data from statements measured in nominal dollars at the end of 1996 are given below.

Balance Sheet		Income and Retained Earnings Statement	
Assets			
Cash	$ 83,840	Sales	$1,100,000
Accounts receivable	72,500	Cost of goods sold	600,000
Inventory	125,000	Gross profit on sales	$ 500,000
Buildings and equipment	120,000	Operating expenses	308,000
Accumulated depreciation	(56,000)	Income before income tax	$ 192,000
Land	50,000	Income tax	85,660
	$395,340	Net income	$ 106,340
		Dividends	20,000
		Increase in retained earnings	$ 86,340
Liabilities and Stockholders' Equity			
Accounts payable	$ 37,000		
Long-term liabilities	40,000		
Capital stock	150,000		
Retained earnings	168,340		
	$395,340		

The following additional information is available at the end of 1996:

(a) Price indexes were as follows for the year:

January 1	150
December 31	153

(b) Sales and purchases were made evenly, and expenses were incurred evenly, throughout the year.

(c) The first-in, first-out method was used to compute inventory cost; average indexes for the year are used in restating inventories.
(d) All the land, buildings, and equipment were acquired when the company was formed.
(e) Dividends were declared and paid at the end of the year.

Instructions: Prepare in terms of end-of-year constant dollars:

1. An income and retained earnings statement accompanied by a schedule summarizing the purchasing power gain or loss for 1996.
2. A balance sheet as of December 31, 1996.

Problem 24—25 (Reporting constant dollar information)

The historical cost income statement for the Colorado Company is presented below.

Colorado Company
Income Statement
For the Year Ended December 31, 1996

Sales		$180,000
Cost of goods sold:		
Beginning inventory	$ 20,000	
Purchases	140,000	
Goods available for sale	$160,000	
Ending inventory	50,000	
Cost of goods sold		110,000
Gross profit		$ 70,000
Operating expenses:		
Depreciation expense	$ 10,000	
Other expenses	20,000	30,000
Net income		$ 40,000

The following additional information is provided:

(a) Sales, purchases, and other expenses were incurred evenly over the year.
(b) The beginning inventory was purchased when the price index was 180. Assume the ending inventory was acquired when the price index was 220.
(c) Price indexes were as follows:

Beginning of year	200
Average for year	220
End of year	240

(d) The equipment on which the depreciation expense is computed was purchased when the price index was 110.

Instructions: Prepare a statement showing income from continuing operations in average-year constant dollars.

Problem 24—26 (Current cost accounting)

Hastings Inc. adopted a current cost system in its first year of operations. At the start of the first year, 1996, the company purchased $168,000 of inventory, and at the end of the year had an inventory of $100,800 on a historical cost basis and $164,500 on a current cost basis. At the time the inventory was sold, the current cost of the inventory was $107,800. Sales for the year were $182,000. Ignore all tax effects and assume that the CPI-U did not change over this period. Other expenses were $8,400 on both historical cost and current cost bases.

Instructions:

1. Prepare a current cost income statement.
2. What is the increase in the specific price of inventory during the year?

Problem 24—27 (Translating foreign currency financial statements)

Anaconda Inc., a multinational producer of computer hardware, has subsidiaries located throughout the world. The company recently received year-end financial statements from its French subsidiary, a company that was purchased on January 1, 1995. Those financial statements are prepared and submitted to company headquarters in French francs. The accountant in charge of translating the financial statements has been unable to locate last year's translated financial statements. Instead, all that is available from last year is the financial statements prepared in francs. The adjusted trial balances as of December 31, 1995 and 1996, in French francs, are as follows:

	Trial Balance Dec. 31, 1996	Trial Balance Dec. 31, 1995
Cash	925,000	750,000
Accounts Receivable	1,875,000	1,215,000
Inventory	2,115,000	1,850,000
Equipment	1,025,000	975,000
Cost of Goods Sold	7,985,000	6,505,000
Expenses	4,234,000	3,156,000
Dividends	900,000	500,000
Total assets	19,059,000	14,951,000
Accounts Payable	2,100,000	1,825,000
Long-Term Debt	1,000,000	1,125,000
Capital Stock	1,200,000	1,200,000
Retained Earnings (balance at beginningof year)	640,000	301,000
Sales	14,119,000	10,500,000
Total liabilities and equity	19,059,000	14,951,000

Relevant exchange rates for 1996 and 1995 are as follows:

	1996	1995
January 1	.196	.175
Date of dividend payment	.205	.188
Average rate for the year	.210	.178
December 31	.228	.196

Instructions: Using the information given, prepare a translated income statement and balance sheet for 1996.

Problem 24—28 (Translating foreign currency financial statements)

Renecko Corp., a company with headquarters in London, England, is a fully owned subsidiary of AmericaWest Inc. The accountant for AmericaWest just received Renecko's financial statements and must translate them in order to prepare consolidated financial statements. Income statement and balance sheet data for the year just ended, along with relevant exchange rates, are as follows:

	(In Pounds)
Revenues	350,000
Cost of goods sold	218,000
Gross margin	132,000
Other expenses	74,000
Net income	58,000

	(In Pounds)
Cash	55,000
Accounts receivable	113,000
Inventory	89,000
Plant and equipment	121,000
Total assets	378,000
Current liabilities	167,000
Long-term debt	48,000
Common stock	100,000
Retained earnings	63,000
Total liabilities and equity	378,000

Exchange rates are:

On date of purchase	$2.15
Average rate for the year	1.98
On the balance sheet date	1.94
On date of dividend payment	1.97

In addition, dividends of 40,000 pounds were paid during the year.

Instructions: If the translated financial statements at year end result in a translation adjustment with a debit balance of $55,000, determine the retained earnings balance at the beginning of the year in dollars.

CHAPTER 25

Financial Reporting and Analysis

CHAPTER TOPICS

- Objectives of Financial Statement Analysis
- Comparative Statement Analysis
- Financial Ratios
    - Liquidity Analysis
    - Activity Analysis
    - Profitability Analysis
    - Capital Structure Analysis
- Segment Information
- Interim Reporting
- The Securities and Exchange Commission
- Expanded Illustration of Statement of Cash Flows (Appendix)

As the world economy becomes more integrated, one question facing financial analysts is whether financial ratios can be compared across national boundaries. For example, the average price-earnings ratio for Japanese companies is around 60, while the average for U.S. companies is about 15. A price-earnings ratio in excess of 20 is considered quite high in the U.S. This dramatic variation is a result of differences in the two national economies and in their accounting methods. One of the accounting differences is that Japanese companies generally depreciate their fixed assets over shorter lives than do U.S. companies.[1] The increasing necessity of cross-border financial comparisons will require financial state-

1. Arthur Andersen & Co. and Salomon Brothers Inc., "Valuing Global Securities: Is Accounting Diversity a Mountain or a Molehill?" (1990).

ment users to be even more aware of the assumptions and methods that accountants have used in preparing the numbers.

Accounting provides information to assist various individuals in making economic decisions. A significant amount of information relevant to this purpose is presented in the primary financial statements of companies. Additional useful information is provided by financial data reported by means other than the financial statements. However, as explained in Chapter 2, financial data are only part of the total information needed by decision makers. Nonfinancial information may also be relevant. Thus, the total information spectrum is broader than just financial reporting. It encompasses financial statements, financial reporting by means other than the financial statements, and additional nonfinancial information.

In Statement of Financial Accounting Concepts No. 5, the FASB outlined the relationship between the financial statements and all other information relevant for investors, creditors, and other parties interested in the performance of a company. This outline is presented in Chapter 2 (see Exhibit 2—3, page 32). Note that the topics covered in your intermediate accounting course fall primarily in the first two categories of information—the financial statements and the notes to the financial statements. This concluding chapter of the text includes coverage of segment disclosure in notes to financial statements, interim reporting requirements, and other means of financial reporting—management discussion and analysis and SEC-mandated disclosures. The bulk of the chapter is devoted to a systematic summary of the techniques of financial statement analysis.

OBJECTIVES OF FINANCIAL STATEMENT ANALYSIS

Financial statement analysis is necessary for intelligent decision making. Nearly all businesses prepare financial statements of some type; the form and complexity of the statements vary according to the decisions to be made by those who use them. The owner of a small business might simply list the firm's cash receipts and disbursements and use this to prepare an income tax return. On the other hand, a large corporation's accounting staff spends considerable time in preparing the company's complex financial statements that can be used for many types of decisions.

Whatever their form, financial statements provide information about a business and its operation to interested users. For example, creditors making a lending decision may have questions concerning matters such as a company's sales, net income, and trends for these items, and the changes in cash flows, the relationship of income to sales, and of income to investments. Identifying these relationships requires analysis of data reported on the income statement, the balance sheet, and the statement of cash flows. Internal management is also concerned with analyzing the general-purpose financial statements, but requires additional special information in setting policies and making decisions. Questions may arise on matters such as the performance of various company divisions, the income from sales of individual products, and whether to make or buy product parts and equipment. Decisions on these matters can be made by establishing internal information systems to provide the necessary data. Thus, in analyzing financial data, the nature of analysis and the information needed depend on the decision needs of users and the issues involved.

The analyses of financial data described in this chapter are directed primarily to the informational needs of external users who usually must rely on the financial reports prepared by a company. Many groups are interested in the data found in financial statements, including:

1. Owners—sole proprietor, partners, or stockholders.
2. Management, including board of directors.

3. Creditors.
4. Government—local, state, and federal (including regulatory, taxing, and statistical units).
5. Prospective owners and prospective creditors.
6. Stock exchanges, investment bankers, and stockbrokers.
7. Trade associations.
8. Employees of a business and their labor unions.
9. The general public.

Questions raised by these groups generally can be answered by analyses that develop comparisons and measure relationships between components of financial statements. The analyses will form a basis for decisions made by the user.

Analyses typically are directed toward evaluating four aspects of a business: (1) liquidity, (2) stability, (3) profitability, and (4) growth potential.

Liquidity relates to the ability of an enterprise to pay its liabilities as they mature. Financial statements are analyzed to determine whether a business currently is liquid and whether it could retain its liquidity in a period of adversity. The analysis includes studies of the relationship of current assets to current liabilities, the size and nature of creditor and ownership interests, the protection afforded creditors and owners through sound asset values, and the amounts and trends of net income. Creditors are especially concerned with the liquidity of their debtors.

Stability is measured by the ability of a business to make interest and principal payments on outstanding debt and to pay regular dividends to its stockholders. In judging stability, data concerning operations and financial position are studied. For example, there must be a regular demand for the goods or services sold, and the gross profit on sales must be sufficient to cover operating expenses, interest, and dividends. There should be a satisfactory turnover of assets, and all business resources should be productively employed.

Profitability is measured by the ability of a business to increase its ownership equity from its operations. The nature and amount of income, as well as its regularity and trend, are significant factors affecting profitability.

The **growth potential** of a company is also of primary importance to stockholders. This element, along with profitability, directly affects future cash flows derived from increased income and/or appreciation in stock values. Growth potential is measured by the expansion and growth into new markets, the rate of growth in existing markets, the rate of growth in earnings per share, and the amount of expenditures for research and development.

An analysis must be directed toward the needs of those for whom it is made. For example, owners are interested in a company's ability to obtain additional capital for current needs and possible expansion. Creditors are interested not only in the position of a business as a going concern but also in its position should it be forced to liquidate.

ANALYTICAL PROCEDURES

Analytical procedures fall into two main categories: (1) comparisons and measurements based on financial data for two or more periods, and (2) comparisons and measurements based on financial data of only the current fiscal period. The first category includes comparative statements, ratios and trends for data on successive statements, and analyses of changes in the balance sheet, income statement, and statement of cash flows. The second category includes determining current balance sheet and income statement relationships and analyzing earnings and earnings potential. A review of financial data usually requires both types of analyses.

The analytical procedures commonly employed may be identified as: comparative statements, index-number trend series, common-size statements, and analysis of financial statement components. These techniques are described and illustrated in the following sections. It should be emphasized that the analyses illustrated herein are simply guides to the evaluation of financial data. Sound conclusions can be reached only through intelligent use and interpretation of such data. The AC&W Corporation is used as an example throughout the chapter.

Comparative Statements

Financial data become more meaningful when compared with similar data for preceding periods. Statements reflecting financial data for two or more periods are called **comparative financial statements.** Annual data can be compared with similar data for prior years. Monthly or quarterly data can be compared with similar data for previous months or quarters or with similar data for the same months or quarters of previous years.

Comparative data allow statement users to analyze trends in a company, thus enhancing the usefulness of information for decision making. The Accounting Principles Board stated that comparisons between financial statements are most informative and useful under the following conditions:

1. The presentations are in good form; that is, the arrangement within the statements is identical.
2. The content of the statements is identical; that is, the same items from the underlying accounting records are classified under the same captions.
3. Accounting principles are not changed or, if they are changed, the financial effects of the changes are disclosed.
4. Changes in circumstances or in the nature of the underlying transactions are disclosed.[2]

To the extent that the foregoing criteria are not met, comparisons may be misleading. Consistent practices and procedures and reporting periods of equal and regular lengths are also important, especially when comparisons are made for a single enterprise.

Comparative financial statements may be even more useful to investors and others when the reporting format highlights absolute changes in dollar amounts as well as relative percentage changes. Statement users will benefit by considering both amounts as they make their analyses. For example, an investor may decide that any change of 10% or more in a financial statement amount should be investigated further. A 10% change in an amount of $1,000, however, is not as significant as a 5% change in an amount of $100,000. When absolute or relative amounts appear out of line, conclusions, favorable or unfavorable, are not justified until investigation has disclosed reasons for the changes.

The development of data measuring changes taking place over a number of periods is known as **horizontal analysis.** Using the AC&W Corporation's income statement as an example and a reporting format that discloses dollar and percentage changes, horizontal analysis is illustrated at the top of page 1062.

Index-Number Trend Series

When comparative financial statements present information for more than two or three years, they become cumbersome and potentially confusing. A technique used to overcome this problem is referred to as an **index-number trend series.**

To compute index numbers, the statement preparer first must choose a base year. This may be the earliest year presented or some other year considered particularly appropriate.

2. *Statement of the Accounting Principles Board No. 4,* "Basic Concepts and Accounting Principles Underlying Financial Statements of Business Enterprises" (New York: American Institute of Certified Public Accountants, 1970), pars. 95-99.

AC&W Corporation
Comparative Income Statement
For Years Ended December 31

				Increase (Decrease)			
				1996-1997		1995-1996	
	1997	1996	1995	Amount	Percent	Amount	Percent
Gross sales	$1,500,000	$1,750,000	$1,000,000	$(250,000)	(14%)	$750,000	75%
Sales returns	75,000	100,000	50,000	(25,000)	(25%)	50,000	100%
Net sales	$1,425,000	$1,650,000	$ 950,000	$(225,000)	(14%)	$700,000	74%
Cost of goods sold	1,000,000	1,200,000	630,000	(200,000)	(17%)	570,000	90%
Gross profit on sales	$ 425,000	$ 450,000	$ 320,000	$ (25,000)	(6%)	$130,000	41%
Selling expense	$ 280,000	$ 300,000	$ 240,000	$ (20,000)	(7%)	$ 60,000	25%
General expense	100,000	110,000	100,000	(10,000)	(9%)	10,000	10%
Total operating expenses	$ 380,000	$ 410,000	$ 340,000	$ (30,000)	(7%)	$ 70,000	21%
Operating income (loss)	$ 45,000	$ 40,000	$ (20,000)	$ 5,000	13%	$ 60,000	—
Other revenue items	85,000	75,000	50,000	10,000	13%	25,000	50%
	$ 130,000	$ 115,000	$ 30,000	$ 15,000	13%	$ 85,000	283%
Other expense items	30,000	30,000	10,000	—	—	20,000	200%
Income before income tax	$ 100,000	$ 85,000	$ 20,000	$ 15,000	18%	$ 65,000	325%
Income tax	30,000	25,000	5,000	5,000	20%	20,000	400%
Net income	$ 70,000	$ 60,000	$ 15,000	$ 10,000	17%	$ 45,000	300%

Next, the base-year amounts are all expressed as 100%. The amounts for all other years are then stated as a percentage of the base-year amounts. Index numbers can be computed only when amounts are positive. The set of percentages for several years may thus be interpreted as trend values or as a series of index numbers relating to a particular item. For example, AC&W Corporation had gross sales of $1,000,000 in 1995, $1,750,000 in 1996, and $1,500,000 in 1997. These amounts, expressed in an index-number trend series with 1995 as the base year, would be 100, 175, and 150, respectively.

The index-number trend series technique is a type of horizontal analysis. It can give statement users a long-range view of a firm's financial position, earnings, and cash flow. The user needs to recognize, however, that long-range trend series are particularly sensitive to changing price levels. For example, in the 10 years from 1975 through 1985, the price level in the United States doubled. A horizontal analysis that ignored such a significant change in the price level might suggest that sales or net income had increased during the period when, in fact, no real growth had occurred.

Data expressed in terms of a base year frequently are useful for comparisons with similar data provided by business or industry sources or government agencies. When information used for making comparisons does not employ the same base period, it will have to be restated. Restatement of a base year calls for the expressing of each value as a percentage of the value for the base-year period.

To illustrate, assume the gross sales data for the AC&W Corporation for 1995-1997 are to be compared with a sales index for its particular industry. The industry sales indexes are as follows:

	1997	**1996**	**1995**
(1991 = 100)	146	157	124

Recognizing 1995 as the base year, industry sales are restated as follows:

1995	100
1996 (157 ÷ 124)	127
1997 (146 ÷ 124)	118

Industry sales and net sales for the AC&W Corporation can now be expressed in comparative form as follows:

	1997	**1996**	**1995**
Industry sales index	118	127	100
AC&W Corporation sales index*	150	175	100

*From comparative income statement on page 1062.

Common-Size Financial Statements

Horizontal analysis measures changes over a number of accounting periods. Statement users also need data that express relationships within a single period, which is known as **vertical analysis.** Preparation of **common-size financial statements** is a widely used vertical analysis technique. The common-size relationships may be stated in terms of percentages or in terms of ratios. Common-size statements may be prepared for the same business as of different dates or periods, or for two or more business units as of the same date or for the same period.

Common-size financial statements are useful in analyzing the internal structure of a financial statement. For example, a common-size balance sheet expresses each amount as a percentage of total assets, usually expressed as a decimal fraction. A common-size income statement usually shows each revenue or expense item as a percentage of net sales. As an illustration, a comparative balance sheet for AC&W Corporation with each item expressed in both dollar amounts and percentages is shown on the next page. Other types of common-size financial statements, e.g., a common-size retained earnings statement or statement of cash flows, may be prepared. When a supporting schedule shows the detail for a group total, individual items may be expressed as percentages of either the base figure or the group total.

Common-size analysis can also be used when comparing a company with other companies or with an entire industry. Differences in sizes of numbers in the financial statements are neutralized by reducing them to common-size ratios. Industry statistics are frequently published in common-size form, which facilitates making these types of comparisons. When comparing a company with other companies or with industry figures, it is important that the financial data for each company reflect comparable price levels. Furthermore, the financial data should be developed using comparable accounting methods, classification procedures, and valuation bases. Comparisons should be limited to companies engaged in similar activities. When the financial policies of two companies are different, these differences should be recognized in evaluating comparative reports. For example, one company may lease its properties while the other may purchase such items; one company may finance its operations using long-term borrowing while the other may rely primarily on funds supplied by stockholders and by earnings. Financial statements for two companies under these circumstances are not wholly comparable.

All this suggests that comparisons between different companies should be evaluated with care, and should be made with a full understanding of the inherent limitations. Reference was made earlier to the criteria that the Accounting Principles Board identified if comparisons are to be meaningful. Comparability between enterprises is more difficult

AC&W Corporation
Comparative Balance Sheet
December 31

	1997		1996		1995	
	Amount	Common-Size Ratio	Amount	Common-Size Ratio	Amount	Common-Size Ratio
Assets						
Current assets	$ 855,000	.38	$ 955,500	.40	$ 673,500	.38
Land, building, and equipment (net)	1,275,000	.56	1,275,000	.54	925,000	.52
Intangible assets	100,000	.04	100,000	.04	100,000	.06
Other assets	48,000	.02	60,500	.02	61,500	.04
Total assets	$2,278,000	1.00	$2,391,000	1.00	$1,760,000	1.00
Liabilities						
Current liabilities	$ 410,000	.18	$ 546,000	.23	$ 130,000	.07
Long-term liabilities–10% bonds	400,000	.18	400,000	.17	300,000	.17
Total liabilities	$ 810,000	.36	$ 946,000	.40	$ 430,000	.24
Stockholders' Equity						
Preferred 6% stock	$ 350,000	.15	$ 350,000	.15	$ 250,000	.14
Common stock	750,000	.33	750,000	.31	750,000	.43
Additional paid-in capital	100,000	.04	100,000	.04	100,000	.06
Retained earnings	268,000	.12	245,000	.10	230,000	.13
Total stockholders' equity	$1,468,000	.64	$1,445,000	.60	$1,330,000	.76
Total liabilities and stockholders' equity	$2,278,000	1.00	$2,391,000	1.00	$1,760,000	1.00

to obtain than comparability within a single enterprise. Ideally, differences in companies' financial reports should arise from basic differences in the companies themselves or from the nature of their transactions and not from differences in accounting practices and procedures.

Other Analytical Procedures

In addition to the financial statement analysis procedures described in the preceding sections, various measures may be developed with respect to specific components of financial statements. Some measurements are of general interest, while others have special significance to particular groups. Creditors, for example, are concerned with the ability of a company to pay its current obligations and seek information about the relationship of current assets to current liabilities. Stockholders are concerned with dividends and seek information relating to earnings that will form the basis for dividends. Managements are concerned with the activity of the merchandise inventory and seek information relating to the number of times goods have turned over during the period. All users are vitally interested in profitability and wish to be informed about the relationship of income to both liabilities and owners' equity.

The computation of percentages, ratios, turnovers, and other measures of financial position and operating results for a period is a form of vertical analysis. Comparison with the same measures for other periods is a form of horizontal analysis. These comparisons can be made within a company's financial statements or with other companies, individually or in industry groups. The measures described and illustrated in the following sections should not be considered all-inclusive; other measures may be useful to various groups, depending on their particular needs. It should be emphasized again that sound conclusions cannot be reached from an individual measurement. But this information, together with adequate investigation and study, may lead to a satisfactory evaluation of financial data.

Many of the ratios discussed in the following sections have been introduced in earlier chapters. For example, the current ratio was introduced in Chapter 5 when the balance sheet was discussed, and cash flow ratios were defined in Chapter 6 in conjunction with the discussion of the statement of cash flows. Accordingly, some of the material in the following sections will be a review of what you already know. The ratio analysis material included in this chapter is intended to serve as a comprehensive summary of the key financial ratios.

Liquidity Analysis

Generally, the first concern of a financial analyst is a firm's liquidity. Will the firm be able to meet its current obligations? If a firm cannot meet its obligations in the short run, it may not have a chance to be profitable or to experience growth in the long run. The two most commonly used measures of liquidity are the current ratio and the acid-test ratio.

Current Ratio. The comparison of current assets with current liabilities is regarded as a fundamental measurement of a company's liquidity. Known as the **current ratio,** or **working capital ratio,** this measurement is computed by dividing total current assets by total current liabilities.

The current ratio is a measure of the ability to meet current obligations. Since it measures liquidity, care must be taken to determine that proper items have been included in the current asset and current liability categories. A ratio of current assets to current liabilities of less than 2 for a trading or manufacturing unit has frequently been considered unsatisfactory. However, because liquidity needs are different for different industries and companies, any such arbitrary measure should not be viewed as meaningful or appropriate in all cases. The table below presents benchmark current ratios for a set of diverse industries:[3]

Industry (number of firms included)	Median Current Ratio
Dairy Farms (148)	2.4
Blast Furnaces and Steel Mills (271)	1.8
Electric Services (1,142)	1.5
Grocery Stores (1,510)	1.9
Jewelry Stores (2,093)	3.2
Personal Credit Institutions (499)	1.7
Legal Services (1,121)	1.9

A comfortable margin of current assets over current liabilities suggests that a company will be able to meet maturing obligations even in the event of unfavorable business conditions or losses on such assets as investment securities, receivables, and inventories.

For the AC&W Corporation, current ratios for December 31, 1997, and December 31, 1996, are developed as follows:[4]

	December 31,	
	1997	1996
Current assets	$855,000	$955,500
Current liabilities	$410,000	$546,000
Current ratio	2.1	1.8

3. The industry ratios in this table, along with others shown later in the chapter, are from "Industry Norms and Key Business Ratios: 1993-94 Edition," Dun and Bradstreet, Inc. (1994).

4. Comparative data for more than two years are generally required in evaluating financial trends. Analyses for only two years are given in the examples in this chapter, since these are sufficient to illustrate the analytical procedures involved.

A current ratio of 2.1 means that AC&W could liquidate its total current liabilities 2.1 times using only its current assets.

The AC&W Corporation increased the current ratio in 1997 from 1.8 to 2.1. If no other information is available, this change may indicate some improvement in AC&W's liquidity position with improved ability to meet its current obligations. This conclusion may be in error, however, since the ratios do not disclose anything about the composition of the current assets. For example, past-due receivables and slow-moving inventories usually are classified as current assets, but they would not represent liquid assets. There is also the possibility, given the business risk in the organization and industry, that these ratios are too high. Assets may be kept unnecessarily liquid and thus not earn the higher returns associated with longer-term investments. Nevertheless, the current ratio is useful in analyzing the liquidity position of the organization. Added meaning is obtained when it is compared with the company's past data and industry standards.

Acid-Test Ratio. A test of a company's immediate liquidity is made by comparing the sum of cash, investment securities, notes receivable, and accounts receivable, commonly referred to as **quick assets,** with current liabilities. The total quick assets divided by current liabilities gives the **acid-test ratio,** or **quick ratio.** Considerable time may be required to convert raw materials, goods in process, and finished goods into receivables and then into cash. A company with a satisfactory current ratio may be in a relatively poor liquidity position when inventories comprise most of the total current assets. This is revealed by the acid-test ratio. In developing the ratio, the receivables and securities included in the total quick assets should be examined closely. In some cases these items actually may be less liquid than inventories.

Usually, a ratio of quick assets to current liabilities of at least 1 is considered desirable. Again, however, special conditions of the particular business must be evaluated. Questions such as the following should be considered: What is the composition of the quick assets? What special requirements are made by current activities upon these assets? How soon are current payables due?

Acid-test ratios for AC&W Corporation are computed as follows:

	December 31,	
	1997	1996
Quick assets:		
Cash	$ 60,000	$100,500
Investment securities	150,000	150,000
Receivables (net)	420,000	375,000
Total quick assets	$630,000	$625,500
Total current liabilities	$410,000	$546,000
Acid-test ratio	1.5	1.1

Cash Flow Adequacy Ratio. Both the current ratio and the acid-test ratio are indirect measures of a company's ability to meet its upcoming obligations. Ratios based on cash flow from operations give a more direct indication of a company's ability to generate sufficient cash to satisfy predictable cash requirements. One overall indicator of cash flow sufficiency is the **cash flow adequacy ratio.**[5] This ratio is computed by dividing cash flow from operating activities by the total primary cash requirements, defined as the sum of dividend payments, long-term asset purchases, and long-term debt repayments. The following information for AC&W Corporation is needed to compute this ratio:

5. See Chapter 6 (Exhibit 6-8, page 213) for a summary of other cash flow ratios.

	1997	1996
Net income	$ 70,000	$ 60,000
Depreciation Expense	100,000	80,000
(Increase) Decrease in non-cash current assets	60,000	(231,500)
Increase (Decrease) in current liabilities	(136,000)	416,000
Cash from operating activities	$ 94,000	$324,500
Long-term asset purchases	$100,000	$430,000
Long-term debt repayments	40,000	30,000
Dividends paid	47,000	45,000
Total primary cash requirements	$187,000	$505,000

Note that long-term asset purchases in 1997 were just enough to offset the depreciation of assets for the year. Long-term debt repayments in both years were for obligations coming due during the year—from AC&W Corporation's balance sheet it can be seen that these amounts were refinanced, resulting in no decrease in long-term debt.

The computation of the cash flow adequacy ratio is as follows:

	1997	1996
Cash from operating activities	$ 94,000	$324,500
Total primary cash requirements	$187,000	$505,000
Cash flow adequacy ratio	0.50	0.64

Since the cash flow adequacy ratio is less than one, AC&W Corporation has not been able to satisfy its primary cash requirements with cash generated by operations. A look at AC&W's balance sheet indicates that the shortfall has been compensated by long-term borrowing and issuance of preferred stock in 1996 and by a decrease in the cash balance in 1997. One study has shown that, for a sample of *Fortune 500* companies, the cash flow adequacy ratio averaged 0.88.[6]

Activity Analysis

There are special tests that may be applied to measure how efficiently a firm is utilizing its assets. Several of these measures also relate to liquidity because they involve significant working capital elements, such as receivables, inventories, and accounts payable.

Accounts Receivable Turnover. The amount of receivables usually bears a close relationship to the volume of credit sales. The receivable position and approximate collection time may be evaluated by computing the **accounts receivable turnover.** This rate is determined by dividing net credit sales (or total net sales if credit sales are unknown) by the average trade accounts receivable outstanding during the year. In developing an average receivables amount, monthly balances should be used if available.

Assume in the case of AC&W Corporation that all sales are made on credit, that receivables arise only from sales, and that receivable totals for only the beginning and the end of the year are available. Receivables turnover rates for 1997 and 1996 are computed as follows:

6. Don E. Giacomino and David E. Mielke, "Cash Flows: Another Approach to Ratio Analysis," *Journal of Accountancy,* March 1993, pp. 55-58.

	1997	1996
Net credit sales	$1,425,000	$1,650,000
Net receivables:		
Beginning of year	$ 375,000	$ 333,500
End of year	$ 420,000	$ 375,000
Average receivables [(beginning balance + ending balance) ÷ 2]	$ 397,500	$ 354,250
Receivables turnover for year	3.6 times	4.7 times

The value computed for receivables turnover represents the average number of sale/collection cycles completed by the firm during the year.

Number of Days' Sales in Receivables. Average receivables are sometimes expressed in terms of the **number of days' sales in receivables,** which shows the average time required to collect receivables. Average receivables outstanding divided by average daily credit sales gives the number of days' sales in average receivables. This measure is computed for AC&W Corporation as illustrated below.

	1997	1996
Average receivables	$ 397,500	$ 354,250
Net credit sales	$1,425,000	$1,650,000
Average daily credit sales (net credit sales ÷ 365)	$3,904	$4,521
Number of days' sales in average receivables (average receivables ÷ average daily credit sales)	102 days	78 days

This same measurement can be obtained by dividing the number of days in the year by the receivables turnover.[7]

In some cases, instead of developing the number of days' sales in average receivables, it may be more useful to report the number of days' credit sales in receivables at the end of the period. This information would be significant in evaluating current position, and particularly the receivable position as of a given date. This information for AC&W Corporation is presented below.

	1997	1996
Receivables at end of year	$420,000	$375,000
Average daily credit sales	$ 3,904	$ 4,521
Number of days' sales in receivables at end of year	108 days	83 days

What constitutes a reasonable number of days in receivables varies with individual businesses. For example, if merchandise is sold on terms of net 60 days, 40 days' sales in receivables would be reasonable; but if terms are net 30 days, a receivable balance equal to 40 days' sales would indicate slow collections. Typical levels for number of days' sales in receivables for several industries are presented on the next page.

7. A 365-day year is used in this chapter because most banks and other financial institutions use 365 days. For simplicity, ratios are sometimes calculated using a 360-day year.

Industry (number of firms included)	Median Number of Days' Sales in Receivables
Dairy Farms (148)	16.8 days
Blast Furnaces and Steel Mills (271)	43.1 days
Electric Services (1,142)	33.6 days
Grocery Stores (1,510)	2.6 days
Jewelry Stores (2,093)	21.9 days
Personal Credit Institutions (499)	367.8 days
Legal Services (1,121)	45.5 days

Sales activity just before the close of a period should be considered when interpreting accounts receivable measurements. If sales are unusually light or heavy just before the end of the fiscal period, this affects total receivables as well as the related measurements. When such unevenness prevails, it may be better to analyze accounts receivable according to their due dates, as was illustrated in Chapter 8.

The problem of minimizing accounts receivable without losing desirable business is important. Receivables often do not earn interest revenue, and the cost of carrying them must be covered by the profit margin. The longer accounts are carried, the smaller will be the percentage return realized on invested capital. In addition, heavier bookkeeping and collection charges and increased bad debts must be considered.

To attract business, credit frequently is granted for relatively long periods. The cost of granting long-term credit should be considered. Assume that a business has average daily credit sales of $5,000 and average accounts receivable of $250,000, which represents 50 days' credit sales. If collections and the credit period can be improved so that accounts receivable represent only 30 days' sales, then accounts receivable will be reduced to $150,000. Assuming a total cost of 10% to carry and service the accounts, the $100,000 decrease would yield annual savings of $10,000.

Inventory Turnover. The amount of inventory carried frequently relates closely to sales volume. The inventory position and the appropriateness of its size may be evaluated by computing the **inventory turnover.** The inventory turnover is computed by dividing cost of goods sold by average inventory. Whenever possible, monthly figures should be used to develop the average inventory balance.

Assume that for AC&W Corporation the inventory balances for only the beginning and the end of the year are available. Inventory turnover rates are computed as follows:

	1997	1996
Cost of goods sold	$1,000,000	$1,200,000
Inventory:		
Beginning of year	$ 330,000	$ 125,000
End of year	$ 225,000	$ 330,000
Average inventory [(beginning balance + ending balance) ÷ 2]	$ 277,500	$ 227,500
Inventory turnover for year	3.6 times	5.3 times

Number of Days' Sales in Inventories. Average inventories are sometimes expressed as the **number of days' sales in inventories.** Information is thus afforded concerning the average time it takes to turn over the inventory. The number of days' sales in inventories is calculated by dividing average inventory by average daily cost of goods sold. The number of days' sales also can be obtained by dividing the number of days in the year by the inventory turnover rate. The latter procedure for AC&W Corporation is illustrated on the next page.

	1997	1996
Inventory turnover for year	3.6 times	5.3 times
Number of days' sales in average inventory (365 ÷ inventory turnover)	101 days	69 days

As was the case with receivables, instead of developing the number of days' sales in average inventories, it may be more useful to report the number of days' sales in ending inventories. The latter measurement is determined by dividing ending inventory by average daily cost of goods sold. This information is helpful in evaluating the current asset position and particularly the inventory position as of a given date.

A company with departmental classifications for inventories might find it desirable to support the company's inventory measurements with individual department measurements, since there can be considerable variation among departments. A manufacturing company can compute separate turnover rates for finished goods, goods in process, and raw materials. The finished goods turnover is computed by dividing cost of goods sold by average finished goods inventory. Goods in process turnover is computed by dividing cost of goods manufactured by average goods in process inventory. Raw materials turnover is computed by dividing the cost of raw materials used by average raw materials inventory.

The same valuation methods must be employed for inventories in successive periods if the inventory measurements are to be comparable. Maximum accuracy is possible if information relating to inventories and amount of goods sold is available in terms of physical units rather than dollar costs.

The effect of seasonal factors on the size of year-end inventories should be considered in inventory analyses. Inventories may be abnormally high or low at the end of a period. Many companies adopt a fiscal year ending when operations are at their lowest point. This is called a **natural business year.** Inventories will normally be lowest at the end of such a period, so that the organization can count inventory and complete year-end closing most conveniently. Under these circumstances, monthly inventory balances should be used to arrive at a representative average inventory figure. When a periodic inventory system is employed, monthly inventories may be estimated using the gross profit method, as explained in Chapter 10.

With an increased inventory turnover, the investment necessary for a given volume of business is smaller, and consequently the return on invested capital is higher. This conclusion assumes an enterprise can acquire goods in smaller quantities sufficiently often at no price disadvantage. If merchandise must be bought in very large quantities in order to get favorable prices, then the savings on quantity purchases must be weighed against the additional investment, increased costs of storage, and other carrying charges.

The financial advantage of an increased turnover rate may be illustrated as follows. Assuming cost of goods sold of $1,000,000 and average inventory at cost of $250,000, inventory turnover is 4 times. Assume further that, through careful buying, the same business volume can be maintained with turnover of 5 times, or an average inventory of only $200,000. If interest on money invested in inventory is 10%, the savings on the $50,000 will be $5,000 annually. Other advantages include decreased inventory spoilage and obsolescence, savings in storage cost, taxes, and insurance, and reduction in risk of losses from price declines.

Inventory investments and turnover rates vary among businesses, and each business must be judged in terms of its financial structure and operations. Management must establish an inventory policy that will avoid the extremes of a dangerously low stock, which may impair sales, and an overstocking of goods, involving a heavy capital investment and risks of spoilage and obsolescence, price declines, and difficulties in meeting purchase obligations.

Asset Turnover. A measure of the overall efficiency of asset utilization is the ratio of net sales to average total assets, called the **asset turnover.** This ratio is calculated by dividing net sales by average total assets. With comparative data, judgments can be made concerning the relative effectiveness of asset utilization. A ratio increase may suggest more efficient asset utilization, although a point may be reached where there is a strain on assets and a company is unable to achieve its full sales potential. An increase in average total assets accompanied by a ratio decrease may suggest overinvestment in assets or inefficient utilization.

In developing the asset turnover rate, long-term investments should be excluded from total assets when they make no contribution to sales. On the other hand, a valuation for leased property should be added to total assets to permit comparability between companies owning their properties and those that lease them. If monthly figures for assets are available, they may be used in developing a representative average for total assets employed during the year. Often, however, the beginning-of-year and end-of-year asset totals are used for computing the average. When sales can be expressed in terms of units sold, ratios of sales units to total assets offer more reliable interpretations than sales dollars, since unit sales are not affected by price changes.

Assume that for AC&W Corporation only asset totals for the beginning and end of the year are available and that sales are not expressed in terms of units. Asset turnover ratio is computed as follows:

	1997	**1996**
Net sales	$1,425,000	$1,650,000
Total assets (excluding long-term investments):		
Beginning of year	$2,391,000	$1,760,000
End of year	$2,278,000	$2,391,000
Average total assets [(beginning balance + ending balance) ÷ 2]	$2,334,500	$2,075,500
Asset turnover	0.6 times	0.8 times

Asset turnover for several industries is presented below.

Industry (number of firms included)	**Median Asset Turnover**
Dairy Farms (148)	1.04 times
Blast Furnaces and Steel Mills (271)	2.13 times
Electric Services (1,142)	0.44 times
Grocery Stores (1,510)	5.65 times
Jewelry Stores (2,093)	1.53 times
Legal Services (1,121)	4.07 times

Other Measures of Activity. Turnover analysis, as illustrated for receivables, inventories, and total assets, can also be applied to other assets or groups of assets. For example, current asset turnover is calculated by dividing net sales by average current assets. This figure may be viewed as the number of times current assets are replenished, or as the number of sales dollars generated per dollar of current assets. Similarly, if net sales are divided by average plant assets (land, buildings, and equipment), a plant asset turnover can be computed. This figure measures the efficiency of plant asset management and indicates the volume of sales generated by the operating assets of a company. Increases in turnover rates generally indicate more efficient utilization of assets.

Similar procedures also can be used to analyze specific liabilities. An accounts payable turnover, for example, may be computed by dividing purchases by average payables; the number of days' purchases in accounts payable may be computed by dividing accounts payable by average daily purchases.

Analysis of liabilities in terms of due dates may assist management in cash planning. Useful relationships also can be obtained by comparing specific assets or liabilities with other assets or liabilities, or with asset or liability totals. For example, data concerning the relationship of cash to accounts payable or of cash to total liabilities may be useful.

Profitability Analysis

Profitability analysis provides evidence concerning the earnings potential of a company and how effectively a firm is being managed. Since the reason most firms exist is to earn profits, the profitability ratios are among the most significant financial ratios. The adequacy of earnings may be measured in terms of (1) the rate earned on sales, (2) the rate earned on average total assets, (3) the rate earned on average common stockholders' equity, and (4) the availability of earnings to common stockholders. Thus, the most popular profitability measurements are profit percentage on sales, return-on-investment ratios, and earnings per share.

Profit Percentage on Sales. The ratio of net income to sales determines the **net profit percentage on sales.** This measurement represents the net income percentage per dollar of sales. The percentage is computed by dividing net income by net sales for a period. For AC&W Corporation, the net profit percentage on sales is:

	1997	1996
Net income	$ 70,000	$ 60,000
Net sales	$1,425,000	$1,650,000
Net profit percentage	4.9%	3.6%

This means that for 1997, AC&W generated almost five cents of profit per dollar of sales revenue. Because net income is used in the computation, any extraordinary or irregular items may distort the profit percentage rate with respect to normal operating activities. Adjustments may be needed in the analysis to account for such items. A sample of profit percentages is presented below.

Industry (number of firms included)	Median Profit Percentage
Dairy Farms (148)	4.9%
Blast Furnaces and Steel Mills (270)	2.9%
Electric Services (1,142)	7.1%
Grocery Stores (1,510)	1.3%
Jewelry Stores (2,093)	4.5%
Legal Services (1,121)	10.1%

For merchandising and manufacturing companies, **gross profit percentage on sales** is often a significant ratio for evaluating the profitability of a company. In these companies, cost of goods sold is the most significant expense, and careful inventory control is necessary to ensure profitable operations. For AC&W, the gross profit percentage on sales is:

	1997	1996
Gross profit on sales	$ 425,000	$ 450,000
Net sales	$1,425,000	$1,650,000
Gross profit percentage	29.8%	27.3%

Rate Earned on Average Total Assets. Overall asset productivity may be expressed as the **rate earned on average total assets,** also referred to as the **return on investment (ROI),** or the asset productivity rate. The rate is computed by dividing net income by the average total assets used to produce net income. This rate measures the efficiency in using resources to generate net income. If total assets by months are available, they should be used to develop an average for the year. Frequently, however, the assets at the beginning of the year or the assets at the end of the year are used. In some cases it may be desirable to use net income from operations by excluding revenue from investments, such as interest, dividends, and rents, or from gains or losses resulting from nonoperating transactions. When this is the case, average total assets should be reduced by the investments or other assets. Sometimes comparisons are developed for the rate of operating income to average total assets or the rate of pretax income to average total assets, so that results are not affected by financial management items or by changes in income tax rates.

Rates earned on average total assets for AC&W Corporation are determined as follows:

	1997	1996
Net income	$ 70,000	$ 60,000
Total assets:		
Beginning of year	$2,391,000	$1,760,000
End of year	$2,278,000	$2,391,000
Average total assets [(beginning balance + ending balance) ÷ 2]	$2,334,500	$2,075,500
Rate earned on average total assets	3.0%	2.9%

An analysis, referred to as the DuPont method, illustrates the factors that affect this ratio. The DuPont method explicitly recognizes that return on average total assets equals the profit margin on sales multiplied by the asset turnover. The formulas for these ratios show clearly why this relationship exists:

Profit margin × Asset turnover = Return on average total assets

$$\frac{\text{Net income}}{\text{Sales}} \times \frac{\text{Sales}}{\text{Average total assets}} = \frac{\text{Net income}}{\text{Average total assets}}$$

Sales cancels out of the formula leaving the return-on-assets ratio. Ratios previously computed for the AC&W Corporation in 1997 further illustrate this analysis:

Profit margin on sales (p. 1072)		Asset turnover (p. 1071)		Rate earned on average total assets (p. 1073)
4.9	×	.6	=	3% (rounded)

This analytical tool helps explain how discount organizations compete with full service companies. Generally, the discount store operates on a relatively small margin and plans for a high turnover of assets, whereas the full service organization has a higher margin but lower turnover.

For example, assume that Company A is a full service organization and Company B is a discount store. Company A has a margin of 22.6% on sales and a total asset turnover of 1.1. Company B has a margin of 4.5% and a turnover of 5.2. Company A's percentage return on assets equals 24.9% (22.6% × 1.1), and Company B's return is 23.4% (4.5% × 5.2). Thus, the return on total assets for Company A is very close to that of Company B, although their asset turnover and profitability ratios are quite different.

Rate Earned on Average Stockholders' Equity. Net income may be expressed as the **rate earned on average stockholders' equity** (or return on stockholders' equity) by dividing net income by average stockholders' equity. In developing this rate, it is preferable to calculate the average stockholders' equity for a year from monthly data, particularly when significant changes have occurred during the year, such as the sale of additional stock, retirement of stock, and accumulation of earnings. Sometimes the beginning or the ending stockholders' equity is used.

For AC&W Corporation, rates earned on average stockholders' equity are as follows:

	1997	1996
Net income	$ 70,000	$ 60,000
Stockholders' equity:		
Beginning of year	$1,445,000	$1,330,000
End of year	$1,468,000	$1,445,000
Average stockholders' equity [beginning balance + ending balance) ÷ 2]	$1,456,500	$1,387,500
Rate earned on average stockholders' equity	4.8%	4.3%

As a company's liabilities increase in relationship to stockholders' equity, the spread between the rate earned on average stockholders' equity and the rate earned on average total assets rises. This difference measures the way a company is using leverage in its business financing. The rate earned on average stockholders' equity is important to investors who must reconcile the risk of debt financing with the potentially greater profitability.

Rate Earned on Average Common Stockholders' Equity. As a refinement to the rate earned on average stockholders' equity, earnings may be measured in terms of the average common stockholders' equity. The **rate earned on average common stockholders' equity** is computed by dividing net income after preferred dividend requirements by average common stockholders' equity.

In the case of AC&W Corporation, preferred dividend requirements are 6%. The rate earned on average common stockholders' equity, then, is calculated as follows:

	1997	1996
Net income	$ 70,000	$ 60,000
Less dividend requirements on preferred stock	21,000	21,000
Net income related to common stock	$ 49,000	$ 39,000
Common stockholders' equity:		
Beginning of year	$1,095,000	$1,080,000
End of year	$1,118,000	$1,095,000
Average common stockholders' equity [(beginning balance + ending balance) ÷ 2]	$1,106,500	$1,087,500
Rate earned on average common stockholders' equity	4.4%	3.6%

Earnings Per Share. The Accounting Principles Board in Opinion No. 15 indicated that **earnings per share** data were of such importance to investors and others that such data should be presented prominently on the income statement. In computing earnings per share on common stock, earnings are first reduced by the prior dividend rights of preferred stock. Computations are made in terms of the weighted average number of common shares outstanding for each period presented. Adjustments are required when a corporation's capital structure includes potentially dilutive securities. If the total potential dilution is material, both primary earnings per share and fully diluted earnings per share must be disclosed. When net income includes below-the-line items, earnings per share should be reported for each major component of income as well as for net income.

For AC&W Corporation, there are no potentially dilutive securities. Earnings per share on common stock is calculated as follows:

	1997	1996
Net income	$70,000	$60,000
Less dividend requirements on preferred stock	21,000	21,000
Income related to common stockholders' equity	$49,000	$39,000
Number of shares of common stock outstanding	75,000	75,000
Earnings per share on common stock	$.65	$.52

Dividends Per Share. In addition to earnings per share, many companies report **dividends per share** in the financial statements. This amount is computed simply by dividing cash dividends for the year by the number of shares of common stock outstanding. When a significant number of common shares have been issued or retired during a period, an average should be computed; otherwise, the number of common shares outstanding at the end of the period normally is used. For AC&W Corporation, the number of shares of common stock outstanding has remained constant for the past 3 years. Therefore, the dividends per share are $.35 for 1997 and $.32 for 1996. Another way of analyzing dividends is to compute the dividend payout ratio, or the percentage of net income paid out in dividends. This may be computed by dividing the dividends per share by the earnings per share, or by dividing dividends paid by net income. The dividend payout ratios for AC&W are 54% in 1997 and 62% in 1996.

Yield on Common Stock. Dividends per share may be used to compute a rate of return on the market value of common stock. Such a rate, referred to as the **yield on common stock,** or dividend yield, is found by dividing the annual dividends per common share by the latest market price per common share. For AC&W Corporation, the yield on the common stock is computed as follows:

	1997	1996
Dividends for year per common share	$ .35	$ .32
Market value per common share at end of year	$10.00	$6.50
Yield on common stock	3.5%	4.9%

Dividend yields are typically quite low (less than five percent) when compared to the interest yield on debt. Investors in common stock are willing to accept a low dividend yield because they anticipate that the stock will increase in price and result in a capital gain.

Price-Earnings Ratio. The market price of common stock may be expressed as a multiple of earnings to evaluate the attractiveness of common stock as an investment. This measurement is referred to as the **price-earnings ratio** and is computed by dividing the market price per share of stock by the annual earnings per share. Instead of using the average market value of shares for the period covered by earnings, the latest market value normally is used. In the United States, price-earnings ratios typically range from 5 to 20. Assuming market values per common share of AC&W Corporation stock at the end of 1997 of $10 and at the end of 1996 of $6.50, price-earnings ratios would be computed as follows:

	1997	1996
Market value per common share at end of year	$10.00	$6.50
Earnings per share (calculated on page 1075)	$ .65	$ .52
Price-earnings ratio	15.4	12.5

As an alternative to the price-earnings ratio, earnings per share can be presented as a percentage of the market price of the stock (earnings-price ratio).

Capital Structure Analysis

The composition of a company's capital structure has significant implications for stockholders, creditors, potential investors, and potential creditors. Creditors look to the stockholders' equity as a margin of safety. As stockholders' equity increases in relation to total liabilities, the margin of protection to creditors also increases. Should a company have financial difficulty and have to terminate its operations through bankruptcy, the higher the margin of safety, the more probable that creditors will recover their investment in the company.

However, from the perspective of the common stockholders, it is often advantageous to use borrowed capital or preferred stock to expand operations rather than issuing additional common stock. If a company can earn a return on the funds obtained through borrowing or from preferred stock that is greater than the cost of the funds, the excess earnings will benefit the common stockholders through an increase in the return on average common stockholders' equity. This result is commonly referred to as **trading on the equity,** or applying **financial leverage.** On the other hand, if the company earns a return that is less than the cost of the funds, the common stockholders must bear the excess cost. There is a legal obligation to pay interest, and preferred stock dividends usually are cumulative; thus, they must be paid before any distribution to the common stockholders.

To illustrate the impact of financial leverage on common stockholders, assume that a company with 10,000 shares of stock outstanding reports average assets of $500,000 and has no liabilities. The company estimates that its income before income taxes will be $80,000 without any borrowed capital. Income taxes are estimated to be 30% of income; therefore, net income is estimated to be $56,000 ($80,000 −$24,000). This would result in a return on average common stockholders' equity of 11.2% ($56,000 ÷ $500,000).

Exhibit 25—1 illustrates the effects of borrowing an extra million dollars at 12% interest under (1) the assumption the extra funds earn 15% before interest and taxes, or more than the cost of the borrowed funds, and (2) the assumption the extra funds earn 5% before interest and taxes, or less than the cost of the borrowed funds. Using financial leverage favorably under the first assumption results in an increase in the return on average common stockholders' equity from 11.2% to 15.4%. The market would probably react to this increase favorably and the market price of the stock would rise. Additional dividends also could be paid with the increase of $21,000 in net income. On the other hand, the unfavorable result of financial leverage can be seen under the second assumption as the return on average common stockholders' equity decreases from 11.2% to 1.4%. The $49,000 decrease in net income will probably have an unfavorable impact on both the stock's market price and the dividend payments.

The illustration uses borrowed funds that had a tax deductible interest cost attached to them. If the funds had been acquired with preferred stock, the computations would have differed because of the nondeductibility of preferred dividends for income tax purposes. However, the same advantages and disadvantages to the common stockholder apply depending on the relationship between the cost of the funds and the amount that can be earned from the funds.

Stockholders, creditors, and other interested parties often make use of capital structure measurements including the debt-to-equity ratio, number of times interest is earned, fixed charge coverage, and book value per share. These methods are illustrated in the following sections.

Exhibit 25—1
Financial Leverage

	Assumption 1 Borrowed Capital Earns 15%	Assumption 2 Borrowed Capital Earns 5%
Income before interest and taxes:		
Without borrowed funds	$ 80,000	$ 80,000
On $1,000,000 borrowed	150,000	50,000
	$230,000	$130,000
Interest (12% × $1,000,000)	120,000	120,000
Income before taxes	$110,000	$ 10,000
Income taxes (30%)	33,000	3,000
Net income	$ 77,000	$ 7,000
Average common stockholders' equity	$500,000	$500,000
Return on average common stockholders' equity	15.4%	1.4%

Ratio of Total Liabilities to Stockholders' Equity. Creditors' and stockholders' equities may be expressed in terms of total assets or in terms of each other. For example, creditors may have a 40% interest in total assets, and stockholders a 60% interest. This can be expressed as a **debt-to-equity ratio** of 0.67 to 1.

For AC&W Corporation, the relationship of total liabilities to stockholders' equity is calculated as follows:

	1997	1996
Total liabilities	$ 810,000	$ 946,000
Stockholders' equity	$1,468,000	$1,445,000
Ratio of total liabilities to stockholders' equity	0.55	0.65

In analyzing the relationship of total liabilities to stockholders' equity, particular note should be made of lease arrangements. Both property rights provided under the leases and the accompanying liabilities should be considered in evaluating the equities and changes in equities from period to period.

Investors generally prefer a higher debt-to-equity ratio to obtain the advantages of financial leverage, while creditors favor a lower ratio to increase the safety of their debt. Typical debt-to-equity ratios are presented below.

Industry (number of firms included)	Median Debt-to-Equity Ratio
Dairy Farms (148)	0.622
Blast Furnaces and Steel Mills (271)	1.201
Electric Services (1,142)	1.626
Grocery Stores (1,510)	0.881
Jewelry Stores (2,093)	0.585
Personal Credit Institutions (499)	2.012
Legal Services (1,121)	0.666

The DuPont analysis on page 1073 can be extended to include the effect of leverage:

$$\text{Profit margin on sales} \times \text{Asset turnover} \times \text{Leverage ratio} = \text{Rate earned on average common stockholders' equity}$$

$$\frac{\text{Net income to common stockholders}}{\text{Sales}} \times \frac{\text{Sales}}{\text{Average total assets}} \times \frac{\text{Average total assets}}{\text{Average common stockholders' equity}} = \frac{\text{Net income to common stockholders}}{\text{Average common stockholders' equity}}$$

This formulation illustrates that the return to common stockholders is a function of operating decisions (margin), investing decisions (turnover), and financing decisions (leverage).[8]

Number of Times Interest Earned. A measure of the debt position of a company in relation to its earnings ability is the **number of times interest is earned.** The calculation is made by dividing income before any charges for interest or income tax by the interest requirements for the period. The resulting figure reflects the company's ability to meet interest payments and the degree of safety afforded the creditors. The number of times interest was earned by AC&W Corporation follows:

	1997	1996
Income before income tax	$100,000	$ 85,000
Add bond interest (10% of $400,000)	40,000	40,000
Amount available in meeting bond interest requirements	$140,000	$125,000
Number of times bond interest requirements were earned	3.5 times	3.1 times

Pretax income was used in the computation, since income tax applies only after interest is deducted, and it is pretax income that protects creditors.

A computation similar to times interest earned, but more inclusive, is the **fixed charge coverage.** Fixed charges include such obligations as interest on bonds and notes, lease obligations, and any other recurring financial commitments. The number of times fixed charges are covered is calculated by adding the fixed charges to pretax income and then dividing the total by the fixed charges.

Book Value Per Share. Stockholders' equity can be measured by calculating the **book value per share,** which is the dollar equity in corporate capital of each share of stock. This amount frequently is used by investors in conjunction with the market value per share to evaluate the attractiveness of the stock for investment purposes.

When there is only one class of stock outstanding, the calculation of book value is relatively simple; the total stockholders' equity is divided by the number of shares of stock outstanding at the close of the reporting period. When a company is holding treasury stock, its cost is deducted from stockholders' equity and the treasury shares are deducted from the shares issued. When more than one class of stock is outstanding, a portion of the stockholders' equity must be allocated to the other classes of stock before the book value of the common stock is computed. Usually the par or liquidation value of the other classes of stock is used to make this allocation.

In the case of AC&W Corporation, the par value of the preferred stock is equal to the liquidation value, and there are no preferred dividends in arrears. The book value per share is computed as follows:

	1997	1996
Common stockholders' equity	$1,118,000	$1,095,000
Number of shares of common stock outstanding	75,000	75,000
Book value per share on common stock	$14.91	$14.60

8. For additional disaggregation suggestions, see Thomas L. Selling and Clyde Stickney, "Disaggregating the Rate of Return on Common Shareholders' Equity: A New Approach," *Accounting Horizons,* December 1990, pp. 9-17.

Since the market value of the stock is lower than the book value, many investors would consider AC&W an attractive investment. However, the nature and limitations of the per share book value measurements must be considered in using these data. Carrying values of assets may vary significantly from their present fair values or immediate realizable values. This would directly affect the per share amount that could be realized in the event of a company liquidation.

Summary of Analytical Measures

Financial ratios, percentages, and other measures are useful tools for analyzing financial statements. They enable statement users to make meaningful judgments about an enterprise's financial condition and operating results. These measures, like financial statements, are more meaningful when compared with similar data for more than one period and with industry averages or other available data. A summary of the major analytical measures discussed in this chapter is presented in Exhibit 25—2.

Exhibit 25—2 Summary of Major Analytical Measures

Measure	Computation	Purpose
Liquidity Analysis		
(1) Current ratio	Current assets / Current liabilities	Measures ability to pay short-term debts.
(2) Acid-test ratio	Quick assets / Current liabilities	Measures immediate ability to pay short-term debts.
(3) Cash flow adequacy	Cash flow from operations / (Purchases of long-term assets + Repayments of long-term debt + Cash dividend payments)	Measures ability to generate sufficient cash to satisfy predictable cash requirements.
Activity Analysis		
(4) Accounts receivable turnover	Net credit sales / Average accounts receivable	Measures receivable position and approximate average collection time.
(5) Number of days' sales in receivables	Average accounts receivable / Average daily credit sales	Measures receivable position and approximate average collection time.
(6) Inventory turnover	Cost of goods sold / Average inventory	Measures appropriateness of inventory levels in terms of time required to sell or "turn over" goods.
(7) Number of days' sales in inventories	Average inventory / Average daily cost of goods sold	Measures appropriateness of inventory levels in terms of time required to sell or "turn over" goods.
(8) Asset turnover	Net sales / Average total assets	Measures effectiveness of asset utilization.
Profitability Analysis		
(9) Net profit margin on sales	Net income / Net sales	Measures profit percentage per dollar of sales.
(10) Gross profit margin on sales	Gross profit / Net sales	Measures gross profit percentage per dollar of sales.
(11) Rate earned on average total assets	Net income / Average total assets	Measures overall asset productivity.
(12) Rate earned on average stockholders' equity	Net income / Average stockholders' equity	Measures rate of return on average stockholders' equity.

Profitability Analysis (Concluded)

(13) Rate earned on average common stockholders' equity	$\frac{\text{Net income} - \text{preferred dividend requirements}}{\text{Average common stockholders' equity}}$	Measures rate of return on average common stockholders' equity.
(14) Earnings per share	$\frac{\text{Net income} - \text{preferred dividend requirements}}{\text{Weighted average number of shares of common stock outstanding}}$	Measures net income per share of common stock.
(15) Dividends per share	$\frac{\text{Dividends on common stock}}{\text{Average number of shares of common stock outstanding}}$	Measures dividends per share of common stock.
(16) Yield on common stock	$\frac{\text{Dividends per share of common stock}}{\text{Market value per share of common stock}}$	Measures rate of cash return to stockholders
(17) Price-earnings ratio	$\frac{\text{Market price per share of common stock}}{\text{Earnings per share of common stock}}$	Measures investor beliefs about stability of earning and growth potential

Capital Structure Analysis

(18) Debt-to-equity ratio	$\frac{\text{Total liabilities}}{\text{Stockholders' equity}}$	Measures use of debt to finance operations.
(19) Number of times interest is earned	$\frac{\text{Income before taxes and interest expense}}{\text{Interest expense}}$	Measures ability to meet interest payments.
(20) Book value per share	$\frac{\text{Common stockholders' equity}}{\text{Number of shares of common stock outstanding}}$	Measures equity per share of common stock.

Market Efficiency

An efficient market is one in which information is reflected rapidly in prices. For example, if the real estate market in a city is efficient, then news of an impending layoff at a major employer in the city should result quickly in lower housing prices because of an anticipated decrease in demand. The major stock exchanges in the United States often are considered to be efficient markets in the sense that information about specific companies or about the economy in general is reflected almost immediately in stock prices. One implication of market efficiency is that, since current stock prices reflect all available information, future movements in stock prices should be unpredictable.

It seems clear that capital markets in the United States are efficient in a general sense, but accumulated evidence suggests the existence of a number of puzzling "anomalies" in the form of predictability in the pattern of stock returns. For example, returns on stock portfolios generally are lower on Monday than on other days of the week. Also, returns are higher than normal on days before holidays and also during the month of January.

From an accounting standpoint, market efficiency relates to the usefulness of so-called "fundamental analysis." Fundamental analysis is the practice of using financial data to calculate the underlying value of a firm and using this underlying value to identify over- and underpriced stocks. The notion of fundamental analysis is in conflict with market efficiency, since the analysis works only if current stock prices do not fully reflect all available accounting information. For this reason, fundamental analysis frequently has been regarded with skepticism by academics. However, recent research has revealed the ability of accounting data to predict future stock returns. Ou and Penman (1989) demonstrate that financial ratios derived from publicly available financial statements can be used to successfully forecast stock returns for the coming year.

Question:

Why might accountants be interested in whether stock prices fully reflect the information contained in the financial statements?

Source: Jane A. Ou and Stephen H. Penman, "Financial Statement Analysis and the Prediction of Stock Returns," *Journal of Accounting and Economics*, November 1989, p. 295.

USE OF INDUSTRY DATA FOR COMPARATIVE ANALYSIS

As indicated earlier in the chapter, comparisons of common-size information or other measurements may be made over time within a company or with similar companies individually or in industry groups. There are many general and industry sources that can be used to obtain comparative information. The major difficulty in using comparative data is the selection of specific companies or an industry that is similar to the company being examined. The government has established a standard for classifying industries known as the **Standard Industrial Code (SIC)**. Over 800 industries are identified, and general survey information is compiled according to these codes.

If the company being analyzed operates only in one general business area, it usually isn't difficult to find a category for comparison. However, many businesses today are large, complex organizations engaged in a variety of activities that bear little relationship to each other. For example, a company might manufacture airplane engines, operate a real estate business, and manage a professional hockey team. Such companies, referred to as **diversified companies,** or **conglomerates,** operate in multiple industries and do not fit into any one specific industry category. Thus, comparative analysis for a highly diversified company requires either an assumption that the company operates primarily in one area or separate data for each subindustry or segment. Generally, comparisons are more meaningful when separate data for segments are analyzed, and many companies are required to include such data with their financial statements.

Segment Reporting

When a company is diversified, the different segments of the company often operate in distinct and separate markets, involve different management teams, and experience different growth patterns, profit potentials, and degrees of risk. In effect, the segments of the company behave almost like, and in some cases are, separate companies within an overall corporate structure. Yet, if only total company information is presented for a highly diversified company, the different degrees of risk, profitability, and growth potential for major segments of the company cannot be analyzed and compared.

Recognizing this problem, the FASB issued Statement No. 14, which requires disclosure of selected information for segments of diversified companies.[9] Information to be reported includes revenues, operating profit, and identifiable assets for each significant industry segment of a company. Essentially, a **segment** is considered significant if its sales, profits, or assets are 10% or more of the respective total company amounts. A practical limit of 10 segments is suggested, and at least 75% of total company sales must be accounted for. The segment data may be reported in the audited financial statements or in a separate schedule considered an integral part of the statements. Other provisions of Statement No. 14 require disclosure of revenues from major customers and information about foreign operations and export sales.

Reporting by lines of business presents several problems. For example, how does one determine which business segments should be reported on? Certainly not all companies are organized in the same manner, even if they are engaged in similar business activities. Reporting on a particular division or profit-center in one company may not be comparable to another company. Another problem relates to transfer pricing. Not all companies use the same method of pricing goods or services that are "sold" among the different divisions or units of a company. This could lead to distorted segment profit data. Another related problem is the allocation of common costs among segments of a company. Certain costs, such as general and administrative expenses, are very difficult to assign to particular segments of a company on anything other than an arbitrary basis. This, again, could result in misleading information.

9. *Statement of Financial Accounting Standards No. 14*, "Financial Reporting for Segments of a Business Enterprise" (Stamford: Financial Accounting Standards Board, 1976).

In spite of these difficulties, the accounting profession has concluded that segment reporting is necessary to assist readers of financial statements in analyzing and understanding an enterprise's past performance and future prospects and making comparisons with other companies. An example of segment reporting, from the 1993 annual report of PepsiCo, is presented in Exhibit 25—3.

Financial statement users always express a desire for more detailed segment information. Ultimately, every user would like unlimited access to the accounting records of all companies. Understandably, companies are reluctant to disclose everything to everyone. The FASB must set accounting standards to balance users' desire for data against firms' legitimate concern over disclosing proprietary information. The topic of reporting disaggregated information is the focus of a recent FASB Research Report and an Invitation to Comment.[10] It is likely that accounting standards adopted in the near future will increase the amount of required segment disclosure.

Interim Reporting

Statements showing financial position and operating results for intervals of less than a year are referred to as **interim financial statements.** Interim reports are considered essential in providing investors and others with more timely information as to the position and progress of an enterprise. This information is most useful in comparative form because of the relationship it shows to data for similar reporting intervals and to data in the annual report.

Notwithstanding the need for interim reports, there are significant difficulties associated with them. One problem is caused by the seasonal factors of certain businesses. For example, in some companies, revenues fluctuate widely among interim periods; in other businesses, significant fixed costs are incurred during a single period but are to benefit several periods. Not only must costs be allocated to appropriate periods of benefit, but they must be matched against the realized revenues for the interim period to determine a reasonable income measurement.

In preparing interim reports, adjustments for accrued items, generally required only at year-end, have to be considered at the end of each interim period. Because of the additional time and extra costs involved to develop complete information, many estimates of expenses are made for interim reports. The increased number of estimates adds an element of subjectivity to these reports.

Another problem is that extraordinary items or the disposal of a business segment will have a greater impact on an interim period's earnings than on the results of operations for an entire year. In analyzing interim financial statements, special attention should be given to these and similar considerations.

Partially because of some of the above problems and partially because of differing views as to the objective of interim reports, there has been a variety of practices in presenting interim financial information. Two prominent viewpoints exist. One viewpoint is that each reporting interval is to be recognized as a separate accounting period. Thus, the results of operations for each interim period are determined in essentially the same manner as for the annual accounting period. Under this approach, the same judgments, estimations, accruals, and deferrals are recognized at the end of each interim period as for the annual period.

The other viewpoint, and the one accepted by the APB in Opinion No. 28, is that the interim period is an integral part of the annual period.[11] Essentially, the revenues and

10. *Research Report* (prepared by Paul Pacter), "Reporting Disaggregated Information" (Norwalk: Financial Accounting Standards Board, February 1993) and *Invitation to Comment,* "Reporting Disaggregated Information by Business Enterprises" (Financial Accounting Standards Board and the Accounting Standards Board of the Canadian Institute of Chartered Accountants, May 1993).

11. *Opinions of the Accounting Principles Board, No. 28,* "Interim Financial Reporting" (New York: American Institute of Certified Public Accountants, 1973), par. 9.

Exhibit 25—3 PepsiCo—Segment Reporting

(in Millions)

Industry Segments:		Net Sales					Operating Profits				
		1993	1992	1991	1990	1989	**1993**	1992	1991	1990	1989
Beverages:	Domestic	**$ 5,918.1**	$ 5,485.2	$ 5,171.5	$ 5,034.5	$ 4,623.3	**$ 936.9**	$ 686.3	$ 746.2	$ 673.8	$ 577.6
	International	**2,720.1**	2,120.4	1,743.7	1,488.5	1,153.4	**172.1**	112.3	117.1	93.8	98.6
		8,638.2	7,605.6	6,915.2	6,523.0	5,776.7	**1,109.0**	798.6	863.3	767.6	676.2
Snack Foods:	Domestic	**4,365.3**	3,950.4	3,737.9	3,471.5	3,211.3	**900.7**	775.5	616.6	732.3	667.8
	International	**2,661.5**	2,181.7	1,512.2	1,295.3	810.5	**288.9**	209.2	140.1	160.3	105.9
		7,026.8	6,132.1	5,250.1	4,766.8	4,021.8	**1,189.6**	984.7	756.7	892.6	773.7
Restaurants:	Domestic	**8,025.7**	7,115.4	6,258.4	5,540.9	4,684.8	**685.1**	597.8	479.4	447.2	356.5
	International	**1,330.0**	1,116.9	868.5	684.8	565.9	**92.9**	120.7	96.2	75.2	57.8
		9,355.7	8,232.3	7,126.9	6,225.7	5,250.7	**778.0**	718.5	575.6	522.4	414.3
Combined Segments:											
	Domestic	**18,309.1**	16,551.0	15,167.8	14,046.9	12,519.4	**2,522.7**	2,059.6	1,842.2	1,853.3	1,601.9
	International	**6,711.6**	5,419.0	4,124.4	3,468.6	2,529.8	**553.9**	442.2	353.4	329.3	262.3
		$25,020.7	$21,970.0	$19,292.2	$17,515.5	$15,049.2	**$3,076.6**	$2,501.8	$2,195.6	$2,182.6	$1,864.2
Unallocated Expenses, net							**(170.1)**	(130.6)	(83.8)	(140.5)	(91.6)
Operating Profit							**$2,906.5**	$2,371.2	$2,111.8	$2,042.1	$1,772.6
Results by Restaurant Chain:											
Pizza Hut		**$ 4,128.7**	$ 3,603.5	$ 3,258.3	$ 2,949.9	$ 2,453.5	**$ 372.1**	$ 335.4	$ 314.5	$ 245.9	$ 205.5
Taco Bell		**2,901.3**	2,460.0	2,038.1	1,745.5	1,465.9	**253.1**	214.3	180.6	149.6	109.4
KFC		**2,325.7**	2,168.8	1,830.5	1,530.3	1,331.3	**152.8**	168.8	80.5	126.9	99.4
		$ 9,355.7	$ 8,232.3	$ 7,126.9	$ 6,225.7	$ 5,250.7	**$ 778.0**	$ 718.5	$ 575.6	$ 522.4	$ 414.3

Geographic Areas[(a)]:	Net Sales			Segment Operating Profits			Identifiable Assets		
	1993	1992	1991	**1993**	1992	1991	**1993**	1992	1991
United States	**$18,309.1**	$16,551.0	$15,167.8	**$2,522.7**	$2,059.6	$1,842.2	**$13,589.5**	$11,957.0	$10,777.8
Canada and Mexico	**2,819.5**	2,214.2	1,434.7	**324.8**	251.0	198.7	**2,581.1**	2,395.2	917.3
Europe	**1,819.0**	1,349.0	1,170.3	**47.4**	52.6	30.9	**2,666.1**	1,948.4	2,367.3
Other	**2,073.1**	1,855.8	1,519.4	**181.7**	138.6	123.8	**1,675.1**	1,282.0	1,138.7
Total	**$25,020.7**	$21,970.0	$19,292.2	**$3,076.6**	$2,501.8	$2,195.6	**$20,511.8**	$17,582.6	$15,201.1

(a) The results of centralized concentrate manufacturing operations in Puerto Rico and Ireland have been allocated based upon sales to the respective areas.

expenses for the total period are allocated among interim periods on some reasonable basis, e.g., time, sales volume, or productive activity.

Under the **integral part of annual period concept,** the same general accounting principles and reporting practices employed for annual reports are to be utilized for interim statements, except modifications may be required so the interim results will better relate to the total results of operations for the annual period. As an example of the type of modification that may be required, assume a company uses the LIFO method of inventory valuation and encounters a situation where liquidation of the base period inventory occurs at an interim date but the inventory is expected to be replaced by the end of the annual period. Under these circumstances, the inventory reported at the interim date should not reflect the

LIFO liquidation, and the cost of goods sold for the interim period should include the expected cost of replacing the liquidated LIFO base.[12]

Another example of a required modification deals with a change in accounting principle during an interim period. In general, these changes should follow the provisions of APB Opinion No. 20.[13] However, the FASB has concluded in Statement No. 3 that for any cumulative effect-type change, other than a change to LIFO, if the change is made "in other than the first interim period of an enterprise's fiscal year, the cumulative effect of the change on retained earnings at the beginning of that year shall be included in the determination of net income of the first interim period of the year of change."[14]

Applying generally accepted accounting practices to interim financial statements can become complex. This is an area that is developing to meet the perceived needs of users. For example, the SEC has adopted rules requiring increased disclosure of interim financial information. Interpretations of old standards and the development of new standards will assist in presenting interim financial data that should help investors and others in analyzing and interpreting the financial picture and operating results of a company.

THE SECURITIES AND EXCHANGE COMMISSION

The focus of this chapter is on financial reporting and analysis. Since the Securities and Exchange Commission (SEC) in the United States plays such a central role in American business, and in financial reporting generally, it is important for accounting and business students to understand something about the SEC. In this section of the chapter, we will address five basic questions:[15]

What is the SEC?
Why was the SEC established?
What is the legal basis of the SEC?
How does the registration process work?
What is the relationship of the SEC to financial reporting?

What Is the SEC?

The Securities and Exchange Commission is an independent, quasi-judicial agency of the United States government. It was established in 1934, in conjunction with the passage of the 1933 and 1934 Securities Acts, to help regulate the U.S. securities markets. A primary purpose of the SEC is to assist in providing investors and other interested parties with reliable information upon which to make sound investment decisions.

The SEC is directed by five commissioners, not more than three of whom may be from the same political party. Members of the Commission are appointed by the President of the United States with the advice and consent of the Senate. Each commissioner is appointed for a five-year term with one member's term expiring each year. The President designates one member to chair the Commission.

The SEC is administered from its Washington, D.C. headquarters and has regional and branch offices in major financial centers of the U.S. The organizational structure is illustrated by Exhibit 25—4. The commissioners are assisted by a staff of professionals, including accountants, engineers, examiners, lawyers, and securities analysts. These professionals are assigned to the various divisions and offices, including the regional offices, as shown in the organization chart.

12. *Ibid.*, par. 14.

13. *Opinions of the Accounting Principles Board, No. 20,* "Accounting Changes" (New York: American Institute of Certified Public Accountants, 1971).

14. *Statement of Financial Accounting Standards No. 3*, "Reporting Accounting Changes in Interim Financial Statements" (Stamford: Financial Accounting Standards Board, 1974), par. 4.

15. For a more complete explanation of the SEC, see *An Introduction to the SEC,* Fifth Edition, by K. Fred Skousen, South-Western Publishing Co., 1991.

Exhibit 25—4 Organizational Structure of SEC

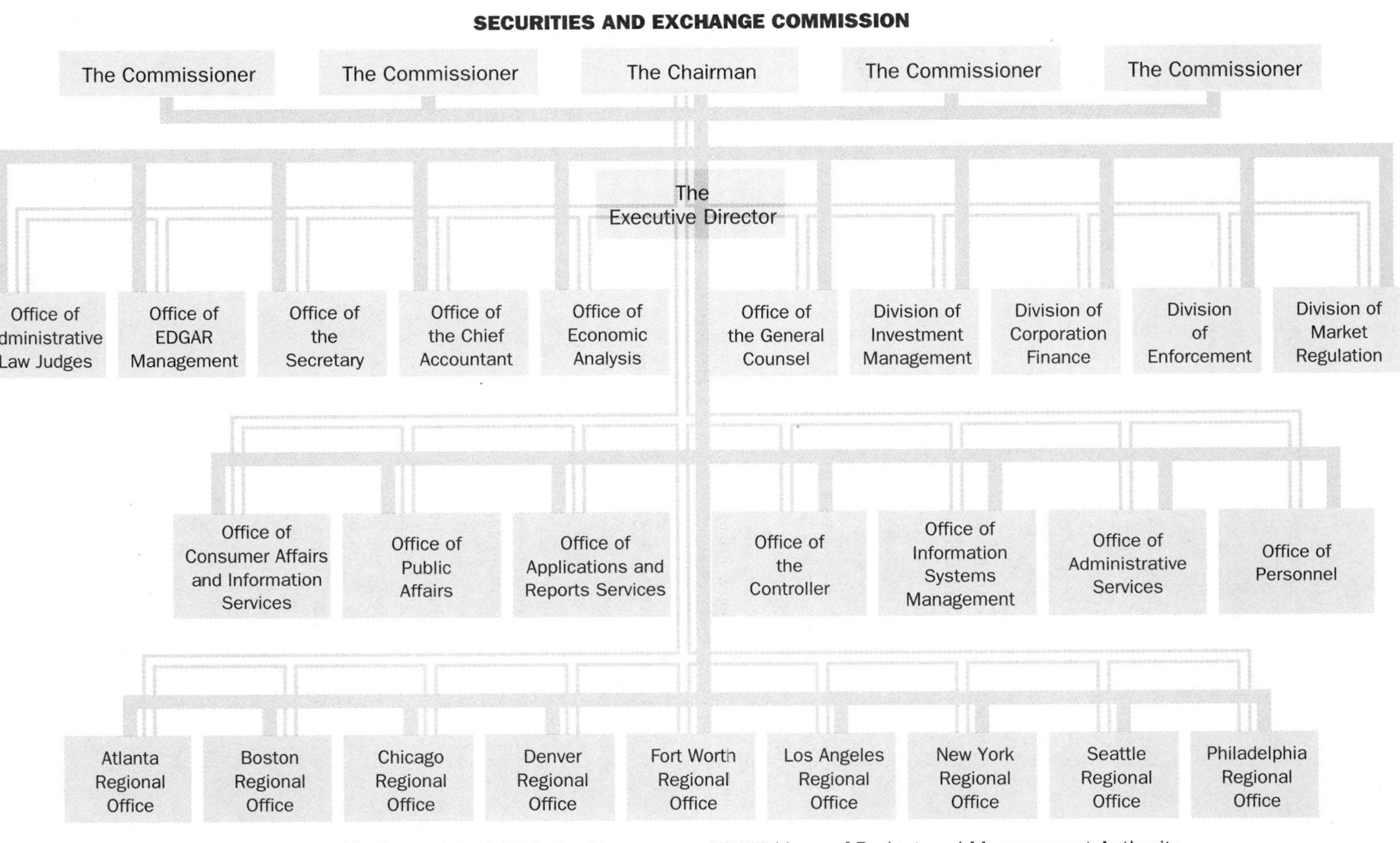

Lines of Policy and Judicial Authority

Lines of Budget and Management Authority

SOURCE: U.S. Securities and Exchange Commission, *The Work of SEC* (Washington, D.C.: U.S. Government Printing Office, 1988). *Federal Securities Law Reports* (Chicago: Commerce Clearing House, Inc., October, (1988), ¶ 301.

Of the main divisions of the SEC, the Division of Corporation Finance is perhaps the most important for individuals in business and specifically for accountants. The division's major responsibilities include: assisting the Commission in establishing and requiring adherence to standards of economic and financial reporting and disclosure by all companies under SEC jurisdiction; setting standards for the disclosure requirements of proxy solicitations; and administering disclosure requirements primarily for the Securities Act of 1933, the Securities Exchange Act of 1934, and the Trust Indenture Act of 1939.

The Division of Corporation Finance reviews selected registration statements (lengthy and often complicated narrations of corporate operations), prospectuses, quarterly and annual reports, proxy statements, and sales literature. Investigations, examinations, formal hearings, and informal conferences are used in the analysis and review of the myriad of reports handled each year by this division.

In addition to its review function, the Division of Corporation Finance also provides a useful interpretative and advisory service to help clarify to issuers, accountants, lawyers, and underwriters the application and requirements of the securities laws it administers. Since substantially all the financial statements submitted for review must be certified by independent accountants, a significant portion of an accountant's work with the SEC will be reviewed by this division. The advisory service has proved effective in avoiding problems by providing instructive guidance concerning registration and reporting procedures.

The Division of Corporation Finance is organized along industry lines. According to the SEC, this structure allows the division to better ascertain the particular disclosure needs of different industries and to more readily identify industry trends. There also has been a shift in emphasis toward greater reliance on periodic disclosures rather than on disclosure documents concerning particular transactions. The expected result is more consistent application of disclosure rules, particularly in the area of management's discussion and analysis of company operations.

Why Was the SEC Established?

In the early days of commerce, the economic system was basically a barter economy. Goods and services were traded directly for other goods and services. Businesses were conducted as proprietorships or sometimes as partnerships and joint ventures. Generally, the managers and the owners of business were the same individuals. External reporting of the results of operations by these closely held commercial entities was simply not needed. Internal information for planning and control was needed, however, and accounting systems were introduced to help provide that information.

As commercial enterprises multiplied, both in size and number, more and more people were attracted to business opportunities, and the investment of capital resources expanded rapidly. The more aggressive businesses soon realized the financial advantage of encouraging capital investment by people who were willing to assume the risks of ownership but in most cases were neither willing nor able to assist in management. An advantage of the developing corporate form of business was that ownership and financial interest could be spread over a broad base by issuing securities. Ownership and management thus became separated, and there was a need for a marketplace where equity and debt securities could be exchanged for invested capital resources. This need led to the establishment of extensive capital markets, first in Europe and then in the United States.

The corporate form of business also increased the need for objective verification of data and created a need for disclosure in the form of more and better information to owners and potential investors. As capital markets increased in size and activity, an irresponsible attitude developed in some corporate officers who took advantage of lax conditions in the securities markets and profited by distortions and manipulations. Governments, sensing some responsibility to protect those who invested in corporations, made faltering attempts to create a working partnership between management and investors and to ensure an adequate supply of capital available for sound economic growth.

The pattern of securities legislation in the United States followed the example of Great Britain: widespread abuses, made obvious by a financial crisis, were followed by a series of retrospective investigations leading to the passage of restrictive laws imposed on securities markets. The stock market crash of 1929 provided the last straw, the final impetus, to the passage of securities legislation in the United States.

In summary, the SEC was established in the U.S. to help regulate its capital markets and to correct certain stock market abuses. One such abuse was price manipulation. It was not uncommon in the 1920s for American stock brokers or dealers to engage in "wash sales" or "matched orders," in which successive buy and sell orders created a false impression of stock activity, resulting in artificially inflated stock prices. This maneuver allowed some individuals to reap huge profits before the price fell back to its true market level. Outright deceit by issuing false and misleading financial statements was another improper practice. These manipulative procedures had as their objective the making of profits at the expense of unwary investors.

One classic example of a major fraud that may have contributed to securities legislation is the Ivar Kreugar case. During the 1920s, the most widely-held securities in the U.S., and perhaps the world, were the stocks and bonds of Kreugar & Toll, Inc., a Swedish match company. These securities were popular because they paid high dividends (over 20 percent annually) and were sold in small denominations, making them attractive to both large and small investors. Ivar Kreugar, known as the "Match King," became famous and wealthy as a financial genius, building his business into a multi-billion-dollar international enterprise. In fact, Kreugar defrauded millions of investors by personally creating false and misleading financial statements. Instead of being paid out of profits, the dividends were paid out of capital that was raised by selling securities to unsuspecting investors. Eventually, the giant pyramid collapsed, Kreugar committed suicide, and Kreugar & Toll, Inc. went bankrupt. On the day Kreugar died, his company's stock was selling for $5 a share. Within weeks, it was selling for five cents a share. The American public was outraged, and some have speculated that this major fraud was instrumental in causing Congress to enact securities legislation to prevent this from happening again.[16]

Another practice undermining securities markets was the excessive use of credit to finance speculative activities. This is commonly referred to as buying stocks "on margin." There was no limit to the amount of credit a broker could extend to a customer. As a result, a slight decline in market prices could start a chain reaction that would gain momentum when an overextended customer sold out because a margin could not be covered. Such a situation became critical when the market began to decline drastically late in 1929 and early in 1930.

The misuse of corporate information by corporate officials and other "insiders" was still another practice that led to instability in the securities markets. While positioning themselves to take advantage of fluctuations in stock prices when the news became public, executive officers and other insiders withheld or released information about corporate activities that caused significant changes in the market.

To correct these abuses and to provide more complete information for current and prospective investors, the U.S. Congress enacted the Securities Act of 1933 and the Securities Exchange Act of 1934. It was under the authority of the latter act that the Securities Exchange Commission was created. The SEC was given the duty to ensure "full

16. Dale L. Flesher and Tonya K. Flesher, "Ivan Kreugar's Contribution to U.S. Financial Reporting," *The Accounting Review*, Vol. 61, No. 3 (Sarasota: American Accounting Association, July 1986), pp. 421-434.

and fair" disclosure of all material facts concerning securities offered for public investment. The Commission's intent was not necessarily to prevent speculative securities from entering the market, but to insist that investors be provided with adequate information. The initiation of litigation in cases of fraud and the provision for proper registration of securities are two additional important objectives of the SEC.

LEGAL BASIS OF THE SEC

The stated purpose of the SEC is to provide "full and fair" disclosure to investors. The two primary Acts administered by the SEC are the Securities Act of 1933 and the Securities Exchange Act of 1934.

The purpose of the 1933 Act is to regulate the initial offering and actual sale of securities through the mail system (interstate commerce). The 1933 Act does not concern itself with the trading of securities after their initial distribution. Thus, the 1933 Act is a "disclosure" statute. Disclosures are provided by means of a registration statement and a prospectus, each of which contains relevant financial and other information deemed useful to investors.

In general, the 1934 Act is a statement of the authority needed to successfully regulate securities trading on the national exchanges. Unlike the 1933 Act, which restricts itself primarily to initial offerings, the 1934 Act is concerned with several aspects of securities trading. The 1934 Act initially extended the full and fair disclosure doctrine to include all companies that had securities registered on the national securities exchanges. In 1964, the Securities Acts Amendments extended the disclosure requirement to the securities of companies that trade on over-the-counter markets. This requirement is limited, however, to companies having over $5 million in total assets and 500 or more stockholders.

In addition to the registration of outstanding securities and the disclosures involved in that process, the 1934 Act requires that updated information be filed with the Commission by means of periodic reports. The annual report to the SEC (Form 10-K) and the quarterly reports (Form 10-Q) are the most widely known and used periodic reports.

As in the case of the 1933 Act, registration and continuous reporting do not guarantee accuracy. However, the SEC can file court proceedings against those who prepare and file (or are associated with the filings of) fraudulent reports and can suspend the trading in securities of companies that fail to make full and accurate reports or repeatedly fail to file on a timely basis.

In summary, the 1933 Act regulates the initial offerings of securities; the 1934 Act provides for continuous reporting requirements for most public companies in the U.S. The two acts are independent of each other, and registration under one Act does not necessarily meet the requirements of the other. The 1933 Act has a narrow scope, the registration of a particular security; the 1934 Act has a broad scope, regulating national stock exchanges, over-the-counter markets, margin trading requirements, and proxy solicitation rules, among other items. The 1933 Act carries with it a strict legal liability allowing plaintiffs to bring legal action even without proving reliance on, or injury from, false and misleading registration statements. The legal liability of the 1934 Act is essentially "common law" liability, requiring gross negligence for liability to third parties and the burden of proof is on the plaintiff to show reliance on misstated financial information that resulted in personal injury.

THE REGISTRATION PROCESS

In reviewing the registration process and SEC reporting requirements, it is important to keep in mind that the SEC's intent is not to judge the merits of securities offered for sale. Furthermore, the SEC's review process does not guarantee completeness or accuracy in the reports filed with the SEC. The securities laws provide for the disclosure of material financial and other information. They also impose severe penalties for presenting false and misleading information and other fraudulent acts. The SEC's role is to determine if the evidence presented in the filed reports indicates satisfactory compliance with the applicable statutes and regulations. Any deficiencies are the responsibility of the company and the individuals involved (management, underwriters, attorneys, accountants, etc.). The final judgment on the investment opportunity presented by the offering rests with the potential investor.

Registration is a major part of the specific Acts administered by the SEC. With some variation because of the differing purposes of the Acts, the process under each Act is quite similar in terms of disclosure requirements and procedures. The various Acts and their respective general registration requirements are:

1. Securities Act of 1933: Registration of new securities offered for public sale.
2. Securities Exchange Act of 1934: Continuous reporting of publicly owned companies and registration of securities, securities exchanges, and certain brokers and dealers.
3. Public Utility Holding Company Act of 1935: Registration of interstate holding companies covered by this law.
4. Trust Indenture Act of 1939: Registration of trust indenture documents and supporting data.
5. Investment Company Act of 1940: Registration of investment companies.
6. Investment Advisers Company Act of 1940 and Securities Investor Protection Act of 1970: Registration of investment advisers.
7. Foreign Corrupt Practices Act of 1977: Affects registration only indirectly through amendment to the Securities Exchange Act of 1934; requires accurate accounting records and adequate internal accounting controls.
8. Insider Trading Sanctions Act of 1984 and Insider Trading and Securities Fraud Enforcement Act of 1988: Alters the penalties and regulations governing insider trading.

In brief, the registration process consists of developing and filing a registration statement with the SEC. A 1933 Act registration statement generally is comprised of two parts, the first part containing information usually included in a prospectus. A prospectus is a rather complete booklet containing information about the company, its history, business, and financial statements. The prospectus includes all information to be presented to prospective investors. A copy of the prospectus customarily is submitted in full satisfaction of the requirements of the first part of the registration statement. Other detailed information not included in a prospectus is filed in the second part of the registration statement. Note that a prospectus is not required in a 1934 Act filing since trading in secondary markets is open to everyone, and companies cannot determine who might be interested in their securities.

Part of the registration process is the selection of the proper form to be used, since the SEC has designed several registration forms for use under each of the Acts. These forms contain no blanks to be filled in as do tax forms. Instead, they are narrative in character, giving general instructions about the items of information to be furnished. Detailed information must be assembled by the companies using the form designed for the type of security being offered as well as the type of company making the offer.

While there are many forms and reports required by the SEC, those that most directly impact financial reporting are:

Forms S-1 to S-16. These forms must be completed and registered with the SEC whenever a company plans to issue new securities to the public. Which of the specific forms is required depends upon whether the company is issuing securities for the first time, what kind of company is involved, size of the offering, and many other factors.

Form 8-K. This report is filed within 15 days of the occurrence of significant events that are of interest to public investors. Such events include a change in outside auditors, a change in officers or directors, or the acquisition or sale of a subsidiary.
Form 10-K. This report must be filed annually within ninety days after the close of each fiscal year. Extensive financial information is contained in this report, including financial statements audited by independent CPAs.
Form 10-Q. This report must be filed quarterly for all publicly-held companies. It contains certain financial information that is unaudited, but that has been reviewed by the company's independent accountants.

The review process at the SEC begins when a completed registration statement is received by the SEC. The statute provides that the registration statement becomes effective 20 days after it is filed. However, the effective date for the registration may be delayed by the review and amendment procedures or it may be accelerated by action of the registrant. Prior to this time the SEC staff is available for prefiling conferences with companies that have questions about registration. Such conferences often avoid lengthy delays once the registration procedures have begun.

A normal examination by the SEC staff consists of a review of the statement and a comparison with other information available about the issuer, the industry, and other companies in the industry. This review usually is made by the Division of Corporation Finance. A branch chief gives a copy of the registration statement to an analyst, an attorney, and an accountant. The analyst reviews for proper form and other nonfinancial information, while the attorney examines the legal aspects, and the accountant reviews the financial statements and schedules. The purpose of this examination, as stated earlier, is to determine compliance with applicable statutes and regulations. The staff of the SEC will try to determine if there is any materially untrue, incomplete, or misleading information in the registration statement; that is, if there is any lack of "full and fair" disclosure. However, this review does not absolve the company or anyone associated with the registration statement from liability under the securities laws.

Memoranda are submitted by each of the three staff experts to the branch chief. A "letter of comments," sometimes known as a "deficiency letter," is then prepared and sent to the company. This letter outlines the deficiencies that the staff has found in the registration statement and makes suggestions for improvements in the document.

The comments letter, which is not part of the public record, is sent to the registrant as soon as possible so that amendments may be made or other appropriate action may be taken. The letter of comments does not delay the effective date of the registration, but if corrections cannot be made within 20 days, the SEC usually asks the issuer to file a delaying amendment. The submission of any amendment usually renews the 20-day waiting period.

Once the deficiencies have been corrected and the issuer and underwriters have properly attended to their concurrent responsibilities, and the SEC staff has informed the Commissioners that they have no significant reservations, the Commission declares the registration statement effective. The issuer and underwriters are then free to proceed with the distribution and sale of the securities.

With certain limited exceptions, all the information compiled as part of the registration statement is public information and may be inspected in the Public Reference Room of the Commission in Washington, D.C. Copies of all documents may be obtained, and prospectuses covering recent public offerings may be examined at any SEC office. There may be lengthy delays in receiving the desired material, however.

RELATIONSHIP OF THE SEC TO FINANCIAL REPORTING

As noted, the SEC has the statutory authority to regulate and to prescribe the form, content, and compilation process of financial statements and other reports. In addition, the

SEC has power to establish rules for any CPA associated with audited financial statements submitted to the Commission. This authority has led to a close and continued interaction between the SEC and the accounting profession. The SEC has traditionally played a significant yet somewhat indirect role in the development of financial accounting and reporting principles and practices as well as auditing standards and procedures. Generally, the SEC has accepted the accounting pronouncements of the Financial Accounting Standards Board, and other accounting bodies such as the AICPA.

The SEC's interaction with the accounting profession is not constant, nor is it a static relationship. The relationship depends on many factors, including the political and economic climate, the philosophy of the chairman of the SEC, and the personality of the SEC's Chief Accountant. There have been periods of great activity and SEC involvement and other times when relatively little interaction has occurred.

At times the SEC has been influential as a *catalyst* to financial reporting. An example is the role the SEC played in encouraging the Financial Executives Institute to conduct a significant study on segment reporting, the results of which were subsequently adopted by the APB and later the FASB as reporting requirements. On other occasions the SEC has served as a *rule maker,* for example in allowing alternative reporting practices for investment tax credits. The SEC has also been an *enforcer,* for example when the SEC suspended trading in the Equity Funding case. Regardless of the role played, it is clear that the SEC is influential, directly or indirectly, over the financial reporting activities of most companies in the United States.

Currently, the environment in the United States is such that the SEC's role appears to be one of oversight rather than regulation. However, if the accounting profession does not meet the challenges and opportunities facing it in an acceptable manner, it is clear that the SEC has the authority and would be required to become more involved as a means of meeting its responsibilities under the federal securities acts.

Disclosures By And About Management

The SEC has focused increasing attention on management disclosures, reflecting an effort to meet the objective of preventing fraud and providing full and fair disclosures to investors. This increased attention to management disclosures also is intended to be responsive to the Treadway Commission's recommendation that top management should communicate its responsibilities for the company's financial reporting. Examples of required management disclosures include: (1) disclosure of responsibilities for an assessment of the internal control system, (2) expanded disclosures in the management's discussion and analysis (MD&A) section of various SEC filings, and (3) disclosures related to management remuneration.

The importance of management's discussion and analysis of the financial condition and results of operations is highlighted by the expanded disclosures required by the SEC. For example, emphasis is being placed on prospective information such as trends, commitments, events or uncertainties that will materially affect the company's liquidity or profitability or its capital resources. Additional disclosures are required for material changes in financial statement line items, interim period disclosures, segment basis analysis, explanations of unusual or highly leveraged transactions, and preliminary merger negotiations. In brief, managements are being asked to provide more information in the analysis and interpretation of the operating results and financial conditions of their companies.

Questions:

1. Why is the SEC focusing on increased management disclosures?
2. What informational items are provided by Microsoft Corporation in the MD&A section of its 1993 Annual Report in Appendix A?

Sources:
An Introduction to the SEC, Skousen, 5th Edition, South-Western Publishing Co., 1991, pp. 138-139.
Report of the National Commission on Fraudulent Financing Reporting [Treadway Commission Report], October 1987.

APPENDIX

Expanded Illustration of Statement of Cash Flows

The basic techniques for preparing a statement of cash flows were explained in Chapter 6. More complex circumstances have been addressed as the topics have come up in subsequent chapters. This appendix presents an expanded problem that illustrates many of the cash flow issues that have been treated in the text.

The following comparative balance sheet for December 31, 1996, and December 31, 1995, is for Willard Company:

Willard Company
Comparative Balance Sheet
December 31, 1996 and 1995

	1996	**1995**
Assets		
Cash and cash equivalents	$ 62,400	$ 180,000
Investment securities (net)	47,000	0
Accounts receivable	400,000	345,000
Allowance for doubtful accounts	(20,000)	(31,000)
Inventories	680,000	643,000
Property, plant, and equipment	810,500	743,400
Accumulated depreciation	(229,000)	(228,000)
Total assets	$1,750,900	$1,652,400
Liabilities		
Accounts payable	$ 46,000	$ 103,000
Short-term notes payable	100,000	120,000
Accrued liabilities	76,500	48,000
Bonds payable	250,000	278,000
Discount on bonds payable	(19,600)	(20,800)
Deferred income tax liability	108,000	97,000
Total liabilities	$ 560,900	$ 625,200
Stockholders' Equity		
Common stock, $10 par	$ 840,000	$ 790,000
Paid-in capital in excess of par	52,000	20,000
Unappropriated retained earnings	268,000	217,200
Appropriated retained earnings	30,000	0
Total stockholders' equity	$1,190,000	$1,027,200
Total liabilities and stockholders' equity	$1,750,900	$1,652,400

Additional information includes:

—Net income for the year ended December 31, 1996, was $172,300. There were no extraordinary items.
—During 1996, uncollectible accounts receivable of $26,400 were written off. Bad debt expense for the year was $32,000.
—During 1996, machinery and land were purchased at a total cost of $115,100.
—Machinery with a cost of $48,000 and a book value of $4,200 was sold for $3,600.
—The bonds payable mature at the rate of $28,000 every year.
—In January 1996, the company issued an additional 1,000 shares of its common stock at $14 per share.
—In May 1996, the company declared and issued a 5% stock dividend on its outstanding stock; there were 80,000 shares of stock outstanding at the time and the market value per share was $17.
—During the year, cash dividends of $20,000 were paid on the common stock.
—The appropriation of retained earnings was in anticipation of an expected future drop in the market related to goods in inventory.
—The notes payable relate to operating activities.
—During 1996, a prior-period adjustment was made to correct an understatement of depreciation on equipment. The amount of the adjustment was $3,500.
—During the year, investment securities were purchased for $50,000. As of December 31, 1996, the securities have a market value of $47,000. The securities are classified as trading securities.
—Depreciation expense for the year totaled $41,300.

The preparation of the statement of cash flows will be illustrated using the indirect method of determining cash flows from operations. The analysis uses T-accounts. The T-accounts are shown on pages 1096 and 1097. Explanations for the individual adjustments and the related entries that are recorded in the T-accounts are presented below and on subsequent pages. Recall that these entries are only presented to aid in the preparation of the statement of cash flows; they are not actually posted to the accounts. The letter preceding each explanation corresponds with that used in the T-accounts.

(a) Net income is recorded as follows:

Cash Flows—Operating	172,300	
Unappropriated Retained Earnings		172,300

(b) Cash dividends paid are recorded as follows:

Unappropriated Retained Earnings	20,000	
Cash Flows—Financing		20,000

(c) The 5% stock dividend results in a transfer of retained earnings to common stock at par and to paid-in capital in excess of par. However, the stock dividend has no effect on cash. The amount of the transfer is the number of new shares (80,000 × .05 = 4,000) multiplied by the market value of the shares at the time of the stock dividend ($17):

Unappropriated Retained Earnings	68,000	
Common Stock, $10 par		40,000
Paid-In Capital in Excess of Par		28,000

(d) The recognition that depreciation had been understated in prior periods is recorded by a debit to Retained Earnings and a credit to Accumulated Depreciation. This correction of earnings of prior periods has no effect on cash:

Unappropriated Retained Earnings	3,500	
Accumulated Depreciation		3,500

(e) The appropriation of Retained Earnings involves no cash and is recorded as follows:

Unappropriated Retained Earnings	30,000	
Appropriated Retained Earnings		30,000

(f) The purchase of the machinery and land is recorded as follows:

Property, Plant, and Equipment	115,100	
Cash Flows—Investing		115,100

(g) The amount of cash received in the sale was $3,600 and this is shown as cash provided by investing activities. The sale of the machinery involved a loss of $600. Since this loss reduced net income but involved no cash effects beyond the $3,600 received, the $600 must be added to cash flows from operating activities to avoid understating the cash effect of the transaction:

Cash Flows—Investing	3,600	
Accumulated Depreciation	43,800	
Cash Flows—Operating	600	
Property, Plant, and Equipment		48,000

(h) Depreciation reduces net income but does not involve cash, so the following adjustment to cash flows is necessary:

Cash Flows—Operating	41,300	
Accumulated Depreciation		41,300

(i) The purchase of the investment securities is shown as follows:

Investment Securities—Trading	50,000	
Cash Flows—Investing		50,000

(j) A decline in the market value of the investment securities caused them to be written down. The $3,000 write-down reduced net income but did not involve cash, so its effect on income must be reversed when preparing the statement of cash flows:

Cash Flows—Operating	3,000	
Investment Securities		3,000

(k) Bonds retired for $28,000 during the year resulted in an outflow of cash for financing activities:

Bonds Payable	28,000	
Cash Flows—Financing		8,000

(l) The amortization of bond discount represents another item that reduced net income but did not involve cash. The necessary adjustment to cash flows is as follows:

Cash Flows—Operating	1,200	
Discount on Bonds Payable		1,200

(m) The $11,000 increase in Deferred Income Tax Liability is added back to cash flows provided by operating activities because it represents income taxes recognized as an expense of the current period for which no cash was paid:

Cash Flows—Operating	11,000	
Deferred Income Tax Liability		11,000

(n) The issuance of new common stock is shown as an increase in cash from financing activities:

Cash Flows—Financing	14,000	
Common Stock, $10 par		10,000
Paid-In Capital in Excess of Par		4,000

Cash flows from operating activities must be adjusted for changes in the levels of current assets and current liabilities. These adjustments are as follows:

(o) The simplest way to handle bad debt expense and account write-offs is to make the adjustment using the net receivable balance. If this is done and the indirect method is used, no special adjustments are required:

	Accounts Receivable (net)	66,000	
	Cash Flows—Operating		66,000
(p)	Inventories	37,000	
	Cash Flows—Operating		37,000
(q)	Accounts Payable	57,000	
	Cash Flows—Operating		57,000
(r)	Short-Term Notes Payable	20,000	
	Cash Flows—Operating		20,000
(s)	Cash Flows—Operating	28,500	
	Accrued Liabilities		28,500

After all changes in account balances for the year have been reconciled, the balances in the three cash flows T-accounts are transferred to a summary account. The $117,600 excess credit amount in this summary account represents a net decrease in cash for the year. The final entry records this decrease in the cash account and completes the analysis:

(t)	Net Decrease in Cash	117,600	
	Cash and Cash Equivalents		117,600

The formal statement of cash flows is prepared using the data in the three cash flows T-accounts.

Willard Company
Statement of Cash Flows
For the Year Ended December 31, 1996

Cash flows from operating activities:		
Net income	$ 172,300	
Adjustments:		
Loss on sale of machinery	600	
Depreciation expense	41,300	
Loss on decline in value of investment securities	3,000	
Amortization of bond discount	1,200	
Increase in deferred income tax liability	11,000	
Increase in net accounts receivable	(66,000)	
Increase in inventories	(37,000)	
Decrease in accounts payable	(57,000)	
Decrease in short-term notes payable	(20,000)	
Increase in accrued liabilities	28,500	
Net cash provided by operating activities		$ 77,900
Cash flows from investing activities:		
Purchase of machinery and land	$(115,100)	
Sale of machinery	3,600	
Purchase of investment securities	(50,000)	
Net cash used in investing activities		(161,500)

Cash flows from financing activities:		
Payment of cash dividends	$ (20,000)	
Retirement of bonds payable	(28,000)	
Issuance of common stock	14,000	
Net cash used in financing activities		(34,000)
Net decrease in cash		$(117,600)
Cash and cash equivalents, beginning of year		180,000
Cash and cash equivalents, end of year		$ 62,400

Cash Flows-Operating

(a)	172,300	(o)	66,000
(g)	600	(p)	37,000
(h)	41,300	(q)	57,000
(j)	3,000	(r)	20,000
(l)	1,200		
(m)	11,000		
(s)	28,500		
	77,900		

Cash Flows-Investing

(g)	3,600	(f)	115,100
		(i)	50,000
			161,500

Cash Flows-Financing

(n)	14,000	(b)	20,000
		(k)	28,000
			34,000

Cash Flows-Summary

	77,900		Operating
		161,500	Investing
		34,000	Financing
(t)	117,600		Net Decrease in Cash
	195,500	195,000	

Cash and Cash Equivalents

Beg. bal.	180,000	(t)	117,600
End bal.	62,400		

Investment Securities (net)

Beg.bal.	0	(j)	3,000
(i)	50,000		
End. bal.	47,000		

Accounts Receivable (net)

Beg. bal.	314,000		
(o)	66,000		
End. bal.	380,000		

Inventories

Beg. bal.	643,000		
(p)	37,000		
End. bal.	680,000		

Property, Plant, and Equipment

Beg. bal.	743,400	(g)	48,000
(f)	115,100		
End. bal.	810,500		

Accumulated Depreciation

(g)	43,800	Beg. bal.	228,000
		(d)	3,500
		(h)	41,300
		End. bal.	229,000

Accounts Payable

(q)	57,000	Beg. bal.	103,000
		End. bal.	46,000

Short-Term Notes Payable

(r)	20,000	Beg. bal.	120,000
		End. bal.	100,000

Accrued Liabilities

		Beg. bal.	48,000
		(s)	28,500
		End. bal.	76,500

Bonds Payable

(k)	28,000	Beg. bal.	278,000
		End. bal.	250,000

Discount on Bonds Payable

Beg. bal.	20,800	(l)	1,200
End. bal.	19,600		

Deferred Income Tax Liability

		Beg. bal.	97,000
		(m)	11,000
		End. bal.	108,000

Common Stock, $10 par

		Beg. bal.	790,000
		(c)	40,000
		(n)	10,000
		End. bal.	840,000

Paid-in Capital in Excess of Par

		Beg. bal.	20,000
		(c)	28,000
		(n)	4,000
		End. bal.	52,000

Unappropriated Retained Earnings

(b)	20,000	Beg. bal.	217,200
(c)	68,000	(a)	172,300
(d)	3,500		
(e)	30,000		
		End. bal.	268,000

Appropriated Retained Earnings

		Beg. bal.	0
		(e)	30,000
		End. bal.	30,000

KEY TERMS

Accounts receivable turnover 1067
Acid-test ratio 1066
Asset turnover 1071
Book value per share 1078
Cash flow adequacy ratio 1066
Common-size financial statements 1063
Comparative financial statements 1061
Conglomerates 1081
Current ratio 1065
Debt-to-equity ratio 1077
Diversified companies 1081
Dividends per share 1075
Earnings per share 1074
Financial leverage 1076
Fixed charge coverage 1078
Gross profit percentage on sales 1072
Growth potential 1060
Horizontal analysis 1061
Integral part of annual period concept 1083
Interim financial statements 1082
Inventory turnover 1069
Liquidity 1060
Natural business year 1070
Net profit percentage on sales 1072
Number of times interest is earned 1078
Price-earnings ratio 1075
Profitability 1060
Quick assets 1066
Quick ratio 1066
Rate earned on average common stockholders' equity 1074
Rate earned on average total assets 1073
Rate earned on average stockholders' equity 1074
Return on investment (ROI) 1073
Segment 1081
Stability 1060
Trading on the equity 1076
Vertical analysis 1063
Working capital ratio 1065
Yield on common stock 1075

QUESTIONS

1. What groups may be interested in a company's financial statements?
2. What types of questions requiring financial statement analysis might be raised by external users, such as investors and creditors, as contrasted to internal management?
3. What are the factors that one would look for in judging a company's (a) liquidity, (b) stability, (c) profitability, and (d) growth potential?
4. Why are comparative financial statements considered more meaningful than statements prepared for a single period? What conditions increase the usefulness of comparative statements?
5. Distinguish between horizontal and vertical analysis. What special purpose does each serve?
6. What information is provided by analysis of comparative statements of cash flows that is not available from analysis of comparative balance sheets and income statements?
7. What is meant by a *common-size* statement? What are its advantages?
8. Mention some factors that may limit the comparability of financial statements of two companies in the same industry.
9. What factors may be responsible for a change in a company's net income from one year to the next?
10. The Black Co. develops the following measurements for 1997 as compared with the year 1996. What additional information would you require before arriving at favorable or unfavorable conclusions for each item?
    (a) Net income has increased by $70,000.
    (b) Sales returns and allowances have increased by $25,000.
    (c) The gross profit rate has increased by 5%.
    (d) Purchase discounts have increased by $5,000.
    (e) Working capital has increased by $85,000.
    (f) Accounts receivable have increased by $150,000.
    (g) Inventories have decreased by $110,000.
    (h) Retained earnings has decreased by $300,000.
11. Distinguish between the current ratio and the acid-test ratio.
12. Balance sheets for the Rich Corporation and the Poor Corporation each show a working capital total of $500,000. Does this indicate that the short-term liquidity of the two corporations is approximately the same? Explain.
13. (a) How is the accounts receivable turnover computed? (b) How is the number of days' purchases in accounts payable computed?
14. (a) How is the merchandise inventory turnover computed? (b) What precautions are necessary in arriving at the basis for the turnover calculation? (c) How would you interpret a rising inventory turnover rate?
15. The ratio of total liabilities to stockholders' equity offers information about the long-term stability of a business. Explain.
16. Indicate how each of the following measurements is calculated and appraise its significance:
    (a) Number of times bond interest requirements were earned.
    (b) Number of times preferred dividend requirements were earned.
    (c) Rate of earnings on average common stockholders' equity.
    (d) Earnings per share on common stock.
    (e) Price-earnings ratio on common stock.

(f) Dividends per share on common stock.
(g) Yield on common stock.

17. Briefly explain how the sources of assets, liabilities, and owners' equity affect the rate of return to the residual owners of the organization.
18. Explain how the turnover of assets can affect return on assets.
19. Identify the major financial relationships that reflect the components of the rate of return to the common stockholders.
20. Under what conditions is the rate of return on average total assets equal to the rate of return to the common shareholder?
21. Under what circumstances is the use of industry ratios beneficial in analyzing a company's activity?
22. (a) What are the principal sources of industry data for use in comparative analysis? (b) What are the advantages and disadvantages of each source?
23. In what ways can segment information assist in the analysis of a company's financial statements?
24. Distinguish between the two primary viewpoints concerning the preparation of interim financial statements.
25. Why must investors be careful in interpreting interim reports?
26. What is the primary function of the SEC? Explain.
27. What major factors led to the establishment of the SEC in the United States?
28. What are the primary differences between the 1933 and 1934 Securities Acts as they impact financial reporting?
29. Who are the major players and what are their respective roles in the SEC registration process?
30. Traditionally, what has been the basic relationship of the SEC to financial reporting, and do you see that relationship changing in the future?

DISCUSSION CASES

Case 25—1 (How should we finance our expansion?)

The Detweiler Co. is considering expanding its operations. The company's balance sheet at December 31, 1996, is presented below.

Detweiler Co.
Balance Sheet
December 31, 1996

Assets		Liabilities	
Cash	$ 325,000	Accounts payable	$ 300,000
Accounts receivable	525,000	Bonds payable	1,100,000
Inventory	1,150,000	Total liabilities	$1,400,000
Land	1,200,000		
Buildings and equipment		Stockholders' Equity	
(net)	2,500,000	Preferred stock, 8%	
		cumulative, $100 par	$ 300,000
		Common stock, $25 par	1,000,000
		Retained earnings	3,000,000
		Total stockholders' equity	$4,300,000
		Total liabilities and	
Total assets	$5,700,000	stockholders' equity	$5,700,000

Each $1,000 bond is convertible at the option of the bondholder to 15 shares of common stock. The bonds carry an interest rate of 12% and are callable at 100. The company's 1996 income before taxes was $2,200,000 and was $1,520,000 after taxes. The preferred stock is callable at par. The common stock has a market price of $60 per share.

The company's management has identified several alternatives to raise $1,000,000.

(a) Issue additional bonds.
(b) Call in the convertible bonds to force conversion and then issue additional bonds.
(c) Issue additional 8% cumulative preferred stock.
(d) Issue additional common stock.

Evaluate the company's leverage position and discuss the advantages and disadvantages of each alternative.

Case 25—2 **(Analyzing earnings)**

Royer Donahoe owns two businesses: a drug store and a retail department store.

	Drug Store	Department Store
Net sales	$1,050,000	$670,000
Cost of goods sold	1,000,000	600,000
Average total assets	50,000	200,000
Other expenses	39,500	36,500

Which business earns more income? Which business earns a higher return on its investment in total assets? Which business would you consider more profitable?

Case 25—3 **(Can a ratio be too good?)**

Tony Christopher is analyzing the financial statements of Shaycole Company and has computed the following ratios:

	Shaycole	Industry Comparison
Current ratio	4.7	1.9
Inventory turnover	14.8 times	6.1 times
Accounts receivable turnover	27.4 times	8.7 times
Debt-to-equity ratio	.117	.864

Andy Martinez, Tony's colleague, tells Tony that Shaycole looks great. Andy points out that, although Shaycole's ratios deviate significantly from the industry norms, all the deviations suggest that Shaycole is doing better than other firms in its industry. Is Andy right?

Case 25—4 **(Evaluating alternative investments)**

Judy Snow is considering investing $10,000 and wishes to know which of two companies offers the better alternative.

The Hoffman Company earned net income of $63,000 last year on average total assets of $280,000 and average stockholders' equity of $210,000. The company's shares are selling on the market at $100 per share; 6,300 shares of common stock are outstanding.

The McMahon Company earned $24,375 last year on average total assets of $125,000 and average stockholders' equity of $100,000. The company's common shares are selling on the market at $78 per share; 2,500 shares are outstanding.

Which stock should Snow buy?

Case 25—5 **(Should the FASB set standards for financial ratios?)**

Financial ratios can be computed using many different formulas. In an article in the *CPA Journal,* one writer recommends that the FASB become involved in identifying common formulas and ratios that would be included in all financial statements. What are the advantages in pursuing such a recommendation? What are the difficulties?

Case 25—6 **(Where do assets go on the income statement?)**

Consider the following excerpt from a magazine article about professional baseball:

I recall a riveting moment during the lockout when NBC began a television interview with George Steinbrenner by presenting its best guess at the Yankees' 1990 budget—a balance sheet that showed roughly forty-five million dollars in expenses against revenues in excess of a hundred million. Mr. Steinbrenner, invited to comment, claimed the figures were out of whack. "You're way out of line," he said. "In cash flow, the Yankees will be lucky if they break even this year."

Comment on this excerpt from an accountant's perspective. Is it possible for both NBC and Mr. Steinbrenner to be right?

Source: Roger Angell, "The Sporting Scene (Baseball)," *The New Yorker,* May 21, 1990, p. 75.

Case 25—7 (Is it necessary to have an SEC?)

Some academic researchers have concluded that there is little justification for the establishment of the SEC. They maintain that there is little evidence of fraud in the financial statements of companies at the time the SEC was established; that the data required by the SEC do not seem to be particularly useful to investors; and that the SEC requirements are not cost beneficial. Others believe there were existing abuses in the capital markets at the time the SEC was established; that the SEC requirements lead to more efficient capital markets; and that the work of the SEC is in the public interest. What is your opinion on this issue?

Case 25—8 (Is the SEC a 500-pound gorilla?)

In a recent class, Bill Barnes heard his professor say that the SEC generally does not prescribe accounting principles, leaving that task to the FASB. Bill is from Texas where his family has a relatively small oil business. Because of this background, Bill is aware that the FASB in Statement No. 19 required all oil and gas companies to use the "successful efforts" method of accounting. Subsequently, the SEC allowed companies to use either the successful efforts method or the full-cost method of accounting for oil and gas exploration. The FASB then issued Statement No. 25, which suspended Statement No. 19 and effectively adopted the SEC standard. Bill asked his professor who really has the final say in the setting of accounting standards. How would you respond to Bill's question?

Case 25—9 (Microsoft's Annual Report)

1. The annual report includes sections on enterprise issues, desktop applications, Microsoft At Work, and Microsoft Home. Most of this sounds like product advertising. Why does Microsoft include this type of material in its report to the shareholders?
2. Find the Management Discussion and Analysis (MD&A) section of the annual report.
   a. The "Results of Operations" section includes a description of the results of three product groups. What are these product groups and which is the largest?
   b. Approximately what percentage of its net revenues does Microsoft spend for research and development? How are these expenditures accounted for? (See the "Significant Accounting Policies" note to the financial statements.)
   c. What are some of the significant risks described in the MD&A?
3. The notes to Microsoft's financial statements contain operating information by geographic segment. Reconcile this information with the statement that in 1993 55% of Microsoft's total revenue was from customers outside the United States.
4. The notes to Microsoft's financial statements also include quarterly information. Is there a seasonal pattern in Microsoft's revenue (i.e. are sales higher around Christmas)?
5. In the notes to its financial statements, Microsoft includes summary data for the past five years and computes values for four key financial ratios. In light of those ratio values, how is Microsoft doing?

EXERCISES

Exercise 25—10 (Index numbers)

Sales for the Montrek Company for a 5-year period and an industry sales index for this period are listed below. Convert both series into indexes employing 1993 as the base year.

	1997	1996	1995	1994	1993
Sales of Montrek Company (in thousands of dollars)	$8,400	$9,205	$8,710	$8,850	$8,530
Industry sales index (1985 = 100)	192	212	200	170	158

Exercise 25—11 (Comparative cost of goods sold schedule)

Cost of goods sold data for P. Lohner Corporation are presented below. The company's fiscal year ends June 30.

	1996-1997	1995-1996
Inventory, July 1	$ 75,000	$ 60,000
Purchases	410,000	320,000
Goods available for sale	$485,000	$380,000
Less inventory, June 30	55,000	75,000
Cost of goods sold	$430,000	$305,000

Prepare a comparative schedule of cost of goods sold showing dollar and percentage changes. Round to nearest whole percentage.

Exercise 25—12 (Vertical analysis)

The financial position of the Islandic Co. at the end of 1997 and 1996 is as follows:

	1997	1996
Assets		
Current assets	$ 70,000	$ 60,000
Long-term investments	15,000	14,000
Land, buildings, and equipment (net)	100,000	75,000
Intangible assets	10,000	10,000
Other assets	5,000	6,000
Total assets	$200,000	$165,000
Liabilities		
Current liabilities	$ 30,000	$ 35,000
Long-term liabilities	88,000	62,000
Total liabilities	$118,000	$ 97,000
Stockholders' Equity		
Preferred 8% stock	$ 10,000	$ 9,000
Common stock	54,000	42,000
Additional paid-in capital	5,000	5,000
Retained earnings	13,000	12,000
Total stockholders' equity	$ 82,000	$ 68,000
Total liabilities and stockholders' equity	$200,000	$165,000

Prepare a comparative balance sheet including a percentage analysis of component items standardizing each item by total assets. Round to nearest whole percentage.

Exercise 25—13 (Liquidity ratios)

The following data are taken from the comparative balance sheet prepared for the McCabe Resources Company:

	1997	1996
Cash	$ 25,000	$ 10,000
Investment securities (net)	9,000	45,000
Trade receivables (net)	43,000	30,000
Inventories	65,000	40,000
Prepaid expenses	3,000	2,000
Land, buildings, and equipment (net)	79,000	75,000
Intangible assets	10,000	15,000
Other assets	2,000	8,000
Total assets	$236,000	$225,000
Current liabilities	$ 80,000	$ 65,000

1. From the data given, compute for 1997 and 1996: (a) the working capital, (b) the current ratio, (c) the acid-test ratio, (d) the ratio of current assets to total assets, and (e) the ratio of cash to current liabilities.
2. Evaluate each of the changes.

Exercise 25—14 (Analysis of inventory position)

Income statements for the Eldermon Sales Co. show the following:

	1997	1996	1995
Sales	$125,000	$100,000	$75,000
Cost of goods sold:			
Beginning inventory	$ 30,000	$ 25,000	$ 5,000
Purchases	105,000	80,000	85,000
	$135,000	$105,000	90,000
Ending inventory	45,000	30,000	25,000
	$ 90,000	$ 75,000	65,000
Gross profit on sales	$ 35,000	$ 25,000	$10,000

Give whatever measurements may be developed in analyzing the inventory position at the end of each year. What conclusions would you make concerning the inventory trend?

Exercise 25—15 (Analysis of accounts payable)

The total purchases of goods by The Gerald Company during 1996 were $720,000. All purchases were on a 2/10, n/30 basis. The average balance in the vouchers payable account was $76,000. Was the company prompt, slow, or average in paying for goods? How many days' average purchases were there in accounts payable, assuming a 365-day year?

Exercise 25—16 (Inventory turnover)

The following data are taken from the Clayburgh Corporation records for the years ending December 31, 1997, 1996, and 1995.

	1997	1996	1995
Finished goods inventory	$ 60,000	$ 40,000	$ 30,000
Goods in process inventory	60,000	65,000	60,000
Raw materials inventory	60,000	40,000	35,000
Sales	400,000	340,000	300,000
Cost of goods sold	225,000	230,000	210,000
Cost of goods manufactured	260,000	250,000	200,000
Raw materials used in production	150,000	130,000	120,000

1. Compute turnover rates for 1997 and for 1996 for (a) finished goods, (b) goods in process, and (c) raw materials.
2. Analyze the turnover results as to reasonableness and the message they provide to a statement reader.

Exercise 25—17 (Inventory turnover)

The controller of the Montoya Manufacturing Co. wishes to analyze the activity of the finished goods, goods in process, and raw materials inventories. The following information is produced for the analysis:

Finished goods inventory, 12/31/96	$112,500
Finished goods inventory, 12/31/97	215,000
Goods in process inventory, 12/31/96	211,000
Goods in process inventory, 12/31/97	239,000
Raw materials inventory, 12/31/96	140,000
Raw materials inventory, 12/31/97	175,000
Cost of goods sold, 1997	245,000
Cost of goods manufactured, 1997	306,000
Cost of materials used, 1997	250,000

1. Compute the inventory turnovers.
2. Based on the foregoing data and the turnover computations, evaluate the company's control over inventories.

Exercise 25—18 (Analysis of capital structure)

The Vijay Corporation estimates that pretax earnings for the year ended December 31, 1996, will be $200,000 if it operates without borrowed capital. Income tax is 30% of earnings. Average stockholders' equity for 1996 is $750,000. Assuming that the company is able to borrow $1,200,000 at 12% interest, indicate the effects on net income and return on average stockholders' equity if borrowed capital earns (1) 20%, and (2) 10%. Explain the cause of the variations.

Exercise 25—19 (Profitability analysis)

The balance sheets for the Fargo Paint Corp. showed long-term liabilities and stockholders' equity balances at the end of each year as follows:

	1997	1996	1995
10% bonds payable	$ 600,000	$600,000	$600,000
Preferred 8% stock, $100 par	600,000	400,000	400,000
Common stock, $25 par	1,200,000	900,000	900,000
Additional paid-in capital	150,000	100,000	100,000
Retained earnings	300,000	100,000	50,000

Net income was: 1997, $280,000; 1996, $130,000. Using the foregoing data, compute the following for each year. (Ignore income tax considerations.)

(a) The rate of earnings on average total stockholders' equity.
(b) The number of times bond interest requirements were earned.
(c) The number of times preferred dividend requirements were earned.
(d) The rate earned on average common stockholders' equity.
(e) The earnings per share on common stock.

Exercise 25—20 (Return on stockholders' equity)

Fay Cutler wishes to know which of two companies will yield the greater rate of return on an investment in common stock. Financial information for 1996 for the Joslyn Co. and the Troy Co. is presented below.

	Joslyn Co.	Troy Co.
Net income	$ 150,000	$ 293,000
Preferred stock (7%)	600,000	970,000
Common stockholders' equity:		
January 1, 1996	1,450,000	2,465,000
December 31, 1996	1,350,000	2,670,000

Determine which company earned the greater return on average common stockholders' equity in 1996.

Exercise 25—21 (Profitability analysis for two companies)

The following information is obtained from the primary financial statements of two retail companies. One company markets its merchandise in a resort area, the other company is a discount household goods store. Neither company has any interest-bearing debt. By analyzing these data, indicate which company is more likely to be the gift shop and which is the discount household goods store. Support your answer.

	Company A	Company B
Revenue	$6,000,000	$6,000,000
Average total assets	$1,200,000	$6,000,000
Net income	$ 125,000	$ 600,000

Exercise 25—22 (Profit margin, asset turnover, and leverage)

Using the data presented below, estimate the rate earned on stockholders' equity for the following industries:

	Leverage Ratio	Asset Turnover	Profit Margin on Sales
Retail jewelry stores	1.578	1.529	0.050
Retail grocery stores	1.832	5.556	0.014
Electric service companies	2.592	0.498	0.069
Legal services firms	1.708	3.534	0.083

Leverage Ratio = Average total assets / Average stockholders' equity
Asset Turnover = Sales / Average total assets
Profit Margin on Sales = Net income / Sales

Exercise 25—23 (Debt covenants and financing alternatives)

Chasebry Company is in need of another factory building. The building will cost $100,000. Chasebry is considering the following possible financing alternatives to acquire the building:

(a) Lease the building under an operating lease.
(b) Issue common stock in the amount of $100,000.
(c) Negotiate a long-term bank loan for $100,000.
(d) Negotiate a long-term bank loan for $60,000 and also increase short-term borrowing by $40,000.

Currently, Chasebry has current assets of $150,000, noncurrent assets of $325,000, current liabilities of $60,000, and noncurrent liabilities of $140,000. Under existing loan covenants, Chasebry must maintain a current ratio of 2.0 or more and a debt-to-equity ratio of less than 0.80. Which, if any, of the financing alternatives will allow Chasebry to avoid violating the loan covenants?

Exercise 25—24 (Analysis of financial data)

For each of the following numbered items, you are to give the lettered financial statement effect(s) for that item. If there is no appropriate response among the effects listed, leave the item blank. If more than one effect is applicable to a particular item, be sure to list *all* applicable letters. (Assume the state statutes do not permit declaration of nonliquidating dividends except from earnings. Also assume that the current ratio is greater than 1:1.)

Item	Effect
1. Declaration of a cash dividend due in one month on preferred stock.	(a) Reduces working capital.
2. Declaration and distribution of a small stock dividend.	(b) Increases working capital.
3. Receipt of a cash dividend, not previously recorded, on stock of another corporation.	(c) Reduces current ratio.
4. Passing of a dividend on preferred cumulative stock.	(d) Increases current ratio.
5. Receipt of preferred shares as a dividend on common stock held as a temporary investment. This was not a regularly recurring dividend. The preferred shares are also a temporary investment.	(e) Reduces the dollar amount of total capital stock.
6. Payment of dividend described in (1).	(f) Increases the dollar amount of total capital stock.
7. Issue of new common shares in a 5-for-1 stock split.	(g) Reduces total retained earnings.
	(h) Increases total retained earnings.
	(i) Reduces equity per share of common stock.
	(j) Reduces equity of each common stockholder.

Exercise 25—25 (Analysis of financial data)

The December 31, 1996, balance sheet of Copepper's Inc. and additional information are presented below. These are the only accounts in Copepper's balance sheet. Amounts indicated by a question mark (?) can be calculated from the additional information given.

Assets		Liabilities and Stockholders' Equity	
Cash	$ 25,000	Accounts payable (trade)	$?
Accounts receivable (net)	?	Income taxes payable (current)	25,000
Inventory	?	Long-term debt	?
Property, plant, and equipment (net)	294,000	Common stock	300,000
		Retained earnings	?
	$432,000		$?

Additional information:

Current ratio (at year-end)	1.5 to 1
Total liabilities divided by total stockholders' equity	.8
Inventory turnover based on sales and ending inventory	15 times
Inventory turnover based on cost of goods sold and ending inventory	10.5 times
Gross margin for 1996	$315,000

1. What was Copepper's December 31, 1996 balance in trade accounts payable?
2. What was Copepper's December 31, 1996 balance in retained earnings?
3. What was Copepper's December 31, 1996 balance in the inventory account?

Exercise 25—26 (Reporting segment information)

Lutz Industries operates in five different industries. From the information given below, determine which segments should be classified as reportable segments according to FASB Statement No. 14. Provide justification for your answer.

Lutz Industries
Information About Company Operations in Different Industries
For the Year Ended December 31, 1996
(In Millions of Dollars)

	Industry 1	Industry 2	Industry 3	Industry 4	Industry 5	Total
Revenues	$ 577	$ 84	$ 93	$117	$ 96	$ 967
Operating profit	66	11	9	10	10	106
Identifiable assets	2,124	298	328	314	353	3,417

Exercise 25—27 (Interim income statements)

The income statement for the year ended December 31, 1996, of Essex Technology Inc. appears on the next page. Using the yearly income statement and the supplemental information, reconstruct the third-quarter interim statement for Essex.

Supplemental information:

(a) Assume a 40% tax rate.
(b) Third-quarter sales were 20% of total sales.
(c) For interim reporting purposes, a gross profit rate of 38% can be justified.
(d) Variable operating expenses are allocated in the same proportion as sales. Fixed operating expenses are allocated based on the expiration of time. Of the total operating expenses, $60,000 relate to variable expenses.
(e) The equipment was sold June 1, 1996.
(f) The extraordinary loss occurred September 1, 1996.

Essex Technology Inc.
Income Statement
For the Year Ended December 31, 1996

Sales	$900,000
Cost of goods sold	560,000
Gross profit on sales	$340,000
Operating expenses	96,000
Operating income	$244,000
Gain on sale of equipment	28,000
Income from continuing operations before income taxes	$272,000
Income taxes	108,800
Income from continuing operations	$163,200
Extraordinary loss (net of income tax savings of $40,000)	(60,000)
Net income	$103,200

Exercise 25—28 (SEC and financial reporting)
Identify and provide a brief description of the major SEC forms and reports that directly impact financial reporting.

Exercise 25—29 (Disclosure of less-than-total company results)
As a result of SEC prodding, the APB and subsequently the FASB adopted rules requiring increased disclosures in financial statements of less-than-total company results. This often takes the form of segment reporting by diversified companies, but also can be by geographic areas, subdivisions of a company that typically have differing degrees of growth potential and risk.

Refer to the annual report of Microsoft and identify the extent of disclosures of less-than-total company results provided by Microsoft. Is this information useful to prospective investors? Why or why not?

PROBLEMS

Problem 25—30 (Comparative statements)
Operations for the Gordo Company for 1997 and 1996 are summarized below:

	1997	1996
Sales	$500,000	$450,000
Sales returns	20,000	10,000
Net sales	$480,000	$440,000
Cost of goods sold	350,000	240,000
Gross profit on sales	$130,000	$200,000
Selling and general expenses	100,000	120,000
Operating income	$ 30,000	$ 80,000
Other expenses	35,000	30,000
Income (loss) before income tax	$ (5,000)	$ 50,000
Income tax (refund)	(2,000)	20,000
Net income (loss)	$ (3,000)	$ 30,000

Instructions:

1. Prepare a comparative income statement showing dollar changes and percentage changes for 1997 as compared with 1996.
2. Prepare a comparative income statement offering a percentage analysis of component revenue and expense items of net sales for each year.
3. Based on the above percentages, prepare an analysis of Gordo's operations for 1997 and 1996.

Problem 25—31 (Common-size statements)

As of December 31, 1996, balance sheet data for the Stay-Trim Company and the Tone-Up Company follows:

	Stay-Trim Company	Tone-Up Company
Assets		
Current assets	$ 51,000	$ 240,000
Long-term investments	5,000	280,000
Land, buildings, and equipment (net)	48,000	520,000
Intangible assets	6,000	100,000
Other assets	5,000	60,000
Total assets	$115,000	$1,200,000
Liabilities		
Current liabilities	$ 15,000	$ 180,000
Long-term liabilities	25,000	300,000
Deferred revenues	5,000	70,000
Total liabilities	$ 45,000	$ 550,000
Stockholders' Equity		
Preferred stock	$ 5,000	$ 100,000
Common stock	30,000	200,000
Additional paid-in capital	25,000	185,000
Retained earnings	10,000	165,000
Total stockholders' equity	$ 70,000	$ 650,000
Total liabilities and stockholders' equity	$115,000	$1,200,000

Instructions:

1. Prepare a comparative common-size statement using the balance sheet data.
2. What analytical conclusions can be drawn from this comparative common-size statement?

Problem 25—32 (Index numbers)

Sales for Leong Mfg. Co. and its chief competitor, La Ultima Company, and the sales index for the industry are as follows:

	1997	1996	1995	1994	1993
Sales of Leong Mfg. Co. (in thousands of dollars)	$ 7,000	$7,280	$7,735	$8,450	$8,385
Sales of La Ultima Company (in thousands of dollars)	$10,100	$9,690	$9,975	$9,785	$9,880
Industry sales index (1988 = 100)	140	152	161	144	133

Instructions:

1. Convert the three series to index numbers using 1993 as the base year.
2. Prepare a short report for the management of Leong Mfg. Co. summarizing your findings.

Problem 25—33 (Computation of various ratios)

The balance sheet data for the Fielding Supply Corp. on December 31, 1996, is as follows:

Assets		Liabilities and Stockholders' Equity	
Cash	$120,000	Notes and accounts payable	$150,000
Investment securities	25,000	Income tax payable	40,000
Notes and accounts receivable (net)	175,000	Wages and interest payable	10,000
Inventories	590,000	Dividends payable	25,000
Prepaid expenses	15,000	Bonds payable	380,000
Bond redemption fund (securities of other companies)	400,000	Deferred revenues	20,000
Land, buildings, and equipment (net)	730,000	Common stock, $20 par	1,200,000
Intangible assets	420,000	Preferred 6% stock, $20 par (noncumulative, liquidating value at par)	200,000
		Retained earnings appropriated for plant expansion	200,000
		Retained earnings	250,000
Total assets	$2,475,000	Total liabilities and stockholders' equity	$2,475,000

Instructions: From the balance sheet data, compute the following:

1. Amount of working capital.
2. Current ratio.
3. Acid-test ratio.
4. Ratio of current assets to total assets.
5. Ratio of total liabilities to stockholders' equity.
6. Ratio of tangible noncurrent assets to bonds payable.
7. Book value per share of common stock.

Problem 25—34 (Liquidity analysis)

The following are comparative data for Sunshine State Equipment, Inc. for the 3-year period 1995-1997.

Income Statement Data

	1997	1996	1995
Net sales	$1,200,000	$ 900,000	$1,020,000
Cost of goods sold	760,000	600,000	610,000
Gross profit on sales	$ 440,000	$ 300,000	$ 410,000
Selling, general, and other expenses	340,000	280,000	250,000
Operating income	$ 100,000	$ 20,000	$ 160,000
Income tax	40,000	9,000	72,000
Net income	$ 60,000	$ 11,000	$ 88,000
Dividends paid	35,000	30,000	88,000
Net increase (decrease) in retained earnings	$ 25,000	$ (19,000)	$ 0

Balance Sheet Data

	1997	1996	1995
Assets			
Cash	$ 50,000	$ 40,000	$ 75,000
Trade notes and accounts receivable (net)	300,000	320,000	250,000
Inventory (at cost)	380,000	420,000	350,000
Prepaid expenses	30,000	10,000	40,000
Land, buildings, and equipment (net)	760,000	600,000	690,000
Intangible assets	110,000	100,000	125,000
Other assets	70,000	10,000	20,000
	$1,700,000	$1,500,000	$1,550,000

Liabilities and Stockholders' Equity

Trade notes and accounts payable	$ 120,000	$ 185,000	$ 220,000
Wages, interest, and dividends payable	25,000	25,000	25,000
Income tax payable	29,000	5,000	30,000
Miscellaneous current liabilities	10,000	4,000	10,000
8% bonds payable	300,000	300,000	250,000
Deferred revenues	10,000	10,000	25,000
Preferred 6% stock, cumulative, $100 par and liquidating value	200,000	200,000	200,000
No-par common stock, $10 stated value	500,000	400,000	400,000
Additional paid-in capital	310,000	200,000	200,000
Retained earnings-appropriated	90,500	60,000	60,000
Retained earnings-unappropriated	105,500	111,000	130,000
	$1,700,000	$1,500,000	$1,550,000

Instructions:

1. From the foregoing data, calculate comparative measurements for the 3 years 1995-1997 as follows (for ratios using averages, assume 1994 figures are the same as 1995):
   (a) Amount of working capital.
   (b) Current ratio.
   (c) Acid-test ratio.
   (d) Average days' sales in trade receivables at the end of the year (assume a 365-day year and all sales on a credit basis).
   (e) Trade payables turnover rate for the year.
   (f) Inventory turnover rate.
   (g) Number of days' sales in the inventory at the end of the year.
   (h) Ratio of total liabilities to stockholders' equity.
   (i) Ratio of land, buildings, and equipment to bonds payable.
   (j) Ratio of stockholders' equity to land, buildings, and equipment.
   (k) Book value per share of common stock.
2. Based on the measurements made in (1), evaluate the liquidity position of Sunshine State Equipment, Inc., at the end of 1997 as compared with the end of 1996.

Problem 25—35 (Profitability analysis)

Use the comparative data for Sunshine State Equipment, Inc., as given in Problem 25—34.

Instructions:

1. Compute comparative measurements for the 3 years 1995-1997 as follows:
   (a) Ratio of net sales to average total assets.
   (b) Ratio of net sales to average land, buildings, and equipment.
   (c) Rate earned on net sales.
   (d) Gross profit rate on net sales.
   (e) Rate earned on average total assets.
   (f) Rate earned on average stockholders' equity.
   (g) Number of times bond interest requirements were earned (before income tax).
   (h) Number of times preferred dividend requirements were earned.
   (i) Rate earned on average common stockholders' equity.
   (j) Earnings per share on common stock.
2. Based on the measurements made in (1), evaluate the profitability of Sunshine State Equipment, Inc., for 1997 as compared with 1996 and 1995.

Problem 25—36 (Analysis of inventory, receivables, and payables)

Inventory and receivable balances and gross profit data for Balboa Arrow Co. appear on the next page.

	1997	1996	1995
Balance sheet data:			
Inventory, December 31	$100,000	$ 90,000	$ 80,000
Accounts receivable, December 31	55,000	50,000	20,000
Accounts payable, December 31	70,000	50,000	45,000
Net purchases	225,000	210,000	160,000
Income statement data:			
Net sales	$320,000	$260,000	$250,000
Cost of goods sold	215,000	200,000	180,000
Gross profit on sales	$105,000	$ 60,000	$ 70,000

Instructions: Assuming a 365-day business year and all sales on a credit basis, compute the following measurements for 1997 and 1996:

1. Receivables turnover rate.
2. Average days' sales in receivables at the end of the year.
3. Inventory turnover rate.
4. Number of days' sales in inventory at the end of the year.
5. Accounts payable turnover rate.

Problem 25—37 (Profitability analysis of three companies)

Financial information (in thousands of dollars) relating to three different companies follows.

Item	Company A	Company B	Company C
Net sales	$ 60,000	$28,000	$21,000
Net income	9,600	1,850	360
Net income to common stockholders*	6,100	1,140	300
Average balances:			
Total assets	155,400	21,500	3,200
Common stockholders' equity	61,000	11,300	1,690

*Net income less preferred stock dividends

Instructions:

1. Compute the following ratios:
   (a) Net profit margin on sales.
   (b) Total asset turnover.
   (c) Rate earned on total assets.
   (d) Rate earned on average stockholders' equity.
2. Assume the three companies are (a) a large department store, (b) a large grocery store, and (c) a large utility. Based on the above information, identify each company. Explain your answer.

Problem 25—38 (Accounting differences and ratio analysis)

The following three ratios have been computed using the financial statements for the year ended December 31, 1996, for Mikemath Company:

Current ratio = (Current assets/Current liabilities)
= $80,000 ÷ $43,000
= 1.86

Debt-to-equity ratio = (Total liabilities/Stockholders' equity)
= $110,000 ÷ $125,000
= 0.88

Profit margin = (Net income/Sales)
= $45,000 ÷ $400,000
= 0.11

The following additional information has been assembled:

(a) Mikemath uses the LIFO method of inventory valuation. Beginning inventory was $36,000 and ending inventory was $43,000. If Mikemath had used FIFO, beginning inventory would have been $48,000 and ending inventory would have been $58,500.

(b) Mikemath's sole depreciable asset was purchased on January 1, 1993. The asset cost $120,000 and is being depreciated over 12 years with no estimated salvage value. Although the 12-year life is within the acceptable range, most firms in Mikemath's industry depreciate similar assets over 7 years.

(c) For 1996, Mikemath adopted FASB Statement No. 106 relating to postretirement benefits other than pensions. As part of the adoption, Mikemath has an $18,000 transition loss. Mikemath has chosen to recognize the entire loss in 1996. Most other firms in Mikemath's industry are amortizing their transition losses over 20 years.

Instructions:

1. How would the values for the three ratios computed above differ if Mikemath had used FIFO, depreciated the asset over 7 years, and amortized the transition loss over 20 years? Do not think of these as accounting changes; compute how the financial statements would differ if the alternate accounting methods had been used to begin with. Ignore any income tax effects.
2. What dangers are there in comparing a company's financial ratios with summary industry ratios?

Problem 25—39 (Reporting segment data)

Abcom Industries operates in several different industries, some of which are appropriately regarded as reportable segments. Total sales for Abcom are $12,000,000 and total common costs are $6,000,000 for 1996. Abcom allocates common costs based on the ratio of a segment's sales to total sales, which is considered an appropriate method of allocation. Additional information regarding the different segments is contained in the following schedule:

	Segment 1	Segment 2	Segment 3	Segment 4	Other Segments
Contribution to total sales	23%	8%	31%	28%	10%
Identifiable assets as percent of total company assets	36%	9%	32%	8%	15%
Traceable costs	$800,000	$350,000	$1,200,000	$1,000,000	$650,000

Instructions: Prepare a schedule from which operating profit is derived for Abcom Industries. The schedule should conform to the reporting criteria set forth in FASB Statement No. 14.

Problem 25—40 (Comprehensive analysis of financial data)

The partially condensed balance sheet and income statement for Maxfield Company are shown below.

Maxfield Company
Balance Sheet
December 31, 1996

Assets	
Cash	$ 63,000
Trade receivables (net of estimated uncollectibles of $12,000)	238,000
Inventories	170,000
Prepaid expenses	7,000
Land, buildings, and equipment (net of accumulated depreciation of $182,000)	390,000
Other assets	13,000
	$881,000

Liabilities and Stockholders' Equity

Accounts and notes payable—trade	$ 98,000
Accrued liabilities payable	17,000
Income tax payable	18,000
First-mortgage, 7% bonds, due in 2003	150,000
$7 preferred stock—no par value (entitled to $110 per share in liquidation); authorized 1,000 shares; in treasury 400 shares; outstanding 600 shares	108,000
Common stock—no par; authorized 100,000 shares, issued and outstanding 10,000 shares at stated value of $10 per share	100,000
Paid-in capital in excess of stated value—common stock	242,000
Retained earnings appropriated for plant expansion	50,000
Retained earnings appropriated for cost of treasury stock	47,000
Retained earnings—unappropriated	98,000
Cost of 400 shares of treasury stock (preferred)	(47,000)
	$881,000

Maxfield Company
Income Statement
For the Year Ended December 31, 1996

	Cash	Credit	Total
Gross sales	$116,000	$876,000	$992,000
Less: Sales discount	$ 3,000	$ 12,000	$ 15,000
Sales returns and allowances	1,000	6,000	7,000
	$ 4,000	$ 18,000	$ 22,000
Net sales	$112,000	$858,000	$970,000
Cost of goods sold:			
Inventory of finished goods, January 1		$ 92,000	
Cost of goods manufactured		680,000	
Inventory of finished goods, December 31		(100,000)	672,000
Gross profit on sales			$298,000
Selling expenses		$ 173,000	
General expenses		70,000	243,000
Income from operations			$ 55,000
Other additions and deductions (net)			3,000
Income before income tax			$ 58,000
Income tax (estimated)			18,000
Net income			$ 40,000

Additional Information:

(a) Working capital at December 31, 1995, was $205,000.
(b) Trade receivables at December 31, 1995, were $220,000 gross, $206,000 net.
(c) Dividends for 1996 have been declared and paid.
(d) There has been no change in amount of bonds outstanding or common stock during 1996.

Instructions: Compute the following:

1. Acid-test ratio.
2. Number of days' sales in receivables.
3. Average finished goods turnover.
4. Number of times bond interest was earned (before tax).
5. Number of times preferred dividend was earned.
6. Earnings per share of common stock.
7. Book value per share of common stock.
8. Current ratio.

(AICPA Adapted)

***Problem 25—41 (Comprehensive statement of cash flows)**

The schedule below shows the account balances of the Beneficio Corporation at the beginning and end of the fiscal year ended October 31, 1996.

Debits	October 31, 1996	October 31, 1995
Cash and Cash Equivalents	$ 222,000	$ 50,000
Investment Securities—Trading	10,000	40,000
Accounts Receivable	148,000	100,000
Inventories	291,000	300,000
Prepaid Insurance	2,500	2,000
Land and Building	195,000	195,000
Equipment	305,000	170,000
Discount on Bonds Payable	8,500	9,000
Treasury Stock (at cost)	5,000	10,000
Cost of Goods Sold	539,000	
Selling and General Expenses	287,000	
Income Taxes	35,000	
Loss on Write-down of Investment Securities	4,000	
Loss on Sale of Equipment	1,000	
Total debits	$2,053,000	$876,000
Credits		
Allowance for Doubtful Accounts	$ 8,000	$ 5,000
Accumulated Depreciation—Building	26,250	22,500
Accumulated Depreciation—Equipment	39,750	27,500
Accounts Payable	55,000	60,000
Notes Payable—Current	70,000	20,000
Miscellaneous Expenses Payable	18,000	8,700
Taxes Payable	35,000	10,000
Unearned Revenue	1,000	9,000
Notes Payable—Long-Term	40,000	60,000
Bonds Payable—Long-Term	250,000	250,000
Deferred Income Tax Liability	47,000	53,300
Common Stock, $2 par	359,400	200,000
Retained Earnings Appropriated for Possible Building Expansion	43,000	33,000
Unappropriated Retained Earnings	34,600	112,000
Paid-In Capital in Excess of Par Value	116,000	5,000
Sales	898,000	
Gain on Sale of Investment Securities	12,000	
Total credits	$2,053,000	$876,000

The following information was also available:

(a) All purchases and sales were on account.
(b) Equipment with an original cost of $15,000 was sold for $7,000.
(c) Selling and general expenses include the following:

Building depreciation	$ 3,750
Equipment depreciation	25,250
Doubtful accounts expense	4,000
Interest expense	18,000

(d) A 6-month note payable for $50,000 was issued toward the purchase of new equipment.
(e) The long-term note payable requires the payment of $20,000 per year plus interest until paid.

(f) Treasury stock was sold for $1,000 more than its cost.
(g) During the year, a 30% stock dividend was declared and issued. At the time, there were 100,000 shares of $2 par common stock outstanding. However, 1,000 of these shares were held as treasury stock at the time and were prohibited from participating in the stock dividend. Market price was $10.00 per share at time the dividend was declared.
(h) Equipment was overhauled, extending its useful life at a cost of $6,000. The cost was debited to Accumulated Depreciation—Equipment.

Instructions: Prepare a statement of cash flows for the year ended October 31, 1996, using the indirect method of reporting cash flow from operations. (AICPA adapted)

*Relates to Appendix

APPENDIX A

Illustrative Financial Statements

Management is responsible for preparing the Company's financial statements and related information that appears in this annual report. Management believes that the financial statements fairly reflect the form and substance of transactions and reasonably present the Company's financial condition and results of operations in conformity with generally accepted accounting principles. Management has included in the Company's financial statements amounts that are based on estimates and judgments, which it believes are reasonable under the circumstances.

The Company maintains a system of internal accounting policies, procedures, and controls intended to provide reasonable assurance, at appropriate cost, that transactions are executed in accordance with Company authorization and are properly recorded and reported in the financial statements, and that assets are adequately safeguarded.

Deloitte & Touche audits the Company's financial statements in accordance with generally accepted auditing standards and provides an objective, independent review of the fairness of reported financial condition and results of operations.

The Board of Directors of the Company has an Audit Committee composed of nonmanagement Directors. The Committee meets with financial management, the internal auditors, and the independent auditors to review internal accounting controls and accounting, auditing, and financial reporting matters.

Michael W. Brown
Vice President, Finance; Treasurer

To the Board of Directors and Stockholders of Microsoft Corporation:

We have audited the accompanying balance sheets of Microsoft Corporation and subsidiaries as of June 30, 1993 and 1992, and the related statements of income, stockholders' equity, and cash flows for each of the three years in the period ended June 30, 1993. These financial statements are the responsibility of the Company's management. Our responsibility is to express an opinion on these financial statements based on our audits.

We conducted our audits in accordance with generally accepted auditing standards. Those standards require that we plan and perform the audit to obtain reasonable assurance about whether the financial statements are free of material misstatement. An audit includes examining, on a test basis, evidence supporting the amounts and disclosures in the financial statements. An audit also includes assessing the accounting principles used and significant estimates made by management, as well as evaluating the overall financial statement presentation. We believe that our audits provide a reasonable basis for our opinion.

In our opinion, such financial statements present fairly, in all material respects, the financial position of Microsoft Corporation and subsidiaries as of June 30, 1993 and 1992, and the results of their operations and their cash flows for each of the three years in the period ended June 30, 1993 in conformity with generally accepted accounting principles.

Deloitte & Touche

Deloitte & Touche
Seattle, Washington
July 28, 1993
(August 20, 1993 as to Contingencies Note)

Results of Operations

Overview

Microsoft's business strategy emphasizes the development and sale of a broad line of microcomputer software products, including operating systems for personal computers, office machines, and personal home devices; languages; and applications programs; as well as personal computer books, hardware, and multimedia products.

Net Revenues

	1993	Change	1992	Change	1991
Net revenues	$3,753	36%	$2,759	50%	$1,843

Product Groups. Operating systems product group sales were $1,267 million, $1,104 million, and $668 million in 1993, 1992, and 1991. Revenues from the Microsoft MS-DOS operating system increased steadily in both 1993 and 1992. Additionally, releases of new retail upgrade versions (MS-DOS 6 Upgrade in 1993 and MS-DOS 5 Upgrade in late 1991) increased revenues year over year. Industry sources indicate the installed base of MS-DOS is approximately 120 million personal computers as of June 30, 1993. The MS® Windows operating system was an increasingly strong contributor to systems revenues during the three-year period. As of June 30, 1993, the installed base of MS Windows is over 30 million PCs.

Applications product group revenues were $2,173 million, $1,363 million, and $935 million in 1993, 1992, and 1991. Increases in applications revenues were led by sales of Windows-based products, particularly The Microsoft Office. The Microsoft Office includes Microsoft Excel, Microsoft Word, a Microsoft Mail license, and the Microsoft PowerPoint® presentation graphics program. Sales of Microsoft Excel and Microsoft Word for Windows also increased in both 1993 and 1992. Microsoft Access, a new database management product released during 1993 with introductory pricing, was a strong contributor to revenue growth. Windows-based software programs represented approximately 75% of applications product group revenues in 1993, up from approximately 65% in 1992 and 50% in 1991.

Versions of The Microsoft Office, Microsoft Excel, and Microsoft Word for the Macintosh also contributed to applications revenue growth, with increased sales in 1993 and 1992. Macintosh products represented approximately 13% of total applications revenues in 1993, and 19% in 1992 and 1991.

Hardware product group revenues were $233 million, $254 million, and $213 million in 1993, 1992, and 1991. The hardware product group's principal products are the Microsoft Mouse and BallPoint® mouse pointing devices. Demand for these and competing products is linked to that for the Windows operating system, which is enhanced by using a mouse.

Sales Channels. The Company has three major channels of distribution: U.S., International, and OEM. Sales in the U.S. and International channels are primarily to distributors and resellers. OEM channel revenues are license fees from original equipment manufacturers.

U.S. channel revenues increased 28% in 1993 to $1,182 million. Revenues were $926 million in 1992 and $563 million in 1991.

Revenues in Europe were $1,259 million, $997 million, and $688 million in 1993, 1992, and 1991. Other international revenues were $504 million, $313 million, and $207 million, respectively.

The Company's operating results are affected by foreign exchange rates. Revenues collected in foreign currencies represented 44%, 46%, and 47% of total revenues in 1993, 1992, and 1991. Since much of the Company's international manufacturing costs and operating expenses are incurred in local currencies, the total impact of exchange rates on net income is less than on revenues.

OEM revenues (primarily operating systems) grew 53% from the prior year to

$731 million. OEM revenues were $477 million in 1992 and $337 million in 1991. MS-DOS continues to be preinstalled on many personal computers sold by OEMs. In addition, many major original equipment manufacturers are preinstalling Windows on personal computers, leading to increased revenues through the OEM channel. During 1993, approximately 75% of total Windows units were sold through the OEM channel, up from approximately 50% in 1992 and 40% in 1991.

Cost of Revenues

	1993	Change	1992	Change	1991
Cost of revenues	$633	36%	$467	29%	$362
Percentage of net revenues	16.9%		16.9%		19.6%

Cost of revenues as a percentage of net revenues was 16.9% in 1993 and 1992, down from 19.6% in 1991. Cost of revenues can vary with the channel mix, product mix within channels, and price changes.

Operating Expenses

	1993	Change	1992	Change	1991
Research and development	$ 470	34%	$352	50%	$235
Percentage of net revenues	12.5%		12.8%		12.8%
Sales and marketing	$1,205	41%	$854	60%	$534
Percentage of net revenues	32.1%		31.0%		29.0%
General and administrative	$ 119	32%	$ 90	45%	$ 62
Percentage of net revenues	3.2%		3.3%		3.4%

Increases in research and development expenses resulted primarily from planned additions to the Company's software development staff and higher levels of third-party development costs. As of June 30, 1993, the Company employed approximately 4,000 people in product research and development, compared to 3,400 in 1992 and 2,700 in 1991.

Increases in sales and marketing expenses have been due to planned hiring of marketing personnel, increased advertising for the launch of new products and marketing programs, including television and radio advertising, and further development of Product Support Services. These increases have occurred in the U.S., in Europe, and in other geographic areas.

Increases in general and administrative expenses are primarily attributable to the growth in the systems and people necessary to support overall increases in the scope of the Company's operations.

Nonoperating Income

	1993	Change	1992	Change	1991
Nonoperating income	$75	67%	$45	114%	$21
Percentage of net revenues	2.0%		1.6%		1.1%

The primary component of nonoperating income is interest income, which was $83 million, $58 million, and $42 million in 1993, 1992, and 1991. Increased interest income is the result of a larger investment portfolio generated by cash from operations, offset in both 1993 and 1992 by declining interest rates.

Provision for Income Taxes

	1993	Change	1992	Change	1991
Provision for income taxes	$448	35%	$333	60%	$208
Percentage of net revenues	11.9%		12.1%		11.3%
Effective tax rate	32.0%		32.0%		31.0%

The effective tax rate was 32% in 1993 and 1992, and 31% in 1991. Notes To Financial Statements describe the differences between the U.S. statutory and effective income tax rates.

Net Income and Earnings Per Share

	1993	Change	1992	Change	1991
Net income	$953	35%	$708	53%	$463
Percentage of net revenues	25.4%		25.7%		25.1%
Earnings per share	$3.15	31%	$2.41	47%	$1.64

Net income as a percentage of net revenues decreased slightly in 1993, primarily due to higher relative sales and marketing expenditures. The increase in net income as a percentage of net revenues in 1992 was attributable to higher gross margin.

(In millions, except earnings per share)	Year Ended June 30		
	1993	1992	1991
Net revenues	$3,753	$2,759	$1,843
Cost of revenues	633	467	362
Gross profit	3,120	2,292	1,481
Operating expenses:			
Research and development	470	352	235
Sales and marketing	1,205	854	534
General and administrative	119	90	62
Total operating expenses	1,794	1,296	831
Operating income	1,326	996	650
Interest income — net	82	56	37
Other	(7)	(11)	(16)
Income before income taxes	1,401	1,041	671
Provision for income taxes	448	333	208
Net income	$ 953	$ 708	$ 463
Earnings per share	$ 3.15	$ 2.41	$ 1.64
Weighted average shares outstanding	303	294	282

See accompanying notes.

Outlook: Issues and Risks

The Company's 1993 Annual Report includes discussions of its long-term growth outlook. The following issues and risks, among others, should be considered in evaluating its outlook.

Rapid technological change. The personal computer software industry is characterized by rapid technological change and uncertainty as to the widespread acceptance of new products.

Long-term investment cycle. Developing, manufacturing, and selling software is expensive and the investment in product development often involves a long pay-back cycle. The Company began investing in the principal products that are significant to its current revenues in the early 1980s. The Company's plans for 1994 include significant investments in software research and development and related product opportunities from which significant revenues are not anticipated for a number of years. Competitors of the Company may clone the Company's products without the cost burden of such long-term investment.

The Microsoft Office. Management expects revenues from The Microsoft Office to increase as a percentage of total revenues in 1994. The price of The Microsoft Office is less than the sum of the prices for the individual application programs included in this product when such programs are sold separately.

Prices. Future prices the Company is able to obtain for its products may decrease from historical levels, depending upon market and other cost factors.

Upgrades. Product upgrades, enabling users to upgrade from earlier versions of the Company's products or from competitors' products, have lower prices than new products. Unit sales represented by product upgrades increased in 1993 and 1992. This trend is expected to continue in 1994.

Introductory pricing. The Company offered certain new products at lower introductory prices during 1993. This practice may continue with other new product offerings.

Channel mix. Average revenue per license is lower from OEM licenses than from retail versions, reflecting the relatively lower direct costs of operations in the OEM channel. An increasingly higher percentage of Windows was sold through the OEM channel during 1993 and 1992. The Company expects this trend to continue in 1994.

Volume discounts. In 1993, unit sales increased under Microsoft Select, a large account program designed to permit large organizations to easily obtain Microsoft products. This program includes volume licensing alternatives and special upgrade, documentation, and installation options. This program has been popular with large enterprises, and revenues under this program are expected to increase in 1994.

Foreign exchange. A large percentage of the Company's sales is transacted in local currencies. As a result, the Company's revenues are subject to foreign exchange rate fluctuations.

Cost of revenues. Although cost of revenues as a percentage of net revenues was relatively consistent in 1993 and 1992, it varies with channel mix and product mix within channels. Changes in channel and product mix, as well as in the cost of the components of the Company's products, may affect cost of revenues as a percentage of net revenues in 1994.

Sales and marketing and support investments. The Company's plans for 1994 include continued investments in its sales and marketing and support groups. Competitors may be able to enter the market without making investments of such scale.

Income taxes. New U.S. tax legislation has been enacted. The new legislation and related regulations and interpretations will increase the Company's effective income tax rate in 1994.

Accounting standards. Accounting standards promulgated by the Financial Accounting Standards Board change periodically. Changes in such standards, including currently proposed changes in the accounting for employee stock option plans, may have a negative impact on the Company's future reported earnings.

Unlicensed copying. Unlicensed copying of software represents a loss of revenues to the Company. The Company is actively educating consumers and lawmakers on this issue. During 1993, new software copyright laws were passed and enforced in Italy, contributing to increased revenues in that country. The Company will continue to devote resources to this issue. However, there can be no assurance that continued efforts will affect revenues positively.

Growth rates. Management does not expect 1994 revenue growth rates to be as high as those for 1993. Operating expenses as a percentage of revenues may increase in 1994 because of the above factors, among others.

Other. See Notes To Financial Statements regarding other factors concerning the Company, including contingencies related to government regulation and legal proceedings.

Financial Condition

The Company's cash and short-term investments totaled $2,290 million at June 30, 1993 and represented 60% of total assets. The portfolio is diversified among security types, industry groups, and individual issuers. The Company's investments are investment grade and liquid.

Microsoft has no material long-term debt. Stockholders' equity at June 30, 1993 was over $3.2 billion.

Cash generated from operations has been sufficient to fund the Company's investment in research and development activities and facilities expansion. As the Company grows, investments will continue in research and development in existing and advanced areas of technology. Cash may also be used to acquire technology or to fund strategic ventures. Additions to property, plant, and equipment are expected to continue, including new facilities and computer systems for development, sales and marketing, product support, and administrative staff.

The exercise of stock options by employees provides additional cash. Funds received have been used to repurchase the Company's common stock on the open market, to provide shares for stock option and stock purchase plans. This practice is expected to continue in 1994.

The Company has available $85 million of standby multicurrency lines of credit. These lines support foreign currency hedging and international cash management.

Management believes existing cash and short-term investments together with funds generated from operations will be sufficient to meet the Company's operating requirements in 1994.

(In millions)	June 30	
	1993	1992
Assets		
Current assets:		
Cash and short-term investments	$2,290	$1,345
Accounts receivable — net of allowances of $76 and $57	338	270
Inventories	127	86
Other	95	69
Total current assets	2,850	1,770
Property, plant, and equipment — net	867	767
Other assets	88	103
Total assets	$3,805	$2,640
Liabilities and stockholders' equity		
Current liabilities:		
Accounts payable	$ 239	$ 196
Accrued compensation	86	62
Income taxes payable	127	73
Other	111	116
Total current liabilities	563	447
Commitments and contingencies	—	—
Stockholders' equity:		
Common stock and paid-in capital — shares authorized 500; issued and outstanding 282 and 272	1,086	657
Retained earnings	2,156	1,536
Total stockholders' equity	3,242	2,193
Total liabilities and stockholders' equity	$3,805	$2,640

See accompanying notes.

(In millions)	Year Ended June 30		
	1993	1992	1991
Common stock and paid-in capital			
Balance, beginning of year	$ 657	$ 395	$ 220
Common stock issued	229	135	95
Common stock repurchased	(7)	(3)	(5)
Stock option income tax benefits	207	130	85
Balance, end of year	1,086	657	395
Retained earnings			
Balance, beginning of year	1,536	956	699
Common stock repurchased	(243)	(132)	(192)
Net income	953	708	463
Translation adjustment	(90)	4	(14)
Balance, end of year	2,156	1,536	956
Total stockholders' equity	$3,242	$2,193	$1,351

See accompanying notes.

(In millions)	Year Ended June 30		
	1993	1992	1991
Cash flows from operations			
Net income	$ 953	$ 708	$463
Depreciation and amortization	151	112	76
Current liabilities	177	167	107
Accounts receivable	(121)	(33)	(65)
Inventories	(51)	(40)	8
Other current assets	(35)	(18)	(18)
Net cash from operations	1,074	896	571
Cash flows from financing			
Common stock issued	229	135	95
Common stock repurchased	(250)	(135)	(197)
Stock option income tax benefits	207	130	85
Net cash from financing	186	130	(17)
Cash flows used for investments			
Additions to property, plant, and equipment	(236)	(317)	(264)
Other assets	(17)	(41)	(40)
Short-term investments	(723)	(284)	(77)
Net cash used for investments	(976)	(642)	(381)
Net change in cash and equivalents	284	384	173
Effect of exchange rates	(62)	(10)	(2)
Cash and equivalents, beginning of year	791	417	246
Cash and equivalents, end of year	1,013	791	417
Short-term investments	1,277	554	269
Cash and short-term investments	$2,290	$1,345	$686

See accompanying notes.

Significant Accounting Policies

Business. The Company develops, produces, markets, and supports a wide range of software for business and personal use, including operating systems, languages, and applications, and also provides personal computer books, hardware, and multimedia products.

Principles of consolidation. The financial statements include the accounts of Microsoft and its wholly owned subsidiaries. Significant intercompany transactions and balances have been eliminated.

Foreign currencies. Current assets and liabilities denominated in foreign currencies are translated at the exchange rate on the balance sheet date. Fixed assets and resulting depreciation are translated at historical rates. Translation adjustments resulting from this process are charged or credited to equity. Revenues, costs, and expenses are translated at average rates of exchange prevailing during the year. The balance in the cumulative translation adjustment account at June 30, 1993 decreased stockholders' equity by $89 million. Gains and losses on foreign currency transactions and hedge contracts are included in other expense.

Revenue recognition. Revenue from sales to distributors or dealers is recognized when related products are shipped. Revenue from products licensed to original equipment manufacturers is recognized ratably over the license period. License fees received prior to product acceptance are recorded as customer deposits.

Warranties and returns. The Company warrants products against defects and has policies permitting the return of products under certain circumstances. The Company's reserve for warranties and returns was $63 million and $41 million at June 30, 1993 and 1992.

Research and development. Research and development costs are expensed as incurred. Financial accounting rules requiring capitalization of certain software development costs do not materially affect the Company.

Income taxes. Income tax expense includes U.S. and international income taxes, plus an accrual for U.S. taxes on undistributed earnings of international subsidiaries. Certain items of income and expense are not reported in tax returns and financial statements in the same year. The tax affected difference is reported as deferred income taxes. Tax credits are accounted for as a reduction of tax expense in the year in which the credits reduce taxes payable.

Earnings per share. Earnings per share is computed on the basis of the weighted average number of common shares outstanding plus the effect of outstanding stock options, computed using the treasury stock method.

Cash and short-term investments. The Company considers all highly liquid investments with a maturity of three months or less at the date of purchase to be cash equivalents. Short-term investments are stated at the lower of cost or market. Cost approximates market value for all classifications of cash and short-term investments.

Inventories. Inventories are stated at the lower of cost or market. Cost is determined using the first-in, first-out method.

Property, plant, and equipment. Property, plant, and equipment is stated at cost and depreciated using the straight-line method over the following estimated useful lives:

Buildings	30 years
Leasehold improvements	Lease term
Computer equipment and other	3–5 years

Diversification of risk. The Company's investment portfolio is diversified and consists of short-term investment grade securities. At June 30, 1993 and 1992 approximately 40% and 35%, respectively, of accounts receivable represented amounts due from ten customers. Two customers each accounted for approximately 10% of revenues in 1993. The Company hedges certain foreign exchange exposures and had $33 million of hedge contracts outstanding at June 30, 1993.

Reclassifications. Certain reclassifications have been made for consistent presentation.

Cash and Short-Term Investments

(In millions)	June 30 1993	1992
Cash and equivalents:		
Cash	$ 225	$ 200
Commercial paper	326	244
Money market preferreds	159	144
Certificates of deposit	160	128
Bank loan participations	143	75
Cash and equivalents	1,013	791
Short-term investments:		
Municipal securities	788	292
Corporate notes and bonds	209	125
U.S. Treasury securities	199	100
Auction rate preferreds	17	22
Commercial paper	64	15
Short-term investments	1,277	554
Cash and short-term investments	$2,290	$1,345

Property, Plant, and Equipment

(In millions)	June 30 1993	1992
Land	$ 144	$142
Buildings	389	345
Computer equipment	415	324
Other	233	166
Property, plant, and equipment—at cost	1,181	977
Accumulated depreciation	(314)	(210)
Property, plant, and equipment—net	$ 867	$767

Leases

The Company has operating leases for most international and U.S. sales and support offices and certain equipment. Certain leases provide for rental adjustments based on a consumer price index. Rental expense for operating leases was $54 million, $44 million, and $28 million in 1993, 1992, and 1991. At June 30, 1993, future minimum rental payments under noncancelable operating leases were (in millions):

Fiscal Year	Minimum Rental Payments
1994	$ 60
1995	52
1996	37
1997	28
1998	24
1999 and thereafter	55
Total minimum payments	$256

Income Taxes

The provision for income taxes was composed of:

(In millions)	1993	1992	1991
Current:			
U.S. and state	$352	$225	$133
International	123	112	102
	475	337	235
Deferred benefit	(27)	(4)	(27)
Provision for income taxes	$448	$333	$208

Deferred taxes related to timing differences were:

(In millions)	1993	1992	1991
International earnings	$ 12	$ 18	$ 2
Revenues	(11)	(13)	(11)
Cost of revenues	(1)	2	(7)
Expenses	(27)	(11)	(11)
Deferred income tax benefit	$(27)	$ (4)	$(27)

Differences between the U.S. statutory and effective tax rates were:

	1993	1992	1991
U.S. statutory rate	34.0%	34.0%	34.0%
Tax exempt income	(0.6)	(0.6)	(0.9)
Foreign Sales Corporation	(1.0)	(1.0)	(0.7)
Tax credits	(0.9)	(1.1)	—
Other—net	0.5	0.7	(1.4)
Effective tax rate	32.0%	32.0%	31.0%

U.S. and international components of income before income taxes were:

(In millions)	1993	1992	1991
U.S.	$ 960	$ 658	$363
International	441	383	308
Income before income taxes	$1,401	$1,041	$671

During 1993, the Internal Revenue Service concluded its examination of the Company's income tax returns for 1988 and 1989 without material adjustments. Income taxes paid were $187 million, $175 million, and $121 million in 1993, 1992, and 1991. Adoption of *Statement of Financial Accounting Standards No. 109—Accounting for Income Taxes* in the first quarter of 1994 will not have a material impact on the financial statements.

Common Stock

Shares of common stock outstanding were as follows:

(In millions)	1993	1992	1991
Balance, beginning of year	272	261	256
Issued	13	13	11
Repurchased	(3)	(2)	(6)
Balance, end of year	282	272	261

The Company repurchases its common stock on the open market to provide shares for issuance to employees under stock option and stock purchase plans. The Company's Board of Directors authorized continuation of this program for 1994.

Employee Stock and Savings Plans

Employee stock purchase plan. The Company has an employee stock purchase plan for all eligible employees. Under the plan, shares of the Company's common stock may be purchased at six-month intervals at 85% of the lower of the fair market value on the first or the last day of each six-month period. Employees may purchase shares having a value not exceeding 10% of their gross compensation during an offering period. During 1993, 1992, and 1991, shares totaling 503,608, 464,519, and 506,038 were issued under the plan at average prices of $66.57, $49.17, and $28.06 per share. At June 30, 1993, 2,131,303 shares were reserved for future issuance.

Savings plan. The Company has a savings plan, which qualifies under Section 401(k) of the Internal Revenue Code. Under the plan, participating U.S. employees may defer up to 15% of their pre-tax salary, but not more than statutory limits. The Company contributes fifty cents for each dollar contributed by a participant, with a maximum contribution of 3% of a participant's earnings. The Company's matching contributions to the savings plan were $6.9 million, $4.9 million, and $3.2 million in 1993, 1992, and 1991.

Stock option plans. The Company has stock option plans for directors, officers, and all employees, which provide for nonqualified and incentive stock options. The Board of Directors determines the option price (not to be less than fair market value for incentive options) at the date of grant. The options generally expire ten years from the date of grant and are exercisable over the period stated in each option. At June 30, 1993, options for 23,176,835 shares were exercisable and 17,043,482 shares were available for future grants under the plans.

Outstanding Options

		Price Per Share	
	Number	Range	Weighted Average
Balance, June 30, 1990	56,318,628	$ 0.16 – 32.00	$11.64
Granted	13,770,737	22.22 – 44.78	29.89
Exercised	(10,823,012)	0.16 – 19.72	8.84
Canceled	(1,767,104)	0.33 – 32.00	11.63
Balance, June 30, 1991	57,499,249	0.61 – 44.78	16.54
Granted	14,870,314	41.17 – 79.58	47.54
Exercised	(10,366,610)	0.61 – 33.22	12.99
Canceled	(1,852,434)	3.00 – 77.67	14.77
Balance, June 30, 1992	60,150,519	0.61 – 79.58	24.87
Granted	12,175,751	61.75 – 88.50	68.59
Exercised	(13,075,582)	0.61 – 73.83	15.90
Canceled	(2,214,755)	9.94 – 88.25	28.46
Balance, June 30, 1993	57,035,933	0.61 – 88.50	36.12

Contingencies

On March 17, 1988, Apple Computer, Inc. brought suit against Microsoft Corporation and Hewlett-Packard Company for alleged copyright infringement in the U.S. District Court, Northern District of California. The complaint includes allegations that the visual displays of Microsoft Windows version 2.03 infringe Apple's copyrights and exceed the scope of a 1985 Settlement Agreement between Microsoft and Apple. The complaint seeks to enjoin Microsoft from marketing Microsoft Windows version 2.03 or any derivative work based on Windows 2.03 and from otherwise infringing Apple's copyrights and seeks damages resulting from the alleged infringement. The complaint also alleges that Microsoft is a contributory infringer as to a Hewlett-Packard product called NewWave™.

The Company answered the complaint, denying Apple's allegations that the visual displays in Microsoft Windows version 2.03 infringe any protectible right of Apple, raising affirmative defenses, asserting counterclaims, and seeking damages in an unspecified amount resulting from Apple's actions. In a July 25, 1989 order, the Court held that: (1) the use in Windows version 2.03 of visual displays that are in Windows version 1.0 and the named application programs is licensed under the 1985 Agreement, and (2) the allegedly infringing visual displays used in Windows version 2.03 are in Windows version 1.0, except for seven displays relating to the use of overlapping main application windows and three displays relating to the appearance and manipulation of icons. This means that 179 of the 189 Windows version 2.03 visual displays that Apple alleges are infringing are covered by the 1985 Agreement.

In a June 14, 1991 order, the Court permitted Apple to supplement its complaint to include Windows version 3.0 as an allegedly infringing work. In a July 25, 1991 order, the Court dismissed Microsoft's remaining counterclaim, wherein Microsoft alleged that Apple had breached an implied covenant not to sue for infringement as to any visual displays covered by the 1985 Agreement.

On February 11, 1992, Microsoft disclosed Apple's written claim for $4.4 billion as damages from Microsoft's alleged infringement of Apple's copyrights. Apple later amended this claim to $5.5 billion and more recently to $4.9 billion. Microsoft considers Apple's damages claim to be insupportable under the copyright law and speculative.

In an April 14, 1992 order, the Court ruled that none of the ten remaining allegedly infringed displays in the Windows version 2.03 case is protectible under Apple's copyrights. The Court also ruled that 26 of the allegedly infringing Windows version 3.0 displays are licensed under the 1985 Agreement.

On August 7, 1992, the Court entered an order on the issue of whether the allegedly infringed visual displays in Apple's works are within the scope of its copyrights. The Court also ruled on Apple's motion for reconsideration of the aspects of its April 14, 1992 order not related to the 1985 Agreement. The Court determined that the 23 remaining allegedly infringed visual displays claimed by Apple to be in Windows 3.0 are unprotectible by copyright, are licensed under the 1985 Agreement, or are not similar in the accused product. The Court affirmed its April 14, 1992 order that none of the ten remaining allegedly infringing Windows 2.03 visual displays is protectible by copyright, with the possible exception of aspects of four of the allegedly infringed visual displays in Apple's works that "could possibly be associated with unlicensed, artistic expression to be compared under a 'virtual identity' standard. . . ."

On April 14, 1993, the Court issued an order that clarified the August 7, 1992 order by ruling one of the remaining four items at issue in Windows to be unprotectible by copyright. The April 14, 1993 order also confirmed the applicability of the virtual identity standard to any analysis of similarity of the works in suit as a whole, and established a June 28, 1993 trial date for all issues that remain to be resolved at the time. In an order dated May 18, 1993, the Court dismissed Apple's copyright infringement claims based on six of its copyrights in their entirety, established that the remaining items at issue in Apple's works were unprotectible or not virtually identical in Windows, and again confirmed that the virtual identity standard must be applied when comparing the similarities of Microsoft's works as a whole to Apple's. Microsoft and Hewlett-Packard moved for summary judgment on the remaining claims, and these motions were not opposed by Apple. On June 8, 1993, the Court entered an order dismissing all of Apple's remaining infringement claims, including its contributory infringement claim against Microsoft. Microsoft anticipates that Apple will take an appeal to the Ninth Circuit Court of Appeals.

In June 1990, Microsoft was notified that it was the subject of a nonpublic investigation being conducted by the staff of the Federal Trade Commission (FTC or Commission). During further communications, the Company learned that the staff wished to determine if Microsoft and the IBM Corporation had entered into an alleged anticompetitive horizontal agreement that was purportedly reflected in a joint press release issued at the COMDEX computer trade show in November 1989.

The existence of this investigation became public knowledge in March 1991 when some third parties disclosed that the FTC staff had contacted them about the investigation. In April 1991, Microsoft learned that, apparently due to complaints from third parties, the staff had decided to broaden the investigation to examine allegations that the Company has monopolized or has attempted to monopolize the market for operating systems, operating environments, computer software, and peripherals for personal computers.

The Company produced documents, witnesses, and other information to the FTC staff in connection with the investigation.

In a Notice of Placement of Commission Action on the Public Record dated August 20, 1993 (the Notice), the FTC disclosed that at a closed meeting on February 5, 1993, Chairman Steiger moved that the FTC staff be authorized to file a complaint in federal court seeking a preliminary injunction against certain alleged Microsoft practices under Section 13(b) of the FTC Act. The motion failed for lack of a majority with two Commissioners voting in favor of the motion, two Commissioners voting against the motion, and one Commissioner recused. The Notice also disclosed that at a closed meeting on July 21, 1993, Chairman Steiger moved that the FTC issue an administrative complaint against the Company. The motion failed for lack of a majority with two Commissioners voting in favor of the motion, two Commissioners voting against the motion, and one Commissioner recused.

In a letter dated August 20, 1993, the Commission notified Microsoft that "it now appears that no further action is warranted by the Commission at this time," and that the investigation had been closed.

The Company was also notified on August 20, 1993 that the U.S. Department of Justice had been granted clearance by the FTC to investigate Microsoft, and would begin its own inquiry.

The Company currently believes that the resolution of these matters will not have a material adverse effect on its financial condition as reported in the accompanying financial statements.

Information by Geographic Area

(In millions)	1993	1992	1991
Net revenues			
U.S. operations	$2,655	$ 1,878	$1,210
European operations	1,289	1,019	708
Other international operations	395	272	187
Eliminations	(586)	(410)	(262)
Total net revenues	$ 3,753	$ 2,759	$1,843
Operating income			
U.S. operations	$ 961	$ 664	$ 373
European operations	360	329	280
Other international operations	18	11	12
Eliminations	(13)	(8)	(15)
Total operating income	$ 1,326	$ 996	$ 650
Identifiable assets			
U.S. operations	$2,944	$ 1,858	$1,278
European operations	1,133	872	578
Other international operations	310	289	208
Eliminations	(582)	(379)	(420)
Total identifiable assets	$3,805	$2,640	$1,644

Intercompany sales between geographic areas are accounted for at prices representative of unaffiliated party transactions. U.S. operations include domestic revenues, exports of finished goods to the Far East and South America, and OEM distribution in the Far East and Europe. Exports and international OEM transactions are in U.S. dollars and totaled $426 million, $255 million, and $188 million in 1993, 1992, and 1991. "Other international operations" primarily include subsidiaries in Australia, Canada, Japan, Korea, and Taiwan. International revenues, which include European operations, other international operations, exports, and OEM distribution, were 55.3%, 55.1%, and 57.3% of total revenues in 1993, 1992, and 1991.

(In millions, except per share data)	Quarter Ended				
	Sept. 30	Dec. 31	Mar. 31	June 30	Year
1993					
Net revenues	$818	$938	$958	$1,039	$3,753
Gross profit	683	781	797	859	3,120
Net income	209	236	243	265	953
Earnings per share	0.70	0.78	0.80	0.87	3.15
Common stock price per share:					
High	82	95	94-1/4	98	98
Low	65-1/2	75-3/4	76-3/4	79-3/4	65-1/2
1992					
Net revenues	$581	$682	$681	$ 815	$2,759
Gross profit	476	567	571	678	2,292
Net income	144	175	179	210	708
Earnings per share	0.50	0.60	0.60	0.71	2.41
Common stock price per share:					
High	60	74-5/8	88-7/8	86-1/8	88-7/8
Low	40-3/8	57-1/2	73	65-3/4	40-3/8
1991					
Net revenues	$369	$460	$487	$ 527	$1,843
Gross profit	293	367	392	429	1,481
Net income	88	113	124	138	463
Earnings per share	0.32	0.41	0.44	0.48	1.64
Common stock price per share:					
High	35-7/8	34-1/8	50-1/4	52-1/4	52-1/4
Low	22-1/2	23-3/4	32-3/8	42-5/8	22-1/2

The Company has not paid cash dividends on its common stock. The Company's common stock is traded on the over-the-counter market and is quoted on the NASDAQ National Market System under the symbol MSFT. On July 30, 1993, there were 27,769 holders of record of the Company's common stock.

(In millions, except employee and per share data)	Year Ended June 30				
	1993	1992	1991	1990	1989
For the year					
Net revenues	$ 3,753	$ 2,759	$1,843	$1,183	$ 804
Cost of revenues	633	467	362	253	204
Research and development	470	352	235	181	110
Sales and marketing	1,205	854	534	317	219
General and administrative	119	90	62	39	28
Operating income	1,326	996	650	393	243
Nonoperating income	75	45	21	17	8
Income before income taxes	1,401	1,041	671	410	251
Provision for income taxes	448	333	208	131	80
Net income	953	708	463	279	171
At year-end					
Working capital	$2,287	$ 1,323	$ 735	$ 533	$ 310
Total assets	$ 3,805	$2,640	$1,644	$1,105	$ 721
Stockholders' equity	$ 3,242	$ 2,193	$1,351	$ 919	$ 562
Number of employees	14,430	11,542	8,226	5,635	4,037
Common stock data					
Earnings per share	$ 3.15	$ 2.41	$ 1.64	$ 1.04	$0.67
Book value per share	$ 11.50	$ 8.06	$ 5.18	$ 3.59	$2.28
Cash and short-term investments per share	$ 8.12	$ 4.94	$ 2.63	$ 1.75	$1.22
Average common and equivalent shares outstanding	303	294	282	269	254
Shares outstanding at year-end	282	272	261	256	246
Key ratios					
Current ratio	5.1	4.0	3.5	3.9	3.0
Return on net revenues	25.4%	25.7%	25.1%	23.6%	21.3%
Return on average total assets	29.6%	33.1%	33.7%	30.6%	28.2%
Return on average stockholders' equity	35.1%	40.0%	40.8%	37.7%	36.5%
Growth percentages — increases					
Net revenues	36%	50%	56%	47%	36%
Net income	35%	53%	66%	63%	38%
Earnings per share	31%	47%	58%	55%	37%
Book value per share	43%	56%	44%	57%	47%

APPENDIX B
Glossary

A

Accelerated Cost Recovery System (ACRS). An alternative to traditional depreciation methods introduced for tax purposes in 1981 and subsequently modified. *See* Modified Accelerated Cost Recovery System (MACRS).

Account. A record used to classify and summarize the effects of transactions; a separate account is maintained for each asset, liability, owners' equity, revenue, and expense item, showing increases, decreases, and the account balance.

Account form of balance sheet. A balance sheet that presents assets on the left-hand side and liabilities and owners' equity on the right-hand side.

Accounting. A service activity whose "function is to provide quantitative information, primarily financial in nature, about economic entities that is intended to be useful in making economic decisions—in making reasoned choices among alternative courses of action" (APB Statement No. 4., par. 40).

Accounting and Audit Guides. Publications by special committees of the AICPA that deal with specific industries. These guides not only contain information concerning the auditing of these entities, but also discuss alternative accounting methods that could be used.

Accounting and Auditing Enforcement Releases (AAERs). SEC reports of substandard or fraudulent reporting in SEC filings and actions taken against the parties involved.

Accounting changes. A general term used to describe the use of different estimates or accounting principles or reporting entities from those used in a prior year.

Accounting cycle. *See* Accounting process.

Accounting Education Change Commission (AECC). A group formed by the American Accounting Association to facilitate improvements in accounting education.

Accounting errors. Incorrect accounting treatment resulting from mathematical mistakes, improper application of accounting principles, or omissions of material facts.

Accounting periods. The time intervals used for financial reporting; due to the need for timely information, the life of a business or other entity is divided into specific accounting periods for external reporting purposes. One year has been established as the normal reporting period, although some entities also provide interim (e.g., quarterly) statements.

Accounting Principles Board (APB). A board of the AICPA that issued opinions establishing accounting standards during the period 1959-1973.

Accounting process. The procedures used for analyzing, recording, classifying, and summarizing the information to be presented in accounting reports; also referred to as the accounting cycle.

Accounting Research Bulletins (ARBs). The publications of the Committee on Accounting Procedure that established accounting standards during the years 1939-1959.

Accounting Series Releases (ASRs). Prior to 1982, the name given to SEC statements dealing with reporting and disclosure requirements in documents filed with the SEC. Such statements are now called Financial Reporting Releases (FRRs).

Accounting system. The procedures and methods used, including use of data processing equipment, to collect and report accounting data.

Accounts receivable. Trade receivables that are not evidenced by a formal agreement or "note"; accounts receivable are usually unsecured "open accounts" and represent an extension of short-term credit to customers.

Accounts receivable turnover. An analytical measurement of how rapidly customers' accounts are being collected. The net accounts receivable formula is net credit sales divided by average accounts receivable for a period.

Accrual accounting. A basic assumption that revenues are recognized when earned and expenses are recognized when incurred, without regard to when cash is received or paid.

Accrued pension cost. The cumulative excess of annual pension costs over annual pension contributions. It is reported as a liability on a company's balance sheet.

Accumulated benefit obligation (ABO). The actuarial present value of pension benefits based on the plan formula for employee service earned to date using the existing salary structure. It is used to compute the minimum liability.

Accumulated postretirement benefit obligation (APBO). The actuarial present value of all future postretirement benefits earned by employees as of a certain date assuming that the benefit plan remains in effect and that assumptions about the future are fulfilled.

Acid-test ratio. An analytical measurement of the short-term liquidity of an entity; also referred to as quick ratio. The ratio formula is quick assets divided by the current liabilities at a specified time.

Actual return on pension plan assets. A component of net periodic pension costs measured by the difference between the fair value of pension plan assets at the end of the period and the fair value at the beginning of the period, adjusted for contributions and payments of benefits during the period.

Actuarial present value. The present value of pension obligations determined by using stated actuarial assumptions and estimates.

Additional markups. Increases that raise prices above original retail.

Additional paid-in capital. The investment by stockholders in excess of the amounts assignable to capital stock as par or stated value as well as invested capital from other sources, such as sale of treasury stock.

Additional pension liability. An additional liability reported for underfunded pension plans. It is computed as the difference between the minimum pension liability and accrued pension cost or as the sum of the minimum pension liability and the prepaid pension cost.

Additions. Expenditures that add to asset usefulness by either extending life or increasing future cash flows. No replacement of components is involved. Additions add to the cost of the asset.

Adjunct account. An account used to record additions to a related account. An example is Freight-In, which is added to the purchases account.

Adjusting entries. Entries required at the end of each accounting period to update the accounts as necessary and to fully recognize, on an accrual basis, revenues and expenses for the period.

Aging receivables. The most commonly used method for establishing an Allowance for Doubtful Accounts based on outstanding receivables. This method involves analyzing individual accounts to determine those not yet due and those past due. Past-due accounts are classified in terms of length of the period past due.

Allowance method. A method of recognizing the estimated losses from uncollectible accounts as expenses during the period in which the sales occur; this method is required by GAAP.

American Accounting Association (AAA). An organization for accounting academicians. Its role in establishing accounting standards includes research projects to help the FASB and a forum for representing different points of view on various issues.

American Institute of Certified Public Accountants (AICPA). A professional organization for CPAs. Membership in the AICPA is voluntary. It publishes a monthly journal, the *Journal of Accountancy*.

Amortization. Periodic cost allocation process for intangible assets.

Annuity. A series of equal payments (receipts) over a specified number of equal time periods.

Annuity due. An annuity that consists of payments (receipts) at the beginning of each period; also known as an annuity in advance.

Antidilution of earnings. Assumed conversion of convertible securities or exercise of stock options that results in an increase in earnings per share or a decrease in loss per share.

Antidilutive securities. Securities whose assumed conversion or exercise results in an antidilution of earnings per share.

Appropriated retained earnings. The restricted portion of retained earnings.

Arm's-length transactions. Exchanges between parties who are independent of each other; a traditional assumption in accounting is that recorded transactions and events are executed between independent parties, each of whom is acting in its own best interests.

Asset and liability method of interperiod tax allocation. A method of income tax allocation that determines deferred tax assets or tax liabilities based on scheduling future expected temporary difference reversals. If tax rates change, the asset or liability balances are adjusted to reflect the tax rates legislated to be in effect in the year when reversal is expected to occur.

Asset turnover. *See* Total asset turnover.

Assets. The resources of an entity: technically defined by the FASB in Concepts Statement No. 6 as "probable future economic benefits obtained or controlled by a particular entity as a result of past transactions or events."

Assignment of receivables. The borrowing of money with receivables pledged as security on the loan.

Available-for-sale securities. Debt and equity securities that are within the scope of FASB Statement No. 115 and are not classified as held-to-maturity or trading securities.

Average amount of accumulated expenditures. A weighted average of the expenditures incurred in the self-construction of an operating asset. Expenditures mean cash disbursements, not accruals. The expenditures are weighted by the portion of the year left after payment is made.

Average cost method. An inventory costing method that assigns the same average cost to each unit sold and each item in the inventory. Under a periodic inventory system, the unit cost is a *weighted average* for the entire period. Under a perpetual inventory system, the unit cost is computed as a *moving average,* which changes with each new purchase of goods.

Average cost retail inventory method. A method of estimating inventory that approximates an average cost valuation.

B

Balance sheet. A statement that reports as of a given point in time the resources (assets) of a business, its obligations (liabilities), and the residual ownership claims against its resources (owners' equity); an alternative title for the statement is the *statement of financial position.*

Bank discounting. The process of transferring negotiable notes to a bank or other financial institution in return for cash.

Bank reconciliation. A process that identifies differences between the cash balance on the depositor's books and the balance reported on the bank statement. The reconciliation provides information needed to adjust the book balance to a corrected cash amount.

Bank service charge. Monthly fee usually charged by a bank to service the depositor's account.

Bargain purchase option. A lease provision that allows for the purchase of a leased asset by the lessee at a price significantly lower than the expected fair market value of the leased asset at the date the bargain purchase option can be exercised.

Bargain renewal option. A lease provision that allows for renewal of the lease by the lessee at significantly reduced lease payments from the original lease. The bargain terms strongly imply that the lease will be renewed, and the lease term is assumed to extend through the bargain renewal period.

Basic earnings per share. An earnings per share computation that considers only common stock issued and outstanding. It is computed as the net income less preferred dividends divided by the weighted-average common shares outstanding for the period.

Betterments. *See* Additions.

Bond certificates. Certificates of indebtedness issued by a company or government agency guaranteeing payment of a principal amount at a specified future date plus periodic interest; usually issued in denominations of $1,000.

Bond discount. The difference between the face value and the sales price when bonds are sold below their face value.

Bond indenture. The contract between the issuing entity and the bondholders specifying the terms, rights, and obligations of the contracting parties.

Bond issuance costs. Costs incurred by the issuer for legal services, printing and engraving, taxes, and underwriting in connection with the sale of a bond.

Bond premium. The difference between the face value and the sales price when bonds are sold above their face value.

Bonds-outstanding method. A variation of the straight-line method of bond premium/discount amortization; applied to serial bonds.

Book value per share. A measure of an entity's value per share of common stock outstanding. The book value per share formula is common stockholders' equity divided by the number of common shares outstanding.

Business combination. The combining of two ongoing business entities, usually by the exchange of capital stock for the net assets acquired.

Business documents. Business records used as the basis for analyzing and recording transactions; examples include invoices, check stubs, receipts, and similar business papers. They are also referred to as source documents.

C

Callable bonds. Bonds for which the issuer reserves the right to pay the obligation prior to the maturity date.

Callable obligation. A debt instrument that is (1) payable on demand or (2) has a specified due date but is payable on demand if the debtor defaults on the provisions of the loan agreement.

Capital lease. A lease that is, in substance, a contract to purchase an asset.

Capital stock. The portion of the contribution by stockholders assignable to the shares of stock as par or stated value.

Capitalized interest. The amount of interest expenditures included as part of the cost of a self-constructed asset.

Cash. Coin, currency, and other items that are acceptable for deposit at face value; serves as a medium of exchange and provides a basis of measurement for accounting.

Cash-basis accounting. A system of accounting in which revenues and expenses are recorded as they are received and paid.

Cash discount. A reduction in the selling price, allowed if payment is received within a specified period, usually offered to customers to encourage prompt payment.

Cash dividend. The payment (receipt) of a dividend in the form of cash.

Cash equivalents. Short-term, highly liquid investments that can be converted easily to cash. Generally, only investments with original maturities of three months or less qualify as cash equivalents; U.S. Treasury bills, money market funds, and commercial paper are examples of instruments that are commonly classified as cash equivalents.

Cash-flow adequacy ratio. An overall indicator of cash flow sufficiency; computed as cash flow from operating activities divided by primary cash requirements (sum of dividend payments, long-term asset purchases, and long-term debt repayments).

Cash overdraft. A credit balance in the cash account; results from checks being written for more than the cash amount on deposit; should be reported as a current liability.

Cash surrender value. The investment portion of a life insurance policy that is available to the policyholder upon cancellation of the policy.

Ceiling limitation. The net realizable value used as an upper limit in defining market when valuing inventory at the lower of cost or market.

Certified Public Accountants (CPAs). Accountants who have met specified professional requirements and who do not work for a single business enterprise but rather provide a variety of professional services for many different individual and business clients. A key service provided by CPAs is the performance of independent audits of financial statements.

Change in accounting estimate. A specific type of accounting change that modifies predictions of future events, e.g., the useful life of a depreciable asset; changes in estimates are to be reflected in current and future periods.

Change in accounting principle. A specific type of accounting change that uses a different accounting principle or method from that used previously, e.g., using straight-line depreciation instead of the declining-balance method; generally, changes in principle require the reporting of a cumulative effect of the change in the current year's income statement, as well as "pro forma" information.

Change in reporting entity. A specific type of accounting change that reflects financial statements for a different unit of accountability, e.g., after a business merger; a change in reporting entity requires restatement of the financial results of prior periods so as to provide comparative data.

Change orders. Modifications to the original terms of a contract.

Chart of accounts. A systematic listing of all accounts used by a particular business entity.

Closing entries. Entries that reduce all nominal, or temporary, accounts to a zero balance at the end of each accounting period, transferring the preclosing balances to real, or permanent, accounts.

Committee on Accounting Procedure (CAP). A committee of the AICPA that issued Accounting Research Bulletins during the period 1939-1959.

Commodity-backed bonds or asset-linked bonds. Bonds that may be redeemed in terms of commodities, such as oil or precious metals.

Common stock. The class of stock issued by corporations that represents the basic residual ownership interest; allows shareholders the right to vote and to receive dividends if declared, although the right to dividends is generally secondary to that of preferred stock.

Common stock equivalent. A security which, because of its terms or the circumstances under which it was issued, is in substance equivalent to common stock.

Common-size financial statements. Financial statements that reflect the components of the financial statement as a percentage of a total, e.g., percentage of total liabilities or total revenues.

Comparability. A secondary quality of useful accounting information, based on the premise that information is more useful when it can be related to a benchmark or standard, such as data for other firms within the same industry.

Comparative financial statements. Financial statements reflecting data for two or more periods.

Compensated absences. Payments by employers for vacation, holiday, illness, or other personal activities.

Compensating balances. The portion of a demand deposit that must be maintained as support for existing borrowing arrangements.

Completed-contract method. An accounting method that recognizes revenues and expenses on long-term construction contracts only when completed.

Complex capital structure. A corporate structure that includes convertible securities and/or stock options, warrants, or rights that could result in the issuance of additional common stock through exercise or conversion.

Composite depreciation. A method of computing depreciation in which dissimilar assets are aggregated and depreciation is computed for the aggregation based on a weighted average life expectancy.

Compound interest. Interest that is computed on the principal amount plus previously accumulated interest.

Comprehensive income. A concept of income measurement and reporting that includes all changes in owners' equity except investments by and distributions to owners. Comprehensive income is specifically defined in FASB Concepts Statement No. 5 and is not currently reported in general-purpose financial statements.

Conceptual framework. A theoretical foundation underlying accounting standards and practice. Today's framework encompasses the objectives, fundamental concepts, and implementation guidelines described in FASB Concepts Statement Nos. 1-6, as well as traditional assumptions. (See Exhibit 2-1, page 31, and Exhibit 2-7, page 47.)

Conglomerates. *See* Diversified companies.

Conservatism. A constraint underlying the reporting of accounting information based on the notion that when doubt exists concerning two or more reporting alternatives, users of information are best served by selecting the alternative with the least favorable impact on owners' equity.

Consigned goods. Inventory that is physically located at a dealer (consignee); however, the title (ownership) is retained by another entity (consignor) until the consignee sells the inventory.

Consignee. An entity that acts as an agent for another party (the consignor) by holding the consignor's inventory in an attempt to sell it. Title to the inventory is retained by the consignor even though physical possession is held by the consignee.

Consignment. A transfer of property without a transfer of title and risk of ownership. The recipient of the property (consignee) acts as a selling agent on behalf of the owner (consignor).

Consignor. A seller that ships merchandise to a third party (the consignee) but retains title until the inventory is sold by the third party. When the merchandise is subsequently sold, the consignee is typically paid a commission on the sale with the balance from the sale being remitted to the seller.

Consistency. A secondary quality of useful accounting information requiring that accounting methods be followed consistently from one period to the next unless conditions indicate that changing to another method would provide more useful information.

Consolidated financial statements. Financial statements that combine the financial results of a parent company and its subsidiaries.

Consolidation method. An accounting method that combines the financial statement balances of the parent and subsidiary companies as if they were one total economic unit; this method is appropriate where the parent company has control (more than 50 percent of the voting stock) over the subsidiary company.

Constant dollar accounting. A method of reporting whereby original costs are adjusted to reflect the changes in the general price level of the economy; with this approach, historical costs are converted to measuring units of equal purchasing power.

Contingent liability. A potential obligation, the existence of which is uncertain because it is dependent on the outcome of a future event, such as a pending lawsuit. The amount of the potential obligation may or may not be determinable.

Contra account. An account used to record subtractions from a related account; sometimes referred to as an "offset account." Examples include Allowance for Doubtful Accounts, which is subtracted from Accounts Receivable, and Accumulated Depreciation, which is subtracted from a plant asset account.

Contributed capital. The portion of corporate capital that represents investments by the owners, or stockholders. Also referred to as Paid-in capital.

Contributory pension plan. A pension plan in which employees make contributions to the plan and thus bear part of the cost.

Control account. A general ledger account that summarizes the detailed information in a subsidiary ledger. For example, Accounts Receivable is the control account for the individual customer accounts in the subsidiary accounts receivable ledger.

Conventional retail inventory method. A method of estimating inventory that approximates a lower of average cost or market valuation.

Convertible bonds. Bonds that provide for conversion into common stock at the option of the bondholder.

Convertible securities. Securities, such as bonds and preferred stock, whose terms permit the holder to convert the investment into common stock of the issuing companies.

Corporation. A business entity that is a separate, legal entity owned by its shareholders, who are given stock certificates as evidence of ownership; the owners' equity is divided between contributed capital (capital stock and paid-in capital accounts) and earned capital (retained earnings account).

Corridor amount. An amount established as a minimum before amortization of pension gains and losses is required. Only amortization of unrecognized pension gains and losses that exceed 10% of the greater of the projected benefit obligation or the market-related asset value as of the beginning of the period is included in the net periodic pension cost. Any systematic method of amortization that exceeds the minimum may be used as long as it is consistently applied to both gains and losses and it is disclosed in the statements.

Cost effectiveness. A pervasive constraint underlying the reporting of accounting information; to be cost effective, information must provide benefits in excess of its cost. Analysis of the cost-benefit relationship is an important consideration in selecting or requiring reporting alternatives.

Cost method. The method of accounting for long-term investments in the stock of another company where significant influence does not exist (generally less than 20 percent ownership); the initial investment is recorded and maintained at cost with dividends being recognized as revenue when received and no adjustment made for a proportionate share of investee earnings.

Cost percentage. Cost of goods available for sale valued at cost divided by the goods available for sale at retail.

Cost recovery method. A revenue recognition method which requires recovery of the total cost (investment) prior to the recognition of revenue.

Cost recovery periods. A period of time defined by tax legislation over which the cost of noncurrent operating assets may be written off (deducted) for tax purposes. Currently, there are six recovery periods for personal property and two for real estate.

Cost-to-cost method. A method for determining the percentage of completion for long-term construction contracts using a ratio of the actual cost incurred to date to the estimated total costs.

Credit. An entry on the right side of an account.

Cumulative effect of a change in accounting principle. An account that summarizes the net effect on the balance sheet of changing from one accounting principle to another. The effect is disclosed on the income statement as an irregular item net of tax.

Cumulative preferred stock. Preferred stock that has a right to receive current dividends as well as any dividends in arrears before common stockholders receive any dividends.

Current assets. Cash and resources that are reasonably expected to be converted into cash during the normal operating cycle of a business or within one year, whichever period is longer.

Current cost. The current value of an asset (i.e., the current exchange price) as measured by its replacement cost, reproduction cost, sales value, net realizable value, or net present value of future cash flows.

Current cost accounting. A method of reporting whereby original costs are adjusted to reflect the changes in the specific prices of individual items; with this approach, historical costs are converted to measurements reflecting the current values of individual items.

Current liabilities. Obligations that are reasonably expected to be paid using current assets or by creating other current liabilities within one year. For operating liabilities, such as accounts payable and accrued liabilities, the time period is extended to cover the operating cycle of a business if the cycle is longer than one year.

Current market value. The cash equivalent price that could be obtained currently by selling an asset in an orderly liquidation.

Current rate. The exchange rate in effect on the date the balance sheet is prepared.

Current ratio. An analytical measurement of the short-term liquidity of an entity. The current ratio formula is current assets divided by current liabilities. Sometimes referred to as the working capital ratio.

Current replacement cost. The cash equivalent price that would be paid currently to purchase or replace goods or services.

Curtailment of a pension plan. An event that significantly reduces the expected years of future services of present employees or eliminates for a significant number of employees the accrual of defined benefits for their future services.

D

Debit. An entry on the left side of an account.

Debt ratio. An indicator of a company's overall ability to repay its debts; computed as total liabilities divided by total assets.

Debt-to-equity ratio. A ratio that measures the relationship between the debt and equity of an entity. The debt-to-equity formula is total debt divided by total stockholders' equity.

Decision usefulness. The overriding quality or characteristic of accounting information.

Declining-balance depreciation methods. Depreciation methods that provide decreasing periodic charges for depreciation by applying a constant percentage to a declining asset book value.

Decreasing-charge deprecation methods. Any method of computing depreciation that provides a decreasing charge against revenue over time. Most common of the decreasing-charge methods are sum-of-the-years-digits depreciation and declining-balance depreciation.

Deductible temporary differences. Differences between financial and taxable income that will result in deductible amounts in future years; expected benefits (tax savings) are reported on the balance sheet as deferred tax assets.

Deferred method of investment tax credit. A method of reporting investment tax credits that defers the credit and recognizes its effect over the life of the asset that gave rise to the credit.

Deferred pension cost. A noncurrent asset resulting from recognition of an additional pension liability for underfunded pension plans. The balance in this account should not exceed the sum of any unrecognized transition loss plus prior service cost.

Deferred tax asset. An expected benefit in the form of tax savings on future deductible amounts resulting from deductible temporary differences between financial and taxable income.

Deferred tax liability. Income taxes expected to be paid on future taxable amounts resulting from taxable temporary differences between financial and taxable income.

Deficit. An excess of dividend payments and losses over net income resulting in a negative (debit) balance in retained earnings.

Defined benefit pension plans. Pension plans that define the benefits that employees will receive at retirement. In these plans, it is necessary to determine what the contribution should be to meet the future benefit requirements. FASB Statement No. 87 deals primarily with this type of pension plan.

Defined contribution pension plans. Pension plans that specify the employer's contributions based on a formula that includes such factors as age, length of service, employer's profits, and compensation levels. FASB Statement No. 87 does not deal with these types of plans except for disclosure requirements. The pension expense is the amount funded each year.

Demand deposits. Funds deposited in a bank that can be withdrawn upon demand.

Denominated currency. The currency in which an invoice is stated. For example, an invoice stating that payment is to be made in American dollars is said to be denominated in American dollars.

Depletion. The periodic allocation of the cost of natural resources; depletion expense represents a charge for the using-up of the resources and is computed in a manner similar to the productive-output method of depreciation, i.e., cost is divided by estimated total resources available to determine the depletion charge per unit removed or extracted.

Deposit in transit. A deposit made near the end of the month and recorded on the depositor's books but that is not received by the bank in time to be reflected on the bank statement.

Deposit method. An accounting method which recognizes the receipt of cash and the unearned revenue prior to the completion of a contract.

Depreciation. Periodic allocation of the cost of tangible noncurrent operating assets over the periods benefited by use of the asset.

Development activities. Application of research findings to develop a plan or design for new or improved products and processes.

Dilution of earnings. A reduction in earnings per share (or increase in loss per share) resulting from the assumption that convertible securities have been converted or that options and warrants have been exercised or other shares have been issued upon the fulfillment of certain conditions.

Dilutive securities. Securities whose assumed exercise or conversion results in a reduction in earnings per share or an increase in loss per share.

Direct financing lease. A lease in which the lessor is primarily engaged in financial activities and views the lease activity as an investment.

Direct method. An approach to calculating and reporting the net cash flow from operating activities that shows the major operating cash receipts and cash payments. The difference between cash receipts and cash payments is the net cash flow provided (used) by operations.

Direct quote. This quote specifies the number of American dollars that can be purchased with one unit of foreign currency. The direct quote for numerous foreign currencies is listed on a daily basis in *The Wall Street Journal.*

Direct write-off method. A method of recognizing the actual losses from uncollectible accounts as expenses during the period in which the receivables are determined to be uncollectible; this method is not in accordance with GAAP.

Discontinued operations. The disposal of a major segment of a business either through sale or abandonment. The segment may be a product line, a division, or a subsidiary company. The assets and related activities of the segment must be clearly distinguishable from other activities of the company, both physically and operationally.

Discussion Memorandum. A document issued by the FASB that identifies the principal issues involved with financial accounting and reporting topics. It includes a discussion of the various points of view as to the resolution of issues, but does not reach a specific conclusion.

Diversified companies. Business entities that have a wide variety of product and service lines of business. Sometimes referred to as conglomerates.

Dividend payout percentage (payout rate). Dividends per share divided by earnings per share.

Dividends. Periodic distributions of earnings in the form of cash, stock, or other property to the stockholders (owners) of a corporation.

Dividends in arrears. Dividends on cumulative preferred stock that are passed or not paid. Dividends in arrears must be paid before any dividends can be paid to common stockholders. Disclosure of the amount of dividends in arrears is made in a note to the balance sheet.

Dividends per share. A measure of the distribution to stockholders by an entity. The dividends per share formula is the dividends paid to the common shareholders divided by the number of common shares issued and outstanding. Dividends are not paid on treasury stock.

Dollar-value LIFO inventory method. An adaptation of the LIFO inventory concept that measures inventory by total dollar amount rather than by individual units. LIFO incremental layers are determined based on total dollar changes.

Dollar-value LIFO retail method. An inventory valuation method in which retail inventory values are classified by total dollar amounts. The retail values are then converted to cost by use of index numbers and LIFO incremental layers are determined based on incremental dollar changes.

Double extension. A method of determining the valuation of inventory using the dollar-value LIFO method by extending all inventory quantities twice: once at a base-year cost and once at current-year cost.

Double extension index. An internal LIFO index computed by double-extending a sample of inventory items at base-year prices and end-of-year prices. The derived index is then used to compute the dollar-value LIFO balance for all inventory items.

Double-declining-balance depreciation. A decreasing charge depreciation method that uses twice the straight-line depreciation rate as the constant percentage to be applied to the decreasing book value.

Double-entry accounting. A system of recording transactions in a way that maintains the equality of the accounting equation: Assets = Liabilities + Owners' Equity.

E

Early extinguishment of debt. The retirement of debt prior to the maturity date of the obligation; any gain or loss arising from early extinguishment of debt must be classified as an extraordinary item on the income statement.

Earnings per share (EPS). Income for the period reported on a per share of common stock basis. The presentation of earnings per share on the income statement is required by generally accepted accounting principles. Separate EPS amounts are required for income from continuing operations and for each irregular or extraordinary component of reported income.

Earnings. A new term found in the FASB's concepts statements that is the equivalent of net income without including the effects of changes in accounting principles.

Economic entity. A specific reporting unit; a traditional assumption in accounting is that the business enterprise or other reporting unit is viewed as separate and distinct from its owners or other entities.

Effective rate of interest. The rate of interest used in compound interest problems; also known as the yield or true rate of interest.

Effective-interest method. An amortization method which provides for recognition of an equal rate of amortization of bond premium or discount each period; uses a constant interest rate times a changing investment balance.

Efforts-expended methods. Methods for determining the percentage of completion for long-term construction contracts using an estimate of work or service performed. The estimates may be based on labor hours, labor dollars, or estimates of experts.

Electronic data processing (EDP) systems. Accounting systems utilizing high-speed computers. Such systems allow great speed and accuracy in processing large amounts of accounting data.

Emerging Issues Task Force (EITF). A task force of representatives from the accounting profession and industry created by the FASB to deal with taking timely action on emerging issues of financial reporting. The task force identifies significant emerging issues and develops consensus positions when possible.

Entry cost. The acquisition cost of an asset.

Equity method. The method of accounting for long-term investments in the stock of another company where significant influence exists (generally 20-50 percent ownership); the initial investment is recorded at cost but is increased by a proportionate share of investor's income and decreased by dividends and a proportionate share of losses to reflect the underlying claim by the investor on the net assets of the investee company.

Executory costs. Costs to maintain property such as repairs, insurance, and taxes. These costs may be paid by the lessee or the lessor. If paid by the lessor, part of each lease payment should be related to the executory costs.

Exit value. The value received for an asset when sold.

Expected postretirement benefit obligation (EPBO). The actuarial present value, as of a certain date, of all future postretirement benefits to be paid to employees.

Expected return on pension plan assets. An amount calculated as a basis for determining the extent of delayed recognition of the effects of changes in the fair value of pension plan assets. The expected return on pension plan assets is determined based on the expected long-term rate of return on pension plan assets and the market-related value of pension plan assets.

Expected service period. Estimated number of years an employee will work before receiving pension benefits. Can be estimated as the average computed life based on the total expected future years of service divided by the number of employees. The expected future years of service may be computed by the formula $[N(N + 1) \div 2] \times D$, where N equals the number of years over which service is to be performed and D is the decrease in number of employees through retirement or termination of services per year.

Expense recognition. The process of determining the period in which expenses are to be recorded. Expense recognition is divided into three categories: (1) direct matching, (2) immediate recognition, and (3) systematic and rational allocation.

Expenses. Outflows or other using-up of assets or incurrences of liabilities (or a combination of both) from delivering or producing goods, rendering services, or carrying out other activities that constitute the entity's ongoing major or central operations.

Exposure Draft. A preliminary statement of a standard that includes specific recommendations made by the FASB. Reaction to the Exposure Draft is requested from the accounting and business community, and the comments received are carefully considered before a Statement of Financial Accounting Standards is issued.

Extraordinary items. Gains or losses resulting from events and transactions that are both unusual in nature and infrequent in occurrence or otherwise defined as an extraordinary item per accounting standards.

F

Face amount, par value, maturity value. The amount that will be paid on a bond at the maturity date.

Factoring receivables. The sale of receivables without recourse for cash to a third party, usually a bank or other financial institution.

Factory overhead. All manufacturing costs other than direct materials and direct labor; alternatively referred to as *manufacturing overhead.*

Fair value of pension plan assets. The amount that could be received from the sale of plan assets in a current sale between a willing buyer and seller. Fair value is used to determine the minimum liability and the transition amount.

Feedback value. A key ingredient of relevant accounting information; helps to confirm or change a decision maker's expectations.

Financial accounting. The activity associated with the development and communication of financial information for external users, primarily in the form of general-purpose financial statements.

Financial Accounting Foundation (FAF). An organization responsible for selecting members of the FASB, GASB, and their Advisory Councils; also responsible for funding the standard-setting bodies.

Financial Accounting Standards Advisory Council. A council that consults with the FASB concerning major policy questions, selects major project task forces to work on specific projects, and conducts such other activities as may be requested by the FASB.

Financial Accounting Standards Board (FASB). An independent private organization consisting of seven full-time members with the responsibility of studying accounting issues and establishing accounting standards to govern financial reporting to external users.

Financial Analysts Federation. An organization of financial analysts who advise the investing public on the meaning of financial reports.

Financial capital maintenance. A concept under which income is defined as the excess of net assets at the end of an accounting period over the net assets at the beginning of the period, excluding effects of transactions with owners.

Financial Executives Institute (FEI). A national organization composed of financial executives employed by large corporations. The FEI membership includes treasurers, controllers, and financial vice-presidents.

Financial income. Income reported on the financial statements as opposed to taxable income that is reported to taxing authorities in accordance with tax regulations.

Financial leverage. A measure of an entity's ability to increase profitability to residual shareholders by using borrowed funds whose cost is less than the profit that can be earned with the borrowed funds.

Financial Reporting Releases (FRRs). SEC statements dealing with reporting and disclosure requirements in documents filed with the SEC.

Financing activities. One of three major categories included in a statement of cash flows; includes transactions and events whereby cash is obtained from or paid to owners and creditors; examples include cash receipts from issuing stocks and bonds and the payment of cash dividends.

Finished goods. Manufactured products for which the manufacturing process is complete.

First-In, First-Out (FIFO) method. An inventory costing method that assigns historical unit costs to expense (cost of goods sold) in the order in which the costs are incurred.

Fixed charge coverage. A measure of the number of times earnings covers the fixed charges of an entity for a period. Fixed charges include interest, lease payments, and specified periodic principal statements.

Fixed stock option plan. A plan in which terms, such as option exercise price and the number of options granted, are fixed on the date the options are granted.

Floor limitation. The net realizable value less a normal profit used as a lower limit in defining market when valuing inventory at the lower of cost or market.

Flow-through method of investment tax credit. A method of reporting investment tax credits that recognizes the full credit from income tax expense in the year it is taken as a deduction from income taxes payable.

Foreign currency transactions. A transaction between two entities wherein the buyer and the seller have different reporting currencies.

FOB (free on board) destination. Terms of sale under which title of goods passes to the purchaser at the point of destination.

FOB (free on board) shipping point. Terms of sale under which title of goods passes to the purchaser at the point of shipment.

Freight-in. Cost of transporting goods from the supplier to the purchaser; part of the cost of inventory.

Full cost approach. An amortization approach in the oil and gas industry that defers all exploratory costs and writes them off against revenues as depletion expense.

Full disclosure principle. A basic accounting concept which requires that all relevant information be presented in an unbiased, understandable, and timely manner.

Full eligibility date. The date at which an employee attains full eligibility for the benefits that employee is expected to earn under the terms of a postretirement benefit plan.

Fully diluted earnings per share. The amount of current earnings per share reflecting the maximum dilution that would have resulted from conversions, exercises, and other contingent issuances of stock that individually would have decreased earnings per share and in the aggregate would have had a dilutive effect.

Functional currency. The currency of the primary economic environment in which an entity operates. In most instances, the functional currency is the currency with which the entity generates and expends cash. Determining a firm's functional currency is necessary before translating foreign currency financial statements.

Funds. Cash and other assets set apart for certain designated purposes.

Future value. The amount of cash that will be accumulated in the future if an investment is made today at a certain interest rate.

G

Gains. Increases in equity (net assets) from peripheral or incidental transactions of an entity and from all other transactions and other events and circumstances affecting the entity except those that result from revenues or investments by owners.

General journal. An accounting record used to record all business activities for which special journals are not maintained.

General ledger. A record of all accounts used by a business. Some accounts in the general ledger, e.g., accounts receivable, are supported by detail contained in subsidiary ledgers. (*See* Control account and Subsidiary ledgers.)

General-purpose financial statements. A balance sheet, income statement, statement of cash flows, and usually a statement of changes in retained earnings or in owners' equity.

Generally accepted accounting principles (GAAP). Accounting standards recognized by the profession as required in the preparation of financial statements for external users. Currently, the Financial Accounting Standards Board is the principal issuer of generally accepted accounting principles.

Going concern. An entity that is expected to continue in existence for the foreseeable future; a traditional assumption in accounting is that an entity is viewed as a going concern in the absence of evidence to the contrary.

Goods in Process. Inventory of a manufacturer that is partly processed and requires further work before it can be sold. Alternatively referred to as Work in process.

Goodwill. The ability of an organization to earn above-normal income. Above-normal income means a rate of return greater than that normally required to attract investors into a particular type of business. Recorded goodwill is the excess amount paid for a company in a business combination over the fair market value of the company's identifiable assets.

Governmental Accounting Standards Board (GASB). An independent private organization responsible for establishing standards in the governmental area. Appointed by the Financial Accounting Foundation.

Gross method. A method of inventory accounting that records inventory cost before considering purchase discounts.

Gross profit on sales. Net sales minus cost of goods sold.

Gross profit percentage on sales. A measure of the profitability of sales in relation to the cost of the goods sold. The gross profit percentage on sales formula is the gross profit for a financial period divided by net sales for the same period.

Gross profit method. An inventory estimation technique based on the relationship between gross profit and revenue (sales). The gross profit, as a percentage of sales, is applied to sales to determine cost of goods sold which, in turn, is used to determine the value of the inventory not yet sold.

Group depreciation. A method of computing depreciation in which like assets are grouped together and depreciation is computed for the group rather than for individual assets.

Growth potential. The capacity of a company to increase sales, net income, and market share in the future. Growth potential is of primary importance to stockholders in valuing a company.

Guaranteed residual value. A guarantee by lessee or a third party of a minimum value for the residual value of a leased asset. If the residual value is less than the guarantee, the guarantor must pay the difference to the lessor.

H

Held-to-maturity securities. Debt securities purchased by a company with both the intent and ability to hold the securities to maturity.**Historical cost.** The cash equivalent price of goods or services at the date of acquisition.

Historical cost/nominal dollar. A method of reporting in terms of the numbers of dollars exchanged at the original transaction date; with this approach, historical costs are not adjusted for any price changes.

Historical rate. The exchange rate in effect on the date of a specific transaction.

Horizontal analysis. Analysis of a company's statements over a number of reporting periods

I

If-converted method. A method used to adjust the earnings per share computation to consider the impact of the possible conversion of convertible securities. Under this method, the earnings per share computation is made as if the convertible securities were converted at the beginning of the year or the date the convertible security was issued, whichever is later.

Impairment. Unexpected reduction in the value of an asset that significantly reduces its current value below its reported value.

Implicit interest rate. The interest rate that would discount the minimum lease payments to the fair market value of the asset at the inception of the lease.

Implicit or effective interest. The actual interest rate earned or paid on a note, bond, or similar instrument.

Imprest petty cash system. A petty cash fund in which all expenditures are documented by vouchers or vendor receipts or invoices.

Imputed interest rate. A rate of interest assigned to a note when there is no current market price for either the property, goods or services or the note. The assigned rate of interest is used to discount future receipts or payments to the present in computing the present value of the note.

Income statement. A statement that reports a firm's net income for a period of time. The statement summarizes revenues, expenses, gains, and losses. The statement is also called the profit and loss statement or the statement of earnings.

Income Summary. A temporary clearing account used at the end of a period to accumulate amounts from closing entries to revenues and expenses. For a corporation, the income summary account is closed to Retained Earnings; for a proprietorship or partnership, it is closed to the appropriate capital accounts.

Incremental borrowing rate. The interest rate at which the lessee could borrow the amount of money necessary to purchase the leased asset, taking into consideration the lessee's financial situation and the current conditions in the marketplace.

Independent audit. The independent examination of the financial statements to be furnished to external users and issuance of an opinion as to the fairness of the presentation in accordance with generally accepted accounting principles.

Indirect method. An approach to calculating and reporting the net cash flow from operating activities that reconciles net income, as reported on the income statement, with net cash flow provided (used) by operations, as shown on the statement of cash flows; net income is adjusted for noncash items, for any gains or losses, and is adjusted from an accrual amount to a cash amount.

Indirect quote. The inverse of the direct quote. It indicates the number of foreign currency units that can be purchased with one American dollar.

Inflation. An increase in the general price level of goods and services.

Initial direct costs. Costs such as commissions, legal fees, and preparation of documents that are incurred by the lessor in negotiating and completing a lease transaction.

Initial markup. The difference between the initial retail price of merchandise and the original historical cost.

Input measures. Measures of the earning process in percentage-of-completion accounting based on cost or efforts devoted to a contract.

Installment sales method. A revenue recognition method which recognizes revenue and related expenses as cash is received.

Institute of Management Accountants (IMA). An organization of management accountants that is concerned with the development and use of accounting data within the business organization.

In-substance defeasance. A process involving the transfer of assets (generally cash and securities) to a trust and the use of the assets and earnings therefrom to satisfy long-term obligations as they come due; a gain or loss is recognized as an extraordinary item and the debt is removed from the balance sheet at the time of transfer.

Intangible noncurrent operating assets. Economic resources with future benefit that are used in the normal operating activity of the organization that cannot be physically observed, e.g., copyrights, patents, trade names, and goodwill.

Integral part of annual period concept. A concept of preparing interim financial statements that utilizes the same accounting principles and practices for the interim statements that would be used for the annual statements, except that modifications are permitted to allow the interim results to relate better to the annual statements. An alternate concept would require the interim period to be treated the same way as an annual statement with no flexibility for interim modifications.

Interest-bearing note. A note written in a form in which the maker promises to pay the face amount plus interest at a specified rate; in this form, the face amount is usually equal to the present value upon issuance of the note.

Interest. The payment (cost) for the use of money; it is the excess cash paid or received over the amount of cash borrowed or loaned.

Interim financial statements. Financial statements for a period of time less than one year. Typically, corporations issue quarterly statements that are subject to limited auditor's review.

Interperiod tax allocation. An accounting method that recognizes the tax effect of temporary differences between financial and taxable income in the financial statement rather than reporting as tax expense the actual tax liability in each year. The allocation may be made either by the (1) deferred method or (2) the asset and liability method. The latter method is currently required by GAAP.

Interpolation. A method of finding future- or present-value table factors when the exact factor does not appear in the table; this method assumes linear relationships.

Interpretation of a Statement of Financial Accounting Standards. A supplemental pronouncement that expands the discussion of an existing Statement of Financial Accounting Standards. These are issued by the FASB, and are considered equal in authority to the Statements issued by the FASB.

Intraperiod tax allocation. A method of income statement presentation of irregular or extraordinary items in which the tax effect of each of these special items is reported with the individual item rather than in the income tax expense related to current operations.

Inventory. Assets held for sale in the normal course of business.

Inventory turnover. An analytical measurement of how rapidly inventories are being used and/or sold during a year. If a company has one inventory, the formula is the cost of goods sold divided by the average inventory. If there are different types of inventory, such as raw materials and work in process, the numerator would be related to the type of inventory. Thus, the numerator for the raw materials inventory would be raw material purchases and the numerator for work in process inventory would be cost of goods completed.

Investing activities. One of three major categories included in a statement of cash flows; includes transactions and events that occur regularly but that relate only indirectly to the central, ongoing operations of an entity; examples include the purchase or sale of securities or other assets not generally held for resale and the making or collecting of loans to other entities.

Investment tax credit. A tax provision that permits taxpayers to deduct a percentage of the cost of new investment in qualifying assets from the income tax liability for a given year.

Involuntary conversions. Retirement of assets caused by uncontrollable events such as fire, earthquake, flood, or condemnation.

J

Journals. Accounting records in which transactions are first entered, providing a chronological record of business activity. (*See* General journal and Special journal.)

Junk bonds. High-risk, high-yield bonds issued by companies in a weak financial condition.

L

Last-In, First-Out (LIFO) method. An inventory costing method that assigns the most recent historical unit costs to expense (cost of goods sold) and the oldest unit cost to the asset inventory.

Lease. A contract specifying the terms under which the owner of the property, the lessor, transfers the right to use the property to a lessee.

Lease term. The noncancellable period of lease designated in the lease contract, plus the period of any bargain renewal periods or other provisions that, at the inception of the lease, strongly indicate that the lease will be renewed.

Ledgers. Records used for summarizing the effects of transactions upon individual accounts. A ledger may be in the form of a book of accounts or a computer printout. (*See* General ledger and Subsidiary ledgers.)

Legal capital. A minimum amount of corporate contributed capital, designated by state incorporation laws, that cannot be impaired by dividends or, in many states, by purchase of treasury stock.

Lessee. The party using property that is owned by another party (lessor).

Lessor. The owner of leased property who transfers the right to use the property to a second party (lessee).

Leveraged buy-out (LBO). An acquisition of a company where a substantial amount of the purchase price, often 90 percent or more, is debt financed.

Leveraged lease. A lease contract usually involving three parties; the lessee, the owner-lessor, and the third-party, a long-term creditor. Only direct financing leases are treated as leveraged leases.

Liabilities. The claims of creditors against an entity's resources: technically defined by the FASB as "probable future sacrifices of economic benefits arising from present obligations of a particular entity to transfer assets or provide services to other entities in the future as a result of past transactions or events."

LIFO allowance (reserve). A valuation account that adjusts a non-LIFO inventory cost to a LIFO cost.

LIFO conformity rule. A federal tax regulation that requires the use of LIFO for financial reporting purposes if LIFO is used for income tax purposes.

LIFO inventory pools. Classification of inventory into groups of items having common characteristics and then assuming the LIFO cost method for each classification or grouping.

Link-chain index. An internal LIFO index computed by double-extending a sample of inventory items at beginning-of-year prices and at end-of-year prices and by multiplying the prior-year index by this current link rate..

Liquidating dividend. A distribution to stockholders representing a return of a portion of contributed capital.

Liquidity. The ability of a company to meet it's obligations as they come due.

Loan value. The amount that an insurance company will lend on a life insurance policy.

Long-term debt. Obligations that are not expected to be paid in cash or other current assets within one year or the normal operating cycle.

Losses. Decreases in equity (net assets) from peripheral or incidental transactions of an entity and from all other transactions and other events and circumstances affecting the entity except those that result from expenses or distributions to owners.

Lower of cost or market (LCM). Generally accepted method for valuation of inventories; this method can be applied to inventories on an aggregate or individual item basis.

M

Maintenance. The normal cost of keeping property in operating condition. Maintenance is charged to expense in the period in which it is incurred.

Management accounting. The activity associated with financial reporting for internal users. Information needed for internal decisions may relate to such items as specific product lines, specific financing alternatives, detailed expense classifications, and differences between actual and budgeted revenues and costs.

Markdown cancellations. Decreases in previously recorded markdowns that do not raise the sales prices above original retail.

Markdowns. Decreases that reduce sales prices below original retail.

Market (in lower of cost or market). The replacement cost adjusted for an upper and/or lower limit that reflects the estimated realizable value.

Market, yield, or effective interest rate. The actual rate of interest earned or paid on a bond.

Market-related value of pension plan assets. Value of pension plan assets used in computing the expected return.

Either of the following can be used as the market-related value: (1) the fair market value of pension plan assets as of the beginning of the year or (2) a weighted average value based on the market value of plan assets over a preceding period not exceeding five years.

Markup cancellations. Decreases in additional markups that do not reduce sales prices below original retail.

Matching principle. A basic accounting concept that is applied to determine when expenses are recognized (recorded). Under this principle, expenses for a period are determined by associating or "matching" them with specific revenues or a particular time period.

Materiality. An important constraint underlying the reporting of accounting information; it determines the threshold for recognition of an item in the financial statements. Materiality decisions focus on the size of a judgment item in a given set of circumstances.

Minimum lease payments. The rental payments required over the lease term plus any amount to be paid for the residual value either through a bargain purchase option or a guarantee of residual value.

Minimum pension liability. The net amount of pension liability that must be reported when a plan is underfunded. The minimum liability is measured as the difference between the accumulated benefit obligation and the fair value of the pension plan assets.

Modified Accelerated Cost Recovery System (MACRS). The accelerated cost recovery system as revised by the Tax Reform Act of 1986. It is applicable for assets acquired after December 31, 1986.

Monetary items. Assets, liabilities, and equities whose balances are fixed in terms of number of dollars regardless of changes in the general price level.

N

Natural business year. A year that ends when a company's operations are at its lowest point. This type of a fiscal year relates primarily to those businesses that have seasonal sales.

Natural resources. Assets produced by nature as opposed to those produced by man. They include such wasting assets as oil, gas, timber, and ore deposits.

Negative goodwill. The excess of fair market values of a company's net assets over the purchase price for the company in a business combination.

Negotiable notes. A note that is legally transferable by endorsement and delivery.

Net assets. *See* Owners' equity.

Net lease investment. The carrying value of a lease on the lessor's books; equals the difference between total lease payments receivable (gross investment) and unearned interest revenue.

Net markdowns. Markdowns less markdown cancellations.

Net markups. Markups less markup cancellations.

Net method. A method of inventory accounting that records inventory net of any purchase discount.

Net monetary position. The difference between a company's monetary assets and its monetary liabilities.

Net operating loss carryback. The amount of operating loss that can be carried back and offset against the income of earlier profitable years to obtain a refund of previously paid income taxes.

Net operating loss carryforward. The amount of operating loss that can be carried forward and offset against income of future profitable years to reduce the tax liability for those years.

Net periodic pension cost. The amount recognized in an employer's financial statements as a cost of a pension plan for a period. Components of net periodic pension cost are service cost, interest cost, actual return on plan assets, pension gain or loss, amortization of unrecognized prior service cost, and amortization of unrecognized transition gain or loss.

Net profit percentage on sales. A measure of the profitability of a company that relates net income to the sales of the company. The formula is net income divided by net sales.

Net realizable value. The amount of cash expected to be received from the conversion of assets in the normal course of business; net realizable value equals selling price less normal selling costs for inventory and equals gross receivables less the allowance for doubtful accounts for accounts receivable.

Neutrality. A key ingredient of reliable accounting information requiring that information be presented in an unbiased manner; relates to the concept of fairness to users.

Nominal accounts. Accounts that are closed to a zero balance at the end of an accounting period; they include all income statement accounts (revenues, expenses, gains, and losses) and the dividends account. They are also referred to as temporary accounts.

Non-interest-bearing note. A note written in a form in which the face amount includes an interest charge; in this form, the difference between the face amount and the present value of the note is the implicit or effective interest.

Noncash investing and financing activities. Investing and financing transactions that affect an entity's financial position but not the entity's cash flows during the period; an example would be the purchase of land by issuing stock. Significant noncash financing and investing activities should be disclosed separately, not reported in the statement of cash flows.

Noncash items. Certain items that are reported on the income statement but that do not affect cash; examples include depreciation on buildings and equipment and amortization of intangibles and bond discount or premium.

Noncontributory pension plans. Plans in which the employer bears the total cost of the plan.

Noncumulative preferred stock. Preferred stock that has no claim on any prior year dividends that may have been "passed."

Nonmonetary items. All items that do not represent rights or obligations to receive or pay a fixed sum regardless of changes in the general price level.

Nonreciprocal transfer of a nonmonetary asset. A transfer of a nonmonetary asset with no sacrifice (cost) incurred by the organization receiving the asset, e.g., donated assets, discovered assets.

Nontrade notes payable. A note issued to nontrade creditors for purposes other than to purchase goods or services.

Nontrade receivables. Any receivables arising from transactions that are not directly associated with the normal operating activities of a business.

Normal operating cycle. The time required for cash to be converted to inventories, inventories into receivables, and receivables ultimately into cash.

Not-sufficient-funds (NSF) check. A check that is not honored by a bank because of insufficient cash in the maker's account.

Notes receivable. Receivables that are evidenced by a formal written promise to pay a certain sum of money at a specified date.

O

Objective acceleration clause. A clause in a debt instrument that identifies specific conditions that will cause the debt to be callable immediately.

Off-balance-sheet financing. Procedures used by companies to avoid disclosing all their debt on the balance sheet in order to make their financial position look stronger.

Operating activities. One of three major categories included in a statement of cash flows; includes transactions and events that normally enter into the determination of operating income; examples include selling goods or services and purchasing inventory.

Operating lease. A simple rental agreement, usually for a relatively short period of time, for one entity (lessee) to use property that is owned by another entity (lessor).

Opinions. Statements of accounting standards issued by the Accounting Principles Board during the period 1959-1973.

Ordinary annuity. An annuity that consists of payments (receipts) at the end of each period; also known as an annuity in arrears.

Original retail. The initial sales price, including the original increase over cost referred to as the initial markup.

Output measures. Measures of the earnings process in percentage-of-completion accounting based on units produced, contract milestones reached, or values added.

Outstanding checks. Checks written near the end of the month that have reduced the depositor's cash balance but have not yet cleared the bank as of the bank statement date.

Owners' equity. The residual interest in the assets of an entity that remains after deducting its liabilities; sometimes referred to as net assets.

P

Paid-in capital. *See* Contributed capital.

Par value. A value that may be assigned to stock by the terms of a corporation's charter; the par value is printed on the stock certificate.

Parent company. A company that exercises control over another company, known as a subsidiary, through majority ownership (more than 50 percent) of the subsidiary's voting stock.

Participating preferred stock. Preferred stock that provides for additional dividends to be paid to preferred stockholders after dividends of a specified amount are paid to common stockholders. Although once quite common, participating preferred stocks are now relatively rare.

Partnership. A business entity owned by two or more people; the owner's equity is recorded in individual partner capital accounts.

Pension gain or loss. A component of net periodic pension costs that is the sum of (a) the difference between the actual return on plan assets and the expected return on plan assets and (b) the amortization of the unrecognized net gain or loss arising in a prior period from a change in the value of either the projected benefit obligation or the plan assets because of an experience different from that assumed or from a change in an actuarial assumption.

Pension plan. An agreement, usually written, that provides for benefits to employees upon retirement from active employment. The plan usually includes provisions as to how the benefits are to be funded, who receives benefits, the amount of benefits to be paid, and restrictions on investments of pension plan assets.

Pension plan assets. Assets arising from contributions to the pension plan. Generally comprised of cash and investments that have been segregated and designated for use of the pension plan only.

Percentage-of-completion accounting. An accounting method for long-term construction contracts which recognizes revenue and related expenses prior to delivery of the goods. Recognition is based on either an input or output measure of the earning process.

Performance-based stock option plan. A plan with terms (option exercise price, number of options, etc.) that depend on how well the individual or company performs after the options are granted.

Period costs. Costs that are recognized as expenses during the period in which cash is spent or liabilities are incurred for goods and services that are used up either simultaneously with acquisition or soon after.

Periodic inventory system. A method of accounting for inventory in which cost of goods sold is determined and inventory is adjusted to the proper balance at the end of the accounting period, not when inventoriable merchandise is bought or sold. Throughout the period, all purchases of inventoriable merchandise are recorded in the purchases account, and ending inventory is determined by a physical count of merchandise on hand.

Permanent accounts. *See* Real (permanent) accounts.

Permanent differences. Nondeductible expenses or nontaxable revenues that are recognized for financial reporting purposes but that are never part of taxable income.

Perpetual inventory system. A method of accounting for inventory in which detailed records of each inventory purchase and sale are maintained. This system provides a current record of inventory on hand and cost of goods sold to date.

Petty cash fund. A small amount of cash kept on hand for the purpose of making miscellaneous payments.

Physical capital maintenance. A concept under which income is defined as the excess of physical productive capacity at the end of an accounting period over the physical productive capacity at the beginning of the period, excluding the effects of transactions with owners.

Pooling of interests. A method of accounting for a business combination whereby all the asset, liability, and owners' equity values are combined; under this approach, the retained earnings amounts are added together to become the total retained earnings for the combined entity.

Post-balance sheet events. *See* Subsequent events.

Post-closing trial balance. A list of all real accounts and their balances after the closing process has been completed.

Posting. The process of summarizing transactions by transferring amounts from the journal to the ledger accounts.

Postretirement benefits other than pensions. Benefits other than pensions provided by an employer to former employees. Includes health insurance, life insurance, and disability payments. Current standards require these benefits to be accrued in a manner similar to pension costs.

Predictive value. A key ingredient of relevant accounting information; helps a decision maker predict future consequences based on information about past transactions and events.

Preferred stock. A class of stock that usually confers dividend and liquidation rights that take precedence over those of common stock; preferred stock is often nonvoting stock.

Prepaid pension cost. The cumulative excess of annual pension contributions over annual pension costs. It is reported as an asset on a company's balance sheet.

Present value. The amount of net future cash inflows or outflows discounted to their present value at an appropriate rate of interest.

Price index. A series of numbers that compares a sample of commodity prices during a base period with equivalent prices at other periods of time; the base period is assigned a value of 100, and the prices of all other periods are expressed as percentages of this amount.

Price-earnings ratio. A measure of the relationship between the market price of a company's stock and its profitability. The formula is the market price per share of common stock divided by the earnings per share of common stock.

Primary earnings per share. The amount of earnings attributable to each share of common stock outstanding, including common stock equivalents.

Principal (or face amount). The amount, excluding interest, that the maker of a note or the issuer of a bond agrees to pay at the maturity date; this amount is printed on the note or bond contract.

Prior-period adjustment. An adjustment made directly to the retained earnings account to correct errors made in prior accounting periods.

Prior service cost. The present value of the increased benefits granted by a pension plan amendment (or initial adoption of a plan). Recognized as a component of net periodic pension cost through amortization over the future service life of the covered employees.

Private Companies Practice Section (PCPS). A section of the AICPA for firms that do not have clients regulated by the SEC. Membership in the section is voluntary. Periodic peer review is required of all firms with membership in the PCPS.

Productive-output depreciation. A use-factor method based on the theory that an asset is acquired for the service it can provide in the form of production output. Depreciable cost is divided by the total estimated output to determine the depreciation rate per unit of output.

Profitability. The ability of a company to earn a satisfactory return on its assets.

Projected benefit obligation (PBO). The actuarial present value of pension benefits using the benefits/years of service approach that requires assumptions about future compensation levels. Increases over time by interest, amendments to plan, additional service years, and changes in actuarial assumptions.

Promissory note. A formal written promise to pay a certain amount of money at a specified future date.

Property dividend. The payment (receipt) of a dividend in the form of some asset other than cash.

Proportional performance method. An accounting method for recording service revenue and related expenses prior to completion of a service contract.

Proprietorship. A business entity owned by one person; the owner's equity is recorded in a single (proprietor) capital account.

Purchase. A method of accounting for a business combination whereby the value of the stock in excess of the net assets acquired is recorded as Goodwill; under this approach, the retained earnings of the acquired company do not become part of the combined retained earnings.

Q

Quasi-reorganization. A procedure by which, when permitted by state law, a company eliminates a deficit in retained earnings by restating its invested capital balance; provides a "fresh start" for a company, changing retained earnings from a negative to a zero balance.

Quick assets. Assets that are very liquid. They include cash, cash equivalents, marketable securities, and usually accounts receivable. Inventories and prepaid expenses do not qualify as quick assets.

Quick ratio. *See* Acid-test ratio.

R

Rate earned on average common stockholders' equity. An analytical measurement of profitability for the residual owners of a company. The formula is net income divided by the average common stockholders' equity.

Rate earned on average total assets. An analytical measurement of profitability for a company as an entity regardless of the source of funds. The formula is net income divided by average total assets.

Rate earned on average stockholders' equity. An analytical measurement of profitability for all stockholders, residual and preferred. The formula is net income divided by average stockholders' equity.

Raw materials. Inventory acquired by a manufacturer for use in the production process. Also referred to as *direct materials*.

Real accounts. Accounts that are not closed to a zero balance at the end of each accounting period; also referred to as Permanent accounts. They include all balance sheet accounts (assets, liabilities, and owners' equity).

Realized holding gains and losses. The differences between the current costs and the historical costs of assets that are sold or used during a period.

Receivables. Claims against others for money, goods, or services; usually, receivable claims are settled by the receipt of cash.

Recognition. The process of formally recording an item in the accounting records and eventually reporting it in the financial statements; includes both the initial recording of an item and any subsequent changes related to that item.

Redeemable preferred stock. Preferred stock that may be redeemed at the option of the holder, or at a fixed price on a specific date, or upon other conditions not solely within the control of the issuer; redemption requirements for this type of stock must be disclosed.

Refundable deposits. An obligation of a company to refund amounts previously collected from customers as deposits.

Registered bonds. Bonds for which the bondholders' names and addresses are kept on file by the issuing company.

Relevance. One of two primary qualities inherent in useful accounting information; essentially information is relevant if it will affect a decision. The key ingredients of relevance are feedback value, predictive value, and timeliness.

Reliability. One of two primary qualities inherent in useful accounting information; to be reliable, information must contain the key ingredients of verifiability, neutrality, and representational faithfulness.

Remeasurement. A method used to convert foreign currency financial statements of a subsidiary into the currency of the parent company. Remeasurement uses both historical and current rates and produces financial statements that appear as if the foreign entity's transactions had been initially recorded in dollars.

Renewals. Unplanned replacements of a component of an asset which may or may not extend the asset's useful life or increase future cash flows. If the asset's life is extended or if future cash flows will increase, then a renewal is properly recorded as an asset. If the life of the asset will not increase and no increased future cash flows are expected as a result of the renewal, then the renewal is charged to expense in the period in which it is incurred.

Repairs. Expenditures to restore assets to good operating condition upon their breakdown or to restore and replace broken parts. Repairs benefit only current operations and are expensed immediately.

Replacement cost. The cost that would be required to replace an existing asset.

Replacements. *See* Renewals.

Report form of balance sheet. A balance sheet that presents assets, liabilities, and owners' equity sections in a vertical arrangement.

Representational faithfulness. A key ingredient of reliable accounting information requiring that the amounts and descriptions reported in the financial statements reflect the actual results of economic transactions and events.

Research activities. Activities undertaken to discover new knowledge that may be used in developing new products, services, or processes or that may result in significant improvements of existing products or processes.

Research and development (R&D). A functional activity engaged in by a company to discover and develop new products, designs, methods, etc.

Reserve Recognition Accounting (RRA). A method of accounting that recognizes the value of oil and gas reserves rather than their historical cost. RRA was proposed as a method by the SEC, but later withdrawn from active consideration.

Residual (salvage) value. Estimated amount that can be realized upon the retirement of a depreciable asset; sometimes referred to as salvage value.

Residual value (leased property). The value of leased property at the end of the lease term. This value may be retained by the lessor, purchased by the lessee, or sold to a third person.

Retail inventory method. A procedure that converts the retail value of inventory to an estimation of cost by using a cost percentage that reflects the relationship of inventory available for sale valued at retail and cost

Retained earnings. The portion of owners' equity that represents the net accumulated earnings of a corporation; generally, equal to total owners' equity less contributed capital.

Retained earnings statement. A supplementary financial statement, often combined with the income statement, that shows the change in retained earnings for the period. The most common changes are net income (or loss) and dividends.

Return on investment (ROI). A general term for various analytical measurements of profitability related to input of resources. *See* Rate earned on average common stockholders' equity and Rate earned on average total assets.

Revenue recognition. The process of determining the period in which revenue is recorded. Revenue is generally recognized when it has been realized or is realizable and when it has been earned through substantial completion of the activities involved in the earnings process.

Revenue recognition principle. A basic accounting concept that is applied to determine when revenue should be recognized (recorded). Generally, under this principle, revenues are recognized when two criteria are met: the earnings process is substantially complete and the revenues are realized or realizable.

Revenues. Inflows or other enhancements of assets of an entity or settlements of its liabilities (or a combination of both) from delivering or producing goods, rendering services, or other activities that constitute the entity's ongoing major or central operations.

Reverse stock split. Replacement of shares outstanding with a smaller number of shares.

Reversing entries. Entries made at the beginning of a period that exactly reverse certain adjusting entries made at the end of the previous period. Reversing entries are optional, and their purpose is to facilitate subsequent recording of transactions.

S

Sale-leaseback. A contractual arrangement in which one party, the seller, sells a leased asset to a second party, and in the same agreement, the seller leases back the property. The seller becomes the seller-lessee and the purchaser the purchaser-lessor. Any profit made on the sale must be deferred and recognized over the lease term. Losses are recognized immediately.

Sales discount. *See* Cash discount.

Sales-type lease. A lease in which the lessor is a manufacturer or dealer utilizing the lease to facilitate the sale of goods.

SEC Practice Section (SECPS). A section of the AICPA for firms that have clients that are subject to government regulations through the Securities and Exchange Commission. Membership in the section is voluntary. Periodic peer review is required of all firms with membership in SECPS. Member firms are subject to more regulation than is true for the member firms belonging to the Private Companies Practice Section.

Secured bonds. Bonds for which assets are pledged to guarantee repayment.

Securities and Exchange Commission (SEC). A governmental body created to regulate the issuance and trading of securities by corporations to the general public. As part of this function, the SEC is vitally interested in financial accounting and reporting standards. While this body has the authority to establish accounting standards, it has historically relied heavily on the private sector to perform this function.

Securities Industry Association. An organization of investment bankers who manage the portfolios of large institutional investors.

Segment. A subdivision of a company that can be identified in relationship to its cash flows, profitability, assets and debt.

Serial bonds. Bonds that mature in a series of installments at future dates.

Service cost. A component of net periodic pension cost representing the actuarial present value of benefits accruing to employees for services rendered during that period.

Service-hours depreciation. A use-factor depreciation method based on the theory that the purchase of an asset represents the purchase of a number of hours of direct service. Depreciable cost is divided by total service hours during the useful life of the asset to determine the depreciation rate per hour.

Settlement interest rate. The interest rate used to compute the interest component of net periodic pension cost and the interest rate used to discount projected and accumulated benefit obligations to their present values. It is the rate at which pension plan obligations could be effectively settled; that is, the rate implicit in the current prices of annuity contracts that could be purchased to settle the benefits owed to employees.

Settlement of a pension plan. An irrevocable action taken by an employer that relieves the employer of primary responsibility for all or part of the pension obligation. Examples include purchasing from an insurance company an annuity that would cover employees' vested benefits, or a lump-sum payment to employees in exchange for their rights to receive specified pension benefits.

Similar assets. Assets that are similar in nature and can be exchanged under certain conditions without recognition of a gain on the transfer.

Simple capital structure. A corporate structure that includes only common and nonconvertible preferred stock and has no convertible securities, stock options, warrants or other rights outstanding.

Simple interest. Interest that is computed on the principal amount only.

Single-employer pension plans. Pension plans established for a single employer. FASB Statement No. 87 primarily refers to this type of plan.

Solvency. The ability of an entity to pay all current and long-term debts as they come due.

Source documents. *See* Business documents.

Special journal. An accounting record used to record a particular type of frequently recurring transaction.

Specific identification method. An inventory costing method that assigns the actual cost of the asset to the inventory (unsold) or cost of goods sold (when sold). The cost flow matches the physical flow of the asset.

Spot rate. The exchange rate at which currencies can be traded immediately.

Stability. The ability of a company to make interest and principal payments on outstanding debt and to pay regular dividends to its stockholders.

Stable monetary units. An accounting assumption that the measuring unit maintains constant purchasing power; based on this assumption, U.S. financial statements have traditionally reported items in nominal dollars without adjustment for changes in purchasing power.

Stated or contract rate. The rate of interest printed on the bond.

Stated value. A value that may be assigned to no-par stock by the board of directors of a corporation; similar in concept to par value.

Statement of cash flows. One of three primary financial statements required to be included in the full set of general-purpose statements presented to external users. The statement provides information about the cash receipts (inflows) and cash payments (outflows) of an entity during a period of time. The statement is separated into cash flows from operating, investing, and financing activities.

Statement of changes in owners' (stockholders') equity. A report that shows the total changes in all owners' equity accounts during a period of time; provides a reconciliation of the beginning and ending owners' equity amounts.

Statements of Financial Accounting Concepts. A set of guidelines established by the FASB to provide a conceptual framework for establishing and administering accounting standards.

Statements of Financial Accounting Standards (SFAS). The official statements of the Financial Accounting Standards Board that govern external financial reporting. These statements are prepared after extensive review and discussion by the FASB with the various groups involved in preparing and using general-purpose financial statements.

Statements of Position. Statements issued by the Accounting Standards Executive Committee of the AICPA that deal with emerging issues that have not yet been placed on the FASB agenda.

Stock appreciation rights (SARs). The right for the holder, typically an employee, to receive an amount equal to the excess of the market value of the issuing company's common stock in excess of a specified price. SARs are often awarded in conjunction with a variable stock option plan.

Stock dividend. The payment (receipt) of a dividend in the form of additional shares of a company's own stock.

Stock options. Rights granted to officers or employees, sometimes as part of compensation plan; term also may be used interchangeably with stock rights and stock warrants.

Stock rights. Rights issued to existing shareholders to permit maintenance of a proportionate ownership interest; term also may be used interchangeably with stock warrants and stock options.

Stock split. A reduction in the par or stated value of stock accompanied by a proportionate increase in number of shares outstanding.

Stock warrants. Rights sold separately for cash, generally in conjunction with another security; term also may be used interchangeably with stock rights and stock options.

Straight-line depreciation. A time-factor method of depreciation that recognizes equal periodic depreciation charges for each year of an asset's useful life.

Straight-line method. An amortization method which provides for recognition of an equal amount of bond premium or discount amortization each period.

Subjective acceleration clause. A clause in a debt instrument that identifies general conditions that can cause the debt to be callable immediately but violation of the conditions cannot be determined objectively.

Subsequent events. Events occurring between the balance sheet date and the date financial statements are issued and made available to external users.

Subsidiary company. A company that is owned or controlled by another company, known as the parent company.

Subsidiary ledgers. A grouping of individual accounts that in total equal the balance of a control account in the general ledger; provides additional detail in support of general ledger balances.

Substantial performance. A criterion for recognizing revenue from a franchising agreement which requires that all provisions of the contract agreement be substantially complete before revenue and related expenses may be recognized.

Successful efforts approach. An amortization method employed in the gas and oil industry that expenses the cost of unsuccessful projects and records as assets only the exploratory costs for successful oil and gas projects.

Sum-of-the-years-digits depreciation method. A depreciation method providing decreasing periodic depreciation charges by applying a series of fractions to the asset cost, where the denominator is the sum of the digits 1 through n, and n equals the asset life in years.

T

Tangible noncurrent operating assets. Economic resources with future benefit that are used in the normal operating activity of the organization that can be physically observed, e.g., land, buildings, and equipment.

Taxable income. Income as defined by income tax regulations as the basis for determining the income tax liability for a given entity.

Taxable temporary differences. Differences between financial and taxable income that result in future taxable amounts; income taxes expected to be paid on future taxable amounts are reported in the balance sheet as a deferred tax liability.

Technical Bulletins. Publications issued by the staff of the FASB that give guidance for specific problems that arise in practice. They are advisory in nature and do not have as much authority as the FASB Statements or Interpretations.

Technological feasibility. The attainment of a detailed program design and working model for computer software.

Temporary accounts. *See* Nominal accounts.

Temporary differences. Differences between pretax financial income and taxable income arising from business events that are recognized for both financial and tax purposes, but in different time periods.

Term bonds. Bonds that mature in one lump sum at a specified future date.

Time deposits. Funds deposited in a bank that legally require prior notification before they can be withdrawn.

Time-factor depreciation methods. Methods of depreciation in which the factor that measures the declining usefulness of an asset is related to time more than to use. The most widely used depreciation methods, such as straight-line, declining-balance, and ACRS, rely on this factor.

Timeliness. A key ingredient of relevant accounting information; to be relevant and therefore useful for decision making, information must be provided on a timely basis.

Times interest earned. An indicator of a company's ability to meet interest payments; calculated as income before interest expense and income taxes divided by interest expense for the period.

Total asset turnover. An analytical measurement of the relationship between asset cost and sales generated by those assets. If a company can generate more sales with the same assets, it will increase its level of profitability. The formula is net sales divided by average total assets.

Trade discount. A reduction in the "list" sales price of an item to the "net" sales price actually charged the customer; trade discounts are generally dependent on the volume of business or size of order from the customer.

Trade notes payable. A note issued to trade creditors for the purchase of goods or services.

Trade receivables. Receivables associated with the normal operating activities of a business, e.g., credit sales of goods or services to customers.

Trading on the equity. *See* Financial leverage.

Trading securities. Debt and equity securities that are within the scope of FASB Statement No. 115 and are purchased with the intent of selling them in the near future to generate profits from short-term changes in market prices.

Transaction. An exchange of goods or services between entities or some other event having an economic impact on a business enterprise.

Transaction approach. A method of determining income by defining the financial statement effects of certain events classified as revenues, gains, expenses, and losses. Also known as the *matching concept,* this is the traditional accounting approach to measuring and defining income.

Translation. A method used to convert foreign currency financial statements of a subsidiary into the currency of the parent company. Translation is used when the foreign subsidiary is a relatively self-contained unit that is independent from the parent company's operations. Current exchange rates are used to convert balance sheet accounts, and average rates are used in converting income statement accounts.

Transfer of receivables with recourse. A hybrid form of receivables financing; depending on the specific circumstances, these may be treated for accounting purposes as a sale (factoring) transaction or as a borrowing (assignment) transaction.

Transition gain or loss. The difference between the projected benefit obligation and the fair value of pension fund assets existing at the time FASB Statement No. 87 is adopted, adjusted by any accrued pension cost or prepaid pension cost at the time of transition. This gain or loss is amortized over the average remaining service life of employees. If average service life is less than 15 years, the employer may use 15 years for amortization purposes.

Treasury stock. Stock issued by a corporation but subsequently reacquired by the corporation and held for possible future reissuance or retirement.

Treasury stock method. A method of recognizing the use of proceeds that would be obtained upon exercise of options and warrants in computing earnings per share. It assumes that any proceeds would be used to purchase common stock at current market prices.

Trial balance. A list of all accounts and their balances; provides a means of testing whether total debits equal total credits for all accounts.

Troubled debt restructuring. A situation involving a concession by creditors to allow debtors to eliminate or significantly modify debt obligations due to the debtor's financial difficulties.

Trust indenture. A legal agreement specifying how a fund should be administered by its trustee(s).

U

Unappropriated (free) retained earnings. The unrestricted portion of retained earnings.

Understandability. An essential, user-specific quality of accounting information.

Unearned revenues. Liabilities resulting from amounts that are received before they have been earned, e.g., advances from customers or unearned rent.

Unguaranteed residual value. A residual value of leased property that remains with the lessor at the end of the lease term. Since there is no guarantee of the residual value, market factors and asset condition determine the value of the leased asset at the end of the lease.

Unit depreciation. Depreciation computed on an individual asset as opposed to computation on groups of assets.

Unrealized holding gains and losses. Increases (decreases) in the current value of assets held during a period but not sold or used.

Unrecognized net pension gain or loss. The cumulative net pension gain or loss that has not been recognized as a part of net periodic pension cost.

Unrecognized prior service cost. That portion of prior service cost that has not been recognized as a part of net periodic pension cost.

Unsecured bonds (debentures). Bonds for which no specific collateral has been pledged.

Use-factor depreciation methods. Methods of depreciation in which the factor that measures the declining usefulness of an asset is related to use more than to time. The units-of-production method is the most common depreciation method that emphasizes the use factor.

Useful life. An estimated measure of time or of production capacity a noncurrent operating asset will yield. All noncurrent operating assets, other than land, have a limited useful life. Physical factors such as wear and tear, deterioration, damage or destruction limit the useful life of an asset. Functional factors such as inadequacy or obsolescence may also limit the useful life of an asset.

V

Valuation allowance. A contra asset account that reduces an asset to its expected realizable value. This type of account is used, for example, in valuing accounts receivable and deferred tax assets.

Verifiability. A key ingredient of reliable accounting information; reported information should be based on objectively determined facts that can be verified by other accountants using the same measurement methods.

Vertical analysis. Analysis of a company's single-year financial statements by comparing elements within the statements with each other and with statement totals.

Vested benefit obligation. The amount of pension benefits that have vested and thus are legally owed to employees as of a certain date.

Vested benefits. The amount of pension benefits an employee will retain if employment with the employer is terminated.

Voucher system. A system that provides for the control of purchases and cash disbursements. Business documents are used to prepare vouchers in support of all payments by check. The voucher identifies the person authorizing the expenditure, explains the nature of the transaction, and names the affected accounts. Checks are written in payment for each individual voucher.

W

Warranties. Obligations of a company to provide free service on units failing to perform satisfactorily or to replace defective goods.

Weighted-average interest rate. An interest rate determined by relating interest expenditures for a period with the amount of weighted borrowings during the same period.

Work in process. *See* Goods in process.

Work sheet. A columnar schedule used to summarize accounting data; often used to facilitate the preparation of adjusting entries and financial statements.

Working capital. Current assets less current liabilities; a measure of liquidity.

Working capital ratio. *See* Current ratio.

Y

Yield on common stock. A measure of the cash return to common stockholders. The formula is dividends per share of common stock divided by market value per share of common stock.

Z

Zero-interest bonds or deep-discount bonds. Bonds that do not bear interest but instead are sold at significant discounts, providing the investor with a total interest payoff at maturity.

APPENDIX C
Index of References to APB and FASB Pronouncements

The following list of pronouncements by the Accounting Principles Board and the Financial Accounting Standards Board (as of July 1, 1994) is provided to give students an overview of the standards issued since 1962 and to reference these standards to the relevant chapters in this book. Earlier pronouncements by the Committee on Accounting Procedure of the AICPA have been largely superseded or amended. In those cases where no change has been made by subsequent standard-setting bodies, the earlier pronouncements are still accepted as official.

Accounting Principles Board Opinions

Date Issued		Opinion Number	Title	Chapter References
Nov.	1962	1	New Depreciation Guidelines and Rules	12
Dec.	1962	2	Accounting for the "Investment Credit"; addendum to Opinion No. 2—Accounting Principles for Regulated Industries	N/A
Oct.	1963	3	The Statement of Source and Application of Funds	6
Mar.	1964	4	Accounting for the "Investment Credit"	20
Sep.	1964	5	Reporting of Leases in Financial Statements of Lessee	19
Oct.	1965	6	Status of Accounting Research Bulletins	17
May	1966	7	Accounting for Leases in Financial Statements of Lessor	19
Nov.	1966	8	Accounting for the Cost of Pension Plans	21
Dec.	1966	9	Reporting the Results of Operations	4
Dec.	1966	10	Omnibus Opinion—1966	20
Dec.	1967	11	Accounting for Income Taxes	20
Dec.	1967	12	Omnibus Opinion—1967	12
Mar.	1969	13	Amending Paragraph 6 of APB Opinion No. 9, Application to Commercial Banks	N/A
Mar.	1969	14	Accounting for Convertible Debt and Debt Issued with Stock Purchase Warrants	15, 16
May	1969	15	Earnings per Share	23
Aug.	1970	16	Business Combinations	N/A
Aug.	1970	17	Intangible Assets	11, 12
Mar.	1971	18	The Equity Method of Accounting for Investments in Common Stock	17
Mar.	1971	19	Reporting Changes in Financial Position	6
July	1971	20	Accounting Changes	22
Aug.	1971	21	Interest on Receivables and Payables	8, 13
Apr.	1972	22	Disclosures of Accounting Policies	5
Apr.	1972	23	Accounting for Income Taxes—Special Areas	20
Apr.	1972	24	Accounting for Income Taxes—Investments in Common Stock Accounted for by the Equity Method (Other than Subsidiaries and Corporate Joint Ventures)	N/A
Oct.	1972	25	Accounting for Stock Issued to Employees	16
Oct.	1972	26	Early Extinguishment of Debt	14
Nov.	1972	27	Accounting for Lease Transactions by Manufacturer or Dealer Lessors	19
May	1973	28	Interim Financial Reporting	25
May	1973	29	Accounting for Nonmonetary Transactions	11, 15, 17
June	1973	30	Reporting the Results of Operations	4, 22
June	1973	31	Disclosures of Lease Commitments by Lessees	19

Accounting Principles Board Statements

Date Issued		Statement Number	Title	Chapter References
Apr.	1962	1	Statement by the Accounting Principles Board (on Accounting Research Studies Nos. 1 and 3)	2
Sep.	1967	2	Disclosure of Supplemental Financial Information by Diversified Companies	25
June	1969	3	Financial Statements Restated for General Price-Level Changes	24
Oct.	1970	4	Basic Concepts and Accounting Principles Underlying Financial Statements of Business Enterprises	2

Financial Accounting Standards Board Statements of Financial Accounting Standards

Date Issued		Statement Number	Title	Chapter References
Dec.	1973	1	Disclosure of Foreign Currency Translation Information	24
Oct.	1974	2	Accounting for Research and Development Costs	11
Dec.	1974	3	Reporting Accounting Changes in Interim Financial Statements	N/A
Mar.	1975	4	Reporting Gains and Losses from Extinguishment of Debt	4, 14
Mar.	1975	5	Accounting for Contingencies	13
May	1975	6	Classification of Short-Term Obligations Expected to be Refinanced	5, 13
June	1975	7	Accounting and Reporting by Development Stage Enterprises	11
Oct.	1975	8	Accounting for the Translation of Foreign Currency Transactions and Foreign Currency Financial Statements	10, 24
Oct.	1975	9	Accounting for Income Taxes—Oil and Gas Producing Companies	N/A
Oct.	1975	10	Extension of "Grandfather" Provisions for Business Combinations	N/A
Dec.	1975	11	Accounting for Contingencies—Transition Method	13
Dec.	1975	12	Accounting for Certain Marketable Securities	17
Nov.	1976	13	Accounting for Leases	19
Dec.	1976	14	Financial Reporting for Segments of a Business Enterprise	25
June	1977	15	Accounting by Debtors and Creditors for Troubled Debt Restructurings	14
June	1977	16	Prior Period Adjustments	16, 22
Nov.	1977	17	Accounting for Leases—Initial Direct Costs	19
Nov.	1977	18	Financial Reporting for Segments of a Business Enterprise—Interim Financial Statements	25
Dec.	1977	19	Financial Accounting and Reporting by Oil and Gas Producing Companies	12
Dec.	1977	20	Accounting for Forward Exchange Contracts	N/A
Apr.	1978	21	Suspension of the Reporting of Earnings Per Share and Segment Information by Nonpublic Enterprises	23, 25
June	1978	22	Changes in the Provisions of Lease Agreements Resulting from Refunding of Tax-Exempt Debt	N/A
Aug.	1978	23	Inception of the Lease	19
Dec.	1978	24	Reporting Segment Information in Financial Statements That Are Presented in Another Enterprise's Financial Report	N/A
Feb.	1979	25	Suspension of Certain Accounting Requirements for Oil and Gas Producing Companies	12
Apr.	1979	26	Profit Recognition on Sales-Type Leases of Real Estate	19
May	1979	27	Classification of Renewals or Extensions of Existing Sales-Type or Direct Financing Leases	19
May	1979	28	Accounting for Sales with Leasebacks	19
June	1979	29	Determining Contingent Rentals	19
Aug.	1979	30	Disclosures of Information About Major Customers	25
Sep.	1979	1	Accounting for Tax Benefits Related to U.K. Tax Legislation Concerning Stock Relief	N/A
Sep.	1979	32	Specialized Accounting and Reporting Principles and Practices in AICPA Statements of Position and Guides on Accounting and Auditing Matters	18

Financial Accounting Standards Board Statements of Financial Accounting Standards (Continued)

Date Issued		Statement Number	Title	Chapter References
Sep.	1979	33	Financial Reporting and Changing Prices	24
Oct.	1979	34	Capitalization of Interest Cost	11
Mar.	1980	35	Accounting and Reporting by Defined Benefit Pension Plans	21
May	1980	36	Disclosure of Pension Information	21
July	1980	37	Balance Sheet Classification of Deferred Income Taxes	20
Sep.	1980	38	Accounting for Preacquisition Contingencies of Purchased Enterprises	N/A
Oct.	1980	39	Financial Reporting and Changing Prices: Specialized Assets—Mining and Oil and Gas	N/A
Nov.	1980	40	Financial Reporting and Changing Prices: Specialized Assets—Timberlands and Growing Timber	N/A
Nov.	1980	41	Financial Reporting and Changing Prices: Specialized Assets—Income-Producing Real Estate	N/A
Nov.	1980	42	Determining Materiality for Capitalization of Interest Costs	11
Nov.	1980	43	Accounting for Compensated Absences	13
Dec.	1980	44	Accounting for Intangible Assets of Motor Carriers	N/A
Mar.	1981	45	Accounting for Franchise Fee Revenue	18
Mar.	1981	46	Financial Reporting and Changing Prices: Motion Picture Films	N/A
Mar.	1981	47	Disclosure of Long-Term Obligations	14
June	1981	48	Revenue Recognition When Right of Return Exists	18
June	1981	49	Accounting for Product Financing Arrangements	N/A
Nov.	1981	50	Financial Reporting in the Record and Music Industry	N/A
Nov.	1981	51	Financial Reporting by Cable Television Companies	N/A
Dec.	1981	52	Foreign Currency Translation	24
Dec.	1981	53	Financial Reporting by Producers and Distributors of Motion Picture Films	N/A
Jan.	1982	54	Financial Reporting and Changing Prices: Investment Companies	N/A
Feb.	1982	55	Determining Whether a Convertible Security Is a Common Stock Equivalent	23
Feb.	1982	56	Designation of AICPA Guide and Statement of Position (SOP) 81-1 on Contractor Accounting and SOP 81-2 Concerning Hospital-Related Organizations as Preferable for Purposes of Applying APB Opinion 20	18
Mar.	1982	57	Related Party Disclosures	N/A
Apr.	1982	58	Capitalization of Interest Cost in Financial Statements That Include Investments Accounted for by the Equity Method	N/A
Apr.	1982	59	Deferral of the Effective Date of Certain Accounting Requirements for Pension Plans of State and Local Governmental Units	N/A
June	1982	60	Accounting and Reporting by Insurance Enterprises	N/A
June	1982	61	Accounting for Title Plant	N/A
June	1982	62	Capitalization of Interest Cost in Situations Involving Certain Tax-Exempt Borrowings and Certain Gifts and Grants	N/A
June	1982	63	Financial Reporting by Broadcasters	N/A
Sep.	1982	64	Extinguishments of Debt Made to Satisfy Sinking-Fund Requirements	14
Sep.	1982	65	Accounting for Certain Mortgage Banking Activities N/A	
Oct.	1982	66	Accounting for Sales of Real Estate	18
Oct.	1982	67	Accounting for Costs and Initial Rental Operations of Real Estate Projects	N/A
Oct.	1982	68	Research and Development Arrangements	14
Nov.	1982	69	Disclosures About Oil and Gas Producing Activities	N/A
Dec.	1982	70	Financial Reporting and Changing Prices: Foreign Currency Translation	N/A
Dec.	1982	71	Accounting for the Effects of Certain Types of Regulation	N/A
Feb.	1983	72	Accounting for Certain Acquisitions of Banking or Thrift Institutions	N/A
Aug.	1983	73	Reporting a Change in Accounting for Railroad Track Structures	N/A
Aug.	1983	74	Accounting for Special Termination Benefits Paid to Employees	21
Nov.	1983	75	Deferral of the Effective Date of Certain Accounting Requirements for Pension Plans of State and Local Governmental Units	N/A

Financial Accounting Standards Board Statements of Financial Accounting Standards (Concluded)

Date Issued	Statement Number	Title	Chapter References
Nov. 1983	76	Extinguishment of Debt	14
Dec. 1983	77	Reporting by Transferors for Transfers of Receivables with Recourse	8
Dec. 1983	78	Classification of Obligations That Are Callable by the Creditor	5, 14
Feb. 1984	79	Elimination of Certain Disclosures for Business Combinations by Nonpublic Enterprises	N/A
Aug. 1984	80	Accounting for Future Contracts	N/A
Nov. 1984	81	Disclosure of Postretirement Health Care and Life Insurance Benefits	21
Nov. 1984	82	Financial Reporting and Changing Prices: Elimination of Certain Disclosures	24
Mar. 1985	83	Designation of AICPA Guides and Statement of Position on Accounting by Brokers and Dealers in Securities, by Employee Benefit Plans, and by Banks as Preferable for Purposes of Applying APB Opinion 20	N/A
Mar. 1985	84	Induced Conversion of Convertible Debt	14
Mar. 1985	85	Yield Test for Determining Whether a Convertible Security Is a Common Stock Equivalent	23
Aug. 1985	86	Accounting for the Costs of Computer Software to Be Sold, Leased, or Otherwise Marketed	11
Dec. 1985	87	Employers' Accounting for Pensions	21
Dec. 1985	88	Employers' Accounting for Settlements and Curtailments of Defined Benefit Pension Plans and for Termination Benefits	21
Dec. 1986	89	Financial Reporting and Changing Prices	24
Dec. 1986	90	Regulated Enterprises—Accounting for Abandonments and Disallowances of Plant Costs	N/A
Dec. 1986	91	Accounting for Nonrefundable Fees and Costs Associated with Originating or Acquiring Loans and Initial Direct Costs of Leases	19
Aug. 1987	92	Regulated Enterprises—Accounting for Phase-In Plans	N/A
Aug. 1987	93	Recognition of Depreciation by Not-for-Profit Organizations	N/A
Oct. 1987	94	Consolidation of all Majority-Owned Subsidiaries	17
Nov. 1987	95	Statement of Cash Flows	6
Dec. 1987	96	Accounting for Income Taxes	20
Dec. 1987	97	Accounting and Reporting by Insurance Enterprises for Certain Insurance Enterprises for Certain Long-Duration Contracts and for Realized Gains and Losses from the Sale of Investments	N/A
May 1988	98	Accounting for Leases: • Sale-Leaseback Transactions Involving Real Estate • Sales-Type Leases of Real Estate • Definition of the Lease Term • Initial Direct Costs of Direct Financial Leases	19
Sep. 1988	99	Deferral of the Effective Date of Recognition of Depreciation by Not-for-Profit Organizations	N/A
Dec. 1988	100	Accounting for Income Taxes—Deferral of the Effective Date FASB Statement No. 96	20
Dec. 1988	101	Regulated Enterprises—Accounting for the Discontinuation of Application of FASB Statement No. 71	N/A
Feb. 1989	102	Statement of Cash Flows—Exemption of Certain Enterprises and Classification of Cash Flows from Certain Securities Acquired for Resale	N/A
Dec. 1989	103	Accounting for Income Taxes—Deferral of Effective Date of FASB Statement No. 96	20
Dec. 1989	104	Statement of Cash Flows—Net Reporting of Certain Cash Receipts and Cash Payments and Classification of Cash Flows from Hedging Transactions	N/A
Mar. 1990	105	Disclosure of Information about Financial Instruments with Off-Balance-Sheet Risk and Financial Instruments with Concentrations of Credit Risk	14

Dec.	1990	106	Employers' Accounting for Postretirement Benefits Other Than Pensions	21
Dec.	1991	107	Disclosures about Fair Value of Financial Instruments	17
Dec.	1991	108	Accounting for Income Taxes—Deferral of the Effective Date of FASB Statement No. 96	20
Feb.	1992	109	Accounting for Income Taxes	20
Aug.	1992	110	Reporting by Defined Benefit Pension Plans Investment Contracts	N/A
Nov.	1992	111	Recision of FASB Statement No. 32 and Technical Corrections	2
Nov.	1992	112	Employers' Accounting for Postemployment Benefits	21
Dec.	1992	113	Accounting and Reporting for Reinsurance of Short-Duration and Long-Duration Contracts	N/A
May	1993	114	Accounting by Creditors for Impairment of a Loan	17
May	1993	115	Accounting for Certain Investments in Debt and Equity Securities	17
June	1993	116	Accounting for Contributions Received and Contributions Made	11, 16
June	1993	117	Financial Statements of Not-for-Profit Organizations	N/A

Financial Accounting Standards Board Statements of Financial Accounting Concepts

Date Issued		Statement Number	Title	Chapter References
Nov.	1978	1	Objectives of Financial Reporting by Business Enterprises	2
May	1980	2	Qualitative Characteristics of Accounting Information	2
Dec.	1980	3	Elements of Financial Statements of Business Enterprises	2
Dec.	1980	4	Objectives of Financial Reporting by Nonbusiness Organizations	N/A
Dec.	1984	5	Recognition and Measurement in Financial Statements of Business Enterprises	2
Dec.	1985	6	Elements of Financial Statements	2

INDEX

D

E

F

Q

R

S

T

U

V

W

Y

Z